Collins
Spanish
Dictionary

This edition printed in 2006 for
Bookmart Ltd
Registered Number 2372865
Trading as Bookmart Ltd
Blaby Road
Wigston
Leicester LE18 4SE

HarperCollins Publishers
Westerhill Road
Bishopbriggs
Glasgow
G64 2QT
Great Britain

First Edition 2006

© HarperCollins Publishers 2006

ISBN-13   978-0-00-777110-3
ISBN-10   0-00-777110-X

www.collins.co.uk

A catalogue record for this book is
available from the British Library

Typeset by Wordcraft, Glasgow

Printed in Great Britian by Clays Ltd, St
Ives plc

Acknowledgements
We would like to thank those authors
and publishers who kindly gave
permission for copyright material to be
used in the Collins Word Web. We
would also like to thank Times
Newspapers Ltd for providing valuable
data.

This book is set in Collins Fedra, a
typeface specially created for Collins
dictionaries by Peter Bil'ak.

MANAGING EDITOR
Michela Clari

CONTRIBUTORS
José Martín Galera
Wendy Lee
José María Ruiz Vaca
Cordelia Lilly
Maree Airlie

EDITORIAL COORDINATION
Joyce Littlejohn
Marianne Noble

SERIES EDITOR
Lorna Knight

ÍNDICE

CONTENTS

William Collins' dream of knowledge for all began with the publication of his first book in 1819. A self-educated mill worker, he not only enriched millions of lives, but also founded a flourishing publishing house. Today, staying true to this spirit, Collins books are packed with inspiration, innovation, and practical expertise. They place you at the centre of a world of possibility and give you exactly what you need to explore it.

Language is the key to this exploration, and at the heart of Collins Dictionaries is language as it is really used. New words, phrases, and meanings spring up every day, and all of them are captured and analysed by the Collins Word Web. Constantly updated, and with over 2.5 billion entries, this living language resource is unique to our dictionaries.

Words are tools for life. And a Collins Dictionary makes them work for you.

Collins. Do more

INTRODUCCIÓN

Estamos muy satisfechos de que hayas decidido comprar
este diccionario y esperamos que lo disfrutes y que te sirva
de gran ayuda ya sea en el colegio, en el trabajo, en tus
vacaciones o en casa.

INTRODUCTION

We are delighted that you have decided to buy this Spanish
dictionary and hope you will enjoy and benefit from using
it at school, at home, on holiday or at work.

ABREVIATURAS

ABBREVIATIONS

abreviatura	*ab(b)r*	abbreviation
adjetivo, locución adjetiva	*adj*	adjective, adjectival phrase
administración	*Admin*	administration
adverbio, locución adverbial	*adv*	adverb, adverbial phrase
agricultura	*Agr*	agriculture
anatomía	*Anat*	anatomy
Argentina	*Arg*	Argentina
arquitectura	*Arq, Arch*	architecture
el automóvil	*Aut(o)*	the motor car and motoring
aviación, viajes aéreos	*Aviac, Aviat*	flying, air travel
biología	*Bio(l)*	biology
botánica, flores	*Bot*	botany
inglés británico	*BRIT*	British English
Centroamérica	*CAM*	Central America
química	*Chem*	chemistry
comercio, finanzas, banca	*Com(m)*	commerce, finance, banking
informática	*Comput*	computing
conjunción	*conj*	conjunction
construcción	*Constr*	building
compuesto	*cpd*	compound element
Cono Sur	*CS*	Southern Cone
cocina	*Culin*	cookery
economía	*Econ*	economics
eletricidad, electrónica	*Elec*	electricity, electronics
enseñanza, sistema escolar y universitario	*Escol*	schooling, schools and universities
España	*ESP*	Spain
especialmente	*esp*	especially
exclamación, interjección	*excl*	exclamation, interjection
femenino	*f*	feminine
lengua familiar (! vulgar)	*fam(!)*	colloquial usage (! particularly offensive)
ferrocarril	*Ferro*	railways
uso figurado	*fig*	figurative use
fotografía	*Foto*	photography
(verbo inglés) del cual la partícula es inseparable	*fus*	(phrasal verb) where the particle is inseparable
generalmente	*gen*	generally
geografía, geología	*Geo*	geography, geology
geometría	*Geom*	geometry
historia	*Hist*	history
uso familiar (! vulgar)	*inf(!)*	colloquial usage (! particularly offensive)
infinitivo	*infin*	infinitive
informática	*Inform*	computing
invariable	*inv*	invariable
irregular	*irreg*	irregular
lo jurídico	*Jur*	law
América Latina	*LAM*	Latin America
gramática, lingüística	*Ling*	grammar, linguistics

ABREVIATURAS

ABBREVIATIONS

masculino	m	masculine
matemáticas	Mat(h)	mathematics
masculino/femenino	m/f	masculine/feminine
medicina	Med	medicine
México	MÉX, MEX	Mexico
lo militar, ejército	Mil	military matters
música	Mús, Mus	music
substantivo, nombre	n	noun
navegación, náutica	Náut, Naut	sailing, navigation
sustantivo numérico	num	numeral noun
complemento	obj	(grammatical) object
	o.s.	oneself
peyorativo	pey, pej	derogatory, pejorative
fotografía	Phot	photography
fisiología	Physiol	physiology
plural	pl	plural
política	Pol	politics
participio de pasado	pp	past participle
preposición	prep	preposition
pronombre	pron	pronoun
psicología, psiquiatría	Psico, Psych	psychology, psychiatry
tiempo pasado	pt	past tense
química	Quím	chemistry
ferrocarril	Rail	railways
religión	Rel	religion
Río de la Plata	RPL	River Plate
	sb	somebody
Cono Sur	SC	Southern Cone
enseñanza, sistema escolar y universitario	Scol	schooling, schools and universities
singular	sg	singular
España	SP	Spain
	sth	something
sujeto	su(b)j	(grammatical) subject
subjuntivo	subjun	subjunctive
tauromaquia	Taur	bullfighting
también	tb	also
técnica, tecnología	Tec(h)	technical term, technology
telecomunicaciones	Telec, Tel	telecommunications
imprenta, tipografía	Tip, Typ	typography, printing
televisión	TV	television
universidad	Univ	university
inglés norteamericano	US	American English
verbo	vb	verb
verbo intransitivo	vi	intransitive verb
verbo pronominal	vr	reflexive verb
verbo transitivo	vt	transitive verb
zoología	Zool	zoology
marca registrada	®	registered trademark
indica un equivalente cultural	≈	introduces a cultural equivalent

SPANISH PRONUNCIATION

VOWELS

a	[a]	pata	not as long as *a* in far. When followed by a consonant in the same syllable (i.e. in a closed syllable), as in *a*mante, the *a* is short, as in b*a*t
e	[e]	me	like *e* in they. In a closed syllable, as in g*e*nte, the *e* is short as in p*e*t
i	[i]	pino	as in m*ea*n or mach*i*ne
o	[o]	lo	as in l*o*cal. In a closed syllable, as in c*o*ntrol, the *o* is short as in c*o*t
u	[u]	lunes	as in r*u*le. It is silent after q, and in gue, gui, unless marked güe, güi e.g. antigüedad, when it is pronounced like *w* in w*o*lf

SEMIVOWELS

i, y	[j]	bien hielo yunta	pronounced like *y* in yes
u	[w]	huevo fuento antigüedad	unstressed *u* between consonant and vowel is pronounced like *w* in well. See notes on *u* above.

DIPHTHONGS

ai, ay	[ai]	baile	as *i* in ride
au	[au]	auto	as *ou* in shout
ei, ey	[ei]	buey	as *ey* in grey
eu	[eu]	deuda	both elements pronounced independently [e] + [u]
oi, oy	[oi]	hoy	as *oy* in toy

CONSONANTS

b	[b,β]	boda bomba labor	see notes on *v* below
c	[k]	caja	*c* before *a, o, u* is pronounced as in cat
ce, ci	[θe,θi]	cero cielo	*c* before *e* or *i* is pronounced as in thin
ch	[tʃ]	chiste	*ch* is pronounced as *ch* in chair
d	[d,ð]	danés ciudad	at the beginning of a phrase or after *l* or *n*, *d* is pronounced as in English. In any other position it is pronounced like *th* in the

g	[g, ɣ]	**g**afas pa**g**a	_g_ before _a_, _o_ or _u_ is pronounced as in _g_ap, if at the beginning of a phrase or after _n_. In other positions the sound is softened
ge, gi	[xe, xi]	**g**ente **g**irar	_g_ before _e_ or _i_ is pronounced similar to _ch_ in Scottish lo_ch_
h		**h**aber	_h_ is always silent in Spanish
j	[x]	**j**ugar	_j_ is pronounced similar to _ch_ in Scottish lo_ch_
ll	[ʎ]	ta**ll**e	_ll_ is pronounced like the _y_ in _y_et or the _lli_ in mi_lli_on
ñ	[ʃ]	ni**ñ**o	_ñ_ is pronounced like the _ni_ in o_ni_on
q	[k]	**q**ue	_q_ is pronounced as _k_ in _k_ing
r, rr	[r, rr]	qui**t**ar ga**rr**a	_r_ is always pronounced in Spanish, unlike the silent _r_ in dance_r_. _rr_ is trilled, like a Scottish _r_
s	[s]	qui**z**ás i**s**la	_s_ is usually pronounced as in pa_ss_, but before _b_, _d_, _g_, _l_, _m_ or _n_ it is pronounced as in ro_s_e
v	[b, β]	**v**ía	_v_ is pronounced something like _b_. At the beginning of a phrase or after _m_ or _n_ it is pronounced as _b_ in _b_oy. In any other position the sound is softened
z	[θ]	tena**z**	_z_ is pronounced as _th_ in _th_in

f, k, l, m, n, p, t and x are pronounced as in English.

STRESS

The rules of stress in Spanish are as follows:

(a)   when a word ends in a vowel or in _n_ or _s_, the second last syllable is stressed:
        pa_ta_ta, pa_ta_tas; _co_me, _co_men
(b)   when a word ends in a consonant other than _n_ or _s_, the stress falls on the last syllable:
        pa_red_, hab_lar_
(c)   when the rules set out in (a) and (b) are not applied, an acute accent appears over the stressed vowel:
        com_ún_, geograf_í_a, ing_lés_

In the phonetic transcription, the symbol ['] precedes the syllable on which the stress falls.

LA PRONUNCIACIÓN INGLESA

VOCALES

	Ejemplo inglés	Explicación
[ɑː]	father	Entre *a* de padre y *o* de noche
[ʌ]	but, come	*a* muy breve
[æ]	man, cat	Con los labios en la posición de *e* en pena y luego se pronuncia el sonido *a* parecido a la *a* de carro
[ə]	father, ago	Vocal neutra parecida a una *e* u *o* casi muda
[əː]	bird, heard	Entre *e* abierta y *o* cerrada, sonido alargado
[ɛ]	get, bed	Como en perro
[ɪ]	it, big	Más breve que en sí
[iː]	tea, see	Como en fino
[ɔ]	hot, wash	Como en torre
[ɔː]	saw, all	Como en por
[u]	put, book	Sonido breve, más cerrado que burro
[uː]	too, you	Sonido largo, como en uno

DIPTONGOS

	Ejemplo inglés	Explicación
[aɪ]	fly, high	Como en fraile
[au]	how, house	Como en pausa
[ɛə]	there, bear	Casi como en vea, pero el sonido *a* se mezcla con el indistinto [ə]
[eɪ]	day, obey	*e* cerrada seguida por una *i* débil
[ɪə]	here, hear	Como en manía, mezclándose el sonido *a* con el indistinto [ə]
[əu]	go, note	[ə] seguido por una breve *u*
[ɔɪ]	boy, oil	Como en voy
[uə]	poor, sure	*u* bastante larga más el sonido indistinto [ə]

CONSONANTES

	Ejemplo inglés	Explicación
[b]	**b**ig, lo**bb**y	Como en tum**b**an
[d]	men**d**e**d**	Como en con**d**e, an**d**ar
[g]	**g**o, **g**et, bi**g**	Como en **g**rande, **g**ol
[dʒ]	**g**in, **j**u**dg**e	Como en la **ll** andaluza y en Generalitat (*catalán*)
[ŋ]	si**ng**	Como en ví**n**culo
[h]	**h**ouse, **h**e	Como la jota hispanoamericana
[j]	**y**oung, **y**es	Como en **y**a
[k]	**c**ome, mo**ck**	Como en **c**aña, Es**c**ocia
[r]	**r**ed, t**r**ead	Se pronuncia con la punta de la lengua hacia atrás y sin hacerla vibrar
[s]	**s**and, ye**s**	Como en **c**asa, se**s**ión
[z]	ro**s**e, **z**ebra	Como en de**s**de, mi**s**mo
[ʃ]	**sh**e, ma**ch**ine	Como en **ch**ambre (*francés*), ro**x**o (*portugués*)
[tʃ]	**ch**in, ri**ch**	Como en **ch**ocolate
[v]	**v**alley	Como **f**, pero se retiran los dientes superiores vibrándolos contra el labio inferior
[w]	**w**ater, **wh**ich	Como la **u** de h**u**evo, p**u**ede
[ʒ]	vi**s**ion	Como en **j**ournal (*francés*)
[θ]	**th**ink, my**th**	Como en re**c**eta, **z**apato
[ð]	**th**is, **th**e	Como en habla**d**o, verda**d**

f, l, m, n, p, t y x iguales que en español.

El signo [*] indica que la r final escrita apenas se pronuncia en inglés británico cuando la palabra siguiente empieza con vocal.
El signo ['] indica la sílaba acentuada.

○ **PALABRA CLAVE**

a [a] (a + el = al) prep **1** (dirección) to; **fueron a Madrid/Grecia** they went to Madrid/Greece; **me voy a casa** I'm going home
2 (distancia): **está a 15 km de aquí** it's 15 kms from here
3 (posición): **a la mesa** at the table; **al lado de** next to, beside; V tb **puerta**
4 (tiempo): **a las 10/a medianoche** at 10/midnight; **a la mañana siguiente** the following morning; **a los pocos días** after a few days; **estamos a 9 de julio** it's the ninth of July; **a los 24 años** at the age of 24; **al año/a la semana** a year/week later
5 (manera): **a la francesa** the French way; **a caballo** on horseback; **a oscuras** in the dark
6 (medio, instrumento): **a lápiz** in pencil; **a mano** by hand; **cocina a gas** gas stove
7 (razón): **a 30 céntimos el kilo** at 30 cents a kilo; **a más de 50 km/h** at more than 50 kms per hour
8 (dativo): **se lo di a él** I gave it to him; **vi a la policía** I saw the policeman; **se lo compré a él** I bought it from him
9 (tras ciertos verbos): **voy a verle** I'm going to see him; **empezó a trabajar** he started working o to work
10 (+ infin): **al verlo, lo reconocí inmediatamente** when I saw him I recognized him at once; **el camino a recorrer** the distance we etc have to travel; **¡a callar!** keep quiet!; **¡a comer!** let's eat!

abad, esa [a'βaδ, 'δesa] nm/f abbot/abbess; **abadía** nf abbey
abajo [a'βaxo] adv (situación) (down) below, underneath; (en edificio) downstairs; (dirección) down, downwards; **el piso de ~** the downstairs flat; **la parte de ~** the lower part; **¡~ el gobierno!** down with the government!; **cuesta/río ~** downhill/downstream; **de arriba ~** from top to bottom; **el ~ firmante** the undersigned; **más ~** lower o further down
abalanzarse [aβalan'θarse] vr: **~ sobre** o **contra** to throw o.s. at

abanderado, -a [aβande'raδo] nm/f (portaestandarte) standard bearer; (de un movimiento) champion, leader; (MÉX: linier) linesman, assistant referee
abandonado, -a [aβando'naδo, a] adj derelict; (desatendido) abandoned; (desierto) deserted; (descuidado) neglected
abandonar [aβando'nar] vt to leave; (persona) to abandon, desert; (cosa) to abandon, leave behind; (descuidar) to neglect; (renunciar a) to give up; (Inform) to quit; **abandonarse** vr: **~se a** to abandon o.s. to; **abandono** nm (acto) desertion, abandonment; (estado) abandon, neglect; (renuncia) withdrawal, retirement; **ganar por abandono** to win by default
abanico [aβa'niko] nm fan; (Náut) derrick
abarcar [aβar'kar] vt to include, embrace; (LAM: acaparar) to monopolize
abarrotado, -a [aβarro'taδo, a] adj packed
abarrotar [aβarro'tar] vt (local, estadio, teatro) to fill, pack
abarrotero, -a [aβarro'tero, a] (MÉX) nm/f grocer; **abarrotes** (MÉX) nmpl groceries; **tienda de abarrotes** (MÉX, CAM) grocery store
abastecer [aβaste'θer] vt: **~ (de)** to supply (with); **abastecimiento** nm supply
abasto [a'βasto] nm supply; **no dar ~ a** to be unable to cope with
abatible [aβa'tiβle] adj: **asiento ~** tip-up seat; (Auto) reclining seat
abatido, -a [aβa'tiδo, a] adj dejected, downcast
abatir [aβa'tir] vt (muro) to demolish; (pájaro) to shoot o bring down; (fig) to depress
abdicar [aβδi'kar] vi to abdicate
abdomen [aβ'δomen] nm abdomen; **abdominales** nmpl (tb: **ejercicios abdominales**) sit-ups
abecedario [aβeθe'δarjo] nm alphabet
abedul [aβe'δul] nm birch
abeja [a'βexa] nf bee
abejorro [aβe'xorro] nm bumblebee
abertura [aβer'tura] nf = **apertura**
abeto [a'βeto] nm fir
abierto, -a [a'βjerto, a] pp de **abrir** ▷ adj open
abismal [aβis'mal] adj (fig) vast, enormous
abismo [a'βismo] nm abyss
ablandar [aβlan'dar] vt to soften; **ablandarse** vr to get soften
abocado, -a [aβo'kaδo, a] adj (vino) smooth, pleasant
abochornar [aβotʃor'nar] vt to embarrass
abofetear [aβofete'ar] vt to slap (in the face)
abogado, -a [aβo'γaδo, a] nm/f lawyer; (notario) solicitor; (en tribunal) barrister (BRIT), attorney (US); **abogado defensor** defence lawyer o (US) attorney
abogar [aβo'γar] vi: **~ por** to plead for; (fig) to advocate
abolir [aβo'lir] vt to abolish; (cancelar) to cancel
abolladura [aβoʎa'δura] nf dent
abollar [aβo'ʎar] vt to dent
abombarse [aβom'barse] (LAM) vr to go bad
abominable [aβomi'naβle] adj abominable
abonado, -a [aβo'naδo, a] adj (deuda) paid(-up) ▷ nm/f subscriber

abonar [aβo'nar] *vt* (*deuda*) to settle; (*terreno*) to fertilize; (*idea*) to endorse; **abonarse** *vr* to subscribe; **abono** *nm* payment; fertilizer; subscription

abordar [aβor'ðar] *vt* (*barco*) to board; (*asunto*) to broach

aborigen [aβo'rixen] *nmf* aborigine

aborrecer [aβorre'θer] *vt* to hate, loathe

abortar [aβor'tar] *vi* (*malparir*) to have a miscarriage; (*deliberadamente*) to have an abortion; **aborto** *nm* miscarriage; abortion

abovedado, -a [aβoβe'ðaðo, a] *adj* vaulted, domed

abrasar [aβra'sar] *vt* to burn (up); (*Agr*) to dry up, parch

abrazar [aβra'θar] *vt* to embrace, hug

abrazo [a'βraθo] *nm* embrace, hug; **un ~** (*en carta*) with best wishes

abrebotellas [aβreβo'teʎas] *nm inv* bottle opener

abrecartas [aβre'kartas] *nm inv* letter opener

abrelatas [aβre'latas] *nm inv* (*BRIT*) o can opener

abreviatura [aβreβja'tura] *nf* abbreviation

abridor [aβri'ðor] *nm* bottle opener; (*de latas*) tin (*BRIT*) o can opener

abrigador, a [aβriga'ðor, a] (*MÉX*) *adj* warm

abrigar [aβri'xar] *vt* (*proteger*) to shelter; (*ropa*) to keep warm; (*fig*) to cherish

abrigo [a'βriɣo] *nm* (*prenda*) coat, overcoat; (*lugar protegido*) shelter

abril [a'βril] *nm* April

abrillantador [aβriʎanta'ðor] *nm* polish

abrillantar [aβriʎan'tar] *vt* to polish

abrir [a'βrir] *vt* to open (up) ▷ *vi* to open; **abrirse** *vr* to open (up); (*extenderse*) to open out; (*cielo*) to clear; **~se paso** to find o force a way through

abrochar [aβro'tʃar] *vt* (*con botones*) to button (up); (*zapato, con broche*) to do up

abrupto, -a [a'βrupto, a] *adj* abrupt; (*empinado*) steep

absoluto, -a [aβso'luto, a] *adj* absolute; **en ~** *adv* not at all

absolver [aβsol'βer] *vt* to absolve; (*Jur*) to pardon; (: *acusado*) to acquit

absorbente [aβsor'βente] *adj* absorbent; (*interesante*) absorbing

absorber [aβsor'βer] *vt* to absorb; (*embeber*) to soak up

absorción [aβsor'θjon] *nf* absorption; (*Com*) takeover

abstemio, -a [aβs'temjo, a] *adj* teetotal

abstención [aβsten'θjon] *nf* abstention

abstenerse [aβste'nerse] *vr*: **~ (de)** to abstain o refrain (from)

abstinencia [aβsti'nenθja] *nf* abstinence; (*ayuno*) fasting

abstracto, -a [aβs'trakto, a] *adj* abstract

abstraer [aβstra'er] *vt* to abstract; **abstraerse** *vr* to be o become absorbed

abstraído, -a [aβstra'iðo, a] *adj* absent-minded

absuelto [aβ'swelto] *pp de* **absolver**

absurdo, -a [aβ'surðo, a] *adj* absurd

abuchear [aβutʃe'ar] *vt* to boo

abuelo, -a [a'βwelo, a] *nm/f* grandfather(-mother); **abuelos** *nmpl* grandparents

abultado, -a [aβul'taðo, a] *adj* bulky

abultar [aβul'tar] *vt* to enlarge

abundancia [aβun'danθja] *nf*: **una ~ de** plenty of; **abundante** *adj* abundant, plentiful

abundar [aβun'dar] *vi* to abound, be plentiful

aburrido, -a [aβu'rriðo, a] *adj* (*hastiado*) bored; (*que aburre*) boring; **aburrimiento** *nm* boredom, tedium

aburrir [aβu'rrir] *vt* to bore; **aburrirse** *vr* to be bored, get bored

abusado, -a [aβu'saðo, a] (*MÉX: fam*) *adj* (*astuto*) sharp, cunning ▷ *excl*: **¡~!** (*inv*) look out!, careful!

abusar [aβu'sar] *vi* to go too far; **~ de** to abuse

abusivo, -a [aβu'siβo, a] *adj* (*precio*) exorbitant

abuso [a'βuso] *nm* abuse

acá [a'ka] *adv* here

acabado, -a [aka'βaðo, a] *adj* finished, complete; (*perfecto*) perfect; (*agotado*) worn out; (*fig*) masterly ▷ *nm* finish

acabar [aka'βar] *vt* (*llevar a su fin*) to finish, complete; (*consumir*) to use up; (*rematar*) to finish off ▷ *vi* to finish, end; **acabarse** *vr* to finish, stop; (*terminarse*) to be over; (*agotarse*) to run out; **~ con** to put an end to; **~ de llegar** to have just arrived; **~ por hacer** to end (up) by doing; **¡se acabó!** it's all over!; (*¡basta!*) that's enough!

acabóse [aka'βose] *nm*: **esto es el ~** this is the last straw

academia [aka'ðemja] *nf* academy; **academia de idiomas** language school; **académico, -a** *adj* academic

acalorado, -a [akalo'raðo, a] *adj* (*discusión*) heated

acampar [akam'par] *vi* to camp

acantilado [akanti'laðo] *nm* cliff

acaparar [akapa'rar] *vt* to monopolize; (*acumular*) to hoard

acariciar [akari'θjar] *vt* to caress; (*esperanza*) to cherish

acarrear [akarre'ar] *vt* to transport; (*fig*) to cause, result in

acaso [a'kaso] *adv* perhaps, maybe; **(por) si ~** (just) in case

acatar [aka'tar] *vt* to respect; (*ley*) obey

acatarrarse [akata'rrarse] *vr* to catch a cold

acceder [akθe'ðer] *vi*: **~ a** (*petición etc*) to agree to; (*tener acceso a*) to have access to; (*Inform*) to access

accesible [akθe'siβle] *adj* accessible

acceso [ak'θeso] *nm* access, entry; (*camino*) access, approach; (*Med*) attack, fit

accesorio, -a [akθe'sorjo, a] *adj, nm* accessory

accidentado, -a [akθiðen'taðo, a] *adj* uneven; (*montañoso*) hilly; (*azaroso*) eventful ▷ *nm/f* accident victim

accidental [akθiðen'tal] *adj* accidental

accidente [akθi'ðente] *nm* accident; **accidentes** *nmpl* (*de terreno*) unevenness *sg*; **accidente laboral o de trabajo/de tráfico** industrial/road o traffic accident

acción [ak'θjon] *nf* action; (*acto*) action, act; (*Com*) share; (*Jur*) action, lawsuit; **accionar** *vt* to work, operate; (*Inform*) to drive

accionista [akθjo'nista] *nmf* shareholder, stockholder

acebo [a'θeβo] *nm* holly; (*árbol*) holly tree

acechar [aθe'tʃar] *vt* to spy on; (*aguardar*) to lie in wait for; **acecho** *nm*: **estar al acecho (de)** to lie in wait (for)

aceite [a'θeite] *nm* oil; **aceite de girasol/oliva** sunflower/olive oil; **aceitera** *nf* oilcan; **aceitoso, -a** *adj* oily

aceituna [aθei'tuna] *nf* olive; **aceituna rellena**

stuffed olive

acelerador [aθelera'ðor] nm accelerator

acelerar [aθele'rar] vt to accelerate

acelga [a'θelɣa] nf chard, beet

acento [a'θento] nm accent; (acentuación) stress

acentuar [aθen'twar] vt to accent; to stress; (fig) to accentuate

acepción [aθep'θjon] nf meaning

aceptable [aθep'taβle] adj acceptable

aceptación [aθepta'θjon] nf acceptance; (aprobación) approval

aceptar [aθep'tar] vt to accept; (aprobar) to approve; ~ **hacer algo** to agree to do sth

acequia [a'θekja] nf irrigation ditch

acera [a'θera] nf pavement (BRIT), sidewalk (US)

acerca [a'θerka]: ~ **de** prep about, concerning

acercar [aθer'kar] vt to bring o move nearer; **acercarse** vr to approach, come near

acero [a'θero] nm steel

acérrimo, -a [a'θerrimo, a] adj (partidario) staunch; (enemigo) bitter

acertado, -a [aθer'taðo, a] adj correct; (apropiado) apt; (sensato) sensible

acertar [aθer'tar] vt (blanco) to hit; (solución) to get right; (adivinar) to guess ▷ vi to get it right, be right; ~ **a** to manage to; ~ **con** to happen o hit on

acertijo [aθer'tixo] nm riddle, puzzle

achacar [atʃa'kar] vt to attribute

achacoso, -a [atʃa'koso, a] adj sickly

achicar [atʃi'kar] vt to reduce; (Náut) to bale out

achicharrar [atʃitʃa'rrar] vt to scorch, burn

achichincle [atʃi'tʃinkle] (MÉX: fam) nmf minion

achicoria [atʃi'korja] nf chicory

achuras [a'tʃuras] (RPL) nfpl offal sg

acicate [aθi'kate] nm spur

acidez [aθi'ðeθ] nf acidity

ácido, -a ['aθiðo, a] adj sour, acid ▷ nm acid

acierto etc [a'θjerto] vb V **acertar** ▷ nm success; (buen paso) wise move; (solución) solution; (habilidad) skill, ability

acitronar [aθitro'nar] (MÉX: fam) vt to brown

aclamar [akla'mar] vt to acclaim; (aplaudir) to applaud

aclaración [aklara'θjon] nf clarification, explanation

aclarar [akla'rar] vt to clarify, explain; (ropa) to rinse ▷ vi to clear up; **aclararse** vr (explicarse) to understand; ~**se la garganta** to clear one's throat

aclimatación [aklimata'θjon] nf acclimatization

aclimatar [aklima'tar] vt to acclimatize; **aclimatarse** vr to become acclimatized

acné [ak'ne] nm acne

acobardar [akoβar'ðar] vt to intimidate

acogedor, a [akoxe'ðor, a] adj welcoming; (hospitalario) hospitable

acoger [ako'xer] vt to welcome; (abrigar) to shelter

acogida [ako'xiða] nf reception; refuge

acomedido, -a [akome'ðiðo, a] (MÉX) adj helpful, obliging

acometer [akome'ter] vt to attack; (emprender) to undertake; **acometida** nf attack, assault

acomodado, -a [akomo'ðaðo, a] adj (persona) well-to-do

acomodador, a [akomoða'ðor, a] nm/f usher(ette)

acomodar [akomo'ðar] vt to adjust; (alojar) to accommodate; **acomodarse** vr to conform;

(instalarse) to install o.s.; (adaptarse): ~**se (a)** to adapt (to)

acompañar [akompa'ɲar] vt to accompany; (documentos) to enclose

acondicionar [akondiθjo'nar] vt to arrange, prepare; (pelo) to condition

aconsejar [akonse'xar] vt to advise, counsel; ~ **a algn hacer o que haga algo** to advise sb to do sth

acontecer [akonte'θer] vi to happen, occur; **acontecimiento** nm event

acopio [a'kopjo] nm store, stock

acoplar [ako'plar] vt to fit; (Elec) to connect; (vagones) to couple

acorazado, -a [akora'θaðo, a] adj armour-plated, armoured ▷ nm battleship

acordar [akor'ðar] vt (resolver) to agree, resolve; (recordar) to remind; **acordarse** vr to agree; ~ **hacer algo** to agree to do sth; ~**se (de algo)** to remember (sth); **acorde** adj (Mús) harmonious; **acorde con** (medidas etc) in keeping with ▷ nm chord

acordeón [akorðe'on] nm accordion

acordonado, -a [akorðo'naðo, a] adj (calle) cordoned-off

acorralar [akorra'lar] vt to round up, corral

acortar [akor'tar] vt to shorten; (duración) to cut short; (cantidad) to reduce; **acortarse** vr to become shorter

acosar [ako'sar] vt to pursue relentlessly; (fig) to hound, pester; **acoso** nm harassment; **acoso sexual** sexual harassment

acostar [akos'tar] vt (en cama) to put to bed; (en suelo) to lay down; **acostarse** vr to go to bed; to lie down; ~**se con algn** to sleep with sb

acostumbrado, -a [akostum'braðo, a] adj usual; ~ **a** used to

acostumbrar [akostum'brar] vt: ~ **a algn a algo** to get sb used to sth ▷ vi: ~ **(a) hacer** to be in the habit of doing; **acostumbrarse** vr: ~**se a** to get used to

acotación [akota'θjon] nf marginal note; (Geo) elevation mark; (de límite) boundary mark; (Teatro) stage direction

acotamiento [akota'mjento] (MÉX) nm hard shoulder (BRIT), berm (US)

acre ['akre] adj (olor) acrid; (fig) biting ▷ nm acre

acreditar [akreði'tar] vt (garantizar) to vouch for, guarantee; (autorizar) to authorize; (dar prueba de) to prove; (Com: abonar) to credit; (embajador) to accredit

acreedor, a [akree'ðor, a] nm/f creditor

acribillar [akriβi'ʎar] vt: ~ **a balazos** to riddle with bullets

acróbata [a'kroβata] nmf acrobat

acta ['akta] nf certificate; (de comisión) minutes pl, record; **acta de matrimonio/nacimiento** (MÉX) marriage/birth certificate; **acta notarial** affidavit

actitud [akti'tuð] nf attitude; (postura) posture

activar [akti'βar] vt to activate; (acelerar) to speed up

actividad [aktiβi'ðað] nf activity

activo, -a [ak'tiβo, a] adj active; (vivo) lively ▷ nm (Com) assets pl

acto ['akto] nm act, action; (ceremonia) ceremony; (Teatro) act; **en el** ~ immediately

actor [ak'tor] nm actor; (Jur) plaintiff ▷ adj: **parte** ~**a** prosecution

actriz [ak'triθ] nf actress

actuación [aktwa'θjon] nf action; (comportamiento) conduct, behaviour; (Jur) proceedings pl; (desempeño) performance

actual [ak'twal] *adj* present(-day), current

actualidad *nf* present; **actualidades** *nfpl* (*noticias*) news *sg*; **en la actualidad** at present; (*hoy día*) nowadays; **actualizar** [aktwaliˈθar] *vt* to update, modernize; **actualmente** [aktwalˈmente] *adv* at present; (*hoy día*) nowadays

actuar [ak'twar] *vi* (*obrar*) to work, operate; (*actor*) to act, perform ▷ *vt* to work, operate; **~ de** to act as

acuarela [akwaˈrela] *nf* watercolour

acuario [aˈkwarjo] *nm* aquarium; (*Astrología*): **A~** Aquarius

acuático, -a [aˈkwatiko, a] *adj* aquatic

acudir [akuˈðir] *vi* (*asistir*) to attend; (*ir*) to go; **~ a** (*fig*) to turn to; **~ a una cita** to keep an appointment; **~ en ayuda de** to go to the aid of

acuerdo *etc* [aˈkwerðo] *vb* V **acordar** ▷ *nm* agreement; **¡de ~!** agreed!; **de ~ con** (*persona*) in agreement with; (*acción, documento*) in accordance with; **estar de ~** to be agreed, agree

acumular [akumuˈlar] *vt* to accumulate, collect

acuñar [akuˈɲar] *vt* (*moneda*) to mint; (*frase*) to coin

acupuntura [akupunˈtura] *nf* acupuncture

acurrucarse [akurruˈkarse] *vr* to crouch; (*ovillarse*) to curl up

acusación [akusaˈθjon] *nf* accusation

acusar [akuˈsar] *vt* to accuse; (*revelar*) to reveal; (*denunciar*) to denounce

acuse [aˈkuse] *nm*: **~ de recibo** acknowledgement of receipt

acústica [aˈkustika] *nf* acoustics *pl*

acústico, -a [aˈkustiko, a] *adj* acoustic

adaptación [aðaptaˈθjon] *nf* adaptation

adaptador [aðaptaˈðor] *nm* (*Elec*) adapter, adaptor; **adaptador universal** universal adapter *o* adaptor

adaptar [aðapˈtar] *vt* to adapt; (*acomodar*) to fit

adecuado, -a [aðeˈkwaðo, a] *adj* (*apto*) suitable; (*oportuno*) appropriate

a. de J.C. *abr* (= *antes de Jesucristo*) B.C.

adelantado, -a [aðelanˈtaðo, a] *adj* advanced; (*reloj*) fast; **pagar por ~** to pay in advance

adelantamiento [aðelantaˈmjento] *nm* (*Auto*) overtaking

adelantar [aðelanˈtar] *vt* to move forward; (*avanzar*) to advance; (*acelerar*) to speed up; (*Auto*) to overtake ▷ *vi* to go forward, advance; **adelantarse** *vr* to go forward, advance

adelante [aðeˈlante] *adv* forward(s), ahead ▷ *excl* come in!; **de hoy en ~** from now on; **más ~** later on; (*más allá*) further on

adelanto [aðeˈlanto] *nm* advance; (*mejora*) improvement; (*progreso*) progress

adelgazar [aðelɣaˈθar] *vt* to thin (down) ▷ *vi* to get thin; (*con régimen*) to slim down, lose weight

ademán [aðeˈman] *nm* gesture; **ademanes** *nmpl* manners

además [aðeˈmas] *adv* besides; (*por otra parte*) moreover; (*también*) also; **~ de** besides, in addition to

adentrarse [aðenˈtrarse] *vr*: **~ en** to go into, get inside; (*penetrar*) to penetrate (into)

adentro [aˈðentro] *adv* inside, in; **mar ~** out at sea; **tierra ~** inland

adepto, -a [aˈðepto, a] *nm/f* supporter

aderezar [aðereˈθar] *vt* (*ensalada*) to dress; (*comida*) to season; **aderezo** *nm* dressing; seasoning

adeudar [aðeuˈðar] *vt* to owe

adherirse [aðeˈrirse] *vr*: **~ a** to adhere to; (*partido*) to join

adhesión [aðeˈsjon] *nf* adhesion; (*fig*) adherence

adicción [aðikˈθjon] *nf* addiction

adición [aðiˈθjon] *nf* addition

adicto, -a [aˈðikto, a] *adj*: **~ a** addicted to; (*dedicado*) devoted to ▷ *nm/f* supporter, follower; (*toxicómano*) addict

adiestrar [aðjesˈtrar] *vt* to train, teach; (*conducir*) to guide, lead

adinerado, -a [aðineˈraðo, a] *adj* wealthy

adiós [aˈðjos] *excl* (*para despedirse*) goodbye!, cheerio!; (*al pasar*) hello!

aditivo [aðiˈtiβo] *nm* additive

adivinanza [aðiβiˈnanθa] *nf* riddle

adivinar [aðiβiˈnar] *vt* to prophesy; (*conjeturar*) to guess; **adivino, -a** *nm/f* fortune-teller

adj *abr* (= *adjetivo*) encl

adjetivo [aðxeˈtiβo] *nm* adjective

adjudicar [aðxuðiˈkar] *vt* to award; **adjudicarse** *vr*: **~se algo** to appropriate sth

adjuntar [aðxunˈtar] *vt* to attach, enclose; **adjunto, -a** *adj* attached, enclosed ▷ *nm/f* assistant

administración [aðministraˈθjon] *nf* administration; (*dirección*) management; **administrador, a** *nm/f* administrator, manager(ess)

administrar [aðminisˈtrar] *vt* to administer; **administrativo, -a** *adj* administrative

admirable [aðmiˈraβle] *adj* admirable

admiración [aðmiraˈθjon] *nf* admiration; (*asombro*) wonder; (*Ling*) exclamation mark

admirar [aðmiˈrar] *vt* to admire; (*extrañar*) to surprise

admisible [aðmiˈsiβle] *adj* admissible

admisión [aðmiˈsjon] *nf* admission; (*reconocimiento*) acceptance

admitir [aðmiˈtir] *vt* to admit; (*aceptar*) to accept

adobar [aðoˈβar] *vt* (*Culin*) to season

adobe [aˈðoβe] *nm* adobe, sun-dried brick

adolecer [aðoleˈθer] *vi*: **~ de** to suffer from

adolescente [aðolesˈθente] *nmf* adolescent, teenager

adonde [aˈðonde] *conj* (to) where

adónde [aˈðonde] *adv* = **dónde**

adopción [aðopˈθjon] *nf* adoption

adoptar [aðopˈtar] *vt* to adopt

adoptivo, -a [aðopˈtiβo, a] *adj* (*padres*) adoptive; (*hijo*) adopted

adoquín [aðoˈkin] *nm* paving stone

adorar [aðoˈrar] *vt* to adore

adornar [aðorˈnar] *vt* to adorn

adorno [aˈðorno] *nm* ornament; (*decoración*) decoration

adosado, -a [aðoˈsaðo, a] *adj*: **casa adosada** semi-detached house

adosar [aðoˈsar] *vt* (*MÉX*) (*adjuntar*) to attach, enclose (*with a letter*)

adquiero *etc* *vb* V **adquirir**

adquirir [aðkiˈrir] *vt* to acquire, obtain

adquisición [aðkisiˈθjon] *nf* acquisition

adrede [aˈðreðe] *adv* on purpose

ADSL *nm abr* broadband

aduana [aˈðwana] *nf* customs *pl*

aduanero, -a [aðwaˈnero, a] *adj* customs *cpd* ▷ *nm/f* customs officer

adueñarse [aðweˈɲarse] *vr*: **~ de** to take possession of

adular [aðu'lar] vt to flatter

adulterar [aðulte'rar] vt to adulterate

adulterio [aðul'terjo] nm adultery

adúltero, -a [a'ðultero, a] adj adulterous ▷ nm/f adulterer/adulteress

adulto, -a [a'ðulto, a] adj, nm/f adult

adverbio [að'βerβjo] nm adverb

adversario, -a [aðβer'sarjo, a] nm/f adversary

adversidad [aðβersi'ðað] nf adversity; (contratiempo) setback

adverso, -a [að'βerso, a] adj adverse

advertencia [aðβer'tenθja] nf warning; (prefacio) preface, foreword

advertir [aðβer'tir] vt to notice; (avisar): ~ a algn de to warn sb about o of

Adviento [að'βjento] nm Advent

advierto etc vb V **advertir**

aéreo, -a [a'ereo, a] adj aerial

aerobic [ae'roβik] nm aerobics sg; **aerobics** (MÉX) nmpl aerobics sg

aeromozo, -a [aero'moθo, a] (LAM) nm/f air steward(ess)

aeronáutica [aero'nautika] nf aeronautics sg

aeronave [aero'naβe] nm spaceship

aeroplano [aero'plano] nm aeroplane

aeropuerto [aero'pwerto] nm airport

aerosol [aero'sol] nm aerosol

afamado, -a [afa'maðo, a] adj famous

afán [a'fan] nm hard work; (deseo) desire

afanador, a [afana'ðor, a] (MÉX) nm/f (de limpieza) cleaner

afanar [afa'nar] vt to harass; (fam) to pinch

afear [afe'ar] vt to disfigure

afección [afek'θjon] nf (Med) disease

afectado, -a [afek'taðo, a] adj affected

afectar [afek'tar] vt to affect

afectísimo, -a [afek'tisimo, a] adj affectionate; **suyo ~** yours truly

afectivo, -a [afek'tiβo, a] adj (problema etc) emotional

afecto [a'fekto] nm affection; **tenerle ~ a algn** to be fond of sb

afectuoso, -a [afek'twoso, a] adj affectionate

afeitar [afei'tar] vt to shave; **afeitarse** vr to shave

afeminado, -a [afemi'naðo, a] adj effeminate

Afganistán [afvanis'tan] nm Afghanistan

afianzar [afjan'θar] vt to strengthen; to secure; **afianzarse** vr to become established

afiche [a'fitʃe] (RPL) nm poster

afición [afi'θjon] nf fondness, liking; **la ~** the fans pl; **pinto por ~** I paint as a hobby; **aficionado, -a** adj keen, enthusiastic; (no profesional) amateur ▷ nm/f enthusiast, fan; amateur; **ser aficionado a algo** to be very keen o fond of sth

aficionar [afiθjo'nar] vt: **~ a algn a algo** to make sb like sth; **aficionarse** vr: **~se a algo** to grow fond of sth

afilado, -a [afi'laðo, a] adj sharp

afilar [afi'lar] vt to sharpen

afiliarse [afi'ljarse] vr to affiliate

afín [a'fin] adj (parecido) similar; (conexo) related

afinar [afi'nar] vt (Tec) to refine; (Mús) to tune ▷ vi (tocar) to play in tune; (cantar) to sing in tune

afincarse [afin'karse] vr to settle

afinidad [afini'ðað] nf affinity; (parentesco) relationship; **por ~** by marriage

afirmación [afirma'θjon] nf affirmation

afirmar [afir'mar] vt to affirm, state; **afirmativo, -a** adj affirmative

afligir [afli'xir] vt to afflict; (apenar) to distress

aflojar [aflo'xar] vt to slacken; (desatar) to loosen, undo; (relajar) to relax ▷ vi to drop; (bajar) to go down; **aflojarse** vr to relax

afluente [aflu'ente] adj flowing ▷ nm tributary

afmo,-a abr (= afectísimo(a) suyo(a)) Yours

afónico, -a [a'foniko, a] adj: **estar ~** to have a sore throat; to have lost one's voice

aforo [a'foro] nm (de teatro etc) capacity

afortunado, -a [afortu'naðo, a] adj fortunate, lucky

África ['afrika] nf Africa; **África del Sur** South Africa; **africano, -a** adj, nm/f African

afrontar [afron'tar] vt to confront; (poner cara a cara) to bring face to face

afrutado, -a [afru'taðo, a] adj fruity

after ['after] (pl ~s) nm after-hours club; **afterhours** [after'aurs] nm inv = **after**

afuera [a'fwera] adv out, outside; **afueras** nfpl outskirts

agachar [aɣa'tʃar] vt to bend, bow; **agacharse** vr to stoop, bend

agalla [a'ɣaʎa] nf (Zool) gill; **tener ~s** (fam) to have guts

agarradera [aɣarra'ðera] (MÉX) nf handle

agarrado, -a [aɣa'rraðo, a] adj mean, stingy

agarrar [aɣa'rrar] vt to grasp, grab; (LAM: tomar) to take, catch; (recoger) to pick up ▷ vi (planta) to take root; **agarrarse** vr to hold on (tightly)

agencia [a'xenθja] nf agency; **agencia de viajes** travel agency; **agencia inmobiliaria** estate (BRIT) o real estate (US) agent's (office)

agenciarse [axen'θjarse] vr to obtain, procure

agenda [a'xenda] nf diary; **~ electronica** PDA

agente [a'xente] nmf agent; (tb: **~ de policía**) policeman/policewoman; **agente de seguros** insurance agent; **agente de tránsito** (MÉX) traffic cop; **agente inmobiliario** estate agent (BRIT), realtor (US)

ágil ['axil] adj agile, nimble; **agilidad** nf agility, nimbleness

agilizar [axili'θar] vt (trámites) to speed up

agiotista [axjo'tista] (MÉX) nmf (usurero) usurer

agitación [axita'θjon] nf (de mano etc) shaking, waving; (de líquido etc) stirring; (fig) agitation

agitado, -a [axi'aðo, a] adj hectic; (viaje) bumpy

agitar [axi'tar] vt to wave, shake; (líquido) to stir; (fig) to stir up, excite; **agitarse** vr to get excited; (inquietarse) to get worried o upset

aglomeración [aɣlomera'θjon] nf agglomeration; **aglomeración de gente/tráfico** mass of people/ traffic jam

agnóstico, -a [aɣ'nostiko, a] adj, nm/f agnostic

agobiar [aɣo'βjar] vt to weigh down; (oprimir) to oppress; (cargar) to burden

agolparse [aɣol'parse] vr to crowd together

agonía [aɣo'nia] nf death throes pl; (fig) agony, anguish

agonizante [aɣoni'θante] adj dying

agonizar [aɣoni'θar] vi to be dying

agosto [a'ɣosto] nm August

agotado, -a [aɣo'taðo, a] adj (persona) exhausted; (libros) out of print; (acabado) finished; (Com) sold out; **agotador, a** [aɣota'ðor, a] adj exhausting

agotamiento [axota'mjento] nm exhaustion

agotar [axo'tar] vt to exhaust; (consumir) to drain; (recursos) to use up, deplete; **agotarse** vr to be exhausted; (acabarse) to run out; (libro) to go out of print

agraciado, -a [axra'θjaðo, a] adj (atractivo) attractive; (en sorteo etc) lucky

agradable [axra'ðaβle] adj pleasant, nice

agradar [axra'ðar] vt: **él me agrada** I like him

agradecer [axraðe'θer] vt to thank; (favor etc) to be grateful for; **agradecido, -a** adj grateful; **¡muy agradecido!** thanks a lot!; **agradecimiento** nm thanks pl; gratitude

agradezco etc vb V **agradecer**

agrado [a'xraðo] nm: **ser de tu etc ~** to be to your etc liking

agrandar [axran'dar] vt to enlarge; (fig) to exaggerate; **agrandarse** vr to get bigger

agrario, -a [a'xrarjo, a] adj agrarian, land cpd; (política) agricultural, farming

agravante [axra'βante] adj aggravating ▷ nm: **con el ~ de que ...** with the further difficulty that ...

agravar [axra'βar] vt (pesar sobre) to make heavier; (irritar) to aggravate; **agravarse** vr to worsen, get worse

agraviar [axra'βjar] vt to offend; (ser injusto con) to wrong

agredir [axre'ðir] vt to attack

agregado, -a [axre'xaðo, a] nm/f: **A~ =** teacher (who is not head of department) ▷ nm aggregate; (persona) attaché

agregar [axre'xar] vt to gather; (añadir) to add; (persona) to appoint

agresión [axre'sjon] nf aggression

agresivo, -a [axre'siβo, a] adj aggressive

agriar [a'xrjar] vt (o turn) sour

agrícola [a'xrikola] adj farming cpd, agricultural

agricultor, a [axrikul'tor, a] nm/f farmer

agricultura [axrikul'tura] nf agriculture, farming

agridulce [axri'ðulθe] adj bittersweet; (Culin) sweet and sour

agrietarse [axrje'tarse] vr to crack; (piel) to chap

agrio, -a [a'xrjo, a] adj bitter

agrupación [axrupa'θjon] nf group; (acto) grouping

agrupar [axru'par] vt to group

agua ['axwa] nf water; (Náut) wake; (Arq) slope of a roof; **aguas** nfpl (de piedra) water sg, sparkle sg; (Med) water sg, urine sg; (Náut) waters; **agua bendita/ destilada/potable** holy/distilled/drinking water; **agua caliente** hot water; **agua corriente** running water; **agua de colonia** eau de cologne; **agua mineral (con/sin gas)** (sparkling/still) mineral water; **agua oxigenada** hydrogen peroxide; **aguas abajo/arriba** downstream/upstream; **aguas jurisdiccionales** territorial waters

aguacate [axwa'kate] nm avocado (pear)

aguacero [axwa'θero] nm (heavy) shower, downpour

aguado, -a [a'xwaðo, a] adj watery, watered down

aguafiestas [axwa'fjestas] nmf inv spoilsport, killjoy

aguamiel [axwa'mjel] (MÉX) nf fermented maguey o agave juice

aguanieve [axwa'njeβe] nf sleet

aguantar [axwan'tar] vt to bear, put up with; (sostener) to hold up ▷ vi to last; **aguantarse** vr to restrain o.s.; **aguante** nm (paciencia) patience; (resistencia) endurance

aguar [a'xwar] vt to water down

aguardar [axwar'ðar] vt to wait for

aguardiente [axwar'ðjente] nm brandy, liquor

aguarrás [axwa'rras] nm turpentine

aguaviva [axwa'βiβa] (RPL) nf jellyfish

agudeza [axu'ðeθa] nf sharpness; (ingenio) wit

agudo, -a [a'xuðo, a] adj sharp; (voz) high-pitched, piercing; (dolor, enfermedad) acute

agüero [a'xwero] nm: **buen/mal ~** good/bad omen

aguijón [axi'xon] nm sting; (fig) spur

águila ['axila] nf eagle; (fig) genius

aguileño, -a [axi'leɲo, a] adj (nariz) aquiline; (rostro) sharp-featured

aguinaldo [axi'naldo] nm Christmas box

aguja [a'xuxa] nf needle; (de reloj) hand; (Arq) spire; (Tec) firing-pin; **agujas** nfpl (Zool) ribs; (Ferro) points

agujerear [axuxere'ar] vt to make holes in

agujero [axu'xero] nm hole

agujetas [axu'xetas] nfpl stitch sg; (rigidez) stiffness sg

ahí [a'i] adv there; **de ~ que** so that, with the result that; **~ llega** here he comes; **por ~** that way; (allá) over there; **200 o por ~** 200 or so

ahijado, -a [ai'xaðo, a] nm/f godson/daughter

ahogar [ao'xar] vt to drown; (asfixiar) to suffocate, smother; (fuego) to put out; **ahogarse** vr (en el agua) to drown; (por asfixia) to suffocate

ahogo [a'oxo] nm breathlessness; (fig) financial difficulty

ahondar [aon'dar] vt to deepen, make deeper; (fig) to study thoroughly ▷ vi: **~ en** to study thoroughly

ahora [a'ora] adv now; (hace poco) a moment ago, just now; (dentro de poco) in a moment; **~ voy** I'm coming; **~ mismo** right now; **~ bien** now then; **por ~** for the present

ahorcar [aor'kar] vt to hang

ahorita [ao'rita] (fam) adv (LAM: en este momento) right now; (MÉX: hace poco) just now; (: dentro de poco) in a minute

ahorrar [ao'rrar] vt (dinero) to save; (esfuerzos) to save, avoid; **ahorro** nm (acto) saving; **ahorros** nmpl (dinero) savings

ahuecar [awe'kar] vt to hollow (out); (voz) to deepen; **ahuecarse** vr to give o.s. airs

ahumar [au'mar] vt to smoke, cure; (llenar de humo) to fill with smoke ▷ vi to smoke; **ahumarse** vr to fill with smoke

ahuyentar [aujen'tar] vt to drive off, frighten off; (fig) to dispel

aire ['aire] nm air; (viento) wind; (corriente) draught; (Mús) tune; **al ~ libre** in the open air; **aire acondicionado** air conditioning; **airear** vt to air; **airearse** vr (persona) to go out for a breath of fresh air; **airoso, -a** adj windy; draughty; (fig) graceful

aislado, -a [ais'laðo, a] adj isolated; (incomunicado) cut-off; (Elec) insulated

aislar [ais'lar] vt to isolate; (Elec) to insulate

ajardinado, -a [axarði'naðo, a] adj landscaped

ajedrez [axe'ðreθ] nm chess

ajeno, -a [a'xeno, a] adj (que pertenece a otro) somebody else's; **~ a** foreign to

ajetreado, -a [axetre'aðo, a] adj busy

ajetreo [axe'treo] nm bustle

ají [a'xi] (cs) nm chil(l)i, red pepper; (salsa) chil(l)i sauce

ajillo [a'xiʎo] nm: **gambas al ~** garlic prawns

ajo ['axo] nm garlic

ajuar [a'xwar] nm household furnishings pl; (de novia) trousseau; (de niño) layette

ajustado, -a [axus'taðo, a] adj (tornillo) tight; (cálculo) right; (ropa) tight(-fitting); (resultado) close

ajustar [axus'tar] vt (adaptar) to adjust; (encajar) to fit; (Tec) to engage; (Imprenta) to make up; (apretar) to tighten; (concertar) to agree (on); (reconciliar) to reconcile; (cuentas, deudas) to settle ▷ vi to fit; **ajustarse** vr: **~se a** (precio etc) to be in keeping with, fit in with; **~ las cuentas a algn** to get even with sb

ajuste [a'xuste] nm adjustment; (Costura) fitting; (acuerdo) compromise; (de cuenta) settlement

al [al] = **a + el; V a**

ala ['ala] nf wing; (de sombrero) brim; winger; **ala delta** nf hang-glider

alabanza [ala'βanθa] nf praise

alabar [ala'βar] vt to praise

alacena [ala'θena] nf kitchen cupboard (BRIT) o closet (US)

alacrán [ala'kran] nm scorpion

alambrada [alam'braða] nf wire fence; (red) wire netting

alambre [a'lambre] nm wire; **alambre de púas** barbed wire

alameda [ala'meða] nf (plantío) poplar grove; (lugar de paseo) avenue, boulevard

álamo ['alamo] nm poplar

alarde [a'larðe] nm show, display; **hacer ~ de** to boast of

alargador [alarxa'ðor] nm (Elec) extension lead

alargar [alar'xar] vt to lengthen, extend; (paso) to hasten; (brazo) to stretch out; (cuerda) to pay out; (conversación) to spin out; **alargarse** vr to get longer

alarma [a'larma] nf alarm; **alarma de incendios** fire alarm; **alarmar** vt to alarm; **alarmarse** vr to get alarmed; **alarmante** [alar'mante] adj alarming

alba ['alβa] nf dawn

albahaca [alβa'aka] nf basil

Albania [al'βanja] nf Albania

albañil [alβa'ɲil] nm bricklayer; (cantero) mason

albarán [alβa'ran] nm (Com) delivery note, invoice

albaricoque [alβari'koke] nm apricot

albedrío [alβe'ðrio] nm: **libre ~** free will

alberca [al'βerka] nf reservoir; (MÉX: piscina) swimming pool

albergar [alβer'xar] vt to shelter

albergue etc [al'βerxe] vb V **albergar** ▷ nm shelter, refuge; **albergue juvenil** youth hostel

albóndiga [al'βondixa] nf meatball

albornoz [alβor'noθ] nm (de los árabes) burnous; (para el baño) bathrobe

alborotar [alβoro'tar] vi to make a row ▷ vt to agitate, stir up; **alborotarse** vr to get excited; (mar) to get rough; **alboroto** nm row, uproar

álbum ['alβum] (pl **~s, ~es**) nm album; **álbum de recortes** scrapbook

albur [al'βur] (MÉX) nm (juego de palabras) pun; (doble sentido) double entendre

alcachofa [alka'tʃofa] nf artichoke

alcalde, -esa [al'kalde, esa] nm/f mayor(ess)

alcaldía [alkal'dia] nf mayoralty; (lugar) mayor's office

alcance etc [al'kanθe] vb V **alcanzar** ▷ nm reach;

(Com) adverse balance; **al ~ de algn** available to sb

alcancía [alkan'θia] (LAM) nf (para ahorrar) money box; (para colectas) collection box

alcantarilla [alkanta'riʎa] nf (de aguas cloacales) sewer; (en la calle) gutter

alcanzar [alkan'θar] vt (algo: con la mano, el pie) to reach; (alcanzarle: en el camino etc) to catch up (with); (autobús) to catch; (bala) to hit, strike ▷ vi (ser suficiente) to be enough; **~ a hacer** to manage to do

alcaparra [alka'parra] nf caper

alcayata [alka'jata] nf hook

alcázar [al'kaθar] nm fortress; (Náut) quarter-deck

alcoba [al'koβa] nf bedroom

alcohol [al'kol] nm alcohol; **alcohol metílico** methylated spirits pl (BRIT), wood alcohol (US); **alcohólico, a** adj, nm/f alcoholic; **alcoholímetro** [alko'limetro] nm Breathalyser® (BRIT), drunkometer (US); **alcoholismo** [alko'lismo] nm alcoholism

alcornoque [alkor'noke] nm cork tree; (fam) idiot

aldea [al'dea] nf village; **aldeano, -a** adj village cpd ▷ nm/f villager

aleación [alea'θjon] nf alloy

aleatorio, -a [alea'torjo, a] adj random

aleccionar [alekθjo'nar] vt to instruct; (adiestrar) to train

alegar [ale'xar] vt to claim; (Jur) to plead ▷ vi (LAM: discutir) to argue

alegoría [alexo'ria] nf allegory

alegrar [ale'xrar] vt (causar alegría) to cheer (up); (fuego) to poke; (fiesta) to liven up; **alegrarse** vr (fam) to get merry o tight; **~se de** to be glad about

alegre [a'lexre] adj happy, cheerful; (fam) merry, tight; (chiste) risqué, blue; **alegría** nf happiness; merriment

alejar [ale'xar] vt to remove; (fig) to estrange; **alejarse** vr to move away

alemán, -ana [ale'man, ana] adj, nm/f German ▷ nm (Ling) German

Alemania [ale'manja] nf Germany

alentador, a [alenta'ðor, a] adj encouraging

alentar [alen'tar] vt to encourage

alergia [a'lerxja] nf allergy

alero [a'lero] nm (de tejado) eaves pl; (guardabarros) mudguard

alerta [a'lerta] adj, nm alert

aleta [a'leta] nf (de pez) fin; (ala) wing; (de foca, Deporte) flipper; (Auto) mudguard

aletear [alete'ar] vi to flutter

alevín [ale'βin] nm fry, young fish

alevosía [aleβo'sia] nf treachery

alfabeto [alfa'βeto] nm alphabet

alfalfa [al'falfa] nf alfalfa, lucerne

alfarería [alfare'ria] nf pottery; (tienda) pottery shop; **alfarero, -a** nm/f potter

alféizar [al'feiθar] nm window-sill

alférez [al'fereθ] nm (Mil) second lieutenant; (Náut) ensign

alfil [al'fil] nm (Ajedrez) bishop

alfiler [alfi'ler] nm pin; (broche) clip

alfombra [al'fombra] nf carpet; (más pequeña) rug; **alfombrilla** nf rug, mat; (Inform) mouse mat o pad

alforja [al'forxa] nf saddlebag

algas ['alxas] nfpl seaweed

álgebra ['alxeβra] nf algebra

algo ['alxo] pron something; anything ▷ adv somewhat, rather; **¿~ más?** anything else?; (en tienda) is that all?; **por ~ será** there must be some reason for it

algodón [alɣo'ðon] nm cotton; (planta) cotton plant; **algodón de azúcar** candy floss (BRIT), cotton candy (US); **algodón hidrófilo** cotton wool (BRIT), absorbent cotton (US)

alguien ['alɣjen] pron someone, somebody; (en frases interrogativas) anyone, anybody

alguno, -a [al'ɣuno, a] adj (delante de nm): **algún** some; (después de n): **no tiene talento ~** he has no talent, he doesn't have any talent ▷ pron (alguien) someone, somebody; **algún que otro libro** some book or other; **algún día iré** I'll go one o some day; **sin interés** without the slightest interest; **~ que otro** an occasional one; **~s piensan** some (people) think

alhaja [a'laxa] nf jewel; (tesoro) precious object, treasure

alhelí [ale'li] nm wallflower, stock

aliado, -a [a'ljaðo, a] adj allied

alianza [a'ljanθa] nf alliance; (anillo) wedding ring

aliar [a'ljar] vt to ally; **aliarse** vr to form an alliance

alias ['aljas] adv alias

alicatado [alika'taðo] nm tiling

alicates [ali'kates] nmpl pliers

aliciente [ali'θjente] nm incentive; (atracción) attraction

alienación [aljena'θjon] nf alienation

aliento [a'ljento] nm breath; (respiración) breathing; **sin ~** breathless

aligerar [alixe'rar] vt to lighten; (reducir) to shorten; (aliviar) to alleviate; (mitigar) to ease; (paso) to quicken

alijo [a'lixo] nm consignment

alimaña [ali'maɲa] nf pest

alimentación [alimenta'θjon] nf (comida) food; (acción) feeding; (tienda) grocer's (shop)

alimentar [alimen'tar] vt to feed; (nutrir) to nourish; **alimentarse** vr to feed

alimenticio, -a [alimen'tiθjo, a] adj food cpd; (nutritivo) nourishing, nutritious

alimento [ali'mento] nm food; (nutrición) nourishment

alineación [alinea'θjon] nf alignment; (Deporte) line-up

alinear [aline'ar] vt to align; (Deporte) to select, pick

aliñar [ali'ɲar] vt (Culin) to season; **aliño** nm (Culin) dressing

alioli [ali'oli] nm garlic mayonnaise

alisar [ali'sar] vt to smooth

alistarse [alis'tarse] vr to enlist; (inscribirse) to enrol

aliviar [ali'βjar] vt (carga) to lighten; (persona) to relieve; (dolor) to relieve, alleviate

alivio [a'liβjo] nm alleviation, relief

aljibe [al'xiβe] nm cistern

allá [a'ʎa] adv (lugar) there; (por ahí) over there; (tiempo) then; **~ abajo** down there; **más ~** further on; **más ~ de** beyond; **¡~ tú!** that's your problem!; **¡~ voy!** I'm coming!

allanamiento [aʎana'mjento] nm (LAM: de policía) raid; **allanamiento de morada** burglary

allanar [aʎa'nar] vt to flatten, level (out); (igualar) to smooth (out); (fig) to subdue; (jur) to burgle, break into

allegado, -a [aʎe'ɣaðo, a] adj near, close ▷ nm/f relation

allí [a'ʎi] adv there; **~ mismo** right there; **por ~** over there; (por ese camino) that way

alma ['alma] nf soul; (persona) person

almacén [alma'θen] nm (depósito) warehouse,

store; (Mil) magazine; (cs: de comestibles) grocer's (shop); **grandes almacenes** department store sg; **almacenaje** nm storage

almacenar [almaθe'nar] vt to store, put in storage; (proveerse) to stock up with

almanaque [alma'nake] nm almanac

almeja [al'mexa] nf clam

almendra [al'mendra] nf almond; **almendro** nm almond tree

almíbar [al'miβar] nm syrup

almidón [almi'ðon] nm starch

almirante [almi'rante] nm admiral

almohada [almo'aða] nf pillow; (funda) pillowcase; **almohadilla** nf cushion; (para alfileres) pincushion; (Tec) pad

almohadón [almoa'ðon] nm large pillow; bolster

almorranas [almo'rranas] nfpl piles, haemorrhoids

almorzar [almor'θar] vt: **~ una tortilla** to have an omelette for lunch ▷ vi to (have) lunch

almuerzo etc [al'mwerθo] vb V **almorzar** ▷ nm lunch

alocado, -a [alo'kaðo, a] adj crazy

alojamiento [aloxa'mjento] nm lodging(s) pl; (viviendas) housing

alojar [alo'xar] vt to lodge; **alojarse** vr to lodge, stay

alondra [a'londra] nf lark, skylark

alpargata [alpar'ɣata] nf rope-soled sandal, espadrille

Alpes ['alpes] nmpl: **los ~** the Alps

alpinismo [alpi'nismo] nm mountaineering, climbing; **alpinista** nmf mountaineer, climber

alpiste [al'piste] nm birdseed

alquilar [alki'lar] vt (propietario: inmuebles) to let, rent (out); (: coche) to hire out; (: TV) to rent (out); (alquilador: inmuebles, TV) to rent; (: coche) to hire; **"se alquila casa"** "house to let (BRIT) o for rent (US)"

alquiler [alki'ler] nm renting; letting; hiring; (arriendo) rent, hire charge; **de ~** for hire; **alquiler de automóviles o coches** car hire

alquimia [al'kimja] nf alchemy

alquitrán [alki'tran] nm tar

alrededor [alreðe'ðor] adv around, about; **~ de** around, about; **mirar a su ~** to look (round) about one; **alrededores** nmpl surroundings

alta ['alta] nf (certificate of) discharge

altar [al'tar] nm altar

altavoz [alta'βoθ] nm loudspeaker; (amplificador) amplifier

alteración [altera'θjon] nf alteration; (alboroto) disturbance

alterar [alte'rar] vt to alter; to disturb; **alterarse** vr (persona) to get upset

altercado [alter'kaðo] nm argument

alternar [alter'nar] vt to alternate ▷ vi to alternate; (turnar) to take turns; **alternarse** vr to alternate; to take turns; **~ con** to mix with; **alternativa** nf alternative; (elección) choice; **alternativo, -a** adj alternative; (alterno) alternating; **alterno, -a** adj alternate; (Elec) alternating

Alteza [al'teθa] nf (tratamiento) Highness

altibajos [alti'βaxos] nmpl ups and downs

altiplano [alti'plano] nm = **altiplanicie**

altisonante [altiso'nante] adj high-flown, high-sounding

altitud [alti'tuð] nf height; (Aviac, Geo) altitude

altivo, -a [al'tiβo, a] adj haughty, arrogant

alto, -a ['alto, a] *adj* high; *(persona)* tall; *(sonido)* high, sharp; *(noble)* high, lofty ▷ *nm* halt; *(Mús)* alto; *(Geo)* hill ▷ *adv (de sitio)* high; *(de sonido)* loud, loudly ▷ *excl* halt!; **la pared tiene 2 metros de ~** the wall is 2 metres high; **en alta mar** on the high seas; **en voz alta** in a loud voice; **las altas horas de la noche** the small owee hours; **en lo ~ de** at the top of; **pasar por ~** to overlook; **altoparlante** [altopar'lante] *(LAM) nm* loudspeaker
altura [al'tura] *nf* height; *(Náut)* depth; *(Geo)* latitude; **la pared tiene 1.80 de ~** the wall is 1 metre 80cm high; **a estas ~s** at this stage; **a estas ~s del año** at this time of the year
alubia [a'luβja] *nf* bean
alucinación [aluθinaˈθjon] *nf* hallucination
alucinar [aluθi'nar] *vi* to hallucinate ▷ *vt* to deceive; *(fascinar)* to fascinate
alud [a'luð] *nm* avalanche; *(fig)* flood
aludir [alu'ðir] *vi*: **~ a** to allude to; **darse por aludido** to take the hint
alumbrado [alum'braðo] *nm* lighting
alumbrar [alum'brar] *vt* to light (up) ▷ *vi (Med)* to give birth
aluminio [alu'minjo] *nm* aluminium *(BRIT)*, aluminum *(US)*
alumno, -a [a'lumno, a] *nm/f* pupil, student
alusión [alu'sjon] *nf* allusion
alusivo, -a [alu'siβo, a] *adj* allusive
aluvión [aluˈβjon] *nm* alluvium; *(fig)* flood
alverja [al'βerxa] *(LAM) nf* pea
alza ['alθa] *nf* rise; *(Mil)* sight
alzamiento [alθa'mjento] *nm (rebelión)* rising
alzar [al'θar] *vt* to lift (up); *(precio, muro)* to raise; *(cuello de abrigo)* to turn up; *(Agr)* to gather in; *(Imprenta)* to gather; **alzarse** *vr* to get up, rise; *(rebelarse)* to revolt; *(Com)* to go fraudulently bankrupt; *(Jur)* to appeal
ama ['ama] *nf* lady of the house; *(dueña)* owner; *(institutriz)* governess; *(madre adoptiva)* foster mother; **ama de casa** housewife; **ama de llaves** housekeeper
amabilidad [amaβili'ðað] *nf* kindness; *(simpatía)* niceness; **amable** *adj* kind; nice; **es usted muy amable** that's very kind of you
amaestrado, -a [amaes'traðo, a] *adj (animal: en circo etc)* performing
amaestrar [amaes'trar] *vt* to train
amago [a'maxo] *nm* threat; *(gesto)* threatening gesture; *(Med)* symptom
amainar [amai'nar] *vi (viento)* to die down
amamantar [amaman'tar] *vt* to suckle, nurse
amanecer [amane'θer] *vi* to dawn ▷ *nm* dawn; **~ afiebrado** to wake up with a fever
amanerado, -a [amane'raðo, a] *adj* affected
amante [a'mante] *adj*: **~ de** fond of ▷ *nmf* lover
amapola [ama'pola] *nf* poppy
amar [a'mar] *vt* to love
amargado, -a [amar'xaðo, a] *adj* bitter
amargar [amar'xar] *vt* to make bitter; *(fig)* to embitter; **amargarse** *vr* to become embittered
amargo, -a [a'maryo, a] *adj* bitter
amarillento, -a [amari'λento, a] *adj* yellowish; *(tez)* sallow; **amarillo, -a** *adj, nm* yellow
amarrado, -a [ama'rraðo, a] *(MÉX: fam) adj* mean, stingy
amarrar [ama'rrar] *vt* to moor; *(sujetar)* to tie up
amarras [a'marras] *nfpl*: **soltar ~** to set sail
amasar [ama'sar] *vt (masa)* to knead; *(mezclar)* to

mix, prepare; *(confeccionar)* to concoct
amateur [ama'ter] *nmf* amateur
amazona [ama'θona] *nf* horsewoman; **Amazonas** *nm*: **el Amazonas** the Amazon
ámbar ['ambar] *nm* amber
ambición [ambi'θjon] *nf* ambition; **ambicionar** *vt* to aspire to; **ambicioso, -a** *adj* ambitious
ambidextro, -a [ambi'ðekstro, a] *adj* ambidextrous
ambientación [ambjenta'θjon] *nf (Cine, Teatro etc)* setting; *(Radio)* sound effects
ambiente [am'bjente] *nm* atmosphere; *(medio)* environment
ambigüedad [ambixwe'ðað] *nf* ambiguity; **ambiguo, -a** *adj* ambiguous
ámbito ['ambito] *nm (rampo)* field; *(fig)* scope
ambos, -as ['ambos, as] *adj pl, pron pl* both
ambulancia [ambu'lanθja] *nf* ambulance
ambulante [ambu'lante] *adj* travelling *cpd*, itinerant
ambulatorio [ambula'torio] *nm* state health-service clinic
amén [a'men] *excl* amen; **~ de** besides
amenaza [ame'naθa] *nf* threat; **amenazar** [amena'θar] *vt* to threaten ▷ *vi*: **amenazar con hacer** to threaten to do
ameno, -a [a'meno, a] *adj* pleasant
América [a'merika] *nf* America; **América Central/Latina** Central/Latin America; **América del Norte/del Sur** North/South America; **americana** *nf* coat, jacket; *V tb* **americano; americano, -a** *adj, nm/f* American
ametralladora [ametraʎa'ðora] *nf* machine gun
amigable [ami'xaβle] *adj* friendly
amígdala [a'mixðala] *nf* tonsil; **amigdalitis** *nf* tonsillitis
amigo, -a [a'mixo, a] *adj* friendly ▷ *nm/f* friend; *(amante)* lover; **ser ~ de algo** to be fond of sth; **ser muy ~s** to be close friends
aminorar [amino'rar] *vt* to diminish; *(reducir)* to reduce; **~ la marcha** to slow down
amistad [amis'tað] *nf* friendship; **amistades** *nfpl (amigos)* friends; **amistoso, -a** *adj* friendly
amnesia [am'nesja] *nf* amnesia
amnistía [amnis'tia] *nf* amnesty
amo ['amo] *nm* owner; *(jefe)* boss
amolar [amo'lar] *(MÉX: fam) vt* to ruin, damage
amoldar [amol'dar] *vt* to mould; *(adaptar)* to adapt
amonestación [amonesta'θjon] *nf* warning; **amonestaciones** *nfpl (Rel)* marriage banns
amonestar [amones'tar] *vt* to warn; *(Rel)* to publish the banns of
amontonar [amonto'nar] *vt* to collect, pile up; **amontonarse** *vr* to crowd together; *(acumularse)* to pile up
amor [a'mor] *nm* love; *(amante)* lover; **hacer el ~** to make love; **amor propio** self-respect
amoratado, -a [amora'taðo, a] *adj* purple
amordazar [amorða'θar] *vt* to muzzle; *(fig)* to gag
amorfo, -a [a'morfo, a] *adj* amorphous, shapeless
amoroso, -a [amo'roso, a] *adj* affectionate, loving
amortiguador [amortigwa'ðor] *nm* shock absorber; *(parachoques)* bumper; **amortiguadores** *nmpl (Auto)* suspension *sg*
amortiguar [amorti'ywar] *vt* to deaden; *(ruido)* to muffle; *(color)* to soften
amotinar [amoti'nar] *vt* to stir up, incite (to riot);

amotinarse *vr* to mutiny

amparar [ampa'rar] *vt* to protect; **ampararse** *vr* to seek protection; *(de la lluvia etc)* to shelter; **amparo** *nm* help, protection; **al amparo de** under the protection of

amperio [am'perjo] *nm* ampère, amp

ampliación [amplja'θjon] *nf* enlargement; *(extensión)* extension

ampliar [am'pljar] *vt* to enlarge; to extend

amplificador [amplifika'ðor] *nm* amplifier

amplificar [amplifi'kar] *vt* to amplify

amplio, -a [am'pljo, a] *adj* spacious; *(de falda etc)* full; *(extenso)* extensive; *(ancho)* wide; **amplitud** *nf* spaciousness; extent; *(fig)* amplitude

ampolla [am'poʎa] *nf* blister; *(Med)* ampoule

amputar [ampu'tar] *vt* to cut off, amputate

amueblar [amwe'βlar] *vt* to furnish

anales [a'nales] *nmpl* annals

analfabetismo [analfaβe'tismo] *nm* illiteracy; **analfabeto, -a** *adj, nm/f* illiterate

analgésico [anal'xesiko] *nm* painkiller, analgesic

análisis [a'nalisis] *nm inv* analysis

analista [ana'lista] *nm/f* (gen) analyst

analizar [anali'θar] *vt* to analyse

analógico, -a [ana'loxiko, a] *adj* (*Inform*) analog; *(reloj)* analogue (*BRIT*), analog (*US*)

análogo, -a [a'nalovo, a] *adj* analogous, similar

ananá [ana'na] (*RPL*) *nm* pineapple

anarquía [anar'kia] *nf* anarchy; **anarquista** *nmf* anarchist

anatomía [anato'mia] *nf* anatomy

anca ['anka] *nf* rump, haunch; **ancas** *nfpl* (*fam*) behind *sg*

ancho, -a ['antʃo, a] *adj* wide; *(falda)* full; *(fig)* liberal ▷ *nm* width; *(Ferro)* gauge; **ponerse ~** to get conceited; **estar a sus anchas** to be at one's ease

anchoa [an'tʃoa] *nf* anchovy

anchura [an'tʃura] *nf* width; *(extensión)* wideness

anciano, -a [an'θjano, a] *adj* old, aged ▷ *nm/f* old man/woman; elder

ancla ['ankla] *nf* anchor

Andalucía [andalu'θia] *nf* Andalusia; **andaluz, -a** *adj, nm/f* Andalusian

andamio [an'damjo] *nm* scaffold(ing)

andar [an'dar] *vt* to go, cover, travel ▷ *vi* to go, walk, travel; *(funcionar)* to go, work; *(estar)* to be ▷ *nm* walk, gait, pace; **andarse** *vr* to go away; **~ a pie/a caballo/en bicicleta** to go on foot/on horseback/by bicycle; **~ haciendo algo** to be doing sth; **¡anda!** *(sorpresa)* go on!; **anda por o en los 40** he's about 40

andén [an'den] *nm* (*Ferro*) platform; *(Náut)* quayside; *(CAM: de la calle)* pavement (*BRIT*), sidewalk (*US*)

Andes ['andes] *nmpl*: **los ~** the Andes

andinismo [andi'nismo] (*LAM*) *nm* mountaineering, climbing

Andorra [an'dorra] *nf* Andorra

andrajoso, -a [andra'xoso, a] *adj* ragged

anduve *etc* vb V **andar**

anécdota [a'nekðota] *nf* anecdote, story

anegar [ane'var] *vt* to flood; *(ahogar)* to drown

anemia [a'nemja] *nf* anaemia

anestesia [anes'tesja] *nf* *(sustancia)* anaesthetic; *(proceso)* anaesthesia; **anestesia general/local** general/local anaesthetic

anexar [anek'sar] *vt* to annex; *(documento)* to attach; **anexión** *nf* annexation; **anexo, -a** *adj* attached ▷ *nm* annexe

anfibio, -a [an'fiβjo, a] *adj* amphibious ▷ *nm* amphibian

anfiteatro [anfite'atro] *nm* amphitheatre; *(Teatro)* dress circle

anfitrión, -ona [anfi'trjon, ona] *nm/f* host(ess)

ánfora ['anfora] *nf* *(cántaro)* amphora; *(MÉX Pol)* ballot box

ángel ['anxel] *nm* angel; **ángel de la guarda** guardian angel

angina [an'xina] *nf* (*Med*) inflammation of the throat; **tener ~s** to have tonsillitis; **angina de pecho** angina

anglicano, -a [angli'kano, a] *adj, nm/f* Anglican

anglosajón, -ona [anglosa'xon, ona] *adj* Anglo-Saxon

anguila [an'gila] *nf* eel

angula [an'gula] *nf* elver, baby eel

ángulo ['angulo] *nm* angle; *(esquina)* corner; *(curva)* bend

angustia [an'gustja] *nf* anguish

anhelar [ane'lar] *vt* to be eager for; *(desear)* to long for, desire ▷ *vi* to pant, gasp; **anhelo** *nm* eagerness; desire

anidar [ani'ðar] *vi* to nest

anillo [a'niʎo] *nm* ring; **anillo de boda/compromiso** wedding/engagement ring

animación [anima'θjon] *nf* liveliness; *(vitalidad)* life; *(actividad)* activity; bustle

animado, -a [ani'maðo, a] *adj* lively; *(vivaz)* animated; **animador, a** *nm/f* (*TV*) host(ess), compère; *(Deporte)* cheerleader

animal [ani'mal] *adj* animal; *(fig)* stupid ▷ *nm* animal; *(fig)* fool; *(bestia)* brute

animar [ani'mar] *vt* (*Bio*) to animate, give life to; *(fig)* to liven up, brighten up, cheer up; *(estimular)* to stimulate; **animarse** *vr* to cheer up; to feel encouraged; *(decidirse)* to make up one's mind

ánimo ['animo] *nm* *(alma)* soul; *(mente)* mind; *(valentía)* courage ▷ *excl* cheer up!

animoso, -a [ani'moso, a] *adj* brave; *(vivo)* lively

aniquilar [aniki'lar] *vt* to annihilate, destroy

anís [a'nis] *nm* aniseed; *(licor)* anisette

aniversario [aniβer'sarjo] *nm* anniversary

anoche [a'notʃe] *adv* last night; **antes de ~** the night before last

anochecer [anotʃe'θer] *vi* to get dark ▷ *nm* nightfall, dark; **al ~** at nightfall

anodino, -a [ano'ðino, a] *adj* dull, anodyne

anomalía [anoma'lia] *nf* anomaly

anonadado, -a [anona'ðaðo, a] *adj*: **estar ~** to be overwhelmed o amazed

anonimato [anoni'mato] *nm* anonymity

anónimo, -a [a'nonimo, a] *adj* anonymous; *(Com)* limited ▷ *nm* *(carta anónima)* anonymous letter; *(: maliciosa)* poison-pen letter

anormal [anor'mal] *adj* abnormal

anotación [anota'θjon] *nf* note; annotation

anotar [ano'tar] *vt* to note down; *(comentar)* to annotate

ansia ['ansja] *nf* anxiety; *(añoranza)* yearning; **ansiar** *vt* to long for

ansiedad [ansje'ðað] *nf* anxiety

ansioso, -a [an'sjoso, a] *adj* anxious; *(anhelante)* eager; **~ de o por algo** greedy for sth

antaño [an'taɲo] *adv* long ago, formerly

Antártico [an'tartiko] *nm*: **el ~** the Antarctic

ante ['ante] *prep* before, in the presence of; *(problema etc)* faced with ▷ *nm (piel)* suede; **~ todo** above all

anteanoche [antea'notʃe] *adv* the night before last

anteayer [antea'jer] *adv* the day before yesterday

antebrazo [ante'βraθo] *nm* forearm

antecedente [anteθe'ðente] *adj* previous ▷ *nm* antecedent; **antecedentes** *nmpl (historial)* record *sg*; **antecedentes penales** criminal record

anteceder [anteθe'ðer] *vt* to precede, go before

antecesor, a [anteθe'sor, a] *nm/f* predecessor

antelación [antela'θjon] *nf*: **con ~** in advance

antemano [ante'mano]: **de ~** *adv* beforehand, in advance

antena [dɪ'tena] *nf* antenna; *(de televisión etc)* aerial; **antena parabólica** satellite dish

antenoche [ante'notʃe] *(LAM) adv* the night before last

anteojo [ante'oxo] *nm* eyeglass; **anteojos** *nmpl (LAM: gafas)* glasses, spectacles

antepasados [antepa'saðos] *nmpl* ancestors

anteponer [antepo'ner] *vt* to place in front; *(fig)* to prefer

anterior [ante'rjor] *adj* preceding, previous; **anterioridad** *nf*: **con anterioridad** a prior to, before

antes ['antes] *adv (con prioridad)* before ▷ *prep*: **~ de** before ▷ *conj*: **~ de ir/de que te vayas** before going/before you go; **~ bien** (but) rather; **dos días ~** two days before o previously; **no quiso venir ~** she didn't want to come any earlier; **tomo el avión ~ que el barco** I take the plane rather than the boat; **~ de o que nada** *(en el tiempo)* first of all; *(indicando preferencia)* above all; **~ que** yo before me; **lo ~ posible** as soon as possible; **cuanto ~ mejor** the sooner the better

antibalas [anti'βalas] *adj inv*: **chaleco ~** bullet-proof jacket

antibiótico [anti'βjotiko] *nm* antibiotic

anticaspa [anti'kaspa] *adj inv* anti-dandruff *cpd*

anticipación [antiθipa'θjon] *nf* anticipation; **con 10 minutos de ~** 10 minutes early

anticipado, -a [antiθi'paðo, a] *adj (pago)* advance; **por ~** in advance

anticipar [antiθi'par] *vt* to anticipate; *(adelantar)* to bring forward; *(Com)* to advance; **anticiparse** *vr*: **~se a su época** to be ahead of one's time

anticipo [anti'θipo] *nm (Com)* advance

anticonceptivo, -a [antikonθep'tiβo, a] *adj, nm* contraceptive

anticongelante [antikonxe'lante] *nm* antifreeze

anticuado, -a [anti'kwaðo, a] *adj* out-of-date, old-fashioned; *(desusado)* obsolete

anticuario [anti'kwarjo] *nm* antique dealer

anticuerpo [anti'kwerpo] *nm (Med)* antibody

antidepresivo [antiðepre'siβo] *nm* antidepressant

antidóping [anti'dopin] *adj inv*: **control ~** drugs test

antídoto [an'tiðoto] *nm* antidote

antiestético, -a [anties'tetiko, a] *adj* unsightly

antifaz [anti'faθ] *nm* mask; *(velo)* veil

antiglobalización [antigloβaliθa'θjon] *nf* anti-globalization; **antiglobalizador, a** *adj* anti-globalization *cpd*

antiguamente [antixwa'mente] *adv* formerly; *(hace mucho tiempo)* long ago

antigüedad [antixwe'ðað] *nf* antiquity; *(artículo)* antique; *(rango)* seniority

antiguo, -a [an'tixwo, a] *adj* old, ancient; *(que fue)* former

Antillas [an'tiʎas] *nfpl*: **las ~** the West Indies

antílope [an'tilope] *nm* antelope

antinatural [antinatu'ral] *adj* unnatural

antipatía [antipa'tia] *nf* antipathy, dislike; **antipático, -a** *adj* disagreeable, unpleasant

antirrobo [anti'troβo] *adj inv (alarma etc)* anti-theft

antisemita [antise'mita] *adj* anti-Semitic ▷ *nmf* anti-Semite

antiséptico, -a [anti'septiko, a] *adj* antiseptic ▷ *nm* antiseptic

antivirus [anti'βirus] *nm inv (Comput)* antivirus program

antojarse [anto'xarse] *vr (desear)*: **se me antoja comprarlo** I have a mind to buy it; *(pensar)*: **se me antoja que ...** I have a feeling that ...

antojitos [anto'xitos] *(MÉX) nmpl* snacks, nibbles

antojo [an'toxo] *nm* caprice, whim; *(rosa)* birthmark; *(lunar)* mole

antología [antolo'xia] *nf* anthology

antorcha [an'tortʃa] *nf* torch

antro ['antro] *nm* cavern

antropología [antropolo'xia] *nf* anthropology

anual [a'nwal] *adj* annual

anuario [a'nwarjo] *nm* yearbook

anulación [anula'θjon] *nf* annulment; *(cancelación)* cancellation

anular [anu'lar] *vt (contrato)* to annul, cancel; *(ley)* to revoke, repeal; *(suscripción)* to cancel ▷ *nm* ring finger

anunciar [anun'θjar] *vt* to announce; *(proclamar)* to proclaim; *(Com)* to advertise

anuncio [a'nunθjo] *nm* announcement; *(señal)* sign; *(Com)* advertisement; *(cartel)* poster

anzuelo [an'θwelo] *nm* hook; *(para pescar)* fish hook

añadidura [aɲaði'ðura] *nf* addition, extra; **por ~** besides, in addition

añadir [aɲa'ðir] *vt* to add

añejo, -a [a'ɲexo, a] *adj* old; *(vino)* mellow

añicos [a'ɲikos] *nmpl*: **hacer ~** to smash, shatter

año ['aɲo] *nm* year; **¡Feliz A~ Nuevo!** Happy New Year!; **tener 15 ~s** to be 15 (years old); **los ~s 90** the nineties; **el ~ que viene** next year; **año bisiesto/escolar/fiscal/sabático** leap/school/tax/sabbatical year

añoranza [aɲo'ranθa] *nf* nostalgia; *(anhelo)* longing

apa [a'pa] *(MÉX) excl* goodness me!, good gracious!

apabullar [apaβu'ʎar] *vt* to crush, squash

apacible [apa'θiβle] *adj* gentle, mild

apaciguar [apaθi'ɣwar] *vt* to pacify, calm (down)

apadrinar [apaðri'nar] *vt* to sponsor, support; *(Rel)* to be godfather to

apagado, -a [apa'ɣaðo, a] *adj (volcán)* extinct; *(color)* dull; *(voz)* quiet; *(sonido)* muted, muffled; *(persona: apático)* listless; **estar ~** *(fuego, luz)* to be out; *(Radio, TV etc)* to be off

apagar [apa'ɣar] *vt* to put out; *(Elec, Radio, TV)* to turn off; *(sonido)* to silence, muffle; *(sed)* to quench

apagón [apa'ɣon] *nm* blackout; power cut

apalabrar [apala'βrar] *vt* to agree to; *(contratar)* to engage

apalear [apale'ar] *vt* to beat, thrash

apantallar [apanta'ʎar] *(MÉX) vt* to impress

apañar [apa'ɲar] *vt* to pick up; *(asir)* to take hold of, grasp; *(reparar)* to mend, patch up; **apañarse** *vr* to manage, get along

apapachar [apapa'tʃar] *(MÉX: fam) vt* to cuddle, hug

aparador [apara'ðor] *nm* sideboard; *(MÉX: escaparate)* shop window

aparato [apa'rato] *nm* apparatus; (*máquina*) machine; (*doméstico*) appliance; (*boato*) ostentation; **aparato digestivo** (*Anat*) digestive system; **aparatoso, -a** *adj* showy, ostentatious

aparcamiento [aparka'mjento] *nm* car park (BRIT), parking lot (US)

aparcar [apar'kar] *vt, vi* to park

aparear [apare'ar] *vt* (*objetos*) to pair, match; (*animales*) to mate; **aparearse** *vr* to make a pair; to mate

aparecer [apare'θer] *vi* to appear; **aparecerse** *vr* to appear

aparejador, a [aparexa'ðor, a] *nm/f* (*Arq*) master builder

aparejo [apa'rexo] *nm* harness; rigging; (*de poleas*) block and tackle

aparentar [aparen'tar] *vt* (*edad*) to look; (*fingir*): **~ tristeza** to pretend to be sad

aparente [apa'rente] *adj* apparent; (*adecuado*) suitable

aparezco *etc vb* V **aparecer**

aparición [apari'θjon] *nf* appearance; (*de libro*) publication; (*espectro*) apparition

apariencia [apa'rjenθja] *nf* (outward) appearance; **en ~** outwardly, seemingly

apartado, -a [apar'taðo, a] *adj* separate; (*lejano*) remote ▷ *nm* (*tipográfico*) paragraph; **apartado de correos** (ESP) post office box; **apartado postal** (LAM) post office box

apartamento [aparta'mento] *nm* apartment, flat (BRIT)

apartar [apar'tar] *vt* to separate; (*quitar*) to remove; **apartarse** *vr* to separate, part; (*irse*) to move away; to keep away

aparte [a'parte] *adv* (*separadamente*) separately; (*además*) besides ▷ *nm* aside; (*tipográfico*) new paragraph

aparthotel [aparto'tel] *nm* serviced apartments

apasionado, -a [apasjo'naðo, a] *adj* passionate

apasionar [apasjo'nar] *vt* to excite; **le apasiona el fútbol** she's crazy about football; **apasionarse** *vr* to get excited

apatía [apa'tia] *nf* apathy

apático, -a [a'patiko, a] *adj* apathetic

Apdo *abr* (= *Apartado (de Correos)*) PO Box

apeadero [apea'ðero] *nm* halt, stop, stopping place

apearse [ape'arse] *vr* (*jinete*) to dismount; (*bajarse*) to get down o out; (*Auto, Ferro*) to get off o out

apechugar [apetʃu'xar] *vr*: **~ con algo** to face up to sth

apegarse [ape'ɣarse] *vr*: **~ a** to become attached to; **apego** *nm* attachment, devotion

apelar [ape'lar] *vi* to appeal; **~ a** (*fig*) to resort to

apellidar [apeʎi'ðar] *vt* to call, name; **apellidarse** *vr*: **se apellida Pérez** her (sur)name's Pérez

apellido [ape'ʎiðo] *nm* surname

apenar [ape'nar] *vt* to grieve, trouble; (LAM: *avergonzar*) to embarrass; **apenarse** *vr* to grieve; (LAM: *avergonzarse*) to be embarrassed

apenas [a'penas] *adv* scarcely, hardly ▷ *conj* as soon as, no sooner

apéndice [a'pendiθe] *nm* appendix; **apendicitis** *nf* appendicitis

aperitivo [aperi'tiβo] *nm* (*bebida*) aperitif; (*comida*) appetizer

apertura [aper'tura] *nf* opening; (*Pol*) liberalization

apestar [apes'tar] *vt* to infect ▷ *vi*: **~ (a)** to stink (of)

apetecer [apete'θer] *vt*: **¿te apetece un café?** do you fancy a (cup of) coffee?; **apetecible** *adj* desirable; (*comida*) appetizing

apetito [ape'tito] *nm* appetite; **apetitoso, -a** *adj* appetizing; (*fig*) tempting

apiadarse [apja'ðarse] *vr*: **~ de** to take pity on

ápice ['apiθe] *nm* whit, iota

apilar [api'lar] *vt* to pile o heap up

apiñarse [api'narse] *vr* to crowd o press together

apio ['apjo] *nm* celery

apisonadora [apisona'ðora] *nf* steamroller

aplacar [apla'kar] *vt* to placate

aplastante [aplas'tante] *adj* overwhelming; (*lógica*) compelling

aplastar [aplas'tar] *vt* to squash (flat); (*fig*) to crush

aplaudir [aplau'ðir] *vt* to applaud

aplauso [a'plauso] *nm* applause; (*fig*) approval, acclaim

aplazamiento [aplaθa'mjento] *nm* postponement

aplazar [apla'θar] *vt* to postpone, defer

aplicación [aplika'θjon] *nf* application; (*esfuerzo*) effort

aplicado, -a [apli'kaðo, a] *adj* diligent, hard-working

aplicar [apli'kar] *vt* (*ejecutar*) to apply; **aplicarse** *vr* to apply o.s.

aplique *etc* [a'plike] *vb* V **aplicar** ▷ *nm* wall light

aplomo [a'plomo] *nm* aplomb, self-assurance

apodar [apo'ðar] *vt* to nickname

apoderado [apoðe'raðo] *nm* agent, representative

apoderarse [apoðe'rarse] *vr*: **~ de** to take possession of

apodo [a'poðo] *nm* nickname

apogeo [apo'xeo] *nm* peak, summit

apoquinar [apoki'nar] (*fam*) *vt* to fork out, cough up

aporrear [aporre'ar] *vt* to beat (up)

aportar [apor'tar] *vt* to contribute ▷ *vi* to reach port; **aportarse** *vr* (LAM: *llegar*) to arrive, come

aposta [a'posta] *adv* deliberately, on purpose

apostar [apos'tar] *vt* to bet, stake; (*tropas etc*) to station, post ▷ *vi* to bet

apóstol [a'postol] *nm* apostle

apóstrofo [a'postrofo] *nm* apostrophe

apoyar [apo'jar] *vt* to lean, rest; (*fig*) to support, back; **apoyarse** *vr*: **~se en** to lean on; **apoyo** *nm* (*gen*) support; backing, help

apreciable [apre'θjaβle] *adj* considerable; (*fig*) esteemed

apreciar [apre'θjar] *vt* to evaluate, assess; (*Com*) to appreciate, value; (*persona*) to respect; (*tamaño*) to gauge, assess; (*detalles*) to notice

aprecio [a'preθjo] *nm* valuation, estimate; (*fig*) appreciation

aprehender [apreen'der] *vt* to apprehend, detain

apremio [a'premjo] *nm* urgency

aprender [apren'der] *vt, vi* to learn; **~ algo de memoria** to learn sth (off) by heart

aprendiz, a [apren'diθ, a] *nm/f* apprentice; (*principiante*) learner; **aprendizaje** *nm* apprenticeship

aprensión [apren'sjon] *nm* apprehension, fear; **aprensivo, -a** *adj* apprehensive

apresar [apre'sar] *vt* to seize; (*capturar*) to capture

apresurado, -a [apresu'raðo, a] *adj* hurried, hasty

apresurar [apresu'rar] *vt* to hurry, accelerate;

apresurarse [apresu'rarse] vr to hurry, make haste
apretado, -a [apre'taðo, a] adj tight; (escritura) cramped
apretar [apre'tar] vt to squeeze; (Tec) to tighten; (presionar) to press together, pack ▷ vi to be too tight
apretón [apre'ton] nm squeeze; **apretón de manos** handshake
aprieto [a'prjeto] nm squeeze; (dificultad) difficulty; **estar en un ~** to be in a fix
aprisa [a'prisa] adv quickly, hurriedly
aprisionar [aprisjo'nar] vt to imprison
aprobación [aproβa'θjon] nf approval
aprobar [apro'βar] vt to approve (of); (examen, materia) to pass ▷ vi to pass
apropiado, -a [apro'pjaðo, a] adj suitable
apropiarse [apro'pjarse] vr: **- de** to appropriate
aprovechado, -a [aproβe'tʃaðo, a] adj industrious, hard-working; (económico) thrifty; (pey) unscrupulous
aprovechar [aproβe'tʃar] vt to use; (explotar) to exploit; (experiencia) to profit from; (oferta, oportunidad) to take advantage of ▷ vi to progress, improve; **aprovecharse** vr: **~se de** to make use of; to take advantage of; **¡que aproveche!** enjoy your meal!
aproximación [aproksima'θjon] nf approximation; (de lotería) consolation prize
aproximar [aproksi'mar] vt to bring nearer; **aproximarse** vr to come near, approach
apruebo etc vb V **aprobar**
aptitud [apti'tuð] nf aptitude
apto, -a ['apto, a] adj suitable
apuesta [a'pwesta] nf bet, wager
apuesto, -a [a'pwesto, a] adj neat, elegant
apuntar [apun'tar] vt (con arma) to aim at; (con dedo) to point at o to; (anotar) to note (down); (Teatro) to prompt; **apuntarse** vr (Deporte: tanto, victoria) to score; (Escol) to enrol
apunte [a'punte] nm note
apuñalar [apuɲa'lar] vt to stab
apurado, -a [apu'raðo, a] adj needy; (difícil) difficult; (peligroso) dangerous; (LAM: con prisa) hurried, rushed
apurar [apu'rar] vt (agotar) to drain; (recursos) to use up; (molestar) to annoy; **apurarse** vr (preocuparse) to worry; (LAM: darse prisa) to hurry
apuro [a'puro] nm (aprieto) fix, jam; (escasez) want, hardship; (vergüenza) embarrassment; (LAM: prisa) haste, urgency
aquejado, -a [ake'xaðo, a] adj: **~ de** (Med) afflicted by
aquel, aquella [a'kel, a'keʎa] adj that; **~los(as)** those
aquél, aquélla [a'kel, a'keʎa] pron that (one); **~los(as)** those (ones)
aquello [a'keʎo] pron that, that business
aquí [a'ki] adv (lugar) here; (tiempo) now; **~ arriba** up here; **~ mismo** right here; **~ yace** here lies; **de ~ a siete días** a week from now
ara ['ara] nf: **en ~s de** for the sake of
árabe ['araβe] adj, nm/f Arab ▷ nm (Ling) Arabic
Arabia [a'raβja] nf Arabia; **Arabia Saudí** o **Saudita** Saudi Arabia
arado [a'raðo] nm plough
Aragón [ara'xon] nm Aragon; **aragonés, -esa** adj, nm/f Aragonese
arancel [aran'θel] nm tariff, duty
arandela [aran'dela] nf (Tec) washer
araña [a'raɲa] nf (Zool) spider; (lámpara) chandelier

arañar [ara'ɲar] vt to scratch
arañazo [ara'ɲaθo] nm scratch
arbitrar [arβi'trar] vt to arbitrate in; (Deporte) to referee ▷ vi to arbitrate
arbitrario, -a [arβi'trarjo, a] adj arbitrary
árbitro ['arβitro] nm arbitrator; (Deporte) referee; (Tenis) umpire
árbol ['arβol] nm (Bot) tree; (Náut) mast; (Tec) axle, shaft; **árbol de Navidad** Christmas tree
arboleda [arβo'leða] nf grove, plantation
arbusto [ar'βusto] nm bush, shrub
arca ['arka] nf chest, box
arcada [ar'kaða] nf arcade; (de puente) arch, span; **arcadas** nfpl (náuseas) retching sg
arcaico, -a [ar'kaiko, a] adj archaic
arce ['arθe] nm maple tree
arcén [ar'θen] nm (de autopista) hard shoulder; (de carretera) verge
archipiélago [artʃi'pjelaxo] nm archipelago
archivador [artʃiβa'ðor] nm filing cabinet
archivar [artʃi'βar] vt to file (away); **archivo** nm file, archive(s) pl; **archivo adjunto** (Inform) attachment; **archivo de seguridad** (Inform) backup file
arcilla [ar'θiʎa] nf clay
arco ['arko] nm (arch; (Mat) arc; (Mil, Mús) bow; **arco iris** rainbow
arder [ar'ðer] vi to burn; **estar que arde** (persona) to fume
ardid [ar'ðið] nm ploy, trick
ardiente [ar'ðjente] adj burning, ardent
ardilla [ar'ðiʎa] nf squirrel
ardor [ar'ðor] nm (calor) heat; (fig) ardour; **ardor de estómago** heartburn
arduo, -a ['arðwo, a] adj arduous
área ['area] nf area; (Deporte) penalty area
arena [a'rena] nf sand; (de una lucha) arena; **arenas movedizas** quicksand sg; **arenal** [are'nal] nm (terreno arenoso) sandy spot
arenisca [are'niska] nf sandstone; (cascajo) grit
arenoso, -a [are'noso, a] adj sandy
arenque [a'renke] nm herring
arete [a'rete] (MÉX) nm earring
Argel [ar'xel] n Algiers; **Argelia** nf Algeria; **argelino, -a** adj, nm/f Algerian
Argentina [arxen'tina] nf (tb: **la ~**) Argentina
argentino, -a [arxen'tino, a] adj Argentinian; (de plata) silvery ▷ nm/f Argentinian
argolla [ar'xoʎa] nf (large) ring
argot [ar'xo](pl **~s**) nm slang
argucia [ar'xuθja] nf subtlety, sophistry
argumentar [arxumen'tar] vt, vi to argue
argumento [arxu'mento] nm argument; (razonamiento) reasoning; (de novela etc) plot; (Cine, TV) storyline
aria ['arja] nf aria
aridez [ari'ðeθ] nf aridity, dryness
árido, -a ['ariðo, a] adj arid, dry
Aries ['arjes] nm Aries
arisco, -a [a'risko, a] adj surly; (insociable) unsociable
aristócrata [aris'tokrata] nmf aristocrat
arma ['arma] nf arm; **armas** nfpl arms; **arma blanca** blade, knife; **arma de doble filo** double-edged sword; **arma de fuego** firearm; **armas de destrucción masiva** weapons of mass destruction
armada [ar'maða] nf armada; (flota) fleet
armadillo [arma'ðiʎo] nm armadillo

armado, -a [ar'maðo, a] *adj* armed; *(Tec)* reinforced
armadura [arma'ðura] *nf* *(Mil)* armour; *(Tec)*
framework; *(Zool)* skeleton; *(Física)* armature
armamento [arma'mento] *nm* armament; *(Náut)*
fitting-out
armar [ar'mar] *vt* *(soldado)* to arm; *(máquina)* to
assemble; *(navío)* to fit out; **-la, ~ un lío** to start a row,
kick up a fuss
armario [ar'marjo] *nm* wardrobe; *(de cocina, baño)*
cupboard; **armario empotrado** built-in cupboard
armatoste [arma'toste] *nm* *(mueble)* monstrosity;
(máquina) contraption
armazón [arma'θon] *nf o m* body, chassis; *(de mueble
etc)* frame; *(Arq)* skeleton
armiño [ar'miɲo] *nm* stoat; *(piel)* ermine
armisticio [armis'tiθjo] *nm* armistice
armonía [armo'nia] *nf* harmony
armónica [ar'monika] *nf* harmonica
armonizar [armoni'θar] *vt* to harmonize; *(diferencias)* to reconcile
aro ['aro] *nm* ring; *(tejo)* quoit; *(cs: pendiente)* earring
aroma [a'roma] *nm* aroma, scent; **aromaterapia**
n aromatherapy; **aromático, -a** [aro'matiko, a] *adj*
aromatic
arpa ['arpa] *nf* harp
arpía [ar'pia] *nf* shrew
arpón [ar'pon] *nm* harpoon
arqueología [arkeolo'xia] *nf* archaeology;
arqueólogo, -a *nm/f* archaeologist
arquetipo [arke'tipo] *nm* archetype
arquitecto [arki'tekto] *nm* architect; **arquitectura**
nf architecture
arrabal [arra'βal] *nm* poor suburb, slum; **arrabales**
nmpl *(afueras)* outskirts
arraigar [arrai'xar] *vt* to establish ▷ *vi* to take root
arrancar [arran'kar] *vt* *(sacar)* to extract, pull out;
(arrebatar) to snatch (away); *(inform)* to boot; *(fig)* to
extract ▷ *vi* *(Auto, máquina)* to start; *(ponerse en marcha)*
to get going; **~ de** to stem from
arranque *etc* [a'rranke] *vb* V **arrancar** ▷ *nm* sudden
start; *(Auto)* start; *(fig)* fit, outburst
arrasar [arra'sar] *vt* *(aplanar)* to level, flatten;
(destruir) to demolish
arrastrar [arras'trar] *vt* to drag (along); *(fig)* to drag
down, degrade; *(agua, viento)* to carry away ▷ *vi* to
drag, trail on the ground; **arrastrarse** *vr* to crawl; *(fig)*
to grovel; **llevar algo arrastrado** to drag sth along
arrear [arre'ar] *vt* to drive on, urge on ▷ *vi* to hurry
along
arrebatar [arreβa'tar] *vt* to snatch (away), seize;
(fig) to captivate
arrebato [arre'βato] *nm* fit of rage, fury; *(éxtasis)*
rapture
arrecife [arre'θife] *nm* reef
arreglado, -a [arre'xlaðo, a] *adj* *(ordenado)* neat,
orderly; *(moderado)* moderate, reasonable
arreglar [arre'xlar] *vt* *(poner orden)* to tidy up; *(algo
roto)* to fix, repair; *(problema)* to solve; **arreglarse** *vr* to
reach an understanding; **arreglárselas** *(fam)* to get
by, manage
arreglo [a'rreylo] *nm* settlement; *(orden)* order;
(acuerdo) agreement; *(Mús)* arrangement, setting
arremangar [arreman'gar] *vt* to roll up, turn up;
arremangarse *vr* to roll up one's sleeves
arremeter [arreme'ter] *vi*: **~ contra** to attack, rush at
arrendamiento [arrenda'mjento] *nm* letting;

(alquilar) hiring; *(contrato)* lease; *(alquiler)* rent;
arrendar *vt* to let, lease; to rent; **arrendatario, -a**
nm/f tenant
arreos [a'rreos] *nmpl* *(de caballo)* harness *sg*, trappings
arrepentimiento [arrepenti'mjento] *nm* regret,
repentance
arrepentirse [arrepen'tirse] *vr* to repent; **~ de** to
regret
arresto [a'rresto] *nm* arrest; *(Mil)* detention; *(audacia)*
boldness, daring; **arresto domiciliario** house arrest
arriar [a'rrjar] *vt* *(velas)* to haul down; *(bandera)* to
lower, strike; *(cable)* to pay out

○ **PALABRA CLAVE**

arriba [a'rriβa] *adv* **1** *(posición)* above; **desde arriba**
from above; **arriba de todo** at the very top, right
on top; **Juan está arriba** Juan is upstairs; **lo arriba
mencionado** the aforementioned
2 *(dirección)*: **calle arriba** up the street
3 de arriba abajo from top to bottom; **mirar a algn
de arriba abajo** to look sb up and down
**4 para arriba: de 5000 euros
para arriba** from 5000 euros up(wards)
▷ *adj*: **de arriba:** **el piso de arriba** the upstairs *(BRIT)*
flat o apartment; **la parte de arriba** the top o upper
part
▷ *prep*: **arriba de** *(LAM: por encima de)* above; **arriba de
200 dólares** more than 200 dollars
▷ *excl*: **¡arriba!** up!; **¡manos arriba!** hands up!; **¡arriba
España!** long live Spain!

arribar [arri'βar] *vi* to put into port; *(llegar)* to arrive
arriendo *etc* [a'rrjendo] *vb* V **arrendar** ▷ *nm* =
arrendamiento
arriesgado, -a [arrjes'xaðo, a] *adj* *(peligroso)* risky;
(audaz) bold, daring
arriesgar [arrjes'xar] *vt* to risk; *(poner en peligro)* to
endanger; **arriesgarse** *vr* to take a risk
arrimar [arri'mar] *vt* *(acercar)* to bring close; *(poner de
lado)* to set aside; **arrimarse** *vr* to come close o closer;
~se a to lean on
arrinconar [arrinko'nar] *vt* *(colocar)* to put in a
corner; *(enemigo)* to corner; *(fig)* to put on one side;
(abandonar) to push aside
arroba [a'rroβa] *nf* *(Internet)* at (sign)
arrodillarse [arroði'ʎarse] *vr* to kneel (down)
arrogante [arro'xante] *adj* arrogant
arrojar [arro'xar] *vt* to throw, hurl; *(humo)* to emit,
give out; *(Com)* to yield, produce; **arrojarse** *vr* to
throw o hurl o.s.
arrojo [a'rroxo] *nm* daring
arrollador, a [arroʎa'ðor, a] *adj* overwhelming
arrollar [arro'ʎar] *vt* *(Auto etc)* to run over, knock
down; *(Deporte)* to crush
arropar [arro'par] *vt* to cover, wrap up; **arroparse** *vr*
to wrap o.s. up
arroyo [a'rrojo] *nm* stream; *(de la calle)* gutter
arroz [a'rroθ] *nm* rice; **arroz con leche** rice pudding
arruga [a'rruxa] *nf* *(de cara)* wrinkle; *(de vestido)*
crease; **arrugar** [arru'xar] *vt* to wrinkle; to crease;
arrugarse *vr* to get creased
arruinar [arrwi'nar] *vt* to ruin, wreck; **arruinarse** *vr*
to be ruined, go bankrupt
arsenal [arse'nal] *nm* naval dockyard; *(Mil)* arsenal

arte ['arte] (gen m en sg y siempre f en pl) nm art; (maña) skill, guile; **artes** nfpl (bellas artes) arts

artefacto [arte'fakto] nm appliance

arteria [ar'terja] nf artery

artesanía [artesa'nia] nf craftsmanship; (artículos) handicrafts pl; **artesano, -a** nm/f artisan, craftsman(-woman)

ártico, -a ['artiko, a] adj Arctic ▷ nm: **el Á~** the Arctic

articulación [artikula'θjon] nf articulation; (Med, Tec) joint

artículo [ar'tikulo] nm article; (cosa) thing, article; **artículos** nmpl (Com) goods; **artículos de escritorio** stationery

artífice [ar'tifiθe] nmf (fig) architect

artificial [artifi'θjal] adj artificial

artillería [artiʎe'ria] nf artillery

artilugio [arti'luxjo] nm gadget

artimaña [arti'maɲa] nf trap, snare; (astucia) cunning

artista [ar'tista] nmf (pintor) artist, painter; (Teatro) artist, artiste; **artista de cine** film actor/actress; **artístico, -a** adj artistic

artritis [ar'tritis] nf arthritis

arveja [ar'βexa] (LAM) nf pea

arzobispo [arθo'βispo] nm archbishop

as [as] nm ace

asa ['asa] nf handle; (fig) lever

asado [a'saðo] nm roast (meat); (LAM: barbacoa) barbecue

asador [asa'ðor] nm spit

asadura [asa'ðura] nf entrails pl, offal

asalariado, -a [asala'rjaðo, a] adj paid, salaried ▷ nm/f wage earner

asaltar [asal'tar] vt to attack, assault; (fig) to assail; **asalto** nm attack, assault; (Deporte) round

asamblea [asam'blea] nf assembly; (reunión) meeting

asar [a'sar] vt to roast

ascendencia [asθen'denθja] nf ancestry; (LAM: influencia) ascendancy; **de ~ francesa** of French origin

ascender [asθen'der] vi (subir) to ascend, rise; (ser promovido) to gain promotion ▷ vt to promote; **~ a** to amount to; **ascendiente** nm influence ▷ nmf ancestor

ascensión [asθen'sjon] nf ascent; (Rel): **la A~** the Ascension

ascenso [as'θenso] nm ascent; (promoción) promotion

ascensor [asθen'sor] nm lift (BRIT), elevator (US)

asco ['asko] nm: **¡qué ~!** how revolting o disgusting; **el ajo me da ~** I hate o loathe garlic; **estar hecho un ~** to be filthy

ascua ['askwa] nf ember

aseado, -a [ase'aðo, a] adj clean; (arreglado) tidy; (pulcro) smart

asear [ase'ar] vt to clean, wash; to tidy (up)

asediar [ase'ðjar] vt (Mil) to besiege, lay siege to; (fig) to chase, pester; **asedio** nm siege; (Com) run

asegurado, -a [aseɣu'raðo, a] adj insured

asegurador, a [aseɣura'ðor, a] nm/f insurer

asegurar [aseɣu'rar] vt (consolidar) to secure, fasten; (dar garantía de) to guarantee; (preservar) to safeguard; (afirmar, dar por cierto) to assure, affirm; (tranquilizar) to reassure; (tomar un seguro) to insure; **asegurarse** vr to assure o.s., make sure

asemejarse [aseme'xarse] vr to be alike; **~ a** to be like, resemble

asentado, -a [asen'taðo, a] adj established, settled

asentar [asen'tar] vt (sentar) to seat, sit down; (poner) to place, establish; (alisar) to level, smooth down o out; (anotar) to note down ▷ vi to be suitable, suit

asentir [asen'tir] vi to assent, agree; **~ con la cabeza** to nod (one's head)

aseo [a'seo] nm cleanliness; **aseos** nmpl (servicios) toilet sg (BRIT), cloakroom sg (BRIT), restroom sg (US)

aséptico, -a [a'septiko, a] adj germ-free, free from infection

asequible [ase'kiβle] adj (precio) reasonable; (meta) attainable; (persona) approachable

asesinar [asesi'nar] vt to murder; (Pol) to assassinate; **asesinato** nm murder; assassination

asesino, -a [ase'sino, a] nm/f murderer, killer; (Pol) assassin

asesor, a [ase'sor, a] nm/f adviser, consultant; **asesorar** [aseso'rar] vt (Jur) to advise, give legal advice to; (Com) to act as consultant to; **asesorarse** vr: **asesorarse con o de** to take advice from, consult; **asesoría** nf (cargo) consultancy; (oficina) consultant's office

asestar [ases'tar] vt (golpe) to deal, strike

asfalto [as'falto] nm asphalt

asfixia [as'fiksja] nf asphyxia, suffocation; **asfixiar** [asfik'sjar] vt to asphyxiate, suffocate; **asfixiarse** vr to be asphyxiated, suffocate

así [a'si] adv (de esta manera) in this way, like this, thus; (aunque) although; (tan pronto como) as soon as; **~ que** so; **~ como** as well as; **~ y todo** even so; **¿no es ~?** isn't it?, didn't you? etc; **~ de grande** this big; **~ ... como** both ... and

Asia ['asja] nf Asia; **asiático, -a** adj, nm/f Asian, Asiatic

asiduo, -a [a'siðwo, a] adj assiduous; (frecuente) frequent ▷ nm/f regular (customer)

asiento [a'sjento] nm (mueble) seat, chair; (de coche, en tribunal etc) seat; (localidad) seat, place; (fundamento) site; **asiento delantero/trasero** front/back seat

asignación [asiɣna'θjon] nf (atribución) assignment; (reparto) allocation; (sueldo) salary; **asignación (semanal)** pocket money

asignar [asiɣ'nar] vt to assign, allocate

asignatura [asiɣna'tura] nf subject; course

asilo [a'silo] nm (refugio) asylum, refuge; (establecimiento) home, institution; **asilo político** political asylum

asimilar [asimi'lar] vt to assimilate

asimismo [asi'mismo] adv in the same way, likewise

asistencia [asis'tenθja] nf audience; (Med) attendance; (ayuda) assistance; **asistencia en carretera** roadside assistance; **asistente** nmf assistant; **los asistentes** those present; **asistente social** social worker

asistido, -a [asis'tiðo, a] adj: **~ por ordenador** computer-assisted

asistir [asis'tir] vt to assist, help ▷ vi: **~ a** to attend, be present at

asma ['asma] nf asthma

asno ['asno] nm donkey; (fig) ass

asociación [asoθja'θjon] nf association; (Com) partnership; **asociado, -a** adj associate ▷ nm/f associate; (Com) partner

asociar [aso'θjar] vt to associate

asomar [aso'mar] vt to show, stick out ▷ vi to

appear; **asomarse** *vr* to appear, show up; **~ la cabeza por la ventana** to put one's head out of the window

asombrar [asom'braɾ] *vt* to amaze, astonish; **asombrarse** *vr* (*sorprenderse*) to be amazed; (*asustarse*) to get a fright; **asombro** *nm* amazement, astonishment; (*susto*) fright; **asombroso, -a** *adj* astonishing, amazing

asomo [a'somo] *nm* hint, sign

aspa ['aspa] *nf* (*cruz*) cross; (*de molino*) sail; **en ~** X-shaped

aspaviento [aspa'βjento] *nm* exaggerated display of feeling; (*fam*) fuss

aspecto [as'pekto] *nm* (*apariencia*) look, appearance; (*fig*) aspect

áspero, -a ['aspero, a] *adj* rough; bitter; sour; harsh

aspersión [asper'sjon] *nf* sprinkling

aspiración [aspira'θjon] *nf* breath, inhalation; (*Mús*) short pause; **aspiraciones** *nfpl* (*ambiciones*) aspirations

aspirador [aspira'ðor] *nm* = **aspiradora**

aspiradora [aspira'ðora] *nf* vacuum cleaner, Hoover®

aspirante [aspi'rante] *nmf* (*candidato*) candidate; (*Deporte*) contender

aspirar [aspi'rar] *vt* to breathe in ⊳ *vi*: **~ a** to aspire to

aspirina [aspi'rina] *nf* aspirin

asqueroso, -a [aske'roso, a] *adj* disgusting, sickening

asta ['asta] *nf* lance; (*arpón*) spear; (*mango*) shaft, handle; (*Zool*) horn; **a media ~** at half mast

asterisco [aste'risko] *nm* asterisk

astilla [as'tiʎa] *nf* splinter; (*pedacito*) chip; **astillas** *nfpl* (*leña*) firewood *sg*

astillero [asti'ʎero] *nm* shipyard

astro ['astro] *nm* star

astrología [astrolo'xia] *nf* astrology; **astrólogo, -a** *nm/f* astrologer

astronauta [astro'nauta] *nmf* astronaut

astronomía [astrono'mia] *nf* astronomy

astucia [as'tuθja] *nf* astuteness; (*ardid*) clever trick

asturiano, -a [astu'rjano, a] *adj, nm/f* Asturian

astuto, -a [as'tuto, a] *adj* astute; (*taimado*) cunning

asumir [asu'mir] *vt* to assume

asunción [asun'θjon] *nf* assumption; (*Rel*): **A~** Assumption

asunto [a'sunto] *nm* (*tema*) matter, subject; (*negocio*) business

asustar [asus'tar] *vt* to frighten; **asustarse** *vr* to be (o become) frightened

atacar [ata'kar] *vt* to attack

atadura [ata'ðura] *nf* bond, tie

atajar [ata'xar] *vt* (*enfermedad, mal*) to stop ⊳ *vi* (*persona*) to take a short cut

atajo [a'taxo] *nm* short cut

atañer [ata'ɲer] *vi*: **~ a** to concern

ataque *etc* [a'take] *vb V* **atacar** ⊳ *nm* attack; **ataque cardíaco** heart attack

atar [a'tar] *vt* to tie, tie up

atarantado, -a [ataran'taðo, a] (*MÉX*) *adj* (*aturdido*) dazed

atardecer [ataɾðe'θeɾ] *vi* to get dark ⊳ *nm* evening; (*crepúsculo*) dusk

atareado, -a [atare'aðo, a] *adj* busy

atascar [atas'kar] *vt* to clog up; (*obstruir*) to jam; (*fig*) to hinder; **atascarse** *vr* to stall; (*cañería*) to get blocked up; **atasco** *nm* obstruction; (*Auto*) traffic jam

ataúd [ata'uð] *nm* coffin

ataviar [ata'βjar] *vt* to deck, array

atemorizar [atemori'θar] *vt* to frighten, scare

Atenas [a'tenas] *n* Athens

atención [aten'θjon] *nf* attention; (*bondad*) kindness ⊳ *excl* (be) careful!, look out!

atender [aten'der] *vt* to attend to, look after; (*Tel*) to answer ⊳ *vi* to pay attention

atenerse [ate'nerse] *vr*: **~ a** to abide by, adhere to

atentado [aten'taðo] *nm* crime, illegal act; (*asalto*) assault; (*tb*: **~ terrorista**) terrorist attack; **~ contra la vida de algn** attempt on sb's life; **atentado suicida** suicide bombing

atentamente [atenta'mente] *adv*: **Le saluda ~** Yours faithfully

atentar [aten'tar] *vi*: **~ a** o **contra** to commit an outrage against

atento, -a [a'tento, a] *adj* attentive, observant; (*cortés*) polite, thoughtful; **estar ~ a** (*explicación*) to pay attention to

atenuar [ate'nwar] *vt* (*disminuir*) to lessen, minimize

ateo, -a [a'teo, a] *adj* atheistic ⊳ *nm/f* atheist

aterrador, a [aterra'ðor, a] *adj* frightening

aterrizaje [aterri'θaxe] *nm* landing; **aterrizaje forzoso** emergency o forced landing

aterrizar [aterri'θar] *vi* to land

aterrorizar [aterrori'θar] *vt* to terrify

atesorar [ateso'rar] *vt* to hoard

atestar [ates'tar] *vt* to pack, stuff; (*Jur*) to attest, testify to

atestiguar [atesti'ɣwar] *vt* to testify to, bear witness to

atiborrar [atiβo'rrar] *vt* to fill, stuff; **atiborrarse** *vr* to stuff o.s.

ático ['atiko] *nm* (*desván*) attic; (*apartamento*) penthouse

atinado, -a [ati'naðo, a] *adj* (*sensato*) wise; (*correcto*) right, correct

atinar [ati'nar] *vi* (*al disparar*): **~ al blanco** to hit the target; (*fig*) to be right

atizar [ati'θar] *vt* to poke; (*horno etc*) to stoke; (*fig*) to stir up, rouse

atlántico, -a [at'lantiko, a] *adj* Atlantic ⊳ *nm*: **el (océano) A~** the Atlantic (Ocean)

atlas ['atlas] *nm inv* atlas

atleta [at'leta] *nm* athlete; **atlético, -a** *adj* athletic; **atletismo** *nm* athletics *sg*

atmósfera [at'mosfera] *nf* atmosphere

atolladero [atoʎa'ðero] *nm* (*fig*) jam, fix

atómico, -a [a'tomiko, a] *adj* atomic

átomo ['atomo] *nm* atom

atónito, -a [a'tonito, a] *adj* astonished, amazed

atontado, -a [aton'taðo, a] *adj* stunned; (*bobo*) silly, daft

atormentar [atormen'tar] *vt* to torture; (*molestar*) to torment; (*acosar*) to plague, harass

atornillar [atorni'ʎar] *vt* to screw on o down

atosigar [atosi'ɣar] *vt* to harass, pester

atracador, a [atraka'ðor, a] *nm/f* robber

atracar [atra'kar] *vt* (*Náut*) to moor; (*robar*) to hold up, rob ⊳ *vi* to moor; **atracarse** *vr*: **~se (de)** to stuff o.s. (with)

atracción [atrak'θjon] *nf* attraction

atraco [a'trako] *nm* holdup, robbery

atracón [atra'kon] *nm*: **darse** o **pegarse un ~ (de)** (*fam*) to stuff o.s. (with)

atractivo, -a [atrak'tiβo, a] *adj* attractive ▷ *nm* appeal

atraer [atra'er] *vt* to attract

atragantarse [atraɣan'tarse] *vr*: **~ (con)** to choke (on); **se me ha atragantado el chico** I can't stand the boy

atrancar [atran'kar] *vt* (*puerta*) to bar, bolt

atrapar [atra'par] *vt* to trap; (*resfriado etc*) to catch

atrás [a'tras] *adv* (*movimiento*) back(-wards); (*lugar*) behind; (*tiempo*) previously; **ir hacia ~** to go back(wards), to go to the rear; **estar ~** to be behind *o* at the back

atrasado, -a [atra'saðo, a] *adj* slow; (*pago*) overdue, late, (*país*) backward

atrasar [atra'sar] *vi* to be slow; **atrasarse** *vr* to remain behind; (*tren*) to be *o* run late; **atraso** *nm* slowness; lateness, delay; (*de país*) backwardness; **atrasos** *nmpl* (*Com*) arrears

atravesar [atraβe'sar] *vt* (*cruzar*) to cross (over); (*traspasar*) to pierce; to go through; (*poner al través*) to lay *o* put across; **atravesarse** *vr* to come in between; (*intervenir*) to interfere

atravieso *etc vb* V **atravesar**

atreverse [atre'βerse] *vr* to dare; (*insolentarse*) to be insolent; **atrevido, -a** *adj* daring; insolent; **atrevimiento** *nm* daring; insolence

atribución [atriβu'θjon] *nf* attribution; **atribuciones** *nfpl* (*Pol*) powers; (*Admin*) responsibilities

atribuir [atriβu'ir] *vt* to attribute; (*funciones*) to confer

atributo [atri'βuto] *nm* attribute

atril [a'tril] *nm* (*para libro*) lectern; (*Mús*) music stand

atropellar [atrope'ʎar] *vt* (*derribar*) to knock over *o* down; (*empujar*) to push (aside); (*Auto*) to run over, run down; (*agraviar*) to insult; **atropello** *nm* (*Auto*) accident; (*empujón*) push; (*agravio*) wrong; (*atrocidad*) outrage

atroz [a'troθ] *adj* atrocious, awful

ATS *nmf abr* (= *Ayudante Técnico Sanitario*) nurse

atuendo [a'twendo] *nm* attire

atún [a'tun] *nm* tuna

aturdir [atur'ðir] *vt* to stun; (*de ruido*) to deafen; (*fig*) to dumbfound, bewilder

audacia [au'ðaθja] *nf* boldness, audacity; **audaz** *adj* bold, audacious

audición [auði'θjon] *nf* hearing; (*Teatro*) audition

audiencia [au'ðjenθja] *nf* audience; (*Jur: tribunal*) court

audífono [au'ðifono] *nm* (*para sordos*) hearing aid

auditor [auði'tor] *nm* (*Jur*) judge advocate; (*Com*) auditor

auditorio [auði'torjo] *nm* audience; (*sala*) auditorium

auge ['auxe] *nm* boom; (*clímax*) climax

augurar [auɣu'rar] *vt* to predict; (*presagiar*) to portend

augurio [au'xurjo] *nm* omen

aula ['aula] *nf* classroom; (*en universidad etc*) lecture room

aullar [au'ʎar] *vi* to howl, yell

aullido [au'ʎiðo] *nm* howl, yell

aumentar [aumen'tar] *vt* to increase; (*precios*) to put up; (*producción*) to step up; (*con microscopio, anteojos*) to magnify ▷ *vi* to increase, be on the increase; **aumentarse** *vr* to increase, be on the increase;

aumento *nm* increase; rise

aun [a'un] *adv* even; **~ así** even so; **~ más** even *o* yet more

aún [a'un] *adv*: **~ está aquí** he's still here; **~ no lo sabemos** we don't know yet; **¿no ha venido ~?** hasn't she come yet?

aunque [a'unke] *conj* though, although, even though

aúpa [a'upa] *excl* come on!

auricular [auriku'lar] *nm* (*Tel*) receiver; **auriculares** *nmpl* (*cascos*) headphones

aurora [au'rora] *nf* dawn

ausencia [au'senθja] *nf* absence

ausentarse [ausen'tarse] *vr* to go away; (*por poco tiempo*) to go out

ausente [au'sente] *adj* absent

austero, -a [aus'tero, a] *adj* austere

austral [aus'tral] *adj* southern ▷ *nm* monetary unit of Argentina

Australia [aus'tralja] *nf* Australia; **australiano, -a** *adj, nm/f* Australian

Austria ['austrja] *nf* Austria; **austríaco, -a** *adj, nm/f* Austrian

auténtico, -a [au'tentiko, a] *adj* authentic

auto ['auto] *nm* (*Jur*) edict, decree; (: *orden*) writ; (*Auto*) car; **autos** *nmpl* (*Jur*) proceedings; (: *acta*) court record *sg*

autoadhesivo [autoaðe'siβo] *adj* self-adhesive; (*sobre*) self-sealing

autobiografía [autoβjoxra'fia] *nf* autobiography

autobomba [auto'βomba] *nf* (*RPL*) fire engine

autobronceador [autoβronθea'ðor] *adj* self-tanning

autobús [auto'βus] *nm* bus; **autobús de línea** long-distance coach

autocar [auto'kar] *nm* coach (*BRIT*), (passenger) bus (*US*)

autóctono, -a [au'toktono, a] *adj* native, indigenous

autodefensa [autoðe'fensa] *nf* self-defence

autodidacta [autoði'ðakta] *adj* self-taught

autoescuela [autoes'kwela] (*ESP*) *nf* driving school

autógrafo [au'toxrafo] *nm* autograph

autómata [au'tomata] *nm* automaton

automático, -a [auto'matiko, a] *adj* automatic ▷ *nm* press stud

automóvil [auto'moβil] *nm* (motor) car (*BRIT*), automobile (*US*); **automovilismo** *nm* (*actividad*) motoring; (*Deporte*) motor racing; **automovilista** *nmf* motorist, driver

autonomía [autono'mia] *nf* autonomy; **autónomo, -a** (*ESP*), **autonómico, -a** (*ESP*) *adj* (*Pol*) autonomous

autopista [auto'pista] *nf* motorway (*BRIT*), freeway (*US*); **autopista de cuota** (*ESP*) *o* **peaje** (*MÉX*) toll (*BRIT*) *o* turnpike (*US*) road

autopsia [au'topsja] *nf* autopsy, postmortem

autor, a [au'tor, a] *nm/f* author

autoridad [autori'ðað] *nf* authority; **autoritario, -a** *adj* authoritarian

autorización [autoriθa'θjon] *nf* authorization; **autorizado, -a** *adj* authorized; (*aprobado*) approved

autorizar [autori'θar] *vt* to authorize; (*aprobar*) to approve

autoservicio [autoser'βiθjo] *nm* (*tienda*) self-service shop (*BRIT*) *o* store (*US*); (*restaurante*) self-service restaurant

autostop [auto'stop] *nm* hitch-hiking; **hacer ~ to** hitch-hike; **autostopista** *nmf* hitch-hiker

autovía [auto'βia] *nf* ≈ Aroad (BRIT), dual carriageway (BRIT), ≈ state highway (US)

auxiliar [auksi'ljar] *vt* to help ▷ *nmf* assistant; **auxilio** *nm* assistance, help; **primeros auxilios** first aid *sg*

Av *abr* (= *Avenida*) Av(e)

aval [a'βal] *nm* guarantee; (*persona*) guarantor

avalancha [aβa'lantʃa] *nf* avalanche

avance [a'βanθe] *nm* advance; (*pago*) advance payment; (*Cine*) trailer

avanzar [aβan'θar] *vt, vi* to advance

avaricia [aβa'riθja] *nf* avarice, greed; **avaricioso, -a** *adj* avaricious, greedy

avaro, -a [a'βaro, a] *adj* miserly, mean ▷ *nm/f* miser

Avda *abr* (= *Avenida*) Av(e)

AVE ['aβe] *nm abr* (= *Alta Velocidad Española*) ≈ bullet train

ave ['aβe] *nf* bird; **ave de rapiña** bird of prey

avecinarse [aβeθi'narse] *vr* (*tormenta: fig*) to be on the way

avellana [aβe'ʎana] *nf* hazelnut; **avellano** *nm* hazel tree

avemaría [aβema'ria] *nm* Hail Mary, Ave Maria

avena [a'βena] *nf* oats *pl*

avenida [aβe'niða] *nf* (*calle*) avenue

aventajar [aβenta'xar] *vt* (*sobrepasar*) to surpass, outstrip

aventón [aβen'ton] (*MÉX: fam*) *nm* ride; **dar ~ a algn** to give sb a ride

aventura [aβen'tura] *nf* adventure; **aventurero, -a** *adj* adventurous

avergonzar [aβerɣon'θar] *vt* to shame; (*desconcertar*) to embarrass; **avergonzarse** *vr* to be ashamed; to be embarrassed

avería [aβe'ria] *nf* (*Tec*) breakdown, fault

averiado, -a [aβe'rjaðo, a] *adj* broken down; "**~**" "out of order"

averiguar [aβeri'ɣwar] *vt* to investigate; (*descubrir*) to find out, ascertain

avestruz [aβes'truθ] *nm* ostrich

aviación [aβja'θjon] *nf* aviation; (*fuerzas aéreas*) air force

aviador, a [aβja'ðor, a] *nm/f* aviator, airman(-woman)

ávido, -a ['aβiðo, a] *adj* avid, eager

avinagrado, -a [aβina'ɣraðo, a] *adj* sour, acid

avión [a'βjon] *nm* aeroplane; (*ave*) martin; **avión de reacción** jet (plane)

avioneta [aβjo'neta] *nf* light aircraft

avisar [aβi'sar] *vt* (*advertir*) to warn, notify; (*informar*) to tell; (*aconsejar*) to advise, counsel; **aviso** *nm* warning; (*noticia*) notice

avispa [a'βispa] *nf* wasp

avispado, -a [aβis'paðo, a] *adj* sharp, clever

avivar [aβi'βar] *vt* to strengthen, intensify

axila [ak'sila] *nf* armpit

ay [ai] *excl* (*dolor*) ow!, ouch!; (*aflicción*) oh!, oh dear!; **¡~ de mí!** poor me!

ayer [a'jer] *adv, nm* yesterday; **antes de ~** the day before yesterday; **~ mismo** only yesterday

ayote [a'jote] (*CAM*) *nm* pumpkin

ayuda [a'juða] *nf* help, assistance ▷ *nm* page; **ayudante** *nmf* assistant, helper; (*Escol*) assistant; (*Mil*) adjutant

ayudar [aju'ðar] *vt* to help, assist

ayunar [aju'nar] *vi* to fast; **ayunas** *nfpl*: **estar en ayunas** to be fasting; **ayuno** *nm* fast; fasting

ayuntamiento [ajunta'mjento] *nm* (*consejo*) town (*o city*) council; (*edificio*) town (*o city*) hall

azafata [aθa'fata] *nf* air stewardess

azafrán [aθa'fran] *nm* saffron

azahar [aθa'ar] *nm* orange/lemon blossom

azar [a'θar] *nm* (*casualidad*) chance, fate; (*desgracia*) misfortune, accident; **por ~** by chance; **al ~** at random

Azores [a'θores] *nfpl*: **las ~** the Azores

azotar [aθo'tar] *vt* to whip, beat; (*pegar*) to spank; **azote** *nm* (*látigo*) whip; (*latigazo*) lash, stroke; (*en las nalgas*) spank; (*calamidad*) calamity

azotea [aθo'tea] *nf* (*flat*) roof

azteca [aθ'teka] *adj, nmf* Aztec

azúcar [a'θukar] *nm* sugar; **azucarado, -a** *adj* sugary, sweet

azucarero, -a [aθuka'rero, a] *adj* sugar *cpd* ▷ *nm* sugar bowl

azucena [aθu'θena] *nf* white lily

azufre [a'θufre] *nm* sulphur

azul [a'θul] *adj, nm* blue; **azul celeste/marino** sky/navy blue

azulejo [aθu'lexo] *nm* tile

azuzar [aθu'θar] *vt* to incite, egg on

B.A. abr (= *Buenos Aires*) B.A.

baba ['baβa] *nf* spittle, saliva; **babear** *vi* to drool, slaver

babero [ba'βero] *nm* bib

babor [ba'βor] *nm* port (side)

babosada [baβo'saða] (*MÉX, CAM: fam*) *nf* drivel; **baboso, -a** [ba'βoso, a] (*LAM: fam*) *adj* silly

baca ['baka] *nf* (*Auto*) luggage o roof rack

bacalao [baka'lao] *nm* cod(fish)

bache ['batʃe] *nm* pothole, rut; (*fig*) bad patch

bachillerato [batʃiʎe'rato] *nm* higher secondary school course

bacinica [baθi'nika] (*LAM*) *nf* potty

bacteria [bak'terja] *nf* bacterium, germ

Bahama [ba'ama]: **las (Islas) ~** *nfpl* the Bahamas

bahía [ba'ia] *nf* bay

bailar [bai'lar] *vt, vi* to dance; **bailarín, -ina** *nm/f* (*ballet*) dancer; **baile** *nm* dance; (*formal*) ball

baja ['baxa] *nf* drop, fall; (*Mil*) casualty; **dar de ~** (*soldado*) to discharge; (*empleado*) to dismiss

bajada [ba'xaða] *nf* descent; (*camino*) slope; (*de aguas*) ebb

bajar [ba'xar] *vi* to go down, come down; (*temperatura, precios*) to drop, fall ▷ *vt* (*cabeza*) to bow; (*escalera*) to go down, come down; (*precio, voz*) to lower; (*llevar abajo*) to take down; **bajarse** *vr* (*de coche*) to get out; (*de autobús, tren*) to get off; **~ de** (*coche*) to get out of; (*autobús, tren*) to get off; **~se algo de Internet** to download sth from the Internet

bajío [ba'xio] (*LAM*) *nm* lowlands *pl*

bajo, -a ['baxo] *adj* (*mueble, número, precio*) low; (*piso*) ground; (*de estatura*) small, short; (*color*) pale; (*sonido*) faint, soft, low; (*voz: en tono*) deep; (*metal*) base; (*humilde*) low, humble ▷ *adv* (*hablar*) softly, quietly; (*volar*) low ▷ *prep* under, below, underneath ▷ *nm* (*Mús*) bass; **~ la lluvia** in the rain

bajón [ba'xon] *nm* fall, drop

bakalao [baka'lao] (*ESP: fam*) *nm* rave (music)

bala ['bala] *nf* bullet

balacear [balaθe'ar] (*MÉX, CAM*) *vt* to shoot

balance [ba'lanθe] *nm* (*Com*) balance; (: *libro*) balance sheet; (: *cuenta general*) stocktaking

balancear [balanθe'ar] *vt* to balance ▷ *vi* to swing

(to and fro); (*vacilar*) to hesitate; **balancearse** *vr* to swing (to and fro), to hesitate

balanza [ba'lanθa] *nf* scales *pl*, balance; **balanza comercial** balance of trade; **balanza de pagos** balance of payments

balaustrada [balaus'traða] *nf* balustrade; (*pasamanos*) banisters *pl*

balazo [ba'laθo] *nm* (*golpe*) shot; (*herida*) bullet wound

balbucear [balβuθe'ar] *vi, vt* to stammer, stutter

balcón [bal'kon] *nm* balcony

balde ['balde] *nm* bucket, pail; **de ~** (for) free, for nothing; **en ~** in vain

baldosa [bal'dosa] *nf* (*azulejo*) floor tile; (*grande*) flagstone; **baldosín** *nm* (small) tile

Baleares [bale'ares] *nfpl*: **las (Islas) ~** the Balearic Islands

balero [ba'lero] (*LAM*) *nm* (*juguete*) cup-and-ball toy

baliza [ba'liθa] *nf* (*Aviac*) beacon; (*Náut*) buoy

ballena [ba'ʎena] *nf* whale

ballet [ba'le] (*pl* **~s**) *nm* ballet

balneario [balne'arjo] *nm* spa; (cs: *en la costa*) seaside resort

balón [ba'lon] *nm* ball

baloncesto [balon'θesto] *nm* basketball

balonmano [balon'mano] *nm* handball

balsa ['balsa] *nf* raft; (*Bot*) balsa wood

bálsamo ['balsamo] *nm* balsam, balm

baluarte [ba'lwarte] *nm* bastion, bulwark

bambú [bam'bu] *nm* bamboo

banana [ba'nana] (*LAM*) *nf* banana; **banano** *nm* (*LAM: árbol*) banana tree; (*CAM: fruta*) banana

banca ['banka] *nf* (*Com*) banking

bancario, -a [ban'karjo, a] *adj* banking *cpd*, bank *cpd*

bancarrota [banka'rrota] *nf* bankruptcy; **hacer ~** to go bankrupt

banco ['banko] *nm* bench; (*Escol*) desk; (*Com*) bank; (*Geo*) stratum; **banco de arena** sandbank; **banco de crédito** credit bank; **banco de datos** databank

banda ['banda] *nf* band; (*pandilla*) gang; (*Náut*) side, edge; **banda ancha** broadband; **banda sonora** soundtrack

bandada [ban'daða] *nf* (*de pájaros*) flock; (*de peces*) shoal

bandazo [ban'daθo] *nm*: **dar ~s** to sway from side to side

bandeja [ban'dexa] *nf* tray

bandera [ban'dera] *nf* flag

banderilla [bande'riʎa] *nf* banderilla

bandido [ban'diðo] *nm* bandit

bando ['bando] *nm* (*edicto*) edict, proclamation; (*facción*) faction; **bandos** *nmpl* (*Rel*) banns

bandolera [bando'lera] *nf*: **llevar en ~** to wear across one's chest

banquero [ban'kero] *nm* banker

banqueta [ban'keta] *nf* stool; (*MÉX: en calle*) pavement (*BRIT*), sidewalk (*US*)

banquete [ban'kete] *nm* banquet; (*para convidados*) formal dinner; **banquete de boda(s)** wedding reception

banquillo [ban'kiʎo] *nm* (*Jur*) dock, prisoner's bench; (*banco*) bench; (*para los pies*) footstool

banquina [ban'kina] (*RPL*) *nf* hard shoulder (*BRIT*), berm (*US*)

bañadera [baɲa'ðera] (*RPL*) *nf* bathtub

bañador [baɲaˈðor] (ESP) nm swimming costume (BRIT), bathing suit (US)

bañar [baˈɲar] vt to bath, bathe (objeto) to dip; (de barniz) to coat; **bañarse** vr (en el mar) to bathe, swim; (en la bañera) to have a bath

bañera [baˈɲera] (ESP) nf bath(tub)

bañero, -a [baˈɲero, a] (CS) nm/f lifeguard

bañista [baˈɲista] nmf bather

baño [ˈbaɲo] nm (en bañera) bath; (en río) dip, swim; (cuarto) bathroom; (bañera) bath(tub); (capa) coating; **darse** o **tomar un ~** (en bañera) to have a take a bath; (en mar, piscina) to have a swim; **baño María** bain-marie

bar [bar] nm bar

barahúnda [baraˈunda] nf uproar, hubbub

baraja [baˈraxa] nf pack (of cards); **barajar** vt (naipes) to shuffle; (fig) to jumble up

baranda [baˈranda] nf = **barandilla**

barandilla [baranˈdiʎa] nf rail, railing

barata [baˈrata] (MÉX) nf (bargain) sale

baratillo [baraˈtiʎo] nm (tienda) junkshop; (subasta) bargain sale; (conjunto de cosas) secondhand goods pl

barato, -a [baˈrato, a] adj cheap ▷ adv cheap, cheaply

barba [ˈbarβa] nf (mentón) chin; (pelo) beard

barbacoa [barβaˈkoa] nf (parrilla) barbecue; (carne) barbecued meat

barbaridad [barβariˈðað] nf barbarity; (acto) barbarism; (atrocidad) outrage; **una ~** (fam) loads; **¡qué ~!** (fam) how awful!

barbarie [barˈβarje] nf barbarism, savagery; (crueldad) barbarity

bárbaro, -a [ˈbarβaro, a] adj barbarous, cruel; (grosero) rough, uncouth ▷ nm/f barbarian ▷ lo **pasamos ~** (fam) we had a great time; **¡qué ~!** (fam) how marvellous!; **un éxito ~** (fam) a terrific success; **es un tipo ~** (fam) he's a great bloke

barbero [barˈβero] nm barber, hairdresser

barbilla [barˈβiʎa] nf chin, tip of the chin

barbudo, -a [barˈβuðo, a] adj bearded

barca [ˈbarka] nf (small) boat; **barcaza** nf barge

Barcelona [barθeˈlona] n Barcelona

barco [ˈbarko] nm boat; (grande) ship; **barco de carga/pesca** cargo/fishing boat; **barco de vela** sailing ship

barda [ˈbarða] (MÉX) nf (de madera) fence

baremo [baˈremo] nm (Mat: fig) scale

barítono [baˈritono] nm baritone

barman [ˈbarman] nm barman

barniz [barˈniθ] nm varnish; (en loza) glaze; (fig) veneer; **barnizar** vt to varnish; (loza) to glaze

barómetro [baˈrometro] nm barometer

barquillo [barˈkiʎo] nm cone, cornet

barra [ˈbarra] nf bar, rod; (de un bar, café) bar; (de pan) French stick; (palanca) lever; **barra de labios** lipstick; **barra libre** free bar

barraca [baˈrraka] nf hut, cabin

barranco [baˈrranko] nm ravine; (fig) difficulty

barrena [baˈrrena] nf drill

barrer [baˈrrer] vt to sweep; (quitar) to sweep away

barrera [baˈrrera] nf barrier

barriada [baˈrrjaða] nf quarter, district

barricada [barriˈkaða] nf barricade

barrida [baˈrriða] nf sweep, sweeping

barriga [baˈrriɣa] nf belly; (panza) paunch; **barrigón, -ona** adj potbellied; **barrigudo, -a** adj potbellied

barril [baˈrril] nm barrel, cask

barrio [ˈbarrjo] nm (vecindad) area, neighbourhood (US); (en afueras) suburb; **barrio chino** (ESP) red-light district

barro [ˈbarro] nm (lodo) mud; (objetos) earthenware; (Med) pimple

barroco, -a [baˈrroko, a] adj, nm baroque

barrote [baˈrrote] nm (de ventana) bar

bártola [barˈtola] nf: **tirarse** o **tumbarse a la ~** to take it easy, be lazy

bártulos [ˈbartulos] nmpl things, belongings

barullo [baˈruʎo] nm row, uproar

basar [baˈsar] vt to base; **basarse** vr: **~se en** to be based on

báscula [ˈbaskula] nf (platform) scales

base [ˈbase] nf base; **a ~ de** on the basis of; (mediante) by means of; **base de datos** (Inform) database

básico, -a [ˈbasiko, a] adj basic

basílica [baˈsilika] nf basilica

básquetbol [basketˈbol] (LAM) nm basketball

○ **PALABRA CLAVE**

bastante [basˈtante] adj 1 (suficiente) enough; **bastante dinero** enough o sufficient money; **bastantes libros** enough books
2 (valor intensivo): **bastante gente** quite a lot of people; **tener bastante calor** to be rather hot
▷ adv: **bastante bueno/malo** quite good/rather bad; **bastante rico** pretty rich; **(lo) bastante inteligente (como) para hacer algo** clever enough o sufficiently clever to do sth

bastar [basˈtar] vi to be enough o sufficient; **bastarse** vr to be self-sufficient; **~ para** to be enough to; **¡basta!** (that's) enough!

bastardo, -a [basˈtarðo, a] adj, nm/f bastard

bastidor [bastiˈðor] nm frame; (de coche) chassis; (Teatro) wing; **entre ~es** (fig) behind the scenes

basto, -a [ˈbasto, a] adj coarse, rough; **bastos** nmpl (Naipes) = clubs

bastón [basˈton] nm stick, staff; (para pasear) walking stick

bastoncillo [bastonˈθiʎo] nm cotton bud

basura [baˈsura] nf rubbish (BRIT), garbage (US) ▷ adj: **comida/televisión ~** junk food/TV

basurero [basuˈrero] nm (hombre) dustman (BRIT), garbage man (US); (lugar) dump; (cubo) (rubbish) bin (BRIT), trash can (US)

bata [ˈbata] nf (gen) dressing gown; (cubretodo) smock, overall; (Med, Tec etc) lab(oratory) coat

batalla [baˈtaʎa] nf battle; **de ~** (fig) for everyday use; **batalla campal** pitched battle

batallón [bataˈʎon] nm battalion

batata [baˈtata] nf sweet potato

batería [bateˈria] nf battery; (Mús) drums; **batería de cocina** kitchen utensils

batido, -a [baˈtiðo, a] adj (camino) beaten, well-trodden ▷ nm (Culin: de leche) milk shake

batidora [batiˈðora] nf beater, mixer; **batidora eléctrica** food mixer, blender

batir [baˈtir] vt to beat, strike; (vencer) to beat, defeat; (revolver) to beat, mix; **batirse** vr to fight; **~ palmas** to applaud

batuta [baˈtuta] nf baton; **llevar la ~** (fig) to be the boss, be in charge

baúl [ba'ul] nm trunk; (Auto) boot (BRIT), trunk (US)

bautismo [bau'tismo] nm baptism, christening

bautizar [bauti'θar] vt to baptize, christen; (fam: diluir) to water down; **bautizo** nm baptism, christening

bayeta [ba'jeta] nf floorcloth

baza ['baθa] nf trick; **meter ~** to butt in

bazar [ba'θar] nm bazaar

bazofia [ba'θofja] nf trash

be [be] nf name of the letter B; **be chica/grande** (MÉX) V/B; **be larga** (LAM) B

beato, -a [be'ato, a] adj blessed; (piadoso) pious

bebé [be'βe] (pl **~s**) nm baby

bebedero [beβe'ðero, a] (MÉX, CS) nm drinking fountain

bebedor, a [beβe'ðor, a] adj hard-drinking

beber [be'βer] vt, vi to drink

bebida [be'βiða] nf drink; **bebido, -a** adj drunk

beca ['beka] nf grant, scholarship; **becario, -a** [be'karjo, a] nm/f scholarship holder, grant holder

bedel [be'ðel] nm (Escol) janitor; (Univ) porter

béisbol ['beisβol] nm baseball

Belén [be'len] nm Bethlehem; **belén** nm (de Navidad) nativity scene, crib

belga ['belγa] adj, nmf Belgian

Bélgica ['belxika] nf Belgium

bélico, -a ['beliko, a] adj (actitud) warlike

belleza [be'λeθa] nf beauty

bello, -a ['beλo, a] adj beautiful, lovely; **Bellas Artes** Fine Art

bellota [be'λota] nf acorn

bemol [be'mol] nm (Mús) flat; **esto tiene ~es** (fam) this is a tough one

bencina [ben'θina] nf (Quím) benzine

bendecir [bende'θir] vt to bless

bendición [bendi'θjon] nf blessing

bendito, -a [ben'dito, a] pp de **bendecir** ▷ adj holy; (afortunado) lucky; (feliz) happy; (sencillo) simple ▷ nm/f simple soul

beneficencia [benefi'θenθja] nf charity

beneficiario, -a [benefi'θjarjo, a] nm/f beneficiary

beneficio [bene'fiθjo] nm (bien) benefit, advantage; (ganancia) profit, gain; **a ~ de algn** in aid of sb; **beneficioso, -a** adj beneficial

benéfico, -a [be'nefiko, a] adj charitable

beneplácito [bene'plaθito] nm approval, consent

benévolo, -a [be'neβolo, a] adj benevolent, kind

benigno, -a [be'niγno, a] adj kind; (suave) mild; (Med: tumor) benign, non-malignant

berberecho [berβe'retʃo] nm (Zool, Culin) cockle

berenjena [beren'xena] nf aubergine (BRIT), eggplant (US)

Berlín [ber'lin] n Berlin

berlinesa [berli'nesa] (RPL) nf doughnut, donut (US)

bermudas [ber'muðas] nfpl Bermuda shorts

berrido [be'rriðo] nm bellow(ing)

berrinche [be'rrintʃe] (fam) nm temper, tantrum

berro ['berro] nm watercress

berza ['berθa] nf cabbage

besamel [besa'mel] nf (Culin) white sauce, bechamel sauce

besar [be'sar] vt to kiss; (fig: tocar) to graze; **besarse** vr to kiss (one another); **beso** nm kiss

bestia ['bestja] nf beast, animal; (fig) idiot; **bestia de carga** beast of burden; **bestial** [bes'tjal] adj bestial; (fam) terrific; **bestialidad** nf bestiality; (fam) stupidity

besugo [be'suxo] nm sea bream; (fam) idiot

besuquear [besuke'ar] vt to cover with kisses; **besuquearse** vr to kiss and cuddle

betabel [beta'βel] (MÉX) nm beetroot (BRIT), beet (US)

betún [be'tun] nm shoe polish; (Quím) bitumen

biberón [biβe'ron] nm feeding bottle

Biblia ['biβlja] nf Bible

bibliografía [biβljoxra'fia] nf bibliography

biblioteca [biβljo'teka] nf library; (mueble) bookshelves; **biblioteca de consulta** reference library; **bibliotecario, -a** nm/f librarian

bicarbonato [bikarβo'nato] nm bicarbonate

bicho ['bitʃo] nm (animal) small animal; (sabandija) bug, insect; (Taur) bull

bici ['biθi] (fam) nf bike

bicicleta [biθi'kleta] nf bicycle, cycle; **ir en ~** to cycle

bidé [bi'ðe] (pl **~s**) nm bidet

bidón [bi'ðon] nm (de aceite) drum; (de gasolina) can

○ PALABRA CLAVE

bien [bjen] nm **1** (bienestar) good; **te lo digo por tu bien** I'm telling you for your own good; **el bien y el mal** good and evil

2 (posesión): **bienes** goods; **bienes de consumo** consumer goods; **bienes inmuebles** o **raíces/bienes muebles** real estate sg/personal property sg ▷ adv **1** (de manera satisfactoria, correcta etc) well; **trabaja/come bien** she works/eats well; **contestó bien** he answered correctly; **me siento bien** I feel fine; **no me siento bien** I don't feel very well; **se está bien aquí** it's nice here

2 (frases): **hiciste bien en llamarme** you were right to call me

3 (valor intensivo) very; **un cuarto bien caliente** a nice warm room; **bien se ve que ...** it's quite clear that ...

4 estar bien: **estoy muy bien aquí** I feel very happy here; **está bien que vengan** it's all right for them to come; **¡está bien! lo haré** oh all right, I'll do it

5 (de buena gana): **yo bien que iría pero ...** I'd gladly go but ... ▷ excl: **¡bien!** (aprobación) O.K.!; **¡muy bien!** well done! ▷ adj inv (matiz despectivo): **gente bien** posh people ▷ conj **1** bien ... bien: **bien en coche bien en tren** either by car or by train

2 (LAM): **no bien: no bien llegue te llamaré** as soon as I arrive I'll call you

3 si bien even though; V tb **más**

bienal [bje'nal] adj biennial

bienestar [bjenes'tar] nm well-being, welfare

bienvenida [bjembe'niða] nf welcome; **dar la ~ a algn** to welcome sb

bienvenido [bjembe'niðo] excl welcome!

bife ['bife] (cs) nm steak

bifurcación [bifurka'θjon] nf fork

bígamo, -a ['biγamo, a] adj bigamous ▷ nm/f bigamist

bigote [bi'γote] nm moustache; **bigotudo, -a** adj with a big moustache

bikini [bi'kini] nm bikini; (Culin) toasted ham and cheese sandwich

bilingüe [bi'lingwe] adj bilingual

billar [bi'λar] nm billiards sg; **billares** nmpl (lugar) billiard hall; (sala de juegos) amusement arcade; **billar americano** pool

billete [bi'λete] nm ticket; (de banco) (bank)note

(BRIT), bill (US); (carta) note; **~ de 20 libras** £20 note; **billete de ida y vuelta** return (BRIT) o round-trip (US) ticket; **billete sencillo** o **de ida** single (BRIT) o one-way (US) ticket, **billete electrónico** e-ticket
billetera [biʎeˈtera] nf wallet
billón [biˈʎon] nm billion
bimensual [bimenˈswal] adj twice monthly
bingo [ˈbiŋɡo] nm bingo
biodegradable [bioðeɣraˈðaβle] adj biodegradable
biografía [bjoɣraˈfia] nf biography
biología [bjoloˈxia] nf biology; **biológico, -a** adj biological; (cultivo, producto) organic; **biólogo, -a** nm/f biologist
biombo [ˈbjombo] nm (folding) screen
bioterrorismo [bjoterroˈrismo] nm bioterrorism
biquini [biˈkini] nm o (RPL) f bikini
birlar [birˈlar] (fam) vt to pinch
Birmania [birˈmanja] nf Burma
birome [biˈrome] (RPL) nf ballpoint (pen)
birria [ˈbirrja] nf: **ser una ~** (película, libro) to be rubbish
bis [bis] excl encore!
bisabuelo, -a [bisaˈβwelo, a] nm/f great-grandfather(-mother)
bisagra [biˈsaɣra] nf hinge
bisiesto [biˈsjesto] adj: **año ~** leap year
bisnieto, -a [bisˈnjeto, a] nm/f great-grandson/daughter
bisonte [biˈsonte] nm bison
bisté [bisˈte] nm = **bistec**
bistec [bisˈtek] nm steak
bisturí [bistuˈri] nm scalpel
bisutería [bisuteˈria] nf imitation o costume jewellery
bit [bit] nm (Inform) bit
bizco, -a [ˈbiθko, a] adj cross-eyed
bizcocho [biθˈkotʃo] nm (Culin) sponge cake
blanca [ˈblanka] nf (Mús) minim; **estar sin ~** (ESP: fam) to be broke; V tb **blanco**
blanco, -a [ˈblanko, a] adj white ▷ nm/f white man/woman, white ▷ nm (color) white; (en texto) blank; (Mil, fig) target; **en ~** blank; **noche en ~** sleepless night
blandir [blanˈdir] vt to brandish
blando, -a [ˈblando, a] adj soft; (tierno) tender, gentle; (carácter) mild; (fam) cowardly
blanqueador [blankeaˈðor] (MÉX) nm bleach
blanquear [blankeˈar] vt to whiten; (fachada) to whitewash; (paño) to bleach ▷ vi to turn white
blanquillo [blanˈkiʎo] (MÉX, CAM) nm egg
blasfemar [blasfeˈmar] vi to blaspheme, curse
bledo [ˈbleðo] nm: **me importa un ~** I couldn't care less
blindado, -a [blinˈdaðo, a] adj (Mil) armour-plated; (antibala) bullet-proof; **coche** (ESP) o **carro** (LAM) **~** armoured car
bloc [blok] (pl **~s**) nm writing pad
blof [blof] (MÉX) nm bluff; **blofear** (MÉX) vi to bluff
blog [bloɣ] (pl **~s**) nm blog
bloque [ˈbloke] nm block; (Pol) bloc
bloquear [blokeˈar] vt to blockade; **bloqueo** nm blockade; (Com) freezing, blocking; **bloqueo mental** mental block
blusa [ˈblusa] nf blouse
bobada [boˈβaða] nf foolish action; foolish statement; **decir ~s** to talk nonsense

bobina [boˈβina] nf (Tec) bobbin, (Foto) spool; (Elec) coil
bobo, -a [ˈboβo, a] adj (tonto) daft, silly; (cándido) naõve ▷ nm/f fool, idiot ▷ nm (Teatro) clown, funny man
boca [ˈboka] nf mouth; (de crustáceo) pincer; (de cañón) muzzle; (entrada) mouth, entrance; **bocas** nfpl (de río) mouth sg; **~ abajo/arriba** face down/up; **se me hace la ~ agua** my mouth is watering; **boca de incendios** hydrant; **boca del estómago** pit of the stomach; **boca de metro** underground (BRIT) o subway (US) entrance
bocacalle [bokaˈkaʎe] nf (entrance to a) street; **la primera ~** the first turning o street
bocadillo [bokaˈðiʎo] nm sandwich
bocado [boˈkaðo] nm mouthful, bite; (de caballo) bridle
bocajarro [bokaˈxarro] nm: **a ~** adv (disparar) point-blank
bocanada [bokaˈnaða] nf (de vino) mouthful, swallow; (de aire) gust, puff
bocata [boˈkata] (fam) nm sandwich
bocazas [boˈkaθas] (fam) nm inv bigmouth
boceto [boˈθeto] nm sketch, outline
bochorno [boˈtʃorno] nm (vergüenza) embarrassment; (calor): **hace ~** it's very muggy
bocina [boˈθina] nf (Mús) trumpet; (Auto) horn; (para hablar) megaphone
boda [ˈboða] nf (tb: **~s**) wedding, marriage; (fiesta) wedding reception; **bodas de oro/plata** golden/silver wedding sg
bodega [boˈðeɣa] nf (de vino) (wine) cellar; (depósito) storeroom; (de barco) hold
bodegón [boðeˈɣon] nm (Arte) still life
bofetada [bofeˈtaða] nf slap (in the face)
boga [ˈboɣa] nf: **en ~** (fig) in vogue
Bogotá [boɣoˈta] n Bogotá
bohemio, -a [boˈemjo, a] adj, nm/f Bohemian
bohío [boˈio] (CAM) nm shack, hut
boicot [boiˈkot] (pl **~s**) nm boycott; **boicotear** vt to boycott
bóiler [ˈboiler] (MÉX) nm boiler
boina [ˈboina] nf beret
bola [ˈbola] nf ball; (canica) marble; (Naipes) (grand) slam; (betún) shoe polish; (mentira) tale, story; **bolas** nfpl (LAM: caza) bolas sg; **bola de billar** billiard ball; **bola de nieve** snowball
boleadoras [boleaˈðoras] nfpl bolas sg
bolear [boleˈar] (MÉX) vt (zapatos) to polish, shine
bolera [boˈlera] nf skittle o bowling alley
bolero, -a [boˈlero, a] nm/f (limpiabotas) shoeshine boy/girl
boleta [boˈleta] (LAM) nf (de rifa) ticket; (cs: recibo) receipt; **boleta de calificaciones** (MÉX) report card
boletería [boleteˈria] (LAM) nf ticket office
boletín [boleˈtin] nm bulletin; (periódico) journal, review; **boletín de noticias** news bulletin
boleto [boˈleto] nm (LAM) ticket; **boleto de ida y vuelta** (LAM) round trip ticket; **boleto electrónico** (LAM) e-ticket; **boleto redondo** (MÉX) round trip ticket
boli [ˈboli] (fam) nm Biro®
bolígrafo [boˈliɣrafo] nm ball-point pen, Biro®
bolilla [boˈliʎa] (RPL) nf topic
bolillo [boˈliʎo] (MÉX) nm (bread) roll
bolita [boˈlita] (cs) nf marble
bolívar [boˈliβar] nm monetary unit of Venezuela
Bolivia [boˈliβja] nf Bolivia; **boliviano, -a** adj, nm/f Bolivian

bollería [boʎeˈria] nf cakes pl and pastries pl

bollo [ˈboʎo] nm (pan) roll; (bulto) bump, lump; (abolladura) dent

bolo [ˈbolo] nm skittle; (píldora) (large) pill; **(juego de) bolos** nmpl skittles sg

bolsa [ˈbolsa] nf (para llevar algo) bag; (MÉX, CAM: bolsillo) pocket; (MÉX: de mujer) handbag; (Anat) cavity, sac; (Com) stock exchange; (Minería) pocket; **de ~** pocket cpd; **bolsa de agua caliente** hot water bottle; **bolsa de aire** air pocket; **bolsa de dormir** (MÉX, RPL) sleeping bag; **bolsa de la compra** shopping bag; **bolsa de papel/plástico** paper/plastic bag

bolsear [bolseˈar] (MÉX, CAM) vt: **a algn** to pick sb's pocket

bolsillo [bolˈsiʎo] nm pocket; (cartera) purse; **de ~** pocket(-size)

bolso [ˈbolso] nm (bolsa) bag; (de mujer) handbag

bomba [ˈbomba] nf (Mil) bomb; (Tec) pump ▷ adj (fam): **noticia ~** bombshell ▷ adv (fam): **pasarlo ~** to have a great time; **bomba atómica/de efecto retardado/de humo** atomic/time/smoke bomb

bombacha [bomˈbatʃa] (RPL) nf panties pl

bombardear [bombardeˈar] vt to bombard; (Mil) to bomb; **bombardeo** nm bombardment; bombing

bombazo [bomˈbaθo] (MÉX) nm (explosión) explosion; (fam: notición) bombshell; (: éxito) smash hit

bombear [bombeˈar] vt (agua) to pump (out o up)

bombero [bomˈbero] nm fireman

bombilla [bomˈbiʎa] (ESP) nf (light) bulb

bombita [bomˈbita] (RPL) nf (light) bulb

bombo [ˈbombo] nm (Mús) bass drum; (Tec) drum

bombón [bomˈbon] nm chocolate; (MÉX: de caramelo) marshmallow

bombona [bomˈbona] (ESP) nf (de butano, oxígeno) cylinder

bonachón, -ona [bonaˈtʃon, ona] adj good-natured, easy-going

bonanza [boˈnanθa] nf (Náut) fair weather; (fig) bonanza; (Minería) rich pocket o vein

bondad [bonˈdað] nf goodness, kindness; **tenga la ~ de** (please) be good enough to

bonito, -a [boˈnito, a] adj pretty; (agradable) nice ▷ nm (atún) tuna (fish)

bono [ˈbono] nm voucher; (Finanzas) bond

bonobús [bonoˈbus] (ESP) nm bus pass

bonoloto [bonoˈloto] nf state-run weekly lottery

boquerón [bokeˈron] nm (pez) (kind of) anchovy; (agujero) large hole

boquete [boˈkete] nm gap, hole

boquiabierto, -a [bokiaˈβjerto, a] adj: **quedarse ~** to be amazed o flabbergasted

boquilla [boˈkiʎa] nf (para riego) nozzle; (para cigarro) cigarette holder; (Mús) mouthpiece

borbotón [borboˈton] nm: **salir a borbotones** to gush out

borda [ˈborða] nf (Náut) (ship's) rail; **tirar algo/caerse por la ~** to throw sth/fall overboard

bordado [borˈðaðo] nm embroidery

bordar [borˈðar] vt to embroider

borde [ˈborðe] nm edge, border; (de camino etc) side; (en la costura) hem; **al ~ de** (fig) on the verge o brink of; **ser ~** (ESP: fam) to be rude; **bordear** vt to border

bordillo [borˈðiʎo] nm kerb (BRIT), curb (US)

bordo [ˈborðo] nm (Náut) side; **a ~** on board

borlote [borˈlote] (MÉX) nm row, uproar

borrachera [boraˈtʃera] nf (ebriedad) drunkenness;

(orgía) spree, binge

borracho, -a [boˈratʃo, a] adj drunk ▷ nm/f (habitual) drunkard, drunk; (temporal) drunk, drunk man/woman

borrador [boraˈðor] nm (escritura) first draft, rough sketch; (goma) rubber (BRIT), eraser

borrar [boˈrrar] vt to erase, rub out

borrasca [boˈraska] nf storm

borrego, -a [boˈrɾexo, a] nm/f (Zool: joven) (yearling) lamb; (adulto) sheep ▷ nm (MÉX: fam) false rumour

borrico, -a [boˈriko, a] nm/f donkey/she-donkey; (fig) stupid man/woman

borrón [boˈron] nm (mancha) stain

borroso, -a [boˈroso, a] adj vague, unclear; (escritura) illegible

bosque [ˈbuske] nm wood; (grande) forest

bostezar [bosteˈθar] vi to yawn; **bostezo** nm yawn

bota [ˈbota] nf (calzado) boot; (para vino) leather wine bottle; **botas de agua o goma** Wellingtons

botana [boˈtana] (MÉX) nf snack, appetizer

botánica [boˈtanika] nf (ciencia) botany; V tb **botánico**

botánico, -a [boˈtaniko, a] adj botanical ▷ nm/f botanist

botar [boˈtar] vt to throw, hurl; (Náut) to launch; (LAM: echar) to throw out o vi (ESP: saltar) to bounce

bote [ˈbote] nm (salto) bounce; (golpe) thrust; (ESP: envase) tin, can; (embarcación) boat; (MÉX, CAM: pey: cárcel) jail; **de ~ en ~** packed, jammed full; **bote de la basura** (MÉX) dustbin (BRIT), trashcan (US); **bote salvavidas** lifeboat

botella [boˈteʎa] nf bottle; **botellín** nm small bottle; **botellón** nm (ESP: fam) outdoor drinking session

botijo [boˈtixo] nm (earthenware) jug

botín [boˈtin] nm (calzado) half boot; (polaina) spat; (Mil) booty

botiquín [botiˈkin] nm (armario) medicine cabinet; (portátil) first-aid kit

botón [boˈton] nm button; (Bot) bud

botones [boˈtones] nm inv (ESP) bellboy (BRIT), bellhop (US)

bóveda [ˈboβeða] nf (Arq) vault

boxeador [bokseaˈðor] nm boxer

boxeo [bokˈseo] nm boxing

boya [ˈboja] nf (Náut) buoy; (de caña) float

boyante [boˈjante] adj prosperous

bozal [boˈθal] nm (para caballos) halter; (de perro) muzzle

bragas [ˈbraɣas] nfpl (de mujer) panties, knickers (BRIT)

bragueta [braˈɣeta] nf fly, flies pl

braille [breil] nm braille

brasa [ˈbrasa] nf live o hot coal

brasero [braˈsero] nm brazier

brasier [braˈsjer] (MÉX) nm bra

Brasil [braˈsil] nm (tb: **el ~**) Brazil; **brasileño, -a** adj, nm/f Brazilian

brassier [braˈsjer] (MÉX) nm V **brasier**

bravo, -a [ˈbraβo, a] adj (valiente) brave; (feroz) ferocious; (salvaje) wild; (mar etc) rough, stormy ▷ excl bravo!; **bravura** nf bravery; ferocity

braza [ˈbraθa] nf fathom; **nadar a ~** to swim breast-stroke

brazalete [braθaˈlete] nm (pulsera) bracelet; (banda) armband

brazo [ˈbraθo] nm arm; (Zool) foreleg; (Bot) limb; branch; **luchar a ~ partido** to fight hand-to-hand; **ir**

cogidos del ~ to walk arm in arm
brebaje [bre'βaxe] nm potion
brecha ['bretʃa] nf (hoyo, vacío) gap, opening; (Mil, fig) breach
brega ['breɣa] nf (lucha) struggle; (trabajo) hard work
breva ['breβa] nf early fig
breve ['breβe] adj short, brief ▷ nf (Mús) breve; **en ~** (pronto) shortly, before long; **brevedad** nf brevity, shortness
bribón, -ona [bri'βon, ona] adj idle, lazy ▷ nm/f (pícaro) rascal, rogue
bricolaje [briko'laxe] nm do-it-yourself, DIY
brida ['briða] nf bridle, rein; (Tec) clamp
bridge [britʃ] nm bridge
brigada [bri'ɣaða] nf (unidad) brigade; (de trabajadores) squad, gang ▷ nm = staff-sergeant, sergeant-major
brillante [bri'ʎante] adj brilliant ▷ nm diamond
brillar [bri'ʎar] vi to shine; (joyas) to sparkle
brillo ['briʎo] nm shine; (brillantez) brilliance; (fig) splendour; **sacar ~ a** to polish
brincar [brin'kar] vi to skip about, hop about, jump about
brinco ['brinko] nm jump, leap
brindar [brin'dar] vi: **~ a o por** to drink (a toast) to ▷ vt to offer, present
brindis ['brindis] nm inv toast
brío ['brio] nm spirit, dash
brisa ['brisa] nf breeze
británico, -a [bri'taniko, a] adj British ▷ nm/f Briton, British person
brizna ['briθna] nf (de hierba, paja) blade; (de tabaco) leaf
broca ['broka] nf (Tec) drill, bit
brocha ['brotʃa] nf (large) paintbrush; **brocha de afeitar** shaving brush
broche ['brotʃe] nm brooch
broma ['broma] nf joke; **de o en ~** in fun, as a joke; **broma pesada** practical joke; **bromear** vi to joke
bromista [bro'mista] adj fond of joking ▷ nm/f joker, wag
bronca ['bronka] nf row; **echar una ~ a algn** to tick sb off
bronce ['bronθe] nm bronze; **bronceado, -a** adj bronze; (por el sol) tanned ▷ nm (sun)tan; (Tec) bronzing
bronceador [bronθea'ðor] nm suntan lotion
broncearse [bronθe'arse] vr to get a suntan
bronquio ['bronkjo] nm (Anat) bronchial tube
bronquitis [bron'kitis] nf inv bronchitis
brotar [bro'tar] vi (Bot) to sprout; (aguas) to gush (forth); (Med) to break out
brote ['brote] nm (Bot) shoot; (Med, fig) outbreak
bruces ['bruθes]: **de bruces** adv: **caer o dar de ~** to fall headlong, fall flat
bruja ['bruxa] nf witch; **brujería** nf witchcraft
brujo ['bruxo] nm wizard, magician
brújula ['bruxula] nf compass
bruma ['bruma] nf mist
brusco, -a ['brusko, a] adj (súbito) sudden; (áspero) brusque
Bruselas [bru'selas] n Brussels
brutal [bru'tal] adj brutal; **brutalidad** [brutali'ðað] nf brutality
bruto, -a ['bruto, a] adj (idiota) stupid; (bestial) brutish; (peso) gross; **en ~** raw, unworked

Bs.As. abr (= Buenos Aires) B.A.
bucal [bu'kal] adj oral; **por vía ~** orally
bucear [buθe'ar] vi to dive ▷ vt to explore; **buceo** nm diving
bucle ['bukle] nm curl
budismo [bu'ðismo] nm Buddhism
buen [bwen] adj m V **bueno**
buenamente [bwena'mente] adv (fácilmente) easily; (voluntariamente) willingly
buenaventura [bwenaβen'tura] nf (suerte) good luck; (adivinación) fortune
buenmozo [bwen'moθo] (MÉX) adj handsome

○ **PALABRA CLAVE**

bueno, -a ['bweno, a] (antes de nmsg: **buen**) adj
1 (excelente etc) good; **es un libro bueno, es un buen libro** it's a good book; **hace bueno, hace buen tiempo** the weather is fine, it is fine; **el bueno de Paco** good old Paco; **fue muy bueno conmigo** he was very nice o kind to me
2 (apropiado): **ser bueno para** to be good for; **creo que vamos por buen camino** I think we're on the right track
3 (irónico): **le di un buen rapapolvo** I gave him a good o real ticking off; **¡buen conductor estás hecho!** some o fine driver you are!; **¡estaría bueno que …!** a fine thing it would be if …!
4 (atractivo, sabroso): **está bueno este bizcocho** this sponge is delicious; **Carmen está muy buena** Carmen is gorgeous
5 (saludos): **¡buen día!, ¡buenos días!** (good) morning!; **¡buenas (tardes)!** (good) afternoon!; (más tarde) (good) evening!; **¡buenas noches!** good night!
6 (otras locuciones): **estar de buenas** to be in a good mood; **por las buenas o por las malas** by hook or by crook; **de buenas a primeras** all of a sudden
▷ excl: **¡bueno!** all right!; **bueno, ¿y qué?** well, so what?

Buenos Aires [bweno'saires] nm Buenos Aires
buey [bwei] nm ox
búfalo ['bufalo] nm buffalo
bufanda [bu'fanda] nf scarf
bufete [bu'fete] nm (despacho de abogado) lawyer's office
bufón [bu'fon] nm clown
buhardilla [buar'ðiʎa] nf attic
búho ['buo] nm owl; (fig) hermit, recluse
buitre ['bwitre] nm vulture
bujía [bu'xia] nf (vela) candle; (Elec) candle (power); (Auto) spark plug
bula ['bula] nf (papal) bull
bulbo ['bulβo] nm bulb
bulevar [bule'βar] nm boulevard
Bulgaria [bul'ɣarja] nf Bulgaria; **búlgaro, -a** adj, nm/f Bulgarian
bulla ['buʎa] nf (ruido) uproar; (de gente) crowd
bullicio [bu'ʎiθjo] nm (ruido) uproar; (movimiento) bustle
bulto ['bulto] nm (paquete) package; (fardo) bundle; (tamaño) size, bulkiness; (Med) swelling, lump; (silueta) vague shape
buñuelo [bu'ɲwelo] nm ≈ doughnut (BRIT), ≈ donut (US); (fruta de sartén) fritter
buque ['buke] nm ship, vessel; **buque de guerra**

warship

burbuja [bur'βuxa] nf bubble

burdel [bur'ðel] nm brothel

burgués, -esa [bur'ɣes, esa] adj middle-class, bourgeois; **burguesía** nf middle class, bourgeoisie

burla ['burla] nf (mofa) gibe; (broma) joke; (engaño) trick; **burlar** [bur'lar] vt (engañar) to deceive ▷ vi to joke; **burlarse** vr to joke; **burlarse de** to make fun of

burlón, -ona [bur'lon, ona] adj mocking

buró [bu'ro] (MÉX) nm bedside table

burocracia [buro'kraθja] nf civil service

burrada [bu'rraða] nf: **decir** o **soltar ~s** to talk nonsense; **hacer ~s** to act stupid; **una ~** (ESP: mucho) a (hell of a) lot

burro, -a ['burro, a] nm/f donkey/she-donkey, (fig) ass, idiot

bursátil [bur'satil] adj stock-exchange cpd

bus [bus] nm bus

busca ['buska] nf search, hunt ▷ nm (Tel) bleeper; **en ~ de** in search of

buscador [buska'ðor] nm (Internet) search engine

buscar [bus'kar] vt to look for, search for, seek ▷ vi to look, search, seek; **se busca secretaria** secretary wanted

busque etc vb V **buscar**

búsqueda ['buskeða] nf = **busca**

busto ['busto] nm (Anat, Arte) bust

butaca [bu'taka] nf armchair; (de cine, teatro) stall, seat

butano [bu'tano] nm butane (gas)

buzo ['buθo] nm diver

buzón [bu'θon] nm (en puerta) letter box; (en calle) pillar box

C

C. abr (= centígrado) C; (compañía) Co.

C/ abr (= calle) St

cabal [ka'βal] adj (exacto) exact; (correcto) right, proper; (acabado) finished, complete; **cabales** nmpl: **no está en sus cabales** she isn't in her right mind

cábalas ['kaβalas] nfpl: **hacer ~** to guess

cabalgar [kaβal'ɣar] vt, vi to ride

cabalgata [kaβal'ɣata] nf procession

caballa [ka'βaʎa] nf mackerel

caballería [kaβaʎe'ria] nf mount; (Mil) cavalry

caballero [kaβa'ʎero] nm gentleman; (de la orden de caballería) knight; (trato directo) sir

caballete [kaβa'ʎete] nm (Arte) easel; (Tec) trestle

caballito [kaβa'ʎito] nm (caballo pequeño) small horse, pony; **caballitos** nmpl (en verbena) roundabout, merry-go-round

caballo [ka'βaʎo] nm horse; (Ajedrez) knight; (Naipes) queen; **ir en ~** to ride; **caballo de carreras** racehorse; **caballo de fuerza** o **vapor** horsepower

cabaña [ka'βaɲa] nf (casita) hut, cabin

cabecear [kaβeθe'ar] vt, vi to nod

cabecera [kaβe'θera] nf head; (Imprenta) headline

cabecilla [kaβe'θiʎa] nm ringleader

cabellera [kaβe'ʎera] nf (head of) hair; (de cometa) tail

cabello [ka'βeʎo] nm (tb: ~s) hair; **cabello de ángel** confectionery and pastry filling made of pumpkin and syrup

caber [ka'βer] vi (entrar) to fit, go; **caben 3 más** there's room for 3 more

cabestrillo [kaβes'triʎo] nm sling

cabeza [ka'βeθa] nf head; (Pol) chief, leader; **cabeza de ajo** bulb of garlic; **cabeza de familia** head of the household; **cabeza rapada** skinhead; **cabezada** nf (golpe) butt; **dar cabezadas** to nod off; **cabezón, -ona** adj (vino) heady; (fam: persona) pig-headed

cabida [ka'βiða] nf space

cabina [ka'βina] nf cabin; (de avión) cockpit; (de camión) cab; **cabina telefónica** telephone (BRIT) box o booth

cabizbajo, -a [kaβiθ'βaxo, a] adj crestfallen, dejected

cable ['kaβle] nm cable

cabo ['kaβo] nm (de objeto) end, extremity; (Mil)

corporal; (*Náut*) rope, cable; (*Geo*) cape; **al ~ de 3 días** after 3 days; **llevar a ~** to carry out

cabra ['kaβra] *nf* goat

cabrú etc *vb* V **caber**

cabrear [kaβre'ar] *vt* to bug; **cabrearse** *vr* (*enfadarse*) to fly off the handle

cabrito [ka'βrito] *nm* kid

cabrón [ka'βron] *nm* cuckold; (*fam!*) bastard (!)

caca ['kaka] (*fam*) *nf* pooh

cacahuete [kaka'wete] (*ESP*) *nm* peanut

cacao [ka'kao] *nm* cocoa; (*Bot*) cacao

cacarear [kakare'ar] *vi* (*persona*) to boast; (*gallina*) to crow

cacería [kaθe'ria] *nf* hunt

cacarizo, -a [kaka'riθo, a] (*MÉX*) *adj* pockmarked

cacerola [kaθe'rola] *nf* pan, saucepan

cachalote [katʃa'lote] *nm* (*Zool*) sperm whale

cacharro [ka'tʃarro] *nm* earthenware pot; **cacharros** *nmpl* pots and pans

cachear [katʃe'ar] *vt* to search, frisk

cachemir [katʃe'mir] *nm* cashmere

cacheada [ka'tʃetaða] (*LAM: fam*) *nf* (*bofetada*) slap

cachete [ka'tʃete] *nm* (*Anat*) cheek; (*ESP: bofetada*) slap (in the face)

cachivache [katʃi'βatʃe] *nm* (*trasto*) piece of junk; **cachivaches** *nmpl* junk *sg*

cacho ['katʃo] *nm* (small) bit; (*LAM: cuerno*) horn

cachondeo [katʃon'deo] (*ESP: fam*) *nm* farce, joke

cachondo, -a [ka'tʃondo, a] *adj* (*Zool*) on heat; (*fam: sexualmente*) randy; (*: gracioso*) funny

cachorro, -a [ka'tʃorro, a] *nm/f* (*perro*) pup, puppy; (*león*) cub

cachucha [ka'tʃuka] (*MÉX: fam*) *nf* cap

cacique [ka'θike] *nm* chief, local ruler; (*Pol*) local party boss

cactus ['kaktus] *nm inv* cactus

cada ['kaða] *adj inv* each; (*antes de número*) every; **~ día** each day, every day; **~ dos días** every other day; **~ uno/a** each one, every one; **~ vez más/menos** more and more/less and less; **~ vez que** ... whenever, every time (that) ...; **uno de ~ diez** one out of every ten

cadáver [ka'ðaβer] *nm* (dead) body, corpse

cadena [ka'ðena] *nf* chain; (*TV*) channel; **trabajo en ~** assembly line work; **cadena montañosa** mountain range; **cadena perpetua** (*Jur*) life imprisonment

cadera [ka'ðera] *nf* hip

cadete [ka'ðete] *nm* cadet

caducar [kaðu'kar] *vi* to expire; **caduco, -a** *adj* expired; (*persona*) very old

caer [ka'er] *vi* to fall (down); **caerse** *vr* to fall (down); **me cae bien/mal** I get on well with him/I can't stand him; **~ en la cuenta** to realize; **dejar ~** to drop; **su cumpleaños cae en viernes** her birthday falls on a Friday

café [ka'fe] (*pl* **~s**) *nm* (*bebida, planta*) coffee; (*lugar*) café ▷ *adj* (*MÉX: color*) brown, tan; **café con leche** white coffee; **café negro** (*LAM*) black coffee; **café solo** (*ESP*) black coffee

cafetera [kafe'tera] *nf* coffee pot

cafetería [kafete'ria] *nf* (*gen*) café

cafetero, -a [kafe'tero, a] *adj* coffee *cpd*; **ser muy ~** to be a coffee addict

cafishio [ka'fiʃjo] (*cs*) *nm* pimp

cagar [ka'ɣar] (*fam!*) *vt* to bungle, mess up ▷ *vi* to have a shit (!)

caída [ka'iða] *nf* fall; (*declive*) slope; (*disminución*)

fall, drop

caído, -a [ka'iðo, a] *adj* drooping

caiga *etc vb* V **caer**

caimán [kai'man] *nm* alligator

caja ['kaxa] *nf* box; (*para reloj*) case; (*de ascensor*) shaft; (*Com*) cashbox; (*donde se hacen los pagos*) cashdesk; (*: en supermercado*) checkout, till; **caja de ahorros** savings bank; **caja de cambios** gearbox; **caja de fusibles** fuse box; **caja fuerte** o **de caudales** safe, strongbox

cajero, -a [ka'xero, a] *nm/f* cashier; **cajero automático** cash dispenser

cajetilla [kaxe'tiʎa] *nf* (*de cigarrillos*) packet

cajón [ka'xon] *nm* big box; (*de mueble*) drawer

cajuela (*MÉX*) *nf* (*Auto*) boot (*BRIT*), trunk (*US*)

cal [kal] *nf* lime

cala ['kala] *nf* (*Geo*) cove, inlet; (*de barco*) hold

calabacín [kalaβa'θin] *nm* (*Bot*) baby marrow; (*: más pequeño*) courgette (*BRIT*), zucchini (*US*)

calabacita [kalaβa'θita] (*MÉX*) *nf* courgette (*BRIT*), zucchini (*US*)

calabaza [kala'βaθa] *nf* (*Bot*) pumpkin

calabozo [kala'βoθo] *nm* (*cárcel*) prison; (*celda*) cell

calada [ka'laða] (*ESP*) *nf* (*de cigarrillo*) puff

calado, -a [ka'laðo, a] *adj* (*prenda*) lace *cpd* ▷ *nm* (*Náut*) draught

calamar [kala'mar] *nm* squid *no pl*

calambre [ka'lambre] *nm* (*Elec*) shock

calar [ka'lar] *vt* to soak, drench; (*penetrar*) to pierce, penetrate; (*comprender*) to see through; (*vela*) to lower; **calarse** *vr* (*Auto*) to stall; **~se las gafas** to stick one's glasses on

calavera [kala'βera] *nf* skull

calcar [kal'kar] *vt* (*reproducir*) to trace; (*imitar*) to copy

calcetín [kalθe'tin] *nm* sock

calcio ['kalθjo] *nm* calcium

calcomanía [kalkoma'nia] *nf* transfer

calculador, a [kalkula'ðor, a] *adj* (*persona*) calculating; **calculadora** [kalkula'ðora] *nf* calculator

calcular [kalku'lar] *vt* (*Mat*) to calculate, compute; **~ que** ... to reckon that ...

caldera [kal'dera] *nf* boiler

calderilla [kalde'riʎa] *nf* (*moneda*) small change

caldo ['kaldo] *nm* stock; (*consomé*) consommé

calefacción [kalefak'θjon] *nf* heating; **calefacción central** central heating

calefón [kale'fon] (*RPL*) *nm* boiler

calendario [kalen'darjo] *nm* calendar

calentador [kalenta'ðor] *nm* heater

calentamiento [kalenta'mjento] *nm* (*Deporte*) warm-up; **calentamiento global** global warming

calentar [kalen'tar] *vt* to heat (up); **calentarse** *vr* to heat up, warm up; (*fig: discusión etc*) to get heated

calentón [kalen'ton] (*RPL: fam*) *adj* (*sexualmente*) horny, randy (*BRIT*)

calentura [kalen'tura] *nf* (*Med*) fever, (high) temperature

calesita [kale'sita] (*RPL*) *nf* merry-go-round, carousel

calibre [ka'liβre] *nm* (*de cañón*) calibre, bore; (*diámetro*) diameter; (*fig*) calibre

calidad [kali'ðað] *nf* quality; **de ~** quality *cpd*; **en ~ de** in the capacity of, as

cálido, -a ['kaliðo, a] *adj* hot; (*fig*) warm

caliente *etc* [ka'ljente] *vb* V **calentar** ▷ *adj* hot; (*fig*) fiery; (*disputa*) heated; (*fam: cachondo*) randy

calificación [kalifika'θjon] *nf* qualification; (*de*

alumno) grade, mark

calificado, -a [kalifi'kaðo, a] (LAM) *adj* (*competente*) qualified; (*obrero*) skilled

calificar [kalifi'kar] *vt* to qualify; (*alumno*) to grade, mark; **~ de** to describe as

calima [ka'lima] *nf* (*cerca del mar*) mist

cáliz ['kaliθ] *nm* chalice

caliza [ka'liθa] *nf* limestone

callado, -a [ka'ʎaðo, a] *adj* quiet

callar [ka'ʎar] *vt* (*asunto delicado*) to keep quiet about, say nothing about; (*persona, opinión*) to silence ▷ *vi* to keep quiet, be silent; **callarse** *vr* to keep quiet, be silent; **¡cállate!** be quiet!, shut up!

calle ['kaʎe] *nf* street; (*Deporte*) lane; **~ arriba/abajo** up/down the street; **calle de sentido único** one-way street; **calle mayor** (ESP) high (BRIT) o main (US) street; **calle peatonal** pedestrianized o pedestrian street; **calle principal** (LAM) high (BRIT) o main (US) street; **callejear** [kaʎe'xear] *vi* to wander (about) the streets; **callejero, -a** *adj* street *cpd* ▷ *nm* street map; **callejón** *nm* alley, passage; **callejón sin salida** cul-de-sac; **callejuela** *nf* side-street, alley

callista [ka'ʎista] *nmf* chiropodist

callo ['kaʎo] *nm* callus; (*en el pie*) corn; **callos** *nmpl* (*Culin*) tripe *sg*

calma ['kalma] *nf* calm

calmante [kal'mante] *nm* sedative, tranquillizer

calmar [kal'mar] *vt* to calm, calm down ▷ *vi* (*tempestad*) to abate; (*mente etc*) to become calm

calor [ka'lor] *nm* heat; (*agradable*) warmth; **hace ~** it's hot; **tener ~** to be hot

caloría [kalo'ria] *nf* calorie

calumnia [ka'lumnja] *nf* calumny, slander

caluroso, -a [kalu'roso, a] *adj* hot; (*sin exceso*) warm; (*fig*) enthusiastic

calva ['kalβa] *nf* bald patch; (*en bosque*) clearing

calvario [kal'βarjo] *nm* stations *pl* of the cross

calvicie [kal'βiθje] *nf* baldness

calvo, -a ['kalβo, a] *adj* bald; (*terreno*) bare, barren; (*tejido*) threadbare

calza ['kalθa] *nf* wedge, chock

calzada [kal'θaða] *nf* roadway, highway

calzado, -a [kal'θaðo, a] *adj* shod ▷ *nm* footwear

calzador [kalθa'ðor] *nm* shoehorn

calzar [kal'θar] *vt* (*zapatos etc*) to wear; (*mueble*) to put a wedge under; **calzarse** *vr*: **~se los zapatos** to put on one's shoes; **¿qué (número) calza?** what size do you take?

calzón [kal'θon] *nm* (ESP: *pantalón corto*) shorts; (LAM: *ropa interior: de hombre*) underpants, pants (BRIT), shorts (US); (: *de mujer*) panties, knickers (BRIT)

calzoncillos [kalθon'θiʎos] *nmpl* underpants

cama ['kama] *nf* bed; **hacer la ~** to make the bed; **cama individual/de matrimonio** single/double bed

camaleón [kamale'on] *nm* chameleon

cámara ['kamara] *nf* chamber; (*habitación*) room; (*sala*) hall; (*Cine*) cine camera; (*fotográfica*) camera; **cámara de aire** (ESP) inner tube; **cámara de comercio** chamber of commerce; **cámara de gas** gas chamber; **cámara digital** digital camera; **cámara frigorífica** cold-storage room

camarada [kama'raða] *nmf* comrade, companion

camarera [kama'rera] *nf* (*en restaurante*) waitress; (*en casa, hotel*) maid

camarero [kama'rero] *nm* waiter

camarógrafo, -a [kama'roɣrafo, a] (LAM) *nm/f*
cameraman/camerawoman

camarón [kama'ron] *nm* shrimp

camarote [kama'rote] *nm* cabin

cambiable [kam'bjaβle] *adj* (*variable*) changeable, variable; (*intercambiable*) interchangeable

cambiante [kam'bjante] *adj* variable

cambiar [kam'bjar] *vt* to change; (*dinero*) to exchange ▷ *vi* to change; **cambiarse** *vr* (*mudarse*) to move; (*de ropa*) to change; **~ de opinión** to change one's mind; **~se de ropa** to change (one's clothes)

cambio ['kambjo] *nm* change; (*trueque*) exchange; (*Com*) rate of exchange; (*oficina*) bureau de change; (*dinero menudo*) small change; **a ~ de** in return o exchange for; **en ~** on the other hand; (*en lugar de*) instead; **cambio climático** climate change; **cambio de divisas** foreign exchange; **cambio de marchas** o **velocidades** gear lever

camelar [kame'lar] *vt* to sweet-talk

camello [ka'meʎo] *nm* camel; (*fam: traficante*) pusher

camerino [kame'rino] *nm* dressing room

camilla [ka'miʎa] *nf* (*Med*) stretcher

caminar [kami'nar] *vi* (*marchar*) to walk, go ▷ *vt* (*recorrer*) to cover, travel

caminata [kami'nata] *nf* long walk; (*por el campo*) hike

camino [ka'mino] *nm* way, road; (*sendero*) track; **a medio ~** halfway (there); **en el ~** on the way, en route; **~ de** on the way to; **Camino de Santiago** Way of St James; **camino particular** private road

camión [ka'mjon] *nm* lorry (BRIT), truck (US); (MÉX: *autobús*) bus; **camión cisterna** tanker; **camión de la basura** dustcart, refuse lorry; **camión de mudanzas** removal (BRIT) o moving (US) van; **camionero, -a** *nm/f* lorry o truck driver

camioneta [kamjo'neta] *nf* van, light truck

camisa [ka'misa] *nf* shirt; (*Bot*) skin; **camisa de fuerza** straitjacket

camiseta [kami'seta] *nf* (*prenda*) tee-shirt; (*ropa interior*) vest; (*de deportista*) top

camisón [kami'son] *nm* nightdress, nightgown

camorra [ka'morra] *nf*: **buscar ~** to look for trouble

camote [ka'mote] *nm* (MÉX, CS: *batata*) sweet potato, yam; (MÉX: *bulbo*) tuber, bulb; (CS: *fam: enamoramiento*) crush

campamento [kampa'mento] *nm* camp

campana [kam'pana] *nf* bell; **campanada** *nf* peal; **campanario** *nm* belfry

campanilla [kampa'niʎa] *nf* small bell

campaña [kam'paɲa] *nf* (*Mil, Pol*) campaign; **campaña electoral** election campaign

campechano, -a [kampe'tʃano, a] *adj* (*franco*) open

campeón, -ona [kampe'on, ona] *nm/f* champion; **campeonato** *nm* championship

cámper ['kamper] (LAM) *nm o f* caravan (BRIT), trailer (US)

campera [kam'pera] (RPL) *nf* anorak

campesino, -a [kampe'sino, a] *adj* country *cpd*, rural; (*gente*) peasant *cpd* ▷ *nm/f* countryman/ woman; (*agricultor*) farmer

campestre [kam'pestre] *adj* country *cpd*, rural

camping ['kampin] (*pl* **~s**) *nm* camping; (*lugar*) campsite; **ir** o **estar de ~** to go camping

campo ['kampo] *nm* (*fuera de la ciudad*) country, countryside; (*Agr, Elec*) field; (*de fútbol*) pitch; (*de golf*) course; (*Mil*) camp; **campo de batalla** battlefield;

campo de concentración concentration camp;
campo de deportes sports ground, playing field;
campo visual field of vision, visual field

camuflaje [kamu'flaxe] nm camouflage

cana ['kana] nf white o grey hair; **tener ~s** to be
going grey

Canadá [kana'ða] nm Canada; **canadiense** adj, nmf
Canadian ▷ nf fur-lined jacket

canal [ka'nal] nm canal; (Geo) channel, strait; (de
televisión) channel; (de tejado) gutter; **canal de Panamá**
Panama Canal

canaleta [kana'leta] (LAM) nf (de tejado) gutter

canalizar [kanali'θar] vt to channel

canalla [ka'naʎa] nf rabble, mob ▷ nm swine

canapé [kana'pe] (pl **~s**) nm sofa, settee; (Culin)
canapé

Canarias [ka'narjas] nfpl (tb: **las Islas ~**) the Canary
Islands, the Canaries

canario, -a [ka'narjo, a] adj, nm/f (native) of the
Canary Isles ▷ nm (Zool) canary

canasta [ka'nasta] nf (round) basket

canasto [ka'nasto] nm large basket

cancela [kan'θela] nf gate

cancelación [kanθela'θjon] nf cancellation

cancelar [kanθe'lar] vt to cancel; (una deuda) to
write off

cáncer ['kanθer] nm (Med) cancer; **C~** (Astrología)
Cancer

cancha ['kantʃa] nf (de baloncesto) court; (LAM: campo)
pitch; **cancha de tenis** (LAM) tennis court

canciller [kanθi'ʎer] nm chancellor

canción [kan'θjon] nf song; **canción de cuna** lullaby

candado [kan'daðo] nm padlock

candente [kan'dente] adj red-hot; (fig: tema) burning

candidato, -a [kandi'ðato, a] nm/f candidate

cándido, -a ['kandiðo, a] adj simple; naive

candil [kan'dil] nm oil lamp; **candilejas** nfpl (Teatro)
footlights

canela [ka'nela] nf cinnamon

canelones [kane'lones] nmpl cannelloni

cangrejo [kan'grexo] nm crab

canguro [kan'guro] nm kangaroo; **hacer de ~** to
babysit

caníbal [ka'niβal] adj, nmf cannibal

canica [ka'nika] nf marble

canijo, -a [ka'nixo, a] adj frail, sickly

canilla [ka'niʎa] (RPL) nf tap (BRIT), faucet (US)

canjear [kanxe'ar] vt to exchange

canoa [ka'noa] nf canoe

canon [ka'non] nm canon; (pensión) rent; (Com) tax

canonizar [kanoni'θar] vt to canonize

canoso, -a [ka'noso, a] adj grey-haired

cansado, -a [kan'saðo, a] adj tired, weary; (tedioso)
tedious, boring

cansancio [kan'sanθjo] nm tiredness, fatigue

cansar [kan'sar] vt (fatigar) to tire; (aburrir)
to bore; (fastidiar) to bother; **cansarse** vr to tire, get
tired; (aburrirse) to get bored

cantábrico, -a [kan'taβriko, a] adj Cantabrian

cantante [kan'tante] adj singing ▷ nmf singer

cantar [kan'tar] vt to sing ▷ vi to sing; (insecto) to
chirp ▷ nm (acción) singing; (canción) song; (poema)
poem

cántaro ['kantaro] nm pitcher, jug; **llover a ~s** to
rain cats and dogs

cante ['kante] nm (Mús) Andalusian folk song; **cante**

jondo flamenco singing

cantera [kan'tera] nf quarry

cantero [kan'tero] (RPL) nm (arriate) border

cantidad [kanti'ðað] nf quantity, amount; **~ de**
lots of

cantimplora [kantim'plora] nf (frasco) water bottle,
canteen

cantina [kan'tina] nf canteen; (de estación) buffet;
(LAM: bar) bar

cantinero, -a [kanti'nero, a] (MÉX) nm/f barman/
barmaid, bartender (US)

canto ['kanto] nm singing; (canción) song; (borde)
edge, rim; (de cuchillo) back; **canto rodado** boulder

cantor, a [kan'tor, a] nm/f singer

canturrear [kanturre'ar] vi to sing softly

canuto [ka'nuto] nm (tubo) small tube; (fam: droga)
joint

caña ['kaɲa] nf (Bot: tallo) stem, stalk; (carrizo)
reed; (vaso) tumbler; (de cerveza) glass of beer; (Anat)
shinbone; **caña de azúcar** sugar cane; **caña de pescar**
fishing rod

cañada [ka'ɲaða] nf (entre dos montañas) gully, ravine;
(camino) cattle track

cáñamo ['kaɲamo] nm hemp

cañería [kaɲe'ria] nf (tubo) pipe

caño ['kaɲo] nm (tubo) tube, pipe; (de albañal) sewer;
(Mús) pipe; (de fuente) jet

cañón [ka'ɲon] nm (Mil) cannon; (de fusil) barrel; (Geo)
canyon, gorge

caoba [ka'oβa] nf mahogany

caos ['kaos] nm chaos

capa ['kapa] nf cloak, cape; (Geo) layer, stratum; **capa**
de ozono ozone layer

capacidad [kapaθi'ðað] nf (medida) capacity;
(aptitud) capacity, ability

caparazón [kapara'θon] nm shell

capataz [kapa'taθ] nm foreman

capaz [ka'paθ] adj able, capable; (amplio) capacious,
roomy

capellán [kape'ʎan] nm chaplain; (sacerdote) priest

capicúa [kapi'kua] adj inv (número, fecha) reversible

capilla [ka'piʎa] nf chapel

capital [kapi'tal] adj capital ▷ nm (Com) capital
▷ nf (ciudad) capital; **capital social** share o authorized
capital

capitalismo [kapita'lismo] nm capitalism;
capitalista adj, nmf capitalist

capitán [kapi'tan] nm captain

capítulo [ka'pitulo] nm chapter

capó [ka'po] nm (Auto) bonnet

capón [ka'pon] nm (gallo) capon

capota [ka'pota] nf (de mujer) bonnet; (Auto) hood
(BRIT), top (US)

capote [ka'pote] nm (abrigo: de militar) greatcoat; (de
torero) cloak

capricho [ka'pritʃo] nm whim, caprice; **caprichoso,**
-a adj capricious

Capricornio [kapri'kornjo] nm Capricorn

cápsula ['kapsula] nf capsule

captar [kap'tar] vt (comprender) to understand; (Radio) to pick up; (atención, apoyo) to attract

captura [kap'tura] nf capture; (Jur) arrest; **capturar**
vt to capture; to arrest

capucha [ka'putʃa] nf hood, cowl

capuchón [kapu'tʃon] (ESP) nm (de bolígrafo) cap

capullo [ka'puʎo] nm (Bot) bud; (Zool) cocoon; (fam)

idiot

caqui ['kaki] nm khaki

cara ['kara] nf (Anat: de moneda) face; (de disco) side; (descaro) boldness; **~ a** facing; **~ de** opposite, facing; **dar la ~ to** face the consequences; **¿~ o cruz?** heads or tails?; **¡qué ~ (más dura)!** what a nerve!

Caracas [ka'rakas] n Caracas

caracol [kara'kol] nm (Zool) snail; (concha) (sea) shell

carácter [ka'rakter] (pl **caracteres**) nm character; **tener buen/mal ~** to be good natured/bad tempered

característica [karakte'ristika] nf characteristic

característico, -a [karakte'ristiko, a] adj characteristic

caracterizar [karakteri'θar] vt to characterize, typify

caradura [kara'ðura] nmf: **es un ~** he's got a nerve

carajillo [kara'xiʎo] nm coffee with a dash of brandy

carajo [ka'raxo] (fam!) nm: **¡~!** shit! (!)

caramba [ka'ramba] excl good gracious!

caramelo [kara'melo] nm (dulce) sweet; (azúcar fundida) caramel

caravana [kara'βana] nf caravan; (fig) group; (Auto) tailback

carbón [kar'βon] nm coal; **papel ~** carbon paper

carbono [kar'βono] nm carbon

carburador [karβura'ðor] nm carburettor

carburante [karβu'rante] nm (para motor) fuel

carcajada [karka'xaða] nf (loud) laugh, guffaw

cárcel [ˈkarθel] nf prison, jail; (Tec) clamp

carcoma [kar'koma] nf woodworm

cardar [kar'ðar] vt (pelo) to backcomb

cardenal [karðe'nal] nm (Rel) cardinal; (Med) bruise

cardíaco, -a [kar'ðiako, a] adj cardiac, heart cpd

cardinal [karði'nal] adj cardinal

cardo [ˈkarðo] nm thistle

carecer [kare'θer] vi: **~ de** to lack, be in need of

carencia [ka'renθja] nf lack; (escasez) shortage; (Med) deficiency

careta [ka'reta] nf mask

carga ['karɣa] nf (peso, Elec) load; (de barco) cargo, freight; (Mil) charge; (responsabilidad) duty, obligation

cargado, -a [kar'ɣaðo, a] adj loaded; (Elec) live; (café, té) strong; (cielo) overcast

cargamento [karɣa'mento] nm (acción) loading; (mercancías) load, cargo

cargar [kar'ɣar] vt (barco, arma) to load; (Elec) to charge; (Com: algo en cuenta) to charge; (Inform) to load ⊳ vi (Mil) to charge; (Auto) to load (up); **~ con** to pick up, carry away; (peso: fig) to shoulder, bear; **cargarse** vr (fam: estropear) to break; (: matar) to bump off

cargo ['karɣo] nm (puesto) post, office; (responsabilidad) duty, obligation; (Jur) charge; **hacerse ~ de** to take charge of o responsibility for

carguero [kar'ɣero] nm freighter, cargo boat; (avión) freight plane

Caribe [ka'riβe] nm: **el ~** the Caribbean; **del ~** Caribbean; **caribeño, -a** [kari'βeɲo, a] adj Caribbean

caricatura [karika'tura] nf caricature

caricia [ka'riθja] nf caress

caridad [kari'ðað] nf charity

caries ['karjes] nf inv tooth decay

cariño [ka'riɲo] nm affection, love; (caricia) caress; (en carta) love ...; **tener ~ a** to be fond of; **cariñoso, -a** adj affectionate

carisma [ka'risma] nm charisma

caritativo, -a [karita'tiβo, a] adj charitable

cariz [ka'riθ] nm: **tener o tomar buen/mal ~** to look good/bad

carmín [kar'min] nm lipstick

carnal [kar'nal] adj carnal; **primo ~** first cousin

carnaval [karna'βal] nm carnival

carne ['karne] nf flesh; (Culin) meat; **se me pone la ~ de gallina sólo verlo** I get the creeps just seeing it; **carne de cerdo/cordero/ternera/vaca** pork/lamb/veal/beef; **carne de gallina** (fig) gooseflesh; **carne molida** (LAM) mince (BRIT), ground meat (US); **carne picada** (ESP, RPL) mince (BRIT), ground meat (US)

carné [kar'ne] (ESP) (pl **~s**) nm: **~ de conducir** driving licence (BRIT), driver's license (US); **~ de identidad** identity card; **~ de socio** membership card

carnero [kar'nero] nm sheep, ram; (carne) mutton

carnet [kar'ne] (FSP) (pl **~s**) nm = **carné**

carnicería [karniθe'ria] nf butcher's (shop), (fig: matanza) carnage, slaughter

carnicero, -a [karni'θero, a] adj carnivorous ⊳ nm/f butcher; (carnívoro) carnivore

carnívoro, -a [kar'niβoro, a] adj carnivorous

caro, -a ['karo, a] adj dear; (Com) dear, expensive ⊳ adv dear, dearly

carpa ['karpa] nf (pez) carp; (de circo) big top; (LAM: tienda de campaña) tent

carpeta [kar'peta] nf folder, file; **carpeta de anillas** ring binder

carpintería [karpinte'ria] nf carpentry, joinery; **carpintero** nm carpenter

carraspear [karraspe'ar] vi to clear one's throat

carraspera [karras'pera] nf hoarseness

carrera [ka'rrera] nf (acción) run(ning); (espacio recorrido) run; (competición) race; (trayecto) course; (profesión) career; (licenciatura) degree; **a la ~** at (full) speed; **carrera de obstáculos** (Deporte) steeplechase

carrete [ka'rrete] nm reel, spool; (Tec) coil

carretera [karre'tera] nf (main) road, highway; **carretera de circunvalación** ring road; **carretera nacional** ≈ A road (BRIT), ≈ state highway (US)

carretilla [karre'tiʎa] nf trolley; (Agr) (wheel)barrow

carril [ka'rril] nm furrow; (de autopista) lane; (Ferro) rail; **carril-bici** cycle lane

carrito [ka'rrito] nm trolley

carro ['karro] nm cart, wagon; (Mil) tank; (LAM: coche) car; **carro patrulla** (LAM) patrol o panda (BRIT) car

carrocería [karroθe'ria] nf bodywork, coachwork

carroña [ka'rroɲa] nf carrion no pl

carroza [ka'rroθa] nf (carruaje) coach

carrusel [karru'sel] nm merry-go-round, roundabout

carta ['karta] nf letter; (Culin) menu; (naipe) card; (mapa) map; (Jur) document; **carta certificada/urgente** registered/special-delivery letter

cartabón [karta'βon] nm set square

cartel [kar'tel] nm (anuncio) poster, placard; (Escol) wall chart; (Com) cartel; **cartelera** nf hoarding, billboard; (en periódico etc) entertainments guide; **"en cartelera"** "showing"

cartera [kar'tera] nf (de bolsillo) wallet; (de colegial, cobrador) satchel; (de señora) handbag; (para documentos) briefcase; (Com) portfolio; **ocupa la ~ de Agricultura** she is Minister of Agriculture

carterista [karte'rista] nmf pickpocket

cartero [kar'tero] nm postman

cartilla [kar'tiʎa] nf primer, first reading book; **cartilla de ahorros** savings book

cartón [kar'ton] nm cardboard; **cartón piedra** papier-mâché

cartucho [kar'tutʃo] nm (Mil) cartridge

cartulina [kartu'lina] nf card

casa ['kasa] nf house; (hogar) home; (Com) firm, company; **en ~** at home; **casa consistorial** town hall; **casa de campo** country house; **casa de huéspedes** boarding house; **casa de socorro** first aid post; **casa rodante** (cs) caravan (BRIT), trailer (US)

casado, -a [ka'saðo, a] adj married ▷ nm/f married man/woman

casar [ka'sar] vt to marry; (Jur) to quash, annul; **casarse** vr to marry, get married

cascabel [kaska'βel] nm (small) bell

cascada [kas'kaða] nf waterfall

cascanueces [kaska'nweθes] nm inv nutcrackers pl

cascar [kas'kar] vt to crack, split, break (open); **cascarse** vr to crack, split, break (open)

cáscara ['kaskara] nf (de huevo, fruta seca) shell; (de fruta) skin; (de limón) peel

casco ['kasko] nm (de bombero, soldado) helmet; (Náut: de barco) hull; (Zool: de caballo) hoof; (botella) empty bottle; (de ciudad): **el ~ antiguo** the old part; **el ~ urbano** the town centre; **los ~s azules** the UN peace-keeping force, the blue berets

cascote [kas'kote] nm rubble

caserío [kase'rio] (ESP) nm farmhouse; (casa) country mansion

casero, -a [ka'sero, a] adj (pan etc) home-made ▷ nm/f (propietario) landlord/lady; **ser muy ~** to be home-loving; **"comida casera"** "home cooking"

caseta [ka'seta] nf hut; (para bañista) cubicle; (de feria) stall

casete [ka'sete] nm o f cassette

casi ['kasi] adv almost, nearly; **~ nada** hardly anything; **~ nunca** hardly ever, almost never; **~ te caes** you almost fell

casilla [ka'siʎa] nf (casita) hut, cabin; (Ajedrez) square; (para cartas) pigeonhole; **casilla de correo** (cs) P.O. Box; **casillero** nm (para cartas) pigeonholes pl

casino [ka'sino] nm club; (de juego) casino

caso ['kaso] nm case; **en ~ de** in case of; **en ~ de que ...** in case ...; **el ~ es que ...** the fact is that ...; **en ese/todo ~** in that/any case; **hacer ~ a** to pay attention to; **venir al ~** to be relevant

caspa ['kaspa] nf dandruff

cassette [ka'sete] nm o f = **casete**

castaña [kas'taɲa] nf chestnut

castaño, -a [kas'taɲo, a] adj chestnut(-coloured), brown ▷ nm chestnut tree

castañuelas [kasta'ɲwelas] nfpl castanets

castellano, -a [kaste'ʎano, a] adj, nm/f Castilian ▷ nm (Ling) Castilian, Spanish

castigar [kasti'ɣar] vt to punish; (Deporte) to penalize; **castigo** nm punishment; (Deporte) penalty

Castilla [kas'tiʎa] nf Castile

castillo [kas'tiʎo] nm castle

castizo, -a [kas'tiθo, a] adj (Ling) pure

casto, -a ['kasto, a] adj chaste, pure

castor [kas'tor] nm beaver

castrar [kas'trar] vt to castrate

casual [ka'swal] adj chance, accidental

casualidad nf chance, accident; (combinación de circunstancias) coincidence; **da la casualidad de que ...** it (just) so happens that ...; **¡qué casualidad!** what a coincidence!

cataclismo [kata'klismo] nm cataclysm

catador, a [kata'ðor, a] nm/f wine taster

catalán, -ana [kata'lan, ana] adj, nm/f Catalan ▷ nm (Ling) Catalan

catalizador [kataliθa'ðor] nm catalyst; (Auto) catalytic convertor

catalogar [katalo'ɣar] vt to catalogue; **~ a algn (de)** (fig) to categorize sb (as)

catálogo [ka'taloɣo] nm catalogue

Cataluña [kata'luɲa] nf Catalonia

catar [ka'tar] vt to taste, sample

catarata [kata'rata] nf (Geo) waterfall; (Med) cataract

catarro [ka'tarro] nm catarrh; (constipado) cold

catástrofe [ka'tastrofe] nf catastrophe

catear [kate'ar] (fam) vt (examen, alumno) to fail

cátedra ['kateðra] nf (Univ) chair, professorship

catedral [kate'ðral] nf cathedral

catedrático, -a [kate'ðratiko, a] nm/f professor

categoría [kateɣo'ria] nf category; (rango) rank, standing; (calidad) quality; **de ~** (hotel) top-class

cateto, -a ['kateto, a] (ESP: pey) nm/f peasant

catolicismo [katoli'θismo] nm Catholicism

católico, -a [ka'toliko, a] adj, nm/f Catholic

catorce [ka'torθe] num fourteen

cauce ['kauθe] nm (de río) riverbed; (fig) channel

caucho ['kautʃo] (ESP) nm rubber

caudal [kau'ðal] nm (de río) volume, flow; (fortuna) wealth; (abundancia) abundance

caudillo [kau'ðiʎo] nm leader, chief

causa ['kausa] nf cause; (razón) reason; (Jur) lawsuit, case; **a ~ de** because of; **causar** [kau'sar] vt to cause

cautela [kau'tela] nf caution, cautiousness; **cauteloso, -a** adj cautious, wary

cautivar [kauti'βar] vt to capture; (atraer) to captivate

cautiverio [kauti'βerjo] nm captivity

cautividad [kautiβi'ðað] nf = **cautiverio**

cautivo, -a [kau'tiβo, a] adj, nm/f captive

cauto, -a ['kauto, a] adj cautious, careful

cava ['kaβa] nm champagne-type wine

cavar [ka'βar] vt to dig

caverna [ka'βerna] nf cave, cavern

cavidad [kaβi'ðað] nf cavity

cavilar [kaβi'lar] vt to ponder

cayendo etc vb V **caer**

caza ['kaθa] nf (acción: gen) hunting; (: con fusil) shooting; (una caza) hunt, chase; (de animales) game ▷ nm (Aviac) fighter; **ir de ~** to go hunting; **caza mayor** game hunting; **cazador, a** [kaθa'ðor, a] nm/f hunter; **cazadora** nf jacket; **cazar** [ka'θar] vt to hunt; (perseguir) to chase; (prender) to catch

cazo ['kaθo] nm saucepan

cazuela [ka'θwela] nf (vasija) pan; (guisado) casserole

CD nm abr (= compact disc) CD

CD-ROM [θeðe'rom] nm abr CD-ROM

CE nf abr (= Comunidad Europea) EC

cebada [θe'βaða] nf barley

cebar [θe'βar] vt (animal) to fatten (up); (anzuelo) to bait; (Mil, Tec) to prime

cebo ['θeβo] nm (para animales) feed, food; (para peces, fig) bait; (de arma) charge

cebolla [θe'βoʎa] nf onion; **cebolleta** nf spring onion

cebra ['θeβra] nf zebra

cecear [θeθe'ar] vi to lisp

ceder [θe'ðer] vt to hand over, give up, part with ▷ vi *(renunciar)* to give in, yield; *(disminuir)* to diminish, decline; *(romperse)* to give way

cedro ['θeðro] nm cedar

cédula ['θeðula] nf certificate, document; **cédula de identidad** (LAM) identity card; **cédula electoral** (LAM) ballot

cegar [θe'ɣar] vt to blind; *(tubería etc)* to block up, stop up ▷ vi *(fig)* to go blind; **cegarse** vr: **~se (de)** to be blinded (by)

ceguera [θe'ɣera] nf blindness

ceja ['θexa] nf eyebrow

cejar [θe'xar] vi *(fig)* to back down

celador, a [θela'ðor, a] nm/f *(de edificio)* watchman; *(de museo etc)* attendant

celda ['θelda] nf cell

celebración [θeleβra'θjon] nf celebration

celebrar [θele'βrar] vt to celebrate; *(alabar)* to praise ▷ vi to be glad; **celebrarse** vr to occur, take place

célebre ['θeleβre] adj famous

celebridad [θeleβri'ðað] nf fame; *(persona)* celebrity

celeste [θe'leste] adj *(azul)* sky-blue

celestial [θeles'tjal] adj celestial, heavenly

celo¹ ['θelo] nm zeal; *(Rel)* fervour; *(Zool)*: **en ~** on heat; **celos** nmpl jealousy sg; **dar ~s a algn** to make sb jealous; **tener ~s** to be jealous

celo²® ['θelo] nm Sellotape®

celofán [θelo'fan] nm cellophane

celoso, -a [θe'loso, a] adj jealous; *(trabajador)* zealous

celta ['θelta] adj Celtic ▷ nmf Celt

célula ['θelula] nf cell

celulitis [θelu'litis] nf cellulite

cementerio [θemen'terjo] nm cemetery, graveyard

cemento [θe'mento] nm cement; *(hormigón)* concrete; (LAM: *cola)* glue

cena ['θena] nf evening meal, dinner; **cenar** [θe'nar] vt to have for dinner ▷ vi to have dinner

cenicero [θeni'θero] nm ashtray

ceniza [θe'niθa] nf ash, ashes pl

censo ['θenso] nm census; **censo electoral** electoral roll

censura [θen'sura] nf *(Pol)* censorship; **censurar** [θensu'rar] vt *(idea)* to censure; *(cortar: película)* to censor

centella [θen'teʎa] nf spark

centenar [θente'nar] nm hundred

centenario, -a [θente'narjo, a] adj centenary; hundred-year-old ▷ nm centenary

centeno [θen'teno] nm *(Bot)* rye

centésimo, -a [θen'tesimo, a] adj hundredth

centígrado [θen'tixraðo] adj centigrade

centímetro [θen'timetro] nm centimetre (BRIT), centimeter (US)

céntimo ['θentimo] nm cent

centinela [θenti'nela] nm sentry, guard

centollo [θen'toʎo] nm spider crab

central [θen'tral] adj central ▷ nf head office; *(Tec)* plant; *(Tel)* exchange; **central eléctrica** power station; **central nuclear** nuclear power station; **central telefónica** telephone exchange

centralita [θentra'lita] nf switchboard

centralizar [θentrali'θar] vt to centralize

centrar [θen'trar] vt to centre

céntrico, -a ['θentriko, a] adj central

centrifugar [θentrifu'ɣar] vt to spin-dry

centro ['θentro] nm centre, **centro comercial** shopping centre; **centro de atención al cliente** call centre; **centro de salud** health centre; **centro escolar** school; **centro juvenil** youth club; **centro turístico** *(lugar muy visitado)* tourist centre; **centro urbano** urban area, city

centroamericano, -a [θentroameri'kano, a] adj, nm/f Central American

ceñido, -a [θe'niðo, a] adj *(chaqueta, pantalón)* tight-(fitting)

ceñir [θe'nir] vt *(rodear)* to encircle, surround; *(ajustar)* to fit (tightly)

ceño ['θeno] nm frown, scowl; **fruncir el ~** to frown, knit one's brow

cepillar [θepi'ʎar] vt to brush; *(madera)* to plane (down)

cepillo [θe'piʎo] nm brush; *(para madera)* plane; **cepillo de dientes** toothbrush

cera ['θera] nf wax

cerámica [θe'ramika] nf pottery; *(arte)* ceramics

cerca ['θerka] nf fence ▷ adv near, nearby, close; **~ de** near, close to

cercanías [θerka'nias] nfpl *(afueras)* outskirts, suburbs

cercano, -a [θer'kano, a] adj close, near

cercar [θer'kar] vt to fence in; *(rodear)* to surround

cerco ['θerko] nm *(Agr)* enclosure; *(LAM: valla)* fence; *(Mil)* siege

cerdo, -a ['θerðo, a] nm/f pig/sow

cereal [θere'al] nm cereal; **cereales** nmpl cereals, grain sg

cerebro [θe'reβro] nm brain; *(fig)* brains pl

ceremonia [θere'monja] nf ceremony; **ceremonioso, -a** adj ceremonious

cereza [θe'reθa] nf cherry

cerilla [θe'riʎa] nf *(fósforo)* match

cerillo [θe'riʎo] nm (MÉX) match

cero ['θero] nm nothing, zero

cerquillo [θer'kiʎo] nm (CAM, RPL) fringe (BRIT), bangs pl (US)

cerrado, -a [θe'rraðo, a] adj closed, shut; *(con llave)* locked; *(tiempo)* cloudy, overcast; *(curva)* sharp; *(acento)* thick, broad

cerradura [θerra'ðura] nf *(acción)* closing; *(mecanismo)* lock

cerrajero [θerra'xero] nm locksmith

cerrar [θe'rrar] vt to close, shut; *(paso, carretera)* to close; *(grifo)* to turn off; *(cuenta, negocio)* to close ▷ vi to close, shut; *(noche)* to come down; **cerrarse** vr to close, shut; **~ con llave** to lock; **~ un trato** to strike a bargain

cerro ['θerro] nm hill

cerrojo [θe'rroxo] nm *(herramienta)* bolt; *(de puerta)* latch

certamen [θer'tamen] nm competition, contest

certero, -a [θer'tero, a] adj *(gen)* accurate

certeza [θer'teθa] nf certainty

certidumbre [θerti'ðumbre] nf = **certeza**

certificado, -a [θertifi'kaðo, a] adj *(carta, paquete)* registered; *(aprobado)* certified ▷ nm certificate; **certificado médico** medical certificate

certificar [θertifi'kar] vt *(asegurar, atestar)* to certify

cervatillo [θerβa'tiʎo] nm fawn

cervecería [θerβeθe'ria] nf *(fábrica)* brewery; *(bar)* public house, pub

cerveza [θer'βeθa] nf beer

cesar [θe'sar] vi to cease, stop ▷ vt (funcionario) to remove from office

cesárea [θe'sarea] nf (Med) Caesarean operation o section

cese ['θese] nm (de trabajo) dismissal; (de pago) suspension

césped ['θespeð] nm grass, lawn

cesta ['θesta] nf basket

cesto ['θesto] nm (large) basket, hamper

cfr abr (= confróntese) cf.

chabacano, -a [tʃaβa'kano, a] adj vulgar, coarse

chabola [tʃa'βola] (ESP) nf shack; **barrio de chabolas** shanty town

chacal [tʃa'kal] nm jackal

chacha ['tʃatʃa] (fam) nf maid

cháchara ['tʃatʃara] nf chatter; **estar de ~** to chatter away

chacra ['tʃakra] (CS) nf smallholding

chafa ['tʃafa] (MÉX: fam) adj useless, dud

chafar [tʃa'far] vt (aplastar) to crush; (plan etc) to ruin

chal [tʃal] nm shawl

chalado, -a [tʃa'lado, a] (fam) adj crazy

chalé [tʃa'le] (pl **-s**) nm villa, ≈ detached house

chaleco [tʃa'leko] nm waistcoat, vest (US); **chaleco de seguridad** (Aut) reflective safety vest; **chaleco salvavidas** life jacket

chalet [tʃa'le] (pl **-s**) nm = **chalé**

chamaco, -a (MÉX) [tʃa'mako, a] nm/f (niño) kid

chambear [tʃambe'ar] (MÉX: fam) vi to earn one's living

champán [tʃam'pan] nm champagne

champiñón [tʃampi'non] nm mushroom

champú [tʃam'pu] (pl **-es, -s**) nm shampoo

chamuscar [tʃamus'kar] vt to scorch, sear, singe

chance ['tʃantʃe] (LAM) nm chance

chancho, -a [tʃantʃo, a] (LAM) nm/f pig

chanchullo [tʃan'tʃuʎo] (fam) nm fiddle

chandal [tʃan'dal] nm tracksuit

chantaje [tʃan'taxe] nm blackmail

chapa ['tʃapa] nf (de metal) plate, sheet; (de madera) board, panel; (RPL Auto) number (BRIT) o license (US) plate; **chapado, -a** adj: **chapado en oro** gold-plated

chaparrón [tʃapa'rron] nm downpour, cloudburst

chaperón [tʃape'ron] (MÉX) nm: **hacer de ~** to play gooseberry, **chaperona** (LAM) nm: **hacer de chaperona** to play gooseberry

chapopote [tʃapo'pote] (MÉX) nm tar

chapulín [tʃapu'lin] (MÉX, CAM) nm grasshopper

chapurrear [tʃapurre'ar] vt (idioma) to speak badly

chapuza [tʃa'puθa] nf botched job

chapuzón [tʃapu'θon] nm: **darse un ~** to go for a dip

chaqueta [tʃa'keta] nf jacket

chaquetón [tʃake'ton] nm long jacket

charca ['tʃarka] nf pond, pool

charco ['tʃarko] nm pool, puddle

charcutería [tʃarkute'ria] nf (tienda) shop selling chiefly pork meat products; (productos) cooked pork meats pl

charla ['tʃarla] nf talk, chat; (conferencia) lecture; **charlar** [tʃar'lar] vi to talk, chat; **charlatán, -ana** [tʃarla'tan, ana] nm/f (hablador) chatterbox; (estafador) trickster

charol [tʃa'rol] nm varnish; (cuero) patent leather

charola [tʃa'rola] (MÉX) nf tray

charro, -a [tʃa'rro, a] (MÉX) nm typical Mexican

chasco ['tʃasko] nm (desengaño) disappointment

chasis ['tʃasis] nm inv chassis

chasquido [tʃas'kiðo] nm crack; click

chat [tʃat] nm (Internet) chat room

chatarra [tʃa'tarra] nf scrap (metal)

chatear [tʃate'ar] vi (Internet) to chat

chato, -a ['tʃato, a] adj flat; (nariz) snub

chaucha ['tʃautʃa] (RPL) nf runner (BRIT) o pole (US) bean

chaval, a [tʃa'βal, a] (ESP) nm/f kid, lad/lass

chavo, -a [tʃa'βo] (MÉX: fam) nm/f guy/girl

checar [tʃe'kar] (MÉX) vt: **~ tarjeta** (al entrar) to clock in o on; (: al salir) to clock off o out

checo, -a ['tʃeko, a] adj, nm/f Czech ▷ nm (Ling) Czech

checoslovaco, -a [tʃekoslo'βako, a] adj, nm/f Czech, Czechoslovak

Checoslovaquia [tʃekoslo'βakja] nf (Hist) Czechoslovakia

cheque ['tʃeke] nm cheque (BRIT), check (US); **cobrar un ~** to cash a cheque; **cheque al portador** cheque payable to bearer; **cheque de viaje** traveller's cheque (BRIT), traveler's check (US); **cheque en blanco** blank cheque

chequeo [tʃe'keo] nm (Med) check-up; (Auto) service

chequera [tʃe'kera] (LAM) nf chequebook (BRIT), checkbook (US)

chévere ['tʃeβere] (LAM: fam) adj great

chícharo ['tʃitʃaro] (MÉX, CAM) nm pea

chichón [tʃi'tʃon] nm bump, lump

chicle ['tʃikle] nm chewing gum

chico, -a ['tʃiko, a] adj small, little ▷ nm/f (niño) child; (muchacho) boy/girl

chiflado, -a [tʃi'flaðo, a] adj crazy

chiflar [tʃi'flar] vt to hiss, boo

chilango, -a [tʃi'lango, a] (MÉX) adj of o from Mexico City

Chile ['tʃile] nm Chile; **chileno, -a** adj, nm/f Chilean

chile ['tʃile] nm chilli pepper

chillar [tʃi'ʎar] vi (persona) to yell, scream; (animal salvaje) to howl; (cerdo) to squeal

chillido [tʃi'ʎiðo] nm (de persona) yell, scream; (de animal) howl

chimenea [tʃime'nea] nf chimney; (hogar) fireplace

China ['tʃina] nf (tb: **la ~**) China

chinche ['tʃintʃe] nf (insecto) (bed)bug; (Tec) drawing pin (BRIT), thumbtack (US) ▷ nmf nuisance, pest

chincheta [tʃin'tʃeta] nf drawing pin (BRIT), thumbtack (US)

chingada [tʃin'gaða] (MÉX: fam!) nf: **hijo de la ~** bastard

chino, -a ['tʃino, a] adj, nm/f Chinese ▷ nm (Ling) Chinese

chipirón [tʃipi'ron] nm (Zool, Culin) squid

Chipre ['tʃipre] nf Cyprus; **chipriota** adj, nmf Cypriot

chiquillo, -a [tʃi'kiʎo, a] nm/f (fam) kid

chirimoya [tʃiri'moja] nf custard apple

chiringuito [tʃirin'xito] nm small open-air bar

chiripa [tʃi'ripa] nf fluke

chirriar [tʃi'rrjar] vi to creak, squeak

chirrido [tʃi'rriðo] nm creak(ing), squeak(ing)

chisme ['tʃisme] nm (habladurías) piece of gossip; (fam: objeto) thingummyjig

chismoso, -a [tʃis'moso, a] adj gossiping ▷ nm/f gossip

chispa ['tʃispa] nf spark; (fig) sparkle; (ingenio) wit; (fam) drunkenness

chispear [tʃispe'ar] vi (*lloviznar*) to drizzle

chiste ['tʃiste] nm joke, funny story

chistoso, -a [tʃis'toso, a] adj funny, amusing

chivo, -a ['tʃiβo, a] nm/f (billy-/nanny-)goat; **chivo expiatorio** scapegoat

chocante [tʃo'kante] adj startling; (*extraño*) odd; (*ofensivo*) shocking

chocar [tʃo'kar] vi (*coches etc*) to collide, crash ▷ vt to shock; (*sorprender*) to startle; **~ con** to collide with; (*fig*) to run into, run up against; **¡chócala!** (*fam*) put it there!

chochear [tʃotʃe'ar] vi to be senile

chocho, -a ['tʃotʃo, a] adj doddering, senile; (*fig*) soft, doting

choclo ['tʃoklo] (cs) nm (*grano*) sweet corn; (*mazorca*) corn on the cob

chocolate [tʃoko'late] adj, nm chocolate; **chocolatina** nf chocolate

chofer [tʃo'fer] nm = **chófer**

chófer ['tʃofer] nm driver

chollo [tʃoʎo] (ESP: fam) nm bargain, snip

choque etc ['tʃoke] vb V **chocar** ▷ nm (*impacto*) impact; (*golpe*) jolt; (*Auto*) crash; (*fig*) conflict; **choque frontal** head-on collision

chorizo [tʃo'riθo] nm hard pork sausage, (type of) salami

chorrada [tʃo'rraða] (ESP: fam) nf: **¡es una ~!** that's crap! (!); **decir ~s** to talk crap (!)

chorrear [tʃorre'ar] vi to gush (out), spout (out); (*gotear*) to drip, trickle

chorro ['tʃorro] nm jet; (*fig*) stream

choza ['tʃoθa] nf hut, shack

chubasco [tʃu'βasko] nm squall

chubasquero [tʃuβas'kero] nm lightweight raincoat

chuchería [tʃutʃe'ria] nf trinket

chuleta [tʃu'leta] nf chop, cutlet

chulo ['tʃulo] nm (*de prostituta*) pimp

chupaleta [tʃupa'leta] (MÉX) nf lollipop

chupar [tʃu'par] vt to suck; (*absorber*) to absorb; **chuparse** vr to grow thin

chupete [tʃu'pete] (ESP, cs) nm dummy (BRIT), pacifier (US)

chupetín [tʃupe'tin] (RPL) nm lollipop

chupito [tʃu'pito] (fam) nm shot

chupón [tʃu'pon] nm (*piruleta*) lollipop; (LAM: chupete) dummy (BRIT), pacifier (US)

churro ['tʃurro] nm (type of) fritter

chusma ['tʃusma] nf rabble, mob

chutar [tʃu'tar] vi to shoot (at goal)

Cía abr (= compañía) Co.

cianuro [θja'nuro] nm cyanide

cibercafé [θiβerka'fe] nm cybercafé

cibernauta [θiβer'nauta] nmf web surfer, Internet user

ciberterrorista [θiβerterro'rista] nmf cyberterrorist

cicatriz [θika'triθ] nf scar; **cicatrizarse** vr to heal (up), form a scar

ciclismo [θi'klismo] nm cycling

ciclista [θi'klista] adj cycle cpd ▷ nmf cyclist

ciclo ['θiklo] nm cycle; **cicloturismo** nm touring by bicycle

ciclón [θi'klon] nm cyclone

ciego, -a ['θjeɣo, a] adj blind ▷ nm/f blind man/woman

cielo ['θjelo] nm sky; (*Rel*) heaven; **¡~s!** good heavens!

ciempiés [θjem'pjes] nm inv centipede

cien [θjen] num V **ciento**

ciencia ['θjenθja] nf science; **ciencias** nfpl (Escol) science sg; **ciencia-ficción** nf science fiction

científico, -a [θjen'tifiko, a] adj scientific ▷ nm/f scientist

ciento ['θjento] num hundred; **pagar al 10 por ~** to pay at 10 per cent; V tb **cien**

cierre etc ['θjerre] vb V **cerrar** ▷ nm closing, shutting; (*con llave*) locking; (LAM: cremallera) zip (fastener)

cierro etc vb V **cerrar**

cierto, -a ['θjerto, a] adj sure, certain; (*un tal*) a certain; (*correcto*) right, correct; **por ~** by the way; **~ hombre** a certain man; **ciertas personas** certain o some people; **sí, es ~** yes, that's correct

ciervo ['θjerβo] nm deer; (*macho*) stag

cifra ['θifra] nf number; (*secreta*) code; **cifrar** [θi'frar] vt to code, write in code

cigala [θi'ɣala] nf Norway lobster

cigarra [θi'ɣarra] nf cicada

cigarrillo [θiɣa'rriʎo] nm cigarette

cigarro [θi'ɣarro] nm cigarette; (*puro*) cigar

cigüeña [θi'ɣweɲa] nf stork

cilíndrico, -a [θi'lindriko, a] adj cylindrical

cilindro [θi'lindro] nm cylinder

cima ['θima] nf (*de montaña*) top, peak; (*de árbol*) top; (*fig*) height

cimentar [θimen'tar] vt to lay the foundations of; (*fig: fundar*) to found

cimiento [θi'mjento] nm foundation

cincel [θin'θel] nm chisel

cinco ['θinko] num five

cincuenta [θin'kwenta] num fifty

cine ['θine] nm cinema; **cinematográfico, -a** [θinemato'ɣrafiko, a] adj cine-, film cpd

cínico, -a ['θiniko, a] adj cynical ▷ nm/f cynic

cinismo [θi'nismo] nm cynicism

cinta ['θinta] nf band, strip; (*de tela*) ribbon; (*película*) reel; (*de máquina de escribir*) ribbon; **cinta adhesiva/aislante** sticky/insulating tape; **cinta de vídeo** videotape; **cinta magnetofónica** tape; **cinta métrica** tape measure

cintura [θin'tura] nf waist

cinturón [θintu'ron] nm belt; **cinturón de seguridad** safety belt

ciprés [θi'pres] nm cypress (tree)

circo ['θirko] nm circus

circuito [θir'kwito] nm circuit

circulación [θirkula'θjon] nf circulation; (*Auto*) traffic

circular [θirku'lar] adj, nf circular ▷ vi, vt to circulate ▷ vi (*Auto*) to drive; **"circule por la derecha"** "keep (to the) right"

círculo ['θirkulo] nm circle; **círculo vicioso** vicious circle

circunferencia [θirkunfe'renθja] nf circumference

circunstancia [θirkuns'tanθja] nf circumstance

cirio ['θirjo] nm (wax) candle

ciruela [θi'rwela] nf plum; **ciruela pasa** prune

cirugía [θiru'xia] nf surgery; **cirugía estética** o **plástica** plastic surgery

cirujano [θiru'xano] nm surgeon

cisne ['θisne] nm swan

cisterna [θis'terna] nf cistern, tank

cita ['θita] nf appointment, meeting; (*de novios*) date;

(*referencia*) quotation

citación [θita'θjon] *nf* (*Jur*) summons *sg*

citar [θi'tar] *vt* (*gen*) to make an appointment with; (*Jur*) to summons; (*un autor, texto*) to quote; **citarse** *vr*: **se ~on en el cine** they arranged to meet at the cinema

cítricos ['θitrikos] *nmpl* citrus fruit *sg*

ciudad [θju'ðað] *nf* town; (*más grande*) city; **ciudadano, -a** *nm/f* citizen

cívico, -a ['θiβiko, a] *adj* civic

civil [θi'βil] *adj* civil ▷ *nm* (*guardia*) policeman; **civilización** [θiβiliθa'θjon] *nf* civilization; **civilizar** [θiβili'θar] *vt* to civilize

cizaña [θi'θaɲa] *nf* (*fig*) discord

cl. *abr* (= *centilitro*) cl.

clamor [kla'mor] *nm* clamour, protest

clandestino, -a [klandes'tino, a] *adj* clandestine; (*Pol*) underground

clara ['klara] *nf* (*de huevo*) egg white

claraboya [klara'βoja] *nf* skylight

clarear [klare'ar] *vi* (*el día*) to dawn; (*el cielo*) to clear up, brighten up; **clarearse** *vr* to be transparent

claridad [klari'ðað] *nf* (*de día*) brightness; (*de estilo*) clarity

clarificar [klarifi'kar] *vt* to clarify

clarinete [klari'nete] *nm* clarinet

claro, -a ['klaro, a] *adj* clear; (*luminoso*) bright; (*color*) light; (*evidente*) clear, evident; (*poco espeso*) thin ▷ *nm* (*en bosque*) clearing ▷ *adv* clearly ▷ *excl*: **¡~ que sí!** of course!; **¡~ que no!** of course not!

clase ['klase] *nf* class; **dar ~(s)** to teach; **clase alta/media/obrera** upper/middle/working class; **clases particulares** private lessons *o* tuition *sg*

clásico, -a ['klasiko, a] *adj* classical

clasificación [klasifika'θjon] *nf* classification; (*Deporte*) league (table)

clasificar [klasifi'kar] *vt* to classify

claustro ['klaustro] *nm* cloister

cláusula ['klausula] *nf* clause

clausura [klau'sura] *nf* closing, closure

clavar [kla'βar] *vt* (*clavo*) to hammer in; (*cuchillo*) to stick, thrust

clave ['klaβe] *nf* key; (*Mús*) clef; **clave de acceso** password; **clave lada** (*MÉX*) dialling (*BRIT*) *o* area (*US*) code

clavel [kla'βel] *nm* carnation

clavícula [kla'βikula] *nf* collar bone

clavija [kla'βixa] *nf* peg, dowel, pin; (*Elec*) plug

clavo ['klaβo] *nm* (*de metal*) nail; (*Bot*) clove

claxon ['klakson] (*pl* **~s**) *nm* horn

clérigo ['kleriɣo] *nm* priest

clero ['klero] *nm* clergy

clicar [kli'kar] *vi* (*Internet*) to click; **~ en el icono** to click on an icon; **~ dos veces** to double-click

cliché [kli'tʃe] *nm* cliché; (*Foto*) negative

cliente, -a ['kljente, a] *nm/f* client, customer; **clientela** [kljen'tela] *nf* clientele, customers *pl*

clima ['klima] *nm* climate; **climatizado, -a** [klimati'θaðo, a] *adj* air-conditioned

clímax ['klimaks] *nm inv* climax

clínica ['klinika] *nf* clinic; (*particular*) private hospital

clip [klip] (*pl* **~s**) *nm* paper clip

clítoris ['klitoris] *nm inv* (*Anat*) clitoris

cloaca [klo'aka] *nf* sewer

clonar [klo'nar] *vt* to clone

cloro ['kloro] *nm* chlorine

clóset ['kloset] (*MÉX*) *nm* cupboard

club [klub] (*pl* **~s** *o* **~es**) *nm* club; **club nocturno** night club

cm *abr* (= *centímetro, centímetros*) cm

coágulo [ko'axulo] *nm* clot

coalición [koali'θjon] *nf* coalition

coartada [koar'taða] *nf* alibi

coartar [koar'tar] *vt* to limit, restrict

coba [ko'βa] *nf*: **dar ~ a algn** (*adular*) to suck up to sb

cobarde [ko'βarðe] *adj* cowardly ▷ *nm* coward; **cobardía** *nf* cowardice

cobaya [ko'βaja] *nf* guinea pig

cobertizo [koβer'tiθo] *nm* shelter

cobertura [koβer'tura] *nf* cover; **aquí no hay ~** (*Tel*) I can't get a signal

cobija [ko'βixa] (*LAM*) *nf* blanket; **cobijar** [koβi'xar] *vt* (*cubrir*) to cover; (*proteger*) to shelter; **cobijo** *nm* shelter

cobra ['koβra] *nf* cobra

cobrador, a [koβra'ðor, a] *nm/f* (*de autobús*) conductor/conductress; (*de impuestos, gas*) collector

cobrar [ko'βrar] *vt* (*cheque*) to cash; (*sueldo*) to collect, draw; (*objeto*) to recover; (*precio*) to charge; (*deuda*) to collect ▷ *vi* to be paid; **cóbrese al entregar** cash on delivery; **¿me cobra, por favor?** how much do I owe you?, can I have the bill, please?

cobre ['koβre] *nm* copper; **cobres** *nmpl* (*Mús*) brass instruments

cobro ['koβro] *nm* (*de cheque*) cashing; **presentar al ~** to cash

cocaína [koka'ina] *nf* cocaine

cocción [kok'θjon] *nf* (*Culin*) cooking; (*en agua*) boiling

cocer [ko'θer] *vt, vi* to cook; (*en agua*) to boil; (*en horno*) to bake

coche ['kotʃe] *nm* (*Auto*) car (*BRIT*), automobile (*US*); (*de tren, de caballos*) coach, carriage; (*para niños*) pram (*BRIT*), baby carriage (*US*); **ir en ~** to drive; **coche celular** police van; **coche de bomberos** fire engine; **coche de carreras** racing car; **coche fúnebre** hearse; **coche-cama** (*pl* **coches-cama**) *nm* (*Ferro*) sleeping car, sleeper

cochera [ko'tʃera] *nf* garage; (*de autobuses, trenes*) depot

coche restaurante (*pl* **coches restaurante**) *nm* (*Ferro*) dining car, diner

cochinillo [kotʃi'niʎo] *nm* (*Culin*) suckling pig, sucking pig

cochino, -a [ko'tʃino, a] *adj* filthy, dirty ▷ *nm/f* pig

cocido [ko'θiðo] *nm* stew

cocina [ko'θina] *nf* kitchen; (*aparato*) cooker, stove; (*acto*) cookery; **cocina eléctrica/de gas** electric/gas cooker; **cocina francesa** French cuisine; **cocinar** *vt, vi* to cook

cocinero, -a [koθi'nero, a] *nm/f* cook

coco ['koko] *nm* coconut

cocodrilo [koko'ðrilo] *nm* crocodile

cocotero [koko'tero] *nm* coconut palm

cóctel ['koktel] *nm* cocktail; **cóctel molotov** petrol bomb, Molotov cocktail

codazo [ko'ðaθo] *nm*: **dar un ~ a algn** to nudge sb

codicia [ko'ðiθja] *nf* greed; **codiciar** *vt* to covet

código ['koðixo] *nm* code; **código civil** common law; **código de barras** bar code; **código de circulación** highway code; **código de la zona** (*LAM*) dialling (*BRIT*) *o* area (*US*) code; **código postal** postcode

codillo [ko'ðiʎo] nm (Zool) knee; (Tec) elbow (joint)
codo ['koðo] nm (Anat, de tubo) elbow; (Zool) knee
codorniz [koðor'niθ] nf quail
coexistir [koe(k)sis'tir] vi to coexist
cofradía [kofra'ðia] nf brotherhood, fraternity
cofre ['kofre] nm (de joyas) case; (de dinero) chest
coger [ko'xer] (ESP) vt to take (hold of); (objeto caído) to pick up; (frutas) to pick, harvest; (resfriado, ladrón, pelota) to catch; **~ por el buen camino** to take the right road; **cogerse** vr (el dedo) to catch; **~se a algo** to get hold of sth
cogollo [ko'ɣoʎo] nm (de lechuga) heart
cogote [ko'ɣote] nm back o nape of the neck
cohabitar [koaβi'tar] vi to live together, cohabit
coherente [koe'rente] adj coherent
cohesión [koe'sjon] nf cohesión
cohete [ko'ete] nm rocket
cohibido, -a [koi'βiðo, a] adj (Psico) inhibited; (tímido) shy
coincidencia [koinθi'ðenθja] nf coincidence
coincidir [koinθi'ðir] vi (en idea) to coincide, agree; (en lugar) to coincide
coito ['koito] nm intercourse, coitus
coja etc vb V **coger**
cojear [koxe'ar] vi (persona) to limp, hobble; (mueble) to wobble, rock
cojera [ko'xera] nf limp
cojín [ko'xin] nm cushion
cojo, -a etc ['koxo, a] vb V **coger** ▷ adj (que no puede andar) lame, crippled; (mueble) wobbly ▷ nm/f lame person, cripple
cojón [ko'xon] (fam!) nm: **¡cojones!** shit! (!); **cojonudo, -a** (fam) adj great, fantastic
col [kol] nf cabbage; **coles de Bruselas** Brussels sprouts
cola ['kola] nf tail; (de gente) queue; (lugar) end, last place; (para pegar) glue, gum; **hacer ~** to queue (up)
colaborador, a [kolaβora'ðor, a] nm/f collaborator
colaborar [kolaβo'rar] vi to collaborate
colada [ko'laða] (ESP) nf: **hacer la ~** to do the washing
colador [kola'ðor] nm (para líquidos) strainer; (para verduras etc) colander
colapso [ko'lapso] nm collapse
colar [ko'lar] vt (líquido) to strain off; (metal) to cast ▷ vi to ooze, seep (through); **colarse** vr to jump the queue; **~se en** to get into without paying; (fiesta) to gatecrash
colcha ['koltʃa] nf bedspread
colchón [kol'tʃon] nm mattress; **colchón inflable** air bed o mattress
colchoneta [koltʃo'neta] nf (en gimnasio) mat; (de playa) air bed
colección [kolek'θjon] nf collection; **coleccionar** vt to collect; **coleccionista** nmf collector
colecta [ko'lekta] nf collection
colectivo, -a [kolek'tiβo, a] adj collective, joint ▷ nm (ARG: autobús) (small) bus
colega [ko'leɣa] nmf colleague; (ESP: amigo) mate
colegial, a [kole'xjal, a] nm/f schoolboy(-girl)
colegio [ko'lexjo] nm college; (escuela) school; (de abogados etc) association; **colegio electoral** polling station; **colegio mayor** hall of residence
cólera [ko'lera] nf (ira) anger; (Med) cholera
colesterol [koleste'rol] nm cholesterol
coleta [ko'leta] nf pigtail
colgante [kol'ɣante] adj hanging ▷ nm (joya) pendant
colgar [kol'ɣar] vt to hang (up); (ropa) to hang out ▷ vi to hang; (Tel) to hang up
cólico [ko'liko] nm colic
coliflor [koli'flor] nf cauliflower
colilla [ko'liʎa] nf cigarette end, butt
colina [ko'lina] nf hill
colisión [koli'sjon] nf collision; **colisión frontal** head-on crash
collar [ko'ʎar] nm necklace; (de perro) collar
colmar [kol'mar] vt to fill to the brim; (fig) to fulfil, realize
colmena [kol'mena] nf beehive
colmillo [kol'miʎo] nm (diente) eye tooth; (de elefante) tusk; (de perro) fang
colmo ['kolmo] nm: **¡es el ~!** it's the limit!
colocación [koloka'θjon] nf (acto) placing; (empleo) job, position
colocar [kolo'kar] vt to place, put, position; (dinero) to invest; (poner en empleo) to find a job for; **colocarse** vr to get a job
Colombia [ko'lombja] nf Colombia; **colombiano, -a** adj, nm/f Colombian
colonia [ko'lonja] nf colony; (agua de colonia) cologne; (MÉX: de casas) residential area; **colonia proletaria** (MÉX) shantytown
colonización [koloniθa'θjon] nf colonization; **colonizador, a** [koloniθa'ðor, a] adj colonizing ▷ nm/f colonist, settler
colonizar [koloni'θar] vt to colonize
coloquio [ko'lokjo] nm conversation; (congreso) conference
color [ko'lor] nm colour
colorado, -a [kolo'raðo, a] adj (rojo) red; (MÉX: chiste) smutty, rude
colorante [kolo'rante] nm colouring
colorear [kolore'ar] vt to colour
colorete [kolo'rete] nm blusher
colorido [kolo'riðo] nm colouring
columna [ko'lumna] nf column; (apoyo) pillar; (apoyo) support; (tb: **~ vertebral**) spine, spinal column; (fig) backbone
columpiar [kolum'pjar] vt to swing; **columpiarse** vr to swing; **columpio** nm swing
coma ['koma] nf comma ▷ nm (Med) coma
comadre [ko'maðre] nf (madrina) godmother; (chismosa) gossip; **comadrona** nf midwife
comal [ko'mal] (MÉX, CAM) nm griddle
comandante [koman'dante] nm commandant
comarca [ko'marka] nf region
comba ['komba] (ESP) nf (cuerda) skipping rope; **saltar a la ~** to skip
combate [kom'bate] nm fight
combatir [komba'tir] vt to fight, combat
combinación [kombina'θjon] nf combination; (Quím) compound; (prenda) slip
combinar [kombi'nar] vt to combine
combustible [kombus'tiβle] nm fuel
comedia [ko'meðja] nf comedy; (Teatro) play, drama; **comediante** [kome'ðjante] nmf (comic) actor/actress
comedido, -a [kome'ðiðo, a] adj moderate
comedor, a [kome'ðor, a] nm (habitación) dining room; (cantina) canteen
comensal [komen'sal] nmf fellow guest (o diner)
comentar [komen'tar] vt to comment on;

comentario [komen'tarjo] nm comment, remark; (literario) commentary; **comentarios** nmpl (chismes) gossip sg; **comentarista** [komenta'rista] nmf commentator

comenzar [komen'θar] vt, vi to begin, start; **~ a hacer algo** to begin o start doing sth

comer [ko'mer] vt to eat; (Damas, Ajedrez) to take, capture ▷ vi to eat; (ESP, MÉX: almorzar) to have lunch; **comerse** vr to eat up

comercial [komer'θjal] adj commercial; (relativo al negocio) business cpd; **comercializar** vt (producto) to market; (pey) to commercialize

comerciante [komer'θjante] nmf trader, merchant

comerciar [komer'θjar] vi to trade, do business

comercio [ko'merθjo] nm commerce, trade; (tienda) shop, store; (negocio) business; (fig) dealings pl; **comercio electrónico** e-commerce; **comercio exterior/interior** foreign/domestic trade

comestible [komes'tiβle] adj eatable, edible; **comestibles** nmpl food sg, foodstuffs

cometa [ko'meta] nm comet ▷ nf kite

cometer [kome'ter] vt to commit

cometido [kome'tiðo] nm task, assignment

cómic ['komik] nm comic

comicios [ko'miθjos] nmpl elections

cómico, -a ['komiko, a] adj comic(al) ▷ nm/f comedian

comida [ko'miða] nf (alimento) food; (almuerzo, cena) meal; (de mediodía) lunch; **comida basura** junk food; **comida chatarra** (MÉX) junk food

comidilla [komi'ðiʎa] nf: **ser la ~ del barrio** o **pueblo** to be the talk of the town

comienzo etc [ko'mjenθo] vb V **comenzar** ▷ nm beginning, start

comillas [ko'miʎas] nfpl quotation marks

comilona [komi'lona] (fam) nf blow-out

comino [ko'mino] nm: **(no) me importa un ~** I don't give a damn

comisaría [komisa'ria] nf (de policía) police station; (Mil) commissariat

comisario [komi'sarjo] nm (Mil etc) commissary; (Pol) commissar

comisión [komi'sjon] nf commission; **Comisiones Obreras** (ESP) Communist trade union

comité [komi'te] (pl **~s**) nm committee

comitiva [komi'tiβa] nf retinue

como ['komo] adv as; (tal ~) like; (aproximadamente) about, approximately ▷ conj (ya que, puesto que) as, since; **¡~ no!** of course!; **~ no lo haga hoy** unless he does it today; **~ si** as if; **es tan alto ~ ancho** it is as high as it is wide

cómo ['komo] adv how?, why? ▷ excl what?, I beg your pardon? ▷ nm: **el ~ y el porqué** the whys and wherefores

cómoda ['komoða] nf chest of drawers

comodidad [komoði'ðað] nf comfort

comodín [komo'ðin] nm joker

cómodo, -a ['komoðo, a] adj comfortable; (práctico, de fácil uso) convenient

compact [kom'pakt] (pl **~s**) nm (tb: **~ disc**) compact disk player

compacto, -a [kom'pakto, a] adj compact

compadecer [kompaðe'θer] vt to pity, be sorry for; **compadecerse** vr: **~se de** to pity, o feel sorry for

compadre [kom'paðre] nm (padrino) godfather; (amigo) friend, pal

compañero, -a [kompa'ɲero, a] nm/f companion; (novio) boy/girlfriend; **compañero de clase** classmate

compañía [kompa'ɲia] nf company; **hacer ~ a algn** to keep sb company

comparación [kompara'θjon] nf comparison; **en ~ con** in comparison with

comparar [kompa'rar] vt to compare

comparecer [kompare'θer] vi to appear (in court)

comparsa [kom'parsa] nmf (Teatro) extra

compartimiento [komparti'mjento] nm (Ferro) compartment

compartir [kompar'tir] vt to share; (dinero, comida etc) to divide (up), share (out)

compás [kom'pas] nm (Mús) beat, rhythm; (Mat) compasses pl; (Náut etc) compass

compasión [kompa'sjon] nf compassion, pity

compasivo, -a [kompa'siβo, a] adj compassionate

compatible [kompa'tiβle] adj compatible

compatriota [kompa'trjota] nmf compatriot, fellow countryman/woman

compenetrarse [kompene'trarse] vr to be in tune

compensación [kompensa'θjon] nf compensation

compensar [kompen'sar] vt to compensate

competencia [kompe'tenθja] nf (incumbencia) domain, field; (Jur, habilidad) competence; (rivalidad) competition

competente [kompe'tente] adj competent

competición [kompeti'θjon] nf competition

competir [kompe'tir] vi to compete

compinche [kom'pintʃe] nmf (LAM) mate, buddy (us)

complacer [kompla'θer] vt to please; **complacerse** vr to be pleased

complaciente [kompla'θjente] adj kind, obliging, helpful

complejo, -a [kom'plexo, a] adj, nm complex

complementario, -a [komplemen'tarjo, a] adj complementary

completar [komple'tar] vt to complete

completo, -a [kom'pleto, a] adj complete; (perfecto) perfect; (lleno) full ▷ nm full complement

complicado, -a [kompli'kaðo, a] adj complicated; **estar ~ en** to be mixed up in

cómplice ['kompliθe] nmf accomplice

complot [kom'plo(t)] (pl **~s**) nm plot

componer [kompo'ner] vt (Mús, Literatura, Imprenta) to compose; (algo roto) to mend, repair; (arreglar) to arrange; **componerse** vr: **~se de** to consist of

comportamiento [komporta'mjento] nm behaviour, conduct

comportarse [kompor'tarse] vr to behave

composición [komposi'θjon] nf composition

compositor, a [komposi'tor, a] nm/f composer

compostura [kompos'tura] nf (actitud) composure

compra ['kompra] nf purchase; **hacer la ~** to do the shopping; **ir de ~s** to go shopping; **comprador, a** nm/f buyer, purchaser; **comprar** [kom'prar] vt to buy, purchase

comprender [kompren'der] vt to understand; (incluir) to comprise, include

comprensión [kompren'sjon] nf understanding; **comprensivo, -a** adj (actitud) understanding

compresa [kom'presa] nf (para mujer) sanitary towel (BRIT) o napkin (us)

comprimido, -a [kompri'miðo, a] adj compressed ▷ nm (Med) pill, tablet

comprimir [kompri'mir] vt to compress; (Internet) to zip

comprobante [kompro'βante] nm proof; (Com) voucher; **comprobante de compra** proof of purchase

comprobar [kompro'βar] vt to check; (probar) to prove; (Tec) to check, test

comprometer [komprome'ter] vt to compromise; (poner en peligro) to endanger; **comprometerse** vr (involucrarse) to get involved

compromiso [kompro'miso] nm (obligación) obligation; (cometido) commitment; (convenio) agreement; (apuro) awkward situation

compuesto, -a [kom'pwesto, a] adj: **~ de** composed of, made up of ▷ nm compound

computadora [komputa'ðora] (LAM) nf computer; **computadora central** mainframe (computer); **computadora personal** personal computer

cómputo ['komputo] nm calculation

comulgar [komul'xar] vi to receive communion

común [ko'mun] adj common ▷ nm: **el ~** the community

comunicación [komunika'θjon] nf communication; (informe) report

comunicado [komuni'kaðo] nm announcement; **comunicado de prensa** press release

comunicar [komuni'kar] vt, vi to communicate; **comunicarse** vr to communicate; **está comunicando** (Tel) the line's engaged (BRIT) o busy (US); **comunicativo, -a** adj communicative

comunidad [komuni'ðað] nf community; **comunidad autónoma** (ESP) autonomous region; **Comunidad (Económica) Europea** European (Economic) Community; **comunidad de vecinos** residents' association

comunión [komu'njon] nf communion

comunismo [komu'nismo] nm communism; **comunista** adj, nmf communist

○ **PALABRA CLAVE**

con [kon] prep **1** (medio, compañía) with; **comer con cuchara** to eat with a spoon; **pasear con algn** to go for a walk with sb

2 (a pesar de): **con todo, merece nuestros respetos** all the same, he deserves our respect

3 (para con): **es muy bueno para con los niños** he's very good with (the) children

4 (+ infin): **con llegar a las seis estará bien** if you come by six it will be fine ▷ conj: **con que: será suficiente con que le escribas** it will be sufficient if you write to her

concebir [konθe'βir] vt, vi to conceive

conceder [konθe'ðer] vt to concede

concejal, a [konθe'xal, a] nm/f town councillor

concentración [konθentra'θjon] nf concentration

concentrar [konθen'trar] vt to concentrate; **concentrarse** vr to concentrate

concepto [kon'θepto] nm concept

concernir [konθer'nir] vi to concern; **en lo que concierne a ...** as far as ... is concerned; **en lo que a mí concierne** as far as I'm concerned

concertar [konθer'tar] vt (Mús) to harmonize; (acordar: precio) to agree; (: tratado) to conclude; (trato) to arrange, fix up; (combinar: esfuerzos) to coordinate

▷ vi to harmonize, be in tune

concesión [konθe'sjon] nf concession

concesionario [konθesjo'narjo] nm (licensed) dealer, agent

concha ['kontʃa] nf shell

conciencia [kon'θjenθja] nf conscience; **tomar ~ de** to become aware of; **tener la ~ tranquila** to have a clear conscience

concienciar [konθjen'θjar] vt to make aware; **concienciarse** vr to become aware

concienzudo, -a [konθjen'θuðo, a] adj conscientious

concierto etc [kon'θjerto] vb V **concertar** ▷ nm concert; (obra) concerto

conciliar [konθi'ljar] vt to reconcile; **~ el sueño** to get to sleep

concilio [kon'θiljo] nm council

conciso, -a [kon'θiso, a] adj concise

concluir [konklu'ir] vt, vi to conclude; **concluirse** vr to conclude

conclusión [konklu'sjon] nf conclusion

concordar [konkor'ðar] vt to reconcile ▷ vi to agree, tally

concordia [kon'korðja] nf harmony

concretar [konkre'tar] vt to make concrete, make more specific; **concretarse** vr to become more definite

concreto, -a [kon'kreto, a] adj, nm (LAM: hormigón) concrete; **en ~** (en resumen) to sum up; (específicamente) specifically; **no hay nada en ~** there's nothing definite

concurrido, -a [konku'rriðo, a] adj (calle) busy; (local, reunión) crowded

concursante [konkur'sante] nmf competitor

concurso [kon'kurso] nm (de público) crowd; (Escol, Deporte, competencia) competition; (ayuda) help, cooperation

condal [kon'dal] adj: **la Ciudad C~** Barcelona

conde ['konde] nm count

condecoración [kondekora'θjon] nf (Mil) medal

condena [kon'dena] nf sentence; **condenación** [kondena'θjon] nf damnation; (Rel) damnation; **condenar** [konde'nar] vt to condemn; (Jur) to convict; **condenarse** vr (Rel) to be damned

condesa [kon'desa] nf countess

condición [kondi'θjon] nf condition; **a ~ de que ...** on condition that ...; **condicional** adj conditional

condimento [kondi'mento] nm seasoning

condominio [kondo'minjo] (LAM) nm condominium

condón [kon'don] nm condom

conducir [kondu'θir] vt to take, convey; (Auto) to drive ▷ vi to drive; (fig) to lead; **conducirse** vr to behave

conducta [kon'dukta] nf conduct, behaviour

conducto [kon'dukto] nm pipe, tube; (fig) channel

conductor, a [konduk'tor, a] adj leading, guiding ▷ nm (Física) conductor; (de vehículo) driver

conduje etc vb V **conducir**

conduzco etc vb V **conducir**

conectado, -a [konek'taðo, a] adj (Inform) on-line

conectar [konek'tar] vt to connect (up); (enchufar) to plug in

conejillo [kone'xiʎo] nm: **~ de Indias** guinea pig

conejo [ko'nexo] nm rabbit

conexión [konek'sjon] nf connection

confección [konfe(k)'θjon] nf preparation;

(*industria*) clothing industry

confeccionar [konfekθjo'nar] *vt* to make (up)

conferencia [konfe'renθja] *nf* conference; (*lección*) lecture; (*ESP Tel*) call; **conferencia de prensa** press conference

conferir [konfe'rir] *vt* to award

confesar [konfe'sar] *vt* to confess, admit

confesión [konfe'sjon] *nf* confession

confesionario [konfesjo'narjo] *nm* confessional

confeti [kon'feti] *nm* confetti

confiado, -a [kon'fjaðo, a] *adj* (*crédulo*) trusting; (*seguro*) confident

confianza [kon'fjanθa] *nf* trust; (*seguridad*) confidence; (*familiaridad*) intimacy, familiarity

confiar [kon'fjar] *vt* to entrust ▷ *vi* to trust; ~ **en algn** to trust sb; ~ **en que ...** to hope that ...

confidencial [konfiðen'θjal] *adj* confidential

confidente [konfi'ðente] *nmf* confidant/e; (*policial*) informer

configurar [konfiɣu'rar] *vt* to shape, form

confín [kon'fin] *nm* limit; **confines** *nmpl* confines, limits

confirmar [konfir'mar] *vt* to confirm

confiscar [konfis'kar] *vt* to confiscate

confite [kon'fite] *nm* sweet (*BRIT*), candy (*US*); **confitería** [konfite'ria] *nf* (*tienda*) confectioner's (shop)

confitura [konfi'tura] *nf* jam

conflictivo, -a [konflik'tiβo, a] *adj* (*asunto, propuesta*) controversial; (*país, situación*) troubled

conflicto [kon'flikto] *nm* conflict; (*fig*) clash

confluir [kon'flwir] *vi* (*ríos*) to meet; (*gente*) to gather

conformar [konfor'mar] *vt* to shape, fashion ▷ *vi* to agree; **conformarse** *vr* to conform; (*resignarse*) to resign o.s.; ~ **se con algo** to be happy with sth

conforme [kon'forme] *adj* (*correspondiente*): ~ **con** in line with; (*de acuerdo*): **estar ~s (con algo)** to be in agreement (with sth) ▷ *adv* as ▷ *excl* agreed! ▷ *prep*: ~ **a** in accordance with; **quedarse ~ (con algo)** to be satisfied (with sth)

confortable [konfor'taβle] *adj* comfortable

confortar [konfor'tar] *vt* to comfort

confrontar [konfron'tar] *vt* to confront; (*dos personas*) to bring face to face; (*cotejar*) to compare

confundir [konfun'dir] *vt* (*equivocar*) to mistake, confuse; (*turbar*) to confuse; **confundirse** *vr* (*turbarse*) to get confused; (*equivocarse*) to make a mistake; (*mezclarse*) to mix

confusión [konfu'sjon] *nf* confusion

confuso, -a [kon'fuso, a] *adj* confused

congelado, -a [konxe'laðo, a] *adj* frozen; **congelados** *nmpl* frozen food(s); **congelador** *nm* (*aparato*) freezer, deep freeze

congelar [konxe'lar] *vt* to freeze; **congelarse** *vr* (*sangre, grasa*) to congeal

congeniar [konxe'njar] *vi* to get on (*BRIT*) o along (*US*) well

congestión [konxes'tjon] *nf* congestion

congestionar [konxestjo'nar] *vt* to congest

congraciarse [kongra'θjarse] *vr* to ingratiate o.s.

congratular [kongratu'lar] *vt* to congratulate

congregar [kongre'ɣar] *vt* to gather together; **congregarse** *vr* to gather together

congresista [kongre'sista] *nmf* delegate, congressman/woman

congreso [kon'greso] *nm* congress

conjetura [konxe'tura] *nf* guess; **conjeturar** *vt* to guess

conjugar [konxu'var] *vt* to combine, fit together; (*Ling*) to conjugate

conjunción [konxun'θjon] *nf* conjunction

conjunto, -a [kon'xunto, a] *adj* joint, united ▷ *nm* whole; (*Mús*) band; **en ~** as a whole

conmemoración [konmemora'θjon] *nf* commemoration

conmemorar [konmemo'rar] *vt* to commemorate

conmigo [kon'miɣo] *pron* with me

conmoción [konmo'θjon] *nf* shock; (*fig*) upheaval; **conmoción cerebral** (*Med*) concussion

conmovedor, a [konmoβe'ðor, a] *adj* touching, moving; (*emocionante*) exciting

conmover [konmo'βer] *vt* to shake, disturb; (*fig*) to move

conmutador [konmuta'ðor] *nm* switch; (*LAM: centralita*) switchboard; (: *central*) telephone exchange

cono ['kono] *nm* cone; **Cono Sur** Southern Cone

conocedor, a [konoθe'ðor, a] *adj* expert, knowledgeable ▷ *nm/f* expert

conocer [kono'θer] *vt* to know; (*por primera vez*) to meet, get to know; (*entender*) to know about; (*reconocer*) to recognize; **conocerse** *vr* (*una persona*) to know o.s.; (*dos personas*) to know each other; ~ **a algn de vista** to know sb by sight

conocido, -a [kono'θiðo, a] *adj* (*well-*)known ▷ *nm/f* acquaintance

conocimiento [konoθi'mjento] *nm* knowledge; (*Med*) consciousness; **conocimientos** *nmpl* (*saber*) knowledge *sg*

conozco *etc vb* V **conocer**

conque ['konke] *conj* and so, so then

conquista [kon'kista] *nf* conquest; **conquistador, a** *adj* conquering ▷ *nm* conqueror; **conquistar** [konkis'tar] *vt* to conquer

consagrar [konsa'xrar] *vt* (*Rel*) to consecrate; (*fig*) to devote

consciente [kons'θjente] *adj* conscious

consecución [konseku'θjon] *nf* acquisition; (*de fin*) attainment

consecuencia [konse'kwenθja] *nf* consequence, outcome; (*coherencia*) consistency

consecuente [konse'kwente] *adj* consistent

consecutivo, -a [konseku'tiβo, a] *adj* consecutive

conseguir [konse'ɣir] *vt* to get, obtain; (*objetivo*) to attain

consejero, -a [konse'xero, a] *nm/f* adviser, consultant; (*Pol*) councillor

consejo [kon'sexo] *nm* advice; (*Pol*) council; **consejo de administración** (*Com*) board of directors; **consejo de guerra** court martial; **consejo de ministros** cabinet meeting

consenso [kon'senso] *nm* consensus

consentimiento [konsenti'mjento] *nm* consent

consentir [konsen'tir] *vt* (*permitir, tolerar*) to consent to; (*mimar*) to pamper, spoil; (*aguantar*) to put up with ▷ *vi* to agree, consent; ~ **que algn haga algo** to allow sb to do sth

conserje [kon'serxe] *nm* caretaker; (*portero*) porter

conservación [konserβa'θjon] *nf* conservation; (*de alimentos, vida*) preservation

conservador, a [konserβa'ðor, a] *adj* (*Pol*) conservative ▷ *nm/f* conservative

conservante [konser'ßante] nm preservative
conservar [konser'ßar] vt to conserve, keep; (alimentos, vida) to preserve; **conservarse** vr to survive
conservas [kon'serßas] nfpl canned food(s) pl
conservatorio [konserßa'torjo] nm (Mús) conservatoire, conservatory
considerable [konsiðe'raßle] adj considerable
consideración [konsiðera'θjon] nf consideration; (estimación) respect
considerado, -a [konsiðe'raðo, a] adj (atento) considerate; (respetado) respected
considerar [konsiðe'rar] vt to consider
consigna [kon'siɣna] nf (orden) order, instruction; (para equipajes) left-luggage office
consigo etc [kon'siɣo] vb V **conseguir** ⊳ pron (m) with him; (f) with her; (Vd) with you; (reflexivo) with o.s.
consiguiendo etc vb V **conseguir**
consiguiente [konsi'ɣjente] adj consequent; **por ~** and so, therefore, consequently
consistente [konsis'tente] adj consistent; (sólido) solid, firm; (válido) sound
consistir [konsis'tir] vi: **~ en** (componerse de) to consist of
consola [kon'sola] nf (mueble) console table; (de videojuegos) console
consolación [konsola'θjon] nf consolation
consolar [konso'lar] vt to console
consolidar [konsoli'ðar] vt to consolidate
consomé [konso'me] (pl **~s**) nm consommé, clear soup
consonante [konso'nante] adj consonant, harmonious ⊳ nf consonant
consorcio [kon'sorθjo] nm consortium
conspiración [konspira'θjon] nf conspiracy
conspirar [konspi'rar] vi to conspire
constancia [kons'tanθja] nf constancy; **dejar ~ de** to put on record
constante [kons'tante] adj, nf constant
constar [kons'tar] vi (evidenciarse) to be clear o evident; **~ de** to consist of
constipado, -a [konsti'paðo, a] adj: **estar ~** to have a cold ⊳ nm cold
constitución [konstitu'θjon] nf constitution
constituir [konstitu'ir] vt (formar, componer) to constitute, make up; (fundar, erigir, ordenar) to constitute, establish
construcción [konstruk'θjon] nf construction, building
constructor, a [konstruk'tor, a] nm/f builder
construir [konstru'ir] vt to build, construct
construyendo etc vb V **construir**
consuelo [kon'swelo] nm consolation, solace
cónsul ['konsul] nm consul; **consulado** nm consulate
consulta [kon'sulta] nf consultation; (Med): **horas de ~** surgery hours; **consultar** [konsul'tar] vt to consult; **consultar algo con algn** to discuss sth with sb; **consultorio** [konsul'torjo] nm (Med) surgery
consumición [konsumi'θjon] nf consumption; (bebida) drink; (comida) food; **consumición mínima** cover charge
consumidor, a [konsumi'ðor, a] nm/f consumer
consumir [konsu'mir] vt to consume; **consumirse** vr to be consumed; (persona) to waste away
consumismo [konsu'mismo] nm consumerism
consumo [kon'sumo] nm consumption

contabilidad [kontaßili'ðað] nf accounting, book-keeping; (profesión) accountancy; **contable** nmf accountant
contacto [kon'takto] nm contact; (Auto) ignition; **estar/ponerse en ~ con algn** to get in touch with sb
contado, -a [kon'taðo, a] adj: **~s** (escasos) numbered, scarce, few ⊳ nm: **pagar al ~** to pay (in) cash
contador [konta'ðor] nm (ESP: aparato) meter ⊳ nmf (LAM Com) accountant
contagiar [konta'xjar] vt (enfermedad) to pass on, transmit; (persona) to infect; **contagiarse** vr to become infected
contagio [kon'taxjo] nm infection; **contagioso, -a** adj infectious; (fig) catching
contaminación [kontamina'θjon] nf contamination; (polución) pollution
contaminar [kontami'nar] vt to contaminate; (aire, agua) to pollute
contante [kon'tante] adj: **dinero ~ (y sonante)** cash
contar [kon'tar] vt (páginas, dinero) to count; (anécdota, chiste etc) to tell ⊳ vi to count; **~ con** to rely on, count on
contemplar [kontem'plar] vt to contemplate; (mirar) to look at
contemporáneo, -a [kontempo'raneo, a] adj, nm/f contemporary
contenedor [kontene'ðor] nm container
contener [konte'ner] vt to contain, hold; (retener) to hold back, contain; **contenerse** vr to control o restrain o.s.
contenido, -a [konte'niðo, a] adj (moderado) restrained; (risa etc) suppressed ⊳ nm contents pl, content
contentar [konten'tar] vt (satisfacer) to satisfy; (complacer) to please; **contentarse** vr to be satisfied
contento, -a [kon'tento, a] adj (alegre) pleased; (feliz) happy
contestación [kontesta'θjon] nf answer, reply
contestador [kontesta'ðor] nm (tb: **~ automático**) answering machine
contestar [kontes'tar] vt to answer, reply; (Jur) to corroborate, confirm
contexto [kon'te(k)sto] nm context
contigo [kon'tiɣo] pron with you
contiguo, -a [kon'tiɣwo, a] adj adjacent, adjoining
continente [konti'nente] adj, nm continent
continuación [kontinwa'θjon] nf continuation; **a ~** then, next
continuar [konti'nwar] vt to continue, go on with ⊳ vi to continue, go on; **~ hablando** to continue talking o to talk
continuidad [kontinwi'ðað] nf continuity
continuo, -a [kon'tinwo, a] adj (sin interrupción) continuous; (acción perseverante) continual
contorno [kon'torno] nm outline; (Geo) contour; **contornos** nmpl neighbourhood sg, surrounding area sg
contra ['kontra] prep, adv against ⊳ nm inv con ⊳ nf: **la C~** (de Nicaragua) the Contras pl
contraataque [kontraa'take] nm counter-attack
contrabajo [kontra'ßaxo] nm double bass
contrabandista [kontraßan'dista] nmf smuggler
contrabando [kontra'ßando] nm (acción) smuggling; (mercancías) contraband
contracción [kontrak'θjon] nf contraction

contracorriente [kontrako'rrjente] nf cross-current

contradecir [kontrađe'θir] vt to contradict

contradicción [kontrađik'θjon] nf contradiction

contradictorio, -a [kontrađik'torjo, a] adj contradictory

contraer [kontra'er] vt to contract; (limitar) to restrict; **contraerse** vr to contract; (limitarse) to limit o.s.

contraluz [kontra'luθ] nm view against the light

contrapartida [kontrapar'tiđa] nf: **como ~ (de)** in return (for)

contrapelo [kontra'pelo]: **a ~** adv the wrong way

contrapeso [kontra'peso] nm counterweight

contraportada [kontrapor'tađa] nf (de revista) back cover

contraproducente [kontraproðu'θente] adj counterproductive

contrario, -a [kon'trarjo, a] adj contrary; (persona) opposed; (sentido, lado) opposite ▷ nm/f enemy, adversary; (Deporte) opponent; **al o por el ~** on the contrary; **de lo ~** otherwise

contrarreloj [kontrarre'lo] nf (tb: **prueba ~**) time trial

contrarrestar [kontrarres'tar] vt to counteract

contrasentido [kontrasen'tiđo] nm (contradicción) contradiction

contraseña [kontra'seɲa] nf (Inform) password

contrastar [kontras'tar] vt, vi to contrast

contraste [kon'traste] nm contrast

contratar [kontra'tar] vt firmar un acuerdo para, to contract for; (empleados, obreros) to hire, engage

contratiempo [kontra'tjempo] nm setback

contratista [kontra'tista] nmf contractor

contrato [kon'trato] nm contract

contraventana [kontraβen'tana] nf shutter

contribución [kontriβu'θjon] nf (municipal etc) tax; (ayuda) contribution

contribuir [kontriβu'ir] vt, vi to contribute; (Com) to pay (in taxes)

contribuyente [kontriβu'jente] nmf (Com) taxpayer; (que ayuda) contributor

contrincante [kontrin'kante] nmf opponent

control [kon'trol] nm control; (inspección) inspection, check; **control de pasaportes** passport inspection; **controlador, a** nm/f controller; **controlador aéreo** air-traffic controller; **controlar** [kontro'lar] vt to control; (inspeccionar) to inspect, check

contundente [kontun'dente] adj (instrumento) blunt; (argumento, derrota) overwhelming

contusión [kontu'sjon] nf bruise

convalecencia [kombale'θenθja] nf convalescence

convalecer [kombale'θer] vi to convalesce, get better

convalidar [kombali'đar] vt (título) to recognize

convencer [komben'θer] vt to convince; **~ a algn (de o para hacer algo)** to persuade sb (to do sth)

convención [komben'θjon] nf convention

conveniente [kombe'njente] adj suitable; (útil) useful

convenio [kom'benjo] nm agreement, treaty

convenir [kombe'nir] vi (estar de acuerdo) to agree; (venir bien) to suit, be suitable

convento [kom'bento] nm convent

convenza etc vb V **convencer**

convergir [komber'xir] vi = **converger**

conversación [kombersa'θjon] nf conversation

conversar [komber'sar] vi to talk, converse

conversión [komber'sjon] nf conversion

convertir [komber'tir] vt to convert

convidar [kombi'đar] vt to invite; **~ a algn a una cerveza** to buy sb a beer

convincente [kombin'θente] adj convincing

convite [kom'bite] nm invitation; (banquete) banquet

convivencia [kombi'βenθja] nf coexistence, living together

convivir [kombi'βir] vi to live together

convocar [kombo'kar] vt to summon, call (together)

convocatoria [komboka'torja] nf (de oposiciones, elecciones) notice; (de huelga) call

cónyuge ['konjuxe] nmf spouse

coñac [ko'ɲa(k)] (pl **-s**) nm cognac, brandy

coño ['koɲo] (fam!) excl (enfado) shit! (!); (sorpresa) bloody hell! (!)

cool [kul] adj (fam) cool

cooperación [koopera'θjon] nf cooperation

cooperar [koope'rar] vi to cooperate

cooperativa [koopera'tiβa] nf cooperative

coordinadora [koorđina'đora] nf (comité) coordinating committee

coordinar [koorđi'nar] vt to coordinate

copa ['kopa] nf cup; (vaso) glass; (bebida): **tomar una ~** (to have a) drink; (de árbol) top; (de sombrero) crown; **copas** nfpl (Naipes) = hearts

copia ['kopja] nf copy; **copia de respaldo o seguridad** (Inform) back-up copy; **copiar** vt to copy

copla ['kopla] nf verse; (canción) (popular) song

copo ['kopo] nm: **~ de nieve** snowflake; **~s de maíz** cornflakes

coqueta [ko'keta] adj flirtatious, coquettish; **coquetear** vi to flirt

coraje [ko'raxe] nm courage; (ánimo) spirit; (ira) anger

coral [ko'ral] adj choral ▷ nf (Mús) choir ▷ nm (Zool) coral

coraza [ko'raθa] nf (armadura) armour; (blindaje) armour-plating

corazón [kora'θon] nm heart

corazonada [koraθo'nađa] nf impulse; (presentimiento) hunch

corbata [kor'βata] nf tie

corchete [kor'tʃete] nm catch, clasp

corcho ['kortʃo] nm cork; (Pesca) float

cordel [kor'đel] nm cord, line

cordero [kor'đero] nm lamb

cordial [kor'đjal] adj cordial

cordillera [korđi'ʎera] nf range (of mountains)

Córdoba ['korđoβa] n Cordova

cordón [kor'đon] nm (cuerda) cord, string; (de zapatos) lace; (Mil etc) cordon; **cordón umbilical** umbilical cord

cordura [kor'đura] nf: **con ~** (obrar, hablar) sensibly

corneta [kor'neta] nf bugle

cornisa [kor'nisa] nf (Arq) cornice

coro ['koro] nm chorus; (conjunto de cantores) choir

corona [ko'rona] nf crown; (de flores) garland

coronel [koro'nel] nm colonel

coronilla [koro'niʎa] nf (Anat) crown (of the head)

corporal [korpo'ral] adj corporal, bodily

corpulento, -a [korpu'lento, a] adj (persona) heavily-built

corral [ko'rral] nm farmyard

correa [ko'rrea] nf strap; (cinturón) belt; (de perro) lead, leash; **correa del ventilador** (Auto) fan belt

corrección [korrek'θjon] nf correction; (reprensión) rebuke; **correccional** nm reformatory

correcto, -a [ko'rrekto, a] adj correct; (persona) well-mannered

corredizo, -a [korre'ðiθo, a] adj (puerta etc) sliding

corredor, a [korre'ðor, a] nm (pasillo) corridor; (balcón corrido) gallery; (Com) agent, broker ▷ nm/f (Deporte) runner

corregir [korre'xir] vt (error) to correct; **corregirse** vr to reform

correo [ko'rreo] nm post, mail; (persona) courier; **Correos** nmpl (ESP) Post Office sg; **correo aéreo** airmail; **correo basura** (Inform) spam; **correo electrónico** e-mail, electronic mail; **correo web** webmail

correr [ko'rrer] vt to run, (cortinas) to draw; (cerrojo) to shoot ▷ vi to run; (líquido) to run, flow; **correrse** vr to slide, move; (colores) to run

correspondencia [korrespon'denθja] nf correspondence; (Ferro) connection

corresponder [korrespon'der] vi to correspond; (convenir) to be suitable; (pertenecer) to belong; (concernir) to concern; **corresponderse** vr (por escrito) to correspond; (amarse) to love one another

correspondiente [korrespon'djente] adj corresponding

corresponsal [korrespon'sal] nmf correspondent

corrida [ko'rriða] nf (de toros) bullfight

corrido, -a [ko'rriðo, a] adj (avergonzado) abashed; **un kilo ~** a good kilo

corriente [ko'rrjente] adj (agua) running; (dinero etc) current; (común) ordinary, normal ▷ nf current ▷ nm current month; **estar al ~ de** to be informed about; **corriente eléctrica** electric current

corrija etc vb V **corregir**

corro [ˈkorro] nm ring, circle (of people)

corromper [korrom'per] vt (madera) to rot; (fig) to corrupt

corrosivo, -a [korro'siβo, a] adj corrosive

corrupción [korrup'θjon] nf rot, decay; (fig) corruption

corsé [kor'se] nm corset

cortacésped [korta'θespeð] nm lawn mower

cortado, -a [kor'taðo, a] adj (gen) cut; (leche) sour; (tímido) shy; (avergonzado) embarrassed ▷ nm coffee (with a little milk)

cortafuegos [korta'fweɣos] nm inv (en el bosque) firebreak, fire lane (us); (Internet) firewall

cortar [kor'tar] vt to cut, cutting; (suministro) to cut off; (un pasaje) to cut out ▷ vi to cut; **cortarse** vr (avergonzarse) to become embarrassed; (leche) to turn, curdle; **~se el pelo** to have one's hair cut

cortauñas [korta'uɲas] nm inv nail clippers pl

corte [ˈkorte] nm cut, cutting; (de tela) piece, length ▷ nf: **las C~s** the Spanish Parliament; **corte de luz** power cut; **corte y confección** dressmaking

cortejo [kor'texo] nm entourage; **cortejo fúnebre** funeral procession

cortés [kor'tes] adj courteous, polite

cortesía [korte'sia] nf courtesy

corteza [kor'teθa] nf (de árbol) bark; (de pan) crust

cortijo [kor'tixo] (ESP) nm farm, farmhouse

cortina [kor'tina] nf curtain

corto, -a [ˈkorto, a] adj (breve) short; (tímido) bashful; **~ de luces** not very bright; **~ de vista** short-sighted; **estar ~ de fondos** to be short of funds; **cortocircuito**

nm short circuit; **cortometraje** nm (Cine) short

cosa [ˈkosa] nf thing; **~ de** about; **eso es ~ mía** that's my business

coscorrón [kosko'rron] nm bump on the head

cosecha [ko'setʃa] nf (Agr) harvest; (de vino) vintage; **cosechar** [kose'tʃar] vt to harvest, gather (in)

coser [ko'ser] vt to sew

cosmético, -a [kos'metiko, a] adj, nm cosmetic

cosquillas [kos'kiʎas] nfpl: **hacer ~** to tickle; **tener ~** to be ticklish

costa [ˈkosta] nf (Geo) coast; **a toda ~** at all costs; **Costa Brava** Costa Brava; **Costa Cantábrica** Cantabrian Coast; **Costa del Sol** Costa del Sol

costado [kos'taðo] nm side

costanera [kos'tanera] (cs) nf promenade, sea front

costar [kos'tar] vt (valer) to cost; **me cuesta hablarle** i find it hard to talk to him

Costa Rica [kosta'rika] nf Costa Rica; **costarricense** adj, nmf Costa Rican; **costarriqueño, -a** adj, nm/f Costa Rican

coste [ˈkoste] nm = **costo**

costear [koste'ar] vt to pay for

costero, -a [kos'tero, a] adj (pueblecito, camino) coastal

costilla [kos'tiʎa] nf rib; (Culin) cutlet

costo [ˈkosto] nm cost, price; **costo de (la) vida** cost of living; **costoso, -a** adj costly, expensive

costra [ˈkostra] nf (corteza) crust; (Med) scab

costumbre [kos'tumbre] nf custom, habit

costura [kos'tura] nf sewing, needlework; (zurcido) seam

costurera [kostu'rera] nf dressmaker

costurero [kostu'rero] nm sewing box o case

cotidiano, -a [koti'ðjano, a] adj daily, day to day

cotilla [ko'tiʎa] (ESP: fam) nmf gossip; **cotillear** (ESP) vi to gossip; **cotilleo** (ESP) nm gossip(ing)

cotizar [koti'θar] vt (Com) to quote, price; **cotizarse** vr: **~se a** to sell at, fetch; (Bolsa) to stand at, be quoted at

coto [ˈkoto] nm (terreno cercado) enclosure; (de caza) reserve

cotorra [ko'torra] nf parrot

coyote [ko'jote] nm coyote, prairie wolf

coz [koθ] nf kick

crack [krak] nm (droga) crack

cráneo [ˈkraneo] nm skull, cranium

cráter [ˈkrater] nm crater

crayón [kra'jon] (MÉX, RPL) nm crayon, chalk

creación [krea'θjon] nf creation

creador, a [krea'ðor, a] adj creative ▷ nm/f creator

crear [kre'ar] vt to create, make

crecer [kre'θer] vi to grow; (precio) to rise

creces [ˈkreθes] con **~** adv amply, fully

crecido, -a [kre'θiðo, a] adj (persona, planta) full-grown; (cantidad) large

crecimiento [kreθi'mjento] nm growth; (aumento) increase

credencial [kreðen'θjal] (LAM: tarjeta) card; **credenciales** nfpl credentials; **credencial de socio** (LAM) membership card

crédito [ˈkreðito] nm credit

credo [ˈkreðo] nm creed

creencia [kre'enθja] nf belief

creer [kre'er] vt, vi to think, believe; **creerse** vr to believe o.s. (to be); **~ en** to believe in; **creo que sí/no** i think/don't think so; **¡ya lo creo!** I should think so!

creído, -a [kre'iðo, a] adj (engreído) conceited

crema ['krema] nf cream; **crema batida** (LAM) whipped cream; **crema pastelera** (confectioner's) custard

cremallera [krema'ʎera] nf zip (fastener)

crepe ['krepe] (ESP) nf pancake

cresta ['kresta] nf (Geo, Zool) crest

creyendo etc vb V **creer**

creyente [kre'jente] nmf believer

creyó etc vb V **creer**

crezco etc vb V **creer**

cría etc ['kria] vb V **criar** ▷ nf (de animales) rearing, breeding; (animal) young; V tb **crío**

criadero [kria'ðero] nm (Zool) breeding place

criado, -a [kri'aðo, a] nm ▷ nf servant, maid

criador [kria'ðor] nm breeder

crianza [kri'anθa] nf rearing, breeding; (fig) breeding

criar [kri'ar] vt (educar) to bring up; (producir) to grow, produce; (animales) to breed

criatura [kria'tura] nf creature; (niño) baby, (small) child

cribar [kri'βar] vt to sieve

crimen ['krimen] nm crime

criminal [krimi'nal] adj, nmf criminal

crines ['krines] nfpl mane

crío, -a ['krio, a] (fam) nm/f (niño) kid

crisis ['krisis] nf inv crisis; **crisis nerviosa** nervous breakdown

crismas ['krismas] (ESP) nm inv Christmas card

cristal [kris'tal] nm crystal; (de ventana) glass, pane; (lente) lens; **cristalino, -a** adj crystalline; (fig) clear ▷ nm lens (of the eye)

cristianismo [kristja'nismo] nm Christianity

cristiano, -a [kris'tjano, a] adj, nm/f Christian

Cristo ['kristo] nm Christ; (crucifijo) crucifix

criterio [kri'terjo] nm criterion; (juicio) judgement

crítica [kritika] nf criticism; V tb **crítico**

criticar [kriti'kar] vt to criticize

crítico, -a ['kritiko, a] adj critical ▷ nm/f critic

Croacia [kro'aθja] nf Croatia

cromo ['kromo] nm chrome

crónica ['kronika] nf chronicle, account

crónico, -a ['kroniko, a] adj chronic

cronómetro [kro'nometro] nm stopwatch

croqueta [kro'keta] nf croquette

cruce etc ['kruθe] vb V **cruzar** ▷ nm (para peatones) crossing; (de carreteras) crossroads

crucero [kru'θero] nm (viaje) cruise

crucificar [kruθifi'kar] vt to crucify

crucifijo [kruθi'fixo] nm crucifix

crucigrama [kruθi'xrama] nm crossword (puzzle)

cruda ['kruða] (MÉX, CAM: fam) nf hangover

crudo, -a ['kruðo, a] adj raw; (no maduro) unripe; (petróleo) crude; (rudo, cruel) cruel ▷ nm crude (oil)

cruel [krwel] adj cruel; **crueldad** nf cruelty

crujiente [kru'xjente] adj (galleta etc) crunchy

crujir [kru'xir] vi (madera etc) to creak; (dedos) to crack; (dientes) to grind; (nieve, arena) to crunch

cruz [kruθ] nf cross; (de moneda) tails sg; **cruz gamada** swastika

cruzada [kru'θaða] nf crusade

cruzado, -a [kru'θaðo, a] adj crossed ▷ nm crusader

cruzar [kru'θar] vt to cross; **cruzarse** vr (líneas etc) to cross; (personas) to pass each other

Cruz Roja nf Red Cross

cuaderno [kwa'ðerno] nm notebook; (de escuela)

exercise book; (Náut) logbook

cuadra ['kwaðra] nf (caballeriza) stable; (LAM: entre calles) block

cuadrado, -a [kwa'ðraðo, a] adj square ▷ nm (Mat) square

cuadrar [kwa'ðrar] vt to square ▷ vi: **~ con** to square with, tally with; **cuadrarse** vr (soldado) to stand to attention

cuadrilátero [kwaðri'latero] nm (Deporte) boxing ring; (Geom) quadrilateral

cuadrilla [kwa'ðriʎa] nf party, group

cuadro ['kwaðro] nm square; (Arte) painting; (Teatro) scene; (diagrama) chart; (Deporte, Med) team; **tela a ~s** checked (BRIT) o chequered (US) material

cuajar [kwa'xar] vt (leche) to curdle; (sangre) to congeal; (Culin) to set; **cuajarse** vr to curdle; to congeal; to set; (llenarse) to fill up

cuajo ['kwaxo] nm: **de ~** (arrancar) by the roots; (cortar) completely

cual [kwal] adv like, as ▷ pron: **el etc ~** which; (persona sujeto) who; (: objeto) whom ▷ adj such as; **cada ~** each one; **déjalo tal ~** leave it just as it is

cuál [kwal] pron interr which (one)

cualesquier, a [kwales'kjer(a)] pl de **cualquier(a)**

cualidad [kwali'ðað] nf quality

cualquier [kwal'kjer] adj V **cualquiera**

cualquiera [kwal'kjera] (pl **cualesquiera**) adj (delante de nm y f **cualquier**) any ▷ pron anybody; **un coche ~ servirá** any car will do; **no es un hombre ~** he isn't just anybody; **cualquier día/libro** any day/book; **eso ~ lo sabe hacer** anybody can do that; **es un ~** he's a nobody

---

cuando ['kwando] adv when; (aún si) if, even if ▷ conj (puesto que) since ▷ prep: **yo, ~ niño ...** when I was a child ...; **~ no sea así** even if it is not so; **~ más** at (the) most; **~ menos** at least; **~ no** if not, otherwise; **de ~ en ~** from time to time

cuándo ['kwando] adv when; **¿desde ~?** since when?

cuantía [kwan'tia] nf extent

○ PALABRA CLAVE

cuanto, -a ['kwanto, a] adj 1 (todo):
tiene todo cuanto desea he's got everything he wants; **le daremos cuantos ejemplares necesite** we'll give him as many copies as o all the copies he needs; **cuantos hombres la ven** all the men who see her

2 unos cuantos: **había unos cuantos periodistas** there were a few journalists

3 (+ más): **cuanto más vino bebes peor te sentirás** the more wine you drink the worse you'll feel

▷ pron: **tiene cuanto desea** he has everything he wants; **tome cuanto/cuantos quiera** take as much/many as you want

▷ adv: **en cuanto: en cuanto profesor** as a teacher; **en cuanto a mí** as for me; V tb **antes**

▷ conj 1 **cuanto más gana más gasta** the more he earns the less he spends; **cuanto más joven más confiado** the younger you are the more trusting you are

2 **en cuanto: en cuanto llegue/llegué** as soon as I arrive/arrived

cuánto, -a ['kwanto, a] adj (exclamación) what a lot

of; (interr: sg) how much? (: pl) how many? ▷ pron, adv how; (: interr: sg) how much? (: pl) how many? **¡cuánta gente!** what a lot of people!; **¿~ cuesta?** how much does it cost?; **¿a ~s estamos?** what's the date?

cuarenta [kwa'renta] num forty

cuarentena [kwaren'tena] nf quarantine

cuaresma [kwa'resma] nf Lent

cuarta ['kwarta] nf (Mat) quarter, fourth; (palmo) span

cuartel [kwar'tel] nm (Mil) barracks pl; **cuartel de bomberos** (RPL) fire station; **cuartel general** headquarters pl

cuarteto [kwar'teto] nm quartet

cuarto, -a ['kwarto, a] adj fourth ▷ nm (Mat) quarter, fourth; (habitación) room; **cuarto de baño** bathroom; **cuarto de estar** living room; **cuarto de hora** quarter (of an) hour; **cuarto de kilo** quarter of a kilo; **cuartos de final** quarter finals

cuatro ['kwatro] num four

Cuba ['kuβa] nf Cuba

cuba ['kuβa] nf cask, barrel

cubano, -a [ku'βano, a] adj, nm/f Cuban

cubata [ku'βata] nm (fam) large drink (of rum and coke etc)

cubeta [ku'βeta] nf (ESP, MÉX) (balde) bucket, tub

cúbico, -a ['kuβiko, a] adj cubic

cubierta [ku'βjerta] nf cover, covering; (neumático) tyre; (Náut) deck

cubierto, -a [ku'βjerto, a] pp de **cubrir** ▷ adj covered ▷ nm cover; (lugar en la mesa) place; **cubiertos** nmpl cutlery sg; **a ~** under cover

cubilete [kuβi'lete] nm (en juegos) cup

cubito [ku'βito] nm (tb: **~ de hielo**) ice-cube

cubo ['kuβo] nm (Mat) cube; (ESP: balde) bucket, tub; (Tec) drum; **cubo de (la) basura** dustbin (BRIT), trash can (US)

cubrir [ku'βrir] vt to cover; **cubrirse** vr (cielo) to become overcast

cucaracha [kuka'ratʃa] nf cockroach

cuchara [ku'tʃara] nf spoon; (Tec) scoop; **cucharada** nf spoonful; **cucharadita** nf teaspoonful

cucharilla [kutʃa'riʎa] nf teaspoon

cucharón [kutʃa'ron] nm ladle

cuchilla [ku'tʃiʎa] nf (large) knife; (de arma blanca) blade; **cuchilla de afeitar** razor blade

cuchillo [ku'tʃiʎo] nm knife

cuchitril [kutʃi'tril] nm hovel

cuclillas [ku'kliʎas] nfpl: **en ~** squatting

cuco, -a ['kuko, a] adj pretty; (astuto) sharp ▷ nm cuckoo

cucurucho [kuku'rutʃo] nm cornet

cueca ['kweka] nf Chilean national dance

cuello ['kweʎo] nm (Anat) neck; (de vestido, camisa) collar

cuenca ['kwenka] nf (Anat) eye socket; (Geo) bowl, deep valley

cuenco ['kwenko] nm bowl

cuenta etc ['kwenta] vb V **contar** ▷ nf (cálculo) count, counting; (en café, restaurante) bill (BRIT), check (US); (Com) account; (de collar) bead; **a fin de ~** in the end; **caer en la ~** to catch on; **darse ~ de** to realize; **tener en ~** to bear in mind; **echar ~s** to take stock; **cuenta atrás** countdown; **cuenta corriente/de ahorros** current/savings account; **cuenta de correo (electrónica)** (Inform) email account; **cuentakilómetros** nm inv ≈ milometer; (de velocidad)

speedometer

cuento etc ['kwento] vb V **contar** ▷ nm story; **cuento chino** tall story; **cuento de hadas** a fairy tale

cuerda ['kwerða] nf rope; (fina) string; (de reloj) spring; **dar ~ a un reloj** to wind up a clock; **cuerda floja** tightrope; **cuerdas vocales** vocal cords

cuerdo, -a ['kwerðo, a] adj sane; (prudente) wise, sensible

cuerno ['kwerno] nm horn

cuero ['kwero] nm leather; **en ~s** stark naked; **cuero cabelludo** scalp

cuerpo ['kwerpo] nm body

cuervo ['kwerβo] nm crow

cuesta etc ['kwesta] vb V **costar** ▷ nf slope; (en camino etc) hill; **~ arriba/abajo** uphill/downhill; **a ~s** on one's back

cueste etc vb V **costar**

cuestión [kwes'tjon] nf matter, question, issue

cuete ['kwete] adj (MÉX: fam) drunk ▷ nm (LAM: cohete) rocket; (MÉX, RPL: fam: embriaguez) drunkenness; (MÉX: Culin) steak

cueva ['kweβa] nf cave

cuidado [kwi'ðaðo] nm care, carefulness; (preocupación) care, worry ▷ excl careful!, look out!; **eso me tiene sin ~** I'm not worried about that

cuidadoso, -a [kwiða'ðoso, a] adj careful; (preocupado) anxious

cuidar [kwi'ðar] vt (Med) to care for; (ocuparse de) to take care of, look after ▷ vi: **~ de** to take care of, look after; **cuidarse** vr to look after o.s.; **~se de hacer algo** to take care to do sth

culata [ku'lata] nf (de fusil) butt

culebra [ku'leβra] nf snake

culebrón [kule'βron] (fam) nm (TV) soap(-opera)

culo ['kulo] nm bottom, backside; (de vaso, botella) bottom

culpa ['kulpa] nf fault; (Jur) guilt; **por ~ de** because of; **echar la ~ a algn** to blame sb for sth; **tener la ~ (de)** to be to blame (for); **culpable** adj ▷ nmf culprit; **culpar** [kul'par] vt to blame; (acusar) to accuse

cultivar [kulti'βar] vt to cultivate

cultivo [kul'tiβo] nm (acto) cultivation; (plantas) crop

culto, -a ['kulto, a] adj (que tiene cultura) cultured, educated ▷ nm (homenaje) worship; (religión) cult

cultura [kul'tura] nf culture

culturismo [kultu'rismo] nm body-building

cumbia ['kumbja] nf popular Colombian dance

cumbre ['kumbre] nf summit, top

cumpleaños [kumple'años] nm inv birthday

cumplido, -a [kum'pliðo, a] adj (abundante) plentiful; (cortés) courteous ▷ nm compliment; **visita de ~** courtesy call

cumplidor, a [kumpli'ðor, a] adj reliable

cumplimiento [kumpli'mjento] nm (de un deber) fulfilment; (acabamiento) completion

cumplir [kum'plir] vt (orden) to carry out, obey; (promesa) to carry out, fulfil; (condena) to serve ▷ vi: **~ con** (deber) to carry out, fulfil; **cumplirse** vr (plazo) to expire; **hoy cumple dieciocho años** he is eighteen today

cuna ['kuna] nf cradle, cot

cundir [kun'dir] vi (noticia, rumor, pánico) to spread; (rendir) to go a long way

cuneta [ku'neta] nf ditch

cuña ['kuña] nf wedge

cuñado, -a [ku'ñaðo, a] nm/f brother-/sister-in-law

cuota ['kwota] nf (parte proporcional) share; (cotización) fee, dues pl

cupe etc vb V **caber**

cupiera etc vb V **caber**

cupo ['kupo] vb V **caber** ▷ nm quota

cupón [ku'pon] nm coupon

cúpula ['kupula] nf dome

cura ['kura] nf (curación) cure; (método curativo) treatment ▷ nm priest

curación [kura'θjon] nf cure; (acción) curing

curandero, -a [kuran'dero, a] nm/f quack

curar [ku'rar] vt (Med: herida) to treat, dress; (: enfermo) to cure; (Culin) to cure, salt; (cuero) to tan; **curarse** vr to get well, recover

curiosear [kurjose'ar] vt to glance at, look over ▷ vi to look round, wander round; (explorar) to poke about

curiosidad [kurjosi'ðað] nf curiosity

curioso, -a [ku'rjoso, a] adj curious ▷ nm/f bystander, onlooker

curita [ku'rita] (LAM) nf (sticking) plaster (BRIT), Bandaid® (US)

currante [ku'rrante] (ESP: fam) nmf worker

currar [ku'rrar] (ESP: fam) vi to work

currículo [ku'rrikulo] = **curriculum**

curriculum [ku'rrikulum] nm curriculum vitae

cursi ['kursi] (fam) adj affected

cursillo [kur'siʎo] nm short course

cursiva [kur'siβa] nf italics pl

curso ['kurso] nm course; **en ~** (año) current; (proceso) going on, under way

cursor [kur'sor] nm (Inform) cursor

curul [ku'rul] (MÉX) nm (escaño) seat

curva ['kurβa] nf curve, bend

custodia [kus'toðja] nf safekeeping; custody

cutis ['kutis] nm inv skin, complexion

cutre ['kutre] (ESP: fam) adj (lugar) grotty

cuyo, -a ['kujo, a] pron (de quien) whose; (de que) whose, of which; **en ~ caso** in which case

C.V. abr (= caballos de vapor) H.P.

d

D. abr (= Don) Esq

dado, -a ['daðo, a] pp de **dar** ▷ nm die; **dados** nmpl dice; **~ que** given that

daltónico, -a [dal'toniko, a] adj colour-blind

dama ['dama] nf (gen) lady; (Ajedrez) queen; **damas** nfpl (juego) draughts sg; **dama de honor** bridesmaid

damasco [da'masko] (RPL) nm apricot

danés, -esa [da'nes, esa] adj Danish ▷ nm/f Dane

dañar [da'nar] vt (objeto) to damage; (persona) to hurt; **dañarse** vr (objeto) to get damaged

dañino, -a [da'nino, a] adj harmful

daño ['dano] nm (objeto) damage; (persona) harm, injury; **~s y perjuicios** (Jur) damages; **hacer ~ a** to damage; (persona) to hurt, injure; **hacerse ~** to hurt o.s.

○ PALABRA CLAVE

dar [dar] vt **1** (gen) to give; (obra de teatro) to put on; (film) to show; (fiesta) to hold; **dar algo a algn** to give sb sth o sth to sb; **dar de beber a algn** to give sb a drink

2 (producir: intereses) to yield; (fruta) to produce

3 (locuciones + n): **da gusto escucharle** it's a pleasure to listen to him; V tb **paseo**

4 (+ n: = perífrasis de verbo): **me da asco** it sickens me

5 (considerar): **dar algo por descontado/entendido** to take
sth for granted/as read; **dar algo
por concluido** to consider sth
finished

6 (hora): **el reloj dio las 6** the clock struck 6 (o'clock)

7: **me da lo mismo** it's all the same to me; V tb **igual, más**

▷ vi **1**: **dar con**: **dimos con él dos horas más tarde** we came across him two hours later; **al final di con la solución** I eventually came up with the answer

2: **dar en** (blanco, suelo) to hit; **el sol me da en la cara** the sun is shining (right) on my face

3: **dar de sí** (zapatos etc) to stretch,
give

darse vr **1**: **darse por vencido** to give up

2 (ocurrir): **se han dado muchos casos** there have been a lot of cases

3: **darse a**: **se ha dado a la bebida** he's taken to

drinking
4: se me dan bien/mal las ciencias I'm good/bad
at science
**5: dárselas de: se las da de
experto** he fancies himself o poses as an expert

dardo ['darðo] nm dart
dátil ['datil] nm date
dato ['dato] nm fact, piece of information; **datos
personales** personal details
dcha. abr (= derecha) r.h.
d. de C. abr (= después de Cristo) A.D.

○ **PALABRA CLAVE**

de [de] (de + el = del) prep **1** (posesión) of; **la casa de
Isabel/mis padres** Isabel's/my parents' house; **es de
ellos** it's theirs
2 (origen, distancia, con números) from; **soy de Gijón** I'm
from Gijón; **de 8 a 20** from 8 to 20; **salir del cine** to go
out o leave the cinema; **de 2 en 2** by 2, 2 at a time
3 (valor descriptivo): **una copa de vino** a glass of wine;
la mesa de la cocina the kitchen table; **un billete
de 10 euros** a 10 euro note; **un niño de tres años**
a three-year-old (child); **una máquina de coser** a
sewing machine; **ir vestido de gris** to be dressed in
grey; **la niña del vestido azul** the girl in the blue dress;
trabaja de profesora she works as a teacher; **de lado**
sideways; **de atrás/delante** rear/front
4 (hora, tiempo): **a las 8 de la mañana** at 8 o'clock in
the morning; **de día/noche** by day/night; **de hoy en
ocho días** a week from now; **de niño era gordo** as a
child he was fat
5 (comparaciones): **más/menos de cien personas**
more/less than a hundred people; **el más caro de la
tienda** the most expensive in the shop; **menos/más
de lo pensado** less/more than expected
6 (causa): **del calor** from the heat
7 (tema) about; **clases de inglés** English classes;
¿sabes algo de él? do you know anything about him?;
un libro de física a physics book
8 (adj + de + infin): **fácil de entender** easy to understand
9 (oraciones pasivas): **fue respetado de todos** he was
loved by all
10 (condicional + infin) if; **de ser
posible** if possible; **de no
terminarlo hoy** if I etc don't finish it today

dé [de] vb V **dar**
debajo [de'βaxo] adv underneath; **~ de** below, under;
por ~ de beneath
debate [de'βate] nm debate; **debatir** vt to debate
deber [de'βer] nm duty ▷ vt to owe ▷ vi: **debe (de)**
it must, it should; **deberes** nmpl (Escol) homework;
deberse vr: **~se a** to owe o be due to; **debo hacerlo**
I must do it; **debe de ir** he should go
debido, -a [de'βiðo, a] adj proper, just; **~ a** due to,
because of
débil ['deβil] adj (persona, carácter) weak; (luz) dim;
debilidad nf weakness; dimness
debilitar [deβili'tar] vt to weaken; **debilitarse** vr
to grow weak
débito ['deβito] nm debit; **débito bancario** (LAM)
direct debit (BRIT) o billing (US)

45 | deformación

debutar [deβu'tar] vi to make one's debut
década ['dekaða] nf decade
decadencia [deka'ðenθja] nf (estado) decadence;
(proceso) decline, decay
decaído, -a [deka'iðo, a] adj: **estar ~** (abatido) to
be down
decano, -a [de'kano, a] nm/f (de universidad etc) dean
decena [de'θena] nf: **una ~** ten (or so)
decente [de'θente] adj decent
decepción [deθep'θjon] nf disappointment
decepcionar [deθepθjo'nar] vt to disappoint
decidir [deθi'ðir] vt, vi to decide; **decidirse** vr: **~se a**
to make up one's mind to
décimo, -a ['deθimo, a] adj tenth ▷ nm tenth
decir [de'θir] vt to say; (contar) to tell; (hablar) to speak
▷ nm saying; **decirse** vr: **es
~** that is (to say); **~ para sí** to say to o.s.; **querer ~** to
mean; **¡dígame!** (Tel) hello!; (en tienda) can I help you?;
decisión [deθi'sjon] nf (resolución) decision; (firmeza)
decisiveness
decisivo, -a [deθi'siβo, a] adj decisive
declaración [deklara'θjon] nf (manifestación)
statement; (de amor) declaration; **declaración fiscal** o
de la renta income-tax return
declarar [dekla'rar] vt to declare ▷ vi to declare; (Jur)
to testify; **declararse** vr to propose
decoración [dekora'θjon] nf decoration
decorado [deko'raðo] nm (Cine, Teatro) scenery, set
decorar [deko'rar] vt to decorate; **decorativo, -a** adj
ornamental, decorative
decreto [de'kreto] nm decree
dedal [de'ðal] nm thimble
dedicación [deðika'θjon] nf dedication
dedicar [deði'kar] vt (libro) to dedicate; (tiempo,
dinero) to devote; (palabras: decir, consagrar) to dedicate,
devote; **dedicatoria** nf (de libro) dedication
dedo ['deðo] nm finger; **hacer ~** (fam) to hitch (a lift);
dedo anular ring finger; **dedo corazón** middle finger;
dedo (del pie) toe; **dedo gordo** (de la mano) thumb; (del
pie) big toe; **dedo índice** index finger; **dedo meñique**
little finger; **dedo pulgar** thumb
deducción [deðuk'θjon] nf deduction
deducir [deðu'θir] vt (concluir) to deduce, infer; (Com)
to deduct
defecto [de'fekto] nm defect, flaw; **defectuoso, -a**
adj defective, faulty
defender [defen'der] vt to defend; **defenderse** vr
(desenvolverse) to get by
defensa [de'fensa] nf defence ▷ nm (Deporte)
defender, back; **defensivo, -a** adj defensive; **a la
defensiva** on the defensive
defensor, a [defen'sor, a] adj defending ▷ nm/f
(abogado defensor) defending counsel; (protector)
protector
deficiencia [defi'θjenθja] nf deficiency
deficiente [defi'θjente] adj (defectuoso) defective;
~ en lacking o deficient in; **ser un ~ mental** to be
mentally handicapped
déficit ['defiθit] (pl **~s**) nm deficit
definición [defini'θjon] nf definition
definir [defi'nir] vt (determinar) to determine,
establish; (decidir) to define; (aclarar) to clarify;
definitivo, -a adj definitive; **en definitiva**
definitively; (en resumen) in short
deformación [deforma'θjon] nf (alteración)
deformation; (Radio etc) distortion

deformar [defor'mar] vt (gen) to deform;
deformarse vr to become deformed; **deforme** adj
(informe) deformed; (feo) ugly; (malhecho) misshapen

defraudar [defrau'ðar] vt (decepcionar) to
disappoint; (estafar) to defraud

defunción [defun'θjon] nf death, demise

degenerar [dexene'rar] vi to degenerate

degradar [deɣra'ðar] vt to debase, degrade;
degradarse vr to demean o.s.

degustación [deɣusta'θjon] nf sampling, tasting

dejar [de'xar] vt to leave; (permitir) to allow, let;
(abandonar) to abandon, forsake; (beneficios) to produce,
yield ▷ vi: ~ **de** (parar) to stop; (no hacer) to fail to; ~ **a un
lado** to leave o set aside; ~ **entrar/salir** to let in/out; ~
pasar to let through

del [del] (= **de** + **el**) V **de**

delantal [delan'tal] nm apron

delante [de'lante] adv in front; (enfrente) opposite;
(adelante) ahead; ~ **de** in front of, before

delantera [delan'tera] nf (de vestido, casa etc) front
part; (Deporte) forward line; **llevar la ~ (a algn)** to be
ahead (of sb)

delantero, -a [delan'tero, a] adj front ▷ nm
(Deporte) forward, striker

delatar [dela'tar] vt to inform on o against, betray;
delator, a nm/f informer

delegación [deleɣa'θjon] nf (acción, delegados)
delegation; (Com: oficina) office, branch; **delegación de
policía** (MÉX) police station

delegado, -a [dele'ɣaðo, a] nm/f delegate; (Com)
agent

delegar [dele'ɣar] vt to delegate

deletrear [deletre'ar] vt to spell (out)

delfín [del'fin] nm dolphin

delgado, -a [del'ɣaðo, a] adj thin; (persona) slim,
thin; (tela etc) light, delicate

deliberar [deliβe'rar] vt to debate, discuss

delicadeza [delika'ðeθa] nf (gen) delicacy;
(refinamiento, sutileza) refinement

delicado, -a [deli'kaðo, a] adj (gen) delicate;
(sensible) sensitive; (quisquilloso) touchy

delicia [de'liθja] nf delight

delicioso, -a [deli'θjoso, a] adj (gracioso) delightful;
(exquisito) delicious

delimitar [delimi'tar] vt (función, responsabilidades)
to define

delincuencia [delin'kwenθja] nf delinquency;
delincuente nmf delinquent; (criminal) criminal

delineante [deline'ante] nmf draughtsman/woman

delirante [deli'rante] adj delirious

delirar [deli'rar] vi to be delirious, rave

delirio [de'lirjo] nm (Med) delirium; (palabras
insensatas) ravings pl

delito [de'lito] nm (gen) crime; (infracción) offence

delta ['delta] nm delta

demacrado, -a [dema'kraðo, a] adj: **estar ~** to look
pale and drawn, be wasted away

demanda [de'manda] nf (pedido, Com) demand;
(petición) request; (Jur) action, lawsuit; **demandar**
[deman'dar] vt (gen) to demand; (Jur) to sue, file a
lawsuit against

demás [de'mas] adj: **los ~ niños** the other o remaining
children ▷ pron: **los/las ~** the others, the rest (of them);
lo ~ the rest (of it)

demasía [dema'sia] nf (exceso) excess, surplus;
comer en ~ to eat to excess

demasiado, -a [dema'sjaðo, a] adj: ~ **vino** too much
wine ▷ adv (antes de adj, adv) too; ~**s libros** too many
books; **¡esto es ~!** that's the limit!; **hace ~ calor** it's too
hot; ~ **despacio** too slowly; ~**s** too many

demencia [de'menθja] nf (locura) madness

democracia [demo'kraθja] nf democracy

demócrata [de'mokrata] nmf democrat;
democrático, -a adj democratic

demoler [demo'ler] vt to demolish; **demolición** nf
demolition

demonio [de'monjo] nm devil, demon; **¡~s!** hell!,
damn!; **¿cómo ~s?** how the hell?

demora [de'mora] nf delay

demos ['demos] vb V **dar**

demostración [demostra'θjon] nf (Mat) proof; (de
afecto) show, display

demostrar [demos'trar] vt (probar) to prove;
(mostrar) to show; (manifestar) to demonstrate

den [den] vb V **dar**

denegar [dene'ɣar] vt (rechazar) to refuse; (Jur) to
reject

denominación [denomina'θjon] nf (acto) naming

densidad [densi'ðað] nf density; (fig) thickness

denso, -a ['denso, a] adj dense; (espeso, pastoso)
thick; (fig) heavy

dentadura [denta'ðura] nf (set of) teeth pl;
dentadura postiza false teeth pl

dentera [den'tera] nf (grima): **dar ~ a algn** to set sb's
teeth on edge

dentífrico, -a [den'tifriko, a] adj dental ▷ nm
toothpaste

dentista [den'tista] nmf dentist

dentro ['dentro] adv inside ▷ prep: ~ **de** in, inside,
within; **por ~** (on the) inside; **mirar por ~** to look
inside; ~ **de tres meses** within three months

denuncia [de'nunθja] nf (delación) denunciation;
(acusación) accusation; (de accidente) report; **denunciar**
vt to report; (delatar) to inform on o against

departamento [departa'mento] nm sección
administrativa, department, section; (LAM: apartamiento)
flat (BRIT), apartment

depender [depen'der] vi: ~ **de** to depend on;
depende it (all) depends

dependienta [depen'djenta] nf saleswoman, shop
assistant

dependiente [depen'djente] adj dependent ▷ nm
salesman, shop assistant

depilar [depi'lar] vt (con cera) to wax; (cejas) to pluck

deportar [depor'tar] vt to deport

deporte [de'porte] nm sport; **hacer ~** to play sports;
deportista adj sports cpd ▷ nmf sportsman/woman;
deportivo, -a adj (club, periódico) sports cpd ▷ nm
sports car

depositar [deposi'tar] vt (dinero) to deposit;
(mercancías) to put away, store; **depositarse** vr to
settle

depósito [de'posito] nm (gen) deposit; (almacén)
warehouse, store; (de agua, gasolina etc) tank; **depósito
de cadáveres** mortuary

depredador, a [depreða'ðor, a] adj predatory ▷ nm
predator

depresión [depre'sjon] nf depression; **depresión
nerviosa** nervous breakdown

deprimido, -a [depri'miðo, a] adj depressed

deprimir [depri'mir] vt to depress; **deprimirse** vr
(persona) to become depressed

deprisa [de'prisa] *adv* quickly, hurriedly

depurar [depu'rar] *vt* to purify; (*purgar*) to purge

derecha [de'retʃa] *nf* right(-hand) side; (*Pol*) right; **a la ~** (*estar*) on the right; (*torcer etc*) (to the) right

derecho, -a [de'retʃo, a] *adj* right, right-hand ▷ *nm* (*privilegio*) right; (*lado*) right(-hand) side; (*leyes*) law ▷ *adv* straight, directly; **derechos** *nmpl* (*de aduana*) duty *sg*; (*de autor*) royalties; **tener ~ a** to have a right to; **derechos de autor** royalties

deriva [de'riβa] *nf*: **ir o estar a la ~** to drift, be adrift

derivado [deri'βaðo] *nm* (*Com*) by-product

derivar [deri'βar] *vt* to derive; (*desviar*) to direct ▷ *vi* to derive, be derived; (*Náut*) to drift; **derivarse** *vr* to derive, be derived; to drift

derramamiento [derrama'mjento] *nm* (*dispersión*) spilling; **derramamiento de sangre** bloodshed

derramar [derra'mar] *vt* to spill; (*verter*) to pour out; (*esparcir*) to scatter; **derramarse** *vr* to pour out

derrame [de'rrame] *nm* (*de líquido*) spilling; (*de sangre*) shedding; (*de tubo etc*) overflow; (*pérdida*) leakage; **derrame cerebral** brain haemorrhage

derredor [derre'ðor] *adv*: **al o en ~ de** around, about

derretir [derre'tir] *vt* (*gen*) to melt; (*nieve*) to thaw; **derretirse** *vr* to melt

derribar [derri'βar] *vt* to knock down; (*construcción*) to demolish; (*persona, gobierno, político*) to bring down

derrocar [derro'kar] *vt* (*gobierno*) to bring down, overthrow

derrochar [derro'tʃar] *vt* to squander; **derroche** *nm* (*despilfarro*) waste, squandering

derrota [de'rrota] *nf* (*Náut*) course; (*Mil, Deporte etc*) defeat, rout; **derrotar** *vt* (*gen*) to defeat; **derrotero** *nm* (*rumbo*) course

derrumbar [derrum'bar] *vt* (*edificio*) to knock down; **derrumbarse** *vr* to collapse

des *etc* *vb* V **dar**

desabrochar [desaβro'tʃar] *vt* (*botones, broches*) to undo, unfasten; **desabrocharse** *vr* (*ropa etc*) to come undone

desacato [desa'kato] *nm* (*falta de respeto*) disrespect; (*Jur*) contempt

desacertado, -a [desaθer'taðo, a] *adj* (*equivocado*) mistaken; (*inoportuno*) unwise

desacierto [desa'θjerto] *nm* mistake, error

desaconsejar [desakonse'xar] *vt* to advise against

desacreditar [desakreði'tar] *vt* (*desprestigiar*) to discredit, bring into disrepute; (*denigrar*) to run down

desacuerdo [desa'kwerðo] *nm* disagreement, discord

desafiar [desa'fjar] *vt* (*retar*) to challenge; (*enfrentarse a*) to defy

desafilado, -a [desafi'laðo, a] *adj* blunt

desafinado, -a [desafi'naðo, a] *adj*: **estar ~** to be out of tune

desafinar [desafi'nar] *vi* (*al cantar*) to be o go out of tune

desafío *etc* [desa'fio] *vb* V **desafiar** ▷ *nm* (*reto*) challenge; (*combate*) duel; (*resistencia*) defiance

desafortunado, -a [desafortu'naðo, a] *adj* (*desgraciado*) unfortunate, unlucky

desagradable [desaɣra'ðaβle] *adj* (*fastidioso, enojoso*) unpleasant; (*irritante*) disagreeable

desagradar [desaɣra'ðar] *vi* (*disgustar*) to displease; (*molestar*) to bother

desagradecido, -a [desaɣraðe'θiðo, a] *adj* ungrateful

desagrado [desa'ɣraðo] *nm* (*disgusto*) displeasure; (*contrariedad*) dissatisfaction

desagüe [des'aɣwe] *nm* (*de un líquido*) drainage; (*cañería*) drainpipe; (*salida*) outlet, drain

desahogar [desao'xar] *vt* (*aliviar*) to ease, relieve; (*ira*) to vent; **desahogarse** *vr* (*relajarse*) to relax; (*desfogarse*) to let off steam

desahogo [desa'oxo] *nm* (*alivio*) relief; (*comodidad*) comfort, ease

desahuciar [desau'θjar] *vt* (*enfermo*) to give up hope for; (*inquilino*) to evict

desairar [desai'rar] *vt* (*menospreciar*) to slight, snub

desalentador, a [desalenta'ðor, a] *adj* discouraging

desaliño [desa'liɲo] *nm* slovenliness

desalmado, -a [desal'maðo, a] *adj* (*cruel*) cruel, heartless

desalojar [desalo'xar] *vt* (*expulsar, echar*) to eject; (*abandonar*) to move out of ▷ *vi* to move out

desamor [desa'mor] *nm* (*frialdad*) indifference; (*odio*) dislike

desamparado, -a [desampa'raðo, a] *adj* (*persona*) helpless; (*lugar: expuesto*) exposed; (*desierto*) deserted

desangrar [desan'grar] *vt* to bleed; (*fig: persona*) to bleed dry; **desangrarse** *vr* to lose a lot of blood

desanimado, -a [desani'maðo, a] *adj* (*persona*) downhearted; (*espectáculo, fiesta*) dull

desanimar [desani'mar] *vt* (*desalentar*) to discourage; (*deprimir*) to depress; **desanimarse** *vr* to lose heart

desapacible [desapa'θiβle] *adj* (*gen*) unpleasant

desaparecer [desapare'θer] *vi* (*gen*) to disappear; (*el sol, el luz*) to vanish; **desaparecido, -a** *adj* missing; **desaparición** *nf* disappearance

desapercibido, -a [desaperθi'βiðo, a] *adj* (*desprevenido*) unprepared; **pasar ~** to go unnoticed

desaprensivo, -a [desapren'siβo, a] *adj* unscrupulous

desaprobar [desapro'βar] *vt* (*reprobar*) to disapprove of; (*condenar*) to condemn; (*no consentir*) to reject

desaprovechado, -a [desaproβe'tʃaðo, a] *adj* (*oportunidad, tiempo*) wasted; (*estudiante*) slack

desaprovechar [desaproβe'tʃar] *vt* to waste

desarmador [desarma'ðor] *nm* (*MÉX*) screwdriver

desarmar [desar'mar] *vt* (*Mil, fig*) to disarm; (*Tec*) to take apart, dismantle; **desarme** *nm* disarmament

desarraigar [desarrai'xar] *vt* to uproot; **desarraigo** *nm* uprooting

desarreglar [desarre'ɣlar] *vt* (*desordenar*) to disarrange; (*trastocar*) to upset, disturb

desarrollar [desarro'ʎar] *vt* (*gen*) to develop; **desarrollarse** *vr* to develop; (*ocurrir*) to take place; (*Foto*) to develop; **desarrollo** *nm* development

desarticular [desartiku'lar] *vt* (*hueso*) to dislocate; (*objeto*) to take apart; (*fig*) to break up

desasosegar [desasose'xar] *vt* (*inquietar*) to disturb, make uneasy

desasosiego *etc* [desaso'sjexo] *vb* V **desasosegar** ▷ *nm* (*intranquilidad*) uneasiness, restlessness; (*ansiedad*) anxiety

desastre [de'sastre] *nm* disaster; **desastroso, -a** *adj* disastrous

desatar [desa'tar] *vt* (*nudo*) to untie; (*paquete*) to undo; (*separar*) to detach; **desatarse** *vr* (*zapatos*) to come untied; (*tormenta*) to break

desatascar [desatas'kar] *vt* (*cañería*) to unblock,

clear

desatender [desaten'der] vt no prestar atención a, to disregard; (abandonar) to neglect

desatino [desa'tino] nm (idiotez) foolishness, folly; (error) blunder

desatornillar [desatorni'ʎar] vt to unscrew

desatrancar [desatran'kar] vt (puerta) to unbolt; (cañería) to clear, unblock

desautorizado, -a [desautori'θaðo, a] adj unauthorized

desautorizar [desautori'θar] vt (oficial) to deprive of authority; (informe) to deny

desayunar [desaju'nar] vi to have breakfast ▷ vt to have for breakfast; **desayuno** nm breakfast

desazón [desa'θon] nf anxiety

desbarajuste [desβara'xuste] nm confusion, disorder

desbaratar [desβara'tar] vt (deshacer, destruir) to ruin

desbloquear [desβloke'ar] vt (negociaciones, tráfico) to get going again; (Com: cuenta) to unfreeze

desbordar [desβor'ðar] vt (sobrepasar) to go beyond; (exceder) to exceed; **desbordarse** vr (río) to overflow; (entusiasmo) to erupt

descabellado, -a [deskaβe'ʎaðo, a] adj (disparatado) wild, crazy

descafeinado, -a [deskafei'naðo, a] adj decaffeinated ▷ nm decaffeinated coffee

descalabro [deska'laβro] nm blow; (desgracia) misfortune

descalificar [deskalifi'kar] vt to disqualify; (desacreditar) to discredit

descalzar [deskal'θar] vt (zapato) to take off; **descalzo, -a** adj barefoot(ed)

descambiar [deskam'bjar] vt to exchange

descaminado, -a [deskami'naðo, a] adj (equivocado) on the wrong road; (fig) misguided

descampado [deskam'paðo] nm open space

descansado, -a [deskan'saðo, a] adj (gen) rested; (que tranquiliza) restful

descansar [deskan'sar] vt (gen) to rest ▷ vi to rest, have a rest; (echarse) to lie down

descansillo [deskan'siʎo] nm (de escalera) landing

descanso [des'kanso] nm (reposo) rest; (alivio) relief; (pausa) break; (Deporte) interval, half time

descapotable [deskapo'taβle] nm (tb: **coche ~**) convertible

descarado, -a [deska'raðo, a] adj shameless; (insolente) cheeky

descarga [des'karɣa] nf (Arq, Elec, Mil) discharge; (Náut) unloading; **descargar** [deskar'ɣar] vt to unload; (golpe) to let fly; **descargarse** vr to unburden o.s.; **descargar algo de Internet** to download sth from the Internet

descaro [des'karo] nm nerve

descarriar [deska'rrjar] vt (descaminar) to misdirect; (fig) to lead astray; **descarriarse** vr (perderse) to lose one's way; (separarse) to stray; (pervertirse) to err, go astray

descarrilamiento [deskarrila'mjento] nm (de tren) derailment

descarrilar [deskarri'lar] vi to be derailed

descartar [deskar'tar] vt (rechazar) to reject; (eliminar) to rule out; **descartarse** vr (Naipes) to discard; **~se de** vr to shirk

descendencia [desθen'denθja] nf (origen) origin,

descent; (hijos) offspring

descender [desθen'der] vt (bajar: escalera) to go down ▷ vi to descend; (temperatura, nivel) to fall, drop; **~ de** to be descended from

descendiente [desθen'djente] nmf descendant

descenso [des'θenso] nm descent; (de temperatura) drop

descifrar [desθi'frar] vt to decipher; (mensaje) to decode

descolgar [deskol'ɣar] vt (bajar) to take down; (teléfono) to pick up; **descolgarse** vr to let o.s. down

descolorido, -a [deskolo'riðo, a] adj faded; (pálido) pale

descompasado, -a [deskompa'saðo, a] adj (sin proporción) out of all proportion; (excesivo) excessive

descomponer [deskompo'ner] vt (desordenar) to disarrange, disturb; (Tec) to put out of order; (dividir) to break down (into parts); (fig) to provoke; **descomponerse** vr (corromperse) to rot, decompose; (LAM Tec) to break down

descomposición [deskomposi'θjon] nf (de un objeto) breakdown; (de fruta etc) decomposition; **descomposición de vientre** (ESP) stomach upset, diarrhoea

descompostura [deskompos'tura] nf (MÉX: avería) breakdown, fault; (LAM: diarrea) diarrhoea

descomprimir [deskompri'mir] (Internet) to unzip

descompuesto, -a [deskom'pwesto, a] adj (corrompido) decomposed; (roto) broken

desconcertado, -a [deskonθer'taðo, a] adj disconcerted, bewildered

desconcertar [deskonθer'tar] vt (confundir) to baffle; (incomodar) to upset, put out; **desconcertarse** vr (turbarse) to be upset

desconchado, -a [deskon'tʃaðo, a] adj (pintura) peeling

desconcierto etc [deskon'θjerto] vb V

desconcertar ▷ nm (gen) disorder; (desorientación) uncertainty; (inquietud) uneasiness

desconectar [deskonek'tar] vt to disconnect

desconfianza [deskon'fjanθa] nf distrust

desconfiar [deskon'fjar] vi to be distrustful; **~ de** to distrust, suspect

descongelar [deskonxe'lar] vt to defrost; (Com, Pol) to unfreeze

descongestionar [deskonxestjo'nar] vt (cabeza, tráfico) to clear

desconocer [deskono'θer] vt (ignorar) not to know, be ignorant of

desconocido, -a [deskono'θiðo, a] adj unknown ▷ nm/f stranger

desconocimiento [deskonoθi'mjento] nm falta de conocimientos, ignorance

desconsiderado, -a [deskonsiðe'raðo, a] adj inconsiderate; (insensible) thoughtless

desconsuelo [deskon'swelo] vb V **desconsolar** ▷ nm (tristeza) distress; (desesperación) despair

descontado, -a [deskon'taðo, a] adj: **dar por ~ (que)** to take (it) for granted (that)

descontar [deskon'tar] vt (deducir) to take away, deduct; (rebajar) to discount

descontento, -a [deskon'tento, a] adj dissatisfied ▷ nm dissatisfaction, discontent

descorchar [deskor'tʃar] vt to uncork

descorrer [desko'rrer] vt (cortinas, cerrojo) to draw back

descortés [deskor'tes] adj (mal educado) discourteous; (grosero) rude

descoser [desko'ser] vt to unstitch; **descoserse** vr to come apart (at the seams)

descosido, -a [desko'siðo, a] adj (Costura) unstitched

descreído, -a [deskre'iðo, a] adj (incrédulo) incredulous; (falto de fe) unbelieving

descremado, -a [deskre'maðo, a] adj skimmed

describir [deskri'βir] vt to describe; **descripción** [deskrip'θjon] nf description

descrito [des'krito] pp de **describir**

descuartizar [deskwarti'θar] vt (animal) to cut up

descubierto, -a [desku'βjerto, a] pp de **descubrir**
▷ adj uncovered, bare; (persona) bareheaded ▷ nm (bancario) overdraft; **al ~** in the open

descubrimiento [deskuβri'mjento] nm (hallazgo) discovery; (revelación) revelation

descubrir [desku'βrir] vt to discover, find; (inaugurar) to unveil; (vislumbrar) to detect; (revelar) to reveal, show; (destapar) to uncover; **descubrirse** vr to reveal o.s.; (quitarse sombrero) to take off one's hat; (confesar) to confess

descuento etc [des'kwento] vb V **descontar** ▷ nm discount

descuidado, -a [deskwi'ðaðo, a] adj (sin cuidado) careless; (desordenado) untidy; (olvidadizo) forgetful; (dejado) neglected; (desprevenido) unprepared

descuidar [deskwi'ðar] vt (dejar) to neglect; (olvidar) to overlook; **descuidarse** vr (distraerse) to be careless; (abandonarse) to let o.s. go; (desprevenirse) to drop one's guard; **¡descuida!** don't worry!; **descuido** nm (dejadez) carelessness; (olvido) negligence

○ PALABRA CLAVE

desde ['desðe] prep **1** (lugar) from; **desde Burgos hasta mi casa hay 30 km** it's 30 km from Burgos to my house

2 (posición): **hablaba desde el balcón** she was speaking from the balcony

3 (tiempo: + adv, n): **desde ahora** from now on; **desde la boda** since the wedding; **desde niño** since I etc was a child; **desde 3 años atrás** since 3 years ago

4 (tiempo: + vb, fecha) since; for; **nos conocemos desde 1992/desde hace 20 años** we've known each other since 1992/for 20 years; **no le veo desde 1997/desde hace 5 años** I haven't seen him since 1997/for 5 years

5 (gama): **desde los más lujosos hasta los más económicos** from the most luxurious to the most reasonably priced

6: **desde luego (que no)** of course (not)

▷ conj: **desde que**: **desde que recuerdo** for as long as I can remember; **desde que llegó no ha salido** he hasn't been out since he arrived

desdén [des'ðen] nm scorn

desdeñar [desðe'ɲar] vt (despreciar) to scorn

desdicha [des'ðitʃa] nf (desgracia) misfortune; (infelicidad) unhappiness; **desdichado, -a** adj (sin suerte) unlucky; (infeliz) unhappy

desear [dese'ar] vt to want, desire, wish for

desechar [dese'tʃar] vt (basura) to throw out o away; (ideas) to reject, discard; **desechos** nmpl rubbish sg, waste sg

desembalar [desemba'lar] vt to unpack

desembarazar [desembara'θar] vt (desocupar) to clear; (desenredar) to free; **desembarazarse** vr: **~se de** to free o.s. of, get rid of

desembarcar [desembar'kar] vt (mercancías etc) to unload ▷ vi to disembark

desembocadura [desemboka'ðura] nf (de río) mouth; (de calle) opening

desembocar [desembo'kar] vi (río) to flow into; (fig) to result in

desembolso [desem'bolso] nm payment

desembrollar [desembro'ʎar] vt (madeja) to unravel; (asunto, malentendido) to sort out

desemejanza [deseme'xanθa] nf dissimilarity

desempaquetar [desempake'tar] vt (regalo) to unwrap; (mercancía) to unpack

desempate [desem'pate] nm (Fútbol) replay, play-off; (Tenis) tie-break(er)

desempeñar [desempe'ɲar] vt (cargo) to hold; (papel) to perform; (lo empeñado) to redeem; **~ un papel** (fig) to play a role)

desempleado, -a [desemple'aðo, a] nm/f unemployed person; **desempleo** nm unemployment

desencadenar [desenkaðe'nar] vt to unchain; (ira) to unleash; **desencadenarse** vr to break loose; (tormenta) to burst; (guerra) to break out

desencajar [desenka'xar] vt (hueso) to dislocate; (mecanismo, pieza) to disconnect, disengage

desencanto [desen'kanto] nm disillusionment

desenchufar [desentʃu'far] vt to unplug

desenfadado, -a [desenfa'ðaðo, a] adj (desenvuelto) uninhibited; (descarado) forward; **desenfado** nm (libertad) freedom; (comportamiento) free and easy manner; (descaro) forwardness

desenfocado, -a [desenfo'kaðo, a] adj (Foto) out of focus

desenfreno [desen'freno] nm wildness; (de las pasiones) lack of self-control

desenganchar [desengan'tʃar] vt (gen) to unhook; (Ferro) to uncouple

desengañar [desenga'ɲar] vt to disillusion; **desengañarse** vr to become disillusioned; **desengaño** nm disillusionment; (decepción) disappointment

desenlace [desen'laθe] nm outcome

desenmascarar [desenmaska'rar] vt to unmask

desenredar [desenre'ðar] vt (pelo) to untangle; (problema) to sort out

desenroscar [desenros'kar] vt to unscrew

desentenderse [desenten'derse] vr: **~ de** to pretend not to know about; (apartarse) to have nothing to do with

desenterrar [desente'rrar] vt to exhume; (tesoro, fig) to unearth, dig up

desentonar [desento'nar] vi (Mús) to sing (o play) out of tune; (color) to clash

desentrañar [desentra'ɲar] vt (misterio) to unravel

desenvoltura [desenβol'tura] nf ease

desenvolver [desenβol'βer] vt (paquete) to unwrap; (fig) to develop; **desenvolverse** vr (desarrollarse) to unfold, develop; (arreglárselas) to cope

deseo [de'seo] nm desire, wish; **deseoso, -a** adj: **estar deseoso de** to be anxious to

desequilibrado, -a [desekili'βraðo, a] adj unbalanced

desertar [deser'tar] vi to desert

desértico, -a [de'sertiko, a] *adj* desert *cpd*

desesperación [desespera'θjon] *nf* (*impaciencia*) desperation, despair; (*irritación*) fury

desesperar [desespe'rar] *vt* to drive to despair; (*exasperar*) to drive to distraction ▷ *vi*: ~ **de** to despair of; **desesperarse** *vr* to despair, lose hope

desestabilizar [desestaβili'θar] *vt* to destabilize

desestimar [desesti'mar] *vt* (*menospreciar*) to have a low opinion of; (*rechazar*) to reject

desfachatez [desfatʃa'teθ] *nf* (*insolencia*) impudence; (*descaro*) rudeness

desfalco [des'falko] *nm* embezzlement

desfallecer [desfaʎe'θer] *vi* (*perder las fuerzas*) to become weak; (*desvanecerse*) to faint

desfasado, -a [desfa'saðo, a] *adj* (*anticuado*) old-fashioned; **desfase** *nm* (*diferencia*) gap

desfavorable [desfaβo'raβle] *adj* unfavourable

desfigurar [desfiɣu'rar] *vt* (*cara*) to disfigure; (*cuerpo*) to deform

desfiladero [desfila'ðero] *nm* gorge

desfilar [desfi'lar] *vi* to parade; **desfile** *nm* procession; **desfile de modelos** fashion show

desgana [des'ɣana] *nf* (*falta de apetito*) loss of appetite; (*apatía*) unwillingness; **desganado, -a** *adj*: **estar desganado** (*sin apetito*) to have no appetite; (*sin entusiasmo*) to have lost interest

desgarrar [desɣa'rrar] *vt* to tear (up); (*fig*) to shatter; **desgarro** (*en tela*) tear; (*aflicción*) grief

desgastar [desɣas'tar] *vt* (*deteriorar*) to wear away o down; (*estropear*) to spoil; **desgastarse** *vr* to get worn out; **desgaste** *nm* wear (and tear)

desglosar [desɣlo'sar] *vt* (*factura*) to break down

desgracia [des'ɣraθja] *nf* misfortune; (*accidente*) accident; (*vergüenza*) disgrace; (*contratiempo*) setback; **por ~** unfortunately; **desgraciado, -a** [desɣra'θjaðo, a] *adj* (*sin suerte*) unlucky, unfortunate; (*miserable*) wretched; (*infeliz*) miserable

desgravar [desɣra'βar] *vt* (*impuestos*) to reduce the tax o duty on

desguace [des'ɣwaθe] (*ESP*) *nm* junkyard

deshabitado, -a [desaβi'taðo, a] *adj* uninhabited

deshacer [desa'θer] *vt* (*casa*) to break up; (*Tec*) to take apart; (*enemigo*) to defeat; (*diluir*) to melt; (*contrato*) to break; (*intriga*) to solve; **deshacerse** *vr* (*disolverse*) to melt; (*despedazarse*) to come apart o undone; **~se de** to get rid of; **~se en lágrimas** to burst into tears

deshecho, -a [des'etʃo, a] *adj* undone; (*roto*) smashed; (*persona*): **estar ~** to be shattered

desheredar [desere'ðar] *vt* to disinherit

deshidratar [desiðra'tar] *vt* to dehydrate

deshielo [des'jelo] *nm* thaw

deshonesto, -a [deso'nesto, a] *adj* indecent

deshonra [des'onra] *nf* (*deshonor*) dishonour; (*vergüenza*) shame

deshora [des'ora]: **a ~** *adv* at the wrong time

deshuesadero [deswesa'ðero] (*MÉX*) *nm* junkyard

deshuesar [deswe'sar] *vt* (*carne*) to bone; (*fruta*) to stone

desierto, -a [de'sjerto, a] *adj* (*casa, calle, negocio*) deserted ▷ *nm* desert

designar [desiɣ'nar] *vt* (*nombrar*) to designate; (*indicar*) to fix

desigual [desi'ɣwal] *adj* (*terreno*) uneven; (*lucha etc*) unequal

desilusión [desilu'sjon] *nf* disillusionment; (*decepción*) disappointment; **desilusionar** *vt* to

disillusion; to disappoint; **desilusionarse** *vr* to become disillusioned

desinfectar [desinfek'tar] *vt* to disinfect

desinflar [desin'flar] *vt* to deflate

desintegración [desinteɣra'θjon] *nf* disintegration

desinterés [desinte'res] *nm* (*desgana*) lack of interest; (*altruismo*) unselfishness

desintoxicarse [desintoksi'karse] *vr* (*drogadicto*) to undergo detoxification

desistir [desis'tir] *vi* (*renunciar*) to stop, desist

desleal [desle'al] *adj* (*infiel*) disloyal; (*Com: competencia*) unfair; **deslealtad** *nf* disloyalty

desligar [desli'ɣar] *vt* (*desatar*) to untie, undo; (*separar*) to separate; **desligarse** *vr* (*de un compromiso*) to extricate o.s.

desliz [des'liθ] *nm* (*fig*) lapse; **deslizar** *vt* to slip, slide

deslumbrar [deslum'brar] *vt* to dazzle

desmadrarse [desma'ðrarse] (*fam*) *vr* (*descontrolarse*) to run wild; (*divertirse*) to let one's hair down; **desmadre** (*fam*) *nm* (*desorganización*) chaos; (*jaleo*) commotion

desmán [des'man] *nm* (*exceso*) outrage; (*abuso de poder*) abuse

desmantelar [desmante'lar] *vt* (*deshacer*) to dismantle; (*casa*) to strip

desmaquillador [desmakiʎa'ðor] *nm* make-up remover

desmayar [desma'jar] *vi* to lose heart; **desmayarse** *vr* (*Med*) to faint; **desmayo** *nm* (*Med: acto*) faint; (: *estado*) unconsciousness

desmemoriado, -a [desmemo'rjaðo, a] *adj* forgetful

desmentir [desmen'tir] *vt* (*contradecir*) to contradict; (*refutar*) to deny

desmenuzar [desmenu'θar] *vt* (*deshacer*) to crumble; (*carne*) to chop; (*examinar*) to examine closely

desmesurado, -a [desmesu'raðo, a] *adj* disproportionate

desmontable [desmon'taβle] *adj* (*que se quita: pieza*) detachable; (*plegable*) collapsible, folding

desmontar [desmon'tar] *vt* (*deshacer*) to dismantle; (*tierra*) to level ▷ *vi* to dismount

desmoralizar [desmorali'θar] *vt* to demoralize

desmoronar [desmoro'nar] *vt* to wear away, erode; **desmoronarse** *vr* (*edificio, dique*) to collapse; (*economía*) to decline

desnatado, -a [desna'taðo, a] *adj* skimmed

desnivel [desni'βel] *nm* (*de terreno*) unevenness

desnudar [desnu'ðar] *vt* (*desvestir*) to undress; (*despojar*) to strip; **desnudarse** *vr* (*desvestirse*) to get undressed; **desnudo, -a** *adj* naked ▷ *nm/f* nude; **desnudo de** devoid o bereft of

desnutrición [desnutri'θjon] *nf* malnutrition; **desnutrido, -a** *adj* undernourished

desobedecer [desoβeðe'θer] *vt, vi* to disobey; **desobediencia** *nf* disobedience

desocupado, -a [desoku'paðo, a] *adj* at leisure; (*desempleado*) unemployed; (*deshabitado*) empty, vacant

desodorante [desoðo'rante] *nm* deodorant

desolación [desola'θjon] *nf* (*de lugar*) desolation; (*fig*) grief

desolar [deso'lar] *vt* to ruin, lay waste

desorbitado, -a [desorβi'taðo, a] *adj* (*excesivo: ambición*) boundless; (*deseos*) excessive; (: *precio*) exorbitant

desorden [des'orðen] *nm* confusion; (*político*) disorder, unrest

desorganización [desorɣaniθa'θjon] *nf* (*de persona*) disorganization; (*en empresa, oficina*) disorder, chaos

desorientar [desorjen'tar] *vt* (*extraviar*) to mislead; (*confundir, desconcertar*) to confuse; **desorientarse** *vr* (*perderse*) to lose one's way

despabilado, -a [despaβi'laðo, a] *adj* (*despierto*) wide-awake; (*fig*) alert, sharp

despachar [despa'tʃar] *vt* (*negocio*) to do, complete; (*enviar*) to send, dispatch; (*vender*) to sell, deal in; (*billete*) to issue; (*mandar ir*) to send away

despacho [des'patʃo] *nm* (*oficina*) office; (*de paquetes*) dispatch; (*venta*) sale; (*comunicación*) message

despacio [des'paθjo] *adv* slowly

desparpajo [despar'paxo] *nm* self-confidence; (*pey*) nerve

desparramar [desparra'mar] *vt* (*esparcir*) to scatter; (*líquido*) to spill

despecho [des'petʃo] *nm* spite

despectivo, -a [despek'tiβo, a] *adj* (*despreciativo*) derogatory; (*Ling*) pejorative

despedida [despe'ðiða] *nf* (*adiós*) farewell; (*de obrero*) sacking

despedir [despe'ðir] *vt* (*visita*) to see off, show out; (*empleado*) to dismiss; (*inquilino*) to evict; (*objeto*) to hurl; (*olor etc*) to give out o off; **despedirse** *vr*: **~se de** to say goodbye to

despegar [despe'ɣar] *vt* to unstick ▷ *vi* (*avión*) to take off; **despegarse** *vr* to come loose, come unstuck; **despego** *nm* detachment

despegue *etc* [des'peɣe] *vb* V **despegar** ▷ *nm* takeoff

despeinado, -a [despei'naðo, a] *adj* dishevelled, unkempt

despejado, -a [despe'xaðo, a] *adj* (*lugar*) clear, free; (*cielo*) clear; (*persona*) wide-awake, bright

despejar [despe'xar] *vt* (*gen*) to clear; (*misterio*) to clear up ▷ *vi* (*el tiempo*) to clear; **despejarse** *vr* (*tiempo, cielo*) to clear (up); (*misterio*) to become clearer; (*cabeza*) to clear

despensa [des'pensa] *nf* larder

despeñarse [despe'narse] *vr* to hurl o.s. down; (*coche*) to tumble over

desperdicio [desper'ðiθjo] *nm* (*despilfarro*) squandering; **desperdicios** *nmpl* (*basura*) rubbish *sg* (*BRIT*), garbage *sg* (*US*); (*residuos*) waste *sg*

desperezarse [despere'θarse] *vr* to stretch

desperfecto [desper'fekto] *nm* (*deterioro*) slight damage; (*defecto*) flaw, imperfection

despertador [desperta'ðor] *nm* alarm clock

despertar [desper'tar] *vt* (*persona*) to wake up; (*recuerdos*) to revive; (*sentimiento*) to arouse ▷ *vi* to awaken, wake up; **despertarse** *vr* to awaken, wake up

despido *etc* [des'piðo] *vb* V **despedir** ▷ *nm* dismissal, sacking

despierto, -a etc [des'pjerto, a] *vb* V **despertar** ▷ *adj* awake; (*fig*) sharp, alert

despilfarro [despil'farro] *nm* (*derroche*) squandering; (*lujo desmedido*) extravagance

despistar [despis'tar] *vt* to throw off the track o scent; (*confundir*) to mislead, confuse; **despistarse** *vr* to take the wrong road; (*confundirse*) to become confused

despiste [des'piste] *nm* absent-mindedness; **un ~ a**

mistake o slip

desplazamiento [desplaθa'mjento] *nm* displacement

desplazar [despla'θar] *vt* to move; (*Náut*) to displace; (*Inform*) to scroll; (*fig*) to oust; **desplazarse** *vr* (*persona*) to travel

desplegar [desple'ɣar] *vt* (*tela, papel*) to unfold, open out; (*bandera*) to unfurl; **despliegue** *etc* [des'pleɣe] *vb* V **desplegar** ▷ *nm* display

desplomarse [desplo'marse] *vr* (*edificio, gobierno, persona*) to collapse

desplumar [desplu'mar] *vt* (*ave*) to pluck; (*fam: estafar*) to fleece

despoblado, -a [despo'βlaðo, a] *adj* (*sin habitantes*) uninhabited

despojar [despo'xar] *vt* (*alguien: de sus bienes*) to divest of, deprive of; (*casa*) to strip, leave bare; (*alguien: de su cargo*) to strip of

despojo [des'poxo] *nm* (*acto*) plundering; (*objetos*) plunder, loot; **despojos** *nmpl* (*de ave, res*) offal *sg*

desposado, -a [despo'saðo, a] *adj, nm/f* newly-wed

despreciar [despre'θjar] *vt* (*desdeñar*) to despise, scorn; (*afrentar*) to slight; **desprecio** *nm* scorn, contempt; slight

desprender [despren'der] *vt* (*broche*) to unfasten; (*olor*) to give off; **desprenderse** *vr* (*botón: caerse*) to fall off; (*broche*) to come unfastened; (*olor, perfume*) to be given off; **~se de algo que ...** to draw from sth that ...

desprendimiento [desprendi'mjento] *nm* (*gen*) loosening; (*generosidad*) disinterestedness; (*de tierra, rocas*) landslide; **desprendimiento de retina** detachment of the retina

despreocupado, -a [despreoku'paðo, a] *adj* (*sin preocupación*) unworried, nonchalant; (*negligente*) careless

despreocuparse [despreoku'parse] *vr* not to worry; **~ de** to have no interest in

desprestigiar [despresti'xjar] *vt* (*criticar*) to run down; (*desacreditar*) to discredit

desprevenido, -a [despreβe'niðo, a] *adj* (*no preparado*) unprepared, unready

desproporcionado, -a [desproporθjo'naðo, a] *adj* disproportionate, out of proportion

desprovisto, -a [despro'βisto, a] *adj*: **~ de** devoid of

después [des'pwes] *adv* afterwards, later; (*próximo paso*) next; **~ de comer** after lunch; **un año ~** a year later; **~ se debatió el tema** the next the matter was discussed; **~ de corregido el texto** after the text had been corrected; **~ de todo** after all

desquiciado, -a [deski'θjaðo, a] *adj* deranged

destacar [desta'kar] *vt* to emphasize, point up; (*Mil*) to detach, detail ▷ *vi* (*resaltarse*) to stand out; (*persona*) to be outstanding o exceptional; **destacarse** *vr* to stand out; to be outstanding o exceptional

destajo [des'taxo] *nm*: **trabajar a ~** to do piecework

destapar [desta'par] *vt* (*botella*) to open; (*cacerola*) to take the lid off; (*descubrir*) to uncover; **destaparse** *vr* (*revelarse*) to reveal one's true character

destartalado, -a [destarta'laðo, a] *adj* (*desordenado*) untidy; (*ruinoso*) tumbledown

destello [des'teʎo] *nm* (*de estrella*) twinkle; (*de faro*) signal light

destemplado, -a [destem'plaðo, a] *adj* (*Mús*) out of tune; (*voz*) harsh; (*Med*) out of sorts; (*tiempo*) unpleasant, nasty

desteñir [deste'nir] *vt* to fade ▷ *vi* to fade;

desteñirse *vr* to fade; **esta tela no destiñe** this fabric will not run

desternillarse [desterniˈʎarse] *vr*: **~ de risa** to split one's sides laughing

desterrar [desteˈrrar] *vt* (*exiliar*) to exile; (*fig*) to banish, dismiss

destiempo [desˈtjempo]: **a ~** *adv* out of turn

destierro *etc* [desˈtjerro] *vb* V **desterrar** ▷ *nm* exile

destilar [destiˈlar] *vt* to distil; **destilería** *nf* distillery

destinar [destiˈnar] *vt* (*funcionario*) to appoint, assign; (*fondos*): **~ (a)** to set aside (for)

destinatario, -a [destinaˈtarjo, a] *nm/f* addressee

destino [desˈtino] *nm* (*suerte*) destiny; (*de avión, viajero*) destination; **con ~ a Londres** (*barco*) (bound) for London; (*avión, carta*) to London

destituir [destiˈtwir] *vt* to dismiss

destornillador [destorniʎaˈðor] *nm* screwdriver

destornillar [destorniˈʎar] *vt* (*tornillo*) to unscrew; **destornillarse** *vr* to unscrew

destreza [desˈtreθa] *nf* (*habilidad*) skill; (*maña*) dexterity

destrozar [destroˈθar] *vt* (*romper*) to smash, break (up); (*estropear*) to ruin; (*nervios*) to shatter

destrozo [desˈtroθo] *nm* (*acción*) destruction; (*desastre*) smashing; **destrozos** *nmpl* (*pedazos*) pieces; (*daños*) havoc *sg*

destrucción [destrukˈθjon] *nf* destruction

destruir [destruˈir] *vt* to destroy

desuso [desˈuso] *nm* disuse; **caer en ~** to become obsolete

desvalijar [desvaliˈxar] *vt* (*persona*) to rob; (*casa, tienda*) to burgle; (*coche*) to break into

desván [desˈβan] *nm* attic

desvanecer [desβaneˈθer] *vt* (*disipar*) to dispel; (*borrar*) to blur; **desvanecerse** *vr* (*humo etc*) to vanish, disappear; (*color*) to fade; (*recuerdo, sonido*) to fade away; (*Med*) to pass out; (*duda*) to be dispelled

desvariar [desβaˈrjar] *vi* (*enfermo*) to be delirious

desvelar [desβeˈlar] *vt* to keep awake; **desvelarse** *vr* (*no poder dormir*) to stay awake; (*preocuparse*) to be vigilant o watchful

desventaja [desβenˈtaxa] *nf* disadvantage

desvergonzado, -a [desβerɣonˈθaðo, a] *adj* shameless

desvestir [desβesˈtir] *vt* to undress; **desvestirse** *vr* to undress

desviación [desβjaˈθjon] *nf* deviation; (*Auto*) diversion, detour

desviar [desˈβjar] *vt* to turn aside; (*río*) to alter the course of; (*navío*) to divert, re-route; (*conversación*) to sidetrack; **desviarse** *vr* (*apartarse del camino*) to turn aside; (: *barco*) to go off course

desvío *etc* [desˈβio] *vb* V **desviar** ▷ *nm* (*desviación*) detour, diversion; (*fig*) indifference

desvivirse [desβiˈβirse] *vr*: **~ por** (*anhelar*) to long for, crave for; (*hacer lo posible por*) to do one's utmost for

detallar [detaˈʎar] *vt* to detail

detalle [deˈtaʎe] *nm* detail; (*gesto*) gesture, token; **al ~ in detail**; (*Com*) retail

detallista [detaˈʎista] *nmf* (*Com*) retailer

detective [detekˈtiβe] *nmf* detective; **detective privado** private detective

detener [deteˈner] *vt* (*gen*) to stop; (*Jur*) to arrest; (*objeto*) to keep; **detenerse** *vr* to stop; (*demorarse*): **~se en** to delay over, linger over

detenidamente [deteniðaˈmente] *adv*

(*minuciosamente*) carefully; (*extensamente*) at great length

detenido, -a [deteˈniðo, a] *adj* (*arrestado*) under arrest ▷ *nm/f* person under arrest, prisoner

detenimiento [deteniˈmjento] *nm*: **con ~** thoroughly; (*observar, considerar*) carefully

detergente [deterˈxente] *nm* detergent

deteriorar [deterjoˈrar] *vt* to spoil, damage; **deteriorarse** *vr* to deteriorate; **deterioro** *nm* deterioration

determinación [determinaˈθjon] *nf* (*empeño*) determination; (*decisión*) decision; **determinado, -a** *adj* specific

determinar [determiˈnar] *vt* (*plazo*) to fix; (*precio*) to settle; **determinarse** *vr* to decide

detestar [detesˈtar] *vt* to detest

detractor, a [detrakˈtor, a] *nm/f* slanderer, libeller

detrás [deˈtras] *adv* (*tb*: **por ~**) behind; (*atrás*) at the back; **~ de** behind

detrimento [detriˈmento] *nm*: **en ~ de** to the detriment of

deuda [ˈdeuða] *nf* debt; **deuda exterior/pública** foreign/national debt

devaluación [deβalwaˈθjon] *nf* devaluation

devastar [deβasˈtar] *vt* (*destruir*) to devastate

deveras [deˈβeras] (*MÉX*) *adj inv*: **un amigo de (a) ~** a true o real friend

devoción [deβoˈθjon] *nf* devotion

devolución [deβoluˈθjon] *nf* (*reenvío*) return, sending back; (*reembolso*) repayment; (*Jur*) devolution

devolver [deβolˈβer] *vt* to return; (*lo extraviado, lo prestado*) to give back; (*carta al correo*) to send back; (*Com*) to repay, refund ▷ *vi* (*vomitar*) to be sick

devorar [deβoˈrar] *vt* to devour

devoto, -a [deˈβoto, a] *adj* devout ▷ *nm/f* admirer

devuelve *pp de* **devolver**

devuelva *etc* *vb* V **devolver**

di *etc* *vb* V **dar; decir**

día [ˈdia] *nm* day; **¿qué ~ es?** what's the date?; **estar/poner al ~** to be/keep up to date; **el ~ de hoy/de mañana** today/tomorrow; **al ~ siguiente** (on) the following day; **vivir al ~** to live from hand to mouth; **de ~** by day, in daylight; **en pleno ~** in full daylight; **Día de la Independencia** Independence Day; **Día de los Muertos** (*MÉX*) All Souls' Day; **Día de Reyes** Epiphany; **día feriado** (*LAM*) holiday; **día festivo** (*ESP*) holiday; **día lectivo** teaching day; **día libre** day off

diabetes [djaˈβetes] *nf* diabetes

diablo [ˈdjaβlo] *nm* devil; **diablura** *nf* prank

diadema [djaˈðema] *nf* tiara

diafragma [djaˈfraɣma] *nm* diaphragm

diagnóstico [djaɣˈnostiko] *nm* = **diagnosis**

diagonal [djaɣoˈnal] *adj* diagonal

diagrama [djaˈɣrama] *nm* diagram

dial [djal] *nm* dial

dialecto [djaˈlekto] *nm* dialect

dialogar [djaloˈɣar] *vi*: **~ con** (*Pol*) to hold talks with

diálogo [ˈdjaloɣo] *nm* dialogue

diamante [djaˈmante] *nm* diamond

diana [ˈdjana] *nf* (*Mil*) reveille; (*de blanco*) centre, bull's-eye

diapositiva [djaposiˈtiβa] *nf* (*Foto*) slide, transparency

diario, -a [ˈdjarjo, a] *adj* daily ▷ *nm* newspaper; **a ~** daily; **de ~** everyday

diarrea [djaˈrrea] *nf* diarrhoea

dibujar [diβu'xar] vt to draw, sketch; **dibujo** nm drawing; **dibujos animados** cartoons

diccionario [dikθjo'narjo] nm dictionary

dice etc vb V **decir**

dicho, -a [ˈditʃo, a] pp de **decir** ▷ adj: **en ~s países** in the aforementioned countries ▷ nm saying

dichoso, -a [di'tʃoso, a] adj happy

diciembre [di'θjembre] nm December

dictado [dik'taðo] nm dictation

dictador [dikta'ðor] nm dictator; **dictadura** nf dictatorship

dictar [dik'tar] vt (carta) to dictate; (Jur: sentencia) to pronounce; (decreto) to issue; (LAM: clase) to give

didáctico, -a [di'ðaktiko, a] adj educational

diecinueve [djeθi'nweβe] num nineteen

dieciocho [djeθi'otʃo] num eighteen

dieciséis [djeθi'seis] num sixteen

diecisiete [djeθi'sjete] num seventeen

diente ['djente] nm (Anat, Tec) tooth; (Zool) fang; (: de elefante) tusk; (de ajo) clove

diera etc vb V **dar**

diesel ['disel] adj: **motor ~** diesel engine

diestro, -a [di'estro, a] adj (derecho) right; (hábil) skilful

dieta ['djeta] nf diet; **estar a ~** to be on a diet

diez [djeθ] num ten

diferencia [dife'renθja] nf difference; **a ~ de** unlike; **diferenciar** vt to differentiate between ▷ vi to differ; **diferenciarse** vr to differ, be different; (distinguirse) to distinguish o.s.

diferente [dife'rente] adj different

diferido [dife'riðo] nm: **en ~** (TV etc) recorded

difícil [di'fiθil] adj difficult

dificultad [difikul'taθ] nf difficulty; (problema) trouble

dificultar [difikul'tar] vt (complicar) to complicate, make difficult; (estorbar) to obstruct

difundir [difun'dir] vt (calor, luz) to diffuse; (Radio, TV) to broadcast; **~ una noticia** to spread a piece of news; **difundirse** vr to spread (out)

difunto, -a [di'funto, a] adj dead, deceased ▷ nm/f deceased (person)

difusión [difu'sjon] nf (Radio, TV) broadcasting

diga etc vb V **decir**

digerir [dixe'rir] vt to digest; (fig) to absorb; **digestión** nf digestion; **digestivo, -a** adj digestive

digital [dixi'tal] adj digital

dignarse [div'narse] vr to deign to

dignidad [divni'ðað] nf dignity

digno, -a ['divno, a] adj worthy

digo etc vb V **decir**

dije etc vb V **decir**

dilatar [dila'tar] vt (cuerpo) to dilate; (prolongar) to prolong

dilema [di'lema] nm dilemma

diluir [dilu'ir] vt to dilute

diluvio [di'luβjo] nm deluge, flood

dimensión [dimen'sjon] nf dimension

diminuto, -a [dimi'nuto, a] adj tiny, diminutive

dimitir [dimi'tir] vi to resign

dimos vb V **dar**

Dinamarca [dina'marka] nf Denmark

dinámico, -a [di'namiko, a] adj dynamic

dinamita [dina'mita] nf dynamite

dínamo ['dinamo] nf dynamo

dineral [dine'ral] nm large sum of money, fortune

dinero [di'nero] nm money; **dinero en efectivo** o **metálico** cash; **dinero suelto** (loose) change

dio vb V **dar**

dios [djos] nm god; **¡D~ mío!** (oh,) my God!; **¡por D~!** for heaven's sake!; **diosa** ['djosa] nf goddess

diploma [di'ploma] nm diploma

diplomacia [diplo'maθja] nf diplomacy; (fig) tact

diplomado, -a [diplo'maðo, a] adj qualified

diplomático, -a [diplo'matiko, a] adj diplomatic ▷ nm/f diplomat

diputación [diputa'θjon] nf (tb: ~ **provincial**) ≈ county council

diputado, -a [dipu'taðo, a] nm/f delegate; (Pol) ≈ member of parliament (BRIT) ≈ representative (US)

dique ['dike] nm dyke

diré etc vb V **decir**

dirección [direk'θjon] nf direction; (señas) address; (Auto) steering; (gerencia) management; (Pol) leadership; **dirección única/prohibida** one-way street/no entry

direccional [direkθjo'nal] (MÉX) nf (Auto) indicator

directa [di'rekta] nf (Auto) top gear

directiva [direk'tiβa] nf (tb: **junta ~**) board of directors

directo, -a [di'rekto, a] adj direct; (Radio, TV) live; **transmitir en ~** to broadcast live

director, a [direk'tor, a] adj leading ▷ nm/f director; (Escol) head(teacher) (BRIT), principal (US); (gerente) manager/ess; (Prensa) editor; **director de cine** film director; **director general** managing director

directorio [direk'torjo] (MÉX) nm (telefónico) phone book

dirigente [diri'xente] nmf (Pol) leader

dirigir [diri'xir] vt to direct; (carta) to address; (obra de teatro, film) to direct; (Mús) to conduct; (negocio) to manage; **dirigirse vr: ~se a** to go towards, make one's way towards; (hablar con) to speak to

dirija etc vb V **dirigir**

disciplina [disθi'plina] nf discipline

discípulo, -a [dis'θipulo, a] nm/f disciple

Discman® ['diskman] nm Discman®

disco ['disko] nm disc; (Deporte) discus; (Tel) dial; (Auto: semáforo) light; (Mús) record; **disco compacto/de larga duración** compact disc/long-playing record; **disco de freno** brake disc; **disco flexible/duro** o **rígido** (Inform) floppy/hard disk

disconforme [diskon'forme] adj differing; **estar ~ (con)** to be in disagreement (with)

discordia [dis'korðja] nf discord

discoteca [disko'teka] nf disco(theque)

discreción [diskre'θjon] nf discretion; (reserva) prudence; **comer a ~** to eat as much as one wishes

discreto, -a [dis'kreto, a] adj discreet

discriminación [diskrimina'θjon] nf discrimination

disculpa [dis'kulpa] nf excuse; (pedir perdón) apology; **pedir ~s a/por** to apologize to/for; **disculpar** vt to excuse, pardon; **disculparse** vr to excuse o.s.; to apologize

discurso [dis'kurso] nm speech

discusión [disku'sjon] nf (diálogo) discussion; (riña) argument

discutir [disku'tir] vt (debatir) to discuss; (pelear) to argue about; (contradecir) to argue against ▷ vi (debatir) to discuss; (pelearse) to argue

disecar [dise'kar] vt (conservar: animal) to stuff;

(: planta) to dry

diseñar [dise'ɲar] vt, vi to design

diseño [di'seɲo] nm design

disfraz [dis'fraθ] nm (máscara) disguise; (excusa) pretext; **disfrazar** vt to disguise; **disfrazarse** vr: **disfrazarse de** to disguise o.s. as

disfrutar [disfru'tar] vt to enjoy ▷ vi to enjoy o.s.; ~ **de** to enjoy, possess

disgustar [disɣus'tar] vt (no gustar) to displease; (contrariar, enojar) to annoy, upset; **disgustarse** vr (enfadarse) to get upset; (dos personas) to fall out

disgusto [dis'ɣusto] nm (contrariedad) annoyance; (tristeza) grief; (riña) quarrel

disimular [disimu'lar] vt (ocultar) to hide, conceal ▷ vi to dissemble

dislocarse [dislo'karse] vr (articulación) to sprain, dislocate

disminución [disminu'θjon] nf decrease, reduction

disminuido, -a [disminu'iðo, a] nm/f: ~ **mental/ físico** mentally/physically handicapped person

disminuir [disminu'ir] vt to decrease, diminish

disolver [disol'βer] vt (gen) to dissolve; **disolverse** vr to dissolve; (Com) to go into liquidation

dispar [dis'par] adj different

disparar [dispa'rar] vt, vi to shoot, fire

disparate [dispa'rate] nm (tontería) foolish remark; (error) blunder; **decir ~s** to talk nonsense

disparo [dis'paro] nm shot

dispersar [disper'sar] vt to disperse; **dispersarse** vr to scatter

disponer [dispo'ner] vt (arreglar) to arrange; (ordenar) to put in order; (preparar) to prepare, get ready ▷ vi: ~ **de** to have, own; **disponerse** vr: **~se a o para hacer** to prepare to do

disponible [dispo'niβle] adj available

disposición [disposi'θjon] nf arrangement, disposition; (voluntad) willingness; (Inform) layout; **a su ~** at your service

dispositivo [disposi'tiβo] nm device, mechanism

dispuesto, -a [dis'pwesto, a] pp de **disponer** ▷ adj (arreglado) arranged; (preparado) disposed

disputar [dispu'tar] vt (carrera) to compete in

disquete [dis'kete] nm floppy disk, diskette

distancia [dis'tanθja] nf distance; **distanciar** [distan'θjar] vt to space out; **distanciarse** vr to become estranged; **distante** [dis'tante] adj distant

diste vb V **dar**

disteis vb V **dar**

distinción [distin'θjon] nf distinction; (elegancia) elegance; (honor) honour

distinguido, -a [distin'giðo, a] adj distinguished

distinguir [distin'ɡir] vt to distinguish; (escoger) to single out; **distinguirse** vr to be distinguished

distintivo [distin'tiβo] nm badge; (fig) characteristic

distinto, -a [dis'tinto, a] adj different; (claro) clear

distracción [distrak'θjon] nf distraction; (pasatiempo) hobby, pastime; (olvido) absent-mindedness, distraction

distraer [distra'er] vt (atención) to distract; (divertir) to amuse; (fondos) to embezzle; **distraerse** vr (entretenerse) to amuse o.s.; (perder la concentración) to allow one's attention to wander

distraído, -a [distra'iðo, a] adj (gen) absent-minded; (entretenido) amusing

distribuidor, a [distriβui'ðor, a] nm/f distributor; **distribuidora** nf (Com) dealer, agent; (Cine) distributor

distribuir [distriβu'ir] vt to distribute

distrito [dis'trito] nm (sector, territorio) region; (barrio) district; **Distrito Federal** (MÉX) Federal District; **distrito postal** postal district

disturbio [dis'turβjo] nm disturbance; (desorden) riot

disuadir [diswa'ðir] vt to dissuade

disuelto [di'swelto] pp de **disolver**

DIU nm abr (= dispositivo intrauterino) IUD

diurno, -a [di'urno, a] adj day cpd

divagar [diβa'ɣar] vi (desviarse) to digress

diván [di'βan] nm divan

diversidad [diβersi'ðað] nf diversity, variety

diversión [diβersi'sjon] nf (gen) entertainment; (actividad) hobby, pastime

diverso, -a [di'βerso, a] adj diverse; **~s libros** several books; **diversos** nmpl sundries

divertido, -a [diβer'tiðo, a] adj (chiste) amusing; (fiesta etc) enjoyable

divertir [diβer'tir] vt (entretener, recrear) to amuse; **divertirse** vr (pasarlo bien) to have a good time; (distraerse) to amuse o.s.

dividendos [diβi'ðendos] nmpl (Com) dividends

dividir [diβi'ðir] vt (gen) to divide; (distribuir) to distribute, share out

divierta etc vb V **divertir**

divino, -a [di'βino, a] adj divine

divirtiendo etc vb V **divertir**

divisa [di'βisa] nf (emblema) emblem, badge; **divisas** nfpl foreign exchange sg

divisar [diβi'sar] vt to make out, distinguish

división [diβi'sjon] nf (gen) division; (de partido) split; (de país) partition

divorciar [diβor'θjar] vt to divorce; **divorciarse** vr to get divorced; **divorcio** nm divorce

divulgar [diβul'ɣar] vt (ideas) to spread; (secreto) to divulge

DNI (ESP) nm abr (= Documento Nacional de Identidad) national identity card

Dña. abr (= doña) Mrs

do [do] nm (Mús) do, C

dobladillo [doβla'ðiʎo] nm (de vestido) hem; (de pantalón: vuelta) turn-up (BRIT), cuff (US)

doblar [do'βlar] vt (to double); (papel) to fold; (caño) to bend; (la esquina) to turn, go round; (film) to dub ▷ vi to turn; (campana) to toll; **doblarse** vr (plegarse) to fold (up), crease; (encorvarse) to bend; **~ a la derecha/ izquierda** to turn right/left

doble ['doβle] adj double; (de dos aspectos) dual; (fig) two-faced ▷ nm double ▷ nmf (Teatro) double, stand-in; **dobles** nmpl (Deporte) doubles sg; **con ~ sentido** with a double meaning

doce ['doθe] num twelve; **docena** nf dozen

docente [do'θente] adj: **centro/personal ~** teaching establishment/staff

dócil ['doθil] adj (pasivo) docile; (obediente) obedient

doctor, a [dok'tor, a] nm/f doctor

doctorado [dokto'raðo] nm doctorate

doctrina [dok'trina] nf doctrine, teaching

documentación [dokumenta'θjon] nf documentation, papers pl

documental [dokumen'tal] adj, nm documentary

documento [doku'mento] nm (certificado) document; **documento adjunto** (Inform) attachment; **documento nacional de identidad** identity card

dólar ['dolar] nm dollar

doler [do'ler] vt, vi to hurt; (fig) to grieve; **dolerse** vr (de su situación) to grieve, feel sorry; (de las desgracias ajenas) to sympathize; **me duele el brazo** my arm hurts

dolor [do'lor] nm pain; (fig) grief, sorrow; **dolor de cabeza/estómago/muelas** headache/stomachache/toothache

domar [do'mar] vt to tame

domesticar [domesti'kar] vt = **domar**

doméstico, -a [do'mestiko, a] adj (vida, servicio) home; (tareas) household; (animal) tame, pet

domicilio [domi'θiljo] nm home; **servicio a ~** home delivery service; **sin ~ fijo** of no fixed abode; **domicilio particular** private residence

dominante [domi'nante] adj dominant; (persona) domineering

dominar [domi'nar] vt (gen) to dominate; (idiomas) to be fluent in ▷ vi to dominate, prevail

domingo [do'miŋgo] nm Sunday; **Domingo de Ramos/Resurrección** Palm/Easter Sunday

dominio [do'minjo] nm (tierras) domain; (autoridad) power, authority; (de las pasiones) grip, hold; (de idiomas) command

don [don] nm (talento) gift; **~ Juan Gómez** Mr Juan Gómez, Juan Gómez Esq (BRIT)

dona ['dona] (MÉX) nf doughnut, donut (US)

donar [do'nar] vt to donate

donativo [dona'tiβo] nm donation

donde ['donde] adv where ▷ prep: **el coche está allí ~ el farol** the car is over there by the lamppost o where the lamppost is; **en ~** where, in which

dónde ['donde] adv where?; **¿a ~ vas?** where are you going (to)?; **¿de ~ vienes?** where have you been?; **¿por ~?** where?, whereabouts?

dondequiera [donde'kjera] adv anywhere; **por ~** everywhere, all over the place ▷ conj: **~ que** wherever

donut® [do'nut] (ESP) nm doughnut, donut (US)

doña ['dona] nf: **~ Alicia** Alicia; **~ Victoria Benito** Mrs Victoria Benito

dorado, -a [do'raðo, a] adj (color) golden; (Tec) gilt

dormir [dor'mir] vt: **~ la siesta** to have an afternoon nap ▷ vi to sleep; **dormirse** vr to fall asleep

dormitorio [dormi'torjo] nm bedroom

dorsal [dor'sal] nm (Deporte) number

dorso ['dorso] nm (de mano) back; (de hoja) other side

dos [dos] num two

dosis ['dosis] nf inv dose, dosage

dotado, -a [do'taðo, a] adj gifted; **~ de** endowed with

dotar [do'tar] vt to endow; **dote** nf dowry; **dotes** nfpl (talentos) gifts

doy [doj] vb V **dar**

drama ['drama] nm drama; **dramaturgo** [drama'turɣo] nm dramatist, playwright

drástico, -a ['drastiko, a] adj drastic

drenaje [dre'naxe] nm drainage

droga ['droɣa] nf drug; **drogadicto, -a** [droɣa'ðikto, a] nm/f drug addict

droguería [droɣe'ria] nf hardware shop (BRIT) o store (US)

ducha ['dutʃa] nf (baño) shower; (Med) douche; **ducharse** vr to take a shower

duda ['duða] nf doubt; **no cabe ~** there is no doubt about it; **dudar** vt, vi to doubt; **dudoso, -a** [du'ðoso, a] adj (incierto) hesitant; (sospechoso) doubtful

duela etc vb V **doler**

duelo ['dwelo] vb V **doler** ▷ nm (combate) duel; (luto) mourning

duende ['dwende] nm imp, goblin

dueño, -a ['dweɲo, a] nm/f (propietario) owner; (de pensión, taberna) landlord/lady; (empresario) employer

duermo etc vb V **dormir**

dulce ['dulθe] adj sweet ▷ adv gently, softly ▷ nm sweet

dulcería [dulθe'ria] (LAM) nf confectioner's (shop)

dulzura [dul'θura] nf sweetness; (ternura) gentleness

dúo ['duo] nm duet

duplicar [dupli'kar] vt (hacer el doble de) to duplicate

duque ['duke] nm duke; **duquesa** nf duchess

duración [dura'θjon] nf (de película, disco etc) length; (de pila etc) life; (curso: de acontecimientos etc) duration

duradero, -a [dura'ðero, a] adj (tela etc) hard-wearing; (fe, paz) lasting

durante [du'rante] prep during

durar [du'rar] vi to last; (recuerdo) to remain

durazno [du'raθno] (LAM) nm (fruta) peach; (árbol) peach tree

durex ['dureks] (MÉX, ARG) nm (tira adhesiva) Sellotape® (BRIT), Scotch tape® (US)

dureza [du'reθa] nf (calidad) hardness

duro, -a ['duro, a] adj hard; (carácter) tough ▷ adv hard ▷ nm (moneda) five-peseta coin o piece

DVD nm abr (= disco de vídeo digital) DVD

e

E abr (= este) E

e [e] conj and

ébano ['eβano] nm ebony

ebrio, -a ['eβrjo, a] adj drunk

ebullición [eβuʎi'θjon] nf boiling

echar [e'tʃar] vt to throw; (agua, vino) to pour (out); (empleado: despedir) to fire, sack; (hojas) to sprout; (cartas) to post; (humo) to emit, give out ▷ vi: **~ a correr** to run off; **echarse** vr to lie down; **~ llave a** to lock (up); **~ abajo** (gobierno) to overthrow; (edificio) to demolish; **~ mano a** to lay hands on; **~ una mano a algn** (ayudar) to give sb a hand; **~ de menos** to miss; **~se atrás** (fig) to back out

eclesiástico, -a [ekle'sjastiko, a] adj ecclesiastical

eco ['eko] nm echo; **tener ~** to catch on

ecología [ekolo'xia] nf ecology; **ecológico, -a** adj (producto, método) environmentally-friendly; (agricultura) organic; **ecologista** adj ecological, environmental ▷ nmf environmentalist

economía [ekono'mia] nf (sistema) economy; (carrera) economics

económico, -a [eko'nomiko, a] adj (barato) cheap, economical; (ahorrativo) thrifty; (Com: año etc) financial; (: situación) economic

economista [ekono'mista] nmf economist

Ecuador [ekwa'ðor] nm Ecuador; **ecuador** nm (Geo) equator

ecuatoriano, -a [ekwato'rjano, a] adj, nm/f Ecuadorian

ecuestre [e'kwestre] adj equestrian

edad [e'ðað] nf age; **¿qué ~ tienes?** how old are you?; **tiene ocho años de ~** he's eight (years old); **de ~ mediana/avanzada** middle-aged/advanced in years; **la E~ Media** the Middle Ages

edición [eði'θjon] nf (acto) publication; (ejemplar) edition

edificar [eðifi'kar] vt, vi to build

edificio [eði'fiθjo] nm building; (fig) edifice, structure

Edimburgo [eðim'burɣo] nm Edinburgh

editar [eði'tar] vt (publicar) to publish; (preparar textos) to edit

editor, a [eði'tor, a] nm/f (que publica) publisher; (redactor) editor ▷ adj publishing cpd; **editorial**

adj editorial ▷ nm leading article, editorial; **casa editorial** publisher

edredón [eðre'ðon] nm duvet

educación [eðuka'θjon] nf education; (crianza) upbringing; (modales) (good) manners pl

educado, -a [eðu'kaðo, a] adj: **bien/mal ~** well/ badly behaved

educar [eðu'kar] vt to educate; (criar) to bring up; (voz) to train

EE. UU. nmpl abr (= Estados Unidos) US(A)

efectivamente [efektiβa'mente] adv (como respuesta) exactly, precisely; (verdaderamente) really; (de hecho) in fact

efectivo, -a [efek'tiβo, a] adj effective; (real) actual, real ▷ nm: **pagar en ~** to pay (in) cash; **hacer ~ un cheque** to cash a cheque

efecto [e'fekto] nm effect, result; **efectos** nmpl (efectos personales) effects; (bienes) goods; (Com) assets; **en ~** in fact; (respuesta) exactly, indeed; **efecto invernadero** greenhouse effect; **efectos especiales/ secundarios/sonoros** special/side/sound effects

efectuar [efek'twar] vt to carry out; (viaje) to make

eficacia [efi'kaθja] nf (de persona) efficiency; (de medicamento etc) effectiveness

eficaz [efi'kaθ] adj (persona) efficient; (acción) effective

eficiente [efi'θjente] adj efficient

egipcio, -a [e'xipθjo, a] adj, nm/f Egyptian

Egipto [e'xipto] nm Egypt

egoísmo [eɣo'ismo] nm egoism

egoísta [eɣo'ista] adj egoistical, selfish ▷ nmf egoist

Eire ['eire] nm Eire

ej. abr (= ejemplo) eg

eje ['exe] nm (Geo, Mat) axis; (de rueda) axle; (de máquina) shaft, spindle

ejecución [exeku'θjon] nf execution; (cumplimiento) fulfilment; (Mús) performance; (Jur: embargo de deudor) attachment

ejecutar [exeku'tar] vt to execute, carry out; (matar) to execute; (cumplir) to fulfil; (Mús) to perform; (Jur: embargar) to attach, distrain (on)

ejecutivo, -a [exeku'tiβo, a] adj executive; **el (poder) ~** the executive (power)

ejemplar [exem'plar] adj exemplary ▷ nm example; (Zool) specimen; (de libro) copy; (de periódico) number, issue

ejemplo [e'xemplo] nm example; **por ~** for example

ejercer [exer'θer] vt to exercise; (influencia) to exert; (un oficio) to practise ▷ vi (practicar): **~ (de)** to practise (as)

ejercicio [exer'θiθjo] nm exercise; (período) tenure; **hacer ~** to take exercise; **ejercicio comercial** financial year

ejército [e'xerθito] nm army; **entrar en el ~** to join the army, join up; **ejército del aire/de tierra** Air Force/Army

ejote [e'xote] (MÉX) nm green bean

○ PALABRA CLAVE

el [el] (f **la**, pl **los, las**, neutro **lo**) art def **1** the; **el libro/la mesa/los estudiantes** the book/table/students
2 (con n abstracto: no se traduce): **el amor/la juventud** love/youth
3 (posesión: se traduce a menudo por adj posesivo): **romperse el brazo** to break one's arm;

levantó la mano he put his hand up; **se puso el sombrero** she put her hat on

4 (*valor descriptivo*): **tener la boca grande/los ojos azules** to have a big mouth/blue eyes

5 (*con días*) on; **me iré el viernes** I'll leave on Friday; **los domingos suelo ir a nadar** on Sundays I generally go swimming

6 (*lo +adj*): **lo difícil/caro** what is difficult/expensive; (*cuán*) **no se da cuenta de lo pesado que es** he doesn't realise how boring he is

▷ *pron demos* **1** : **mi libro y el de usted** my book and yours; **las de Pepe son mejores** Pepe's are better; **no la(s) blanca(s) sino la(s) gris(es)** not the white one(s) but the grey one(s)

2 : **lo de: lo de ayer** what happened yesterday; **lo de las facturas** that business about the invoices

▷ *pron relativo* **1** (*indef*): **el que: el(los) que quiera(n) que se vaya(n)** anyone who wants to can leave; **llévese el que más le guste** take the one you like best

2 (*def*): **el que: el que compré ayer** the one I bought yesterday; **los que se vayan** those who leave

3 : **lo que: lo que pienso yo/más me gusta** what I think/like most

▷ *conj*: **el que: el que lo diga** the fact that he says so; **el que sea tan vago me molesta** his being so lazy bothers me

▷ *excl*: **el susto que me diste!** what a fright you gave me!

▷ *pron personal* **1** (*persona*: m) him; (: f) her; (: pl) them; **lo/las veo** I can see him/them

2 (*animal, cosa*: sg) it; (: pl) them; **lo (o la) veo** I can see it; **los (o las) veo** I can see them

3 (*como sustituto de frase*): **lo: no lo sabía** I didn't know; **ya lo entiendo** I understand now

él [el] *pron* (*persona*) he; (*cosa*) it; (*después de prep*: *persona*) him; (: *cosa*) it; **de ~** his

elaborar [elaβo'rar] *vt* (*producto*) to make, manufacture; (*preparar*) to prepare; (*madera, metal etc*) to work; (*proyecto etc*) to work on o out

elástico, -a [e'lastiko, a] *adj* (*flexible*) flexible ▷ *nm* elastic; (*un elástico*) elastic band

elección [elek'θjon] *nf* election; (*selección*) choice, selection; **elecciones generales** general election *sg*

electorado [elekto'raðo] *nm* electorate, voters *pl*

electricidad [elektriθi'ðað] *nf* electricity

electricista [elektri'θista] *nmf* electrician

eléctrico, -a [e'lektriko, a] *adj* electric

electro... [elektro] *prefijo* electro...;
electrocardiograma *nm* electrocardiogram;
electrocutar *vt* to electrocute; **electrodo** *nm* electrode; **electrodomésticos** *nmpl* (*electrical*) household appliances

electrónica [elek'tronika] *nf* electronics *sg*

electrónico, -a [elek'troniko, a] *adj* electronic

elefante [ele'fante] *nm* elephant

elegancia [ele'ɣanθja] *nf* elegance, grace; (*estilo*) stylishness

elegante [ele'ɣante] *adj* elegant, graceful; (*estiloso*) stylish, fashionable

elegir [ele'xir] *vt* (*escoger*) to choose, select; (*optar*) to opt for; (*presidente*) to elect

elemental [elemen'tal] *adj* (*claro, obvio*) elementary; (*fundamental*) elemental, fundamental

elemento [ele'mento] *nm* element; (*fig*) ingredient;

elementos *nmpl* elements, rudiments

elevación [eleβa'θjon] *nf* elevation; (*acto*) raising, lifting; (*de precios*) rise; (*Geo etc*) height, altitude

elevar [ele'βar] *vt* to raise, lift (up); (*precio*) to put up; **elevarse** *vr* (*edificio*) to rise; (*precios*) to go up

eligiendo *etc* vb V **elegir**

elija *etc* vb V **elegir**

eliminar [elimi'nar] *vt* to eliminate, remove

eliminatoria [elimina'torja] *nf* heat, preliminary (round)

élite ['elite] *nf* elite

ella ['eʎa] *pron* (*persona*) she; (*cosa*) it; (*después de prep*: *persona*) her; (: *cosa*) it; **de ~** hers

ellas ['eʎas] *pron* (*personas y cosas*) they; (*después de prep*) them; **de ~** theirs

ello ['eʎo] *pron* it

ellos ['eʎos] *pron* they; (*después de prep*) them; **de ~** theirs

elogiar [elo'xjar] *vt* to praise; **elogio** *nm* praise

elote [e'lote] (*Méx*) *nm* corn on the cob

eludir [elu'ðir] *vt* to avoid

email [i'mel] *nm* email; (*dirección*) email address; **mandar un ~ a algn** to email sb, send sb an email

embajada [emba'xaða] *nf* embassy

embajador, a [embaxa'ðor, a] *nm/f* ambassador/ambassadress

embalar [emba'lar] *vt* to parcel, wrap (up); **embalarse** *vr* to go fast

embalse [em'balse] *nm* (*presa*) dam; (*lago*) reservoir

embarazada [embara'θaða] *adj* pregnant ▷ *nf* pregnant woman

embarazo [emba'raθo] *nm* (*de mujer*) pregnancy; (*impedimento*) obstacle, obstruction; (*timidez*) embarrassment; **embarazoso, -a** *adj* awkward, embarrassing

embarcación [embarka'θjon] *nf* (*barco*) boat, craft; (*acto*) embarkation, boarding

embarcadero [embarka'ðero] *nm* pier, landing stage

embarcar [embar'kar] *vt* (*cargamento*) to ship, stow; (*persona*) to embark, put on board; **embarcarse** *vr* to embark, go on board

embargar [embar'ɣar] *vt* (*Jur*) to seize, impound

embargo [em'barɣo] *nm* (*Jur*) seizure; (*Com, Pol*) embargo

embargue *etc* vb V **embargar**

embarque *etc* [em'barke] vb V **embarcar** ▷ *nm* shipment, loading

embellecer [embeʎe'θer] *vt* to embellish, beautify

embestida [embes'tiða] *nf* attack, onslaught; (*carga*) charge

embestir [embes'tir] *vt* to attack, assault; to charge, attack ▷ *vi* to attack

emblema [em'blema] *nm* emblem

embobado, -a [embo'βaðo, a] *adj* (*atontado*) stunned, bewildered

embolia [em'bolja] *nf* (*Med*) clot

émbolo ['embolo] *nm* (*Auto*) piston

emborrachar [emborra'tʃar] *vt* to make drunk, intoxicate; **emborracharse** *vr* to get drunk

emboscada [embos'kaða] *nf* ambush

embotar [embo'tar] *vt* to blunt, dull

embotellamiento [emboteʎa'mjento] *nm* (*Auto*) traffic jam

embotellar [embote'ʎar] *vt* to bottle

embrague [em'braɣe] *nm* (*tb*: **pedal de ~**) clutch

embrión [em'brjon] nm embryo

embrollo [em'broʎo] nm (enredo) muddle, confusion; (aprieto) fix, jam

embrujado, -a [embru'xaðo, a] adj bewitched; **casa embrujada** haunted house

embrutecer [embrute'θer] vt (atontar) to stupefy

embudo [em'buðo] nm funnel

embuste [em'buste] nm (mentira) lie; **embustero, -a** adj lying, deceitful ▷ nm/f (mentiroso) liar

embutido [embu'tiðo] nm (Culin) sausage; (Tec) inlay

emergencia [emer'xenθja] nf emergency; (surgimiento) emergence

emerger [emer'xer] vi to emerge, appear

emigración [emixra'θjon] nf emigration; (de pájaros) migration

emigrar [emi'rrar] vi (personas) to emigrate; (pájaros) to migrate

eminente [emi'nente] adj eminent, distinguished; (elevado) high

emisión [emi'sjon] nf (acto) emission; (Com etc) issue; (Radio, TV: acto) broadcasting; (: programa) broadcast, programme (BRIT), program (US)

emisora [emi'sora] nf radio o broadcasting station

emitir [emi'tir] vt (olor etc) to emit, give off; (moneda etc) to issue; (opinión) to express; (Radio) to broadcast

emoción [emo'θjon] nf emotion; (excitación) excitement; (sentimiento) feeling

emocionante [emoθjo'nante] adj (excitante) exciting, thrilling

emocionar [emoθjo'nar] vt (excitar) to excite, thrill; (conmover) to move, touch; (impresionar) to impress

emoticón [emoti'kon], **emoticono** [emoti'kono] nm smiley

emotivo, -a [emo'tiβo, a] adj emotional

empacho [em'patʃo] nm (Med) indigestion; (fig) embarrassment

empalagoso, -a [empala'yoso, a] adj cloying; (fig) tiresome

empalmar [empal'mar] vt to join, connect ▷ vi (dos caminos) to meet, join; **empalme** nm joint, connection; (de trenes) connection

empanada [empa'naða] nf pie, pasty

empañarse [empa'narse] vr (cristales etc) to steam up

empapar [empa'par] vt (mojar) to soak, saturate; (absorber) to soak up, absorb; **empaparse** vr: **~se de** to soak up

empapelar [empape'lar] vt (paredes) to paper

empaquetar [empake'tar] vt to pack, parcel up

empastar [empas'tar] vt (embadurnar) to paste; (diente) to fill

empaste [em'paste] nm (de diente) filling

empatar [empa'tar] vi to draw, tie; **~on a dos** they drew two-all; **empate** nm draw, tie

empecé etc vb V **empezar**

empedernido, -a [empeðer'niðo, a] adj hard, heartless; (fumador) inveterate

empeine [em'peine] nm (de pie, zapato) instep

empeñado, -a [empe'naðo, a] adj (persona) determined; (objeto) pawned

empeñar [empe'nar] vt (objeto) to pawn, pledge; (persona) to compel; **empeñarse** vr (endeudarse) to get into debt; **~se en** to be set on, be determined to

empeño [em'peno] nm (determinación, insistencia) determination, insistence; **casa de ~s** pawnshop

empeorar [empeo'rar] vt to make worse, worsen

▷ vi to get worse, deteriorate

empezar [empe'θar] vt, vi to begin, start

empiece etc vb V **empezar**

empiezo etc vb V **empezar**

emplasto [em'plasto] nm (Med) plaster

emplazar [empla'θar] vt (ubicar) to site, place, locate; (Jur) to summons; (convocar) to summon

empleado, -a [emple'aðo, a] nm/f (gen) employee; (de banco etc) clerk

emplear [emple'ar] vt (usar) to use, employ; (dar trabajo a) to employ; **emplearse** vr (conseguir trabajo) to be employed; (ocuparse) to occupy o.s.

empleo [em'pleo] nm (puesto) job; (puestos: colectivamente) employment; (uso) use, employment

empollar [empo'ʎar] (ESP: fam) vt, vi to swot (up); **empollón, -ona** (ESP: fam) nm/f swot

emporio [em'porjo] (LAM) nm (gran almacén) department store

empotrado, -a [empo'traðo, a] adj (armario etc) built-in

emprender [empren'der] vt (empezar) to begin, embark on; (acometer) to tackle, take on

empresa [em'presa] nf (de espíritu etc) enterprise; (Com) company, firm; **empresariales** nfpl business studies; **empresario, -a** nm/f (Com) businessman(-woman)

empujar [empu'xar] vt to push, shove

empujón [empu'xon] nm push, shove

empuñar [empu'nar] vt (asir) to grasp, take (firm) hold of

○ **PALABRA CLAVE**

en [en] prep **1** (posición) in; (: sobre) on; **está en el cajón** it's in the drawer; **en Argentina/La Paz** in Argentina/La Paz; **en la oficina/el colegio** at the office/school; **está en el suelo/quinto piso** it's on the floor/the fifth floor

2 (dirección) into; **entró en el aula** she went into the classroom; **meter algo en el bolso** to put sth into one's bag

3 (tiempo) in; on; **en 1605/3 semanas/invierno** in 1605/3 weeks/winter; **en (el mes de) enero** in (the month of) January; **en aquella ocasión/época** on that occasion/at that time

4 (precio) for; **lo vendió en 20 dólares** he sold it for 20 dollars

5 (diferencia) by; **reducir/aumentar en una tercera parte/un 20 por ciento** to reduce/increase by a third/20 per cent

6 (manera): **en avión/autobús** by plane/bus; **escrito en inglés** written in English

7 (después de vb que indica gastar etc) on; **han cobrado demasiado en dietas** they've charged too much to expenses; **se le va la mitad del sueldo en comida** he spends half his salary on food

8 (tema, ocupación): **experto en la materia** expert on the subject; **trabaja en la construcción** he works in the building industry

9 (adj + en + infin): **lento en reaccionar** slow to react

enaguas [e'naɣwas] nfpl petticoat sg, underskirt sg

enajenación [enaxena'θjon] nf (Psico: tb: ~ **mental**) mental derangement

enamorado, -a [enamo'raðo, a] *adj* in love ▷ *nm/f* lover; **estar ~ (de)** to be in love (with)

enamorar [enamo'rar] *vt* to win the love of; **enamorarse** *vr*: **~de algn** to fall in love with sb

enano, -a [e'nano, a] *adj* tiny ▷ *nm/f* dwarf

encabezamiento [enkaβeθa'mjento] *nm* (*de carta*) heading; (*de periódico*) headline

encabezar [enkaβe'θar] *vt* (*movimiento, revolución*) to lead, head; (*lista*) to head, be at the top of; (*carta*) to put a heading to

encadenar [enkaðe'nar] *vt* to chain (together); (*poner grilletes a*) to shackle

encajar [enka'xar] *vt* (*ajustar*): **~(en)** to fit (into); (*fam: golpe*) to give ▷ *vi* to fit (well); (*fig: corresponder a*) to match

encaje [en'kaxe] ɪɪɪɪ (*labor*) lace

encallar [enka'ʎar] *vi* (*Náut*) to run aground

encaminar [enkami'nar] *vt* to direct, send

encantado, -a [enkan'taðo, a] *adj* (*hechizado*) bewitched; (*muy contento*) delighted; **¡~!** how do you do, pleased to meet you

encantador, a [enkanta'ðor, a] *adj* charming, lovely ▷ *nm/f* magician, enchanter/enchantress

encantar [enkan'tar] *vt* (*agradar*) to charm, delight; (*hechizar*) to bewitch, cast a spell on; **me encanta eso** I love that; **encanto** *nm* (*hechizo*) spell, charm; (*fig*) charm, delight

encarcelar [enkarθe'lar] *vt* to imprison, jail

encarecer [enkare'θer] *vt* to put up the price of; **encarecerse** *vr* to get dearer

encargado, -a [enkar'xaðo, a] *adj* in charge ▷ *nm/f* agent, representative; (*responsable*) person in charge

encargar [enkar'xar] *vt* to entrust; (*recomendar*) to urge, recommend; **encargarse** *vr*: **~se de** to look after, take charge of; **~a algn a algn** to put sb in charge of sth; **~a algn que haga algo** to ask sb to do sth

encargo [en'karxo] *nm* (*tarea*) assignment, job; (*responsabilidad*) responsibility; (*Com*) order

encariñarse [enkari'narse] *vr*: **~con** to grow fond of, get attached to

encarnación [enkarna'θjon] *nf* incarnation, embodiment

encarrilar [enkarri'lar] *vt* (*tren*) to put back on the rails; (*fig*) to correct, put on the right track

encasillar [enkasi'ʎar] *vt* (*fig*) to pigeonhole; (*actor*) to typecast

encendedor [enθende'ðor] *nm* lighter

encender [enθen'der] *vt* (*con fuego*) to light; (*luz, radio*) to put on, switch on; (*avivar: pasión*) to inflame; **encenderse** *vr* to catch fire; (*excitarse*) to get excited; (*de cólera*) to flare up; (*el rostro*) to blush

encendido [enθen'diðo] *nm* (*Auto*) ignition

encerado [enθe'raðo] *nm* (*Escol*) blackboard

encerrar [enθe'rrar] *vt* (*confinar*) to shut in, shut up; (*comprender, incluir*) to contain, include

encharcado, -a [entʃar'kaðo, a] *adj* (*terreno*) flooded

encharcarse [entʃar'karse] *vr* to get flooded

enchufado, -a [entʃu'faðo, a] (*fam*) *nm/f* well-connected person

enchufar [entʃu'far] *vt* (*Elec*) to plug in; (*Tec*) to connect, fit together; **enchufe** *nm* (*Elec: clavija*) plug; (: *toma*) socket; (*do dos tubos*) joint, connection; (*fam: influencia*) contact, connection; (: *puesto*) cushy job

encía [en'θia] *nf* gum

encienda *etc vb* V **encender**

encierro *etc* [en'θjerro] *vb* V **encerrar** ▷ *nm* shutting in, shutting up; (*calabozo*) prison

encima [en'θima] *adv* (*sobre*) above, over; (*además*) besides; **~de** (*en*) on, on top of; (*sobre*) above, over; (*además de*) besides, on top of; **por ~ de** over; **¿llevas dinero ~?** have you (got) any money on you?; **se me vino ~** it took me by surprise

encina [en'θina] *nf* holm oak

encinta [en'θinta] *adj* pregnant

enclenque [en'klenke] *adj* weak, sickly

encoger [enko'xer] *vt* to shrink, contract; **encogerse** *vr* to shrink, contract; (*fig*) to cringe; **~se de hombros** to shrug one's shoulders

encomendar [enkomen'dar] *vt* to entrust, commend; **encomendarse** *vr*: **~se a** to put one's trust in

encomienda *etc* [enko'mjenda] *vb* V **encomendar** ▷ *nf* (*encargo*) charge, commission; (*elogio*) tribute; **encomienda postal** (*LAM*) package

encontrar [enkon'trar] *vt* (*hallar*) to find; (*inesperadamente*) to meet, run into; **encontrarse** *vr* to meet (each other); (*situarse*) to be (situated); **~se con** to meet; **~se bien (de salud)** to feel well

encrucijada [enkruθi'xaða] *nf* crossroads *sg*

encuadernación [enkwaðerna'θjon] *nf* binding

encuadrar [enkwa'ðrar] *vt* (*retrato*) to frame; (*ajustar*) to fit, insert; (*contener*) to contain

encubrir [enku'βrir] *vt* (*ocultar*) to hide, conceal; (*criminal*) to harbour, shelter

encuentro *etc* [en'kwentro] *vb* V **encontrar** ▷ *nm* (*de personas*) meeting; (*Auto etc*) collision, crash; (*Deporte*) match, game; (*Mil*) encounter

encuerado, -a [(*MÉX*) enkwe'raðo, a] *adj* nude, naked

encuesta [en'kwesta] *nf* inquiry, investigation; (*sondeo*) (public) opinion poll

encumbrar [enkum'brar] *vt* (*persona*) to exalt

endeble [en'deβle] *adj* (*persona*) weak; (*argumento, excusa, persona*) weak

endemoniado, -a [endemo'njaðo, a] *adj* possessed (of the devil); (*travieso*) devilish

enderezar [endere'θar] *vt* (*poner derecho*) to straighten (out); (: *verticalmente*) to set upright; (*situación*) to straighten o sort out; (*dirigir*) to direct; **enderezarse** *vr* (*persona sentada*) to straighten up

endeudarse [endeu'ðarse] *vr* to get into debt

endiablado, -a [endja'βlaðo, a] *adj* devilish, diabolical; (*travieso*) mischievous

endilgar [endil'xar] (*fam*) *vt*: **~le algo a algn** to lumber sb with sth

endiñar [endi'nar] (*ESP: fam*) *vt* (*bofetón*) to land, belt

endosar [endo'sar] *vt* (*cheque etc*) to endorse

endulzar [endul'θar] *vt* to sweeten; (*suavizar*) to soften

endurecer [endure'θer] *vt* to harden; **endurecerse** *vr* to harden, grow hard

enema [e'nema] *nf* (*Med*) enema

enemigo, -a [ene'miɣo, a] *adj* enemy, hostile ▷ *nm/f* enemy

enemistad [enemis'taθ] *nf* enmity

enemistar [enemis'tar] *vt* to make enemies of, cause a rift between; **enemistarse** *vr* to become enemies; (*amigos*) to fall out

energía [ener'xia] *nf* (*vigor*) energy, drive; (*empuje*) push; (*Tec, Elec*) energy, power; **energía eólica** wind

power; **energía solar** solar energy o power
enérgico, -a [e'nerxiko, a] *adj* (*gen*) energetic; (*voz, modales*) forceful
energúmeno, -a [ener'ɣumeno, a] (*fam*) *nm/f* (*fig*) madman(-woman)
enero [e'nero] *nm* January
enfadado, -a [enfa'ðaðo, a] *adj* angry, annoyed
enfadar [enfa'ðar] *vt* to anger, annoy; **enfadarse** *vr* to get angry o annoyed
enfado [en'faðo] *nm* (*enojo*) anger, annoyance; (*disgusto*) trouble, bother
énfasis ['enfasis] *nm* emphasis, stress
enfático, -a [en'fatiko, a] *adj* emphatic
enfermar [enfer'mar] *vt* to make ill ▷ *vi* to fall ill, be taken ill
enfermedad [enferme'ðað] *nf* illness; **enfermedad venérea** venereal disease
enfermera [enfer'mera] *nf* nurse
enfermería [enferme'ria] *nf* infirmary; (*de colegio etc*) sick bay
enfermero [enfer'mero] *nm* (male) nurse
enfermizo, -a [enfer'miθo, a] *adj* (*persona*) sickly, unhealthy; (*fig*) unhealthy
enfermo, -a [en'fermo, a] *adj* ill, sick ▷ *nm/f* invalid, sick person; (*en hospital*) patient; **caer** o **ponerse ~** to fall ill
enfocar [enfo'kar] *vt* (*foto etc*) to focus; (*problema etc*) to approach
enfoque *etc* [en'foke] *vb* V **enfocar** ▷ *nm* focus
enfrentar [enfren'tar] *vt* (*peligro*) to face (up to), confront; (*oponer*) to bring face to face; **enfrentarse** *vr* (*dos personas*) to face o confront each other; (*Deporte: dos equipos*) to meet; **~se a** o **con** to face up to, confront
enfrente [en'frente] *adv* opposite; **la casa de ~** the house opposite, the house across the street; **~ de** opposite, facing
enfriamiento [enfria'mjento] *nm* chilling, refrigeration; (*Med*) cold, chill
enfriar [enfri'ar] *vt* (*alimentos*) to cool, chill; (*algo caliente*) to cool down; **enfriarse** *vr* to cool down; (*Med*) to catch a chill; (*amistad*) to cool
enfurecer [enfure'θer] *vt* to enrage, madden; **enfurecerse** *vr* to become furious, fly into a rage; (*mar*) to get rough
enganchar [engan'tʃar] *vt* to hook; (*dos vagones*) to hitch up; (*Tec*) to couple, connect; (*Mil*) to recruit; **engancharse** *vr* (*Mil*) to enlist, join up
enganche [en'gantʃe] *nm* hook; (*ESP Tec*) coupling, connection; (*acto*) hooking (up); (*Mil*) recruitment, enlistment; (*MÉX: depósito*) deposit
engañar [enga'ɲar] *vt* to deceive; (*estafar*) to cheat, swindle; **engañarse** *vr* (*equivocarse*) to be wrong; (*disimular la verdad*) to deceive o.s.
engaño [en'gaɲo] *nm* deceit; (*estafa*) trick, swindle; (*error*) mistake, misunderstanding; (*ilusión*) delusion; **engañoso, -a** *adj* (*tramposo*) crooked; (*mentiroso*) dishonest, deceitful; (*aspecto*) deceptive; (*consejo*) misleading
engatusar [engatu'sar] (*fam*) *vt* to coax
engendro [en'xendro] *nm* (*Bio*) foetus; (*fig*) monstrosity
englobar [englo'βar] *vt* to include, comprise
engordar [engor'ðar] *vt* to fatten ▷ *vi* to get fat, put on weight
engorroso, -a [engo'rroso, a] *adj* bothersome,

trying
engranaje [engra'naxe] *nm* (*Auto*) gear
engrasar [engra'sar] *vt* (*Tec: poner grasa*) to grease; (*: lubricar*) to lubricate, oil; (*manchar*) to make greasy
engreído, -a [engre'iðo, a] *adj* vain, conceited
enhebrar [ene'βrar] *vt* to thread
enhorabuena [enora'βwena] *excl* **¡~!** congratulations! ▷ *nf*: **dar la ~** to congratulate
enigma [e'niɣma] *nm* enigma; (*problema*) puzzle; (*misterio*) mystery
enjambre [en'xambre] *nm* swarm
enjaular [enxau'lar] *vt* to (put in a) cage; (*fam*) to jail, lock up
enjuagar [enxwa'ɣar] *vt* (*ropa*) to rinse (out)
enjuague *etc* [en'xwaɣe] *vb* V **enjuagar** ▷ *nm* (*Med*) mouthwash; (*de ropa*) rinse, rinsing
enlace [en'laθe] *nm* link, connection; (*relación*) relationship; (*tb: ~ matrimonial*) marriage; (*de carretera, trenes*) connection; **enlace sindical** shop steward
enlatado, -a [enla'taðo, a] *adj* (*alimentos, productos*) tinned, canned
enlazar [enla'θar] *vt* (*unir con lazos*) to bind together; (*atar*) to tie; (*conectar*) to link, connect; (*LAM: caballo*) to lasso
enloquecer [enloke'θer] *vt* to drive mad ▷ *vi* to go mad
enmarañar [enmara'ɲar] *vt* (*enredar*) to tangle (up), entangle; (*complicar*) to complicate; (*confundir*) to confuse
enmarcar [enmar'kar] *vt* (*cuadro*) to frame
enmascarar [enmaska'rar] *vt* to mask; **enmascararse** *vr* to put on a mask
enmendar [enmen'dar] *vt* to emend, correct; (*constitución etc*) to amend; (*comportamiento*) to reform; **enmendarse** *vr* to reform, mend one's ways; **enmienda** *nf* correction; amendment; reform
enmudecer [enmuðe'θer] *vi* (*perder el habla*) to fall silent; (*guardar silencio*) to remain silent
ennoblecer [ennoβle'θer] *vt* to ennoble
enojado, -a [eno'xaðo, a] (*LAM*) *adj* angry
enojar [eno'xar] *vt* (*encolerizar*) to anger; (*disgustar*) to annoy, upset; **enojarse** *vr* to get angry; to get annoyed
enojo [e'noxo] *nm* (*cólera*) anger; (*irritación*) annoyance
enorme [e'norme] *adj* enormous, huge; (*fig*) monstrous
enredadera [enreða'ðera] *nf* (*Bot*) creeper, climbing plant
enredar [enre'ðar] *vt* (*cables, hilos etc*) to tangle (up), entangle; (*situación*) to complicate, confuse; (*meter cizaña*) to sow discord among o between; (*implicar*) to embroil, implicate; **enredarse** *vr* to get entangled, get tangled (up); (*situación*) to get complicated; (*persona*) to get embroiled; (*LAM: fam*) to meddle
enredo [en'reðo] *nm* (*maraña*) tangle; (*confusión*) mix-up, confusion; (*intriga*) intrigue
enriquecer [enrike'θer] *vt* to make rich, enrich; **enriquecerse** *vr* to get rich
enrojecer [enroxe'θer] *vt* to redden ▷ *vi* (*persona*) to blush; **enrojecerse** *vr* to blush
enrollar [enro'ʎar] *vt* to roll (up), wind (up)
ensalada [ensa'laða] *nf* salad; **ensaladilla (rusa)** *nf* Russian salad
ensanchar [ensan'tʃar] *vt* (*hacer más ancho*) to

widen; (*agrandar*) to enlarge, expand; (*Costura*) to let out; **ensancharse** *vr* to get wider, expand

ensayar [ensa'jar] *vt* to test, try (out); (*Teatro*) to rehearse

ensayo [en'sajo] *nm* test, trial; (*Quím*) experiment; (*Teatro*) rehearsal; (*Deporte*) try; (*Escol, Literatura*) essay

enseguida [ense'ɣiða] *adv* at once, right away

ensenada [ense'naða] *nf* inlet, cove

enseñanza [ense'nanθa] *nf* (*educación*) education; (*acción*) teaching; (*doctrina*) teaching, doctrine; **enseñanza (de) primaria/secundaria** elementary/secondary education

enseñar [ense'nar] *vt* (*educar*) to teach; (*mostrar, señalar*) to show

enseres [en'seres] *nmpl* belongings

ensuciar [ensu'θjar] *vt* (*manchar*) to dirty, soil; (*fig*) to defile; **ensuciarse** *vr* to get dirty; (*bebé*) to dirty one's nappy

entablar [enta'βlar] *vt* (*recubrir*) to board (up); (*Ajedrez, Damas*) to set up; (*conversación*) to strike up; (*Jur*) to file ▷ *vi* to draw

ente ['ente] *nm* (*organización*) body, organization; (*fam: persona*) odd character

entender [enten'der] *vt* (*comprender*) to understand; (*darse cuenta*) to realize ▷ *vi* to understand; (*creer*) to think, believe; **entenderse** *vr* (*comprenderse*) to be understood; (*ponerse de acuerdo*) to agree, reach an agreement; ~ **algo de** to know a little about; ~ **en** to deal with, have to do with; ~ **mal** to misunderstand; ~**se con algn** (*llevarse bien*) to get on o along with sb; ~**se mal** (*dos personas*) to get on badly

entendido, -a [enten'diðo, a] *adj* (*comprendido*) understood; (*hábil*) skilled; (*inteligente*) knowledgeable ▷ *nm/f* (*experto*) expert ▷ *excl* agreed!; **entendimiento** *nm* (*comprensión*) understanding; (*inteligencia*) mind, intellect; (*juicio*) judgment

enterado, -a [ente'raðo, a] *adj* well-informed; **estar ~ de** to know about, be aware of

enteramente [entera'mente] *adv* entirely, completely

enterar [ente'rar] *vt* (*informar*) to inform, tell; **enterarse** *vr* to find out, get to know

enterito [ente'rito] (RPL) *nm* boiler suit (BRIT), overalls (US)

entero, -a [en'tero, a] *adj* (*total*) whole, entire; (*fig: honesto*) honest; (: *firme*) firm, resolute ▷ *nm* (*Com: punto*) point

enterrar [ente'rrar] *vt* to bury

entidad [enti'ðað] *nf* (*empresa*) firm, company; (*organismo*) body; (*sociedad*) society; (*Filosofía*) entity

entiendo *etc vb* V **entender**

entierro [en'tjerro] *nm* (*acción*) burial; (*funeral*) funeral

entonación [entona'θjon] *nf* (*Ling*) intonation

entonar [ento'nar] *vt* (*canción*) to intone; (*colores*) to tone; (*Med*) to tone up ▷ *vi* to be in tune

entonces [en'tonθes] *adv* then, at that time; **desde ~** since then; **en aquel ~** at that time; **(pues) ~** and so

entornar [entor'nar] *vt* (*puerta, ventana*) to half-close, leave ajar; (*los ojos*) to screw up

entorpecer [entorpe'θer] *vt* (*entendimiento*) to dull; (*impedir*) to obstruct, hinder; (: *tránsito*) to slow down, delay

entrada [en'traða] *nf* (*acción*) entry, access; (*sitio*) entrance, way in; (*Inform*) input; (*Com*) receipts *pl*, takings *pl*; (*Culin*) starter; (*Deporte*) innings *sg*; (*Teatro*)

house, audience; (*billete*) ticket; ~**s y salidas** (*Com*) income and expenditure; **de ~** from the outset; **entrada de aire** (*Tec*) air intake o inlet

entrado, -a [en'traðo, a] *adj*: ~ **en años** elderly; **una vez ~ el verano** in the summer(time), when summer comes

entramparse [entram'parse] *vr* to get into debt

entrante [en'trante] *adj* next, coming; **mes/año ~** next month/year; **entrantes** *nmpl* starters

entraña [en'trana] *nf* (*fig: centro*) heart, core; (*raíz*) root; **entrañas** *nfpl* (*Anat*) entrails; (*fig*) heart *sg*; **entrañable** *adj* close, intimate; **entrañar** *vt* to entail

entrar [en'trar] *vt* (*introducir*) to bring in; (*Inform*) to input ▷ *vi* (*meterse*) to go in, come in, enter; (*comenzar*): ~ **diciendo** to begin by saying; **hacer ~** to show in; **me entró sed/sueño** I started to feel thirsty/sleepy; **no me entra** I can't get the hang of it

entre ['entre] *prep* (*dos*) between; (*más de dos*) among(st)

entreabrir [entrea'βrir] *vt* to half-open, open halfway

entrecejo [entre'θexo] *nm*: **fruncir el ~** to frown

entredicho [entre'ðitʃo] *nm* (*Jur*) injunction; **poner en ~** to cast doubt on; **estar en ~** to be in doubt

entrega [en'treɣa] *nf* (*de mercancías*) delivery; (*de novela etc*) instalment; **entregar** [entre'ɣar] *vt* (*dar*) to hand (over), deliver; **entregarse** *vr* (*rendirse*) to surrender, give in, submit; (*dedicarse*) to devote o.s.

entremeses [entre'meses] *nmpl* hors d'œuvres

entremeter [entreme'ter] *vt* to insert, put in; **entremeterse** *vr* to meddle, interfere; **entremetido, -a** *adj* meddling, interfering

entremezclar [entremeθ'klar] *vt* to intermingle; **entremezclarse** *vr* to intermingle

entrenador, a [entrena'ðor, a] *nm/f* trainer, coach

entrenarse [entre'narse] *vr* to train

entrepierna [entre'pjerna] *nf* crotch

entresuelo [entre'swelo] *nm* mezzanine

entretanto [entre'tanto] *adv* meanwhile, meantime

entretecho [entre'tetʃo] (CS) *nm* attic

entretejer [entrete'xer] *vt* to interweave

entretener [entrete'ner] *vt* (*divertir*) to entertain, amuse; (*detener*) to hold up, delay; **entretenerse** *vr* (*divertirse*) to amuse o.s.; (*retrasarse*) to delay, linger; **entretenido, -a** *adj* entertaining, amusing; **entretenimiento** *nm* entertainment, amusement

entrever [entre'βer] *vt* to glimpse, catch a glimpse of

entrevista [entre'βista] *nf* interview; **entrevistar** *vt* to interview; **entrevistarse** *vr* to have an interview

entristecer [entriste'θer] *vt* to sadden, grieve; **entristecerse** *vr* to grow sad

entrometerse [entrome'terse] *vr*: ~ **(en)** to interfere (in o with)

entumecer [entume'θer] *vt* to numb, benumb; **entumecerse** *vr* (*por el frío*) to go o become numb

enturbiar [entur'βjar] *vt* (*el agua*) to make cloudy; (*fig*) to confuse; **enturbiarse** *vr* (*oscurecerse*) to become cloudy; (*fig*) to get confused, become obscure

entusiasmar [entusjas'mar] *vt* to excite, fill with enthusiasm; (*gustar mucho*) to delight; **entusiasmarse** *vr*: ~**se con** o **por** to get enthusiastic o excited about

entusiasmo [entu'sjasmo] *nm* enthusiasm; (*excitación*) excitement

entusiasta [entu'sjasta] *adj* enthusiastic ▷ *nmf*

enthusiast

enumerar [enume'rar] vt to enumerate

envainar [embai'nar] vt to sheathe

envalentonar [embalento'nar] vt to give courage to; **envalentonarse** vr (pey: jactarse) to boast, brag

envasar [emba'sar] vt (empaquetar) to pack, wrap; (enfrascar) to bottle; (enlatar) to can; (embolsar) to pocket

envase [em'base] nm (en paquete) packing, wrapping; (en botella) bottling; (en lata) canning; (recipiente) container; (paquete) package; (botella) bottle; (lata) tin (BRIT), can

envejecer [embexe'θer] vt to make old, age ▷ vi (volverse viejo) to grow old; (parecer viejo) to age

envenenar [embene'nar] vt to poison; (fig) to embitter

envergadura [emberɣa'ðura] nf (fig) scope, compass

enviar [em'bjar] vt to send; **~ un mensaje a algn** (por movil) to text sb, to send sb a text message

enviciarse [embi'θjarse] vr: **~ (con)** to get addicted (to)

envidia [em'biðja] nf envy; **tener ~ a** to envy, be jealous of; **envidiar** vt to envy

envío [em'bio] nm (acción) sending; (de mercancías) consignment; (de dinero) remittance

enviudar [embju'ðar] vi to be widowed

envoltura [embol'tura] nf (cobertura) cover; (embalaje) wrapper, wrapping; **envoltorio** nm package

envolver [embol'βer] vt to wrap (up); (cubrir) to cover; (enemigo) to surround; (implicar) to involve, implicate

envuelto [em'bwelto] pp de **envolver**

enyesar [enje'sar] vt (pared) to plaster; (Med) to put in plaster

enzarzarse [enθar'θarse] vr: **~ en** (pelea) to get mixed up in; (disputa) to get involved in

épica ['epika] nf epic

epidemia [epi'ðemja] nf epidemic

epilepsia [epi'lepsja] nf epilepsy

episodio [epi'soðjo] nm episode

época ['epoka] nf period, time; (Hist) age, epoch; **hacer ~** to be epoch-making

equilibrar [ekili'βrar] vt to balance; **equilibrio** nm balance, equilibrium; **mantener/perder el equilibrio** to keep/lose one's balance; **equilibrista** nmf (funámbulo) tightrope walker; (acróbata) acrobat

equipaje [eki'paxe] nm luggage; (avíos): **hacer el ~** to pack; **equipaje de mano** hand luggage

equipar [eki'par] vt (proveer) to equip

equipararse [ekipa'rarse] vr: **~ con** to be on a level with

equipo [e'kipo] nm (conjunto de cosas) equipment; (Deporte) team; (de obreros) shift

equis ['ekis] nf inv (the letter) X

equitación [ekita'θjon] nf horse riding

equivalente [ekiβa'lente] adj, nm equivalent

equivaler [ekiβa'ler] vi to be equivalent o equal

equivocación [ekiβoka'θjon] nf mistake, error

equivocado, -a [ekiβo'kaðo, a] adj wrong, mistaken

equivocarse [ekiβo'karse] vr to be wrong, make a mistake; **~ de camino** to take the wrong road

era ['era] vb V **ser** ▷ nf era, age

erais vb V **ser**

éramos vb V **ser**

eran vb V **ser**

eras vb V **ser**

erección [erek'θjon] nf erection

eres vb V **ser**

erigir [eri'xir] vt to erect, build; **erigirse** vr: **~se en** to set o.s. up as

erizo [e'riθo] nm (Zool) hedgehog; **erizo de mar** sea-urchin

ermita [er'mita] nf hermitage; **ermitaño, -a** [ermi'taɲo, a] nm/f hermit

erosión [ero'sjon] nf erosion

erosionar [erosjo'nar] vt to erode

erótico, -a [e'rotiko, a] adj erotic; **erotismo** nm eroticism

errante [e'rrante] adj wandering, errant

erróneo, -a [e'rroneo, a] adj (equivocado) wrong, mistaken

error [e'rror] nm error, mistake; (Inform) bug; **error de imprenta** misprint

eructar [eruk'tar] vt to belch, burp

erudito, -a [eru'ðito, a] adj erudite, learned

erupción [erup'θjon] nf eruption; (Med) rash

es vb V **ser**

esa ['esa] (pl **~s**) adj demos V **ese**

ésa ['esa] (pl **~s**) pron V **ése**

esbelto, -a [es'βelto, a] adj slim, slender

esbozo [es'βoθo] nm sketch, outline

escabeche [eska'βetʃe] nm brine; (de aceitunas etc) pickle; **en~** pickled

escabullirse [eskaβu'ʎirse] vr to slip away, to clear out

escafandra [eska'fandra] nf (buzo) diving suit; (escafandra espacial) space suit

escala [es'kala] nf (proporción, Mús) scale; (de mano) ladder; (Aviac) stopover; **hacer ~ en** to stop o call in at

escalafón [eskala'fon] nm (escala de salarios) salary scale, wage scale

escalar [eska'lar] vt to climb, scale

escalera [eska'lera] nf stairs pl, staircase; (escala) ladder; (Naipes) run; **escalera de caracol** spiral staircase; **escalera de incendios** fire escape; **escalera mecánica** escalator

escalfar [eskal'far] vt (huevos) to poach

escalinata [eskali'nata] nf staircase

escalofriante [eskalo'frjante] adj chilling

escalofrío [eskalo'frio] nm (Med) chill; **escalofríos** nmpl (fig) shivers

escalón [eska'lon] nm step, stair; (de escalera) rung

escalope [eska'lope] nm (Culin) escalope

escama [es'kama] nf (de pez, serpiente) scale; (de jabón) flake; (fig) resentment

escampar [eskam'par] vb impers to stop raining

escandalizar [eskandali'θar] vt to scandalize, shock; **escandalizarse** vr to be shocked; (ofenderse) to be offended

escándalo [es'kandalo] nm scandal; (alboroto, tumulto) row, uproar; **escandaloso, -a** adj scandalous, shocking

escandinavo, -a [eskandi'naβo, a] adj, nm/f Scandinavian

escanear [eskane'ar] vt to scan

escaño [es'kaɲo] nm (escaño) (Pol) seat

escapar [eska'par] vi (gen) to escape, run away; (Deporte) to break away; **escaparse** vr to escape, get away; (agua, gas) to leak (out) escaparate [eskapa'rate] nm shop window

escape [es'kape] nm (de agua, gas) leak; (de motor) exhaust

escarabajo [eskara'βaxo] nm beetle

escaramuza [eskara'muθa] nf skirmish

escarbar [eskar'βar] vt (tierra) to scratch

escarceos [eskar'θeos] nmpl: en mis ~ con la política ... in my dealings with politics ...; escarceos amorosos love affairs

escarcha [es'kartʃa] nf frost; escarchado, -a [eskar'tʃaðo, a] adj (Culin: fruta) crystallized

escarlata [eskar'lata] adj inv scarlet

escarlatina [eskarla'tina] nf scarlet fever

escarmentar [eskarmen'tar] vt to punish severely ▷ vi to learn one's lesson

escarmiento etc [eskar'mjento] vb V escarmentar ▷ nm (ejemplo) lesson; (castigo) punishment

escarola [eska'rola] nf endive

escarpado, -a [eskar'paðo, a] adj (pendiente) sheer, steep; (rocas) craggy

escasear [eskase'ar] vi to be scarce

escasez [eska'seθ] nf (falta) shortage, scarcity; (pobreza) poverty

escaso, -a [es'kaso, a] adj (poco) scarce; (raro) rare; (ralo) thin, sparse; (limitado) limited

escatimar [eskati'mar] vt to skimp (on), be sparing with

escayola [eska'jola] nf plaster

escena [es'θena] nf scene; escenario [esθe'narjo] nm (Teatro) stage; (Cine) set; (fig) scene; escenografía nf set design

escéptico, -a [es'θeptiko, a] adj sceptical ▷ nm/f sceptic

esclarecer [esklare'θer] vt (misterio, problema) to shed light on

esclavitud [esklaβi'tuð] nf slavery

esclavizar [esklaβi'θar] vt to enslave

esclavo, -a [es'klaβo, a] nm/f slave

escoba [es'koβa] nf broom; escobilla nf brush

escocer [esko'θer] vi to burn, sting; escocerse vr to chafe, get chafed

escocés, -esa [esko'θes, esa] adj Scottish ▷ nm/f Scotsman(-woman), Scot

Escocia [es'koθja] nf Scotland

escoger [esko'xer] vt to choose, pick, select; escogido, -a adj chosen, selected

escolar [esko'lar] adj school cpd ▷ nmf schoolboy(-girl), pupil

escollo [es'koʎo] nm (obstáculo) pitfall

escolta [es'kolta] nf escort; escoltar vt to escort

escombros [es'kombros] nmpl (basura) rubbish sg; (restos) debris sg

esconder [eskon'der] vt to hide, conceal; esconderse vr to hide; escondidas (LAM) nfpl: a escondidas secretly; escondite nm hiding place; (ESP: juego) hide-and-seek; escondrijo nm hiding place, hideout

escopeta [esko'peta] nf shotgun

escoria [es'korja] nf (de alto horno) slag; (fig) scum, dregs pl

Escorpio [es'korpjo] nm Scorpio

escorpión [eskor'pjon] nm scorpion

escotado, -a [esko'taðo, a] adj low-cut

escote [es'kote] nm (de vestido) low neck; pagar a ~ to share the expenses

escotilla [esko'tiʎa] nf (Náut) hatch(way)

escozor [esko'θor] nm (dolor) sting(ing)

escribible [eskri'βiβle] adj writable

escribir [eskri'βir] vt, vi to write; ~ a máquina to type; ¿cómo se escribe? how do you spell it?

escrito, -a [es'krito, a] pp de escribir ▷ nm (documento) document; (manuscrito) text, manuscript; por ~ in writing

escritor, -a [eskri'tor, a] nm/f writer

escritorio [eskri'torjo] nm desk

escritura [eskri'tura] nf (acción) writing; (caligrafía) (hand)writing; (Jur: documento) deed

escrúpulo [es'krupulo] nm scruple; (minuciosidad) scrupulousness; escrupuloso, -a adj scrupulous

escrutinio [eskru'tinjo] nm (examen atento) scrutiny; (Pol: recuento de votos) count(ing)

escuadra [es'kwaðra] nf (Mil etc) squad; (Náut) squadron; (flota: de coches etc) fleet; escuadrilla nf (de aviones) squadron; (LAM: de obreros) gang

escuadrón [eskwa'ðron] nm squadron

escuálido, -a [es'kwaliðo, a] adj skinny, scraggy; (sucio) squalid

escuchar [esku'tʃar] vt to listen to ▷ vi to listen

escudo [es'kuðo] nm shield

escuela [es'kwela] nf school; escuela de artes y oficios (ESP) ≈ technical college; escuela de choferes (LAM) driving school; escuela de manejo (MÉX) driving school

escueto, -a [es'kweto, a] adj plain; (estilo) simple

escuincle, -a [es'kwinkle, a] (MÉX: fam) nm/f kid

esculpir [eskul'pir] vt to sculpt; (grabar) to engrave; (tallar) to carve; escultor, -a nm/f sculptor(-tress); escultura nf sculpture

escupidera [eskupi'ðera] nf spittoon

escupir [esku'pir] vt, vi to spit (out)

escurreplatos [eskurre'platos] (ESP) nm inv draining board (BRIT), drainboard (US)

escurridero [eskurri'ðero] (LAM) nm draining board (BRIT), drainboard (US)

escurridizo, -a [eskurri'ðiθo, a] adj slippery

escurridor [eskurri'ðor] nm colander

escurrir [esku'rrir] vt (ropa) to wring out; (verduras, platos) to drain ▷ vi (líquidos) to drip; escurrirse vr (secarse) to drain; (resbalarse) to slip, slide; (escaparse) to slip away

ese¹ ['ese] (f esa, pl esos, esas) adj demos (sg) that; (pl) those

ése¹ ['ese] (f ésa, pl ésos, ésas) pron (sg) that (one); (pl) those (ones); ~ ... éste ... the former ... the latter ...; no me vengas con ésas don't give me any more of that nonsense

esencia [e'senθja] nf essence; esencial adj essential

esfera [es'fera] nf sphere; (de reloj) face; esférico, -a adj spherical

esforzarse [esfor'θarse] vr to exert o.s., make an effort

esfuerzo etc [es'fwerθo] vb V esforzarse ▷ nm effort

esfumarse [esfu'marse] vr (apoyo, esperanzas) to fade away

esgrima [es'rrima] nf fencing

esguince [es'ɣinθe] nm (Med) sprain

eslabón [esla'βon] nm link

eslip [ez'lip] nm pants pl (BRIT), briefs pl

eslovaco, -a [eslo'βako, a] adj, nm/f Slovak, Slovakian ▷ nm (Ling) Slovak, Slovakian

Eslovaquia [eslo'βakja] nf Slovakia

esmalte [es'malte] nm enamel; esmalte de uñas nail varnish o polish

esmeralda [esme'ralda] nf emerald
esmerarse [esme'rarse] vr (aplicarse) to take great pains, exercise great care; (afanarse) to work hard
esmero [es'mero] nm (great) care
esnob [es'nob] (pl ~s) adj (persona) snobbish ▷ nmf snob
eso ['eso] pron that, that thing o matter; ~ **de su coche** that business about his car; ~ **de ir al cine** all that about going to the cinema; **a** ~ **de las cinco** at about five o'clock; **en** ~ thereupon, at that point; ~ **es** that's it; **¡~ sí que es vida!** now that's really living!; **por ~ te lo dije** that's why I told you; **y** ~ **que llovía** in spite of the fact it was raining
esos adj demos V **ese**
ésos pron V **ése**
espabilar etc [espaβi'lar] = **despabilar** etc
espacial [espa'θjal] adj (del espacio) space cpd
espaciar [espa'θjar] vt to space (out)
espacio [es'paθjo] nm space; (Mús) interval; (Radio, TV) programme (BRIT), program (US); **el** ~ space; **espacio aéreo/exterior** air/outer space; **espacioso, -a** adj spacious, roomy
espada [es'paða] nf sword; **espadas** nfpl (Naipes) spades
espaguetis [espa'ɣetis] nmpl spaghetti sg
espalda [es'palda] nf (gen) back; **espaldas** nfpl (hombros) shoulders; **a ~s de algn** behind sb's back; **estar de ~s** to have one's back turned; **tenderse de ~s** to lie (down) on one's back; **volver la ~ a algn** to cold-shoulder sb
espantajo [espan'taxo] nm = **espantapájaros**
espantapájaros [espanta'paxaros] nm inv scarecrow
espantar [espan'tar] vt (asustar) to frighten, scare; (ahuyentar) to frighten off; (asombrar) to horrify, appal; **espantarse** vr to get frightened o scared; to be appalled
espanto [es'panto] nm (susto) fright; (terror) terror; (asombro) astonishment; **espantoso, -a** adj frightening; terrifying; astonishing
España [es'paɲa] nf Spain; **español, a** adj Spanish ▷ nm/f Spaniard ▷ nm (Ling) Spanish
esparadrapo [espara'ðrapo] nm (sticking) plaster (BRIT), adhesive tape (US)
esparcir [espar'θir] vt to spread; (diseminar) to scatter; **esparcirse** vr to spread (out), to scatter; (divertirse) to enjoy o.s.
espárrago [es'parraɣo] nm asparagus
esparto [es'parto] nm esparto (grass)
espasmo [es'pasmo] nm spasm
espátula [es'patula] nf spatula
especia [es'peθja] nf spice
especial [espe'θjal] adj special; **especialidad** nf speciality (BRIT), specialty (US)
especie [es'peθje] nf (Bio) species; (clase) kind, sort; **en** ~ in kind
especificar [espeθifi'kar] vt to specify; **específico, -a** adj specific
espécimen [es'peθimen] (pl **especímenes**) nm specimen
espectáculo [espek'takulo] nm (gen) spectacle; (Teatro etc) show
espectador, a [espekta'ðor, a] nm/f spectator
especular [espeku'lar] vt, vi to speculate
espejismo [espe'xismo] nm mirage
espejo [es'pexo] nm mirror; **(espejo) retrovisor**
rear-view mirror
espeluznante [espeluθ'nante] adj horrifying, hair-raising
espera [es'pera] nf (pausa, intervalo) wait; (Jur: plazo) respite; **en** ~ **de** waiting for; (con expectativa) expecting
esperanza [espe'ranθa] nf (confianza) hope; (expectativa) expectation; **hay pocas ~s de que venga** there is little prospect of his coming; **esperanza de vida** life expectancy
esperar [espe'rar] vt (aguardar) to wait for; (tener expectativa de) to expect; (desear) to hope for ▷ vi to wait; to expect; to hope; **hacer a algn** to keep sb waiting; ~ **un bebé** to be expecting (a baby)
esperma [es'perma] nf sperm
espeso, -a [es'peso, a] adj thick; **espesor** nm thickness
espía [es'pia] nmf spy; **espiar** vt (observar) to spy on
espiga [es'piɣa] nf (Bot: de trigo etc) ear
espigón [espi'ɣon] nm (Bot) ear; (Náut) breakwater
espina [es'pina] nf thorn; (de pez) bone; **espina dorsal** (Anat) spine
espinaca [espi'naka] nf spinach
espinazo [espi'naθo] nm spine, backbone
espinilla [espi'niʎa] nf (Anat: tibia) shin(bone); (grano) blackhead
espinoso, -a [espi'noso, a] adj (planta) thorny, prickly; (asunto) difficult
espionaje [espjo'naxe] nm spying, espionage
espiral [espi'ral] adj, nf spiral
espirar [espi'rar] vt to breathe out, exhale
espiritista [espiri'tista] adj, nmf spiritualist
espíritu [es'piritu] nm spirit; **Espíritu Santo** Holy Ghost o Spirit; **espiritual** adj spiritual
espléndido, -a [es'plendiðo, a] adj (magnífico) magnificent, splendid; (generoso) generous
esplendor [esplen'dor] nm splendour
espolvorear [espolβore'ar] vt to dust, sprinkle
esponja [es'ponxa] nf sponge; (fig) sponger; **esponjoso, -a** adj spongy
espontaneidad [espontanei'ðað] nf spontaneity; **espontáneo, -a** adj spontaneous
esposa [es'posa] nf wife; **esposas** nfpl handcuffs; **esposar** vt to handcuff
esposo [es'poso] nm husband
espray [es'prai] nm spray
espuela [es'pwela] nf spur
espuma [es'puma] nf foam; (de cerveza) froth, head; (de jabón) lather; **espuma de afeitar** shaving foam; **espumadera** nf (utensilio) skimmer; **espumoso, -a** adj frothy, foamy; (vino) sparkling
esqueleto [eske'leto] nm skeleton
esquema [es'kema] nm (diagrama) diagram; (dibujo) plan; (Filosofía) schema
esquí [es'ki] (pl ~s) nm (objeto) ski; (Deporte) skiing; **esquí acuático** water-skiing; **esquiar** vi to ski
esquilar [eski'lar] vt to shear
esquimal [eski'mal] adj, nmf Eskimo
esquina [es'kina] nf corner; **esquinazo** [eski'naθo] nm: **dar esquinazo a algn** to give sb the slip
esquirol [eski'rol] (ESP) nm strikebreaker, scab
esquivar [eski'βar] vt to avoid
esta ['esta] adj demos V **este²**
está vb V **estar**
ésta pron V **éste**
estabilidad [estaβili'ðað] nf stability; **estable** adj stable

establecer [estaβle'θer] vt to establish; **establecerse** vr to establish o.s.; (echar raíces) to settle (down); **establecimiento** nm establishment

establo [es'taβlo] nm (Agr) stable

estaca [es'taka] nf stake, post; (de tienda de campaña) peg

estacada [esta'kaða] nf fence, fencing; (palenque) stockade

estación [esta'θjon] nf station; (del año) season; **estación balnearia** seaside resort; **estación de autobuses** bus station; **estación de servicio** service station

estacionamiento [estaθjona'mjento] nm (Auto) parking; (Mil) stationing

estacionar [estaθjo'nar] vt (Auto) to park; (Mil) to station

estadía [esta'ðia] (LAM) nf stay

estadio [es'taðjo] nm (fase) stage, phase; (Deporte) stadium

estadista [esta'ðista] nm (Pol) statesman; (Mat) statistician

estadística [esta'ðistika] nf figure, statistic; (ciencia) statistics sg

estado [es'taðo] nm (Pol: condición) state; **estar en ~** to be pregnant; **estado civil** marital status; **estado de ánimo** state of mind; **estado de cuenta** bank statement; **estado de sitio** state of siege; **estado mayor** staff; **Estados Unidos** United States (of America)

estadounidense [estaðouni'ðense] adj United States cpd, American ▷ nm/f American

estafa [es'tafa] nf swindle, trick; **estafar** vt to swindle, defraud

estáis vb V **estar**

estallar [esta'ʎar] vi to burst; (bomba) to explode, go off; (epidemia, guerra, rebelión) to break out; **~ en llanto** to burst into tears; **estallido** nm explosion; (fig) outbreak

estampa [es'tampa] nf print, engraving; **estampado, -a** [estam'paðo, a] adj printed ▷ nm (impresión: acción) printing; (: efecto) print; (marca) stamping

estampar [estam'par] vt (imprimir) to print; (marcar) to stamp; (metal) to engrave; (poner sello en) to stamp; (fig) to stamp, imprint

estampida [estam'piða] nf stampede

estampido [estam'piðo] nm bang, report

estampilla [estam'piʎa] (LAM) nf (postage) stamp

están vb V **estar**

estancado, -a [estan'kaðo, a] adj stagnant

estancar [estan'kar] vt (aguas) to hold up, hold back; (Com) to monopolize; (fig) to block, hold up; **estancarse** vr to stagnate

estancia [es'tanθja] nf (ESP, MÉX: permanencia) stay; (sala) room; (RPL: de ganado) farm, ranch; **estanciero** (RPL) nm farmer, rancher

estanco, -a [es'tanko, a] adj watertight ▷ nm tobacconist's (shop), cigar store (us)

estándar [es'tandar] adj, nm standard

estandarte [estan'darte] nm banner, standard

estanque [es'tanke] nm (lago) pool, pond; (Agr) reservoir

estanquero, -a [estan'kero, a] nm/f tobacconist

estante [es'tante] nm (armario) rack, stand; (biblioteca) bookcase; (anaquel) shelf; **estantería** nf shelving, shelves pl

---

○ PALABRA CLAVE

estar [es'tar] vi 1 (posición) to be; **está en la plaza** it's in the square; **¿está Juan?** is Juan in?; **estamos a 30 km de Junín** we're 30 kms from Junín

2 (+ adj: estado) to be; **estar enfermo** to be ill; **está muy elegante** he's looking very smart; **¿cómo estás?** how are you keeping?

3 (+ gerundio): **estoy leyendo** I'm reading

4 (uso pasivo): **está condenado a muerte** he's been condemned to death; **está envasado en ...** it's packed in ...

5 (con fechas): **¿a cuántos estamos?** what's the date today?; **estamos a 5 de mayo** it's the 5th of May

6 (locuciones): **¿estamos?** (¿de acuerdo?) okay?; (¿listo?) ready?

7: **estar de: estar de vacaciones/viaje** to be on holiday/away o on a trip; **está de camarero** he's working as a waiter

8: **estar para: está para salir** he's about to leave; **no estoy para bromas** I'm not in the mood for jokes

9: **estar por** (propuesta etc) to be in favour of; (persona etc) to support, side with; **está por limpiar** it still has to be cleaned

10: **estar sin: estar sin dinero** to have no money; **está sin terminar** it isn't finished yet

estarse vr: **se estuvo en la cama toda la tarde** he stayed in bed all afternoon

---

estas ['estas] adj demos V **este²**

éstas pron V **éste**

estatal [esta'tal] adj state cpd

estático, -a [es'tatiko, a] adj static

estatua [es'tatwa] nf statue

estatura [esta'tura] nf stature, height

este¹ ['este] nm east

este² ['este] (f **esta**, pl **estos, estas**) adj demos (sg) this; (pl) these

esté etc vb V **estar**

éste ['este] (f **ésta**, pl **éstos, éstas**) pron (sg) this (one); (pl) these (ones); **ése ... ~ ...** the former ... the latter ...

estén etc vb V **estar**

estepa [es'tepa] nf (Geo) steppe

estera [es'tera] nf mat(ting)

estéreo [es'tereo] adj inv, nm stereo; **estereotipo** nm stereotype

estéril [es'teril] adj sterile, barren; (fig) vain, futile; **esterilizar** vt to sterilize

esterlina [ester'lina] adj: **libra ~** pound sterling

estés etc vb V **estar**

estética [es'tetika] nf aesthetics sg

estético, -a [es'tetiko, a] adj aesthetic

estiércol [es'tjerkol] nm dung, manure

estigma [es'tixma] nm stigma

estilo [es'tilo] nm style; (Tec) stylus; (Natación) stroke; **algo por el ~** something along those lines

estima [es'tima] nf esteem, respect; **estimación** [estima'θjon] nf (evaluación) estimation; (aprecio, afecto) esteem, regard; **estimado, a** adj esteemed; **E~ señor** Dear Sir

estimar [esti'mar] vt (evaluar) to estimate; (valorar) to value; (apreciar) to esteem, respect; (pensar, considerar) to think, reckon

estimulante [estimu'lante] adj stimulating ▷ nm stimulant

estimular [estimu'lar] vt to stimulate; (excitar) to excite

estímulo [es'timulo] nm stimulus; (ánimo) encouragement

estirar [esti'rar] vt to stretch; (dinero, suma etc) to stretch out; **estirarse** vr to stretch

estirón [esti'ron] nm pull, tug; (crecimiento) spurt, sudden growth; **dar o pegar un ~** (fam: niño) to shoot up (inf)

estirpe [es'tirpe] nf stock, lineage

estival [esti'βal] adj summer cpd

esto ['esto] pron this, this thing o matter; **~ de la boda** this business about the wedding

Estocolmo [esto'kolmo] nm Stockholm

estofado [esto'faðo] nm stew

estómago [es'tomaxo] nm stomach; **tener ~** to be thick-skinned

estorbar [estor'βar] vt to hinder, obstruct; (molestar) to bother, disturb ▷ vi to be in the way; **estorbo** nm (molestia) bother, nuisance; (obstáculo) hindrance, obstacle

estornudar [estornu'ðar] vi to sneeze

estos ['estos] adj demos V **este²**

éstos pron V **éste**

estoy vb V **estar**

estrado [es'traðo] nm platform

estrafalario, -a [estrafa'larjo, a] adj odd, eccentric

estrago [es'traxo] nm ruin, destruction; **hacer ~s en** to wreak havoc among

estragón [estra'ɣon] nm tarragon

estrambótico, -a [estram'botiko, a] adj (persona) eccentric; (peinado, ropa) outlandish

estrangular [estraŋgu'lar] vt (persona) to strangle; (Med) to strangulate

estratagema [estrata'xema] nf (Mil) stratagem; (astucia) cunning

estrategia [estra'texja] nf strategy; **estratégico, -a** adj strategic

estrato [es'trato] nm stratum, layer

estrechar [estre'tʃar] vt (reducir) to narrow; (Costura) to take in; (abrazar) to hug, embrace; **estrecharse** vr (reducirse) to narrow, grow narrow; (abrazarse) to embrace; **~ la mano** to shake hands

estrechez [estre'tʃeθ] nf narrowness; (de ropa) tightness; **estrecheces** nfpl (dificultades económicas) financial difficulties

estrecho, -a [es'tretʃo, a] adj narrow; (apretado) tight; (íntimo) close, intimate; (miserable) mean ▷ nm strait; **~ de miras** narrow-minded

estrella [es'treʎa] nf star; **estrella de mar** (Zool) starfish; **estrella fugaz** shooting star

estrellar [estre'ʎar] vt (hacer añicos) to smash (to pieces); (huevos) to fry; **estrellarse** vr to smash; (chocarse) to crash; (fracasar) to fail

estremecer [estreme'θer] vt to shake; **estremecerse** vr to shake, tremble

estrenar [estre'nar] vt (vestido) to wear for the first time; (casa) to move into; (película, obra de teatro) to premiere; **estrenarse** vr (persona) to make one's début; (película, Cine etc) première

estreñido, -a [estre'niðo, a] adj constipated

estreñimiento [estreni'mjento] nm constipation

estrepitoso, -a [estrepi'toso, a] adj noisy; (fiesta) rowdy

estría [es'tria] nf groove

estribar [estri'βar] vi: **~ en** to lie on

estribillo [estri'βiʎo] nm (Literatura) refrain; (Mús) chorus

estribo [es'triβo] nm (de jinete) stirrup; (de coche, tren) step; (de puente) support; (Geo) spur; **perder los ~s** to fly off the handle

estribor [estri'βor] nm (Náut) starboard

estricto, -a [es'trikto, a] adj (riguroso) strict; (severo) severe

estridente [estri'ðente] adj (color) loud; (voz) raucous

estropajo [estro'paxo] nm scourer

estropear [estrope'ar] vt to spoil; (dañar) to damage; **estropearse** vr (objeto) to get damaged; (persona, piel) to be ruined

estructura [estruk'tura] nf structure

estrujar [estru'xar] vt (apretar) to squeeze; (aplastar) to crush; (fig) to drain, bleed

estuario [es'twarjo] nm estuary

estuche [es'tutʃe] nm box, case

estudiante [estu'ðjante] nmf student; **estudiantil** adj student cpd

estudiar [estu'ðjar] vt to study

estudio [es'tuðjo] nm study; (Cine, Arte, Radio) studio; **estudios** nmpl studies; (erudición) learning sg; **estudioso, -a** adj studious

estufa [es'tufa] nf heater, fire

estupefaciente [estupefa'θjente] nm drug, narcotic

estupefacto, -a [estupe'fakto, a] adj speechless, thunderstruck

estupendo, -a [estu'pendo, a] adj wonderful, terrific; (fam) great; **¡~!** that's great!, fantastic!

estupidez [estupi'ðeθ] nf (torpeza) stupidity; (acto) stupid thing (to do)

estúpido, -a [es'tupiðo, a] adj stupid, silly

estuve etc vb V **estar**

ETA ['eta] (ESP) nf abr (= Euskadi ta Askatasuna) ETA

etapa [e'tapa] nf (de viaje) stage; (Deporte) leg; (parada) stopping place; (fase) stage, phase

etarra [e'tarra] nmf member of ETA

etc. abr (= etcétera) etc

etcétera [et'θetera] adv etcetera

eternidad [eterni'ðað] nf eternity; **eterno, -a** adj eternal, everlasting

ética ['etika] nf ethics pl

ético, -a ['etiko, a] adj ethical

etiqueta [eti'keta] nf (modales) etiquette; (rótulo) label, tag

Eucaristía [eukaris'tia] nf Eucharist

euforia [eu'forja] nf euphoria

euro ['euro] nm (moneda) euro

eurodiputado, -a [euroðipu'taðo, a] nm/f Euro MP, MEP

Europa [eu'ropa] nf Europe; **europeo, -a** adj, nm/f European

Euskadi [eus'kaði] nm the Basque Country o Provinces pl

euskera [eus'kera] nm (Ling) Basque

evacuación [eβakwa'θjon] nf evacuation

evacuar [eβa'kwar] vt to evacuate

evadir [eβa'ðir] vt to evade, avoid; **evadirse** vr to escape

evaluar [eβa'lwar] vt to evaluate

evangelio [eβan'xeljo] nm gospel

evaporar [eβapo'rar] vt to evaporate; **evaporarse** vr to vanish

evasión [eβa'sjon] *nf* escape, flight; *(fig)* evasion; **evasión de capitales** flight of capital

evasiva [eβa'siβa] *nf (pretexto)* excuse

evento [e'βento] *nm* event

eventual [eβen'twal] *adj* possible, conditional (upon circumstances); *(trabajador)* casual, temporary

evidencia [eβi'ðenθja] *nf* evidence, proof

evidente [eβi'ðente] *adj* obvious, clear, evident

evitar [eβi'tar] *vt (evadir)* to avoid; *(impedir)* to prevent; **~ hacer algo** to avoid doing sth

evocar [eβo'kar] *vt* to evoke, call forth

evolución [eβolu'θjon] *nf (desarrollo)* evolution, development; *(cambio)* change; *(Mil)* manoeuvre; **evolucionar** *vi* to evolve; to manoeuvre

ex [eks] *adj* ex-; **el ~ ministro** the former minister, the ex-minister

exactitud [eksakti'tuð] *nf* exactness, *(precisión)* accuracy; *(puntualidad)* punctuality; **exacto, -a** *adj* exact; accurate; punctual; **¡exacto!** exactly!

exageración [eksaxera'θjon] *nf* exaggeration

exagerar [eksaxe'rar] *vt, vi* to exaggerate

exaltar [eksal'tar] *vt* to exalt, glorify; **exaltarse** *vr (excitarse)* to get excited o worked up

examen [ek'samen] *nm* examination; **examen de conducir** driving test; **examen de ingreso** entrance examination

examinar [eksami'nar] *vt* to examine; **examinarse** *vr* to be examined, take an examination

excavadora [ekskaβa'ðora] *nf* excavator

excavar [ekska'βar] *vt* to excavate

excedencia [eksθe'ðenθja] *nf*: **estar en ~** to be on leave; **pedir o solicitar la ~** to ask for leave

excedente [eksθe'ðente] *adj, nm* excess, surplus

exceder [eksθe'ðer] *vt* to exceed, surpass; **excederse** *vr (extralimitarse)* to go too far

excelencia [eksθe'lenθja] *nf* excellence; **su E~** his Excellency; **excelente** *adj* excellent

excéntrico, -a [eks'θentriko, a] *adj, nm/f* eccentric

excepción [eksθep'θjon] *nf* exception; **a ~ de** with the exception of, except for; **excepcional** *adj* exceptional

excepto [eks'θepto] *adv* excepting, except (for)

exceptuar [eksθep'twar] *vt* to except, exclude

excesivo, -a [eksθe'siβo, a] *adj* excessive

exceso [eks'θeso] *nm (gen)* excess; *(Com)* surplus; **exceso de equipaje/peso** excess luggage/weight; **exceso de velocidad** speeding

excitado, -a [eksθi'taðo, a] *adj* excited; *(emociones)* aroused

excitar [eksθi'tar] *vt* to excite; *(incitar)* to urge; **excitarse** *vr* to get excited

exclamación [eksklama'θjon] *nf* exclamation

exclamar [ekskla'mar] *vi* to exclaim

excluir [eksklu'ir] *vt* to exclude; *(dejar fuera)* to shut out; *(descartar)* to reject

exclusiva [eksklu'siβa] *nf (Prensa)* exclusive, scoop; *(Com)* sole right

exclusivo, -a [eksklu'siβo, a] *adj* exclusive; **derecho ~** sole o exclusive right

Excmo. *abr* = **excelentísimo**

excomulgar [ekskomul'γar] *vt (Rel)* to excommunicate

excomunión [ekskomu'njon] *nf* excommunication

excursión [ekskur'sjon] *nf* excursion, outing; **excursionista** *nmf (turista)* sightseer

excusa [eks'kusa] *nf* excuse; *(disculpa)* apology;

excusar [eksku'sar] *vt* to excuse

exhaustivo, -a [eksaus'tiβo, a] *adj (análisis)* thorough; *(estudio)* exhaustive

exhausto, -a [ek'sausto, a] *adj* exhausted

exhibición [eksiβi'θjon] *nf* exhibition, display, show

exhibir [eksi'βir] *vt* to exhibit, display, show

exigencia [eksi'xenθja] *nf* demand, requirement; **exigente** *adj* demanding

exigir [eksi'xir] *vt (gen)* to demand, require; **~ el pago** to demand payment

exiliado, -a [eksi'ljaðo, a] *adj* exiled ▷ *nm/f* exile

exilio [ek'siljo] *nm* exile

eximir [eksi'mir] *vt* to exempt

existencia [eksis'tenθja] *nf* existence; **existencias** *nfpl* stock(s) *pl*

existir [eksis'tir] *vi* to exist, be

éxito ['eksito] *nm (triunfo)* success; *(Mús etc)* hit; **tener ~** to be successful

exorbitante [eksorβi'tante] *adj (precio)* exorbitant; *(cantidad)* excessive

exótico, -a [ek'sotiko, a] *adj* exotic

expandir [ekspan'dir] *vt* to expand

expansión [ekspan'sjon] *nf* expansion

expansivo, -a [ekspan'siβo, a] *adj*: **onda expansiva** shock wave

expatriarse [ekspa'trjarse] *vr* to emigrate; *(Pol)* to go into exile

expectativa [ekspekta'tiβa] *nf (espera)* expectation; *(perspectiva)* prospect

expedición [ekspeði'θjon] *nf (excursión)* expedition

expediente [ekspe'ðjente] *nm* expedient; *(Jur: procedimiento)* action, proceedings *pl*; *(: papeles)* dossier, file, record

expedir [ekspe'ðir] *vt (despachar)* to send, forward; *(pasaporte)* to issue

expensas [eks'pensas] *nfpl*: **a ~ de** at the expense of

experiencia [ekspe'rjenθja] *nf* experience

experimentado, -a [eksperimen'taðo, a] *adj* experienced

experimentar [eksperimen'tar] *vt (en laboratorio)* to experiment with; *(probar)* to test, try out; *(notar, observar)* to experience; *(deterioro, pérdida)* to suffer; **experimento** *nm* experiment

experto, -a [eks'perto, a] *adj* expert, skilled ▷ *nm/f* expert

expirar [ekspi'rar] *vi* to expire

explanada [ekspla'naða] *nf (llano)* plain

explayarse [ekspla'jarse] *vr (en discurso)* to speak at length; **~ con algn** to confide in sb

explicación [eksplika'θjon] *nf* explanation

explicar [ekspli'kar] *vt* to explain; **explicarse** *vr* to explain (o.s.)

explícito, -a [eks'pliθito, a] *adj* explicit

explique *etc vb* V **explicar**

explorador, a [eksplora'ðor, a] *nm/f (pionero)* explorer; *(Mil)* scout ▷ *nm (Med)* probe; *(Tec)* radar scanner

explorar [eksplo'rar] *vt* to explore; *(Med)* to probe; *(radar)* to scan

explosión [eksplo'sjon] *nf* explosion; **explosivo, -a** *adj* explosive

explotación [eksplota'θjon] *nf* exploitation; *(de planta etc)* running

explotar [eksplo'tar] *vt* to exploit; to run, operate ▷ *vi* to explode

exponer [ekspo'ner] *vt* to expose; *(cuadro)* to display;

(vida) to risk; (idea) to explain; **exponerse** vr: **~se a
(hacer) algo** to run the risk of (doing) sth
exportación [eksporta'θjon] nf (acción) export;
(mercancías) exports pl
exportar [ekspor'tar] vt to export
exposición [eksposi'θjon] nf (gen) exposure; (de arte)
show, exhibition; (explicación) explanation; (declaración)
account, statement
expresamente [ekspresa'mente] adv (decir) clearly;
(a propósito) expressly
expresar [ekspre'sar] vt to express; **expresión** nf
expression
expresivo, -a [ekspre'siβo, a] adj (persona, gesto,
palabras) expressive; (cariñoso) affectionate
expreso, -a [eks'preso, a] pp de **expresar** ▷ adj
(explícito) express; (claro) specific, clear; (tren) fast
▷ adv: **enviar ~** to send by express (delivery)
express [eks'pres] (LAM) adv: **enviar algo ~** to send
sth special delivery
exprimidor [eksprimi'ðor] nm squeezer
exprimir [ekspri'mir] vt (fruta) to squeeze; (zumo)
to squeeze out
expuesto, -a [eks'pwesto, a] pp de **exponer** ▷ adj
exposed; (cuadro etc) on show, on display
expulsar [ekspul'sar] vt (echar) to eject, throw out;
(alumno) to expel; (despedir) to sack, fire; (Deporte) to
send off; **expulsión** nf expulsion; sending-off
exquisito, -a [ekski'sito, a] adj exquisite; (comida)
delicious
éxtasis ['ekstasis] nm ecstasy
extender [eksten'der] vt to extend; (los brazos) to
stretch out, hold out; (mapa, tela) to spread (out), open
(out); (mantequilla) to spread; (certificado) to issue;
(cheque, recibo) to make out; (documento) to draw up;
extenderse vr (gen) to extend; (persona: en el suelo)
to stretch out; (epidemia) to spread; **extendido, -a**
adj (abierto) spread out, open; (brazos) outstretched;
(costumbre) widespread
extensión [eksten'sjon] nf (de terreno, mar) expanse,
stretch; (de tiempo) length, duration; (Tel) extension; **en
toda la ~ de la palabra** in every sense of the word
extenso, -a [eks'tenso, a] adj extensive
exterior [ekste'rjor] adj (de fuera) external; (afuera)
outside, exterior; (apariencia) outward; (deuda,
relaciones) foreign ▷ nm (gen) exterior, outside;
(aspecto) outward appearance; (Deporte) wing(er);
(países extranjeros) abroad; **en el ~** abroad; **al ~**
outwardly, on the surface
exterminar [ekstermi'nar] vt to exterminate
externo, -a [eks'terno, a] adj (exterior) external,
outside; (superficial) outward ▷ nm/f day pupil
extinguir [ekstin'gir] vt (fuego) to extinguish, put
out; (raza, población) to wipe out; **extinguirse** vr
(fuego) to go out; (Bio) to die out, become extinct
extintor [ekstin'tor] nm (fire) extinguisher
extirpar [ekstir'par] vt (Med) to remove (surgically)
extra ['ekstra] adj inv (tiempo) extra; (chocolate, vino)
good-quality ▷ nm/f extra ▷ nm extra; (bono) bonus
extracción [ekstrak'θjon] nf extraction; (en lotería)
draw
extracto [eks'trakto] nm extract
extradición [ekstraði'θjon] nf extradition
extraer [ekstra'er] vt to extract, take out
extraescolar [ekstraesko'lar] adj: **actividad ~**
extracurricular activity
extranjero, -a [ekstran'xero, a] adj foreign ▷ nm/f

foreigner ▷ nm foreign countries pl; **en el ~** abroad
extrañar [ekstra'nar] vt (sorprender) to find strange
o odd; (echar de menos) to miss; **extrañarse** vr
(sorprenderse) to be amazed, be surprised; **me extraña**
I'm surprised
extraño, -a [eks'trano, a] adj (extranjero) foreign;
(raro, sorprendente) strange, odd
extraordinario, -a [ekstraorði'narjo, a] adj
extraordinary; (edición, número) special ▷ nm (de
periódico) special edition; **horas extraordinarias**
overtime sg
extrarradio [ekstra'rraðjo] nm suburbs
extravagante [ekstraβa'xante] adj (excéntrico)
eccentric; (estrafalario) outlandish
extraviado, -a [ekstra'βjaðo, a] adj lost, missing
extraviar [ekstra'βjar] vt (persona: desorientar)
to mislead, misdirect; (perder) to lose, misplace;
extraviarse vr to lose one's way, get lost
extremar [ekstre'mar] vt to carry to extremes
extremaunción [ekstremaun'θjon] nf extreme
unction
extremidad [ekstremi'ðað] nf (punta) extremity;
extremidades nfpl (Anat) extremities
extremo, -a [eks'tremo, a] adj extreme; (último)
last ▷ nm end; (límite, grado sumo) extreme; **en último
~** as a last resort
extrovertido, -a [ekstroβer'tiðo, a] adj, nm/f
extrovert
exuberante [eksuβe'rante] adj exuberant; (fig)
luxuriant, lush
eyacular [ejaku'lar] vt, vi to ejaculate
o lose one's way, get lost
extremar [ekstre'mar] vt to carry to extremes
extremaunción [ekstremaun'θjon] nf extreme
unction
extremidad [ekstremi'ðað] nf (punta) extremity;
extremidades nfpl (Anat) extremities
extremo, -a [eks'tremo, a] adj extreme; (último)
last ▷ nm end; (límite, grado sumo) extreme; **en último
~** as a last resort
extrovertido, -a [ekstroβer'tiðo, a] adj, nm/f
extrovert
exuberante [eksuβe'rante] adj exuberant; (fig)
luxuriant, lush
eyacular [ejaku'lar] vt, vi to ejaculate

f

fa [fa] nm (Mús) fa, F

fabada [fa'βaða] nf bean and sausage stew

fábrica [fa'βrika] nf factory; **marca de ~** trademark; **precio de ~** factory price

fabricación [faβrika'θjon] nf (manufactura) manufacture; (producción) production; **de ~ casera** home-made; **fabricación en serie** mass production

fabricante [faβri'kante] nmf manufacturer

fabricar [faβri'kar] vt (manufacturar) to manufacture, make; (construir) to build; (cuento) to fabricate, devise

fábula ['faβula] nf (cuento) fable; (chisme) rumour; (mentira) fib

fabuloso, -a [faβu'loso, a] adj (oportunidad, tiempo) fabulous, great

facción [fak'θjon] nf (Pol) faction; **facciones** nfpl (de rostro) features

faceta [fa'θeta] nf facet

facha [fatʃa] (fam) nf (aspecto) look; (cara) face

fachada [fa'tʃaða] nf (Arq) façade, front

fácil ['faθil] adj (simple) easy; (probable) likely

facilidad [faθili'ðað] nf (capacidad) ease; (sencillez) simplicity; (de palabra) fluency; **facilidades** nfpl facilities; **facilidades de pago** credit facilities

facilitar [faθili'tar] vt (hacer fácil) to make easy; (proporcionar) to provide

factor [fak'tor] nm factor

factura [fak'tura] nf (cuenta) bill; **facturación** nf (de equipaje) check-in; **facturar** vt (Com) to invoice, charge for; (equipaje) to check in

facultad [fakul'tað] nf (aptitud, Escol etc) faculty; (poder) power

faena [fa'ena] nf (trabajo) work; (quehacer) task, job

faisán [fai'san] nm pheasant

faja ['faxa] nf (para la cintura) sash; (de mujer) corset; (de tierra) strip

fajo ['faxo] nm (de papeles) bundle; (de billetes) wad

falda ['falda] nf (prenda de vestir) skirt; **falda pantalón** culottes pl, split skirt

falla ['faʎa] nf (defecto) fault, flaw; **falla humana** (LAM) human error

fallar [fa'ʎar] vt (Jur) to pronounce sentence on ▷ vi (memoria) to fail; (motor) to miss

Fallas ['faʎas] nfpl Valencian celebration of the feast of St Joseph

fallecer [taʎe'θer] vi to pass away, die; **fallecimiento** nm decease, demise

fallido, -a [fa'ʎiðo, a] adj (gen) frustrated, unsuccessful

fallo ['faʎo] nm (Jur) verdict, ruling; (fracaso) failure; **fallo cardíaco** heart failure; **fallo humano** (ESP) human error

falsificar [falsifi'kar] vt (firma etc) to forge; (moneda) to counterfeit

falso, -a ['falso, a] adj false; (documento, moneda etc) fake; **en ~** falsely

falta ['falta] nf (defecto) fault, flaw; (privación) lack, want; (ausencia) absence; (carencia) shortage; (equivocación) mistake; (Deporte) foul; **echar en ~** to miss; **hacer ~ hacer algo** to be necessary to do sth; **me hace ~ una pluma** I need a pen; **falta de educación** bad manners pl; **falta de ortografía** spelling mistake

faltar [fal'tar] vi (escasear) to be lacking, be wanting; (ausentarse) to be absent, be missing; **faltan 2 horas para llegar** there are 2 hours to go till arrival; **~ al respeto a algn** to be disrespectful to sb; **¡no faltaba más!** (no hay de qué) don't mention it!

fama ['fama] nf (renombre) fame; (reputación) reputation

familia [fa'milja] nf family; **familia numerosa** large family; **familia política** in-laws pl

familiar [fami'ljar] adj (relativo a la familia) family cpd; (conocido, informal) familiar ▷ nm relative, relation

famoso, -a [fa'moso, a] adj (renombrado) famous

fan [fan] (pl ~s) nmf fan

fanático, -a [fa'natiko, a] adj fanatical ▷ nm/f fanatic; (Cine, Deporte) fan

fanfarrón, -ona [fanfa'rron, ona] adj boastful

fango ['fango] nm mud

fantasía [fanta'sia] nf fantasy, imagination; **joyas de ~** imitation jewellery sg

fantasma [fan'tasma] nm (espectro) ghost, apparition; (fanfarrón) show-off

fantástico, -a [fan'tastiko, a] adj fantastic

farmacéutico, -a [farma'θeutiko, a] adj pharmaceutical ▷ nm/f chemist (BRIT), pharmacist

farmacia [far'maθja] nf chemist's (shop) (BRIT), pharmacy; **farmacia de guardia** all-night chemist

fármaco ['farmako] nm drug

faro ['faro] nm (Náut: torre) lighthouse; (Auto) headlamp; **faros antiniebla** fog lamps; **faros delanteros/traseros** headlights/rear lights

farol [fa'rol] nm lantern, lamp

farola [fa'rola] nf street lamp (BRIT) o light (US)

farra ['farra] (LAM: fam) nf party; **ir de ~** to go on a binge

farsa ['farsa] nf (gen) farce

farsante [far'sante] nmf fraud, fake

fascículo [fas'θikulo] nm (de revista) part, instalment

fascinar [fasθi'nar] vt (gen) to fascinate

fascismo [fas'θismo] nm fascism; **fascista** adj, nmf fascist

fase ['fase] nf phase

fashion ['faʃon] adj (fam) trendy

fastidiar [fasti'ðjar] vt (molestar) to annoy, bother; (estropear) to spoil; **fastidiarse** vr: **¡que se fastidie!** (fam) he'll just have to put up with it!

fastidio [fas'tiðjo] nm (molestia) annoyance; **fastidioso, -a** adj (molesto) annoying

fatal [fa'tal] adj (gen) fatal; (desgraciado) ill-fated;

(fam: malo, pésimo) awful; **fatalidad** nf *(destino)* fate; *(mala suerte)* misfortune

fatiga [fa'tiɣa] nf *(cansancio)* fatigue, weariness
fatigar [fati'ɣar] vt to tire, weary
fatigoso, -a [fati'ɣoso, a] adj *(cansador)* tiring
fauna ['fauna] nf fauna
favor [fa'ßor] nm favour; **estar a ~ de** to be in favour of; **haga el ~ de ...** would you be so good as to ..., kindly ...; **por ~** please; **favorable** adj favourable
favorecer [faßore'θer] vt to favour; *(vestido etc)* to become, flatter; **este peinado le favorece** this hairstyle suits him
favorito, -a [faßo'rito, a] adj, nm/f favourite
fax [faks] nm inv fax; **mandar por ~** to fax
fe [fe] nf *(Rel)* faith; *(documento)* certificate; **actuar con buena/mala ~** to act in good/bad faith
febrero [fe'ßrero] nm February
fecha ['fetʃa] nf date; **con ~ adelantada** postdated; **en ~ próxima** soon; **hasta la ~** to date, so far; **poner ~** to date; **fecha de caducidad** *(de producto alimenticio)* sell-by date; *(de contrato etc)* expiry date; **fecha de nacimiento** date of birth; **fecha límite o tope** deadline
fecundo, -a [fe'kundo, a] adj *(fértil)* fertile; *(fig)* prolific; *(productivo)* productive
federación [feðera'θjon] nf federation
felicidad [feliθi'ðað] nf happiness; **¡~es!** *(deseos)* best wishes, congratulations!; *(en cumpleaños)* happy birthday!
felicitación [feliθita'θjon] nf *(tarjeta)* greeting(s) card
felicitar [feliθi'tar] vt to congratulate
feliz [fe'liθ] adj happy
felpudo [fel'puðo] nm doormat
femenino, -a [feme'nino, a] adj, nm feminine
feminista [femi'nista] adj, nmf feminist
fenómeno [fe'nomeno] nm phenomenon; *(fig)* freak, accident ▷ adj great ▷ excl great!, marvellous!; **fenomenal** adj = **fenómeno**
feo, -a ['feo, a] adj *(gen)* ugly; *(desagradable)* bad, nasty
féretro ['feretro] nm *(ataúd)* coffin; *(sarcófago)* bier
feria ['ferja] nf *(gen)* fair; *(descanso)* holiday, rest day; *(méx: cambio)* small o loose change; *(cs: mercado)* village market
feriado [fe'rjaðo] *(LAM)* nm holiday
fermentar [fermen'tar] vi to ferment
feroz [fe'roθ] adj *(cruel)* cruel; *(salvaje)* fierce
férreo, -a ['ferreo, a] adj iron
ferretería [ferrete'ria] nf *(tienda)* ironmonger's (shop) *(BRIT)*, hardware store *(US)*
ferrocarril [ferroka'rril] nm railway
ferroviario, -a [ferro'ßjarjo, a] adj rail cpd
ferry ['ferri] *(pl* **~s o ferries**) nm ferry
fértil ['fertil] adj *(productivo)* fertile; *(rico)* rich; **fertilidad** nf *(gen)* fertility; *(productividad)* fruitfulness
fervor [fer'ßor] nm fervour
festejar [feste'xar] vt *(celebrar)* to celebrate; **festejo** [fes'texo] nm celebration; **festejos** nmpl *(fiestas)* festivals
festín [fes'tin] nm feast, banquet
festival [festi'ßal] nm festival
festividad [festißi'ðað] nf festivity
festivo, -a [fes'tißo, a] adj *(de fiesta)* festive; *(Cine, Literatura)* humorous; **día ~** holiday
feto ['feto] nm foetus
fiable ['fjaßle] adj *(persona)* trustworthy; *(máquina)* reliable

fiambre ['fjambre] nm cold meat
fiambrera [fjam'brera] nf *(para almuerzo)* lunch box
fianza ['fjanθa] nf surety; *(Jur)*: **libertad bajo ~** release on bail
fiar [fi'ar] vt *(salir garante de)* to guarantee; *(vender a crédito)* to sell on credit ▷ vi to trust; **fiarse** vr to trust (in), rely on; **~ a** *(secreto)* to confide (to); **~se de algn** to rely on sb
fibra ['fißra] nf fibre; **fibra óptica** optical fibre
ficción [fik'θjon] nf fiction
ficha ['fitʃa] nf *(Tel)* token; *(en juegos)* counter, marker; *(tarjeta)* (index) card; **fichaje** nm *(Deporte)* signing; **fichar** vt *(archivar)* to file, index; *(Deporte)* to sign; **estar fichado** to have a record; **fichero** nm box file; *(Inform)* file
ficticio, -a [fik'tiθjo, a] adj *(imaginario)* fictitious; *(falso)* fabricated
fidelidad [fiðeli'ðað] nf *(lealtad)* fidelity, loyalty; **alta ~** high fidelity, hi-fi
fideos [fi'ðeos] nmpl noodles
fiebre ['fjeßre] nf *(Med)* fever; *(fig)* fever, excitement; **tener ~** to have a temperature; **fiebre aftosa** foot-and-mouth disease
fiel [fjel] adj *(leal)* faithful, loyal; *(fiable)* reliable; *(exacto)* accurate, faithful ▷ nm: **los ~es** the faithful
fieltro ['fjeltro] nm felt
fiera ['fjera] nf *(animal feroz)* wild animal o beast; *(fig)* dragon; V tb **fiero**
fiero, -a ['fjero, a] adj *(cruel)* cruel; *(feroz)* fierce; *(duro)* harsh
fierro ['fjerro] *(LAM)* nm *(hierro)* iron
fiesta ['fjesta] nf *(gen)* party; *(de pueblo)* festival; *(vacaciones: tb: ~s)* holiday sg; **fiesta mayor** annual festival; **fiesta patria** *(LAM)* independence day
figura [fi'ɣura] nf *(gen)* figure; *(forma, imagen)* shape, form; *(Naipes)* face card
figurar [fiɣu'rar] vt *(representar)* to represent; *(fingir)* to figure ▷ vi to figure; **figurarse** vr *(imaginarse)* to imagine; *(suponer)* to suppose
fijador [fixa'ðor] nm *(Foto etc)* fixative; *(de pelo)* gel
fijar [fi'xar] vt *(gen)* to fix; *(estampilla)* to affix, stick (on); **fijarse** vr: **~se en** to notice
fijo, -a ['fixo, a] adj *(gen)* fixed; *(firme)* firm; *(permanente)* permanent ▷ adv: **mirar ~** to stare
fila ['fila] nf row; *(Mil)* rank; **ponerse en ~** to line up, get into line; **fila india** single file
filatelia [fila'telja] nf philately, stamp collecting
filete [fi'lete] nm *(de carne)* fillet steak; *(de pescado)* fillet
filiación [filja'θjon] nf *(Pol)* affiliation
filial [fi'ljal] adj filial ▷ nf subsidiary
Filipinas [fili'pinas] nfpl: **las (Islas) ~** the Philippines; **filipino, -a** adj, nm/f Philippine
filmar [fil'mar] vt to film, shoot
filo ['filo] nm *(gen)* edge; **sacar ~ a** to sharpen; **al ~ del mediodía** at about midday; **de doble ~** double-edged
filología [filolo'ria] nf philology; **filología inglesa** *(Univ)* English Studies
filón [fi'lon] nm *(Minería)* vein, lode; *(fig)* goldmine
filosofía [filoso'fia] nf philosophy; **filósofo, -a** nm/f philosopher
filtrar [fil'trar] vt, vi to filter, strain; **filtrarse** vr to filter; **filtro** *(Tec, utensilio)* filter
fin [fin] nm end; *(objetivo)* aim, purpose; **al ~ y al cabo** when all's said and done; **a ~ de** in order to; **por ~** finally; **en ~** in short; **fin de semana** weekend

final [fi'nal] adj final ▷ nm end, conclusion ▷ nf final; **al ~ in** the end; **a ~es de** at the end of; **finalidad** nf (propósito) purpose, intention; **finalista** nmf finalist; **finalizar** vt to end, finish; (Inform) to log out o off ▷ vi to end, come to an end

financiar [finan'θjar] vt to finance; **financiero, -a** adj financial ▷ nm/f financier

finca ['finka] nf (casa de campo) country house; (ESP: bien inmueble) property, land; (LAM: granja) farm

finde ['finde] nm abr (fam: fin de semana) weekend

fingir [fin'xir] vt (simular) to simulate, feign ▷ vi (aparentar) to pretend

finlandés, -esa [finlan'des, esa] adj Finnish ▷ nm/f Finn ▷ nm (Ling) Finnish

Finlandia [fin'landja] nf Finland

fino, -a ['fino, a] adj fine; (delgado) slender; (de buenas maneras) polite, refined; (jerez) fino, dry

firma ['firma] nf signature; (Com) firm, company

firmamento [firma'mento] nm firmament

firmar [fir'mar] vt to sign

firme ['firme] adj firm; (estable) stable; (sólido) solid; (constante) steady; (decidido) resolute ▷ nm road (surface); **firmeza** nf firmness; (constancia) steadiness; (solidez) solidity

fiscal [fis'kal] adj fiscal ▷ nmf public prosecutor; **año ~** tax o fiscal year

fisgonear [fisɣone'ar] vt to poke one's nose into ▷ vi to pry, spy

física ['fisika] nf physics sg; V tb **físico**

físico, -a ['fisiko, a] adj physical ▷ nm physique ▷ nm/f physicist

fisura [fi'sura] nf crack; (Med) fracture

flác(c)ido, -a ['fla(k)θido, a] adj flabby

flaco, -a ['flako, a] adj (muy delgado) skinny, thin; (débil) weak, feeble

flagrante [fla'ɣrante] adj flagrant

flama ['flama] (MÉX) nf flame; **flamable** (MÉX) adj flammable

flamante [fla'mante] (fam) adj brilliant; (nuevo) brand-new

flamenco, -a [fla'menko, a] adj (de Flandes) Flemish; (baile, música) flamenco ▷ nm (baile, música) flamenco; (Zool) flamingo

flamingo [fla'minɡo] (MÉX) nm flamingo

flan [flan] nm creme caramel

flash [flaʃ] (pl ~ o -es) nm (Foto) flash

flauta ['flauta] nf (Mús) flute

flecha ['fletʃa] nf arrow

flechazo [fle'tʃaθo] nm love at first sight

fleco ['fleko] nm fringe

flema ['flema] nm phlegm

flequillo [fle'kiʎo] nm (pelo) fringe

flexible [flek'siβle] adj flexible

flexión [flek'sjon] nf press-up

flexo ['flekso] nm adjustable table-lamp

flirtear [flirte'ar] vi to flirt

flojera [flo'xera] (LAM: fam) nf: **me da ~** I can't be bothered

flojo, -a ['floxo, a] adj (gen) loose; (sin fuerzas) limp; (débil) weak

flor [flor] nf flower; **a ~ de** on the surface of; **flora** nf flora; **florecer** vi (Bot) to flower, bloom; (fig) to flourish; **florería** (LAM) nf florist's (shop); **florero** nm vase; **floristería** nf florist's (shop)

flota ['flota] nf fleet

flotador [flota'ðor] nm (para nadar) float; (para nadar)

rubber ring

flotar [flo'tar] vi (gen) to float; **flote** nm: **a flote** afloat; **salir a flote** (fig) to get back on one's feet

fluidez [flui'ðeθ] nf fluidity; (fig) fluency

fluido, -a [flu'iðo, a] adj, nm fluid

fluir [flu'ir] vi to flow

flujo ['fluxo] nm flow; **flujo y reflujo** ebb and flow

flúor ['fluor] nm fluoride

fluorescente [flwores'θente] adj fluorescent ▷ nm fluorescent light

fluvial [flu'βjal] adj (navegación, cuenca) fluvial, river cpd

fobia ['fobja] nf phobia; **fobia a las alturas** fear of heights

foca ['foka] nf seal

foco ['foko] nm focus; (Elec) floodlight; (MÉX: bombilla) (light) bulb

fofo, -a ['fofo, a] adj soft, spongy; (carnes) flabby

fogata [fo'ɣata] nf bonfire

fogón [fo'ɣon] nm (de cocina) ring, burner

folio ['foljo] nm folio, page

follaje [fo'ʎaxe] nm foliage

folleto [fo'ʎeto] nm (Pol) pamphlet

follón [fo'ʎon] (ESP: fam) nm (lío) mess; (conmoción) fuss; **armar un ~** to kick up a row

fomentar [fomen'tar] vt (Med) to foment

fonda ['fonda] nf inn

fondo ['fondo] nm (de mar) bottom; (de coche, sala) back; (Arte etc) background; (reserva) fund; **fondos** nmpl (Com) funds, resources; **una investigación a ~** a thorough investigation; **en el ~** at bottom, deep down

fonobuzón [fonoβu'θon] nm voice mail

fontanería [fontane'ria] nf plumbing; **fontanero, -a** nm/f plumber

footing ['futin] nm jogging; **hacer ~** to jog, go jogging

forastero, -a [foras'tero, a] nm/f stranger

forcejear [forθexe'ar] vi (luchar) to struggle

forense [fo'rense] nmf pathologist

forma ['forma] nf (figura) form, shape; (método) way, means; **las ~s** the conventions; **estar en ~** to be fit; **de ~ que ...** so that ...; **de todas ~s** in any case

formación [forma'θjon] nf (gen) formation; (educación) education; **formación profesional** vocational training

formal [for'mal] adj (gen) formal; (fig: serio) serious; (: de fiar) reliable; **formalidad** nf formality; seriousness; **formalizar** vt (Jur) to formalize; (situación) to put in order, regularize; **formalizarse** vr (situación) to put in order, be regularized

formar [for'mar] vt (componer) to form, shape; (constituir) to make up, constitute; (Escol) to train, educate; **formarse** vr (Escol) to be trained, educated; (cobrar forma) to form, take form; (desarrollarse) to develop

formatear [formate'ar] vt to format

formato [for'mato] nm format

formidable [formi'ðaβle] adj (temible) formidable; (estupendo) tremendous

fórmula ['formula] nf formula

formulario [formu'larjo] nm form

fornido, -a [for'niðo, a] adj well-built

foro ['foro] nm (Pol, Inform etc) forum

forrar [fo'rrar] vt (abrigo) to line; (libro) to cover; **forro** nm (de cuaderno) cover; (Costura) lining; (de sillón)

upholstery; **forro polar** fleece
fortalecer [fortale'θer] vt to strengthen
fortaleza [forta'leθa] nf (Mil) fortress, stronghold; (fuerza) strength; (determinación) resolution
fortuito, -a [for'twito, a] adj accidental
fortuna [for'tuna] nf (suerte) fortune, (good) luck; (riqueza) fortune, wealth
forzar [for'θar] vt (puerta) to force (open); (compeler) to compel
forzoso, -a [for'θoso, a] adj necessary
fosa ['fosa] nf (sepultura) grave; (en tierra) pit; **fosas nasales** nostrils
fósforo ['fosforo] nm (Quím) phosphorus; (cerilla) match
fósil ['fosil] nm fossil
foso ['foso] nm ditch; (Teatro) pit; (Auto) inspection pit
foto ['foto] nf photo, snap(shot); **sacar una ~** to take a photo o picture; **foto (de) carné** passport(-size) photo
fotocopia [foto'kopja] nf photocopy; **fotocopiadora** nf photocopier; **fotocopiar** vt to photocopy
fotografía [fotoɣra'fia] nf (Arte) photography; (una fotografía) photograph; **fotografiar** vt to photograph
fotógrafo, -a [fo'toɣrafo, a] nm/f photographer
fotomatón [fotoma'ton] nm photo booth
FP (ESP) nf abr (= Formación Profesional) vocational courses for 14- to 18-year-olds
fracasar [fraka'sar] vi (gen) to fail
fracaso [fra'kaso] nm failure
fracción [frak'θjon] nf fraction, break
fractura [frak'tura] nf fracture, break
fragancia [fra'ɣanθja] nf (olor) fragrance, perfume
frágil ['fraxil] adj (débil) fragile; (Com) breakable
fragmento [fraɣ'mento] nm (pedazo) fragment
fraile ['fraile] nm (Rel) friar; (: monje) monk
frambuesa [fram'bwesa] nf raspberry
francés, -esa [fran'θes, esa] adj French ▷ nm/f Frenchman(-woman) ▷ nm (Ling) French
Francia ['franθja] nf France
franco, -a ['franko, a] adj (cándido) frank, open; (Com: exento) free ▷ nm (moneda) franc
francotirador, a [frankotira'ðor, a] nm/f sniper
franela [fra'nela] nf flannel
franja ['franxa] nf fringe
franquear [franke'ar] vt (camino) to clear; (carta, paquete postal) to frank, stamp; (obstáculo) to overcome
franqueo [fran'keo] nm postage
franqueza [fran'keθa] nf (candor) frankness
frasco ['frasko] nm bottle, flask
frase ['frase] nf sentence; **frase hecha** set phrase; (pey) stock phrase
fraternal [fra'ternal, a] adj brotherly, fraternal
fraude ['frauðe] nm (cualidad) dishonesty; (acto) fraud
frazada [fra'saða] (LAM) nf blanket
frecuencia [fre'kwenθja] nf frequency; **con ~** frequently, often
frecuentar [frekwen'tar] vt to frequent
frecuente [fre'kwente] adj (gen) frequent
fregadero [freɣa'ðero] nm (kitchen) sink
fregar [fre'ɣar] vt (frotar) to scrub; (platos) to wash (up); (LAM: fam: fastidiar) to annoy; (: malograr) to screw up
fregona [fre'ɣona] nf mop
freír [fre'ir] vt to fry
frenar [fre'nar] vt to brake; (fig) to check
frenazo [fre'naθo] nm: **dar un ~** to brake sharply

frenesí [frene'si] nm frenzy
freno ['freno] nm (Tec, Auto) brake; (de cabalgadura) bit; (fig) check; **freno de mano** handbrake
frente ['frente] nm (Arq, Pol) front; (de objeto) front part ▷ nf forehead, brow; **~ a** in front of; (en situación opuesta de) opposite; **al ~ de** (fig) at the head of; **chocar de ~** to crash head-on; **hacer ~ a** to face up to
fresa ['fresa] (ESP) nf strawberry
fresco, -a ['fresko, a] adj (nuevo) fresh; (frío) cool; (descarado) cheeky ▷ nm (aire) fresh air; (Arte) fresco; (LAM: jugo) fruit drink ▷ nm/f (fam): **ser un ~** to have a nerve; **tomar el ~** to get some fresh air; **frescura** nf freshness; (descaro) cheek, nerve
frialdad [frial'dað] nf (gen) coldness; (indiferencia) indifference
frigidez [frixi'ðeθ] nf frigidity
frigorífico [friɣo'rifiko] nm refrigerator
frijol [fri'xol] nm kidney bean
frío, -a etc ['frio, a] vb V **freír** ▷ adj cold; (indiferente) indifferent ▷ nm cold; indifference; **hace ~** it's cold; **tener ~** to be cold
frito, -a ['frito, a] adj fried; **me trae ~ ese hombre** I'm sick and tired of that man; **fritos** nmpl fried food
frívolo, -a ['friβolo, a] adj frivolous
frontal [fron'tal] adj frontal; **choque ~** head-on collision
frontera [fron'tera] nf frontier; **fronterizo, -a** adj frontier cpd; (contiguo) bordering
frontón [fron'ton] nm (Deporte: cancha) pelota court; (: juego) pelota
frotar [fro'tar] vt to rub; **frotarse** vr: **~se las manos** to rub one's hands
fructífero, -a [fruk'tifero, a] adj fruitful
fruncir [frun'θir] vt to pucker; (Costura) to pleat; **~ el ceño** to knit one's brow
frustrar [frus'trar] vt to frustrate
fruta ['fruta] nf fruit; **frutería** nf fruit shop; **frutero, -a** adj fruit cpd ▷ nm/f fruiterer ▷ nm fruit bowl
frutilla [fru'tiʎa] (CS) nf strawberry
fruto ['fruto] nm fruit; (fig: resultado) result; (: beneficio) benefit; **frutos secos** nuts and dried fruit pl
fucsia ['fuksja] nf fuchsia
fue [fwe] vb V **ser; ir**
fuego ['fweɣo] nm (gen) fire; **a ~ lento** on a low heat; **¿tienes ~?** have you (got) a light?; **fuego amigo** friendly fire; **fuegos artificiales** fireworks
fuente ['fwente] nf (fuente) fountain; (manantial: fig) spring; (origen) source; (plato) large dish
fuera etc ['fwera] vb V **ser; ir** ▷ adv out(side); (en otra parte) away; (excepto, salvo) except, save ▷ prep: **~ de** (fig) besides; **~ de sí** beside o.s.; **por ~** (on the) outside
fuera-borda [fwera'βorða] nm speedboat
fuerte ['fwerte] adj strong; (golpe) hard; (ruido) loud; (comida) rich; (lluvia) heavy; (dolor) intense ▷ adv strongly; hard; loud(ly)
fuerza etc ['fwerθa] vb V **forzar** ▷ nf (fortaleza) strength; (Tec, Elec) power; (coacción) force; (Mil, Pol) force; **a ~ de** by dint of; **cobrar ~s** to recover one's strength; **tener ~s para** to have the strength to; **a la ~** forcibly, by force; **por ~** of necessity; **fuerza de voluntad** willpower; **fuerzas aéreas** air force sg; **fuerzas armadas** armed forces
fuga ['fuɣa] nf (huida) flight, escape; (de gas etc) leak
fugarse [fu'ɣarse] vr to flee, escape
fugaz [fu'ɣaθ] adj fleeting

fugitivo, a [fuxi'tiβo, a] *adj, nm/f* fugitive
fui [fwi] *vb V* **ser; ir**
fulano, -a [fu'lano, a] *nm/f* so-and-so, what's-his-name/what's-her-name
fulminante [fulmi'nante] *adj (fig: mirada)* fierce; *(Med: enfermedad, ataque)* sudden; *(fam: éxito, golpe)* sudden
fumador, a [fuma'ðor, a] *nm/f* smoker
fumar [fu'mar] *vt, vi* to smoke; **~ en pipa** to smoke a pipe
función [fun'θjon] *nf* function; *(en trabajo)* duties *pl; (espectáculo)* show; **entrar en funciones** to take up one's duties
funcionar [funθjo'nar] *vi (gen)* to function; *(máquina)* to work; **"no funciona"** "out of order"
funcionario, -a [funθjo'narjo, a] *nm/f* civil servant
funda ['funda] *nf (gen)* cover; *(de almohada)* pillowcase
fundación [funda'θjon] *nf* foundation
fundamental [fundamen'tal] *adj* fundamental, basic
fundamento [funda'mento] *nm (base)* foundation
fundar [fun'dar] *vt* to found; **fundarse** *vr:* **~se en** to be founded on
fundición [fundi'θjon] *nf* fusing; *(fábrica)* foundry
fundir [fun'dir] *vt (gen)* to fuse; *(metal)* to smelt, melt down; *(nieve etc)* to melt; *(Com)* to merge; *(estatua)* to cast; **fundirse** *vr (colores etc)* to merge, blend; *(unirse)* to fuse together; *(Elec: fusible, lámpara etc)* to fuse, blow; *(nieve etc)* to melt
fúnebre ['funeβre] *adj* funeral *cpd*, funereal
funeral [fune'ral] *nm* funeral; **funeraria** *nf* undertaker's
funicular [funiku'lar] *nm (tren)* funicular; *(teleférico)* cable car
furgón [fur'xon] *nm* wagon; **furgoneta** *nf (Auto, Com)* (transit) van (BRIT), pick-up (truck) (US)
furia ['furja] *nf (ira)* fury; *(violencia)* violence; **furioso, -a** *adj (iracundo)* furious; *(violento)* violent
furtivo, -a [fur'tiβo, a] *adj* furtive ▷ *nm* poacher
fusible [fu'siβle] *nm* fuse
fusil [fu'sil] *nm* rifle; **fusilar** *vt* to shoot
fusión [fu'sjon] *nf (gen)* melting; *(unión)* fusion; *(Com)* merger
fútbol ['futβol] *nm* football (BRIT), soccer (US); **fútbol americano** American football (BRIT), football (US); **fútbol sala** indoor football (BRIT) o soccer (US); **futbolín** *nm* table football; **futbolista** *nmf* footballer
futuro, -a [fu'turo, a] *adj, nm* future

gabardina [gaβar'ðina] *nf* raincoat, gabardine
gabinete [gaβi'nete] *nm (Pol)* cabinet; *(estudio)* study; *(de abogados etc)* office
gachas ['gatʃas] *nfpl* porridge *sg*
gafas ['gafas] *nfpl* glasses; **gafas de sol** sunglasses
gafe ['gafe] *(ESP) nmf* jinx
gaita ['gaita] *nf* bagpipes *pl*
gajes ['gaxes] *nmpl:* **~ del oficio** occupational hazards
gajo ['gaxo] *nm (de naranja)* segment
gala ['gala] *nf (traje de etiqueta)* full dress; **galas** *nfpl (ropa)* finery *sg;* **estar de ~** to be in one's best clothes; **hacer ~ de** to display
galápago [ga'lapaxo] *nm (Zool)* turtle
galardón [galar'ðon] *nm* award, prize
galaxia [ga'laksja] *nf* galaxy
galera [ga'lera] *nf (nave)* galley; *(carro)* wagon; *(Imprenta)* galley
galería [gale'ria] *nf (gen)* gallery; *(balcón)* veranda(h); *(pasillo)* corridor; **galería comercial** shopping mall
Gales ['gales] *nm (tb:* **País de ~)** Wales; **galés, -esa** *adj* Welsh ▷ *nm/f* Welshman(-woman) ▷ *nm (Ling)* Welsh
galgo, -a [ˈgalxo, a] *nm/f* greyhound
gallego, -a [ga'ʎexo, a] *adj, nm/f* Galician
galleta [ga'ʎeta] *nf* biscuit (BRIT), cookie (US)
gallina [ga'ʎina] *nf* hen ▷ *nm (fam: cobarde)* chicken; **gallinero** *nm* henhouse; *(Teatro)* top gallery
gallo ['gaʎo] *nm* cock, rooster
galopar [galo'par] *vi* to gallop
gama ['gama] *nf (fig)* range
gamba ['gamba] *nf* prawn (BRIT), shrimp (US)
gamberro, -a [gam'berro, a] *(ESP) nm/f* hooligan, lout
gamuza [ga'muθa] *nf* chamois
gana ['gana] *nf (deseo)* desire, wish; *(apetito)* appetite; *(voluntad)* will; *(añoranza)* longing; **de buena ~** willingly; **de mala ~** reluctantly; **me da ~s de** I feel like, I want to; **no me da la ~** I don't feel like it; **tener ~s de** to feel like
ganadería [ganaðe'ria] *nf (ganado)* livestock; *(ganado vacuno)* cattle *pl; (cría, comercio)* cattle raising
ganadero, -a [gana'ðero, a] *(ESP) nm/f (hacendado)* rancher
ganado [ga'naðo] *nm* livestock; **ganado porcino**

pigs pl

ganador, a [gana'ðor, a] adj winning ▷ nm/f winner

ganancia [ga'nanθja] nf (lo ganado) gain; (aumento) increase; (beneficio) profit; **ganancias** nfpl (ingresos) earnings; (beneficios) profit sg, winnings

ganar [ga'nar] vt (obtener) to get, obtain; (sacar ventaja) to gain; (salario etc) to earn; (Deporte, premio) to win; (derrotar a) to beat; (alcanzar) to reach ▷ vi (Deporte) to win; **ganarse** vr: **~se la vida** to earn one's living

ganchillo [gan'tʃiʎo] nm crochet

gancho ['gantʃo] nm (gen) hook; (colgador) hanger

gandul, a [a gan'dul, a] adj, nm/f good-for-nothing, layabout

ganga ['ganga] nf bargain

gangrena [gan'grena] nf gangrene

ganso, -a ['ganso, a] nm/f (Zool) goose; (fam) idiot

ganzúa [gan'θua] nf skeleton key

garabato [gara'βato] nm (escritura) scrawl, scribble

garaje [ga'raxe] nm garage

garantía [garan'tia] nf guarantee

garantizar [garanti'θar] vt to guarantee

garbanzo [gar'βanθo] nm chickpea (BRIT), garbanzo (US)

garfio ['garfjo] nm grappling iron

garganta [gar'ɣanta] nf (Anat) throat; (de botella) neck; **gargantilla** nf necklace

gárgaras ['garɣaras] nfpl: **hacer ~** to gargle

gargarear [garɣare'ar] (LAM) vi to gargle

garita [ga'rita] nf cabin, hut; (Mil) sentry box

garra ['garra] nf (de gato, Tec) claw; (de ave) talon; (fam: mano) hand, paw

garrafa [ga'rrafa] nf carafe, decanter

garrapata [garra'pata] nf tick

gas [gas] nm gas; **gases lacrimógenos** tear gas sg

gasa ['gasa] nf gauze

gaseosa [gase'osa] nf lemonade

gaseoso, -a [gase'oso, a] adj gassy, fizzy

gasoil [ga'soil] nm diesel (oil)

gasóleo [ga'soleo] nm = **gasoil**

gasolina [gaso'lina] nf petrol (BRIT), gas(oline) (US); **gasolinera** nf petrol (BRIT), gas (US) station

gastado, -a [gas'tado, a] adj (dinero) spent; (ropa) worn out; (usado: frase etc) trite

gastar [gas'tar] vt (dinero, tiempo) to spend; (fuerzas) to use up; (desperdiciar) to waste; (llevar) to wear; **gastarse** vr to wear out; (estropearse) to waste; **~ en** to spend on; **~ bromas** to crack jokes; **¿qué número gastas?** what size (shoe) do you take?

gasto ['gasto] nm (desembolso) expenditure, spending; (consumo, uso) use; **gastos** nmpl (desembolsos) expenses; (cargos) charges, costs

gastronomía [gastrono'mia] nf gastronomy

gatear [gate'ar] vi (andar a gatas) to go on all fours

gatillo [ga'tiʎo] nm (de arma de fuego) trigger; (de dentista) forceps

gato, -a ['gato, a] nm/f (gen) cat ▷ nm (Tec) jack; **andar a gatas** to go on all fours

gaucho ['gautʃo] nm gaucho

gaviota [ga'βjota] nf seagull

gay [ge] adj inv, nm gay, homosexual

gazpacho [gaθ'patʃo] nm gazpacho

gel [xel] nm: **~ de baño/ducha** bath/shower gel

gelatina [xela'tina] nf jelly; (polvos etc) gelatine

gema ['xema] nf gem

gemelo, -a [xe'melo, a] adj, nm/f twin; **gemelos** nmpl (de camisa) cufflinks; (prismáticos) field glasses, binoculars

gemido [xe'miðo] nm (quejido) moan, groan; (aullido) howl

Géminis ['xeminis] nm Gemini

gemir [xe'mir] vi (quejarse) to moan, groan; (aullar) to howl

generación [xenera'θjon] nf generation

general [xene'ral] adj general ▷ nm general; **por lo o en ~** in general; **Generalitat** nf Catalan parliament; **generalizar** vt to generalize; **generalizarse** vr to become generalized, spread

generar [xene'rar] vt to generate

género ['xenero] nm (clase) kind, sort; (tipo) type; (Bio) genus; (Ling) gender; (Com) material; **género humano** human race

generosidad [xenerosi'ðað] nf generosity; **generoso, -a** adj generous

genial [xe'njal] adj inspired; (idea) brilliant; (estupendo) wonderful

genio ['xenjo] nm (carácter) nature, disposition; (humor) temper; (facultad creadora) genius; **de mal ~** bad-tempered

genital [xeni'tal] adj genital; **genitales** nmpl genitals

genoma [xe'noma] nm genome

gente ['xente] nf (personas) people pl; (parientes) relatives pl

gentil [xen'til] adj (elegante) graceful; (encantador) charming

genuino, -a [xe'nwino, a] adj genuine

geografía [xeoɣra'fia] nf geography

geología [xeolo'xia] nf geology

geometría [xeome'tria] nf geometry

gerente [xe'rente] nmf (supervisor) manager; (jefe) director

geriatría [xeria'tria] nf (Med) geriatrics sg

germen ['xermen] nm germ

gesticular [xestiku'lar] vi to gesticulate; (hacer muecas) to grimace; **gesticulación** nf gesticulation; (mueca) grimace

gestión [xes'tjon] nf management; (diligencia, acción) negotiation

gesto ['xesto] nm (mueca) grimace; (ademán) gesture

Gibraltar [xiβral'tar] nm Gibraltar; **gibraltareño, -a** adj, nm/f Gibraltarian

gigante [xi'ɣante] adj, nm giant; **gigantesco, -a** adj gigantic

gilipollas [xili'poʎas] (fam) adj inv daft ▷ nmf inv wally

gimnasia [xim'nasja] nf gymnastics pl; **gimnasio** nm gymnasium; **gimnasta** nmf gymnast

ginebra [xi'neβra] nf gin

ginecólogo, -a [xine'koloɣo, a] nm/f gynaecologist

gira ['xira] nf tour, trip

girar [xi'rar] vt (dar la vuelta) to turn (around); (: rápidamente) to spin; (Com: giro postal) to draw; (: letra de cambio) to issue ▷ vi to turn (round); (rápido) to spin

girasol [xira'sol] nm sunflower

giratorio, -a [xira'torjo, a] adj revolving

giro ['xiro] nm (movimiento) turn, revolution; (Ling) expression; (Com) draft; **giro bancario/postal** bank draft/money order

gis [xis] (MÉX) nm chalk

gitano, -a [xi'tano, a] adj, nm/f gypsy

glacial [gla'θjal] *adj* icy, freezing
glaciar [gla'θjar] *nm* glacier
glándula ['glandula] *nf* gland
global [glo'βal] *adj* global; **globalización** *nf* globalization
globo ['gloβo] *nm* (*esfera*) globe, sphere; (*aerostato, juguete*) balloon
glóbulo ['gloβulo] *nm* globule; (*Anat*) corpuscle
gloria ['glorja] *nf* glory
glorieta [glo'rjeta] *nf* (*de jardín*) bower, arbour; (*plazoleta*) roundabout (BRIT), traffic circle (US)
glorioso, -a [glo'rjoso, a] *adj* glorious
glotón, -ona [glo'ton, ona] *adj* gluttonous, greedy ▷ *nm/f* glutton
glucosa [glu'kosa] *nf* glucose
gobernador, a [goβerna'ðor, a] *adj* governing ▷ *nm/f* governor; **gobernante** *adj* governing
gobernar [goβer'nar] *vt* (*dirigir*) to guide, direct; (*Pol*) to rule, govern ▷ *vi* to govern; (*Náut*) to steer
gobierno *etc* [go'βjerno] *vb* V **gobernar** ▷ *nm* (*Pol*) government; (*dirección*) guidance, direction; (*Náut*) steering
goce *etc* ['goθe] *vb* V **gozar** ▷ *nm* enjoyment
gol [gol] *nm* goal
golf [golf] *nm* golf
golfa ['golfa] (*fam!*) *nf* (*mujer*) slut, whore
golfo, -a ['golfo, a] *nm* (*Geo*) gulf ▷ *nm/f* (*fam: niño*) urchin; (*gamberro*) lout
golondrina [golon'drina] *nf* swallow
golosina [golo'sina] *nf* (*dulce*) sweet; **goloso, -a** *adj* sweet-toothed
golpe ['golpe] *nm* blow; (*de puño*) punch; (*de mano*) smack; (*de remo*) stroke; (*fig: choque*) clash; **no dar ~** to be bone idle; **de un ~** with one blow; **de ~** suddenly; **golpe (de estado)** coup d'état; **golpear** *vt, vi* to strike, knock; (*asestar*) to beat; (*de puño*) to punch; (*golpetear*) to tap
goma ['goma] *nf* (*caucho*) rubber; (*elástico*) elastic; (*una goma*) elastic band; **goma de borrar** eraser, rubber (BRIT); **goma espuma** foam rubber
gomina [go'mina] *nf* hair gel
gomita [go'mita] (RPL) *nf* rubber band
gordo, -a ['gorðo, a] *adj* (*gen*) fat; (*fam*) enormous; **el (premio) ~** (*en lotería*) first prize
gorila [go'rila] *nm* gorilla
gorra ['gorra] *nf* cap; (*de bebé*) bonnet; (*militar*) bearskin; **entrar de ~** (*fam*) to gatecrash; **ir de ~** to sponge
gorrión [go'rrjon] *nm* sparrow
gorro ['gorro] *nm* (*gen*) cap; (*de bebé, mujer*) bonnet
gorrón, -ona [go'rron, ona] *nm/f* scrounger; **gorronear** (*fam*) vi to scrounge
gota ['gota] *nf* (*gen*) drop; (*de sudor*) bead; (*Med*) gout; **gotear** vi to drip; (*lloviznar*) to drizzle; **gotera** *nf* leak
gozar [go'θar] vi to enjoy o.s.; **~ de** (*disfrutar*) to enjoy; (*poseer*) to possess
gr. *abr* (= *gramo, gramos*) g
grabación [graβa'θjon] *nf* recording
grabado [gra'βaðo] *nm* print, engraving
grabadora [graβa'ðora] *nf* tape-recorder; **grabadora de CD/DVD** CD/DVD writer
grabar [gra'βar] *vt* to engrave; (*discos, cintas*) to record
gracia ['graθja] *nf* (*encanto*) grace, gracefulness; (*humor*) humour, wit; **¡(muchas) ~s!** thanks (very much)!; **~s a** thanks to; **dar las ~s a algn por algo** to

thank sb for sth; **tener ~** (*chiste etc*) to be funny; **no me hace ~** I am not keen; **gracioso, -a** *adj* (*divertido*) funny, amusing; (*cómico*) comical ▷ *nm/f* (*Teatro*) comic character
grada ['graða] *nf* (*de escalera*) step; (*de anfiteatro*) tier, row; **gradas** *nfpl* (*Deporte: de estadio*) terraces
grado ['graðo] *nm* degree; (*de aceite, vino*) grade; (*grada*) step; (*Mil*) rank; **de buen ~** willingly; **grado centígrado/Fahrenheit** degree centigrade/Fahrenheit
graduación [graðwa'θjon] *nf* (*del alcohol*) proof, strength; (*Escol*) graduation; (*Mil*) rank
gradual [gra'ðwal] *adj* gradual
graduar [gra'ðwar] *vt* (*gen*) to graduate; (*Mil*) to commission; **graduarse** *vr* to graduate; **~se la vista** to have one's eyes tested
gráfica ['grafika] *nf* graph
gráfico, -a ['grafiko, a] *adj* graphic ▷ *nm* diagram; **gráficos** *nmpl* (*Inform*) graphics
grajo ['graxo] *nm* rook
gramática [gra'matika] *nf* grammar
gramo ['gramo] *nm* gramme (BRIT), gram (US)
gran [gran] *adj* V **grande**
grana ['grana] *nf* (*color, tela*) scarlet
granada [gra'naða] *nf* pomegranate; (*Mil*) grenade
granate [gra'nate] *adj* deep red
Gran Bretaña [-bre'taɲa] *nf* Great Britain
grande ['grande] (*antes de nmsg* **gran**) *adj* (*de tamaño*) big, large; (*alto*) tall; (*distinguido*) great; (*impresionante*) grand ▷ *nm* grandee
granel [gra'nel]: **a ~** (*Com*) in bulk
granero [gra'nero] *nm* granary, barn
granito [gra'nito] *nm* (*Agr*) small grain; (*roca*) granite
granizado [grani'θaðo] *nm* iced drink
granizar [grani'θar] vi to hail; **granizo** *nm* hail
granja ['granxa] *nf* (*gen*) farm; **granjero, -a** *nm/f* farmer
grano ['grano] *nm* grain; (*semilla*) seed; (*de café*) bean; (*Med*) pimple, spot
granuja [gra'nuxa] *nmf* rogue; (*golfillo*) urchin
grapa ['grapa] *nf* staple; (*Tec*) clamp; **grapadora** *nf* stapler
grasa ['grasa] *nf* (*gen*) grease; (*de cocinar*) fat, lard; (*sebo*) suet; (*mugre*) filth; **grasiento, -a** *adj* greasy; (*de aceite*) oily; **graso, -a** *adj* (*leche, queso, carne*) fatty; (*pelo, piel*) greasy
gratinar [grati'nar] *vt* to cook au gratin
gratis ['gratis] *adv* free
grato, -a ['grato, a] *adj* (*agradable*) pleasant, agreeable
gratuito, -a [gra'twito, a] *adj* (*gratis*) free; (*sin razón*) gratuitous
grave ['graβe] *adj* heavy; (*serio*) grave, serious; **gravedad** *nf* gravity
Grecia ['greθja] *nf* Greece
gremio ['gremjo] *nm* trade, industry
griego, -a ['grjeɣo, a] *adj, nm/f* Greek
grieta ['grjeta] *nf* crack
grifo ['grifo] (ESP) *nm* tap (BRIT), faucet (US)
grillo ['griʎo] *nm* (*Zool*) cricket
gripa ['gripa] (MÉX) *nf* flu, influenza
gripe ['gripe] *nf* flu, influenza; **gripe aviar** bird flu
gris [gris] *adj* (*color*) grey
gritar [gri'tar] *vt, vi* to shout, yell; **grito** *nm* shout, yell; (*de horror*) scream
grosella [gro'seʎa] *nf* (red)currant

grosero, -a [gro'sero, a] *adj (poco cortés)* rude, bad-mannered; *(ordinario)* vulgar, crude

grosor [gro'sor] *nm* thickness

grúa ['grua] *nf (Tec)* crane; *(de petróleo)* derrick

grueso, -a ['grweso, a] *adj* thick; *(persona)* stout ▷ *nm* bulk; **el ~ de** the bulk of

grulla ['gruʎa] *nf* crane

grumo ['grumo] *nm* clot, lump

gruñido [gru'niðo] *nm* grunt; *(de persona)* grumble

gruñir [gru'nir] *vi (animal)* to growl; *(persona)* to grumble

grupo ['grupo] *nm* group; *(Tec)* unit, set; **grupo de presión** pressure group; **grupo sanguíneo** blood group

gruta ['gruta] *nf* grotto

guacho, -a ['gwatʃo, a] *(cs) nm/f* homeless child

guajolote [gwaxo'lote] *(MÉX) nm* turkey

guante ['gwante] *nm* glove; **guantes de goma** rubber gloves; **guantera** *nf* glove compartment

guapo, -a ['gwapo, a] *adj* good-looking, attractive; *(elegante)* smart

guarda ['gwarða] *nmf (persona)* guard, keeper ▷ *nf (acto)* guarding; *(custodia)* custody; **guarda jurado** (armed) security guard; **guardabarros** *nm inv* mudguard *(BRIT)*, fender *(US)*; **guardabosques** *nm inv* gamekeeper; **guardacostas** *nm inv* coastguard vessel ▷ *nmf* guardian, protector; **guardaespaldas** *nmf inv* bodyguard; **guardameta** *nmf* goalkeeper; **guardar** *vt (gen)* to keep; *(vigilar)* to guard, watch over; *(dinero: ahorrar)* to save; **guardarse** *vr (preservarse)* to protect o.s.; *(evitar)* to avoid; **guardar cama** to stay in bed; **guardarropa** *nm (armario)* wardrobe; *(en establecimiento público)* cloakroom

guardería [gwarðe'ria] *nf* nursery

guardia ['gwarðja] *nf (Mil)* guard; *(cuidado)* care, custody ▷ *nmf* guard; *(policía)* policeman(-woman); **estar de ~** to be on guard; **montar ~** to mount guard; **Guardia Civil** Civil Guard

guardián, -ana [gwar'ðjan, ana] *nm/f (gen)* guardian, keeper

guarida [gwa'riða] *nf (de animal)* den, lair; *(refugio)* refuge

guarnición [gwarni'θjon] *nf (de vestimenta)* trimming; *(de piedra)* mount; *(Culin)* garnish; *(arneses)* harness; *(Mil)* garrison

guarro, -a ['gwarro, a] *nm/f* pig

guasa ['gwasa] *nf* joke; **guasón, -ona** *adj (bromista)* joking ▷ *nm/f* wit; joker

Guatemala [gwate'mala] *nf* Guatemala

guay [gwai] *(fam) adj* super, great

güero, -a ['gwero, a] *(MÉX) adj* blond(e)

guerra ['gerra] *nf* war; **dar ~** to annoy; **guerra civil** civil war; **guerra fría** cold war; **guerrero, -a** *adj (carácter)* warlike ▷ *nm/f* warrior

guerrilla [ge'rriʎa] *nf* guerrilla warfare; *(tropas)* guerrilla band o group

guía *etc* ['gia] *vb* V **guiar** ▷ *nmf (persona)* guide; *(nf: libro)* guidebook; **guía telefónica** telephone directory; **guía turística** tourist guide

guiar [gi'ar] *vt* to guide, direct; *(Auto)* to steer; **guiarse** *vr*: **~se por** to be guided by

guinda ['ginda] *nf* morello cherry

guindilla [gin'diʎa] *nf* chilli pepper

guiñar [gi'nar] *vt* to wink

guión [gi'on] *nm (Ling)* hyphen, dash; *(Cine)* script; **guionista** *nmf* scriptwriter

guiri ['giri] *(ESP: fam, pey) nmf* foreigner

guirnalda [gir'nalda] *nf* garland

guisado [gi'saðo] *nm* stew

guisante [gi'sante] *nm* pea

guisar [gi'sar] *vt, vi* to cook; **guiso** *nm* cooked dish

guitarra [gi'tarra] *nf* guitar

gula ['gula] *nf* gluttony, greed

gusano [gu'sano] *nm* worm; *(lombriz)* earthworm

gustar [gus'tar] *vt* to taste, sample ▷ *vi* to please, be pleasing; **~ de algo** to like o enjoy sth; **me gustan las uvas** I like grapes; **le gusta nadar** she likes o enjoys swimming

gusto ['gusto] *nm (sentido, sabor)* taste; *(placer)* pleasure; **tiene ~ a menta** it tastes of mint; **tener buen ~** to have good taste; **coger el o tomar ~ a algo** to take a liking to sth; **sentirse a ~** to feel at ease; **mucho ~ (en conocerle)** pleased to meet you; **el ~ es mío** the pleasure is mine; **con ~** willingly, gladly

h

ha vb V **haber**
haba ['aβa] nf bean
Habana [a'βana] nf: **la ~** Havana
habano [a'βano] nm Havana cigar
habéis vb V **haber**

○ **PALABRA CLAVE**

haber [a'βer] vb aux **1** (tiempos compuestos) to have; **había comido** I had eaten; **antes/después de haberlo visto** before seeing/after seeing o having seen it
2: **¡haberlo dicho antes!** you should have said so before!
3: **haber de:** he de hacerlo I have to do it; **ha de llegar mañana** it should arrive tomorrow
▷ vb impers **1** (existencia: sg) there is; (: pl) there are; **hay un hermano/dos hermanos** there is one brother/ there are two brothers; **¿cuánto hay de aquí a Sucre?** how far is it from here to Sucre?
2 (obligación): **hay que hacer algo** something must be done; **hay que apuntarlo para acordarse** you have to write it down to remember
3: **¡hay que ver!** well I never!
4: **¡no hay de o por (LAM) qué!** don't mention it!, not at all!
5: **¿qué hay?** (¿qué pasa?) what's up?, what's the matter?; (¿qué tal?) how's it going?
▷ vb: **he aquí unas sugerencias** here are some suggestions; **no hay cintas blancas pero sí las hay rojas** there aren't any white ribbons but there are some red ones
▷ nm (en cuenta) credit side; **haberes** nmpl assets; **¿cuánto tengo en el haber?** how much do I have in my account?; **tiene varias novelas en su haber** he has several novels to his credit
haberse vr: **habérselas con algn** to have it out with sb

habichuela [aβi'tʃwela] nf kidney bean
hábil ['aβil] adj (listo) clever, smart; (capaz) fit, capable; (experto) expert; **día ~** working day; **habilidad** nf skill, ability

habitación [aβita'θjon] nf (cuarto) room; (Bio: morada) habitat; **habitación doble o de matrimonio** double room; **habitación individual o sencilla** single room
habitante [aβi'tante] nmf inhabitant
habitar [aβi'tar] vt (residir en) to inhabit; (ocupar) to occupy ▷ vi to live
hábito ['aβito] nm habit
habitual [aβi'twal] adj usual
habituar [aβi'twar] vt to accustom; **habituarse** vr: **~se a** to get used to
habla ['aβla] nf (capacidad de hablar) speech; (idioma) language; (dialecto) dialect; **perder el ~** to become speechless; **de ~ francesa** French-speaking; **estar al ~** to be in contact; (Tel) to be on the line; **¡González al ~!** (Tel) González speaking!
hablador, a [aβla'ðor, a] adj talkative ▷ nm/f chatterbox
habladuría [aβlaðu'ria] nf rumour; **habladurías** nfpl gossip sg
hablante [a'βlante] adj speaking ▷ nmf speaker
hablar [a'βlar] vt to speak, talk ▷ vi to speak; **hablarse** vr to speak to each other; **~ con** to speak to; **~ de** to speak o about; **¡ni ~!** it's out of the question!; **"se habla inglés"** "English spoken here"
habré etc [a'βre] vb V **haber**
hacendado [aθen'daðo] (LAM) nm rancher, farmer
hacendoso, -a [aθen'doso, a] adj industrious

○ **PALABRA CLAVE**

hacer [a'θer] vt **1** (fabricar, producir) to make; (construir) to build; **hacer una película/un ruido** to make a film/ noise; **el guisado lo hice yo** I made o cooked the stew
2 (ejecutar: trabajo etc) to do; **hacer la colada** to do the washing; **hacer la comida** to do the cooking; **¿qué haces?** what are you doing?; **hacer el malo o el papel del malo** (Teatro) to play the villain
3 (estudios, algunos deportes) to do; **hacer español/ económicas** to do o study Spanish/economics; **hacer yoga/gimnasia** to do yoga/go to gym
4 (transformar, incidir en): **esto lo hará más difícil** this will make it more difficult; **salir te hará sentir mejor** going out will make you feel better
5 (cálculo): **2 y 2 hacen 4** 2 and 2 make 4; **éste hace 100** this one makes 100
6 (+ sub): **esto hará que ganemos** this will make us win; **harás que no quiera venir** you'll stop him wanting to come
7 (como sustituto de vb) to do; **él bebió y yo hice lo mismo** he drank and I did likewise
8 no hace más que criticar all he does is criticize
▷ vb semi-aux (directo): **hacer +infin: les hice venir** I made o had them come; **hacer trabajar a los demás** to get others to work
▷ vi **1 haz como que no lo sabes** act as if you don't know
2 (ser apropiado): **si os hace** if it's alright with you
3 hacer de: **hacer de Otelo** to play Othello
▷ vb impers **1 hace calor/frío** it's hot/cold; V tb **bueno, sol, tiempo**
2 (tiempo): **hace 3 años** 3 years ago; **hace un mes que voy/no voy** I've been going/I haven't been for a month
3 ¿cómo has hecho para llegar tan rápido? how did you manage to get here so quickly?
hacerse vr **1** (volverse) to become; **se hicieron amigos**

they became friends
2 (*acostumbrarse*): **hacerse a** to get used to
3 se hace con huevos y leche it's made out of eggs and milk; **eso no se hace** that's not done
4 (*obtener*): **hacerse de** o **con algo** to get hold of sth
5 (*fingirse*): **hacerse el sueco** to turn a deaf ear

hacha ['atʃa] *nf* axe; (*antorcha*) torch
hachís [a'tʃis] *nm* hashish
hacia ['aθja] *prep* (*en dirección de*) towards; (*cerca de*) near; (*actitud*) towards; **~ adelante/atrás** forwards/backwards; **~ arriba/abajo** up(wards)/down(wards); **~ mediodía/las cinco** about noon/five
hacienda [a'θjenda] *nf* (*propiedad*) property; (*finca*) farm; (LAM: *rancho*) ranch; (**Ministerio de** H~ Exchequer (BRIT), Treasury Department (US); **hacienda pública** public finance
hada ['aða] *nf* fairy
hago *etc vb* V **hacer**
Haití [ai'ti] *nm* Haiti
halagar [ala'ɣar] *vt* to flatter
halago [a'laɣo] *nm* flattery
halcón [al'kon] *nm* falcon, hawk
hallar [a'ʎar] *vt* (*gen*) to find; (*descubrir*) to discover; (*toparse con*) to run into; **hallarse** *vr* to be (situated)
halterofilia [altero'filja] *nf* weightlifting
hamaca [a'maka] *nf* hammock
hambre ['ambre] *nf* hunger; (*plaga*) famine; (*deseo*) longing; **tener ~** to be hungry; **¡me muero de ~!** I'm starving!; **hambriento, -a** *adj* hungry, starving
hamburguesa [ambur'ɣesa] *nf* hamburger; **hamburguesería** *nf* burger bar
han *vb* V **haber**
harapos [a'rapos] *nmpl* rags
haré *vb* V **hacer**
harina [a'rina] *nf* flour; **harina de maíz** cornflour (BRIT), cornstarch (US); **harina de trigo** wheat flour
hartar [ar'tar] *vt* to satiate, glut; (*fig*) to tire, sicken; **hartarse** *vr* (*de comida*) to fill o.s., gorge o.s.; (*cansarse*): **~se (de)** to get fed up (with); **harto, -a** *adj* (*lleno*) full; (*cansado*) fed up ▷ *adv* (*bastante*) enough; (*muy*) very; **estar harto de hacer algo/de algn** to be fed up of doing sth/with sb
has *vb* V **haber**
hasta ['asta] *adv* even ▷ *prep* (*alcanzando a*) as far as; up to; down to; (*de tiempo: a tal hora*) till, until; (*antes de*) before ▷ *conj*: **~ que ...** until; **~ luego/el sábado** see you soon/on Saturday; **~ ahora** (*al despedirse*) see you in a minute; **~ pronto** see you soon
hay *vb* V **haber**
Haya ['aja] *nf*: **la ~** The Hague
haya *etc* ['aja] *vb* V **haber** ▷ *nf* beech tree
haz [aθ] *vb* V **hacer** ▷ *nm* (*de luz*) beam
hazaña [a'θaɲa] *nf* feat, exploit
hazmerreír [aθmerre'ir] *nm inv* laughing stock
he *vb* V **haber**
hebilla [e'βiʎa] *nf* buckle, clasp
hebra ['eβra] *nf* thread; (Bot: *fibra*) fibre, grain
hebreo, -a [e'βreo, a] *adj, nm/f* Hebrew ▷ *nm* (Ling) Hebrew
hechizar [etʃi'θar] *vt* to cast a spell on, bewitch
hechizo [e'tʃiθo] *nm* witchcraft, magic; (*acto de magia*) spell, charm
hecho, -a ['etʃo, a] *pp de* **hacer** ▷ *adj* (*carne*) done; (Costura) ready-to-wear ▷ *nm* deed, act; (*dato*) fact;

(*cuestión*) matter; (*suceso*) event ▷ *excl* agreed!, done!; **de ~** in fact, as a matter of fact; **el ~ es que ...** the fact is that ...; **¡bien ~!** well done!
hechura [e'tʃura] *nf* (*forma*) form, shape; (*de persona*) build
hectárea [ek'tarea] *nf* hectare
helada [e'laða] *nf* frost
heladera [ela'ðera] (LAM) *nf* (*refrigerador*) refrigerator
helado, -a [e'lado, a] *adj* frozen; (*glacial*) icy; (*fig*) chilly, cold ▷ *nm* ice cream
helar [e'lar] *vt* to freeze, ice (up); (*dejar atónito*) to amaze; (*desalentar*) to discourage ▷ *vi* to freeze; **helarse** *vr* to freeze
helecho [e'letʃo] *nm* fern
hélice ['eliθe] *nf* (Tec) propeller
helicóptero [eli'koptero] *nm* helicopter
hembra ['embra] *nf* (Bot, Zool) female; (*mujer*) woman; (Tec) nut
hemorragia [emo'rraxja] *nf* haemorrhage
hemorroides [emo'rroiðes] *nfpl* haemorrhoids, piles
hemos *vb* V **haber**
heno ['eno] *nm* hay
heredar [ere'ðar] *vt* to inherit; **heredero, -a** *nm/f* heir(ess)
hereje [e'rexe] *nmf* heretic
herencia [e'renθja] *nf* inheritance
herida [e'riða] *nf* wound, injury; V *tb* **herido**
herido, -a [e'riðo, a] *adj* injured, wounded ▷ *nm/f* casualty
herir [e'rir] *vt* to wound, injure; (*fig*) to offend
hermanastro, -a [erma'nastro, a] *nm/f* stepbrother/sister
hermandad [erman'dað] *nf* brotherhood
hermano, -a [er'mano, a] *nm/f* brother/sister; **hermano(-a) gemelo(-a)**, twin brother/sister; **hermano(-a) político(-a)**, brother-in-law/sister-in-law
hermético, -a [er'metiko, a] *adj* hermetic; (*fig*) watertight
hermoso, -a [er'moso, a] *adj* beautiful, lovely; (*estupendo*) splendid; (*guapo*) handsome; **hermosura** *nf* beauty
hernia ['ernja] *nf* hernia; **hernia discal** slipped disc
héroe ['eroe] *nm* hero
heroína [ero'ina] *nf* (*mujer*) heroine; (*droga*) heroin
herradura [erra'ðura] *nf* horseshoe
herramienta [erra'mjenta] *nf* tool
herrero [e'rrero] *nm* blacksmith
hervidero [erβi'ðero] *nm* (*fig*) swarm; (Pol *etc*) hotbed
hervir [er'βir] *vt* to boil; (*burbujear*) to bubble; **~ a fuego lento** to simmer; **hervor** *nm* boiling; (*fig*) ardour, fervour
heterosexual [eterosek'swal] *adj* heterosexual
hice *etc vb* V **hacer**
hidratante [iðra'tante] *adj*: **crema ~** moisturizing cream, moisturizer; **hidratar** *vt* (*piel*) to moisturize; **hidrato** *nm* hydrate; **hidratos de carbono** carbohydrates
hidráulico, -a [i'ðrauliko, a] *adj* hydraulic
hidro... [iðro] *prefijo* hydro..., water-...;
hidroeléctrico, -a *adj* hydroelectric; **hidrógeno** *nm* hydrogen
hiedra ['jeðra] *nf* ivy
hiel [jel] *nf* gall, bile; (*fig*) bitterness
hiela *etc vb* V **helar**
hielo ['jelo] *nm* (*gen*) ice; (*escarcha*) frost; (*fig*) coldness,

reserve

hiena ['jena] nf hyena

hierba ['jerβa] nf (pasto) grass; (Culin, Med: planta) herb; **mala ~** weed; (fig) evil influence; **hierbabuena** nf mint

hierro ['jerro] nm (metal) iron; (objeto) iron object

hígado ['iɣaðo] nm liver

higiene [i'xjene] nf hygiene; **higiénico, -a** adj hygienic

higo ['iɣo] nm fig; **higo seco** dried fig; **higuera** nf fig tree

hijastro, -a [i'xastro, a] nm/f stepson/daughter

hijo, -a ['ixo, a] nm/f son/daughter, child; **hijos** nmpl children, sons and daughters; **hijo adoptivo** adopted child; **hijo de papá/mamá** daddy's/mummy's boy; **hijo de puta** (fam!) bastard (!), son of a bitch (!); **hijo/a político/a** son-/daughter-in-law

hilera [i'lera] nf row, file

hilo ['ilo] nm thread; (Bot) fibre; (metal) wire; (de agua) trickle, thin stream

hilvanar [ilβa'nar] vt (Costura) to tack (BRIT), baste (US); (fig) to do hurriedly

himno ['imno] nm hymn; **himno nacional** national anthem

hincapié [inka'pje] nm: **hacer ~ en** to emphasize

hincar [in'kar] vt to drive (in), thrust (in)

hincha ['intʃa] (fam) nmf fan

hinchado, -a [in'tʃaðo, a] adj (gen) swollen; (persona) pompous

hinchar [in'tʃar] vt (gen) to swell; (inflar) to blow up, inflate; (fig) to exaggerate; **hincharse** vr (inflarse) to swell up; (fam: de comer) to stuff o.s.; **hinchazón** nf (Med) swelling; (altivez) arrogance

hinojo [i'noxo] nm fennel

hipermercado [ipermer'kaðo] nm hypermarket, superstore

hípico, -a ['ipiko, a] adj horse cpd

hipnotismo [ipno'tismo] nm hypnotism; **hipnotizar** vt to hypnotize

hipo ['ipo] nm hiccups pl

hipocresía [ipokre'sia] nf hypocrisy; **hipócrita** adj hypocritical ▷ nmf hypocrite

hipódromo [i'poðromo] nm racetrack

hipopótamo [ipo'potamo] nm hippopotamus

hipoteca [ipo'teka] nf mortgage

hipótesis [i'potesis] nf inv hypothesis

hispánico, -a [is'paniko, a] adj Hispanic

hispano, -a [is'pano, a] adj Hispanic, Spanish, Hispano- ▷ nm/f Spaniard; **Hispanoamérica** nf Latin America; **hispanoamericano, -a** adj, nm/f Latin American

histeria [is'terja] nf hysteria

historia [is'torja] nf history; (cuento) story, tale; **historias** nfpl (chismes) gossip sg; **dejarse de ~s** to come to the point; **pasar a la ~** to go down in history; **historiador, a** nm/f historian; **historial** nm (profesional) curriculum vitae, C.V.; (Med) case history; **histórico, -a** adj historical; (memorable) historic

historieta [isto'rjeta] nf tale, anecdote; (dibujos) comic strip

hito ['ito] nm (fig) landmark

hizo vb V hacer

hocico [o'θiko] nm snout

hockey ['xokei] nm hockey; **hockey sobre hielo/patines** ice/roller hockey

hogar [o'ɣar] nm fireplace, hearth; (casa) home;

(vida familiar) home life; **hogareño, -a** adj home cpd; (persona) home-loving

hoguera [o'ɣera] nf (gen) bonfire

hoja ['oxa] nf (gen) leaf; (de flor) petal; (de papel) sheet; (página) page; **hoja de afeitar** (LAM) razor blade; **hoja electrónica** o **de cálculo** spreadsheet; **hoja informativa** leaflet, handout

hojalata [oxa'lata] nf tin(plate)

hojaldre [o'xaldre] nm (Culin) puff pastry

hojear [oxe'ar] vt to leaf through, turn the pages of

hojuela [o'xwela] (MÉX) nf flake

hola ['ola] excl hello!

holá [o'la] (RPL) excl hello!

Holanda [o'landa] nf Holland; **holandés, -esa** adj Dutch ▷ nm/f Dutchman(-woman) ▷ nm (Ling) Dutch

holgado, -a [ol'ɣaðo, a] adj (ropa) loose, baggy; (rico) comfortable

holgar [ol'ɣar] vi (descansar) to rest; (sobrar) to be superfluous

holgazán, -ana [olɣa'θan, ana] adj idle, lazy ▷ nm/f loafer

hollín [o'ʎin] nm soot

hombre ['ombre] nm (gen) man; (raza humana): **el ~** man(kind) ▷ excl: **¡sí ~!** (claro) of course!; (para énfasis) man, old boy; **hombre de negocios** businessman; **hombre de pro** honest man; **hombre-rana** frogman; **hombrera** [om'brera] nf shoulder strap

hombro ['ombro] nm shoulder

homenaje [ome'naxe] nm (gen) homage; (tributo) tribute

homicida [omi'θiða] adj homicidal ▷ nmf murderer; **homicidio** nm murder, homicide

homologar [omolo'ɣar] vt (Com: productos, tamaños) to standardize

homólogo, -a [o'moloɣo, a] nm/f: **su** etc **~** his etc counterpart o opposite number

homosexual [omosek'swal] adj, nmf homosexual

honda ['onda] (cs) nf catapult

hondo, -a ['ondo, a] adj deep; **lo ~** the depth(s) pl, the bottom; **hondonada** nf hollow, depression; (cañón) ravine

Honduras [on'duras] nf Honduras

hondureño, -a [ondu'reɲo, a] adj, nm/f Honduran

honestidad [onesti'ðað] nf purity, chastity; (decencia) decency; **honesto, -a** adj chaste; decent; (justo) just

hongo ['ongo] nm (Bot: gen) fungus; (: comestible) mushroom; (: venenoso) toadstool

honor [o'nor] nm (gen) honour; **en ~ a la verdad** to be fair; **honorable** adj honourable

honorario, -a [ono'rarjo, a] adj honorary; **honorarios** nmpl fees

honra ['onra] nf (gen) honour; (renombre) good name; **honradez** nf honesty; (de persona) integrity; **honrado, -a** adj honest, upright; **honrar** [on'rar] vt to honour

hora ['ora] nf (una hora) hour; (tiempo) time; **¿qué ~ es?** what time is it?; **¿a qué ~?** at what time?; **media ~** half an hour; **a la ~ de recreo** at playtime; **a primera ~** first thing (in the morning); **a última ~** at the last moment; **a altas ~s** in the small hours; **¡a buena ~!** about time too!; **pedir ~** to make an appointment; **dar la ~** to strike the hour; **horas de oficina/trabajo** office/working hours; **horas de visita** visiting times; **horas extras** o **extraordinarias** overtime sg; **horas pico** (LAM) rush o peak hours; **horas punta** (ESP) rush hours

horario, -a [o'rarjo, a] *adj* hourly, hour *cpd* ▷ *nm*
timetable; **horario comercial** business hours *pl*
horca ['orka] *nf* gallows *sg*
horcajadas [orka'xaðas]: **a ~** *adv* astride
horchata [or'tʃata] *nf* cold drink made from tiger nuts
and water, tiger nut milk
horizontal [oriθon'tal] *adj* horizontal
horizonte [ori'θonte] *nm* horizon
horma ['orma] *nf* mould
hormiga [or'miɣa] *nf* ant; **hormigas** *nfpl* (*Med*) pins
and needles
hormigón [ormi'ɣon] *nm* concrete; **hormigón
armado/pretensado** reinforced/prestressed
concrete; **hormigonera** *nf* cement mixer
hormigueo [ormi'ɣeo] *nm* (*comezón*) itch
hormona [or'mona] *nf* hormone
hornillo [or'niʎo] *nm* (*cocina*) portable stove; **hornillo
de gas** gas ring
horno ['orno] *nm* (*Culin*) oven; (*Tec*) furnace; **alto ~**
blast furnace
horóscopo [o'roskopo] *nm* horoscope
horquilla [or'kiʎa] *nf* hairpin; (*Agr*) pitchfork
horrendo, -a [o'rrendo, a] *adj* horrendous, frightful
horrible [o'rriβle] *adj* horrible, dreadful
horripilante [orripi'lante] *adj* hair-raising,
horrifying
horror [o'rror] *nm* horror, dread; (*atrocidad*) atrocity;
¡qué ~! (*fam*) how awful!; **horrorizar** *vt* to horrify,
frighten; **horrorizarse** *vr* to be horrified; **horroroso,
-a** *adj* horrifying, ghastly
hortaliza [orta'liθa] *nf* vegetable
hortelano, -a [orte'lano, a] *nm/f* (market) gardener
hortera [or'tera] (*fam*) *adj* tacky
hospedar [ospe'ðar] *vt* to put up; **hospedarse** *vr*
to stay, lodge
hospital [ospi'tal] *nm* hospital
hospitalario, -a [ospita'larjo, a] *adj* (*acogedor*)
hospitable; **hospitalidad** *nf* hospitality
hostal [os'tal] *nm* small hotel
hostelería [ostele'ria] *nf* hotel business o trade
hostia ['ostja] *nf* (*Rel*) host, consecrated wafer;
(*fam!: golpe*) whack, punch ▷ *excl* (*fam!*): **¡~(s)!** damn!
hostil [os'til] *adj* hostile
hotdog [ot'dog] (*LAM*) *nm* hot dog
hotel [o'tel] *nm* hotel; **hotelero, -a** *adj* hotel *cpd*
▷ *nm/f* hotelier
hoy [oi] *adv* (*este día*) today; (*la actualidad*) now(adays)
▷ *nm* present time; **~ (en) día** now(adays)
hoyo ['ojo] *nm* hole, pit
hoz [oθ] *nf* sickle
hube *etc vb* V **haber**
hucha ['utʃa] *nf* money box
hueco, -a ['weko, a] *adj* (*vacío*) hollow, empty;
(*resonante*) booming ▷ *nm* hollow, cavity
huelga *etc* ['welɣa] *vb* V **holgar** ▷ *nf* strike;
declararse en ~ to go on strike, come out on strike;
huelga de hambre hunger strike; **huelga general**
general strike
huelguista [wel'ɣista] *nmf* striker
huella ['weʎa] *nf* (*pisada*) tread; (*marca del paso*)
footprint, footstep; (: *de animal, máquina*) track; **huella
dactilar** fingerprint
huelo *etc vb* V **oler**
huérfano, -a ['werfano, a] *adj* orphan(ed) ▷ *nm/f*
orphan
huerta ['werta] *nf* market garden; (*en Murcia y*

Valencia) irrigated region
huerto ['werto] *nm* kitchen garden; (*de árboles
frutales*) orchard
hueso ['weso] *nm* (*Anat*) bone; (*de fruta*) stone
huésped ['wespeð] *nmf* guest
hueva ['weβa] *nf* roe
huevera [we'βera] *nf* eggcup
huevo ['weβo] *nm* egg; **huevo a la copa** (*cs*) soft-
boiled egg; **huevo duro/escalfado** hard-boiled/
poached egg; **huevo estrellado** (*LAM*) fried egg; **huevo
frito** (*ESP*) fried egg; **huevo pasado por agua** soft-
boiled egg; **huevos revueltos** scrambled eggs; **huevo
tibio** (*MÉX*) soft-boiled egg
huida [u'iða] *nf* escape, flight
huir [u'ir] *vi* (*escapar*) to flee, escape; (*evitar*) to avoid
hule ['ule] *nm* oilskin; (*MÉX: goma*) rubber
hulera [u'lera] (*MÉX*) *nf* catapult
humanidad [umani'ðað] *nf* (*género humano*)
man(kind); (*cualidad*) humanity
humanitario, -a [umani'tarjo, a] *adj*
humanitarian
humano, -a [u'mano, a] *adj* (*gen*) human;
(*humanitario*) humane ▷ *nm* human; **ser ~** human
being
humareda [uma'reða] *nf* cloud of smoke
humedad [ume'ðað] *nf* (*de clima*) humidity; (*de
pared etc*) dampness; **a prueba de ~** damp-proof;
humedecer *vt* to moisten, wet; **humedecerse** *vr*
to get wet
húmedo, -a ['umeðo, a] *adj* (*mojado*) damp, wet;
(*tiempo etc*) humid
humilde [u'milde] *adj* humble, modest
humillación [umiʎa'θjon] *nf* humiliation;
humillante *adj* humiliating
humillar [umi'ʎar] *vt* to humiliate
humo ['umo] *nm* (*de fuego*) smoke; (*gas nocivo*) fumes
pl; (*vapor*) steam, vapour; **humos** *nmpl* (*fig*) conceit *sg*
humor [u'mor] *nm* (*disposición*) mood, temper; (*lo que
divierte*) humour; **de buen/mal ~** in a good/bad mood;
humorista *nmf* comic; **humorístico, -a** *adj* funny,
humorous
hundimiento [undi'mjento] *nm* (*gen*) sinking;
(*colapso*) collapse
hundir [un'dir] *vt* to sink; (*edificio, plan*) to ruin,
destroy; **hundirse** *vr* to sink, collapse
húngaro, -a ['ungaro, a] *adj, nm/f* Hungarian
Hungría [un'gria] *nf* Hungary
huracán [ura'kan] *nm* hurricane
huraño, -a [u'raɲo, a] *adj* (*antisocial*) unsociable
hurgar [ur'ɣar] *vt* to poke, jab; (*remover*) to stir (up);
hurgarse *vr*: **~se (las narices)** to pick one's nose
hurón, -ona [u'ron, ona] *nm* (*Zool*) ferret
hurtadillas [urta'ðiʎas]: **a ~** *adv* stealthily, on the sly
hurtar [ur'tar] *vt* to steal; **hurto** *nm* theft, stealing
husmear [usme'ar] *vt* (*oler*) to sniff out, scent; (*fam*)
to pry into
huyo *etc vb* V **huir**

I

iba etc vb V **ir**

ibérico, -a [i'βeriko, a] adj Iberian

iberoamericano, -a [iβeroameri'kano, a] adj, nm/f Latin American

Ibiza [i'βiθa] nf Ibiza

iceberg [iθe'βer] nm iceberg

icono [i'kono] nm ikon, icon

ida ['iða] nf going, departure; **~ y vuelta** round trip, return

idea [i'ðea] nf idea; **no tengo la menor ~** I haven't a clue

ideal [iðe'al] adj, nm ideal; **idealista** nmf idealist; **idealizar** vt to idealize

ídem ['iðem] pron ditto

idéntico, -a [i'ðentiko, a] adj identical

identidad [iðenti'ðað] nf identity

identificación [iðentifika'θjon] nf identification

identificar [iðentifi'kar] vt to identify; **identificarse** vr: **~se con** to identify with

ideología [iðeolo'xia] nf ideology

idilio [i'ðiljo] nm love-affair

idioma [i'ðjoma] nm (gen) language

idiota [i'ðjota] adj idiotic ⊳ nmf idiot

ídolo [i'ðolo] nm (tb fig) idol

idóneo, -a [i'ðoneo, a] adj suitable

iglesia [i'ɣlesja] nf church

ignorante [iɣno'rante] adj ignorant, uninformed ⊳ nmf ignoramus

ignorar [iɣno'rar] vt not to know, be ignorant of; (no hacer caso a) to ignore

igual [i'ɣwal] adj (gen) equal; (similar) like, similar; (mismo) (the) same; (constante) constant; (temperatura) even ⊳ nmf like; **~ que** like, the same as; **me da** o **es ~** I don't care; **son ~es** they're the same; **al ~ que** (prep, conj) like, just like

igualar [iɣwa'lar] vt (gen) to equalize, make equal; (allanar, nivelar) to level (off), even (out); **igualarse** vr (platos de balanza) to balance out

igualdad [iɣwal'dað] nf equality; (similaridad) sameness; (uniformidad) uniformity

igualmente [iɣwal'mente] adv equally; (también) also, likewise ⊳ excl the same to you!

ilegal [ile'ɣal] adj illegal

ilegítimo, -a [ile'xitimo, a] adj illegitimate

ileso, -a [i'leso, a] adj unhurt

ilimitado, -a [ilimi'taðo, a] adj unlimited

iluminación [ilumina'θjon] nf illumination; (alumbrado) lighting

iluminar [ilumi'nar] vt to illuminate, light (up); (fig) to enlighten

ilusión [ilu'sjon] nf illusion; (quimera) delusion; (esperanza) hope; **hacerse ilusiones** to build up one's hopes; **ilusionado, -a** adj excited; **ilusionar** vi: **le ilusiona ir de vacaciones** he's looking forward to going on holiday; **ilusionarse** vr: **ilusionarse (con)** to get excited (about)

iluso, -a [i'luso, a] adj easily deceived ⊳ nm/f dreamer

ilustración [ilustra'θjon] nf illustration; (saber) learning, erudition; **la I~** the Enlightenment; **ilustrado, -a** adj illustrated; learned

ilustrar [ilus'trar] vt to illustrate; (instruir) to instruct; (explicar) to explain, make clear

ilustre [i'lustre] adj famous, illustrious

imagen [i'maxen] nf (gen); (dibujo) picture

imaginación [imaxina'θjon] nf imagination

imaginar [imaxi'nar] vt (gen) to imagine; (idear) to think up; (suponer) to suppose; **imaginarse** vr to imagine; **imaginario, -a** adj imaginary; **imaginativo, -a** adj imaginative

imán [i'man] nm magnet

imbécil [im'beθil] nmf imbecile, idiot

imitación [imita'θjon] nf imitation; **de ~** imitation cpd

imitar [imi'tar] vt to imitate; (parodiar, remedar) to mimic, ape

impaciente [impa'θjente] adj impatient; (nervioso) anxious

impacto [im'pakto] nm impact

impar [im'par] adj odd

imparcial [impar'θjal] adj impartial, fair

impecable [impe'kaβle] adj impeccable

impedimento [impeðim'ento] nm impediment, obstacle

impedir [impe'ðir] vt (obstruir) to impede, obstruct; (estorbar) to prevent; **~ a algn hacer** o **que algn haga algo** to prevent sb (from) doing sth, stop sb doing sth

imperativo, -a [impera'tiβo, a] adj (urgente, Ling) imperative

imperdible [imper'ðiβle] nm safety pin

imperdonable [imperðo'naβle] adj unforgivable, inexcusable

imperfecto, -a [imper'fekto, a] adj imperfect

imperio [im'perjo] nm empire; (autoridad) rule, authority; (fig) pride, haughtiness

impermeable [imperme'aβle] adj waterproof ⊳ nm raincoat, mac (BRIT)

impersonal [imperso'nal] adj impersonal

impertinente [imperti'nente] adj impertinent

ímpetu ['impetu] nm (impulso) impetus, impulse; (impetuosidad) impetuosity; (violencia) violence

implantar [implan'tar] vt to introduce

implemento [imple'mento] nm (LAM) tool, implement

implicar [impli'kar] vt to involve; (entrañar) to imply

implícito, -a [im'pliθito, a] adj (tácito) implicit; (sobreentendido) implied

imponente [impo'nente] adj (impresionante) impressive, imposing; (solemne) grand

imponer [impo'ner] vt (gen) to impose; (exigir) to exact; **imponerse** vr to assert o.s.; (prevalecer) to prevail; **imponible** adj (Com) taxable

impopular [impopu'lar] adj unpopular

importación [importa'θjon] nf (acto) importing; (mercancías) imports pl

importancia [impor'tanθja] nf importance; (valor) value, significance; (extensión) size, magnitude; **no tiene ~** it's nothing; **importante** adj important; valuable, significant

importar [impor'tar] vt (del extranjero) to import; (costar) to amount to ▷ vi to be important, matter; **me importa un rábano** I couldn't care less; **no importa** it doesn't matter; **¿le importa que fume?** do you mind if I smoke?

importe [im'porte] nm (total) amount; (valor) value

imposible [impo'siβle] adj (gen) impossible; (insoportable) unbearable, intolerable

imposición [imposi'θjon] nf imposition; (Com: impuesto) tax; (: inversión) deposit

impostor, a [impos'tor, a] nm/f impostor

impotencia [impo'tenθja] nf impotence; **impotente** adj impotent

impreciso, -a [impre'θiso, a] adj imprecise, vague

impregnar [impreɣ'nar] vt to impregnate; **impregnarse** vr to become impregnated

imprenta [im'prenta] nf (acto) printing; (aparato) press; (casa) printer's; (letra) print

imprescindible [impresθin'diβle] adj essential, vital

impresión [impre'sjon] nf (gen) impression; (Imprenta) printing; (edición) edition; (Foto) print; (marca) imprint; **impresión digital** fingerprint

impresionante [impresjo'nante] adj impressive; (tremendo) tremendous; (maravilloso) great, marvellous

impresionar [impresjo'nar] vt (conmover) to move; (afectar) to impress, strike; (película fotográfica) to expose; **impresionarse** vr to be impressed; (conmoverse) to be moved

impreso, -a [im'preso, a] pp de **imprimir** ▷ adj printed; **impresos** nmpl printed matter; **impresora** nf printer

imprevisto, -a [impre'βisto, a] adj (gen) unforeseen; (inesperado) unexpected

imprimir [impri'mir] vt to imprint, impress, stamp; (textos) to print; (Inform) to output, print out

improbable [impro'βaβle] adj improbable; (inverosímil) unlikely

impropio, -a [im'propjo, a] adj improper

improvisado, -a [improβi'saðo, a] adj improvised

improvisar [improβi'sar] vt to improvise

improviso, -a [impro'βiso, a] adj: **de ~** unexpectedly, suddenly

imprudencia [impru'ðenθja] nf imprudence; (indiscreción) indiscretion; (descuido) carelessness; **imprudente** adj unwise, imprudent; (indiscreto) indiscreet

impuesto, -a [im'pwesto, a] adj imposed ▷ nm tax; **impuesto al valor agregado** o **añadido** (LAM) value added tax (BRIT) ≈ sales tax (US); **impuesto sobre el valor añadido** (ESP) value added tax (BRIT) ≈ sales tax (US)

impulsar [impul'sar] vt to drive; (promover) to promote, stimulate

impulsivo, -a [impul'siβo, a] adj impulsive; **impulso** nm impulse; (fuerza, empuje) thrust, drive;

(fig: sentimiento) urge, impulse

impureza [impu'reθa] nf impurity; **impuro, -a** adj impure

inaccesible [inakθe'siβle] adj inaccessible

inaceptable [inaθep'taβle] adj unacceptable

inactivo, -a [inak'tiβo, a] adj inactive

inadecuado, -a [inaðe'kwaðo, a] adj (insuficiente) inadequate; (inapto) unsuitable

inadvertido, -a [inaðβer'tiðo, a] adj (no visto) unnoticed

inaguantable [inaɣwan'taβle] adj unbearable

inanimado, -a [inani'maðo, a] adj inanimate

inaudito, -a [inau'ðito, a] adj unheard-of

inauguración [inauɣura'θjon] nf inauguration; opening

inaugurar [inauɣu'rar] vt to inaugurate; (exposición) to open

inca ['inka] nmf Inca

incalculable [inkalku'laβle] adj incalculable

incandescente [inkandes'θente] adj incandescent

incansable [inkan'saβle] adj tireless, untiring

incapacidad [inkapaθi'ðað] nf incapacity; (incompetencia) incompetence; **incapacidad física/ mental** physical/mental disability

incapacitar [inkapaθi'tar] vt (inhabilitar) to incapacitate, render unfit; (descalificar) to disqualify

incapaz [inka'paθ] adj incapable

incautarse [inkau'tarse] vr: **~ de** to seize, confiscate

incauto, -a [in'kauto, a] adj (imprudente) incautious, unwary

incendiar [inθen'djar] vt to set fire to; (fig) to inflame; **incendiarse** vr to catch fire; **incendiario, -a** adj incendiary

incendio [in'θendjo] nm fire

incentivo [inθen'tiβo] nm incentive

incertidumbre [inθerti'ðumbre] nf (inseguridad) uncertainty; (duda) doubt

incesante [inθe'sante] adj incessant

incesto [in'θesto] nm incest

incidencia [inθi'ðenθja] nf (Mat) incidence

incidente [inθi'ðente] nm incident

incidir [inθi'ðir] vi (influir) to influence; (afectar) to affect

incienso [in'θjenso] nm incense

incierto, -a [in'θjerto, a] adj uncertain

incineración [inθinera'θjon] nf incineration; (de cadáveres) cremation

incinerar [inθine'rar] vt to burn; (cadáveres) to cremate

incisión [inθi'sjon] nf incision

incisivo, -a [inθi'siβo, a] adj sharp, cutting; (fig) incisive

incitar [inθi'tar] vt to incite, rouse

inclemencia [inkle'menθja] nf (severidad) harshness, severity; (del tiempo) inclemency

inclinación [inklina'θjon] nf (gen) inclination; (de tierras) slope, incline; (de cabeza) nod, bow; (fig) leaning, bent

inclinar [inkli'nar] vt to incline; (cabeza) to nod, bow ▷ vi to lean, slope; **inclinarse** vr to bow; (encorvarse) to stoop; **~se a** (parecerse a) to take after, resemble; **~se ante** to bow down to; **me inclino a pensar que ...** I'm inclined to think that ...

incluir [inklu'ir] vt to include; (incorporar) to incorporate; (meter) to enclose

inclusive [inklu'siβe] adv inclusive ▷ prep including

incluso [inˈkluso] *adv* even

incógnita [inˈkoɣnita] *nf* (Mat) unknown quantity

incógnito [inˈkoɣnito] *nm*: **de ~** incognito

incoherente [inkoeˈrente] *adj* incoherent

incoloro, -a [inkoˈloro, a] *adj* colourless

incomodar [inkomoˈðar] *vt* to inconvenience; (*molestar*) to bother, trouble; (*fastidiar*) to annoy

incomodidad [inkomoðiˈðað] *nf* inconvenience; (*fastidio, enojo*) annoyance; (*de vivienda*) discomfort

incómodo, -a [inˈkomoðo, a] *adj* (*inconfortable*) uncomfortable; (*molesto*) annoying; (*inconveniente*) inconvenient

incomparable [inkompaˈraβle] *adj* incomparable

incompatible [inkompaˈtiβle] *adj* incompatible

incompetente [inkompeˈtente] *adj* incompetent

incompleto, -a [inkomˈpleto, a] *adj* incomplete, unfinished

incomprensible [inkomprenˈsiβle] *adj* incomprehensible

incomunicado, -a [inkomuniˈkaðo, a] *adj* (*aislado*) cut off, isolated; (*confinado*) in solitary confinement

incondicional [inkondiθjoˈnal] *adj* unconditional; (*apoyo*) wholehearted; (*partidario*) staunch

inconfundible [inkonfunˈdiβle] *adj* unmistakable

incongruente [inkonˈɣrwente] *adj* incongruous

inconsciente [inkonsˈθjente] *adj* unconscious; thoughtless

inconsecuente [inkonseˈkwente] *adj* inconsistent

inconstante [inkonsˈtante] *adj* inconstant

incontable [inkonˈtaβle] *adj* countless, innumerable

inconveniencia [inkombeˈnjenθja] *nf* unsuitability, inappropriateness; (*descortesía*) impoliteness; **inconveniente** *adj* unsuitable; impolite ▷ *nm* obstacle; (*desventaja*) disadvantage; **el inconveniente es que ...** the trouble is that ...

incordiar [inkorˈðjar] (*fam*) *vt* to bug, annoy

incorporar [inkorpoˈrar] *vt* to incorporate; **incorporarse** *vr* to sit up; **~se a** to join

incorrecto, -a [inkoˈrrekto, a] *adj* (*gen*) incorrect, wrong; (*comportamiento*) bad-mannered

incorregible [inkorreˈxiβle] *adj* incorrigible

incrédulo, -a [inˈkreðulo, a] *adj* incredulous, unbelieving; sceptical

increíble [inkreˈiβle] *adj* incredible

incremento [inkreˈmento] *nm* increment; (*aumento*) rise, increase

increpar [inkreˈpar] *vt* to reprimand

incruento, -a [inˈkrwento, a] *adj* bloodless

incrustar [inkrusˈtar] *vt* to incrust; (*piedras: en joya*) to inlay

incubar [inkuˈβar] *vt* to incubate

inculcar [inkulˈkar] *vt* to inculcate

inculto, -a [inˈkulto, a] *adj* (*persona*) uneducated; (*grosero*) uncouth ▷ *nm/f* ignoramus

incumplimiento [inkumpliˈmjento] *nm* non-fulfilment; **incumplimiento de contrato** breach of contract

incurrir [inkuˈrrir] *vi*: **~ en** to incur; (*crimen*) to commit

indagar [indaˈɣar] *vt* to investigate; to search; (*averiguar*) to ascertain

indecente [indeˈθente] *adj* indecent, improper; (*lascivo*) obscene

indeciso, -a [indeˈθiso, a] *adj* (*por decidir*) undecided; (*vacilante*) hesitant

indefenso, -a [indeˈfenso, a] *adj* defenceless

indefinido, -a [indefiˈniðo, a] *adj* indefinite; (*vago*) vague, undefined

indemne [inˈdemne] *adj* (*objeto*) undamaged; (*persona*) unharmed, unhurt

indemnizar [indemniˈθar] *vt* to indemnify; (*compensar*) to compensate

independencia [independˈenθja] *nf* independence

independiente [indepenˈdjente] *adj* (*libre*) independent; (*autónomo*) self-sufficient

indeterminado, -a [indetermiˈnaðo, a] *adj* indefinite; (*desconocido*) indeterminate

India [ˈindja] *nf*: **la ~** India

indicación [indikaˈθjon] *nf* indication; (*señal*) sign; (*sugerencia*) suggestion, hint

indicado, -a [indiˈkaðo, a] *adj* (*momento, método*) right; (*tratamiento*) appropriate; (*solución*) likely

indicador [indikaˈðor] *nm* indicator; (*Tec*) gauge, meter

indicar [indiˈkar] *vt* (*mostrar*) to indicate, show; (*termómetro etc*) to read, register; (*señalar*) to point to

índice [ˈindiθe] *nm* index; (*catálogo*) catalogue; (*Anat*) index finger, forefinger; **índice de materias** table of contents

indicio [inˈdiθjo] *nm* indication, sign; (*en pesquisa etc*) clue

indiferencia [indifeˈrenθja] *nf* indifference; (*apatía*) apathy; **indiferente** *adj* indifferent

indígena [inˈdixena] *adj* indigenous, native ▷ *nmf* native

indigestión [indixesˈtjon] *nf* indigestion

indigesto, -a [indiˈxesto, a] *adj* (*alimento*) indigestible; (*fig*) turgid

indignación [indiɣnaˈθjon] *nf* indignation

indignar [indiɣˈnar] *vt* to anger, make indignant; **indignarse** *vr*: **~se por** to get indignant about

indigno, -a [inˈdiɣno, a] *adj* (*despreciable*) low, contemptible; (*inmerecido*) unworthy

indio, -a [ˈindjo, a] *adj, nm/f* Indian

indirecta [indiˈrekta] *nf* insinuation, innuendo; (*sugerencia*) hint

indirecto, -a [indiˈrekto, a] *adj* indirect

indiscreción [indiskreˈθjon] *nf* (*imprudencia*) indiscretion; (*irreflexión*) tactlessness; (*acto*) gaffe, faux pas

indiscreto, -a [indisˈkreto, a] *adj* indiscreet

indiscutible [indiskuˈtiβle] *adj* indisputable, unquestionable

indispensable [indispenˈsaβle] *adj* indispensable, essential

indispuesto, -a [indisˈpwesto, a] *adj* (*enfermo*) unwell, indisposed

indistinto, -a [indisˈtinto, a] *adj* indistinct; (*vago*) vague

individual [indiβiˈðwal] *adj* individual; (*habitación*) single ▷ *nm* (*Deporte*) singles *sg*

individuo, -a [indiˈβiðwo, a] *adj, nm* individual

índole [ˈindole] *nf* (*naturaleza*) nature; (*clase*) sort, kind

inducir [induˈθir] *vt* to induce; (*inferir*) to infer; (*persuadir*) to persuade

indudable [induˈðaβle] *adj* undoubted; (*incuestionable*) unquestionable

indultar [indulˈtar] *vt* (*perdonar*) to pardon, reprieve; (*librar de pago*) to exempt; **indulto** *nm* pardon; exemption

industria [in'dustrja] nf industry; (habilidad) skill;
industrial adj industrial ▷ nm industrialist
inédito, -a [in'eðito, a] adj (texto) unpublished;
(nuevo) new
ineficaz [inefi'kaθ] adj (inútil) ineffective; (ineficiente)
inefficient
ineludible [inelu'ðiβle] adj inescapable,
unavoidable
ineptitud [inepti'tuð] nf ineptitude, incompetence;
inepto, -a adj inept, incompetent
inequívoco, -a [ine'kiβoko, a] adj unequivocal;
(inconfundible) unmistakable
inercia [in'erθja] nf inertia; (pasividad) passivity
inerte [in'erte] adj inert; (inmóvil) motionless
inesperado, -a [inespe'raðo, a] adj unexpected,
unforeseen
inestable [ines'taβle] adj unstable
inevitable [ineβi'taβle] adj inevitable
inexacto, -a [inek'sakto, a] adj inaccurate; (falso)
untrue
inexperto, -a [inek'sperto, a] adj (novato)
inexperienced
infalible [infa'liβle] adj infallible; (plan) foolproof
infame [in'fame] adj infamous; (horrible) dreadful;
infamia nf infamy; (deshonra) disgrace
infancia [in'fanθja] nf infancy, childhood
infantería [infante'ria] nf infantry
infantil [infan'til] adj (pueril, aniñado) infantile;
(cándido) childlike; (literatura, ropa etc) children's
infarto [in'farto] nm (tb: ~ **de miocardio**) heart
attack
infatigable [infati'ɣaβle] adj tireless, untiring
infección [infek'θjon] nf infection; **infeccioso, -a**
adj infectious
infectar [infek'tar] vt to infect; **infectarse** vr to
become infected
infeliz [infe'liθ] adj unhappy, wretched ▷ nmf
wretch
inferior [infe'rjor] adj inferior; (situación) lower ▷ nmf
inferior, subordinate
inferir [infe'rir] vt (deducir) to infer, deduce; (causar)
to cause
infidelidad [infiðeli'ðað] nf (gen) infidelity,
unfaithfulness
infiel [in'fjel] adj unfaithful, disloyal; (erróneo)
inaccurate ▷ nmf infidel, unbeliever
infierno [in'fjerno] nm hell
infiltrarse [infil'trarse] vr: **~ en** to infiltrate in(to);
(persona) to work one's way in(to)
ínfimo, -a ['infimo, a] adj (más bajo) lowest;
(despreciable) vile, mean
infinidad [infini'ðað] nf infinity; (abundancia) great
quantity
infinito, -a [infi'nito, a] adj, nm infinite
inflación [infla'θjon] nf (hinchazón) swelling;
(monetaria) inflation; (fig) conceit
inflamable [infl'maβle] adj flammable
inflamar [infla'mar] vt (Med: fig) to inflame;
inflamarse vr to catch fire; to become inflamed
inflar [in'flar] vt (hinchar) to inflate, blow up; (fig)
to exaggerate; **inflarse** vr to swell (up); (fig) to get
conceited
inflexible [inflek'siβle] adj inflexible; (fig)
unbending
influencia [influ'enθja] nf influence
influir [influ'ir] vt to influence

influjo [in'fluxo] nm influence
influya etc vb V **influir**
influyente [influ'jente] adj influential
información [informa'θjon] nf information;
(noticias) news sg; (Jur) inquiry; **I~** (oficina) Information
Office; (mostrador) Information Desk; (Tel) Directory
Enquiries
informal [infor'mal] adj (gen) informal
informar [infor'mar] vt (gen) to inform; (revelar) to
reveal, make known ▷ vi (Jur) to plead; (denunciar) to
inform; (dar cuenta de) to report on; **informarse** vr to
find out; **~se de** to inquire into
informática [infor'matika] nf computer science,
information technology
informe [in'forme] adj shapeless ▷ nm report
infracción [infrak'θjon] nf infraction, infringement
infravalorar [infraβalo'rar] vt to undervalue,
underestimate
infringir [infrin'xir] vt to infringe, contravene
infundado, -a [infun'daðo, a] adj groundless,
unfounded
infundir [infun'dir] vt to infuse, instil
infusión [infu'sjon] nf infusion; **infusión de
manzanilla** camomile tea
ingeniería [inxenje'ria] nf engineering; **ingeniería
genética** genetic engineering; **ingeniero, -a** nm/f
engineer; **ingeniero civil o de caminos** civil engineer
ingenio [in'xenjo] nm (talento) talent; (agudeza)
wit; (habilidad) ingenuity, inventiveness; **ingenio
azucarero** (LAM) sugar refinery; **ingenioso, -a**
[inxe'njoso, a] adj ingenious, clever; (divertido) witty;
ingenuo, -a adj ingenuous
ingerir [inxe'rir] vt to ingest; (tragar) to swallow;
(consumir) to consume
Inglaterra [ingla'terra] nf England
ingle ['ingle] nf groin
inglés, -esa [in'gles, esa] adj English ▷ nm/f
Englishman(-woman) ▷ nm (Ling) English
ingrato, -a [in'grato, a] adj (gen) ungrateful
ingrediente [ingre'ðjente] nm ingredient
ingresar [ingre'sar] vt (dinero) to deposit ▷ vi to
come in; **~ en el hospital** to go into hospital
ingreso [in'greso] nm (entrada) entry; (en hospital etc)
admission; **ingresos** nmpl (dinero) income sg; (Com)
takings pl
inhabitable [inaβi'taβle] adj uninhabitable
inhalar [ina'lar] vt to inhale
inhibir [ini'βir] vt to inhibit
inhóspito, -a [i'nospito, a] adj (región, paisaje)
inhospitable
inhumano, -a [inu'mano, a] adj inhuman
inicial [ini'θjal] adj, nf initial
iniciar [ini'θjar] vt (persona) to initiate; (empezar) to
begin, commence; (conversación) to start up
iniciativa [iniθja'tiβa] nf initiative; **iniciativa
privada** private enterprise
ininterrumpido, -a [ininterrum'piðo, a] adj
uninterrupted
injertar [inxer'tar] vt to graft; **injerto** nm graft
injuria [in'xurja] nf (agravio, ofensa) offence; (insulto)
insult
injusticia [inxus'tiθja] nf injustice
injusto, -a [in'xusto, a] adj unjust, unfair
inmadurez [inmaðu'reθ] nf immaturity
inmediaciones [inmeðja'θjones] nfpl
neighbourhood sg, environs

inmediato, -a [inme'ðjato, a] *adj* immediate; (*contiguo*) adjoining; (*rápido*) prompt; (*próximo*) neighbouring, next; **de ~** immediately

inmejorable [inmexo'raβle] *adj* unsurpassable; (*precio*) unbeatable

inmenso, -a [in'menso, a] *adj* immense, huge

inmigración [inmixra'θjon] *nf* immigration

inmobiliaria [inmoβil'jarja] *nf* estate agency

inmolar [inmo'lar] *vt* to immolate, sacrifice

inmoral [inmo'ral] *adj* immoral

inmortal [inmor'tal] *adj* immortal; **inmortalizar** *vt* to immortalize

inmóvil [in'moβil] *adj* immobile

inmueble [in'mweβle] *adj*: **bienes ~s** real estate, landed property ▷ *nm* property

inmundo, -a [in'mundo, a] *adj* filthy

inmune [in'mune] *adj*: **~ (a)** (*Med*) immune (to)

inmunidad [inmuni'ðað] *nf* immunity

inmutarse [inmu'tarse] *vr* to turn pale; **no se inmutó** he didn't turn a hair

innato, -a [in'nato, a] *adj* innate

innecesario, -a [inneθe'sarjo, a] *adj* unnecessary

innovación [innoβa'θjon] *nf* innovation

innovar [inno'βar] *vt* to introduce

inocencia [ino'θenθja] *nf* innocence

inocentada [inoθen'taða] *nf* practical joke

inocente [ino'θente] *adj* (*ingenuo*) naive, innocent; (*inculpable*) innocent; (*sin malicia*) harmless ▷ *nmf* simpleton; **el día de los (Santos) I~s** = April Fools' Day

inodoro, -a [ino'ðoro] *nm* toilet, lavatory (*BRIT*)

inofensivo, -a [inofen'siβo, a] *adj* inoffensive, harmless

inolvidable [inolβi'ðaβle] *adj* unforgettable

inoportuno, -a [inopor'tuno, a] *adj* untimely; (*molesto*) inconvenient

inoxidable [inoksi'ðaβle] *adj*: **acero ~** stainless steel

inquietar [inkje'tar] *vt* to worry, trouble; **inquietarse** *vr* to worry, get upset; **inquieto, -a** *adj* anxious, worried; **inquietud** *nf* anxiety, worry

inquilino, -a [inki'lino, a] *nm/f* tenant

insaciable [insa'θjaβle] *adj* insatiable

inscribir [inskri'βir] *vt* to inscribe; **~ a algn en** (*lista*) to put sb on; (*censo*) to register sb on

inscripción [inskrip'θjon] *nf* inscription; (*Escol etc*) enrolment; (*en censo*) registration

insecticida [insekti'θiða] *nm* insecticide

insecto [in'sekto] *nm* insect

inseguridad [insexuri'ðað] *nf* insecurity; **inseguridad ciudadana** lack of safety in the streets

inseguro, -a [inse'xuro, a] *adj* insecure; (*inconstante*) unsteady; (*incierto*) uncertain

insensato, -a [insen'sato, a] *adj* foolish, stupid

insensible [insen'siβle] *adj* (*gen*) insensitive; (*movimiento*) imperceptible; (*sin sentido*) numb

insertar [inser'tar] *vt* to insert

inservible [inser'βiβle] *adj* useless

insignia [in'sixnja] *nf* (*señal distintiva*) badge; (*estandarte*) flag

insignificante [insixnifi'kante] *adj* insignificant

insinuar [insi'nwar] *vt* to insinuate, imply

insípido, -a [in'sipiðo, a] *adj* insipid

insistir [insis'tir] *vi* to insist; **~ en algo** to insist on sth; (*enfatizar*) to stress sth

insolación [insola'θjon] *nf* (*Med*) sunstroke

insolente [inso'lente] *adj* insolent

insólito, -a [in'solito, a] *adj* unusual

insoluble [inso'luβle] *adj* insoluble

insomnio [in'somnjo] *nm* insomnia

insonorizado, -a [insonori'θaðo, a] *adj* (*cuarto etc*) soundproof

insoportable [insopor'taβle] *adj* unbearable

inspección [inspek'θjon] *nf* inspection, check; **inspeccionar** *vt* (*examinar*) to inspect, examine; (*controlar*) to check

inspector, a [inspek'tor, a] *nm/f* inspector

inspiración [inspira'θjon] *nf* inspiration

inspirar [inspi'rar] *vt* to inspire; (*Med*) to inhale; **inspirarse** *vr*: **~se en** to be inspired by

instalación [instala'θjon] *nf* (*equipo*) fittings *pl*, equipment; **instalación eléctrica** wiring

instalar [insta'lar] *vt* (*establecer*) to instal; (*erguir*) to set up, erect; **instalarse** *vr* to establish o.s.; (*en una vivienda*) to move into

instancia [ins'tanθja] *nf* (*Jur*) petition; (*ruego*) request; **en última ~** as a last resort

instantáneo, -a [instan'taneo, a] *adj* instantaneous; **café ~** instant coffee

instante [ins'tante] *nm* instant, moment; **al ~** right now

instar [ins'tar] *vt* to press, urge

instaurar [instau'rar] *vt* (*costumbre*) to establish; (*normas, sistema*) to bring in, introduce; (*gobierno*) to instal

instigar [insti'xar] *vt* to instigate

instinto [ins'tinto] *nm* instinct; **por ~** instinctively

institución [institu'θjon] *nf* institution, establishment

instituir [institu'ir] *vt* to establish; (*fundar*) to found; **instituto** *nm* (*gen*) institute; (*ESP Escol*) ≈ comprehensive (*BRIT*) o high (*US*) school

institutriz [institu'triθ] *nf* governess

instrucción [instruk'θjon] *nf* instruction

instruir [instru'ir] *vt* (*gen*) to instruct; (*enseñar*) to teach, educate

instrumento [instru'mento] *nm* (*gen*) instrument; (*herramienta*) tool, implement

insubordinarse [insuβorði'narse] *vr* to rebel

insuficiente [insufi'θjente] *adj* (*gen*) insufficient; (*Escol: calificación*) unsatisfactory

insular [insu'lar] *adj* insular

insultar [insul'tar] *vt* to insult; **insulto** *nm* insult

insuperable [insupe'raβle] *adj* (*excelente*) unsurpassable; (*problema etc*) insurmountable

insurrección [insurrek'θjon] *nf* insurrection, rebellion

intachable [inta'tʃaβle] *adj* irreproachable

intacto, -a [in'takto, a] *adj* intact

integral [inte'xral] *adj* integral; (*completo*) complete; **pan ~** wholemeal (*BRIT*) o wholewheat (*US*) bread

integrar [inte'xrar] *vt* to make up, compose; (*Mat: fig*) to integrate

integridad [intexri'ðað] *nf* wholeness; (*carácter*) integrity; **íntegro, -a** *adj* whole, entire; (*honrado*) honest

intelectual [intelek'twal] *adj*, *nmf* intellectual

inteligencia [inteli'xenθja] *nf* intelligence; (*ingenio*) ability; **inteligente** *adj* intelligent

intemperie [intem'perje] *nf*: **a la ~** out in the open, exposed to the elements

intención [inten'θjon] *nf* (*gen*) intention, purpose; **con segundas intenciones** maliciously; **con ~** deliberately

intencionado, -a [intenθjo'naðo, a] *adj* deliberate; **mal ~** ill-disposed, hostile

intensidad [intensi'ðað] *nf* (*gen*) intensity; (*Elec, Tec*) strength; **llover con ~** to rain hard

intenso, -a [in'tenso, a] *adj* intense; (*sentimiento*) profound, deep

intentar [inten'tar] *vt* (*tratar*) to try, attempt; **intento** *nm* attempt

interactivo, -a [interak'tiβo, a] *adj* (*Inform*) interactive

intercalar [interka'lar] *vt* to insert

intercambio [inter'kambjo] *nm* exchange, swap

interceder [interθe'ðer] *vi* to intercede

interceptar [interθep'tar] *vt* to intercept

interés [inte'res] *nm* (*gen*) interest; (*parte*) share, part; (*pey*) self-interest; **intereses creados** vested interests

interesado, -a [intere'saðo, a] *adj* interested; (*prejuiciado*) prejudiced; (*pey*) mercenary, self-seeking

interesante [intere'sante] *adj* interesting

interesar [intere'sar] *vt, vi* to interest, be of interest to; **interesarse** *vr*: **~se en** o **por** to take an interest in

interferir [interfe'rir] *vt* to interfere with; (*Tel*) to jam ▷ *vi* to interfere

interfón [inter'fon] (*MÉX*) *nm* entry phone

interino, -a [inte'rino, a] *adj* temporary ▷ *nm/f* temporary holder of a post; (*Med*) locum; (*Escol*) supply teacher

interior [inte'rjor] *adj* inner, inside; (*Com*) domestic, internal ▷ *nm* interior, inside; (*fig*) soul, mind; **Ministerio del I~ ≈** Home Office (*BRIT*) ≈ Department of the Interior (*US*); **interiorista** (*ESP*) *nmf* interior designer

interjección [interxek'θjon] *nf* interjection

interlocutor, a [interloku'tor, a] *nm/f* speaker

intermedio, -a [inter'meðjo, a] *adj* intermediate ▷ *nm* interval

interminable [intermi'naβle] *adj* endless

intermitente [intermi'tente] *adj* intermittent ▷ *nm* (*Auto*) indicator

internacional [internaθjo'nal] *adj* international

internado [inter'naðo] *nm* boarding school

internar [inter'nar] *vt* to intern; (*en un manicomio*) to commit; **internarse** *vr* (*penetrar*) to penetrate

internauta [inter'nauta] *nmf* web surfer, Internet user

Internet, internet [inter'net] *nm* o *f* Internet

interno, -a [in'terno, a] *adj* internal, interior; (*Pol etc*) domestic ▷ *nm/f* (*alumno*) boarder

interponer [interpo'ner] *vt* to interpose, put in; **interponerse** *vr* to intervene

interpretación [interpreta'θjon] *nf* interpretation

interpretar [interpre'tar] *vt* to interpret; (*Teatro, Mús*) to perform, play; **intérprete** *nmf* (*Ling*) interpreter, translator; (*Mús, Teatro*) performer, artist(e)

interrogación [interroxa'θjon] *nf* interrogation; (*Ling*: *tb*: **signo de ~**) question mark

interrogar [interro'xar] *vt* to interrogate, question

interrumpir [interrum'pir] *vt* to interrupt

interrupción [interrup'θjon] *nf* interruption

interruptor [interrup'tor] *nm* (*Elec*) switch

intersección [intersek'θjon] *nf* intersection

interurbano, -a [interur'βano, a] *adj*: **llamada interurbana** long-distance call

intervalo [inter'βalo] *nm* interval; (*descanso*) break

intervenir [interβe'nir] *vt* (*controlar*) to control, supervise; (*Med*) to operate on ▷ *vi* (*participar*) to take part, participate; (*mediar*) to intervene

interventor, a [interβen'tor, a] *nm/f* inspector; (*Com*) auditor

intestino [intes'tino] *nm* (*Med*) intestine

intimar [inti'mar] *vi* to become friendly

intimidad [intimi'ðað] *nf* intimacy; (*familiaridad*) familiarity; (*vida privada*) private life; (*Jur*) privacy

íntimo, -a ['intimo, a] *adj* intimate

intolerable [intole'raβle] *adj* intolerable, unbearable

intoxicación [intoksika'θjon] *nf* poisoning; **intoxicación alimenticia** food poisoning

intranet [intra'net] *nf* intranet

intranquilo, -a [intran'kilo, a] *adj* worried

intransitable [intransi'taβle] *adj* impassable

intrépido, -a [in'trepiðo, a] *adj* intrepid

intriga [in'trixa] *nf* intrigue; (*plan*) plot; **intrigar** *vt, vi* to intrigue

intrínseco, -a [in'trinseko, a] *adj* intrinsic

introducción [introðuk'θjon] *nf* introduction

introducir [introðu'θir] *vt* (*gen*) to introduce; (*moneda etc*) to insert; (*Inform*) to input, enter

intromisión [intromi'sjon] *nf* interference, meddling

introvertido, -a [introβer'tiðo, a] *adj, nm/f* introvert

intruso, -a [in'truso, a] *adj* intrusive ▷ *nm/f* intruder

intuición [intwi'θjon] *nf* intuition

inundación [inunda'θjon] *nf* flood(ing); **inundar** *vt* to flood; (*fig*) to swamp, inundate

inusitado, -a [inusi'taðo, a] *adj* unusual, rare

inútil [in'util] *adj* useless; (*esfuerzo*) vain, fruitless

inutilizar [inutili'θar] *vt* to make o render useless

invadir [imba'ðir] *vt* to invade

inválido, -a [im'baliðo, a] *adj* invalid ▷ *nm/f* invalid

invasión [imba'sjon] *nf* invasion

invasor, a [imba'sor, a] *adj* invading ▷ *nm/f* invader

invención [imben'θjon] *nf* invention

inventar [imben'tar] *vt* to invent

inventario [imben'tarjo] *nm* inventory

invento [im'bento] *nm* invention

inventor, a [imben'tor, a] *nm/f* inventor

invernadero [imberna'ðero] *nm* greenhouse

inverosímil [imbero'simil] *adj* implausible

inversión [imber'sjon] *nf* (*Com*) investment

inverso, -a [im'berso, a] *adj* inverse, opposite; **en el orden ~** in reverse order; **a la inversa** inversely, the other way round

inversor, a [imber'sor, a] *nm/f* (*Com*) investor

invertir [imber'tir] *vt* (*Com*) to invest; (*volcar*) to turn upside down; (*tiempo etc*) to spend

investigación [imbestiɣa'θjon] *nf* investigation; (*Escol*) research; **investigación y desarrollo** research and development

investigar [imbesti'ɣar] *vt* to investigate; (*Escol*) to do research into

invierno [im'bjerno] *nm* winter

invisible [imbi'siβle] *adj* invisible

invitado, -a [imbi'taðo, a] *nm/f* guest

invitar [imbi'tar] *vt* to invite; (*incitar*) to entice; (*pagar*) to buy, pay for

invocar [imbo'kar] *vt* to invoke, call on

involucrar [imbolu'krar] vt: ~ **en** to involve in; **involucrarse** vr (persona): **~se en** to get mixed up in

involuntario, -a [imbolun'tarjo, a] adj (movimiento, gesto) involuntary; (error) unintentional

inyección [injek'θjon] nf injection

inyectar [injek'tar] vt to inject

iPod® ['ipoð] (pl ~s) nm iPod®

○ PALABRA CLAVE

ir [ir] vi 1 to go; (a pie) to walk; (viajar) to travel; **ir caminando** to walk; **fui en tren** I went o travelled by train; **¡(ahora) voy!** (I'm just) coming!

2: **ir (a) por: ir (a) por el médico** to fetch the doctor

3 (progresar: persona, cosa) to go; **el trabajo va muy bien** work is going very well; **¿cómo te va?** how are things going?; **me va muy bien** I'm getting on very well; **le fue fatal** it went awfully badly for him

4 (funcionar): **el coche no va muy bien** the car isn't running very well

5: **te va estupendamente ese color** that colour suits you fantastically well

6 (locuciones): **¿vino? – ¡que va!** did he come? – of course not!; **vamos, no llores** come on, don't cry; **¡vaya coche!** what a car!, that's some car!

7: **no vaya a ser: tienes que correr, no vaya a ser que pierdas el tren** you'll have to run so as not to miss the train

8 (+ pp): **iba vestido muy bien** he was very well dressed

9: **ni me** etc **va ni me** etc **viene** I etc don't care

▷ vb aux 1 **ir a: voy/iba a hacerlo hoy** I am/was going to do it today

2 (+ gerundio): **iba anocheciendo** it was getting dark; **todo se me iba aclarando** everything was gradually becoming clearer to me

3 (+ pp: = pasivo): **van vendidos 300 ejemplares** 300 copies have been sold so far

irse vr 1: **¿por dónde se va al zoológico?** which is the way to the zoo?

2 (marcharse) to leave; **ya se habrán ido** they must already have left o gone

ira ['ira] nf anger, rage

Irak [i'rak] nm = **Iraq**

Irán [i'ran] nm Iran; **iraní** adj, nmf Iranian

Iraq [i'rak] nm Iraq; **iraquí** adj, nmf Iraqi

iris ['iris] nm inv (tb: **arco ~**) rainbow; (Anat) iris

Irlanda [ir'landa] nf Ireland; **irlandés, -esa** adj Irish ▷ nm/f Irishman(-woman); **los irlandeses** the Irish

ironía [iro'nia] nf irony; **irónico, -a** adj ironic(al)

IRPF nm abr (= Impuesto sobre la Renta de las Personas Físicas) (personal) income tax

irreal [irre'al] adj unreal

irregular [irrexu'lar] adj (gen) irregular; (situación) abnormal

irremediable [irreme'ðjaβle] adj irremediable; (vicio) incurable

irreparable [irrepa'raβle] adj (daños) irreparable; (pérdida) irrecoverable

irrespetuoso, -a [irrespe'twoso, a] adj disrespectful

irresponsable [irrespon'saβle] adj irresponsible

irreversible [irreβer'sible] adj irreversible

irrigar [irri'var] vt to irrigate

irrisorio, -a [irri'sorjo, a] adj derisory, ridiculous

irritar [irri'tar] vt to irritate, annoy

irrupción [irrup'θjon] nf irruption; (invasión) invasion

isla ['isla] nf island

Islam [is'lam] nm Islam; **las enseñanzas del ~** the teachings of Islam; **islámico, -a** adj Islamic

islandés, -esa [islan'des, esa] adj Icelandic ▷ nm/f Icelander

Islandia [is'landja] nf Iceland

isleño, -a [is'leɲo, a] adj island cpd ▷ nm/f islander

Israel [isra'el] nm Israel; **israelí** adj, nmf Israeli

istmo ['istmo] nm isthmus

Italia [i'talja] nf Italy; **italiano, -a** adj, nm/f Italian

itinerario [itine'rarjo] nm itinerary, route

ITV (ESP) nf abr (= inspección técnica de vehículos) roadworthiness test, ≈ MOT (BRIT)

IVA ['iβa] nm abr (= impuesto sobre el valor añadido) VAT

izar [i'θar] vt to hoist

izdo, -a abr (= izquierdo, a) l

izquierda [iθ'kjerda] nf left; (Pol) left (wing); **a la ~** (estar) on the left; (torcer etc) (to the) left

izquierdo, -a [iθ'kjerðo, a] adj left

j

jabalí [xaβa'li] nm wild boar
jabalina [xaβa'lina] nf javelin
jabón [xa'βon] nm soap
jaca ['xaka] nf pony
jacal [xa'kal] (MÉX) nm shack
jacinto [xa'θinto] nm hyacinth
jactarse [xak'tarse] vr to boast, brag
jadear [xaðe'ar] vi to pant, gasp for breath
jaguar [xa'ɣwar] nm jaguar
jaiba [xaiβa] (LAM) nf crab
jalar [xa'lar] (LAM) vt to pull
jalea [xa'lea] nf jelly
jaleo [xa'leo] nm racket, uproar; **armar un ~** to kick
  up a racket
jalón [xa'lon] (LAM) nm tug
jamás [xa'mas] adv never
jamón [xa'mon] nm ham; **jamón dulce** o **de York**
  cooked ham; **jamón serrano** cured ham
Japón [xa'pon] nm Japan; **japonés, -esa** adj, nm/f
  Japanese ▷ nm (Ling) Japanese
jaque ['xake] nm (Ajedrez) check; **jaque mate**
  checkmate
jaqueca [xa'keka] nf (very bad) headache, migraine
jarabe [xa'raβe] nm syrup
jardín [xar'ðin] nm garden; **jardín infantil** o **de
  infancia** nursery (school); **jardinería** nf gardening;
  jardinero, -a nm/f gardener
jarra ['xarra] nf jar; (jarro) jug
jarro ['xarro] nm jug
jarrón [xa'rron] nm vase
jaula ['xaula] nf cage
jauría [xau'ria] nf pack of hounds
jazmín [xaθ'min] nm jasmine
J.C. abr (= Jesucristo) J.C.
jeans [jins, dʒins] (LAM) nmpl jeans, denims; **unos
  ~** a pair of jeans
jefatura [xefa'tura] nf (tb: **~ de policía**) police
  headquarters sg
jefe, -a ['xefe, a] nm/f (gen) chief, head; (patrón) boss;
  jefe de cocina chef; **jefe de estación** stationmaster;
  jefe de Estado head of state; **jefe de estudios**
  (Escol) director of studies; **jefe de gobierno** head of
  government

jengibre [xen'xiβre] nm ginger
jeque ['xeke] nm sheik
jerárquico, -a [xe'rarkiko, a] adj hierarchic(al)
jerez [xe'reθ] nm sherry
jerga ['xerɣa] nf jargon
jeringa [xe'ringa] nf syringe; (LAM: molestia)
  annoyance, bother; **jeringuilla** nf syringe
jeroglífico [xero'ɣlifiko] nm hieroglyphic
jersey [xer'sei] (pl **~s**) nm jersey, pullover, jumper
Jerusalén [xerusa'len] n Jerusalem
Jesucristo [xesu'kristo] nm Jesus Christ
jesuita [xe'swita] adj, nm Jesuit
Jesús [xe'sus] nm Jesus; **¡~!** good heavens!; (al
  estornudar) bless you!
jinete [xi'nete] nmf horseman(-woman), rider
jipijapa [xipi'xapa] (LAM) nm straw hat
jirafa [xi'rafa] nf giraffe
jirón [xi'ron] nm rag, shred
jitomate [xito'mate] (MÉX) nm tomato
joder [xo'ðer] (fam!) vt, vi to fuck (!)
jogging ['joxin] (RPL) nm tracksuit (BRIT), sweat
  suit (US)
jornada [xor'naða] nf (viaje de un día) day's journey;
  (camino o viaje entero) journey; (día de trabajo) working
  day
jornal [xor'nal] nm (day's) wage; **jornalero** nm (day)
  labourer
joroba [xo'roβa] nf hump, hunched back; **jorobado,
  -a** adj hunchbacked ▷ nm/f hunchback
jota ['xota] nf (the letter) J; (danza) Aragonese dance; **no
  saber ni ~** to have no idea
joven ['xoβen] (pl **jóvenes**) adj young ▷ nm young
  man, youth ▷ nf young woman, girl
joya ['xoja] nf jewel, gem; (fig: persona) gem; **joyas
  de fantasía** costume o imitation jewellery; **joyería** nf
  (joyas) jewellery; (tienda) jeweller's (shop); **joyero** nm
  (persona) jeweller; (caja) jewel case
juanete [xwa'nete] nm (del pie) bunion
jubilación [xuβila'θjon] nf (retiro) retirement
jubilado, -a [xuβi'laðo, a] adj retired ▷ nm/f
  pensioner (BRIT), senior citizen
jubilar [xuβi'lar] vt to pension off, retire; (fam) to
  discard; **jubilarse** vr to retire
júbilo ['xuβilo] nm joy, rejoicing; **jubiloso, -a** adj
  jubilant
judía [xu'ðia] (ESP) nf (Culin) bean; **judía blanca/
  verde** haricot/French bean; V tb **judío**
judicial [xuði'θjal] adj judicial
judío, -a [xu'ðio, a] adj Jewish ▷ nm/f Jew(ess)
judo ['juðo] nm judo
juego etc ['xweɣo] vb V **jugar** ▷ nm (gen) play;
  (pasatiempo, partido) game; (en casino) gambling;
  (conjunto) set; **fuera de ~** (Deporte: persona) offside;
  (: pelota) out of play; **juego de palabras** pun, play on
  words; **Juegos Olímpicos** Olympic Games
juerga ['xwerɣa] (ESP: fam) nf binge; (fiesta) party; **ir
  de ~** to go out on a binge
jueves ['xweβes] nm inv Thursday
juez [xweθ] nmf judge; **juez de instrucción**
  examining magistrate; **juez de línea** linesman; **juez
  de salida** starter
jugada [xu'ɣaða] nf play; **buena ~** good move o shot
  o stroke etc
jugador, a [xuɣa'ðor, a] nm/f player; (en casino)
  gambler
jugar [xu'ɣar] vt, vi to play; (en casino) to gamble;

(apostar) to bet; **~ al fútbol** to play football

juglar [xuˈɣlar] *nm* minstrel

jugo [ˈxuɣo] *nm* (Bot) juice; *(fig)* essence, substance; **jugo de naranja** (LAM) orange juice; **jugoso, -a** *adj* juicy; *(fig)* substantial, important

juguete [xuˈɣete] *nm* toy; **juguetear** *vi* to play; **juguetería** *nf* toyshop

juguetón, -ona [xuɣeˈton, ona] *adj* playful

juicio [ˈxwiθjo] *nm* judgement; *(razón)* sanity, reason; *(opinión)* opinion

julio [ˈxuljo] *nm* July

jumper [ˈdʒumper] (LAM) *nm* pinafore dress (BRIT), jumper (US)

junco [ˈxunko] *nm* rush, reed

jungla [ˈxungla] *nf* jungle

junio [ˈxunjo] *nm* June

junta [ˈxunta] *nf* (asamblea) meeting, assembly; *(comité, consejo)* council, committee; *(Com, Finanzas)* board; *(Tec)* joint; **junta directiva** board of directors

juntar [xunˈtar] *vt* to join, unite; *(maquinaria)* to assemble, put together; *(dinero)* to collect; **juntarse** *vr* to join, meet; *(reunirse: personas)* to meet, assemble; *(arrimarse)* to approach, draw closer; **~se con algn** to join sb

junto, -a [ˈxunto, a] *adj* joined; *(unido)* united; *(anexo)* near, close; *(contiguo, próximo)* next, adjacent ▷ *adv:* **todo ~** all at once; **~s** together; **~ a** near (to), next to; **~ con** (together) with

jurado [xuˈraðo] *nm* (Jur: individuo) juror; *(: grupo)* jury; *(de concurso: grupo)* panel (of judges); *(: individuo)* member of a panel

juramento [xuraˈmento] *nm* oath; *(maldición)* oath, curse; **prestar ~** to take the oath; **tomar ~ a** to swear in, administer the oath to

jurar [xuˈrar] *vt, vi* to swear; **~ en falso** to commit perjury; **tenérsela jurada a algn** to have it in for sb

jurídico, -a [xuˈriðiko, a] *adj* legal

jurisdicción [xurisðikˈθjon] *nf* (poder, autoridad) jurisdiction; *(territorio)* district

justamente [xustaˈmente] *adv* justly, fairly; *(precisamente)* just, exactly

justicia [xusˈtiθja] *nf* justice; *(equidad)* fairness, justice

justificación [xustifikaˈθjon] *nf* justification; **justificar** *vt* to justify

justo, -a [ˈxusto, a] *adj* (equitativo) just, fair, right; *(preciso)* exact, correct; *(ajustado)* tight ▷ *adv* *(precisamente)* exactly, precisely; *(LAM: apenas a tiempo)* just in time

juvenil [xuβeˈnil] *adj* youthful

juventud [xuβenˈtuð] *nf* (adolescencia) youth; *(jóvenes)* young people *pl*

juzgado [xuθˈɣaðo] *nm* tribunal; *(Jur)* court

juzgar [xuθˈɣar] *vt* to judge; **a ~ por ...** to judge by ..., judging by ...

kárate [ˈkarate] *nm* karate

kg *abr* (= kilogramo) kg

kilo [ˈkilo] *nm* kilo; **kilogramo** *nm* kilogramme; **kilometraje** *nm* distance in kilometres ≈ mileage; **kilómetro** *nm* kilometre; **kilovatio** *nm* kilowatt

kiosco [ˈkjosko] *nm* = **quiosco**

kleenex® [kliˈneks] *nm* paper handkerchief, tissue

Kosovo [koˈsoβo] *nm* Kosovo

km *abr* (= kilómetro) km

kv *abr* (= kilovatio) kw

l *abr* (= litro) l

la [la] *art def the* ▷ *pron* her; (Ud.) you; (cosa) it ▷ *nm* (Mús) la; **~ del sombrero rojo** the girl in the red hat; V tb **el**

laberinto [laβe'rinto] *nm* labyrinth

labio ['laβjo] *nm* lip

labor [la'βor] *nf* labour; (Agr) farm work; (tarea) job, task; (Costura) needlework; **labores domésticas** o **del hogar** household chores; **laborable** *adj* (Agr) workable; **día laborable** working day; **laboral** *adj* (accidente) at work; (jornada) working

laboratorio [laβora'torjo] *nm* laboratory

laborista [laβo'rista] *adj*: **Partido L~** Labour Party

labrador, a [laβra'ðor, a] *adj* farming *cpd* ▷ *nm/f* farmer

labranza [la'βranθa] *nf* (Agr) cultivation

labrar [la'βrar] *vt* (gen) to work; (madera etc) to carve; (fig) to cause, bring about

laca ['laka] *nf* lacquer

lacio, -a ['laθjo, a] *adj* (pelo) straight

lacón [la'kon] *nm* shoulder of pork

lactancia [lak'tanθja] *nf* lactation

lácteo, -a ['lakteo, a] *adj*: **productos ~s** dairy products

ladear [laðe'ar] *vt* to tip, tilt ▷ *vi* to tilt; **ladearse** *vr* to lean

ladera [la'ðera] *nf* slope

lado ['laðo] *nm* (gen) side; (fig) protection; (Mil) flank; **al ~ de** beside; **poner de ~** to put on its side; **poner a un ~** to put aside; **por todos ~s** on all sides, all round (BRIT)

ladrar [la'ðrar] *vi* to bark; **ladrido** *nm* bark, barking

ladrillo [la'ðriʎo] *nm* (gen) brick; (azulejo) tile

ladrón, -ona [la'ðron, ona] *nm/f* thief

lagartija [laɣar'tixa] *nf* (Zool) (small) lizard

lagarto [la'ɣarto] *nm* (Zool) lizard

lago ['laɣo] *nm* lake

lágrima ['laɣrima] *nf* tear

laguna [la'ɣuna] *nf* (lago) lagoon; (hueco) gap

lamentable [lamen'taβle] *adj* lamentable, regrettable; (miserable) pitiful

lamentar [lamen'tar] *vt* (sentir) to regret; (deplorar) to lament; **lamentarse** *vr* to lament; **lo lamento**

mucho I'm very sorry

lamer [la'mer] *vt* to lick

lámina ['lamina] *nf* (plancha delgada) sheet; (para estampar, estampa) plate

lámpara ['lampara] *nf* lamp; **lámpara de alcohol/ gas** spirit/gas lamp; **lámpara de pie** standard lamp

lana ['lana] *nf* wool

lancha ['lantʃa] *nf* launch; **lancha motora** motorboat, speedboat

langosta [lan'gosta] *nf* (crustáceo) lobster; (: de río) crayfish; **langostino** *nm* Dublin Bay prawn

lanza ['lanθa] *nf* (arma) lance, spear

lanzamiento [lanθa'mjento] *nm* (gen) throwing; (Náut, Com) launch, launching; **lanzamiento de peso** putting the shot

lanzar [lan'θar] *vt* (gen) to throw; (Deporte: pelota) to bowl; (Náut, Com) to launch; (Jur) to evict; **lanzarse** *vr* to throw o.s.

lapa ['lapa] *nf* limpet

lapicero [lapi'θero] *nm* (bolígrafo) ballpoint pen, Biro®

lápida ['lapiða] *nf* stone; **lápida mortuoria** headstone

lápiz ['lapiθ] *nm* pencil; **lápiz de color** coloured pencil; **lápiz de labios** lipstick; **lápiz de ojos** eyebrow pencil

largar [lar'ɣar] *vt* (soltar) to release; (aflojar) to loosen; (lanzar) to launch; (fam) to let fly; (velas) to unfurl; (LAM: lanzar) to throw; **largarse** *vr* (fam) to beat it; **~se a** (CS: empezar) to start to

largo, -a ['larɣo, a] *adj* (longitud) long; (tiempo) lengthy; (fig) generous ▷ *nm* length; (Mús) largo; **dos años ~s** two long years; **tiene 9 metros de ~** it is 9 metres long; **a la larga** in the long run; **a lo ~ de** along; (tiempo) all through, throughout; **largometraje** *nm* feature film

laringe [la'rinxe] *nf* larynx; **laringitis** *nf* laryngitis

las [las] *art def the* ▷ *pron* them; **~ que cantan** the ones o women o girls who sing; V tb **el**

lasaña [la'saɲa] *nf* lasagne, lasagna

láser ['laser] *nm* laser

lástima ['lastima] *nf* (pena) pity; **dar ~** to be pitiful; **es una ~ que ...** it's a pity that ...; **¡qué ~!** what a pity!; **está hecha una ~** she looks pitiful

lastimar [lasti'mar] *vt* (herir) to wound; (ofender) to offend; **lastimarse** *vr* to hurt o.s.

lata ['lata] *nf* (metal) tin; (caja) tin can; (fam) nuisance; **en ~** tinned (BRIT), canned; **dar la ~** to be a nuisance

latente [la'tente] *adj* latent

lateral [late'ral] *adj* side *cpd*, lateral ▷ *nm* (Teatro) wings

latido [la'tiðo] *nm* (de corazón) beat

latifundio [lati'fundjo] *nm* large estate

latigazo [lati'ɣaθo] *nm* (golpe) lash; (sonido) crack

látigo ['latiɣo] *nm* whip

latín [la'tin] *nm* Latin

latino, -a [la'tino, a] *adj* Latin; **latinoamericano, -a** *adj, nm/f* Latin-American

latir [la'tir] *vi* (corazón, pulso) to beat

latitud [lati'tuð] *nf* (Geo) latitude

latón [la'ton] *nm* brass

laurel [lau'rel] *nm* (Bot) laurel; (Culin) bay

lava ['laβa] *nf* lava

lavabo [la'βaβo] *nm* (pila) washbasin; (tb: **~s**) toilet

lavado [la'βaðo] *nm* washing; (de ropa) laundry; (Arte) wasli, **lavado de cerebro** brainwashing; **lavado en seco** dry-cleaning

lavadora [laβa'ðora] nf washing machine

lavanda [la'βanda] nf lavender

lavandería [laβande'ria] nf laundry; (automática) launderette

lavaplatos [laβa'platos] nm inv dishwasher

lavar [la'βar] vt to wash; (borrar) to wipe away; **lavarse** vr to wash o.s.; **~se las manos** to wash one's hands; **~se los dientes** to brush one's teeth; **~ y marcar** (pelo) to shampoo and set; **~ en seco** to dry-clean; **~ los platos** to wash the dishes

lavarropas [laβa'rropas] (RPL) nm inv washing machine

lavavajillas [laβaβa'xiʎas] nm inv dishwasher

laxante [lak'sante] nm laxative

lazarillo [laθa'riʎo] nm (tb: **perro ~**) guide dog

lazo [la'βo] nm knot; (lazada) bow; (para animales) lasso; (trampa) snare; (vínculo) tie

le [le] pron (directo) him (o her); (: usted) you; (indirecto) to him (o her o it); (: usted) to you

leal [le'al] adj loyal; **lealtad** nf loyalty

lección [lek'θjon] nf lesson

leche ['letʃe] nf milk; **tiene mala ~** (fam!) he's a swine (!); **leche condensada** condensed milk; **leche desnatada** skimmed milk

lecho ['letʃo] nm (cama: de río) bed; (Geo) layer

lechón [le'tʃon] nm sucking (BRIT) o suckling (US) pig

lechoso, -a [le'tʃoso, a] adj milky

lechuga [le'tʃuɣa] nf lettuce

lechuza [le'tʃuθa] nf owl

lector, a [lek'tor, a] nm/f reader ⊳ nm: **~ de discos compactos** CD player

lectura [lek'tura] nf reading

leer [le'er] vt to read

legado [le'ɣaðo] nm (don) bequest; (herencia) legacy; (enviado) legate

legajo [le'ɣaxo] nm file

legal [le'ɣal] adj (gen) legal; (persona) trustworthy; **legalizar** [leɣali'θar] vt to legalize; (documento) to authenticate

legaña [le'ɣaɲa] nf sleep (in eyes)

legión [le'xjon] nf legion; **legionario, -a** adj legionary ⊳ nm legionnaire

legislación [lexisla'θjon] nf legislation

legislar [lexis'lar] vi to legislate

legislatura [lexisla'tura] nf (Pol) period of office

legítimo, -a [le'xitimo, a] adj (genuino) authentic; (legal) legitimate

legua ['leɣwa] nf league

legumbres [le'ɣumbres] nfpl pulses

leído, -a [le'iðo, a] adj well-read

lejanía [lexa'nia] nf distance; **lejano, -a** adj far-off; (en el tiempo) distant; (fig) remote

lejía [le'xia] nf bleach

lejos ['lexos] adv far, far away; **a lo ~** in the distance; **de** o **desde ~** from afar; **~ de** far from

lema ['lema] nm motto; (Pol) slogan

lencería [lenθe'ria] nf linen, drapery

lengua ['leŋgwa] nf tongue; (Ling) language; **morderse la ~** to hold one's tongue

lenguado [leŋ'gwaðo] nm sole

lenguaje [len'gwaxe] nm language; **lenguaje de programación** program(m)ing language

lengüeta [len'gweta] nf (Anat) epiglottis; (zapatos) tongue; (Mús) reed

lente ['lente] nf lens; (lupa) magnifying glass; **lentes** nfpl lenses ⊳ nm (LAM: gafas) glasses; **lentes bifocales/de sol** (LAM) bifocals/sunglasses; **lentes de contacto** contact lenses

lenteja [len'texa] nf lentil; **lentejuela** nf sequin

lentilla [len'tiʎa] nf contact lens

lentitud [lenti'tuð] nf slowness; **con ~** slowly

lento, -a ['lento, a] adj slow

leña ['leɲa] nf firewood; **leñador, a** nm/f woodcutter

leño ['leɲo] nm (trozo de árbol) log; (madero) timber; (fig) blockhead

Leo ['leo] nm Leo

león [le'on] nm lion; **león marino** sea lion

leopardo [leo'parðo] nm leopard

leotardos [leo'tarðos] nmpl tights

lepra ['lepra] nf leprosy; **leproso, -a** nm/f leper

les [les] pron (directo) them; (: ustedes) you; (indirecto) to them; (: ustedes) to you

lesbiana [les'βjana] adj, nf lesbian

lesión [le'sjon] nf wound, lesion; (Deporte) injury; **lesionado, -a** adj injured ⊳ nm/f injured person

letal [le'tal] adj lethal

letanía [leta'nia] nf litany

letra ['letra] nf letter; (escritura) handwriting; (Mús) lyrics pl; **letra de cambio** bill of exchange; **letra de imprenta** print; **letrado, -a** adj learned ⊳ nm/f lawyer; **letrero** nm (cartel) sign; (etiqueta) label

letrina [le'trina] nf latrine

leucemia [leu'θemja] nf leukaemia

levadura [leβa'ðura] nf (para el pan) yeast; (de cerveza) brewer's yeast

levantar [leβan'tar] vt (gen) to raise; (del suelo) to pick up; (hacia arriba) to lift (up); (plan) to make, draw up; (mesa) to clear; (campamento) to strike; (fig) to cheer up, hearten; **levantarse** vr to get up; (enderezarse) to straighten up; (rebelarse) to rebel; **~ el ánimo** to cheer up

levante [le'βante] nm east coast; **el L~** region of Spain extending from Castellón to Murcia

levar [le'βar] vt to weigh

leve ['leβe] adj light; (fig) trivial

levita [le'βita] nf frock coat

léxico ['leksiko] nm (vocabulario) vocabulary

ley [lei] nf (gen) law; (metal) standard

leyenda [le'jenda] nf legend

leyó etc vb V **leer**

liar [li'ar] vt to tie (up); (unir) to bind; (envolver) to wrap (up); (enredar) to confuse; (cigarrillo) to roll; **liarse** vr (fam) to get involved; **~se a palos** to get involved in a fight

Líbano ['liβano] nm: **el ~** the Lebanon

libélula [li'βelula] nf dragonfly

liberación [liβera'θjon] nf liberation; (de la cárcel) release

liberal [liβe'ral] adj, nmf liberal

liberar [liβe'rar] vt to liberate

libertad [liβer'tað] nf liberty, freedom; **libertad bajo fianza** bail; **libertad bajo palabra** parole; **libertad condicional** probation; **libertad de culto/de prensa/de comercio** freedom of worship/of the press/of trade

libertar [liβer'tar] vt (preso) to set free; (de una obligación) to release; (eximir) to exempt

libertino, -a [liβer'tino, a] adj permissive ⊳ nm/f permissive person

libra ['liβra] nf pound; **L~** (Astrología) Libra; **libra esterlina** pound sterling

libramiento [liβra'mjento] (MÉX) nm ring road (BRIT), beltway (US)

librar [li'βrar] vt (de peligro) to save; (batalla) to wage, fight; (de impuestos) to exempt; (cheque) to make out; (Jur) to exempt; **librarse** vr: **~se de** to escape from, free o.s. from

libre ['liβre] adj free; (lugar) unoccupied; (asiento) vacant; (de deudas) free of debts; **~ de impuestos** free of tax; **tiro ~** free kick; **los 100 metros ~s** the 100 metres free-style (race); **al aire ~** in the open air

librería [liβre'ria] nf (tienda) bookshop; **librero, -a** nm/f bookseller

libreta [li'βreta] nf notebook

libro ['liβro] nm book; **libro de bolsillo** paperback; **libro de texto** textbook; **libro electrónico** e-book

Lic. abr = **licenciado, a**

licencia [li'θenθja] nf (gen) licence; (permiso) permission; **licencia de caza** game licence; **licencia por enfermedad** (MÉX, RPL) sick leave; **licenciado, -a** adj licensed ▷nm/f graduate; **licenciar** vt (empleado) to dismiss; (permitir) to permit, allow; (soldado) to discharge; (estudiante) to confer a degree upon; **licenciarse** vr: **licenciarse en Derecho** to graduate in law

lícito, -a ['liθito, a] adj (legal) lawful; (justo) fair, just; (permisible) permissible

licor [li'kor] nm spirits pl (BRIT), liquor (US); (de frutas etc) liqueur

licuadora [likwa'ðora] nf blender

líder ['liðer] nmf leader; **liderato** nm leadership; **liderazgo** nm leadership

lidia ['liðja] nf bullfighting; (una lidia) bullfight; **toros de ~** fighting bulls; **lidiar** vt, vi to fight

liebre ['ljeβre] nf hare

lienzo ['ljenθo] nm linen; (Arte) canvas; (Arq) wall

liga ['liɣa] nf (de medias) garter, suspender; (LAM: goma) rubber band; (confederación) league

ligadura [liɣa'ðura] nf bond, tie; (Med, Mús) ligature

ligamento [liɣa'mento] nm ligament

ligar [li'ɣar] vt (atar) to tie; (unir) to join; (Med) to bind up; (Mús) to slur ▷vi to mix, blend; (fam): **(él) liga mucho** he pulls a lot of women; **ligarse** vr to commit o.s.

ligero, -a [li'xero, a] adj (de peso) light; (tela) thin; (rápido) swift, quick; (ágil) agile, nimble; (de importancia) slight; (de carácter) flippant, superficial ▷adv: **a la ligera** superficially

liguero [li'xero] nm suspender (BRIT) o garter (US) belt

lija ['lixa] nf (Zool) dogfish; (tb: **papel de ~**) sandpaper

lila ['lila] nf lilac

lima ['lima] nf file; (Bot) lime; **lima de uñas** nailfile; **limar** vt to file

limitación [limita'θjon] nf limitation, limit

limitar [limi'tar] vt to limit; (reducir) to reduce, cut down ▷vi: **~ con** to border on; **limitarse** vr: **~se a** to limit o.s. to

límite ['limite] nm (gen) limit; (fin) end; (frontera) border; **límite de velocidad** speed limit

limítrofe [li'mitrofe] adj neighbouring

limón [li'mon] nm lemon ▷adj: **amarillo ~** lemon-yellow; **limonada** nf lemonade

limosna [li'mosna] nf alms pl; **vivir de ~** to live on charity

limpiador [limpja'ðor] (MÉX) nm = **limpiaparabrisas**

limpiaparabrisas [limpjapara'βrisas] nm inv

windscreen (BRIT) o windshield (US) wiper

limpiar [lim'pjar] vt to clean; (con trapo) to wipe; (quitar) to wipe away; (zapatos) to shine, polish; (fig) to clean up

limpieza [lim'pjeθa] nf (estado) cleanliness; (acto) cleaning; (: de las calles) cleansing; (: de zapatos) polishing; (habilidad) skill; (fig: Policía) clean-up; (pureza) purity; (Mil): **operación de ~** mopping-up operation; **limpieza en seco** dry cleaning

limpio, -a ['limpjo, a] adj clean; (moralmente) pure; (Com) clear, net; (fam) honest ▷adv: **jugar ~** to play fair; **pasar a** (ESP) o **en** (LAM) **~** to make a clean copy of

lince ['linθe] nm lynx

linchar [lin'tʃar] vt to lynch

lindar [lin'dar] vi to adjoin; **~ con** to border on

lindo, -a ['lindo, a] adj pretty, lovely ▷adv: **nos divertimos de lo ~** we had a marvellous time; **canta muy ~** (LAM) he sings beautifully

línea ['linea] nf (gen) line; **en ~** (Inform) on line; **línea aérea** airline; **línea de meta** goal line; (en carrera) finishing line; **línea discontinua** (Auto) broken line; **línea recta** straight line

lingote [lin'ɡote] nm ingot

lingüista [lin'ɡwista] nmf linguist; **lingüística** nf linguistics sg

lino ['lino] nm linen; (Bot) flax

linterna [lin'terna] nf torch (BRIT), flashlight (US)

lío ['lio] nm bundle; (fam) fuss; (desorden) muddle, mess; **armar un ~** to make a fuss

liquen ['liken] nm lichen

liquidación [likiða'θjon] nf liquidation; **venta de ~** clearance sale

liquidar [liki'ðar] vt (mercancías) to liquidate; (deudas) to pay off; (empresa) to wind up

líquido, -a ['likiðo, a] adj liquid; (ganancia) net ▷nm liquid; **líquido imponible** net taxable income

lira ['lira] nf (Mús) lyre; (moneda) lira

lírico, -a ['liriko, a] adj lyrical

lirio ['lirjo] nm (Bot) iris

lirón [li'ron] nm (Zool) dormouse; (fig) sleepyhead

Lisboa [lis'βoa] n Lisbon

lisiar [li'sjar] vt to maim

liso, -a ['liso, a] adj (terreno) flat; (cabello) straight; (superficie) even; (tela) plain

lista ['lista] nf list; (de alumnos) school register; (de libros) catalogue; (de platos) menu; (de precios) price list; **pasar ~** to call the roll; **tela de ~s** striped material; **lista de espera** waiting list; **lista de precios** price list; **listín** nm (tb: **listín telefónico** o **de teléfonos**) telephone directory

listo, -a ['listo, a] adj (perspicaz) smart, clever; (preparado) ready

listón [lis'ton] nm (de madera, metal) strip

litera [li'tera] nf (en barco, tren) berth; (en dormitorio) bunk, bunk bed

literal [lite'ral] adj literal

literario, -a [lite'rarjo, a] adj literary

literato, -a [lite'rato, a] adj literary ▷nm/f writer

literatura [litera'tura] nf literature

litigio [li'tixjo] nm (Jur) lawsuit; (fig): **en ~ con** in dispute with

litografía [litoɣra'fia] nf lithography; (una litografía) lithograph

litoral [lito'ral] adj coastal ▷nm coast, seaboard

litro ['litro] nm litre

lívido, -a ['liβiðo, a] adj livid

llaga ['ʎaɣa] *nf* wound
llama ['ʎama] *nf* flame; (*Zool*) llama
llamada [ʎa'maða] *nf* call; **llamada a cobro revertido** reverse-charge (*BRIT*) o collect (*US*) call; **llamada al orden** call to order; **llamada de atención** warning; **llamada local** (*LAM*) local call; **llamada metropolitana** (*ESP*) local call; **llamada por cobrar** (*MÉX*) reverse-charge (*BRIT*) o collect (*US*) call
llamamiento [ʎama'mjento] *nm* call
llamar [ʎa'mar] *vt* to call; (*atención*) to attract ▷ *vi* (*por teléfono*) to telephone; (*a la puerta*) to knock (o ring); (*por señas*) to beckon; (*Mil*) to call up; **llamarse** *vr* to be called, be named; **¿cómo se llama (usted)?** what's your name?
llamativo, -a [ʎama'tiβo, a] *adj* showy; (*color*) loud
llano, -a ['ʎano, a] *adj* (*superficie*) flat; (*persona*) straightforward; (*estilo*) clear ▷ *nm* plain, flat ground
llanta ['ʎanta] *nf* (*ESP*) (*wheel*) rim; **llanta (de goma)** (*LAM: neumático*) tyre; (*: cámara*) inner (tube); **llanta de repuesto** (*LAM*) spare tyre
llanto ['ʎanto] *nm* weeping
llanura [ʎa'nura] *nf* plain
llave ['ʎaβe] *nf* key; (*del agua*) tap; (*Mecánica*) spanner; (*de la luz*) switch; (*Mús*) key; **echar la ~** to lock up; **llave de contacto** (*ESP Auto*) ignition key; **llave de encendido** (*LAM Auto*) ignition key; **llave de paso** stopcock; **llave inglesa** monkey wrench; **llave maestra** master key; **llavero** *nm* keyring
llegada [ʎe'ɣaða] *nf* arrival
llegar [ʎe'ɣar] *vi* to arrive; (*alcanzar*) to reach; (*bastar*) to be enough; **llegarse** *vr*: **~se a** to approach; **~ a** to manage to, succeed in; **~ a saber** to find out; **~ a ser** to become; **~ a las manos de** to come into the hands of
llenar [ʎe'nar] *vt* to fill; (*espacio*) to cover; (*formulario*) to fill in o up; (*fig*) to heap
lleno, -a ['ʎeno, a] *adj* full, filled; (*repleto*) full up ▷ *nm* (*Teatro*) full house; **dar ~ contra un muro** to hit a wall head-on
llevadero, -a [ʎeβa'ðero, a] *adj* bearable, tolerable
llevar [ʎe'βar] *vt* to take; (*ropa*) to wear; (*cargar*) to carry; (*quitar*) to take away; (*en coche*) to drive; (*transportar*) to transport; (*traer: dinero*) to carry; (*conducir*) to lead; (*Mat*) to carry ▷ *vi* (*suj: camino etc*): **~ a** to lead to; **llevarse** *vr* to carry off, take away; **llevamos dos días aquí** we have been here for two days; **él me lleva 2 años** he's 2 years older than me; **~ los libros** (*Com*) to keep the books; **~se bien** to get on well (together)
llorar [ʎo'rar] *vt, vi* to cry, weep; **~ de risa** to cry with laughter
llorón, -ona [ʎo'ron, ona] *adj* tearful ▷ *nm/f* cry-baby
lloroso, -a [ʎo'roso, a] *adj* (*gen*) weeping, tearful; (*triste*) sad, sorrowful
llover [ʎo'βer] *vi* to rain
llovizna [ʎo'βiθna] *nf* drizzle; **lloviznar** *vi* to drizzle
llueve *etc vb V* **llover**
lluvia ['ʎuβja] *nf* rain; **lluvia radioactiva** (*radioactive*) fallout; **lluvioso, -a** *adj* rainy
lo [lo] *art def*: **~ bel~** the beautiful, what is beautiful, that which is beautiful ▷ *pron* (*persona*) him; (*cosa*) it; **~ que sea** whatever; *V tb* **el**
loable [lo'aβle] *adj* praiseworthy
lobo ['loβo] *nm* wolf; **lobo de mar** (*fig*) sea dog
lóbulo ['loβulo] *nm* lobe
local [lo'kal] *adj* local ▷ *nm* place, site; (*oficinas*)

premises *pl*; **localidad** *nf* (*barrio*) locality; (*lugar*) location; (*Teatro*) seat, ticket; **localizar** *vt* (*ubicar*) to locate, find; (*restringir*) to localize; (*situar*) to place
loción [lo'θjon] *nf* lotion
loco, -a ['loko, a] *adj* mad ▷ *nm/f* lunatic, mad person; **estar ~ con** o **por algo/por algn** to be mad about sth/sb
locomotora [lokomo'tora] *nf* engine, locomotive
locuaz [lo'kwaθ] *adj* loquacious
locución [loku'θjon] *nf* expression
locura [lo'kura] *nf* madness; (*acto*) crazy act
locutor, a [loku'tor, a] *nm/f* (*Radio*) announcer; (*comentarista*) commentator; (*TV*) newsreader
locutorio [loku'torjo] *nm* (*en telefónica*) telephone booth
lodo ['loðo] *nm* mud
lógica ['loxika] *nf* logic
lógico, -a ['loxiko, a] *adj* logical
login ['loxin] login
logística [lo'xistika] *nf* logistics *sg*
logotipo [loðo'tipo] *nm* logo
logrado, -a [lo'ðraðo, a] *adj* (*interpretación, reproducción*) polished, excellent
lograr [lo'ðrar] *vt* to achieve; (*obtener*) to get, obtain; **~ hacer** to manage to do; **~ que algn venga** to manage to get sb to come
logro ['loxro] *nm* achievement, success
lóker ['loker] (*LAM*) *nm* locker
loma ['loma] *nf* hillock (*BRIT*), small hill
lombriz [lom'briθ] *nf* worm
lomo ['lomo] *nm* (*de animal*) back; (*Culin: de cerdo*) pork loin; (*: de vaca*) rib steak; (*de libro*) spine
lona ['lona] *nf* canvas
loncha ['lontʃa] *nf* = **lonja**
lonchería [lontʃe'ria] (*LAM*) *nf* snack bar, diner (*US*)
Londres ['londres] *n* London
longaniza [longa'niθa] *nf* pork sausage
longitud [lonxi'tuð] *nf* length; (*Geo*) longitude; **tener 3 metros de ~** to be 3 metres long; **longitud de onda** wavelength
lonja ['lonxa] *nf* slice; (*de tocino*) rasher; **lonja de pescado** fish market
loro ['loro] *nm* parrot
los [los] *art def* the ▷ *pron* them; (*ustedes*) you; **mis libros y ~ tuyos** my books and yours; *V tb* **el**
losa ['losa] *nf* stone
lote ['lote] *nm* portion; (*Com*) lot
lotería [lote'ria] *nf* lottery; (*juego*) lotto
loza ['loθa] *nf* crockery
lubina [lu'βina] *nf* sea bass
lubricante [luβri'kante] *nm* lubricant
lubricar [luβri'kar] *vt* to lubricate
lucha ['lutʃa] *nf* fight, struggle; **lucha de clases** class struggle; **lucha libre** wrestling; **luchar** *vi* to fight
lúcido, -a ['luθiðo, a] *adj* (*persona*) lucid; (*mente*) logical; (*idea*) crystal-clear
luciérnaga [lu'θjernaxa] *nf* glow-worm
lucir [lu'θir] *vt* to illuminate, light (up); (*ostentar*) to show off ▷ *vi* (*brillar*) to shine; **lucirse** *vr* (*irónico*) to make a fool of o.s.
lucro ['lukro] *nm* profit, gain
lúdico, -a ['luðiko, a] *adj* (*aspecto, actividad*) play *cpd*
luego ['lwexo] *adv* (*después*) next; (*más tarde*) later, afterwards
lugar [lu'ɣar] *nm* place; (*sitio*) spot; **en primer ~** in the first place, firstly; **en ~ de** instead of; **hacer ~** to make

room; **fuera de ~** out of place; **sin ~ a dudas** without doubt, undoubtedly; **dar ~ a** to give rise to; **tener ~** to take place; **yo en su ~** if I were him; **lugar común** commonplace

lúgubre ['luɣuβre] *adj* mournful

lujo ['luxo] *nm* luxury; (*fig*) profusion, abundance; **de ~** luxury *cpd*, de luxe; **lujoso, -a** *adj* luxurious

lujuria [lu'xurja] *nf* lust

lumbre ['lumbre] *nf* fire; (*para cigarrillo*) light

luminoso, -a [lumi'noso, a] *adj* luminous, shining

luna ['luna] *nf* moon; (*de un espejo*) glass; (*de gafas*) lens; (*fig*) crescent; **estar en la ~** to have one's head in the clouds; **luna de miel** honeymoon; **luna llena/nueva** full/new moon

lunar [lu'nar] *adj* lunar ⊳ *nm* (*Anat*) mole; **tela de ~es** spotted material

lunes ['lunes] *nm inv* Monday

lupa ['lupa] *nf* magnifying glass

lustre ['lustre] *nm* polish; (*fig*) lustre; **dar ~ a** to polish

luto ['luto] *nm* mourning; **llevar el** o **vestirse de ~** to be in mourning

Luxemburgo [luksem'burxo] *nm* Luxembourg

luz [luθ] (*pl* **luces**) *nf* light; **dar a ~ un niño** to give birth to a child; **sacar a la ~** to bring to light; **dar** o **encender** (*ESP*) o **prender** (*LAM*)**/apagar la ~** to switch the light on/off; **tener pocas luces** to be dim o stupid; **traje de luces** bullfighter's costume; **luces de tráfico** traffic lights; **luz de freno** brake light; **luz roja/verde** red/green light

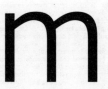

m *abr* (= *metro*) m; (= *minuto*) m

macana [ma'kana] (*MÉX*) *nf* truncheon (*BRIT*), billy club (*US*)

macarrones [maka'rrones] *nmpl* macaroni *sg*

macedonia [maθe'ðonja] *nf* (*tb*: **~ de frutas**) fruit salad

maceta [ma'θeta] *nf* (*de flores*) pot of flowers; (*para plantas*) flowerpot

machacar [matʃa'kar] *vt* to crush, pound ⊳ *vi* (*insistir*) to go on, keep on

machete [ma'tʃete] *nm* machete, (large) knife

machetear [matʃete'ar] (*MÉX*) *vt* to swot (*BRIT*), grind away (*US*)

machismo [ma'tʃismo] *nm* male chauvinism; **machista** *adj, nm* sexist

macho ['matʃo] *adj* male; (*fig*) virile ⊳ *nm* male; (*fig*) he-man

macizo, -a [ma'θiθo, a] *adj* (*grande*) massive; (*fuerte, sólido*) solid ⊳ *nm* mass, chunk

madeja [ma'ðexa] *nf* (*de lana*) skein, hank; (*de pelo*) mass, mop

madera [ma'ðera] *nf* wood; (*fig*) nature, character; **una ~** a piece of wood

madrastra [ma'ðrastra] *nf* stepmother

madre ['maðre] *adj* mother *cpd* ⊳ *nf* mother; (*de vino etc*) dregs *pl*; **madre política/soltera** mother-in-law/unmarried mother

Madrid [ma'ðrið] *n* Madrid

madriguera [maðri'ɣera] *nf* burrow

madrileño, -a [maðri'leɲo, a] *adj* of o from Madrid ⊳ *nm/f* native of Madrid

madrina [ma'ðrina] *nf* godmother; (*Arq*) prop, shore; (*Tec*) brace; (*de boda*) bridesmaid

madrugada [maðru'ɣaða] *nf* early morning; (*alba*) dawn, daybreak

madrugador, a [maðruɣa'ðor, a] *adj* early-rising

madrugar [maðru'ɣar] *vi* to get up early; (*fig*) to get ahead

madurar [maðu'rar] *vt, vi* (*fruta*) to ripen; (*fig*) to mature; **madurez** *nf* ripeness; maturity; **maduro, -a** *adj* ripe; mature

maestra *nf* V **maestro**

maestría [maes'tria] *nf* mastery; (*habilidad*) skill,

expertise

maestro, -a [ma'estro, a] *adj* masterly; (*principal*) main ⊳ *nm/f* master/mistress; (*profesor*) teacher ⊳ *nm* (*autoridad*) authority; (*Mús*) maestro; (*experto*) master; **maestro albañil** master mason

magdalena [maɣða'lena] *nf* fairy cake

magia ['maxja] *nf* magic; **mágico, -a** *adj* magic(al) ⊳ *nm/f* magician

magisterio [maxis'terjo] *nm* (*enseñanza*) teaching; (*profesión*) teaching profession; (*maestros*) teachers *pl*

magistrado [maxis'traðo] *nm* magistrate

magistral [maxis'tral] *adj* magisterial; (*fig*) masterly

magnate [maɣ'nate] *nm* magnate, tycoon

magnético, -a [maɣ'netiko, a] *adj* magnetic

magnetofón [maɣneto'fon] *nm* tape recorder

magnetófono [maɣne'tofono] *nm* = **magnetofón**

magnífico, -a [maɣ'nifiko, a] *adj* splendid, magnificent

magnitud [maɣni'tuð] *nf* magnitude

mago, -a ['maɣo, a] *nm/f* magician; **los Reyes M~s** the Three Wise Men

magro, -a ['maɣro, a] *adj* (*carne*) lean

mahonesa [mao'nesa] *nf* mayonnaise

maître ['metre] *nm* head waiter

maíz [ma'iθ] *nm* maize (*BRIT*), corn (*US*); sweet corn

majestad [maxes'tað] *nf* majesty

majo, -a ['maxo, a] *adj* nice; (*guapo*) attractive, good-looking; (*elegante*) smart

mal [mal] *adv* badly; (*equivocadamente*) wrongly ⊳ *adj* = **malo** ⊳ *nm* evil; (*desgracia*) misfortune; (*daño*) harm, damage; (*Med*) illness; **~ que bien** rightly or wrongly; **ir de ~ en peor** to get worse and worse

malabarista [malaβa'rista] *nmf* juggler

malaria [ma'larja] *nf* malaria

malcriado, -a [mal'krjaðo, a] *adj* spoiled

maldad [mal'dað] *nf* evil, wickedness

maldecir [malde'θir] *vt* to curse

maldición [maldi'θjon] *nf* curse

maldito, -a [mal'dito, a] *adj* (*condenado*) damned; (*perverso*) wicked; **¡~ sea!** damn it!

malecón [male'kon] (*LAM*) *nm* sea front, promenade

maleducado, -a [maleðu'kaðo, a] *adj* bad-mannered, rude

malentendido [malenten'diðo] *nm* misunderstanding

malestar [males'tar] *nm* (*gen*) discomfort; (*fig: inquietud*) uneasiness; (*Pol*) unrest

maleta [ma'leta] *nf* case, suitcase; (*Auto*) boot (*BRIT*), trunk (*US*); **hacer las ~s** to pack; **maletero** *nm* (*Auto*) boot (*BRIT*), trunk (*US*); **maletín** *nm* small case, bag

maleza [ma'leθa] *nf* (*malas hierbas*) weeds *pl*; (*arbustos*) thicket

malgastar [malɣas'tar] *vt* (*tiempo, dinero*) to waste; (*salud*) to ruin

malhechor, a [male'tʃor, a] *nm/f* delinquent

malhumorado, -a [malumo'raðo, a] *adj* bad-tempered

malicia [ma'liθja] *nf* (*maldad*) wickedness; (*astucia*) slyness, guile; (*mala intención*) malice, spite; (*carácter travieso*) mischievousness

maligno, -a [ma'liɣno, a] *adj* evil; (*malévolo*) malicious; (*Med*) malignant

malla ['maʎa] *nf* mesh; (*de baño*) swimsuit; (*de ballet, gimnasia*) leotard; **mallas** *nfpl* tights; **malla de alambre** wire mesh

Mallorca [ma'ʎorka] *nf* Majorca

malo, -a ['malo, a] *adj* bad, false ⊳ *nm/f* villain; **estar ~** to be ill

malograr [malo'ɣrar] *vt* to spoil; (*plan*) to upset; (*ocasión*) to waste

malparado, -a [malpa'raðo, a] *adj*: **salir ~** to come off badly

malpensado, -a [malpen'saðo, a] *adj* nasty

malteada [malte'aða] (*LAM*) *nf* milkshake

maltratar [maltra'tar] *vt* to ill-treat, mistreat

malvado, -a [mal'βaðo, a] *adj* evil, villainous

Malvinas [mal'βinas] *nfpl* (*tb*: **Islas ~**) Falklands, Falkland Islands

mama ['mama] *nf* (*de animal*) teat; (*de mujer*) breast

mamá [ma'ma] (*pl* **~s**) (*fam*) *nf* mum, mummy

mamar [ma'mar] *vt, vi* to suck

mamarracho [mama'rratʃo] *nm* sight, mess

mameluco [mame'luko] (*RPL*) *nm* dungarees *pl* (*BRIT*), overalls *pl* (*US*)

mamífero [ma'mifero] *nm* mammal

mampara [mam'para] *nf* (*entre habitaciones*) partition; (*biombo*) screen

mampostería [mamposte'ria] *nf* masonry

manada [ma'naða] *nf* (*Zool*) herd; (*: de leones*) pride; (*: de lobos*) pack

manantial [manan'tjal] *nm* spring

mancha ['mantʃa] *nf* stain, mark; (*Zool*) patch; **manchar** *vt* (*gen*) to stain, mark; (*ensuciar*) to soil, dirty

manchego, -a [man'tʃeɣo, a] *adj* of o from La Mancha

manco, -a ['manko, a] *adj* (*de un brazo*) one-armed; (*de una mano*) one-handed; (*fig*) defective, faulty

mancuernas [man'kwernas] (*MÉX*) *nfpl* cufflinks

mandado [man'daðo] (*LAM*) *nm* errand

mandamiento [manda'mjento] *nm* (*orden*) order, command; (*Rel*) commandment

mandar [man'dar] *vt* (*ordenar*) to order; (*dirigir*) to lead, command; (*enviar*) to send; (*pedir*) to order, ask for ⊳ *vi* to be in charge; (*pey*) to be bossy; **¿mande?** (*MÉX: ¿cómo dice?*) pardon?, excuse me?; **~ hacer un traje** to have a suit made

mandarina [manda'rina] (*ESP*) *nf* tangerine, mandarin (orange)

mandato [man'dato] *nm* (*orden*) order; (*Pol: período*) term of office; (*: territorio*) mandate

mandíbula [man'diβula] *nf* jaw

mandil [man'dil] *nm* apron

mando ['mando] *nm* (*Mil*) command; (*de país*) rule; (*el primer lugar*) lead; (*Pol*) term of office; (*Tec*) control; **~ a la izquierda** left-hand drive; **mando a distancia** remote control

mandón, -ona [man'don, ona] *adj* bossy, domineering

manejar [mane'xar] *vt* to manage; (*máquina*) to work, operate; (*caballo etc*) to handle; (*casa*) to run, manage; (*LAM: coche*) to drive; **manejarse** *vr* (*comportarse*) to act, behave; (*arreglárselas*) to manage; **manejo** *nm* (*de bicicleta*) handling; (*de negocio*) management, running; (*LAM Auto*) driving; (*facilidad de trato*) ease, confidence; **manejos** *nmpl* (*intrigas*) intrigues

manera [ma'nera] *nf* way, manner, fashion; **maneras** *nfpl* (*modales*) manners; **su ~ de ser** the way he is; (*aire*) his manner; **de ninguna ~** by no means, on no account; **de otra ~** otherwise; **de todas ~s** at any rate; **no hay ~ de persuadirle** there's no way of convincing him

manga ['maŋa] nf (de camisa) sleeve; (de riego) hose

mango ['maŋgo] nm handle; (Bot) mango

manguera [maŋ'gera] nf hose

maní [ma'ni] (LAM) nm peanut

manía [ma'nia] nf (Med) mania; (fig: moda) rage, craze; (disgusto) dislike; (malicia) spite; **coger ~ a algn** to take a dislike to sb; **tener ~ a algn** to dislike sb; **maníaco, -a** adj maniac(al) ▷ nm/f maniac

maniático, -a [ma'njatiko, a] adj maniac(al) ▷ nm/f maniac

manicomio [mani'komjo] nm mental hospital (BRIT), insane asylum (US)

manifestación [manifesta'θjon] nf (declaración) statement, declaration; (de emoción) show, display; (Pol: desfile) demonstration; (de concentración) mass meeting

manifestar [manifes'tar] vt to show, manifest; (declarar) to state, declare; **manifiesto, -a** adj clear, manifest ▷ nm manifesto

manillar [mani'ʎar] nm handlebars pl

maniobra [ma'njoβra] nf manoeuvre; **maniobras** nfpl (Mil) manoeuvres; **maniobrar** vt to manoeuvre

manipulación [manipula'θjon] nf manipulation

manipular [manipu'lar] vt to manipulate; (manejar) to handle

maniquí [mani'ki] nm dummy ▷ nmf model

manivela [mani'βela] nf crank

manjar [man'xar] nm (tasty) dish

mano ['mano] nf hand; (Zool) foot, paw; (de pintura) coat; (serie) lot, series; **a ~** by hand; **a ~ derecha/izquierda** on the right(-hand side)/left(-hand side); **de primera ~** (at) first hand; **de segunda ~** (at) second hand; **robo a ~ armada** armed robbery; **estrechar la ~ a algn** to shake sb's hand; **mano de obra** labour, manpower; **manos libres** adj inv (teléfono, dispositivo) hands-free ▷ nm inv hands-free kit

manojo [ma'noxo] nm handful, bunch; (de llaves) bunch

manopla [ma'nopla] nf mitten

manosear [manose'ar] vt (tocar) to handle, touch; (desordenar) to mess up, rumple; (insistir en) to overwork; (LAM: acariciar) to caress, fondle

manotazo [mano'taθo] nm slap, smack

mansalva [man'salβa]: **a ~** adv indiscriminately

mansión [man'sjon] nf mansion

manso, -a ['manso, a] adj gentle, mild; (animal) tame

manta ['manta] nf blanket

manteca [man'teka] nf fat; (cs: mantequilla) butter; **manteca de cerdo** lard

mantecado [mante'kaðo] (ESP) nm Christmas sweet made from flour, almonds and lard

mantel [man'tel] nm tablecloth

mantendré etc vb V **mantener**

mantener [mante'ner] vt to support, maintain; (alimentar) to sustain; (conservar) to keep; (Tec) to maintain, service; **mantenerse** vr (seguir de pie) to be still standing; (no ceder) to hold one's ground; (subsistir) to sustain o.s., keep going; **mantenimiento** nm maintenance; sustenance; (sustento) support

mantequilla [mante'kiʎa] nf butter

mantilla [man'tiʎa] nf mantilla; **mantillas** nfpl (de bebé) baby clothes

manto ['manto] nm (capa) cloak; (de ceremonia) robe, gown

mantuve etc vb V **mantener**

manual [ma'nwal] adj manual ▷ nm manual, handbook

manuscrito, -a [manus'krito, a] adj handwritten ▷ nm manuscript

manutención [manuten'θjon] nf maintenance; (sustento) support

manzana [man'θana] nf apple; (Arq) block (of houses)

manzanilla [manθa'niʎa] nf (planta) camomile; (infusión) camomile tea

manzano [man'θano] nm apple tree

maña ['maɲa] nf (gen) skill, dexterity; (pey) guile; (destreza) trick, knack

mañana [ma'ɲana] adv tomorrow ▷ nm future ▷ nf morning; **de o por la ~** in the morning; **¡hasta ~!** see you tomorrow!; **~ por la ~** tomorrow morning

mapa ['mapa] nm map

maple ['maple] (LAM) nm maple

maqueta [ma'keta] nf (scale) model

maquiladora [makila'ðora] (MÉX) nf (Com) bonded assembly plant

maquillaje [maki'ʎaxe] nm make-up; (acto) making up

maquillar [maki'ʎar] vt to make up; **maquillarse** vr to put on (some) make-up

máquina ['makina] nf machine; (de tren) locomotive, engine; (Foto) camera; (fig) machinery; **escrito a ~** typewritten; **máquina de coser** sewing machine; **máquina de escribir** typewriter; **máquina fotográfica** camera

maquinaria [maki'narja] nf (máquinas) machinery; (mecanismo) mechanism, works pl

maquinilla [maki'niʎa] (ESP) nf (tb: ~ de afeitar) razor

maquinista [maki'nista] nmf (de tren) engine driver; (Tec) operator; (Náut) engineer

mar [mar] nm o f sea; **~ adentro** o **afuera** out at sea; **en alta ~** on the high seas; **la ~ de** (fam) lots of; **el Mar Negro/Báltico** the Black/Baltic Sea

maraña [ma'raɲa] nf (maleza) thicket; (confusión) tangle

maravilla [mara'βiʎa] nf marvel, wonder; (Bot) marigold; **maravillar** vt to astonish, amaze; **maravillarse** vr to be astonished, be amazed; **maravilloso, -a** adj wonderful, marvellous

marca ['marka] nf (gen) mark; (sello) stamp; (Com) make, brand; **de ~** excellent, outstanding; **marca de fábrica** trademark; **marca registrada** registered trademark

marcado, -a [mar'kaðo, a] adj marked, strong

marcador [marka'ðor] nm (Deporte) scoreboard; (: persona) scorer

marcapasos [marka'pasos] nm inv pacemaker

marcar [mar'kar] vt (gen) to mark; (número de teléfono) to dial; (gol) to score; (números) to record, keep a tally of; (pelo) to set ▷ vi (Deporte) to score; (Tel) to dial

marcha ['martʃa] nf march; (Tec) running, working; (Auto) gear; (velocidad) speed; (fig) progress; (dirección) course; **poner en ~** to put into gear; (fig) to set in motion, get going; **dar ~ atrás** to reverse, put into reverse; **estar en ~** to be under way, be in motion

marchar [mar'tʃar] vi (ir) to go; (funcionar) to work, go; **marcharse** vr to go (away), leave

marchitar [martʃi'tar] vt to wither, dry up; **marchitarse** vr (Bot) to wither; (fig) to fade away;

marchito, -a adj withered, faded; (fig) in decline
marciano, -a [mar'θjano, a] adj, nm/f Martian
marco ['marko] nm frame; (moneda) mark; (fig) framework
marea [ma'rea] nf tide; **marea negra** oil slick
marear [mare'ar] vt (fig) to annoy, upset; (Med): **~ a algn** to make sb feel sick; **marearse** vr (tener náuseas) to feel sick; (desvanecerse) to feel faint; (aturdirse) to feel dizzy; (fam: emborracharse) to get tipsy
maremoto [mare'moto] nm tidal wave
mareo [ma'reo] nm (náusea) sick feeling; (en viaje) travel sickness; (aturdimiento) dizziness; (fam: lata) nuisance
marfil [mar'fil] nm ivory
margarina [marɣa'rina] nf margarine
margarita [marɣa'rita] nf (Bot) daisy; (Tip) daisywheel
margen ['marxen] nm (borde) edge, border; (fig) margin, space ▷ nf (de río etc) bank; **dar ~ para** to give an opportunity for; **mantenerse al ~** to keep out (of things)
marginar [marxi'nar] vt (socialmente) to marginalize, ostracize
mariachi [ma'rjatʃi] nm (persona) mariachi musician; (grupo) mariachi band
marica [ma'rika] (fam) nm sissy
maricón [mari'kon] (fam) nm queer
marido [ma'riðo] nm husband
marihuana [mari'wana] nf marijuana, cannabis
marina [ma'rina] nf navy; **marina mercante** merchant navy
marinero, -a [mari'nero, a] adj sea cpd ▷ nm sailor, seaman
marino, -a [ma'rino, a] adj sea cpd, marine ▷ nm sailor
marioneta [marjo'neta] nf puppet
mariposa [mari'posa] nf butterfly
mariquita [mari'kita] nf ladybird (BRIT), ladybug (US)
marisco [ma'risko] (ESP) nm shellfish inv, seafood; **mariscos** (LAM) nmpl = **marisco**
marítimo, -a [ma'ritimo, a] adj sea cpd, maritime
mármol ['marmol] nm marble
marqués, -esa [mar'kes, esa] nm/f marquis/marchioness
marrón [ma'rron] adj brown
marroquí [marro'ki] adj, nm/f Moroccan ▷ nm Morocco (leather)
Marruecos [ma'rrwekos] nm Morocco
martes ['martes] nm inv Tuesday; **~ y trece** ≈ Friday 13th
martillo [mar'tiʎo] nm hammer
mártir ['martir] nm/f martyr; **martirio** nm martyrdom; (fig) torture, torment
marxismo [mark'sismo] nm Marxism
marzo ['marθo] nm March

⊙ PALABRA CLAVE

más [mas] adj, adv 1: **más (que o de)** (compar) more (than), ...+er (than); **más grande/inteligente** bigger/more intelligent; **trabaja más (que yo)** he works more (than me) ▷ Vb **cada**
2 (superl): **el más** the most, ...+est; **el más grande/inteligente (de)** the biggest/most intelligent (in)
3 (negativo): **no tengo más dinero** I haven't got any

more money; **no viene más por aquí** he doesn't come round here any more
4 (adicional): **no le veo más solución que ...** I see no other solution than to ...; **¿quién más?** anybody else?
5 (+ adj: valor intensivo): **¡qué perro más sucio!** what a filthy dog!; **¡es más tonto!** he's so stupid!
6 (locuciones): **más o menos** more or less; **los más** most people; **es más** furthermore; **más bien** rather; **¡qué más da!** what does it matter!; V tb **no**
7: **por más: por más que te esfuerces** no matter how hard you try; **por más que quisiera ...** much as I should like to ...
8: **de más: veo que aquí estoy de más** I can see I'm not needed here; **tenemos uno de más** we've got one extra ▷ prep: **2 más 2 son 4** 2 and 0 plus 2 are 4
▷ nm inv: **este trabajo tiene sus más y sus menos** this job's got its good points and its bad points

mas [mas] conj but
masa ['masa] nf (mezcla) dough; (volumen) volume, mass; (Física) mass; **en ~** en masse; **las ~s** (Pol) the masses
masacre [ma'sakre] nf massacre
masaje [ma'saxe] nm massage
máscara ['maskara] nf mask; **máscara antigás/de oxígeno** gas/oxygen mask; **mascarilla** nf (de belleza, Med) mask
masculino, -a [masku'lino, a] adj masculine; (Bio) male
masía [ma'sia] nf farmhouse
masivo, -a [ma'siβo, a] adj mass cpd
masoquista [maso'kista] nmf masochist
máster ['master] (ESP) nm master
masticar [masti'kar] vt to chew
mástil ['mastil] nm (de navío) mast; (de guitarra) neck
mastín [mas'tin] nm mastiff
masturbarse [mastur'βarse] vr to masturbate
mata ['mata] nf (arbusto) bush, shrub; (de hierba) tuft
matadero [mata'ðero] nm slaughterhouse, abattoir
matamoscas [mata'moskas] nm inv (pala) fly swat
matanza [ma'tanθa] nf slaughter
matar [ma'tar] vt, vi to kill; **matarse** vr (suicidarse) to kill o.s., commit suicide; (morir) to be o get killed; **~ el hambre** to stave off hunger
matasellos [mata'seʎos] nm inv postmark
mate ['mate] adj matt ▷ nm (en ajedrez) (check)mate; (LAM: hierba) maté; (: vasija) gourd
matemáticas [mate'matikas] nfpl mathematics; **matemático, -a** adj mathematical ▷ nm/f mathematician
materia [ma'terja] nf (gen) matter; (Tec) material; (Escol) subject; **en ~ de** on the subject of; **materia prima** raw material; **material** adj material ▷ nm material; (Tec) equipment; **materialista** adj materialist(ic); **materialmente** adv materially; (fig) absolutely
maternal [mater'nal] adj motherly, maternal
maternidad [materni'ðað] nf motherhood, maternity; **materno, -a** adj maternal; (lengua) mother cpd
matinal [mati'nal] adj morning cpd
matiz [ma'tiθ] nm shade; **matizar** vt (variar) to vary; (Arte) to blend; **matizar de** to tinge with
matón [ma'ton] nm bully
matorral [mato'rral] nm thicket

matrícula [ma'trikula] nf (registro) register; (Auto) registration number; (: placa) number plate; **matrícula de honor** (Univ) top marks in a subject at university with the right to free registration the following year; **matricular** vt to register, enrol

matrimonio [matri'monjo] nm (pareja) (married) couple; (unión) marriage

matriz [ma'triθ] nf (Anat) womb; (Tec) mould

matrona [ma'trona] nf (persona de edad) matron; (comadrona) midwife

matufia [ma'tufja] (RPL: fam) nf put-up job

maullar [mau'ʎar] vi to mew, miaow

maxilar [maksi'lar] nm jaw(bone)

máxima ['maksima] nf maxim

máximo, -a ['maksimo, a] adj maximum; (más alto) highest; (más grande) greatest ▷ nm maximum; **como ~** at most

mayo ['majo] nm May

mayonesa [majo'nesa] nf mayonnaise

mayor [ma'jor] adj main, chief; (adulto) adult; (de edad avanzada) elderly; (Mús) major; (compar: de tamaño) bigger; (: de edad) older; (superl: de tamaño) biggest; (: de edad) oldest ▷ nm (adulto) adult; **mayores** nmpl (antepasados) ancestors; **al por ~** wholesale; **mayor de edad** adult

mayoral [majo'ral] nm foreman

mayordomo [major'ðomo] nm butler

mayoría [majo'ria] nf majority, greater part

mayorista [majo'rista] nmf wholesaler

mayoritario, -a [majori'tarjo, a] adj majority cpd

mayúscula [ma'juskula] nf capital letter

mazapán [maθa'pan] nm marzipan

mazo ['maθo] nm (martillo) mallet; (de flores) bunch; (Deporte) bat

me [me] pron (directo) me; (indirecto) (to) me; (reflexivo) (to) myself; **¡dá-lo!** give it to me!

mear [me'ar] (fam) vi to pee, piss (!)

mecánica [me'kanika] nf (Escol) mechanics sg; (mecanismo) mechanism; V tb **mecánico**

mecánico, -a [me'kaniko, a] adj mechanical ▷ nm/f mechanic

mecanismo [meka'nismo] nm mechanism; (marcha) gear

mecanografía [mekanoɣra'fia] nf typewriting; **mecanógrafo, -a** nm/f typist

mecate [me'kate] (MÉX, CAM) nm rope

mecedora [meθe'ðora] nf rocking chair

mecer [me'θer] vt (cuna) to rock; **mecerse** vr to rock; (rama) to sway

mecha ['metʃa] nf (de vela) wick; (de bomba) fuse

mechero [me'tʃero] nm (cigarette) lighter

mechón [me'tʃon] nm (gen) tuft; (de pelo) lock

medalla [me'ðaʎa] nf medal

media ['meðja] nf stocking; (LAM: calcetín) sock; (promedio) average

mediado, -a [me'ðjaðo, a] adj half-full; (trabajo) half-completed; **a ~s de** in the middle of, halfway through

mediano, -a [me'ðjano, a] adj (regular) medium, average; (mediocre) mediocre

medianoche [meðja'notʃe] nf midnight

mediante [me'ðjante] adv by (means of), through

mediar [me'ðjar] vi (interceder) to mediate, intervene

medicamento [meðika'mento] nm medicine, drug

medicina [meði'θina] nf medicine

médico, -a ['meðiko, a] adj medical ▷ nm/f doctor

medida [me'ðiða] nf measure; (medición) measurement; (prudencia) moderation, prudence; **en cierta/gran ~** up to a point/to a great extent; **un traje a la ~** a made-to-measure suit; **~ de cuello** collar size; **a ~ de** in proportion to; (de acuerdo con) in keeping with; **a ~ que** (conforme) as; **medidor** (LAM) nm meter

medio, -a ['meðjo, a] adj half(a); (punto) mid, middle; (promedio) average ▷ adv half ▷ nm (centro) middle, centre; (promedio) average; (método) means, way; (ambiente) environment; **medios** nmpl means, resources; **~ litro** half a litre; **las tres y media** half past three; **a ~ terminar** half finished; **pagar a medias** to share the cost; **medio ambiente** environment; **medio de transporte** means of transport; **Medio Oriente** Middle East; **medios de comunicación** media; **medioambiental** adj (política, efectos) environmental

mediocre [me'ðjokre] adj mediocre

mediodía [meðjo'ðia] nm midday, noon

medir [me'ðir] vt, vi (gen) to measure

meditar [meði'tar] vt to ponder, think over, meditate on; (planear) to think out

mediterráneo, -a [meðite'rraneo, a] adj Mediterranean ▷ nm: **el M~** the Mediterranean

médula ['meðula] nf (Anat) marrow; **médula espinal** spinal cord

medusa [me'ðusa] (ESP) nf jellyfish

megáfono [me'ɣafono] nm megaphone

megapíxel [mexa'piksel] (pl **megapixels** or **~es**) nm megapixel

mejilla [me'xiʎa] nf cheek

mejillón [mexi'ʎon] nm mussel

mejor [me'xor] adj, adv (compar) better; (superl) best; **a lo ~** probably; (quizá) maybe; **~ dicho** rather; **tanto ~** so much the better

mejora [me'xora] nf improvement; **mejorar** vt to improve, make better ▷ vi to improve, get better; **mejorarse** vr to improve, get better

melancólico, -a [melan'koliko, a] adj (triste) sad, melancholy; (soñador) dreamy

melena [me'lena] nf (de persona) long hair; (Zool) mane

mellizo, -a [me'ʎiθo, a] adj, nm/f twin

melocotón [meloko'ton] (ESP) nm peach

melodía [melo'ðia] nf melody, tune

melodrama [melo'ðrama] nm melodrama; **melodramático, -a** adj melodramatic

melón [me'lon] nm melon

membrete [mem'brete] nm letterhead

membrillo [mem'briʎo] nm quince; **(carne de) ~** quince jelly

memoria [me'morja] nf (gen) memory; **memorias** nfpl (de autor) memoirs; **memorizar** vt to memorize

menaje [me'naxe] nm (tb: **artículos de ~**) household items

mencionar [menθjo'nar] vt to mention

mendigo, -a [men'diɣo, a] nm/f beggar

menear [mene'ar] vt to move; **menearse** vr to shake; (balancearse) to sway; (moverse) to move; (fig) to get a move on

menestra [me'nestra] nf (tb: **~ de verduras**) vegetable stew

menopausia [meno'pausja] nf menopause

menor [me'nor] adj (más pequeño: compar) smaller; (: superl) smallest; (más joven: compar) younger; (: superl) youngest; (Mús) minor ▷ nmf (joven) young person, juvenile; **no tengo la ~ idea** I haven't the faintest idea;

al por ~ retail; **menor de edad** person under age
Menorca [me'norka] nf Minorca

○ **PALABRA CLAVE**

menos [menos] adj **1: menos
(que** o **de)** (compar: cantidad) less
(than); (: número) fewer (than); **con menos
entusiasmo** with less enthusiasm; **menos gente**
fewer people; V tb **cada**
2 (superl): **es el que menos culpa tiene** he is the least
to blame
▷ adv **1** (compar): **menos (que** o **de)** less (than); **me
gusta menos que el otro** I like it less than the other
one
2 (superl): **es el menos listo (de su clase)** he's the least
bright in his class; **de todas ellas es la que menos me
agrada** out of all of them she's the one I like least
3 (locuciones): **no quiero verle y menos visitarle** I don't
want to see him, let alone visit him; **tenemos siete de
menos** we're seven short; **(por) lo menos** at (the very)
least; **¡menos mal!** thank goodness!
▷ prep except; (cifras) minus; **todos menos él** everyone
except (for) him; **5 menos 2** 5 minus 2
▷ conj: **a menos que: a menos que venga mañana**
unless he comes tomorrow

menospreciar [menospre'θjar] vt to underrate,
undervalue; (despreciar) to scorn, despise
mensaje [men'saxe] nm message; **enviar un ~ a
algn** (por móvil) to text sb, send sb a text message;
mensaje de texto text message; **mensajero, -a** nm/f
messenger
menso, -a ['menso, a] (MÉX: fam) adj stupid
menstruación [menstrwa'θjon] nf menstruation
mensual [men'swal] adj monthly; **100 euros ~es**
100 euros a month; **mensualidad** nf (salario) monthly
salary; (Com) monthly payment, monthly instalment
menta ['menta] nf mint
mental [men'tal] adj mental; **mentalidad** nf
mentality; **mentalizar** vt (sensibilizar) to make
aware; (convencer) to convince; (preparar) to prepare
(mentally); **mentalizarse** vr (concienciarse) to become
aware; **mentalizarse (de)** to get used to the idea (of);
mentalizarse de que ... (convencerse) to get it into
one's head that ...
mente ['mente] nf mind
mentir [men'tir] vi to lie
mentira [men'tira] nf (una mentira) lie; (acto) lying;
(invención) fiction; **parece mentira que ...** it seems
incredible that ..., I can't believe that ...; **mentiroso, -a**
[menti'roso, a] adj lying ▷ nm/f liar
menú [me'nu] (pl **~s**) nm menu; **menú del día** set
menu; **menú turístico** tourist menu
menudencias [menu'ðenθjas] (LAM) nfpl giblets
menudo, -a [me'nuðo, a] adj (pequeño) small, tiny;
(sin importancia) petty, insignificant; **¡~ negocio!** (fam)
some deal!; **a ~** often, frequently
meñique [me'ɲike] nm little finger
mercadillo [merka'ðiʎo] (ESP) nm flea market
mercado [mer'kaðo] nm market; **mercado de
pulgas** (LAM) flea market
mercancía [merkan'θia] nf commodity;
mercancías nfpl goods, merchandise sg
mercenario, -a [merθe'narjo, a] adj, nm mercenary

mercería [merθe'ria] nf haberdashery (BRIT),
notions pl (US); (tienda) haberdasher's (BRIT), notions
store (US)
mercurio [mer'kurjo] nm mercury
merecer [mere'θer] vt to deserve, merit ▷ vi to be
deserving, be worthy; **merece la pena** it's worthwhile;
merecido, -a adj (well) deserved; **llevar su merecido**
to get one's deserts
merendar [meren'dar] vt to have for tea ▷ vi to
have tea; (en el campo) to have a picnic; **merendero** nm
open-air cafe
merengue [me'renge] nm meringue
meridiano [meri'ðjano] nm (Geo) meridian
merienda [me'rjenda] nf (light) tea, afternoon
snack; (de campo) picnic
mérito ['merito] nm merit; (valor) worth, value
merluza [mer'luθa] nf hake
mermelada [merme'laða] nf jam
mero, -a ['mero, a] adj mere; (MÉX, CAM: fam) very
merodear [meroðe'ar] vi: **~ por** to prowl about
mes [mes] nm month
mesa ['mesa] nf table; (de trabajo) desk; (Geo) plateau;
poner/quitar la ~ to lay/clear the table; **mesa
electoral** officials in charge of a polling station; **mesa
redonda** (reunión) round table; **mesero, -a** (LAM) nm/f
waiter/waitress
meseta [me'seta] nf (Geo) plateau, tableland
mesilla [me'siʎa] nf (tb: **~ de noche**) bedside table
mesón [me'son] nm inn
mestizo, -a [mes'tiθo, a] adj half-caste, of mixed
race ▷ nm/f half-caste
meta ['meta] nf goal; (de carrera) finish
metabolismo [metaβo'lismo] nm metabolism
metáfora [me'tafora] nf metaphor
metal [me'tal] nm (materia) metal; (Mús) brass;
metálico, -a adj metallic; (de metal) metal ▷ nm
(dinero contante) cash
meteorología [meteorolo'xia] nf meteorology
meter [me'ter] vt (colocar) to put, place; (introducir) to
put in, insert; (involucrar) to involve; (causar) to make,
cause; **meterse** vr: **~se en** to go into, enter; (fig) to
interfere in, meddle in; **~se a** to start; **~se a escritor**
to become a writer; **~se con algn** to provoke sb, pick a
quarrel with sb
meticuloso, -a [metiku'loso, a] adj meticulous,
thorough
metódico, -a [me'toðiko, a] adj methodical
método [me'toðo] nm method
metralleta [metra'ʎeta] nf sub-machine-gun
métrico, -a [me'triko, a] adj metric
metro ['metro] nm metre; (tren) underground (BRIT),
subway (US)
metrosexual [metrosek'swal] adj, nm metrosexual
mexicano, -a [mexi'kano, a] adj, nm/f Mexican
México ['mexiko] nm Mexico; **Ciudad de ~** Mexico
City
mezcla ['meθkla] nf mixture; **mezcladora** (MÉX)
nf (tb: **mezcladora de cemento**) cement mixer;
mezclar vt to mix (up); **mezclarse** vr to mix, mingle;
mezclarse en to get mixed up in, get involved in
mezquino, -a [meθ'kino, a] adj mean
mezquita [meθ'kita] nf mosque
mg. abr (= miligramo) mg
mi [mi] adj pos my ▷ nm (Mús) E
mí [mi] pron me; myself
mía pron V **mío**

michelín [mitʃe'lin] (fam) nm (de grasa) spare tyre
microbio [mi'kroβjo] nm microbe
micrófono [mi'krofono] nm microphone
microondas [mikro'ondas] nm inv (tb: **horno ~**) microwave (oven)
microscopio [mikro'skopjo] nm microscope
miedo ['mjeðo] nm fear; (nerviosismo) apprehension, nervousness; **tener ~** to be afraid; **de ~** wonderful, marvellous; **hace un frío de ~** (fam) it's terribly cold; **miedoso, -a** adj fearful, timid
miel [mjel] nf honey
miembro ['mjembro] nm limb; (socio) member; **miembro viril** penis
mientras ['mjentras] conj while; (duración) as long as ▷ adv meanwhile; **~ tanto** meanwhile
miércoles ['mjerkoles] nm inv Wednesday
mierda ['mjerða] (fam!) nf shit(!)
miga ['miɣa] nf crumb; (fig: meollo) essence; **hacer buenas ~s** (fam) to get on well
mil [mil] num thousand; **dos ~ libras** two thousand pounds
milagro [mi'laɣro] nm miracle; **milagroso, -a** adj miraculous
milésima [mi'lesima] nf (de segundo) thousandth
mili ['mili] (ESP: fam) nf: **hacer la ~** to do one's military service
milímetro [mi'limetro] nm millimetre
militante [mili'tante] adj militant
militar [mili'tar] adj military ▷ nmf soldier ▷ vi (Mil) to serve; (en un partido) to be a member
milla ['miʎa] nf mile
millar [mi'ʎar] nm thousand
millón [mi'ʎon] num million; **millonario, -a** nm/f millionaire
miluso [mi'luso] (MÉX) nm inv odd-job man
mimar [mi'mar] vt to spoil, pamper
mimbre ['mimbre] nm wicker
mímica [mimika] nf (para comunicarse) sign language; (imitación) mimicry
mimo ['mimo] nm (caricia) caress; (de niño) spoiling; (Teatro) mime; (: actor) mime artist
mina ['mina] nf mine
mineral [mine'ral] adj mineral ▷ nm (Geo) mineral; (mena) ore
minero, -a [mi'nero, a] adj mining cpd ▷ nm/f miner
miniatura [minja'tura] adj inv, nf miniature
minidisco [mini'disko] nm MiniDisc®
minifalda [mini'falda] nf miniskirt
mínimo, -a ['minimo, a] adj, nm minimum
minino, -a [mi'nino, a] (fam) nm/f puss, pussy
ministerio [minis'terjo] nm Ministry; **Ministerio de Hacienda/de Asuntos Exteriores** Treasury (BRIT), Treasury Department (US)/Foreign Office (BRIT), State Department (US)
ministro, -a [mi'nistro, a] nm/f minister
minoría [mino'ria] nf minority
minúscula [mi'nuskula] nf small letter
minúsculo, -a [mi'nuskulo, a] adj tiny, minute
minusválido, -a [minus'βaliðo, a] adj (physically) handicapped ▷ nm/f (physically) handicapped person
minuta [mi'nuta] nf (de comida) menu
minutero [minu'tero] nm minute hand
minuto [mi'nuto] nm minute
mío, -a ['mio, a] pron: **el ~/la mía** mine; **un amigo ~** a friend of mine; **lo ~** what is mine

miope [mi'ope] adj short-sighted
mira ['mira] nf (de arma) sight(s) (pl); (fig) aim, intention
mirada [mi'raða] nf look, glance; (expresión) look, expression; **clavar la ~ en** to stare at; **echar una ~ a** to glance at
mirado, -a [mi'raðo, a] adj (sensato) sensible; (considerado) considerate; **bien/mal ~** (estimado) well/ not well thought of; **bien ~ ...** all things considered ...
mirador [mira'ðor] nm viewpoint, vantage point
mirar [mi'rar] vt to look at; (observar) to watch; (considerar) to consider, think over; (vigilar, cuidar) to watch, look after ▷ vi to look; (Arq) to face; **mirarse** vr (dos personas) to look at each other; **~ bien/mal** to think highly of/have a poor opinion of; **~se al espejo** to look at o.s. in the mirror
mirilla [mi'riʎa] nf spyhole, peephole
mirlo ['mirlo] nm blackbird
misa ['misa] nf mass
miserable [mise'raβle] adj (avaro) mean, stingy; (nimio) miserable, paltry; (lugar) squalid; (fam) vile, despicable ▷ nmf (malvado) rogue
miseria [mi'serja] nf (pobreza) poverty; (tacañería) meanness, stinginess; (condiciones) squalor; **una ~** a pittance
misericordia [miseri'korðja] nf (compasión) compassion, pity; (piedad) mercy
misil [mi'sil] nm missile
misión [mi'sjon] nf mission; **misionero, -a** nm/f missionary
mismo, -a ['mismo, a] adj (semejante) same; (después de pron) -self; (para énfasis) very ▷ adv: **aquí/hoy ~** right here/this very day; **ahora ~** right now ▷ conj: **lo ~ que** just like o as; **el ~ traje** the same suit; **en ese ~ momento** at that very moment; **vino el ~ ministro** the minister himself came; **yo ~ lo vi** I saw it myself; **lo ~ the same (thing); da lo ~ it's all the same; quedamos en las mismas** we're no further forward; **por lo ~ for the same reason
misterio [mis'terjo] nm mystery; **misterioso, -a** adj mysterious
mitad [mi'tað] nf (medio) half; (centro) middle; **a ~ de precio** (at) half-price; **en o a ~ del camino** halfway along the road; **cortar por la ~** to cut through the middle
mitin ['mitin] (pl mítines) nm meeting
mito ['mito] nm myth
mixto, -a ['miksto, a] adj mixed
ml. abr (= mililitro) ml
mm. abr (= milímetro) mm
mobiliario [moβi'ljarjo] nm furniture
mochila [mo'tʃila] nf rucksack (BRIT), back-pack
moco ['moko] nm mucus; **mocos** nmpl (fam) snot; **limpiarse los ~s de la nariz** (fam) to wipe one's nose
moda ['moða] nf fashion; (estilo) style; **a la o de ~** in fashion, fashionable; **pasado de ~** out of fashion
modales [mo'ðales] nmpl manners
modelar [moðe'lar] vt to model
modelo [mo'ðelo] adj inv, nmf model
módem ['moðem] nm (Inform) modem
moderado, -a [moðe'raðo, a] adj moderate
moderar [moðe'rar] vt to moderate; (violencia) to restrain, control; (velocidad) to reduce; **moderarse** vr to restrain o.s., control o.s.
modernizar [moðerni'θar] vt to modernize
moderno, -a [mo'ðerno, a] adj modern; (actual)

present-day

modestia [mo'ðestja] nf modesty; **modesto, -a** adj modest

modificar [moðifi'kar] vt to modify

modisto, -a [mo'ðisto, a] nm/f (diseñador) couturier, designer; (que confecciona) dressmaker

modo ['moðo] nm way, manner; (Mús) mode; **modos** nmpl manners; **de ningún ~** in no way; **de todos ~s** at any rate; **modo de empleo** directions pl (for use)

mofarse [mo'farse] vr: **~ de** to mock, scoff at

mofle ['mofle] (MÉX, CAM) nm silencer (BRIT), muffler (US)

mogollón [moɣo'ʎon] (ESP: fam) adv a hell of a lot

moho ['moo] nm mould, mildew; (en metal) rust

mojar [mo'xar] vt to wet; (humedecer) to damp(en), moisten; (calar) to soak; **mojarse** vr to get wet

molcajete [molka'xete] (MÉX) nm mortar

molde ['molde] nm mould; (Costura) pattern; (fig) model; **moldeado** nm soft perm; **moldear** vt to mould

mole ['mole] nf mass, bulk; (edificio) pile

moler [mo'ler] vt to grind, crush

molestar [moles'tar] vt to bother; (fastidiar) to annoy; (incomodar) to inconvenience, put out ▷ vi to be a nuisance; **molestarse** vr to bother; (incomodarse) to go to trouble; (ofenderse) to take offence; **¿(no) te molesta si ...?** do you mind if ...?

molestia [mo'lestja] nf bother, trouble; (incomodidad) inconvenience; (Med) discomfort; **es una ~** it's a nuisance; **molesto, -a** adj (que fastidia) annoying; (incómodo) inconvenient; (inquieto) uncomfortable, ill at ease; (enfadado) annoyed

molido, -a [mo'liðo, a] adj: **estar ~** (fig) to be exhausted o dead beat

molinillo [moli'niʎo] nm hand mill; **molinillo de café** coffee grinder

molino [mo'lino] nm (edificio) mill; (máquina) grinder

momentáneo, -a [momen'taneo, a] adj momentary

momento [mo'mento] nm moment; **de ~** at o for the moment

momia ['momja] nf mummy

monarca [mo'narka] nmf monarch, ruler; **monarquía** nf monarchy

monasterio [monas'terjo] nm monastery

mondar [mon'dar] vt to peel; **mondarse** vr (ESP): **~se de risa** (fam) to split one's sides laughing

mondongo [mon'dongo] (LAM) nm tripe

moneda [mo'neða] nf (tipo de dinero) currency, money; (pieza) coin; **una ~ de 2 euros** a 2 euro piece; **monedero** nm purse

monitor, a [moni'tor, a] nm/f instructor, coach ▷ nm (TV) set; (Inform) monitor

monja ['monxa] nf nun

monje ['monxe] nm monk

mono, -a ['mono, a] adj (bonito) lovely, pretty; (gracioso) nice, charming ▷ nm/f monkey, ape ▷ nm dungarees pl; (overoles) overalls pl

monopatín [monopa'tin] nm skateboard

monopolio [mono'poljo] nm monopoly; **monopolizar** vt to monopolize

monótono, -a [mo'notono, a] adj monotonous

monstruo ['monstrwo] nm monster ▷ adj inv fantastic; **monstruoso, -a** adj monstrous

montaje [mon'taxe] nm assembly; (Teatro) décor; (Cine) montage

montaña [mon'taɲa] nf (monte) mountain; (sierra) mountains pl, mountainous area; **montaña rusa** roller coaster; **montañero, -a** nm/f mountaineer; **montañismo** nm mountaineering

montar [mon'tar] vt (subir a) to mount, get on; (Tec) to assemble, put together; (negocio) to set up; (arma) to cock; (colocar) to lift on to; (Culin) to beat ▷ vi to mount, get on; (sobresalir) to overlap; **~ en bicicleta** to ride a bicycle; **~ en cólera** to get angry; **~ a caballo** to ride, go horseriding

monte ['monte] nm (montaña) mountain; (bosque) woodland; (área sin cultivar) wild area, wild country; **monte de piedad** pawnshop

montón [mon'ton] nm heap, pile; (fig): **un ~ de** heaps o lots of

monumento [monu'mento] nm monument

moqueta [mo'keta] nf fitted carpet

mora ['mora] nf blackberry; V tb **moro**

morado, -a [mo'raðo, a] adj purple, violet ▷ nm bruise

moral [mo'ral] adj moral ▷ nf (ética) ethics pl; (moralidad) morals pl, morality; (ánimo) morale

moraleja [mora'lexa] nf moral

morboso, -a [mor'βoso, a] adj morbid

morcilla [mor'θiʎa] nf blood sausage = black pudding (BRIT)

mordaza [mor'ðaθa] nf (para la boca) gag; (Tec) clamp

morder [mor'ðer] vt to bite; (fig: consumir) to eat away, eat into; **mordisco** nm bite

moreno, -a [mo'reno, a] adj (color) dark brown; (de tez) dark; (de pelo moreno) dark-haired; (negro) black

morfina [mor'fina] nf morphine

moribundo, -a [mori'βundo, a] adj dying

morir [mo'rir] vi to die; (fuego) to die down; (luz) to go out; **morirse** vr to die; (fig) to be dying; **murió en un accidente** he was killed in an accident; **~se por algo** to be dying for sth

moro, -a ['moro, a] adj Moorish ▷ nm/f Moor

moroso, -a [mo'roso, a] nm/f bad debtor, defaulter

morraña [mo'rraɲa] (MÉX) nf (cambio) small o loose change

morro ['morro] nm (Zool) snout, nose; (Auto, Aviac) nose

morsa ['morsa] nf walrus

mortadela [morta'ðela] nf mortadella

mortal [mor'tal] adj mortal; (golpe) deadly; **mortalidad** nf mortality

mortero [mor'tero] nm mortar

mosca ['moska] nf fly

Moscú [mos'ku] n Moscow

mosquearse [moske'arse] (fam) vr (enojarse) to get cross; (ofenderse) to take offence

mosquitero [moski'tero] nm mosquito net

mosquito [mos'kito] nm mosquito

mostaza [mos'taθa] nf mustard

mosto ['mosto] nm (unfermented) grape juice

mostrador [mostra'ðor] nm (de tienda) counter; (de café) bar

mostrar [mos'trar] vt to show; (exhibir) to display, exhibit; (explicar) to explain; **mostrarse** vr: **~se amable** to be kind; to prove to be kind; **no se muestra muy inteligente** he doesn't seem (to be) very intelligent

mota ['mota] nf speck, tiny piece; (en diseño) dot

mote ['mote] nm nickname

motín [mo'tin] nm (del pueblo) revolt, rising; (del

ejército) mutiny

motivar [moti'βar] vt (*causar*) to cause, motivate; (*explicar*) to explain, justify; **motivo** nm motive, reason

moto ['moto] (*fam*) nf = **motocicleta**

motocicleta [motoθi'kleta] nf motorbike (BRIT), motorcycle

motoneta [moto'neta] (cs) nf scooter

motor [mo'tor] nm motor, engine; **motor a chorro** o **de reacción/de explosión** jet engine/internal combustion engine

motora [mo'tora] nf motorboat

movedizo, -a adj V **arena**

mover [mo'βer] vt to move; (*cabeza*) to shake; (*accionar*) to drive; (fig) to cause, provoke; **moverse** vr to move; (fig) to get a move on

móvil ['moβil] adj mobile; (*pieza de máquina*) moving; (*mueble*) movable ▷ nm (*motivo*) motive; (*teléfono*) mobile

movimiento [moβi'mjento] nm movement; (Tec) motion; (*actividad*) activity

mozo, -a ['moθo, a] adj (*joven*) young ▷ nm/f youth, young man/girl; (cs: *mesero*) waiter/waitress

MP3 nm MP3; **reproductor (de) ~** MP3 player

mucama [mu'kama] (RPL) nf maid

muchacho, -a [mu'tʃatʃo, a] nm/f (*niño*) boy/girl; (*criado*) servant; (*criada*) maid

muchedumbre [mutʃe'ðumbre] nf crowd

○ PALABRA CLAVE

mucho, -a ['mutʃo, a] adj **1** (*cantidad*) a lot of, much; (*número*) lots of, a lot of, many; **mucho dinero** a lot of money; **hace mucho calor** it's very hot; **muchas amigas** lots o a lot of friends

2 (sg: *grande*): **ésta es mucha casa para él** this house is much too big for him

▷ pron: **tengo mucho que hacer** I've got a lot to do; **muchos dicen que ...** a lot of people say that ...; V tb **tener**

▷ adv **1 me gusta mucho** I like it a lot; **lo siento mucho** I'm very sorry; **come mucho** he eats a lot; **¿te vas a quedar mucho?** are you going to be staying long?

2 (*respuesta*) very; **¿estás cansado? – ¡mucho!** are you tired? – very!

3 (*locuciones*): **como mucho** at (the) most; **con mucho: el mejor con mucho** by far the best; **ni mucho menos: no es rico ni mucho menos** he's far from being rich

4: **por mucho que: por mucho que le creas** no matter how o however much you believe her

muda ['muða] nf change of clothes

mudanza [mu'ðanθa] nf (*de casa*) move

mudar [mu'ðar] vt to change; (Zool) to shed ▷ vi to change; **mudarse** vr (*ropa*) to change; **~se de casa** to move house

mudo, -a ['muðo, a] adj dumb; (*callado, Cine*) silent

mueble ['mweβle] nm piece of furniture; **muebles** nmpl furniture sg

mueca ['mweka] nf face, grimace; **hacer ~s a** to make faces at

muela ['mwela] nf back tooth; **muela del juicio** wisdom tooth

muelle ['mweʎe] nm spring; (Náut) wharf; (*malecón*)

pier

muero etc vb V **morir**

muerte ['mwerte] nf death; (*homicidio*) murder; **dar ~ a** to kill

muerto, -a ['mwerto, a] pp de **morir** ▷ adj dead ▷ nm/f dead man/woman; (*difunto*) deceased; (*cadáver*) corpse; **estar ~ de cansancio** to be dead tired; **Día de los Muertos** (MÉX) All Souls' Day

muestra ['mwestra] nf (*señal*) indication, sign; (*demostración*) demonstration; (*prueba*) proof; (*estadística*) sample; (*modelo*) model, pattern; (*testimonio*) token

muestro etc vb V **mostrar**

muevo etc vb V **mover**

mugir [mu'xir] vi (*vaca*) to moo

mugre ['muxre] nf dirt, filth

mujer [mu'xer] nf woman; (*esposa*) wife; **mujeriego** nm womanizer

mula ['mula] nf mule

muleta [mu'leta] nf (*para andar*) crutch; (Taur) stick with red cape attached

multa ['multa] nf fine; **poner una ~ a** to fine; **multar** vt to fine

multicines [multi'θines] nmpl multiscreen cinema sg

multinacional [multinaθjo'nal] nf multinational

múltiple ['multiple] adj multiple; (pl) many, numerous

multiplicar [multipli'kar] vt (Mat) to multiply; (fig) to increase; **multiplicarse** vr (Bio) to multiply; (fig) to be everywhere at once

multitud [multi'tuð] nf (*muchedumbre*) crowd; **~ de** lots of

mundial [mun'djal] adj world-wide, universal; (*guerra, récord*) world cpd

mundo ['mundo] nm world; **todo el ~** everybody; **tener ~** to be experienced, know one's way around

munición [muni'θjon] nf ammunition

municipal [muniθi'pal] adj municipal, local

municipio [muni'θipjo] nm (*ayuntamiento*) town council, corporation; (*territorio administrativo*) town, municipality

muñeca [mu'neka] nf (Anat) wrist; (*juguete*) doll

muñeco [mu'neko] nm (*figura*) figure; (*marioneta*) puppet; (fig) puppet, pawn

mural [mu'ral] adj mural, wall cpd ▷ nm mural

muralla [mu'raʎa] nf (*city*) wall(s) (pl)

murciélago [mur'θjelaxo] nm bat

murmullo [mur'muʎo] nm murmur(ing); (*cuchicheo*) whispering

murmurar [murmu'rar] vi to murmur, whisper; (*cotillear*) to gossip

muro ['muro] nm wall

muscular [musku'lar] adj muscular

músculo ['muskulo] nm muscle

museo [mu'seo] nm museum; **museo de arte** art gallery

musgo ['musxo] nm moss

música ['musika] nf music; V tb **músico**

músico, -a ['musiko, a] adj musical ▷ nm/f musician

muslo ['muslo] nm thigh

musulmán, -ana [musul'man, ana] nm/f Moslem

mutación [muta'θjon] nf (Bio) mutation; (*cambio*) (sudden) change

mutilar [muti'lar] vt to mutilate; (a una persona)

to maim

mutuo, -a ['mutwo, a] *adj* mutual
muy [mwi] *adv* very; (*demasiado*) too; **M~ Señor mío**
Dear Sir; **~ de noche** very late at night; **eso es ~ de él**
that's just like him

N *abr* (= *norte*) N
nabo ['naβo] *nm* turnip
nacer [na'θer] *vi* to be born; (*de huevo*) to hatch;
(*vegetal*) to sprout; (*río*) to rise; **nací en Barcelona** I was
born in Barcelona; **nacido, -a** *adj* born; **recién nacido**
newborn; **nacimiento** *nm* birth; (*de Navidad*) Nativity;
(*de río*) source
nación [na'θjon] *nf* nation; **nacional** *adj* national;
nacionalismo *nm* nationalism
nada ['naða] *pron* nothing ⊳ *adv* not at all, in no way;
no decir ~ to say nothing, not to say anything; **~ más**
nothing else; **de ~** don't mention it
nadador, a [naða'ðor, a] *nm/f* swimmer
nadar [na'ðar] *vi* to swim
nadie ['naðje] *pron* nobody, no-one; **~ habló** nobody
spoke; **no había ~** there was nobody there, there
wasn't anybody there
nado ['naðo] **a nado**: *adv*: **pasar a ~** to swim across
nafta ['nafta] (*RPL*) *nf* petrol (*BRIT*), gas (*US*)
naipe ['naipe] *nm* (playing) card; **naipes** *nmpl* cards
nalgas ['nalɣas] *nfpl* buttocks
nalguear [nalɣe'ar] (*MÉX*, *CAM*) *vt* to spank
nana ['nana] (*ESP*) *nf* lullaby
naranja [na'ranxa] *adj inv*, *nf* orange; **media ~** (*fam*)
better half; **naranjada** *nf* orangeade; **naranjo** *nm*
orange tree
narciso [nar'θiso] *nm* narcissus
narcótico, -a [nar'kotiko, a] *adj*, *nm* narcotic;
narcotizar *vt* to drug; **narcotráfico** *nm* drug
trafficking o running
nariz [na'riθ] *nf* nose; **nariz chata/respingona**
snub/turned-up nose
narración [narra'θjon] *nf* narration
narrar [na'rrar] *vt* to narrate, recount; **narrativa**
nf narrative
nata ['nata] *nf* cream; **nata montada** whipped
cream
natación [nata'θjon] *nf* swimming
natal [na'tal] *adj*: **ciudad ~** home town; **natalidad**
nf birth rate
natillas [na'tiʎas] *nfpl* custard *sg*
nativo, -a [na'tiβo, a] *adj*, *nm/f* native
natural [natu'ral] *adj* natural; (*fruta etc*) fresh ⊳ *nmf*

native ▷ nm (disposición) nature

naturaleza [natura'leθa] nf nature; (género) nature, kind; **naturaleza muerta** still life

naturalmente [natural'mente] adv (de modo natural) in a natural way; ¡~! of course!

naufragar [naufra'xar] vi to sink; **naufragio** nm shipwreck

nauseabundo, -a [nausea'βundo, a] adj nauseating, sickening

náuseas ['nauseas] nfpl nausea sg; **me da ~** it makes me feel sick

náutico, -a ['nautiko, a] adj nautical

navaja [na'βaxa] nf knife; (de barbero, peluquero) razor

naval [na'βal] adj naval

Navarra [na'βarra] n Navarre

nave ['naβe] nf (barco) ship, vessel; (Arq) nave; **nave espacial** spaceship; **nave industrial** factory premises pl

navegador [naβexa'ðor] nm (Inform) browser

navegante [naβe'ɣante] nm/f navigator

navegar [naβe'ɣar] vi (barco) to sail; (avión) to fly; ~ **por Internet** to surf the Net

Navidad [naβi'ðað] nf Christmas; **Navidades** nfpl Christmas time; ¡**Feliz ~!** Merry Christmas!; **navideño, -a** adj Christmas cpd

nazca etc vb V **nacer**

nazi ['naθi] adj, nm/f Nazi

NE abr (= nor(d)este) NE

neblina [ne'βlina] nf mist

necesario, -a [neθe'sarjo, a] adj necessary

neceser [neθe'ser] nm toilet bag; (bolsa grande) holdall

necesidad [neθesi'ðað] nf need; (lo inevitable) necessity; (miseria) poverty; **en caso de ~** in case of need o emergency; **hacer sus ~es** to relieve o.s.

necesitado, -a [neθesi'taðo, a] adj needy, poor; ~ **de** in need of

necesitar [neθesi'tar] vt to need, require

necio, -a ['neθjo, a] adj foolish

nectarina [nekta'rina] nf nectarine

nefasto, -a [ne'fasto, a] adj ill-fated, unlucky

negación [neɣa'θjon] nf negation; (rechazo) refusal, denial

negar [ne'ɣar] vt (renegar, rechazar) to refuse; (prohibir) to refuse, deny; (desmentir) to deny; **negarse** vr: ~**se a** to refuse to

negativa [neɣa'tiβa] nf negative; (rechazo) refusal, denial

negativo, -a [neɣa'tiβo, a] adj, nm negative

negociante [neɣo'θjante] nm/f businessman/ woman

negociar [neɣo'θjar] vt, vi to negotiate; ~ **en** to deal o trade in

negocio [ne'ɣoθjo] nm (Com) business; (asunto) affair, business; (operación comercial) deal, transaction; (lugar) place of business; **los ~s** business sg; **hacer ~** to do business

negra ['neɣra] nf (Mús) crotchet; V tb **negro**

negro, -a ['neɣro, a] adj black; (suerte) awful ▷ nm black ▷ nm/f black man/woman

nene, -a ['nene, a] nm/f baby, small child

neón [ne'on] nm: **luces/lámpara de ~** neon lights/lamp

neoyorquino, -a [neojor'kino, a] adj (of) New York

nervio ['nerβjo] nm nerve; **nerviosismo** nm nervousness, nerves pl; **nervioso, -a** adj nervous

neto, -a ['neto, a] adj net

neumático, -a [neu'matiko, a] adj pneumatic ▷ nm (ESP) tyre (BRIT), tire (US); **neumático de recambio** spare tyre

neurólogo, -a [neu'roloxo, a] nm/f neurologist

neurona [neu'rona] nf nerve cell

neutral [neu'tral] adj neutral; **neutralizar** vt to neutralize; (contrarrestar) to counteract

neutro, -a ['neutro, a] adj (Bio, Ling) neuter

neutrón [neu'tron] nm neutron

nevada [ne'βaða] nf snowstorm; (caída de nieve) snowfall

nevar [ne'βar] vi to snow

nevera [ne'βera] (ESP) nf refrigerator (BRIT), icebox (US)

nevería [neβe'ria] (MÉX) nf ice-cream parlour

nexo ['nekso] nm link, connection

ni [ni] conj nor, neither; (tb: ~ **siquiera**) not ... even; ~ **aunque** not even if; ~ **blanco** ~ **negro** neither white nor black

Nicaragua [nika'raɣwa] nf Nicaragua; **nicaragüense** adj, nm/f Nicaraguan

nicho ['nitʃo] nm niche

nicotina [niko'tina] nf nicotine

nido ['niðo] nm nest

niebla ['njeβla] nf fog; (neblina) mist

niego etc vb V **negar**

nieto, -a ['njeto, a] nm/f grandson/daughter; **nietos** nmpl grandchildren

nieve etc ['njeβe] vb V **nevar** ▷ nf snow; (MÉX: helado) ice cream

NIF nm abr (= Número de Identificación Fiscal) personal identification number used for financial and tax purposes

ninfa ['ninfa] nf nymph

ningún adj V **ninguno**

ninguno, -a [nin'guno, a] (adj **ningún**) no pron (nadie) nobody; (ni uno) none, not one; (ni uno ni otro) neither; **de ninguna manera** by no means, not at all

niña ['niɲa] nf (Anat) pupil; V tb **niño**

niñera [ni'ɲera] nf nursemaid, nanny

niñez [ni'ɲeθ] nf childhood; (infancia) infancy

niño, -a ['niɲo, a] adj (joven) young; (inmaduro) immature ▷ nm/f child, boy/girl

nipón, -ona [ni'pon, ona] adj, nm/f Japanese

níquel ['nikel] nm nickel

níspero ['nispero] nm medlar

nítido, -a ['nitiðo, a] adj clear; sharp

nitrato [ni'trato] nm nitrate

nitrógeno [ni'troxeno] nm nitrogen

nivel [ni'βel] nm (Geo) level; (norma) level, standard; (altura) height; **nivel de aceite** oil level; **nivel de aire** spirit level; **nivel de vida** standard of living; **nivelar** vt to level out; (fig) to even up; (Com) to balance

no [no] adv no; not ▷ excl no!; ~ **tengo nada** I don't have anything, I have nothing; ~ **es el mío** it's not mine; **ahora ~** not now; ¿~ **lo sabes?** don't you know?; ~ **mucho** not much; ~ **bien termine, lo entregaré** as soon as I finish, I'll hand it over; ~ **más: ayer ~ más** just yesterday; ¡**pase ~ más!** come in!; ¡**a que ~ lo sabes!** I bet you don't know!; ¡**cómo ~!** of course!; **la ~ intervención** non-intervention

noble ['noβle] adj, nmf noble; **nobleza** nf nobility

noche ['notʃe] nf night, night-time; (la tarde) evening; **de ~, por la ~** at night; **es de ~** it's dark

nochebuena [notʃe'βwena] nf Christmas Eve

nochevieja [notʃe'βjexa] nf New Year's Eve

nocivo, -a [no'θiβo, a] *adj* harmful
noctámbulo, -a [nok'tambulo, a] *nm/f* sleepwalker
nocturno, -a [nok'turno, a] *adj* (*de la noche*) nocturnal, night *cpd*; (*de la tarde*) evening *cpd* ⊳ *nm* nocturne
nogal [no'ɣal] *nm* walnut tree
nómada ['nomaða] *adj* nomadic ⊳ *nmf* nomad
nombrar [nom'βrar] *vt* (*designar*) to name; (*mencionar*) to mention; (*dar puesto a*) to appoint
nombre ['nombre] *nm* name; (*sustantivo*) noun; **~ y apellidos** name in full; **poner ~ a** to call, name; **nombre común/propio** common/proper noun; **nombre de pila/de soltera** Christian/maiden name
nómina ['nomina] *nf* (*lista*) payroll; (*hoja*) payslip
nominal [nomi'nal] *adj* nominal
nominar [nomi'nar] *vt* to nominate
nominativo, -a [nomina'tiβo, a] *adj* (*Com*): **cheque ~ a X** cheque made out to X
nordeste [nor'ðeste] *adj* north-east, north-eastern, north-easterly ⊳ *nm* north-east
nórdico, -a ['norðiko, a] *adj* Nordic
noreste [no'reste] *adj*, *nm* = **nordeste**
noria ['norja] *nf* (*Agr*) waterwheel; (*de carnaval*) big (*BRIT*) o Ferris (*US*) wheel
norma ['norma] *nf* rule (of thumb)
normal [nor'mal] *adj* (*corriente*) normal; (*habitual*) usual, natural; **normalizarse** *vr* to return to normal; **normalmente** *adv* normally
normativa [norma'tiβa] *nf* (set of) rules *pl*, regulations *pl*
noroeste [noro'este] *adj* north-west, north-western, north-westerly ⊳ *nm* north-west
norte ['norte] *adj* north, northern, northerly ⊳ *nm* north; (*fig*) guide
norteamericano, -a [norteameri'kano, a] *adj*, *nm/f* (North) American
Noruega [no'rweɣa] *nf* Norway
noruego, -a [no'rweɣo, a] *adj*, *nm/f* Norwegian
nos [nos] *pron* (*directo*) us; (*indirecto*) us; to us; for us; from us; (*reflexivo*) (to) ourselves; (*recíproco*) (to) each other; **~ levantamos a las 7** we get up at 7
nosotros, -as [no'sotros, as] *pron* (*sujeto*) we; (*después de prep*) us
nostalgia [nos'talxja] *nf* nostalgia
nota ['nota] *nf* note; (*Escol*) mark
notable [no'taβle] *adj* notable; (*Escol*) outstanding
notar [no'tar] *vt* to notice, note; **notarse** *vr* to be obvious; **se nota que ...** one observes that ...
notario [no'tarjo] *nm* notary
noticia [no'tiðja] *nf* (*información*) piece of news; **las ~s** the news *sg*; **tener ~s de algn** to hear from sb
noticiero [noti'θjero] (*LAM*) *nm* news bulletin
notificar [notifi'kar] *vt* to notify, inform
notorio, -a [no'torjo, a] *adj* (*público*) well-known; (*evidente*) obvious
novato, -a [no'βato, a] *adj* inexperienced ⊳ *nm/f* beginner, novice
novecientos, -as [noβe'θjentos, as] *num* nine hundred
novedad [noβe'ðað] *nf* (*calidad de nuevo*) newness; (*noticia*) piece of news; (*cambio*) change, (new) development
novel [no'βel] *adj* new; (*inexperto*) inexperienced ⊳ *nmf* beginner
novela [no'βela] *nf* novel

noveno, -a [no'βeno, a] *adj* ninth
noventa [no'βenta] *num* ninety
novia *nf* V **novio**
novicio, -a [no'βiθjo, a] *nm/f* novice
noviembre [no'βjembre] *nm* November
novillada [noβi'ʎaða] *nf* (*Taur*) bullfight with young bulls; **novillero** *nm* novice bullfighter; **novillo** *nm* young bull, bullock; **hacer novillos** (*fam*) to play truant
novio, -a [no'βjo, a] *nm/f* boyfriend/girlfriend; (*prometido*) fiancé/fiancée; (*recién casado*) bridegroom/bride; **los ~s** the newly-weds
nube ['nuβe] *nf* cloud
nublado, -a [nu'βlaðo, a] *adj* cloudy; **nublarse** *vr* to grow dark
nubosidad [nuβosi'ðað] *nf* cloudiness; **había mucha ~** it was very cloudy
nuca ['nuka] *nf* nape of the neck
nuclear [nukle'ar] *adj* nuclear
núcleo ['nukleo] *nm* (*centro*) core; (*Física*) nucleus; **núcleo urbano** city centre
nudillo [nu'ðiʎo] *nm* knuckle
nudista [nu'ðista] *adj* nudist
nudo ['nuðo] *nm* knot; (*de carreteras*) junction
nuera ['nwera] *nf* daughter-in-law
nuestro, -a ['nwestro, a] *adj pos* our ⊳ *pron* ours; **~ padre** our father; **un amigo ~** a friend of ours; **es el ~** it's ours
Nueva York [-jɔrk] *n* New York
Nueva Zelanda [-θe'landa] *nf* New Zealand
nueve ['nweβe] *num* nine
nuevo, -a ['nweβo, a] *adj* (*gen*) new; **de ~** again
nuez [nweθ] *nf* walnut; (*Anat*) Adam's apple; **nuez moscada** nutmeg
nulo, -a ['nulo, a] *adj* (*inepto, torpe*) useless; (*inválido*) (null and) void; (*Deporte*) drawn, tied
núm. *abr* (= *número*) no.
numerar [nume'rar] *vt* to number
número ['numero] *nm* (*gen*) number; (*tamaño: de zapato*) size; (*ejemplar: de diario*) number, issue; **sin ~** numberless, unnumbered; **número atrasado** back number; **número de matrícula/teléfono** registration/telephone number; **número impar/par** odd/even number; **número romano** Roman numeral
numeroso, -a [nume'roso, a] *adj* numerous
nunca ['nunka] *adv* (*jamás*) never; **~ lo pensé** I never thought it; **no viene ~** he never comes; **~ más** never again; **más que ~** more than ever
nupcias ['nupθjas] *nfpl* wedding *sg*, nuptials
nutria ['nutrja] *nf* otter
nutrición [nutri'θjon] *nf* nutrition
nutrir [nu'trir] *vt* (*alimentar*) to nourish; (*dar de comer*) to feed; (*fig*) to strengthen; **nutritivo, -a** *adj* nourishing, nutritious
nylon [ni'lon] *nm* nylon

ñ o

ñango, -a ['ɲaŋɡo, a] (*MÉX*) *adj* puny

ñapa ['ɲapa] (*LAM*) *nf* extra

ñata ['ɲata] (*LAM: fam*) *nf* nose; *V tb* **ñato**

ñato, -a ['ɲato, a] (*LAM*) *adj* snub-nosed

ñoñería [ɲoɲe'ria] *nf* insipidness

ñoño, -a ['ɲoɲo, a] *adj* (*fam: tonto*) silly, stupid; (*soso*) insipid; (*persona*) spineless; (*ESP: película, novela*) sentimental

O *abr* (= *oeste*) W

o [o] *conj* or

oasis [o'asis] *nm inv* oasis

obcecarse [oβθe'karse] *vr* to get o become stubborn

obedecer [oβeðe'θer] *vt* to obey; **obediente** *adj* obedient

obertura [oβer'tura] *nf* overture

obeso, -a [o'βeso, a] *adj* obese

obispo [o'βispo] *nm* bishop

obituario [oβi'twarjo] (*LAM*) *nm* obituary

objetar [oβxe'tar] *vt, vi* to object

objetivo, -a [oβxe'tiβo, a] *adj, nm* objective

objeto [oβ'xeto] *nm* (*cosa*) object; (*fin*) aim

objetor, a [oβxe'tor, a] *nm/f* objector

obligación [oβliɣa'θjon] *nf* obligation; (*Com*) bond

obligar [oβli'ɣar] *vt* to force; **obligarse** *vr* to bind o.s.; **obligatorio, -a** *adj* compulsory, obligatory

oboe [o'βoe] *nm* oboe

obra ['oβra] *nf* work; (*Arq*) construction, building; (*Teatro*) play; **por ~ de** thanks to (the efforts of); **obra maestra** masterpiece; **obras públicas** public works; **obrar** *vt* to work; (*tener efecto*) to have an effect on ▷ *vi* to act, behave; (*tener efecto*) to have an effect; **la carta obra en su poder** the letter is in his/her possession

obrero, -a [o'βrero, a] *adj* (*clase*) working; (*movimiento*) labour *cpd* ▷ *nm/f* (*gen*) worker; (*sin oficio*) labourer

obsceno, -a [oβs'θeno, a] *adj* obscene

obscu... = oscu...

obsequiar [oβse'kjar] *vt* (*ofrecer*) to present with; (*agasajar*) to make a fuss of, lavish attention on; **obsequio** *nm* (*regalo*) gift; (*cortesía*) courtesy, attention

observación [oβserβa'θjon] *nf* observation; (*reflexión*) remark

observador, a [oβserβa'ðor, a] *nm/f* observer

observar [oβser'βar] *vt* to observe; (*anotar*) to notice; **observarse** *vr* to keep to, observe

obsesión [oβse'sjon] *nf* obsession; **obsesivo, -a** *adj* obsessive

obstáculo [oβs'takulo] *nm* obstacle; (*impedimento*) hindrance, drawback

obstante [oβs'tante]: **no ~** *adv* nevertheless

obstinado, -a [oβsti'naðo, a] *adj* obstinate, stubborn

obstinarse [oβsti'narse] *vr* to be obstinate; **~ en** to persist in

obstruir [oβstru'ir] *vt* to obstruct

obtener [oβte'ner] *vt* (*gen*) to obtain; (*premio*) to win

obturador [oβtura'ðor], nm Foto shutter

obvio, -a [oββjo, a] *adj* obvious

oca ['oka] *nf* (*animal*) goose; (*juego*) ≈ snakes and ladders

ocasión [oka'sjon] *nf* (*oportunidad*) opportunity, chance; (*momento*) occasion, time; (*causa*) cause; **de ~** secondhand; **ocasionar** *vt* to cause

ocaso [o'kaso] *nm* (*fig*) decline

occidente [okθi'ðente] *nm* west

OCDE *nf abr* (= *Organización de Cooperación y Desarrollo Económico*) OECD

océano [o'θeano] *nm* ocean; **Océano índico** Indian Ocean

ochenta [o'tʃenta] *num* eighty

ocho ['otʃo] *num* eight; **dentro de ~ días** within a week

ocio ['oθjo] *nm* (*tiempo*) leisure; (*pey*) idleness

octavilla [okta'viʎa] *nf* leaflet, pamphlet

octavo, -a [ok'taβo, a] *adj* eighth

octubre [ok'tuβre] *nm* October

oculista [oku'lista] *nmf* oculist

ocultar [okul'tar] *vt* (*esconder*) to hide; (*callar*) to conceal; **oculto, -a** *adj* hidden; (*fig*) secret

ocupación [okupa'θjon] *nf* occupation

ocupado, -a [oku'paðo, a] *adj* (*persona*) busy; (*plaza*) occupied, taken; (*teléfono*) engaged; **ocupar** *vt* (*gen*) to occupy; **ocuparse** *vr*: **ocuparse de o en** (*gen*) to concern o.s. with; (*cuidar*) to look after

ocurrencia [oku'rrenθja] *nf* (*idea*) bright idea

ocurrir [oku'rrir] *vi* to happen; **ocurrirse** *vr*: **se me ocurrió que ...** it occurred to me that ...

odiar [o'ðjar] *vt* to hate; **odio** *nm* hate, hatred; **odioso, -a** *adj* hateful; (*malo*) nasty

odontólogo, -a [oðon'toloxo, a] *nm/f* dentist, dental surgeon

oeste [o'este] *nm* west; **una película del ~** a western

ofender [ofen'der] *vt* (*agraviar*) to offend; (*insultar*) to insult; **ofenderse** *vr* to take offence; **ofensa** *nf* offence; **ofensiva** *nf* offensive; **ofensivo, -a** *adj* offensive

oferta [o'ferta] *nf* offer; (*propuesta*) proposal; **la ~ y la demanda** supply and demand; **artículos en ~** goods on offer

oficial [ofi'θjal] *adj* official ▷ *nm* (*Mil*) officer

oficina [ofi'θina] *nf* office; **oficina de correos** post office; **oficina de información** information bureau; **oficina de turismo** tourist office; **oficinista** *nmf* clerk

oficio [o'fiθjo] *nm* (*profesión*) profession; (*puesto*) post; (*Rel*) service; **ser del ~** to be an old hand; **tener mucho ~** to have a lot of experience; **oficio de difuntos** funeral service

ofimática [ofi'matika] *nf* office computing

ofrecer [ofre'θer] *vt* (*dar*) to offer; (*proponer*) to propose; **ofrecerse** *vr* (*persona*) to offer o.s., volunteer; (*situación*) to present itself; **¿qué se le ofrece?, ¿se le ofrece algo?** what can I do for you?, can I get you anything?

ofrecimiento [ofreθi'mjento] *nm* offer

oftalmólogo, -a [oftal'moloxo, a] *nm/f* ophthalmologist

oída [o'iða] *nf*: **de ~s** by hearsay

oído [o'iðo] *nm* (*Anat*) ear; (*sentido*) hearing

oigo *etc vb* V **oír**

oír [o'ir] *vt* (*gen*) to hear; (*atender a*) to listen to; **¡oiga!** listen!; **~ misa** to attend mass

OIT *nf abr* (= *Organización Internacional del Trabajo*) ILO

ojal [o'xal] *nm* buttonhole

ojalá [oxa'la] *excl* if only (it were so)!, some hope! ▷ *conj* if only ...!, would that ...!; **~ (que) venga hoy** I hope he comes today

ojeada [oxe'aða] *nf* glance

ojera [o'xera] *nf*: **tener ~s** to have bags under one's eyes

ojo ['oxo] *nm* eye; (*de puente*) span; (*de cerradura*) keyhole ▷ *excl* careful!; **tener ~ para** to have an eye for; **ojo de buey** porthole

okey [o'kei] (*LAM*) *excl* O.K.

okupa [o'kupa] (*ESP: fam*) *nmf* squatter

ola ['ola] *nf* wave

olé [o'le] *excl* bravo!, olé!

oleada [ole'aða] *nf* big wave, swell; (*fig*) wave

oleaje [ole'axe] *nm* swell

óleo ['oleo] *nm* oil; **oleoducto** *nm* (*oil*) pipeline

oler [o'ler] *vt* (*gen*) to smell; (*inquirir*) to pry into; (*fig: sospechar*) to sniff out ▷ *vi* to smell; **~ a** to smell of

olfatear [olfate'ar] *vt* to smell; (*inquirir*) to pry into; **olfato** *nm* sense of smell

olimpiada [olim'piaða] *nf*: **las O~s** the Olympics; **olímpico, -a** [o'limpiko, a], *adj* Olympic

oliva [o'liβa] *nf* (*aceituna*) olive; **aceite de ~** olive oil; **olivo** *nm* olive tree

olla ['oʎa] *nf* pan; (*comida*) stew; **olla exprés** o **a presión** (*ESP*) pressure cooker; **olla podrida** *type of Spanish stew*

olmo ['olmo] *nm* elm (tree)

olor [o'lor] *nm* smell; **oloroso, -a** *adj* scented

olvidar [olβi'ðar] *vt* to forget; (*omitir*) to omit; **olvidarse** *vr* (*fig*) to forget o.s.; **se me olvidó** I forgot

olvido [ol'βiðo] *nm* oblivion; (*despiste*) forgetfulness

ombligo [om'bliɣo] *nm* navel

omelette [ome'lete] (*LAM*) *nf* omelet(te)

omisión [omi'sjon] *nf* (*abstención*) omission; (*descuido*) neglect

omiso, -a [o'miso, a], *adj*: **hacer caso ~ de** to ignore, pass over

omitir [omi'tir] *vt* to omit

omnipotente [omnipo'tente] *adj* omnipotent

omóplato [o'moplato] *nm* shoulder blade

OMS *nf abr* (= *Organización Mundial de la Salud*) WHO

once ['onθe] *num* eleven; **onces** (*cs*) *nfpl* tea break *sg*

onda ['onda] *nf* wave; **onda corta/larga/media** short/long/medium wave; **ondear** *vi* to wave; (*tener ondas*) to be wavy; (*agua*) to ripple

ondulación [ondula'θjon] *nf* undulation; **ondulado, -a** *adj* wavy

ONG *nf abr* (= *organización no gubernamental*) NGO

ONU ['onu] *nf abr* (= *Organización de las Naciones Unidas*) UNO

opaco, -a [o'pako, a] *adj* opaque

opción [op'θjon] *nf* (*gen*) option; (*derecho*) right, option

OPEP ['opep] *nf abr* (= *Organización de Países Exportadores de Petróleo*) OPEC

ópera ['opera] *nf* opera; **ópera bufa** o **cómica** comic opera

operación [opera'θjon] *nf* (*gen*) operation; (*Com*)

transaction, deal

operador, a [opera'ðor, a] nm/f operator; (Cine: de proyección) projectionist; (: de rodaje) cameraman

operar [ope'rar] vt (producir) to produce, bring about; (Med) to operate on ▷ vi (Com) to operate, deal; **operarse** vr to occur; (Med) to have an operation

opereta [ope'reta] nf operetta

opinar [opi'nar] vt to think ▷ vi to give one's opinion; **opinión** nf (creencia) belief; (criterio) opinion

opio ['opjo] nm opium

oponer [opo'ner] vt (resistencia) to put up, offer; **oponerse** vr (objetar) to object; (estar frente a frente) to be opposed; (dos personas) to oppose each other; ~ **A a B** to set A against B; **me opongo a pensar que ...** I refuse to believe o think that ...

oportunidad [oportuni'ðað] nf (ocasión) opportunity; (posibilidad) chance

oportuno, -a [opor'tuno, a] adj (en su tiempo) opportune, timely; (respuesta) suitable; **en el momento ~** at the right moment

oposición [oposi'θjon] nf opposition; **oposiciones** nfpl (Escol) public examinations

opositor, a [oposi'tor, a] nm/f (adversario) opponent; (candidato): ~ **(a)** candidate (for)

opresión [opre'sjon] nf oppression; **opresor, a** nm/f oppressor

oprimir [opri'mir] vt to squeeze; (fig) to oppress

optar [op'tar] vi (elegir) to choose; ~ **por** to opt for; **optativo, -a** adj optional

óptico, -a ['optiko, a] adj optic(al) ▷ nm/f optician; **óptica** nf optician's (shop); **desde esta óptica** from this point of view

optimismo [opti'mismo] nm optimism; **optimista** nmf optimist

opuesto, -a [o'pwesto, a] adj (contrario) opposite; (antagónico) opposing

oración [ora'θjon] nf (Rel) prayer; (Ling) sentence

orador, a [ora'ðor, a] nm/f (conferenciante) speaker, orator

oral [o'ral] adj oral

orangután [orangu'tan] nm orangutan

orar [o'rar] vi to pray

oratoria [ora'torja] nf oratory

órbita ['orβita] nf orbit

orden ['orðen] nm (gen) order ▷ nf (gen) order; (Inform) command; **en ~ de prioridad** in order of priority; **orden del día** agenda

ordenado, -a [orðe'naðo, a] adj (metódico) methodical; (arreglado) orderly

ordenador [orðena'ðor] nm computer; **ordenador central** mainframe computer

ordenar [orðe'nar] vt (mandar) to order; (poner orden) to put in order, arrange; **ordenarse** vr (Rel) to be ordained

ordeñar [orðe'nar] vt to milk

ordinario, -a [orði'narjo, a] adj (común) ordinary, usual; (vulgar) vulgar, common

orégano [o'reɣano] nm oregano

oreja [o'rexa] nf ear; (Mecánica) lug, flange

orfanato [orfa'nato] nm orphanage

orfebrería [orfeβre'ria] nf gold/silver work

orgánico, -a [or'ɣaniko, a] adj organic

organismo [orɣa'nismo] nm (Bio) organism; (Pol) organization

organización [orɣaniθa'θjon] nf organization; **organizar** vt to organize

órgano ['orɣano] nm organ

orgasmo [or'ɣasmo] nm orgasm

orgía [or'xia] nf orgy

orgullo [or'ɣuʎo] nm pride; **orgulloso, -a** adj (gen) proud; (altanero) haughty

orientación [orjenta'θjon] nf (posición) position; (dirección) direction

oriental [orjen'tal] adj eastern; (del Extremo Oriente) oriental

orientar [orjen'tar] vt (situar) to orientate; (señalar) to point; (dirigir) to direct; (guiar) to guide; **orientarse** vr to get one's bearings

oriente [o'rjente] nm east; **el O~ Medio** the Middle East; **el Próximo/Extremo O~** the Near/Far East

origen [o'rixen] nm origin

original [orixi'nal] adj (nuevo) original; (extraño) odd, strange; **originalidad** nf originality

originar [orixi'nar] vt to start, cause; **originarse** vr to originate; **originario, -a** adj original; **originario de** native of

orilla [o'riʎa] nf (borde) border; (de río) bank; (de bosque, tela) edge; (de mar) shore

orina [o'rina] nf urine; **orinal** nm (chamber) pot; **orinar** vi to urinate; **orinarse** vr to wet o.s.

oro ['oro] nm gold; **oros** nmpl (Naipes) hearts

orquesta [or'kesta] nf orchestra; **orquesta sinfónica** symphony orchestra

orquídea [or'kiðea] nf orchid

ortiga [or'tiɣa] nf nettle

ortodoxo, -a [orto'ðokso, a] adj orthodox

ortografía [ortoɣra'fia] nf spelling

ortopedia [orto'peðja] nf orthopaedics sg; **ortopédico, -a** adj orthopaedic

oruga [o'ruɣa] nf caterpillar

orzuelo [or'θwelo] nm stye

os [os] pron (gen) you; (a vosotros) to you

osa ['osa] nf (she-)bear; **Osa Mayor/Menor** Great/ Little Bear

osadía [osa'ðia] nf daring

osar [o'sar] vi to dare

oscilación [osθila'θjon] nf (movimiento) oscillation; (fluctuación) fluctuation

oscilar [osθi'lar] vi to oscillate; to fluctuate

oscurecer [oskure'θer] vt to darken ▷ vi to grow dark; **oscurecerse** vr to grow o get dark

oscuridad [oskuri'ðað] nf obscurity; (tinieblas) darkness

oscuro, -a [os'kuro, a] adj dark; (fig) obscure; **a oscuras** in the dark

óseo, -a ['oseo, a] adj bone cpd

oso ['oso] nm bear; **oso de peluche** teddy bear; **oso hormiguero** anteater

ostentar [osten'tar] vt (gen) to show; (pey) to flaunt, show off; (poseer) to have, possess

ostión [os'tjon] nm (MÉX) nm = **ostra**

ostra ['ostra] nf oyster

OTAN ['otan] nf abr (= Organización del Tratado del Atlántico Norte) NATO

otitis [o'titis] nf earache

otoñal [oto'nal] adj autumnal

otoño [o'tono] nm autumn

otorgar [otor'ɣar] vt (conceder) to concede; (dar) to grant

otorrino, -a [oto'rrino, a], **otorrinolaringólogo, -a** [otorrinolarin'ɣoloɣo, a] nm/f ear, nose and throat specialist

○ **PALABRA CLAVE**

otro, -a ['otro, a] *adj* **1** *(distinto: sg)* another; *(: pl)* other; **con otros amigos** with other o different friends **2** *(adicional)*: **tráigame otro café (más), por favor** can I have another coffee please; **otros diez días más** another ten days
▷ *pron* **1 el otro** the other one; **(los) otros** (the) others; **de otro** somebody else's; **que lo haga otro** let somebody else do it
2 *(recíproco)*: **se odian (la) una a (la) otra** they hate one another o each other
3: **otro tanto: comer otro tanto** to eat the same o as much again; **recibió una decena de telegramas y otras tantas llamadas** he got about ten telegrams and as many calls

ovación [oβa'θjon] *nf* ovation
oval [o'βal] *adj* oval; **ovalado, -a** *adj* oval; **óvalo** *nm* oval
ovario [o'βarjo] *nm* ovary
oveja [o'βexa] *nf* sheep
overol [oβe'rol] (LAM) *nm* overalls *pl*
ovillo [o'βiʎo] *nm (de lana)* ball of wool
OVNI ['oβni] *nm abr (= objeto volante no identificado)* UFO
ovulación [oβula'θjon] *nf* ovulation; **óvulo** *nm* ovum
oxidación [oksiða'θjon] *nf* rusting
oxidar [oksi'ðar] *vt* to rust; **oxidarse** *vr* to go rusty
óxido ['oksiðo] *nm* oxide
oxigenado, -a [oksixe'naðo, a] *adj (Quím)* oxygenated; *(pelo)* bleached
oxígeno [ok'sixeno] *nm* oxygen
oyente [o'jente] *nmf* listener
oyes *etc vb* V **oír**
ozono [o'θono] *nm* ozone

p

pabellón [paβe'ʎon] *nm* bell tent; *(Arq)* pavilion; *(de hospital etc)* block, section; *(bandera)* flag
pacer [pa'θer] *vi* to graze
paciencia [pa'θjenθja] *nf* patience
paciente [pa'θjente] *adj, nmf* patient
pacificación [paθifika'θjon] *nf* pacification
pacífico, -a [pa'θifiko, a] *adj (persona)* peaceable; *(existencia)* peaceful; **el (Océano) P~** the Pacific (Ocean)
pacifista [paθi'fista] *nmf* pacifist
pacotilla [pako'tiʎa] *nf*: **de ~** *(actor, escritor)* third-rate
pactar [pak'tar] *vt* to agree to o on ▷ *vi* to come to an agreement
pacto ['pakto] *nm (tratado)* pact; *(acuerdo)* agreement
padecer [paðe'θer] *vt (sufrir)* to suffer; *(soportar)* to endure, put up with; **padecimiento** *nm* suffering
padrastro [pa'ðrastro] *nm* stepfather
padre ['paðre] *nm* father ▷ *adj (fam)*: **un éxito ~** a tremendous success; **padres** *nmpl* parents; **padre político** father-in-law
padrino [pa'ðrino] *nm (Rel)* godfather; *(tb*: **~ de boda)** best man; *(fig)* sponsor, patron; **padrinos** *nmpl* godparents
padrón [pa'ðron] *nm (censo)* census, roll
padrote [pa'ðrote] (MÉX: fam) *nm* pimp
paella [pa'eʎa] *nf* paella, *dish of rice with meat, shellfish etc*
paga ['paxa] *nf (pago)* payment; *(sueldo)* pay, wages *pl*
pagano, -a [pa'xano, a] *adj, nm/f* pagan, heathen
pagar [pa'xar] *vt* to pay; *(las compras, crimen)* to pay for; *(fig: favor)* to repay ▷ *vi* to pay; **~ al contado/a plazos** to pay (in) cash/in instalments
pagaré [paxa're] *nm* I.O.U.
página ['paxina] *nf* page; **página de inicio** *(Inform)* home page; **página web** *(Inform)* web page
pago ['paxo] *nm (dinero)* payment; **en ~ de** in return for; **pago anticipado/a cuenta/contra reembolso/ en especie** advance payment/payment on account/ cash on delivery/payment in kind
pág(s). *abr (= página(s))* p(p).
pague *etc vb* V **pagar**
país [pa'is] *nm (gen)* country; *(región)* land; **los P~es Bajos** the Low Countries; **el P~ Vasco** the Basque

Country

paisaje [pai'saxe] nm landscape, scenery

paisano, -a [pai'sano, a] adj of the same country ▷ nm/f (compatriota) fellow countryman/woman; **vestir de ~** (soldado) to be in civvies; (guardia) to be in plain clothes

paja ['paxa] nf straw; (fig) rubbish (BRIT), trash (US)

pajarita [paxa'rita] nf (corbata) bow tie

pájaro ['paxaro] nm bird; **pájaro carpintero** woodpecker

pajita [pa'xita] nf (drinking) straw

pala ['pala] nf spade, shovel; (raqueta etc) bat; (: de tenis) racquet; (Culin) slice; **pala mecánica** power shovel

palabra [pa'laβra] nf word; (facultad) (power of) speech; (derecho de hablar) right to speak; **tomar la ~** (en mitin) to take the floor

palabrota [pala'βrota] nf swearword

palacio [pa'laθjo] nm palace; (mansión) mansion, large house; **palacio de justicia** courthouse; **palacio municipal** town o city hall

paladar [pala'ðar] nm palate; **paladear** vt to taste

palanca [pa'lanka] nf lever; (fig) pull, influence

palangana [palan'gana] nf washbasin

palco ['palko] nm box

Palestina [pales'tina] nf Palestine; **palestino, -a** nm/f Palestinian

paleta [pa'leta] nf (de pintor) palette; (de albañil) trowel; (de ping-pong) bat; (MÉX, CAM: helado) ice lolly (BRIT), Popsicle® (US)

palidecer [paliðe'θer] vi to turn pale; **palidez** nf paleness; **pálido, -a** adj pale

palillo [pa'liʎo] nm (mondadientes) toothpick; (para comer) chopstick

palito [pa'lito] (RPL) nm (helado) ice lolly (BRIT), Popsicle® (US)

paliza [pa'liθa] nf beating, thrashing

palma [pal'ma] nf (Anat) palm; (árbol) palm tree; **batir** o **dar ~s** to clap, applaud; **palmada** nf slap; **palmadas** nfpl clapping sg, applause sg

palmar [pal'mar] (fam) vi (tb: ~**la**) to die, kick the bucket

palmear [palme'ar] vi to clap

palmera [pal'mera] nf (Bot) palm tree

palmo ['palmo] nm (medida) span; (fig) small amount; **~ a ~** inch by inch

palo ['palo] nm stick; (poste) post; (de tienda de campaña) pole; (mango) handle, shaft; (golpe) blow, hit; (de golf) club; (de béisbol) bat; (Náut) mast; (Naipes) suit

paloma [pa'loma] nf dove, pigeon

palomitas [palo'mitas] nfpl popcorn sg

palpar [pal'par] vt to touch, feel

palpitar [palpi'tar] vi to palpitate; (latir) to beat

palta ['palta] (cs) nf avocado

paludismo [palu'ðismo] nm malaria

pamela [pa'mela] nf picture hat, sun hat

pampa ['pampa] nf pampas, prairie

pan [pan] nm bread; (una barra) loaf; **pan integral** wholemeal (BRIT) o wholewheat (US) bread; **pan rallado** breadcrumbs pl; **pan tostado** (MÉX: tostada) toast

pana ['pana] nf corduroy

panadería [panaðe'ria] nf baker's (shop); **panadero, -a** nm/f baker

Panamá [pana'ma] nm Panama; **panameño, -a** adj Panamanian

pancarta [pan'karta] nf placard, banner

panceta [pan'θeta] (ESP, RPL) nf bacon

pancho ['pantʃo] (RPL) nm hot dog

pancito [pan'θito] nm (bread) roll

panda ['panda] nm (Zool) panda

pandereta [pande'reta] nf tambourine

pandilla [pan'diʎa] nf set, group; (de criminales) gang; (pey: camarilla) clique

panecillo [pane'θiʎo] (ESP) nm (bread) roll

panel [pa'nel] nm panel; **panel solar** solar panel

panfleto [pan'fleto] nm pamphlet

pánico ['paniko] nm panic

panorama [pano'rama] nm panorama; (vista) view

panqueque [pan'keke] (LAM) nm pancake

pantalla [pan'taʎa] nf (de cine) screen; (de lámpara) lampshade

pantalón [panta'lon] nm trousers; **pantalones** nmpl trousers; **pantalones cortes** shorts

pantano [pan'tano] nm (ciénaga) marsh, swamp; (depósito: de agua) reservoir; (fig) jam, difficulty

panteón [pante'on] nm (monumento) pantheon

pantera [pan'tera] nf panther

pantimedias [panti'meðjas] (MÉX) nfpl = **pantis**

pantis ['pantis] nmpl tights (BRIT), pantyhose (US)

pantomima [panto'mima] nf pantomime

pantorrilla [panto'rriʎa] nf calf (of the leg)

pants [pants] (MÉX) nmpl tracksuit (BRIT), sweat suit (US)

pantufla [pan'tufla] nf slipper

panty(s) ['panti(s)] nm(pl) tights (BRIT), pantyhose (US)

panza ['panθa] nf belly, paunch

pañal [pa'ɲal] nm nappy (BRIT), diaper (US); **pañales** nmpl (fig) early stages, infancy sg

paño ['paɲo] nm (tela) cloth; (pedazo de tela) (piece of) cloth; (trapo) duster, rag; **paños menores** underclothes

pañuelo [pa'ɲwelo] nm handkerchief, hanky; (fam: para la cabeza) (head)scarf

papa ['papa] nm: **el P~** the Pope ▷ nf (LAM: patata) potato; **papas fritas** (LAM) French fries, chips (BRIT); (de bolsa) crisps (BRIT), potato chips (US)

papá [pa'pa] (fam) nm dad(dy), pa (US)

papada [pa'paða] nf double chin

papagayo [papa'ɣajo] nm parrot

papalote [papa'lote] (MÉX, CAM) nm kite

papanatas [papa'natas] (fam) nm inv simpleton

papaya [pa'paja] nf papaya

papear [pape'ar] (fam) vt, vi to scoff

papel [pa'pel] nm paper; (hoja de papel) sheet of paper; (Teatro: fig) role; **papel de aluminio** aluminium (BRIT) o aluminum (US) foil; **papel de arroz/envolver/fumar** rice/wrapping/cigarette paper; **papel de estaño** o **plata** tinfoil; **papel de lija** sandpaper; **papel higiénico** toilet paper; **papel moneda** paper money; **papel secante** blotting paper

papeleo [pape'leo] nm red tape

papelera [pape'lera] nf wastepaper basket; (en la calle) litter bin; **papelera (de reciclaje)** (Inform) wastebasket

papelería [papele'ria] nf stationer's (shop)

papeleta [pape'leta] (ESP) nf (Pol) ballot paper

paperas [pa'peras] nfpl mumps sg

papilla [pa'piʎa] nf (de bebé) baby food

paquete [pa'kete] nm (de cigarrillos etc) packet; (Correos etc) parcel

par [par] adj (igual) like, equal; (Mat) even ▷ nm equal;

(de guantes) pair; (de veces) couple; (Pol) peer: (Golf. Com)
par; **abrir de ~ en ~** to open wide

para ['para] prep for; **no es ~ comer** it's not for eating;
decir ~ sí to say to o.s.; **¿~ qué lo quieres?** what do you
want it for?; **se casaron ~ separarse otra vez** they
married only to separate again; **lo tendré ~ mañana**
I'll have it (for) tomorrow; **ir ~ casa** to go home, head
for home; **profesor es muy estúpido** he's very stupid
for a teacher; **¿quién es usted ~ gritar así?** who are
you to shout like that?; **tengo bastante ~ vivir** I have
enough to live on; V tb **con**

parabién [para'βjen] nm congratulations pl

parábola [pa'raβola] nf parable; (Mat) parabola;
parabólica nf (tb: **antena parabólica**) satellite dish

parabrisas [para'βrisas] nm inv windscreen (BRIT),
windshield (US)

paracaídas [paraka'iðas] nm inv parachute;
paracaidista nmf parachutist; (Mil) paratrooper

parachoques [para'tʃokes] nm inv (Auto) bumper;
(Mecánica etc) shock absorber

parada [pa'raða] nf (acto) stopping; (de
industria) shutdown, stoppage; (lugar) stopping place;
parada de autobús bus stop; **parada de taxis** taxi
stand o rank (BRIT)

paradero [para'ðero] nm stopping-place; (situación)
whereabouts

parado, -a [pa'raðo, a] adj (persona) motionless,
standing still; (fábrica) closed, at a standstill; (coche)
stopped; (LAM: de pie) standing (up); (ESP: sin empleo)
unemployed, idle

paradoja [para'ðoxa] nf paradox

parador [para'ðor] nm parador, state-run hotel

paragolpes [para'golpes] (RPL) nm inv (Auto)
bumper, fender (US)

paraguas [pa'raxwas] nm inv umbrella

Paraguay [para'xwai] nm Paraguay; **paraguayo, -a**
adj, nm/f Paraguayan

paraíso [para'iso] nm paradise, heaven

paraje [pa'raxe] nm place, spot

paralelo, -a [para'lelo, a] adj parallel

parálisis [pa'ralisis] nf inv paralysis; **paralítico, -a**
adj, nm/f paralytic

paralizar [parali'θar] vt to paralyse; **paralizarse** vr
to become paralysed; (fig) to come to a standstill

páramo ['paramo] nm bleak plateau

paranoico, -a [para'noiko, a] nm/f paranoiac

parapente [para'pente] nm (deporte) paragliding;
(aparato) paraglider

parapléjico, -a [para'plexiko, a] adj, nm/f
paraplegic

parar [pa'rar] vt to stop; (golpe) to ward off ▷ vi to
stop; **pararse** vr to stop; (LAM: ponerse de pie) to stand
up; **ha parado de llover** it has stopped raining; **van a
ir a ~ a comisaría** they're going to end up in the police
station; **~se** to pay attention to

pararrayos [para'rrajos] nm inv lightning conductor

parásito, -a [pa'rasito, a] nm/f parasite

parcela [par'θela] nf plot, piece of ground

parche ['partʃe] nm (gen) patch

parchís [par'tʃis] nm ludo

parcial [par'θjal] adj (pago) part-; (eclipse) partial; (Jur)
prejudiced, biased; (Pol) partisan

parecer [pare'θer] nm (opinión) opinion, view;
(aspecto) looks pl ▷ vi (tener apariencia) to seem, look;
(asemejarse) to look o seem like; (aparecer, llegar) to
appear; **parecerse** vr to look alike, resemble each

other; **al ~** apparently; **según parece** evidently,
apparently; **~se a** to look like, resemble; **me parece
que** I think (that), it seems to me that

parecido, -a [pare'θiðo, a] adj similar ▷ nm
similarity, likeness, resemblance; **bien ~** good-looking,
nice-looking

pared [pa'reð] nf wall

pareja [pa'rexa] nf (par) pair; (dos personas) couple;
(otro: de un par) other one (of a pair); (persona) partner

parentesco [paren'tesko] nm relationship

paréntesis [pa'rentesis] nm inv parenthesis; (en
escrito) bracket

parezco etc vb V **parecer**

pariente [pa'rjente] nmf relative, relation

parir [pa'rir] vt to give birth to ▷ vi (mujer) to give
birth, have a baby

París [pa'ris] n Paris

parka ['parka] (LAM) nf anorak

parking ['parkin] nm car park (BRIT), parking lot (US)

parlamentar [parlamen'tar] vi to parley

parlamentario, -a [parlamen'tarjo, a] adj
parliamentary ▷ nm/f member of parliament

parlamento [parla'mento] nm parliament

parlanchín, -ina [parlan'tʃin, ina] adj indiscreet
▷ nm/f chatterbox

parlar [par'lar] vi to chatter (away)

paro ['paro] nm (huelga) stoppage (of work),
strike; (ESP: desempleo) unemployment; (: subsidio)
unemployment benefit; **estar en ~** (ESP) to be
unemployed; **paro cardíaco** cardiac arrest

parodia [pa'roðja] nf parody; **parodiar** vt to parody

parpadear [parpaðe'ar] vi (ojos) to blink; (luz) to
flicker

párpado ['parpaðo] nm eyelid

parque ['parke] nm (lugar verde) park; (MÉX: munición)
ammunition; **parque de atracciones** fairground;
parque de bomberos (ESP) fire station; **parque
infantil/temático/zoológico** playground/theme
park/zoo

parqué [par'ke] nm parquet (flooring)

parquímetro [par'kimetro] nm parking meter

parra ['parra] nf (grape)vine

párrafo ['parrafo] nm paragraph; **echar un ~** (fam)
to have a chat

parranda [pa'rranda] (fam) nf spree, binge

parrilla [pa'rriʎa] nf (Culin) grill; (de coche) grille;
(carne a la) **~** barbecue; **parrillada** nf barbecue

párroco ['parroko] nm parish priest

parroquia [pa'rrokja] nf parish; (iglesia) parish
church; (Com) clientele, customers pl; **parroquiano, -a**
nm/f parishioner; (Com) client, customer

parte ['parte] nm message; (informe) report ▷ nf part;
(lado, cara) side; (de reparto) share; (Jur) party; **en alguna
~ de Europa** somewhere in Europe; **en o por todas ~s**
everywhere; **en gran ~** to a large extent; **la mayor ~ de
los españoles** most Spaniards; **de un tiempo a esta
~** for some time past; **de ~ de algn** on sb's behalf; **¿de
de quién?** (Tel) who is speaking?; **por ~ de** on the part
of; **yo por mi ~** I for my part; **por otra ~** on the other
hand; **dar ~** to inform; **tomar ~** to take part; **parte
meteorológico** weather forecast o report

participación [partiθipa'θjon] nf (acto)
participation, taking part; (parte, Com) share; (de
lotería) shared prize; (aviso) notice, notification

participante [partiθi'pante] nmf participant

participar [partiθi'par] vt to notify, inform ▷ vi to

take part, participate

partícipe [par'tiθipe] nmf participant

particular [partiku'lar] adj (especial) particular, special; (individual, personal) private, personal ▷ nm (punto, asunto) particular, point; (individuo) individual; **tiene coche** ~ he has a car of his own

partida [par'tiða] nf (salida) departure; (Com) entry, item; (juego) game; (grupo de personas) band, group; **mala** ~ dirty trick; **partida de nacimiento/matrimonio/defunción** (ESP) birth/marriage/death certificate

partidario, -a [parti'ðarjo, a] adj partisan ▷ nm/f supporter, follower

partido [par'tiðo] nm (Pol) party; (Deporte) game, match; **sacar ~ de** to profit o benefit from; **tomar ~** to take sides

partir [par'tir] vt (dividir) to split, divide; (compartir, distribuir) to share (out), distribute; (romper) to break open, split open; (rebanada) to cut (off) ▷ vi (ponerse en camino) to set off o out; (comenzar) to start (off o out); **partirse** vr to crack o split o break (in two etc); **a ~ de** (starting) from

partitura [parti'tura] nf (Mús) score

parto ['parto] nm birth; (fig) product, creation; **estar de ~** to be in labour

parvulario [parβu'larjo] (ESP) nm nursery school, kindergarten

pasa ['pasa] nf raisin; **pasa de Corinto** currant

pasacintas [pasa'θintas] (LAM) nm cassette player

pasada [pa'saða] nf passing, passage; **de ~** in passing, incidentally; **una mala ~** a dirty trick

pasadizo [pasa'ðiθo] nm (pasillo) passage, corridor; (callejuela) alley

pasado, -a [pa'saðo, a] adj past; (malo: comida, fruta) bad; (muy cocido) overdone; (anticuado) out of date ▷ nm past; ~ **mañana** the day after tomorrow; **el mes** ~ last month

pasador [pasa'ðor] nm (cerrojo) bolt; (de pelo) hair slide; (horquilla) grip

pasaje [pa'saxe] nm (paso) passage; (pago de viaje) fare; (los pasajeros) passengers pl; (pasillo) passageway

pasajero, -a [pasa'xero, a] adj passing; (situación, estado) temporary; (amor, enfermedad) brief ▷ nm/f passenger

pasamontañas [pasamon'taɲas] nm inv balaclava helmet

pasaporte [pasa'porte] nm passport

pasar [pa'sar] vt to pass; (tiempo) to spend; (desgracias) to suffer, endure; (noticia) to give, pass on; (río) to cross; (barrera) to pass through; (falta) to overlook, tolerate; (contrincante) to surpass, do better than; (coche) to overtake; (Cine) to show; (enfermedad) to give, infect with ▷ vi (gen) to pass; (terminarse) to be over; (ocurrir) to happen; **pasarse** vr (flores) to fade; (comida) to go bad o off; (fig) to overdo it, go too far; ~ **de** to go beyond, exceed; ~ **por** (LAM) to fetch; **~lo bien/mal** to have a good/bad time; **¡pase!** come in!; **hacer ~** to show in; **lo que pasa es que ...** the thing is ...; ~ **se al enemigo** to go over to the enemy; **se me pasó** I forgot; **no se la pasa nada** here's nothing; **pase lo que pase** come what may; **¿qué pasa?** what's going on?, what's up?; **¿qué te pasa?** what's wrong?

pasarela [pasa'rela] nf footbridge; (en barco) gangway

pasatiempo [pasa'tjempo] nm pastime, hobby

Pascua ['paskwa] nf (en Semana Santa) Easter;

Pascuas nfpl Christmas (time); **¡felices ~s!** Merry Christmas!

pase ['pase] nm pass; (Cine) performance, showing

pasear [pase'ar] vt to take for a walk; (exhibir) to parade, show off ▷ vi to walk, go for a walk; **pasearse** vr to walk, go for a walk; ~ **en coche** to go for a drive; **paseo** nm (avenida) avenue; (distancia corta) walk, stroll; **dar un** o **ir de paseo** to go for a walk; **paseo marítimo** (ESP) promenade

pasillo [pa'siʎo] nm passage, corridor

pasión [pa'sjon] nf passion

pasivo, -a [pa'siβo, a] adj passive; (inactivo) inactive ▷ nm (Com) liabilities pl, debts pl

pasmoso, -a [pas'moso, a] adj amazing, astonishing

paso, -a ['paso, a] adj dried ▷ nm step; (modo de andar) walk; (huella) footprint; (rapidez) speed, pace, rate; (camino accesible) way through, passage; (cruce) crossing; (pasaje) passing, passage; (Geo) pass; (estrecho) strait; **a ese** ~ (fig) at that rate; **salir al** ~ **de** o a to waylay; **estar de** ~ to be passing through; **prohibido el** ~ no entry; **ceda el** ~ give way; **paso a nivel** (Ferro) level-crossing; **paso (de) cebra** (ESP) zebra crossing; **paso de peatones** pedestrian crossing; **paso elevado** flyover

pasota [pa'sota] (ESP: fam) adj, nmf dropout; **ser un** ~ to be a bit of a dropout; (ser indiferente) not to care about anything

pasta ['pasta] nf paste; (Culin: masa) dough; (: de bizcochos etc) pastry; (fam) dough; **pastas** nfpl (bizcochos) pastries, small cakes; (fideos, espaguetis etc) pasta; **pasta dentífrica** o **de dientes** toothpaste

pastar [pas'tar] vt, vi to graze

pastel [pas'tel] nm (dulce) cake; (Arte) pastel; **pastel de carne** meat pie; **pastelería** nf cake shop

pastilla [pas'tiʎa] nf (de jabón, chocolate) bar; (píldora) tablet, pill

pasto ['pasto] nm (hierba) grass; (lugar) pasture, field; **pastor, a** [pas'tor, a] nm/f shepherd/ess ▷ nm (Rel) clergyman, pastor; **pastor alemán** Alsatian

pata ['pata] nf (pierna) leg; (pie) foot; (de muebles) leg; ~**s arriba** upside down; **metedura de ~** (fam) gaffe; **meter la ~** (fam) to put one's foot in it; **tener buena/mala ~** to be lucky/unlucky; **pata de cabra** (Tec) crowbar; **patada** nf kick; (en el suelo) stamp

patata [pa'tata] nf potato; **patatas fritas** chips, French fries; (de bolsa) crisps

paté [pa'te] nm pâté

patente [pa'tente] adj obvious, evident; (Com) patent ▷ nf patent

paternal [pater'nal] adj fatherly, paternal; **paterno, -a** adj paternal

patético, -a [pa'tetiko, a] adj pathetic, moving

patilla [pa'tiʎa] nf (de gafas) side(piece); **patillas** nfpl sideburns

patín [pa'tin] nm skate; (de trineo) runner; **patín de ruedas** roller skate; **patinaje** nm skating; **patinar** vi to skate; (resbalarse) to skid, slip; (fam) to slip up, blunder

patineta [pati'neta] nf (MÉX: patinete) scooter; (CS: monopatín) skateboard

patinete [pati'nete] nm scooter

patio ['patjo] nm (de casa) patio, courtyard; **patio de recreo** playground

pato ['pato] nm duck; **pagar el** ~ (fam) to take the blame, carry the can

patoso, -a [pa'toso, a] (fam) adj clumsy
patotero [pato'tero] (cs) nm hooligan, lout
patraña [pa'traɲa] nf story, fib
patria ['patrja] nf native land, mother country
patrimonio [patri'monjo] nm inheritance; (fig) heritage
patriota [pa'trjota] nmf patriot
patrocinar [patroθi'nar] vt to sponsor
patrón, -ona [pa'tron, ona] nm/f (jefe) boss, chief, master(mistress); (propietario) landlord/lady; (Rel) patron saint ▷ nm (Tec, Costura) pattern
patronato [patro'nato] nm sponsorship; (acto) patronage; (fundación benéfica) trust, foundation
patrulla [pa'truʎa] nf patrol
pausa ['pausa] nf pause, break
pauta ['pauta] nf line, guide line
pava ['paβa] (nɾl) nf kettle
pavimento [paβi'mento] nm (de losa) pavement, paving
pavo ['paβo] nm turkey; **pavo real** peacock
payaso, -a [pa'jaso, a] nm/f clown
payo, -a ['pajo, a] nm/f non-gipsy
paz [paθ] nf peace; (tranquilidad) peacefulness, tranquillity; **hacer las paces** to make peace; (fig) to make up; **¡déjame en ~!** leave me alone!
PC nm PC, personal computer
P.D. abr (= posdata) P.S., p.s.
peaje [pe'axe] nm toll
peatón [pea'ton] nm pedestrian; **peatonal** adj pedestrian
peca ['peka] nf freckle
pecado [pe'kaðo] nm sin; **pecador, a** adj ▷ nm/f sinner
pecaminoso, -a [pekami'noso, a] adj sinful
pecar [pe'kar] vi (Rel) to sin; **peca de generoso** he is generous to a fault
pecera [pe'θera] nf fish tank; (redonda) goldfish bowl
pecho ['petʃo] nm (Anat) chest; (de mujer) breast; **dar el ~ a** to breast-feed; **tomar algo a ~** to take sth to heart
pechuga [pe'tʃuɣa] nf breast
peculiar [peku'ljar] adj special, peculiar; (característico) typical, characteristic
pedal [pe'ðal] nm pedal; **pedalear** vi to pedal
pedante [pe'ðante] adj pedantic ▷ nmf pedant
pedazo [pe'ðaθo] nm piece, bit; **hacerse ~s** to smash, shatter
pediatra [pe'ðjatra] nmf paediatrician
pedido [pe'ðiðo] nm (Com) order; (petición) request
pedir [pe'ðir] vt to ask for, request; (comida, Com: mandar) to order; (necesitar) to need, demand, require ▷ vi to ask; **me pidió que cerrara la puerta** he asked me to shut the door; **¿cuánto piden por el coche?** how much are they asking for the car?
pedo ['peðo] (fam!) nm fart
pega ['peɣa] nf snag; **poner ~s (a)** to complain (about)
pegadizo, -a [peɣa'ðiθo, a] adj (Mús) catchy
pegajoso, -a [peɣa'xoso, a] adj sticky, adhesive
pegamento [peɣa'mento] nm gum, glue
pegar [pe'ɣar] vt (papel, sellos) to stick (on); (cartel) to stick up; (coser) to sew (on); (unir: partes) to join, fix together; (Comput) to paste; (Med) to give, infect with; (dar: golpe) to give, deal ▷ vi (adherirse) to stick, adhere; (ir juntos: colores) to match, go together; (golpear) to hit; (quemar: el sol) to strike hot, burn; **pegarse** vr (gen) to

stick; (dos personas) to hit each other, fight; (fam): **~ un grito** to let out a yell; **~ un salto** to jump (with fright); **~ en** to touch; **~se un tiro** to shoot o.s.
pegatina [peɣa'tina] nf sticker
pegote [pe'ɣote] (fam) nm eyesore, sight
peinado [pei'naðo] nm hairstyle
peinar [pei'nar] vt to comb; (hacer estilo) to style; **peinarse** vr to comb one's hair
peine ['peine] nm comb; **peineta** nf ornamental comb
p.ej. abr (= por ejemplo) e.g.
Pekín [pe'kin] n Peking(g)
pelado, -a [pe'laðo, a] adj (fruta, patata etc) peeled; (cabeza) shorn; (campo, fig) bare; (fam: sin dinero) broke
pelar [pe'lar] vt (fruta, patatas etc) to peel; (cortar el pelo a) to cut the hair of; (quitar la piel: animal) to skin; **pelarse** vr (la piel) to peel off; **voy a ~me** I'm going to get my hair cut
peldaño [pel'daɲo] nm step
pelea [pe'lea] nf (lucha) fight; (discusión) quarrel, row; **peleado, -a** [pele'aðo, a] adj: **estar peleado (con algn)** to have fallen out (with sb); **pelear** [pele'ar] vi to fight; **pelearse** vr to fight; (reñirse) to fall out, quarrel
pelela [pe'lela] (cs) nf potty
peletería [pelete'ria] nf furrier's, fur shop
pelícano [pe'likano] nm pelican
película [pe'likula] nf film; (cobertura ligera) thin covering; (Foto: rollo) roll or reel of film; **película de dibujos (animados)/del oeste** cartoon/western
peligro [pe'lixro] nm danger; (riesgo) risk; **correr ~ de** to run the risk of; **peligroso, -a** adj dangerous; risky
pelirrojo, -a [peli'rroxo, a] adj red-haired, red-headed ▷ nm/f redhead
pellejo [pe'ʎexo] nm (de animal) skin, hide
pellizcar [peʎiθ'kar] vt to pinch, nip
pelma ['pelma] (ESP: fam) nmf pain (in the neck)
pelmazo [pel'maθo] (ESP: fam) nm = **pelma**
pelo ['pelo] nm (cabellos) hair; (de barba, bigote) whisker; (de animal: pelaje) hair, fur, coat; **venir al ~** to be exactly what one needs; **un hombre de ~ en pecho** a brave man; **por los ~s** by the skin of one's teeth; **no tener ~s en la lengua** to be outspoken, not to mince one's words; **con ~s y señales** in minute detail; **tomar el ~ a algn** to pull sb's leg
pelota [pe'lota] nf ball; **en ~** stark naked; **hacer la ~ (a algn)** (ESP: fam) to creep (to sb); **pelota vasca** pelota
pelotón [pelo'ton] nm (Mil) squad, detachment
peluca [pe'luka] nf wig
peluche [pe'lutʃe] nm: **oso/muñeco de ~** teddy bear/soft toy
peludo, -a [pe'luðo, a] adj hairy, shaggy
peluquería [peluke'ria] nf hairdresser's; **peluquero, -a** nm/f hairdresser
pelusa [pe'lusa] nf (Bot) down; (en tela) fluff
pena ['pena] nf (congoja) grief, sadness; (remordimiento) regret; (dificultad) trouble; (dolor) pain; (Jur) sentence; **merecer o valer la ~** to be worthwhile; **a duras ~s** with great difficulty; **¡qué ~!** what a shame!; **pena capital** capital punishment; **pena de muerte** death penalty
penal [pe'nal] adj penal ▷ nm (cárcel) prison
penalidad [penali'ðað] nf (problema, dificultad) trouble, hardship; (Jur) penalty, punishment; **penalidades** nfpl trouble sg, hardship sg
penalti [pe'nalti] nm = **penalty**

penalty [pe'nalti] (pl **~s** o **penalties**) nm penalty (kick)

pendiente [pen'djente] adj pending, unsettled ▷ nm earring ▷ nf hill, slope

pene ['pene] nm penis

penetrante [pene'trante] adj (herida) deep; (persona, arma) sharp; (sonido) penetrating, piercing; (mirada) searching; (viento, ironía) biting

penetrar [pene'trar] vt to penetrate, pierce; (entender) to grasp ▷ vi to penetrate, go in; (entrar) to enter, go in; (líquido) to soak in; (fig) to pierce

penicilina [peniθi'lina] nf penicillin

península [pe'ninsula] nf peninsula; **peninsular** adj peninsular

penique [pe'nike] nm penny

penitencia [peni'tenθja] nf penance

penoso, -a [pe'noso, a] adj (lamentable) distressing; (difícil) arduous, difficult

pensador, a [pensa'ðor, a] nm/f thinker

pensamiento [pensa'mjento] nm thought; (mente) mind; (idea) idea

pensar [pen'sar] vt to think; (considerar) to think over, think out; (proponerse) to intend, plan; (imaginarse) to think up, invent ▷ vi to think; **~ en** to aim at, aspire to; **pensativo, -a** adj thoughtful, pensive

pensión [pen'sjon] nf (casa) boarding o guest house; (dinero) pension; (cama y comida) board and lodging; **media ~** half-board; **pensión completa** full board; **pensionista** nmf (jubilado) (old-age) pensioner; (huésped) lodger

penúltimo, -a [pe'nultimo, a] adj penultimate, last but one

penumbra [pe'numbra] nf half-light

peña ['peɲa] nf (roca) rock; (cuesta) cliff, crag; (grupo) group, circle; (LAM: club) folk club

peñasco [pe'ɲasko] nm large rock, boulder

peñón [pe'ɲon] nm wall of rock; **el P~** the Rock (of Gibraltar)

peón [pe'on] nm labourer; (LAM Agr) farm labourer, farmhand; (Ajedrez) pawn

peonza [pe'onθa] nf spinning top

peor [pe'or] adj (comparativo) worse; (superlativo) worst ▷ adv worse; worst; **de mal en ~** from bad to worse

pepinillo [pepi'niʎo] nm gherkin

pepino [pe'pino] nm cucumber; **(no) me importa un ~** I don't care one bit

pepita [pe'pita] nf (Bot) pip; (Minería) nugget

pepito [pe'pito] (ESP) nm (tb: **~ de ternera**) steak sandwich

pequeño, -a [pe'keɲo, a] adj small, little

pera ['pera] nf pear; **peral** nm pear tree

percance [per'kanθe] nm setback, misfortune

percatarse [perka'tarse] vr: **~ de** to notice, take note of

percebe [per'θeβe] nm barnacle

percepción [perθep'θjon] nf (vista) perception; (idea) notion, idea

percha ['pertʃa] nf (coat)hanger; (ganchos) coat hooks pl; (de ave) perch

percibir [perθi'βir] vt to perceive, notice; (Com) to earn, get

percusión [perku'sjon] nf percussion

perdedor, a [perðe'ðor, a] adj losing ▷ nm/f loser

perder [per'ðer] vt (tiempo, palabras) to waste; (oportunidad) to lose, miss; (tren) to miss ▷ vi to lose;

perderse vr (extraviarse) to get lost; (desaparecer) to disappear, be lost to view; (arruinarse) to be ruined; **echar a ~** (comida) to spoil, ruin; (oportunidad) to waste

pérdida ['perðiða] nf loss; (de tiempo) waste; **pérdidas** nfpl (Com) losses

perdido, -a [per'ðiðo, a] adj lost

perdiz [per'ðiθ] nf partridge

perdón [per'ðon] nm (disculpa) pardon, forgiveness; (clemencia) mercy; **¡~!** sorry!, I beg your pardon!; **perdonar** vt to pardon, forgive; (la vida) to spare; (excusar) to exempt, excuse; **¡perdone (usted)!** sorry!, I beg your pardon!

perecedero, -a [pereθe'ðero, a] adj perishable

perecer [pere'θer] vi to perish, die

peregrinación [perexrina'θjon] nf (Rel) pilgrimage

peregrino, -a [pere'xrino, a] adj (idea) strange, absurd ▷ nm/f pilgrim

perejil [pere'xil] nm parsley

perenne [pe'renne] adj everlasting, perennial

pereza [pe'reθa] nf laziness, idleness; **perezoso, -a** adj lazy, idle

perfección [perfek'θjon] nf perfection; **perfeccionar** vt to perfect; (mejorar) to improve; (acabar) to complete, finish

perfecto, -a [per'fekto, a] adj perfect; (total) complete

perfil [per'fil] nm profile; (contorno) silhouette, outline; (Arq) (cross) section; **perfiles** nmpl features

perforación [perfora'θjon] nf perforation; (con taladro) drilling; **perforadora** nf punch

perforar [perfo'rar] vt to perforate; (agujero) to drill, bore; (papel) to punch a hole in ▷ vi to drill, bore

perfume [per'fume] nm perfume, scent

periferia [peri'ferja] nf periphery; (de ciudad) outskirts pl

periférico [peri'feriko] (LAM) nm ring road (BRIT), beltway (US)

perilla [pe'riʎa] nf (barba) goatee; (LAM: de puerta) doorknob, door handle

perímetro [pe'rimetro] nm perimeter

periódico, -a [pe'rjoðiko, a] adj periodic(al) ▷ nm newspaper

periodismo [perjo'ðismo] nm journalism; **periodista** nmf journalist

periodo [pe'rjoðo] nm period

período [pe'rioðo] nm = **periodo**

periquito [peri'kito] nm budgerigar, budgie

perito, -a [pe'rito, a] adj (experto) expert; (diestro) skilled, skilful ▷ nm/f expert; skilled worker; (técnico) technician

perjudicar [perxuði'kar] vt (gen) to damage, harm; **perjudicial** adj damaging, harmful; (en detrimento) detrimental; **perjuicio** nm damage, harm

perjurar [perxu'rar] vi to commit perjury

perla ['perla] nf pearl; **me viene de ~s** it suits me fine

permanecer [permane'θer] vi (quedarse) to stay, remain; (seguir) to continue to be

permanente [perma'nente] adj permanent, constant ▷ nf perm

permiso [per'miso] nm permission; (licencia) permit, licence; **con ~** excuse me; **estar de ~** (Mil) to be on leave; **permiso de conducir** driving licence (BRIT), driver's license (US); **permiso por enfermedad** (LAM) sick leave

permitir [permi'tir] vt to permit, allow

pernera [per'nera] nf trouser leg

pero ['pero] conj but; (aún) yet ▷ nm (defecto) flaw, defect; (reparo) objection
perpendicular [perpendiku'lar] adj perpendicular
perpetuo, -a [per'petwo, a] adj perpetual
perplejo, -a [per'plexo, a] adj perplexed, bewildered
perra ['perra] nf (Zool) bitch; **estar sin una ~** (ESP: fam) to be flat broke
perrera [pe'rrera] nf kennel
perrito [pe'rrito] nm (tb: **~ caliente**) hot dog
perro ['perro] nm dog
persa ['persa] adj, nmf Persian
persecución [perseku'θjon] nf pursuit, chase; (Rel, Pol) persecution
perseguir [perse'ɣir] vt to pursue, hunt; (cortejar) to chase after; (molestar) to pester, annoy; (Rel, Pol) to persecute
persiana [per'sjana] nf (Venetian) blind
persistente [persis'tente] adj persistent
persistir [persis'tir] vi to persist
persona [per'sona] nf person; **persona mayor** elderly person
personaje [perso'naxe] nm important person, celebrity; (Teatro etc) character
personal [perso'nal] adj (particular) personal; (para una persona) single, for one person ▷ nm personnel, staff; **personalidad** nf personality
personarse [perso'narse] vr to appear in person
personificar [personifi'kar] vt to personify
perspectiva [perspek'tiβa] nf perspective; (vista, panorama) view, panorama; (posibilidad futura) outlook, prospect
persuadir [perswa'ðir] vt (gen) to persuade; (convencer) to convince; **persuadirse** vr to become convinced; **persuasión** nf persuasion
pertenecer [pertene'θer] vi to belong; (fig) to concern; **perteneciente** adj: **perteneciente a** belonging to; **pertenencia** nf ownership; **pertenencias** nfpl (bienes) possessions, property sg
pertenezca etc vb V **pertenecer**
pértiga ['pertiɣa] nf: **salto de ~** pole vault
pertinente [perti'nente] adj relevant, pertinent; (apropiado) appropriate; **~ a** concerning, relevant to
perturbación [perturβa'θjon] nf (Pol) disturbance; (Med) upset, disturbance
Perú [pe'ru] nm Peru; **peruano, -a** adj, nm/f Peruvian
perversión [perβer'sjon] nf perversion; **perverso, -a** adj perverse; (depravado) depraved
pervertido, -a [perβer'tiðo, a] adj perverted ▷ nm/f pervert
pervertir [perβer'tir] vt to pervert, corrupt
pesa ['pesa] nf weight; (Deporte) shot
pesadez [pesa'ðeθ] nf (peso) heaviness; (lentitud) slowness; (aburrimiento) tediousness
pesadilla [pesa'ðiʎa] nf nightmare, bad dream
pesado, -a [pe'saðo, a] adj heavy; (lento) slow; (difícil, duro) tough, hard; (aburrido) boring, tedious; (tiempo) sultry
pésame ['pesame] nm expression of condolence, message of sympathy; **dar el ~** to express one's condolences
pesar [pe'sar] vt to weigh ▷ vi to weigh; (ser pesado) to weigh a lot, be heavy; (fig: opinión) to carry weight; **no pesa mucho** it's not very heavy ▷ nm (arrepentimiento) regret; (pena) grief, sorrow; **a ~ de** **pese a (que)** in spite of, despite
pesca ['peska] nf (acto) fishing; (lo pescado) catch; **ir**

de ~ to go fishing
pescadería [peskaðe'ria] nf fish shop, fishmonger's (BRIT)
pescadilla [peska'ðiʎa] nf whiting
pescado [pes'kaðo] nm fish
pescador, a [peska'ðor, a] nm/f fisherman/woman
pescar [pes'kar] vt (tomar) to catch; (intentar tomar) to fish for; (conseguir: trabajo) to manage to get ▷ vi to fish, go fishing
pesebre [pe'seβre] nm manger
peseta [pe'seta] nf (Hist) peseta
pesimista [pesi'mista] adj pessimistic ▷ nmf pessimist
pésimo, -a ['pesimo, a] adj awful, dreadful
peso ['peso] nm weight; (balanza) scales pl; (moneda) peso; **vender al ~** to sell by weight; **peso bruto/neto** gross/net weight; **peso pesado/pluma** heavyweight/ featherweight
pesquero, -a [pes'kero, a] adj fishing cpd
pestaña [pes'taɲa] nf (Anat) eyelash; (borde) rim
peste ['peste] nf plague; (mal olor) stink, stench
pesticida [pesti'θiða] nm pesticide
pestillo [pes'tiʎo] nm (cerrojo) bolt; (picaporte) door handle
petaca [pe'taka] nf (de cigarros) cigarette case; (de pipa) tobacco pouch; (MÉX: maleta) suitcase
pétalo ['petalo] nm petal
petardo [pe'tardo] nm firework, firecracker
petición [peti'θjon] nf (pedido) request, plea; (memorial) petition; (Jur) plea
peto ['peto] nm (ESP) nm dungarees pl, overalls pl (US)
petróleo [pe'troleo] nm oil, petroleum; **petrolero, -a** adj petroleum cpd ▷ nm (oil) tanker
peyorativo, -a [pejora'tiβo, a] adj pejorative
pez [peθ] nm fish; **pez espada** swordfish
pezón [pe'θon] nm teat, nipple
pezuña [pe'θuɲa] nf hoof
pianista [pja'nista] nmf pianist
piano ['pjano] nm piano
piar [pjar] vi to cheep
pibe, -a ['piβe, a] (RPL) nm/f boy/girl
picadero [pika'ðero] nm riding school
picadillo [pika'ðiʎo] nm mince, minced meat
picado, -a [pi'kaðo, a] adj pricked, punctured; (Culin) minced, chopped; (mar) choppy; (diente) bad; (tabaco) cut; (enfadado) cross
picador [pika'ðor] nm (Taur) picador; (minero) faceworker
picadura [pika'ðura] nf (pinchazo) puncture; (de abeja) sting; (de mosquito) bite; (tabaco picado) cut tobacco
picante [pi'kante] adj hot; (comentario) racy, spicy
picaporte [pika'porte] nm (manija) doorhandle; (pestillo) latch
picar [pi'kar] vt (agujerear, perforar) to prick, puncture; (abeja) to sting; (mosquito, serpiente) to bite; (Culin) to mince, chop; (incitar) to incite, goad; (dañar, irritar) to annoy, bother; (quemar: lengua) to burn, sting ▷ vi (pez) to bite, take the bait; (sol) to burn, scorch; (abeja, Med) to sting; (mosquito) to bite; **picarse** vr (agriarse) to turn sour, go off; (ofenderse) to take offence
picardía [pikar'ðia] nf villainy; (astucia) slyness, craftiness; (una picardía) dirty trick; (palabra) rude/bad word o expression
pícaro, -a ['pikaro, a] adj (malicioso) villainous; (travieso) mischievous ▷ nm (astuto) crafty sort;

(sinvergüenza) rascal, scoundrel

pichi ['pitʃi] (ESP) nm pinafore dress (BRIT); jumper (US)

pichón [pi'tʃon] nm young pigeon

pico ['piko] nm (de ave) beak; (punta) sharp point; (Tec) pick, pickaxe; (Geo) peak, summit; **y ~ and a bit; las seis y ~** six and a bit

picor [pi'kor] nm itch

picoso, -a [pi'koso, a] (MÉX) adj (comida) hot

picudo, -a [pi'kuðo, a] adj pointed, with a point

pidió etc vb V **pedir**

pido etc vb V **pedir**

pie [pje] (pl ~s) nm foot; (fig: motivo) motive, basis; (: fundamento) foothold; **ir a ~** to go on foot, walk; **estar de ~** to be standing (up); **ponerse de ~** to stand up; **de ~s a cabeza** from top to bottom; **al ~ de la letra** (citar) literally, verbatim; (copiar) exactly, word for word; **en ~ de guerra** on a war footing; **dar ~ a** to give cause for; **hacer ~** (en el agua) to touch (the) bottom

piedad [pje'ðað] nf (lástima) pity, compassion; (clemencia) mercy; (devoción) piety, devotion

piedra ['pjeðra] nf stone; (roca) rock; (de mechero) flint; (Meteorología) hailstone; **piedra preciosa** precious stone

piel [pjel] nf (Anat) skin; (Zool) skin, hide, fur; (cuero) leather; (Bot) skin, peel

pienso etc vb V **pensar**

pierdo etc vb V **perder**

pierna ['pjerna] nf leg

pieza ['pjeθa] nf piece; (habitación) room; **pieza de recambio o repuesto** spare (part)

pigmeo, -a [pix'meo, a] adj, nm/f pigmy

pijama [pi'xama] nm pyjamas pl (BRIT), pajamas pl (US)

pila ['pila] nf (Elec) battery; (montón) heap, pile; (lavabo) sink

píldora ['pildora] nf pill; **la ~ (anticonceptiva)** the (contraceptive) pill

pileta [pi'leta] (RPL) nf (fregadero) (kitchen) sink; (piscina) swimming pool

pillar [pi'ʎar] vt (saquear) to pillage, plunder; (fam: coger) to catch; (: agarrar) to grasp, seize; (: entender) to grasp, catch on to; **pillarse** vr: **~se un dedo con la puerta** to catch one's finger in the door

pillo, -a [pi'ʎo, a] adj villainous; (astuto) sly, crafty ▷ nm/f rascal, rogue, scoundrel

piloto [pi'loto] nm pilot; (de aparato) (pilot) light; (Auto: luz) tail o rear light; (: conductor) driver; **piloto automático** automatic pilot

pimentón [pimen'ton] nm paprika

pimienta [pi'mjenta] nf pepper

pimiento [pi'mjento] nm pepper, pimiento

pin [pin] (pl ~s) nm badge

pinacoteca [pinako'teka] nf art gallery

pinar [pi'nar] nm pine forest (BRIT), pine grove (US)

pincel [pin'θel] nm paintbrush

pinchadiscos [pintʃa'ðiskos] (ESP) nm inv disc-jockey, DJ

pinchar [pin'tʃar] vt (perforar) to prick, pierce; (neumático) to puncture; (fig) to prod; (Inform) to click

pinchazo [pin'tʃaθo] nm (perforación) prick; (de neumático) puncture; (fig) prod

pincho ['pintʃo] nm savoury (snack); **pincho de tortilla** small slice of omelette; **pincho moruno** shish kebab

ping-pong ['pin'pon] nm table tennis

pingüino [pin'gwino] nm penguin

pino ['pino] nm pine (tree)

pinta ['pinta] nf spot; (de líquidos) spot, drop; (aspecto) appearance, look(s) (pl); **pintado, -a** adj spotted; (de colores) colourful; **pintadas** nfpl graffiti sg

pintalabios [pinta'laβjos] (ESP) nm inv lipstick

pintar [pin'tar] vt to paint ▷ vi to paint; (fam) to count, be important; **pintarse** vr to put on make-up

pintor, -a [pin'tor, a] nm/f painter

pintoresco, -a [pinto'resko, a] adj picturesque

pintura [pin'tura] nf painting; **pintura al óleo** oil painting

pinza ['pinθa] nf (Zool) claw; (para colgar ropa) clothes peg; (Tec) pincers pl; **pinzas** nfpl (para depilar etc) tweezers pl

piña ['piɲa] nf (de pino) pine cone; (fruta) pineapple; (fig) group

piñata [pi'ɲata] nf container hung up at parties to be beaten with sticks until sweets or presents fall out

piñón [pi'ɲon] nm (fruto) pine nut; (Tec) pinion

pío, -a ['pio, a] adj (devoto) pious, devout; (misericordioso) merciful

piojo [pi'joxo] nm louse

pipa ['pipa] nf pipe; **pipas** nfpl (Bot) (edible) sunflower seeds

pipí [pi'pi] (fam) nm: **hacer ~** to have a wee(-wee) (BRIT), to have to go (wee-wee) (US)

pique [pi'ke] nm (resentimiento) pique, resentment; (rivalidad) rivalry, competition; **irse a ~** to sink; (esperanza, familia) to be ruined

piqueta [pi'keta] nf pick(axe)

piquete [pi'kete] nm (Mil) squad, party; (de obreros) picket; (MÉX: de insecto) bite; **piquetear** (LAM) vt to picket

pirado, -a [pi'raðo, a] (fam) adj round the bend ▷ nm/f nutter

piragua [pi'raɣwa] nf canoe; **piragüismo** nm canoeing

pirámide [pi'ramiðe] nf pyramid

pirata [pi'rata] adj, nmf pirate; **pirata informático** hacker

Pirineo(s) [piri'neo(s)] nm(pl) Pyrenees pl

pirómano, -a [pi'romano, a] nm/f (Med, Jur) arsonist

piropo [pi'ropo] nm compliment, (piece of) flattery

pirueta [pi'rweta] nf pirouette

piruleta [piru'leta] (ESP) nf lollipop

pis [pis] (fam) nm pee, piss; **hacer ~** to have a pee; (para niños) to wee-wee

pisada [pi'saða] nf (paso) footstep; (huella) footprint

pisar [pi'sar] vt (caminar sobre) to walk on, tread on; (apretar con el pie) to press; (fig) to trample on, walk all over ▷ vi to tread, step, walk

piscina [pis'θina] nf swimming pool

Piscis ['pisθis] nm Pisces

piso ['piso] nm (suelo, planta) floor; (ESP: apartamento) flat (BRIT), apartment; **primer ~** (ESP) first floor; (LAM: planta baja) ground floor

pisotear [pisote'ar] vt to trample (on o underfoot)

pista ['pista] nf track, trail; (indicio) clue; **pista de aterrizaje** runway; **pista de baile** dance floor; **pista de hielo** ice rink; **pista de tenis** (ESP) tennis court

pistola [pis'tola] nf pistol; (Tec) spray-gun

pistón [pis'ton] nm (Tec) piston; (Mús) key

pitar [pi'tar] vt (silbato) to blow; (rechiflar) to whistle at, boo ▷ vi to whistle; (Auto) to sound o toot one's horn; (LAM: fumar) to smoke

pitillo [pi'tiʎo] nm cigarette

pito ['pito] nm whistle; (de coche) horn

pitón [pi'ton] nm (Zool) python

pitonisa [pito'nisa] nf fortune-teller

pitorreo [pito'rreo] nm joke; **estar de ~** to be joking

píxel ['piksel] (pl **pixels** or **-es**) nm pixel

piyama [pi'jama] (LAM) nm pyjamas pl (BRIT), pajamas pl (US)

pizarra [pi'θarra] nf (piedra) slate; (ESP: encerado) blackboard; **pizarra blanca** whiteboard; **pizarra interactiva** interactive whiteboard

pizarrón [piθa'rron] (LAM) nm blackboard

pizca ['piθka] nf pinch, spot; (fig) spot, speck; **ni ~** not a bit

placa ['plaka] nf plate; (distintivo) badge, insignia; **placa de matrícula** (LAM) number plate

placard [pla'kar] (RPL) nm cupboard

placer [pla'θer] nm pleasure ▷ vt to please

plaga ['playa] nf pest; (Med) plague; (abundancia) abundance

plagio ['plaxjo] nm plagiarism

plan [plan] nm (esquema, proyecto) plan; (idea, intento) idea, intention; **tener ~** (fam) to have a date; **tener un ~** (fam) to have an affair; **en ~ económico** (fam) on the cheap; **vamos en ~ de turismo** we're going as tourists; **si te pones en ese ~ ...** if that's your attitude ...

plana ['plana] nf sheet (of paper), page; (Tec) trowel; **en primera ~** on the front page

plancha ['plantʃa] nf (para planchar) iron; (rótulo) plate, sheet; (Náut) gangway; **a la ~** (Culin) grilled; **planchar** vt to iron ▷ vi to do the ironing

planear [plane'ar] vt to plan ▷ vi to glide

planeta [pla'neta] nm planet

plano, -a ['plano, a] adj flat, level, even ▷ nm (Mat, Tec) plane; (Foto) shot; (Arq) plan; (Geo) map; (de ciudad) map, street plan; **primer ~** close-up

planta ['planta] nf (Bot, Tec) plant; (Anat) sole of the foot; (piso) floor; (Com: personal) staff; **planta baja** ground floor

plantar [plan'tar] vt (Bot) to plant; (levantar) to erect, set up; **plantarse** vr to stand firm; **~ a algn en la calle** to throw sb out; **dejar plantado a algn** (fam) to stand sb up

plantear [plante'ar] vt (problema) to pose; (dificultad) to raise

plantilla [plan'tiʎa] nf (de zapato) insole; (ESP: personal) personnel; **ser de ~** (ESP) to be on the staff

plantón [plan'ton] nm (Mil) guard, sentry; (fam) long wait; **dar (un) ~ a algn** to stand sb up

plasta ['plasta] (ESP: fam) adj inv boring ▷ nmf bore

plástico, -a ['plastiko, a] adj plastic ▷ nm plastic

Plastilina® [plasti'lina] nf Plasticine®

plata ['plata] nf (metal) silver; (cosas hechas de plata) silverware; (cs: dinero) cash, dough

plataforma [plata'forma] nf platform; **plataforma de lanzamiento/perforación** launch(ing) pad/drilling rig

plátano ['platano] nm (fruta) banana; (árbol) plane tree; banana tree

platea [pla'tea] nf (Teatro) pit

plática ['platika] nf talk, chat; **platicar** vi to talk, chat

platillo [pla'tiʎo] nm saucer; **platillos** nmpl (Mús) cymbals; **platillo volante** flying saucer

platino [pla'tino] nm platinum; **platinos** nmpl (Auto) contact points

plato ['plato] nm plate, dish; (parte de comida) course; (comida) dish; **primer ~** first course; **plato combinado** set main course (served on one plate); **plato fuerte** main course

playa ['plaja] nf beach; (costa) seaside; **playa de estacionamiento** (cs) car park (BRIT), parking lot (US)

playera [pla'jera] nf (MÉX: camiseta) T-shirt; **playeras** nfpl (zapatos) canvas shoes

plaza ['plaθa] nf square; (mercado) market(place); (sitio) room, space; (de vehículo) seat, place; (colocación) post, job; **plaza de toros** bullring

plazo ['plaθo] nm (lapso de tiempo) time, period; (fecha de vencimiento) expiry date; (pago parcial) instalment; **a corto/largo ~** short-/long-term; **comprar algo a ~s** to buy sth on hire purchase (BRIT) o on time (US)

plazoleta [plaθo'leta] nf small square

plebeyo, -a [ple'βejo, a] adj plebeian; (pey) coarse, common

plegable [ple'yaβle] adj collapsible; (silla) folding

pleito ['pleito] nm (Jur) lawsuit, case; (fig) dispute, feud

plenitud [pleni'tuð] nf plenitude, fullness; (abundancia) abundance

pleno, -a ['pleno, a] adj full; (completo) complete ▷ nm plenum; **en ~ día** in broad daylight; **en ~ verano** at the height of summer; **en plena cara** full in the face

pliego etc ['pljexo] vb V **plegar** ▷ nm (hoja) sheet (of paper); (carta) sealed letter/document; **pliego de condiciones** details pl, specifications pl

pliegue etc ['pljexe] vb V **plegar** ▷ nm fold, crease; (de vestido) pleat

plomería [plome'ria] (LAM) nf plumbing; **plomero** (LAM) nm plumber

plomo ['plomo] nm (metal) lead; (Elec) fuse; **sin ~** unleaded

pluma ['pluma] nf feather; (para escribir): **~ (estilográfica)** ink pen; **~ fuente** (LAM) fountain pen

plumero [plu'mero] nm (para el polvo) feather duster

plumón [plu'mon] nm (de ave) down

plural [plu'ral] adj plural

pluriempleo [pluriem'pleo] nm having more than one job

plus [plus] nm bonus

población [poβla'θjon] nf population; (pueblo, ciudad) town, city

poblado, -a [po'βlaðo, a] adj inhabited ▷ nm (aldea) village; (pueblo) (small) town; **densamente ~** densely populated

poblador, a [poβla'ðor, a] nm/f settler, colonist

pobre ['poβre] adj poor ▷ nmf poor person; **pobreza** nf poverty

pocilga [po'θilya] nf pigsty

○ **PALABRA CLAVE**

poco, -a ['poko, a] adj **1** (sg) little, not much; **poco tiempo** little o not much time; **de poco interés** of little interest, not very interesting; **poca cosa** not much

2 (pl) few, not many; **unos pocos** a few, some; **pocos niños comen lo que les conviene** few children eat what they should

▷ adv **1** little, not much; **cuesta poco** it doesn't cost much

2 (+ adj: negativo, antónimo): **poco amable/inteligente**

not very nice/intelligent
3: **por poco me caigo** I almost fell
4: **a poco: a poco de haberse casado** shortly after getting married
5: **poco a poco** little by little
▷ *nm* a little, a bit; **un poco triste/de dinero** a little sad/money

podar [po'ðar] *vt* to prune

○ **PALABRA CLAVE**

poder [po'ðer] *vi* **1** (*tener capacidad*) can, be able to; **no puedo hacerlo** I can't do it, I'm unable to do it
2 (*tener permiso*) can, may, be allowed to; **¿se puede?** may I (o we)?; **puedes irte ahora** you may go now; **no se puede fumar en este hospital** smoking is not allowed in this hospital
3 (*tener posibilidad*) may, might, could; **puede llegar mañana** he may o might arrive tomorrow; **pudiste haberte hecho daño** you might o could have hurt yourself; **¡podías habérmelo dicho antes!** you might have told me before!
4: **puede ser** perhaps; **puede ser que lo sepa Tomás** Tomás may o might know
5: **¡no puedo más!** I've had enough!; **es tonto a más no poder** he's as stupid as they come
6: **poder con: no puedo con este crío** this kid's too much for me
▷ *nm* power; **detentar** o **ocupar** o **estar en el poder** to be in power; **poder adquisitivo/ejecutivo/legislativo** purchasing/executive/legislative power; **poder judicial** judiciary

poderoso, -a [poðe'roso, a] *adj* (*político, país*) powerful
podio ['poðjo] *nm* (*Deporte*) podium
podium ['poðjum] = **podio**
podrido, -a [po'ðriðo, a] *adj* rotten, bad; (*fig*) rotten, corrupt
podrir [po'ðrir] = **pudrir**
poema [po'ema] *nm* poem
poesía [poe'sia] *nf* poetry
poeta [po'eta] *nmf* poet; **poético, -a** *adj* poetic(al)
poetisa [poe'tisa] *nf* (woman) poet
póker ['poker] *nm* poker
polaco, -a [po'lako, a] *adj* Polish ▷ *nm/f* Pole
polar [po'lar] *adj* polar
polea [po'lea] *nf* pulley
polémica [po'lemika] *nf* polemics *sg*; (*una polémica*) controversy, polemic
polen ['polen] *nm* pollen
policía [poli'θia] *nmf* policeman/woman ▷ *nf* police; **policíaco, -a** *adj* police *cpd*; **novela policíaca** detective story; **policial** *adj* police *cpd*
polideportivo [poliðepor'tiβo] *nm* sports centre o complex
polígono [po'liɣono] *nm* (*Mat*) polygon; **polígono industrial** (*ESP*) industrial estate
polilla [po'liʎa] *nf* moth
polio ['poljo] *nf* polio
política [po'litika] *nf* politics *sg*; (*económica, agraria etc*) policy; V *tb* **político**

político, -a [po'litiko, a] *adj* political; (*discreto*) tactful; (*de familia*) ...-in-law ▷ *nm/f* politician; **padre ~** father-in-law
póliza ['poliθa] *nf* certificate, voucher; (*impuesto*) tax stamp; **póliza de seguro(s)** insurance policy
polizón [poli'θon] *nm* stowaway
pollera [po'ʎera] (*cs*) *nf* skirt
pollo ['poʎo] *nm* chicken
polo ['polo] *nm* (*Geo, Elec*) pole; (*helado*) ice lolly (*BRIT*), Popsicle® (*US*); (*Deporte*) polo; (*suéter*) polo-neck; **polo Norte/Sur** North/South Pole
Polonia [po'lonja] *nf* Poland
poltrona [pol'trona] *nf* easy chair
polución [polu'θjon] *nf* pollution
polvera [pol'βera] *nf* powder compact
polvo ['polβo] *nm* dust; (*Quím, Culin, Med*) powder; **polvos** *nmpl* (*maquillaje*) powder *sg*; **en ~** powdered; **quitar el ~** to dust; **estar hecho ~** (*fam*) to be worn out o exhausted; **polvos de talco** talcum powder *sg*
pólvora ['polβora] *nf* gunpowder
polvoriento, -a [polβo'rjento, a] *adj* (*superficie*) dusty; (*sustancia*) powdery
pomada [po'maða] *nf* cream, ointment
pomelo [po'melo] *nm* grapefruit
pómez ['pomeθ] *nf*: **piedra ~** pumice stone
pomo ['pomo] *nm* doorknob
pompa ['pompa] *nf* (*burbuja*) bubble; (*bomba*) pump; (*esplendor*) pomp, splendour
pómulo ['pomulo] *nm* cheekbone
pon [pon] *vb* V **poner**
ponchadura [pontʃa'ðura] (*MÉX*) *nf* puncture (*BRIT*), flat (*US*); **ponchar** (*MÉX*) *vt* (*llanta*) to puncture
ponche ['pontʃe] *nm* punch
poncho ['pontʃo] *nm* poncho
pondré *etc vb* V **poner**

○ **PALABRA CLAVE**

poner [po'ner] *vt* **1** (*colocar*) to put; (*telegrama*) to send; (*obra de teatro*) to put on; (*película*) to show; **ponlo más fuerte** turn it up; **¿qué ponen en el Excelsior?** what's on at the Excelsior?
2 (*tienda*) to open; (*instalar: gas etc*) to put in; (*radio, TV*) to switch o turn on
3 (*suponer*) **pongamos que ...** let's suppose that ...
4 (*contribuir*) **el gobierno ha puesto otro millón** the government has contributed another million
5 (*Tel*) **póngame con el Sr. López** can you put me through to Mr. López
6: **poner de: le han puesto de director general** they've appointed him general manager
7 (+ *adj*) to make; **me estás poniendo nerviosa** you're making me nervous
8 (*dar nombre*): **al hijo le pusieron Diego** they called their son Diego
▷ *vi* (*gallina*) to lay
ponerse *vr* **1** (*colocarse*): **se puso a mi lado** he came and stood beside me; **tú ponte en esa silla** you go and sit on that chair
2 (*vestido, cosméticos*) to put on; **¿por qué no te pones el vestido nuevo?** why don't you put on o wear your new dress?
3 (+ *adj*) to turn; to get, become; **se puso muy serio** he got very serious; **después de lavarla la tela se puso azul** after washing it the material turned blue

4: ponerse a: se puso a llorar he started to cry;
tienes que ponerte a estudiar you must get down
to studying

pongo etc vb V **poner**

poniente [po'njente] nm (occidente) west; (viento)
west wind

pontífice [pon'tifiθe] nm pope, pontiff

popa ['popa] nf stern

popote [po'pote] (MÉX) nm straw

popular [popu'lar] adj popular; (cultura) of the
people, folk cpd; **popularidad** nf popularity

○ **PALABRA CLAVE**

por [por] prep **1** (objetivo) for; **luchar por la patria** to
fight for one's
country

2 (+ infin): **por no llegar tarde** so as not to arrive late;
por citar unos ejemplos to give a few examples
3 (causa) out of, because of; **por escasez de fondos**
through o for lack of funds

4 (tiempo): **por la mañana/noche** in the morning/at
night; **se queda por una semana** she's staying (for)
a week

5 (lugar): **pasar por Madrid** to pass through Madrid;
ir a Guayaquil por Quito to go to Guayaquil via
Quito; **caminar por la calle** to walk along the street;
V tb **todo**

6 (cambio, precio): **te doy uno nuevo por el que tienes**
I'll give you a new one (in return) for the one you've got
7 (valor distributivo): **6 euros por hora/cabeza** 6 euros
an o per hour/a o per head

8 (modo, medio) by; **por correo/avión** by post/air;
entrar por la entrada principal to go in through the
main entrance

9: 10 por 10 son 100 10 times 10 is 100

10 (en lugar de): **vino él por su jefe** he came instead
of his boss

11 (por mí que revienten** as far as I'm concerned they
can drop dead

12: ¿por qué? why?; **¿por qué no?** why not?

porcelana [porθe'lana] nf porcelain; (china) china

porcentaje [porθen'taxe] nm percentage

porción [por'θjon] nf (parte) portion, share; (cantidad)
quantity, amount

porfiar [por'fjar] vi to persist, insist; (disputar) to
argue stubbornly

pormenor [porme'nor] nm detail, particular

pornografía [pornoxra'fia] nf pornography

poro ['poro] nm pore

pororó [poro'ro] (RPL) nm popcorn

poroso, -a [po'roso, a] adj porous

poroto [po'roto] (CS) nm bean

porque ['porke] conj (a causa de) because; (ya que)
since; (con el fin de) so that, in order that

porqué [por'ke] nm reason, cause

porquería [porke'ria] nf (suciedad) filth, dirt; (acción)
dirty trick; (objeto) small thing, trifle; (fig) rubbish

porra ['porra] (ESP) nf (arma) stick, club

porrazo [po'rraθo] nm blow, bump

porro ['porro] (fam) nm (droga) joint (fam)

porrón [po'rron] nm glass wine jar with a long spout

portaaviones [porta'(a)βjones] nm inv aircraft
carrier

portada [por'taða] nf (de revista) cover

portador, a [porta'ðor, a] nm/f carrier, bearer; (Com)
bearer, payee

portaequipajes [portaeki'paxes] nm inv
(Auto: maletero) boot; (: baca) luggage rack

portafolio [porta'foljo] (LAM) nm briefcase

portal [por'tal] nm (entrada) vestibule, hall; (portada)
porch, doorway; (puerta de entrada) main door; (Internet)
portal; **portales** nmpl arcade sg

portamaletas [portama'letas] nm inv
(Auto: maletero) boot; (: baca) roof rack

portarse [por'tarse] vr to behave, conduct o.s.

portátil [por'tatil] adj portable

portavoz [porta'βoθ] nmf spokesman/woman

portazo [por'taθo] nm: **dar un ~** to slam the door

porte ['porte] nm (Com) transport; (precio) transport
charges pl

portentoso, -a [porten'toso, a] adj marvellous,
extraordinary

porteño, -a [por'teno, a] adj o f from Buenos Aires

portería [porte'ria] nf (oficina) porter's office;
(Deporte) goal

portero, -a [por'tero, a] nm/f porter; (conserje)
caretaker; (ujier) doorman; (Deporte) goalkeeper;
portero automático (ESP) entry phone

pórtico [por'tiko] nm (patio) portico, porch; (fig)
gateway; (arcada) arcade

portorriqueño, -a [portorri'keno, a] adj Puerto
Rican

Portugal [portu'xal] nm Portugal; **portugués, -esa**
adj, nm/f Portuguese ▷nm (Ling) Portuguese

porvenir [porβe'nir] nm future

pos [pos] prep: **en ~ de** after, in pursuit of

posaderas [posa'ðeras] nfpl backside sg, buttocks

posar [po'sar] vt (en el suelo) to lay down, put down;
(la mano) to place, put gently ▷vi (modelo) to sit, pose;
posarse vr to settle; (pájaro) to perch; (avión) to land,
come down

posavasos [posa'basos] nm inv coaster; (para cerveza)
beermat

posdata [pos'ðata] nf postscript

pose ['pose] nf pose

poseedor, a [posee'ðor, a] nm/f owner, possessor;
(de récord, puesto) holder

poseer [pose'er] vt to possess, own; (ventaja) to enjoy;
(récord, puesto) to hold

posesivo, -a [pose'siβo, a] adj possessive

posibilidad [posiβili'ðað] nf possibility;
(oportunidad) chance; **posibilitar** vt to make possible;
(hacer realizable) to make feasible

posible [po'siβle] adj (posible) feasible; **de
ser ~** if possible; **en lo ~** as far as possible

posición [posi'θjon] nf position; (rango social) status

positivo, -a [posi'tiβo, a] adj positive

poso ['poso] nm sediment; (heces) dregs pl

posponer [pospo'ner] vt (relegar) to put behind/
below; (aplazar) to postpone

posta ['posta] nf: **a ~** deliberately, on purpose

postal [pos'tal] adj postal ▷nf postcard

poste ['poste] nm (de telégrafos etc) post, pole;
(columna) pillar

póster ['poster] (pl **~es, ~s**) nm poster

posterior [poste'rjor] adj back, rear; (siguiente)
following, subsequent; (más tarde) later

postgrado [post'graðo] nm = **posgrado**

postizo, -a [pos'tiθo, a] adj false, artificial ▷ nm
hairpiece

postre ['postre] nm sweet, dessert

póstumo, -a ['postumo, a] adj posthumous

postura [pos'tura] nf (del cuerpo) posture, position;
(fig) attitude, position

potable [po'taβle] adj drinkable; **agua ~** drinking
water

potaje [po'taxe] nm thick vegetable soup

potencia [po'tenθja] nf power; **potencial**
[poten'θjal] adj, nm potential

potente [po'tente] adj powerful

potro, -a ['potro, a] nm/f (Zool) colt/filly ▷ nm (de
gimnasia) vaulting horse

pozo ['poθo] nm well; (de río) deep pool; (de mina) shaft

PP (ESP) nm abr = **Partido Popular**

práctica ['praktika] nf practice; (método): (arte,
capacidad) skill; **en la ~** in practice

practicable [prakti'kaβle] adj practicable; (camino)
passable

practicante [prakti'kante] nmf (Med: ayudante de
doctor) medical assistant; (': enfermero) nurse; (quien
practica algo) practitioner ▷ adj practising

practicar [prakti'kar] vt to practise; (Deporte) to
play; (realizar) to carry out, perform

práctico, -a ['praktiko, a] adj practical;
(instruido: persona) skilled, expert

practique etc vb V **practicar**

pradera [pra'ðera] nf meadow; (us etc) prairie

prado ['praðo] nm (campo) meadow, field; (pastizal)
pasture

Praga ['praɣa] n Prague

pragmático, -a [praɣ'matiko, a] adj pragmatic

precario, -a [pre'karjo, a] adj precarious

precaución [prekau'θjon] nf (medida preventiva)
preventive measure, precaution; (prudencia) caution,
wariness

precedente [preθe'ðente] adj preceding; (anterior)
former ▷ nm precedent

preceder [preθe'ðer] vt, vi to precede, go before,
come before

precepto [pre'θepto] nm precept

precinto [pre'θinto] nm (tb: **~ de garantía**) seal

precio ['preθjo] nm price; (costo) cost; (valor) value,
worth; (de viaje) fare; **precio al contado/de coste/de
oportunidad** cash/cost/bargain price; **precio al por
menor** retail price; **precio de ocasión** bargain price;
precio de venta al público retail price; **precio tope**
top price

preciosidad [preθjosi'ðað] nf (valor) (high) value,
(great) worth; (encanto) charm; (cosa bonita) beautiful
thing; **es una ~** it's lovely, it's really beautiful

precioso, -a [pre'θjoso, a] adj precious; (de mucho
valor) valuable; (fam) lovely

precipicio [preθi'piθjo] nm cliff, precipice; (fig) abyss

precipitación [preθipita'θjon] nf haste; (lluvia)
rainfall

precipitado, -a [preθipi'taðo, a] adj (conducta)
hasty, hasty; (salida) hasty, sudden

precipitar [preθipi'tar] vt (arrojar) to hurl down,
throw; (apresurar) to hasten; (acelerar) to speed up,
accelerate; **precipitarse** vr to throw o.s.; (apresurarse)
to rush; (actuar sin pensar) to act rashly

precisamente [preθisa'mente] adv precisely;
(exactamente) precisely, exactly

precisar [preθi'sar] vt (necesitar) to need, require;
(fijar) to determine exactly, fix; (especificar) to specify

precisión [preθi'sjon] nf (exactitud) precision

preciso, -a [pre'θiso, a] adj (exacto) precise;
(necesario) necessary, essential

preconcebido, -a [prekonθe'βiðo, a] adj
preconceived

precoz [pre'koθ] adj (persona) precocious; (calvicie
etc) premature

predecir [preðe'θir] vt to predict, forecast

predestinado, -a [preðesti'naðo, a] adj
predestined

predicar [preði'kar] vt, vi to preach

predicción [preðik'θjon] nf prediction

predilecto, -a [preði'lekto, a] adj favourite

predisposición [preðisposi'θjon] nf inclination;
prejudice, bias

predominar [preðomi'nar] vt to dominate ▷ vi to
predominate; (prevalecer) to prevail; **predominio** nm
predominance, prevalence

preescolar [pre(e)sko'lar] adj preschool

prefabricado, -a [prefaβri'kaðo, a] adj
prefabricated

prefacio [pre'faθjo] nm preface

preferencia [prefe'renθja] nf preference; **de ~**
preferably, for preference

preferible [prefe'riβle] adj preferable

preferir [prefe'rir] vt to prefer

prefiero etc vb V **preferir**

prefijo [pre'fixo] nm (Tel) (dialling) code

pregunta [pre'ɣunta] nf question; **hacer una
~** to ask a question; **preguntas frecuentes** FAQs,
frequently asked questions

preguntar [preɣun'tar] vt to ask; (cuestionar) to
question ▷ vi to ask; **preguntarse** vr to wonder;
preguntar por algn to ask for sb; **preguntón, -ona**
[preɣun'ton, ona] adj inquisitive

prehistórico, -a [preis'toriko, a] adj prehistoric

prejuicio [pre'xwiθjo] nm (acto) prejudgement; (idea
preconcebida) preconception; (parcialidad) prejudice,
bias

preludio [pre'luðjo] nm prelude

prematuro, -a [prema'turo, a] adj premature

premeditar [premeði'tar] vt to premeditate

premiar [pre'mjar] vt to reward; (en un concurso) to
give a prize to

premio ['premjo] nm reward; prize; (Com) premium

prenatal [prena'tal] adj antenatal, prenatal

prenda ['prenda] nf (ropa) garment, article of
clothing; (garantía) pledge; **prendas** nfpl (talentos)
talents, gifts

prender [pren'der] vt (captar) to catch, capture;
(detener) to arrest; (Costura) to pin, attach; (sujetar) to
fasten ▷ vi to catch; (arraigar) to take root; **prenderse**
vr (encenderse) to catch fire

prendido, -a [pren'diðo, a] (LAM) adj (luz etc) on

prensa ['prensa] nf press; **la ~** the press

preñado, -a [pre'ɲaðo, a] adj pregnant; **~ de**
pregnant with, full of

preocupación [preokupa'θjon] nf worry, concern;
(ansiedad) anxiety

preocupado, -a [preoku'paðo, a] adj worried,
concerned; (ansioso) anxious

preocupar [preoku'par] vt to worry; **preocuparse**
vr to worry; **~se de algo** (hacerse cargo) to take care
of sth

preparación [prepara'θjon] *nf* (*acto*) preparation; (*estado*) readiness; (*entrenamiento*) training

preparado, -a [prepa'raðo, a] *adj* (*dispuesto*) prepared; (*Culin*) ready (to serve) ▷ *nm* preparation

preparar [prepa'rar] *vt* (*disponer*) to prepare, get ready; (*Tec: tratar*) to prepare, process; (*entrenar*) to teach, train; **prepararse** *vr*: **~se a** o **para** to prepare to o for, get ready to o for; **preparativo, -a** *adj* preparatory, preliminary; **preparativos** *nmpl* preparations; **preparatoria** (*MÉX*) *nf* sixth-form college (*BRIT*), senior high school (*US*)

presa ['presa] *nf* (*cosa apresada*) catch; (*víctima*) victim; (*de animal*) prey; (*de agua*) dam

presagiar [presa'xjar] *vt* to presage, forebode; **presagio** *nm* omen

prescindir [presθin'dir] *vi*: **~ de** (*privarse de*) to do o go without; (*descartar*) to dispense with

prescribir [preskri'βir] *vt* to prescribe

presencia [pre'senθja] *nf* presence; **presenciar** *vt* to be present at; (*asistir a*) to attend; (*ver*) to see, witness

presentación [presenta'θjon] *nf* presentation; (*introducción*) introduction

presentador, a [presenta'ðor, a] *nm/f* presenter, compère

presentar [presen'tar] *vt* to present; (*ofrecer*) to offer; (*mostrar*) to show, display; (*a una persona*) to introduce; **presentarse** *vr* (*llegar inesperadamente*) to appear, turn up; (*ofrecerse: como candidato*) to run, stand; (*aparecer*) to show, appear; (*solicitar empleo*) to apply

presente [pre'sente] *adj* present ▷ *nm* present; **hacer ~** to state, declare; **tener ~** to remember, bear in mind

presentimiento [presenti'mjento] *nm* premonition, presentiment

presentir [presen'tir] *vt* to have a premonition of

preservación [preserβa'θjon] *nf* protection, preservation

preservar [preser'βar] *vt* to protect, preserve; **preservativo** *nm* sheath, condom

presidencia [presi'ðenθja] *nf* presidency; (*de comité*) chairmanship

presidente [presi'ðente] *nmf* president; (*de comité*) chairman/woman

presidir [presi'ðir] *vt* (*dirigir*) to preside at, preside over; (: *comité*) to take the chair at; (*dominar*) to dominate, rule ▷ *vi* to preside; to take the chair

presión [pre'sjon] *nf* pressure; **presión atmosférica** atmospheric o air pressure; **presionar** *vt* to press; (*fig*) to press, put pressure on ▷ *vi*: **presionar para** to press for

preso, -a ['preso, a] *nm/f* prisoner; **tomar** o **llevar a algn** to arrest sb, take sb prisoner

prestación [presta'θjon] *nf* service; (*subsidio*) benefit; **prestaciones** *nfpl* (*Tec, Auto*) performance features

prestado, -a [pres'taðo, a] *adj* on loan; **pedir ~** to borrow

prestamista [presta'mista] *nmf* moneylender

préstamo ['prestamo] *nm* loan; **préstamo hipotecario** mortgage

prestar [pres'tar] *vt* to lend, loan; (*atención*) to pay; (*ayuda*) to give

prestigio [pres'tixjo] *nm* prestige; **prestigioso, -a** *adj* (*honorable*) prestigious; (*famoso, renombrado*) renowned, famous

presumido, -a [presu'miðo, a] *adj* (*persona*) vain

presumir [presu'mir] *vt* to presume ▷ *vi* (*tener aires*) to be conceited; **presunto, -a** *adj* (*supuesto*) supposed, presumed; (*así llamado*) so-called; **presuntuoso, -a** *adj* conceited, presumptuous

presupuesto [presu'pwesto] *pp de* **presuponer** ▷ *nm* (*Finanzas*) budget; (*estimación: de costo*) estimate

pretencioso, -a [preten'θjoso, a] *adj* pretentious

pretender [preten'der] *vt* (*intentar*) to try to, seek to; (*reivindicar*) to claim; (*buscar*) to seek, try for; (*cortejar*) to woo, court; **~ que** to expect that

pretendiente *nmf* (*amante*) suitor; (*al trono*) pretender; **pretensión** *nf* (*aspiración*) aspiration; (*reivindicación*) claim; (*orgullo*) pretension

pretexto [pre'teksto] *nm* pretext; (*excusa*) excuse

prevención [preβen'θjon] *nf* prevention; (*precaución*) precaution

prevenido, -a [preβe'niðo, a] *adj* prepared, ready; (*cauteloso*) cautious

prevenir [preβe'nir] *vt* (*impedir*) to prevent; (*predisponer*) to prejudice, bias; (*avisar*) to warn; (*preparar*) to prepare, get ready; **prevenirse** *vr* to get ready, prepare; **~se contra** to take precautions against; **preventivo, -a** *adj* preventive, precautionary

prever [pre'βer] *vt* to foresee

previo, -a ['preβjo, a] *adj* (*anterior*) previous; (*preliminar*) preliminary ▷ *prep*: **~ acuerdo de los otros** subject to the agreement of the others

previsión [preβi'sjon] *nf* (*perspicacia*) foresight; (*predicción*) forecast; **previsto, -a** *adj* anticipated, forecast

prima ['prima] *nf* (*Com*) bonus; (*de seguro*) premium; *V tb* **primo**

primario, -a [pri'marjo, a] *adj* primary

primavera [prima'βera] *nf* spring(-time)

primera [pri'mera] *nf* (*Auto*) first gear; (*Ferro: tb*: **~ clase**) first class; **de ~** (*fam*) first-class, first-rate

primero, -a [pri'mero, a] *adj* (*tb*: **primer**) first; (*principal*) prime *adv* first; (*más bien*) sooner, rather; **primera plana** front page

primitivo, -a [primi'tiβo, a] *adj* (*primitive*) (*original*) original

primo, -a ['primo, a] *adj* prime ▷ *nm/f* cousin; (*fam*) fool, idiot; **materias primas** raw materials; **primo hermano** first cousin

primogénito, -a [primo'xenito, a] *adj* first-born

primoroso, -a [primo'roso, a] *adj* exquisite, delicate

princesa [prin'θesa] *nf* princess

principal [prinθi'pal] *adj* principal, main ▷ *nm* (*jefe*) chief, principal

príncipe ['prinθipe] *nm* prince

principiante [prinθi'pjante] *nmf* beginner

principio [prin'θipjo] *nm* (*comienzo*) beginning, start; (*origen*) origin; (*primera etapa*) rudiment, basic idea; (*moral*) principle; **desde el ~** from the first; **en un ~** at first; **a ~s de** at the beginning of

pringue ['pringe] *nm* (*grasa*) grease, fat, dripping

prioridad [priori'ðað] *nf* priority

prisa ['prisa] *nf* (*apresuramiento*) hurry, haste; (*rapidez*) speed; (*urgencia*) (sense of) urgency; **a o de ~** quickly; **correr ~** to be urgent; **darse ~** to hurry up; **tener ~** to be in a hurry

prisión [pri'sjon] *nf* (*cárcel*) prison; (*período de cárcel*) imprisonment; **prisionero, -a** *nm/f* prisoner

prismáticos [pris'matikos] *nmpl* binoculars

privado, -a [pri'βaðo, a] *adj* private

privar [pri'βar] *vt* to deprive; **privativo, -a** *adj* exclusive

privilegiar [priβile'xjar] *vt* to grant a privilege to; *(favorecer)* to favour

privilegio [priβi'lexjo] *nm* privilege; *(concesión)* concession

pro [pro] *nm of* profit, advantage ▷ *prep:* **asociación ~ ciegos** association for the blind ▷ *prefijo:* **~ americano** pro-American; **en ~ de** on behalf of, for; **los ~s y los contras** the pros and cons

proa ['proa] *nf* bow, prow; **de ~** bow *cpd*, fore

probabilidad [proβaβili'ðað] *nf* probability, likelihood; *(oportunidad, posibilidad)* chance, prospect; **probable** *adj* probable, likely

probador [proβa'ðor] *nm* (*en tienda*) fitting room

probar [pro'βar] *vt* (*demostrar*) to prove; (*someter a prueba*) to test, try out; (*ropa*) to try on; (*comida*) to taste ▷ *vi* to try; **~se un traje** to try on a suit

probeta [pro'βeta] *nf* test tube

problema [pro'βlema] *nm* problem

procedente [proθe'ðente] *adj* (*razonable*) reasonable; (*conforme a derecho*) proper, fitting; **~ de** coming from, originating in

proceder [proθe'ðer] *vi* (*avanzar*) to proceed; (*actuar*) to act; (*ser correcto*) to be right (and proper), be fitting ▷ *nm* (*comportamiento*) behaviour, conduct; **~ de** to come from, originate in; **procedimiento** *nm* procedure; (*proceso*) process; (*método*) means *pl*, method

procesador [proθesa'ðor] *nm* processor; **procesador de textos** word processor

procesar [proθe'sar] *vt* to try, put on trial

procesión [proθe'sjon] *nf* procession

proceso [pro'θeso] *nm* process; (*Jur*) trial

proclamar [prokla'mar] *vt* to proclaim

procrear [prokre'ar] *vt, vi* to procreate

procurador, a [prokura'ðor, a] *nm/f* attorney

procurar [proku'rar] *vt* (*intentar*) to try, endeavour; (*conseguir*) to get, obtain; (*asegurar*) to secure; (*producir*) to produce

prodigio [pro'ðixjo] *nm* prodigy; (*milagro*) wonder, marvel; **prodigioso, -a** *adj* prodigious, marvellous

pródigo, -a ['proðixo, a] *adj:* **hijo ~** prodigal son

producción [proðuk'θjon] *nf* (*gen*) production; (*producto*) output; **producción en serie** mass production

producir [proðu'θir] *vt* to produce; (*causar*) to cause, bring about; **producirse** *vr* (*cambio*) to come about; (*accidente*) to take place; (*problema etc*) to arise; (*hacerse*) to be produced, be made; (*estallar*) to break out

productividad [proðuktiβi'ðað] *nf* productivity; **productivo, -a** *adj* productive; (*provechoso*) profitable

producto [pro'ðukto] *nm* product

productor, a [proðuk'tor, a] *adj* productive, producing ▷ *nm/f* producer

proeza [pro'eθa] *nf* exploit, feat

profano, -a [pro'fano, a] *adj* profane ▷ *nm/f* layman/woman

profecía [profe'θia] *nf* prophecy

profesión [profe'sjon] *nf* profession; (*en formulario*) occupation; **profesional** *adj* professional

profesor, a [profe'sor, a] *nm/f* teacher; **profesorado** *nm* teaching profession

profeta [pro'feta] *nmf* prophet

prófugo, -a ['profuxo, a] *nm/f* fugitive; (*Mil: desertor*) deserter

profundidad [profundi'ðað] *nf* depth; **profundizar** *vi:* **profundizar en** to go deeply into; **profundo, -a** *adj* deep; (*misterio, pensador*) profound

progenitor [proxeni'tor] *nm* ancestor; **progenitores** *nmpl* (*padres*) parents

programa [pro'xrama] *nm* programme (BRIT), program (US); **programa de estudios** curriculum, syllabus; **programación** *nf* programming; **programador, a** *nm/f* programmer; **programar** *vt* to program

progresar [proxre'sar] *vi* to progress, make progress; **progresista** *adj, nmf* progressive; **progresivo, -a** *adj* progressive; (*gradual*) gradual; (*continuo*) continuous; **progreso** *nm* progress

prohibición [proiβi'θjon] *nf* prohibition, ban

prohibir [proi'βir] *vt* to prohibit, ban, forbid; **prohibido o se prohibe fumar** no smoking; **"prohibido el paso"** "no entry"

prójimo, -a ['proximo, a] *nm/f* fellow man; (*vecino*) neighbour

prólogo ['proloxo] *nm* prologue

prolongar [prolon'xar] *vt* to extend; (*reunión etc*) to prolong; (*calle, tubo*) to extend

promedio [pro'meðjo] *nm* average; (*de distancia*) middle, mid-point

promesa [pro'mesa] *nf* promise

prometer [prome'ter] *vt* to promise ▷ *vi* to show promise; **prometerse** *vr* (*novios*) to get engaged; **prometido, -a** *adj* promised; engaged ▷ *nm/f* fiancé/fiancée

prominente [promi'nente] *adj* prominent

promoción [promo'θjon] *nf* promotion

promotor [promo'tor] *nm* promoter; (*instigador*) instigator

promover [promo'βer] *vt* to promote; (*causar*) to cause; (*instigar*) to instigate, stir up

promulgar [promul'xar] *vt* to promulgate; (*anunciar*) to proclaim

pronombre [pro'nombre] *nm* pronoun

pronosticar [pronosti'kar] *vt* to predict, foretell, forecast; **pronóstico** *nm* prediction, forecast; **pronóstico del tiempo** weather forecast

pronto, -a ['pronto, a] *adj* (*rápido*) prompt, quick; (*preparado*) ready ▷ *adv* quickly, promptly; (*en seguida*) at once, right away; (*dentro de poco*) soon; (*temprano*) early ▷ *nm:* **tiene unos ~s muy malos** he gets ratty all of a sudden (*inf*); **de ~** suddenly; **por lo ~** meanwhile, for the present

pronunciación [pronunθja'θjon] *nf* pronunciation

pronunciar [pronun'θjar] *vt* to pronounce; (*discurso*) to make, deliver; **pronunciarse** *vr* to revolt, rebel; (*declararse*) to declare o.s.

propagación [propaxa'θjon] *nf* propagation

propaganda [propa'xanda] *nf* (*Pol*) propaganda; (*Com*) advertising

propenso, -a [pro'penso, a] *adj* inclined to; **ser ~ a** to be inclined to, have a tendency to

propicio, -a [pro'piθjo, a] *adj* favourable, propitious

propiedad [propje'ðað] *nf* property; (*posesión*) possession, ownership; **propiedad particular** private property

propietario, -a [propje'tarjo, a] *nm/f* owner, proprietor

propina [pro'pina] *nf* tip

propio, -a ['propjo, a] *adj* own, of one's own;

(*característico*) characteristic, typical; (*debido*) proper; (*mismo*) selfsame, very; **el ~ ministro** the minister himself; **¿tienes casa propia?** have you a house of your own?

proponer [propo'ner] vt to propose, put forward; (*problema*) to pose; **proponerse** vr to propose, intend

proporción [propor'θjon] nf proportion; (*Mat*) ratio; **proporciones** nfpl (*dimensiones*) dimensions sg; **proporcionado, -a** adj proportionate; (*regular*) medium, middling; (*justo*) just right; **proporcionar** vt (*dar*) to give, supply, provide

proposición [proposi'θjon] nf proposition; (*propuesta*) proposal

propósito [pro'posito] nm purpose; (*intento*) aim, intention ▷ adv: **a ~** by the way, incidentally; (*a posta*) on purpose, deliberately; **a ~ de** about, with regard to

propuesta etc [pro'pwesta] vb V **proponer** ▷ nf proposal

propulsar [propul'sar] vt to drive, propel; (*fig*) to promote, encourage; **propulsión** nf propulsion; **propulsión a chorro o por reacción** jet propulsion

prórroga ['prorroxa] nf extension; (*Jur*) stay; (*Com*) deferment; (*Deporte*) extra time; **prorrogar** vt (*período*) to extend; (*decisión*) to defer, postpone

prosa ['prosa] nf prose

proseguir [prose'xir] vt to continue, carry on ▷ vi to continue, go on

prospecto [pros'pekto] nm prospectus

prosperar [prospe'rar] vi to prosper, thrive, flourish; **prosperidad** nf prosperity; (*éxito*) success; **próspero, -a** adj prosperous, flourishing; (*que tiene éxito*) successful

prostíbulo [pros'tiβulo] nm brothel (BRIT), house of prostitution (US)

prostitución [prostitu'θjon] nf prostitution

prostituir [prosti'twir] vt to prostitute; **prostituirse** vr to prostitute o.s., become a prostitute

prostituta [prosti'tuta] nf prostitute

protagonista [protaxo'nista] nmf protagonist

protección [protek'θjon] nf protection

protector, a [protek'tor, a] adj protective, protecting ▷ nm/f protector

proteger [prote'xer] vt to protect; **protegido, -a** nm/f protégé/protégée

proteína [prote'ina] nf protein

protesta [pro'testa] nf protest; (*declaración*) protestation

protestante [protes'tante] adj Protestant

protestar [protes'tar] vt to protest, declare ▷ vi to protest

protocolo [proto'kolo] nm protocol

prototipo [proto'tipo] nm prototype

provecho [pro'βetʃo] nm advantage, benefit; (*Finanzas*) profit; **¡buen ~!** bon appétit!; **en ~ de** to the benefit of; **sacar ~ de** to benefit from, profit by

provenir [proβe'nir] vi: **~ de** to come o stem from

proverbio [pro'βerβjo] nm proverb

providencia [proβi'ðenθja] nf providence

provincia [pro'βinθja] nf province

provisión [proβi'sjon] nf provision; (*abastecimiento*) provision, supply; (*medida*) measure, step

provisional [proβisjo'nal] adj provisional

provocar [proβo'kar] vt to provoke; (*alentar*) to tempt, invite; (*causar*) to bring about, lead to; (*promover*) to promote; (*estimular*) to rouse, stimulate; **¿te provoca un café?** (CAM) would you like a coffee?;

provocativo, -a adj provocative

proxeneta [prokse'neta] nm pimp

próximamente [proksima'mente] adv shortly, soon

proximidad [proksimi'ðað] nf closeness, proximity; **próximo, -a** adj near, close; (*vecino*) neighbouring; (*siguiente*) next

proyectar [projek'tar] vt (*objeto*) to hurl, throw; (*luz*) to cast, shed; (*Cine*) to screen, show; (*planear*) to plan

proyectil [projek'til] nm projectile, missile

proyecto [pro'jekto] nm plan; (*estimación de costo*) detailed estimate

proyector [projek'tor] nm (*Cine*) projector

prudencia [pru'ðenθja] nf (*sabiduría*) wisdom; (*cuidado*) care; **prudente** adj sensible, wise; (*conductor*) careful

prueba etc ['prweβa] vb V **probar** ▷ nf proof; (*ensayo*) test, trial; (*degustación*) tasting, sampling; (*de ropa*) fitting; **a ~** on trial; **a ~ de** proof against; **a ~ de agua/fuego** waterproof/fireproof; **someter a ~** to put to the test

psico... [siko] prefijo psycho...; **psicología** nf psychology; **psicológico, -a** adj psychological; **psicólogo, -a** nm/f psychologist; **psicópata** nmf psychopath; **psicosis** nf inv psychosis

psiquiatra [si'kjatra] nmf psychiatrist; **psiquiátrico, -a** adj psychiatric

PSOE [pe'soe] (ESP) nm abr = **Partido Socialista Obrero Español**

púa ['pua] nf (*Bot, Zool*) prickle, spine; (*para guitarra*) plectrum (BRIT), pick (US); **alambre de ~** barbed wire

pubertad [puβer'tað] nf puberty

publicación [puβlika'θjon] nf publication

publicar [puβli'kar] vt (*editar*) to publish; (*hacer público*) to publicize; (*divulgar*) to make public, divulge

publicidad [puβliθi'ðað] nf publicity; (*Com: propaganda*) advertising; **publicitario, -a** adj publicity cpd; advertising cpd

público, -a ['puβliko, a] adj public ▷ nm public; (*Teatro etc*) audience

puchero [pu'tʃero] nm (*Culin: guiso*) stew; (: *olla*) cooking pot; **hacer ~s** to pout

pucho ['putʃo] (CS: fam) nm cigarette, fag (BRIT)

pude etc vb V **poder**

pudiente [pu'ðjente] adj (*rico*) wealthy, well-to-do

pudiera etc vb V **poder**

pudor [pu'ðor] nm modesty

pudrir [pu'ðrir] vt to rot; **pudrirse** vr to rot, decay

pueblo ['pweβlo] nm people; (*nación*) nation; (*aldea*) village

puedo etc vb V **poder**

puente ['pwente] nm bridge; **hacer ~** (*fam*) to take extra days off work between 2 public holidays; to take a long weekend; **puente aéreo** shuttle service; **puente colgante** suspension bridge; **puente levadizo** drawbridge

puerco, -a ['pwerko, a] nm/f pig/sow ▷ adj (*sucio*) dirty, filthy; (*obsceno*) disgusting; **puerco espín** porcupine

pueril [pwe'ril] adj childish

puerro ['pwerro] nm leek

puerta ['pwerta] nf door; (*de jardín*) gate; (*portal*) doorway; (*fig*) gateway; (*portería*) goal; **a la ~** at the door; **a ~ cerrada** behind closed doors; **puerta giratoria** revolving door

puerto ['pwerto] nm port; (*paso*) pass; (*fig*) haven,

refuge

Puerto Rico [pwerto'riko] nm Puerto Rico; **puertorriqueño, -a** adj, nm/f Puerto Rican

pues [pwes] adv (entonces) then; (bueno) well, well then; (así que) so ▷ conj (ya que) since; **¡~ sí!** yes!, certainly!

puesta ['pwesta] nf (apuesta) bet, stake; **puesta al día** updating; **puesta a punto** fine tuning; **puesta de sol** sunset; **puesta en marcha** starting

puesto, -a ['pwesto, a] pp de **poner** ▷ adj: **tener algo ~** to have sth on, be wearing sth ▷ nm (lugar, posición) place; (trabajo) post, job; (Com) stall ▷ conj: **~ que** since, as

púgil ['puxil] nm boxer

pulga ['pulɣa] nf flea

pulgada [pul'ɣaða] nf inch

pulgar [pul'ɣar] nm thumb

pulir [pu'lir] vt to polish; (alisar) to smooth; (fig) to polish up, touch up

pulmón [pul'mon] nm lung; **pulmonía** nf pneumonia

pulpa ['pulpa] nf pulp; (de fruta) flesh, soft part

pulpería [pulpe'ria] (LAM) nf (tienda) small grocery store

púlpito ['pulpito] nm pulpit

pulpo ['pulpo] nm octopus

pulque ['pulke] nm pulque

pulsación [pulsa'θjon] nf beat; **pulsaciones** pulse rate

pulsar [pul'sar] vt (tecla) to touch, tap; (Mús) to play; (botón) to press, push ▷ vi to pulsate; (latir) to beat, throb

pulsera [pul'sera] nf bracelet

pulso ['pulso] nm (Anat) pulse; (fuerza) strength; (firmeza) steadiness, steady hand

pulverizador [pulβeriθa'ðor] nm spray, spray gun

pulverizar [pulβeri'θar] vt to pulverize; (líquido) to spray

puna ['puna] (CAM) nf mountain sickness

punta ['punta] nf point, tip; (extremo) end; (fig) touch, trace; **horas ~** peak o rush hours; **sacar ~ a** to sharpen

puntada [pun'taða] nf (Costura) stitch

puntal [pun'tal] nm prop, support

puntapié [punta'pje] nm kick

puntería [punte'ria] nf (de arma) aim, aiming; (destreza) marksmanship

puntero, -a [pun'tero, a] adj leading ▷ nm (palo) pointer

puntiagudo, -a [puntja'ɣuðo, a] adj sharp, pointed

puntilla [pun'tiʎa] nf (encaje) lace edging o trim; (andar) **de ~s** (to walk) on tiptoe

punto ['punto] nm (gen) point; (señal diminuta) spot, dot; (Costura, Med) stitch; (lugar) spot, place; (momento) point, moment; **a ~** ready; **estar a ~ de** to be on the point of o about to; **en ~** on the dot; **hasta cierto ~** to some extent; **hacer ~** (ESP: tejer) to knit; **dos ~s** (Ling) colon; **punto de interrogación** question mark; **punto de vista** point of view, viewpoint; **punto final** full stop (BRIT), period (US); **punto muerto** dead center; (Auto) neutral (gear); **punto y aparte** (en dictado) full stop, new paragraph; **punto y coma** semicolon

puntocom [punto'kom] adj inv, nf inv dotcom

puntuación [puntwa'θjon] nf punctuation; (puntos: en examen) mark(s) (pl); (Deporte) score

puntual [pun'twal] adj (a tiempo) punctual; (exacto) exact, accurate; **puntualidad** nf punctuality;

exactness, accuracy

puntuar [pun'twar] vi (Deporte) to score, count

punzante [pun'θante] adj (dolor) shooting, sharp; (herramienta) sharp

puñado [pu'ɲaðo] nm handful

puñal [pu'ɲal] nm dagger; **puñalada** nf stab

puñetazo [puɲe'taðo] nm punch

puño ['puɲo] nm (Anat) fist; (cantidad) fistful, handful; (Costura) cuff; (de herramienta) handle

pupila [pu'pila] nf pupil

pupitre [pu'pitre] nm desk

puré [pu're] nm purée; (sopa) (thick) soup; **puré de papas** (LAM) mashed potatoes; **puré de patatas** (ESP) mashed potatoes

purga ['purɣa] nf purge; **purgante** adj, nm purgative

purgatorio [purɣa'torjo] nm purgatory

purificar [purifi'kar] vt to purify; (refinar) to refine

puritano, -a [puri'tano, a] adj (actitud) puritanical; (iglesia, tradición) puritan ▷ nm/f puritan

puro, -a ['puro, a] adj pure; (verdad) simple, plain ▷ nm cigar

púrpura ['purpura] nf purple

pus [pus] nm pus

puse etc vb V **poder**

pusiera etc vb V **poder**

puta ['puta] (fam!) nf whore, prostitute

putrefacción [putrefak'θjon] nf rotting, putrefaction

PVP nm abr (= precio de venta al público) RRP

pyme, PYME ['pime] nf abr (= Pequeña y Mediana Empresa) SME

to be; (haber aún) to remain, be left; **quedarse** vr to remain, stay (behind); **~se (con) algo** to keep sth; **~ en** (acordar) to agree on/to; **~ en nada** to come to nothing; **~ por hacer** to be still to be done; **~ ciego/mudo** to be left blind/dumb; **no te queda bien ese vestido** that dress doesn't suit you; **eso queda muy lejos** that's a long way (away); **quedamos a las seis** we agreed to meet at six

quedo, -a ['keðo, a] adj still ▷ adv softly, gently
quehacer [kea'θer] nm task, job; **quehaceres (domésticos)** nmpl household chores
queja ['kexa] nf complaint; **quejarse** vr (enfermo) to moan, groan; (protestar) to complain; **quejarse de que** to complain (about the fact) that; **quejido** nm moan
quemado, -a [ke'maðo, a] adj burnt
quemadura [kema'ðura] nf burn, scald
quemar [ke'mar] vt to burn; (fig: malgastar) to burn up, squander ▷ vi to be burning hot; **quemarse** vr (consumirse) to burn (up); (del sol) to get sunburnt
quemarropa [kema'rropa]: **a ~** adv point-blank
quepo etc vb V **caber**
querella [ke'reʎa] nf (Jur) charge; (disputa) dispute

---

que [ke] conj **1** (con oración subordinada: muchas veces no se traduce) that; **dijo que vendría** he said (that) he would come; **espero que lo encuentres** I hope (that) you'll find it; V tb **el**
2 (en oración independiente): **¡que entre!** send him in; **¡que aproveche!** enjoy your meal!; **¡que se mejore tu padre!** I hope your father gets better
3 (enfático): **¿me quieres? – ¡que sí!** do you love me? – of course!
4 (consecutivo: muchas veces no se traduce) that; **es tan grande que no lo puedo levantar** it's so big (that) I can't lift it
5 (comparaciones) than; **yo que tú/él** if I were you/him; V tb **más, menos, mismo**
6 (valor disyuntivo): **que le guste o no** whether he likes it or not; **que venga o que no venga** whether he comes or not
7 (porque): **no puedo, que tengo que quedarme en casa** I can't, I've got to stay in
▷ pron **1** (cosa) that, which; (+ prep) which; **el sombrero que te compraste** the hat (that o which) you bought; **la cama en que dormí** the bed (that o which) I slept in
2 (persona: suj) that, who; (: objeto) that, whom; **el amigo que me acompañó al museo** the friend that o who went to the museum with me; **la chica que invité** the girl (that o whom) I invited

qué [ke] adj what?, which? ▷ pron what?; **¡~ divertido!** how funny!; **¿~ edad tienes?** how old are you?; **¿de ~ me hablas?** what are you saying to me?; **¿~ tal?** how are you?, how are things?; **¿~ hay (de nuevo)?** what's new?
quebrado, -a [ke'βraðo, a] adj (roto) broken ▷ nm/f bankrupt ▷ nm (Mat) fraction
quebrantar [keβran'tar] vt (infringir) to violate, transgress
quebrar [ke'βrar] vt to break, smash ▷ vi to go bankrupt
quedar [ke'ðar] vi to stay, remain; (encontrarse: sitio)

---

querer [ke'rer] vt **1** (desear) to want; **quiero más dinero** I want more money; **quisiera o querría un té** I'd like a tea; **sin querer** unintentionally; **quiero ayudar/que vayas** I want to help/you to go
2 (preguntas: para pedir algo): **¿quiere abrir la ventana?** could you open the window?; **¿quieres echarme una mano?** can you give me a hand?
3 (amar) to love; (tener cariño a) to be fond of; **te quiero** I love you; **quiere mucho a sus hijos** he's very fond of his children
4 **le pedí que me dejara ir pero no quiso** I asked him to let me go but he refused

querido, -a [ke'riðo, a] adj dear ▷ nm/f darling; (amante) lover
queso ['keso] nm cheese; **queso crema** (LAM) cream cheese; **queso de untar** (ESP) cream cheese; **queso manchego** sheep's milk cheese made in La Mancha; **queso rallado** grated cheese
quicio ['kiθjo] nm hinge; **sacar a algn de ~** to get on sb's nerves
quiebra ['kjeβra] nf break, split; (Com) bankruptcy; (Econ) slump
quiebro ['kjeβro] nm (del cuerpo) swerve
quien [kjen] pron who; **hay ~ piensa que** there are those who think that; **no hay ~ lo haga** no-one will do it
quién [kjen] pron who, whom; **¿~ es?** who's there?
quienquiera [kjen'kjera] (pl **quienesquiera**) pron whoever

quiero etc vb V **querer**
quieto, -a ['kjeto, a] adj still; (carácter) placid; **quietud** nf stillness
quilate [ki'late] nm carat
químico, -a ['kimiko, a] adj chemical ▷ nm/f chemist ▷ nf chemistry
quincalla [kin'kaʎa] nf hardware, ironmongery (BRIT)
quince ['kinθe] num fifteen; **~ días** a fortnight; **quinceañero, -a** nm/f teenager; **quincena** nf

fortnight; (*pago*) fortnightly pay; **quincenal** *adj*
fortnightly

quiniela [ki'njela] *nf* football pools *pl*; **quinielas** *nfpl*
(*impreso*) pools coupon *sg*

quinientos, -as [ki'njentos, as] *adj, num* five
hundred

quinto, -a ['kinto, a] *adj* fifth ▷ *nf* country house;
(*Mil*) call-up, draft

quiosco ['kjosko] *nm* (*de música*) bandstand; (*de
periódicos*) news stand

quirófano [ki'rofano] *nm* operating theatre

quirúrgico, -a [ki'rurxiko, a] *adj* surgical

quise *etc vb* V **querer**

quisiera *etc vb* V **querer**

quisquilloso, -a [kiski'ʎoso, a] *adj* (*susceptible*)
touchy; (*meticuloso*) pernickety

quiste ['kiste] *nm* cyst

quitaesmalte [kitaes'malte] *nm* nail-polish
remover

quitamanchas [kita'mantʃas] *nm inv* stain remover

quitanieves [kita'njeβes] *nm inv* snowplough
(*BRIT*), snowplow (*US*)

quitar [ki'tar] *vt* to remove, take away; (*ropa*) to
take off; (*dolor*) to relieve; **¡quita de ahí!** get away!;
quitarse *vr* to withdraw; (*ropa*) to take off; **se quitó el
sombrero** he took off his hat

Quito ['kito] *n* Quito

quizá(s) [ki'θa(s)] *adv* perhaps, maybe

rábano ['raβano] *nm* radish; **me importa un ~** I don't
give a damn

rabia ['raβja] *nf* (*Med*) rabies *sg*; (*ira*) fury, rage; **rabiar**
vi to have rabies; to rage, be furious; **rabiar por algo**
to long for sth

rabieta [ra'βjeta] *nf* tantrum, fit of temper

rabino [ra'βino] *nm* rabbi

rabioso, -a [ra'βjoso, a] *adj* rabid; (*fig*) furious

rabo ['raβo] *nm* tail

racha ['ratʃa] *nf* gust of wind; **buena/mala ~** spell of
good/bad luck

racial [ra'θjal] *adj* racial, race *cpd*

racimo [ra'θimo] *nm* bunch

ración [ra'θjon] *nf* portion; **raciones** *nfpl* rations

racional [raθjo'nal] *adj* (*razonable*) reasonable;
(*lógico*) rational

racionar [raθjo'nar] *vt* to ration (out)

racismo [ra'θismo] *nm* racism; **racista** *adj, nm*
racist

radar [ra'ðar] *nm* radar

radiador [raðja'ðor] *nm* radiator

radiante [ra'ðjante] *adj* radiant

radical [raði'kal] *adj, nmf* radical

radicar [raði'kar] *vi*: **~ en** (*dificultad, problema*) to lie in;
(*solución*) to consist in

radio ['raðjo] *nf* radio; (*aparato*) radio (set) ▷ *nm*
(*Mat*) radius; (*Quím*) radium; **radioactividad** *nf*
radioactivity; **radioactivo, -a** *adj* radioactive;
radiografía *nf* X-ray; **radioterapia** *nf* radiotherapy;
radioyente *nmf* listener

ráfaga ['rafaxa] *nf* gust; (*de luz*) flash; (*de tiros*) burst

raíz [ra'iθ] *nf* root; **a ~ de** as a result of; **raíz cuadrada**
square root

raja ['raxa] *nf* (*de melón etc*) slice; (*grieta*) crack; **rajar**
vt to split; (*fam*) to slash; **rajarse** *vr* to split, crack;
rajarse de to back out of

rajatabla [raxa'taβla]: **a ~** *adv* (*estrictamente*) strictly,
to the letter

rallador [raʎa'ðor] *nm* grater

rallar [ra'ʎar] *vt* to grate

rama ['rama] *nf* branch; **ramaje** *nm* branches *pl*,
foliage; **ramal** *nm* (*de cuerda*) strand; (*Ferro*) branch
line (*BRIT*); (*Auto*) branch (road) (*BRIT*)

rambla ['rambla] nf (avenida) avenue

ramo ['ramo] nm branch; (sección) department, section

rampa ['rampa] nf ramp; **rampa de acceso** entrance ramp

rana ['rana] nf frog; **salto de ~** leapfrog

ranchero [ran'tʃero] (MÉX) nm (hacendado) rancher; smallholder

rancho ['rantʃo] nm (grande) ranch; (pequeño) small farm

rancio, -a ['ranθjo, a] adj (comestibles) rancid; (vino) aged, mellow; (fig) ancient

rango ['rango] nm rank, standing

ranura [ra'nura] nf groove; (de teléfono etc) slot

rapar [ra'par] vt to shave; (los cabellos) to crop

rapaz [ra'paθ] (nf-a) nmf young boy/girl ▷ adj (Zool) predatory

rape ['rape] nm (pez) monkfish; **al ~** cropped

rapé [ra'pe] nm snuff

rapidez [rapi'ðeθ] nf speed, rapidity; **rápido, -a** adj fast, quick ▷ adv quickly ▷ nm (Ferro) express; **rápidos** nmpl rapids

rapiña [ra'pina] nm robbery; **ave de ~** bird of prey

raptar [rap'tar] vt to kidnap; **rapto** nm kidnapping; (impulso) sudden impulse; (éxtasis) ecstasy, rapture

raqueta [ra'keta] nf racquet

raquítico, -a [ra'kitiko, a] adj stunted; (fig) poor, inadequate

rareza [ra'reθa] nf rarity; (fig) eccentricity

raro, -a ['raro, a] adj (poco común) rare; (extraño) odd, strange; (excepcional) remarkable

ras [ras] nm: **a ~ de** level with; **a ~ de tierra** at ground level

rasar [ra'sar] vt (igualar) to level

rascacielos [raska'θjelos] nm inv skyscraper

rascar [ras'kar] vt (con las uñas etc) to scratch; (raspar) to scrape; **rascarse** vr to scratch (o.s.)

rasgar [ras'ɣar] vt to tear, rip (up)

rasgo ['rasɣo] nm (con pluma) stroke; **rasgos** nmpl (facciones) features, characteristics; **a grandes ~s** in outline, broadly

rasguño [ras'ɣuno] nm scratch

raso, -a ['raso, a] adj (liso) flat, level; (a baja altura) very low ▷ nm satin; **cielo ~** clear sky

raspadura [raspa'ðura] nf (acto) scrape, scraping; (marca) scratch; **raspaduras** nfpl (de papel etc) scrapings

raspar [ras'par] vt to scrape; (arañar) to scratch; (limar) to file

rastra ['rastra] nf (Agr) rake; **a ~s** by dragging; (fig) unwillingly

rastrear [rastre'ar] vt (seguir) to track

rastrero, -a [ras'trero, a] adj (Bot, Zool) creeping; (fig) despicable, mean

rastrillo [ras'triʎo] nm rake

rastro ['rastro] nm (Agr) rake; (pista) track, trail; (vestigio) trace; **el R~** (ESP) the Madrid fleamarket

rasurado [rasu'raðo] (MÉX) nm shaving; **rasuradora** [rasura'ðora] (MÉX) nf electric shaver; **rasurar** [rasu'rar] (MÉX) vt to shave; **rasurarse** vr to shave

rata ['rata] nf rat

ratear [rate'ar] vt (robar) to steal

ratero, -a [ra'tero, a] adj light-fingered ▷ nm/f (carterista) pickpocket; (ladrón) petty thief

rato ['rato] nm while, short time; **a ~s** from time to time; **hay para ~** there's still a long way to go; **al poco ~ soon afterwards; pasar el ~** to kill time; **pasar un buen/mal ~** to have a good/rough time; **en mis ~s libres** in my spare time

ratón [ra'ton] nm mouse; **ratonera** nf mousetrap

raudal [rau'ðal] nm torrent; **a ~es** in abundance

raya ['raja] nf line; (marca) scratch; (en tela) stripe; (de pelo) parting; (límite) boundary; (pez) ray; (puntuación) dash; **a ~s** striped; **pasarse de la ~** to go too far; **tener a ~** to keep in check; **raza** vt to line; to scratch; (subrayar) to underline ▷ vi: **rayar en o con** to border on

rayo ['rajo] nm (del sol) ray, beam; (de luz) shaft; (en una tormenta) (flash of) lightning; **rayos X** X-rays

raza ['raθa] nf race; **raza humana** human race

razón [ra'θon] nf reason; (justicia) right, justice; (razonamiento) reasoning; (motivo) reason, motive; (Mat) ratio; **a ~ de to cada día** at the rate of 10 a day; **en ~ de** with regard to; **dar ~ a algn** to agree that sb is right; **tener ~** to be right; **razón de ser** raison d'être; **razón directa/inversa** direct/inverse proportion; **razonable** adj reasonable; (justo, moderado) fair; **razonamiento** nm (juicio) judg(e)ment; (argumento) reasoning; **razonar** vt, vi to reason, argue

re [re] nm (Mús) D

reacción [reak'θjon] nf reaction; **avión a ~** jet plane; **reacción en cadena** chain reaction; **reaccionar** vi to react

reacio, -a [re'aθjo, a] adj stubborn

reactivar [reakti'βar] vt to revitalize

reactor [reak'tor] nm reactor

real [re'al] adj real; (del rey, fig) royal

realidad [reali'ðað] nf reality, fact; (verdad) truth

realista [rea'lista] nmf realist

realización [realiθa'θjon] nf fulfilment

realizador, a [realiθa'ðor, a] nm/f film-maker

realizar [reali'θar] vt to achieve; (plan) to carry out; (viaje) to make, undertake; **realizarse** vr to come about, come true

realmente [real'mente] adv really, actually

realzar [real'θar] vt to enhance; (acentuar) to highlight

reanimar [reani'mar] vt to revive; (alentar) to encourage; **reanimarse** vr to revive

reanudar [reanu'ðar] vt (renovar) to renew; (historia, viaje) to resume

reaparición [reapari'θjon] nf reappearance

rearme [re'arme] nm rearmament

rebaja [re'βaxa] nf (Com) reduction; (: descuento) discount; **rebajas** nfpl (Com) sale; **rebajar** vt (bajar) to lower; (reducir) to reduce; (disminuir) to lessen; (humillar) to humble

rebanada [reβa'naða] nf slice

rebañar [reβa'nar] vt (comida) to scrape up; (plato) to scrape clean

rebaño [re'βano] nm herd; (de ovejas) flock

rebatir [reβa'tir] vt to refute

rebeca [re'βeka] nf cardigan

rebelarse [reβe'larse] vr to rebel, revolt

rebelde [re'βelde] adj rebellious; (niño) unruly ▷ nmf rebel; **rebeldía** nf rebelliousness; (desobediencia) disobedience

rebelión [reβe'ljon] nf rebellion

reblandecer [reβlande'θer] vt to soften

rebobinar [reβoβi'nar] vt (cinta, película de video) to rewind

rebosante [reβo'sante] adj overflowing

rebosar [reβo'sar] vi (líquido, recipiente) to overflow;

(abundar) to abound, be plentiful

rebotar [reβo'tar] *vt* to bounce; *(rechazar)* to repel ▷ *vi (pelota)* to bounce; *(bala)* to ricochet; **rebote** *nm* rebound; **de rebote** on the rebound

rebozado, -a [reβo'θaðo, a] *adj* fried in batter o breadcrumbs

rebozar [reβo'θar] *vt* to wrap up; *(Culin)* to fry in batter o breadcrumbs

rebuscado, -a [reβus'kaðo, a] *adj (amanerado)* affected; *(palabra)* recherché; *(idea)* far-fetched

rebuscar [reβus'kar] *vi:* ~ **(en/por)** to search carefully (in/for)

recado [re'kaðo] *nm (mensaje)* message; *(encargo)* errand; **tomar un** ~ *(Tel)* to take a message

recaer [reka'er] *vi* to relapse; ~ **en** to fall to o on; *(criminal etc)* to fall back into, relapse into; **recaída** *nf* relapse

recalcar [rekal'kar] *vt (fig)* to stress, emphasize

recalentar [rekalen'tar] *vt (volver a calentar)* to reheat; *(calentar demasiado)* to overheat

recámara [re'kamara] *(MÉX)* *nf* bedroom

recambio [re'kambjo] *nm* spare; *(de pluma)* refill

recapacitar [rekapaθi'tar] *vi* to reflect

recargado, -a [rekar'xaðo, a] *adj* overloaded

recargar [rekar'xar] *vt* to overload; *(batería)* to recharge; ~ **el saldo de** *(Tel)* to top up; **recargo** *nm* surcharge; *(aumento)* increase

recatado, -a [reka'taðo, a] *adj (modesto)* modest, demure; *(prudente)* cautious

recaudación [rekauða'θjon] *nf (acción)* collection; *(cantidad)* takings *pl*; *(en deporte)* gate; **recaudador, a** *nm/f* tax collector

recelar [reθe'lar] *vt:* ~ **que ...** *(sospechar)* to suspect that ...; *(temer)* to fear that ... ▷ *vi:* ~ **de** to distrust; **recelo** *nm* distrust, suspicion

recepción [reθep'θjon] *nf* reception; **recepcionista** *nmf* receptionist

receptor, a [reθep'tor, a] *nm/f* recipient ▷ *nm (Tel)* receiver

recesión [reθe'sjon] *nf (Com)* recession

receta [re'θeta] *nf (Culin)* recipe; *(Med)* prescription

rechazar [retʃa'θar] *vt* to reject; *(oferta)* to turn down; *(ataque)* to repel

rechazo [re'tʃaθo] *nm* rejection

rechinar [retʃi'nar] *vi* to creak; *(dientes)* to grind

rechistar [retʃis'tar] *vi:* **sin** ~ without a murmur

rechoncho, -a [re'tʃontʃo, a] *(fam)* *adj* thickset (BRIT), heavy-set *(US)*

rechupete [retʃu'pete]: **de** ~ *adj (comida)* delicious, scrumptious

recibidor [reθiβi'ðor] *nm* entrance hall

recibimiento [reθiβi'mjento] *nm* reception, welcome

recibir [reθi'βir] *vt* to receive; *(dar la bienvenida)* to welcome ▷ *vi* to entertain; **recibo** *nm* receipt

reciclable [reθi'klaβle] *adj* recyclable

reciclar [reθi'klar] *vt* to recycle

recién [re'θjen] *adv* recently, newly; **los** ~ **casados** the newly-weds; **el** ~ **llegado** the newcomer; **el** ~ **nacido** the newborn child

reciente [re'θjente] *adj* recent; *(fresco)* fresh

recinto [re'θinto] *nm* enclosure; *(área)* area, place

recio, -a ['reθjo, a] *adj* strong, tough; *(voz)* loud ▷ *adv* hard, loud(ly)

recipiente [reθi'pjente] *nm* receptacle

recíproco, -a [re'θiproco, a] *adj* reciprocal

recital [reθi'tal] *nm (Mús)* recital; *(Literatura)* reading

recitar [reθi'tar] *vt* to recite

reclamación [reklama'θjon] *nf* claim, demand; *(queja)* complaint

reclamar [rekla'mar] *vt* to claim, demand ▷ *vi:* ~ **contra** to complain about; **reclamo** *nm (anuncio)* advertisement; *(tentación)* attraction

reclinar [rekli'nar] *vt* to recline, lean; **reclinarse** *vr* to lean back

reclusión [reklu'sjon] *nf (prisión)* prison; *(refugio)* seclusion

recluta [re'kluta] *nmf* recruit ▷ *nf* recruitment; **reclutar** *vt (datos)* to collect; *(dinero)* to collect up; **reclutamiento** *nm* recruitment

recobrar [reko'βrar] *vt (salud)* to recover; *(rescatar)* to get back; **recobrarse** *vr* to recover

recodo [re'koðo] *nm (de río, camino)* bend

recogedor [rekoxe'ðor] *nm* dustpan

recoger [reko'xer] *vt* to collect; *(Agr)* to harvest; *(levantar)* to pick up; *(juntar)* to gather; *(pasar a buscar)* to come for, get; *(dar asilo)* to give shelter to; *(faldas)* to gather up; *(pelo)* to put up; **recogerse** *vr (retirarse)* to retire; **recogido, -a** *adj (lugar)* quiet, secluded; *(pequeño)* small ▷ *nf (Correos)* collection; *(Agr)* harvest

recolección [rekolek'θjon] *nf (Agr)* harvesting; *(colecta)* collection

recomendación [rekomenda'θjon] *nf (sugerencia)* suggestion, recommendation; *(referencia)* reference

recomendar [rekomen'dar] *vt* to suggest, recommend; *(confiar)* to entrust

recompensa [rekom'pensa] *nf* reward, recompense; **recompensar** *vt* to reward, recompense

reconciliación [rekonθilja'θjon] *nf* reconciliation

reconciliar [rekonθi'ljar] *vt* to reconcile; **reconciliarse** *vr* to become reconciled

recóndito, -a [re'kondito, a] *adj (lugar)* hidden, secret

reconocer [rekono'θer] *vt* to recognize; *(registrar)* to search; *(Med)* to examine; **reconocido, -a** *adj* recognized; *(agradecido)* grateful; **reconocimiento** *nm* recognition; search; examination; gratitude; *(confesión)* admission

reconquista [rekon'kista] *nf* reconquest; **la R~** the Reconquest (of Spain)

reconstituyente [rekonstitu'jente] *nm* tonic

reconstruir [rekonstru'ir] *vt* to reconstruct

reconversión [rekonβer'sjon] *nf (reestructuración)* restructuring; **reconversión industrial** industrial rationalization

recopilación [rekopila'θjon] *nf (resumen)* summary; *(compilación)* compilation; **recopilar** *vt* to compile

récord ['rekorð] *(pl* ~**s)** *adj inv, nm* record

recordar [rekor'ðar] *vt (acordarse de)* to remember; *(acordar a otro)* to remind ▷ *vi* to remember

recorrer [reko'rrer] *vt (país)* to cross, travel through; *(distancia)* to cover; *(registrar)* to search; *(repasar)* to look over; **recorrido** *nm* run, journey; **tren de largo recorrido** main-line train

recortar [rekor'tar] *vt* to cut out; **recorte** *nm (acción, de prensa)* cutting; *(de telas, chapas)* trimming; **recorte presupuestario** budget cut

recostar [rekos'tar] *vt* to lean; **recostarse** *vr* to lie down

recoveco [reko'βeko] *nm (de camino, río etc)* bend; *(en casa)* cubby hole

recreación [rekrea'θjon] *nf* recreation

recrear [rekre'ar] vt (entretener) to entertain; (volver a crear) to recreate; **recreativo, -a** adj recreational; **recreo** nm (Escol) break, playtime

recriminar [rekrimi'nar] vt to reproach ▷ vi to recriminate; **recriminarse** vr to reproach each other

recrudecer [rekruðe'θer] vt, vi to worsen; **recrudecerse** vr to worsen

recta ['rekta] nf straight line

rectángulo, -a [rek'tangulo, a] adj rectangular ▷ nm rectangle

rectificar [rektifi'kar] vt to rectify; (volverse recto) to straighten ▷ vi to correct o.s.

rectitud [rekti'tuð] nf straightness

recto, -a ['rekto, a] adj straight; (persona) honest, upright; **siga todo** - go straight on ▷ nm rectum

rector, a [rek'tor, a] nm/f rector

recuadro [re'kwaðro] nm box; (Tip) inset

recubrir [reku'βrir] vt: ~ **(con)** (pintura, crema) to cover (with)

recuento [re'kwento] nm inventory; **hacer el ~ de** to count o reckon up

recuerdo [re'kwerðo] nm souvenir; **recuerdos** nmpl (memorias) memories; **¡~s a tu madre!** give my regards to your mother!

recular [reku'lar] vi to back down

recuperación [rekupera'θjon] nf recovery

recuperar [rekupe'rar] vt to recover; (tiempo) to make up; **recuperarse** vr to recuperate

recurrir [reku'rrir] vi (Jur) to appeal; **~ a** to resort to; (persona) to turn to; **recurso** nm resort; (medios) means pl, resources pl; (Jur) appeal

red [reð] nf net, mesh; (Ferro etc) network; (trampa) trap; **la R~** (Internet) the Net

redacción [reðak'θjon] nf (acción) editing; (personal) editorial staff; (Escol) essay, composition

redactar [reðak'tar] vt to draw up, draft; (periódico) to edit

redactor, a [reðak'tor, a] nm/f editor

redada [re'ðaða] nf (de policía) raid, round-up

rededor [reðe'ðor] nm: **al o en ~** around, round about

redoblar [reðo'βlar] vt to redouble ▷ vi (tambor) to roll

redonda [re'ðonda] nf: **a la ~** around, round about

redondear [reðonde'ar] vt to round, round off

redondel [reðon'del] nm (círculo) circle; (Taur) bullring, arena

redondo, -a [re'ðondo, a] adj (circular) round; (completo) complete

reducción [reðuk'θjon] nf reduction

reducido, -a [reðu'θiðo, a] adj reduced; (limitado) limited; (pequeño) small

reducir [reðu'θir] vt to reduce; to limit; **reducirse** vr to diminish

redundancia [reðun'danθja] nf redundancy

reembolsar [re(e)mbol'sar] vt (persona) to reimburse; (dinero) to repay, pay back; (depósito) to refund; **reembolso** nm reimbursement; refund

reemplazar [re(e)mpla'θar] vt to replace; **reemplazo** nm replacement; **de reemplazo** (Mil) reserve

reencuentro [re(e)n'kwentro] nm reunion

reescribible [reeskri'βiβle] adj rewritable

refacción [refak'θjon] (MÉX) nf spare (part)

referencia [refe'renθja] nf reference; **con ~ a** with reference to

referéndum [refe'rendum] (pl **~s**) nm referendum

referente [refe'rente] adj: **~ a** concerning, relating to

réferi ['referi] (LAM) nmf referee

referir [refe'rir] vt (contar) to tell, recount; (relacionar) to refer, relate; **referirse** vr: **~se a** to refer to

refilón [refi'lon]: **de ~** adv obliquely

refinado, -a [refi'naðo, a] adj refined

refinar [refi'nar] vt to refine; **refinería** nf refinery

reflejar [refle'xar] vt to reflect; **reflejo, -a** adj reflected; (movimiento) reflex ▷ nm reflection; (Anat) reflex

reflexión [reflek'sjon] nf reflection; **reflexionar** vt to reflect on ▷ vi to reflect; (detenerse) to pause (to think)

reflexivo, -a [reflek'siβo, a] adj thoughtful; (Ling) reflexive

reforma [re'forma] nf reform; (Arq etc) repair; **reforma agraria** agrarian reform

reformar [refor'mar] vt to reform; (modificar) to change, alter; (Arq) to repair; **reformarse** vr to mend one's ways

reformatorio [reforma'torjo] nm reformatory

reforzar [refor'θar] vt to strengthen; (Arq) to reinforce; (fig) to encourage

refractario, -a [refrak'tarjo, a] adj (Tec) heat-resistant

refrán [re'fran] nm proverb, saying

refregar [refre'xar] vt to scrub

refrescante [refres'kante] adj refreshing, cooling

refrescar [refres'kar] vt to refresh ▷ vi to cool down; **refrescarse** vr to get cooler; (tomar aire fresco) to go out for a breath of fresh air; (beber) to have a drink

refresco [re'fresko] nm soft drink, cool drink; **"~s"** "refreshments"

refriega [re'frjexa] nf scuffle, brawl

refrigeración [refrixera'θjon] nf refrigeration; (de sala) air-conditioning

refrigerador [refrixera'ðor] nm refrigerator (BRIT), icebox (US)

refrigerar [refrixe'rar] vt to refrigerate; (sala) to air-condition

refuerzo [re'fwerθo] nm reinforcement; (Tec) support

refugiado, -a [refu'xjaðo, a] nm/f refugee

refugiarse [refu'xjarse] vr to take refuge, shelter

refugio [re'fuxjo] nm refuge; (protección) shelter

refunfuñar [refunfu'ɲar] vi to grunt, growl; (quejarse) to grumble

regadera [rexa'ðera] nf watering can

regadío [rexa'ðio] nm irrigated land

regalado, -a [rexa'laðo, a] adj comfortable, luxurious; (gratis) free, for nothing

regalar [rexa'lar] vt (dar) to give (as a present); (entregar) to give away; (mimar) to pamper, make a fuss of

regaliz [rexa'liθ] nm liquorice

regalo [re'xalo] nm (obsequio) gift, present; (gusto) pleasure

regañadientes [rexaɲa'ðjentes]: **a ~** adv reluctantly

regañar [rexa'ɲar] vt to scold ▷ vi to grumble; **regañón, -ona** adj nagging

regar [re'xar] vt to water, irrigate; (fig) to scatter, sprinkle

regatear [rexate'ar] vt (Com) to bargain over; (escatimar) to be mean with ▷ vi to bargain, haggle; (Deporte) to dribble; **regateo** nm bargaining; dribbling; (del cuerpo) swerve, dodge

regazo [re'raθo] nm lap

regenerar [rexene'rar] vt to regenerate

régimen ['reximen] (pl **regímenes**) nm regime; (Med) diet

regimiento [rexi'mjento] nm regiment

regio, -a ['rexjo, a] adj royal, regal; (fig: suntuoso) splendid; (cs: fam) great, terrific

región [re'xjon] nf region

regir [re'xir] vt (gobernar, ruler) to manage, to run ▷ vi to apply, be in force

registrar [rexis'trar] vt (buscar) to search; (: en cajón) to look through; (inspeccionar) to inspect; (anotar) to register, record; (Inform) to log; **registrarse** vr to register; (ocurrir) to happen

registro [re'xistro] nm (acto) registration; (Mús, libro) register; (inspección) inspection, search; **registro civil** registry office

regla ['rexla] nf (ley) rule, regulation; (de medir) ruler, rule; (Med: período) period; **en ~** in order

reglamentación [reɣlamenta'θjon] nf (acto) regulation; (lista) rules pl

reglamentar [reɣlamen'tar] vt to regulate; **reglamentario, -a** adj statutory; **reglamento** nm rules pl, regulations pl

regocijarse [reɣoθi'xarse] vr (alegrarse) to rejoice; **regocijo** joy, happiness

regrabadora [reɣraβa'ðora] nf rewriter; **regrabadora de DVD** DVD rewriter

regresar [reɣre'sar] vi to come back, go back, return; **regreso** nm return

reguero [re'ɣero] nm (de sangre etc) trickle; (de humo) trail

regulador [reɣula'ðor] nm regulator; (de radio etc) knob, control

regular [reɣu'lar] adj regular; (normal) normal, usual; (común) ordinary; (organizado) regular, orderly; (mediano) average; (fam) not bad, so-so ▷ adv so-so, alright ▷ vt (controlar) to control, regulate; (Tec) to adjust; **por lo ~** as a rule; **regularidad** nf regularity; **regularizar** to regularize

rehabilitación [reaβilita'θjon] nf rehabilitation; (Arq) restoration

rehabilitar [reaβili'tar] vt to rehabilitate; (Arq) to restore; (reintegrar) to reinstate

rehacer [rea'θer] vt (reparar) to mend, repair; (volver a hacer) to redo, repeat; **rehacerse** vr (Med) to recover

rehén [re'en] nm hostage

rehuir [reu'ir] vt to avoid, shun

rehusar [reu'sar] vt, vi to refuse

reina ['reina] nf queen; **reinado** nm reign

reinar [rei'nar] vi to reign

reincidir [reinθi'ðir] vi to relapse

reincorporarse [reinkorpo'rarse] vr: **~ a** to rejoin

reino ['reino] nm kingdom; **reino animal/vegetal** animal/plant kingdom; **el Reino Unido** the United Kingdom

reintegrar [reinte'ɣrar] vt (reconstituir) to reconstruct; (persona) to reinstate; (dinero) to refund, pay back; **reintegrarse** vr: **~se a** to return to

reír [re'ir] vi to laugh; **reírse** vr to laugh; **~se de** to laugh at

reiterar [reite'rar] vt to reiterate

reivindicación [reiβindika'θjon] nf (demanda) claim, demand; (justificación) vindication

reivindicar [reiβindi'kar] vt to claim

reja ['rexa] nf (de ventana) grille, bars pl; (en la calle) grating

rejilla [re'xiʎa] nf grating, grille; (muebles) wickerwork; (de ventilación) vent; (de coche etc) luggage rack

rejoneador [rexonea'ðor] nm mounted bullfighter

rejuvenecer [rexuβene'θer] vt, vi to rejuvenate

relación [rela'θjon] nf relation, relationship; (Mat) ratio; (narración) report; **con ~ a, en ~ con** in relation to; **relaciones públicas** public relations; **relacionar** vt to relate, connect; **relacionarse** vr to be connected, be linked

relajación [relaxa'θjon] nf relaxation

relajar [rela'xar] vt to relax; **relajarse** vr to relax

relamerse [rela'merse] vr to lick one's lips

relámpago [re'lampaɣo] nm flash of lightning; **visita ~** lightning visit

relatar [rela'tar] vt to tell, relate

relativo, -a [rela'tiβo, a] adj relative; **en lo ~ a** concerning

relato [re'lato] nm (narración) story, tale

relegar [rele'ɣar] vt to relegate

relevante [rele'βante] adj eminent, outstanding

relevar [rele'βar] vt (sustituir) to relieve; **relevarse** vr to relay; **~ a algn de un cargo** to relieve sb of his post

relevo [re'leβo] nm relief; **carrera de ~s** relay race

relieve [re'ljeβe] nm (Arte, Tec) relief; (fig) prominence, importance; **bajo ~** bas-relief

religión [reli'xjon] nf religion; **religioso, -a** adj religious ▷ nm/f monk/nun

relinchar [relin'tʃar] vi to neigh

reliquia [re'likja] nf relic; **reliquia de familia** heirloom

rellano [re'ʎano] nm (Arq) landing

rellenar [reʎe'nar] vt (llenar) to fill up; (Culin) to stuff; (Costura) to pad; **relleno, -a** adj full up; stuffed ▷ nm stuffing; (de tapicería) padding

reloj [re'lo(x)] nm clock; **poner el ~ (en hora)** to set one's watch (o the clock); **reloj (de pulsera)** wristwatch; **reloj despertador** alarm (clock); **reloj digital** digital watch; **relojero, -a** nm/f clockmaker; watchmaker

reluciente [relu'θjente] adj brilliant, shining

relucir [relu'θir] vi to shine; (fig) to excel

remachar [rema'tʃar] vt to rivet; (fig) to hammer home, drive home; **remache** nm rivet

remangar [reman'gar] vt to roll up

remanso [re'manso] nm pool

remar [re'mar] vi to row

rematado, -a [rema'taðo, a] adj complete, utter

rematar [rema'tar] vt to finish off; (Com) to sell off cheap ▷ vi to end, finish off; (Deporte) to shoot

remate [re'mate] nm end, finish; (punta) tip; (Deporte) shot; (Arq) top; **de o para ~** to crown it all (BRIT), to top it off

remedar [reme'ðar] vt to imitate

remediar [reme'ðjar] vt to remedy; (subsanar) to make good, repair; (evitar) to avoid

remedio [re'meðjo] nm remedy; (alivio) relief, help; (Jur) recourse, remedy; **poner ~ a** to correct, stop; **no tener más ~** to have no alternative; **¡qué ~!** there's no choice!; **sin ~** hopeless

remendar [remen'dar] vt to repair; (con parche) to patch

remiendo [re'mjendo] nm mend; (con parche) patch; (cosido) darn

remilgado, -a [remil'ɣaðo, a] adj prim; (afectado)

affected

remiso, -a [re'miso, a] *adj* slack, slow

remite [re'mite] *nm (en sobre)* name and address of sender

remitir [remi'tir] *vt* to remit, send ▷ *vi* to slacken; *(en carta)*: **remite: X** sender: X; **remitente** *nmf* sender

remo ['remo] *nm (de barco)* oar; *(Deporte)* rowing

remojar [remo'xar] *vt* to steep, soak; *(galleta etc)* to dip, dunk

remojo [re'moxo] *nm*: **dejar la ropa en ~** to leave clothes to soak

remolacha [remo'latʃa] *nf* beet, beetroot

remolcador [remolka'ðor] *nm (Náut)* tug; *(Auto)* breakdown lorry

remolcar [remol'kar] *vt* to tow

remolino [remo'lino] *nm* eddy; *(de agua)* whirlpool; *(de viento)* whirlwind; *(de gente)* crowd

remolque [re'molke] *nm* tow, towing; *(cuerda)* towrope; **llevar a ~** to tow

remontar [remon'tar] *vt* to mend; **remontarse** *vr* to soar; **~se a** *(Com)* to amount to; **~ el vuelo** to soar

remorder [remor'ðer] *vt* to distress, disturb; **~le la conciencia a algn** to have a guilty conscience; **remordimiento** *nm* remorse

remoto, -a [re'moto, a] *adj* remote

remover [remo'ßer] *vt* to stir; *(tierra)* to turn over; *(objetos)* to move round

remuneración [remunera'θjon] *nf* remuneration

remunerar [remune'rar] *vt* to remunerate; *(premiar)* to reward

renacer [rena'θer] *vi* to be reborn; *(fig)* to revive; **renacimiento** *nm* rebirth; **el Renacimiento** the Renaissance

renacuajo [rena'kwaxo] *nm (Zool)* tadpole

renal [re'nal] *adj* renal, kidney *cpd*

rencilla [ren'θiʎa] *nf* quarrel

rencor [ren'kor] *nm* rancour, bitterness; **rencoroso, -a** *adj* spiteful

rendición [rendi'θjon] *nf* surrender

rendido, -a [ren'diðo, a] *adj (sumiso)* submissive; *(cansado)* worn-out, exhausted

rendija [ren'dixa] *nf (hendedura)* crack, cleft

rendimiento [rendi'mjento] *nm (producción)* output; *(Tec, Com)* efficiency

rendir [ren'dir] *vt (vencer)* to defeat; *(producir)* to produce; *(dar beneficio)* to yield; *(agotar)* to exhaust ▷ *vi* to pay; **rendirse** *vr (someterse)* to surrender; *(cansarse)* to wear o.s. out; **~ homenaje o culto a** to pay homage to

renegar [rene'ɣar] *vi (renunciar)* to renounce; *(blasfemar)* to blaspheme; *(quejarse)* to complain

RENFE ['renfe] *nf abr (= Red Nacional de los Ferrocarriles Españoles)*

renglón [ren'ɡlon] *nm (línea)* line; *(Com)* item, article; **a ~ seguido** immediately after

renombre [re'nombre] *nm* renown

renovación [renoβa'θjon] *nf (de contrato)* renewal; *(Arq)* renovation

renovar [reno'βar] *vt* to renew; *(Arq)* to renovate

renta ['renta] *nf (ingresos)* income; *(beneficio)* profit; *(alquiler)* rent; **renta vitalicia** annuity; **rentable** *adj* profitable

renuncia [re'nunθja] *nf* resignation; **renunciar** [renun'θjar] *vt* to renounce; *(tabaco, alcohol etc)*: **renunciar a** to give up; *(oferta, oportunidad)* to turn down; *(puesto)* to resign ▷ *vi* to resign

---

reñido, -a [re'niðo, a] *adj (batalla)* bitter, hard-fought; **estar ~ con algn** to be on bad terms with sb

reñir [re'nir] *vt (regañar)* to scold ▷ *vi (estar peleado)* to quarrel, fall out; *(combatir)* to fight

reo ['reo] *nmf* culprit, offender; *(acusado)* accused, defendant

reojo [re'oxo] *nm*: **de ~** *adv* out of the corner of one's eye

reparación [repara'θjon] *nf (acto)* mending, repairing; *(Tec)* repair; *(fig)* amends *pl*, reparation

reparar [repa'rar] *vt* to repair; *(fig)* to make amends for; *(observar)* to observe ▷ *vi*: **~ en** *(darse cuenta de)* to notice; *(prestar atención a)* to pay attention to

reparo [re'paro] *nm (advertencia)* observation; *(duda)* doubt; *(dificultad)* difficulty; **poner ~s (a)** to raise objections (to)

repartidor, a [reparti'ðor, a] *nm/f* distributor

repartir [repar'tir] *vt* to distribute, share out; *(Correos)* to deliver; **reparto** *nm* distribution; delivery; *(Teatro, Cine)* cast; *(CAM: urbanización)* housing estate *(BRIT)*, real estate development *(US)*

repasar [repa'sar] *vt (Escol)* to revise; *(Mecánica)* to check, overhaul; *(Costura)* to mend; **repaso** *nm* revision; overhaul, checkup; mending

repecho [re'petʃo] *nm* steep incline

repelente [repe'lente] *adj* repellent, repulsive

repeler [repe'ler] *vt* to repel

repente [re'pente] *nm*: **de ~** suddenly

repentino, -a [repen'tino, a] *adj* sudden

repercusión [reperku'sjon] *nf* repercussion

repercutir [reperku'tir] *vi (objeto)* to rebound; *(sonido)* to echo; **~ en** *(fig)* to have repercussions on

repertorio [reper'torjo] *nm* list; *(Teatro)* repertoire

repetición [repeti'θjon] *nf* repetition

repetir [repe'tir] *vt* to repeat; *(plato)* to have a second helping of ▷ *vi* to repeat; *(sabor)* to come back; **repetirse** *vr (volver sobre un tema)* to repeat o.s.

repetitivo, -a [repeti'tiβo, a] *adj* repetitive, repetitious

repique [re'pike] *nm* pealing, ringing; **repiqueteo** *nm* pealing; *(de tambor)* drumming

repisa [re'pisa] *nf* ledge, shelf; *(de ventana)* windowsill; **la ~ de la chimenea** the mantelpiece

repito *etc vb* **V repetir**

replantearse [replante'arse] *vr*: **~ un problema** to reconsider a problem

repleto, -a [re'pleto, a] *adj* replete, full up

réplica ['replika] *nf* answer; *(Arte)* replica

replicar [repli'kar] *vi* to answer; *(objetar)* to argue, answer back

repliegue [re'pljeɣe] *nm (Mil)* withdrawal

repoblación [repoβla'θjon] *nf* repopulation; *(de río)* restocking; **repoblación forestal** reafforestation

repoblar [repo'βlar] *vt* to repopulate; *(con árboles)* to reafforest

repollito [repo'ʎito] *(cs) nm*: **~s de Bruselas** (Brussels) sprouts

repollo [re'poʎo] *nm* cabbage

reponer [repo'ner] *vt* to replace, put back; *(Teatro)* to revive; **reponerse** *vr* to recover; **~ que ...** to reply that ...

reportaje [repor'taxe] *nm* report, article

reportero, -a [repor'tero, a] *nm/f* reporter

reposacabezas [reposaka'βeθas] *nm inv* headrest

reposar [repo'sar] *vi* to rest, repose

reposera [repo'sera] *(RPL) nf* deck chair

reposición [reposi'θjon] *nf* replacement; *(Cine)*

remake

reposo [re'poso] nm rest

repostar [repos'tar] vt to replenish; (Auto) to fill up (with petrol (BRIT) o gasoline (US))

repostería [reposte'ria] nf confectioner's (shop)

represa [re'presa] nf dam; (lago artificial) lake, pool

represalia [repre'salja] nf reprisal

representación [representa'θjon] nf representation; (Teatro) performance; **representante** nmf representative; performer

representar [represen'tar] vt to represent; (Teatro) to perform; (edad) to look; **representarse** vr to imagine; **representativo, -a** adj representative

represión [repre'sjon] nf repression

reprimenda [repri'menda] nf reprimand, rebuke

reprimir [repri'mir] vt to repress

reprobar [repro'βar] vt to censure, reprove

reprochar [repro'tʃar] vt to reproach; **reproche** nm reproach

reproducción [reproðuk'θjon] nf reproduction

reproducir [reproðu'θir] vt to reproduce; **reproducirse** vr to breed; (situación) to recur

reproductor, a [reproðuk'tor, a] adj reproductive ▷ nm player; **reproductor de CD** CD player

reptil [rep'til] nm reptile

república [re'puβlika] nf republic; **República Dominicana** Dominican Republic; **republicano, -a** adj, nm republican

repudiar [repu'ðjar] vt to repudiate; (fe) to renounce

repuesto [re'pwesto] nm (pieza de recambio) spare (part); (abastecimiento) supply; **rueda de ~** spare wheel

repugnancia [repuɣ'nanθja] nf repugnance; **repugnante** adj repugnant, repulsive

repugnar [repuɣ'nar] vt to disgust

repulsa [re'pulsa] nf rebuff

repulsión [repul'sjon] nf repulsion, aversion; **repulsivo, -a** adj repulsive

reputación [reputa'θjon] nf reputation

requerir [reke'rir] vt (pedir) to ask, request; (exigir) to require; (llamar) to send for, summon

requesón [reke'son] nm cottage cheese

requete... [re'kete] prefijo extremely

réquiem ['rekjem] (pl ~s) nm requiem

requisito [reki'sito] nm requirement, requisite

res [res] nf beast, animal

resaca [re'saka] nf (de mar) undertow, undercurrent; (fam) hangover

resaltar [resal'tar] vi to project, stick out; (fig) to stand out

resarcir [resar'θir] vt to compensate; **resarcirse** vr to make up for

resbaladero [resβala'ðero] (MÉX) nm slide

resbaladizo, -a [resβala'ðiθo, a] adj slippery

resbalar [resβa'lar] vi to slip, slide; (fig) to slip (up); **resbalarse** vr to slip, slide; to slip (up); **resbalón** nm (acción) slip

rescatar [reska'tar] vt (salvar) to save, rescue; (objeto) to get back, recover; (cautivos) to ransom

rescate [res'kate] nm rescue; (de objeto) recovery; **pagar un ~** to pay a ransom

rescindir [resθin'dir] vt to rescind

rescisión [resθi'sjon] nf cancellation

resecar [rese'kar] vt to dry thoroughly; (Med) to cut out, remove; **resecarse** vr to dry up

reseco, -a [re'seko, a] adj very dry; (fig) skinny

resentido, -a [resen'tiðo, a] adj resentful

resentimiento [resenti'mjento] nm resentment, bitterness

resentirse [resen'tirse] vr (debilitarse: persona) to suffer; **~ de** (consecuencias) to feel the effects of; **~ de (o por) algo** to resent sth, be bitter about sth

reseña [re'seɲa] nf (cuenta) account; (informe) report; (Literatura) review

reseñar [rese'ɲar] vt to describe; (Literatura) to review

reserva [re'serβa] nf reserve; (reservación) reservation

reservado, -a [reser'βaðo, a] adj reserved; (retraído) cold, distant ▷ nm private room

reservar [reser'βar] vt (guardar) to keep; (habitación, entrada) to reserve; **reservarse** vr to save o.s.; (callar) to keep to o.s.

resfriado [resfri'aðo] nm cold; **resfriarse** vr to cool; (Med) to catch a cold

resguardar [resɣwar'ðar] vt to protect, shield; **resguardarse** vr: **~se de** to guard against; **resguardo** nm defence; (vale) voucher; (recibo) receipt, slip

residencia [resi'ðenθja] nf residence; **residencia de ancianos** residential home, old people's home; **residencia universitaria** hall of residence; **residencial** nf (urbanización) housing estate

residente [resi'ðente] adj, nmf resident

residir [resi'ðir] vi to reside, live; **~ en** to reside in, lie in

residuo [re'siðwo] nm residue

resignación [resiɣna'θjon] nf resignation; **resignarse** vr: **resignarse a o con** to resign o.s. to, be resigned to

resina [re'sina] nf resin

resistencia [resis'tenθja] nf (dureza) endurance, strength; (oposición, Elec) resistance; **resistente** adj strong, hardy; resistant

resistir [resis'tir] vt (soportar) to bear; (oponerse a) to resist, oppose; (aguantar) to put up with ▷ vi to resist; (aguantar) to last, endure; **resistirse** vr: **~se a** to refuse to, resist

resoluto, -a [reso'luto, a] adj resolute

resolver [resol'βer] vt to resolve; (solucionar) to solve, resolve; (decidir) to decide, settle; **resolverse** vr to make up one's mind

resonar [reso'nar] vi to ring, echo

resoplar [reso'plar] vi to snort; **resoplido** nm heavy breathing

resorte [re'sorte] nm (muelle) spring; (fig) lever

resortera [resor'tera] (MÉX) nf catapult

respaldar [respal'dar] vt to back (up), support; **respaldarse** vr to lean back; **~se con o en** (fig) to take one's stand on; **respaldo** nm (de sillón) back; (fig) support, backing

respectivo, -a [respek'tiβo, a] adj respective; **en lo ~a** with regard to

respecto [res'pekto] nm: **al ~** on this matter; **con ~ a, ~ de** with regard to, in relation to

respetable [respe'taβle] adj respectable

respetar [respe'tar] vt to respect; **respeto** nm respect; (acatamiento) deference; **respetos** nmpl respects; **respetuoso, -a** adj respectful

respingo [res'pingo] nm start, jump

respiración [respira'θjon] nf breathing; (Med) respiration; (ventilación) ventilation; **respiración asistida** artificial respiration (by machine)

respirar [respi'rar] vi to breathe; **respiratorio, -a** adj respiratory; **respiro** nm breathing; (fig: descanso)

resplue

resplandecer [resplande'θer] vi to shine;
resplandeciente adj resplendent, shining;
resplandor nm brilliance, brightness; (de luz, fuego)
blaze

responder [respon'der] vt to answer ▷ vi to answer;
(fig) to respond; (pey) to answer back; **~ de o por** to
answer for; **respondón, -ona** adj cheeky

responsabilidad [responsaβili'ðað] nf
responsibility

responsabilizarse [responsaβili'θarse] vr to make
o.s. responsible, take charge

responsable [respon'saβle] adj responsible

respuesta [res'pwesta] nf answer, reply

resquebrajar [reskeβra'xar] vt to crack, split;
resquebrajarse vr to crack, split

resquicio [res'kiθjo] nm chink, (hendedura) crack

resta [resta] nf (Mat) remainder

restablecer [restaβle'θer] vt to re-establish, restore;
restablecerse vr to recover

restante [res'tante] adj remaining; **lo ~** the
remainder

restar [res'tar] vt (Mat) to subtract; (fig) to take away
▷ vi to remain, be left

restauración [restaura'θjon] nf restoration

restaurante [restau'rante] nm restaurant

restaurar [restau'rar] vt to restore

restituir [restitu'ir] vt (devolver) to return, give back;
(rehabilitar) to restore

resto [resto] nm (residuo) rest, remainder; (apuesta)
stake; **restos** nmpl remains

restorán [resto'ran] nm (Lam) restaurant

restregar [restre'xar] vt to scrub, rub

restricción [restrik'θjon] nf restriction

restringir [restrin'xir] vt to restrict, limit

resucitar [resuθi'tar] vt, vi to resuscitate, revive

resuelto, -a [re'swelto, a] pp de **resolver** ▷ adj
resolute, determined

resultado [resul'taðo] nm result; (conclusión)
outcome; **resultante** adj resulting, resultant

resultar [resul'tar] vi (ser) to be; (llegar a ser) to turn
out to be; (salir bien) to turn out well; (Com) to amount
to; **~ de** to stem from; **me resulta difícil hacerlo** it's
difficult for me to do it

resumen [re'sumen] (pl **resúmenes**) nm summary,
résumé; **en ~** in short

resumir [resu'mir] vt to sum up; (cortar) to abridge,
cut down; (condensar) to summarize

resurgir [resur'xir] vi (reaparecer) to reappear

resurrección [resurre(k)'θjon] nf resurrection

retablo [re'taβlo] nm altarpiece

retaguardia [reta'xwarðja] nf rearguard

retahíla [reta'ila] nf series, string

retal [re'tal] nm remnant

retar [re'tar] vt to challenge; (desafiar) to defy, dare

retazo [re'taθo] nm snippet (BRIT), fragment

retención [reten'θjon] nf (tráfico) hold-up;
retención fiscal deduction for tax purposes

retener [rete'ner] vt (intereses) to withhold

reticente [reti'θente] adj (como) insinuating;
(postura) reluctant; **ser ~ a hacer algo** to be reluctant o
unwilling to do sth

retina [re'tina] nf retina

retintín [retin'tin] nm jangle, jingle

retirada [reti'raða] nf (Mil, refugio) retreat; (de dinero)
withdrawal; (de embajador) recall; **retirado, -a** adj

(lugar) remote; (vida) quiet; (jubilado) retired

retirar [reti'rar] vt to withdraw; (quitar) to remove;
(jubilar) to retire, pension off; **retirarse** vr to retreat,
withdraw; to retire; (acostarse) to retire, go to bed;
retiro nm retreat; retirement; (pago) pension

reto [reto] nm dare, challenge

retocar [reto'kar] vt (fotografía) to touch up, retouch

retoño [re'tono] nm sprout, shoot; (fig) offspring,
child

retoque [re'toke] nm retouching

retorcer [retor'θer] vt to twist; (manos, lavado) to
wring; **retorcerse** vr to become twisted; (mover el
cuerpo) to writhe

retorcido, -a [retor'θiðo, a] adj (persona) devious

retorcijón [retorθi'xon] (Lam) nm (tb: **~ de tripas**)
stomach cramp

retórica [re'torika] nf rhetoric; (pey) affectedness

retorno [re'torno] nm return

retortijón [retorti'xon] (ESP) nm (tb: **~ de tripas**)
stomach cramp

retozar [reto'θar] vi (juguetear) to frolic, romp; (saltar)
to gambol

retracción [retrak'θjon] nf retraction

retraerse [retra'erse] vr to retreat, withdraw;
retraído, -a adj shy, retiring; **retraimiento** nm
retirement; (timidez) shyness

retransmisión [retransmi'sjon] nf repeat
(broadcast)

retransmitir [retransmi'tir] vt (mensaje) to relay;
(TV etc) to repeat, retransmit; (: en vivo) to broadcast
live

retrasado, -a [retra'saðo, a] adj late; (Med) mentally
retarded; (país etc) backward, underdeveloped

retrasar [retra'sar] vt (demorar) to postpone, put off;
(retardar) to slow down ▷ vi (atrasarse) to be late; (reloj)
to be slow; (producción) to fall (off); (quedarse atrás) to
lag behind; **retrasarse** vr to be late; to be slow; to fall
(off); to lag behind

retraso [re'traso] nm (demora) delay; (lentitud)
slowness; (tardanza) lateness; (atraso) backwardness;
retrasos nmpl (Finanzas) arrears; **llegar con ~** to arrive
late; **retraso mental** mental deficiency

retratar [retra'tar] vt (Arte) to paint the portrait of;
(fotografiar) to photograph; (fig) to depict, describe;
retrato nm portrait; (fig) likeness; **retrato-robot**
(ESP) nm Identikit®

retrete [re'trete] nm toilet

retribuir [retri'βwir] vt (recompensar) to reward;
(pagar) to pay

retro... [retro] prefijo retro...

retroceder [retroθe'ðer] vi (echarse atrás) to move
back(wards); (fig) to back down

retroceso [retro'θeso] nm backward movement;
(Med) relapse; (fig) backing down

retrospectivo, -a [retrospek'tiβo, a] adj
retrospective

retrovisor [retroβi'sor] nm (tb: **espejo ~**) rear-view
mirror

retumbar [retum'bar] vi to echo, resound

reúma [re'uma], **reuma** [reuma] nm rheumatism

reunión [reu'njon] nf (asamblea) meeting; (fiesta)
party

reunir [reu'nir] vt (juntar) to reunite, join
(together); (recoger) to gather (together); (personas)
to get together; (cualidades) to combine; **reunirse** vr
(personas: en asamblea) to meet, gather

revalidar [reβali'ðar] vt (ratificar) to confirm, ratify

revalorizar [reβalori'θar] vt to revalue, reassess

revancha [re'βantʃa] nf revenge

revelación [reβela'θjon] nf revelation

revelado [reβe'laðo] nm developing

revelar [reβe'lar] vt to reveal; (Foto) to develop

reventa [re'βenta] nf (de entradas: para concierto) touting

reventar [reβen'tar] vt to burst, explode

reventón [reβen'ton] nm (Auto) blow-out (BRIT), flat (US)

reverencia [reβe'renθja] nf reverence; **reverenciar** vt to revere

reverendo, -a [reβe'rendo, a] adj reverend

reverente [reβe'rente] adj reverent

reversa [re'βersa] (MÉX, CAM) nf reverse (gear)

reversible [reβer'siβle] adj (prenda) reversible

reverso [re'βerso] nm back, other side; (de moneda) reverse

revertir [reβer'tir] vi to revert

revés [re'βes] nm back, wrong side; (fig) reverse, setback; (Deporte) backhand; **al ~** the wrong way round; (de arriba abajo) upside down; (ropa) inside out; **volver algo del ~** to turn sth round; (ropa) to turn sth inside out

revisar [reβi'sar] vt (examinar) to check; (texto etc) to revise; **revisión** nf revision; **revisión salarial** wage review

revisor, a [reβi'sor, a] nm/f inspector; (Ferro) ticket collector

revista [re'βista] nf magazine, review; (Teatro) revue; (inspección) inspection; **pasar - a** to review, inspect; **revista del corazón** magazine featuring celebrity gossip and real-life romance stories

revivir [reβi'βir] vi to revive

revolcarse [reβol'karse] vr to roll about

revoltijo [reβol'tixo] nm mess, jumble

revoltoso, -a [reβol'toso, a] adj (travieso) naughty, unruly

revolución [reβolu'θjon] nf revolution; **revolucionario, -a** adj, nm/f revolutionary

revólver [reβol'βer] vt (desordenar) to disturb, mess up; (mover) to move about ⊳ vi: **~ en** to go through, rummage (about) in; **revolverse** vr (volver contra) to turn on o against

revólver [re'βolβer] nm revolver

revuelo [re'βwelo] nm fluttering; (fig) commotion

revuelta [re'βwelta] nf (motín) revolt; (agitación) commotion

revuelto, -a [re'βwelto, a] pp de **revolver** ⊳ adj (mezclado) mixed-up, in disorder

rey [rei] nm king; **Día de R~es** Twelfth Night; **los R~es Magos** the Three Wise Men, the Magi

reyerta [re'jerta] nf quarrel, brawl

rezagado, -a [reθa'ɣaðo, a] nm/f straggler

rezar [re'θar] vi to pray; **~ con** (fam) to concern, have to do with; **rezo** nm prayer

rezumar [reθu'mar] vt to ooze

ría ['ria] nf estuary

riada [ri'aða] nf flood

ribera [ri'βera] nf (de río) bank; (: área) riverside

ribete [ri'βete] nm (de vestido) border; (fig) addition

ricino [ri'θino] nm: **aceite de ~** castor oil

rico, -a ['riko, a] adj rich; (adinerado) wealthy, rich; (lujoso) luxurious; (comida) delicious; (niño) lovely, cute ⊳ nm/f rich person

ridiculez [riðiku'leθ] nf absurdity

ridiculizar [riðikuli'θar] vt to ridicule

ridículo, -a [ri'ðikulo, a] adj ridiculous; **hacer el ~** to make a fool of o.s.; **poner a algn en ~** to make a fool of sb

riego ['rjexo] nm (aspersión) watering; (irrigación) irrigation; **riego sanguíneo** blood flow o circulation

riel [rjel] nm rail

rienda ['rjenda] nf rein; **dar ~ suelta a** to give free rein to

riesgo ['rjesxo] nm risk; **correr el ~ de** to run the risk of

rifa ['rifa] nf (lotería) raffle; **rifar** vt to raffle

rifle ['rifle] nm rifle

rigidez [rixi'ðeθ] nf rigidity, stiffness; (fig) strictness; **rígido, -a** adj rigid, stiff; strict, inflexible

rigor [ri'xor] nm strictness, rigour; (inclemencia) harshness; **de ~** de rigueur, essential; **riguroso, -a** adj rigorous; harsh; (severo) severe

rimar [ri'mar] vi to rhyme

rimbombante [rimbom'bante] adj pompous

rímel ['rimel] nm mascara

rímmel ['rimel] nm = **rímel**

rin [rin] (MÉX) nm (wheel) rim

rincón [rin'kon] nm corner (inside)

rinoceronte [rinoθe'ronte] nm rhinoceros

riña ['riɲa] nf (disputa) argument; (pelea) brawl

riñón [ri'ɲon] nm kidney

río etc ['rio] vb V **reír** ⊳ nm river; (fig) torrent, stream; **río abajo/arriba** downstream/upstream; **Río de la Plata** River Plate

rioja [ri'oxa] nm (vino) rioja (wine)

rioplatense [riopla'tense] adj of o from the River Plate region

riqueza [ri'keθa] nf wealth, riches pl; (cualidad) richness

risa ['risa] nf laughter; (una risa) laugh; **¡qué ~!** what a laugh!

risco ['risko] nm crag, cliff

ristra ['ristra] nf string

risueño, -a [ri'sweɲo, a] adj (sonriente) smiling; (contento) cheerful

ritmo ['ritmo] nm rhythm; **a ~ lento** slowly; **trabajar a ~ lento** to go slow; **ritmo cardíaco** heart rate

rito ['rito] nm rite

ritual [ri'twal] adj, nm ritual

rival [ri'βal] adj, nm/f rival; **rivalidad** nf rivalry; **rivalizar** vi: **rivalizar con** to rival, vie with

rizado, -a [ri'θaðo, a] adj curly ⊳ nm curls pl

rizar [ri'θar] vt to curl; **rizarse** vr (pelo) to curl; (agua) to ripple; **rizo** nm curl; ripple

RNE nf abr = **Radio Nacional de España**

robar [ro'βar] vt to rob; (objeto) to steal; (casa etc) to break into; (Naipes) to draw

roble ['roβle] nm oak; **robledal** nm oakwood

robo ['roβo] nm robbery, theft

robot [ro'βot] nm robot; **robot (de cocina)** (ESP) food processor

robustecer [roβuste'θer] vt to strengthen

robusto, -a [ro'βusto, a] adj robust, strong

roca ['roka] nf rock

roce ['roθe] nm (caricia) brush; (Tec) friction; (en la piel) graze; **tener ~ con** to be in close contact with

rociar [ro'θjar] vt to spray

rocín [ro'θin] nm nag, hack

rocío [ro'θio] nm dew

rocola [ro'kola] (LAM) nf jukebox

rocoso, -a [ro'koso, a] adj rocky

rodaballo [roða'baʎo] nm turbot

rodaja [ro'ðaxa] nf slice

rodaje [ro'ðaxe] nm (Cine) shooting, filming; (Auto): **en ~** running in

rodar [ro'ðar] vt (vehículo) to wheel (along); (escalera) to roll down; (viajar por) to travel (over) ▷ vi to roll; (coche) to go, run; (Cine) to shoot, film

rodear [roðe'ar] vt to surround ▷ vi to go round; **rodearse** vr: **~ de amigos** to surround o.s. with friends

rodeo [ro'ðeo] nm (ruta indirecta) detour; (evasión) evasion; (Deporte) rodeo; **hablar sin ~s** to come to the point, speak plainly

rodilla [ro'ðiʎa] nf knee; **de ~s** kneeling; **ponerse de ~s** to kneel (down)

rodillo [ro'ðiʎo] nm roller; (Culin) rolling-pin

roedor, a [roe'ðor, a] adj gnawing ▷ nm rodent

roer [ro'er] vt (masticar) to gnaw; (corroer, fig) to corrode

rogar [ro'xar] vt, vi (pedir) to ask for; (suplicar) to beg, plead; **se ruega no fumar** please do not smoke

rojizo, -a [ro'xiθo, a] adj reddish

rojo, -a ['roxo, a] adj, nm red; **al ~ vivo** red-hot

rol [rol] nm list, roll; (papel) role

rollito [ro'ʎito] nm (tb: **~ de primavera**) spring roll

rollizo, -a [ro'ʎiθo, a] adj (objeto) cylindrical; (persona) plump

rollo ['roʎo] nm roll; (de cuerda) coil; (madera) log; (ESP: pey) bore; **¡qué ~!** (ESP: fam) what a carry-on!

Roma ['roma] n Rome

romance [ro'manθe] nm (amoroso) romance; (Literatura) ballad

romano, -a [ro'mano, a] adj, nm/f Roman; **a la romana** in batter

romanticismo [romanti'θismo] nm romanticism

romántico, -a [ro'mantiko, a] adj romantic

rombo ['rombo] nm (Geom) rhombus

romería [rome'ria] nf (Rel) pilgrimage; (excursión) trip, outing

romero, -a [ro'mero, a] nm/f pilgrim ▷ nm rosemary

romo, -a ['romo, a] adj blunt; (fig) dull

rompecabezas [rompeka'βeθas] nm inv riddle, puzzle; (juego) jigsaw (puzzle)

rompehuelgas [rompe'welxas] (LAM) nm inv strikebreaker, scab

rompeolas [rompe'olas] nm inv breakwater

romper [rom'per] vt to break; (hacer pedazos) to smash; (papel, tela etc) to tear, rip ▷ vi (olas) to break; (sol, diente) to break through; **romperse** vr to break; **~ un contrato** to break a contract; **~ a** (empezar a) to start (suddenly) to; **~ a llorar** to burst into tears; **~ con algn** to fall out with sb

ron [ron] nm rum

roncar [ron'kar] vi to snore

ronco, -a ['ronko, a] adj (afónico) hoarse; (áspero) raucous

ronda ['ronda] nf (gen) round; (patrulla) patrol; **rondar** vt to patrol ▷ vi to patrol; (fig) to prowl round

ronquido [ron'kiðo] nm snore, snoring

ronronear [ronrone'ar] vi to purr

roña ['roɲa] nf (Veterinaria) mange; (mugre) dirt, grime; (óxido) rust

roñoso, -a [ro'ɲoso, a] adj (mugriento) filthy; (tacaño)

mean

ropa ['ropa] nf clothes pl, clothing; **ropa blanca** linen; **ropa de cama** bed linen; **ropa de color** coloureds pl; **ropa interior** underwear; **ropa sucia** dirty washing; **ropaje** nm gown, robes pl

ropero [ro'pero] nm linen cupboard; (guardarropa) wardrobe

rosa ['rosa] adj pink ▷ nf rose

rosado, -a [ro'saðo, a] adj pink ▷ nm rosé

rosal [ro'sal] nm rosebush

rosario [ro'sarjo] nm (Rel) rosary; **rezar el ~** to say the rosary

rosca ['roska] nf (de tornillo) thread; (de humo) coil, spiral; (pan, postre) ring-shaped roll/pastry

rosetón [rose'ton] nm rosette; (Arq) rose window

rosquilla [ros'kiʎa] nf doughnut-shaped fritter

rostro ['rostro] nm (cara) face

rotativo, -a [rota'tiβo, a] adj rotary

roto, -a ['roto, a] pp de **romper** ▷ adj broken

rotonda [ro'tonda] nf roundabout

rótula ['rotula] nf kneecap; (Tec) ball-and-socket joint

rotulador [rotula'ðor] nm felt-tip pen

rótulo ['rotulo] nm heading, title; label; (letrero) sign

rotundamente [rotunda'mente] adv (negar) flatly; (responder, afirmar) emphatically; **rotundo, -a** adj round; (enfático) emphatic

rotura [ro'tura] nf (acto) breaking; (Med) fracture

rozadura [roθa'ðura] nf abrasion, graze

rozar [ro'θar] vt (frotar) to rub; (arañar) to scratch; (tocar ligeramente) to shave, touch lightly; **rozarse** vr to rub (together); **~se con** (fam) to rub shoulders with

rte. abr (= remite, remitente) sender

RTVE nf abr = **Radiotelevisión Española**

rubí [ru'βi] nm ruby; (de reloj) jewel

rubio, -a ['ruβjo, a] adj fair-haired, blond(e) ▷ nm/f blond/blonde; **tabaco ~** Virginia tobacco

rubor [ru'βor] nm (sonrojo) blush; (timidez) bashfulness; **ruborizarse** vr to blush

rúbrica ['ruβrika] nf (de la firma) flourish; **rubricar** vt (firmar) to sign with a flourish; (concluir) to sign and seal

rudimentario, -a [ruðimen'tarjo, a] adj rudimentary

rudo, -a ['ruðo, a] adj (sin pulir) unpolished; (grosero) coarse; (violento) violent; (sencillo) simple

rueda ['rweða] nf wheel; (círculo) ring, circle; (rodaja) slice, round; **rueda de auxilio** (RPL) spare tyre; **rueda delantera/trasera/de repuesto** front/back/spare wheel; **rueda de prensa** press conference; **rueda gigante** (LAM) big (BRIT) o Ferris (US) wheel

ruedo ['rweðo] nm (círculo) circle; (Taur) arena, bullring

ruego etc ['rwexo] vb V **rogar** ▷ nm request

rugby ['ruxβi] nm rugby

rugido [ru'xiðo] nm roar

rugir [ru'xir] vi to roar

rugoso, -a [ru'xoso, a] adj (arrugado) wrinkled; (áspero) rough; (desigual) ridged

ruido ['rwiðo] nm noise; (sonido) sound; (alboroto) racket, row; (escándalo) commotion, rumpus; **ruidoso, -a** adj noisy, loud; (fig) sensational

ruin [rwin] adj contemptible, mean

ruina ['rwina] nf (ruin; (colapso) collapse; (de persona) ruin, downfall

ruinoso, -a [rwi'noso, a] adj ruinous; (destartalado) dilapidated, tumbledown; (Com) disastrous

ruiseñor [rwise'ɲor] nm nightingale
rulero [ru'lero] (RPL) nm roller
ruleta [ru'leta] nf roulette
rulo ['rulo] nm (para el pelo) curler
Rumanía [ruma'nia] nf Rumania
rumba ['rumba] nf rumba
rumbo ['rumbo] nm (ruta) route, direction; (ángulo de dirección) course, bearing; (fig) course of events; **ir con ~ a** to be heading for
rumiante [ru'mjante] nm ruminant
rumiar [ru'mjar] vt to chew; (fig) to chew over ▷ vi to chew the cud
rumor [ru'mor] nm (ruido sordo) low sound; (murmuración) murmur, buzz; **rumorearse** vr: **se rumorea que ...** it is rumoured that ...
rupestre [ru'pestre] adj rock cpd
ruptura [rup'tura] nf rupture
rural [ru'ral] adj rural
Rusia ['rusja] nf Russia; **ruso, -a** adj, nm/f Russian
rústico, -a ['rustiko, a] adj rustic; (ordinario) coarse, uncouth ▷ nm/f yokel
ruta ['ruta] nf route
rutina [ru'tina] nf routine

S

S abr (= santo, a) St; (= sur) S
s. abr (= siglo) C.; (= siguiente) foll
S.A. abr (= Sociedad Anónima) Ltd. (BRIT), Inc. (US)
sábado ['saβaðo] nm Saturday
sábana ['saβana] nf sheet
sabañón [saβa'ɲon] nm chilblain
saber [sa'βer] vt to know; (llegar a conocer) to find out, learn; (tener capacidad de) to know how to ▷ vi: **~ a** to taste of, taste like ▷ nm knowledge, learning; **a ~** namely; **¿sabes conducir/nadar?** can you drive/swim?; **¿sabes francés?** do you speak French?; **~ de memoria** to know by heart; **hacer ~ algo a algn** to inform sb of sth, let sb know sth
sabiduría [saβiðu'ria] nf (conocimientos) wisdom; (instrucción) learning
sabiendas [sa'βjendas]: **a ~** adv knowingly
sabio, -a ['saβjo, a] adj (docto) learned; (prudente) wise, sensible
sabor [sa'βor] nm taste, flavour; **saborear** vt to taste, savour; (fig) to relish
sabotaje [saβo'taxe] nm sabotage
sabré etc vb V **saber**
sabroso, -a [sa'βroso, a] adj tasty; (fig: fam) racy, salty
sacacorchos [saka'kortʃos] nm inv corkscrew
sacapuntas [saka'puntas] nm inv pencil sharpener
sacar [sa'kar] vt to take out; (fig: extraer) to get (out); (quitar) to remove, get out; (hacer salir) to bring out; (conclusión) to draw; (novela etc) to publish, bring out; (ropa) to take off; (obra) to make; (premio) to receive; (entradas) to get; (Tenis) to serve; **~ adelante** (niño) to bring up; (negocio) to carry on, go on with; **~ a algn a bailar** to get sb up to dance; **~ una foto** to take a photo; **~ la lengua** to stick out one's tongue; **~ buenas/malas notas** to get good/bad marks
sacarina [saka'rina] nf saccharin(e)
sacerdote [saθer'ðote] nm priest
saciar [sa'θjar] vt (hambre, sed) to satisfy; **saciarse** vr (de comida) to get full up
saco ['sako] nm bag; (grande) sack; (su contenido) bagful; (LAM: chaqueta) jacket; **saco de dormir** sleeping bag
sacramento [sakra'mento] nm sacrament

sacrificar [sakrifi'kar] vt to sacrifice; **sacrificio** nm sacrifice

sacristía [sakris'tia] nf sacristy

sacudida [saku'ðiða] nf (agitación) shake, shaking; (sacudimiento) jolt, bump; **sacudida eléctrica** electric shock

sacudir [saku'ðir] vt to shake; (golpear) to hit

Sagitario [saxi'tarjo] nm Sagittarius

sagrado, -a [sa'ɣraðo, a] adj sacred, holy

Sáhara [ˈsaara] nm: **el ~** the Sahara (desert)

sal [sal] vb V **salir** ▷ nf salt; **sales de baño** bath salts

sala [ˈsala] nf room; (tb: **~ de estar**) living room; (Teatro) house, auditorium; (de hospital) ward; **sala de espera** waiting room; **sala de estar** living room; **sala de fiestas** dance hall

salado, -a [sa'laðo, a] adj salty; (fig) witty, amusing; **agua salada** salt water

salar [sa'lar] vt to salt, add salt to

salario [sa'larjo] nm wage, pay

salchicha [sal'tʃitʃa] nf (pork) sausage; **salchichón** nm (salami-type) sausage

saldo [ˈsaldo] nm (pago) settlement; (de una cuenta) balance; (lo restante) remnant(s) (pl), remainder; (de móvil) credit; **saldos** nmpl (en tienda) sale

saldré etc vb V **salir**

salero [sa'lero] nm salt cellar

salgo etc vb V **salir**

salida [sa'liða] nf (puerta etc) exit, way out; (acto) leaving, going out; (de tren, Aviac) departure; (Tec) output, production; (fig) way out; (Com) opening; (Geo, Informát) outlet; (de gas) escape; **calle sin ~** cul-de-sac; **salida de baño** (RPL) bathrobe; **salida de emergencia/incendios** emergency exit/fire escape

salir [sa'lir] vi **1** (partir: tb: **salir de**) to leave; **Juan ha salido** Juan is out; **salió de la cocina** he came out of the kitchen

2 (aparecer) to appear; (disco, libro) to come out; **anoche salió en la tele** she appeared o was on TV last night; **salió en todos los periódicos** it was in all the papers

3 (resultar): **la muchacha nos salió muy trabajadora** the girl turned out to be a very hard worker; **la comida te ha salido exquisita** the food was delicious; **sale muy caro** it's very expensive

4: **salirle a uno algo: la entrevista que hice me salió bien/mal** the interview I did went o turned out well/badly

5: **salir adelante: no sé como haré para salir adelante** I don't know how I'll get by

salirse vr (líquido) to spill; (animal) to escape

saliva [sa'liβa] nf saliva

salmo [ˈsalmo] nm psalm

salmón [sal'mon] nm salmon

salmonete [salmo'nete] nm red mullet

salón [sa'lon] nm (de casa) living room, lounge; (muebles) lounge suite; **salón de baile** dance hall; **salón de belleza** beauty parlour

salpicadera [salpika'ðera] (MÉX) nf mudguard (BRIT), fender (US)

salpicadero [salpika'ðero] nm (Auto) dashboard

salpicar [salpi'kar] vt (rociar) to sprinkle, spatter; (esparcir) to scatter

salpicón [salpi'kon] nm (tb: **~ de marisco**) seafood salad

salsa [ˈsalsa] nf sauce; (con carne asada) gravy; (fig) spice

saltamontes [salta'montes] nm inv grasshopper

saltar [sal'tar] vt to jump (over), leap (over); (dejar de lado) to skip, miss out ▷ vi to jump, leap; (pelota) to bounce; (al aire) to fly up; (quebrarse) to break; (al agua) to dive; (fig) to explode, blow up

salto [ˈsalto] nm jump, leap; (al agua) dive; **salto de agua** waterfall; **salto de altura/longitud** high/long jump

salud [sa'luð] nf health; **¡(a su) ~!** cheers!, good health!; **saludable** adj (de buena salud) healthy; (provechoso) good, beneficial

saludar [salu'ðar] vt to greet; (Mil) to salute; **saludo** nm greeting; **"saludos"** (en carta) "best wishes", "regards"

salvación [salβa'θjon] nf salvation; (rescate) rescue

salvado [sal'βaðo] nm bran

salvaje [sal'βaxe] adj wild; (tribu) savage

salvamanteles [salβaman'teles] nm inv table mat

salvamento [salβa'mento] nm rescue

salvapantallas [salβapan'taʎas] nm inv screen saver

salvar [sal'βar] vt (rescatar) to save, rescue; (resolver) to overcome, resolve; (cubrir distancias) to cover, travel; (hacer excepción) to except, exclude; (barco) to salvage

salvavidas [salβa'βiðas] adj inv: **bote/chaleco ~** lifeboat/life jacket

salvo, -a [ˈsalβo, a] adj safe ▷ adv except (for), save; **a ~** out of danger; **~ que** unless

san [san] adj saint; **S~ Juan** St John

sanar [sa'nar] vt (herida) to heal; (persona) to cure ▷ vi (persona) to get well, recover; (herida) to heal

sanatorio [sana'torjo] nm sanatorium

sanción [san'θjon] nf sanction

sancochado, -a [sanko'tʃado, a] (MÉX) adj (Culin) underdone, rare

sandalia [san'dalja] nf sandal

sandía [san'dia] nf watermelon

sandwich [ˈsandwitʃ] (pl **~s, ~es**) nm sandwich

sanfermines [sanfer'mines] nmpl festivities in celebration of San Fermín (Pamplona)

sangrar [san'grar] vt, vi to bleed; **sangre** nf blood

sangría [san'gria] nf sangria, sweetened drink of red wine with fruit

sangriento, -a [san'grjento, a] adj bloody

sanguíneo, -a [san'gineo, a] adj blood cpd

sanidad [sani'ðað] nf (tb: **~ pública**) public health

San Isidro [sani'sidro] nm patron saint of Madrid

sanitario, -a [sani'tarjo, a] adj health cpd; **sanitarios** nmpl toilets (BRIT), washroom (US)

sano, -a [ˈsano, a] adj healthy; (sin daños) sound; (comida) wholesome; (entero) whole, intact; **~ y salvo** safe and sound

Santiago [san'tjaxo] nm: **~ (de Chile)** Santiago

santiamén [santja'men] nm: **en un ~** in no time at all

santidad [santi'ðað] nf holiness, sanctity

santiguarse [santi'ɣwarse] vr to make the sign of the cross

santo, -a [ˈsanto, a] adj holy; (fig) wonderful, miraculous ▷ nm/f saint ▷ nm saint's day; **~ y seña** password

santuario [san'twarjo] nm sanctuary, shrine

sapo [ˈsapo] nm toad

saque ['sake] nm (Tenis) service, serve; (Fútbol) throw-in; **saque de esquina** corner (kick)

saquear [sake'ar] vt (Mil) to sack; (robar) to loot, plunder; (fig) to ransack

sarampión [saram'pjon] nm measles sg

sarcástico, -a [sar'kastiko, a] adj sarcastic

sardina [sar'ðina] nf sardine

sargento [sar'xento] nm sergeant

sarmiento [sar'mjento] nm (Bot) vine shoot

sarna ['sarna] nf itch; (Med) scabies

sarpullido [sarpu'ʎiðo] nm (Med) rash

sarro ['sarro] nm (en dientes) tartar, plaque

sartén [sar'ten] nf frying pan

sastre ['sastre] nm tailor; **sastrería** nf (arte) tailoring; (tienda) tailor's (shop)

Satanás [sata'nas] nm Satan

satélite [sa'telite] nm satellite

sátira ['satira] nf satire

satisfacción [satisfak'θjon] nf satisfaction

satisfacer [satisfa'θer] vt to satisfy; (gastos) to meet; (pérdida) to make good; **satisfacerse** vr to satisfy o.s., be satisfied; (vengarse) to take revenge; **satisfecho, -a** adj satisfied; (contento) content(ed), happy; (tb: **satisfecho de sí mismo**) self-satisfied, smug

saturar [satu'rar] vt to saturate; **saturarse** vr (mercado, aeropuerto) to reach saturation point

sauce ['sauθe] nm willow; **sauce llorón** weeping willow

sauna ['sauna] nf sauna

savia ['saβja] nf sap

saxofón [sakso'fon] nm saxophone

sazonar [saθo'nar] vt to ripen; (Culin) to flavour, season

scooter [e'skuter] (ESP) nf scooter

Scotch® [skotʃ] (LAM) nm Sellotape® (BRIT), Scotch tape® (US)

SE abr (= sudeste) SE

○ **PALABRA CLAVE**

se [se] pron **1** (reflexivo: sg: m) himself; (: f) herself; (: pl) themselves; (: cosa) itself; (: de Vd) yourself; (: de Vds) yourselves; **se está preparando** she's preparing herself

2 (con complemento indirecto) to him; to her; to them; to it; to you; **a usted se lo dije ayer** I told you yesterday; **se compró un sombrero** he bought himself a hat; **se rompió la pierna** he broke his leg

3 (uso recíproco) each other, one another; **se miraron (el uno al otro)** they looked at each other o one another

4 (en oraciones pasivas): **se han vendido muchos libros** a lot of books have been sold

5 (impers): **se dice que ...** people say that ..., it is said that ...; **allí se come muy bien** the food there is very good, you can eat very well there

sé etc [se] vb V **saber; ser**

sea etc vb V **ser**

sebo ['seβo] nm fat, grease

secador [seka'ðor] nm: **~ de pelo** hair-dryer

secadora [seka'ðora] nf tumble dryer

secar [se'kar] vt to dry; **secarse** vr to dry (off); (río, planta) to dry up

sección [sek'θjon] nf section

seco, -a ['seko, a] adj dry; (carácter) cold; (respuesta)

sharp, curt; **parar en ~** to stop dead; **decir algo a secas** to say sth curtly

secretaría [sekreta'ria] nf secretariat

secretario, -a [sekre'tarjo, a] nm/f secretary

secreto, -a [se'kreto, a] adj secret; (persona) secretive ▷ nm secret; (calidad) secrecy

secta ['sekta] nf sect

sector [sek'tor] nm sector

secuela [se'kwela] nf consequence

secuencia [se'kwenθja] nf sequence

secuestrar [sekwes'trar] vt to kidnap; (bienes) to seize, confiscate; **secuestro** nm kidnapping; seizure, confiscation

secundario, -a [sekun'darjo, a] adj secondary

sed [seð] nf thirst; **tener ~** to be thirsty

seda ['seða] nf silk

sedal [se'ðal] nm fishing line

sedán [se'ðan] (LAM) nm saloon (BRIT), sedan (US)

sedante [se'ðante] nm sedative

sede ['seðe] nf (de gobierno) seat; (de compañía) headquarters pl; **Santa S~** Holy See

sedentario, -a [seðen'tarjo, a] adj sedentary

sediento, -a [se'ðjento, a] adj thirsty

sedimento [seði'mento] nm sediment

seducción [seðuk'θjon] nf seduction

seducir [seðu'θir] vt to seduce; (cautivar) to charm, fascinate; (atraer) to attract; **seductor, a** adj seductive; charming, fascinating; attractive ▷ nm/f seducer

segar [se'xar] vt (mies) to reap, cut; (hierba) to mow, cut

seglar [se'xlar] adj secular, lay

seguida [se'xiða] nf: **en ~** at once, right away

seguido, -a [se'xiðo, a] adj (continuo) continuous, unbroken; (recto) straight ▷ adv (directo) straight (on); (después) after; (LAM) often; **~s** consecutive, successive; **5 días ~s** 5 days running, 5 days in a row

seguir [se'xir] vt to follow; (venir después) to follow on, come after; (proseguir) to continue; (perseguir) to chase, pursue ▷ vi (gen) to follow; (continuar) to continue, carry o go on; **seguirse** vr to follow; **sigo sin comprender** I still don't understand; **sigue lloviendo** it's still raining

según [se'xun] prep according to ▷ adv: **¿irás? - ~** are you going? - it all depends ▷ conj as; **~ caminamos** while we walk

segundo, -a [se'xundo, a] adj second ▷ nm second ▷ nf second meaning; **de segunda mano** second-hand; **segunda (clase)** second class; **segunda (marcha)** (Auto) second (gear)

seguramente [sexura'mente] adv surely; (con certeza) for sure, with certainty

seguridad [sexuri'ðað] nf safety; (del estado, de casa etc) security; (certidumbre) certainty; (confianza) confidence; (estabilidad) stability; **seguridad social** social security

seguro, -a [se'xuro, a] adj (cierto) sure, certain; (fiel) trustworthy; (libre de peligro) safe; (bien defendido, firme) secure ▷ adv for sure, certainly ▷ nm (Com) insurance; **seguro contra terceros/a todo riesgo** third party/comprehensive insurance; **seguros sociales** social security sg

seis [seis] num six

seísmo [se'ismo] nm tremor, earthquake

selección [selek'θjon] nf selection; **seleccionar** vt to pick, choose, select

selectividad [selektiβi'ðað] (ESP) nf university entrance examination

selecto, -a [se'lekto, a] adj select, choice; (escogido) selected

sellar [se'ʎar] vt (documento oficial) to seal; (pasaporte, visado) to stamp

sello ['seʎo] nm stamp; (precinto) seal

selva ['selβa] nf (bosque) forest, woods pl; (jungla) jungle

semáforo [se'maforo] nm (Auto) traffic lights pl; (Ferro) signal

semana [se'mana] nf week; **entre ~** during the week; **Semana Santa** Holy Week; **semanal** adj weekly; **semanario** nm weekly magazine

sembrar [sem'brar] vt to sow; (objetos) to sprinkle, scatter about; (noticias etc) to spread

semejante [seme'xante] adj (parecido) similar ▷ nm fellow man, fellow creature; **~s** alike, similar; **nunca hizo cosa ~** he never did any such thing; **semejanza** nf similarity, resemblance

semejar [seme'xar] vi to seem like, resemble; **semejarse** vr to look alike, be similar

semen ['semen] nm semen

semestral [semes'tral] adj half-yearly, bi-annual

semicírculo [semi'θirkulo] nm semicircle

semidesnatado, -a [semiðesna'taðo, a] adj semi-skimmed

semifinal [semifi'nal] nf semifinal

semilla [se'miʎa] nf seed

seminario [semi'narjo] nm (Rel) seminary; (Escol) seminar

sémola ['semola] nf semolina

senado [se'naðo] nm senate; **senador, a** nm/f senator

sencillez [senθi'ʎeθ] nf simplicity; (de persona) naturalness; **sencillo, -a** adj simple; natural, unaffected

senda ['senda] nf path, track

senderismo [sende'rismo] nm hiking

sendero [sen'dero] nm path, track

sendos, -as ['sendos, as] adj pl: **les dio ~ golpes** he hit both of them

senil [se'nil] adj senile

seno ['seno] nm (Anat) bosom, bust; (fig) bosom; **~s** breasts

sensación [sensa'θjon] nf sensation; (sentido) sense; (sentimiento) feeling; **sensacional** adj sensational

sensato, -a [sen'sato, a] adj sensible

sensible [sen'sible] adj sensitive; (apreciable) perceptible, appreciable; (pérdida) considerable; **sensiblero, -a** adj sentimental

sensitivo, -a [sensi'tiβo, a] adj sense cpd

sensorial [senso'rjal] adj sensory

sensual [sen'swal] adj sensual

sentada [sen'taða] nf sitting; (protesta) sit-in

sentado, -a [sen'taðo, a] adj: **estar ~** to sit, be sitting (down); **dar por ~** to take for granted, assume

sentar [sen'tar] vt to set, seat; (fig) to establish ▷ vi (vestido) to suit; (alimento): **~ bien/mal a** to agree/ disagree with; **sentarse** vr (persona) to sit, sit down; (los depósitos) to settle

sentencia [sen'tenθja] nf (máxima) maxim, saying; (Jur) sentence; **sentenciar** vt to sentence

sentido, -a [sen'tiðo, a] adj (pérdida) regrettable; (carácter) sensitive ▷ nm sense; (sentimiento) feeling; (significado) sense, meaning; (dirección) direction; **mi**

más ~ pésame my deepest sympathy; **tener ~** to make sense; **sentido común** common sense; **sentido del humor** sense of humour; **sentido único** one-way (street)

sentimental [sentimen'tal] adj sentimental; **vida ~** love life

sentimiento [senti'mjento] nm feeling

sentir [sen'tir] vt to feel; (percibir) to perceive, sense; (lamentar) to regret, be sorry for ▷ vi (tener la sensación) to feel; (lamentarse) to feel sorry ▷ nm opinion, judgement; **~se bien/mal** to feel well/ill; **lo siento** I'm sorry

seña ['seɲa] nf sign; (Mil) password; **señas** nfpl (dirección) address sg; **señas personales** personal description sg

señal [se'ɲal] nf sign; (síntoma) symptom; (Ferro, Tel) signal; (marca) mark; (Com) deposit; **en ~ de** as a token o sign of; **señalar** vt to mark; (indicar) to point out, indicate

señor [se'ɲor] nm (hombre) man; (caballero) gentleman; (dueño) owner, master; (trato: antes de nombre propio) Mr; (: hablando directamente) sir; **muy ~ mío** Dear Sir; **el ~ alcalde/presidente** the mayor/president

señora [se'ɲora] nf (dama) lady; (trato: antes de nombre propio) Mrs; (: hablando directamente) madam; (esposa) wife; **Nuestra S~** Our Lady

señorita [seɲo'rita] nf (con nombre y/o apellido) Miss; (mujer joven) young lady

señorito [seɲo'rito] nm young gentleman; (pey) rich kid

sepa etc vb V **saber**

separación [separa'θjon] nf separation; (división) division; (hueco) gap

separar [sepa'rar] vt to separate; (dividir) to divide; **separarse** vr (parte) to come away; (partes) to come apart; (persona) to leave, go away; (matrimonio) to separate; **separatismo** nm separatism

sepia ['sepja] nf cuttlefish

septentrional [septentrjo'nal] adj northern

septiembre [sep'tjembre] nm September

séptimo, -a ['septimo, a] adj, num seventh

sepulcral [sepul'kral] adj (fig: silencio, atmósfera) deadly; **sepulcro** nm tomb, grave

sepultar [sepul'tar] vt to bury; **sepultura** nf (acto) burial; (tumba) grave, tomb

sequía [se'kia] nf drought

séquito ['sekito] nm (de rey etc) retinue; (seguidores) followers pl

---

○ **PALABRA CLAVE**

ser [ser] vi **1** (descripción) to be; **es médica/muy alta** she's a doctor/very tall; **la familia es de Cuzco** his (o her etc) family is from Cuzco; **soy Ana** (Tel) Ana speaking o here

2 (propiedad): **es de Joaquín** it's Joaquín's, it belongs to Joaquín

3 (horas, fechas, números): **es la una** it's one o'clock; **son las seis y media** it's half-past six; **es el 1 de junio** it's the first of June; **somos/son seis** there are six of us/them

4 (en oraciones pasivas): **ha sido descubierto ya** it's already been discovered

5: **es de esperar que ...** it is to be hoped o I etc hope that ...

6 (*locuciones con subj*): **o sea** that is to say; **sea él sea su hermana** either him or his sister
7: a no ser por él ... but for him ...
8: a no ser que: a no ser que tenga uno ya unless he's got one already ▷ *nm* being; **ser humano** human being

sereno, -a [se'reno, a] *adj* (*persona*) calm, unruffled; (*el tiempo*) fine, settled; (*ambiente*) calm, peaceful ▷ *nm* night watchman
serial [se'rjal] *nm* serial
serie [serje] *nf* series; (*cadena*) sequence, succession; **fuera de ~** out of order; (*fig*) special, out of the ordinary; **fabricación en ~** mass production
seriedad [serje'ðað] *nf* seriousness; (*formalidad*) reliability; **serio, -a** *adj* serious; reliable, dependable; grave, serious; **en serio** *adv* seriously
serigrafía [serixra'fia] *nf* silk-screen printing
sermón [ser'mon] *nm* (*Rel*) sermon
seropositivo, -a [seroposi'tiβo] *adj* HIV positive
serpentear [serpente'ar] *vi* to wriggle; (*camino, río*) to wind, snake
serpentina [serpen'tina] *nf* streamer
serpiente [ser'pjente] *nf* snake; **serpiente de cascabel** rattlesnake
serranía [serra'nia] *nf* mountainous area
serrar [se'rrar] *vt* = **aserrar**
serrín [se'rrin] *nm* sawdust
serrucho [se'rrutʃo] *nm* saw
service ['serβis] (*RPL*) *nm* (*Auto*) service
servicio [ser'βiθjo] *nm* service; (*LAM Auto*) service; **servicios** *nmpl* (*ESP*) toilet(s); **servicio incluido** service charge included; **servicio militar** military service
servidumbre [serβi'ðumbre] *nf* (*sujeción*) servitude; (*criados*) servants *pl*, staff
servil [ser'βil] *adj* servile
servilleta [serβi'ʎeta] *nf* serviette, napkin
servir [ser'βir] *vt* to serve ▷ *vi* to serve; (*tener utilidad*) to be of use, be useful; **servirse** *vr* to serve o help o.s.; **~se de algo** to make use of sth, use sth; **sírvase pasar** please come in
sesenta [se'senta] *num* sixty
sesión [se'sjon] *nf* (*Pol*) session, sitting; (*Cine*) showing
seso ['seso] *nm* brain; **sesudo, -a** *adj* sensible, wise
seta ['seta] *nf* mushroom; **seta venenosa** toadstool
setecientos, -as [sete'θjentos, as] *adj, num* seven hundred
setenta [se'tenta] *num* seventy
seto ['seto] *nm* hedge
severo, -a [se'βero, a] *adj* severe
Sevilla [se'βiʎa] *n* Seville; **sevillano, -a** *adj* of o from Seville ▷ *nm/f* native o inhabitant of Seville
sexo ['sekso] *nm* sex
sexto, -a ['seksto, a] *adj, num* sixth
sexual [sek'swal] *adj* sexual; **vida ~** sex life
si [si] *conj* if ▷ *nm* (*Mús*) B; **me pregunto ~** ... I wonder of whether ...
sí [si] *adv* yes ▷ *nm* consent ▷ *pron* (*uso impersonal*) oneself; (*sg: m*) himself; (: *f*) herself; (: *de cosa*) itself; (*de usted*) yourself; (*pl*) themselves; (*de ustedes*) yourselves; (*recíproco*) each other; **él no quiere pero yo ~** he doesn't want to but I do; **ella ~ vendrá** she will certainly come, she is sure to come; **claro que ~** of

course; **creo que ~** I think so
siamés, -esa [sja'mes, esa] *adj, nm/f* Siamese
SIDA ['siða] *nm abr* (= *Síndrome de Inmunodeficiencia Adquirida*) AIDS
siderúrgico, -a [siðe'rurxico, a] *adj* iron and steel *cpd*
sidra ['siðra] *nf* cider
siembra ['sjembra] *nf* sowing
siempre ['sjempre] *adv* always; (*todo el tiempo*) all the time; **~ que** (*cada vez*) whenever; (*dado que*) provided that; **como ~** as usual; **para ~** for ever
sien [sjen] *nf* temple
siento *etc* ['sjento] *vb* V **sentar**; **sentir**
sierra ['sjerra] *nf* (*Tec*) saw; (*cadena de montañas*) mountain range
siervo, -a ['sjerβo, a] *nm/f* slave
siesta ['sjesta] *nf* siesta, nap; **echar la ~** to have an afternoon nap o a siesta
siete ['sjete] *num* seven
sifón [si'fon] *nm* syphon
sigla ['siɣla] *nf* abbreviation; acronym
siglo ['siɣlo] *nm* century; (*fig*) age
significado [siɣnifi'kaðo] *nm* (*de palabra etc*) meaning
significar [siɣnifi'kar] *vt* to mean, signify; (*notificar*) to make known, express
signo ['siɣno] *nm* sign; **signo de admiración** *o* **exclamación** exclamation mark; **signo de interrogación** question mark
sigo *etc vb* V **seguir**
siguiente [si'ɣjente] *adj* next, following
siguió *etc vb* V **seguir**
sílaba ['silaβa] *nf* syllable
silbar [sil'βar] *vt, vi* to whistle; **silbato** *nm* whistle; **silbido** *nm* whistle, whistling
silenciador [silenθja'ðor] *nm* silencer
silenciar [silen'θjar] *vt* (*persona*) to silence; (*escándalo*) to hush up; **silencio** *nm* silence, quiet; **silencioso, -a** *adj* silent, quiet
silla ['siʎa] *nf* (*asiento*) chair; (*tb:* **~ de montar**) saddle; **silla de ruedas** wheelchair
sillón [si'ʎon] *nm* armchair, easy chair
silueta [si'lweta] *nf* silhouette; (*de edificio*) outline; (*figura*) figure
silvestre [sil'βestre] *adj* wild
simbólico, -a [sim'boliko, a] *adj* symbolic(al)
simbolizar [simboli'θar] *vt* to symbolize
símbolo ['simbolo] *nm* symbol
similar [simi'lar] *adj* similar
simio ['simjo] *nm* ape
simpatía [simpa'tia] *nf* liking; (*afecto*) affection; (*amabilidad*) kindness; **simpático, -a** *adj* nice, pleasant; kind
simpatizante [simpati'θante] *nmf* sympathizer
simpatizar [simpati'θar] *vi:* **~ con** to get on well with
simple ['simple] *adj* simple; (*elemental*) simple, easy; (*mero*) mere; (*puro*) pure, sheer ▷ *nmf* simpleton; **simpleza** *nf* simpleness; (*necedad*) silly thing; **simplificar** *vt* to simplify
simposio [sim'posjo] *nm* symposium
simular [simu'lar] *vt* to simulate
simultáneo, -a [simul'taneo, a] *adj* simultaneous
sin [sin] *prep* without; **la ropa está ~ lavar** the clothes are unwashed; **~ que** without; **~ embargo** however, still

sinagoga [sina'soxa] *nf* synagogue
sinceridad [sinθeri'ðað] *nf* sincerity; **sincero, -a** *adj* sincere
sincronizar [sinkroni'θar] *vt* to synchronize
sindical [sindi'kal] *adj* union *cpd*, trade-union *cpd*; **sindicalista** *adj*, *nmf* trade unionist
sindicato [sindi'kato] *nm* (de trabajadores) trade(s) union; (de negociantes) syndicate
síndrome ['sindrome] *nm* (Med) syndrome; **síndrome de abstinencia** (Med) withdrawal symptoms; **síndrome de la clase turista** (Med) economy-class syndrome
sinfín [sin'fin] *nm*: **un ~ de** a great many, no end of
sinfonía [sinfo'nia] *nf* symphony
singular [singu'lar] *adj* singular; (fig) outstanding, exceptional; (raro) peculiar, odd
siniestro, -a [si'njestro, a] *adj* sinister ▷ *nm* (accidente) accident
sinnúmero [sin'numero] *nm* = **sinfín**
sino [sino] *nm* fate, destiny ▷ *conj* (pero) but; (salvo) except, save
sinónimo, -a [si'nonimo, a] *adj* synonymous ▷ *nm* synonym
síntesis ['sintesis] *nf* synthesis; **sintético, -a** *adj* synthetic
sintió *vb* V **sentir**
síntoma ['sintoma] *nm* symptom
sintonía [sinto'nia] *nf* (Radio, Mús: de programa) tuning; **sintonizar** *vt* (Radio: emisora) to tune (in)
sinvergüenza [simber'ɣwenθa] *nmf* rogue, scoundrel; **¡es un ~!** he's got a nerve!
siquiera [si'kjera] *conj* even if, even though ▷ *adv* at least; **ni ~** not even
Siria ['sirja] *nf* Syria
sirviente, -a [sir'βjente, a] *nm/f* servant
sirvo *etc vb* V **servir**
sistema [sis'tema] *nm* system; (método) method; **sistema educativo** education system; **sistemático, -a** *adj* systematic
sitiar [si'tjar] *vt* to besiege, lay siege to
sitio ['sitjo] *nm* (lugar) place; (espacio) room, space; (Mil) siege; **sitio de taxis** (MÉX: parada) taxi stand o rank (BRIT); **sitio web** (Inform) website
situación [sitwa'θjon] *nf* situation, position; (estatus) position, standing
situado, -a [situ'aðo] *adj* situated, placed
situar [si'twar] *vt* to place, put; (edificio) to locate, situate
slip [slip] *nm* pants *pl*, briefs *pl*
smoking ['smokin, es'mokin] (*pl* ~s) *nm* dinner jacket (BRIT), tuxedo (US)
SMS *nm* (mensaje) text message, SMS message
snob [es'nob] = **esnob**
SO *abr* (= suroeste) SW
sobaco [so'βako] *nm* armpit
sobar [so'βar] *vt* (ropa) to rumple; (comida) to play around with
soberanía [soβera'nia] *nf* sovereignty; **soberano, -a** *adj* sovereign; (fig) supreme ▷ *nm/f* sovereign
soberbia [so'βerβja] *nf* pride; haughtiness, arrogance; magnificence
soberbio, -a [so'βerβjo, a] *adj* (orgulloso) proud; (altivo) arrogant; (estupendo) magnificent, superb
sobornar [soβor'nar] *vt* to bribe; **soborno** *nm* bribe
sobra [so'βra] *nf* excess, surplus; **sobras** *nfpl* left-overs, scraps; **de ~** surplus, extra; **tengo de ~** I've more

than enough; **sobrado, -a** *adj* (más que suficiente) more than enough; (superfluo) excessive; **sobrante** *adj* remaining, extra ▷ *nm* surplus, remainder
sobrar [so'βrar] *vt* to exceed, surpass ▷ *vi* (tener de más) to be more than enough; (quedar) to remain, be left (over)
sobrasada [soβra'saða] *nf* pork sausage spread
sobre ['soβre] *prep* (gen) on; (encima) on (top of); (por encima de, arriba de) over, above; (más que) more than; (además) in addition to, besides; (alrededor de) about ▷ *nm* envelope; **~ todo** above all
sobrecama [soβre'kama] *nf* bedspread
sobrecargar [soβrekar'ɣar] *vt* (camión) to overload; (Com) to surcharge
sobredosis [soβre'ðosis] *nf inv* overdose
sobreentender [soβre(e)nten'der] *vt* to deduce, infer; **sobreentenderse** *vr*: **se sobreentiende que ...** it is implied that ...
sobrehumano, -a [soβreu'mano, a] *adj* superhuman
sobrellevar [soβreʎe'βar] *vt* to bear, endure
sobremesa [soβre'mesa] *nf*: **durante la ~** after dinner
sobrenatural [soβrenatu'ral] *adj* supernatural
sobrenombre [soβre'nombre] *nm* nickname
sobrepasar [soβrepa'sar] *vt* to exceed, surpass
sobreponerse [soβrepo'nerse] *vr*: **~ a** to overcome
sobresaliente [soβresa'ljente] *adj* outstanding, excellent
sobresalir [soβresa'lir] *vi* to project, jut out; (fig) to stand out, excel
sobresaltar [soβresal'tar] *vt* (asustar) to scare, frighten; (sobrecoger) to startle; **sobresalto** *nm* (movimiento) start; (susto) scare; (turbación) sudden shock
sobretodo [soβre'toðo] *nm* overcoat
sobrevenir [soβreβe'nir] *vi* (ocurrir) to happen (unexpectedly); (resultar) to follow, ensue
sobrevivir [soβreβi'βir] *vi* to survive
sobrevolar [soβreβo'lar] *vt* to fly over
sobriedad [soβrje'ðað] *nf* sobriety, soberness; (moderación) moderation, restraint
sobrino, -a [so'βrino, a] *nm/f* nephew/niece
sobrio, -a ['soβrjo, a] *adj* sober; (moderado) moderate, restrained
socarrón, -ona [soka'rron, ona] *adj* (sarcástico) sarcastic, ironic(al)
socavón [soka'βon] *nm* (hoyo) hole
sociable [so'θjaβle] *adj* (persona) sociable, friendly; (animal) social
social [so'θjal] *adj* social; (Com) company *cpd*
socialdemócrata [soθjalde'mokrata] *nmf* social democrat
socialista [soθja'lista] *adj*, *nm* socialist
socializar [soθjali'θar] *vt* to socialize
sociedad [soθje'ðað] *nf* society; (Com) company; **sociedad anónima** limited company; **sociedad de consumo** consumer society
socio, -a [so'θjo, a] *nm/f* (miembro) member; (Com) partner
sociología [soθjolo'xia] *nf* sociology; **sociólogo, -a** *nm/f* sociologist
socorrer [soko'rrer] *vt* to help; **socorrista** *nmf* first aider; (en piscina, playa) lifeguard; **socorro** *nm* (ayuda) help, aid; (Mil) relief; **¡socorro!** help!
soda ['soða] *nf* (sosa) soda; (bebida) soda (water)

sofá [so'fa] (*pl* **~s**) *nm* sofa, settee; **sofá-cama** *nm* studio couch; sofa bed

sofocar [sofo'kar] *vt* to suffocate; (*apagar*) to smother, put out; **sofocarse** *vr* to suffocate; (*fig*) to blush, feel embarrassed; **sofoco** *nm* suffocation; embarrassment

sofreír [sofre'ir] *vt* (*Culin*) to fry lightly

soga ['soɣa] *nf* rope

sois *etc vb* V **ser**

soja ['soxa] *nf* soya

sol [sol] *nm* sun; (*luz*) sunshine, sunlight; (*Mús*) G; **hace ~** it's sunny

solamente [sola'mente] *adv* only, just

solapa [so'lapa] *nf* (*de chaqueta*) lapel; (*de libro*) jacket

solapado, -a [sola'paðo, a] *adj* (*intenciones*) underhand; (*gestos, movimiento*) sly

solar [so'lar] *adj* solar, sun *cpd*

soldado [sol'daðo] *nm* soldier; **soldado raso** private

soldador [solda'ðor] *nm* soldering iron; (*persona*) welder

soldar [sol'dar] *vt* to solder, weld

soleado, -a [sole'aðo, a] *adj* sunny

soledad [sole'ðað] *nf* solitude; (*estado infeliz*) loneliness

solemne [so'lemne] *adj* solemn

soler [so'ler] *vi* to be in the habit of, be accustomed to; **suele salir a las ocho** she usually goes out at eight o'clock

solfeo [sol'feo] *nm* solfa

solicitar [soliθi'tar] *vt* (*permiso*) to ask for, seek; (*puesto*) to apply for; (*votos*) to canvass for; (*atención*) to attract

solícito, -a [so'liθito, a] *adj* (*diligente*) diligent; (*cuidadoso*) careful; **solicitud** *nf* (*calidad*) great care; (*petición*) request; (*a un puesto*) application

solidaridad [soliðari'ðað] *nf* solidarity; **solidario, -a** *adj* (*participación*) joint, common; (*compromiso*) mutually binding

sólido, -a [so'liðo, a] *adj* solid

soliloquio [soli'lokjo] *nm* soliloquy

solista [so'lista] *nmf* soloist

solitario, -a [soli'tarjo, a] *adj* (*persona*) lonely, solitary; (*lugar*) lonely, desolate ▷ *nm/f* (*recluso*) recluse; (*en la sociedad*) loner ▷ *nm* solitaire

sollozar [soλo'θar] *vi* to sob; **sollozo** *nm* sob

solo, -a ['solo, a] *adj* (*único*) single, sole; (*sin compañía*) alone; (*solitario*) lonely; **hay una sola dificultad** there is just one difficulty; **a solas** alone, by oneself

sólo ['solo] *adv* only, just

solomillo [solo'miʎo] *nm* sirloin

soltar [sol'tar] *vt* (*dejar ir*) to let go of; (*desprender*) to unfasten, loosen; (*librar*) to release, set free; (*risa etc*) to let out

soltero, -a [sol'tero, a] *adj* single, unmarried ▷ *nm/f* bachelor/single woman; **solterón, -ona** *nm/f* old bachelor/spinster

soltura [sol'tura] *nf* looseness, slackness; (*de los miembros*) agility, ease of movement; (*en el hablar*) fluency, ease

soluble [so'luβle] *adj* (*Quím*) soluble; (*problema*) solvable; **~ en agua** soluble in water

solución [solu'θjon] *nf* solution; **solucionar** *vt* (*problema*) to solve; (*asunto*) to settle, resolve

solventar [solβen'tar] *vt* (*pagar*) to settle, pay; (*resolver*) to resolve; **solvente** *adj* (*Econ: empresa, persona*) solvent

sombra ['sombra] *nf* shadow; (*como protección*) shade; **sombras** *nfpl* (*oscuridad*) darkness *sg*, shadows; **tener buena/mala ~** to be lucky/unlucky

sombrero [som'brero] *nm* hat

sombrilla [som'briʎa] *nf* parasol, sunshade

sombrío, -a [som'brio, a] *adj* (*oscuro*) dark; (*triste*) sombre, sad; (*persona*) gloomy

someter [some'ter] *vt* (*país*) to conquer; (*persona*) to subject to one's will; (*informe*) to present, submit; **someterse** *vr* to give in, yield, submit; **~ a** to subject to

somier [so'mjer] (*pl* **~s**) *n* spring mattress

somnífero [som'nifero] *nm* sleeping pill

somos *vb* V **ser**

son [son] *vb* V **ser** ▷ *nm* sound

sonaja [so'naxa] (*MÉX*) *nf* = **sonajero**

sonajero [sona'xero] *nm* (baby's) rattle

sonambulismo [sonambu'lismo] *nm* sleepwalking; **sonámbulo, -a** *nm/f* sleepwalker

sonar [so'nar] *vt* to ring ▷ *vi* to sound; (*hacer ruido*) to make a noise; (*pronunciarse*) to be sounded, be pronounced; (*ser conocido*) to sound familiar; (*campana*) to ring; (*reloj*) to strike, chime; **sonarse** *vr* **~se (las narices)** to blow one's nose; **me suena ese nombre** that name rings a bell

sonda ['sonda] *nf* (*Náut*) sounding; (*Tec*) bore, drill; (*Med*) probe

sondear [sonde'ar] *vt* to sound; to bore (into), drill; to probe, sound; (*fig*) to sound out; **sondeo** *nm* sounding; boring, drilling; (*fig*) poll, enquiry

sonido [so'niðo] *nm* sound

sonoro, -a [so'noro, a] *adj* sonorous; (*resonante*) loud, resonant

sonreír [sonre'ir] *vi* to smile; **sonreírse** *vr* to smile; **sonriente** *adj* smiling; **sonrisa** *nf* smile

sonrojarse [sonro'xarse] *vr* to blush, go red; **sonrojo** *nm* blush

soñador, a [soɲa'ðor, a] *nm/f* dreamer

soñar [so'ɲar] *vt, vi* to dream; **~ con** to dream about o of

soñoliento, -a [soɲo'ljento, a] *adj* sleepy, drowsy

sopa ['sopa] *nf* soup

soplar [so'plar] *vt* (*polvo*) to blow away, blow off; (*inflar*) to blow up; (*vela*) to blow out ▷ *vi* to blow; **soplo** *nm* blow, puff; (*de viento*) puff, gust

soplón, -ona [so'plon, ona] (*fam*) *nm/f* (*niño*) telltale; (*de policía*) grass (*fam*)

soporífero [sopo'rifero] *nm* sleeping pill

soportable [sopor'taβle] *adj* bearable

soportar [sopor'tar] *vt* to bear, carry; (*fig*) to bear, put up with; **soporte** *nm* support; (*fig*) pillar, support

soprano [so'prano] *nf* soprano

sorber [sor'βer] *vt* (*chupar*) to sip; (*absorber*) to soak up, absorb

sorbete [sor'βete] *nm* iced fruit drink

sorbo ['sorβo] *nm* (*trago: grande*) gulp, swallow; (*: pequeño*) sip

sordera [sor'ðera] *nf* deafness

sórdido, -a ['sorðiðo, a] *adj* dirty, squalid

sordo, -a ['sorðo, a] *adj* (*persona*) deaf ▷ *nm/f* deaf person; **sordomudo, -a** *adj* deaf and dumb

sorna ['sorna] *nf* sarcastic tone

soroche [so'rotʃe] (*CAM*) *nm* mountain sickness

sorprendente [sorpren'dente] *adj* surprising

sorprender [sorpren'der] *vt* to surprise; **sorpresa** *nf* surprise

sortear [sorte'ar] vt to draw lots for; (*rifar*) to raffle; (*dificultad*) to avoid; **sorteo** nm (*en lotería*) draw; (*rifa*) raffle

sortija [sor'tixa] nf ring; (*rizo*) ringlet, curl

sosegado, -a [sose'ɣaðo, a] adj quiet, calm

sosiego [so'sjeɣo] nm quiet(ness), calm(ness)

soso, -a ['soso, a] adj (*Culin*) tasteless; (*aburrido*) dull, uninteresting

sospecha [sos'petʃa] nf suspicion; **sospechar** vt to suspect; **sospechoso, -a** adj suspicious; (*testimonio, opinión*) suspect ▷ nm/f suspect

sostén [sos'ten] nm (*apoyo*) support; (*sujetador*) bra; (*alimentación*) sustenance, food

sostener [soste'ner] vt to support; (*mantener*) to keep up, maintain; (*alimentar*) to sustain, keep going; **sostenerse** vr to support o.s.; (*seguir*) to continue, remain; **sostenido, -a** adj continuous, sustained; (*prolongado*) prolonged

sotana [so'tana] nf (*Rel*) cassock

sótano ['sotano] nm basement

soy [soi] vb V **ser**

soya ['soja] (*LAM*) nf soya (*BRIT*), soy (*US*)

Sr. abr (= *Señor*) Mr

Sra. abr (= *Señora*) Mrs

Sres. abr (= *Señores*) Messrs

Srta. abr (= *Señorita*) Miss

Sta. abr (= *Santa*) St

Sto. abr (= *Santo*) St

su [su] pron (*de él*) his; (*de ella*) her; (*de una cosa*) its; (*de ellos, ellas*) their; (*de usted, ustedes*) your

suave ['swaβe] adj gentle; (*superficie*) smooth; (*trabajo*) easy; (*música, voz*) soft, sweet; **suavidad** nf gentleness; smoothness; softness, sweetness; **suavizante** nm (*de ropa*) softener; (*del pelo*) conditioner; **suavizar** vt to soften; (*quitar la aspereza*) to smooth (out)

subasta [su'βasta] nf auction; **subastar** vt to auction (off)

subcampeón, -ona [subkampe'on, ona] nm/f runner-up

subconsciente [subkon'sθjente] adj, nm subconscious

subdesarrollado, -a [subðesarro'ʎaðo, a] adj underdeveloped

subdesarrollo [subðesa'rroʎo] nm underdevelopment

subdirector, -a [subðirek'tor, a] nm/f assistant director

súbdito, -a ['suβðito, a] nm/f subject

subestimar [subesti'mar] vt to underestimate, underrate

subida [su'βiða] nf (*de montaña etc*) ascent, climb; (*de precio*) rise, increase; (*pendiente*) slope, hill

subir [su'βir] vt (*objeto*) to raise, lift up; (*cuesta, calle*) to go up; (*colina, montaña*) to climb; (*precio*) to raise, put up ▷ vi to go up, come up; (*a un coche*) to get in; (*a un autobús, tren o avión*) to get on, board; (*precio*) to rise, go up; (*río, marea*) to rise; **subirse** vr to get up, climb

súbito, -a ['suβito, a] adj (*repentino*) sudden; (*imprevisto*) unexpected

subjetivo, -a [subxe'tiβo, a] adj subjective

sublevar [suβle'βar] vt to rouse to revolt; **sublevarse** vr to revolt, rise

sublime [su'βlime] adj sublime

submarinismo [submari'nismo] nm scuba diving

submarino, -a [subma'rino, a] adj underwater

▷ nm submarine

subnormal [subnor'mal] adj subnormal ▷ nmf subnormal person

subordinado, -a [suβorði'naðo, a] adj, nm/f subordinate

subrayar [suβra'jar] vt to underline

subsanar [subsa'nar] vt to rectify

subsidio [suβ'siðjo] nm (*ayuda*) aid, financial help; (*subvención*) subsidy, grant; (*de enfermedad, paro etc*) benefit, allowance

subsistencia [subsis'tenθja] nf subsistence

subsistir [subsis'tir] vi to subsist; (*sobrevivir*) to survive, endure

subte ['suβte] (*RPL*) nm underground (*BRIT*), subway (*US*)

subterráneo, -a [suβte'rraneo, a] adj underground, subterranean ▷ nm underpass, underground passage

subtítulo [suβ'titulo] nm (*Cine*) subtitle

suburbio [su'βurβjo] nm (*barrio*) slum quarter

subvención [subβen'θjon] nf (*Econ*) subsidy, grant; **subvencionar** vt to subsidize

sucedáneo, -a [suθe'ðaneo, a] adj substitute ▷ nm substitute (food)

suceder [suθe'ðer] vt, vi to happen; (*seguir*) to succeed, follow; **lo que sucede es que ...** the fact is that ...; **sucesión** nf succession; (*serie*) sequence, series

sucesivamente [suθesiβa'mente] adv: **y así ~** and so on

sucesivo, -a [suθe'siβo, a] adj successive, following; **en lo ~** in future, from now on

suceso [su'θeso] nm (*hecho*) event, happening; (*incidente*) incident

suciedad [suθje'ðað] nf (*estado*) dirtiness; (*mugre*) dirt, filth

sucio, -a ['suθjo, a] adj dirty

suculento, -a [suku'lento, a] adj succulent

sucumbir [sukum'bir] vi to succumb

sucursal [sukur'sal] nf branch (office)

sudadera [suða'ðera] nf sweatshirt

Sudáfrica [suð'afrika] nf South Africa

Sudamérica [suða'merika] nf South America; **sudamericano, -a** adj, nm/f South American

sudar [su'ðar] vt, vi to sweat

sudeste [su'ðeste] nm south-east

sudoeste [suðo'este] nm south-west

sudor [su'ðor] nm sweat; **sudoroso, -a** adj sweaty, sweating

Suecia ['sweθja] nf Sweden; **sueco, -a** adj Swedish ▷ nm/f Swede

suegro, -a ['sweɣro, a] nm/f father-/mother-in-law

suela ['swela] nf sole

sueldo ['sweldo] nm pay, wage(s) (*pl*)

suele etc vb V **soler**

suelo ['swelo] nm (*tierra*) ground; (*de casa*) floor

suelto, -a ['swelto, a] adj loose; (*libre*) free; (*separado*) detached; (*ágil*) quick, agile ▷ nm (*loose*) change, small change

sueñito [swe'ɲito] (*LAM*) nm nap

sueño etc ['sweɲo] vb V **soñar** ▷ nm sleep; (*somnolencia*) sleepiness, drowsiness; (*lo soñado, fig*) dream; **tener ~** to be sleepy

suero ['swero] nm (*Med*) serum; (*de leche*) whey

suerte ['swerte] nf (*fortuna*) luck; (*azar*) chance; (*destino*) fate, destiny; (*especie*) sort, kind; **tener ~** to be lucky

suéter ['sweter] nm sweater

suficiente [sufi'θjente] adj enough, sufficient ▷ nm (Escol) pass

sufragio [su'fraxjo] nm (voto) vote; (derecho de voto) suffrage

sufrido, -a [su'friðo, a] adj (persona) tough; (paciente) long-suffering, patient

sufrimiento [sufri'mjento] nm (dolor) suffering

sufrir [su'frir] vt (padecer) to suffer; (soportar) to bear, put up with; (apoyar) to hold up, support ▷ vi to suffer

sugerencia [suxe'renθja] nf suggestion

sugerir [suxe'rir] vt to suggest; (sutilmente) to hint

sugestión [suxes'tjon] nf suggestion; (sutil) hint; **sugestionar** vt to influence

sugestivo, -a [suxes'tiβo, a] adj stimulating; (fascinante) fascinating

suicida [sui'θiða] adj suicidal ▷ nmf suicidal person; (muerto) suicide, person who has committed suicide; **suicidarse** vr to commit suicide, kill o.s.; **suicidio** nm suicide

Suiza ['swiθa] nf Switzerland; **suizo, -a** adj, nm/f Swiss

sujeción [suxe'θjon] nf subjection

sujetador [suxeta'ðor] nm (sostén) bra

sujetar [suxe'tar] vt (fijar) to fasten; (detener) to hold down; **sujetarse** vr to subject o.s.; **sujeto, -a** adj fastened, secure ▷ nm subject; (individuo) individual; **sujeto a** subject to

suma ['suma] nf (cantidad) total, sum; (de dinero) sum; (acto) adding (up), addition; **en ~** in short

sumamente [suma'mente] adv extremely, exceedingly

sumar [su'mar] vt to add (up) ▷ vi to add up

sumergir [sumer'xir] vt to submerge; (hundir) to sink

suministrar [suminis'trar] vt to supply, provide; **suministro** nm supply; (acto) supplying, providing

sumir [su'mir] vt to sink, submerge; (fig) to plunge

sumiso, -a [su'miso, a] adj submissive, docile

sumo, -a ['sumo, a] adj great, extreme; (autoridad) highest, supreme

suntuoso, -a [sun'twoso, a] adj sumptuous, magnificent

supe etc vb V **saber**

super... [super] prefijo super..., over...

superbueno, -a [super'bweno, a] adj great, fantastic

súper ['super] nf (gasolina) four-star (petrol)

superar [supe'rar] vt (sobreponerse a) to overcome; (rebasar) to surpass, do better than; (pasar) to go beyond; **superarse** vr to excel o.s.

superficial [superfi'θjal] adj superficial; (medida) surface cpd, of the surface

superficie [super'fiθje] nf surface; (área) area

superfluo, -a [su'perflwo, a] adj superfluous

superior [supe'rjor] adj (piso, clase) upper; (temperatura, número, nivel) higher; (mejor: calidad, producto) superior, better ▷ nmf superior; **superioridad** nf superiority

supermercado [supermer'kaðo] nm supermarket

superponer [superpo'ner] vt to superimpose

superstición [supersti'θjon] nf superstition; **supersticioso, -a** adj superstitious

supervisar [superβi'sar] vt to supervise

supervivencia [superβi'βenθja] nf survival

superviviente [superβi'βjente] adj surviving

supiera etc vb V **saber**

suplantar [suplan'tar] vt to supplant

suplemento [suple'mento] nm supplement

suplente [su'plente] adj, nm substitute

supletorio, -a [suple'torjo, a] adj supplementary ▷ nm supplement; **teléfono ~** extension

súplica ['suplika] nf request; (Jur) petition

suplicar [supli'kar] vt (cosa) to beg (for), plead for; (persona) to beg, plead with

suplicio [su'pliθjo] nm torture

suplir [su'plir] vt (compensar) to make good, make up for; (reemplazar) to replace, substitute ▷ vi: **~ a** to take the place of, substitute for

supo etc vb V **saber**

suponer [supo'ner] vt to suppose; **suposición** nf supposition

suprimir [supri'mir] vt to suppress; (derecho, costumbre) to abolish; (palabra etc) to delete; (restricción) to cancel, lift

supuesto, -a [su'pwesto, a] pp de **suponer** ▷ adj (hipotético) supposed ▷ nm assumption, hypothesis; **~ que** since; **por ~** of course

sur [sur] nm south

surcar [sur'kar] vt to plough; **surco** nm (en metal, disco) groove; (Agr) furrow

surgir [sur'xir] vi to arise, emerge; (dificultad) to come up, crop up

suroeste [suro'este] nm south-west

surtido, -a [sur'tiðo, a] adj mixed, assorted ▷ nm (selección) selection, assortment; (abastecimiento) supply, stock; **surtidor** nm (tb: **surtidor de gasolina**) petrol pump (BRIT), gas pump (US)

surtir [sur'tir] vt to supply, provide ▷ vi to spout, spurt

susceptible [susθep'tiβle] adj susceptible; (sensible) sensitive; **~ de** capable of

suscitar [susθi'tar] vt to cause, provoke; (interés, sospechas) to arouse

suscribir [suskri'βir] vt (firmar) to sign; (respaldar) to subscribe to, endorse; **suscribirse** vr to subscribe; **suscripción** nf subscription

susodicho, -a [suso'ðitʃo, a] adj above-mentioned

suspender [suspen'der] vt (objeto) to hang (up), suspend; (trabajo) to stop, suspend; (Escol) to fail; (interrumpir) to suspend; (atrasar) to postpone

suspense [sus'pense] (ESP) nm suspense; **película/ novela de ~** thriller

suspensión [suspen'sjon] nf suspension; (fig) stoppage, suspension

suspenso, -a [sus'penso, a] adj hanging, suspended; (ESP Escol) failed ▷ nm (ESP Escol) fail; **película o novela de ~** (LAM) thriller; **quedar o estar en ~** to be pending

suspicaz [suspi'kaθ] adj suspicious, distrustful

suspirar [suspi'rar] vi to sigh; **suspiro** nm sigh

sustancia [sus'tanθja] nf substance

sustento [sus'tento] nm support; (alimento) sustenance, food

sustituir [sustitu'ir] vt to substitute, replace; **sustituto, -a** nm/f substitute, replacement

susto ['susto] nm fright, scare

sustraer [sustra'er] vt to remove, take away; (Mat) to subtract

susurrar [susu'rrar] vi to whisper; **susurro** nm whisper

sutil [su'til] adj (aroma, diferencia) subtle; (tenue) thin;

(inteligencia, persona) sharp
suyo, -a ['sujo, a] (con artículo o después del verbo
ser) adj (de él) his; (de ella) hers; (de ellos, ellas) theirs;
(de Ud, Uds) yours; **un amigo ~** a friend of his (o hers o
theirs o yours)

Tabacalera [taβaka'lera] nf Spanish state tobacco
monopoly
tabaco [ta'βako] nm tobacco; (ESP: fam) cigarettes pl
tabaquería [tabake'ria] (LAM) nf tobacconist's
(shop) (BRIT), smoke shop (US); **tabaquero, -a** (LAM)
nm/f tobacconist
taberna [ta'βerna] nf bar, pub (BRIT)
tabique [ta'βike] nm partition (wall)
tabla ['taβla] nf (de madera) plank; (estante) shelf; (de
vestido) pleat; (Arte) panel; **tablas** nfpl: **estar o quedar
en ~s** to draw; **tablado** nm (plataforma) platform;
(Teatro) stage
tablao [ta'βlao] nm (tb: **~ flamenco**) flamenco show
tablero [ta'βlero] nm (de madera) plank, board; (de
ajedrez, damas) board; **tablero de mandos** (LAM Auto)
dashboard
tableta [ta'βleta] nf (Med) tablet; (de chocolate) bar
tablón [ta'βlon] nm (de suelo) plank; (de techo) beam;
tablón de anuncios notice (BRIT) o bulletin (US) board
tabú [ta'βu] nm taboo
taburete [taβu'rete] nm stool
tacaño, -a [ta'kaɲo, a] adj mean
tacha ['tatʃa] nf flaw; (Tec) stud; **tachar** vt (borrar) to
cross out; **tachar de** to accuse of
tacho ['tatʃo] nm (cs) (balde) bucket; **tacho de la
basura** rubbish bin (BRIT), trash can (US)
taco ['tako] nm (Billar) cue; (de billetes) book; (cs: de
zapato) heel; (tarugo) peg; (palabrota) swear word
tacón [ta'kon] nm heel; **de ~ alto** high-heeled
táctica ['taktika] nf tactics pl
táctico, -a ['taktiko, a] adj tactical
tacto ['takto] nm touch; (fig) tact
tajada [ta'xaða] nf slice
tajante [ta'xante] adj sharp
tajo ['taxo] nm (corte) cut; (Geo) cleft
tal [tal] adj such ▷ pron (persona) someone, such a
one; (cosa) something, such a thing ▷ adv: **~ como**
(igual) just as ▷ conj: **con ~ de que** provided that; **~
cual** (como es) just as it is; **~ vez** perhaps; **~ como** such
as; **~ para cual** (dos iguales) two of a kind; **¿qué ~?** how
are things?; **¿qué ~ te gusta?** how do you like it?
taladrar [tala'ðrar] vt to drill; **taladro** nm drill
talante [ta'lante] nm (humor) mood; (voluntad) will,

willingness

talar [ta'lar] *vt* to fell, cut down; (*devastar*) to devastate

talco ['talko] *nm* (*polvos*) talcum powder

talento [ta'lento] *nm* talent; (*capacidad*) ability

TALGO ['talɣo] (ESP) *nm abr* (= *tren articulado ligero Goicoechea-Oriol*) = HST (BRIT)

talismán [talis'man] *nm* talisman

talla ['taʎa] *nf* (*estatura, fig, Med*) height, stature; (*palo*) measuring rod; (*Arte*) carving; (*medida*) size

tallar [ta'ʎar] *vt* (*madera*) to carve; (*metal etc*) to engrave; (*medir*) to measure

tallarines [taʎa'rines] *nmpl* noodles

talle ['taʎe] *nm* (*Anat*) waist; (*fig*) appearance

taller [ta'ʎer] *nm* (*Tec*) workshop; (*de artista*) studio

tallo ['taʎo] *nm* (*de planta*) stem; (*de hierba*) blade; (*brote*) shoot

talón [ta'lon] *nm* (*Anat*) heel; (*Com*) counterfoil; (*cheque*) cheque (BRIT), check (US)

talonario [talo'narjo] *nm* (*de cheques*) chequebook (BRIT), checkbook (US); (*de recibos*) receipt book

tamaño, -a [ta'maɲo, a] *adj* (*tan grande*) such a big; (*tan pequeño*) such a small ▷ *nm* size; **de ~ natural** full-size

tamarindo [tama'rindo] *nm* tamarind

tambalearse [tambale'arse] *vr* (*persona*) to stagger; (*vehículo*) to sway

también [tam'bjen] *adv* (*igualmente*) also, too, as well; (*además*) besides

tambor [tam'bor] *nm* drum; (*Anat*) eardrum; **tambor del freno** brake drum

tamizar [tami'θar] *vt* to sieve

tampoco [tam'poko] *adv* nor, neither; **yo ~ lo compré** I didn't buy it either

tampón [tam'pon] *nm* tampon

tan [tan] *adv* so; **~ es así que ...** so much so that ...

tanda ['tanda] *nf* (*gen*) series; (*turno*) shift

tangente [tan'xente] *nf* tangent

tangerina [tanxe'rina] (LAM) *nf* tangerine

tangible [tan'xiβle] *adj* tangible

tanque ['tanke] *nm* (*cisterna, Mil*) tank; (*Auto*) tanker

tantear [tante'ar] *vt* (*calcular*) to reckon (up); (*medir*) to take the measure of; (*probar*) to test, try out; (*tomar la medida: persona*) to take the measurements of; (*situación*) to weigh up; (*persona: opinión*) to sound out ▷ *vi* (*Deporte*) to score; **tanteo** *nm* (*cálculo*) (rough) calculation; (*prueba*) test, trial; (*Deporte*) scoring

tanto, -a ['tanto, a] *adj* (*cantidad*) so much, as much ▷ *adv* (*cantidad*) so much, as much; (*tiempo*) so long, as long ▷ *conj*: **en ~ que** while ▷ *nm* (*suma*) certain amount; (*proporción*) so much; (*punto*) point; (*gol*) goal; **un ~ perezoso** somewhat lazy ▷ *pron*: **cada uno paga ~** each one pays so much; **~s so** many, as many; **20 y ~s** 20-odd; **hasta ~ (que)** until such time as; **~ tú como yo** both you and I; **~ como eso** as much as that; **~ más ... cuanto que** all the more ... because; **~ mejor/peor** so much the better/the worse; **~ si viene como si va** whether he comes or whether he goes; **~ es así que** so much so that; **por (lo) ~** therefore; **entre ~** meanwhile; **estar al ~** to be up to date; **me he vuelto ronco de o con ~ hablar** I have become hoarse with so much talking; **a ~s de agosto** on such and such a day in August

tapa ['tapa] *nf* (*de caja, olla*) lid; (*de botella*) top; (*de libro*) cover; (*comida*) snack

tapadera [tapa'ðera] *nf* lid, cover

tapar [ta'par] *vt* (*cubrir*) to cover; (*envolver*) to wrap o cover up; (*la vista*) to obstruct; (*persona, falta*) to conceal; (*MÉX, CAM: diente*) to fill; **taparse** *vr* to wrap o.s. up

taparrabo [tapa'rraβo] *nm* loincloth

tapete [ta'pete] *nm* table cover

tapia [ta'pja] *nf* (*garden*) wall

tapicería [tapiθe'ria] *nf* tapestry, (*para muebles*) upholstery; (*tienda*) upholsterer's (shop)

tapiz [ta'piθ] *nm* (*alfombra*) carpet; (*tela tejida*) tapestry; **tapizar** *vt* (*muebles*) to upholster

tapón [ta'pon] *nm* (*de botella*) top; (*de lavabo*) plug; **tapón de rosca** screw-top

taquigrafía [takiɣra'fia] *nf* shorthand; **taquígrafo, -a** *nm/f* shorthand writer, stenographer

taquilla [ta'kiʎa] *nf* (*donde se compra*) booking office; (*suma recogida*) takings *pl*

tarántula [ta'rantula] *nf* tarantula

tararear [tarare'ar] *vi* to hum

tardar [tar'ðar] *vi* (*tomar tiempo*) to take a long time; (*llegar tarde*) to be late; (*demorar*) to delay; **¿tarda mucho el tren?** does the train take (very) long?; **a más ~ at** the latest; **no tardes en venir** come soon

tarde ['tarðe] *adv* late ▷ *nf* (*de día*) afternoon; (*al anochecer*) evening; **de ~ en ~** from time to time; **¡buenas ~s!** good afternoon!; **a o por la ~** in the afternoon; in the evening

tardío, -a [tar'ðio, a] *adj* (*retrasado*) late; (*lento*) slow (to arrive)

tarea [ta'rea] *nf* task; (*faena*) chore; (*Escol*) homework

tarifa [ta'rifa] *nf* (*lista de precios*) price list; (*precio*) tariff

tarima [ta'rima] *nf* (*plataforma*) platform

tarjeta [tar'xeta] *nf* card; **tarjeta de crédito/de Navidad/postal/telefónica** credit card/Christmas card/postcard/phonecard; **tarjeta de embarque** boarding pass; **tarjeta de memoria** memory card; **tarjeta prepago** top-up card; **tarjeta SIM** SIM card

tarro ['tarro] *nm* jar, pot

tarta ['tarta] *nf* (*pastel*) cake; (*de base dura*) tart

tartamudear [tartamuðe'ar] *vi* to stammer; **tartamudo, -a** *adj* stammering ▷ *nm/f* stammerer

tártaro, -a ['tartaro, a] *adj*: **salsa tártara** tartar(e) sauce

tasa ['tasa] *nf* (*precio*) (fixed) price, rate; (*valoración*) valuation; (*medida, norma*) measure, standard; **tasa de cambio/interés** exchange/interest rate; **tasas de aeropuerto** airport tax; **tasas universitarias** university fees

tasar [ta'sar] *vt* (*arreglar el precio*) to fix a price for; (*valorar*) to value, assess

tasca ['taska] (*fam*) *nf* pub

tatarabuelo, -a [tatara'βwelo, a] *nm/f* great-great-grandfather/mother

tatuaje [ta'twaxe] *nm* (*dibujo*) tattoo; (*acto*) tattooing

tatuar [ta'twar] *vt* to tattoo

taurino, -a [tau'rino, a] *adj* bullfighting *cpd*

Tauro ['tauro] *nm* Taurus

tauromaquia [tauro'makja] *nf* tauromachy, (art of) bullfighting

taxi ['taksi] *nm* taxi; **taxista** [tak'sista] *nmf* taxi driver

taza ['taθa] *nf* cup; (*de retrete*) bowl; **~ para café** coffee cup; **taza de café** cup of coffee; **tazón** *nm* (*taza grande*) mug, large cup; (*de fuente*) basin

te [te] *pron* (*complemento de objeto*) you; (*complemento indirecto*) (to) you; (*reflexivo*) (to) yourself; **¿~ duele mucho el brazo?** does your arm hurt a lot?; **~ equivocas** you're wrong; **¡cálma~!** calm down!

té [te] *nm* tea

teatral [tea'tral] *adj* theatre *cpd*; (*fig*) theatrical

teatro [te'atro] *nm* theatre; (*Literatura*) plays *pl*, drama

tebeo [te'βeo] *nm* comic

techo ['tetʃo] *nm* (*externo*) roof; (*interno*) ceiling; **techo corredizo** sunroof

tecla ['tekla] *nf* key; **teclado** *nm* keyboard; **teclear** *vi* (*Mús*) to strum; (*con los dedos*) to tap ▷ *vt* (*Inform*) to key in

técnica ['teknika] *nf* technique; (*tecnología*) technology; V *tb* **técnico**

técnico, -a ['tekniko, a] *adj* technical ▷ *nm/f* technician; (*experto*) expert

tecnología [teknolo'xia] *nf* technology; **tecnológico, -a** *adj* technological

tecolote [teko'lote] (*MÉX*) *nm* owl

tedioso, -a [te'ðjoso, a] *adj* boring, tedious

teja ['texa] *nf* tile; (*Bot*) lime (tree); **tejado** *nm* (tiled) roof

tejemaneje [texema'nexe] *nm* (*lío*) fuss; (*intriga*) intrigue

tejer [te'xer] *vt* to weave; (*hacer punto*) to knit; (*fig*) to fabricate; **tejido** *nm* (*tela*) material, fabric; (*telaraña*) web; (*Anat*) tissue

tel [tel] *abr* (= *teléfono*) tel

tela ['tela] *nf* (*tejido*) material; (*telaraña*) web; (*en líquido*) skin; **telar** *nm* (*máquina*) loom

telaraña [tela'raɲa] *nf* cobweb

tele ['tele] (*fam*) *nf* telly (BRIT), TV (US)

tele... ['tele] *prefijo* tele...; **telebasura** *nf* trash TV; **telecomunicación** *nf* telecommunication; **telediario** *nm* television news; **teledirigido, -a** *adj* remote-controlled

teleférico [tele'feriko] *nm* (*de esquí*) ski-lift

telefonear [telefone'ar] *vi* to telephone

telefónico, -a [tele'foniko, a] *adj* telephone *cpd*

telefonillo [telefo'niʎo] *nm* (*de puerta*) intercom

telefonista [telefo'nista] *nmf* telephonist

teléfono [te'lefono] *nm* (tele)phone; **estar hablando a ~** to be on the phone; **llamar a algn por ~** to ring sb (up) o phone sb (up); **teléfono celular** (LAM) mobile phone; **teléfono con cámara** camera phone; **teléfono inalámbrico** cordless phone; **teléfono móvil** (ESP) mobile phone

telégrafo [te'leɣrafo] *nm* telegraph

telegrama [tele'ɣrama] *nm* telegram

tele: telenovela *nf* soap (opera); **teleobjetivo** *nm* telephoto lens; **telepatía** *nf* telepathy; **telepático, -a** *adj* telepathic; **telerrealidad** *nf* reality TV; **telescopio** *nm* telescope; **telesilla** *nf* chairlift; **telespectador, a** *nm/f* viewer; **telesquí** *nm* ski-lift; **teletarjeta** *nf* phonecard; **teletipo** *nm* teletype; **teletrabajador, a** *nm/f* teleworker; **teletrabajo** *nm* teleworking; **televentas** *nfpl* telesales

televidente [teleβi'ðente] *nmf* viewer

televisar [teleβi'sar] *vt* to televise

televisión [teleβi'sjon] *nf* television; **televisión digital** digital television

televisor [teleβi'sor] *nm* television set

télex ['teleks] *nm inv* telex

telón [te'lon] *nm* curtain; **telón de acero** (*Pol*) iron curtain; **telón de fondo** backcloth, background

tema ['tema] *nm* (*asunto*) subject, topic; (*Mús*) theme; **temático, -a** *adj* thematic

temblar [tem'blar] *vi* to shake, tremble; (*por frío*) to shiver; **temblor** *nm* trembling; (*de tierra*) earthquake; **tembloroso, -a** *adj* trembling

temer [te'mer] *vt* to fear ▷ *vi* to be afraid; **temo que llegue tarde** I am afraid he may be late

temible [te'miβle] *adj* fearsome

temor [te'mor] *nm* (*miedo*) fear; (*duda*) suspicion

témpano ['tempano] *nm* (*tb*: **~ de hielo**) ice-floe

temperamento [tempera'mento] *nm* temperament

temperatura [tempera'tura] *nf* temperature

tempestad [tempes'tað] *nf* storm

templado, -a [tem'plaðo, a] *adj* (*moderado*) moderate; (*frugal*) frugal; (*agua*) lukewarm; (*clima*) mild; (*Mús*) well-tuned; **templanza** *nf* moderation; mildness

templar [tem'plar] *vt* (*moderar*) to moderate; (*furia*) to restrain; (*calor*) to reduce; (*afinar*) to tune (up); (*acero*) to temper; (*tuerca*) to tighten up; **temple** *nm* (*ajuste*) tempering; (*afinación*) tuning; (*pintura*) tempera

templo ['templo] *nm* (*iglesia*) church; (*pagano etc*) temple

temporada [tempo'raða] *nf* time, period; (*estación*) season

temporal [tempo'ral] *adj* (*no permanente*) temporary ▷ *nm* storm

temprano, -a [tem'prano, a] *adj* early; (*demasiado pronto*) too soon, too early

ten *vb* V **tener**

tenaces [te'naθes] *adj pl* V **tenaz**

tenaz [te'naθ] *adj* (*material*) tough; (*persona*) tenacious; (*creencia, resistencia*) stubborn

tenaza(s) [te'naθa(s)] *nf*(*pl*) (*Med*) forceps; (*Tec*) pliers; (*Zool*) pincers

tendedero [tende'ðero] *nm* (*para ropa*) drying place; (*cuerda*) clothes line

tendencia [ten'denθja] *nf* tendency; **tener ~ a** to tend to, have a tendency to

tender [ten'der] *vt* (*extender*) to spread out; (*colgar*) to hang out; (*vía férrea, cable*) to lay; (*estirar*) to stretch ▷ *vi*: **~ a** to tend to, have a tendency towards; **tenderse** *vr* to lie down; **~ la cama/mesa** (LAM) to make the bed/lay (BRIT) o set (US) the table

tenderete [tende'rete] *nm* (*puesto*) stall; (*exposición*) display of goods

tendero, -a [ten'dero, a] *nm/f* shopkeeper

tendón [ten'don] *nm* tendon

tendré *etc vb* V **tener**

tenebroso, -a [tene'βroso, a] *adj* (*oscuro*) dark; (*fig*) gloomy

tenedor [tene'ðor] *nm* (*Culin*) fork

tenencia [te'nenθja] *nf* (*de casa*) tenancy; (*de oficio*) tenure; (*de propiedad*) possession

○ **PALABRA CLAVE**

tener [te'ner] *vt* **1** (*poseer, gen*) to have; (*en la mano*) to hold; **¿tienes un boli?** have you got a pen?; **va a tener un niño** she's going to have a baby; **¡ten** (*o* **tenga**)!, **¡aquí tienes** (*o* **tiene**)!** here you are!

2 (*edad, medidas*) to be; **tiene 7 años** she's 7 (years old); **tiene 15 cm de largo** it's 15 cm long; V **calor; hambre etc**

3 (*considerar*): **lo tengo por brillante** I consider him to be brilliant; **tener en mucho a algn** to think very highly of sb

4 (*+ pp: = pretérito*): **tengo terminada ya la mitad del trabajo** I've done half the work already

5: tener que hacer algo to have to do sth; **tengo que acabar este trabajo hoy** I have to finish this job today

6: ¿qué tienes, estás enfermo? what's the matter with you, are you ill?

tenerse *vr* **1 tenerse en pie** to stand up

2 tenerse por to think o.s.

tengo *etc vb* V **tener**
tenia ['tenja] *nf* tapeworm
teniente [te'njente] *nm* (*rango*) lieutenant; (*ayudante*) deputy
tenis ['tenis] *nm* tennis; **tenis de mesa** table tennis; **tenista** *nmf* tennis player
tenor [te'nor] *nm* (*sentido*) meaning; (*Mús*) tenor; **a ~ de** on the lines of
tensar [ten'sar] *vt* to tighten; (*arco*) to draw
tensión [ten'sjon] *nf* tension; (*Tec*) stress; **tener la ~ alta** to have high blood pressure; **tensión arterial** blood pressure
tenso, -a ['tenso, a] *adj* tense
tentación [tenta'θjon] *nf* temptation
tentáculo [ten'takulo] *nm* tentacle
tentador, a [tenta'ðor, a] *adj* tempting
tentar [ten'tar] *vt* (*seducir*) to tempt; (*atraer*) to attract
tentempié [tentem'pje] *nm* snack
tenue ['tenwe] *adj* (*delgado*) thin, slender; (*neblina*) light; (*lazo, vínculo*) slight
teñir [te'ɲir] *vt* to dye; (*fig*) to tinge; **teñirse** *vr* to dye; **~se el pelo** to dye one's hair
teología [teolo'xia] *nf* theology
teoría [teo'ria] *nf* theory; **en ~** in theory; **teórico, -a** *adj* theoretic(al) ▷ *nm/f* theoretician, theorist; **teorizar** *vi* to theorize
terapéutico, -a [tera'peutiko, a] *adj* therapeutic
terapia [te'rapja] *nf* therapy
tercer *adj* V **tercero**
tercermundista [terθermun'dista] *adj* Third World *cpd*
tercero, -a [ter'θero, a] (*delante de nmsg*: **tercer**) *adj* third ▷ *nm* (*Jur*) third party
terceto [ter'θeto] *nm* trio
terciar [ter'θjar] *vi* (*participar*) to take part; (*hacer de árbitro*) to mediate; **terciario, -a** *adj* tertiary
tercio [ter'θjo] *nm* third
terciopelo [terθjo'pelo] *nm* velvet
terco, -a ['terko, a] *adj* obstinate
tergal® [ter'ɣal] *nm* type of polyester
tergiversar [terxiβer'sar] *vt* to distort
termal [ter'mal] *adj* thermal
termas ['termas] *nfpl* hot springs
térmico, -a ['termiko, a] *adj* thermal
terminal [termi'nal] *adj, nm, nf* terminal
terminante [termi'nante] *adj* (*final*) final, definitive; (*tajante*) categorical; **terminantemente** *adv:* **terminantemente prohibido** strictly forbidden
terminar [termi'nar] *vt* (*completar*) to complete, finish; (*concluir*) to end ▷ *vi* (*llegar a su fin*) to end; (*parar*) to stop; (*acabar*) to finish; **terminarse** *vr* to come to an end; **~ por hacer algo** to end up (by)

doing sth

término ['termino] *nm* end, conclusion; (*parada*) terminus; (*límite*) boundary; **en último ~** (*a fin de cuentas*) in the last analysis; (*como último recurso*) as a last resort; **término medio** average; (*fig*) middle way
termómetro [ter'mometro] *nm* thermometer
termo(s)® ['termo(s)] *nm* Thermos®
termostato [termo'stato] *nm* thermostat
ternero, -a [ter'nero, a] *nm/f* (*animal*) calf ▷ *nf* (*carne*) veal
ternura [ter'nura] *nf* (*trato*) tenderness; (*palabra*) endearment; (*cariño*) fondness
terrado [te'rraðo] *nm* terrace
terraplén [terra'plen] *nm* embankment
terrateniente [terrate'njente] *nmf* landowner
terraza [te'rraθa] *nf* (*balcón*) balcony; (*tejado*) (flat) roof; (*Agr*) terrace
terremoto [terre'moto] *nm* earthquake
terrenal [terre'nal] *adj* earthly
terreno [te'rreno] *nm* (*tierra*) land; (*parcela*) plot; (*suelo*) soil; (*fig*) field; **un ~** a piece of land
terrestre [te'rrestre] *adj* terrestrial; (*ruta*) land *cpd*
terrible [te'rriβle] *adj* terrible, awful
territorio [terri'torjo] *nm* territory
terrón [te'rron] *nm* (*de azúcar*) lump; (*de tierra*) clod, lump
terror [te'rror] *nm* terror; **terrorífico, -a** *adj* terrifying; **terrorista** *adj, nmf* terrorist; **terrorista suicida** suicide bomber
terso, -a ['terso, a] *adj* (*liso*) smooth; (*pulido*) polished
tertulia [ter'tulja] *nf* (*reunión informal*) social gathering; (*grupo*) group, circle
tesis ['tesis] *nf inv* thesis
tesón [te'son] *nm* (*firmeza*) firmness; (*tenacidad*) tenacity
tesorero, -a [teso'rero, a] *nm/f* treasurer
tesoro [te'soro] *nm* treasure; (*Com, Pol*) treasury
testamento [testa'mento] *nm* will
testarudo, -a [testa'ruðo, a] *adj* stubborn
testículo [tes'tikulo] *nm* testicle
testificar [testifi'kar] *vt* to testify; (*fig*) to attest ▷ *vi* to give evidence
testigo [tes'tiɣo] *nmf* witness; **testigo de cargo/descargo** witness for the prosecution/defence; **testigo ocular** eye witness
testimonio [testi'monjo] *nm* testimony
teta ['teta] *nf* (*de biberón*) teat; (*Anat: fam*) breast
tétanos ['tetanos] *nm* tetanus
tetera [te'tera] *nf* teapot
tétrico, -a ['tetriko, a] *adj* gloomy, dismal
textil [teks'til] *adj* textile
texto ['teksto] *nm* text; **textual** *adj* textual
textura [teks'tura] *nf* (*de tejido*) texture
tez [teθ] *nf* (*cutis*) complexion
ti [ti] *pron* you; (*reflexivo*) yourself
tía ['tia] *nf* (*pariente*) aunt; (*fam*) chick, bird
tibio, -a ['tiβjo, a] *adj* lukewarm
tiburón [tiβu'ron] *nm* shark
tic [tik] *nm* (*ruido*) click; (*de reloj*) tick; (*Med*): **~ nervioso** nervous tic
tictac [tik'tak] *nm* (*de reloj*) tick tock
tiempo ['tjempo] *nm* time; (*época, período*) age, period; (*Meteorología*) weather; (*Ling*) tense; (*Deporte*) half; **a ~** in time; **a un o al mismo ~** at the same time; **al poco ~** very soon (after); **se quedó poco ~** he didn't stay very long; **hace poco ~** not long ago; **mucho ~** a

long time; **dé ~ en ~** from time to time; **hace buen/mal ~** the weather is fine/bad; **estar a ~** to be in time; **hace ~** some time ago; **hacer ~** to while away the time; **motor de 2 ~s** two-stroke engine; **primer ~** first half

tienda ['tjenda] *nf* shop, store; **tienda de abarrotes** (MÉX, CAM) grocer's (BRIT), grocery store (US); **tienda de alimentación o comestibles** grocer's (BRIT), grocery store (US); **tienda de campaña** tent

tienes *etc vb* V **tener**

tienta *etc* ['tjenta] *vb* V **tentar** ▷ *nf*: **andar a ~s** to grope one's way along

tiento *etc* ['tjento] *vb* V **tentar** ▷ *nm* (tacto) touch; (precaución) wariness

tierno, -a ['tjerno, a] *adj* (blando) tender; (fresco) fresh; (amable) sweet

tierra ['tjerra] *nf* earth; (suelo) soil; (mundo) earth, world; (país) country, land; **~ adentro** inland

tieso, -a ['tjeso, a] *adj* (rígido) rigid; (duro) stiff; (fam: orgulloso) conceited

tiesto ['tjesto] *nm* flowerpot

tifón [ti'fon] *nm* typhoon

tifus ['tifus] *nm* typhus

tigre ['tiɣre] *nm* tiger

tijera [ti'xera] *nf* scissors *pl*; (Zool) claw; **tijeras** *nfpl* scissors; (para plantas) shears

tila ['tila] *nf* lime blossom tea

tildar [til'dar] *vt*: **~ de** to brand as

tilde ['tilde] *nf* (Tip) tilde

tilín [ti'lin] *nm* tinkle

timar [ti'mar] *vt* (estafar) to swindle

timbal [tim'bal] *nm* small drum

timbre ['timbre] *nm* (sello) stamp; (campanilla) bell; (tono) timbre; (Com) stamp duty

timidez [timi'ðeθ] *nf* shyness; **tímido, -a** *adj* shy

timo ['timo] *nm* swindle

timón [ti'mon] *nm* helm, rudder; **timonel** *nm* helmsman

tímpano ['timpano] *nm* (Anat) eardrum; (Mús) small drum

tina ['tina] *nf* tub; (baño) bath(tub); **tinaja** *nf* large jar

tinieblas [ti'njeβlas] *nfpl* darkness *sg*; (sombras) shadows

tino ['tino] *nm* (habilidad) skill; (juicio) insight

tinta ['tinta] *nf* ink; (Tec) dye; (Arte) colour

tinte ['tinte] *nm* dye

tintero [tin'tero] *nm* inkwell

tinto ['tinto] *nm* red wine

tintorería [tintore'ria] *nf* dry cleaner's

tío ['tio] *nm* (pariente) uncle; (fam: individuo) bloke (BRIT), guy

tiovivo [tio'βiβo] *nm* merry-go-round

típico, -a ['tipiko, a] *adj* typical

tipo ['tipo] *nm* (clase) type, kind; (hombre) fellow; (Anat: de hombre) build; (: de mujer) figure; (Imprenta) type; **tipo bancario/de descuento/de interés/de cambio** bank/discount/interest/exchange rate

tipografía [tipoɣra'fia] *nf* printing *cpd*

tiquet ['tiket] (*pl* **~s**) *nm* ticket; (en tienda) cash slip

tiquismiquis [tikis'mikis] *nm inv* fussy person ▷ *nmpl* (querellas) squabbling *sg*; (escrúpulos) silly scruples

tira ['tira] *nf* strip; (fig) abundance; **tira y afloja** give and take

tirabuzón [tiraβu'θon] *nm* (rizo) curl

tirachinas [tira'tʃinas] *nm inv* catapult

tirada [ti'raða] *nf* (acto) cast, throw; (serie) series;

(Tip) printing, edition; **de una ~** at one go

tirado, -a [ti'raðo, a] *adj* (barato) dirt-cheap; (fam: fácil) very easy

tirador [tira'ðor] *nm* (mango) handle

tirano, -a [ti'rano, a] *adj* tyrannical ▷ *nm/f* tyrant

tirante [ti'rante] *adj* (cuerda etc) tight, taut; (relaciones) strained ▷ *nm* (Arq) brace; (Tec) stay; **tirantes** *nmpl* (de pantalón) braces (BRIT), suspenders (US); **tirantez** *nf* tightness; (fig) tension

tirar [ti'rar] *vt* to throw; (dejar caer) to drop; (volcar) to upset; (derribar) to knock down o over; (desechar) to throw out o away; (dinero) to squander; (imprimir) to print ▷ *vi* (disparar) to shoot; (de la puerta etc) to pull; (fam: andar) to go; (tender a, buscar realizar) to tend to; (Deporte) to shoot; **tirarse** *vr* to throw o.s.; **~ abajo** to bring down, destroy; **tira más a su padre** he takes more after his father; **ir tirando** to manage

tirita [ti'rita] *nf* (sticking) plaster (BRIT), Bandaid® (US)

tiritar [tiri'tar] *vi* to shiver

tiro ['tiro] *nm* (lanzamiento) throw; (disparo) shot; (Deporte) shot; (Golf, Tenis) drive; (alcance) range; **caballo de ~** cart-horse; **tiro al blanco** target practice

tirón [ti'ron] *nm* (sacudida) pull, tug; **de un ~** in one go, all at once

tiroteo [tiro'teo] *nm* exchange of shots, shooting

tisis ['tisis] *nf inv* consumption, tuberculosis

títere ['titere] *nm* puppet

titubear [tituβe'ar] *vi* to stagger; to stammer; (fig) to hesitate; **titubeo** *nm* staggering; stammering; hesitation

titulado, -a [titu'laðo, a] *adj* (libro) entitled; (persona) titled

titular [titu'lar] *adj* titular ▷ *nmf* holder ▷ *nm* headline ▷ *vt* to title; **titularse** *vr* to be entitled; **título** *nm* title; (de diario) headline; (certificado) professional qualification; (universitario) (university) degree; **a título de** in the capacity of

tiza ['tiθa] *nf* chalk

toalla [to'aʎa] *nf* towel

tobillo [to'βiʎo] *nm* ankle

tobogán [toβo'ɣan] *nm* (montaña rusa) roller-coaster; (de niños) chute, slide

tocadiscos [toka'ðiskos] *nm inv* record player

tocado, -a [to'kaðo, a] *adj* (fam) touched ▷ *nm* headdress

tocador [toka'ðor] *nm* (mueble) dressing table; (cuarto) boudoir; (fam) ladies' toilet (BRIT) o room (US)

tocar [to'kar] *vt* to touch; (Mús) to play; (referirse a) to allude to; (timbre) to ring ▷ *vi* (a la puerta) to knock (on o at the door); (ser de turno) to fall to, be the turn of; (ser hora) to be due; **tocarse** *vr* (cubrirse la cabeza) to cover one's head; (tener contacto) to touch (each other); **por lo que a mí me toca** as far as I am concerned; **te toca a ti** it's your turn

tocayo, -a [to'kajo, a] *nm/f* namesake

tocino [to'θino] *nm* bacon

todavía [toða'βia] *adv* (aun) even; (aún) still, yet; **~ más** yet more; **~ no** not yet

---

O PALABRA CLAVE

todo, -a ['toðo, a] *adj* **1** (con artículo sg) all; **toda la carne** all the meat; **toda la noche** all night, the whole night; **todo el libro** the whole book; **toda una botella** a whole bottle; **todo lo contrario** quite the opposite;

está toda sucia she's all dirty; **por todo el país** throughout the whole country

2 (con artículo pl) all; every; **todos los libros** all the books; **todas las noches** every night; **todos los que quieran salir** all those who want to leave ▷ pron **1** everything, all; **todos** everyone, everybody; **lo sabemos todo** we know everything; **todos querían más tiempo** everybody or everyone wanted more time; **nos marchamos todos** all of us left

2: **con todo**: **con todo él me sigue gustando** even so I still like him

▷ adv **all**; **ir todo seguido** keep straight on or ahead ▷ nm: **como un todo** as a whole; **del todo**: **no me agrada del todo** I don't entirely like it

todopoderoso, -a [toðopoðeˈroso, a] adj all powerful; (Rel) almighty

todoterreno [todoteˈrreno] sm inv four-wheel drive, SUV (ESP US)

toga [ˈtoɣa] nf toga; (Escol) gown

Tokio [ˈtokjo] n Tokyo

toldo [ˈtoldo] nm (para el sol) sunshade (BRIT), parasol; (tienda) marquee

tolerancia [toleˈranθja] nf tolerance; **tolerante** adj (sociedad) liberal; (persona) open-minded

tolerar [toleˈrar] vt to tolerate; (resistir) to endure

toma [ˈtoma] nf (acto) taking; (Med) dose; **toma de corriente** socket; **toma de tierra** earth (wire); **tomacorriente** (LAM) nm socket

tomar [toˈmar] vt to take; (aspecto) to take on; (beber) to drink ▷ vi to take; (LAM: beber) to drink; **tomarse** vr to take; **~se por** to consider o.s. to be; **~ a bien/mal** to take well/badly; **~ en serio** to take seriously; **~ el pelo a algn** to pull sb's leg; **~la con algn** to pick a quarrel with sb; **¡tome!** here you are!; **~ el sol** to sunbathe

tomate [toˈmate] nm tomato

tomillo [toˈmiʎo] nm thyme

tomo [ˈtomo] nm (libro) volume

ton [ton] abr = **tonelada** ▷ nm: **sin ~ ni son** without rhyme or reason

tonalidad [tonaliˈðað] nf tone

tonel [toˈnel] nm barrel

tonelada [toneˈlaða] nf ton; **tonelaje** nm tonnage

tónica [ˈtonika] nf (Mús) tonic; (fig) keynote

tónico, -a [ˈtoniko, a] adj tonic ▷ nm (Med) tonic

tono [ˈtono] nm tone; **fuera de ~** inappropriate

tontería [tonteˈria] nf (estupidez) foolishness; (cosa) stupid thing; (acto) foolish act; **tonterías** nfpl (disparates) rubbish sg, nonsense sg

tonto, -a [ˈtonto, a] adj stupid, silly ▷ nm/f fool

topar [toˈpar] vi: **~ contra o en** to run into; **~ con** to run up against

tope [ˈtope] adj maximum ▷ nm (fin) end; (límite) limit; (Ferro) buffer; (Auto) bumper; **al ~** end to end

tópico, -a [ˈtopiko, a] adj topical ▷ nm platitude

topo [ˈtopo] nm (Zool) mole; (fig) blunderer

toque etc [ˈtoke] vb V **tocar** ▷ nm touch; (Mús) beat; (de campana) peal; **dar un ~ a** to warn; **toque de queda** curfew

toqué etc vb V **tocar**

toquetear [toketeˈar] vt to finger

toquilla [toˈkiʎa] nf (pañuelo) headscarf; (chal) shawl

tórax [ˈtoraks] nm thorax

torbellino [torbeˈʎino] nm whirlwind; (fig) whirl

torcedura [torθeˈðura] nf twist; (Med) sprain

torcer [torˈθer] vt to twist; (la esquina) to turn; (Med) to sprain ▷ vi (desviar) to turn off; **torcerse** vr (ladearse) to bend; (desviarse) to go astray; (fracasar) to go wrong; **torcido, -a** adj twisted; (fig) crooked ▷ nm curl

tordo, -a [ˈtorðo, a] adj dappled ▷ nm thrush

torear [toreˈar] vt (fig: evadir) to avoid; (jugar con) to tease ▷ vi to fight bulls; **toreo** nm bullfighting; **torero, -a** nm/f bullfighter

tormenta [torˈmenta] nf storm; (fig: confusión) turmoil

tormento [torˈmento] nm torture; (fig) anguish

tornar [torˈnar] vt (devolver) to return, give back; (transformar) to transform ▷ vi to go back

tornasolado, -a [tornasoˈlaðo, a] adj (brillante) iridescent; (reluciente) shimmering

torneo [torˈneo] nm tournament

tornillo [torˈniʎo] nm screw

torniquete [torniˈkete] nm (Med) tourniquet

torno [ˈtorno] nm (Tec) winch; (tambor) drum; **en ~ (a)** round, about

toro [ˈtoro] nm bull; (fam) he-man; **los ~s** bullfighting

toronja [toˈronxa] nf grapefruit

torpe [ˈtorpe] adj (poco hábil) clumsy, awkward; (necio) dim; (lento) slow

torpedo [torˈpeðo] nm torpedo

torpeza [torˈpeθa] nf (falta de agilidad) clumsiness; (lentitud) slowness; (error) mistake

torre [ˈtorre] nf tower; (de petróleo) derrick

torrefacto, -a [torreˈfakto, a] adj roasted

torrente [toˈrrente] nm torrent

torrija [toˈrrixa] nf French toast

torsión [torˈsjon] nf twisting

torso [ˈtorso] nm torso

torta [ˈtorta] nf cake; (fam) slap

tortícolis [torˈtikolis] nm inv stiff neck

tortilla [torˈtiʎa] nf omelette; (LAM: de maíz) maize pancake; **tortilla de papas** (LAM) potato omelette; **tortilla de patatas** (ESP) potato omelette; **tortilla francesa** (ESP) plain omelette

tórtola [ˈtortola] nf turtledove

tortuga [torˈtuɣa] nf tortoise

tortuoso, -a [torˈtwoso, a] adj winding

tortura [torˈtura] nf torture; **torturar** vt to torture

tos [tos] nf cough; **tos ferina** whooping cough

toser [toˈser] vi to cough

tostada [tosˈtaða] nf piece of toast; **tostado, -a** adj toasted; (por el sol) dark brown; (piel) tanned

tostador [tostaˈðor] (ESP) nm toaster; **tostadora** (LAM) nf = **tostador**

tostar [tosˈtar] vt to toast; (café) to roast; (persona) to tan; **tostarse** vr to get brown

total [toˈtal] adj total ▷ adv in short; (al fin y al cabo) when all is said and done ▷ nm total; **en ~** in all; **~ que** ... to cut (BRIT) o make (US) a long story short ...

totalidad [totaliˈðað] nf whole

totalitario, -a [totaliˈtarjo, a] adj totalitarian

tóxico, -a [ˈtoksiko, a] adj toxic ▷ nm poison; **toxicómano, -a** nm/f drug addict

toxina [toˈksina] nf toxin

tozudo, -a [toˈθuðo, a] adj obstinate

trabajador, a [traβaxaˈðor, a] adj hard-working ▷ nm/f worker; **trabajador autónomo o por cuenta propia** self-employed person

trabajar [traβaˈxar] vt to work; (Agr) to till;

(*empeñarse en*) to work at; (*convencer*) to persuade ▷ vi to work; (*esforzarse*) to strive; **trabajo** *nm* work; (*tarea*) task; (*Pol*) labour; (*fig*) effort; **tomarse el trabajo de** to take the trouble to; **trabajo a destajo** piecework; **trabajo en equipo** teamwork; **trabajo por turnos** shift work; **trabajos forzados** hard labour *sg*
trabalenguas [traβa'lenɣwas] *nm inv* tongue twister
tracción [trak'θjon] *nf* traction; **tracción delantera/trasera** front-wheel/rear-wheel drive
tractor [trak'tor] *nm* tractor
tradición [traði'θjon] *nf* tradition; **tradicional** *adj* traditional
traducción [traðuk'θjon] *nf* translation
traducir [traðu'θir] *vt* to translate; **traductor, a** *nm/f* translator
traer [tra'er] *vt* to bring; (*llevar*) to carry; (*llevar puesto*) to wear; (*incluir*) to carry; (*causar*) to cause; **traerse** *vr*: **~se algo** to be up to sth
traficar [trafi'kar] *vi* to trade
tráfico ['trafiko] *nm* (*Com*) trade; (*Auto*) traffic
tragaluz [traɣa'luθ] *nm* skylight
tragamonedas [traɣamo'neðas] (*LAM*) *nm inv* slot machine
tragaperras [traɣa'perras] (*ESP*) *nf inv* slot machine
tragar [tra'ɣar] *vt* to swallow; (*devorar*) to devour, bolt down; **tragarse** *vr* to swallow
tragedia [tra'xeðja] *nf* tragedy; **trágico, -a** *adj* tragic
trago ['traɣo] *nm* (*líquido*) drink; (*bocado*) gulp; (*fam: de bebida*) swig; (*desgracia*) blow; **echar un ~** to have a drink
traición [trai'θjon] *nf* treachery; (*Jur*) treason; (*una traición*) act of treachery; **traicionar** *vt* to betray
traidor, a [trai'ðor, a] *adj* treacherous ▷ *nm/f* traitor
traigo *etc vb* V **traer**
traje ['traxe] *etc vb* V **traer** ▷ *nm* (*de hombre*) suit; (*de mujer*) dress; (*vestido típico*) costume; **traje de baño/ chaqueta** swimsuit/suit; **traje de etiqueta** dress suit; **traje de luces** bullfighter's costume
trajera *etc vb* V **traer**
trajín [tra'xin] *nm* (*fam: movimiento*) bustle; **trajinar** *vi* (*moverse*) to bustle about
trama ['trama] *nf* (*intriga*) plot; (*de tejido*) weft (*BRIT*), woof (*US*); **tramar** *vt* to plot; (*Tec*) to weave
tramitar [trami'tar] *vt* (*asunto*) to transact; (*negociar*) to negotiate
trámite ['tramite] *nm* (*paso*) step; (*Jur*) transaction; **trámites** *nmpl* (*burocracia*) procedure *sg*; (*Jur*) proceedings
tramo ['tramo] *nm* (*de tierra*) plot; (*de escalera*) flight; (*de vía*) section
trampa ['trampa] *nf* trap; (*en el suelo*) trapdoor; (*truco*) trick; (*engaño*) fiddle; **trampear** *vt, vi* to cheat
trampolín [trampo'lin] *nm* (*de piscina etc*) diving board
tramposo, -a [tram'poso, a] *adj* crooked, cheating ▷ *nm/f* crook, cheat
tranca ['tranka] *nf* (*palo*) stick; (*de puerta, ventana*) bar; **trancar** *vt* to bar
trance [tranθe] *nm* (*momento difícil*) difficult moment o juncture; (*estado hipnotizado*) trance
tranquilidad [trankili'ðað] *nf* (*calma*) calmness, stillness; (*paz*) peacefulness
tranquilizar [trankili'θar] *vt* (*calmar*) to calm

(down); (*asegurar*) to reassure; **tranquilizarse** *vr* to calm down; **tranquilo, -a** *adj* (*calmado*) calm; (*apacible*) peaceful; (*mar*) calm; (*mente*) untroubled
transacción [transak'θjon] *nf* transaction
transbordador [transβorða'ðor] *nm* ferry
transbordo [trans'βorðo] *nm* transfer; **hacer ~** to change (trains *etc*)
transcurrir [transku'rrir] *vi* (*tiempo*) to pass; (*hecho*) to take place
transcurso [trans'kurso] *nm*: **~ del tiempo** lapse (of time)
transeúnte [transe'unte] *nmf* passer-by
transferencia [transfe'renθja] *nf* transference; (*Com*) transfer
transferir [transfe'rir] *vt* to transfer
transformador [transforma'ðor] *nm* (*Elec*) transformer
transformar [transfor'mar] *vt* to transform; (*convertir*) to convert
transfusión [transfu'sjon] *nf* transfusion
transgénico, -a [trans'xeniko, a] *adj* genetically modified, GM
transición [transi'θjon] *nf* transition
transigir [transi'xir] *vi* to compromise, make concessions
transitar [transi'tar] *vi* to go (from place to place); **tránsito** *nm* transit; (*Auto*) traffic; **transitorio, -a** *adj* transitory
transmisión [transmi'sjon] *nf* (*Tec*) transmission; (*transferencia*) transfer; **transmisión exterior/en directo** outside/live broadcast
transmitir [transmi'tir] *vt* to transmit; (*Radio, TV*) to broadcast
transparencia [transpa'renθja] *nf* transparency; (*claridad*) clearness, clarity; (*foto*) slide
transparentar [transparen'tar] *vt* to reveal ▷ *vi* to be transparent; **transparente** *adj* transparent; (*claro*) clear
transpirar [transpi'rar] *vi* to perspire
transportar [transpor'tar] *vt* to transport; (*llevar*) to carry; **transporte** *nm* transport; (*Com*) haulage
transversal [transβer'sal] *adj* transverse, cross
tranvía [tram'bia] *nm* tram
trapeador [trapea'ðor] (*LAM*) *nm* mop; **trapear** (*LAM*) *vt* to mop
trapecio [tra'peθjo] *nm* trapeze; **trapecista** *nmf* trapeze artist
trapero, -a [tra'pero, a] *nm/f* ragman
trapicheo [trapi'tʃeo] (*fam*) *nm* scheme, fiddle
trapo ['trapo] *nm* (*tela*) rag; (*de cocina*) cloth
tráquea ['trakea] *nf* windpipe
traqueteo [trake'teo] *nm* rattling
tras [tras] *prep* (*detrás*) behind; (*después*) after
trasatlántico [trasat'lantiko] *nm* (*barco*) (cabin) cruiser
trascendencia [trasθen'denθja] *nf* (*importancia*) importance; (*Filosofía*) transcendence
trascendental [trasθenden'tal] *adj* important; (*Filosofía*) transcendental
trasero, -a [tra'sero, a] *adj* back, rear ▷ *nm* (*Anat*) bottom
trasfondo [tras'fondo] *nm* background
trasgredir [trasɣre'ðir] *vt* to contravene
trashumante [trasu'mante] *adj* (*animales*) migrating
trasladar [trasla'ðar] *vt* to move; (*persona*) to

transfer; (postergar) to postpone; (copiar) to copy;
trasladarse vr (mudarse) to move; **traslado** nm
move; (mudanza) move, removal
traslucir [traslu'θir] vt to show
trasluz [tras'luθ] nm reflected light; **al ~** against o
up to the light
trasnochador, a [trasnotʃa'ðor, a] nm/f night owl
trasnochar [trasno'tʃar] vi (acostarse tarde) to stay
up late
traspapelar [traspape'lar] vt (documento, carta) to
mislay, misplace
traspasar [traspa'sar] vt (suj: bala etc) to pierce, go
through; (propiedad) to sell, transfer; (calle) to cross
over; (límites) to go beyond; (ley) to break; **traspaso** nm
(venta) transfer, sale
traspatio [tras'patjo] (LAM) nm backyard
traspié [tras'pje] nm (tropezón) trip; (error) blunder
trasplantar [trasplan'tar] vt to transplant
traste ['traste] nm (Mús) fret; **dar al ~ con algo** to
ruin sth
trastero [tras'tero] nm storage room
trastienda [tras'tjenda] nf back of shop
trasto ['trasto] (pey) nm (cosa) piece of junk; (persona)
dead loss
trastornado, -a [trastor'naðo, a] adj (loco) mad,
crazy
trastornar [trastor'nar] vt (fig: planes) to disrupt;
(: nervios) to shatter; (: persona) to drive crazy;
trastornarse vr (volverse loco) to go mad o crazy;
trastorno nm (acto) overturning; (confusión)
confusion
tratable [tra'taβle] adj friendly
tratado [tra'taðo] nm (Pol) treaty; (Com) agreement
tratamiento [trata'mjento] nm treatment;
tratamiento de textos (Inform) word processing cpd
tratar [tra'tar] vt (ocuparse de) to treat; (manejar,
Tec) to handle; (Med) to treat; (dirigirse a: persona)
to address ▷ vi: **~ de** (hablar sobre) to deal with, be
about; (intentar) to try to; **tratarse** vr to treat each
other; **~ con** (Com) to trade in; (negociar) to negotiate
with; (tener contactos) to have dealings with; **¿de qué
se trata?** what's it about?; **trato** nm dealings pl;
(relaciónes) relationship; (comportamiento) manner;
(Com) agreement
trauma ['trauma] nm trauma
través [tra'βes] nm (fig) reverse; **al ~** across,
crossways; **a ~ de** across; (sobre) over; (por) through
travesaño [traβe'saɲo] nm (Arq) crossbeam;
(Deporte) crossbar
travesía [traβe'sia] nf (calle) cross-street; (Náut)
crossing
travesura [traβe'sura] nf (broma) prank; (ingenio) wit
travieso, -a [tra'βjeso, a] adj (niño) naughty
trayecto [tra'jekto] nm (ruta) road, way; (viaje)
journey; (tramo) stretch; **trayectoria** nf trajectory;
(fig) path
traza ['traθa] nf (aspecto) looks pl; (señal) sign;
trazado, -a adj: **bien trazado** shapely, well-formed
▷ nm (Arq) plan, design; (fig) outline
trazar [tra'θar] vt (Arq) to plan; (Arte) to sketch;
(fig) to trace; (plan) to draw up; **trazo** nm (línea) line;
(bosquejo) sketch
trébol ['treβol] nm (Bot) clover
trece ['treθe] num thirteen
trecho ['tretʃo] nm (distancia) distance; (tiempo) while
tregua ['treɣwa] nf (Mil) truce; (fig) respite

treinta ['treinta] num thirty
tremendo, -a [tre'mendo, a] adj (terrible) terrible;
(imponente: cosa) imposing; (fam: fabuloso) tremendous
tren [tren] nm train; **tren de aterrizaje**
undercarriage; **tren de cercanías** suburban train
trenca ['trenka] nf duffel coat
trenza ['trenθa] nf (de pelo) plait (BRIT), braid (US)
trepadora [trepa'ðora] nf (Bot) climber
trepar [tre'par] vt, vi to climb
tres [tres] num three
tresillo [tre'siʎo] nm three-piece suite; (Mús) triplet
treta ['treta] nf trick
triángulo [tri'angulo] nm triangle
tribu ['triβu] nf tribe
tribuna [tri'βuna] nf (plataforma) platform; (Deporte)
(grand)stand
tribunal [triβu'nal] nm (Jur) court; (comisión, fig)
tribunal; **~ popular** jury
tributo [tri'βuto] nm (Com) tax
trigal [tri'ɣal] nm wheat field
trigo ['triɣo] nm wheat
trigueño, -a [tri'ɣeɲo, a] adj (pelo) corn-coloured
trillar [tri'ʎar] vt (Agr) to thresh
trimestral [trimes'tral] adj quarterly; (Escol) termly
trimestre [tri'mestre] nm (Escol) term
trinar [tri'nar] vi (pájaros) to sing; (rabiar) to fume,
be angry
trinchar [trin'tʃar] vt to carve
trinchera [trin'tʃera] nf (fosa) trench
trineo [tri'neo] nm sledge
trinidad [trini'ðað] nf trio; (Rel): **la T~** the Trinity
tripa ['tripa] nf (Anat) intestine; (fam: tb: **~s**) insides pl
triple ['triple] adj triple
triplicado, -a [tripli'kaðo, a] adj: **por ~** in triplicate
tripulación [tripula'θjon] nf crew
tripulante [tripu'lante] nmf crewman/woman
tripular [tripu'lar] vt (barco) to man; (Auto) to drive
triquiñuela [triki'nwela] nf trick
tris [tris] nm inv crack
triste ['triste] adj sad; (lamentable) sorry, miserable;
tristeza nf (aflicción) sadness; (melancolía) melancholy
triturar [tritu'rar] vt (moler) to grind; (mascar) to
chew
triunfar [triun'far] vi (tener éxito) to triumph; (ganar)
to win; **triunfo** nm triumph
trivial [tri'βjal] adj trivial
triza ['triθa] nf: **hacer ~s** to smash to bits; (papel) to
tear to shreds
trocear [troθe'ar] vt (carne, manzana) to cut up, cut
into pieces
trocha ['trotʃa] nf short cut
trofeo [tro'feo] nm (premio) trophy; (éxito) success
tromba ['tromba] nf downpour
trombón [trom'bon] nm trombone
trombosis [trom'bosis] nf inv thrombosis
trompa ['trompa] nf (Mús) horn; (trompa) humming top;
(hocico) snout; (fam): **cogerse una ~** to get tight
trompazo [trom'paθo] nm bump, bang
trompeta [trom'peta] nf trumpet; (clarín) bugle
trompicón [trompi'kon]: **a trompicones** adv in fits
and starts
trompo ['trompo] nm spinning top
trompón [trom'pon] nm bump
tronar [tro'nar] vt (MÉX, CAM: fusilar) to shoot;
(MÉX: examen) to flunk ▷ vi to thunder; (fig) to rage
tronchar [tron'tʃar] vt (árbol) to chop down; (fig: vida)

to cut short; (: *esperanza*) to shatter; (*persona*) to tire out; **troncharse** *vr* to fall down

tronco ['tronko] *nm* (*de árbol*, Anat) trunk

trono ['trono] *nm* throne

tropa ['tropa] *nf* (Mil) troop; (*soldados*) soldiers pl

tropezar [trope'θar] *vi* to trip, stumble; (*error*) to slip up; **~ con** to run into; (*topar con*) to bump into; **tropezón** *nm* trip; (*fig*) blunder

tropical [tropi'kal] *adj* tropical

trópico ['tropiko] *nm* tropic

tropiezo [tro'pjeθo] *vb* V **tropezar** ▷ *nm* (*error*) slip, blunder; (*desgracia*) misfortune; (*obstáculo*) snag

trotamundos [trota'mundos] *nm inv* globetrotter

trotar [tro'tar] *vi* to trot; **trote** *nm* trot; (*fam*) travelling; **de mucho trote** hard-wearing

trozar [tro'θar] (LAM) *vt* to cut up, cut into pieces

trozo ['troθo] *nm* bit, piece

trucha ['trutʃa] *nf* trout

truco ['truko] *nm* (*habilidad*) knack; (*engaño*) trick

trueno ['trweno] *nm* thunder; (*estampido*) bang

trueque *etc* ['trweke] *vb* V **trocar** ▷ *nm* exchange; (Com) barter

trufa ['trufa] *nf* (Bot) truffle

truhán, -ana [tru'an, ana] *nm/f* rogue

truncar [trun'kar] *vt* (*cortar*) to truncate; (*fig: la vida etc*) to cut short; (: *el desarrollo*) to stunt

tu [tu] *adj* your

tú [tu] *pron* you

tubérculo [tu'βerkulo] *nm* (Bot) tuber

tuberculosis [tuβerku'losis] *nf inv* tuberculosis

tubería [tuβe'ria] *nf* pipes pl; (*conducto*) pipeline

tubo ['tuβo] *nm* tube, pipe; **tubo de ensayo** test tube; **tubo de escape** exhaust (pipe)

tuerca ['twerka] *nf* nut

tuerto, -a ['twerto, a] *adj* blind in one eye ▷ *nm/f* one-eyed person

tuerza *etc vb* V **torcer**

tuétano ['twetano] *nm* marrow; (Bot) pith

tufo ['tufo] *nm* (*hedor*) stench

tul [tul] *nm* tulle

tulipán [tuli'pan] *nm* tulip

tullido, -a [tu'ʎiðo, a] *adj* crippled

tumba ['tumba] *nf* (*sepultura*) tomb

tumbar [tum'bar] *vt* to knock down; **tumbarse** *vr* (*echarse*) to lie down; (*extenderse*) to stretch out

tumbo ['tumbo] *nm*: **dar ~s** to stagger

tumbona [tum'bona] *nf* (*butaca*) easy chair; (*de playa*) deckchair (BRIT), beach chair (US)

tumor [tu'mor] *nm* tumour

tumulto [tu'multo] *nm* turmoil

tuna ['tuna] *nf* (Mús) student music group; V tb **tuno**

tunante [tu'nante] *nmf* rascal

tunear [tune'ar] *vt* (Auto) to style, mod (inf)

túnel ['tunel] *nm* tunnel

tuning ['tunin] *nm* (Auto) car styling, modding (inf)

tuno, -a ['tuno, a] *nm/f* (*fam*) rogue ▷ *nm* member of student music group

tupido, -a [tu'piðo, a] *adj* (*denso*) dense; (*tela*) close-woven

turbante [tur'βante] *nm* turban

turbar [tur'βar] *vt* (*molestar*) to disturb; (*incomodar*) to upset

turbina [tur'βina] *nf* turbine

turbio, -a ['turβjo, a] *adj* cloudy; (*tema etc*) confused

turbulencia [turβu'lenθja] *nf* turbulence; (*fig*) restlessness; **turbulento, -a** *adj* turbulent;

(*fig: intranquilo*) restless; (: *ruidoso*) noisy

turco, -a ['turko, a] *adj* Turkish ▷ *nm/f* Turk

turismo [tu'rismo] *nm* tourism; (*coche*) car; **turista** *nmf* tourist; **turístico, -a** *adj* tourist *cpd*

turnar [tur'nar] *vi* to take (it in) turns; **turnarse** *vr* to take (it in) turns; **turno** *nm* (*de trabajo*) shift; (*en juegos etc*) turn

turquesa [tur'kesa] *nf* turquoise

Turquía [tur'kia] *nf* Turkey

turrón [tu'rron] *nm* (*dulce*) nougat

tutear [tute'ar] *vt* to address as familiar "tú"; **tutearse** *vr* to be on familiar terms

tutela [tu'tela] *nf* (*legal*) guardianship; **tutelar** *adj* tutelary ▷ *vt* to protect

tutor, a [tu'tor, a] *nm/f* (*legal*) guardian; (*Escol*) tutor

tuve *etc vb* V **tener**

tuviera *etc vb* V **tener**

tuyo, -a ['tuʝo, a] *adj* yours, of yours ▷ *pron* yours; **un amigo ~** a friend of yours; **los ~s** (*fam*) your relations o family

TV *nf abr* (= *televisión*) TV

TVE *nf abr* = **Televisión Española**

u

u [u] *conj* or

ubicar [uβi'kar] *vt* to place, situate; (LAM: *encontrar*) to find; **ubicarse** *vr* (LAM: *encontrarse*) to lie, be located

ubre ['uβre] *nf* udder

UCI *nf abr* (= Unidad de Cuidados Intensivos) ICU

Ud(s) *abr* = **usted(es)**

UE *nf abr* (= Unión Europea) EU

ufanarse [ufa'narse] *vr* to boast; **ufano, -a** *adj* (*arrogante*) arrogant; (*presumido*) conceited

UGT (ESP) *nf abr* = **Unión General de Trabajadores**

úlcera ['ulθera] *nf* ulcer

ulterior [ulte'rjor] *adj* (*más allá*) farther, further; (*subsecuente, siguiente*) subsequent

últimamente ['ultimamente] *adv* (*recientemente*) lately, recently

ultimar [ulti'mar] *vt* to finish; (*finalizar*) to finalize; (LAM: *matar*) to kill

ultimátum [ulti'matum] (*pl* **-s**) *nm* ultimatum

último, -a ['ultimo, a] *adj* last; (*más reciente*) latest, most recent; (*más bajo*) bottom; (*más alto*) top; **en las últimas** on one's last legs; **por -** finally

ultra ['ultra] *adj* ultra ▷ *nmf* extreme right-winger

ultraje [ul'traxe] *nm* outrage; insult

ultramar [ultra'mar] *nm*: **de** o **en -** abroad, overseas

ultramarinos [ultrama'rinos] *nmpl* groceries; **tienda de -** grocer's (shop)

ultranza [ul'tranθa]: **a -** *adv* (*a todo trance*) at all costs; (*completo*) outright

umbral [um'bral] *nm* (*gen*) threshold

un, una [un, 'una] *art indef* a; (*antes de vocal*) an; **una mujer/naranja** a woman/an orange

▷ *adj*: **unos** (o **unas**): **hay unos regalos para ti** there are some presents for you; **hay unas cervezas en la nevera** there are some beers in the fridge

unánime [u'nanime] *adj* unanimous; **unanimidad** *nf* unanimity

undécimo, -a [un'deθimo, a] *adj* eleventh

ungir [un'xir] *vt* to anoint

ungüento [un'gwento] *nm* ointment

único, -a ['uniko, a] *adj* only, sole; (*sin par*) unique

unidad [uni'ðað] *nf* unity; (Com, Tec etc) unit

unido, -a [u'niðo, a] *adj* joined, linked; (*fig*) united

unificar [unifi'kar] *vt* to unite, unify

uniformar [unifor'mar] *vt* to make uniform, level up; (*persona*) to put into uniform

uniforme [uni'forme] *adj* uniform, equal; (*superficie*) even ▷ *nm* uniform

unilateral [unilate'ral] *adj* unilateral

unión [u'njon] *nf* union; (*acto*) uniting, joining; (*unidad*) unity; (Tec) joint; **Unión Europea** European Union

unir [u'nir] *vt* (*juntar*) to join, unite; (*atar*) to tie, fasten; (*combinar*) to combine; **unirse** *vr* to join together, unite; (*empresas*) to merge

unísono [u'nisono] *nm*: **al -** in unison

universal [uniβer'sal] *adj* universal; (*mundial*) world *cpd*

universidad [uniβersi'ðað] *nf* university

universitario, -a [uniβersi'tarjo, a] *adj* university *cpd* ▷ *nm/f* (*profesor*) lecturer; (*estudiante*) (university) student; (*graduado*) graduate

universo [uni'βerso] *nm* universe

uno, -a ['uno, a] *adj* one; **unos pocos** a few; **unos cien** about a hundred ▷ *pron* **1** one; **quiero sólo uno** I only want one; **uno de ellos** one of them

2 (*alguien*) somebody, someone; **conozco a uno que se te parece** I know somebody o someone who looks like you; **uno mismo** oneself; **unos querían quedarse** some (people) wanted to stay

3 (los) **unos ... (los) otros ...** some ... others

▷ *nf* one; **es la una** it's one o'clock

▷ *nm* (number) one

untar [un'tar] *vt* (*mantequilla*) to spread; (*engrasar*) to grease, oil

uña ['uɲa] *nf* (Anat) nail; (*garra*) claw; (*casco*) hoof; (*arrancaclavos*) claw

uranio [u'ranjo] *nm* uranium

urbanización [urβaniθa'θjon] *nf* (*barrio, colonia*) housing estate

urbanizar [urβani'θar] *vt* (*zona*) to develop, urbanize

urbano, -a [ur'βano, a] *adj* (*de ciudad*) urban; (*cortés*) courteous, polite

urbe ['urβe] *nf* large city

urdir [ur'ðir] *vt* to warp; (*complot*) to plot, contrive

urgencia [ur'xenθja] *nf* urgency; (*prisa*) haste, rush; (*emergencia*) emergency; **servicios de -** emergency services; **"U-s"** "Casualty"; **urgente** *adj* urgent

urgir [ur'xir] *vi* to be urgent; **me urge** I'm in a hurry for it

urinario, -a [uri'narjo, a] *adj* urinary ▷ *nm* urinal

urna ['urna] *nf* urn; (Pol) ballot box

urraca [u'rraka] *nf* magpie

URSS [urs] *nf* (Hist): **la URSS** the USSR

Uruguay [uru'xwai] *nm* (tb: **el -**) Uruguay; **uruguayo, -a** *adj, nm/f* Uruguayan

usado, -a [u'saðo, a] *adj* used; (*de segunda mano*) secondhand

usar [u'sar] *vt* to use; (*ropa*) to wear; (*tener costumbre*) to be in the habit of; **usarse** *vr* to be used; **uso** *nm*

use; wear; (*costumbre*) usage, custom; (*moda*) fashion;
al uso in keeping with custom; **al uso de** in the style
of; **de uso externo** (*Med*) for external use
usted [us'teð] *pron* (*sg*) you *sg*; (*pl*): **~es** you *pl*
usual [u'swal] *adj* usual
usuario, -a [usu'arjo, a] *nm/f* user
usura [u'sura] *nf* usury; **usurero, -a** *nm/f* usurer
usurpar [usur'par] *vt* to usurp
utensilio [uten'siljo] *nm* tool; (*Culin*) utensil
útero ['utero] *nm* uterus, womb
útil ['util] *adj* useful ▷ *nm* tool; **utilidad** *nf*
usefulness; (*Com*) profit; **utilizar** *vt* to use, utilize
utopía [uto'pia] *nf* Utopia; **utópico, -a** *adj* Utopian
uva ['uβa] *nf* grape

v *abr* (= voltio) v
va *vb* V **ir**
vaca ['baka] *nf* (*animal*) cow; **carne de ~** beef
vacaciones [baka'θjones] *nfpl* holidays
vacante [ba'kante] *adj* vacant, empty ▷ *nf* vacancy
vaciar [ba'θjar] *vt* to empty out; (*ahuecar*) to hollow
out; (*moldear*) to cast; **vaciarse** *vr* to empty
vacilar [baθi'lar] *vi* to be unsteady; (*al hablar*) to
falter; (*dudar*) to hesitate, waver; (*memoria*) to fail
vacío, -a [ba'θio, a] *adj* empty; (*puesto*) vacant;
(*desocupado*) idle; (*vano*) vain ▷ *nm* emptiness; (*Física*)
vacuum; (*un vacío*) (empty) space
vacuna [ba'kuna] *nf* vaccine; **vacunar** *vt* to
vaccinate
vacuno, -a [ba'kuno, a] *adj* cow *cpd*; **ganado ~**
cattle
vadear [baðe'ar] *vt* (*río*) to ford; **vado** *nm* ford
vagabundo, -a [baɣa'βundo, a] *adj* wandering
▷ *nm* tramp
vagancia [ba'ɣanθja] *nf* (*pereza*) idleness, laziness
vagar [ba'ɣar] *vi* to wander; (*no hacer nada*) to idle
vagina [ba'xina] *nf* vagina
vago, -a ['baɣo, a] *adj* vague; (*perezoso*) lazy ▷ *nm/f*
(*vagabundo*) tramp; (*flojo*) lazybones *sg*, idler
vagón [ba'ɣon] *nm* (*Ferro: de pasajeros*) carriage; (: *de
mercancías*) wagon
vaho ['bao] *nm* (*vapor*) vapour, steam; (*respiración*)
breath
vaina ['baina] *nf* sheath
vainilla [bai'niʎa] *nf* vanilla
vais *vb* V **ir**
vaivén [bai'βen] *nm* to-and-fro movement; (*de
tránsito*) coming and going; **vaivenes** *nmpl* (*fig*) ups
and downs
vajilla [ba'xiʎa] *nf* crockery, dishes *pl*; (*juego*) service,
set
valdré *etc vb* V **valer**
vale ['bale] *nm* voucher; (*recibo*) receipt; (*pagaré*) IOU
valedero, -a [bale'ðero, a] *adj* valid
valenciano, -a [balen'θjano, a] *adj* Valencian
valentía [balen'tia] *nf* courage, bravery
valer [ba'ler] *vt* to be worth; (*Mat*) to equal; (*costar*)
to cost ▷ *vi* (*ser útil*) to be useful; (*ser válido*) to be valid;

valerse vr to take care of oneself; **~se de** to make use of, take advantage of; **~ la pena** to be worthwhile; **¿vale?** (ESP) OK?; **más vale que nos vayamos** we'd better go; **¡eso a mí no me vale!** (MÉX: fam: no importar) I couldn't care less about that

valeroso, -a [bale'roso, a] adj brave, valiant

valgo etc vb V **valer**

valía [ba'lia] nf worth, value

validar [bali'ðar] vt to validate; **validez** nf validity; **válido, -a** adj valid

valiente [ba'ljente] adj brave, valiant ▷ nm hero

valija [ba'lixa] (CS) nf (suit)case

valioso, -a [ba'ljoso, a] adj valuable

valla [ˈbaʎa] nf fence; (Deporte) hurdle; **valla publicitaria** hoarding; **vallar** vt to fence in

valle [ˈbaʎe] nm valley

valor [ba'lor] nm value, worth; (precio) price; (valentía) valour, courage; (importancia) importance; **valores** nmpl (Com) securities; **valorar** vt to value

vals [bals] nm inv waltz

válvula [ˈbalβula] nf valve

vamos vb V **ir**

vampiro, -resa [bam'piro, 'resa] nm/f vampire

van vb V **ir**

vanguardia [ban'gwardja] nf vanguard; (Arte etc) avant-garde

vanidad [bani'ðað] nf vanity; **vanidoso, -a** adj vain, conceited

vano, -a [ˈbano, a] adj vain

vapor [ba'por] nm vapour; (vaho) steam; **al ~** (Culin) steamed; **vapor de agua** water vapour; **vaporizador** nm atomizer; **vaporizar** vt to vaporize; **vaporoso, -a** adj vaporous

vaquero, -a [ba'kero, a] adj cattle cpd ▷ nm cowboy; **vaqueros** nmpl (pantalones) jeans

vaquilla [ba'kiʎa] nf (Zool) heifer

vara [ˈbara] nf stick; (Tec) rod

variable [ba'rjaβle] adj, nf variable

variación [barja'θjon] nf variation

variar [bar'jar] vt to vary; (modificar) to modify; (cambiar de posición) to switch around ▷ vi to vary

varicela [bari'θela] nf chickenpox

varices [ba'riθes] nfpl varicose veins

variedad [barje'ðað] nf variety

varilla [ba'riʎa] nf stick; (Bot) twig; (Tec) rod; (de rueda) spoke

vario, -a [ˈbarjo, a] adj varied; **~s** various, several

varita [ba'rita] nf (tb: **~ mágica**) magic wand

varón [ba'ron] nm male, man; **varonil** adj manly, virile

Varsovia [bar'soβja] n Warsaw

vas vb V **ir**

vasco, -a [ˈbasko, a] adj, nm/f Basque; **vascongado, -a** [baskon'gaðo, a] adj Basque; **las Vascongadas** the Basque Country

vaselina [base'lina] nf Vaseline®

vasija [ba'sixa] nf container, vessel

vaso [ˈbaso] nm glass, tumbler; (Anat) vessel

vástago [ˈbastaxo] nm (Bot) shoot; (Tec) rod; (fig) offspring

vasto, -a [ˈbasto, a] adj vast, huge

Vaticano [bati'kano] nm: **el ~** the Vatican

vatio [ˈbatjo] nm (Elec) watt

vaya etc vb V **ir**

Vd(s) abr = **usted(es)**

ve [be] vb V **ir**; **ver**

vecindad [beθin'dað] nf neighbourhood; (habitantes) residents pl

vecindario [beθin'darjo] nm neighbourhood; residents pl

vecino, -a [be'θino, a] adj neighbouring ▷ nm/f neighbour; (residente) resident

veda [ˈbeða] nf prohibition; **vedar** [be'ðar] vt (prohibir) to ban, prohibit; (impedir) to stop, prevent

vegetación [bexeta'θjon] nf vegetation

vegetal [bexe'tal] adj, nm vegetable

vegetariano, -a [bexeta'rjano, a] adj, nm/f vegetarian

vehículo [be'ikulo] nm vehicle; (Med) carrier

veía etc vb V **ver**

veinte [ˈbeinte] num twenty

vejar [be'xar] vt (irritar) to annoy, vex; (humillar) to humiliate

vejez [be'xeθ] nf old age

vejiga [be'xixa] nf (Anat) bladder

vela [ˈbela] nf (de cera) candle; (Náut) sail; (insomnio) sleeplessness; (vigilia) vigil; (Mil) sentry duty; **estar a dos ~s** (fam: sin dinero) to be skint

velado, -a [be'laðo, a] adj veiled; (sonido) muffled; (Foto) blurred ▷ nf soirée

velar [be'lar] vt (vigilar) to keep watch over ▷ vi to stay awake; **~ por** to watch over, look after

velatorio [bela'torjo] nm (funeral) wake

velero [be'lero] nm (Náut) sailing ship; (Aviac) glider

veleta [be'leta] nf weather vane

veliz [be'lis] (MÉX) nm (suit)case

vello [ˈbeʎo] nm down, fuzz

velo [ˈbelo] nm veil

velocidad [beloθi'ðað] nf speed; (Tec, Auto) gear

velocímetro [belo'θimetro] nm speedometer

velorio [be'lorjo] (LAM) nm (funeral) wake

veloz [be'loθ] adj fast

ven vb V **venir**

vena [ˈbena] nf vein

venado [be'naðo] nm deer

vencedor, a [benθe'ðor, a] adj victorious ▷ nm/f victor, winner

vencer [ben'θer] vt (dominar) to defeat, beat; (derrotar) to vanquish; (superar, controlar) to overcome, master ▷ vi (triunfar) to win (through), triumph; (plazo) to expire; **vencido, -a** adj (derrotado) defeated, beaten; (Com) due ▷ adv: **pagar vencido** to pay in arrears

venda [ˈbenda] nf bandage; **vendaje** nm bandage, dressing; **vendar** vt to bandage; **vendar los ojos** to blindfold

vendaval [benda'βal] nm (viento) gale

vendedor, a [bende'ðor, a] nm/f seller

vender [ben'der] vt to sell; **venderse** vr (estar a la venta) to be on sale; **~ al contado/al por mayor/al por menor** to sell for cash/wholesale/retail; **"se vende"** "for sale"

vendimia [ben'dimja] nf grape harvest

vendré etc vb V **venir**

veneno [be'neno] nm poison; (de serpiente) venom; **venenoso, -a** adj poisonous; venomous

venerable [bene'raβle] adj venerable; **venerar** vt (respetar) to revere; (adorar) to worship

venéreo, -a [be'nereo, a] adj: **enfermedad venérea** venereal disease

venezolano, -a [beneθo'lano, a] adj Venezuelan

Venezuela [bene'θwela] nf Venezuela

venganza [ben'ganθa] nf vengeance, revenge;

vengar vt to avenge; **vengarse** vr to take revenge; **vengativo, -a** adj (persona) vindictive

vengo etc vb V **venir**

venia [ˈbenja] nf (perdón) pardon; (permiso) consent

venial [beˈnjal] adj venial

venida [beˈniða] nf (llegada) arrival; (regreso) return

venidero, -a [beniˈðero, a] adj coming, future

venir [beˈnir] vi to come; (llegar) to arrive; (ocurrir) to happen; (fig): ~ **de** to stem from; ~ **bien/mal** to be suitable/unsuitable; **el año que viene** next year; ~**se abajo** to collapse

venta [ˈbenta] nf (Com) sale; **"en ~"** "for sale"; **estar a la ~** en ~ to be (up) for sale o on the market; **venta a domicilio** door-to-door selling; **venta a plazos** hire purchase; **venta al contado/al por mayor/al por menor** cash sale/wholesale/retail

ventaja [benˈtaxa] nf advantage; **ventajoso, -a** adj advantageous

ventana [benˈtana] nf window; **ventanilla** nf (de taquilla) window (of booking office etc)

ventilación [bentilaˈθjon] nf ventilation; (corriente) draught

ventilador [bentilaˈðor] nm fan

ventilar [bentiˈlar] vt to ventilate; (para secar) to put out to dry; (asunto) to air, discuss

ventisca [benˈtiska] nf blizzard

ventrílocuo, -a [benˈtrilokwo, a] nm/f ventriloquist

ventura [benˈtura] nf (felicidad) happiness; (buena suerte) luck; (destino) fortune; **a la (buena) ~** at random; **venturoso, -a** adj happy; (afortunado) lucky, fortunate

veo etc vb V **ver**

ver [ber] vt to see; (mirar) to look at, watch; (entender) to understand; (investigar) to look into ▷ vi to see; to understand; **verse** vr (encontrarse) to meet; (dejarse ver) to be seen; (hallarse: en un apuro) to find o.s., be; **(vamos) a ~** let's see; **no tener nada que ~ con** to have nothing to do with; **a mi modo de ~** as I see it; **ya ~emos** we'll see

vera [ˈbera] nf edge, verge; (de río) bank

veranear [beraneˈar] vi to spend the summer; **veraneo** nm summer holiday; **veraniego, -a** adj summer cpd

verano [beˈrano] nm summer

veras [ˈberas] nfpl truth sg; **de ~** really, truly

verbal [berˈβal] adj verbal

verbena [berˈβena] nf (baile) open-air dance

verbo [ˈberβo] nm verb

verdad [berˈðað] nf truth; (fiabilidad) reliability; **de ~** real, proper; **a decir ~** to tell the truth; **verdadero, -a** adj (veraz) true, truthful; (fiable) reliable; (fig) real

verde [ˈberðe] adj green; (chiste) blue, dirty ▷ nm green; **viejo ~** dirty old man; **verdear** vi to turn green; **verdor** nm greenness

verdugo [berˈðuxo] nm executioner

verdulero, -a [berðuˈlero, a] nm/f greengrocer

verduras [berˈðuras] nfpl (Culin) greens

vereda [beˈreða] nf path; (cs: acera) pavement (BRIT), sidewalk (US)

veredicto [bereˈðikto] nm verdict

vergonzoso, -a [berɣonˈθoso, a] adj shameful; (tímido) timid, bashful

vergüenza [berˈɣwenθa] nf shame, sense of shame; (timidez) bashfulness; (pudor) modesty; **me da ~** I'm ashamed

verídico, -a [beˈriðiko, a] adj true, truthful

verificar [berifiˈkar] vt to check; (corroborar) to verify; (llevar a cabo) to carry out: **verificarse** vr (predicción) to prove to be true

verja [ˈberxa] nf (cancela) iron gate; (valla) iron railings pl; (de ventana) grille

vermut [berˈmut] (pl ~s) nm vermouth

verosímil [beroˈsimil] adj likely, probable; (relato) credible

verruga [beˈrruɣa] nf wart

versátil [berˈsatil] adj versatile

versión [berˈsjon] nf version

verso [ˈberso] nm verse; **un ~** a line of poetry

vértebra [ˈberteβra] nf vertebra

verter [berˈter] vt (líquido: adrede) to empty, pour (out); (: sin querer) to spill; (basura) to dump ▷ vi to flow

vertical [bertiˈkal] adj vertical

vértice [ˈbertiθe] nm vertex, apex

vertidos [berˈtiðos] nmpl waste sg

vertiente [berˈtjente] nf slope; (fig) aspect

vértigo [ˈbertiɣo] nm vertigo; (mareo) dizziness

vesícula [beˈsikula] nf blister

vespino® [besˈpino] nm o nf moped

vestíbulo [besˈtiβulo] nm hall; (de teatro) foyer

vestido [besˈtiðo] nm (ropa) clothes pl, clothing; (de mujer) dress, frock ▷ pp de **vestir**; ~ **de azul/marinero** dressed in blue/as a sailor

vestidor [bestiˈðor] (MÉX) nm (Deporte) changing (BRIT) o locker (US) room

vestimenta [bestiˈmenta] nf clothing

vestir [besˈtir] vt (poner: ropa) to put on; (llevar: ropa) to wear; (proveer de ropa a) to clothe; (sastre) to make clothes for ▷ vi to dress; (verse bien) to look good; **vestirse** vr to get dressed, dress o.s.

vestuario [besˈtwarjo] nm clothes pl, wardrobe; (Teatro: cuarto) dressing room; (Deporte) changing (BRIT) o locker (US) room

vetar [beˈtar] vt to veto

veterano, -a [beteˈrano, a] adj, nm veteran

veterinaria [beteriˈnarja] nf veterinary science; V tb **veterinario**

veterinario, -a [beteriˈnarjo, a] nm/f vet(erinary surgeon)

veto [ˈbeto] nm veto

vez [beθ] nf time; (turno) turn; **a la ~ que** at the same time as; **a su ~** in its turn; **otra ~** again; **una ~** once; **de una ~** in one go; **de una ~ para siempre** once and for all; **en ~ de** instead of; **a o algunas veces** sometimes; **una y otra ~** repeatedly; **de ~ en cuando** from time to time; **7 veces 9** 7 times 9; **hacer las veces de** to stand in for; **tal ~** perhaps

vía [ˈbia] nf track, route; (Ferro) line; (fig) way; (Anat) passage, tube ▷ prep via, by way of; **por ~ judicial** by legal means; **en ~s de** in the process of; **vía aérea** airway; **Vía Láctea** Milky Way; **vía pública** public road o thoroughfare

viable [ˈbjaβle] adj (solución, plan, alternativa) feasible

viaducto [bjaˈðukto] nm viaduct

viajante [bjaˈxante] nm commercial traveller

viajar [bjaˈxar] vi to travel; **viaje** nm journey; (gira) tour; (Náut) voyage; **estar de viaje** to be on a trip; **viaje de ida y vuelta** round trip; **viaje de novios** honeymoon; **viajero, -a** adj travelling; (Zool) migratory ▷ nm/f (quien viaja) traveller; (pasajero) passenger

víbora [ˈbiβora] nf (Zool) viper; (: (MÉX: venenoso) poisonous snake

vibración [biβra'θjon] nf vibration

vibrar [bi'βrar] vt, vi to vibrate

vicepresidente [biθepresi'ðente] nmf vice-president

viceversa [biθe'βersa] adv vice versa

vicio ['biθjo] nm (gen) vice; (mala costumbre) bad habit; **vicioso, -a** adj (muy malo) vicious; (corrompido) depraved ▷ nm/f depraved person

víctima ['biktima] nf victim

victoria [bik'torja] nf victory; **victorioso, -a** adj victorious

vid [bið] nf vine

vida ['biða] nf (gen) life; (duración) lifetime; **de por ~** for life; **en la o mí ~** never; **estar con ~** to be still alive; **ganarse la ~** to earn one's living

video ['biðeo] nm video ▷ adj inv: **película de ~** video film; **videocámara** nf camcorder; **videocasete** nm video cassette, videotape; **videoclub** nm video club; **videojuego** nm video game; **videollamada** nf video call; **videoteléfono** nm videophone

vidrio ['biðrjo] nm glass

vieira ['bjeira] nf scallop

viejo, -a ['bjexo, a] adj old ▷ nm/f old man/woman; **hacerse ~** to get old

Viena ['bjena] n Vienna

vienes etc vb V **venir**

vienés, -esa [bje'nes, esa] adj Viennese

viento ['bjento] nm wind; **hacer ~** to be windy

vientre ['bjentre] nm belly; (matriz) womb

viernes ['bjernes] nm inv Friday; **Viernes Santo** Good Friday

Vietnam [bjet'nam] nm Vietnam; **vietnamita** adj Vietnamese

viga ['biɣa] nf beam, rafter; (de metal) girder

vigencia [bi'xenθja] nf validity; **estar en ~** to be in force; **vigente** adj valid, in force; (imperante) prevailing

vigésimo, -a [bi'xesimo, a] adj twentieth

vigía [bi'xia] nm look-out

vigilancia [bixi'lanθja] nf: **tener a algn bajo ~** to keep watch on sb

vigilar [bixi'lar] vt to watch over ▷ vi (gen) to be vigilant; (hacer guardia) to keep watch; **~ por** to take care of

vigilia [vi'xilja] nf wakefulness, being awake; (Rel) fast

vigor [bi'ɣor] nm vigour, vitality; **en ~** in force; **entrar/poner en ~** to come/put into effect; **vigoroso, -a** adj vigorous

VIH nm abr (= virus de la inmunodeficiencia humana) HIV; **VIH negativo/positivo** HIV-negative/-positive

vil [bil] adj vile, low

villa ['biʎa] nf (casa) villa; (pueblo) small town; (municipalidad) municipality

villancico [biʎan'θiko] nm (Christmas) carol

vilo ['bilo]: **en ~** adv in the air, suspended; (fig) on tenterhooks, in suspense

vinagre [bi'naɣre] nm vinegar

vinagreta [bina'ɣreta] nf vinaigrette, French dressing

vinculación [binkula'θjon] nf (lazo) link, bond; (acción) linking

vincular [binku'lar] vt to link, bind; **vínculo** nm link, bond

vine etc vb V **venir**

vinicultura [binikul'tura] nf wine growing

viniera etc vb V **venir**

vino ['bino] vb V **venir** ▷ nm wine; **vino blanco/tinto** white/red wine

viña ['biɲa] nf vineyard; **viñedo** nm vineyard

viola ['bjola] nf viola

violación [bjola'θjon] nf violation; (sexual) rape

violar [bjo'lar] vt to violate; (sexualmente) to rape

violencia [bjo'lenθja] nf violence, force; (incomodidad) embarrassment; (acto injusto) unjust act; **violentar** vt to force; (casa) to break into; (agredir) to assault; (violar) to violate; **violento, -a** adj violent; (furioso) furious; (situación) embarrassing; (acto) forced, unnatural

violeta [bjo'leta] nf violet

violín [bjo'lin] nm violin

violón [bjo'lon] nm double bass

virar [bi'rar] vi to change direction

virgen ['birxen] adj, nf virgin

Virgo ['birɣo] nm Virgo

viril [bi'ril] adj virile; **virilidad** nf virility

virtud [bir'tuð] nf virtue; **en ~ de** by virtue of; **virtuoso, -a** adj virtuous ▷ nm/f virtuoso

viruela [bi'rwela] nf smallpox

virulento, -a [biru'lento, a] adj virulent

virus ['birus] nm inv virus

visa ['bisa] (LAM) nf = **visado**

visado [bi'saðo] (ESP) nm visa

víscera ['bisθera] nf (Anat, Zool) gut, bowel; **vísceras** nfpl entrails

visceral [bisθe'ral] adj (odio) intense; **reacción ~** gut reaction

visera [bi'sera] nf visor

visibilidad [bisiβili'ðað] nf visibility; **visible** adj visible; (fig) obvious

visillos [bi'siʎos] nmpl lace curtains

visión [bi'sjon] nf (Anat) vision, (eye)sight; (fantasía) vision, fantasy

visita [bi'sita] nf call, visit; (persona) visitor; **hacer una ~** to pay a visit; **visitar** [bisi'tar] vt to visit, call on

visón [bi'son] nm mink

visor [bi'sor] nm (Foto) viewfinder

víspera ['bispera] nf: **la ~ de ...** the day before ...

vista ['bista] nf sight, vision; (capacidad de ver) (eye)sight; (mirada) look(s) (pl); **a primera ~** at first glance; **hacer la ~ gorda** to turn a blind eye; **volver la ~** to look back; **está a la ~ que** it's obvious that; **en ~ de** in view of; **en ~ de que** in view of the fact that; **¡hasta la ~!** so long!, see you!; **con ~s a** with a view to; **vistazo** nm glance; **dar o echar un vistazo a** to glance at

visto, -a ['bisto, a] pp de **ver** ▷ vb V **vestir** ▷ adj seen; (considerado) considered ▷ nm: **~ bueno** approval; **por lo ~** apparently; **está ~ que** it's clear that; **está bien/mal ~** it's acceptable/unacceptable; **~ que** since, considering that

vistoso, -a [bis'toso, a] adj colourful

visual [bi'swal] adj visual

vital [bi'tal] adj (de) life cpd, living cpd; (fig) vital; (persona) lively, vivacious; **vitalicio, -a** adj for life; **vitalidad** nf (de persona, negocio) energy; (de ciudad) liveliness

vitamina [bita'mina] nf vitamin

vitorear [bitore'ar] vt to cheer, acclaim

vitrina [bi'trina] nf show case; (LAM: escaparate) shop window

viudo, -a ['bjuðo, a] nm/f widower/widow

viva ['biβa] excl hurrah!; **~ el rey!** long live the king!

vivaracho, -a [biβa'ratʃo, a] adj jaunty, lively; (ojos) bright, twinkling

vivaz [bi'βaθ] adj lively
víveres ['biβeres] nmpl provisions
vivero [bi'βero] nm (para plantas) nursery; (para peces) fish farm; (fig) hotbed
viveza [bi'βeθa] nf liveliness; (agudeza: mental) sharpness
vivienda [bi'βjenda] nf housing; (una vivienda) house; (piso) flat (BRIT), apartment (US)
viviente [bi'βjente] adj living
vivir [bi'βir] vt, vi to live ▷ nm life, living
vivo, -a ['biβo, a] adj alive, living; (fig: descripción) vivid; (persona: astuto) smart, clever; **en ~** (transmisión etc) live
vocablo [bo'kaβlo] nm (palabra) word; (término) term
vocabulario [bokaβu'larjo] nm vocabulary
vocación [boka'θjon] nf vocation; **vocacional** (LAM) nf ≈ technical college
vocal [bo'kal] adj vocal ▷ nf vowel; **vocalizar** vt to vocalize
vocero [bo'θero] (LAM) nm spokesman/woman
voces ['boθes] pl de **voz**
vodka ['boðka] nm o f vodka
vol abr = **volumen**
volado [bo'laðo] (MÉX) adv in a rush, hastily
volador, a [bola'ðor, a] adj flying
volandas [bo'landas]: **en ~** adv in the air
volante [bo'lante] adj flying ▷ nm (de coche) steering wheel; (de reloj) balance
volar [bo'lar] vt (edificio) to blow up ▷ vi to fly
volátil [bo'latil] adj volatile
volcán [bol'kan] nm volcano; **volcánico, -a** adj volcanic
volcar [bol'kar] vt to upset, overturn; (tumbar, derribar) to knock over; (vaciar) to empty out ▷ vi to overturn; **volcarse** vr to tip over
voleibol [bolei'βol] nm volleyball
volqué etc vb V **volcar**
voltaje [bol'taxe] nm voltage
voltear [bolte'ar] vt to turn over; (volcar) to turn upside down
voltereta [bolte'reta] nf somersault
voltio ['boltjo] nm volt
voluble [bo'luβle] adj fickle
volumen [bo'lumen] (pl **volúmenes**) nm volume; **voluminoso, -a** adj voluminous; (enorme) massive
voluntad [bolun'taθ] nf will; (resolución) willpower; (deseo) desire, wish
voluntario, -a [bolun'tarjo, a] adj voluntary ▷ nm/f volunteer
volver [bol'βer] vt (gen) to turn; (dar vuelta a) to turn (over); (voltear) to turn round, turn upside down; (poner al revés) to turn inside out; (devolver) to return ▷ vi to return, go back, come back; **volverse** vr to turn round; **~ la espalda** to turn one's back; **~ triste** etc **a algn** to make sb sad etc; **~ a hacer** to do again; **~ en sí** to come to; **~se insoportable/muy caro** to get o become unbearable/very expensive; **~se loco** to go mad
vomitar [bomi'tar] vt, vi to vomit; **vómito** nm vomit
voraz [bo'raθ] adj voracious
vos [bos] (LAM) pron you
vosotros, -as [bo'sotros, as] (ESP) pron you; (reflexivo): **entre/para ~** among/for yourselves
votación [bota'θjon] nf (acto) voting; (voto) vote
votar [bo'tar] vi to vote; **voto** nm vote; (promesa) vow; **votos** nmpl (good) wishes

voy vb V **ir**
voz [boθ] nf voice; (grito) shout; (rumor) rumour; (Ling) word; **dar voces** to shout, yell; **de viva ~** verbally; **en ~ alta** aloud; **en ~ baja** in a low voice, in a whisper; **voz de mando** command
vuelco ['bwelko] vb V **volcar** ▷ nm spill, overturning
vuelo ['bwelo] vb V **volar** ▷ nm flight; (encaje) lace, frill; **coger al ~** to catch in flight; **vuelo chárter/regular** charter/scheduled flight; **vuelo libre** (Deporte) hang-gliding
vuelque etc vb V **volcar**
vuelta ['bwelta] nf (gen) turn; (curva) bend, curve; (regreso) return; (revolución) revolution; (de circuito) lap; (de papel, tela) reverse; (cambio) change; **a la ~** on one's return; **a la ~ (de la esquina)** round the corner; **a ~ de correo** by return of post; **dar ~s** (cabeza) to spin; **dar(se) la ~** (volverse) to turn round; **estar dé ~** to be back; **dar una ~** to go for a walk; (en coche) to go for a drive; **vuelta ciclista** (Deporte) (cycle) tour
vuelto ['bwelto] pp de **volver**
vuelvo etc vb V **volver**
vuestro, -a ['bwestro, a] adj pos your; **un amigo ~** a friend of yours ▷ pron: **el ~/la vuestra, los ~s/las vuestras** yours
vulgar [bul'xar] adj (ordinario) vulgar; (común) common; **vulgaridad** nf commonness; (acto) vulgarity; (expresión) coarse expression
vulnerable [bulne'raβle] adj vulnerable
vulnerar [bulne'rar] vt (ley, acuerdo) to violate, breach; (derechos, intimidad) to violate; (reputación) to damage

W X

walkie-talkie [walki-'talki] (*pl* **~s**) *nm* walkie-talkie
Walkman® ['walkman] *nm* Walkman®
wáter ['bater] *nm* (*taza*) toilet; (*LAM: lugar*) toilet (*BRIT*), rest room (*US*)
web [web] *nm o f* (*página*) website; (*red*) (World Wide) Web; **webcam** *nf* webcam; **webmaster** *nmf* webmaster; **website** *nm* website
western ['western] (*pl* **~s**) *nm* western
whisky ['wiski] *nm* whisky, whiskey
windsurf ['winsurf] *nm* windsurfing; **hacer ~** to go windsurfing

xenofobia [kseno'foβja] *nf* xenophobia
xilófono [ksi'lofono] *nm* xylophone
xocoyote, -a [ksoko'yote, a] (*MÉX*) *nm/f* baby of the family, youngest child

Y Z

y [i] *conj* and
ya [ja] *adv* (*gen*) already; (*ahora*) now; (*en seguida*) at
once; (*pronto*) soon ▷ *excl* all right! **¡~ voy!** coming!
now that; **~ lo sé** I know; **~ que** since; **¡~ está bien!**
that's (quite) enough!; **¡~ voy!** coming!
yacaré [jaka're] (*CS*) *nm* cayman
yacer [ja'θer] *vi* to lie
yacimiento [jaθi'mjento] *nm* (*de mineral*) deposit;
(*arqueológico*) site
yanqui ['janki] *adj, nmf* Yankee
yate ['jate] *nm* yacht
yazco *etc vb* V **yacer**
yedra ['jeðra] *nf* ivy
yegua ['jeɣwa] *nf* mare
yema ['jema] *nf* (*del huevo*) yolk; (*Bot*) leaf bud; (*fig*)
best part; **yema del dedo** fingertip
yerno ['jerno] *nm* son-in-law
yeso ['jeso] *nm* plaster
yo [jo] *pron* I; **soy ~** it's me
yodo ['joðo] *nm* iodine
yoga ['joɣa] *nm* yoga
yogur(t) [jo'ɣur(t)] *nm* yoghurt
yuca ['juka] *nf* (*alimento*) cassava, manioc root
Yugoslavia [juɣos'laβja] *nf* (*Hist*) Yugoslavia
yugular [juɣu'lar] *adj* jugular
yunque ['junke] *nm* anvil
yuyo ['jujo] (*RPL*) *nm* (*mala hierba*) weed

zafar [θa'far] *vt* (*soltar*) to untie; (*superficie*) to clear;
zafarse *vr* (*escaparse*) to escape; (*Tec*) to slip off
zafiro [θa'firo] *nm* sapphire
zaga ['θaɣa] *nf*: **a la ~** behind
zaguán [θa'ɣwan] *nm* hallway
zalamero, -a [θala'mero, a] *adj* flattering; (*cobista*)
suave
zamarra [θa'marra] *nf* (*chaqueta*) sheepskin jacket
zambullirse [θambu'ʎirse] *vr* to dive
zampar [θam'par] *vt* to gobble down
zanahoria [θana'orja] *nf* carrot
zancadilla [θanka'ðiʎa] *nf* trip
zanco ['θanko] *nm* stilt
zanja ['θanxa] *nf* ditch; **zanjar** *vt* (*resolver*) to resolve
zapata [θa'pata] *nf* (*Mecánica*) shoe
zapatería [θapate'ria] *nf* (*oficio*) shoemaking;
(*tienda*) shoe shop; (*fábrica*) shoe factory; **zapatero, -a**
nm/f shoemaker
zapatilla [θapa'tiʎa] *nf* slipper; **zapatilla de
deporte** training shoe
zapato [θa'pato] *nm* shoe
zapping ['θapin] *nm* channel-hopping; **hacer ~** to
channel-hop
zar [θar] *nm* tsar, czar
zarandear [θarande'ar] (*fam*) *vt* to shake vigorously
zarpa ['θarpa] *nf* (*garra*) claw
zarpar [θar'par] *vi* to weigh anchor
zarza ['θarθa] *nf* (*Bot*) bramble; **zarzamora** *nf*
blackberry
zarzuela [θar'θwela] *nf* Spanish light opera
zigzag [θiɣ'θax] *nm* zigzag
zinc [θink] *nm* zinc
zíper ['θiper] (*MÉX, CAM*) *nm* zip (fastener) (*BRIT*),
zipper (*US*)
zócalo ['θokalo] *nm* (*Arq*) plinth, base; (*de pared*)
skirting board (*BRIT*), baseboard (*US*); (*MÉX: plaza*) main
o public square
zoclo ['θoklo] (*MÉX*) *nm* skirting board (*BRIT*),
baseboard (*US*)
zodíaco [θo'ðiako] *nm* zodiac
zona ['θona] *nf* zone; **zona fronteriza** border area;
zona roja (*LAM*) red-light district
zonzo, -a (*LAM: fam*) ['θonθo, a] *adj* silly ▷ *nm/f* fool

zoo ['θoo] nm zoo
zoología [θoolo'xia] nf zoology; **zoológico, -a** adj
zoological ▷ nm (tb: **parque zoológico**) zoo; **zoólogo,**
-a nm/f zoologist
zoom [θum] nm zoom lens
zopilote [θopi'lote] (MÉX, CAM) nm buzzard
zoquete [θo'kete] nm (fam) blockhead
zorro, -a ['θorro, a] adj crafty ▷ nm/f fox/vixen
zozobrar [θoθo'βrar] vi (hundirse) to capsize; (fig)
to fail
zueco ['θweko] nm clog
zumbar [θum'bar] vt (golpear) to hit ▷ vi to buzz;
zumbido nm buzzing
zumo ['θumo] nm juice
zurcir [θur'θir] vt (coser) to darn
zurdo, -a ['θurðo, a] adj left-handed
zurrar [θu'rrar] (fam) vt to wallop

A [eɪ] n (Mus) la m

○ **KEYWORD**

a [ə] (before vowel or silent h: an) indef art
1 un(a); **a book** un libro; **an apple** una manzana; **she's a doctor** (ella) es médica
2 (instead of the number "one") un(a); **a year ago** hace un año; **a hundred/thousand** etc **pounds** cien/mil etc libras
3 (in expressing ratios, prices etc): **3 a day/week** 3 al día/a la semana; **10 km an hour** 10 km por hora; **£5 a person** £5 por persona; **30p a kilo** 30p el kilo

A2 (BRIT: Scol) n segunda parte de los "A levels"
A.A. n abbr (BRIT: = Automobile Association) ≈ RACE m (SP); (= Alcoholics Anonymous) Alcohólicos Anónimos
A.A.A. (US) n abbr (= American Automobile Association) ≈ RACE m (SP)
aback [ə'bæk] adv: **to be taken ~** quedar desconcertado
abandon [ə'bændən] vt abandonar; (give up) renunciar a
abattoir ['æbətwɑ:*] (BRIT) n matadero
abbey ['æbɪ] n abadía
abbreviation [ə'bri:vɪ'eɪʃən] n (short form) abreviatura
abdomen ['æbdəmən] n abdomen m
abduct [æb'dʌkt] vt raptar, secuestrar
abide [ə'baɪd] vt: **I can't ~ it/him** no lo/le puedo ver; **abide by** vt fus atenerse a
ability [ə'bɪlɪtɪ] n habilidad f, capacidad f; (talent) talento
able ['eɪbl] adj capaz; (skilled) hábil; **to be ~ to do sth** poder hacer algo
abnormal [æb'nɔ:məl] adj anormal
aboard [ə'bɔ:d] adv a bordo ▷ prep a bordo de
abolish [ə'bɒlɪʃ] vt suprimir, abolir
abolition [æbəu'lɪʃən] n supresión f, abolición f

abort [ə'bɔ:t] vt, vi abortar; **abortion** [ə'bɔ:ʃən] n aborto; **to have an abortion** abortar, hacerse abortar

○ **KEYWORD**

about [ə'baut] adv 1 (approximately) más o menos, aproximadamente; **about a hundred/thousand** etc unos(unas) cien/mil etc; **it takes about 10 hours** se tarda unas o más o menos 10 horas; **at about 2 o'clock** sobre las dos; **I've just about finished** casi he terminado
2 (referring to place) por todas partes; **to leave things lying about** dejar las cosas (tiradas) por ahí; **to run about** correr por todas partes; **to walk about** pasearse, ir y venir
3: **to be about to do sth** estar a punto de hacer algo
▷ prep 1 (relating to) de, sobre, acerca de; **a book about London** un libro sobre or acerca de Londres; **what is it about?** ¿de qué se trata?; **we talked about it** hablamos de eso or ello; **what** or **how about doing this?** ¿qué tal si hacemos esto?
2 (referring to place) por; **to walk about the town** caminar por la ciudad

above [ə'bʌv] adv encima, por encima, arriba ▷ prep encima de; (greater than: in number) más de; (: in rank) superior a; **mentioned ~** susodicho; **~ all** sobre todo
abroad [ə'brɔːd] adv (to be) en el extranjero; (to go) al extranjero
abrupt [ə'brʌpt] adj (sudden) brusco; (curt) áspero
abscess ['æbsɪs] n absceso
absence ['æbsəns] n ausencia
absent ['æbsənt] adj ausente; **absent-minded** adj distraído
absolute ['æbsəlu:t] adj absoluto; **absolutely** [-'lu:tlɪ] adv (totally) totalmente; (certainly!) ¡por supuesto (que sí)!
absorb [əb'zɔ:b] vt absorber; **to be ~ed in a book** estar absorto en un libro; **absorbent cotton** (US) n algodón m hidrófilo; **absorbing** adj absorbente
abstain [əb'steɪn] vi: **to ~ (from)** abstenerse (de)
abstract ['æbstrækt] adj abstracto
absurd [əb'sə:d] adj absurdo
abundance [ə'bʌndəns] n abundancia
abundant [ə'bʌndənt] adj abundante
abuse [n ə'bju:s, vb ə'bju:z] n (insults) insultos mpl, injurias fpl; (ill-treatment) malos tratos mpl; (misuse) abuso ▷ vt insultar; maltratar; abusar de; **abusive** adj ofensivo
abysmal [ə'bɪzməl] adj pésimo; (failure) garrafal; (ignorance) supino
academic [ækə'demɪk] adj académico, universitario; (pej: issue) puramente teórico ▷ n estudioso/a, profesor(a) m/f universitario/a; **academic year** n (Univ) año m académico; (Scol) año m escolar
academy [ə'kædəmɪ] n (learned body) academia; (school) instituto, colegio; **~ of music** conservatorio
accelerate [æk'seləreɪt] vt, vi acelerar; **acceleration** [ækselə'reɪʃən] n aceleración f; **accelerator** (BRIT) n acelerador m

accent ['æksɛnt] n acento; (fig) énfasis m

accept [ək'sɛpt] vt aceptar; (responsibility, blame) admitir; **acceptable** adj aceptable; **acceptance** n aceptación f

access ['æksɛs] n acceso; **to have ~ to** tener libre acceso a; **accessible** [-'sɛsəbl] adj (place, person) accesible; (knowledge etc) asequible

accessory [æk'sɛsərɪ] n accesorio; (Law): **~ to** cómplice de

accident ['æksɪdənt] n accidente m; (chance event) casualidad f; **by ~** (unintentionally) sin querer; (by chance) por casualidad; **accidental** [-'dɛntl] adj accidental, fortuito; **accidentally** [-'dɛntəlɪ] adv sin querer; por casualidad; **Accident and Emergency Department** n (BRIT) Urgencias fpl; **accident insurance** n seguro contra accidentes

acclaim [ə'kleɪm] vt aclamar, aplaudir ▷ n aclamación f, aplausos mpl

accommodate [ə'kɔmədeɪt] vt (person) alojar, hospedar; (: car, hotel etc) tener cabida para; (oblige, help) complacer

accommodation [əkɔmə'deɪʃən] (US **accommodations**) n alojamiento

accompaniment [ə'kʌmpənɪmənt] n acompañamiento

accompany [ə'kʌmpənɪ] vt acompañar

accomplice [ə'kʌmplɪs] n cómplice mf

accomplish [ə'kʌmplɪʃ] vt (finish) concluir; (achieve) lograr; **accomplishment** n (skill: gen pl) talento; (completion) realización f

accord [ə'kɔːd] n acuerdo ▷ vt conceder; **of his own ~** espontáneamente; **accordance** n: **in accordance with** de acuerdo con; **according** ▷ **according to** prep según; (in accordance with) conforme a; **accordingly** adv (appropriately) de acuerdo con esto; (as a result) en consecuencia

account [ə'kaunt] n (Comm) cuenta; (report) informe m; **accounts** npl (Comm) cuentas fpl; **of no ~** de ninguna importancia; **on ~** a cuenta; **on no ~** bajo ningún concepto; **on ~ of** a causa de, por motivo de; **to take into ~, take ~ of** tener en cuenta; **account for** vt fus (explain) explicar; (represent) representar; **accountable** adj: **accountable (to)** responsable (ante); **accountant** n contable mf, contador(a) m/f; **account number** n (at bank etc) número de cuenta

accumulate [ə'kjuːmjuleɪt] vt acumular ▷ vi acumularse

accuracy ['ækjurəsɪ] n (of total) exactitud f; (of description etc) precisión f

accurate ['ækjurɪt] adj (total) exacto; (description) preciso; (person) cuidadoso; (device) de precisión; **accurately** adv con precisión

accusation [ækju'zeɪʃən] n acusación f

accuse [ə'kjuːz] vt: **to ~ sb (of sth)** acusar a algn (de algo); **accused** n (Law) acusado/a

accustomed [ə'kʌstəmd] adj: **~ to** acostumbrado a

ace [eɪs] n as m

ache [eɪk] n dolor m ▷ vi doler; **my head ~s** me duele la cabeza

achieve [ə'tʃiːv] vt (aim, result) alcanzar; (success) lograr, conseguir; **achievement** n (completion) realización f; (success) éxito

acid ['æsɪd] adj ácido; (taste) agrio ▷ n (Chem, inf: LSD) ácido

acknowledge [ək'nɔlɪdʒ] vt (letter: also: **~ receipt of**) acusar recibo de; (fact, situation, person) reconocer;

acknowledgement n acuse m de recibo

acne ['æknɪ] n acné m

acorn ['eɪkɔːn] n bellota

acoustic [ə'kuːstɪk] adj acústico

acquaintance [ə'kweɪntəns] n (person) conocido/a; (with person, subject) conocimiento

acquire [ə'kwaɪə*] vt adquirir; **acquisition** [ækwɪ'zɪʃən] n adquisición f

acquit [ə'kwɪt] vt absolver, exculpar; **to ~ o.s. well** salir con éxito

acre ['eɪkə*] n acre m

acronym ['ækrənɪm] n siglas fpl

across [ə'krɔs] prep (on the other side of) al otro lado de, del otro lado de; (crosswise) a través de ▷ adv de un lado a otro, de una parte a otra; a través, al través; (measurement): **the road is 10m ~** la carretera tiene 10m de ancho; **to run/swim ~** atravesar corriendo/nadando; **~ from** enfrente de

acrylic [ə'krɪlɪk] adj acrílico ▷ n acrílica

act [ækt] n acto, acción f; (of play) acto; (in music hall etc) número; (Law) decreto, ley f ▷ vi (behave) comportarse; (have effect: drug, chemical) hacer efecto; (Theatre) actuar; (pretend) fingir; (take action) obrar ▷ vt (part) hacer el papel de; **in the ~ of:** **to catch sb in the ~ of ...** pillar a algn en el momento en que ...; **to ~ as** actuar o hacer de; **act up** (inf) vi (person) portarse mal; **acting** adj suplente ▷ n (activity) actuación f; (profession) profesión f de actor

action ['ækʃən] n acción f, acto; (Mil) acción f, batalla; (Law) proceso, demanda; **out of ~** (person) fuera de combate; (thing) estropeado; **to take ~** tomar medidas; **action replay** n (TV) repetición f

activate ['æktɪveɪt] vt activar

active ['æktɪv] adj activo, enérgico; (volcano) en actividad; **actively** adv (participate) activamente; (discourage, dislike) enérgicamente

activist ['æktɪvɪst] n activista m/f

activity [-'tɪvɪtɪ] n actividad f; **activity holiday** n vacaciones con actividades organizadas

actor ['æktə*] n actor m

actress ['æktrɪs] n actriz f

actual ['æktjuəl] adj verdadero, real; (emphatic use) propiamente dicho

actually ['æktjuəlɪ] adv realmente, en realidad; (even) incluso

acupuncture ['ækjupʌŋktʃə*] n acupuntura

acute [ə'kjuːt] adj agudo

ad [æd] n abbr = **advertisement**

A.D. adv abbr (= anno Domini) DC

adamant ['ædəmənt] adj firme, inflexible

adapt [ə'dæpt] vt adaptar ▷ vi: **to ~ (to)** adaptarse (a), ajustarse (a); **adapter** (US **adaptor**) n (Elec) adaptador m; (for several plugs) ladrón m

add [æd] vt añadir, agregar; **add up** vt (figures) sumar ▷ vi (fig): **it doesn't add up** no tiene sentido; **add up to** vt fus (Math) sumar, ascender a; (fig: mean) querer decir, venir a ser

addict ['ædɪkt] n adicto/a; (enthusiast) entusiasta mf; **addicted** [ə'dɪktɪd] adj: **to be addicted to** ser adicto a, ser fanático de; **addiction** [ə'dɪkʃən] n (to drugs etc) adicción f; **addictive** [ə'dɪktɪv] adj que causa adicción

addition [ə'dɪʃən] n (adding up) adición f; (thing added) añadidura, añadido; **in ~** además, por añadidura; **in ~ to** además de; **additional** adj adicional

additive ['ædɪtɪv] n aditivo

address [ə'drɛs] n dirección f, señas fpl; (speech) discurso ▷vt (letter) dirigir; (speak to) dirigir la palabra a; (problem) tratar; **address book** n agenda (de direcciones)

adequate [ˈædɪkwɪt] adj (satisfactory) adecuado; (enough) suficiente

adhere [ədˈhɪə*] vi: **to ~** (stick to) pegarse a; (fig: abide by) observar; (: belief etc) ser partidario de

adhesive [ədˈhiːzɪv] n adhesivo; **adhesive tape** n (BRIT) cinta adhesiva; (US Med) esparadrapo

adjacent [əˈdʒeɪsənt] adj: **~ to** contiguo a, inmediato a

adjective [ˈædʒɛktɪv] n adjetivo

adjoining [əˈdʒɔɪnɪŋ] adj contiguo, vecino

adjourn [əˈdʒɜːn] vt aplazar ▷vi suspenderse

adjust [əˈdʒʌst] vt (change) modificar; (clothing) arreglar; (machine) ajustar ▷vi: **to ~ (to)** adaptarse (a); **adjustable** adj ajustable; **adjustment** n adaptación f; (to machine, prices) ajuste m

administer [ədˈmɪnɪstə*] vt administrar; **administration** [-ˈtreɪʃən] n (management) administración f; (government) gobierno; **administrative** [-trətɪv] adj administrativo

administrator [ədˈmɪnɪstreɪtə*] n administrador(a) m/f

admiral [ˈædmərəl] n almirante m

admiration [ædməˈreɪʃən] n admiración f

admire [ədˈmaɪə*] vt admirar; **admirer** n (fan) admirador(a) m/f

admission [ədˈmɪʃən] n (to university, club) ingreso; (entry fee) entrada; (confession) confesión f

admit [ədˈmɪt] vt (confess) confesar; (permit to enter) dejar entrar, dar entrada a; (to club, organization) admitir; (accept: defeat) reconocer; **to be ~ted to hospital** ingresar en el hospital; **admit to** vt fus confesarse culpable de; **admittance** n entrada; **admittedly** adv es cierto o verdad que

adolescent [ædəʊˈlɛsnt] adj, n adolescente mf

adopt [əˈdɔpt] vt adoptar; **adopted** adj adoptivo; **adoption** [əˈdɔpʃən] n adopción f

adore [əˈdɔː*] vt adorar

adorn [əˈdɔːn] vt adornar

Adriatic [eɪdrɪˈætɪk] n: **the ~ (Sea)** el (Mar) Adriático

adrift [əˈdrɪft] adv a la deriva

adult [ˈædʌlt] n adulto/a ▷adj (grown-up) adulto; (for adults) para adultos; **adult education** n educación f para adultos

adultery [əˈdʌltərɪ] n adulterio

advance [ədˈvɑːns] n (in progress) adelanto, progreso; (money) anticipo, préstamo; (Mil) avance m ▷adj: **~ booking** reserva anticipada; **~ notice, ~ warning** previo aviso ▷vt (money) anticipar; (theory, idea) proponer (para la discusión) ▷vi avanzar, adelantarse; **to make ~s (to sb)** hacer proposiciones (a algn); **in ~** por adelantado; **advanced** adj avanzado; (Scol: studies) adelantado

advantage [ədˈvɑːntɪdʒ] n (also Tennis) ventaja; **to take ~ of** (person) aprovecharse de; (opportunity) aprovechar

advent [ˈædvənt] n advenimiento; **A~** Adviento

adventure [ədˈvɛntʃə*] n aventura; **adventurous** [-tʃərəs] adj atrevido; aventurero

adverb [ˈædvɜːb] n adverbio

adversary [ˈædvəsərɪ] n adversario, contrario

adverse [ˈædvɜːs] adj adverso, contrario

advert [ˈædvɜːt] (BRIT) n abbr = **advertisement**

advertise [ˈædvətaɪz] vi (in newspaper etc) anunciar, hacer publicidad; **~ for** (staff, accommodation etc) buscar por medio de anuncios ▷vt anunciar; **advertisement** [ədˈvɜːtɪsmənt] n (Comm) anuncio; **advertiser** n anunciante mf; **advertising** n publicidad f, anuncios mpl; (industry) industria publicitaria

advice [ədˈvaɪs] n consejo, consejos mpl; (notification) aviso; **a piece of ~** un consejo; **to take legal ~** consultar con un abogado

advisable [ədˈvaɪzəbl] adj aconsejable, conveniente

advise [ədˈvaɪz] vt aconsejar; (inform): **to ~ sb of sth** informar a algn de algo; **to ~ sb against sth/doing sth** desaconsejar algo a algn/aconsejar a algn que no haga algo; **adviser, advisor** n consejero/a; (consultant) asesor(a) m/f; **advisory** adj consultivo

advocate [vb ˈædvəkeɪt, n -kɪt] vt abogar por ▷n (lawyer) abogado/a; (supporter): **~ of** defensor(a) m/f de

Aegean [iːˈdʒiːən] n: **the ~ (Sea)** el (Mar) Egeo

aerial [ˈɛərɪəl] n antena ▷adj aéreo

aerobics [ɛəˈrəʊbɪks] n aerobic m

aeroplane [ˈɛərəpleɪn] (BRIT) n avión m

aerosol [ˈɛərəsɔl] n aerosol m

affair [əˈfɛə*] n asunto; (also: **love ~**) aventura (amorosa)

affect [əˈfɛkt] vt (influence) afectar, influir en; (afflict, concern) afectar; (move) conmover; **affected** adj afectado; **affection** n afecto, cariño; **affectionate** adj afectuoso, cariñoso

afflict [əˈflɪkt] vt afligir

affluent [ˈæfluənt] adj (wealthy) acomodado; **the ~ society** la sociedad opulenta

afford [əˈfɔːd] vt (provide) proporcionar; **can we ~ to buy) it?** ¿tenemos bastante dinero para comprarlo?; **affordable** adj asequible

Afghanistan [æfˈgænɪstæn] n Afganistán m

afraid [əˈfreɪd] adj: **to be ~ of** (person) tener miedo a; (thing) tener miedo de; **to be ~ to** tener miedo de, temer; **I am ~ that** me temo que; **I am ~ not/so** lo siento, pero no/es así

Africa [ˈæfrɪkə] n África; **African** adj, n africano/a m/f; **African-American** adj, n afroamericano/a

after [ˈɑːftə*] prep (time) después de; (place, order) detrás de, tras ▷adv después ▷conj después (de) que; **what/who are you ~?** ¿qué/a quién busca usted?; **~ having done/he left** después de haber hecho/ después de que se marchó; **to name sb ~ sb** llamar a algn por algn; **it's twenty ~ eight** (US) son las ocho y veinte; **to ask ~ sb** preguntar por algn; **~ all** después de todo, al fin y al cabo; **~ you!** ¡pase usted!; **after-effects** npl consecuencias fpl, efectos mpl; **aftermath** n consecuencias fpl, resultados mpl; **afternoon** n tarde f; **after-shave (lotion)** n aftershave m; **aftersun (lotion/cream)** n loción f/crema para después del sol, aftersun m; **afterwards** (US **afterward**) adv después, más tarde

again [əˈgɛn] adv otra vez, de nuevo; **to do sth ~** volver a hacer algo; **~ and ~** una y otra vez

against [əˈgɛnst] prep (in opposition to) en contra de; (leaning on, touching) contra, junto a

age [eɪdʒ] n edad f; (period) época ▷vi envejecer(se) ▷vt envejecer; **she is 20 years of ~** tiene 20 años; **to come of ~** llegar a la mayoría de edad; **it's been ~s since I saw you** hace siglos que no te veo; **~d 10** de 10 años de edad; **age group** n: **to be in the same age group** tener la misma edad; **age limit** n edad f mínima (or máxima)

agency ['eɪdʒənsɪ] n agencia

agenda [ə'dʒɛndə] n orden m del día

agent ['eɪdʒənt] n agente mf; (Comm: holding concession) representante mf, delegado/a; (Chem, fig) agente m

aggravate ['ægrəveɪt] vt (situation) agravar; (person) irritar

aggression [ə'grɛʃən] n agresión f

aggressive [ə'grɛsɪv] adj (belligerent) agresivo; (assertive) enérgico

agile ['ædʒaɪl] adj ágil

agitated ['ædʒɪteɪtɪd] adj agitado

AGM n abbr (= annual general meeting) asamblea anual

ago [ə'gəʊ] adv: **2 days** ~ hace 2 días; **not long** ~ hace poco; **how long** ~? ¿hace cuánto tiempo?

agony ['ægənɪ] n (pain) dolor m agudo; (distress) angustia; **to be in** ~ retorcerse de dolor

agree [ə'griː] vt (price, date) acordar, quedar en ▷ vi (have same opinion) **to** ~ **(with/that)** estar de acuerdo (con/que); (correspond) coincidir, concordar; (consent) acceder; **to** ~ **with** (person) estar de acuerdo con, ponerse de acuerdo con; (: food) sentar bien a; (Ling) concordar con; **to** ~ **to sth/to do sth** consentir en algo/aceptar hacer algo; **to** ~ **that** (admit) estar de acuerdo en que; **agreeable** adj (sensation) agradable; (person) simpático; (willing) de acuerdo, conforme; **agreed** adj (time, place) convenido; **agreement** n acuerdo; (contract) contrato; **in agreement** de acuerdo, conforme

agricultural [ægrɪ'kʌltʃərəl] adj agrícola

agriculture ['ægrɪkʌltʃə*] n agricultura

ahead [ə'hɛd] adv (in front) delante; (into the future): **she had no time to think** ~ no tenía tiempo de hacer planes para el futuro; ~ **of** (in front of, advance of) antes de; ~ **of time** antes de la hora; **go right** or **straight** ~ (direction) siga adelante; (permission) hazlo (or hágalo)

aid [eɪd] n ayuda, auxilio; (device) aparato ▷ vt ayudar, auxiliar; **in** ~ **of** a beneficio de

aide [eɪd] n (person, also Mil) ayudante mf

AIDS [eɪdz] n abbr (= acquired immune deficiency syndrome) SIDA m

ailing ['eɪlɪŋ] adj (person, economy) enfermizo

ailment ['eɪlmənt] n enfermedad f, achaque m

aim [eɪm] vt (gun, camera) apuntar; (missile, remark) dirigir; (blow) asestar ▷ vi (also: **take** ~) apuntar ▷ n (in shooting) puntería; (objective) propósito, meta; **to** ~ **at** (with weapon) apuntar a; (objective) aspirar a, pretender; **to** ~ **to do** tener la intención de hacer

ain't [eɪnt] (inf) = **am not**; **aren't**; **isn't**

air [ɛə*] n aire m; (appearance) aspecto ▷ vt (room) ventilar; (clothes, ideas) airear ▷ cpd aéreo; **to throw sth into the** ~ (ball etc) lanzar algo al aire; **by** ~ (travel) en avión; **to be on the** ~ (Radio, TV) estar en antena; **airbag** n airbag m inv; **airbed** (BRIT) n colchón m neumático; **airborne** adj (in the air) en el aire; **as soon as the plane was airborne** tan pronto como el avión estuvo en el aire; **air-conditioned** adj climatizado; **air conditioning** n aire acondicionado; **aircraft** n inv avión m; **airfield** n campo de aviación; **Air Force** n fuerzas fpl aéreas, aviación f; **air hostess** (BRIT) n azafata; **airing cupboard** (BRIT) armario m para oreo; **airlift** n puente m aéreo; **airline** n línea aérea; **airliner** n avión m de pasajeros; **airmail** n: **by airmail** por avión; **airplane** (US) n avión m; **airport** n

aeropuerto; **air raid** n ataque m aéreo; **airsick** adj: **to be airsick** marearse (en avión); **airspace** n espacio aéreo; **airstrip** n pista de aterrizaje; **air terminal** n terminal f; **airtight** adj hermético; **air-traffic controller** n controlador(a) m/f aéreo/a; **airy** adj (room) bien ventilado; (fig: manner) desenfadado

aisle [aɪl] n (of church) nave f; (of theatre, supermarket) pasillo; **aisle seat** n (on plane) asiento de pasillo

ajar [ə'dʒɑː*] adj entreabierto

à la carte [ælæ'kɑːt] adv a la carta

alarm [ə'lɑːm] n (in shop, bank) alarma; (anxiety) inquietud f ▷ vt asustar, inquietar; **alarm call** n (in hotel etc) alarma; **alarm clock** n despertador m; **alarmed** adj (person) alarmado, asustado; (house, car etc) con alarma; **alarming** adj alarmante

Albania [æl'beɪnɪə] n Albania

albeit [ɔːl'biːɪt] conj aunque

album ['ælbəm] n álbum m; (L.P.) elepé m

alcohol ['ælkəhɒl] n alcohol m; **alcohol-free** adj sin alcohol; **alcoholic** [-'hɒlɪk] adj, n alcohólico/a m/f

alcove ['ælkəʊv] n nicho, hueco

ale [eɪl] n cerveza

alert [ə'lɜːt] adj (attentive) atento; (to danger, opportunity) alerta ▷ n alerta m, alarma ▷ vt poner sobre aviso; **to be on the** ~ (also Mil) estar alerta or sobre aviso

algebra ['ældʒɪbrə] n álgebra

Algeria [æl'dʒɪərɪə] n Argelia

alias ['eɪlɪəs] adv alias, conocido por ▷ n (of criminal) apodo; (of writer) seudónimo

alibi ['ælɪbaɪ] n coartada

alien ['eɪlɪən] n (foreigner) extranjero/a; (extraterrestrial) extraterrestre mf ▷ adj: ~ **to** ajeno a; **alienate** vt enajenar, alejar

alight [ə'laɪt] adj ardiendo; (eyes) brillante ▷ vi (person) apearse, bajar; (bird) posarse

align [ə'laɪn] vt alinear

alike [ə'laɪk] adj semejantes, iguales ▷ adv igualmente, del mismo modo; **to look** ~ parecerse

alive [ə'laɪv] adj vivo; (lively) alegre

○ **KEYWORD**

all [ɔːl] adj (sg) todo/a; (pl) todos/as; **all day** todo el día; **all night** toda la noche; **all men** todos los hombres; **all five came** vinieron los cinco; **all the books** todos los libros; **all his life** toda su vida
▷ pron **1** todo; **I ate it all, I ate all of it** me lo comí todo; **all of us went** fuimos todos; **all the boys went** fueron todos los chicos; **is that all?** ¿eso es todo?, ¿algo más? (in shop) ¿algo más?, ¿alguna cosa más?
2 (in phrases): **above all** sobre todo; por encima de todo; **after all** después de todo; **at all: not at all** (in answer to question) en absoluto; (in answer to thanks) ¡de nada!, ¡no hay de qué!; **I'm not at all tired** no estoy nada cansado/a; **anything at all will do** cualquier cosa viene bien; **all in all** a fin de cuentas
▷ adv: **all alone** completamente solo/a; **it's not as hard as all that** no es tan difícil como lo pintas; **all the more the better** tanto más/mejor; **all but** casi; **the score is 2 all** están empatados a 2

Allah ['ælə] n Alá m

allegation [ælɪ'geɪʃən] n alegato

alleged [ə'lɛdʒd] adj supuesto, presunto; **allegedly**

adv supuestamente, según se afirma

allegiance [ə'liːdʒəns] *n* lealtad *f*

allergic [ə'lɜːdʒɪk] *adj*: **~ to** alérgico a

allergy ['ælədʒɪ] *n* alergia

alleviate [ə'liːvɪeɪt] *vt* aliviar

alley ['ælɪ] *n* callejuela

alliance [ə'laɪəns] *n* alianza

allied ['ælaɪd] *adj* aliado

alligator ['ælɪɡeɪtə*] *n* (Zool) caimán *m*

all-in (BRIT) ['ɔːlɪn] *adj, adv* (charge) todo incluido

allocate ['æləkeɪt] *vt* (money etc) asignar

allot [ə'lɒt] *vt* asignar

all-out ['ɔːl] *adj* (effort etc) supremo

allow [ə'lau] *vt* permitir, dejar; (a claim) admitir; (sum, time etc) dar, conceder; (concede): **to ~ that** reconocer que; **to ~ sb to do** permitir a algn hacer; **he is ~ed to se le permite...; **allow for** *vt fus* tener en cuenta; **allowance** [ə'lauəns] *n* subvención *f*; (welfare payment) pensión *f*; (pocket money) dinero de bolsillo; (tax allowance) desgravación *f*; **to make allowances for** (person) disculpar a; (thing) tener en cuenta

all right *adv* bien; (as answer) ¡conforme!, ¡está bien!

ally ['ælaɪ] *n* aliado/a ▷ *vt*: **to ~ o.s. with** aliarse con

almighty [ɔːl'maɪtɪ] *adj* todopoderoso; (row etc) imponente

almond ['ɑːmənd] *n* almendra

almost ['ɔːlməust] *adv* casi

alone [ə'ləun] *adj, adv* solo; **to leave sb ~** dejar a algn en paz; **to leave sth ~** no tocar algo, dejar algo sin tocar; **let ~ ...** y mucho menos ...

along [ə'lɒŋ] *prep* a lo largo de, por ▷ *adv*: **is he coming ~ with us?** ¿viene con nosotros?; **he was limping ~** iba cojeando; **~ with** junto con; **all ~** (all the time) desde el principio; **alongside** *prep* al lado de ▷ *adv* al lado

aloof [ə'luːf] *adj* reservado ▷ *adv*: **to stand ~** mantenerse apartado

aloud [ə'laud] *adv* en voz alta

alphabet ['ælfəbet] *n* alfabeto

Alps [ælps] *npl*: **the ~** los Alpes

already [ɔːl'redɪ] *adv* ya

alright [ɔːl'raɪt] (BRIT) *adv* = **all right**

also ['ɔːlsəu] *adv* también, además

altar ['ɒltə*] *n* altar *m*

alter ['ɒltə*] *vt* cambiar, modificar ▷ *vi* cambiar; **alteration** [ɒltə'reɪʃən] *n* cambio; (to clothes) arreglo; (to building) arreglos *mpl*

alternate [adj ɒl'tɜːnɪt, vb 'ɒltəneɪt] *adj* (actions etc) alternativo; (events) alterno; (us) = **alternative** ▷ *vi*: **to ~ (with)** alternar (con); **on ~ days** un día sí y otro no

alternative [ɒl'tɜːnətɪv] *adj* alternativo ▷ *n* alternativa; **~ medicine** medicina alternativa; **alternatively** *adv*: **alternatively one could ...** por otra parte se podría ...

although [ɔːl'ðəu] *conj* aunque

altitude ['æltɪtjuːd] *n* altura

altogether [ɔːltə'ɡeðə*] *adv* completamente, del todo; (on the whole) en total, en conjunto

aluminium [ælju'mɪnɪəm] (BRIT), **aluminum** [ə'luːmɪnəm] (US) *n* aluminio

always ['ɔːlweɪz] *adv* siempre

Alzheimer's (disease) ['æltshaɪməz-] *n* enfermedad *f* de Alzheimer

am [æm] *vb* see **be**

amalgamate [ə'mælɡəmeɪt] *vi* amalgamarse ▷ *vt* amalgamar, unir

amass [ə'mæs] *vt* amontonar, acumular

amateur ['æmətə*] *n* aficionado/a, amateur *mf*

amaze [ə'meɪz] *vt* asombrar, pasmar; **to be ~d (at)** quedar pasmado (de); **amazed** *adj* asombrado; **amazement** *n* asombro, sorpresa; **amazing** *adj* extraordinario; (fantastic) increíble

Amazon ['æməzən] *n* (Geo) Amazonas *m*

ambassador [æm'bæsədə*] *n* embajador(a) *m/f*

amber ['æmbə*] *n* ámbar *m*; **at ~** (BRIT Aut) en el amarillo

ambiguous [æm'bɪɡjuəs] *adj* ambiguo

ambition [æm'bɪʃən] *n* ambición *f*; **ambitious** [-əs] *adj* ambicioso

ambulance ['æmbjuləns] *n* ambulancia

ambush ['æmbuʃ] *n* emboscada ▷ *vt* tender una emboscada a

amen [ɑː'men] *excl* amén

amend [ə'mend] *vt* enmendar; **to make ~s** dar cumplida satisfacción; **amendment** *n* enmienda

amenities [ə'miːnɪtɪz] *npl* comodidades *fpl*

America [ə'merɪkə] *n* (USA) Estados *mpl* Unidos; **American** *adj*, *n* norteamericano/a; estadounidense *mf*; **American football** *n* (BRIT) fútbol *m* americano

amicable ['æmɪkəbl] *adj* amistoso, amigable

amid(st) [ə'mɪd(st)] *prep* entre, en medio de

ammunition [æmju'nɪʃən] *n* municiones *fpl*

amnesty ['æmnɪstɪ] *n* amnistía

among(st) [ə'mʌŋ(st)] *prep* entre, en medio de

amount [ə'maunt] *n* (gen) cantidad *f*; (of bill etc) suma, importe *m* ▷ *vi*: **to ~ to** sumar; (be same as) equivaler a, significar

amp(ère) ['æmp(eə*)] *n* amperio

ample ['æmpl] *adj* (large) grande; (abundant) abundante; (enough) bastante, suficiente

amplifier ['æmplɪfaɪə*] *n* amplificador *m*

amputate ['æmpjuteɪt] *vt* amputar

Amtrak ['æmtræk] (US) *n* empresa nacional de ferrocarriles de los EEUU

amuse [ə'mjuːz] *vt* divertir; (distract) distraer, entretener; **amusement** *n* diversión *f*; (pastime) pasatiempo; (laughter) risa; **amusement arcade** *n* salón *m* de juegos; **amusement park** *n* parque *m* de atracciones

amusing [ə'mjuːzɪŋ] *adj* divertido

an [æn] *indef art* see **a**

anaemia [ə'niːmɪə] (US **anemia**) *n* anemia

anaemic [ə'niːmɪk] (US **anemic**) *adj* anémico; (fig) soso, insípido

anaesthetic [ænɪs'θetɪk] (US **anesthetic**) *n* anestesia

analog(ue) ['ænəlɒɡ] *adj* (computer, watch) analógico

analogy [ə'nælədʒɪ] *n* analogía

analyse ['ænəlaɪz] (US **analyze**) *vt* analizar; **analysis** [ə'næləsɪs] (pl **analyses** [-siːz]) *n* análisis *m inv*; **analyst** [-lɪst] *n* (political analyst, psychoanalyst) analista *mf*

analyze ['ænəlaɪz] (US) *vt* = **analyse**

anarchy ['ænəkɪ] *n* anarquía, desorden *m*

anatomy [ə'nætəmɪ] *n* anatomía

ancestor ['ænsɪstə*] *n* antepasado

anchor ['æŋkə*] *n* ancla, áncora ▷ *vi* (also: **to drop ~**) anclar ▷ *vt* anclar; **to weigh ~** levar anclas

anchovy ['æntʃəvɪ] *n* anchoa

ancient ['eɪnʃənt] *adj* antiguo

and [ænd] *conj* y; (before i-, hi- + consonant) e; **men~women** hombres y mujeres; **father ~ son** padre e hijo;

trees ~ grass árboles y hierba; **~ so on** etcétera, y así sucesivamente; **try ~ come** procura venir; **he talked ~ talked** habló sin parar; **better ~ better** cada vez mejor

Andes [ˈændiːz] *npl:* **the ~** los Andes

Andorra [ænˈdɔːrə] *n* Andorra

anemia *etc* [əˈniːmɪə] (*us*) = **anaemia** *etc*

anesthetic [ænɪsˈθetɪk] (*us*) = **anaesthetic**

angel [ˈeɪndʒəl] *n* ángel *m*

anger [ˈæŋɡəʳ] *n* cólera

angina [ænˈdʒaɪnə] *n* angina (del pecho)

angle [ˈæŋɡl] *n* ángulo; **from their ~** desde su punto de vista

angler [ˈæŋɡləʳ] *n* pescador/a *m/f* (de caña)

Anglican [ˈæŋɡlɪkən] *adj, n* anglicano/a *m/f*

angling [ˈæŋɡlɪŋ] *n* pesca con caña

angrily [ˈæŋɡrɪlɪ] *adv* coléricamente, airadamente

angry [ˈæŋɡrɪ] *adj* enfadado, airado; (*wound*) inflamado; **to be ~ with sb/at sth** estar enfadado con algn/por algo; **to get ~** enfadarse, enojarse

anguish [ˈæŋɡwɪʃ] *n* (*physical*) tormentos *mpl*; (*mental*) angustia

animal [ˈænɪməl] *n* animal *m*; (*pej: person*) bestia ▷ *adj* animal

animated [-meɪtɪd] *adj* animado

animation [ænɪˈmeɪʃən] *n* animación *f*

aniseed [ˈænɪsiːd] *n* anís *m*

ankle [ˈæŋkl] *n* tobillo

annex [*n* ˈæneks, *vb* æˈneks] *n* (*brit: also:* **~e:** *building*) edificio anexo ▷ *vt* (*territory*) anexionar

anniversary [ænɪˈvɜːsərɪ] *n* aniversario

announce [əˈnauns] *vt* anunciar; **announcement** *n* anuncio; (*official*) declaración *f*; **announcer** *n* (*Radio*) locutor/a *m/f*; (*TV*) presentador/a *m/f*

annoy [əˈnɔɪ] *vt* molestar, fastidiar; **don't get ~ed!** ¡no se enfade!; **annoying** *adj* molesto, fastidioso; (*person*) pesado

annual [ˈænjuəl] *adj* anual ▷ *n* (*Bot*) anual *m*; (*book*) anuario; **annually** *adv* anualmente, cada año

annum [ˈænəm] *n see* **per**

anonymous [əˈnɒnɪməs] *adj* anónimo

anorak [ˈænəræk] *n* anorak *m*

anorexia [ænəˈreksɪə] *n* (*Med: also:* **~ nervosa**) anorexia

anorexic [ænəˈreksɪk] *adj, n* anoréxico/a *m/f*

another [əˈnʌðəʳ] *adj* (*one more, a different one*) otro ▷ *pron* otro; *see* **one**

answer [ˈɑːnsəʳ] *n* contestación *f*, respuesta; (*to problem*) solución *f* ▷ *vi* contestar, responder ▷ *vt* (*reply to*) contestar a, responder a; (*problem*) resolver; (*prayer*) escuchar; **in ~ to your letter** contestando or en contestación a su carta; **to ~ the phone** contestar or coger el teléfono; **to ~ the bell** *or* **the door** acudir a la puerta; **answer back** *vi* replicar, ser respondón/ona; **answerphone** *n* (*esp brit*) contestador *m* (automático)

ant [ænt] *n* hormiga

Antarctic [æntˈɑːktɪk] *n:* **the ~** el Antártico

antelope [ˈæntɪləup] *n* antílope *m*

antenatal [ˈæntɪˈneɪtl] *adj* antenatal, prenatal

antenna [ænˈtɛnə, *pl* -niː] (*pl* **antennae**) *n* antena

anthem [ˈænθəm] *n:* **national ~** himno nacional

anthology [ænˈθɒlədʒɪ] *n* antología

anthrax [ˈænθræks] *n* ántrax *m*

anthropology [ænθrəˈpɒlədʒɪ] *n* antropología

anti [ˈæntɪ] *prefix* anti; **antibiotic** [-baɪˈɒtɪk] *n* antibiótico; **antibody** [ˈæntɪbɒdɪ] *n* anticuerpo

anticipate [ænˈtɪsɪpeɪt] *vt* prever; (*expect*) esperar, contar con; (*look forward to*) esperar con ilusión; (*do first*) anticiparse a, adelantarse a; **anticipation** [-ˈpeɪʃən] *n* (*expectation*) previsión *f*; (*eagerness*) ilusión *f*, expectación *f*

anticlimax [æntɪˈklaɪmæks] *n* decepción *f*

anticlockwise [æntɪˈklɔkwaɪz] (*brit*) *adv* en dirección contraria a la de las agujas del reloj

antics [ˈæntɪks] *npl* gracias *fpl*

anti: antidote [ˈæntɪdəut] *n* antídoto; **antifreeze** [ˈæntɪfriːz] *n* anticongelante *m*; **antihistamine** [-ˈhɪstəmiːn] *n* antihistamínico; **antiperspirant** [æntɪpəˈspɪrənt] *n* antitranspirante *m*

antique [ænˈtiːk] *n* antigüedad *f* ▷ *adj* antiguo; **antique shop** *n* tienda de antigüedades

antiseptic [æntɪˈseptɪk] *adj, n* antiséptico

antisocial [æntɪˈsəuʃəl] *adj* antisocial

antivirus [ˈæntɪˈvaɪərəs] *adj* (*program, software*) antivirus *inv*

antlers [ˈæntləz] *npl* cuernas *fpl*, cornamenta *sg*

anxiety [æŋˈzaɪətɪ] *n* inquietud *f*; (*Med*) ansiedad *f*; **~ to do** deseo de hacer

anxious [ˈæŋkʃəs] *adj* inquieto, preocupado; (*worrying*) preocupante; (*keen*): **to be ~ to do** tener muchas ganas de hacer

○ **KEYWORD**

any [ˈenɪ] *adj* **1** (*in questions etc*) algún/alguna; **have you any butter/children?** ¿tienes mantequilla/hijos?; **if there are any tickets left** si quedan billetes, si queda algún billete

2 (*with negative*): **I haven't any money/books** no tengo dinero/libros

3 (*no matter which*) cualquier; **any excuse will do** valdrá *or* servirá cualquier excusa; **choose any book you like** escoge el libro que quieras

4 (*in phrases*): **in any case** de todas formas, en cualquier caso; **any day now** cualquier día (de estos); **at any moment** en cualquier momento, de un momento a otro; **at any rate** en todo caso; **any time: come (at) any time** ven cuando quieras; **he might come (at) any time** podría llegar de un momento a otro

▷ *pron* **1** (*in questions etc*): **have you got any?** ¿tienes alguno(s)/a(s)?; **can any of you sing?** ¿sabe cantar alguno de vosotros/ustedes?

2 (*with negative*): **I haven't any (of them)** no tengo ninguno

3 (*no matter which one(s)*): **take any of those books (you like)** toma el libro que quieras de ésos

▷ *adv* **1** (*in questions etc*): **do you want any more soup/sandwiches?** ¿quieres más sopa/bocadillos?; **are you feeling any better?** ¿te sientes algo mejor?

2 (*with negative*): **I can't hear him any more** ya no le oigo; **don't wait any longer** no esperes más

any: anybody *pron* cualquiera; (*in interrogative sentences*) alguien; (*in negative sentences*) nadie; **I don't see anybody** no veo a nadie; **if anybody should phone ...** si llama alguien ...; **anyhow** *adv* (*at any rate*) de todos modos, de todas formas; (*haphazard*): **do it anyhow you like** hazlo como quieras; **she leaves things just anyhow** deja las cosas como quiera *or* de cualquier modo; **I shall go anyhow** de todos modos iré; **anyone**

pron = **anybody, anything** *pron* (*in questions etc*) algo, alguna cosa; (*with negative*) nada; **can you see anything?** ¿ves algo?; **if anything happens to me ...** si algo me ocurre ...; (*no matter what*): **you can say anything you like** puedes decir lo que quieras; **anything will do** vale todo o cualquier cosa; **he'll eat anything** come de todo o lo que sea; **anytime** *adv* (*at any moment*) en cualquier momento, de un momento a otro; (*whenever*) no importa cuándo, cuando quieras; **anyway** *adv* (*at any rate*) de todos modos, de todas formas; **I shall go anyway** iré de todos modos; (*besides*): **anyway, I couldn't come even if I wanted to** además, no podría venir aunque quisiera; **why are you phoning, anyway?** ¿entonces, por qué llamas?, ¿por qué llamas, pues?; **anywhere** *adv* (*in questions etc*): **can you see him anywhere?** ¿le ves por algún lado?; **are you going anywhere?** ¿vas a algún sitio?; (*with negative*): **I can't see him anywhere** no le veo por ninguna parte; **anywhere in the world** (*no matter where*) en cualquier parte (del mundo); **put the books down anywhere** deja tus libros donde quieras

apart [ə'pɑːt] *adv* (*aside*) aparte; (*situation*): ~ (**from**) separado (de); (*movement*): **to pull** ~ separar; **10 miles** ~ separados por 10 millas; **to take** ~ desmontar; ~ **from** *prep* aparte de

apartment [ə'pɑːtmənt] *n* (*US*) piso (*SP*), departamento (*LAM*), apartamento; (*room*) cuarto; **apartment building** (*US*) *n* edificio de apartamentos

apathy ['æpəθɪ] *n* apatía, indiferencia

ape [eɪp] *n* mono ▷ *vt* imitar, remedar

aperitif [ə'perɪtɪf] *n* aperitivo

aperture ['æpətʃjʊə*] *n* rendija, resquicio; (*Phot*) abertura

APEX ['eɪpeks] *n abbr* (= *Advanced Purchase Excursion Fare*) tarifa *f* APEX

apologize [ə'pɒlədʒaɪz] *vi*: **to** ~ (**for sth to sb**) disculparse (con algn de algo)

apology [ə'pɒlədʒɪ] *n* disculpa, excusa

apostrophe [ə'pɒstrəfɪ] *n* apóstrofo

appal [ə'pɔːl] (*US* **appall**) *vt* horrorizar, espantar; **appalling** *adj* espantoso; (*awful*) pésimo

apparatus [æpə'reɪtəs] *n* (*equipment*) equipo; (*organization*) aparato; (*in gymnasium*) aparatos *mpl*

apparent [ə'pærənt] *adj* aparente; (*obvious*) evidente; **apparently** *adv* por lo visto, al parecer

appeal [ə'piːl] *vi* (*Law*) apelar ▷ *n* (*Law*) apelación *f*; (*request*) llamamiento; (*plea*) petición *f*; (*charm*) atractivo; ~ **for** reclamar; **to** ~ **to** (*be attractive to*) atraer; **it doesn't** ~ **to me** no me atrae, no me llama la atención; **appealing** *adj* (*attractive*) atractivo

appear [ə'pɪə*] *vi* aparecer, presentarse; (*Law*) comparecer; (*publication*) salir (a luz), publicarse; (*seem*) parecer; **to** ~ **on TV/in "Hamlet"** salir por la tele/hacer un papel en "Hamlet"; **it would** ~ **that** parecería que; **appearance** *n* aparición *f*; (*look*) apariencia, aspecto

appendices [ə'pendɪsiːz] *npl of* **appendix**

appendicitis [əpendɪ'saɪtɪs] *n* apendicitis *f*

appendix [ə'pendɪks] (*pl* **appendices**) *n* apéndice *m*

appetite ['æpɪtaɪt] *n* apetito; (*fig*) deseo, anhelo

appetizer ['æpɪtaɪzə*] *n* (*drink*) aperitivo; (*food*) tapas *fpl* (*SP*)

applaud [ə'plɔːd] *vt, vi* aplaudir

applause [ə'plɔːz] *n* aplausos *mpl*

apple ['æpl] *n* manzana; **apple pie** *n* pastel *m* de manzana, pay *m* de manzana (*LAM*)

appliance [ə'plaɪəns] *n* aparato

applicable [ə'plɪkəbl] *adj* (*relevant*): **to be** ~ (**to**) referirse (a)

applicant ['æplɪkənt] *n* candidato/a; solicitante *mf*

application [æplɪ'keɪʃən] *n* aplicación *f*; (*for a job etc*) solicitud *f*, petición *f*; **application form** *n* solicitud *f*

apply [ə'plaɪ] *vt* (*paint etc*) poner; (*law etc: put into practice*) poner en vigor ▷ *vi*: **to** ~ (**to**) (*ask*) dirigirse a; (*be applicable*) ser aplicable a; **to** ~ **for** (*permit, grant, job*) solicitar; **to** ~ **o.s. to** aplicarse a, dedicarse a

appoint [ə'pɔɪnt] *vt* (*to post*) nombrar a

appointment *n* (*with client*) cita; (*act*) nombramiento; (*post*) puesto; (*at hairdresser etc*): **to have an appointment** tener hora; **to make an appointment (with sb)** citarse (con algn)

appraisal [ə'preɪzl] *n* valoración *f*

appreciate [ə'priːʃɪeɪt] *vt* apreciar, tener en mucho; (*be grateful for*) agradecer; (*be aware*) comprender ▷ *vi* (*Comm*) aumentar(se) en valor; **appreciation** [-'eɪʃən] *n* apreciación *f*; (*gratitude*) reconocimiento, agradecimiento; (*Comm*) aumento en valor

apprehension [æprɪ'henʃən] *n* (*fear*) aprensión *f*

apprehensive [æprɪ'hensɪv] *adj* aprensivo

apprentice [ə'prentɪs] *n* aprendiz/a *m/f*

approach [ə'prəʊtʃ] *vi* acercarse ▷ *vt* acercarse a; (*ask, apply to*) dirigirse a; (*situation, problem*) abordar ▷ *n* acercamiento; (*access*) acceso; (*to problem, situation*): ~ (**to**) actitud *f* (ante)

appropriate [*adj* ə'prəʊprɪɪt, *vb* ə'prəʊprɪeɪt] *adj* apropiado, conveniente ▷ *vt* (*take*) apropiarse de

approval [ə'pruːvəl] *n* aprobación *f*, visto bueno; (*permission*) consentimiento; **on** ~ (*Comm*) a prueba

approve [ə'pruːv] *vt* aprobar; **approve of** *vt fus* (*thing*) aprobar; (*person*): **they don't approve of her** (ella) no les parece bien

approximate [ə'prɒksɪmɪt] *adj* aproximado; **approximately** *adv* aproximadamente, más o menos

Apr. *abbr* (= *April*) abr

apricot ['eɪprɪkɒt] *n* albaricoque *m*, chabacano (*MEX*), damasco (*RPL*)

April ['eɪprəl] *n* abril *m*; **April Fools' Day** *n* el primero de abril, ≈ día *m* de los Inocentes (*28 December*)

apron ['eɪprən] *n* delantal *m*

apt [æpt] *adj* acertado, apropiado; (*likely*): ~ **to do** propenso a hacer

aquarium [ə'kweərɪəm] *n* acuario

Aquarius [ə'kweərɪəs] *n* Acuario

Arab ['ærəb] *adj, n* árabe *mf*

Arabia [ə'reɪbɪə] *n* Arabia; **Arabian** *adj* árabe; **Arabic** ['ærəbɪk] *adj* árabe; (*numerals*) arábigo ▷ *n* árabe *m*

arbitrary ['ɑːbɪtrərɪ] *adj* arbitrario

arbitration [ɑːbɪ'treɪʃən] *n* arbitraje *m*

arc [ɑːk] *n* arco

arcade [ɑː'keɪd] *n* (*round a square*) soportales *mpl*; (*shopping mall*) galería comercial

arch [ɑːtʃ] *n* arco; (*of foot*) arco del pie ▷ *vt* arquear

archaeology [ɑːkɪ'ɒlədʒɪ] (*US* **archeology**) *n* arqueología

archbishop [ɑːtʃ'bɪʃəp] *n* arzobispo

archeology [ɑːkɪ'ɒlədʒɪ] (*US*) *n* = **archaeology**

architect ['ɑːkɪtekt] *n* arquitecto/a; **architectural** [ɑːkɪ'tektʃərəl] *adj* arquitectónico; **architecture** *n* arquitectura

archive ['ɑːkaɪv] *n* (*often pl: also Comput*) archivo

Arctic ['ɑːktɪk] *adj* ártico ▷ *n*: **the** ~ el Ártico

are [ɑː*] *vb see* **be**

area ['eərɪə] *n* área, región *f*; (*part of place*) zona; (*Math* *etc*) área, superficie *f*; (*in room: e.g. dining area*) parte *f*; (*of knowledge, experience*) campo; **area code** (*us*) *n* (*Tel*) prefijo

arena [ə'ri:nə] *n* estadio; (*of circus*) pista

aren't [ɑ:nt] = **are not**

Argentina [ɑ:dʒən'ti:nə] *n* Argentina; **Argentinian** [-'tɪnɪən] *adj, n* argentino/a *m/f*

arguably ['ɑ:gjuəblɪ] *adv* posiblemente

argue ['ɑ:gju:] *vi* (*quarrel*) discutir, pelearse; (*reason*) razonar, argumentar; **to ~ that** sostener que

argument ['ɑ:gjumənt] *n* discusión *f*, pelea; (*reasons*) argumento

Aries ['eərɪz] *n* Aries

arise [ə'raɪz] (*pt* **arose**, *pp* **arisen**) *vi* surgir, presentarse

arithmetic [ə'rɪθmətɪk] *n* aritmética

arm [ɑ:m] *n* brazo ▷ *vt* armar; **arms** *npl* armas *fpl*; **~ in ~** cogidos del brazo; **armchair** ['ɑ:mtʃeə*] *n* sillón *m*, butaca

armed [ɑ:md] *adj* armado; **armed robbery** *n* robo a mano armada

armour [ɑ:mə*] (*us* **armor**) *n* armadura; (*Mil: tanks*) blindaje *m*

armpit ['ɑ:mpɪt] *n* sobaco, axila

armrest ['ɑ:mrest] *n* apoyabrazos *m inv*

army ['ɑ:mɪ] *n* ejército; (*fig*) multitud *f*

A road *n* (*BRIT*) = carretera *f* nacional

aroma [ə'rəumə] *n* aroma *m*, fragancia; **aromatherapy** *n* aromaterapia

arose [ə'rəuz] *pt of* **arise**

around [ə'raund] *adv* alrededor; (*in the area*) **there is no one else ~** no hay nadie más por aquí ▷ *prep* alrededor de

arouse [ə'rauz] *vt* despertar; (*anger*) provocar

arrange [ə'reɪndʒ] *vt* arreglar, ordenar; (*organize*) organizar; **to ~ to do sth** quedar en hacer algo; **arrangement** *n* arreglo; (*agreement*) acuerdo; **arrangements** *npl* (*preparations*) preparativos *mpl*

array [ə'reɪ] *n*: **~ of** (*things*) serie *f* de; (*people*) conjunto de

arrears [ə'rɪəz] *npl* atrasos *mpl*; **to be in ~ with one's rent** estar retrasado en el pago del alquiler

arrest [ə'rest] *vt* detener; (*sb's attention*) llamar ▷ *n* detención *f*; **under ~** detenido

arrival [ə'raɪvəl] *n* llegada; **new ~** recién llegado/a; (*baby*) recién nacido

arrive [ə'raɪv] *vi* llegar; (*baby*) nacer; **arrive at** *vt fus* (*decision, solution*) llegar a

arrogance ['ærəgəns] *n* arrogancia, prepotencia (*LAM*)

arrogant ['ærəgənt] *adj* arrogante

arrow ['ærəu] *n* flecha

arse [ɑ:s] (*BRIT: inf!*) *n* culo, trasero

arson ['ɑ:sn] *n* incendio premeditado

art [ɑ:t] *n* arte *m*; (*skill*) destreza; **art college** *n* escuela *f* de Bellas Artes

artery ['ɑ:tərɪ] *n* arteria

art gallery *n* pinacoteca; (*saleroom*) galería de arte

arthritis [ɑ:'θraɪtɪs] *n* artritis *f*

artichoke ['ɑ:tɪtʃəuk] *n* alcachofa; **Jerusalem ~** aguaturma

article ['ɑ:tɪkl] *n* artículo

articulate [*adj* ɑ:'tɪkjulɪt, *vb* ɑ:'tɪkjuleɪt] *adj* claro, bien expresado ▷ *vt* expresar

artificial [ɑ:tɪ'fɪʃəl] *adj* artificial; (*affected*) afectado

artist ['ɑ:tɪst] *n* artista *mf*; (*Mus*) intérprete *mf*;

artistic [ɑ:'tɪstɪk] *adj* artístico

art school *n* escuela de bellas artes

○ **KEYWORD**

as [æz] *conj* **1** (*referring to time*) cuando, mientras; a medida que; **as the years went by** con el paso de los años; **he came in as I was leaving** entró cuando me marchaba; **as from tomorrow** desde *or* a partir de mañana

2 (*in comparisons*): **as big as** tan grande como; **twice as big as** el doble de grande que; **as much money/many books as** tanto dinero/tantos libros como; **as soon as** en cuanto

3 (*since, because*) como, ya que; **he left early as he had to be home by 10** se fue temprano ya que tenía que estar en casa a las 10

4 (*referring to manner, way*): **do as you wish** haz lo que quieras; **as she said** como dijo; **he gave it to me as a present** me lo dio de regalo

5 (*in the capacity of*): **he works as a barman** trabaja de barman; **as chairman of the company, he ...** como presidente de la compañía ...

6 (*concerning*): **as for** *or* **to that** por *or* en lo que respecta a eso

7: **as if** *or* **though** como si; **he looked as if he was ill** parecía como si estuviera enfermo, tenía aspecto de enfermo; *see also* **long**; **such**; **well**

a.s.a.p. *abbr* (= *as soon as possible*) cuanto antes

asbestos [æz'bestəs] *n* asbesto, amianto

ascent [ə'sent] *n* subida; (*slope*) cuesta, pendiente *f*

ash [æʃ] *n* ceniza; (*tree*) fresno

ashamed [ə'feɪmd] *adj* avergonzado, apenado (*LAM*); **to be ~ of** avergonzarse de

ashore [ə'ʃɔ:*] *adv* en tierra; (*swim etc*) a tierra

ashtray ['æʃtreɪ] *n* cenicero

Ash Wednesday *n* miércoles *m* de Ceniza

Asia ['eɪʃə] *n* Asia; **Asian** *adj, n* asiático/a *m/f*

aside [ə'saɪd] *adv* a un lado ▷ *n* aparte *m*

ask [ɑ:sk] *vt* (*question*) preguntar; (*invite*) invitar; **to ~ sb sth/to do sth** preguntar algo a algn/pedir a algn que haga algo; **to ~ sb about sth** preguntar algo a algn; **to ~ (sb) a question** hacer una pregunta (a algn); **to ~ sb out to dinner** invitar a cenar a algn; **ask for** *vt fus* pedir; (*trouble*) buscar

asleep [ə'sli:p] *adj* dormido; **to fall ~** dormirse, quedarse dormido

asparagus [əs'pærəgəs] *n* (*plant*) espárrago; (*food*) espárragos *mpl*

aspect ['æspekt] *n* aspecto, apariencia; (*direction in which a building etc faces*) orientación *f*

aspirations [æspə'reɪʃənz] *npl* aspiraciones *fpl*; (*ambition*) ambición *f*

aspire [əs'paɪə*] *vi*: **to ~ to** aspirar a, ambicionar

aspirin ['æsprɪn] *n* aspirina

ass [æs] *n* asno, burro; (*inf: idiot*) imbécil *mf*; (*us: inf!*) culo, trasero

assassin [ə'sæsɪn] *n* asesino/a; **assassinate** *vt* asesinar

assault [ə'sɔ:lt] *n* asalto; (*Law*) agresión *f* ▷ *vt* asaltar, atacar; (*sexually*) violar

assemble [ə'sembl] *vt* reunir, juntar; (*Tech*) montar ▷ *vi* reunirse, juntarse

assembly [ə'semblɪ] *n* reunión *f*, asamblea;

(parliament) parlamento; *(construction)* montaje *m*

assert [əˈsəːt] *vt* afirmar; *(authority)* hacer valer; **assertion** [-ʃən] *n* afirmación *f*

assess [əˈses] *vt* valorar, calcular; *(tax, damages)* fijar; *(for tax)* gravar; **assessment** *n* valoración *f*; *(for tax)* gravamen *m*

asset [ˈæset] *n* ventaja; **assets** *npl (Comm)* activo; *(property, funds)* fondos *mpl*

assign [əˈsaɪn] *vt*: **to ~ (to)** *(date)* fijar (para); *(task)* asignar (a); *(resources)* destinar (a); **assignment** *n* tarea

assist [əˈsɪst] *vt* ayudar; **assistance** *n* ayuda, auxilio; **assistant** *n* ayudante *mf*; *(BRIT: also:* **shop assistant)** dependiente/a *m/f*

associate [*adj, n* əˈsəʊʃɪt, *vb* əˈsəʊʃɪeɪt] *adj* asociado ▷ *n (at work)* colega *mf* ▷ *vt* asociar; *(ideas)* relacionar ▷ *vi*: **to ~ with sb** tratar con algn

association [əsəʊsɪˈeɪʃən] *n* asociación *f*

assorted [əˈsɔːtɪd] *adj* surtido, variado

assortment [əˈsɔːtmənt] *n (of shapes, colours)* surtido; *(of books)* colección *f*; *(of people)* mezcla

assume [əˈsjuːm] *vt* suponer; *(responsibilities)* asumir; *(attitude)* adoptar, tomar

assumption [əˈsʌmpʃən] *n* suposición *f*, presunción *f*; *(of power etc)* toma

assurance [əˈʃʊərəns] *n* garantía, promesa; *(confidence)* confianza, aplomo; *(insurance)* seguro

assure [əˈʃʊə*] *vt* asegurar

asterisk [ˈæstərɪsk] *n* asterisco

asthma [ˈæsmə] *n* asma

astonish [əˈstɒnɪʃ] *vt* asombrar, pasmar; **astonished** *adj* estupefacto, pasmado; **to be astonished (at)** asombrarse (de); **astonishing** *adj* asombroso, pasmoso; **I find it astonishing that ...** me asombra or pasma que ...; **astonishment** *n* asombro, sorpresa

astound [əˈstaʊnd] *vt* asombrar, pasmar

astray [əˈstreɪ] *adv*: **to go ~** extraviarse; **to lead ~** *(morally)* llevar por mal camino

astrology [æsˈtrɒlədʒɪ] *n* astrología

astronaut [ˈæstrənɔːt] *n* astronauta *mf*

astronomer [əsˈtrɒnəmə*] *n* astrónomo/a

astronomical [æstrəˈnɒmɪkəl] *adj* astronómico

astronomy [æsˈtrɒnəmɪ] *n* astronomía

astute [əsˈtjuːt] *adj* astuto

asylum [əˈsaɪləm] *n (refuge)* asilo; *(mental hospital)* manicomio

○ **KEYWORD**

at [æt] *prep* **1** *(referring to position)* en; *(direction)* a; **at the top** en lo alto; **at home/school** en casa/la escuela; **to look at sth/sb** mirar algo/a algn
2 *(referring to time)*: **at 4 o'clock** a las 4; **at night** por la noche; **at Christmas** en Navidad; **at times** a veces
3 *(referring to rates, speed etc)*: **at £1 a kilo** a una libra el kilo; **two at a time** de dos en dos; **at 50 km/h** a 50 km/h
4 *(referring to manner)*: **at a stroke** de un golpe; **at peace** en paz
5 *(referring to activity)*: **to be at work** estar trabajando; *(in the office etc)* estar en el trabajo; **to play at cowboys** jugar a los vaqueros; **to be good at sth** ser bueno en algo
6 *(referring to cause)*: **shocked/surprised/annoyed at sth** asombrado/sorprendido/fastidiado por algo/

I went at his suggestion fui a instancias suyas

7 *(symbol)* arroba

ate [eɪt] *pt of* **eat**

atheist [ˈeɪθɪɪst] *n* ateo/a

Athens [ˈæθɪnz] *n* Atenas

athlete [ˈæθliːt] *n* atleta *mf*

athletic [æθˈletɪk] *adj* atlético; **athletics** *n* atletismo

Atlantic [ətˈlæntɪk] *adj* atlántico ▷ *n*: **the ~ (Ocean)** el (Océano) Atlántico

atlas [ˈætləs] *n* atlas *m inv*

A.T.M. *n abbr* (= *automated telling machine*) cajero automático

atmosphere [ˈætməsfɪə*] *n* atmósfera; *(of place)* ambiente *m*

atom [ˈætəm] *n* átomo; **atomic** [əˈtɒmɪk] *adj* atómico; **atom(ic) bomb** *n* bomba atómica

A to Z® *n (map)* callejero

atrocity [əˈtrɒsɪtɪ] *n* atrocidad *f*

attach [əˈtætʃ] *vt (fasten)* atar; *(join)* unir, sujetar; *(document, letter)* adjuntar; *(importance etc)* dar, conceder; **to be ~ed to sb/sth** *(to like)* tener cariño a algn/algo; **attachment** *n (tool)* accesorio; *(Comput)* archivo, documento adjunto; *(love)*: **attachment (to)** apego (a)

attack [əˈtæk] *vt (Mil)* atacar; *(criminal)* agredir, asaltar; *(criticize)* criticar; *(task)* emprender ▷ *n* ataque *m*, asalto; *(on sb's life)* atentado; *(fig: criticism)* crítica; *(of illness)* ataque *m*; **heart ~** infarto (de miocardio); **attacker** *n* agresor(a) *m/f*, asaltante *mf*

attain [əˈteɪn] *vt (also:* **~ to)** alcanzar; *(achieve)* lograr, conseguir

attempt [əˈtempt] *n* tentativa, intento; *(attack)* atentado ▷ *vt* intentar

attend [əˈtend] *vt* asistir a; *(patient)* atender; **attend to** *vt fus* ocuparse de; *(customer, patient)* atender a; **attendance** *n* asistencia, presencia; *(people present)* concurrencia; **attendant** *n* ayudante *mf*; *(in garage etc)* encargado/a ▷ *adj (dangers)* concomitante

attention [əˈtenʃən] *n* atención *f*; *(care)* atenciones *fpl* ▷ *excl (Mil)* ¡firme(s)!; **for the ~ of ...** *(Admin)* atención ...

attic [ˈætɪk] *n* desván *m*

attitude [ˈætɪtjuːd] *n* actitud *f*; *(disposition)* disposición *f*

attorney [əˈtəːnɪ] *n (lawyer)* abogado/a; **Attorney General** *n (BRIT)* = Presidente *m* del Consejo del Poder Judicial *(SP)*; *(US)* = ministro de Justicia

attract [əˈtrækt] *vt* atraer; *(sb's attention)* llamar; **attraction** [əˈtrækʃən] *n* encanto; *(gen pl: amusements)* diversiones *fpl*; *(Physics)* atracción *f*; *(fig: towards sb, sth)* atractivo; **attractive** *adj* guapo; *(interesting)* atrayente

attribute [*n* ˈætrɪbjuːt, *vb* əˈtrɪbjuːt] *n* atributo ▷ *vt*: **to ~ sth to** atribuir algo a

aubergine [ˈəʊbəʒiːn] *n (BRIT)* berenjena; *(colour)* morado

auburn [ˈɔːbən] *adj* color castaño rojizo

auction [ˈɔːkʃən] *n (also:* **sale by ~)** subasta ▷ *vt* subastar

audible [ˈɔːdɪbl] *adj* audible, que se puede oír

audience [ˈɔːdɪəns] *n* público; *(Radio)* radioescuchas *mpl*; *(TV)* telespectadores *mpl*; *(interview)* audiencia

audit [ˈɔːdɪt] *vt* revisar, intervenir

audition [ɔː'dɪʃən] n audición f
auditor ['ɔːdɪtə*] n interventor(a) m/f, censor(a) m/f
de cuentas
auditorium [ɔːdɪ'tɔːrɪəm] n auditorio
Aug. abbr (=August) ag
August ['ɔːɡəst] n agosto
aunt [ɑːnt] n tía; **auntie** n diminutive of **aunt**; **aunty**
n diminutive of **aunt**
au pair ['au'pea*] n (also: ~ **girl**) (chica) au pair f
aura ['ɔːrə] n aura; (atmosphere) ambiente m
austerity [ɔ'sterɪtɪ] n austeridad f
Australia [ɔs'treɪlɪə] n Australia; **Australian** adj, n
australiano/a m/f
Austria ['ɔstrɪə] n Austria; **Austrian** adj, n
austríaco/a m/f
authentic [ɔ'θentɪk] adj auténtico
author ['ɔːθə*] n autor(a) m/f
authority [ɔ'θɔrɪtɪ] n autoridad f; (official permission)
autorización f; **the authorities** npl las autoridades
authorize ['ɔːθəraɪz] vt autorizar
auto ['ɔːtəu] (us) n coche m (SP), carro (LAM),
automóvil m
auto: autobiography [ɔːtəbaɪ'ɒɡrəfɪ] n
autobiografía; **autograph** ['ɔːtəɡrɑːf] n autógrafo
▷ vt (photo etc) dedicar; (programme) firmar; **automatic**
[ɔːtə'mætɪk] adj automático ▷ n (gun) pistola
automática; (car) coche m automático; **automatically**
adv automáticamente; **automobile** ['ɔːtəməbiːl] (us)
n coche m (SP), carro (LAM), automóvil m; **autonomous**
[ɔ'tɒnəməs] adj autónomo; **autonomy** [ɔ'tɒnəmɪ]
n autonomía
autumn ['ɔːtəm] n otoño
auxiliary [ɔːɡ'zɪlɪərɪ] adj, n auxiliar mf
avail [ə'veɪl] vt: **to ~ o.s. of** aprovechar(se) de ▷ n: **to**
no ~ en vano, sin resultado
availability [əveɪlə'bɪlɪtɪ] n disponibilidad f
available [ə'veɪləbl] adj disponible; (unoccupied)
libre; (person: unattached) soltero y sin compromiso
avalanche ['ævəlɑːnʃ] n alud m, avalancha
Ave. abbr = **avenue**
avenue ['ævənjuː] n avenida; (fig) camino
average ['ævərɪdʒ] n promedio, término medio ▷ adj
medio, de término medio; (ordinary) regular, corriente
▷ vt sacar un promedio de; **on ~** por regla general
avert [ə'vɜːt] vt prevenir; (blow) desviar; (one's eyes)
apartar
avid ['ævɪd] adj ávido
avocado [ævə'kɑːdəu] n (also BRIT: ~ **pear**) aguacate
m, palta (sc)
avoid [ə'vɔɪd] vt evitar, eludir
await [ə'weɪt] vt esperar, aguardar
awake [ə'weɪk] (pt awoke, pp awoken or awaked)
adj despierto ▷ vt despertar ▷ vi despertarse; **to be**
~ estar despierto
award [ə'wɔːd] n premio; (Law: damages)
indemnización f ▷ vt otorgar, conceder;
(Law: damages) adjudicar
aware [ə'weə*] adj: **~ (of)** consciente (de); **to become**
~ of/that (realize) darse cuenta de/de que; (learn)
enterarse de/de que; **awareness** n conciencia;
(knowledge) conocimiento
away [ə'weɪ] adv fuera; (movement): **she went ~** se
marchó; **far ~** lejos; **two kilometres ~** a dos kilómetros
de distancia; **two hours ~ by car** a dos horas en coche;
the holiday was two weeks ~ faltaban dos semanas
para las vacaciones; **he's ~ for a week** estará ausente

una semana; **to take ~ (from)** quitar (a); (subtract)
substraer (de); **to work/pedal ~** seguir trabajando/
pedaleando; **to fade ~** (colour) desvanecerse; (sound)
apagarse
awe [ɔː] n admiración f respetuosa; **awesome**
['ɔːsəm] (us) adj (excellent) formidable
awful ['ɔːfəl] adj horroroso; (quantity): **an ~ lot (of)**
cantidad (de); **awfully** adv (very) terriblemente
awkward ['ɔːkwəd] adj desmañado, torpe; (shape)
incómodo; (embarrassing) delicado, difícil
awoke [ə'wəuk] pt of **awake**
awoken [ə'wəukən] pp of **awake**
axe [æks] (us **ax**) n hacha ▷ vt (project) cortar; (jobs)
reducir
axle ['æksl] n eje m, árbol m
ay(e) [aɪ] excl sí
azalea [ə'zeɪlɪə] n azalea

B [biː] n (Mus) si m

B.A. abbr = Bachelor of Arts

baby ['beɪbɪ] n bebé m f; (us: inf: darling) mi amor; **baby carriage** (us) n cochecito; **baby-sit** vi hacer de canguro; **baby-sitter** n canguro/a; **baby wipe** n toallita húmeda (para bebés)

bachelor ['bætʃələ*] n soltero; **B~ of Arts/Science** licenciado/a en Filosofía y Letras/Ciencias

back [bæk] n (of person) espalda; (of animal) lomo; (of hand) dorso; (as opposed to front) parte f de atrás; (of chair) respaldo; (of page) reverso; (of book) final m; (Football) defensa m; (of crowd): **the ones at the ~** los del fondo ▷ vt (candidate: also: **~ up**) respaldar, apoyar; (horse: at races) apostar a; (car) dar marcha atrás a or con ▷ vi (car etc) ir (or salir or entrar) marcha atrás ▷ adj (payment, rent) atrasado; (seats, wheels) de atrás ▷ adv (not forward) hacia) atrás; (returned): **he's ~ está** de vuelta, ha vuelto; **he ran ~** volvió corriendo; (restitution): **can I have it ~?** ¿me lo devuelve?; (again): **he called ~** llamó de nuevo; **back down** vi echarse atrás; **back out** vi (of promise) volverse atrás; **back up** vt (person) apoyar, respaldar; (theory) defender; (Comput) hacer una copia preventiva or de reserva; **backache** n dolor m de espalda; **backbencher** (BRIT) n miembro del parlamento sin cargo relevante; **backbone** n columna vertebral; **back door** n puerta f trasera; **backfire** vi (Aut) petardear; (plans) fallar, salir mal; **backgammon** n backgammon m; **background** n fondo; (of events) antecedentes mpl; (basic knowledge) bases fpl; (experience) conocimientos mpl, educación f; **family background** n origen m, antecedentes mpl; **backing** n (fig) apoyo, respaldo; **backlog** n: **backlog of work** trabajo atrasado; **backpack** n mochila; **backpacker** n mochilero/a; **backslash** n pleca, barra inversa; **backstage** adv entre bastidores; **backstroke** n espalda; **backup** adj suplementario; (Comput) de reserva ▷ n (support) apoyo; (also: **backup file**) copia preventiva or de reserva; **backward** adj (person, country) atrasado; **backwards** adv hacia atrás; (read a list) al revés; (fall) de espaldas; **backyard** n traspatio

bacon ['beɪkən] n tocino, beicon m

bacteria [bæk'tɪərɪə] npl bacterias fpl

bad [bæd] adj malo; (mistake, accident) grave; (food) podrido, pasado; **his ~ leg** su pierna lisiada; **to go ~** (food) pasarse

badge [bædʒ] n insignia; (policeman's) chapa, placa

badger ['bædʒə*] n tejón m

badly ['bædlɪ] adv mal; **to reflect ~ on sb** influir negativamente en la reputación de algn; **~ wounded** gravemente herido; **he needs it ~** le hace gran falta; **to be ~ off (for money)** andar mal de dinero

bad-mannered ['bæd'mænəd] adj mal educado

badminton ['bædmɪntən] n bádminton m

bad-tempered ['bæd'tempəd] adj de mal genio or carácter; (temporarily) de mal humor

bag [bæg] n bolsa; (handbag) bolso; (satchel) mochila; (case) maleta; **~s of** (inf) un montón de; **baggage** n equipaje m; **baggage allowance** n límite m de equipaje; **baggage reclaim** n recogida de equipajes; **baggy** adj amplio; **bagpipes** npl gaita

bail [beɪl] n fianza ▷ vt (prisoner: gen: grant bail to) poner en libertad bajo fianza; (boat: also: **~ out**) achicar; **on ~** (prisoner) bajo fianza; **to ~ sb out** obtener la libertad de algn bajo fianza

bait [beɪt] n cebo ▷ vt poner cebo en; (tease) tomar el pelo a

bake [beɪk] vt cocer (al horno) ▷ vi cocerse; **baked beans** npl judías fpl en salsa de tomate; **baked potato** n patata al horno; **baker** n panadero; **bakery** n panadería; (for cakes) pastelería; **baking** n (act) amasar m; (batch) hornada; **baking powder** n levadura (en polvo)

balance ['bæləns] n equilibrio; (Comm: sum) balance m; (remainder) resto; (scales) balanza ▷ vt equilibrar; (budget) nivelar; (account) saldar; (make equal) equilibrar; **~ of trade/payments** balanza de comercio/pagos; **balanced** adj (personality, diet) equilibrado; (report) objetivo; **balance sheet** n balance m

balcony ['bælkənɪ] n (open) balcón m; (closed) galería; (in theatre) anfiteatro

bald [bɔːld] adj calvo; (tyre) liso

Balearics [bælɪ'ærɪks] npl: **the ~** las Baleares

ball [bɔːl] n pelota; (football) balón m; (of wool, string) ovillo; (dance) baile m; **to play ~** (fig) cooperar

ballerina [bælə'riːnə] n bailarina

ballet ['bæleɪ] n ballet m; **ballet dancer** n bailarín/ ina m/f

balloon [bə'luːn] n globo

ballot ['bælət] n votación f

ballpoint (pen) ['bɔːlpɔɪnt-] n bolígrafo

ballroom ['bɔːlrum] n salón m de baile

Baltic [bɔːltɪk] n: **the ~ (Sea)** el (Mar) Báltico

bamboo [bæm'buː] n bambú m

ban [bæn] n prohibición f, proscripción f ▷ vt prohibir, proscribir

banana [bə'nɑːnə] n plátano, banana (LAM), banano (CAM)

band [bænd] n grupo; (strip) faja, tira; (stripe) lista; (Mus: jazz) orquesta; (: rock) grupo; (Mil) banda

bandage ['bændɪdʒ] n venda, vendaje m ▷ vt vendar

Band-Aid® ['bændeɪd] (us) n tirita

bandit ['bændɪt] n bandido

bang [bæŋ] n (of gun, exhaust) estallido, detonación f; (of door) portazo; (blow) golpe m ▷ vt (door) cerrar de golpe; (one's head) golpear ▷ vi estallar; (door) cerrar de golpe

Bangladesh [bɑːŋglə'deʃ] n Bangladesh m

bangle ['bæŋgl] n brazalete m, ajorca
bangs [bæŋz] (US) npl flequillo
banish ['bænɪʃ] vt desterrar
banister(s) ['bænɪstə(z)] n(pl) barandilla,
pasamanos m inv
banjo ['bændʒəu] (pl **~es** or **~s**) n banjo
bank [bæŋk] n (Comm) banco; (of river, lake) ribera,
orilla; (of earth) terraplén m ▷ vi (Aviat) ladearse; **bank
on** vt fus contar con; **bank account** n cuenta de
banco; **bank balance** n saldo; **bank card** n tarjeta
bancaria; **bank charges** npl comisión fsg; **banker**
n banquero; **bank holiday** n (BRIT) día m festivo
or de fiesta; **banking** n banca; **bank manager** n
director(a) m/f (de sucursal) de banco; **banknote** n
billete m de banco
bankrupt ['bæŋkrʌpt] adj quebrado, insolvente;
to go ~ hacer bancarrota; **to be ~** estar en quiebra;
bankruptcy n quiebra
bank statement n balance m or detalle m de cuenta
banner ['bænə*] n pancarta
bannister(s) ['bænɪstə(z)] n(pl) = **banister(s)**
banquet ['bæŋkwɪt] n banquete m
baptism ['bæptɪzəm] n bautismo; (act) bautizo
baptize [bæp'taɪz] vt bautizar
bar [ba:*] n (pub) bar m; (counter) mostrador m; (rod)
barra; (of window, cage) reja; (of soap) pastilla; (of
chocolate) tableta; (fig: hindrance) obstáculo; (prohibition)
proscripción f; (Mus) barra ▷ vt (road) obstruir; (person)
excluir; (activity) prohibir; **the B~** (Law) la abogacía;
behind ~s entre rejas; **~ none** sin excepción
barbaric [ba:'bærɪk] adj bárbaro
barbecue ['ba:bɪkju:] n barbacoa
barbed wire ['ba:bd-] n alambre m de púas
barber ['ba:bə*] n peluquero, barbero; **barber's
(shop)** (US **barber shop**) n peluquería
bar code n código de barras
bare [bɛə*] adj desnudo; (trees) sin hojas; (necessities
etc) básico ▷ vt desnudar; (teeth) enseñar; **barefoot**
adj, adv descalzo; **barely** adv apenas
bargain ['ba:gɪn] n pacto, negocio; (good buy) ganga
▷ vi negociar; (haggle) regatear; **into the ~** además, por
añadidura; **bargain for** vt fus: **he got more than he
bargained for** le resultó peor de lo que esperaba
barge [ba:dʒ] n barcaza; **barge in** vi irrumpir;
(interrupt: conversation) interrumpir
bark [ba:k] n (of tree) corteza; (of dog) ladrido ▷ vi
ladrar
barley ['ba:lɪ] n cebada
barmaid ['ba:meɪd] n camarera
barman ['ba:mən] (irreg) n camarero, barman m
barn [ba:n] n granero
barometer [bə'rɔmɪtə*] n barómetro
baron ['bærən] n barón m; (press baron etc) magnate
m; **baroness** n baronesa
barracks ['bærəks] npl cuartel m
barrage ['bæra:ʒ] n (Mil) descarga, bombardeo; (dam)
presa; (of criticism) lluvia, aluvión m
barrel ['bærəl] n barril m; (of gun) cañón m
barren ['bærən] adj estéril
barrette [bə'ret] (US) n pasador m (LAM, SP), broche
m (MEX)
barricade [bærɪ'keɪd] n barricada
barrier ['bærɪə*] n barrera
barring ['ba:rɪŋ] prep excepto, salvo
barrister ['bærɪstə*] (BRIT) n abogado/a
barrow ['bærəu] n (cart) carretilla (de mano)

bartender ['ba:tendə*] (US) n camarero, barman m
base [beɪs] n base f ▷ vt: **to ~ sth on** basar or fundar
algo en ▷ adj bajo, infame
baseball ['beɪsbɔ:l] n béisbol m; **baseball cap** n
gorra f de béisbol
basement ['beɪsmənt] n sótano
bases¹ ['beɪsi:z] npl of **basis**
bases² ['beɪsiz] npl of **base**
bash [bæʃ] (inf) vt golpear
basic ['beɪsɪk] adj básico; **basically** adv
fundamentalmente, en el fondo; (simply)
sencillamente; **basics** npl: **the basics** los fundamentos
basil ['bæzl] n albahaca
basin ['beɪsn] n cuenco, tazón m; (Geo) cuenca; (also:
wash~) lavabo
basis ['beɪsɪs] (pl **bases**) n base f; **on a part-time/
trial ~** a tiempo parcial/a prueba
basket ['ba:skɪt] n cesta, cesto; canasta; **basketball**
n baloncesto
bass [beɪs] n (Mus: instrument) bajo; (double bass)
contrabajo; (singer) bajo
bastard ['ba:stəd] n bastardo; (inf!) hijo de puta (!)
bat [bæt] n (Zool) murciélago; (for ball games) palo;
(BRIT: for table tennis) pala ▷ vt: **he didn't ~ an eyelid**
ni pestañeó
batch [bætʃ] n (of bread) hornada; (of letters etc) lote m
bath [ba:θ, pl ba:ðz] n (action) baño; (bathtub) bañera
(SP), tina (LAM), bañadera (RPL) ▷ vt bañar; **to have a ~**
bañarse, tomar un baño; see also **baths**
bathe [beɪð] vi bañarse ▷ vt (wound) lavar
bathing ['beɪðɪŋ] n el bañarse; **bathing costume** (US
bathing suit) n traje m de baño
bath: bathrobe n (man's) batín m; (woman's) bata;
bathroom n (cuarto de) baño; **baths** [ba:ðz] npl
(also: **swimming baths**) piscina; **bath towel** n toalla
de baño; **bathtub** n bañera
baton ['bætən] n (Mus) batuta; (Athletics) testigo;
(weapon) porra
batter ['bætə*] vt maltratar; (rain etc) azotar
▷ n masa (para rebozar); **battered** adj (hat, pan)
estropeado
battery ['bætərɪ] n (Aut) batería; (of torch) pila;
battery farming n cría intensiva
battle ['bætl] n batalla; (fig) lucha ▷ vi luchar;
battlefield n campo m de batalla
bay [beɪ] n (Geo) bahía; **B~ of Biscay** = mar
Cantábrico; **to hold sb at ~** mantener a algn a raya
bazaar [bə'za:*] n bazar m; (fete) venta con fines
benéficos
B. & B. n abbr = **bed and breakfast**; (place) pensión f;
(terms) cama y desayuno
BBC n abbr (= British Broadcasting Corporation) cadena de
radio y televisión estatal británica
B.C. adv abbr (= before Christ) a. de C.

○ KEYWORD

be [bi:] (pt was, were, pp been) aux vb **1** (with present
participle: forming continuous tenses): **what are you
doing?** ¿qué estás haciendo?, ¿qué haces?; **they're
coming tomorrow** vienen mañana; **I've been
waiting for hours** llevo horas esperándote
2 (with pp: forming passives) ser (but often replaced by
active or reflexive constructions): **to be murdered** ser
asesinado; **the box had been opened** habían abierto
la caja; **the thief was nowhere to be seen** no se veía

al ladrón por ninguna parte

3 (in tag questions): **it was fun, wasn't it?** fue divertido, ¿no? or ¿verdad?; **he's good-looking, isn't he?** es guapo, ¿no te parece?; **she's back again, is she?** entonces, ¿ha vuelto?

4 (+to +infin): **the house is to be sold** (necessity) hay que vender la casa; (future) van a vender la casa; **he's not to open it** no tiene que abrirlo ▷ vb +complement **1** (with n or num complement, but see also **3, 4, 5** and impers vb below) ser; **he's a doctor** es médico; **2 and 2 are 4** 2 y 2 son 4 **2** (with adj complement: expressing permanent or inherent quality) ser; (: expressing state seen as temporary or reversible) estar; **I'm English** soy inglés/esa; **she's tall/pretty** es alta/bonita; **he's young** es joven; **be careful/good/quiet** ten cuidado/pórtate bien/cállate; **I'm tired** estoy cansado/a; **it's dirty** está sucio/a

3 (of health) estar; **how are you?** ¿cómo estás?; **he's very ill** está muy enfermo; **I'm better now** ya estoy mejor

4 (of age) tener; **how old are you?** ¿cuántos años tienes?; **I'm sixteen (years old)** tengo dieciséis años **5** (cost) costar; ser; **how much was the meal?** ¿cuánto fue or costó la comida?; **that'll be £5.75, please** son £5.75, por favor; **this shirt is £17** esta camisa cuesta £17 ▷ vi (exist, occur etc) existir, haber; **the best singer that ever was** el mejor cantante que existió jamás; **is there a God?** ¿hay un Dios?, ¿existe Dios?; **be that as it may** sea como sea; **so be it** así sea

2 (referring to place) estar; **I won't be here tomorrow** no estaré aquí mañana

3 (referring to movement): **where have you been?** ¿dónde has estado?

▷ impers vb **1** (referring to time): **it's 5 o'clock** son las 5; **it's the 28th of April** estamos a 28 de abril **2** (referring to distance): **it's 10 km to the village** el pueblo está a 10 km

3 (referring to the weather): **it's too hot/cold** hace demasiado calor/frío; **it's windy today** hace viento hoy

4 (emphatic): **it's me** soy yo; **it was Maria who paid the bill** fue María la que pagó la cuenta

beach [biːtʃ] n playa ▷ vt varar
beacon ['biːkən] n (lighthouse) faro; (marker) guía
bead [biːd] n cuenta; (of sweat etc) gota; **beads** npl (necklace) collar m
beak [biːk] n pico
beam [biːm] n (Arch) viga, travesaño; (of light) rayo, haz m de luz ▷ vi brillar; (smile) sonreír
bean [biːn] n judía; **runner/broad ~** habichuela/ haba; **coffee ~** grano de café; **beansprouts** npl brotes mpl de soja
bear [bɛə*] (pt **bore**, pp **borne**) n oso ▷ vt (weight etc) llevar; (cost) pagar; (responsibility) tener; (endure) soportar, aguantar; (children) parir, tener; (fruit) dar ▷ vi: **to ~ right/left** torcer a la derecha/izquierda
beard [biəd] n barba
bearer ['bɛərə*] n portador(a) m/f
bearing ['bɛərɪŋ] n porte m, comportamiento; (connection) relación f
beast [biːst] n bestia; (inf) bruto, salvaje m
beat [biːt] (pt ~, pp **beaten**) n (of heart) latido; (Mus) ritmo, compás m; (of policeman) ronda ▷ vt pegar, golpear; (eggs) batir; (defeat: opponent) vencer, derrotar;

(: record) sobrepasar ▷ vi (heart) latir; (drum) redoblar; (rain, wind) azotar; **off the ~en track** aislado; **to ~ it** (inf) largarse; **beat up** vt (attack) dar una paliza a; **beating** n paliza
beautiful ['bjuːtɪful] adj precioso, hermoso, bello; **beautifully** adv maravillosamente
beauty ['bjuːtɪ] n belleza; **beauty parlour** (us **beauty parlor**) n salón m de belleza; **beauty salon** n salón m de belleza; **beauty spot** n (Tourism) lugar m pintoresco
beaver ['biːvə*] n castor m
became [bɪˈkeɪm] pt of **become**
because [bɪˈkɒz] conj porque; **~ of** debido a, a causa de
beckon ['bɛkən] vt (also: **~ to**) llamar con señas
become [bɪˈkʌm] (pt **became**, pp ~) vt (suit) favorecer, sentar bien a ▷ vi (+ n) hacerse, llegar a ser; (+ adj) ponerse, volverse; **to ~ fat** engordar
bed [bɛd] n cama; (of flowers) macizo; (of coal, clay) capa; (of river) lecho; (of sea) fondo; **to go to ~** acostarse; **bed and breakfast** n (place) pensión f; (terms) cama y desayuno; **bedclothes** npl ropa de cama; **bedding** n ropa de cama; **bed linen** n (BRIT) ropa f de cama
bed: bedroom n dormitorio; **bedside** n: **at the bedside of** a la cabecera de; **bedside lamp** n lámpara de noche; **bedside table** n mesilla de noche; **bedsit(ter)** (BRIT) n cuarto de alquiler; **bedspread** n cubrecama m, colcha; **bedtime** n hora de acostarse
bee [biː] n abeja
beech [biːtʃ] n haya
beef [biːf] n carne f de vaca; **roast ~** rosbif m; **beefburger** n hamburguesa; **Beefeater** n alabardero de la Torre de Londres
been [biːn] pp of **be**
beer [biə*] n cerveza; **beer garden** n (BRIT) terraza f de verano, jardín m (de un bar)
beet [biːt] (us) n (also: **red ~**) remolacha
beetle ['biːtl] n escarabajo
beetroot ['biːtruːt] (BRIT) n remolacha
before [bɪˈfɔː*] prep (of time) antes de; (of space) delante de ▷ conj antes (de) que ▷ adv antes, anteriormente; delante, adelante; **~ going** antes de marcharse; **~ she goes** antes de que se vaya; **the week ~** la semana anterior; **I've never seen it ~** no lo he visto nunca; **beforehand** adv de antemano, con anticipación
beg [bɛg] vi pedir limosna ▷ vt pedir, rogar; (entreat) suplicar; **to ~ sb to do sth** rogar a algn que haga algo; see also **pardon**
began [bɪˈgæn] pt of **begin**
beggar ['bɛgə*] n mendigo/a
begin [bɪˈgɪn] (pt **began**, pp **begun**) vt, vi empezar, comenzar; **to ~ doing** or **to do sth** empezar a hacer algo; **beginner** n principiante mf; **beginning** n principio, comienzo
begun [bɪˈgʌn] pp of **begin**
behalf [bɪˈhaːf] n: **on ~ of** en nombre de, por; (for benefit of) en beneficio de; **on my/his ~** por mí/él
behave [bɪˈheɪv] vi (person) portarse, comportarse; (well: also: **~ o.s.**) portarse bien; **behaviour** (us **behavior**) n comportamiento, conducta
behind [bɪˈhaɪnd] prep detrás de; (supporting): **to be ~ sb** apoyar a algn ▷ adv detrás, por detrás, atrás ▷ n trasero; **to be ~ (schedule)** ir retrasado; **~ the scenes** (fig) entre bastidores

beige [beɪʒ] *adj* color beige

Beijing [beɪˈdʒɪŋ] *n* Pekín *m*

being [ˈbiːɪŋ] *n* ser *m*; (*existence*): **in ~** existente; **to come into ~** aparecer

belated [bɪˈleɪtɪd] *adj* atrasado, tardío

belch [bɛltʃ] *vi* eructar ▷ *vt* (*gen*: belch out: smoke etc) arrojar

Belgian [ˈbɛldʒən] *adj, n* belga *mf*

Belgium [ˈbɛldʒəm] *n* Bélgica

belief [bɪˈliːf] *n* opinión *f*; (*faith*) fe *f*

believe [bɪˈliːv] *vt, vi* creer; **to ~ in** creer en; **believer** *n* partidario/a; (*Rel*) creyente *mf*, fiel *mf*

bell [bɛl] *n* campana; (*small*) campanilla; (*on door*) timbre *m*

bellboy [ˈbɛlbɔɪ] (*BRIT*) *n* botones *m inv*

bellhop [ˈbɛlhɔp] (*US*) *n* =**bellboy**

bellow [ˈbɛləu] *vi* bramar; (*person*) rugir

bell pepper *n* (*esp US*) pimiento, pimentón *m* (*LAM*)

belly [ˈbɛlɪ] *n* barriga, panza; **belly button** (*inf*) *n* ombligo

belong [bɪˈlɔŋ] *vi*: **to ~ to** pertenecer a; (*club etc*) ser socio de; **this book ~s here** este libro va aquí; **belongings** *npl* pertenencias *fpl*

beloved [bɪˈlʌvɪd] *adj* querido/a

below [bɪˈləu] *prep* bajo, debajo de; (*less than*) inferior a ▷ *adv* abajo, (por) debajo; **see ~** véase más abajo

belt [bɛlt] *n* cinturón *m*; (*Tech*) correa, cinta ▷ *vt* (*thrash*) pegar con correa; **beltway** (*US*) *n* (*Aut*) carretera de circunvalación

bemused [bɪˈmjuːzd] *adj* perplejo

bench [bɛntʃ] *n* banco; (*BRIT Pol*): **the Government/ Opposition ~es** (los asientos de) los miembros del Gobierno/de la Oposición; **the B~** (*Law: judges*) magistratura

bend [bɛnd] (*pt, pp* **bent**) *vt* doblar ▷ *vi* inclinarse ▷ *n* (*BRIT: in road, river*) curva; (*in pipe*) codo; **bend down** *vi* inclinarse, doblarse; **bend over** *vi* inclinarse

beneath [bɪˈniːθ] *prep* bajo, debajo de; (*unworthy*) indigno de ▷ *adv* abajo, (por) debajo

beneficial [bɛnɪˈfɪʃəl] *adj* beneficioso

benefit [ˈbɛnɪfɪt] *n* beneficio; (*allowance of money*) subsidio ▷ *vt* beneficiar ▷ *vi*: **he'll ~ from it** lo sacará provecho

benign [bɪˈnaɪn] *adj* benigno; (*smile*) afable

bent [bɛnt] *pt, pp* of **bend** ▷ *n* inclinación *f* ▷ *adj*: **to be ~ on** estar empeñado en

bereaved [bɪˈriːvd] *npl*: **the ~** los íntimos de una persona afligidos por su muerte

beret [ˈbɛreɪ] *n* boina

Berlin [bəˈlɪn] *n* Berlín *m*

Bermuda [bəːˈmjuːdə] *n* las Bermudas

berry [ˈbɛrɪ] *n* baya

berth [bəːθ] *n* (*bed*) litera; (*cabin*) camarote *m*; (*for ship*) amarradero ▷ *vi* atracar, amarrar

beside [bɪˈsaɪd] *prep* junto a, al lado de; **to be ~ o.s. with anger** estar fuera de sí; **that's ~ the point** eso no tiene nada que ver; **besides** *adv* además ▷ *prep* además de

best [bɛst] *adj* (el/la) mejor ▷ *adv* (lo) mejor; **the ~ part of** (*quantity*) la mayor parte de; **at ~** en el mejor de los casos; **to make the ~ of sth** sacar el mejor partido de algo; **to do one's ~** hacer todo lo posible; **to the ~ of my knowledge** que yo sepa; **to the ~ of my ability** como mejor puedo; **best-before date** *n* fecha de consumo preferente; **best man** (*irreg*) *n* padrino de boda; **bestseller** *n* éxito de librería, bestseller *m*

bet [bɛt] (*pt, pp* or **~ted**) *n* apuesta ▷ *vt*: **to ~ money on** apostar dinero por ▷ *vi* apostar; **to ~ sb sth** apostar algo a algn

betray [bɪˈtreɪ] *vt* traicionar; (*trust*) faltar a

better [ˈbɛtə*] *adj, adv* mejor ▷ *vt* superar ▷ *n*: **to get the ~ of sb** quedar por encima de algn; **you had ~ do it** más vale que lo hagas; **he thought ~ of it** cambió de parecer; **to get ~** (*Med*) mejorar(se)

betting [ˈbɛtɪŋ] *n* juego, el apostar; **betting shop** (*BRIT*) *n* agencia de apuestas

between [bɪˈtwiːn] *prep* entre ▷ *adv* (*time*) mientras tanto; (*place*) en medio

beverage [ˈbɛvərɪdʒ] *n* bebida

beware [bɪˈwɛə*] *vi*: **to ~ (of)** tener cuidado (con); **"~ of the dog"** "perro peligroso"

bewildered [bɪˈwɪldəd] *adj* aturdido, perplejo

beyond [bɪˈjɔnd] *prep* más allá de; (*past: understanding*) fuera de; (*after: date*) después de, más allá de; (*above*) superior a ▷ *adv* (*in space*) más allá; (*in time*) posteriormente; **~ doubt** fuera de toda duda; **~ repair** irreparable

bias [ˈbaɪəs] *n* (*prejudice*) prejuicio, pasión *f*; (*preference*) predisposición *f*; **bias(s)ed** *adj* parcial

bib [bɪb] *n* babero

Bible [ˈbaɪbl] *n* Biblia

bicarbonate of soda [baɪˈkɑːbənɪt-] *n* bicarbonato sódico

biceps [ˈbaɪsɛps] *n* bíceps *m*

bicycle [ˈbaɪsɪkl] *n* bicicleta; **bicycle pump** *n* bomba de bicicleta

bid [bɪd] (*pt* **bade** or *, pp* **bidden** or **~**) *n* oferta, postura; (*in tender*) licitación *f*; (*attempt*) tentativa, conato ▷ *vi* hacer una oferta ▷ *vt* (*offer*) ofrecer; **to ~ sb good day** decir a algn los buenos días; **bidder** *n*: **the highest bidder** el mejor postor

bidet [ˈbiːdeɪ] *n* bidet *m*

big [bɪg] *adj* grande; (*brother, sister*) mayor; **bigheaded** *adj* engreído; **big toe** *n* dedo gordo (del pie)

bike [baɪk] *n* bici *f*; **bike lane** *n* carril-bici *m*

bikini [bɪˈkiːnɪ] *n* bikini *m*

bilateral [baɪˈlætərəl] *adj* (*agreement*) bilateral

bilingual [baɪˈlɪŋgwəl] *adj* bilingüe

bill [bɪl] *n* cuenta; (*invoice*) factura; (*Pol*) proyecto de ley; (*US: banknote*) billete *m*; (*of bird*) pico; (*of show*) programa *m*; **"post no ~s"** "prohibido fijar carteles"; **to fit** or **fill the ~** (*fig*) cumplir con los requisitos; **billboard** (*US*) *n* cartelera; **billfold** [ˈbɪlfəuld] (*US*) *n* cartera

billiards [ˈbɪljədz] *n* billar *m*

billion [ˈbɪljən] *n* (*BRIT*) billón *m* (*millón de millones*); (*US*) mil millones *mpl*

bin [bɪn] *n* (*for rubbish*) cubo or bote *m* (*MEX*) or tacho (*SC*) de la basura; (*container*) recipiente *m*

bind [baɪnd] (*pt, pp* **bound**) *vt* atar; (*book*) encuadernar; (*oblige*) obligar ▷ *n* (*inf: nuisance*) lata

binge [bɪndʒ] (*inf*) *n*: **to go on a ~** ir de juerga

bingo [ˈbɪŋgəu] *n* bingo *m*

binoculars [bɪˈnɔkjuləz] *npl* prismáticos *mpl*

bio... *prefix*: **biochemistry** *n* bioquímica; **biodegradable** [baɪəudɪˈgreɪdəbl] *adj* biodegradable; **biography** [baɪˈɔgrəfɪ] *n* biografía; **biological** *adj* biológico; **biology** [baɪˈɔlədʒɪ] *n* biología; **biometric** [baɪəˈmɛtrɪk] *adj* biométrico

birch [bəːtʃ] *n* (*tree*) abedul *m*

bird [bəːd] *n* ave *f*, pájaro; (*BRIT: inf: girl*) chica; **bird flu** *n* gripe *f* aviar; **bird of prey** *n* ave *f* de presa; **birdwatching** *n*: **he likes to go birdwatching on**

Sundays los domingos le gusta ir a ver pájaros

Biro® ['baɪrəʊ] n bóli

birth [bɜːθ] n nacimiento; **to give ~ to** parir, dar a luz; **birth certificate** n partida de nacimiento; **birth control** n (policy) control m de natalidad; (methods) métodos mpl anticonceptivos; **birthday** n cumpleaños m inv ⊳ cpd (cake, card etc) de cumpleaños; **birthmark** n antojo, marca de nacimiento; **birthplace** n lugar m de nacimiento

biscuit ['bɪskɪt] (BRIT) n galleta

bishop ['bɪʃəp] n obispo; (Chess) alfil m

bistro ['biːstrəʊ] n café-bar m

bit [bɪt] pt of **bite** n trozo, pedazo, pedacito; (Comput) bit m, bitio; (for horse) freno, bocado; **a ~ of** un poco de; **a ~ mad** un poco loco; **~ by ~** poco a poco

bitch [bɪtʃ] n perra; (inf!: woman) zorra (!)

bite [baɪt] (pt **bit**, pp **bitten**) vt, vi morder; (insect etc) picar ⊳ n (insect bite) picadura; (mouthful) bocado; **to ~ one's nails** comerse las uñas; **let's have a ~ (to eat)** (inf) vamos a comer algo

bitten ['bɪtn] pp of **bite**

bitter ['bɪtə*] adj amargo; (wind) cortante, penetrante; (battle) encarnizado ⊳ n (BRIT: beer) cerveza típica británica a base de lúpulos

bizarre [bɪ'zɑː*] adj raro, extraño

black [blæk] adj negro; (tea, coffee) solo ⊳ n color m negro; (person): **B~** negro/a ⊳ vt (BRIT Industry) boicotear; **to give sb a ~ eye** ponerle a algn el ojo morado; **~ and blue** (bruised) amoratado; **to be in the ~** (bank account) estar en números negros; **black out** vi (faint) desmayarse; **blackberry** n zarzamora; **blackbird** n mirlo; **blackboard** n pizarra; **black coffee** n café m solo; **blackcurrant** n grosella negra; **black ice** n hielo invisible en la carretera; **blackmail** n chantaje m ⊳ vt chantajear; **black market** n mercado negro; **blackout** n (Mil) oscurecimiento; (power cut) apagón m; (TV, Radio) interrupción f de programas; (fainting) desvanecimiento; **black pepper** n pimienta f negra; **black pudding** n morcilla; **Black Sea** n: **the Black Sea** el Mar Negro

bladder ['blædə*] n vejiga

blade [bleɪd] n hoja; (of propeller) paleta; **a ~ of grass** una brizna de hierba

blame [bleɪm] n culpa ⊳ vt: **to ~ sb for sth** echar a algn la culpa de algo; **to be to ~ (for)** tener la culpa (de)

bland [blænd] adj (music, taste) soso

blank [blæŋk] adj en blanco; (look) sin expresión ⊳ n (of memory): **my mind is a ~** no puedo recordar nada; (on form) blanco, espacio en blanco; (cartridge) cartucho sin bala o de fogueo

blanket ['blæŋkɪt] n manta (SP), cobija (LAM); (of snow) capa; (of fog) manto

blast [blɑːst] n (of wind) ráfaga, soplo; (of explosive) explosión f ⊳ vt (blow up) volar

blatant ['bleɪtənt] adj descarado

blaze [bleɪz] n (fire) hoguera; (fig: of colour) despliegue m; (: of glory) esplendor m ⊳ vi arder en llamas; (fig) brillar ⊳ vt: **to ~ a trail** (fig) abrir (un) camino; **in a ~ of publicity** con gran publicidad

blazer ['bleɪzə*] n chaqueta de uniforme de colegial o de socio de club

bleach [bliːtʃ] n (also: **household ~**) lejía ⊳ vt blanquear; **bleachers** (us) npl (Sport) gradas fpl al sol

bleak [bliːk] adj (countryside) desierto; (prospect) poco prometedor(a); (weather) crudo; (smile) triste

bled [bled] pt, pp of **bleed**

bleed [bliːd] (pt, pp **bled**) vt, vi sangrar; **my nose is ~ing** me está sangrando la nariz

blemish ['blemɪʃ] n marca, mancha; (on reputation) tacha

blend [blend] n mezcla ⊳ vt mezclar; (colours etc) combinar, mezclar ⊳ vi (colours etc: also: **~ in**) combinarse, mezclarse; **blender** n (Culin) batidora

bless [bles] (pt, pp **~ed** or **blest**) vt bendecir; **~ you!** (after sneeze) ¡Jesús!; **blessing** n (approval) aprobación f; (godsend) don m del cielo, bendición f; (advantage) beneficio, ventaja

blew [bluː] pt of **blow**

blight [blaɪt] vt (hopes etc) frustrar, arruinar

blind [blaɪnd] adj ciego; (fig): **~ (to)** ciego (a) ⊳ n (for window) persiana ⊳ vt cegar; (dazzle) deslumbrar; (deceive): **to ~ sb to ...** cegar a algn a ...; **the blind** npl los ciegos; **blind alley** n callejón m sin salida; **blindfold** n venda ⊳ adv con los ojos vendados ⊳ vt vendar los ojos a

blink [blɪŋk] vi parpadear, pestañear; (light) oscilar

bliss [blɪs] n felicidad f

blister ['blɪstə*] n ampolla ⊳ vi (paint) ampollarse

blizzard ['blɪzəd] n ventisca

bloated ['bləʊtɪd] adj hinchado; (person: full) ahíto

blob [blɒb] n (drop) gota; (indistinct object) bulto

block [blɒk] n bloque m; (in pipes) obstáculo; (of buildings) manzana (SP), cuadra (LAM) ⊳ vt obstruir, cerrar; (progress) estorbar; **~ of flats** (BRIT) bloque m de pisos; **mental ~** bloqueo mental; **block up** vt tapar, obstruir; (pipe) atascar; **blockade** [-'keɪd] n bloqueo ⊳ vt bloquear; **blockage** n estorbo, obstrucción f; **blockbuster** n (book) bestseller m; (film) éxito de público; **block capitals** npl mayúsculas fpl; **block letters** npl mayúsculas fpl

blog [blɒg] n blog m

bloke [bləʊk] (BRIT: inf) n tipo, tío

blond(e) [blɒnd] adj, n rubio a m/f

blood [blʌd] n sangre f; **blood donor** n donante mf de sangre; **blood group** n grupo sanguíneo; **blood poisoning** n envenenamiento de la sangre; **blood pressure** n presión f sanguínea; **bloodshed** n derramamiento de sangre; **bloodshot** adj inyectado en sangre; **bloodstream** n corriente f sanguínea; **blood test** n análisis m inv de sangre; **blood transfusion** n transfusión f de sangre; **blood type** n grupo sanguíneo; **blood vessel** n vaso sanguíneo; **bloody** adj sangriento; (BRIT: inf!) lleno de sangre; (BRIT: inf!): **this bloody ...** este condenado o puñetero ... (!) ⊳ adv: **bloody strong/good** (BRIT: inf!) terriblemente fuerte/bueno

bloom [bluːm] n flor f ⊳ vi florecer

blossom ['blɒsəm] n flor f ⊳ vi florecer

blot [blɒt] n borrón m; (fig) mancha ⊳ vt (stain) manchar

blouse [blauz] n blusa

blow [bləʊ] (pt **blew**, pp **blown**) n golpe m; (with sword) espadazo ⊳ vi soplar; (dust, sand etc) volar; (fuse) fundirse ⊳ vt (wind) llevarse; (fuse) quemar; (instrument) tocar; **to ~ one's nose** sonarse; **blow away** vt llevarse, arrancar; **blow out** vi (candle) apagarse; **blow up** vi estallar ⊳ vt volar; (tyre) inflar; (Phot) ampliar; **blow-dry** n moldeado (con secador)

blown [bləʊn] pp of **blow**

blue [bluː] adj azul; (depressed) deprimido; **~ film/joke** película/chiste m verde; **out of the ~** (fig) de repente; **bluebell** n campanilla, campánula azul; **blueberry** n arándano; **blue cheese** n queso azul; **blues** npl: **the blues** (Mus) el blues; **to have the blues** estar triste; **bluetit** n herrerillo m (común)

bluff [blʌf] vi tirarse un farol, farolear ▷ n farol m: **to call sb's ~** coger a algn la palabra

blunder ['blʌndə*] n patinazo, metedura de pata ▷ vi cometer un error, meter la pata

blunt [blʌnt] adj (pencil) despuntado; (knife) desafilado, romo; (person) franco, directo

blur [blə:*] n (shape): **to become a ~** hacerse borroso ▷ vt (vision) enturbiar; (distinction) borrar; **blurred** adj borroso

blush [blʌʃ] vi ruborizarse, ponerse colorado ▷ n rubor m; **blusher** n colorete m

board [bɔ:d] n (cardboard) cartón m; (wooden) tabla, tablero; (on wall) tablón m; (for chess etc) tablero; (committee) junta, consejo; (in firm) mesa or junta directiva; (Naut, Aviat): **on ~** a bordo ▷ vt (ship) embarcarse en; (train) subir a; **full ~** (BRIT) pensión completa; **half ~** (BRIT) media pensión; **to go by the ~** (fig) ser abandonado or olvidado; **board game** n juego de tablero; **boarding card** (BRIT) n tarjeta de embarque; **boarding pass** (US) n = **boarding card**; **boarding school** n internado; **board room** n sala de juntas

boast [bəust] vi: **to ~** (about or of) alardear (de)

boat [bəut] n barco, buque m; (small) barca, bote m

bob [bɔb] vi (also: **~ up and down**) menearse, balancearse

bobby pin ['bɔbɪ-] (US) n horquilla

body ['bɔdɪ] n cuerpo; (corpse) cadáver m; (of car) caja, carrocería; (fig: group) grupo; (: organization) organismo; **body-building** n culturismo; **bodyguard** n guardaespaldas m inv; **bodywork** n carrocería

bog [bɔg] n pantano, ciénaga ▷ vt: **to get ~ged down** (fig) empantanarse, atascarse

bogus ['bəugəs] adj falso, fraudulento

boil [bɔɪl] vt (water) hervir; (: egg, potato) pasar por agua, cocer ▷ vi hervir; (fig: with anger) estar furioso; (: with heat) asfixiarse ▷ n (Med) furúnculo, divieso; **to come to the ~, to come to a ~** (US) comenzar a hervir; **to ~ down to** (fig) reducirse a; **boil over** vi salirse, rebosar; **boiled egg** n (soft) huevo tibio (MEX) or pasado por agua or a la copa (SC); (hard) huevo duro; **boiled potatoes** npl patatas fpl (SP) or papas fpl (LAM) cocidas; **boiler** n caldera; **boiling** ['bɔɪlɪŋ] adj: **I'm boiling (hot)** (inf) estoy asado; **boiling point** n punto de ebullición

bold [bəuld] adj valiente, audaz; (pej) descarado; (colour) llamativo

Bolivia [bə'lɪvɪə] n Bolivia; **Bolivian** adj, n boliviano/a m/f

bollard ['bɔləd] (BRIT) n (Aut) poste m

bolt [bəult] n (lock) cerrojo; (with nut) perno, tornillo ▷ adv: **~ upright** rígido, erguido ▷ vt (door) echar el cerrojo a; (also: **~ together**) sujetar con tornillos; (food) engullir ▷ vi fugarse; (horse) desbocarse

bomb [bɔm] n bomba ▷ vt bombardear; **bombard** [bɔm'bɑ:d] vt bombardear; (fig) asediar; **bomber** n (Aviat) bombardero; **bomb scare** n amenaza de bomba

bond [bɔnd] n (promise) fianza; (Finance) bono; (link) vínculo, lazo; (Comm): **in ~** en depósito bajo fianza; **bonds** npl (chains) cadenas fpl

bone [bəun] n hueso; (of fish) espina ▷ vt deshuesar; quitar las espinas a

bonfire ['bɔnfaɪə*] n hoguera, fogata

bonnet ['bɔnɪt] n gorra; (BRIT: of car) capó m

bonus ['bəunəs] n (payment) paga extraordinaria, plus m; (fig) bendición f

boo [bu:] excl ¡uh! ▷ vt abuchear, rechiflar

book [buk] n libro; (of tickets) taco; (of stamps etc) librito ▷ vt (ticket) sacar; (seat, room) reservar; **books** npl (Comm) cuentas fpl, contabilidad f; **book in** vi (at hotel) registrarse; **book up** vt: **to be booked up** (hotel) estar completo; **bookcase** n librería, estante m para libros; **booking** n reserva; **booking office** n (BRIT Rail) despacho de billetes (SP) or boletos (LAM); (Theatre) taquilla (SP), boletería (LAM); **book-keeping** n contabilidad f; **booklet** n folleto; **bookmaker** n corredor m de apuestas; **bookmark** n (also Comput) marcador; **bookseller** n librero; **bookshelf** n estante m (para libros); **bookshop, book store** n librería

boom [bu:m] n (noise) trueno, estampido; (in prices etc) alza rápida; (Econ, in population) boom m ▷ vi (cannon) hacer gran estruendo, retumbar; (Econ) estar en alza

boost [bu:st] n estímulo, empuje m ▷ vt estimular, empujar

boot [bu:t] n bota; (of car) maletero, maletero ▷ vt (Comput) arrancar; **to ~** (in addition) además, por añadidura

booth [bu:ð] n (telephone booth, voting booth) cabina

booze [bu:z] (inf) n bebida

border ['bɔ:də*] n borde m, margen m; (of a country) frontera; (for flowers) arriate m ▷ vt (road) bordear; (another country: also: **~ on**) lindar con; **borderline** n: **on the borderline** en el límite

bore [bɔ:*] pt of **bear** ▷ vt (hole) hacer un agujero en; (well) perforar; (person) aburrir ▷ n (person) pelmazo, pesado; (of gun) calibre m; **bored** adj aburrido; **he's bored to tears** or **death** or **stiff** está aburrido como una ostra, está muerto de aburrimiento; **boredom** n aburrimiento

boring ['bɔ:rɪŋ] adj aburrido

born [bɔ:n] adj: **to be ~** nacer; **I was ~ in 1960** nací en 1960

borne [bɔ:n] pp of **bear**

borough ['bʌrə] n municipio

borrow ['bɔrəu] vt: **to ~ sth (from sb)** tomar algo prestado (a algn)

Bosnia(-Herzegovina) ['bɔ:snɪə(herzə'gəuvi:nə)] n Bosnia(-Herzegovina); **Bosnian** ['bɔznɪən] adj, n bosnio/a

bosom ['buzəm] n pecho

boss [bɔs] n jefe m ▷ vt (also: **~ about or around**) mangonear; **bossy** adj mandón/ona

both [bəuθ] adj, pron ambos/as, los dos (las dos); **~ of us went, we ~ went** fuimos los dos, ambos fuimos ▷ adv: **~ A and B** tanto A como B

bother ['bɔðə*] vt (worry) preocupar; (disturb) molestar, fastidiar ▷ vi (also: **~ o.s.**) molestarse ▷ n (trouble) dificultad f; (nuisance) molestia, lata; **to ~ doing** tomarse la molestia de hacer

bottle ['bɔtl] n botella; (small) frasco; (baby's) biberón m ▷ vt embotellar; **bottle bank** n contenedor m de vidrio; **bottle-opener** n abrebotellas m inv

bottom ['bɔtəm] n (of box, sea) fondo; (buttocks) trasero, culo; (of page) pie m; (of list) final m; (of class) último/a ▷ adj (lowest) más bajo; (last) último

bought [bɔ:t] pt, pp of **buy**

boulder ['bəuldə*] n canto rodado

bounce [bauns] vi (ball) (re)botar; (cheque) ser rechazado ▷ vt hacer (re)botar; (rebound) (re)bote m; **bouncer** (inf) n gorila m (que echa a los alborotadores de un bar, club etc)

bound [baund] pt, pp of **bind** ▷ n (leap) salto; (gen pl: limit) límite m ▷ vi (leap) saltar ▷ vt (border) rodear ▷ adj: **- by** rodeado de; **to be - to do sth** (obliged) tener el deber de hacer algo; **he's - to come** es seguro que vendrá; **out of -s** prohibido el paso; **- for** con destino a

boundary ['baundrɪ] n límite m

bouquet ['bukeɪ] n (of flowers) ramo

bourbon ['buəbən] (us) n (also: **- whiskey**) whisky m americano, bourbon m

bout [baut] n (of malaria etc) ataque m; (of activity) período; (Boxing etc) combate m, encuentro

boutique [bu:'ti:k] n boutique f, tienda de ropa

bow¹ [bəu] n (knot) lazo; (weapon, Mus) arco

bow² [bau] n (of the head) reverencia; (Naut: also: **-s**) proa ▷ vi inclinarse, hacer una reverencia

bowels [bauəlz] npl intestinos mpl, vientre m; (fig) entrañas fpl

bowl [bəul] n tazón m, cuenco; (ball) bola ▷ vi (Cricket) arrojar la pelota; see also **bowls**; **bowler** n (Cricket) lanzador m (de la pelota); (BRIT: also: **bowler hat**) hongo, bombín m; **bowling** n (game) bochas fpl, bolos mpl; **bowling alley** n bolera; **bowling green** n pista para bochas; **bowls** n juego de las bochas, bolos mpl

bow tie [bəu-] n corbata de lazo, pajarita

box [bɒks] n (also: **cardboard -**) caja, cajón m; (Theatre) palco ▷ vt encajonar ▷ vi (Sport) boxear; **boxer** ['bɒksə*] n (person) boxeador m; **boxer shorts** ['bɒksəfɔːts] pl n bóxers; **a pair of boxer shorts** unos bóxers; **boxing** ['bɒksɪŋ] n (Sport) boxeo; **Boxing Day** (BRIT) n día en que se dan los aguinaldos, 26 de diciembre; **boxing gloves** npl guantes mpl de boxeo; **boxing ring** n ring m, cuadrilátero; **box office** n taquilla (sP), boletería (LAM)

boy [bɔɪ] n (young) niño; (older) muchacho, chico; (son) hijo; **boy band** n boy band m (grupo musical de chicos)

boycott ['bɔɪkɒt] n boicot m ▷ vt boicotear

boyfriend ['bɔɪfrɛnd] n novio

bra [brɑː] n sostén m, sujetador m

brace [breɪs] n (BRIT: also: **-s**: on teeth) corrector m, aparato; (tool) berbiquí m ▷ vt (knees, shoulders) tensionar; **braces** npl (BRIT) tirantes mpl; **to - o.s.** (fig) prepararse

bracelet ['breɪslɪt] n pulsera, brazalete m

bracket ['brækɪt] n (Tech) soporte m, puntal m; (group) clase f, categoría; (also: **brace -**) soporte m, abrazadera; (also: **round -**) paréntesis m inv; (also: **square -**) corchete m ▷ vt (word etc) poner entre paréntesis

brag [bræg] vi jactarse

braid [breɪd] n (trimming) galón m; (of hair) trenza

brain [breɪn] n cerebro; **brains** npl sesos mpl; **she's got -s** es muy lista

braise [breɪz] vt cocer a fuego lento

brake [breɪk] n (on vehicle) freno ▷ vi frenar; **brake light** n luz f de frenado

bran [bræn] n salvado

branch [brɑːntʃ] n rama; (Comm) sucursal f; **branch off** vi: **a small road branches off to the right** hay una carretera pequeña que sale hacia la derecha; **branch out** vi (fig) extenderse

brand [brænd] n marca; (fig: type) tipo ▷ vt (cattle)

marcar con hierro candente; **brand name** n marca; **brand-new** adj flamante, completamente nuevo

brandy ['brændɪ] n coñac m

brash [bræʃ] adj (forward) descarado

brass [brɑːs] n latón m; **the -** (Mus) los cobres; **brass band** n banda de metal

brat [bræt] (pej) n mocoso/a

brave [breɪv] adj valiente, valeroso ▷ vt (face up to) desafiar; **bravery** n valor m, valentía

brawl [brɔːl] n pelea, reyerta

Brazil [brə'zɪl] n (el) Brasil; **Brazilian** adj, n brasileño/a m/f

breach [briːtʃ] vt abrir brecha en ▷ n (gap) brecha; (breaking): **- of contract** infracción f de contrato; **- of the peace** perturbación f del orden público

bread [brɛd] n pan m; **breadbin** n panera; **breadbox** (us) n panera; **breadcrumbs** npl migajas fpl; (Culin) pan rallado

breadth [brɛtθ] n anchura; (fig) amplitud f

break [breɪk] (pt **broke**, pp **broken**) vt romper; (promise) faltar a; (law) violar, infringir; (record) batir ▷ vi romperse, quebrarse; (storm) estallar; (weather) cambiar; (dawn) despuntar; (news etc) darse a conocer ▷ n (gap) abertura; (fracture) fractura; (time) intervalo; (: at school) (período del) recreo; (chance) oportunidad f, to **- the news to** comunicar la noticia a algn; **break down** vt (figures, data) analizar, descomponer ▷ vi (machine) estropearse; (Aut) averiarse; (person) romper a llorar; (talks) fracasar; **break in** vt (horse etc) domar ▷ vi (burglar) forzar una entrada; (interrupt) interrumpir; **break into** vt fus (house) forzar; **break off** vi (speaker) pararse, detenerse; (branch) partir; **break out** vi estallar; (prisoner) escaparse; **to break out in spots** salirle a algn granos; **break up** vi (ship) hacerse pedazos; (crowd, meeting) disolverse; (marriage) deshacerse; (Scol) terminar (el curso); (line) cortarse ▷ vt (rocks etc) romper; (journey) partir; (fight etc) acabar con; **the line's or you're breaking up** se corta; **breakdown** n (Aut) avería; (in communications) interrupción f; (Med: also: **nervous breakdown**) colapso, crisis f nerviosa; (of marriage, talks) fracaso; (of statistics) análisis m inv; **breakdown truck, breakdown van** n (camión m) grúa

breakfast ['brɛkfəst] n desayuno

break: break-in n robo con allanamiento de morada; **breakthrough** n (also fig) avance m

breast [brɛst] n (of woman) pecho, seno; (chest) pecho; (of bird) pechuga; **breast-feed** (pt, pp **breast-fed**) vt, vi amamantar, criar a los pechos; **breast-stroke** n braza (de pecho)

breath [brɛθ] n aliento, respiración f; **to take a deep - respirar hondo; out of - sin aliento, sofocado

Breathalyser® ['brɛθəlaɪzə*] (BRIT) n alcoholímetro

breathe [briːð] vt, vi respirar; **breathe in** vt, vi aspirar; **breathe out** vt, vi espirar; **breathing** n respiración f

breath: breathless adj sin aliento, jadeante; **breathtaking** adj imponente, pasmoso; **breath test** n prueba de la alcoholemia

bred [brɛd] pt, pp of **breed**

breed [briːd] (pt, pp **bred**) vt criar ▷ vi reproducirse, procrear ▷ n (Zool) raza, casta; (type) tipo

breeze [briːz] n brisa

breezy ['briːzɪ] adj de mucho viento, ventoso; (person) despreocupado

brew [bruː] vt (tea) hacer; (beer) elaborar ▷ vi

(fig: trouble) prepararse; *(storm)* amenazar; **brewery** n fábrica de cerveza, cervecería
bribe [braɪb] n soborno ▷ vt sobornar, cohechar; **bribery** n soborno, cohecho
bric-a-brac ['brɪkəbræk] n inv baratijas fpl
brick [brɪk] n ladrillo; **bricklayer** n albañil m
bride [braɪd] n novia; **bridegroom** n novio; **bridesmaid** n dama de honor
bridge [brɪdʒ] n puente m; *(Naut)* puente m de mando; *(of nose)* caballete m; *(Cards)* bridge m ▷ vt *(fig)*: **to ~ a gap** llenar un vacío
bridle ['braɪdl] n brida, freno
brief [briːf] adj breve, corto ▷ n *(Law)* escrito; *(task)* cometido, encargo ▷ vt informar; **briefs** npl *(for men)* calzoncillos mpl; *(for women)* bragas fpl; **briefcase** n cartera (SP), portafolio (LAM); **briefing** n *(Press)* informe m; **briefly** adv *(glance)* fugazmente; *(say)* en pocas palabras
brigadier [brɪgə'dɪə*] n general m de brigada
bright [braɪt] adj brillante; *(room)* luminoso; *(day)* de sol; *(person: clever)* listo, inteligente; (: *lively*) alegre; *(colour)* vivo; *(future)* prometedor(a)
brilliant ['brɪljənt] adj brillante; *(inf)* fenomenal
brim [brɪm] n borde m; *(of hat)* ala
brine [braɪn] n *(Culin)* salmuera
bring [brɪŋ] *(pt, pp brought)* vt *(thing, person: with you)* traer; (: *to sb*) llevar, conducir; *(trouble, satisfaction)* causar; **bring about** vt ocasionar, producir; **bring back** vt volver a traer; *(return)* devolver; **bring down** vt *(government, plane)* derribar; *(price)* rebajar; **bring in** vt *(harvest)* recoger; *(person)* hacer entrar or pasar; *(object)* traer; *(Pol: bill, law)* presentar; *(produce: income)* producir, rendir; **bring on** vt *(illness, attack)* producir, causar; *(player, substitute)* sacar (de la reserva), hacer salir; **bring out** vt sacar; *(book etc)* publicar; *(meaning)* subrayar; **bring up** vt subir; *(person)* educar, criar; *(question)* sacar a colación; *(food: vomit)* devolver, vomitar
brink [brɪŋk] n borde m
brisk [brɪsk] adj *(abrupt: tone)* brusco; *(person)* enérgico, vigoroso; *(pace)* rápido; *(trade)* activo
bristle ['brɪsl] n cerda ▷ vi: **to ~ in anger** temblar de rabia
Brit [brɪt] n abbr *(inf: = Briton)* británico/a
Britain ['brɪtən] n *(also: Great ~)* Gran Bretaña
British ['brɪtɪʃ] adj británico ▷ npl: **the ~** los británicos; **British Isles** npl: **the British Isles** las Islas Británicas
Briton ['brɪtən] n británico/a
brittle ['brɪtl] adj quebradizo, frágil
broad [brɔːd] adj ancho; *(range)* amplio; *(accent)* cerrado; **in ~ daylight** en pleno día; **broadband** n banda ancha; **broad bean** n haba; **broadcast** *(pt, pp ~)* n emisión f, ▷ vt *(Radio)* emitir; *(TV)* transmitir ▷ vi emitir; transmitir; **broaden** vt ampliar ▷ vi ensancharse; **to broaden one's mind** hacer más tolerante a algn; **broadly** adv en general; **broad-minded** adj tolerante, liberal
broccoli ['brɔkəlɪ] n brécol m
brochure ['brəʊʃjʊə*] n folleto
broil [brɔɪl] vt *(Culin)* asar a la parrilla
broiler ['brɔɪlə*] n *(grill)* parrilla
broke [brəʊk] pt of **break** ▷ adj *(inf)* pelado, sin blanca
broken ['brəʊkən] pp of **break** ▷ adj roto;

(machine: also: ~ down) averiado; **~ leg** pierna rota; **in ~ English** en un inglés imperfecto
broker ['brəʊkə*] n agente mf, bolsista mf; *(insurance broker)* agente de seguros
bronchitis [brɔŋ'kaɪtɪs] n bronquitis f
bronze [brɔnz] n bronce m
brooch [brəʊtʃ] n prendedor m, broche m
brood [bruːd] n camada, cría ▷ vi *(person)* dejarse obsesionar
broom [brum] n escoba; *(Bot)* retama
Bros. abbr *(= Brothers)* Hnos
broth [brɔθ] n caldo
brothel ['brɔθl] n burdel m
brother ['brʌðə*] n hermano; **brother-in-law** n cuñado
brought [brɔːt] pt, pp of **bring**
brow [brau] n *(forehead)* frente m; *(eyebrow)* ceja; *(of hill)* cumbre f
brown [braun] adj *(colour)* marrón; *(hair)* castaño; *(tanned)* bronceado, moreno ▷ n *(colour)* color m marrón or pardo ▷ vt *(Culin)* dorar; **brown bread** n pan integral
Brownie ['braunɪ] n niña exploradora
brown rice n arroz m integral
brown sugar n azúcar m terciado
browse [brauz] vi *(through book)* hojear; *(in shop)* mirar; **browser** n *(Comput)* navegador m
bruise [bruːz] n cardenal m (SP), moretón m ▷ vt magullar
brunette [bruː'net] n morena
brush [brʌʃ] n cepillo; *(for painting, shaving etc)* brocha; *(artist's)* pincel m; *(with police etc)* roce m ▷ vt *(sweep)* barrer; *(groom)* cepillar; *(also: ~ against)* rozar al pasar
Brussels ['brʌslz] n Bruselas
Brussels sprout n col f de Bruselas
brutal ['bruːtl] adj brutal
B.Sc. abbr *(= Bachelor of Science)* licenciado en Ciencias
BSE n abbr *(= bovine spongiform encephalopathy)* encefalopatía espongiforme bovina
bubble ['bʌbl] n burbuja ▷ vi burbujear, borbotar; **bubble bath** n espuma para el baño; **bubble gum** n chicle m de globo; **bubblejet printer** ['bʌbldʒet-] n impresora de inyección por burbujas
buck [bʌk] n *(rabbit)* conejo macho; *(deer)* gamo; *(US: inf)* dólar m ▷ vi corcovear; **to pass the ~ (to sb)** echar (a algn) el muerto
bucket ['bʌkɪt] n cubo, balde m
buckle ['bʌkl] n hebilla ▷ vt abrochar con hebilla ▷ vi combarse
bud [bʌd] n *(of plant)* brote m, yema; *(of flower)* capullo ▷ vi brotar, echar brotes
Buddhism ['budɪzm] n Budismo
Buddhist ['budɪst] adj, n budista m/f
buddy ['bʌdɪ] *(US)* n compañero, compinche m
budge [bʌdʒ] vt mover; *(fig)* hacer ceder ▷ vi moverse, ceder
budgerigar ['bʌdʒərɪgaː*] n periquito
budget ['bʌdʒɪt] n presupuesto ▷ vi: **to ~ for sth** presupuestar algo
budgie ['bʌdʒɪ] n = **budgerigar**
buff [bʌf] adj *(colour)* color de ante ▷ n *(inf: enthusiast)* entusiasta mf
buffalo ['bʌfələu] *(pl ~ or ~es)* n *(BRIT)* búfalo; *(US: bison)* bisonte m
buffer ['bʌfə*] n *(Comput)* memoria intermedia; *(Rail)* tope m

buffet¹ ['bʌfɪt] vt golpear

buffet² ['bufeɪ] n (BRIT: *in station*) bar m, cafetería; (*food*) buffet m; **buffet car** (BRIT) n (Rail) coche-comedor m

bug [bʌg] n (*esp US: insect*) bicho, sabandija; (Comput) error m; (*germ*) microbio, bacilo; (*spy device*) micrófono oculto ▷ vt (*inf: annoy*) fastidiar; (*room*) poner micrófono oculto en

buggy ['bʌgɪ] n cochecito de niño

build [bɪld] (pt, pp **built**) n (*of person*) tipo ▷ vt construir, edificar; **build up** vt (*morale, forces, production*) acrecentar; (*stocks*) acumular; **builder** n (*contractor*) contratista mf; **building** n construcción f; (*structure*) edificio; **building site** n obra; **building society** (BRIT) n sociedad f inmobiliaria

built [bɪlt] pt, pp of **build**; **built-in** adj (*cupboard*) empotrado; (*device*) interior, incorporado; **built-up** adj (*area*) urbanizado

bulb [bʌlb] n (Bot) bulbo; (Elec) bombilla, foco (MEX), bujía (CAM), bombita (RPL)

Bulgaria [bʌl'geərɪə] n Bulgaria; **Bulgarian** adj, n búlgaro/a m/f

bulge [bʌldʒ] n bulto, protuberancia ▷ vi bombearse, pandearse; (*pocket etc*) **to ~ (with)** rebosar (de)

bulimia [bəˈliːmɪə] n bulimia

bulimic [bjuːˈlɪmɪk] adj, n bulímico/a m/f

bulk [bʌlk] n masa, mole f; **in ~** (Comm) a granel; **the ~ of** la mayor parte de; **bulky** adj voluminoso, abultado

bull [bʊl] n toro; (*male elephant, whale*) macho

bulldozer ['bʊldəʊzə*] n bulldozer m

bullet ['bʊlɪt] n bala

bulletin ['bʊlɪtɪn] n anuncio, parte m; (*journal*) boletín m; **bulletin board** n (US) tablón m de anuncios; (Comput) tablero de noticias

bullfight ['bʊlfaɪt] n corrida de toros; **bullfighter** n torero; **bullfighting** n los toros, el toreo

bully ['bʊlɪ] n valentón m, matón m ▷ vt intimidar, tiranizar

bum [bʌm] n (*inf: backside*) culo; (*esp US: tramp*) vagabundo

bumblebee ['bʌmblbiː] n abejorro

bump [bʌmp] n (*blow*) tope m, choque m; (*jolt*) sacudida; (*on road etc*) bache m; (*on head etc*) chichón m ▷ vt (*strike*) chocar contra; **bump into** vt fus chocar contra, tropezar con; (*person*) topar con; **bumper** n (Aut) parachoques m inv ▷ adj: **bumper crop** or **harvest** cosecha abundante; **bumpy** adj (*road*) lleno de baches

bun [bʌn] n (BRIT: *cake*) pastel m; (US: *bread*) bollo; (*of hair*) moño

bunch [bʌntʃ] n (*of flowers*) ramo; (*of keys*) manojo; (*of bananas*) piña; (*of people*) grupo; (*pej*) pandilla; **bunches** npl (*in hair*) coletas fpl

bundle ['bʌndl] n bulto, fardo; (*of sticks*) haz m; (*of papers*) legajo ▷ vt (*also: ~ up*) atar, envolver; **to ~ sth/sb into** meter algo/a algn precipitadamente en

bungalow ['bʌŋgələu] n bungalow m, chalé m

bungee jumping ['bʌndʒi:'dʒʌmpɪŋ] n puenting m, banyi m

bunion ['bʌnjən] n juanete m

bunk [bʌŋk] n litera; **bunk beds** npl literas fpl

bunker ['bʌŋkə*] n (*coal store*) carbonera; (Mil) refugio; (Golf) bunker m

bunny ['bʌnɪ] n (*inf: also: ~ rabbit*) conejito

buoy [bɔɪ] n boya; **buoyant** adj (*ship*) capaz de flotar; (*economy*) boyante; (*person*) optimista

burden ['bəːdn] n carga ▷ vt cargar

bureau [bjuəˈrəu] n (BRIT: *writing desk*) escritorio, buró m; (US: *chest of drawers*) cómoda; (*office*) oficina, agencia

bureaucracy [bjuəˈrɒkrəsɪ] n burocracia

bureaucrat ['bjuərəkræt] n burócrata m/f

bureau de change [-də'ʃɑ̃ʒ] (pl **bureaux de change**) n caja f de cambio

bureaux ['bjuərəuz] npl of **bureau**

burger ['bəːgə*] n hamburguesa

burglar ['bəːglə*] n ladrón/ona m/f; **burglar alarm** n alarma f antirrobo; **burglary** n robo con allanamiento, robo de una casa

burial ['berɪəl] n entierro

burn [bəːn] (pt, pp **~ed** or **~t**) vt quemar; (*house*) incendiar ▷ vi quemarse, arder; incendiarse; (*sting*) escocer ▷ vi quemadura; **burn down** vi incendiar; **burn out** vi (*writer etc*): **to burn o.s. out** agotarse; **burning** adj (*building etc*) en llamas; (*hot: sand etc*) abrasador(a); (*ambition*) ardiente

burnt [bəːnt] pt, pp of **burn**

burp [bəːp] (*inf*) n eructo ▷ vi eructar

burrow ['bʌrəu] n madriguera ▷ vi hacer una madriguera; (*rummage*) hurgar

burst [bəːst] (pt, pp **~**) vt reventar; (*river: banks etc*) romper ▷ vi reventarse; (*tyre*) pincharse ▷ n (*of gunfire*) ráfaga; (*also: ~ pipe*) reventón m; **a ~ of energy/speed/ enthusiasm** una explosión de energía/un ímpetu de velocidad/un arranque deentusiasmo; **to ~ into flames** estallar en llamas; **to ~ into tears** deshacerse en lágrimas; **to ~ out laughing** soltar la carcajada; **to ~ open** abrirse de golpe; **to be ~ing with** (*container*) estar lleno a rebosar de; (: *person*) reventar por or de; **burst into** vt fus (*room etc*) irrumpir en

bury ['berɪ] vt enterrar; (*body*) enterrar, sepultar

bus [bʌs] (pl **~es**) n autobús m; **bus conductor** n cobrador(a) m/f

bush [bʊʃ] n arbusto; (*scrub land*) monte m; **to beat about the ~** andar(se) con rodeos

business ['bɪznɪs] n (*matter*) asunto; (*trading*) comercio, negocios mpl; (*firm*) empresa, casa; (*occupation*) oficio; **to be away on ~** estar en viaje de negocios; **it's my ~ to ...** me toca or corresponde ...; **it's none of my ~** yo no tengo nada que ver; **he means ~** habla en serio; **business class** n (Aer) clase f preferente; **businesslike** adj eficiente; **businessman** (*irreg*) n hombre m de negocios; **business trip** n viaje m de negocios; **businesswoman** (*irreg*) n mujer f de negocios

busker ['bʌskə*] (BRIT) n músico/a ambulante

bus: bus pass n bonobús; **bus shelter** n parada cubierta; **bus station** n estación f de autobuses; **bus-stop** n parada de autobús

bust [bʌst] n (Anat) pecho; (*sculpture*) busto ▷ adj (*inf: broken*) roto, estropeado; **to go ~** quebrar

bustling ['bʌslɪŋ] adj (*town*) animado, bullicioso

busy ['bɪzɪ] adj ocupado, atareado; (*shop, street*) concurrido, animado; (Tel: *line*) comunicando ▷ vt: **to ~ o.s. with** ocuparse en; **busy signal** (US) n (Tel) señal f de comunicando

○ **KEYWORD**

but [bʌt] conj 1 pero; **he's not very bright, but he's hard-working** no es muy inteligente, pero es trabajador

2 (*in direct contradiction*) sino; **he's not English but French** no es inglés sino francés; **he didn't sing but he shouted** no cantó sino que gritó
3 (*showing disagreement, surprise etc*): **but that's far too expensive!** ¡pero eso es carísimo!; **but it does work!** ¡(pero) sí que funciona!
▷ *prep* (*apart from, except*) menos, salvo; **we've had nothing but trouble** no hemos tenido más que problemas; **no-one but him can do it** nadie más que él puede hacerlo; **who but a lunatic would do such a thing?** ¡sólo un loco haría una cosa así!; **but for you/your help** si no fuera por ti/tu ayuda; **anything but that** cualquier cosa menos eso
▷ *adv* (*just, only*): **she's but a child** no es más que una niña; **had I but known** si lo hubiera sabido; **I can but try** al menos lo puedo intentar; **it's all but finished** está casi acabado

butcher ['butʃə*] *n* carnicero ▷ *vt* hacer una carnicería con; (*cattle etc*) matar; **butcher's (shop)** *n* carnicería
butler ['bʌtlə*] *n* mayordomo
butt [bʌt] *n* (*barrel*) tonel *m*; (*of gun*) culata; (*of cigarette*) colilla; (*BRIT: fig: target*) blanco ▷ *vt* dar cabezadas contra, top(et)ar
butter ['bʌtə*] *n* mantequilla ▷ *vt* untar con mantequilla; **buttercup** *n* botón *m* de oro
butterfly ['bʌtəflaɪ] *n* mariposa; (*Swimming: also: ~ stroke*) braza de mariposa
buttocks ['bʌtəks] *npl* nalgas *fpl*
button ['bʌtn] *n* botón *m*; (*us*) placa, chapa ▷ *vt* (*also: ~ up*) abotonar, abrochar ▷ *vi* abrocharse
buy [baɪ] (*pt, pp* **bought**) *vt* comprar ▷ *n* compra; **to ~ sb sth/sth from sb** comprarle algo a algn; **to ~ sb a drink** invitar a algn a tomar algo; **buy out** *vt* (*partner*) comprar la parte de; **buy up** *vt* (*property*) acaparar; (*stock*) comprar todas las existencias de; **buyer** *n* comprador(a) *m/f*
buzz [bʌz] *n* zumbido; (*inf: phone call*) llamada (por teléfono) ▷ *vi* zumbar; **buzzer** *n* timbre *m*

○ **KEYWORD**

by [baɪ] *prep* **1** (*referring to cause, agent*) por; de; **killed by lightning** muerto por un relámpago; **a painting by Picasso** un cuadro de Picasso
2 (*referring to method, manner, means*): **by bus/car/train** en autobús/coche/tren; **to pay by cheque** pagar con un cheque; **by moonlight/candlelight** a la luz de la luna/una vela; **by saving hard he ...** ahorrando ...
3 (*via, through*) por; **we came by Dover** vinimos por Dover
4 (*close to, past*): **the house by the river** la casa junto al río; **she rushed by me** pasó a mi lado como una exhalación; **I go by the post office every day** paso por delante de Correos todos los días
5 (*time: not later than*) para; (: *during*): **by daylight** de día; **by 4 o'clock** para las cuatro; **by this time tomorrow** mañana a estas horas; **by the time I got here it was too late** cuando llegué ya era demasiado tarde
6 (*amount*): **by the metre/kilo** por metro/kilo; **paid by the hour** pagado por hora
7 (*Math, measure*): **to divide/multiply by 3** dividir/multiplicar por 3; **a room 3 metres by 4** una habitación de 3 metros por 4; **it's broader by a metre**
es un metro más ancho
8 (*according to*) según, de acuerdo con; **it's 3 o'clock by my watch** según mi reloj, son las tres; **it's all right by me** por mí, está bien
9: **(all) by oneself** *etc* todo solo; **he did it (all) by himself** lo hizo él solo; **he was standing (all) by himself in a corner** estaba de pie solo en un rincón
10: **by the way** a propósito, por cierto; **this wasn't my idea, by the way** pues, no fue idea mía
▷ *adv* **1** *see* **go**; **pass** *etc*
2: **by and by** finalmente; **they'll come back by and by** acabarán volviendo; **by and large** en líneas generales, en general

bye(-bye) ['baɪ('baɪ)] *excl* adiós, hasta luego
by-election (*BRIT*) *n* elección *f* parcial
bypass ['baɪpɑːs] *n* carretera de circunvalación; (*Med*) (operación *f* de) by-pass *f* ▷ *vt* evitar
byte [baɪt] *n* (*Comput*) byte *m*, octeto

C

C [siː] n (Mus) do m
cab [kæb] n taxi m; (of truck) cabina
cabaret ['kæbəreɪ] n cabaret m
cabbage ['kæbɪdʒ] n col f, berza
cabin ['kæbɪn] n cabaña; (on ship) camarote m; (on plane) cabina; **cabin crew** n tripulación f de cabina
cabinet ['kæbɪnɪt] n (Pol) consejo de ministros; (furniture) armario; (also: **display ~**) vitrina; **cabinet minister** n ministro/a (del gabinete)
cable ['keɪbl] n cable m ⊳ vt cablegrafiar; **cable car** n teleférico; **cable television** n televisión f por cable
cactus ['kæktəs] (pl **cacti**) n cacto
café ['kæfeɪ] n café m
cafeteria [kæfɪ'tɪərɪə] n cafetería
caffein(e) ['kæfiːn] n cafeína
cage [keɪdʒ] n jaula
cagoule [kə'guːl] n chubasquero
cake [keɪk] n (Culin: large) tarta; (: small) pastel m; (of soap) pastilla
calcium ['kælsɪəm] n calcio
calculate ['kælkjuleɪt] vt calcular; **calculation** [-'leɪʃən] n cálculo, cómputo; **calculator** n calculadora
calendar ['kæləndə*] n calendario
calf [kɑːf] (pl **calves**) n (of cow) ternero, becerro; (of other animals) cría; (also: **~skin**) piel f de becerro; (Anat) pantorrilla
calibre ['kælɪbə*] (US **caliber**) n calibre m
call [kɔːl] vt llamar; (meeting) convocar ⊳ vi (shout) llamar; (Tel) llamar (por teléfono); (visit: also: **~ in, ~ round**) hacer una visita ⊳ n llamada; (of bird) canto; **to be ~ed** llamarse; **on ~** (on duty) de guardia; **call back** vi (return) volver; (Tel) volver a llamar; **call for** vt fus (demand) pedir, exigir; (fetch) pasar a recoger; **call in** vt (doctor, expert, police) llamar; **call off** vt (cancel: meeting, race) cancelar; (: deal) anular; (: strike) desconvocar; **call on** vt fus (visit) visitar; (turn to) acudir a; **call out** vi gritar; **call up** vt (Mil) llamar al servicio militar; (Tel) llamar; **callbox** (BRIT) n cabina telefónica; **call centre** (US **call center**) n centro de atención al cliente; **caller** n visita; (Tel) usuario/a
callous ['kæləs] adj insensible, cruel
calm [kɑːm] adj tranquilo; (sea) liso, en calma ⊳ n calma, tranquilidad f ⊳ vt calmar, tranquilizar; **calm down** vi calmarse, tranquilizarse ⊳ vt calmar, tranquilizar; **calmly** ['kɑːmlɪ] adv tranquilamente, con calma
Calor gas® ['kælə*-] n butano
calorie ['kælərɪ] n caloría
calves [kɑːvz] npl of **calf**
camcorder ['kæmkɔːdə*] n videocámara
came [keɪm] pt of **come**
camel ['kæməl] n camello
camera ['kæmərə] n máquina fotográfica; (Cinema, TV) cámara; **in ~** (Law) a puerta cerrada; **cameraman** (irreg) n cámara m; **camera phone** n teléfono con cámara
camouflage ['kæməflɑːʒ] n camuflaje m ⊳ vt camuflar
camp [kæmp] n campamento, camping m; (Mil) campamento; (for prisoners) campo; (fig: faction) bando ⊳ vi acampar ⊳ adj afectado, afeminado
campaign [kæm'peɪn] n (Mil, Pol etc) campaña ⊳ vi hacer campaña; **campaigner** n: **campaigner for** defensor(a) m/f de
camp: campbed (BRIT) n cama de campaña; **camper** n campista mf; (vehicle) caravana; **campground** (US) n camping m, campamento; **camping** n camping m; **to go camping** hacer camping; **campsite** n camping m
campus ['kæmpəs] n ciudad f universitaria
can¹ [kæn] n (of oil, water) bidón m; (tin) lata, bote m ⊳ vt enlatar

can² [kæn] (negative **cannot, can't**, conditional and pt **could**) aux vb 1 (be able to) poder; **you can do it if you try** puedes hacerlo si lo intentas; **I can't see you** no te veo
2 (know how to) saber; **I can swim/play tennis/drive** sé nadar/jugar al tenis/conducir; **can you speak French?** ¿hablas o sabes hablar francés?
3 (may) poder; **can I use your phone?** ¿me dejas o puedo usar tu teléfono?
4 (expressing disbelief, puzzlement etc): **it can't be true!** ¡no puede ser (verdad)!; **what can he want?** ¿qué querrá?
5 (expressing possibility, suggestion etc): **he could be in the library** podría estar en la biblioteca; **she could have been delayed** pudo haberse retrasado

Canada ['kænədə] n (el) Canadá; **Canadian** [kə'neɪdɪən] adj, n canadiense mf
canal [kə'næl] n canal m
canary [kə'nɛərɪ] n canario
Canary Islands [kə'nɛərɪ'aɪləndz] npl: **the ~** las (Islas) Canarias
cancel ['kænsəl] vt cancelar; (train) suprimir; (cross out) tachar, borrar; **cancellation** [-'leɪʃən] n cancelación f; supresión f
Cancer ['kænsə*] n (Astrology) Cáncer m
cancer ['kænsə*] n cáncer m
candidate ['kændɪdeɪt] n candidato/a
candle ['kændl] n vela; (in church) cirio; **candlestick** n (single) candelero; (low) palmatoria; (bigger, ornate) candelabro
candy ['kændɪ] n azúcar m cande; (US) caramelo; **candy bar** (US) n barrita (dulce); **candyfloss** (BRIT) n

algodón m (azucarado)

cane [keɪn] n (Bot) caña; (stick) vara, pálmeta; (for furniture) mimbre f ▷ vt (BRIT: Scol) castigar (con vara)

canister ['kænɪstə*] n bote m, lata; (of gas) bombona

cannabis ['kænəbɪs] n marijuana

canned [kænd] adj en lata, de lata

cannon ['kænən] (pl ~ or -s) n cañón m

cannot ['kænɔt] = can not

canoe [kə'nuː] n canoa; (Sport) piragua; **canoeing** n piragüismo

canon ['kænən] n (clergyman) canónigo; (standard) canon m

can-opener ['kænəupnə*] n abrelatas m inv

can't [kænt] = can not

canteen [kæn'tiːn] n (eating place) cantina; (BRIT: of cutlery) juego

canter ['kæntə*] vi ir a medio galope

canvas ['kænvəs] n (material) lona; (painting) lienzo; (Naut) velas fpl

canvass ['kænvəs] vi (Pol): **to ~ for** solicitar votos por ▷ vt (Comm) sondear

canyon ['kænjən] n cañón m

cap [kæp] n (hat) gorra; (of pen) capuchón m; (of bottle) tapa, tapón m; (contraceptive) diafragma m; (for toy gun) cápsula ▷ vt (outdo) superar; (limit) recortar

capability [keɪpə'bɪlɪtɪ] n capacidad f

capable ['keɪpəbl] adj capaz

capacity [kə'pæsɪtɪ] n capacidad f; (position) calidad f

cape [keɪp] n capa; (Geo) cabo

caper ['keɪpə*] n (Culin: gen pl) alcaparra; (prank) broma

capital ['kæpɪtl] n (also: ~ city) capital f; (money) capital m; (also: ~ letter) mayúscula; **capitalism** n capitalismo; **capitalist** adj, n capitalista mf; **capital punishment** n pena de muerte

Capricorn ['kæprɪkɔːn] n Capricornio

capsize [kæp'saɪz] vt volcar, hacer zozobrar ▷ vi volcarse, zozobrar

capsule ['kæpsjuːl] n cápsula

captain ['kæptɪn] n capitán m

caption ['kæpʃən] n (heading) título; (to picture) leyenda

captivity [kæp'tɪvɪtɪ] n cautiverio

capture ['kæptʃə*] vt prender, apresar; (animal, Comput) capturar; (place) tomar; (attention) captar, llamar ▷ n apresamiento; captura; toma; (data capture) formulación f de datos

car [kɑː*] n coche m, carro (LAM), automóvil m; (US Rail) vagón m

carafe [kə'ræf] n jarra

caramel ['kærəməl] n caramelo

carat ['kærət] n quilate m

caravan ['kærəvæn] n (BRIT) caravana, rulof; (in desert) caravana; **caravan site** (BRIT) n camping m para caravanas

carbohydrate [kɑːbəu'haɪdreɪt] n hidrato de carbono; (food) fécula

carbon ['kɑːbən] n carbono; **carbon dioxide** n dióxido de carbono, anhídrido carbónico; **carbon monoxide** n monóxido de carbono

car boot sale n mercadillo organizado en un aparcamiento, en el que se exponen las mercancías en el maletero del coche

carburettor [kɑːbju'retə*] (US **carburetor**) n carburador m

card [kɑːd] n (material) cartulina; (index card etc) ficha;

(playing card) carta, naipe m; (visiting card, greetings card etc) tarjeta; **cardboard** n cartón m; **card game** n juego de naipes o cartas

cardigan ['kɑːdɪgən] n rebeca

cardinal ['kɑːdɪnl] adj cardinal; (importance, principal) esencial ▷ n cardenal m

cardphone ['kɑːdfəun] n cabina que funciona con tarjetas telefónicas

care [keə*] n cuidado; (worry) inquietud f; (charge) cargo, custodia ▷ vi: **to ~ about** (person, animal) tener cariño a; (thing, idea) preocuparse por; **~ of** en casa de, al cuidado de; **in sb's ~** a cargo de algn; **to take ~ to** cuidarse de, tener cuidado de; **to take ~ of** cuidar; (problem etc) ocuparse de; **I don't ~** no me importa; **I couldn't ~ less** eso me trae sin cuidado; **care for** vt fus cuidar a; (like) querer

career [kə'rɪə*] n profesión f; (in work, school) carrera ▷ vi (also: **~ along**) correr a toda velocidad

care: carefree adj despreocupado; **careful** adj cuidadoso; (cautious) cauteloso; **(be) careful!** ¡tenga cuidado!; **carefully** adv con cuidado, cuidadosamente; con cautela; **caregiver** (US) n (professional) enfermero/a m/f; (unpaid) persona que cuida a un pariente o vecino; **careless** adj descuidado; (heedless) poco atento; **carelessness** n descuido, falta de atención; **carer** ['keərə*] n (professional) enfermero/a m/f; (unpaid) persona que cuida a un pariente o vecino; **caretaker** n portero/a, conserje mf

car-ferry ['kɑːferɪ] n transbordador m para coches

cargo ['kɑːgəu] (pl **-es**) n cargamento, carga

car hire n alquiler m de automóviles

Caribbean [kærɪ'biːən] n: **the ~ (Sea)** el (Mar) Caribe

caring ['keərɪŋ] adj humanitario; (behaviour) afectuoso

carnation [kɑː'neɪʃən] n clavel m

carnival ['kɑːnɪvəl] n carnaval m; (US: funfair) parque m de atracciones

carol ['kærəl] n: **(Christmas) ~** villancico

carousel [kærə'sel] (US) n tiovivo, caballitos mpl

car park (BRIT) n aparcamiento, parking m

carpenter ['kɑːpɪntə*] n carpintero/a

carpet ['kɑːpɪt] n alfombra; (fitted) moqueta ▷ vt alfombrar

car rental (US) n alquiler m de coches

carriage ['kærɪdʒ] n (BRIT Rail) vagón m; (horse-drawn) coche m; (of goods) transporte m; (: cost) porte m, flete m; **carriageway** (BRIT) n (part of road) calzada

carrier ['kærɪə*] n (transport company) transportista, empresa de transportes; (Med) portador(a) m/f; **carrier bag** (BRIT) n bolsa de papel o plástico

carrot ['kærət] n zanahoria

carry ['kærɪ] vt (person) llevar; (transport) transportar; (involve: responsibilities etc) entrañar, implicar; (Med) ser portador de ▷ vi (sound) oírse; **to get carried away** (fig) entusiasmarse; **carry on** vi (continue) seguir (adelante), continuar ▷ vt proseguir, continuar; **carry out** vt (orders) cumplir; (investigation) llevar a cabo, realizar

cart [kɑːt] n carro, carreta ▷ vt (inf: transport) acarrear

carton ['kɑːtən] n (box) caja (de cartón); (of milk etc) bote m; (of yogurt) tarrina

cartoon [kɑː'tuːn] n (Press) caricatura; (comic strip) tira cómica; (film) dibujos mpl animados

cartridge ['kɑːtrɪdʒ] n cartucho; (of pen) recambio

carve [kɑːv] vt (meat) trinchar; (wood, stone) cincelar, esculpir; (*initials etc*) grabar; **carving** n (*object*) escultura; (*design*) talla; (*art*) tallado

car wash n lavado de coches

case [keɪs] n (*container*) caja; (*Med*) caso; (*for jewels etc*) estuche m; (*Law*) causa, proceso; (*BRIT: also: suit~*) maleta; **in ~ of** en caso de; **in any ~** en todo caso; **just in ~** por si acaso

cash [kæʃ] n dinero en efectivo, dinero contante ▷ vt cobrar, hacer efectivo; **to pay (in) ~** pagar al contado; **~ on delivery** cóbrese al entregar; **cashback** n (*discount*) devolución f; (*at supermarket etc*) retirada de dinero en efectivo de un establecimiento donde se ha pagado con tarjeta; también dinero retirado; **cash card** n tarjeta f dinero; **cash desk** (*BRIT*) n caja; **cash dispenser** n cajero automático

cashew [kæˈʃuː] n (*also: ~ nut*) anacardo

cashier [kæˈʃɪə*] n cajero/a

cashmere [ˈkæʃmɪə*] n cachemira

cash point n cajero automático

cash register n caja

casino [kəˈsiːnəu] n casino

casket [ˈkɑːskɪt] n cofre m, estuche m; (*US: coffin*) ataúd m

casserole [ˈkæsərəul] n (*food, pot*) cazuela

cassette [kæˈset] n casete f; **cassette player, cassette recorder** n casete m

cast [kɑːst] (*pt, pp ~*) vt (*throw*) echar, arrojar, lanzar; (*glance, eyes*) dirigir; (*Theatre*): **to ~ sb as Othello** dar a algn el papel de Otelo ▷ vi (*Fishing*) lanzar ▷ n (*Theatre*) reparto; (*also: plaster ~*) vaciado; **to ~ one's vote** votar; **to ~ doubt on** suscitar dudas acerca de; **cast off** vi (*Naut*) desamarrar; (*Knitting*) cerrar (los puntos)

castanets [kæstəˈnets] npl castañuelas fpl

caster sugar [ˈkɑːstə*-] (*BRIT*) n azúcar m extrafino

Castile [kæsˈtiːl] n Castilla; **Castilian** adj, n castellano/a m/f

cast-iron [ˈkɑːstaɪən] adj (*lit*) (hecho) de hierro fundido; (*fig: case*) irrebatible

castle [ˈkɑːsl] n castillo; (*Chess*) torre f

casual [ˈkæʒjul] adj fortuito; (*irregular: work etc*) eventual, temporero; (*unconcerned*) despreocupado; (*clothes*) informal

casualty [ˈkæʒjultɪ] n víctima, herido/a; (*dead*) muerto/a; (*Med: department*) urgencias fpl

cat [kæt] n gato; (*big cat*) felino

Catalan [ˈkætəlæn] adj, n catalán/ana m/f

catalogue [ˈkætəlɔɡ] (*US* **catalog**) n catálogo ▷ vt catalogar

Catalonia [kætəˈləunɪə] n Cataluña

catalytic converter [kætəˈlɪtɪkkənˈvɜːtə*] n catalizador m

cataract [ˈkætərækt] n (*Med*) cataratas fpl

catarrh [kəˈtɑː*] n catarro

catastrophe [kəˈtæstrəfɪ] n catástrofe f

catch [kætʃ] (*pt, pp* **caught**) vt coger (SP), agarrar (LAM); (*arrest*) detener; (*grasp*) asir; (*breath*) contener; (*surprise: person*) sorprender; (*attract: attention*) captar; (*hear*) oír; (*Med*) contagiarse de, coger; (*also: ~ up*) alcanzar ▷ vi (*fire*) encenderse; (*in branches etc*) enredarse ▷ n (*fish etc*) pesca; (*act of catching*) cogida; (*hidden problem*) dificultad f; (*game*) pilla-pilla; (*of lock*) pestillo, cerradura; **to ~ fire** encenderse; **to ~ sight of** divisar; **catch up** vi (*fig*) ponerse al día; **catching** [ˈkætʃɪŋ] adj (*Med*) contagioso

category [ˈkætɪɡərɪ] n categoría, clase f

cater [ˈkeɪtə*] vi: **to ~ for** (*BRIT*) abastecer a; (*needs*)

atender a; (*Comm: parties etc*) proveer comida a

caterpillar [ˈkætəpɪlə*] n oruga, gusano

cathedral [kəˈθiːdrəl] n catedral f

Catholic [ˈkæθəlɪk] adj, n (*Rel*) católico/a m/f

Catseye® [ˈkætsaɪ] (*BRIT*) n (*Aut*) catafoto

cattle [ˈkætl] npl ganado

catwalk [ˈkætwɔːk] n pasarela

caught [kɔːt] pt, pp of **catch**

cauliflower [ˈkɒlɪflauə*] n coliflor f

cause [kɔːz] n causa, motivo, razón f; (*principle: also Pol*) causa ▷ vt causar

caution [ˈkɔːʃən] n cautela, prudencia; (*warning*) advertencia, amonestación f ▷ vt amonestar; **cautious** adj cauteloso, prudente, precavido

cave [keɪv] n cueva, caverna; **cave in** vi (*roof etc*) derrumbarse, hundirse

caviar(e) [ˈkævɪɑː*] n caviar m

cavity [ˈkævɪtɪ] n hueco, cavidad f

cc abbr (*= cubic centimetres*) c.c.; (*= carbon copy*) copia hecha con papel del carbón

CCTV n abbr (*= closed-circuit television*) circuito cerrado de televisión

CD n abbr (*= compact disc*) CD m; (*player*) (reproductor m de) CD; **CD player** n reproductor m de CD; **CD-ROM** [siːdiːˈrɒm] n abbr CD-ROM m; **CD writer** n grabadora de CD

cease [siːs] vt, vi cesar; **ceasefire** n alto el fuego

cedar [ˈsiːdə*] n cedro

ceilidh [ˈkeɪlɪ] n baile con música y danzas tradicionales escocesas o irlandesas

ceiling [ˈsiːlɪŋ] n techo; (*fig*) límite m

celebrate [ˈsɛlɪbreɪt] vt celebrar ▷ vi divertirse; **celebration** [-ˈbreɪʃən] n fiesta, celebración f

celebrity [sɪˈlɛbrɪtɪ] n celebridad f

celery [ˈsɛlərɪ] n apio

cell [sɛl] n celda; (*Biol*) célula; (*Elec*) elemento

cellar [ˈsɛlə*] n sótano; (*for wine*) bodega

cello [ˈtʃɛləu] n violoncelo

Cellophane® [ˈsɛləfeɪn] n celofán m

cellphone [ˈsɛlfəun] n teléfono celular

Celsius [ˈsɛlsɪəs] adj centígrado

Celtic [ˈkɛltɪk] adj celta

cement [səˈmɛnt] n cemento

cemetery [ˈsɛmɪtrɪ] n cementerio

censor [ˈsɛnsə*] n censor m ▷ vt (*cut*) censurar; **censorship** n censura

census [ˈsɛnsəs] n censo

cent [sɛnt] n (*unit of dollar*) centavo, céntimo; (*unit of euro*) céntimo; see also **per**

centenary [sɛnˈtiːnərɪ] n centenario

centennial [sɛnˈtɛnɪəl] (*US*) n centenario

center [ˈsɛntə*] (*US*) = **centre**

centi... [ˈsɛntɪ] prefix: **centigrade** adj centígrado; **centimetre** (*US* **centimeter**) n centímetro; **centipede** [ˈsɛntɪpiːd] n ciempiés m inv

central [ˈsɛntrəl] adj central; (*of house etc*) céntrico; **Central America** n Centroamérica; **central heating** n calefacción f central; **central reservation** n (*BRIT Aut*) mediana

centre [ˈsɛntə*] (*US* **center**) n centro; (*fig*) núcleo ▷ vt centrar; **centre-forward** n (*Sport*) delantero centro; **centre-half** n (*Sport*) medio centro

century [ˈsɛntjurɪ] n siglo; **20th ~** siglo veinte

CEO n abbr = **chief executive officer**

ceramic [sɪˈræmɪk] adj cerámico

cereal [ˈsiːrɪəl] n cereal m

ceremony ['sɛrɪmənɪ] n ceremonia; **to stand on ~** hacer ceremonias, estar de cumplido

certain ['sɜːtən] adj seguro; (person): **a ~ Mr Smith** un tal Sr. Smith; (particular, some) cierto; **for ~** a ciencia cierta; **certainly** adv (undoubtedly) ciertamente; (of course) desde luego, por supuesto; **certainty** n certeza, certidumbre f, seguridad f; (inevitability) certeza

certificate [sə'tɪfɪkɪt] n certificado

certify ['sɜːtɪfaɪ] vt certificar; (award diploma to) conceder un diploma a; (declare insane) declarar loco

cf. abbr (=compare) cfr

CFC n abbr (=chlorofluorocarbon) CFC m

chain [tʃeɪn] n cadena; (of mountains) cordillera; (of events) sucesión f ▷ vt (also: **~ up**) encadenar; **chain-smoke** vi fumar un cigarrillo tras otro

chair [tʃeə*] n silla; (armchair) sillón m, butaca; (of university) cátedra; (of meeting etc) presidencia ▷ vt (meeting) presidir; **chairlift** n telesilla; **chairman** (irreg) n presidente m; **chairperson** n presidente/a m/f; **chairwoman** (irreg) n presidenta

chalet ['ʃæleɪ] n chalet m (de madera)

chalk [tʃɔːk] n (Geo) creta; (for writing) tiza, gis m (MEX); **chalkboard** (US) n pizarrón (LAM), pizarra (SP)

challenge ['tʃælɪndʒ] n desafío, reto ▷ vt desafiar, retar; (statement, right) poner en duda; **to ~ sb to do sth** retar a algn a que haga algo; **challenging** adj exigente; (tone) desafío

chamber ['tʃeɪmbə*] n cámara, sala; (Pol) cámara; (BRIT Law: gen pl) despacho; **~ of commerce** cámara de comercio; **chambermaid** n camarera

champagne [ʃæm'peɪn] n champaña m, champán m

champion ['tʃæmpɪən] n campeón/ona m/f; (of cause) defensor/a m/f; **championship** n campeonato

chance [tʃɑːns] n (opportunity) ocasión f, oportunidad f; (likelihood) posibilidad f; (risk) riesgo ▷ vt arriesgar, probar ▷ adj fortuito, casual; **to ~ it** arriesgarse, intentarlo; **to take a ~** arriesgarse; **by ~** por casualidad

chancellor ['tʃɑːnsələ*] n canciller m; **Chancellor of the Exchequer** (BRIT) n Ministro de Hacienda

chandelier [ʃændə'lɪə*] n araña (de luces)

change [tʃeɪndʒ] vt cambiar; (replace) cambiar, reemplazar; (gear, clothes, job) cambiar de; (transform) transformar ▷ vi cambiar(se); (change trains) hacer transbordo; (traffic lights) cambiar de color; (be transformed): **to ~ into** transformarse en ▷ n cambio; (alteration) modificación f; (transformation) transformación f; (of clothes) muda; (coins) suelto, sencillo; (money returned) vuelta; **to ~ gear** (Aut) cambiar de marcha; **to ~ one's mind** cambiar de opinión o idea; **for a ~** para variar; **change over** vi (from sth to sth) cambiar; (players etc) cambiar(se) ▷ vt cambiar; **changeable** adj (weather) cambiable; (BRIT) n máquina de cambio; **changing room** (BRIT) n vestuario

channel ['tʃænl] n (TV) canal m; (of river) cauce m; (groove) conducto; (fig: medium) medio ▷ vt (river etc) encauzar; **the (English) C~** el Canal de la Mancha; **the C~ Islands** las Islas Normandas; **Channel Tunnel** n: **the Channel Tunnel** el túnel del Canal de la Mancha, el Eurotúnel

chant [tʃɑːnt] n (of crowd) gritos mpl; (Rel) canto ▷ vt (slogan, word) repetir a gritos

chaos ['keɪɔs] n caos m

chaotic [keɪ'ɔtɪk] adj caótico

chap [tʃæp] (BRIT: inf) n (man) tío, tipo

chapel ['tʃæpəl] n capilla

chapped [tʃæpt] adj agrietado

chapter ['tʃæptə*] n capítulo

character ['kærɪktə*] n carácter m, naturaleza, índole f; (moral strength, personality) carácter; (in novel, film) personaje m; **characteristic** [-'rɪstɪk] adj característico ▷ n característica; **characterize** ['kærɪktəraɪz] vt caracterizar

charcoal ['tʃɑːkəul] n carbón m vegetal; (Art) carboncillo

charge [tʃɑːdʒ] n (Law) cargo, acusación f; (cost) precio, coste m; (responsibility) cargo ▷ vt (Law): **to ~ (with)** acusar (de); (battery) cargar; (price) pedir; (customer) cobrar ▷ vi precipitarse; (Mil) cargar, atacar; **charge card** n tarjeta de cuenta; **charger** n (also: **battery charger**) cargador m (de baterías)

charismatic [kærɪz'mætɪk] adj carismático

charity ['tʃærɪtɪ] n caridad f; (organization) sociedad f benéfica; (money, gifts) limosnas fpl; **charity shop** (BRIT) n tienda de artículos de segunda mano que dedica su recaudación a causas benéficas

charm [tʃɑːm] n encanto, atractivo; (talisman) hechizo; (on bracelet) dije m ▷ vt encantar; **charming** adj encantador(a)

chart [tʃɑːt] n (diagram) cuadro; (graph) gráfica; (map) carta de navegación ▷ vt (course) trazar; (progress) seguir; **charts** npl (Top 40): **the ~s** los 40 principales (SP)

charter ['tʃɑːtə*] vt (plane) alquilar; (ship) fletar ▷ n (document) carta; (of university, company) estatutos mpl; **chartered accountant** (BRIT) n contable m/f diplomado/a; **charter flight** n vuelo chárter

chase [tʃeɪs] vt (pursue) perseguir; (also: **~ away**) ahuyentar ▷ n persecución f

chat [tʃæt] vi (also: **have a ~**) charlar; (on Internet) chatear ▷ n charla; **chat up** vt (inf: girl) ligar con, enrollarse con; **chat room** n (Internet) canal m, canal m de charla; **chat show** (BRIT) n programa m de entrevistas

chatter ['tʃætə*] vi (person) charlar; (teeth) castañetear ▷ n (of birds) parloteo; (of people) charla, cháchara

chauffeur ['ʃəufə*] n chófer m

chauvinist ['ʃəuvɪnɪst] n (male chauvinist) machista m; (nationalist) chovinista m/f

cheap [tʃiːp] adj barato; (joke) de mal gusto; (poor quality) de mala calidad ▷ adv barato; **cheap day return** n billete de ida y vuelta del mismo día; **cheaply** adv barato, a bajo precio

cheat [tʃiːt] vi hacer trampa ▷ vt: **to ~ sb (out of sth)** estafar (algo) a algn ▷ n (person) tramposo/a; **cheat on** vt fus engañar

Chechnya [tʃɪtʃ'njɑː] n Chechenia

check [tʃek] vt (examine) controlar; (facts) comprobar; (halt) parar, detener; (restrain) refrenar, restringir ▷ n (inspection) control m, inspección f; (curb) freno; (US: bill) nota, cuenta; (US) =**cheque**; (pattern: gen pl) cuadro; **check in** vi (at hotel) firmar el registro; (at airport) facturar el equipaje ▷ vt (luggage) facturar; **check off** vt (esp US: check) comprobar; (tick off) tachar; **check out** vi (of hotel) marcharse; **check up** vi: **to check up on sth** comprobar algo; **to check up on sb** investigar a algn; **checkbook** (US) n =**chequebook**; **checked** adj a cuadros; **checkers** (US) n juego de damas; **check-in** n (also: **check-in desk**: at airport) mostrador m de facturación; **checking account** (US) n cuenta corriente; **checklist** n lista (de control); **checkmate** n jaque m mate; **checkout** n caja; **checkpoint** n (punto de) control m; **checkroom** (us) n consigna; **checkup** n (Med) reconocimiento general

cheddar ['tʃedə*] n (also: **~ cheese**) queso m cheddar

cheek [tʃiːk] n mejilla; (impudence) descaro; **what a ~!** ¡qué cara!; **cheekbone** n pómulo; **cheeky** adj fresco, descarado

cheer [tʃiə*] vt vitorear, aplaudir; (gladden) alegrar, animar ▷ vi dar vivas ▷ n viva m; **cheer up** vi animarse ▷ vt alegrar, animar; **cheerful** adj alegre

cheerio [tʃiəri'əu] (BRIT) excl ¡hasta luego!

cheerleader ['tʃiəliːdə*] n animador(a) m/f

cheese [tʃiːz] n queso; **cheeseburger** n hamburguesa con queso; **cheesecake** n pastel m de queso

chef [ʃef] n jefe/a m/f de cocina

chemical ['kemikəl] adj químico ▷ n producto químico

chemist ['kemist] n (BRIT: pharmacist) farmacéutico/a; (scientist) químico/a; **chemistry** n química; **chemist's (shop)** (BRIT) n farmacia

cheque [tʃek] (us **check**) n cheque m; **chequebook** n talonario de cheques (SP), chequera (LAM); **cheque card** n tarjeta de cheque

cherry ['tʃeri] n cereza; (also: **~ tree**) cerezo

chess [tʃes] n ajedrez m

chest [tʃest] n (Anat) pecho; (box) cofre m, cajón m

chestnut ['tʃesnʌt] n castaña; (also: **~ tree**) castaño

chest of drawers n cómoda

chew [tʃuː] vt mascar, masticar; **chewing gum** n chicle m

chic [ʃiːk] adj elegante

chick [tʃik] n pollito, polluelo; (inf: girl) chica

chicken ['tʃikin] n gallina, pollo; (food) pollo; (inf: coward) gallina mf; **chicken out** (inf) vi rajarse; **chickenpox** n varicela

chickpea ['tʃikpiː] n garbanzo

chief [tʃiːf] n jefe/a m/f ▷ adj principal; **chief executive (officer)** n director(a) m/f general; **chiefly** adv principalmente

child [tʃaild] (pl **~ren**) n niño/a; (offspring) hijo/a; **child abuse** n (with violence) malos tratos mpl a niños; (sexual) abuso m sexual de niños; **child benefit** n (BRIT) subsidio por cada hijo pequeño; **childbirth** n parto; **child-care** n cuidado de los niños; **childhood** n niñez f, infancia; **childish** adj pueril, aniñado; **child minder** (BRIT) n madre f de día; **children** ['tʃildrən] npl of **child**

Chile ['tʃili] n Chile m; **Chilean** adj, n chileno/a m/f

chill [tʃil] n frío; (Med) resfriado ▷ vt enfriar; (Culin) congelar; **chill out** vi (esp us: inf) tranquilizarse

chil(l)i ['tʃili] (BRIT) n chile m, ají m (SC)

chilly ['tʃili] adj frío

chimney ['tʃimni] n chimenea

chimpanzee [tʃimpæn'ziː] n chimpancé m

chin [tʃin] n mentón m, barbilla

China ['tʃainə] n China

china ['tʃainə] n porcelana; (crockery) loza

Chinese [tʃai'niːz] adj chino ▷ n inv chino/a m/f; (Ling) chino

chip [tʃip] n (gen pl: Culin: BRIT) patata (SP) or papa (LAM) frita; (: us: also: **potato ~**) patata or papa frita; (of wood) astilla; (of glass, stone) lasca; (at poker) ficha; (Comput) chip m ▷ vt (cup, plate) desconchar; **chip shop** pescadería (donde se vende principalmente pescado rebozado y patatas fritas)

chiropodist [ki'rɔpədist] (BRIT) n pedicuro/a, callista m/f

chisel ['tʃizl] n (for wood) escoplo; (for stone) cincel m

chives [tʃaivz] npl cebollinos mpl

chlorine ['klɔːriːn] n cloro

choc-ice ['tʃɔkais] n (BRIT) helado m cubierto de chocolate

chocolate ['tʃɔklit] n chocolate m; (sweet) bombón m

choice [tʃɔis] n elección f, selección f; (option) opción f; (preference) preferencia ▷ adj escogido

choir ['kwaiə*] n coro

choke [tʃəuk] vi ahogarse; (on food) atragantarse ▷ vt estrangular, ahogar; (block): **to be ~d with** estar atascado de ▷ n (Aut) estárter m

cholesterol [kə'lestərəl] n colesterol m

choose [tʃuːz] (pt **chose**, pp **chosen**) vt escoger, elegir; (team) seleccionar; **to ~ to do sth** optar por hacer algo

chop [tʃɔp] vt (wood) cortar, tajar; (Culin: also: **~ up**) picar ▷ n (Culin) chuleta; **chop down** vt (tree) talar; **chop off** vt cortar (de un tajo); **chopsticks** ['tʃɔpstiks] npl palillos mpl

chord [kɔːd] n (Mus) acorde m

chore [tʃɔː*] n faena, tarea; (routine task) trabajo rutinario

chorus ['kɔːrəs] n coro; (repeated part of song) estribillo

chose [tʃəuz] pt of **choose**

chosen ['tʃəuzn] pp of **choose**

Christ [kraist] n Cristo

christen ['krisn] vt bautizar; **christening** n bautizo

Christian ['kristiən] adj, n cristiano/a m/f; **Christianity** [-'æniti] n cristianismo; **Christian name** n nombre m de pila

Christmas ['krisməs] n Navidad f; **Merry ~!** ¡Felices Pascuas!; **Christmas card** n crismas m inv, tarjeta de Navidad; **Christmas carol** n villancico m; **Christmas Day** n día m de Navidad; **Christmas Eve** n Nochebuena; **Christmas pudding** n (esp BRIT) pudín m de Navidad; **Christmas tree** n árbol m de Navidad

chrome [krəum] n cromo

chronic ['krɔnik] adj crónico

chrysanthemum [kri'sænθəməm] n crisantemo

chubby ['tʃʌbi] adj regordete

chuck [tʃʌk] (inf) vt lanzar, arrojar; (BRIT: also: **~ up**) abandonar; **chuck out** vt (person) echar (fuera); (rubbish etc) tirar

chuckle ['tʃʌkl] vi reírse entre dientes

chum [tʃʌm] n compañero/a

chunk [tʃʌŋk] n pedazo, trozo

church [tʃəːtʃ] n iglesia; **churchyard** n cementerio

churn [tʃəːn] n (for butter) mantequera; (for milk) lechera

chute [ʃuːt] n (also: **rubbish ~**) vertedero; (for coal etc) rampa de caída

chutney ['tʃʌtni] n condimento a base de frutas de la India

CIA (us) n abbr (= Central Intelligence Agency) CIA f

CID (BRIT) n abbr (= Criminal Investigation Department) = B.I.C. f(SP)

cider ['saidə*] n sidra

cigar [si'gɑː*] n puro

cigarette [sigə'ret] n cigarrillo; **cigarette lighter** n mechero

cinema ['sinəmə] n cine m

cinnamon ['sɪnəmən] n canela
circle ['səːkl] n círculo; (in theatre) anfiteatro ▷vi dar vueltas ▷vt (surround) rodear, cercar; (move round) dar la vuelta a
circuit ['səːkɪt] n circuito; (tour) gira; (track) pista; (lap) vuelta
circular ['səːkjulə*] adj circular ▷n circular f
circulate ['səːkjulert] vi circular; (person: at party etc) hablar con los invitados ▷vt poner en circulación; **circulation** [-'leɪʃən] n circulación f; (of newspaper) tirada
circumstances ['səːkəmstənsɪz] npl circunstancias fpl; (financial condition) situación f económica
circus ['səːkəs] n circo
cite [saɪt] vt citar
citizen ['sɪtɪzn] n (Pol) ciudadano/a; (of city) vecino/a, habitante mf; **citizenship** n ciudadanía; (BRIT: Scol) civismo
citrus fruits ['sɪtrəs-] npl agrios mpl
city ['sɪtɪ] n ciudad f; **the C~** centro financiero de Londres; **city centre** (BRIT) n centro de la ciudad; **city technology college** n centro de formación profesional (centro de enseñanza secundaria que da especial importancia a la ciencia y tecnología.)
civic ['sɪvɪk] adj cívico; (authorities) municipal
civil ['sɪvɪl] adj (civil) atento, cortés; **civilian** [sɪ'vɪlɪən] adj civil (no military) ▷n civil mf, paisano/a
civilization [sɪvɪlaɪ'zeɪʃən] n civilización f
civilized ['sɪvɪlaɪzd] adj civilizado
civil: civil law n derecho civil; **civil rights** npl derechos mpl civiles; **civil servant** n funcionario/a del Estado; **Civil Service** n administración f pública; **civil war** n guerra civil
CJD n abbr (= Creutzfeldt-Jakob disease) enfermedad de Creutzfeldt-Jakob
claim [kleɪm] vt exigir, reclamar; (rights etc) reivindicar; (assert) pretender ▷vi (for insurance) reclamar ▷n reclamación f; pretensión f; **claim form** n solicitud f
clam [klæm] n almeja
clamp [klæmp] n abrazadera, grapa ▷vt (two things together) cerrar fuertemente; (one thing on another) afianzar (con abrazadera); (Aut: wheel) poner el cepo a
clan [klæn] n clan m
clap [klæp] vi aplaudir
claret ['klærət] n burdeos m inv
clarify ['klærɪfaɪ] vt aclarar
clarinet ['klærɪ'net] n clarinete m
clarity ['klærɪtɪ] n claridad f
clash [klæʃ] n enfrentamiento; choque m; desacuerdo; estruendo ▷vi (fight) enfrentarse; (beliefs) chocar; (disagree) estar en desacuerdo; (colours) desentonar; (two events) coincidir
clasp [klɑːsp] n (hold) apretón m; (of necklace, bag) cierre m ▷vt apretar; abrazar
class [klɑːs] n clase f ▷vt clasificar
classic ['klæsɪk] adj, n clásico; **classical** adj clásico
classification [klæsɪfɪ'keɪʃən] n clasificación f
classify ['klæsɪfaɪ] vt clasificar
classmate ['klɑːsmeɪt] n compañero/a de clase
classroom ['klɑːsrum] n aula; **classroom assistant** n profesor(a) m/f de apoyo
classy ['klɑːsɪ] adj (inf) elegante, con estilo
clatter ['klætə*] n estrépito ▷vi hacer ruido or estrépito
clause [klɔːz] n cláusula; (Ling) oración f

claustrophobic [klɔːstrə'fəubɪk] adj claustrofóbico; **I feel ~** me entra claustrofobia
claw [klɔː] n (of cat) uña; (of bird of prey) garra; (of lobster) pinza
clay [kleɪ] n arcilla
clean [kliːn] adj limpio; (record, reputation) bueno, intachable; (joke) decente ▷vt limpiar; (hands etc) lavar; **clean up** vt limpiar, asear; **cleaner** n (person) asistenta; (substance) producto para la limpieza; **cleaner's** n tintorería; **cleaning** n limpieza
cleanser ['klenzə*] n (for face) crema limpiadora
clear [klɪə*] adj claro; (road, way) libre; (conscience) limpio, tranquilo; (skin) terso; (sky) despejado ▷vt (space) despejar, limpiar; (Law: suspect) absolver; (obstacle) salvar, saltar por encima de; (cheque) aceptar ▷vi (fog etc) despejarse ▷adv: **~ of** a distancia de; **to ~ the table** recoger or levantar la mesa; **clear away** vt (things, clothes etc) quitar (de en medio); (dishes) retirar; **clear up** vt limpiar; (mystery) aclarar, resolver; **clearance** n (removal) despeje m; (permission) acreditación f; **clear-cut** adj bien definido, nítido; **clearing** n (in wood) claro m; **clearly** adv claramente; (evidently) sin duda; **clearway** (BRIT) n carretera donde no se puede parar
clench [klentʃ] vt apretar, cerrar
clergy ['kləːdʒɪ] n clero
clerk [klɑːk, (US) kləːrk] n (BRIT) oficinista mf; (US) dependiente/a m/f
clever ['klevə*] adj (intelligent) inteligente, listo; (skilful) hábil; (device, arrangement) ingenioso
cliché ['kliːʃeɪ] n cliché m, frase f hecha
click [klɪk] vt (tongue) chasquear; (heels) taconear ▷vi (Comput) hacer clic; **to ~ on an icon** hacer clic en un icono
client ['klaɪənt] n cliente m/f
cliff [klɪf] n acantilado
climate ['klaɪmɪt] n clima m; **climate change** n cambio climático
climax ['klaɪmæks] n (of battle, career) apogeo; (of film, book) punto culminante; (sexual) orgasmo
climb [klaɪm] vi subir; (plant) trepar; (move with effort): **to ~ over a wall/into a car** trepar a una tapia/subir a un coche ▷vt (stairs) subir; (tree) trepar a; (mountain) escalar ▷n subida; **climb down** vi (fig) volverse atrás; **climber** n alpinista mf (SP, MEX), andinista m/f (LAM); **climbing** n alpinismo (SP, MEX), andinismo (LAM)
clinch [klɪntʃ] vt (deal) cerrar; (argument) remachar
cling [klɪŋ] (pt, pp **clung**) vi: **to ~** agarrarse a; (clothes) pegarse a
Clingfilm® ['klɪŋfɪlm] n plástico adherente
clinic ['klɪnɪk] n clínica
clip [klɪp] n (for hair) horquilla; (also: **paper ~**) sujetapapeles m inv, clip m; (TV, Cinema) fragmento ▷vt (cut) cortar; (also: **~ together**) unir; **clipping** n (newspaper) recorte m
cloak [kləuk] n capa, manto ▷vt (fig) encubrir, disimular; **cloakroom** n guardarropa; (BRIT: WC) lavabo (SP), aseos mpl (SP), baño (LAM)
clock [klɔk] n reloj m; **clock in** or **on** vi (with card) fichar, picar; (start work) entrar a trabajar; **clock off** or **out** vi (with card) fichar or picar la salida; (leave work) salir del trabajar; **clockwise** adv en el sentido de las agujas del reloj; **clockwork** n aparato de relojería ▷adj (toy) de cuerda
clog [klɔg] n zueco, chanclo ▷vt atascar ▷vi (also: **~**

up) atascarse

clone [kləun] n clon m ▷ vt clonar
close¹ [kləus] adj (near): ~ **(to)** cerca (de); (friend) íntimo; (connection) estrecho; (examination) detallado, minucioso; (weather) bochornoso ▷ adv cerca; ~ **by**, ~ **at hand** muy cerca; **to have a ~ shave** (fig) escaparse por un pelo
close² [kləuz] vt (shut) cerrar; (end) concluir, terminar ▷ vi (shop etc) cerrarse; (end) concluirse, terminarse ▷ n (end) fin m, final m, conclusión f; **close down** vi cerrarse definitivamente; **closed** adj (shop etc) cerrado
closely ['kləuslı] adv (study) con detalle; (watch) de cerca; (resemble) estrechamente
closet ['klɔzıt] n armario
close-up ['kləusʌp] n primer plano
closing time n hora de cierre
closure ['kləuʒə*] n cierre m
clot [klɔt] n (gen) coágulo; (inf: idiot) imbécil m/f ▷ vi (blood) coagularse
cloth [klɔθ] n (material) tela, paño; (rag) trapo
clothes [kləuðz] npl ropa; **clothes line** n cuerda (para tender la ropa); **clothes peg** (us **clothes pin**) n pinza
clothing ['kləuðıŋ] n = **clothes**
cloud [klaud] n nube f; **cloud over** vi (also fig) nublarse; **cloudy** adj nublado, nubloso; (liquid) turbio
clove [kləuv] n clavo; ~ **of garlic** diente m de ajo
clown [klaun] n payaso ▷ vi (also: ~ **about**, ~ **around**) hacer el payaso
club [klʌb] n (society) club m; (weapon) porra, cachiporra; (also: **golf** ~) palo ▷ vt aporrear ▷ vi: **to ~ together** (for gift) comprar entre todos; **clubs** npl (Cards) tréboles mpl; **club class** n (Aviat) clase f preferente
clue [klu:] n pista; (in crosswords) indicación f; **I haven't a ~** no tengo ni idea
clump [klʌmp] n (of trees) grupo
clumsy ['klʌmzı] adj (person) torpe, desmañado; (tool) difícil de manejar; (movement) desgarbado
clung [klʌŋ] pt, pp of **cling**
cluster ['klʌstə*] n grupo ▷ vi agruparse, apiñarse
clutch [klʌtʃ] n (Aut) embrague m; (grasp): ~**es** garras fpl ▷ vt asir; agarrar
cm abbr (= centimetre) cm
Co. abbr = **county**; **company**
c/o abbr (= care of) c/a, a/c
coach [kəutʃ] n (bus) autocar m (SP), coche m de línea; (horse-drawn) coche m; (of train) vagón m, coche m; (Sport) entrenador(a) m/f, instructor(a) m/f; (tutor) profesor(a) m/f particular ▷ vt (Sport) entrenar; (student) preparar, enseñar; **coach station** n (BRIT) estación f de autobuses etc; **coach trip** n excursión f en autocar
coal [kəul] n carbón m
coalition [kəuə'lıʃən] n coalición f
coarse [kɔːs] adj basto, burdo; (vulgar) grosero, ordinario
coast [kəust] n costa, litoral m ▷ vi (Aut) ir en punto muerto; **coastal** adj costero, costanero; **coastguard** n guardacostas m inv; **coastline** n litoral m
coat [kəut] n abrigo; (of animal) pelaje m, lana; (of paint) mano f, capa ▷ vt cubrir, revestir; **coat hanger** n percha (SP), gancho (LAM); **coating** n capa, baño
coax [kəuks] vt engatusar
cob [kɔb] n see **corn**
cobbled ['kɔbld] adj: ~ **street** calle f empedrada, calle

fadoquinada
cobweb ['kɔbwɛb] n telaraña
cocaine [kə'keın] n cocaína
cock [kɔk] n (rooster) gallo; (male bird) macho ▷ vt (gun) amartillar; **cockerel** n gallito
cockney ['kɔknı] n habitante de ciertos barrios de Londres
cockpit ['kɔkpıt] n cabina
cockroach ['kɔkrəutʃ] n cucaracha
cocktail ['kɔkteıl] n coctel m, cóctel m
cocoa ['kəukəu] n cacao; (drink) chocolate m
coconut ['kəukənʌt] n coco
cod [kɔd] n bacalao
C.O.D. abbr (= cash on delivery) C.A.E.
code [kəud] n código; (cipher) clave f; (dialling code) prefijo; (post code) código postal
coeducational [kəuɛdju'keıʃənl] adj mixto
coffee ['kɔfı] n café m; **coffee bar** (BRIT) n cafetería; **coffee bean** n grano de café; **coffee break** n descanso (para tomar café); **coffee maker** n máquina de hacer café, cafetera; **coffeepot** n cafetera; **coffee shop** n café m; **coffee table** n mesita (para servir el café)
coffin ['kɔfın] n ataúd m
cog [kɔg] n (wheel) rueda dentada; (tooth) diente m
cognac ['kɔnjæk] n coñac m
coherent [kəu'hıərənt] adj coherente
coil [kɔıl] n rollo; (Elec) bobina, carrete m; (contraceptive) espiral f ▷ vt enrollar
coin [kɔın] n moneda ▷ vt (word) inventar, idear
coincide [kəuın'saıd] vi coincidir; (agree) estar de acuerdo; **coincidence** [kəu'ınsıdəns] n casualidad f
Coke® [kəuk] n Coca-Cola®
coke [kəuk] n (coal) coque m
colander ['kɔləndə*] n colador m, escurridor m
cold [kəuld] adj frío ▷ n frío; (Med) resfriado; **it's ~** hace frío; **to be ~** (person) tener frío; **to catch (a) ~** resfriarse; **in ~ blood** a sangre fría; **cold sore** n herpes mpl or fpl
coleslaw ['kəulslɔ:] n especie de ensalada de col
colic ['kɔlık] n cólico
collaborate [kə'læbəreıt] vi colaborar
collapse [kə'læps] vi hundirse, derrumbarse; (Med) sufrir un colapso ▷ n hundimiento, derrumbamiento; (Med) colapso
collar ['kɔlə*] n (of coat, shirt) cuello; (of dog etc) collar; **collarbone** n clavícula
colleague ['kɔli:g] n colega mf; (at work) compañero/a
collect [kə'lekt] vt (litter, mail etc) recoger; (as a hobby) coleccionar; (BRIT: call and pick up) recoger; (debts, subscriptions etc) recaudar ▷ vi reunirse; (dust) acumularse; **to call ~** (us Tel) llamar a cobro revertido; **collection** [kə'lekʃən] n colección f; (of mail, for charity) recogida; **collective** [kə'lektıv] adj colectivo; **collector** n coleccionista mf
college ['kɔlıdʒ] n colegio mayor; (of agriculture, technology) escuela universitaria
collide [kə'laıd] vi chocar
collision [kə'lıʒən] n choque m
cologne [kə'ləun] n (also: **eau de ~**) (agua de) colonia
Colombia [kə'lɔmbıə] n Colombia; **Colombian** adj, n colombiano/a
colon ['kəulən] n (sign) dos puntos; (Med) colon m
colonel ['kɜ:nl] n coronel m
colonial [kə'ləunıəl] adj colonial

colony ['kɒlənɪ] n colonia
colour etc ['kʌlə*] (us **color** etc) n color m ▷ vt color(e)ar; (dye) teñir; (fig: account) adornar; (: judgement) distorsionar ▷ vi (blush) sonrojarse; **colour in** vt colorear; **colour-blind** adj daltónico; **coloured** adj de color; (photo) en color; **colour film** n película en color; **colourful** adj lleno de color; (story) fantástico; (person) excéntrico; **colouring** n (complexion) tez f; (in food) colorante m; **colour television** n televisión f en color
column ['kɒləm] n columna
coma ['kəumə] n coma m
comb [kəum] n peine m; (ornamental) peineta ▷ vt (hair) peinar; (area) registrar a fondo
combat ['kɒmbæt] n combate m ▷ vt combatir
combination [kɒmbɪ'neɪʃən] n combinación f
combine [vb kəm'baɪn, n 'kɒmbaɪn] vt combinar; (qualities) reunir ▷ vi combinarse ▷ n (Econ) cartel m

○ KEYWORD

come [kʌm] (pt **came**, pp **come**) vi **1** (movement towards) venir; **to come running** venir corriendo
2 (arrive) llegar; **he's come here to work** ha venido aquí para trabajar; **to come home** volver a casa
3 (reach): **to come to** llegar a; **the bill came to £40** la cuenta ascendía a cuarenta libras
4 (occur): **an idea came to me** se me ocurrió una idea
5 (be, become): **to come loose/undone** etc aflojarse/ desabrocharse/desatarse etc; **I've come to like him** por fin ha llegado a gustarme
come across vt fus (person) topar con; (thing) dar con
come along vi (BRIT: progress) ir
come back vi (return) volver
come down vi (price) bajar; (tree, building) ser derribado
come from vt fus (place, source) ser de
come in vi (visitor) entrar; (train, report) llegar; (fashion) ponerse de moda; (on deal etc) entrar
come off vi (button) soltarse, desprenderse; (attempt) salir bien
come on vi (pupil) progresar; (work, project) desarrollarse; (lights) encenderse; (electricity) volver; **come on!** ¡vamos!
come out vi (fact) salir a la luz; (book, sun) salir; (stain) quitarse
come round vi (after faint, operation) volver en sí
come to vi (wake) volver en sí
come up vi (sun) salir; (problem) surgir; (event) aproximarse; (in conversation) mencionarse
come up with vt fus (idea) sugerir; (money) conseguir

comeback ['kʌmbæk] n: **to make a ~** (Theatre) volver a las tablas
comedian [kə'miːdɪən] n humorista mf
comedy ['kɒmɪdɪ] n comedia; (humour) comicidad f
comet ['kɒmɪt] n cometa m
comfort ['kʌmfət] n bienestar m; (relief) alivio ▷ vt consolar; **comfortable** adj cómodo; (financially) acomodado; (easy) fácil; **comfort station** (US) n servicios mpl
comic ['kɒmɪk] adj (also: **~al**) cómico ▷ n (comedian) cómico; (BRIT: for children) tebeo; (BRIT: for adults) comic m; **comic book** (US) n libro m de cómics; **comic strip** n tira cómica

comma ['kɒmə] n coma
command [kə'mɑːnd] n orden f, mandato; (Mil: authority) mando; (mastery) dominio ▷ vt (troops) mandar; (give orders to): **to ~ sb to do** mandar or ordenar a algn hacer; **commander** n (Mil) comandante mf, jefe a m/f
commemorate [kə'meməreɪt] vt conmemorar
commence [kə'mens] vt, vi comenzar, empezar; **commencement** (US) n (Univ) (ceremonia de) graduación f
commend [kə'mend] vt elogiar, alabar; (recommend) recomendar
comment ['kɒment] n comentario ▷ vi: **to ~ on** hacer comentarios sobre; **"no ~"** (written) "sin comentarios"; (spoken) "no tengo nada que decir"; **commentary** ['kɒməntərɪ] n comentario; **commentator** ['kɒmənteɪtə*] n comentarista mf
commerce ['kɒmɜːs] n comercio
commercial [kə'mɜːʃəl] adj comercial ▷ n (TV, Radio) anuncio; **commercial break** n intermedio para publicidad
commission [kə'mɪʃən] n (committee, fee) comisión f ▷ vt (work of art) encargar; **out of ~** fuera de servicio; **commissioner** n (Police) comisario de policía
commit [kə'mɪt] vt (act) cometer; (resources) dedicar; (to sb's care) entregar; **to ~ o.s. (to do)** comprometerse (a hacer); **to ~ suicide** suicidarse; **commitment** n compromiso; (to ideology etc) entrega
committee [kə'mɪtɪ] n comité m
commodity [kə'mɒdɪtɪ] n mercancía
common ['kɒmən] adj común; (pej) ordinario ▷ n campo común; **commonly** adv comúnmente; **commonplace** adj de lo más común; **Commons** (BRIT) npl (Pol): **the Commons** (la Cámara de) los Comunes; **common sense** n sentido común; **Commonwealth** n: **the Commonwealth** la Commonwealth
communal ['kɒmjuːnl] adj (property) comunal; (kitchen) común
commune [n 'kɒmjuːn, vb kə'mjuːn] n (group) comuna ▷ vi: **to ~ with** comulgar or conversar con
communicate [kə'mjuːnɪkeɪt] vt comunicar ▷ vi: **to ~ (with)** comunicarse (con); (in writing) estar en contacto (con)
communication [kəmjuːnɪ'keɪʃən] n comunicación f
communion [kə'mjuːnɪən] n (also: **Holy ~**) comunión f
communism ['kɒmjunɪzəm] n comunismo; **communist** adj, n comunista mf
community [kə'mjuːnɪtɪ] n comunidad f; (large group) colectividad f; **community centre** (US **community center**) n centro social; **community service** n trabajo m comunitario (prestado en lugar de cumplir una pena de prisión)
commute [kə'mjuːt] vi viajar a diario de la casa al trabajo ▷ vt conmutar; **commuter** n persona que viaja a diario de la casa al trabajo
compact [adj kəm'pækt, n 'kɒmpækt] adj compacto ▷ n (also: **powder ~**) polvera; **compact disc** n compact disc m; **compact disc player** n reproductor m de disco compacto, compact disc m
companion [kəm'pænɪən] n compañero/a
company ['kʌmpənɪ] n compañía; (Comm) sociedad f, compañía; **to keep sb ~** acompañar a algn; **company car** n coche m de la empresa; **company director** n director(a) m/f de empresa

comparable ['kɒmpərəbl] adj comparable

comparative [kəm'pærətɪv] adj relativo; (study) comparativo; **comparatively** adv (relatively) relativamente

compare [kəm'pɛə*] vt: **to ~ sth/sb with** or **to** comparar algo/a algn con ▷ vi: **to ~ (with)** compararse (con); **comparison** n comparación f

compartment [kəm'pɑ:tmənt] n (also: Rail) compartim(i)ento

compass ['kʌmpəs] n brújula; **compasses** npl (Math) compás m

compassion [kəm'pæʃən] n compasión f

compatible [kəm'pætɪbl] adj compatible

compel [kəm'pɛl] vt obligar; **compelling** adj (fig: argument) convincente

compensate ['kɒmpənseɪt] vt compensar ▷ vi: **to ~ for** compensar; **compensation** [-'seɪʃən] n (for loss) indemnización f

compete [kəm'pi:t] vi (take part) tomar parte, concurrir; (vie with): **to ~ with** competir con, hacer competencia a

competent ['kɒmpɪtənt] adj competente, capaz

competition [kɒmpɪ'tɪʃən] n (contest) concurso; (rivalry) competencia

competitive [kəm'pɛtɪtɪv] adj (Econ, Sport) competitivo

competitor [kəm'pɛtɪtə*] n (rival) competidor(a) m/f; (participant) concursante mf

complacent [kəm'pleɪsənt] adj autocomplaciente

complain [kəm'pleɪn] vi quejarse; (Comm) reclamar; **complaint** n queja; reclamación f; (Med) enfermedad f

complement [n 'kɒmplɪmənt, vb 'kɒmplɪmənt] n complemento; (esp of ship's crew) dotación f ▷ vt (enhance) complementar; **complementary** [kɒmplɪ'mɛntərɪ] adj complementario

complete [kəm'pli:t] adj (full) completo; (finished) acabado ▷ vt (fulfil) completar; (finish) acabar; (a form) llenar; **completely** adv completamente; **completion** [-'pli:ʃn] n terminación f; (of contract) realización f

complex ['kɒmplɛks] adj, n complejo

complexion [kəm'plɛkʃən] n (of face) tez f, cutis m

compliance [kəm'plaɪəns] n (submission) sumisión f; (agreement) conformidad f; **in ~ with** de acuerdo con

complicate ['kɒmplɪkeɪt] vt complicar; **complicated** adj complicado; **complication** [-'keɪʃən] n complicación f

compliment ['kɒmplɪmənt] n (formal) cumplido ▷ vt felicitar; **complimentary** [-'mɛntərɪ] adj lisonjero; (free) de favor

comply [kəm'plaɪ] vi: **to ~ with** cumplir con

component [kəm'pəʊnənt] adj componente ▷ n (Tech) pieza

compose [kəm'pəʊz] vt: **to be ~d of** componerse de; (music etc) componer; **to ~ o.s.** tranquilizarse; **composer** n (Mus) compositor(a) m/f; **composition** [kɒmpə'zɪʃən] n composición f

composure [kəm'pəʊʒə*] n serenidad f, calma

compound ['kɒmpaʊnd] n (Chem) compuesto; (Ling) palabra compuesta; (enclosure) recinto ▷ adj compuesto; (fracture) complicado

comprehension [-'hɛnʃən] n comprensión f

comprehensive [kɒmprɪ'hɛnsɪv] adj exhaustivo; (insurance) contra todo riesgo; **comprehensive (school)** n centro estatal de enseñanza secundaria ≈ Instituto Nacional de Bachillerato (SP)

compress [vb kəm'prɛs, n 'kɒmprɛs] vt comprimir;

(information) condensar ▷ n (Med) compresa

comprise [kəm'praɪz] vt (also: **be ~d of**) comprender, constar de; (constitute) constituir

compromise ['kɒmprəmaɪz] n (agreement) arreglo ▷ vt comprometer ▷ vi transigir

compulsive [kəm'pʌlsɪv] adj compulsivo; (viewing, reading) obligado

compulsory [kəm'pʌlsərɪ] adj obligatorio

computer [kəm'pju:tə*] n ordenador m, computador m, computadora; **computer game** n juego para ordenador; **computer-generated** adj realizado por ordenador, creado por ordenador; **computerize** vt (data) computerizar; (system) informatizar; **we're computerized now** ya nos hemos informatizado; **computer programmer** n programador(a) m/f; **computer programming** n programación f; **computer science** n informática; **computer studies** npl informática fsg, computación f fsg (LAM); **computing** [kəm'pju:tɪŋ] n (activity, science) informática

con [kɒn] vt (deceive) engañar; (cheat) estafar ▷ n estafa

conceal [kən'si:l] vt ocultar

concede [kən'si:d] vt (point, argument) reconocer; (territory) ceder; **to ~ (defeat)** darse por vencido; **to ~ that** admitir que

conceited [kən'si:tɪd] adj presumido

conceive [kən'si:v] vt, vi concebir

concentrate ['kɒnsəntreɪt] vi concentrarse ▷ vt concentrar

concentration [kɒnsən'treɪʃən] n concentración f

concept ['kɒnsɛpt] n concepto

concern [kən'sɜ:n] n (matter) asunto; (Comm) empresa; (anxiety) preocupación f ▷ vt (worry) preocupar; (involve) afectar; (relate to) tener que ver con; **to be ~ed (about)** interesarse (por), preocuparse (por); **concerning** prep sobre, acerca de

concert ['kɒnsət] n concierto; **concert hall** n sala de conciertos

concerto [kən'tʃɜ:təu] n concierto

concession [kən'sɛʃən] n concesión f; **tax ~** privilegio fiscal

concise [kən'saɪs] adj conciso

conclude [kən'klu:d] vt (treaty etc) firmar; (agreement) llegar a; (decide) llegar a la conclusión de; **conclusion** [-'klu:ʒən] n conclusión f; firma

concrete ['kɒnkri:t] n hormigón m ▷ adj de hormigón; (fig) concreto

concussion [kən'kʌʃən] n conmoción f cerebral

condemn [kən'dɛm] vt condenar; (building) declarar en ruina

condensation [kɒndɛn'seɪʃən] n condensación f

condense [kən'dɛns] vi condensarse ▷ vt condensar, abreviar

condition [kən'dɪʃən] n condición f, estado; (requirement) condición f ▷ vt condicionar; **on ~ that** a condición (de) que; **conditional** [kən'dɪʃənl] adj condicional; **conditioner** n suavizante

condo ['kɒndəu] (US) n (inf) = **condominium**

condom ['kɒndəm] n condón m

condominium [kɒndə'mɪnɪəm] (US) n (building) bloque m de pisos or apartamentos (propiedad de quienes lo habitan), condominio (LAM); (apartment) piso or apartamento (en propiedad), condominio (LAM)

condone [kən'dəun] vt condonar

conduct [n 'kɒndʌkt, vb kən'dʌkt] n conducta,

comportamiento ▷ *vt* (*lead*) conducir; (*manage*) llevar a cabo, dirigir; (*Mus*) dirigir; **to ~ o.s.** comportarse; **conducted tour** (BRIT) *n* visita acompañada; **conductor** *n* (*of orchestra*) director *m*; (*us: on train*) revisor(a) *m/f*; (*on bus*) cobrador *m*; (*Elec*) conductor *m*

cone [kəun] *n* cono; (*pine cone*) piña; (*on road*) pivote *m*; (*for ice-cream*) cucurucho

confectionery [kən'fɛkʃənrɪ] *n* dulces *mpl*

confer [kən'fəː*] *vt*: **to ~ sth on** otorgar algo a ▷ *vi* conferenciar

conference ['kɒnfərns] *n* (*meeting*) reunión *f*; (*convention*) congreso

confess [kən'fɛs] *vt* confesar ▷ *vi* admitir; **confession** [-'fɛʃən] *n* confesión *f*

confide [kən'faɪd] *vi*: **to ~ in** confiar en

confidence ['kɒnfɪdns] *n* (*also:* **self-~**) confianza; (*secret*) confidencia; **in ~** (*speak, write*) en confianza; **confident** *adj* seguro de sí mismo; (*certain*) seguro; **confidential** [kɒnfɪ'dɛnʃəl] *adj* confidencial

confine [kən'faɪn] *vt* (*limit*) limitar; (*shut up*) encerrar; **confined** *adj* (*space*) reducido

confirm [kən'fəːm] *vt* confirmar; **confirmation** [kɒnfə'meɪʃən] *n* confirmación *f*

confiscate ['kɒnfɪskeɪt] *vt* confiscar

conflict [*n* 'kɒnflɪkt, *vb* kən'flɪkt] *n* conflicto ▷ *vi* (*opinions*) chocar

conform [kən'fɔːm] *vi* conformarse; **to ~ to** ajustarse a

confront [kən'frʌnt] *vt* (*problems*) hacer frente a; (*enemy, danger*) enfrentarse con; **confrontation** [kɒnfrən'teɪʃən] *n* enfrentamiento

confuse [kən'fjuːz] *vt* (*perplex*) aturdir, desconcertar; (*mix up*) confundir; (*complicate*) complicar; **confused** *adj* confuso; (*person*) perplejo; **confusing** *adj* confuso; **confusion** [-'fjuːʒən] *n* confusión *f*

congestion [kən'dʒɛstʃən] *n* congestión *f*

congratulate [kən'grætjuleɪt] *vt*: **to ~ sb (on)** felicitar a algn (por); **congratulations** [-'leɪʃənz] *npl* felicitaciones *fpl*; **congratulations!** ¡enhorabuena!

congregation [-'geɪʃən] *n* (*of a church*) feligreses *mpl*

congress ['kɒŋgres] *n* congreso; (*us*): **C~** Congreso; **congressman** (*irreg: us*) *n* miembro del Congreso; **congresswoman** (*irreg: us*) *n* diputada, miembro *f* del Congreso

conifer ['kɒnɪfə*] *n* conífera

conjugate ['kɒndʒugeɪt] *vt* conjugar

conjugation [kɒndʒə'geɪʃən] *n* conjugación *f*

conjunction [kən'dʒʌŋkʃən] *n* conjunción *f*; **in ~ with** junto con

conjure ['kʌndʒə*] *vi* hacer juegos de manos

connect [kə'nɛkt] *vt* juntar, unir, unir; (*Elec*) conectar; (*Tel: subscriber*) poner; (*: caller*) poner al habla; (*fig*) relacionar, asociar ▷ *vt*: **to ~ with** (*train*) enlazar con; **to be ~ed with** (*associated*) estar relacionado con; **connecting flight** *n* vuelo *m* de enlace; **connection** [-ʃən] *n* juntura, unión *f*; (*Elec*) conexión *f*; (*Rail*) enlace *m*; (*Tel*) comunicación *f*; (*fig*) relación *f*

conquer ['kɒŋkə*] *vt* (*territory*) conquistar; (*enemy, feelings*) vencer

conquest ['kɒŋkwɛst] *n* conquista

cons [kɒnz] *npl see* **convenience**; **pro**; **mod**

conscience ['kɒnʃəns] *n* conciencia

conscientious [kɒnʃɪ'ɛnʃəs] *adj* concienzudo; (*objection*) de conciencia

conscious ['kɒnʃəs] *adj* (*deliberate*) deliberado; (*awake, aware*) consciente; **consciousness** *n*

conciencia; (*Med*) conocimiento

consecutive [kən'sɛkjutɪv] *adj* consecutivo; **on 3 ~ occasions** en 3 ocasiones consecutivas

consensus [kən'sɛnsəs] *n* consenso

consent [kən'sɛnt] *n* consentimiento ▷ *vi*: **to ~ (to)** consentir (en)

consequence ['kɒnsɪkwəns] *n* consecuencia; (*significance*) importancia

consequently ['kɒnsɪkwəntlɪ] *adv* por consiguiente

conservation [kɒnsə'veɪʃən] *n* conservación *f*

conservative [kən'səːvətɪv] *adj* conservador(a); (*estimate etc*) cauteloso; **Conservative** (BRIT) *adj, n* (*Pol*) conservador(a) *m/f*

conservatory [kən'səːvətrɪ] *n* invernadero; (*Mus*) conservatorio

consider [kən'sɪdə*] *vt* considerar; (*take into account*) tener en cuenta; (*study*) estudiar, examinar; **to ~ doing sth** pensar en (la posibilidad de) hacer algo; **considerable** *adj* considerable; **considerably** *adv* notablemente; **considerate** *adj* considerado; **consideration** [-'reɪʃən] *n* consideración *f*; (*factor*) factor *m*; **to give sth further consideration** estudiar algo más a fondo; **considering** *prep* teniendo en cuenta

consignment [kən'saɪnmənt] *n* envío

consist [kən'sɪst] *vi*: **to ~ of** consistir en

consistency [kən'sɪstənsɪ] *n* (*of argument etc*) coherencia; consecuencia; (*thickness*) consistencia

consistent [kən'sɪstənt] *adj* (*person*) consecuente; (*argument etc*) coherente

consolation [kɒnsə'leɪʃən] *n* consuelo

console¹ [kən'səul] *vt* consolar

console² ['kɒnsəul] *n* consola

consonant ['kɒnsənənt] *n* consonante *f*

conspicuous [kən'spɪkjuəs] *adj* (*visible*) visible

conspiracy [kən'spɪrəsɪ] *n* conjura, complot *m*

constable ['kʌnstəbl] (BRIT) *n* policía *mf*; **chief ~** ≈ jefe *m* de policía

constant ['kɒnstənt] *adj* constante; **constantly** *adv* constantemente

constipated ['kɒnstɪpeɪtəd] *adj* estreñido; **constipation** [kɒnstɪ'peɪʃən] *n* estreñimiento

constituency [kən'stɪtjuənsɪ] *n* (*Pol: area*) distrito electoral; (*: electors*) electorado

constitute ['kɒnstɪtjuːt] *vt* constituir

constitution [kɒnstɪ'tjuːʃən] *n* constitución *f*

constraint [kən'streɪnt] *n* obligación *f*; (*limit*) restricción *f*

construct [kən'strʌkt] *vt* construir; **construction** [-ʃən] *n* construcción *f*; **constructive** *adj* constructivo

consul ['kɒnsl] *n* cónsul *mf*; **consulate** ['kɒnsjulɪt] *n* consulado

consult [kən'sʌlt] *vt* consultar; **consultant** *n* (BRIT Med) especialista *mf*; (*other specialist*) asesor(a) *m/f*; **consultation** [kɒnsəl'teɪʃən] *n* consulta; **consulting room** (BRIT) *n* consultorio

consume [kən'sjuːm] *vt* (*eat*) comerse; (*drink*) beberse; (*fire etc, Comm*) consumir; **consumer** *n* consumidor(a) *m/f*

consumption [kən'sʌmpʃən] *n* consumo

cont. *abbr* (= *continued*) sigue

contact ['kɒntækt] *n* contacto; (*person*) contacto; (*: pej*) enchufe *m* ▷ *vt* ponerse en contacto con; **contact lenses** *npl* lentes *fpl* de contacto

contagious [kən'teɪdʒəs] adj contagioso

contain [kən'teɪn] vt contener; **to ~ o.s.** contenerse; **container** n recipiente m; (for shipping etc) contenedor m

contaminate [kən'tæmɪneɪt] vt contaminar

cont'd abbr (= continued) sigue

contemplate ['kɔntəmpleɪt] vt contemplar; (reflect upon) considerar

contemporary [kən'tempərərɪ] adj, n contemporáneo a m/f

contempt [kən'tempt] n desprecio; **~ of court** (Law) desacato (a los tribunales)

contend [kən'tend] vt (argue) afirmar ▷ vi: **to ~ with/for** luchar contra/por

content [adj, vb kən'tent, n kɔntent] adj (happy) contento; (satisfied) satisfecho ▷ vt contentar; satisfacer ▷ n contenido; **contents** npl contenido; **(table of) ~s** índice m de materias; **contented** adj contento; satisfecho

contest [n 'kɔntest, vb kən'test] n lucha; (competition) concurso ▷ vt (dispute) impugnar; (Pol) presentarse como candidato/a en; **contestant** [kən'testənt] n concursante mf; (in fight) contendiente mf

context ['kɔntekst] n contexto

continent ['kɔntɪnənt] n continente m; **the C~** (BRIT) el continente europeo; **continental** [-'nentl] adj continental; **continental breakfast** n desayuno estilo europeo; **continental quilt** (BRIT) n edredón m

continual [kən'tɪnjuəl] adj continuo; **continually** adv constantemente

continue [kən'tɪnju:] vi, vt seguir, continuar

continuity [kɔntɪ'njuɪtɪ] n (also Cine) continuidad f

continuous [kən'tɪnjuəs] adj continuo; **continuous assessment** (BRIT) evaluación f continua; **continuously** adv continuamente

contour ['kɔntuə*] n contorno; (also: **~ line**) curva de nivel

contraception [kɔntrə'sepʃən] n contracepción f

contraceptive [kɔntrə'septɪv] adj, n anticonceptivo f

contract [n 'kɔntrækt, vb kən'trækt] n contrato ▷ vi (Comm): **to ~ to do sth** comprometerse por contrato a hacer algo; (become smaller) contraerse, encogerse ▷ vt contraer; **contractor** n contratista mf

contradict [kɔntrə'dɪkt] vt contradecir; **contradiction** [-ʃən] n contradicción f

contrary[1] ['kɔntrərɪ] adj contrario ▷ n lo contrario; **on the ~** al contrario; **unless you hear to the ~** a no ser que le digan lo contrario

contrary[2] [kən'treərɪ] adj (perverse) terco

contrast [n 'kɔntra:st, vb kən'tra:st] n contraste m ▷ vt comparar; **in ~ to** en contraste con

contribute [kən'trɪbju:t] vi contribuir ▷ vt: **to ~ £10/an article to** contribuir con 10 libras/un artículo a; **to ~ to** (charity) donar a; (newspaper) escribir para; (discussion) intervenir en; **contribution** [kɔntrɪ'bju:ʃən] n (donation) donativo; (BRIT: for social security) cotización f; (to debate) intervención f; (to journal) colaboración f; **contributor** n contribuyente mf; (to newspaper) colaborador(a) m/f

control [kən'trəul] vt controlar; (process etc) dirigir; (machinery) manejar; (temper) dominar; (disease) contener ▷ n control m; **controls** npl (of vehicle) instrumentos mpl de mando; (of radio) controles mpl; (governmental) medidas fpl de control; **under ~** bajo control; **to be in ~ of** tener el mando de; **the car went out of ~** se perdió el control del coche; **control tower**

n (Aviat) torre f de control

controversial [kɔntrə'və:ʃl] adj polémico

controversy ['kɔntrəvə:sɪ] n polémica

convenience [kən'vi:nɪəns] n (easiness) comodidad f; (suitability) idoneidad f; (advantage) ventaja; **at your ~** cuando le sea conveniente; **all modern ~s, all mod cons** (BRIT) todo confort

convenient [kən'vi:nɪənt] adj (useful) útil; (place, time) conveniente

convent ['kɔnvənt] n convento

convention [kən'venʃən] n convención f; (meeting) asamblea; (agreement) convenio; **conventional** adj convencional

conversation [kɔnvə'seɪʃən] n conversación f

conversely [-'və:slɪ] adv a la inversa

conversion [kən'və:ʃən] n conversión f

convert [vb kən'və:t, n 'kɔnvə:t] vt (Rel, Comm) convertir; (alter): **to ~ sth into/to** transformar algo en/convertir algo a ▷ n converso/a; **convertible** adj convertible ▷ n descapotable m

convey [kən'veɪ] vt llevar; (thanks) comunicar; (idea) expresar; **conveyor belt** n cinta transportadora

convict [vb kən'vɪkt, n 'kɔnvɪkt] vt (find guilty) declarar culpable a ▷ n presidiario/a; **conviction** [-ʃən] n condena; (belief, certainty) convicción f

convince [kən'vɪns] vt convencer; **convinced** adj: **convinced of/that** convencido de/de que; **convincing** adj convincente

convoy ['kɔnvɔɪ] n convoy m

cook [kuk] vt (stew etc) guisar; (meal) preparar ▷ vi cocer; (person) cocinar ▷ n cocinero/a; **cook book** n libro de cocina; **cooker** n cocina; **cookery** n cocina; **cookery book** (BRIT) n = **cook book**; **cookie** (US) n galleta; **cooking** n cocina

cool [ku:l] adj fresco; (not afraid) tranquilo; (unfriendly) frío ▷ vt enfriar ▷ vi enfriarse; **cool down** vi enfriarse; (fig: person, situation) calmarse; **cool off** vi (become calmer) calmarse, apaciguarse; (lose enthusiasm) perder (el) interés, enfriarse

cop [kɔp] (inf) n poli mf (SP), tira mf (MEX)

cope [kəup] vi: **to ~ with** (problem) hacer frente a

copper ['kɔpə*] n (metal) cobre m; (BRIT: inf) poli mf, tira mf (MEX)

copy ['kɔpɪ] n copia; (of book etc) ejemplar m ▷ vt copiar; **copyright** n derechos mpl de autor

coral ['kɔrəl] n coral m

cord [kɔ:d] n cuerda; (Elec) cable m; (fabric) pana; **cords** npl (trousers) pantalones mpl de pana; **cordless** adj sin hilos

corduroy ['kɔ:dərɔɪ] n pana

core [kɔ:*] n centro, núcleo; (of fruit) corazón m; (of problem) meollo ▷ vt quitar el corazón de

coriander [kɔrɪ'ændə*] n culantro

cork [kɔ:k] n corcho; (tree) alcornoque m; **corkscrew** n sacacorchos m inv

corn [kɔ:n] n (BRIT: cereal crop) trigo; (US: maize) maíz m; (on foot) callo; **~ on the cob** (Culin) mazorca, elote m (MEX), choclo (SC)

corned beef ['kɔ:nd-] n carne f acecinada (en lata)

corner ['kɔ:nə*] n (outside) esquina; (inside) rincón m; (in road) curva; (Football) córner m; (Boxing) esquina ▷ vt (trap) arrinconar; (Comm) acaparar ▷ vi (in car) tomar las curvas; **corner shop** (BRIT) tienda de la esquina

cornflakes ['kɔ:nfleɪks] npl copos mpl de maíz, cornflakes mpl

cornflour ['kɔ:nflauə*] (BRIT) n harina de maíz

cornstarch [ˈkɔːnstɑːtʃ] (US) n = **cornflour**

Cornwall [ˈkɔːnwəl] n Cornualles m

coronary [ˈkɒrənərɪ] n (also: ~ **thrombosis**) infarto

coronation [kɒrəˈneɪʃən] n coronación f

coroner [ˈkɒrənə*] n juez mf de instrucción

corporal [ˈkɔːpərl] n cabo ▷ adj: ~ **punishment** castigo corporal

corporate [ˈkɔːpərɪt] adj (action, ownership) colectivo; (finance, image) corporativo

corporation [kɔːpəˈreɪʃən] n (of town) ayuntamiento m; (Comm) corporación f

corps [kɔː*, pl kɔːz] n inv cuerpo; **diplomatic ~** cuerpo diplomático; **press ~** gabinete m de prensa

corpse [kɔːps] n cadáver m

correct [kəˈrekt] adj justo, exacto; (proper) correcto ▷ vt corregir; (exam) corregir, calificar; **correction** [-ʃən] n (act) corrección f; (instance) rectificación f

correspond [kɒrɪsˈpɒnd] vi (write): **to ~ (with)** escribirse con; (be equivalent to): **to ~ (to)** corresponder (a); (be in accordance): **to ~ (with)** corresponder (con); **correspondence** n correspondencia; **correspondent** n corresponsal mf; **corresponding** adj correspondiente

corridor [ˈkɒrɪdɔː*] n pasillo

corrode [kəˈrəʊd] vt corroer ▷ vi corroerse

corrupt [kəˈrʌpt] adj (person) corrupto; (Comput) corrompido ▷ vt corromper; (Comput) degradar; **corruption** n corrupción f; (of data) alteración f

Corsica [ˈkɔːsɪkə] n Córcega

cosmetic [kɒzˈmetɪk] adj, n cosmético; **cosmetic surgery** n cirugía estética

cosmopolitan [kɒzməˈpɒlɪtn] adj cosmopolita

cost [kɒst] (pt, pp ~) n (price) precio ▷ vi costar, valer ▷ vt preparar el presupuesto de; **how much does it ~?** ¿cuánto cuesta?; **to ~ sb time/effort** costarle a algn tiempo/esfuerzo; **it ~ him his life** le costó la vida; **at all ~s** cueste lo que cueste; **costs** npl (Comm) costes mpl; (Law) costas fpl

co-star [ˈkəʊstɑː*] n coprotagonista mf

Costa Rica [ˈkɒstəˈriːkə] n Costa Rica; **Costa Rican** adj, n costarriqueño/a

costly [ˈkɒstlɪ] adj costoso

cost of living n costo o coste m (Sp) de la vida

costume [ˈkɒstjuːm] n traje m; (BRIT: also: **swimming ~**) traje de baño

cosy [ˈkəʊzɪ] (US **cozy**) adj (person) cómodo; (room) acogedor, a

cot [kɒt] n (BRIT: child's) cuna; (US: campbed) cama de campaña

cottage [ˈkɒtɪdʒ] n casita de campo; (rustic) barraca; **cottage cheese** n requesón m

cotton [ˈkɒtn] n algodón m; (thread) hilo; **cotton on** vi (inf): **to cotton on (to sth)** caer en la cuenta (de algo); **cotton bud** n (BRIT) bastoncillo m de algodón; **cotton candy** n (US) algodón m (azucarado); **cotton wool** (BRIT) n algodón m (hidrófilo)

couch [kautʃ] n sofá m; (doctor's etc) diván m

cough [kɒf] vi toser ▷ n tos f; **cough mixture** n jarabe m para la tos

could [kʊd] pt of **can²**; **couldn't** = **could not**

council [ˈkaunsl] n consejo; **city** o **town ~** consejo municipal; **council estate** n (BRIT) n urbanización de viviendas municipales de alquiler; **council house** (BRIT) n vivienda municipal de alquiler; **councillor** (US **councilor**) n concejal/a m/f; **council tax** n (BRIT) contribución f municipal (dependiente del valor de la vivienda)

counsel [ˈkaunsl] n (advice) consejo; (lawyer) abogado/a ▷ vt aconsejar; **counselling** (US **counseling**) n (Psych) asistencia f psicológica; **counsellor** (US **counselor**) n consejero/a, abogado/a

count [kaunt] vt contar; (include) incluir ▷ vi contar ▷ n cuenta; (of votes) escrutinio; (level) nivel m; (nobleman) conde m; **count in** (inf) vt: **to count sb in on sth** contar con algn para algo; **count on** vt fus contar con; **countdown** n cuenta atrás

counter [ˈkauntə*] n (in shop) mostrador m; (in games) ficha ▷ vt contrarrestar ▷ adv: **to run ~ to** ser contrario a, ir en contra de; **counter clockwise** (US) adv en sentido contrario al de las agujas del reloj

counterfeit [ˈkauntəfɪt] n falsificación f, simulación f ▷ vt falsificar ▷ adj falso, falsificado

counterpart [ˈkauntəpɑːt] n homólogo/a

countess [ˈkauntɪs] n condesa

countless [ˈkauntlɪs] adj innumerable

country [ˈkʌntrɪ] n país m; (native land) patria; (as opposed to town) campo; (region) región f, tierra; **country and western (music)** n música country; **country house** n casa de campo; **countryside** n campo

county [ˈkauntɪ] n condado

coup [kuː] (pl ~s) n (also: ~ **d'état**) golpe m (de estado); (achievement) éxito

couple [ˈkʌpl] n (of things) par m; (of people) pareja; (married couple) matrimonio; **a ~ of** un par de

coupon [ˈkuːpɒn] n cupón m; (voucher) valé m

courage [ˈkʌrɪdʒ] n valor m, valentía; **courageous** [kəˈreɪdʒəs] adj valiente

courgette [kuəˈʒet] (BRIT) n calabacín m, calabacita (MEX)

courier [ˈkurɪə*] n mensajero/a; (for tourists) guía mf (de turismo)

course [kɔːs] n (direction) dirección f; (of river, Scol) curso; (process) transcurso; (Med): ~ **of treatment** tratamiento; (of ship) rumbo; (part of meal) plato; (Golf) campo; **of ~** desde luego, naturalmente; **of ~!** ¡claro!

court [kɔːt] n (royal) corte f; (Law) tribunal m, juzgado; (Tennis etc) pista, cancha; **to ~ (a woman)** cortejar a; **to take to ~** demandar

courtesy [ˈkɜːtəsɪ] n cortesía; **(by) ~ of** por cortesía de; **courtesy bus, courtesy coach** n autobús m gratuito

court: **court-house** [ˈkɔːthaus] (US) n palacio de justicia; **courtroom** [ˈkɔːtrum] n sala de justicia; **courtyard** [ˈkɔːtjɑːd] n patio

cousin [ˈkʌzn] n primo/a; **first ~** primo/a carnal, primo/a hermano/a

cover [ˈkʌvə*] vt cubrir; (feelings, mistake) ocultar; (with lid) tapar; (book etc) forrar; (distance) recorrer; (include) abarcar; (protect: also: Insurance) cubrir; (Press) investigar; (discuss) tratar ▷ n cubierta; (lid) tapa; (for chair etc) funda; (envelope) sobre m; (for book) forro; (of magazine) portada; (shelter) abrigo; (Insurance) cobertura; (of spy) cobertura; **covers** npl (on bed) sábanas; mantas; **to take ~** (shelter) protegerse, resguardarse; **under ~** (indoors) bajo techo; **under ~ of darkness** al amparo de la oscuridad; **under separate ~** (Comm) por separado; **cover up** vi: **to cover up for sb** encubrir a algn; **coverage** n (TV, Press) cobertura; **cover charge** n precio del cubierto; **cover-up** n encubrimiento

cow [kau] n vaca; (inf!: woman) bruja ▷ vt intimidar

coward [ˈkauəd] n cobarde mf; **cowardly** adj

cobarde
cowboy ['kaubɔɪ] n vaquero
cozy ['kəuzɪ] (us) adj = **cosy**
crab [kræb] n cangrejo
crack [kræk] n grieta; (noise) crujido; (drug) crack m ▷ vt agrietar, romper; (nut) cascar; (solve: problem) resolver; (: code) descifrar; (whip etc) chasquear; (knuckles) crujir; (joke) contar ▷ adj (expert) de primera; **crack down on** vt fus adoptar fuertes medidas contra; **cracked** adj (cup, window) rajado; (wall) resquebrajado; **cracker** n (biscuit) crácker m; (Christmas cracker) petardo sorpresa
crackle ['krækl] vi crepitar
cradle ['kreɪdl] n cuna
craft [krɑːft] n (skill) arte m; (trade) oficio; (cunning) astucia; (boat: pl inv) barco; (plane: pl inv) avión m; **craftsman** (irreg) n artesano; **craftsmanship** n (quality) destreza
cram [kræm] vt (fill): **to ~ sth with** llenar algo (a reventar) de; (put): **to ~ sth into** meter algo a la fuerza en ▷ vi (for exams) empollar
cramp [kræmp] n (Med) calambre m; **cramped** adj apretado, estrecho
cranberry ['krænbərɪ] n arándano agrio
crane [kreɪn] n (Tech) grúa; (bird) grulla
crap [kræp] n (inf!) mierda (!)
crash [kræʃ] n (noise) estrépito; (of cars etc) choque m; (of plane) accidente m de aviación; (Comm) quiebra ▷ vt (car, plane) estrellar ▷ vi (car, plane) estrellarse; (two cars) chocar; (Comm) quebrar; **crash course** n curso acelerado; **crash helmet** n casco (protector)
crate [kreɪt] n cajón m de embalaje; (for bottles) caja
crave [kreɪv] vt, vi: **to ~ (for)** ansiar, anhelar
crawl [krɔːl] vi (drag o.s.) arrastrarse; (child) andar a gatas, gatear; (vehicle) avanzar (lentamente) ▷ n (Swimming) crol m
crayfish ['kreɪfɪʃ] n inv (freshwater) cangrejo de río; (saltwater) langosta
crayon ['kreɪən] n lápiz m de color
craze [kreɪz] n (fashion) moda
crazy ['kreɪzɪ] adj (person) loco; (idea) disparatado; (inf: keen): **~ about sb/sth** loco por algn/algo
creak [kriːk] vi (floorboard) crujir; (hinge etc) chirriar, rechinar
cream [kriːm] n (of milk) nata, crema; (lotion) crema; (fig) flor f y nata ▷ adj (colour) color crema; **cream cheese** n queso blanco; **creamy** adj cremoso; (colour) color crema
crease [kriːs] n (fold) pliegue m; (in trousers) raya; (wrinkle) arruga ▷ vt (wrinkle) arrugar ▷ vi (wrinkle up) arrugarse
create [kriː'eɪt] vt crear; **creation** [-ʃən] n creación f; **creative** adj creativo; **creator** n creador(a) m/f
creature ['kriːtʃə*] n (animal) animal m, bicho; (person) criatura
crèche [krɛʃ] n guardería (infantil)
credentials [krɪ'dɛnʃlz] npl (references) referencias fpl; (identity papers) documentos mpl de identidad
credibility [krɛdɪ'bɪlɪtɪ] n credibilidad f
credible ['krɛdɪbl] adj creíble; (trustworthy) digno de confianza
credit ['krɛdɪt] n (of merit) honor m, mérito ▷ vt (Comm) abonar; (believe: also: **give ~ to**) creer, prestar fe a ▷ adj crediticio; **credits** npl (Cinema) fichas fpl técnicas; **to be in ~** (person) tener saldo a favor; **to ~ sb with** (fig) reconocer a algn el mérito de; **credit card** n

tarjeta de crédito
creek [kriːk] n cala, ensenada; (us) riachuelo
creep [kriːp] (pt, pp **crept**) vi arrastrarse
cremate [krɪ'meɪt] vt incinerar
crematorium [krɛmə'tɔːrɪəm] (pl **crematoria**) n crematorio
crept [krɛpt] pt, pp of **creep**
crescent ['krɛsnt] n media luna; (street) calle f (en forma de semicírculo)
cress [krɛs] n berro
crest [krɛst] n (of bird) cresta; (of hill) cima, cumbre f; (of coat of arms) blasón m
crew [kruː] n (of ship etc) tripulación f; (TV, Cinema) equipo; **crew-neck** n cuello a la caja
crib [krɪb] n cuna ▷ vt (inf) plagiar
cricket ['krɪkɪt] n (insect) grillo; (game) críquet m; **cricketer** n jugador(a) m/f de críquet
crime [kraɪm] n (no pl: illegal activities) crimen m; (illegal action) delito; **criminal** ['krɪmɪnl] n criminal mf, delincuente mf ▷ adj criminal; (illegal) delictivo; (law) penal
crimson ['krɪmzn] adj carmesí
cringe [krɪndʒ] vi agacharse, encogerse
cripple ['krɪpl] n lisiado/a, cojo/a ▷ vt lisiar, mutilar
crisis ['kraɪsɪs] (pl **crises**) n crisis f inv
crisp [krɪsp] adj fresco; (vegetables etc) crujiente; (manner) seco; **crispy** adj crujiente
criterion [kraɪ'tɪərɪən] (pl **criteria**) n criterio
critic ['krɪtɪk] n crítico/a; **critical** adj crítico; (illness) grave; **criticism** ['krɪtɪsɪzm] n crítica; **criticize** ['krɪtɪsaɪz] vt criticar
Croat ['krəuæt] adj, n = **Croatian**
Croatia [krəu'eɪʃə] n Croacia; **Croatian** adj, n croata m/f ▷ n (Ling) croata m
crockery ['krɔkərɪ] n loza, vajilla
crocodile ['krɔkədaɪl] n cocodrilo
crocus ['krəukəs] n croco, crocus m
croissant ['krwasɑ̃] n croissant m, medialuna (esp LAM)
crook [kruk] n ladrón/ona m/f; (of shepherd) cayado; **crooked** ['krukɪd] adj torcido; (dishonest) nada honrado
crop [krɔp] n (produce) cultivo; (amount produced) cosecha; (riding crop) látigo de montar ▷ vt cortar, recortar; **crop up** vi surgir, presentarse
cross [krɔs] n cruz f; (hybrid) cruce m ▷ vt (street etc) cruzar, atravesar ▷ adj de mal humor, enojado; **cross off** vt tachar; **cross out** vt tachar; **cross over** vi cruzar; **cross-Channel ferry** ['krɔs'tʃænl-] n transbordador m que cruza el Canal de la Mancha; **crosscountry (race)** n carrera a campo traviesa, cross m; **crossing** n (sea passage) travesía; (also: pedestrian crossing) paso para peatones; **crossing guard** (us) n persona encargada de ayudar a los niños a cruzar la calle; **crossroads** n cruce m, encrucijada; **crosswalk** (us) n paso de peatones; **crossword** n crucigrama m
crotch [krɔtʃ] n (Anat, of garment) entrepierna
crouch [krautʃ] vi agacharse, acurrucarse
crouton ['kruːtɒn] n cubito de pan frito
crow [krəu] n (bird) cuervo; (of cock) canto, cacareo ▷ vi (cock) cantar
crowd [kraud] n muchedumbre f, multitud f ▷ vt (fill) llenar ▷ vi (gather): **to ~ round** reunirse en torno a; (cram): **to ~ in** entrar en tropel; **crowded** adj (full) atestado; (densely populated) superpoblado

crown [kraun] n corona; (of head) coronilla; (for tooth) funda; (of hill) cumbre f ⊳ vt coronar; (fig) completar, rematar; **crown jewels** npl joyas fpl reales

crucial ['kru:ʃl] adj decisivo

crucifix ['kru:sɪfɪks] n crucifijo

crude [kru:d] adj (materials) bruto; (fig: basic) tosco; (: vulgar) ordinario; **crude (oil)** n (petróleo) crudo

cruel ['kruəl] adj cruel; **cruelty** n crueldad f

cruise [kru:z] n crucero ⊳ vi (ship) hacer un crucero; (car) ir a velocidad de crucero

crumb [krʌm] n miga, migaja

crumble ['krʌmbl] vt desmenuzar ⊳ vi (building, also fig) desmoronarse

crumpet ['krʌmpɪt] n ≈ bollo para tostar

crumple ['krʌmpl] vt (paper) estrujar; (material) arrugar

crunch [krʌntʃ] vt (with teeth) mascar; (underfoot) hacer crujir ⊳ n (fig) hora or momento de la verdad; **crunchy** adj crujiente

crush [krʌʃ] n (crowd) aglomeración f; (infatuation): **to have a ~ on sb** estar loco por algn; (drink): **lemon ~** limonada ⊳ vt aplastar; (paper) estrujar; (cloth) arrugar; (fruit) exprimir; (opposition) aplastar; (hopes) destruir

crust [krʌst] n corteza; (of snow, ice) costra; **crusty** adj (bread) crujiente; (person) de mal carácter

crutch [krʌtʃ] n muleta

cry [kraɪ] vi llorar ⊳ n (shriek) chillido; (shout) grito; **cry out** vi (call out, shout) lanzar un grito, echar un grito ⊳ vt gritar

crystal ['krɪstl] n cristal m

cub [kʌb] n cachorro; (also: ~ scout) niño explorador

Cuba ['kju:bə] n Cuba; **Cuban** adj, n cubano/a m/f

cube [kju:b] n cubo ⊳ vt (Math) cubicar

cubicle ['kju:bɪkl] n (at pool) caseta; (for bed) cubículo

cuckoo ['kuku:] n cuco

cucumber ['kju:kʌmbə*] n pepino

cuddle ['kʌdl] vt abrazar ⊳ vi abrazarse

cue [kju:] n (snooker cue) taco; (Theatre etc) señal f

cuff [kʌf] n (of sleeve) puño; (us: of trousers) vuelta; (blow) bofetada ⊳ **off the ~** adv de improviso; **cufflinks** npl gemelos mpl

cuisine [kwɪ'zi:n] n cocina

cul-de-sac ['kʌldəsæk] n callejón m sin salida

cull [kʌl] vt (idea) sacar ⊳ n (of animals) matanza selectiva

culminate ['kʌlmɪneɪt] vi: **to ~ in** terminar en

culprit ['kʌlprɪt] n culpable mf

cult [kʌlt] n culto

cultivate ['kʌltɪveɪt] vt cultivar

cultural ['kʌltʃərəl] adj cultural

culture ['kʌltʃə*] n (also fig) cultura; (Biol) cultivo

cumin ['kʌmɪn] n (spice) comino

cunning ['kʌnɪŋ] n astucia ⊳ adj astuto

cup [kʌp] n taza; (as prize) copa

cupboard ['kʌbəd] n armario; (in kitchen) alacena

cup final n (Football) final f de copa

curator [kjuə'reɪtə*] n director/a m/f

curb [kə:b] vt refrenar; (person) reprimir ⊳ n freno; (us) bordillo

curdle ['kə:dl] vi cuajarse

cure [kjuə*] vt curar ⊳ n cura, curación f; (fig: solution) remedio

curfew ['kə:fju:] n toque m de queda

curiosity [kjuərɪ'ɒsɪtɪ] n curiosidad f

curious ['kjuərɪəs] adj curioso; (person: interested): **to**

be ~ sentir curiosidad

curl [kə:l] n rizo ⊳ vt (hair) rizar ⊳ vi rizarse; **curl up** vi (person) hacerse un ovillo; **curler** n rulo; **curly** adj rizado

currant ['kʌrnt] n pasa (de Corinto); (blackcurrant, redcurrant) grosella

currency ['kʌrnsɪ] n moneda; **to gain ~** (fig) difundirse

current ['kʌrnt] n corriente f ⊳ adj (accepted) corriente; (present) actual; **current account** (BRIT) n cuenta corriente; **current affairs** npl noticias fpl de actualidad; **currently** adv actualmente

curriculum [kə'rɪkjuləm] (pl ~s or **curricula**) n plan m de estudios; **curriculum vitae** n currículum m

curry ['kʌrɪ] n curry m ⊳ vt: **to ~ favour with** buscar favores con; **curry powder** n curry m en polvo

curse [kə:s] vi soltar tacos ⊳ vt maldecir ⊳ n maldición f; (swearword) palabrota, taco

cursor ['kə:sə*] n (Comput) cursor m

curt [kə:t] adj corto, seco

curtain ['kə:tn] n cortina; (Theatre) telón m

curve [kə:v] n curva ⊳ vi (road) hacer una curva; (line etc) curvarse; **curved** adj curvo

cushion ['kuʃən] n cojín m; (of air) colchón m ⊳ vt (shock) amortiguar

custard ['kʌstəd] n natillas fpl

custody ['kʌstədɪ] n custodia; **to take into ~** detener

custom ['kʌstəm] n costumbre f; (Comm) clientela

customer ['kʌstəmə*] n cliente m/f

customized ['kʌstəmaɪzd] adj (car etc) hecho a encargo

customs ['kʌstəmz] npl aduana; **customs officer** n aduanero/a

cut [kʌt] (pt, pp ~) vt cortar; (price) rebajar; (text, programme) acortar; (reduce) reducir ⊳ vi cortar ⊳ n (of garment) corte m; (in skin) cortadura; (in salary etc) rebaja; (in spending) reducción f, recorte m; (slice of meat) tajada; **to ~ a tooth** echar un diente; **to ~ and paste** (Comput) cortar y pegar; **cut back** vt (plants) podar; (production, expenditure) reducir; **cut down** vt (tree) derribar; (reduce) reducir; **cut off** vt cortar; (person, place) aislar; (Tel) desconectar; **cut out** vt (shape) recortar; (stop: activity etc) dejar; (remove) quitar; **cut up** vt cortar (en pedazos); **cutback** n reducción f

cute [kju:t] adj mono

cutlery ['kʌtlərɪ] n cubiertos mpl

cutlet ['kʌtlɪt] n chuleta; (nut etc cutlet) plato vegetariano hecho con nueces y verdura en forma de chuleta

cut-price ['kʌt'praɪs] (BRIT) adj a precio reducido

cut-rate ['kʌt'reɪt] (US) adj = **cut-price**

cutting ['kʌtɪŋ] adj mordaz ⊳ n (BRIT: from newspaper) recorte m; (from plant) esqueje m

CV n abbr = **curriculum vitae**

cwt abbr = **hundredweight(s)**

cybercafé ['saɪbəkæfeɪ] n cibercafé m

cyberspace ['saɪbəspeɪs] n ciberespacio

cycle ['saɪkl] n ciclo; (bicycle) bicicleta ⊳ vi ir en bicicleta; **cycle hire** n alquiler m de bicicletas; **cycle lane** n carril-bici m; **cycle path** n carril-bici m; **cycling** n ciclismo; **cyclist** n ciclista m/f

cyclone ['saɪkləun] n ciclón m

cylinder ['sɪlɪndə*] n cilindro; (of gas) bombona

cymbal ['sɪmbl] n címbalo, platillo

cynical ['sɪnɪkl] adj cínico

Cypriot ['sɪprɪət] adj, n chipriota m/f

Cyprus ['saɪprəs] n Chipre f

cyst [sɪst] n quiste m; **cystitis** [-'taɪtɪs] n cistitis f
czar [zɑ:*] n zar m
Czech [tʃek] adj, n checo/a m/f; **Czech Republic**
n: **the Czech Republic** la República Checa

D [di:] n (Mus) re m
dab [dæb] vt (eyes, wound) tocar (ligeramente); (paint,
cream) poner un poco de
dad [dæd] n = **daddy**
daddy ['dædɪ] n papá m
daffodil ['dæfədɪl] n narciso
daft [dɑ:ft] adj tonto
dagger ['dægə*] n puñal m, daga
daily ['deɪlɪ] adj diario, cotidiano ▷ adv todos los
días, cada día
dairy ['deərɪ] n (shop) lechería; (on farm) vaquería;
dairy produce n productos mpl lácteos
daisy ['deɪzɪ] n margarita
dam [dæm] n presa ▷ vt construir una presa sobre,
represar
damage ['dæmɪdʒ] n lesión f; daño; (dents etc)
desperfectos mpl; (fig) perjuicio ▷ vt dañar, perjudicar;
(spoil, break) estropear; **damages** npl (Law) daños mpl
y perjuicios
damn [dæm] vt condenar; (curse) maldecir ▷ n (inf): **I
don't give a ~** me importa un pito ▷ adj (inf: also: **~ed**)
maldito; **~ (it)!** ¡maldito sea!
damp [dæmp] adj húmedo, mojado ▷ n humedad f
▷ vt (also: **~en**: cloth, rag) mojar; (: enthusiasm) enfriar
dance [dɑ:ns] n baile m ▷ vi bailar; **dance floor** n
pista f de baile; **dancer** n bailador(a) m/f; (professional)
bailarín/ina m/f; **dancing** n baile m
dandelion ['dændɪlaɪən] n diente m de león
dandruff ['dændrəf] n caspa
Dane [deɪn] n danés/esa m/f
danger ['deɪndʒə*] n peligro; (risk) riesgo; **~!** (on
sign) ¡peligro de muerte!; **to be in ~ of** correr riesgo de;
dangerous adj peligroso
dangle ['dæŋgl] vt colgar ▷ vi pender, colgar
Danish ['deɪnɪʃ] adj danés/esa ▷ n (Ling) danés m
dare [deə*] vt: **to ~ sb to do** desafiar a algn a hacer
▷ vi: **to ~ (to) do sth** atreverse a hacer algo; **I ~ say** (I
suppose) puede ser (que); **daring** adj atrevido, osado
▷ n atrevimiento, osadía
dark [dɑ:k] adj oscuro; (hair, complexion) moreno
▷ n: **in the ~** a oscuras; **to be in the ~ about** (fig)
no saber nada de; **after ~** después del anochecer;
darken vt (colour) hacer más oscuro ▷ vi oscurecerse;

darkness n oscuridad f; **darkroom** n cuarto oscuro
darling ['dɑːlɪŋ] adj, n querido/a m/f
dart [dɑːt] n dardo; (in sewing) sisa ▷ vi precipitarse;
dartboard n diana; **darts** n (game) dardos mpl
dash [dæʃ] n (small quantity: of liquid) gota, chorrito;
(sign) raya ▷ vt (throw) tirar; (hopes) defraudar ▷ vi
precipitarse, ir de prisa
dashboard ['dæʃbɔːd] n (Aut) salpicadero
data ['deɪtə] npl datos mpl; **database** n base f de
datos; **data processing** n proceso de datos
date [deɪt] n (day) fecha; (with friend) cita; (fruit)
dátil m ▷ vt fechar; (person) salir con; **~ of birth** fecha
de nacimiento; **to~** adv hasta la fecha; **dated** adj
anticuado
daughter ['dɔːtə*] n hija; **daughter-in-law** n nuera,
hija política
daunting ['dɔːntɪŋ] adj desalentador(a)
dawn [dɔːn] n alba, amanecer m; (fig) nacimiento ▷ vi
(day) amanecer; (fig): **it ~ed on him that ...** cayó en la
cuenta de que ...
day [deɪ] n (working day) jornada; (heyday)
tiempos mpl, días mpl; **the ~ before/after** el día
anterior/siguiente; **the ~ after tomorrow** pasado
mañana; **the ~ before yesterday** anteayer; **the
following ~** el día siguiente; **by ~** de día; **day-care
centre** ['deɪkeə~] n centro de día; (for children)
guardería infantil; **daydream** vi soñar despierto;
daylight n luz f (del día); **day return** (BRIT) n billete m
de ida y vuelta (en un día); **daytime** n día m; **day-to-
day** adj cotidiano; **day trip** n excursión f (de un día)
dazed [deɪzd] adj aturdido
dazzle ['dæzl] vt deslumbrar; **dazzling** adj (light,
smile) deslumbrante; (career) fuerte
DC abbr (= direct current) corriente f continua
dead [dɛd] adj muerto; (limb) dormido; (telephone)
cortado; (battery) agotado ▷ adv (completely)
totalmente; (exactly) exactamente; **to shoot sb ~**
matar a algn a tiros; **~ tired** muerto (de cansancio); **to
stop ~** parar en seco; **dead end** n callejón m sin salida;
deadline n fecha (or hora) tope; **deadly** adj mortal,
fatal; **Dead Sea** n: **the Dead Sea** el Mar Muerto
deaf [dɛf] adj sordo; **deafen** vt ensordecer;
deafening adj ensordecedor/a
deal [diːl] (pt, pp ~t) n (agreement) pacto, convenio;
(business deal) trato ▷ vt dar; (card) repartir; **a great ~
(of)** bastante, mucho; **deal with** vt fus (people) tratar
con; (problem) ocuparse de; (subject) tratar de; **dealer** n
comerciante m/f; (Cards) mano f; **dealings** npl (Comm)
transacciones fpl; (relations) relaciones fpl
dealt [dɛlt] pt, pp of **deal**
dean [diːn] n (Rel) deán m; (Scol: BRIT) decano; (: US)
decano m; rector m
dear [dɪə*] adj querido; (expensive) caro ▷ n: **my ~** mi
querido/a ▷ excl: **~ me!** ¡Dios mío!; **D~ Sir/Madam**
(in letter) Muy Señor Mío, Estimado Señor/Estimada
Señora; **D~ Mr/Mrs X** Estimado/a Señor(a) X; **dearly**
adv (love) mucho; (pay) caro
death [dɛθ] n muerte f; **death penalty** n pena de
muerte; **death sentence** n condena a muerte
debate [dɪ'beɪt] n debate m ▷ vt discutir
debit ['dɛbɪt] n debe m ▷ vt: **to ~ a sum to sb or to
sb's account** cargar una suma en cuenta a algn; **debit
card** n tarjeta f de débito
debris ['dɛbriː] n escombros mpl
debt [dɛt] n deuda; **to be in ~** tener deudas
debut ['deɪbjuː] n presentación f

Dec. abbr (= December) dic
decade ['dɛkeɪd] n decenio, década
decaffeinated [dɪ'kæfɪneɪtɪd] adj descafeinado
decay [dɪ'keɪ] n (of building) desmoronamiento; (of
tooth) caries f inv ▷ vi (rot) pudrirse
deceased [dɪ'siːst] n: **the ~** el(la) difunto/a
deceit [dɪ'siːt] n engaño; **deceive** [dɪ'siːv] vt
engañar
December [dɪ'sɛmbə*] n diciembre m
decency ['diːsənsɪ] n decencia
decent ['diːsənt] adj (proper) decente; (person: kind)
amable, bueno
deception [dɪ'sɛpʃən] n engaño
deceptive [dɪ'sɛptɪv] adj engañoso
decide [dɪ'saɪd] vt (person) decidir; (question,
argument) resolver ▷ vi decidir; **to ~ to/that** decidir
hacer/que; **to ~ on sth** decidirse por algo
decimal ['dɛsɪməl] adj decimal ▷ n decimal m
decision [dɪ'sɪʒən] n decisión f
decisive [dɪ'saɪsɪv] adj decisivo; (person) decidido
deck [dɛk] n (Naut) cubierta; (of bus) piso; (record deck)
platina; (of cards) baraja; **deckchair** n tumbona
declaration [dɛklə'reɪʃən] n declaración f
declare [dɪ'kleə*] vt declarar
decline [dɪ'klaɪn] n disminución f, descenso ▷ vt
rehusar ▷ vi (person, business) decaer; (strength)
disminuir
decorate ['dɛkəreɪt] vt (adorn): **to ~ (with)** adornar
(de), decorar (de); (paint) pintar; (paper) empapelar;
decoration [-'reɪʃən] n adorno; (act) decoración
f; (medal) condecoración f; **decorator** n (workman)
pintor m (decorador)
decrease [n 'diːkriːs, vb diː'kriːs] n: **~ (in)** disminución
f (de) ▷ vt disminuir, reducir ▷ vi reducirse
decree [dɪ'kriː] n decreto
dedicate ['dɛdɪkeɪt] vt dedicar; **dedicated** adj
dedicado; (Comput) especializado; **dedicated word
processor** procesador m de textos especializado
or dedicado; **dedication** [-'keɪʃən] n (devotion)
dedicación f; (in book) dedicatoria
deduce [dɪ'djuːs] vt deducir
deduct [dɪ'dʌkt] vt restar; descontar; **deduction**
[dɪ'dʌkʃən] n (amount deducted) descuento; (conclusion)
deducción f, conclusión f
deed [diːd] n hecho, acto; (feat) hazaña; (Law)
escritura
deem [diːm] vt (formal) juzgar, considerar
deep [diːp] adj profundo; (expressing measurements)
de profundidad; (voice) bajo; (breath) profundo;
(colour) intenso ▷ adv: **the spectators stood 20 ~**
los espectadores se formaron de 20 en fondo; **to be 4
metres ~** tener 4 metros de profundidad; **deep-fry** vt
freír en aceite abundante; **deeply** adv (breathe) a pleno
pulmón; (interested, moved, grateful) profundamente,
hondamente
deer [dɪə*] n inv ciervo
default [dɪ'fɔːlt] n: **by ~ (win)** por incomparecencia
▷ adj (Comput) por defecto
defeat [dɪ'fiːt] n derrota ▷ vt derrotar, vencer
defect [n 'diːfɛkt, vb dɪ'fɛkt] n defecto ▷ vi: **to ~ to
the enemy** pasarse al enemigo; **defective** [dɪ'fɛktɪv]
adj defectuoso
defence [dɪ'fɛns] (US **defense**) n defensa
defend [dɪ'fɛnd] vt defender; **defendant** n acusado/
a; (in civil case) demandado/a; **defender** n defensor(a)
m/f; (Sport) defensa mf

defense [dɪˈfɛns] (*us*) = **defence**

defensive [dɪˈfɛnsɪv] *adj* defensivo ⊳ *n*: **on the ~** a la defensiva

defer [dɪˈfəː*] *vt* aplazar

defiance [dɪˈfaɪəns] *n* desafío; **in ~ of** en contra de; **defiant** [dɪˈfaɪənt] *adj* (*challenging*) desafiante, retador(a)

deficiency [dɪˈfɪʃənsɪ] *n* (*lack*) falta; (*defect*) defecto; **deficient** [dɪˈfɪʃənt] *adj* deficiente

deficit [ˈdɛfɪsɪt] *n* déficit *m*

define [dɪˈfaɪn] *vt* (*word etc*) definir; (*limits etc*) determinar

definite [ˈdɛfɪnɪt] *adj* (*fixed*) determinado; (*obvious*) claro; (*certain*) indudable; **he was ~ about it** no dejó lugar a dudas (sobre ello); **definitely** *adv* desde luego, por supuesto

definition f [dɛfɪˈnɪʃən] *n* definición f; (*clearness*) nitidez f

deflate [diːˈfleɪt] *vt* desinflar

deflect [dɪˈflɛkt] *vt* desviar

defraud [dɪˈfrɔːd] *vt*: **to ~ sb of sth** estafar algo a algn

defrost [diːˈfrɔst] *vt* descongelar

defuse [diːˈfjuːz] *vt* desactivar; (*situation*) calmar

defy [dɪˈfaɪ] *vt* (*resist*) oponerse a; (*challenge*) desafiar; (*fig*): **it defies description** resulta imposible describirlo

degree [dɪˈɡriː] *n* grado; (*Scol*) título; **to have a ~ in maths** tener una licenciatura en matemáticas; **by ~s** (*gradually*) poco a poco, por etapas; **to some ~** hasta cierto punto

dehydrated [diːhaɪˈdreɪtɪd] *adj* deshidratado; (*milk*) en polvo

de-icer [diːˈaɪsə*] *n* descongelador *m*

delay [dɪˈleɪ] *vt* demorar, aplazar; (*person*) entretener; (*train*) retrasar ⊳ *vi* tardar ⊳ *n* demora, retraso; **to be ~ed** retrasarse; **without ~** en seguida, sin tardar

delegate [*n* ˈdɛlɪɡɪt, *vb* ˈdɛlɪɡeɪt] *n* delegado/a ⊳ *vt* (*person*) delegar en; (*task*) delegar

delete [dɪˈliːt] *vt* suprimir, tachar

deli [ˈdɛlɪ] *n* = **delicatessen**

deliberate [*adj* dɪˈlɪbərɪt, *vb* dɪˈlɪbəreɪt] *adj* (*intentional*) intencionado; (*slow*) pausado, lento ⊳ *vi* deliberar; **deliberately** *adv* (*on purpose*) a propósito

delicacy [ˈdɛlɪkəsɪ] *n* delicadeza; (*choice food*) manjar *m*

delicate [ˈdɛlɪkɪt] *adj* delicado; (*fragile*) frágil

delicatessen [dɛlɪkəˈtɛsn] *n* ultramarinos *mpl* finos

delicious [dɪˈlɪʃəs] *adj* delicioso

delight [dɪˈlaɪt] *n* (*feeling*) placer *m*, deleite *m*; (*person, experience etc*) encanto, delicia ⊳ *vt* encantar, deleitar; **to take ~ in** deleitarse en; **delighted** *adj*: **delighted (at or with/to do)** encantado (con/de hacer); **delightful** *adj* encantador(a), delicioso

delinquent [dɪˈlɪŋkwənt] *adj, n* delincuente *mf*

deliver [dɪˈlɪvə*] *vt* (*distribute*) repartir; (*hand over*) entregar; (*message*) comunicar; (*speech*) pronunciar; (*Med*) asistir al parto de; **delivery** *n* reparto, entrega; (*of speaker*) modo de expresarse; (*Med*) parto, alumbramiento; **to take delivery of** recibir

delusion [dɪˈluːʒən] *n* ilusión f, engaño

de luxe [dəˈlʌks] *adj* de lujo

delve [dɛlv] *vi*: **to ~ into** hurgar en

demand [dɪˈmɑːnd] *vt* (*gen*) exigir; (*rights*) reclamar ⊳ *n* exigencia; (*claim*) reclamación f; (*Econ*) demanda; **to be in ~** ser muy solicitado; **on ~** a solicitud; **demanding** *adj* (*boss*) exigente; (*work*) absorbente

demise [dɪˈmaɪz] *n* (*death*) fallecimiento

demo [ˈdɛməʊ] (*inf*) *n abbr* (= *demonstration*) manifestación f

democracy [dɪˈmɔkrəsɪ] *n* democracia; **democrat** [ˈdɛməkræt] *n* demócrata *mf*; **democratic** [dɛməˈkrætɪk] *adj* democrático; (*us*) demócrata

demolish [dɪˈmɔlɪʃ] *vt* derribar, demoler; (*fig: argument*) destruir

demolition [dɛməˈlɪʃən] *n* derribo, demolición f

demon [ˈdiːmən] *n* (*evil spirit*) demonio

demonstrate [ˈdɛmənstreɪt] *vt* demostrar; (*skill, appliance*) mostrar ⊳ *vi* manifestarse; **demonstration** [-ˈstreɪʃən] *n* (*Pol*) manifestación f; (*proof, exhibition*) demostración f; **demonstrator** *n* (*Pol*) manifestante *mf*; (*Comm*) demostrador(a) *m/f*, vendedor(a) *m/f*

demote [dɪˈməʊt] *vt* degradar

den [dɛn] *n* (*of animal*) guarida; (*room*) habitación f

denial [dɪˈnaɪəl] *n* (*refusal*) negativa; (*of report etc*) negación f

denim [ˈdɛnɪm] *n* tela vaquera; **denims** *npl* vaqueros *mpl*

Denmark [ˈdɛnmɑːk] *n* Dinamarca

denomination [dɪnɔmɪˈneɪʃən] *n* valor *m*; (*Rel*) confesión f

denounce [dɪˈnauns] *vt* denunciar

dense [dɛns] *adj* (*crowd*) denso; (*thick*) espeso; (: *foliage etc*) tupido; (*inf: stupid*) torpe

density [ˈdɛnsɪtɪ] *n* densidad f ⊳ **single/double-~ disk** *n* (*Comput*) disco de densidad sencilla/de doble densidad

dent [dɛnt] *n* abolladura ⊳ *vt* (*also*: **make a ~ in**) abollar

dental [ˈdɛntl] *adj* dental; **dental floss** [-flɔs] *n* seda dental; **dental surgery** *n* clínica f dental, consultorio *m* dental

dentist [ˈdɛntɪst] *n* dentista *mf*

dentures [ˈdɛntʃəz] *npl* dentadura (postiza)

deny [dɪˈnaɪ] *vt* negar; (*charge*) rechazar

deodorant [diːˈəʊdərənt] *n* desodorante *m*

depart [dɪˈpɑːt] *vi* irse, marcharse; (*train*) salir; **to ~ from** (*fig: differ from*) apartarse de

department [dɪˈpɑːtmənt] *n* (*Comm*) sección f; (*Scol*) departamento, (*Pol*) ministerio; **department store** *n* gran almacén *m*

departure [dɪˈpɑːtʃə*] *n* partida, ida; (*of train*) salida; (*of employee*) marcha; **a new ~** un nuevo rumbo; **departure lounge** *n* (*at airport*) sala de embarque

depend [dɪˈpɛnd] *vi*: **to ~ on** depender de; (*rely on*) contar con; **it ~s** depende, según; **~ing on the result** según el resultado; **dependant** *n* dependiente *mf*; **dependent** *adj*: **to be dependent on** depender de ⊳ *n* = **dependant**

depict [dɪˈpɪkt] *vt* (*in picture*) pintar; (*describe*) representar

deport [dɪˈpɔːt] *vt* deportar

deposit [dɪˈpɔzɪt] *n* depósito; (*Chem*) sedimento; (*of ore, oil*) yacimiento ⊳ *vt* (*gen*) depositar; **deposit account** (*BRIT*) *n* cuenta de ahorros

depot [ˈdɛpəʊ] *n* (*storehouse*) depósito; (*for vehicles*) parque *m*; (*us*) estación f

depreciate [dɪˈpriːʃɪeɪt] *vi* depreciarse, perder valor

depress [dɪˈprɛs] *vt* deprimir; (*wages etc*) hacer bajar; (*press down*) apretar; **depressed** *adj* deprimido; **depressing** *adj* deprimente; **depression** [dɪˈprɛʃən] *n* depresión f

deprive [dɪˈpraɪv] *vt*: **to ~ sb of** privar a algn de;

deprived adj necesitado
dept. abbr (=department) dto
depth [depθ] n profundidad f; (of cupboard) fondo; **to be in the ~s of despair** sentir la mayor desesperación; **to be out of one's ~** (in water) no hacer pie; (fig) sentirse totalmente perdido
deputy ['depjʊtɪ] adj: **~ head** subdirector(a) m/f ▷ n sustituto/a, suplente mf; (us Pol) diputado/a; (us: also: **~ sheriff**) agente m del sheriff
derail [dɪ'reɪl] vt: **to be ~ed** descarrilarse
derelict ['derɪlɪkt] adj abandonado
derive [dɪ'raɪv] vt (benefit etc) obtener ▷ vi: **to ~ from** derivarse de
descend [dɪ'send] vt, vi descender, bajar; **to ~ from** descender de; **to ~ to** rebajarse a; **descendant** n descendiente mf
descent [dɪ'sent] n descenso; (origin) descendencia
describe [dɪs'kraɪb] vt describir; **description** ['-krɪpʃən] n descripción f; (sort) clase f, género
desert [n 'dezət, vb dɪ'zəːt] n desierto ▷ vt abandonar ▷ vi (Mil) desertar; **deserted** [dɪ'zəːtɪd] adj desierto
deserve [dɪ'zəːv] vt merecer, ser digno de
design [dɪ'zaɪn] n (sketch) bosquejo; (layout, shape) diseño; (pattern) dibujo; (intention) intención f ▷ vt diseñar; **design and technology** (BRIT: Scol) ≈ dibujo y tecnología
designate [vb 'dezɪgneɪt, adj 'dezɪgnɪt] vt (appoint) nombrar; (destine) designar ▷ adj designado
designer [dɪ'zaɪnə*] n diseñador(a) m/f; (fashion designer) modisto/a, diseñador(a) m/f de moda
desirable [dɪ'zaɪərəbl] adj (proper) deseable; (attractive) atractivo
desire [dɪ'zaɪə*] n deseo ▷ vt desear
desk [desk] n (in office) escritorio; (for pupil) pupitre m; (in hotel, at airport) recepción f; (BRIT: in shop, restaurant) caja; **desk-top publishing** ['desktɒp-] n autoedición f
despair [dɪs'pɛə*] n desesperación f ▷ vi: **to ~** perder la esperanza de
despatch [dɪs'pætʃ] n, vt =**dispatch**
desperate ['despərɪt] adj desesperado; (fugitive) peligroso; **to be ~ for sth/to do** necesitar urgentemente algo/hacer; **desperately** adv desesperadamente; (very) terriblemente, gravemente
desperation [despə'reɪʃən] n desesperación f; **in (sheer) ~** (absolutamente) desesperado
despise [dɪs'paɪz] vt despreciar
despite [dɪs'paɪt] prep a pesar de, pese a
dessert [dɪ'zəːt] n postre m; **dessertspoon** n cuchara (de postre)
destination [destɪ'neɪʃən] n destino
destined ['destɪnd] adj: **~ for London** con destino a Londres
destiny ['destɪnɪ] n destino
destroy [dɪs'trɔɪ] vt destruir; (animal) sacrificar
destruction [dɪs'trʌkʃən] n destrucción f
destructive [dɪs'trʌktɪv] adj destructivo, destructor(a)
detach [dɪ'tætʃ] vt separar; (unstick) despegar; **detached** adj (attitude) objetivo, imparcial; **detached house** n ≈ chalé m, ≈ chalet m
detail ['diːteɪl] n detalle m; (no pl; (: in picture etc) detalles mpl; (trifle) pequeñez f ▷ vt detallar; (Mil) destacar; **in ~** detalladamente; **detailed** adj detallado
detain [dɪ'teɪn] vt retener; (in captivity) detener
detect [dɪ'tekt] vt descubrir; (Med, Police) identificar;

(Mil, Radar, Tech) detectar; **detection** [dɪ'tekʃən] n descubrimiento; identificación f; **detective** [dɪ'tektɪv] n detective mf; **detective story** n novela policíaca
detention [dɪ'tenʃən] n detención f, arresto; (Scol) castigo
deter [dɪ'təː*] vt (dissuade) disuadir
detergent [dɪ'təːdʒənt] n detergente m
deteriorate [dɪ'tɪərɪəreɪt] vi deteriorarse
determination [dɪtəːmɪ'neɪʃən] n resolución f
determine [dɪ'təːmɪn] vt determinar; **determined** adj (person) resuelto, decidido; **determined to do** resuelto a hacer
deterrent [dɪ'terənt] n (Mil) fuerza de disuasión
detest [dɪ'test] vt aborrecer
detour ['diːtuə*] n (gen, us Aut) desviación f
detract [dɪ'trækt] vt: **to ~ from** quitar mérito a, desvirtuar
detrimental [detrɪ'mentl] adj: **~ (to)** perjudicial (a)
devastating ['devəsteɪtɪŋ] adj devastador(a); (fig) arrollador(a)
develop [dɪ'veləp] vt desarrollar; (Phot) revelar; (disease) coger; (habit) adquirir; (fault) empezar a tener ▷ vi desarrollarse; (advance) progresar; (facts, symptoms) aparecer; **developing country** n país m en (vías de) desarrollo; **development** n desarrollo; (advance) progreso; (of affair, case) desenvolvimiento; (of land) urbanización f
device [dɪ'vaɪs] n (apparatus) aparato, mecanismo
devil ['devl] n diablo, demonio
devious ['diːvɪəs] adj taimado
devise [dɪ'vaɪz] vt idear, inventar
devote [dɪ'vəʊt] vt: **to ~ sth to** dedicar algo a; **devoted** adj (loyal) leal, fiel; **to be devoted to sb** querer con devoción a algn; **the book is devoted to politics** el libro trata de la política; **devotion** n dedicación f; (Rel) devoción f
devour [dɪ'vaʊə*] vt devorar
devout [dɪ'vaʊt] adj devoto
dew [djuː] n rocío
diabetes [daɪə'biːtiːz] n diabetes f
diabetic [daɪə'betɪk] adj, n diabético/a m/f
diagnose ['daɪəgnəʊz] vt diagnosticar
diagnosis [daɪəg'nəʊsɪs] (pl **-ses**) n diagnóstico
diagonal [daɪ'ægənl] adj, n diagonal f
diagram ['daɪəgræm] n diagrama m, esquema m
dial ['daɪəl] n esfera (SP), cara (LAM); (on radio etc) dial m; (of phone) disco ▷ vt (number) marcar
dialect ['daɪəlekt] n dialecto
dialling code ['daɪəlɪŋ-] n prefijo
dialling tone (us **dial tone**) n (BRIT) señal f or tono de marcar
dialogue ['daɪəlɒg] (us **dialog**) n diálogo
diameter [daɪ'æmɪtə*] n diámetro
diamond ['daɪəmənd] n diamante m; (shape) rombo; **diamonds** npl (Cards) diamantes mpl
diaper ['daɪəpə*] (us) n pañal m
diarrhoea [daɪə'riːə] (us **diarrhea**) n diarrea
diary ['daɪərɪ] n (daily account) diario; (book) agenda
dice [daɪs] n inv dados mpl ▷ vt (Culin) cortar en cuadritos
dictate [dɪk'teɪt] vt dictar; (conditions) imponer; **dictation** ['-teɪʃən] n dictado; (giving of orders) órdenes fpl
dictator [dɪk'teɪtə*] n dictador m
dictionary ['dɪkʃənrɪ] n diccionario
did [dɪd] pt of **do**

didn't ['dɪdənt] = **did not**

die [daɪ] vi morir, (fig: fade) desvanecerse, desaparecer; **to be dying for sth/to do sth** morirse por algo/de ganas de hacer algo; **die down** vi apagarse; (wind) amainar; **die out** vi desaparecer

diesel ['di:zəl] n vehículo con motor Diesel

diet ['daɪət] n dieta; (restricted food) régimen m ▷ vi (also: **be on a ~**) estar a dieta, hacer régimen

differ ['dɪfə*] vi: **to ~ (from)** (be different) ser distinto (a), diferenciarse (de); (disagree) discrepar (de); **difference** n diferencia; (disagreement) desacuerdo; **different** adj diferente, distinto; **differentiate** [-'renʃɪeɪt] vi: **to differentiate (between)** distinguir (entre); **differently** adv de otro modo, en forma distinta

difficult ['dɪfɪkəlt] adj difícil; **difficulty** n dificultad f

dig [dɪg] (pt, pp **dug**) vt (hole, ground) cavar ▷ n (prod) empujón m; (archaeological) excavación f; (remark) indirecta; **to ~ one's nails into** clavar las uñas en; **dig up** vt (information) desenterrar; (plant) desarraigar

digest [vb daɪ'dʒest, n 'daɪdʒest] vt (food) digerir; (facts) asimilar ▷ n resumen m; **digestion** [dɪ'dʒestʃən] n digestión f

digit ['dɪdʒɪt] n (number) dígito; (finger) dedo; **digital** adj digital; **digital camera** n cámara digital; **digital TV** n televisión f digital

dignified ['dɪgnɪfaɪd] adj grave, solemne

dignity ['dɪgnɪtɪ] n dignidad f

digs [dɪgz] (BRIT: inf) npl pensión f, alojamiento

dilemma [daɪ'lemə] n dilema m

dill [dɪl] n eneldo

dilute [daɪ'lu:t] vt diluir

dim [dɪm] adj (light) débil; (outline) indistinto; (room) oscuro; (inf: stupid) lerdo ▷ vt (light) bajar

dime [daɪm] (US) n moneda de diez centavos

dimension [dɪ'menʃən] n dimensión f

diminish [dɪ'mɪnɪʃ] vt, vi disminuir

din [dɪn] n estruendo, estrépito

dine [daɪn] vi cenar; **diner** n (person) comensal mf

dinghy ['dɪŋgɪ] n bote m; (also: **rubber ~**) lancha (neumática)

dingy ['dɪndʒɪ] adj (room) sombrío; (colour) sucio

dining car ['daɪnɪŋ-] (BRIT) n (Rail) coche-comedor m

dining room ['daɪnɪŋ-] n comedor m

dining table n mesa f de comedor

dinner ['dɪnə*] n (evening meal) cena; (lunch) comida; (public) cena, banquete m; **dinner jacket** n smoking m; **dinner party** n cena; **dinner time** n (evening) hora de cenar; (midday) hora de comer

dinosaur ['daɪnəsɔ:*] n dinosaurio

dip [dɪp] n (slope) pendiente m; (in sea) baño; (Culin) salsa ▷ vt (in water) mojar; (ladle etc) meter; (BRIT Aut): **to ~ one's lights** poner luces de cruce ▷ vi (road etc) descender, bajar

diploma [dɪ'pləumə] n diploma m

diplomacy [dɪ'pləuməsɪ] n diplomacia

diplomat ['dɪpləmæt] n diplomático/a; **diplomatic** [dɪplə'mætɪk] adj diplomático

dipstick ['dɪpstɪk] (BRIT) n (Aut) varilla de nivel (del aceite)

dire [daɪə*] adj calamitoso

direct [daɪ'rekt] adj directo; (challenge) claro; (person) franco ▷ vt dirigir; (order): **to ~ sb to do sth** mandar a algn hacer algo ▷ adv directo; **can you ~ me to ...?** ¿puede indicarme dónde está ...?; **direct debit** n domiciliación f bancaria de recibos

direction [dɪ'rekʃən] n dirección f; **sense of ~** sentido de la dirección; **directions** npl (instructions) instrucciones fpl; **~s for use** modo de empleo

directly [dɪ'rektlɪ] adv (in straight line) directamente; (at once) en seguida

director [dɪ'rektə*] n director(a) m/f

directory [dɪ'rektərɪ] n (Tel) guía (telefónica); (Comput) directorio; **directory enquiries** (US **directory assistance**) n (servicio de) información f

dirt [də:t] n suciedad f; (earth) tierra; **dirty** adj sucio; (joke) verde, colorado (MEX) ▷ vt ensuciar; (stain) manchar

disability [dɪsə'bɪlɪtɪ] n incapacidad f

disabled [dɪs'eɪbld] adj: **to be physically ~** ser minusválido/a; **to be mentally ~** ser deficiente mental

disadvantage [dɪsəd'vɑ:ntɪdʒ] n desventaja, inconveniente m

disagree [dɪsə'gri:] vi (differ) discrepar; **to ~ (with)** no estar de acuerdo (con); **disagreeable** adj desagradable; (person) antipático; **disagreement** n desacuerdo

disappear [dɪsə'pɪə*] vi desaparecer; **disappearance** n desaparición f

disappoint [dɪsə'pɔɪnt] vt decepcionar, defraudar; **disappointed** adj decepcionado; **disappointing** adj decepcionante; **disappointment** n decepción f

disapproval [dɪsə'pru:vəl] n desaprobación f

disapprove [dɪsə'pru:v] vi: **to ~ of** ver mal

disarm [dɪs'ɑ:m] vt desarmar; **disarmament** [dɪs'ɑ:məmənt] n desarme m

disaster [dɪ'zɑ:stə*] n desastre m

disastrous [dɪ'zɑ:strəs] adj desastroso

disbelief [dɪsbə'li:f] n incredulidad f

disc [dɪsk] n disco; (Comput) = **disk**

discard [vb dɪs'kɑ:d, n 'dɪskɑ:d] vt (old things) tirar; (fig) descartar

discharge [vb dɪs'tʃɑ:dʒ, n 'dɪstʃɑ:dʒ] vt (task, duty) cumplir; (waste) verter; (patient) dar de alta; (employee) despedir; (soldier) licenciar; (defendant) poner en libertad ▷ n (Elec) descarga; (Med) supuración f; (dismissal) despedida; (of duty) desempeño; (of debt) pago, descargo

discipline ['dɪsɪplɪn] n disciplina ▷ vt disciplinar; (punish) castigar

disc jockey n pinchadiscos mf inv

disclose [dɪs'kləuz] vt revelar

disco ['dɪskəu] n abbr discoteca

discoloured [dɪs'kʌləd] (US **discolored**) adj descolorido

discomfort [dɪs'kʌmfət] n incomodidad f; (unease) inquietud f; (physical) malestar m

disconnect [dɪskə'nekt] vt separar; (Elec etc) desconectar

discontent [dɪskən'tent] n descontento

discontinue [dɪskən'tɪnju:] vt interrumpir; (payments) suspender; **"~d"** (Comm) "ya no se fabrica"

discount [n 'dɪskaunt, vb dɪs'kaunt] n descuento ▷ vt descontar

discourage [dɪs'kʌrɪdʒ] vt desalentar; (advise against): **to ~ sb from doing** disuadir a algn de hacer

discover [dɪs'kʌvə*] vt descubrir; (error) darse cuenta de; **discovery** n descubrimiento

discredit [dɪs'kredɪt] vt desacreditar

discreet [dɪs'kri:t] adj (tactful) discreto; (careful) prudente

discrepancy [dɪs'krepənsɪ] n diferencia

discretion [dɪ'skreʃən] n (tact) discreción f; **at the ~**

of a criterio de

discriminate [dɪ'skrɪmɪneɪt] vi: **to ~ between**
distinguir entre; **to ~ against** discriminar contra;
discrimination [-'neɪʃən] f (*discernment*) perspicacia;
(*bias*) discriminación f

discuss [dɪ'skʌs] vt discutir; (*a theme*) tratar;
discussion [dɪ'skʌʃən] n discusión f

disease [dɪ'ziːz] n enfermedad f

disembark [dɪsɪm'baːk] vt, vi desembarcar

disgrace [dɪs'greɪs] n ignominia; (*shame*) vergüenza,
escándalo ▷ vt deshonrar; **disgraceful** adj
vergonzoso

disgruntled [dɪs'grʌntld] adj disgustado,
descontento

disguise [dɪs'gaɪz] n disfraz m ▷ vt disfrazar; **in ~**
disfrazado

disgust [dɪs'gʌst] n repugnancia ▷ vt repugnar,
dar asco a

disgusted [dɪs'gʌstɪd] adj indignado

disgusting [dɪs'gʌstɪŋ] adj repugnante, asqueroso;
(*behaviour etc*) vergonzoso

dish [dɪʃ] n (*gen*) plato; **to do** or **wash the ~es** fregar
los platos; **dishcloth** n estropajo

dishonest [dɪs'ɒnɪst] adj (*person*) poco honrado,
tramposo; (*means*) fraudulento

dishtowel ['dɪʃtauəl] (us) n estropajo

dishwasher ['dɪʃwɒʃə*] n lavaplatos m inv

disillusion [dɪsɪ'luːʒən] vt desilusionar

disinfectant [dɪsɪn'fɛktənt] n desinfectante m

disintegrate [dɪs'ɪntɪgreɪt] vi disgregarse,
desintegrarse

disk [dɪsk] n (*esp us*) = **disc**; (*Comput*) disco, disquete
m; **single-/double-sided ~** disco de una cara/dos
caras; **disk drive** n disc drive m; **diskette** n = **disk**

dislike [dɪs'laɪk] n antipatía, aversión f ▷ vt tener
antipatía a

dislocate ['dɪsləkeɪt] vt dislocar

disloyal [dɪs'lɔɪəl] adj desleal

dismal ['dɪzml] adj (*gloomy*) deprimente, triste; (*very
bad*) malísimo, fatal

dismantle [dɪs'mæntl] vt desmontar, desarmar

dismay [dɪs'meɪ] n consternación f ▷ vt consternar

dismiss [dɪs'mɪs] vt (*worker*) despedir; (*pupils*) dejar
marchar; (*soldiers*) dar permiso para irse; (*idea, Law*)
rechazar; (*possibility*) descartar; **dismissal** n despido

disobedient [dɪsə'biːdɪənt] adj desobediente

disobey [dɪsə'beɪ] vt desobedecer

disorder [dɪs'ɔːdə*] n desorden m; (*rioting*) disturbios
mpl; (*Med*) trastorno

disorganized [dɪs'ɔːgənaɪzd] adj desorganizado

disown [dɪs'əun] vt (*action*) renegar de; (*person*) negar
cualquier tipo de relación con

dispatch [dɪs'pætʃ] vt enviar ▷ n (*sending*) envío;
(*Press*) informe m; (*Mil*) parte m

dispel [dɪs'pɛl] vt disipar

dispense [dɪs'pɛns] vt (*medicines*) preparar; **dispense
with** vt fus prescindir de; **dispenser** n (*container*)
distribuidor m automático

disperse [dɪs'pɜːs] vt dispersar ▷ vi dispersarse

display [dɪs'pleɪ] n (*in shop window*) escaparate m;
(*exhibition*) exposición f; (*Comput*) visualización f; (*of
feeling*) manifestación f ▷ vt exponer; manifestar;
(*ostentatiously*) lucir

displease [dɪs'pliːz] vt (*offend*) ofender; (*annoy*)
fastidiar

disposable [dɪs'pəuzəbl] adj desechable; (*income*)

disponible

disposal [dɪs'pəuzl] n (*of rubbish*) destrucción f; **at
one's ~** a su disposición

dispose [dɪs'pəuz] vi: **to ~ of** (*unwanted goods*)
deshacerse de; (*problem etc*) resolver; **disposition**
[dɪspə'zɪʃən] n (*nature*) temperamento; (*inclination*)
propensión f

disproportionate [dɪsprə'pɔːʃənət] adj
desproporcionado

dispute [dɪs'pjuːt] n disputa; (*also*: **industrial ~**)
conflicto (laboral) ▷ vt (*argue*) disputar, discutir;
(*question*) cuestionar

disqualify [dɪs'kwɒlɪfaɪ] vt (*Sport*) desclasificar; **to
~ sb for sth/from doing sth** incapacitar a algn para
algo/hacer algo

disregard [dɪsrɪ'gɑːd] vt (*ignore*) no hacer caso de

disrupt [dɪs'rʌpt] vt (*plans*) desbaratar, trastornar;
(*conversation*) interrumpir; **disruption** [dɪs'rʌpʃən] n
trastorno, desbaratamiento; interrupción f

dissatisfaction [dɪssætɪsfækʃən] n disgusto,
descontento

dissatisfied [dɪs'sætɪsfaɪd] adj insatisfecho

dissect [dɪ'sɛkt] vt disecar

dissent [dɪ'sɛnt] n disensión f

dissertation [dɪsə'teɪʃən] n tesina

dissolve [dɪ'zɒlv] vt disolver ▷ vi disolverse; **to ~
in(to) tears** deshacerse en lágrimas

distance ['dɪstəns] n distancia; **in the ~** a lo lejos

distant ['dɪstənt] adj lejano; (*manner*) reservado, frío

distil [dɪs'tɪl] (us **distill**) vt destilar; **distillery** n
destilería

distinct [dɪs'tɪŋkt] adj (*different*) distinto; (*clear*) claro;
(*unmistakeable*) inequívoco; **as ~ from** a diferencia
de; **distinction** [dɪs'tɪŋkʃən] n distinción f; (*honour*)
honor m; (*in exam*) sobresaliente m; **distinctive** adj
distintivo

distinguish [dɪs'tɪŋgwɪʃ] vt distinguir; **to ~ o.s.**
destacarse; **distinguished** adj (*eminent*) distinguido

distort [dɪs'tɔːt] vt distorsionar; (*shape, image*)
deformar

distract [dɪs'trækt] vt distraer; **distracted** adj
distraído; **distraction** [dɪs'trækʃən] n distracción f;
(*confusion*) aturdimiento

distraught [dɪs'trɔːt] adj loco de inquietud

distress [dɪs'trɛs] n (*anguish*) angustia, aflicción f
▷ vt afligir; **distressing** adj angustioso; doloroso

distribute [dɪs'trɪbjuːt] vt distribuir; (*share out*)
repartir; **distribution** [-'bjuːʃən] n distribución f,
reparto; **distributor** n (*Aut*) distribuidor m; (*Comm*)
distribuidora

district ['dɪstrɪkt] n (*of country*) zona, región f; (*of
town*) barrio; (*Admin*) distrito; **district attorney** (us)
n fiscal mf

distrust [dɪs'trʌst] n desconfianza ▷ vt desconfiar
de

disturb [dɪs'tɜːb] vt (*person: bother, interrupt*)
molestar; (: *upset*) perturbar, inquietar; (*disorganize*)
alterar; **disturbance** n (*upheaval*) perturbación f;
(*political etc: gen pl*) disturbio; (*of mind*) trastorno;
disturbed adj (*worried, upset*) preocupado,
angustiado; **emotionally disturbed** trastornado;
(*childhood*) inseguro; **disturbing** adj inquietante,
perturbador(a) f

ditch [dɪtʃ] n zanja; (*irrigation ditch*) acequia ▷ vt
(*inf: partner*) deshacerse de; (: *plan, car etc*) abandonar

ditto ['dɪtəu] adv ídem, lo mismo

dive [daɪv] n (from board) salto; (underwater) buceo; (of submarine) sumersión f ▷ vi (swimmer: into water) saltar; (: under water) zambullirse, bucear; (fish, submarine) sumergirse; (bird) lanzarse en picado; **to ~ into** (bag etc) meter la mano en; (place) meterse de prisa en; **diver** n (underwater) buzo

diverse [daɪˈvɜːs] adj diversos/as, varios/as

diversion [daɪˈvəːʃən] n (BRIT Aut) desviación f; (distraction, Mil) diversión f; (of funds) distracción f

diversity [daɪˈvɜːsɪtɪ] n diversidad f

divert [daɪˈvɜːt] vt (turn aside) desviar

divide [dɪˈvaɪd] vt dividir; (separate) separar ▷ vi dividirse; (road) bifurcarse; **divided highway** (us) n carretera de doble calzada

divine [dɪˈvaɪn] adj (also fig) divino

diving [ˈdaɪvɪŋ] n (Sport) salto; (underwater) buceo; **diving board** n trampolín m

division [dɪˈvɪʒən] n división f; (sharing out) reparto; (disagreement) diferencias fpl; (Comm) sección f

divorce [dɪˈvɔːs] n divorcio ▷ vt divorciarse de; **divorced** adj divorciado/a; **divorcee** [-ˈsiː] n divorciado/a

D.I.Y. (BRIT) adj, n abbr = **do-it-yourself**

dizzy [ˈdɪzɪ] adj (spell) de mareo; **to feel ~** marearse

DJ n abbr = **disc jockey**

DNA n abbr (= deoxyribonucleic acid) ADN m

○ KEYWORD

do [duː] (pt **did**, pp **done**) n (inf: party etc): **we're having a little do on Saturday** damos una fiestecita el sábado; **it was rather a grand do** fue un acontecimiento a lo grande
▷ aux vb **1** (in negative constructions: not translated): **I don't understand** no entiendo
2 (to form questions: not translated):
didn't you know? ¿no lo sabías?; **what do you think?** ¿qué opinas?
3 (for emphasis, in polite expressions):
people do make mistakes sometimes sí que se cometen errores a veces; **she does seem rather late** a mí también me parece que se ha retrasado; **do sit down/help yourself** siéntate/sírvete por favor; **do take care!** ¡ten cuidado!, ¡te pido!)
4 (used to avoid repeating vb): **she sings better than I do** canta mejor que yo; **do you agree? – yes, I do/no, I don't** ¿estás de acuerdo? – sí (lo estoy)/no (lo estoy); **she lives in Glasgow – so do I** vive en Glasgow – yo también; **he didn't like it and neither did we** no le gustó y a nosotros tampoco; **who made this mess? – I did** ¿quién hizo esta chapuza? – yo; **he asked me to help him and I did** me pidió que le ayudara y lo hice
5 (in question tags): **you like him, don't you?** te gusta, ¿verdad? or ¿no?; **I don't know him, do I?** creo que no le conozco
▷ vt **1** (gen, carry out, perform etc): **what are you doing tonight?** ¿qué haces esta noche?; **what can I do for you?** ¿en qué puedo servirle?; **to do the washing-up/cooking** fregar los platos/cocinar; **to do one's teeth/hair/nails** lavarse los dientes/arreglarse el pelo/arreglarse las uñas
2 (Aut etc): **the car was doing 100** el coche iba a 100; **we've done 200 km already** ya hemos hecho 200 km; **he can do 100 in that car** puede ir a 100 en ese coche
▷ vi **1** (act, behave) hacer; **do as I do** haz como yo
2 (get on, fare): **he's doing well/badly at school** va

bien/mal en la escuela; **the firm is doing well** la empresa anda or va bien; **how do you do?** mucho gusto; (less formal) ¿qué tal?
3 (suit): **will it do?** ¿sirve?, ¿está or va bien?
4 (be sufficient) bastar; **will £10 do?** ¿será bastante con £10?; **that'll do** así está bien; **that'll do!** (in annoyance) ¡ya está bien!, ¡basta ya!; **to make do (with)** arreglárselas (con)

do up vt (laces) atar; (zip, dress, shirt) abrochar; (renovate: room, house) renovar

do with vt fus (need): **I could do with a drink/some help** no me vendría mal un trago/un poco de ayuda; (be connected) tener que ver con; **what has it got to do with you?** ¿qué tiene que ver contigo?

do without vi pasar sin; **if you're late for tea then you'll do without** si llegas tarde tendrás que quedarte sin cenar
▷ vt fus pasar sin; **I can do without a car** puedo pasar sin coche

dock [dɒk] n (Naut) muelle m; (Law) banquillo (de los acusados) ▷ vi (enter dock) atracar (la) muelle; (Space) acoplarse; **docks** npl (Naut) muelles mpl, puerto sg

doctor [ˈdɒktə*] n médico/a; (Ph.D. etc) doctor(a) m/f ▷ vt (drink etc) adulterar; **Doctor of Philosophy** n Doctor en Filosofía y Letras

document [ˈdɒkjʊmənt] n documento; **documentary** [-ˈmentərɪ] adj documental ▷ n documental m; **documentation** [-menˈteɪʃən] n documentación f

dodge [dɒdʒ] n (fig) truco ▷ vt evadir; (blow) esquivar

dodgy [ˈdɒdʒɪ] adj (inf: uncertain) dudoso; (suspicious) sospechoso; (risky) arriesgado

does [dʌz] vb see **do**

doesn't [ˈdʌznt] = **does not**

dog [dɒg] n perro ▷ vt seguir los pasos de; (bad luck) perseguir; **doggy bag** [ˈdɒgɪ-] n bolsa para llevarse las sobras de la comida

do-it-yourself [ˈduːɪtjɔːˈsɛlf] n bricolaje m

dole [dəʊl] (BRIT) n (payment) subsidio de paro; **on the ~** parado

doll [dɒl] n muñeca; (us: inf: woman) muñeca, gachí f

dollar [ˈdɒlə*] n dólar m

dolphin [ˈdɒlfɪn] n delfín m

dome [dəʊm] n (Arch) cúpula

domestic [dəˈmestɪk] adj (animal, duty) doméstico; (flight, policy) nacional; **domestic appliance** n aparato m doméstico, aparato m de uso doméstico

dominant [ˈdɒmɪnənt] adj dominante

dominate [ˈdɒmɪneɪt] vt dominar

domino [ˈdɒmɪnəʊ] (pl **~es**) n ficha de dominó; **dominoes** n (game) dominó

donate [dəˈneɪt] vt donar; **donation** [dəˈneɪʃən] n donativo

done [dʌn] pp of **do**

donkey [ˈdɒŋkɪ] n burro

donor [ˈdəʊnə*] n donante mf; **donor card** n carnet m de donante

don't [dəʊnt] = **do not**

donut [ˈdəʊnʌt] (us) n = **doughnut**

doodle [ˈduːdl] vi hacer dibujitos or garabatos

doom [duːm] n (fate) suerte f ▷ vt: **to be ~ed to failure** estar condenado al fracaso

door [dɔː*] n puerta; **doorbell** n timbre m; **door handle** n tirador m; (of car) manija f; **doorknob** n pomo m de la puerta, manilla f (LAM); **doorstep** n peldaño; **doorway** n entrada, puerta

dope [dəʊp] n (inf: illegal drug) droga; (: person) imbécil mf ⊳ vt (horse etc) drogar

dormitory ['dɔ:mɪtrɪ] n (BRIT) dormitorio; (US) colegio mayor

DOS n abbr (= disk operating system) DOS m

dosage ['dəʊsɪdʒ] n dosis f inv

dose [dəʊs] n dosis f inv

dot [dɒt] n punto ⊳ vi: **~ted with** salpicado de; **on the ~** en punto; **dotcom** [dɒt'kɒm] n puntocom f inv; **dotted line** n: **to sign on the dotted line** firmar

double ['dʌbl] adj doble ⊳ adv (twice): **to cost ~** costar el doble ⊳ n doble m ⊳ vt doblar ⊳ vi doblarse; **on the ~**, **at the ~** (BRIT) corriendo; **double back** vi (person) volver sobre sus pasos; **double bass** n contrabajo; **double bed** n cama de matrimonio; **double-check** vt volver a revisar ⊳ vi: **I'll double-check** voy a revisarlo otra vez; **double-click** vi (Comput) hacer doble clic; **double-cross** vt (trick) engañar; (betray) traicionar; **doubledecker** n autobús m de dos pisos; **double glazing** (BRIT) n doble acristalamiento; **double room** n habitación f doble; **doubles** n (Tennis) juego de dobles; **double yellow lines** npl (BRIT: Aut) línea doble amarilla de prohibido aparcar, ≈ línea f sg amarilla continua

doubt [daʊt] n duda ⊳ vt dudar; (suspect) dudar de; **to ~ that** dudar que; **doubtful** adj dudoso; (person): **to be doubtful about sth** tener dudas sobre algo; **doubtless** adv sin duda

dough [dəʊ] n masa, pasta; **doughnut** (US **donut**) n ≈ rosquilla

dove [dʌv] n paloma

down [daʊn] n (feathers) plumón m, flojel m ⊳ adv (downwards) abajo, hacia abajo; (on the ground) por o en tierra ⊳ prep abajo ⊳ vt (inf: drink) beberse; **~ with X!** ¡abajo X!; **down-and-out** n vagabundo/a; **downfall** n caída, ruina; **downhill** adv: **to go downhill** (also fig) ir cuesta abajo

Downing Street ['daʊnɪŋ-] n (BRIT) Downing Street f

down: download vt (Comput) bajar; **downright** adj (nonsense, lie) manifiesto; (refusal) terminante

Down's syndrome ['daʊnz-] n síndrome m de Down

down: downstairs adv (below) (en el piso de) abajo; (downwards) escaleras abajo; **down-to-earth** adj práctico; **downtown** adv en el centro de la ciudad; **down under** adv en Australia (or Nueva Zelanda); **downward** ['-wəd] adj, adv hacia abajo; **downwards** ['-wədz] adv hacia abajo

doz. abbr = **dozen**

doze [dəʊz] vi dormitar

dozen ['dʌzn] n docena; **a ~ books** una docena de libros; **~s of** cantidad de

Dr. abbr = **doctor**; **drive**

drab [dræb] adj gris, monótono

draft [drɑ:ft] n (first copy) borrador m; (Pol: of bill) anteproyecto; (US: call-up) quinta ⊳ vt (plan) preparar; (write roughly) hacer un borrador de; see also **draught**

drag [dræg] vt arrastrar; (river) dragar, rastrear ⊳ n (time) pasar despacio; (play, film etc) hacerse pesado ⊳ n (inf) lata; (women's clothing): **in ~** vestido de travesti; **to ~ and drop** (Comput) arrastrar y soltar

dragon ['drægən] n dragón m

dragonfly ['drægənflaɪ] n libélula

drain [dreɪn] n desaguadero; (in street) sumidero; (source of loss): **to be a ~ on** consumir, agotar ⊳ vt (land, marshes) desaguar; (reservoir) desecar; (vegetables) escurrir ⊳ vi escurrirse; **drainage** n (act) desagüe m; (Med, Agr) drenaje m; (sewage) alcantarillado; **drainpipe** n tubo de desagüe

drama ['drɑ:mə] n (art) teatro; (play) drama m; (excitement) emoción f; **dramatic** [drə'mætɪk] adj dramático; (sudden, marked) espectacular

drank [dræŋk] pt of **drink**

drape [dreɪp] vt (cloth) colocar; (flag) colgar; **drapes** npl (US) cortinas fpl

drastic ['dræstɪk] adj (measure) severo; (change) radical, drástico

draught [drɑ:ft] (US **draft**) n (of air) corriente f de aire; (Naut) calado; **on ~** (beer) de barril; **draught beer** n cerveza de barril; **draughts** (BRIT) n (game) juego de damas

draw [drɔ:] (pt **drew**, pp **drawn**) vt (picture) dibujar; (cart) tirar de; (curtain) correr; (take out) sacar; (attract) atraer; (money) retirar; (wages) cobrar ⊳ vi (Sport) empatar ⊳ n (Sport) empate m; (lottery) sorteo; **draw out** vi (lengthen) alargarse ⊳ vt sacar; **draw up** vi (stop) pararse ⊳ vt (chair) acercar; (document) redactar; **drawback** n inconveniente m, desventaja

drawer [drɔ:*] n cajón m

drawing ['drɔ:ɪŋ] n dibujo; **drawing pin** (BRIT) n chincheta; **drawing room** n salón m

drawn [drɔ:n] pp of **draw**

dread [dred] n pavor m, terror m ⊳ vt temer, tener miedo or pavor a; **dreadful** adj horroroso

dream [dri:m] (pt, pp **-ed** or **-t**) n sueño ⊳ vt, vi soñar; **dreamer** n soñador(a) m/f

dreamt [dremt] pt, pp of **dream**

dreary ['drɪərɪ] adj monótono

drench [drentʃ] vt empapar

dress [dres] n vestido; (clothing) ropa ⊳ vt vestir; (wound) vendar ⊳ vi vestirse; **to get ~ed** vestirse; **dress up** vi vestirse de etiqueta; (in fancy dress) disfrazarse; **dress circle** (BRIT) n principal m; **dresser** n (furniture) aparador m; (: US) cómoda (con espejo); **dressing** n (Med) vendaje m; (Culin) aliño; **dressing gown** (BRIT) n bata; **dressing room** n (Theatre) camarín m; (Sport) vestuario; **dressing table** n tocador m; **dressmaker** n modista, costurera

drew [dru:] pt of **draw**

dribble ['drɪbl] vi (baby) babear ⊳ vt (ball) regatear

dried [draɪd] adj (fruit) seco; (milk) en polvo

drier ['draɪə*] n = **dryer**

drift [drɪft] n (of current etc) flujo; (of snow) ventisquero; (meaning) significado ⊳ vi (boat) ir a la deriva; (sand, snow) amontonarse

drill [drɪl] n (drill bit) broca; (tool for DIY etc) taladro; (of dentist) fresa; (for mining etc) perforadora, barrena; (Mil) instrucción f ⊳ vt perforar, taladrar; (troops) enseñar la instrucción a ⊳ vi (for oil) perforar

drink [drɪŋk] (pt **drank**, pp **drunk**) n bebida; (sip) trago ⊳ vt, vi beber; **to have a ~** tomar algo; tomar una copa or un trago; **a ~ of water** un trago de agua; **drink-driving** n: **to be charged with drink-driving** ser acusado de conducir borracho or en estado de embriaguez; **drinker** n bebedor/a m/f; **drinking water** n agua potable

drip [drɪp] n (act) goteo; (one drip) gota; (Med) gota a gota m ⊳ vi gotear

drive [draɪv] (pt **drove**, pp **driven**) n (journey) viaje m (en coche); (also: **~way**) entrada; (energy) energía, vigor m; (Comput: also: **disk ~**) drive m ▷ vt (car) conducir (SP), manejar (LAM); (nail) clavar; (push) empujar; (Tech: motor) impulsar ▷ vi (Aut: at controls) conducir; (: travel) pasearse en coche; **left-/right-hand ~** conducción f a la izquierda/derecha; **to ~ sb mad** volverle loco a algn; **drive out** vt (force out) expulsar, echar; **drive-in** adj (esp US): **drive-in cinema** autocine m

driven [drɪvn] pp of **drive**

driver ['draɪvə*] n conductor(a) m/f (SP), chofer mf (LAM); (of taxi, bus) chófer mf (SP), chofer mf (LAM); **driver's license** (US) n carnet m de conducir

driveway ['draɪvweɪ] n entrada

driving ['draɪvɪŋ] n el conducir (SP), el manejar (LAM); **driving instructor** n profesor(a) m/f de autoescuela (SP), instructor(a) m/f de manejar (LAM); **driving lesson** n clase f de conducir (SP) or manejar (LAM); **driving licence** (BRIT) n licencia de manejo (LAM), carnet m de conducir (SP); **driving test** n examen m de conducir (SP) or manejar (LAM)

drizzle ['drɪzl] n llovizna

droop [druːp] vi (flower) marchitarse; (shoulders) encorvarse; (head) inclinarse

drop [drɒp] n (of water) gota; (lessening) baja; (fall) caída ▷ vt dejar caer; (voice, eyes, price) bajar; (passenger) dejar; (omit) omitir ▷ vi (object) caer; (wind) amainar; **drop in** vi (inf: visit): **to drop in (on)** pasar por casa (de); **drop off** vi (sleep) dormirse ▷ vt (passenger) dejar; **drop out** vi (withdraw) retirarse

drought [draut] n sequía

drove [drəuv] pt of **drive**

drown [draun] vt ahogar ▷ vi ahogarse

drowsy ['drauzɪ] adj soñoliento; **to be ~** tener sueño

drug [drʌg] n medicamento; (narcotic) droga ▷ vt drogar; **to be on ~s** drogarse; **drug addict** n drogadicto/a; **drug dealer** n traficante mf de drogas; **druggist** (US) n farmacéutico; **drugstore** (US) n farmacia

drum [drʌm] n tambor m; (for oil, petrol) bidón m; **drums** npl batería; **drummer** n tambor m

drunk [drʌŋk] pp of **drink** ▷ adj borracho ▷ n (also: **~ard**) borracho/a; **drunken** adj borracho; (laughter, party) de borrachos

dry [draɪ] adj seco; (day) sin lluvia; (climate) árido, seco ▷ vt secar; (tears) enjugarse ▷ vi secarse; **dry off** vi secarse ▷ vt secar; **dry up** vi (river) secarse; **dry-cleaner's** n tintorería; **dry-cleaning** n lavado en seco; **dryer** n (for hair) secador m; (US: for clothes) secadora

DSS n abbr = **Department of Social Security**

D & T (BRIT: Scol) n abbr (= design and technology) = dibujo y tecnología

DTP n abbr (= desk-top publishing) autoedición f

dual ['djuəl] adj doble; **dual carriageway** (BRIT) n carretera de doble calzada

dubious ['djuːbɪəs] adj indeciso; (reputation, company) sospechoso

duck [dʌk] n pato ▷ vi agacharse

due [djuː] adj (owed): **he is ~ £10** se le deben 10 libras; (expected: event): **the meeting is ~ on Wednesday** la reunión tendrá lugar el miércoles; (: arrival): **the train is ~ at 8am** el tren tiene su llegada para las 8; (proper) debido ▷ n: **to give sb his (or her) ~** ser justo con algn ▷ adv: **~ north** derecho al norte

duel ['djuəl] n duelo

duet [djuː'ɛt] n dúo

dug [dʌg] pt, pp of **dig**

duke [djuːk] n duque m

dull [dʌl] adj (light) débil; (stupid) torpe; (boring) pesado; (sound, pain) sordo; (weather, day) gris ▷ vt (pain, grief) aliviar; (mind, senses) entorpecer

dumb [dʌm] adj mudo; (pej: stupid) estúpido

dummy ['dʌmɪ] n (tailor's dummy) maniquí m; (mock-up) maqueta; (BRIT: for baby) chupete m ▷ adj falso, postizo

dump [dʌmp] n (also: **rubbish ~**) basurero, vertedero; (inf: place) cuchitril m ▷ vt (put down) dejar; (get rid of) deshacerse de; (Comput: data) transferir

dumpling ['dʌmplɪŋ] n bola de masa hervida

dune [djuːn] n duna

dungarees [dʌŋgə'riːz] npl mono

dungeon ['dʌndʒən] n calabozo

duplex ['djuːplɛks] n dúplex m

duplicate [n 'djuːplɪkət, vb 'djuːplɪkeɪt] n duplicado ▷ vt duplicar; (photocopy) fotocopiar; (repeat) repetir; **in ~** por duplicado

durable ['djuərəbl] adj duradero

duration [djuə'reɪʃən] n duración f

during ['djuərɪŋ] prep durante

dusk [dʌsk] n crepúsculo, anochecer m

dust [dʌst] n polvo ▷ vt quitar el polvo a, desempolvar; (cake etc) to ~ **with** espolvorear de; **dustbin** (BRIT) n cubo or bote m (MEX) or tacho (SC) de la basura; **duster** n paño, trapo; **dustman** (BRIT: irreg) n basurero; **dustpan** n cogedor m; **dusty** adj polvoriento

Dutch [dʌtʃ] adj holandés/esa ▷ n (Ling) holandés m; **the Dutch** npl los holandeses; **to go ~** (inf) pagar cada uno lo suyo; **Dutchman** (irreg) n holandés m; **Dutchwoman** (irreg) n holandesa

duty ['djuːtɪ] n deber m; (tax) derechos mpl de aduana; **on ~** de servicio; (at night etc) de guardia; **off ~** libre (de servicio); **duty-free** adj libre de impuestos

duvet ['duːveɪ] (BRIT) n edredón m

DVD n abbr (= digital versatile or video disc) DVD m; **DVD player** n lector m de DVD; **DVD writer** n grabadora de DVD

dwarf [dwɔːf] (pl **dwarves**) n enano/a ▷ vt empequeñecer

dwell [dwɛl] (pt, pp **dwelt**) vi morar; **dwell on** vt fus explayarse en

dwelt [dwɛlt] pt, pp of **dwell**

dwindle ['dwɪndl] vi disminuir

dye [daɪ] n tinte m ▷ vt teñir

dying ['daɪɪŋ] adj moribundo

dynamic [daɪ'næmɪk] adj dinámico

dynamite ['daɪnəmaɪt] n dinamita

dyslexia [dɪs'lɛksɪə] n dislexia

dyslexic [dɪs'lɛksɪk] adj, n disléxico/a m/f

e

E [iː] n (Mus) mi m

E111 n abbr (= form E111) impreso E111

each [iːtʃ] adj cada inv ▷ pron cada uno; **~ other** el uno al otro; **they hate ~ other** se odian (entre ellos o mutuamente); **they have 2 books ~** tienen 2 libros por persona

eager ['iːgə*] adj (keen) entusiasmado; **to be ~ to do sth** tener muchas ganas de hacer algo, impacientarse por hacer algo; **to be ~ for** tener muchas ganas de

eagle ['iːgl] n águila

ear [ɪə*] n oreja; oído; (of corn) espiga; **earache** n dolor m de oídos; **eardrum** n tímpano

earl [əːl] n conde m

earlier ['əːlɪə*] adj anterior ▷ adv antes

early ['əːlɪ] adv temprano; (before time) con tiempo, con anticipación ▷ adj temprano; (settlers etc) primitivo; (death, departure) prematuro; (reply) pronto; **to have an ~ night** acostarse temprano; **in the ~ or ~ in the spring/19th century** a principios de primavera/del siglo diecinueve; **early retirement** n jubilación f anticipada

earmark ['ɪəmɑːk] vt: **to ~ (for)** reservar (para), destinar (a)

earn [əːn] vt (salary) percibir; (interest) devengar; (praise) merecerse

earnest ['əːnɪst] adj (wish) fervoroso; (person) serio, formal; **in ~** en serio

earnings ['əːnɪŋz] npl (personal) sueldo, ingresos mpl; (company) ganancias fpl

ear: earphones ['ɪəfəʊnz] npl auriculares mpl; **earplugs** npl tapones mpl para los oídos; **earring** n pendiente m, arete m

earth [əːθ] n tierra; (BRIT Elec) cable m de toma de tierra ▷ vt (BRIT Elec) conectar a tierra; **earthquake** n terremoto

ease [iːz] n facilidad f; (comfort) comodidad f ▷ vt (lessen: problem) mitigar; (: pain) aliviar; (: tension) reducir; **to ~ sth in/out** meter/sacar algo con cuidado; **at ~!** (Mil) ¡descansen!

easily ['iːzɪlɪ] adv fácilmente

east [iːst] n este m ▷ adj del este, oriental; (wind) del este ▷ adv al este, hacia el este; **the E~** el Oriente; (Pol) los países del Este; **eastbound** adj en dirección este

Easter ['iːstə*] n Pascua (de Resurrección); **Easter egg** n huevo de Pascua

eastern ['iːstən] adj del este, oriental; (oriental) oriental

Easter Sunday n Domingo de Resurrección

easy ['iːzɪ] adj fácil; (simple) sencillo; (comfortable) holgado, cómodo; (relaxed) tranquilo ▷ adv: **to take it** or **things ~** (not worry) tomarlo con calma; (rest) descansar; **easy-going** adj acomodadizo

eat [iːt] (pt **ate**, pp **eaten**) vt comer; **eat out** vi comer fuera

eavesdrop ['iːvzdrɔp] vi: **to ~ (on)** escuchar a escondidas

e-book ['iːbuk] n libro electrónico

e-business ['iːbɪznɪs] n (company) negocio electrónico; (commerce) comercio electrónico

EC n abbr (= European Community) CE f

eccentric [ɪk'sɛntrɪk] adj, n excéntrico/a m/f

echo ['ɛkəʊ] (pl **~es**) n eco ▷ vt (sound) repetir ▷ vi resonar, hacer eco

eclipse [ɪ'klɪps] n eclipse m

eco-friendly ['iːkəʊfrɛndlɪ] adj ecológico

ecological [iːkə'lɔdʒɪkl] adj ecológico

ecology [ɪ'kɔlədʒɪ] n ecología

e-commerce n abbr comercio electrónico

economic [iːkə'nɔmɪk] adj económico; (business etc) rentable; **economical** adj económico; **economics** n (Scol) economía ▷ npl (of project etc) rentabilidad f

economist [ɪ'kɔnəmɪst] n economista m/f

economize [ɪ'kɔnəmaɪz] vi economizar, ahorrar

economy [ɪ'kɔnəmɪ] n economía; **economy class** n (Aviat) clase f económica; **economy class syndrome** n síndrome m de la clase turista

ecstasy ['ɛkstəsɪ] n éxtasis m inv; (drug) éxtasis m inv; **ecstatic** [ɛks'tætɪk] adj extático

eczema ['ɛksɪmə] n eczema m

edge [ɛdʒ] n (of knife) filo; (of object) borde m; (of lake) orilla ▷ vt (Sewing) ribetear; **on ~** (fig) = **edgy; to ~ away from** alejarse poco a poco de

edgy ['ɛdʒɪ] adj nervioso, inquieto

edible ['ɛdɪbl] adj comestible

Edinburgh ['ɛdɪnbərə] n Edimburgo

edit ['ɛdɪt] vt (be editor of) dirigir; (text, report) corregir, preparar; **edition** [ɪ'dɪʃən] n edición f; **editor** n (of newspaper) director(a) m/f; (of column) **foreign/ political editor** n encargado de la sección de extranjero/ política; (of book) redactor(a) m/f; **editorial** [-'tɔːrɪəl] adj editorial ▷ n editorial m

educate ['ɛdjukeɪt] vt (gen) educar; (instruct) instruir; **educated** ['ɛdjukeɪtɪd] adj culto

education [ɛdju'keɪʃən] n educación f; (schooling) enseñanza; (Scol) pedagogía; **educational** adj (policy etc) educacional; (experience) docente; (toy) educativo

eel [iːl] n anguila

eerie ['ɪərɪ] adj misterioso

effect [ɪ'fɛkt] n efecto ▷ vt efectuar, llevar a cabo; **to take ~** (law) entrar en vigor or vigencia; (drug) surtir efecto; **in ~** en realidad; **effects** npl (property) efectos mpl; **effective** adj eficaz; (actual) verdadero; **effectively** adv eficazmente; (in reality) efectivamente

efficiency [ɪ'fɪʃənsɪ] n eficiencia; rendimiento

efficient [ɪ'fɪʃənt] adj eficiente; (machine) de buen rendimiento; **efficiently** adv eficientemente, de manera eficiente

effort ['ɛfət] n esfuerzo; **effortless** adj sin ningún esfuerzo; (style) natural

e.g. adv abbr (= exempli gratia) p. ej.
egg [ɛg] n huevo; **hard-boiled/soft-boiled ~** huevo duro/pasado por agua; **eggcup** n huevera; **eggplant** (esp us) n berenjena; **eggshell** n cáscara de huevo; **egg white** n clara de huevo; **egg yolk** n yema de huevo

ego [ˈiːgəu] n ego
Egypt [ˈiːdʒɪpt] n Egipto; **Egyptian** [ɪˈdʒɪpʃən] adj, n egipcio/a m/f
eight [eɪt] num ocho; **eighteen** num diez y ocho, dieciocho; **eighteenth** adj decimoctavo; **the eighteenth floor** la planta dieciocho; **the eighteenth of August** el dieciocho de agosto; **eighth** num octavo; **eightieth** [ˈeɪtɪɪθ] adj octogésimo
eighty [ˈeɪtɪ] num ochenta
Eire [ˈeərə] n Eire m
either [ˈaɪðə*] adj cualquiera de los dos; (both, each) cada ⊳ pron: **~ (of them)** cualquiera (de los dos) ⊳ adv tampoco ⊳ conj: **~ yes or no** sí o no; **on ~ side** en ambos lados; **I don't like ~** no me gusta ninguno/a de los(las) dos; **no, I don't ~** no, yo tampoco
eject [ɪˈdʒɛkt] vt echar, expulsar; (tenant) desahuciar
elaborate [adj ɪˈlæbərɪt, vb ɪˈlæbəreɪt] adj (complex) complejo ⊳ vt (expand) ampliar; (refine) refinar ⊳ vi explicar con más detalles
elastic [ɪˈlæstɪk] n elástico ⊳ adj elástico; (fig) flexible; **elastic band** (BRIT) n gomita
elbow [ˈɛlbəu] n codo
elder [ˈɛldə*] adj mayor ⊳ n (tree) saúco; (person) mayor; **elderly** adj de edad, mayor ⊳ npl: **the elderly** los mayores
eldest [ˈɛldɪst] adj, n el/la mayor
elect [ɪˈlɛkt] vt elegir ⊳ adj: **the president ~** el presidente electo; **to ~ to do** optar por hacer; **election** n elección f; **electoral** adj electoral; **electorate** n electorado
electric [ɪˈlɛktrɪk] adj eléctrico; **electrical** adj eléctrico; **electric blanket** n manta eléctrica; **electric fire** n estufa eléctrica; **electrician** [ɪlɛkˈtrɪʃən] n electricista mf; **electricity** [ɪlɛkˈtrɪsɪtɪ] n electricidad f; **electric shock** n electrochoque m; **electrify** [ɪˈlɛktrɪfaɪ] vt (Rail) electrificar; (fig: audience) electrizar
electronic [ɪlɛkˈtrɔnɪk] adj electrónico; **electronic mail** n correo electrónico; **electronics** n electrónica
elegance [ˈɛlɪgəns] n elegancia
elegant [ˈɛlɪgənt] adj elegante
element [ˈɛlɪmənt] n elemento; (of kettle etc) resistencia
elementary [ɛlɪˈmɛntərɪ] adj elemental; (primitive) rudimentario; **elementary school** (us) n escuela de enseñanza primaria
elephant [ˈɛlɪfənt] n elefante m
elevate [ˈɛlɪveɪt] vt (gen) elevar; (in rank) ascender
elevator [ˈɛlɪveɪtə*] n (us) ascensor m; (in warehouse etc) montacargas m inv
eleven [ɪˈlɛvn] num once; **eleventh** num undécimo
eligible [ˈɛlɪdʒəbl] adj: **an ~ young man/woman** un buen partido; **to be ~ for sth** llenar los requisitos para algo
eliminate [ɪˈlɪmɪneɪt] vt (suspect, possibility) descartar
elm [ɛlm] n olmo
eloquent [ˈɛləkwənt] adj elocuente
else [ɛls] adv: **something ~** otra cosa; **somewhere ~** en otra parte; **everywhere ~** en todas partes menos

aquí; **where ~?** ¿dónde más?, ¿en qué otra parte?; **there was little ~ to do** apenas quedaba otra cosa que hacer; **nobody ~ spoke** no habló nadie más; **elsewhere** adv (be) en otra parte; (go) a otra parte
elusive [ɪˈluːsɪv] adj esquivo; (quality) difícil de encontrar
e-mail [ˈiːmeɪl] n abbr (= electronic mail) correo electrónico, e-mail m; **e-mail address** n dirección f electrónica, email m
embankment [ɪmˈbæŋkmənt] n terraplén m
embargo [ɪmˈbɑːgəu] (pl **~es**) n (Comm, Naut) embargo; (prohibition) prohibición f; **to put an ~ on sth** poner un embargo en algo
embark [ɪmˈbɑːk] vi embarcarse ⊳ vt embarcar; **to ~ on** (journey) emprender; (course of action) lanzarse a
embarrass [ɪmˈbærəs] vt avergonzar; (government etc) dejar en mal lugar; **embarrassed** adj (laugh, silence) embarazoso; **embarrassing** adj (situation) violento; (question) embarazoso; **embarrassment** n (shame) vergüenza; (problem): **to be an embarrassment for sb** poner en un aprieto a algn
embassy [ˈɛmbəsɪ] n embajada
embrace [ɪmˈbreɪs] vt abrazar, dar un abrazo a; (include) abarcar ⊳ vi abrazarse ⊳ n abrazo
embroider [ɪmˈbrɔɪdə*] vt bordar; **embroidery** n bordado
embryo [ˈɛmbrɪəu] n embrión m
emerald [ˈɛmərəld] n esmeralda
emerge [ɪˈməːdʒ] vi salir; (arise) surgir
emergency [ɪˈməːdʒənsɪ] n crisis f inv; **in an ~** en caso de urgencia; **state of ~** estado de emergencia; **emergency brake** (us) n freno de mano; **emergency exit** n salida de emergencia; **emergency landing** n aterrizaje m forzoso; **emergency room** (us: Med) n sala f de urgencias; **emergency services** npl (fire, police, ambulance) servicios mpl de urgencia or emergencia
emigrate [ˈɛmɪgreɪt] vi emigrar; **emigration** [ɛmɪˈgreɪʃən] n emigración f
eminent [ˈɛmɪnənt] adj eminente
emissions [ɪˈmɪʃənz] npl emisión f
emit [ɪˈmɪt] vt emitir; (smoke) arrojar; (smell) despedir; (sound) producir
emotion [ɪˈməuʃən] n emoción f; **emotional** adj (needs) emocional; (person) sentimental; (scene) conmovedor(a), emocionante; (speech) emocionado
emperor [ˈɛmpərə*] n emperador m
emphasis [ˈɛmfəsɪs] (pl **-ses**) n énfasis m inv
emphasize [ˈɛmfəsaɪz] vt (word, point) subrayar, recalcar; (feature) hacer resaltar
empire [ˈɛmpaɪə*] n imperio
employ [ɪmˈplɔɪ] vt emplear; **employee** [-ˈiː] n empleado/a; **employer** n patrón/ona m/f; empresario; **employment** n (work) trabajo; **employment agency** n agencia de colocaciones
empower [ɪmˈpauə*] vt: **to ~ sb to do sth** autorizar a algn para hacer algo
empress [ˈɛmprɪs] n emperatriz f
emptiness [ˈɛmptɪnɪs] n vacío; (of life etc) vaciedad f
empty [ˈɛmptɪ] adj vacío; (place) desierto; (house) desocupado; (threat) vano ⊳ vt vaciar; (place) dejar vacío ⊳ vi vaciarse; (house etc) quedar desocupado; **empty-handed** adj con las manos vacías
EMU n abbr (= European Monetary Union) UME f
emulsion [ɪˈmʌlʃən] n emulsión f; (also: **~ paint**) pintura emulsión

enable [ɪ'neɪbl] vt: **to ~ sb to do sth** permitir a algn hacer algo

enamel [ɪ'næməl] n esmalte m; (also: **~ paint**) pintura esmaltada

enchanting [ɪn'tʃɑːntɪŋ] adj encantador(a)

encl. abbr (= enclosed) adj

enclose [ɪn'kləʊz] vt (land) cercar; (letter etc) adjuntar; **please find ~d** le mandamos adjunto

enclosure [ɪn'kləʊʒə*] n cercado, recinto

encore [ɔŋ'kɔː*] excl ¡otra!, ¡bis! ▷ n bis m

encounter [ɪn'kaʊntə*] n encuentro ▷ vt encontrar, encontrarse con; (difficulty) tropezar con

encourage [ɪn'kʌrɪdʒ] vt alentar, animar; (activity) fomentar; (growth) estimular; **encouragement** n estímulo; (of industry) fomento

encouraging [ɪn'kʌrɪdʒɪŋ] adj alentador(a)

encyclop(a)edia [ensaɪkləʊ'piːdɪə] n enciclopedia

end [end] n fin m; (of table) extremo; (of street/line) n; (Sport) lado ▷ vt terminar, acabar; (also: **bring to an ~, put an ~ to**) acabar con ▷ vi terminar, acabar; **in the ~** al fin; **on ~** (object) de punta, de cabeza; **to stand on ~** (hair) erizarse; **for hours on ~** hora tras hora; **end up** vi: **to end up in** terminar en; (place) ir a parar en

endanger [ɪn'deɪndʒə*] vt poner en peligro; **an ~ed species** una especie en peligro de extinción

endearing [ɪn'dɪərɪŋ] adj simpático, atractivo

endeavour [ɪn'devə*] (us **endeavor**) n esfuerzo ▷ vi: **to ~ to do** esforzarse por hacer; (try) procurar hacer

ending [ɪn'endɪŋ] n (of book) desenlace m; (Ling) terminación f

endless ['endlɪs] adj interminable, inacabable

endorse [ɪn'dɔːs] vt (cheque) endosar; (approve) aprobar; **endorsement** n (on driving licence) nota de inhabilitación

endurance [ɪn'djʊərəns] n resistencia

endure [ɪn'djʊə*] vt (bear) aguantar, soportar ▷ vi (last) durar

enemy ['enəmɪ] adj, n enemigo/a m/f

energetic [enə'dʒetɪk] adj enérgico

energy ['enədʒɪ] n energía

enforce [ɪn'fɔːs] vt (Law) hacer cumplir

engaged [ɪn'geɪdʒd] adj (BRIT: busy, in use) ocupado; (betrothed) prometido; **to get ~** prometerse; **engaged tone** (BRIT) n (Tel) señal f de comunicado

engagement [ɪn'geɪdʒmənt] n (appointment) compromiso, cita; (booking) contratación f; (to marry) compromiso; (period) noviazgo; **engagement ring** n anillo de prometida

engaging [ɪn'geɪdʒɪŋ] adj atractivo

engine ['endʒɪn] n (Aut) motor m; (Rail) locomotora

engineer [endʒɪ'nɪə*] n ingeniero; (BRIT: for repairs) mecánico; (on ship, us Rail) maquinista m; **engineering** n ingeniería

England ['ɪŋɡlənd] n Inglaterra

English ['ɪŋɡlɪʃ] adj inglés/esa ▷ n (Ling) inglés m; **the English** npl los ingleses mpl; **English Channel** n: **the English Channel** (el Canal de) la Mancha; **Englishman** (irreg) n inglés m; **Englishwoman** (irreg) n inglesa

engrave [ɪn'greɪv] vt grabar

engraving [ɪn'greɪvɪŋ] n grabado

enhance [ɪn'hɑːns] vt (gen) aumentar; (beauty) realzar

enjoy [ɪn'dʒɔɪ] vt (health, fortune) disfrutar de, gozar de; (like) gustarle a algn; **to ~ o.s.** divertirse; **enjoyable**

adj agradable; (amusing) divertido; **enjoyment** n (joy) placer m; (activity) diversión f

enlarge [ɪn'lɑːdʒ] vt aumentar; (broaden) extender; (Phot) ampliar ▷ vi: **to ~ on** (subject) tratar con más detalles; **enlargement** n (Phot) ampliación f

enlist [ɪn'lɪst] vt alistar; (support) conseguir ▷ vi alistarse

enormous [ɪ'nɔːməs] adj enorme

enough [ɪ'nʌf] adj: **~ time/books** bastante tiempo/bastantes libros ▷ pron bastante(s) ▷ adv: **big ~** bastante grande; **he has not worked ~** no ha trabajado bastante; **have you got ~?** ¿tiene usted bastante(s)?; **~ to eat** (lo) suficiente de (lo) bastante para comer; **~!** ¡basta ya! **that's ~, thanks** con eso basta, gracias; **I've had ~ of him** estoy harto de él; **... which, funnily or oddly ~ ...** ... lo que, por extraño que parezca ...

enquire [ɪn'kwaɪə*] vt, vi = **inquire**

enquiry [ɪn'kwaɪərɪ] n (official investigation) investigación

enrage [ɪn'reɪdʒ] vt enfurecer

enrich [ɪn'rɪtʃ] vt enriquecer

enrol [ɪn'rəʊl] (us **enroll**) vt (members) inscribir; (Scol) matricular ▷ vi inscribirse; matricularse; **enrolment** (us **enrollment**) n inscripción f; matriculación f

en route [ɔn'ruːt] adv durante el viaje

en suite [ɔn'swiːt] adj: **with ~ bathroom** con baño

ensure [ɪn'ʃʊə*] vt asegurar

entail [ɪn'teɪl] vt suponer

enter ['entə*] vt (room) entrar en; (club) hacerse socio de; (army) alistarse en; (sb for a competition) inscribir; (write down) anotar, apuntar; (Comput) meter ▷ vi entrar

enterprise ['entəpraɪz] n empresa; (spirit) iniciativa; **free ~** la libre empresa; **private ~** la iniciativa privada; **enterprising** adj emprendedor(a)

entertain [entə'teɪn] vt (amuse) divertir; (invite: guest) invitar (a casa); (idea) abrigar; **entertainer** n artista mf; **entertaining** adj divertido, entretenido; **entertainment** n (amusement) diversión f; (show) espectáculo

enthusiasm [ɪn'θuːzɪæzəm] n entusiasmo

enthusiast [ɪn'θuːzɪæst] n entusiasta mf; **enthusiastic** [-'æstɪk] adj entusiasta; **to be enthusiastic about** entusiasmarse por

entire [ɪn'taɪə*] adj entero; **entirely** adv totalmente

entitle [ɪn'taɪtl] vt: **to ~ sb to sth** dar a algn derecho a algo; **entitled** adj (book) titulado; **to be entitled to do** tener derecho a hacer

entrance [n 'entrəns, vb ɪn'trɑːns] n entrada ▷ vt encantar, hechizar; **to gain ~ to** (university etc) ingresar en; **entrance examination** n examen m de ingreso; **entrance fee** n cuota; **entrance ramp** (us) n (Aut) rampa de acceso

entrant ['entrənt] n (in race, competition) participante mf; (in examination) candidato/a

entrepreneur [ɔntrəprə'nə:] n empresario

entrust [ɪn'trʌst] vt: **to ~ sth to sb** confiar algo a algn

entry ['entrɪ] n entrada; (in competition) participación f; (in register) apunte m; (in account) partida; (in reference book) artículo; **"no ~"** prohibido el paso"; (Aut) "dirección prohibida"; **entry phone** n portero automático

envelope ['envələʊp] n sobre m

envious ['envɪəs] adj envidioso; (look) de envidia

environment [ɪn'vaɪərnmənt] n (surroundings)

entorno; (*natural world*): **the ~** el medio ambiente;
environmental [-'mentl] *adj* ambiental;
medioambiental; **environmentally** [-'mentəli]
adv: **environmentally sound/friendly** ecológico
envisage [ɪn'vɪzɪdʒ] *vt* prever
envoy ['ɛnvɔɪ] *n* enviado
envy ['ɛnvɪ] *n* envidia ▷ *vt* tener envidia a; **to ~ sb
sth** envidiar algo a algn
epic ['ɛpɪk] *n* épica ▷ *adj* épico
epidemic [ɛpɪ'dɛmɪk] *n* epidemia
epilepsy ['ɛpɪlɛpsɪ] *n* epilepsia
epileptic [ɛpɪ'lɛptɪk] *adj*, *n* epiléptico/a *m/f*;
epileptic fit [ɛpɪ'lɛptɪk-] *n* ataque *m* de epilepsia,
acceso *m* epiléptico
episode ['ɛpɪsəud] *n* episodio
equal ['iːkwl] *adj* igual; (*treatment*) equitativo ▷ *n*
igual *mf* ▷ *vt* ser igual a; (*fig*) igualar; **to be ~ to** (*task*)
estar a la altura de; **equality** [iː'kwɔlɪtɪ] *n* igualdad *f*;
equalize *vi* (*Sport*) empatar; **equally** *adv* igualmente;
(*share etc*) a partes iguales
equation [ɪ'kweɪʒən] *n* (*Math*) ecuación *f*
equator [ɪ'kweɪtə*] *n* ecuador *m*
equip [ɪ'kwɪp] *vt* equipar; (*person*) proveer; **to be well
~ped** estar bien equipado; **equipment** *n* equipo;
(*tools*) avíos *mpl*
equivalent [ɪ'kwɪvələnt] *adj*: **~ (to)** equivalente (a)
▷ *n* equivalente *m*
ER *abbr* (*BRIT*: = *Elizabeth Regina*) la reina Isabel; (*US*: *Med*)
= **emergency room**
era ['ɪərə] *n* era, época
erase [ɪ'reɪz] *vt* borrar; **eraser** *n* goma de borrar
erect [ɪ'rɛkt] *adj* erguido ▷ *vt* erigir, levantar;
(*assemble*) montar; **erection** [-ʃən] *n* construcción *f*;
(*assembly*) montaje *m*; (*Physiol*) erección *f*
ERM *n abbr* (= *Exchange Rate Mechanism*) tipo de cambio
europeo
erode [ɪ'rəud] *vt* (*Geo*) erosionar; (*metal*) corroer,
desgastar; (*fig*) desgastar
erosion [ɪ'rəuʒən] *n* erosión *f*; desgaste *m*
erotic [ɪ'rɔtɪk] *adj* erótico
errand ['ɛrnd] *n* recado (*SP*), mandado (*LAM*)
erratic [ɪ'rætɪk] *adj* desigual, poco uniforme
error ['ɛrə*] *n* error *m*, equivocación *f*
erupt [ɪ'rʌpt] *vi* entrar en erupción; (*fig*) estallar;
eruption [ɪ'rʌpʃən] *n* erupción *f*; (*of war*) estallido
escalate ['ɛskəleɪt] *vi* extenderse, intensificarse
escalator ['ɛskəleɪtə*] *n* escalera móvil
escape [ɪ'skeɪp] *n* fuga ▷ *vi* escaparse; (*flee*) huir,
evadirse; (*leak*) fugarse ▷ *vt* (*responsibility etc*) evitar,
eludir; (*consequences*) escapar a; (*elude*): **his name ~s
me** no me sale su nombre; **to ~ from** (*place*) escaparse
de; (*person*) escaparse a
escort [*n* 'ɛskɔːt, *vb* ɪ'skɔːt] *n* acompañante *mf*; (*Mil*)
escolta *mf* ▷ *vt* acompañar
especially [ɪ'spɛʃlɪ] *adv* (*above all*) sobre todo;
(*particularly*) en particular, especialmente
espionage ['ɛspɪənɑːʒ] *n* espionaje *m*
essay ['ɛseɪ] *n* (*Literature*) ensayo; (*Scol*: *short*)
redacción *f*; (: *long*) trabajo
essence ['ɛsns] *n* esencia
essential [ɪ'sɛnʃl] *adj* (*necessary*) imprescindible;
(*basic*) esencial; **essentially** *adv* esencialmente;
essentials *npl* lo imprescindible, lo esencial
establish [ɪ'stæblɪʃ] *vt* establecer; (*prove*)
demostrar; (*relations*) entablar; (*reputation*)
ganarse; **establishment** *n* establecimiento; **the**

Establishment la clase dirigente
estate [ɪ'steɪt] *n* (*land*) finca, hacienda; (*inheritance*)
herencia; (*BRIT*: *also*: **housing ~**) urbanización *f*; **estate
agent** (*BRIT*) *n* agente *mf* inmobiliario/a; **estate car**
(*BRIT*) *n* furgoneta
estimate [*n* 'ɛstɪmət, *vb* 'ɛstɪmeɪt] *n* estimación
f, apreciación *f*; (*assessment*) tasa, cálculo; (*Comm*)
presupuesto ▷ *vt* estimar, tasar, calcular
etc *abbr* (= *et cetera*) etc
eternal [ɪ'tɜːnl] *adj* eterno
eternity [ɪ'tɜːnɪtɪ] *n* eternidad *f*
ethical ['ɛθɪkl] *adj* ético; **ethics** ['ɛθɪks] *n* ética
▷ *npl* moralidad *f*
Ethiopia [iːθɪ'əupɪə] *n* Etiopia
ethnic ['ɛθnɪk] *adj* étnico; **ethnic minority** *n*
minoría étnica
e-ticket ['iːtɪkɪt] *n* billete *m* electrónico (*SP*), boleto
electrónico (*LAM*)
etiquette ['ɛtɪkɛt] *n* etiqueta
EU *n abbr* (= *European Union*) UE *f*
euro *n* euro
Europe ['juərəp] *n* Europa; **European** [-'piːən] *adj*, *n*
europeo/a *m/f*; **European Community** *n* Comunidad
f Europea; **European Union** *n* Unión *f* Europea
Eurostar® ['juərəustɑː*] *n* Eurostar® *m*
evacuate [ɪ'vækjueɪt] *vt* (*people*) evacuar; (*place*)
desocupar
evade [ɪ'veɪd] *vt* evadir, eludir
evaluate [ɪ'væljueɪt] *vt* evaluar; (*value*) tasar;
(*evidence*) interpretar
evaporate [ɪ'væpəreɪt] *vi* evaporarse; (*fig*)
desvanecerse
eve [iːv] *n*: **on the ~ of** en vísperas de
even ['iːvn] *adj* (*level*) llano; (*smooth*) liso; (*speed*,
temperature) uniforme; (*number*) par ▷ *adv* hasta,
incluso; (*introducing a comparison*) aún, todavía; **~ if, ~
though** aunque +*subjun*; **~ more** aun más; **~ so** aun así;
not ~ ni siquiera; **~ he was** hasta él estuvo allí;
~ on Sundays incluso los domingos; **to get ~ with sb**
ajustar cuentas con algn
evening ['iːvnɪŋ] *n* tarde *f*; (*late*) noche *f*; **in the ~** por
la tarde; **evening class** *n* clase *f* nocturna; **evening
dress** *n* (*no pl*: *formal clothes*) traje *m* de etiqueta;
(*woman's*) traje *m* de noche
event [ɪ'vɛnt] *n* suceso, acontecimiento; (*Sport*)
prueba; **in the ~ of** en caso de; **eventful** *adj* (*life*)
activo; (*day*) ajetreado
eventual [ɪ'vɛntʃuəl] *adj* final; **eventually** *adv*
(*finally*) finalmente; (*in time*) con el tiempo
ever ['ɛvə*] *adv* (*at any time*) nunca, jamás; (*at all times*)
siempre; (*in question*): **why ~ not?** ¿y por qué no?; **the
best ~** lo nunca visto; **have you ~ seen it?** ¿lo ha visto
usted alguna vez?; **better than ~** mejor que nunca; **~
since** *adv* desde entonces ▷ *conj* después de que;
evergreen *n* árbol *m* de hoja perenne

○ **KEYWORD**

every ['ɛvrɪ] *adj* **1** (*each*) cada; **every one of them**
(*persons*) todos ellos/as; (*objects*) cada uno de ellos/as;
every shop in the town was closed todas
las tiendas de la ciudad estaban cerradas
2 (*all possible*) todo/a; **I gave you every assistance**
te di toda la ayuda posible; **I have every confidence
in him** tiene toda mi confianza; **we wish you every
success** te deseamos toda suerte de éxitos

3 (showing recurrence) todo/a; **every day/week** todos los días/todas las semanas; **every other car had been broken into** habían forzado uno de cada dos coches; **she visits me every other/third day** me visita cada dos/tres días; **every now and then** de vez en cuando

every: everybody pron = **everyone**; **everyday** adj (daily) cotidiano, de todos los días; (usual) acostumbrado; **everyone** pron todos/as, todo el mundo; **everything** pron todo; **this shop sells everything** esta tienda vende de todo; **everywhere** adv: **I've been looking for you everywhere** te he estado buscando por todas partes; **everywhere you go you meet ...** en todas partes encuentras ...

evict [ɪ'vɪkt] vt desahuciar

evidence ['evɪdəns] n (proof) prueba f; (of witness) testimonio; (sign) indicios mpl; **to give** ~ prestar declaración, dar testimonio

evident ['evɪdənt] adj evidente, manifiesto; **evidently** adv por lo visto

evil ['iːvl] adj malo; (influence) funesto ▷ n mal m

evoke [ɪ'vəuk] vt evocar

evolution [iːvə'luːʃən] n evolución f

evolve [ɪ'vɒlv] vt desarrollar ▷ vi evolucionar, desarrollarse

ewe [juː] n oveja

ex [eks] (inf) n: **my** ~ mi ex

ex- [eks] prefix ex

exact [ɪg'zækt] adj exacto; (person) meticuloso ▷ vt: **to** ~ **sth (from)** exigir algo (de); **exactly** adv exactamente; (indicating agreement) exacto

exaggerate [ɪg'zædʒəreɪt] vt, vi exagerar; **exaggeration** [-'reɪʃən] n exageración f

exam [ɪg'zæm] n abbr (Scol) = **examination**

examination [ɪgzæmɪ'neɪʃən] n examen m; (Med) reconocimiento

examine [ɪg'zæmɪn] vt examinar; (inspect) inspeccionar, escudriñar; (Med) reconocer; **examiner** n examinador(a) m/f

example [ɪg'zɑːmpl] n ejemplo; **for** ~ por ejemplo

exasperated [ɪg'zɑːspəreɪtd] adj exasperado

excavate ['ekskəveɪt] vt excavar

exceed [ɪk'siːd] vt (amount) exceder; (number) pasar de; (speed limit) sobrepasar; (powers) excederse en; (hopes) superar; **exceedingly** adv sumamente, sobremanera

excel [ɪk'sel] vi sobresalir; **to** ~ **o.s** lucirse

excellence ['eksələns] n excelencia

excellent ['eksələnt] adj excelente

except [ɪk'sept] prep (also: ~ **for**, ~**ing**) excepto, salvo ▷ vt exceptuar, excluir; ~ **if/when** excepto si/cuando; ~ **that** salvo que; **exception** [ɪk'sepʃən] n excepción f; **to take exception to** ofenderse por; **exceptional** [ɪk'sepʃənl] adj excepcional; **exceptionally** [ɪk'sepʃənəlɪ] adv excepcionalmente, extraordinariamente

excerpt ['eksɜːpt] n extracto

excess [ɪk'ses] n exceso; **excess baggage** n exceso de equipaje; **excessive** [ɪg'zæ] adj excesivo

exchange [ɪks'tʃeɪndʒ] n intercambio; (conversation) diálogo; (also: **telephone** ~) central f (telefónica) ▷ vt: **to** ~ **(for)** cambiar (por); **exchange rate** n tipo de cambio

excite [ɪk'saɪt] vt (stimulate) estimular; (arouse) excitar; **excited** adj: **to get excited** emocionarse;

excitement n (agitation) excitación f; (exhilaration) emoción f; **exciting** adj emocionante

exclaim [ɪk'skleɪm] vi exclamar; **exclamation** [ekskla'meɪʃən] n exclamación f; **exclamation mark** n punto de admiración; **exclamation point** (us) = **exclamation mark**

exclude [ɪk'skluːd] vt excluir; exceptuar

excluding [ɪks'kluːdɪŋ] prep: ~ **VAT** IVA no incluido

exclusion [ɪk'skluːʒən] n exclusión f; **to the** ~ **of** con exclusión de

exclusive [ɪk'skluːsɪv] adj exclusivo; (club, district) selecto; ~ **of tax** excluyendo impuestos; **exclusively** adv únicamente

excruciating [ɪk'skruːʃɪeɪtɪŋ] adj (pain) agudísimo, atroz; (noise, embarrassment) horrible

excursion [ɪk'skəːʃən] n (tourist excursion) excursión f

excuse [n ɪk'skjuːs, vb ɪk'skjuːz] n disculpa, excusa; (pretext) pretexto ▷ vt (justify) justificar; (forgive) disculpar, perdonar; **to** ~ **sb from doing sth** dispensar a algn de hacer algo; ~ **me!** (attracting attention) ¡por favor!; (apologizing) ¡perdón!; **if you will** ~ **me** con su permiso

ex-directory ['eksdɪ'rektərɪ] (Brit) adj que no consta en la guía

execute ['eksɪkjuːt] vt (plan) realizar; (order) cumplir; (person) ajusticiar, ejecutar; **execution** [-'kjuːʃən] n realización f; cumplimiento; ejecución f

executive [ɪg'zekjutɪv] n (person, committee) ejecutivo; (Pol: committee) poder m ejecutivo ▷ adj ejecutivo

exempt [ɪg'zempt] adj: ~ **from** exento de ▷ vt: **to** ~ **sb from** eximir a algn de

exercise ['eksəsaɪz] n ejercicio ▷ vt (patience) usar de; (right) valerse de; (dog) llevar de paseo; (mind) preocupar ▷ vi (also: **to take** ~) hacer ejercicio(s); **exercise book** n cuaderno

exert [ɪg'zəːt] vt ejercer; **to** ~ **o.s.** esforzarse; **exertion** [-ʃən] n esfuerzo

exhale [eks'heɪl] vt despedir ▷ vi exhalar

exhaust [ɪg'zɔːst] n (Aut: also: ~ **pipe**) escape m; (: fumes) gases mpl de escape ▷ vt agotar; **exhausted** adj agotado; **exhaustion** [ɪg'zɔːstʃən] n agotamiento; **nervous exhaustion** postración f nerviosa

exhibit [ɪg'zɪbɪt] n (Art) obra expuesta; (Law) objeto expuesto ▷ vt (show: emotions) manifestar; (: courage, skill) demostrar; (paintings) exponer; **exhibition** [eksɪ'bɪʃən] n exposición f; (of talent etc) demostración f

exhilarating [ɪg'zɪləreɪtɪŋ] adj estimulante, tónico

exile ['eksaɪl] n exilio; (person) exiliado/a ▷ vt desterrar, exiliar

exist [ɪg'zɪst] vi existir; (live) vivir; **existence** n existencia; **existing** adj existente, actual

exit ['eksɪt] n salida ▷ vi (Theatre) hacer mutis; (Comput) salir (del sistema); **exit ramp** (us) n (Aut) vía de acceso

exotic [ɪg'zɒtɪk] adj exótico

expand [ɪk'spænd] vt ampliar; (number) aumentar ▷ vi (population) aumentar; (trade etc) expandirse; (gas, metal) dilatarse

expansion [ɪk'spænʃən] n (of population) aumento; (of trade) expansión f

expect [ɪk'spekt] vt esperar; (require) contar con; (suppose) suponer ▷ vi: **to be** ~**ing** (pregnant woman) estar embarazada; **expectation** [ekspek'teɪʃən] n *(hope)* esperanza; *(belief)* expectativa

expedition [ɛkspə'dɪʃən] n expedición f

expel [ɪk'spɛl] vt arrojar; *(from place)* expulsar

expenditure [ɪks'pɛndɪtʃə*] n gastos mpl, desembolso; consumo

expense [ɪk'spɛns] n gasto, gastos mpl; *(high cost)* costa; **expenses** npl *(Comm)* gastos mpl; **at the ~ of** a costa de; **expense account** n cuenta de gastos

expensive [ɪk'spɛnsɪv] adj caro, costoso

experience [ɪk'spɪərɪəns] n experiencia ▷vt experimentar; *(suffer)* sufrir; **experienced** adj experimentado

experiment [ɪk'spɛrɪmənt] n experimento ▷vi hacer experimentos; **experimental** [-'mɛntl] adj experimental; **the process is still at the experimental stage** el proceso está todavía en prueba

expert ['ɛkspə:t] adj experto, perito ▷n experto/a, perito/a; *(specialist)* especialista mf; **expertise** [-'ti:z] n pericia

expire [ɪk'spaɪə*] vi caducar, vencer; **expiry** n vencimiento; **expiry date** n *(of medicine, food item)* fecha de caducidad

explain [ɪk'spleɪn] vt explicar; **explanation** [ɛksplə'neɪʃən] n explicación f

explicit [ɪk'splɪsɪt] adj explícito

explode [ɪk'spləud] vi estallar, explotar; *(population)* crecer rápidamente; *(with anger)* reventar

exploit [n 'ɛksplɔɪt, vb ɪk'splɔɪt] n hazaña ▷vt explotar; **exploitation** [-'teɪʃən] n explotación f

explore [ɪk'splɔ:*] vt explorar; *(fig)* examinar, investigar; **explorer** n explorador(a) m/f

explosion [ɪk'spləuʒən] n explosión f; **explosive** [ɪks'pləusɪv] adj, n explosivo

export [vb ɛk'spɔ:t, n, cpd 'ɛkspɔ:t] vt exportar ▷n *(process)* exportación f; *(product)* producto de exportación ▷cpd de exportación; **exporter** n exportador m

expose [ɪk'spəuz] vt exponer; *(unmask)* desenmascarar; **exposed** adj expuesto

exposure [ɪk'spəuʒə*] n exposición f; *(publicity)* publicidad f; *(Phot: speed)* velocidad f de obturación; *(: shot)* fotografía; **to die from ~** *(Med)* morir de frío

express [ɪk'sprɛs] adj *(definite)* expreso, explícito; *(BRIT: letter etc)* urgente ▷n *(train)* rápido ▷vt expresar; **expression** [ɪk'sprɛʃən] n expresión f; *(of actor etc)* sentimiento; **expressway** (us) n *(urban motorway)* autopista

exquisite [ɛk'skwɪzɪt] adj exquisito

extend [ɪk'stɛnd] vt *(visit, street)* prolongar; *(building)* ampliar; *(invitation)* ofrecer ▷vi *(land)* extenderse; *(period of time)* prolongarse

extension [ɪk'stɛnʃən] n extensión f; *(building)* ampliación f; *(of time)* prolongación f; *(Tel: in private house)* línea derivada; *(: in office)* extensión f; **extension lead** n alargador m, alargadera

extensive [ɪk'stɛnsɪv] adj extenso; *(damage)* importante; *(knowledge)* amplio

extent [ɪk'stɛnt] n *(breadth)* extensión f; *(scope)* alcance m; **to some ~** hasta cierto punto; **to the ~ of ...** hasta el punto de ...; **to such an ~ that ...** hasta tal punto que ...; **to what ~?** ¿hasta qué punto?

exterior [ɛk'stɪərɪə*] adj exterior, externo ▷n exterior m

external [ɛk'stə:nl] adj externo

extinct [ɪk'stɪŋkt] adj *(volcano)* extinguido; *(race)* extinto; **extinction** n extinción f

extinguish [ɪk'stɪŋgwɪʃ] vt extinguir, apagar

extra ['ɛkstrə] adj adicional ▷adv *(in addition)* de más ▷n *(luxury, addition)* extra m; *(Cinema, Theatre)* extra mf, comparsa mf

extract [vb ɪk'strækt, n 'ɛkstrækt] vt sacar; *(tooth)* extraer; *(money, promise)* obtener ▷n extracto

extradite ['ɛkstrədaɪt] vt extraditar

extraordinary [ɪk'strɔ:dnrɪ] adj extraordinario; *(odd)* raro

extravagance [ɪk'strævəgəns] n derroche m, despilfarro; *(thing bought)* extravagancia

extravagant [ɪk'strævəgənt] adj *(lavish: person)* pródigo; *(: gift)* (demasiado) caro; *(wasteful)* despilfarrador(a)

extreme [ɪk'stri:m] adj extremo, extremado ▷n extremo; **extremely** adv sumamente, extremadamente

extremist [ɪk'stri:mɪst] adj, n extremista m/f

extrovert ['ɛkstrəvə:t] n extrovertido/a

eye [aɪ] n ojo ▷vt mirar de soslayo, ojear; **to keep an ~ on** vigilar; **eyeball** n globo ocular; **eyebrow** n ceja; **eyedrops** npl gotas fpl para los ojos, colirio; **eyelash** n pestaña; **eyelid** n párpado; **eyeliner** n delineador m *(de ojos)*; **eyeshadow** n sombreador m de ojos; **eyesight** n vista; **eye witness** n testigo mf presencial

f

F [ɛf] n (Mus) fa m

fabric ['fæbrɪk] n tejido, tela

fabulous ['fæbjuləs] adj fabuloso

face [feɪs] n (Anat) cara, rostro; (of clock) esfera (SP), cara (LAM); (of mountain) cara, ladera; (of building) fachada ▷ vt (direction) estar de cara a; (situation) hacer frente a; (facts) aceptar; (person, card) boca abajo; **to lose** ~ desprestigiarse; **to make or pull a** ~ hacer muecas; **in the** ~ **of** (difficulties etc) ante; **on the** ~ **of it** a primera vista; ~ **to** ~ cara a cara; **face up to** vt fus hacer frente a, arrostrar; **face cloth** (BRIT) n manopla; **face pack** n (BRIT) mascarilla

facial ['feɪʃəl] adj de la cara ▷ n (also: **beauty** ~) tratamiento facial, limpieza

facilitate [fə'sɪlɪteɪt] vt facilitar

facilities [fə'sɪlɪtɪz] npl (buildings) instalaciones fpl; (equipment) servicios mpl; **credit** ~ facilidades fpl de crédito

fact [fækt] n hecho; **in** ~ en realidad

faction ['fækʃən] n facción f

factor ['fæktə*] n factor m

factory ['fæktərɪ] n fábrica

factual ['fæktjuəl] adj basado en los hechos

faculty ['fækəltɪ] n facultad f; (US: teaching staff) personal m docente

fad [fæd] n novedad f, moda

fade [feɪd] vi desteñirse; (sound, smile) desvanecerse; (light) apagarse; (flower) marchitarse; (hope, memory) perderse; **fade away** vi (sound) apagarse

fag [fæg] (BRIT: inf) n (cigarette) pitillo (SP), cigarro

Fahrenheit ['fɑ:rənhaɪt] n Fahrenheit m

fail [feɪl] vt (candidate, test) suspender (SP), reprobar (LAM); (memory etc) fallar a ▷ vi suspender (SP), reprobar (LAM); (be unsuccessful) fracasar; (strength, brakes) fallar; (light) acabarse; **to** ~ **to do sth** (neglect) dejar de hacer algo; (be unable) no poder hacer algo; **without** ~ sin falta; **failing** n falta, defecto ▷ prep a falta de; **failure** ['feɪljə*] n fracaso; (person) fracasado/a; (mechanical etc) fallo

faint [feɪnt] adj débil; (recollection) vago; (mark) apenas visible ▷ n desmayo ▷ vi desmayarse; **to feel** ~ estar mareado, marearse; **faintest** adj: **I haven't the faintest idea** no tengo la más remota idea; **faintly** adv débilmente; (vaguely) vagamente

fair [fɛə*] adj justo; (hair, person) rubio; (weather) bueno; (good enough) regular; (considerable) considerable ▷ adv (play) limpio ▷ n feria; (BRIT: funfair) parque m de atracciones; **fairground** n recinto ferial; **fair-haired** adj (person) rubio; **fairly** adv (justly) con justicia; (quite) bastante; **fair trade** n comercio justo; **fairway** n (Golf) calle f

fairy ['fɛərɪ] n hada; **fairy tale** n cuento de hadas

faith [feɪθ] n fe f; (trust) confianza; (sect) religión f; **faithful** adj (loyal: troops etc) leal; (: spouse) fiel; (: account) exacto; **faithfully** adv fielmente; **yours faithfully** (BRIT: in letters) le saluda atentamente

fake [feɪk] n (painting etc) falsificación f; (person) impostor(a) m/f ▷ adj falso ▷ vt fingir; (painting etc) falsificar

falcon ['fɔːlkən] n halcón m

fall [fɔːl] (pt fell, pp fallen) n caída; (in price etc) descenso; (US) otoño ▷ vi caer(se); (price) bajar, descender; **falls** npl (waterfall) cascada, salto de agua; **to** ~ **flat** (on one's face) caerse (boca abajo); (plan) fracasar; (joke, story) no hacer gracia; **fall apart** vi deshacerse; **fall down** vi (person) caerse; (building, hopes) derrumbarse; **fall for** vt fus (trick) dejarse engañar por; (person) enamorarse de; **fall off** vi caerse; (diminish) disminuir; **fall out** vi (friends etc) reñir; (hair, teeth) caerse; **fall over** vi caer(se); **fall through** vi (plan, project) fracasar

fallen ['fɔːlən] pp of **fall**

fallout ['fɔːlaut] n lluvia radioactiva

false [fɔːls] adj falso; **under** ~ **pretences** con engaños; **false alarm** n falsa alarma; **false teeth** (BRIT) npl dentadura postiza

fame [feɪm] n fama

familiar [fə'mɪlɪə*] adj conocido, familiar; (tone) de confianza; **to be** ~ **with** (subject) conocer (bien); **familiarize** [fə'mɪlɪəraɪz] vt: **to familiarize o.s. with** familiarizarse con

family ['fæmɪlɪ] n familia; **family doctor** n médico/a de cabecera; **family planning** n planificación f familiar

famine ['fæmɪn] n hambre f, hambruna

famous ['feɪməs] adj famoso, célebre

fan [fæn] n abanico; (Elec) ventilador m; (of pop star) fan mf; (Sport) hincha mf ▷ vt abanicar; (fire, quarrel) atizar

fan belt n correa del ventilador

fan club n club m de fans

fancy ['fænsɪ] n (whim) capricho, antojo; (imagination) imaginación f ▷ adj (luxury) lujoso, de lujo ▷ vt (feel like, want) tener ganas de; (imagine) imaginarse; (think) creer; **to take a** ~ **to sb** tomar cariño a algn; **he fancies her** (inf) le gusta (ella) mucho; **fancy dress** n disfraz m

fan heater n calefactor m de aire

fantasize ['fæntəsaɪz] vi fantasear, hacerse ilusiones

fantastic [fæn'tæstɪk] adj (enormous) enorme; (strange, wonderful) fantástico

fantasy ['fæntəzɪ] n (dream) sueño; (unreality) fantasía

fanzine ['fænziːn] n fanzine m

FAQs abbr (= frequently asked questions) preguntas frecuentes

far [fɑː*] adj (distant) lejano ▷ adv lejos; (much, greatly) mucho; ~ **away**, ~ **off** (a lo) lejos; ~ **better** mucho mejor; **~ from** lejos de; **by ~** con mucho; **go as ~ as the farm** vaya hasta la granja; **as ~ as I know** que yo sepa; **how ~?** ¿hasta dónde?; (fig) ¿hasta qué punto?

farce [fɑːs] n farsa

fare [fɛə*] n (on trains, buses) precio (del billete); (in taxi: cost) tarifa; (food) comida; **half ~** medio pasaje m; **full ~** pasaje completo

Far East n: **the ~** el Extremo Oriente

farewell [fɛəˈwel] excl, n adiós m

farm [fɑːm] n cortijo (SP), hacienda (LAM), rancho (MEX), estancia (RPL) ▷ vt cultivar; **farmer** n granjero, hacendado (LAM), ranchero (MEX), estanciero (RPL); **farmhouse** n granja, casa del hacendado (LAM), rancho (MEX), casco de la estancia (RPL); **farming** n agricultura; (of crops) cultivo; (of animals) cría; **farmyard** n corral m

far-reaching [fɑːˈriːtʃɪŋ] adj (reform, effect) de gran alcance

fart [fɑːt] (inf!) vi tirarse un pedo (!)

farther [ˈfɑːðə*] adv más lejos, más allá ▷ adj más lejano

farthest [ˈfɑːðɪst] superlative of **far**

fascinate [ˈfæsɪneɪt] vt fascinar; **fascinated** adj fascinado

fascinating [ˈfæsɪneɪtɪŋ] adj fascinante

fascination [-ˈneɪʃən] n fascinación f

fascist [ˈfæʃɪst] adj, n fascista m/f

fashion [ˈfæʃən] n moda; (fashion industry) industria de la moda; (manner) manera ▷ vt formar; **in ~** a la moda; **out of ~** pasado de moda; **fashionable** adj de moda; **fashion show** n desfile m de modelos

fast [fɑːst] adj rápido; (dye, colour) resistente; (clock): **to be ~** estar adelantado ▷ adv rápidamente, de prisa; (stuck, held) firmemente ▷ n ayuno ▷ vi ayunar; **~ asleep** profundamente dormido

fasten [ˈfɑːsn] vt atar, sujetar; (coat, belt) abrochar ▷ vi atarse; abrocharse

fast food n comida rápida, platos mpl preparados

fat [fæt] adj gordo; (book) grueso; (profit) grande, pingüe ▷ n grasa; (on person) carnes fpl; (lard) manteca

fatal [ˈfeɪtl] adj (mistake) fatal; (injury) mortal; **fatality** [fəˈtælɪtɪ] n (road death etc) víctima; **fatally** adv fatalmente; mortalmente

fate [feɪt] n destino; (of person) suerte f

father [ˈfɑːðə*] n padre m; **Father Christmas** n Papá m Noel; **father-in-law** n suegro

fatigue [fəˈtiːg] n fatiga, cansancio

fattening [ˈfætnɪŋ] adj (food) que hace engordar

fatty [ˈfætɪ] adj (food) graso ▷ n (inf) gordito/a, gordinflón/ona m/f

faucet [ˈfɔːsɪt] (US) n grifo (SP), llave f, canilla (RPL)

fault [fɔːlt] n (blame) culpa; (defect: in person, machine) defecto; (Geo) falla ▷ vt criticar; **it's my ~** es culpa mía; **to find ~ with** criticar, poner peros a; **at ~** culpable; **faulty** adj defectuoso

fauna [ˈfɔːnə] n fauna

favour etc [ˈfeɪvə*] (US **favor** etc) n favor m; (approval) aprobación f ▷ vt (proposition) estar a favor de, aprobar; (assist) ser propicio a; **to do sb a ~** hacer un favor a algn; **to find ~ with sb** caer en gracia a algn; **in ~ of** a favor de; **favourable** adj favorable; **favourite** [ˈfeɪvrɪt] adj, n favorito, preferido

fawn [fɔːn] n cervato m ▷ vi: **to ~ (up)on** adular de cervato, leonado ▷ adj (also: **~-coloured**) color

fax [fæks] n (document) fax m; (machine) telefax m ▷ vt mandar por telefax

FBI (US) n abbr (= Federal Bureau of Investigation) ≈ BIC f (SP)

fear [fɪə*] n miedo, temor m ▷ vt tener miedo de, temer; **for ~ of** por si; **fearful** adj temeroso, miedoso; (awful) terrible; **fearless** adj audaz

feasible [ˈfiːzəbl] adj factible

feast [fiːst] n banquete m; (Rel: also: **~ day**) fiesta ▷ vi festejar

feat [fiːt] n hazaña

feather [ˈfeðə*] n pluma

feature [ˈfiːtʃə*] n característica; (article) artículo de fondo ▷ vt (film) presentar ▷ vi: **to ~ in** tener un papel destacado en; **features** npl (of face) facciones fpl; **feature film** n largometraje m

Feb. abbr (= February) feb

February [ˈfebruərɪ] n febrero

fed [fed] pt, pp of **feed**

federal [ˈfedərəl] adj federal

federation [fedəˈreɪʃən] n federación f

fed up [fedˈʌp] adj: **to be ~ (with)** estar harto (de)

fee [fiː] n pago; (professional) derechos mpl, honorarios mpl; (of club) cuota; school **~s** matrícula

feeble [ˈfiːbl] adj débil; (joke) flojo

feed [fiːd] (pt, pp **fed**) n comida; (of animal) pienso; (on printer) dispositivo de alimentación ▷ vt alimentar; (BRIT: baby: breastfeed) dar el pecho a; (animal) dar de comer a; (data, information): **to ~ into** meter en; **feedback** n reacción f, feedback m

feel [fiːl] (pt, pp **felt**) n (sensation) sensación f; (sense of touch) tacto; (impression): **to have the ~ of** parecerse a ▷ vt tocar; (cold etc) sentir; (think, believe) creer; **to ~ hungry/cold** tener hambre/frío; **to ~ lonely/better** sentirse solo/mejor; **I don't ~ well** no me siento bien; **it ~s soft** es suave al tacto; **to ~ like** (want) tener ganas de; **feeling** n (physical) sensación f; (foreboding) presentimiento; (emotion) sentimiento

feet [fiːt] npl of **foot**

fell [fel] pt of **fall** ▷ vt (tree) talar

fellow [ˈfeləu] n tipo, tío (SP); (comrade) compañero; (of learned society) socio/a; **fellow citizen** n conciudadano/a; **fellow countryman** (irreg) n compatriota m; **fellow men** npl semejantes mpl; **fellowship** n compañerismo; (grant) beca

felony [ˈfelənɪ] n crimen m

felt [felt] pt, pp of **feel** ▷ n fieltro; **felt-tip** n (also: **felt-tip pen**) rotulador m

female [ˈfiːmeɪl] n (Zool) hembra; (pej: woman) mujer f, tía; (Zool) hembra ▷ adj femenino; hembra

feminine [ˈfemɪnɪn] adj femenino

feminist [ˈfemɪnɪst] n feminista

fence [fens] n valla, cerca ▷ vt (also: **~ in**) cercar ▷ vi (Sport) hacer esgrima; **fencing** n esgrima

fend [fend] vi: **to ~ for o.s.** valerse por sí mismo; **fend off** vt (attack) rechazar; (questions) evadir

fender [ˈfendə*] (US) n guardafuego; (Aut) parachoques m inv

fennel [ˈfenl] n hinojo

ferment [vb fəˈment, n ˈfɜːment] vi fermentar ▷ n (fig) agitación f

fern [fɜːn] n helecho

ferocious [fəˈrəuʃəs] adj feroz

ferret [ˈferɪt] n hurón m

ferry [ˈferɪ] n (small) barca (de pasaje), balsa; (large: also: **~boat**) transbordador m, ferry m ▷ vt transportar

fertile [ˈfɜːtaɪl] adj fértil; (Biol) fecundo; **fertilize**

['fɜːtɪlaɪz] vt (Biol) fecundar; (Agr) abonar; **fertilizer** n abono

festival ['festɪvəl] n (Rel) fiesta; (Art, Mus) festival m

festive ['festɪv] adj festivo; **the ~ season** (BRIT: Christmas) las Navidades

fetch [fetʃ] vt ir a buscar; (sell for) venderse por

fête [feɪt] n fiesta

fetus ['fiːtəs] (US) = **foetus**

feud [fjuːd] n (hostility) enemistad f; (quarrel) disputa

fever ['fiːvə*] n fiebre f; **feverish** adj febril

few [fjuː] adj (not many) pocos ▷ pron pocos; algunos; **a ~** adj unos pocos, algunos; **fewer** adj menos; **fewest** adj los(las) menos

fiancé [fɪˈɒnseɪ] n novio, prometido; **fiancée** n novia, prometida

fiasco [fɪˈæskəʊ] n fiasco

fib [fɪb] n mentirilla

fibre ['faɪbə*] (US **fiber**) n fibra; **fibreglass** (US **Fiberglass®**) n fibra de vidrio

fickle ['fɪkl] adj inconstante

fiction ['fɪkʃən] n ficción f; **fictional** adj novelesco

fiddle ['fɪdl] n (Mus) violín m; (cheating) trampa ▷ vt (BRIT: accounts) falsificar; **fiddle with** vt fus juguetear con

fidelity [fɪˈdelɪtɪ] n fidelidad f

field [fiːld] n campo; (fig) campo, esfera; (Sport) campo (SP), cancha (LAM); **field marshal** n mariscal m

fierce [fɪəs] adj feroz; (wind, heat) fuerte; (fighting, enemy) encarnizada

fifteen [fɪfˈtiːn] num quince; **fifteenth** adj decimoquinto; **the fifteenth floor** la planta quince; **the fifteenth of August** el quince de agosto

fifth [fɪfθ] num quinto

fiftieth ['fɪftɪɪθ] adj quincuagésimo

fifty ['fɪftɪ] num cincuenta; **fifty-fifty** adj (deal, split) a medias ▷ adv a medias, mitad por mitad

fig [fɪg] n higo

fight [faɪt] (pt, pp **fought**) n (gen) pelea; (Mil) combate m; (struggle) lucha ▷ vt luchar contra; (cancer, alcoholism) combatir; (election) intentar ganar; (emotion) resistir ▷ vi pelear, luchar; **fight back** vi defenderse; (after illness) recuperarse ▷ vt (tears) contener; **fight off** vt (attack, attacker) rechazar; (disease, sleep, urge) luchar contra; **fighting** n combate m, pelea

figure ['fɪgə*] n (Drawing, Geom) figura, dibujo; (number, cipher) cifra; (body, outline) tipo; (personality) figura ▷ vt (esp US) imaginar ▷ vi (appear) figurar; **figure out** vt (work out) resolver

file [faɪl] n (tool) lima; (dossier) expediente m; (folder) carpeta; (Comput) fichero; (row) fila ▷ vt limar; (Law: claim) presentar; (store) archivar; **filing cabinet** n fichero, archivador m

Filipino [fɪlɪˈpiːnəʊ] adj filipino ▷ n (person) filipino/a m/f; (Ling) tagalo

fill [fɪl] vt (space): **to ~ (with)** llenar (de); (vacancy, need) cubrir ▷ n: **to eat one's ~** llenarse; **fill in** vt rellenar; **fill out** vt (form, receipt) rellenar; **fill up** vt llenar (hasta el borde) ▷ vi (Aut) poner gasolina

fillet ['fɪlɪt] n filete m; **fillet steak** n filete m de ternera

filling ['fɪlɪŋ] n (Culin) relleno; (for tooth) empaste m; **filling station** n estación f de servicio

film [fɪlm] n película ▷ vt (scene) filmar ▷ vi rodar (una película); **film star** n astro, estrella de cine

filter ['fɪltə*] n filtro ▷ vt filtrar; **filter lane** (BRIT) n carril m de selección

filth [fɪlθ] n suciedad f; **filthy** adj sucio; (language) obsceno

fin [fɪn] n (gen) aleta

final ['faɪnl] adj (last) final, último; (definitive) definitivo, terminante ▷ n (BRIT Sport) final f; **finals** npl (Scol) examen m final; (US Sport) final f

finale [fɪˈnɑːlɪ] n final m

final: finalist n (Sport) finalista mf; **finalize** vt concluir, completar; **finally** adv (lastly) por último, finalmente; (eventually) por fin

finance [faɪˈnæns] n (money) fondos mpl ▷ vt financiar; **finances** npl finanzas fpl; (personal finances) situación f económica; **financial** [-ˈnænʃəl] adj financiero; **financial year** n ejercicio (financiero)

find [faɪnd] (pt, pp **found**) vt encontrar, hallar; (come upon) descubrir ▷ n hallazgo; descubrimiento; **to ~ sb guilty** (Law) declarar culpable a algn; **find out** vt averiguar; (truth, secret) descubrir; **to find out about** (subject) informarse sobre; (by chance) enterarse de; **findings** npl (Law) veredicto, fallo; (of report) recomendaciones fpl

fine [faɪn] adj excelente; (thin) fino ▷ adv (well) bien ▷ n (Law) multa ▷ vt (Law) multar; **to be ~** (person) estar bien; (weather) hacer buen tiempo; **fine arts** npl bellas artes fpl

finger ['fɪŋgə*] n dedo ▷ vt (touch) manosear; **little/index ~** (dedo) meñique m/índice m; **fingernail** n uña; **fingerprint** n huella dactilar; **fingertip** n yema f del dedo

finish ['fɪnɪʃ] n (end) fin m; (Sport) meta; (polish etc) acabado ▷ vt, vi terminar; **to ~ doing sth** acabar de hacer algo; **to ~ third** llegar el tercero; **finish off** vt acabar, terminar; (kill) acabar con; **finish up** vt acabar, terminar ▷ vi ir a parar, terminar

Finland ['fɪnlənd] n Finlandia

Finn [fɪn] n finlandés/esa m/f; **Finnish** adj finlandés/esa ▷ n (Ling) finlandés m

fir [fɜː*] n abeto

fire ['faɪə*] n fuego; (in hearth) lumbre f; (accidental) incendio; (heater) estufa ▷ vt (gun) disparar; (interest) despertar; (inf: dismiss) despedir ▷ vi (shoot) disparar; **on ~** ardiendo, en llamas; **fire alarm** n alarma de incendios; **firearm** n arma de fuego; **fire brigade** (US **fire department**) n (cuerpo de) bomberos mpl; **fire engine** (BRIT) n coche m de bomberos; **fire escape** n escalera de incendios; **fire exit** n salida de incendios; **fire extinguisher** n extintor m (de incendios); **fireman** (irreg) n bombero; **fireplace** n chimenea; **fire station** n parque m de bomberos; **firetruck** (US) n **= fire engine**; **firewall** n (Internet) firewall m; **firewood** n leña; **fireworks** npl fuegos mpl artificiales

firm [fɜːm] adj firme; (look, voice) resuelto ▷ n firma, empresa; **firmly** adv firmemente; resueltamente

first [fɜːst] adj primero; (before others) primero; (when listing reasons etc) en primer lugar, primeramente ▷ n (person: in race) primero/a; (Aut) primera; (BRIT Scol) título de licenciado con calificación de sobresaliente; **at ~** al principio; **~ of all** ante todo; **first aid** n primera ayuda, primeros auxilios mpl; **first-aid kit** n botiquín m; **first-class** adj (excellent) de primera (categoría); (ticket etc) de primera clase; **first-hand** adj de primera mano; **first lady** n (esp US) primera dama; **firstly** adv en primer lugar; **first name** n nombre m (de pila); **first-rate** adj estupendo

fiscal ['fɪskəl] adj fiscal; **fiscal year** n año fiscal, ejercicio

fish [fɪʃ] n inv pez m; (food) pescado ▷ vt, vi pescar; **to go ~ing** ir de pesca; **~ and chips** pescado frito con patatas fritas; **fisherman** (irreg) n pescador m; **fish fingers** (BRIT) npl croquetas fpl de pescado; **fishing** n pesca; **fishing boat** n barca de pesca; **fishing line** n sedal m; **fishmonger** n (BRIT) pescadero/a; **fishmonger's (shop)** (BRIT) n pescadería; **fish sticks** (US) npl =**fish fingers**; **fishy** (inf) adj sospechoso

fist [fɪst] n puño

fit [fɪt] adj (healthy) en (buena) forma; (proper) adecuado, apropiado ▷ vt (clothes) estar or sentar bien a; (instal) poner; (equip) proveer, dotar; (facts) cuadrar or corresponder con ▷ vi (clothes) sentar bien; (in space, gap) caber; (facts) coincidir ▷ n (Med) ataque m; **~ to** (ready) a punto de; **~ for** apropiado para; **a ~ of anger/pride** un arranque de cólera/orgullo; **this dress is a good ~** este vestido me sienta bien; **by ~s and starts** a rachas; **fit in** vi (fig: person) llevarse bien (con todos); **fitness** n (Med) salud f; **fitted** adj (jacket, shirt) entallado; (sheet) de cuatro picos; **fitted carpet** n moqueta; **fitted kitchen** n cocina amueblada; **fitting** adj apropiado ▷ n (of dress) prueba; (of piece of equipment) instalación f; **fitting room** n probador m; **fittings** npl instalaciones fpl

five [faɪv] num cinco; **fiver** (inf) n (BRIT) billete m de cinco libras; (US) billete m de cinco dólares

fix [fɪks] vt (secure) fijar, asegurar; (mend) arreglar; (prepare) preparar ▷ n **to be in a ~** estar en un aprieto; **fix up** vt (meeting) arreglar; **to fix sb up with sth** proveer a algn de algo; **fixed** adj (prices etc) fijo; **fixture** n (Sport) encuentro

fizzy ['fɪzɪ] adj (drink) gaseoso

flag [flæg] n bandera; (stone) losa ▷ vi decaer ▷ vt: **to ~ sb down** hacer señas a algn para que se pare; **flagpole** n asta de bandera

flair [fleə*] n aptitud especial

flak [flæk] n (Mil) fuego antiaéreo; (inf: criticism) lluvia de críticas

flake [fleɪk] n (of rust, paint) escama; (of snow, soap powder) copo ▷ vi (also: **~ off**) desconcharse

flamboyant [flæm'bɔɪənt] adj (dress) vistoso; (person) extravagante

flame [fleɪm] n llama

flamingo [flə'mɪŋɡəu] n flamenco

flammable ['flæməbl] adj inflamable

flan [flæn] (BRIT) n tarta

flank [flæŋk] n (of animal) ijar m; (of army) flanco ▷ vt flanquear

flannel ['flænl] n (BRIT: also: **face ~**) manopla; (fabric) franela

flap [flæp] n (of pocket, envelope) solapa ▷ vt (wings, arms) agitar ▷ vi (sail, flag) ondear

flare [fleə*] n llamarada; (Mil) bengala; (in skirt etc) vuelo; **flares** npl (trousers) pantalones mpl de campana; **flare up** vi encenderse; (fig: person) encolerizarse; (: revolt) estallar

flash [flæʃ] n relámpago; (also: **news ~**) noticias fpl de última hora; (Phot) flash m ▷ vt (light, headlights) lanzar un destello con; (news, message) transmitir; (smile) lanzar ▷ vi brillar; (hazard light etc) lanzar destellos; **in a ~** en un instante; **he ~ed by** or **past** pasó como un rayo; **flashback** n (Cinema) flashback m; **flashbulb** n bombilla fusible; **flashlight** n linterna

flask [flɑːsk] n frasco; (also: **vacuum ~**) termo

flat [flæt] adj llano; (smooth) liso; (tyre) desinflado;

(battery) descargado; (beer) muerto; (refusal etc) rotundo; (Mus) desafinado; (rate) fijo ▷ n (BRIT: apartment) piso (SP), departamento (LAM), apartamento; (Aut) pinchazo; (Mus) bemol m; **to work ~ out** trabajar a toda mecha; **flatten** vt (also: **flatten out**) allanar; (smooth out) alisar; (building, plants) arrasar

flatter ['flætə*] vt adular, halagar; **flattering** adj halagüeño; (dress) que favorece

flaunt [flɔːnt] vt ostentar, lucir

flavour etc ['fleɪvə*] (US **flavor** etc) n sabor m, gusto ▷ vt sazonar, condimentar; **strawberry-flavoured** con sabor a fresa; **flavouring** n (in product) aromatizante m

flaw [flɔː] n defecto; **flawless** adj impecable

flea [fliː] n pulga; **flea market** n rastro, mercadillo

flee [fliː] (pt, pp **fled**) vt huir de ▷ vi huir, fugarse

fleece [fliːs] n vellón n; (wool) lana; (top) forro polar ▷ vt (inf) desplumar

fleet [fliːt] n flota; (of lorries etc) escuadra

fleeting ['fliːtɪŋ] adj fugaz

Flemish ['flemɪʃ] adj flamenco

flesh [fleʃ] n carne f; (skin) piel f; (of fruit) pulpa

flew [fluː] pt of **fly**

flex [fleks] n cordón m ▷ vt (muscles) tensar; **flexibility** n flexibilidad f; **flexible** adj flexible; **flexitime** (US **flextime**) n horario flexible

flick [flɪk] n capirotazo; chasquido ▷ vt (with hand) dar un capirotazo a; (whip etc) chasquear; (switch) accionar; **flick through** vt fus hojear

flicker ['flɪkə*] vi (light) parpadear; (flame) vacilar

flies [flaɪz] npl of **fly**

flight [flaɪt] n vuelo; (escape) huida, fuga; (also: **~ of steps**) tramo (de escaleras); **flight attendant** n auxiliar mf de vuelo

flimsy ['flɪmzɪ] adj (thin) muy ligero; (building) endeble; (excuse) flojo

flinch [flɪntʃ] vi encogerse; **to ~ from** retroceder ante

fling [flɪŋ] (pt, pp **flung**) vt arrojar

flint [flɪnt] n pedernal m; (in lighter) piedra

flip [flɪp] vt dar la vuelta a; (switch: turn on) encender; (turn) apagar; (coin) echar a cara o cruz

flip-flops ['flɪpflɔps] npl esp BRIT chancletas fpl

flipper ['flɪpə*] n aleta

flirt [fləːt] vi coquetear, flirtear ▷ n coqueta

float [fləut] n (for fishing) flotador m; (in procession) carroza; (money) reserva ▷ vi flotar; (swimmer) hacer la plancha

flock [flɔk] n (of sheep) rebaño; (of birds) bandada ▷ vi: **to ~ to** acudir en tropel a

flood [flʌd] n inundación f; (of letters, imports etc) avalancha ▷ vt inundar ▷ vi (place) inundarse; (people): **to ~ into** inundar; **flooding** n inundaciones fpl; **floodlight** n foco

floor [flɔː*] n suelo; (storey) piso; (of sea) fondo ▷ vt (question) dejar sin respuesta; (: blow) derribar; **ground ~, first ~** (US) planta baja; **first ~, second ~** (US) primer piso; **floorboard** n tabla; **flooring** n suelo; (material) solería; **floor show** n cabaret m

flop [flɔp] n fracaso ▷ vi (fail) fracasar; (plop) derrumbarse; **floppy** adj flojo ▷ n (Comput: also: **floppy disk**) floppy m

flora ['flɔːrə] n flora

floral ['flɔːrl] adj (pattern) floreado

florist ['flɔrɪst] n florista mf; **florist's (shop)** n floristería

flotation [fləu'teɪʃən] n (of shares) emisión f; (of company) lanzamiento

flour ['flauə*] n harina
flourish ['flʌrɪʃ] vi florecer ▷ n ademán m, movimiento (ostentoso)
flow [fləu] n (movement) flujo; (of traffic) circulación f; (tide) corriente f ▷ vi (river, blood) fluir; (traffic) circular
flower ['flauə*] n flor f ▷ vi florecer; **flower bed** n macizo; **flowerpot** n tiesto
flown [fləun] pp of **fly**
fl. oz. abbr (= fluid ounce)
flu [flu:] n: **to have ~** tener la gripe
fluctuate ['flʌktjueɪt] vi fluctuar
fluent ['flu:ənt] adj (linguist) que habla perfectamente; (speech) elocuente; **he speaks ~ French, he's ~ in French** domina el francés
fluff [flʌf] n pelusa; **fluffy** adj de pelo suave
fluid ['flu:ɪd] adj (movement) fluido, líquido; (situation) inestable ▷ n fluido, líquido; **fluid ounce** n onza f líquida
fluke [flu:k] (inf) n chiripa
flung [flʌŋ] pt, pp of **fling**
fluorescent [fluə'resnt] adj fluorescente
fluoride ['fluəraɪd] n fluoruro
flurry ['flʌrɪ] n (of snow) temporal m; **~ of activity** frenesí m de actividad
flush [flʌʃ] n rubor m; (fig: of youth etc) resplandor m ▷ vt limpiar con agua ▷ vi ruborizarse ▷ adj: **~ with** a ras de; **to ~ the toilet** hacer funcionar la cisterna
flute [flu:t] n flauta
flutter ['flʌtə*] n (of wings) revoloteo, aleteo; (fig): **a ~ of panic/excitement** una oleada de pánico/excitación ▷ vi revolotear
fly [flaɪ] (pt **flew**, pp **flown**) n mosca; (on trousers: also: **flies**) bragueta ▷ vt (plane) pilot(e)ar; (cargo) transportar (en avión); (distances) recorrer (en avión) ▷ vi volar; (passengers) ir en avión; (escape) evadirse; (flag) ondear; **fly away, fly off** vi emprender el vuelo; **fly-drive** n: **fly-drive holiday** vacaciones que incluyen vuelo y alquiler de coche; **flying** n (activity) (el) volar; (action) vuelo ▷ adj: **with flying colours** con lucimiento; **flying saucer** n platillo volante; **flying visit** visita relámpago; **flyover** (BRIT) n paso a desnivel or superior
FM abbr (Radio) (= frequency modulation) FM
foal [fəul] n potro
foam [fəum] n espuma ▷ vi hacer espuma
focus ['fəukəs] (pl **~es**) n foco; (centre) centro ▷ vt (field glasses etc) enfocar ▷ vi: **to ~ (on)** enfocar (a); (issue etc) centrarse en; **in/out of ~** enfocado/desenfocado
foetus ['fi:təs] (US **fetus**) n feto
fog [fɔg] n niebla; **foggy** adj: **it's foggy** hay niebla, está brumoso; **fog lamp** (US **fog light**) n (Aut) faro de niebla
foil [fɔɪl] vt frustrar ▷ n hoja; (kitchen foil) papel m (de) aluminio; (complement) complemento; (Fencing) florete m
fold [fəuld] n (bend, crease) pliegue m; (Agr) redil m ▷ vt doblar; (arms) cruzar; **fold up** vi plegarse, doblarse; (business) quebrar ▷ vt (map etc) plegar; **folder** n (for papers) carpeta; (Comput) directorio; **folding** adj (chair, bed) plegable
foliage ['fəulɪdʒ] n follaje m
folk [fəuk] npl gente f ▷ adj popular, folklórico; **folks** npl (family) familia sg, parientes mpl; **folklore** ['fəuklɔ:*] n folklore m; **folk music** n música folk; **folk song** n canción f popular

follow ['fɔləu] vt seguir ▷ vi seguir; (result) resultar; **to ~ suit** hacer lo mismo; **follow up** vt (letter, offer) responder a; (case) investigar; **follower** n (of person, belief) partidario a; **following** adj siguiente ▷ n afición f, partidarios mpl; **follow-up** n continuación f
fond [fɔnd] adj (memory, smile etc) cariñoso; (hopes) ilusorio; **to be ~ of** tener cariño a; (pastime, food) ser aficionado a
food [fu:d] n comida; **food mixer** n batidora; **food poisoning** n intoxicación f alimenticia; **food processor** n robot m de cocina; **food stamp** (US) n vale m para comida
fool [fu:l] n tonto a; (Culin) puré m de frutas con nata ▷ vt engañar ▷ vi (gen) bromear; **fool about, fool around** vi hacer el tonto; **foolish** adj tonto; (careless) imprudente; **foolproof** adj (plan etc) infalible
foot [fut] (pl **feet**) n pie m; (measure) pie m (= 304 mm); (of animal) pata ▷ vt (bill) pagar; **on ~** a pie; **footage** n (Cinema) imágenes fpl; **foot-and-mouth (disease)** [futənd'mauθ-] n fiebre f aftosa; **football** n balón m; (game: BRIT) fútbol m; (: US) fútbol americano; **footballer** n (BRIT) = **football player**; **football match** n partido de fútbol; **football player** n (BRIT) futbolista mf; (US) jugador m de fútbol americano; **footbridge** n puente m para peatones; **foothills** npl estribaciones fpl; **foothold** n pie m firme; **footing** n (fig) posición f; **to lose one's footing** perder el pie; **footnote** n nota (al pie de la página); **footpath** n sendero; **footprint** n huella, pisada; **footstep** n paso; **footwear** n calzado

⊙ **KEYWORD**

for [fɔ:] prep **1** (indicating destination, intention) para; **the train for London** el tren con destino a or de Londres; **he left for Rome** marchó para Roma; **he went for the paper** fue por el periódico; **is this for me?** ¿es esto para mí?; **it's time for lunch** es la hora de comer
2 (indicating purpose) para; **what('s it) for?** ¿para qué (es)?; **to pray for peace** rezar por la paz
3 (on behalf of, representing): **the MP for Hove** el diputado por Hove; **he works for the government/a local firm** trabaja para el gobierno/en una empresa local; **I'll ask him for you** se
lo pediré por ti; **G for George** G de Gerona
4 (because of) por esta razón; **for fear of being criticized** por temor a ser criticado
5 (with regard to) para; **it's cold for July** hace frío para julio; **he has a gift for languages** tiene don de lenguas
6 (in exchange for) por; **I sold it for £5** lo vendí por £5; **to pay 50 pence for a ticket** pagar 50 peniques por un billete
7 (in favour of): **are you for or against us?** ¿estás con nosotros o contra nosotros?; **I'm all for it** estoy totalmente a favor; **vote for X** vote (a) X
8 (referring to distance): **there are roadworks for 5 km** hay obras en 5 km; **we walked for miles** caminamos kilómetros y kilómetros
9 (referring to time): **he was away for two years** estuvo fuera (durante) dos años; **it hasn't rained for 3 weeks** no ha llovido durante or en 3 semanas; **I have known her for years** la conozco desde hace años; **can you do it for tomorrow?** ¿lo podrás hacer para mañana?
10 (with infinitive clauses): **it is not for me to decide** la

decisión no es cosa mía; **it would be best for you to leave** sería mejor que te fueras; **there is still time for you to do it** todavía te queda tiempo para hacerlo; **for this to be possible ...** para que esto sea posible ... **11** (*in spite of*) a pesar de; **for all his complaints** a pesar de sus quejas ▷ *conj* (*since, as: rather formal*) puesto que

forbid [fə'bɪd] (*pt* forbad(e), *pp* forbidden) *vt* prohibir; **to ~ sb to do sth** prohibir a algn hacer algo; **forbidden** *pt of* forbid ▷ *adj* (*food, area*) prohibido; (*word, subject*) tabú

force [fɔːs] *n* fuerza ▷ *vt* forzar; (*push*) meter a la fuerza; **to ~ o.s. to do** hacer un esfuerzo por hacer; **forced** *adj* forzado; **forceful** *adj* enérgico

ford [fɔːd] *n* vado

fore [fɔː*] *n*: **to come to the ~** empezar a destacar; **forearm** *n* antebrazo; **forecast** (*pt, pp* **forecast**) *n* pronóstico ▷ *vt* pronosticar; **forecourt** *n* patio; **forefinger** *n* (*dedo*) índice *m*; **forefront** *n*: **in the forefront of** en la vanguardia de; **foreground** *n* primer plano; **forehead** ['fɔrɪd] *n* frente*f*

foreign ['fɔrɪn] *adj* extranjero; (*trade*) exterior; (*object*) extraño; **foreign currency** *n* divisas *fpl*; **foreigner** *n* extranjero/a; **foreign exchange** *n* divisas *fpl*; **Foreign Office** (BRIT) *n* Ministerio de Asuntos Exteriores; **Foreign Secretary** (BRIT) *n* Ministro de Asuntos Exteriores

fore: **foreman** (*irreg*) *n* capataz *m*; (*in construction*) maestro de obras; **foremost** *adj* principal ▷ *adv*: **first and foremost** ante todo; **forename** *n* nombre *m* (de pila)

forensic [fə'rɛnsɪk] *adj* forense

foresee [fɔː'siː] (*pt* foresaw, *pp* foreseen) *vt* prever; **foreseeable** *adj* previsible

forest ['fɔrɪst] *n* bosque *m*; **forestry** *n* silvicultura

forever [fə'rɛvə*] *adv* para siempre; (*endlessly*) constantemente

foreword ['fɔːwəd] *n* prefacio

forfeit ['fɔːfɪt] *vt* perder

forgave [fə'geɪv] *pt of* forgive

forge [fɔːdʒ] *n* herrería ▷ *vt* (*signature, money*) falsificar; (*metal*) forjar; **forger** *n* falsificador(a) *m/f*; **forgery** *n* falsificación *f*

forget [fə'gɛt] (*pt* forgot, *pp* forgotten) *vt* olvidar ▷ *vi* olvidarse; **forgetful** *adj* despistado

forgive [fə'gɪv] (*pt* forgave, *pp* forgiven) *vt* perdonar; **to ~ sb for sth** perdonar algo a algn

forgot [fə'gɔt] *pt of* forget

forgotten [fə'gɔtn] *pp of* forget

fork [fɔːk] *n* (*for eating*) tenedor *m*; (*for gardening*) horca; (*of roads*) bifurcación *f* ▷ *vi* (*road*) bifurcarse

forlorn [fə'lɔːn] *adj* (*person*) triste, melancólico; (*place*) abandonado; (*attempt, hope*) desesperado

form [fɔːm] *n* forma; (BRIT Scol) clase *f*; (*document*) formulario ▷ *vt* formar; (*idea*) concebir; (*habit*) adquirir; **in top ~** en plena forma; **to ~ a queue** hacer cola

formal ['fɔːməl] *adj* (*offer, receipt*) por escrito; (*person etc*) correcto; (*occasion, dinner*) de etiqueta; (*dress*) correcto; (*garden*) (de estilo) clásico; **formality** [-'mælɪtɪ] *n* (*procedure*) trámite *m*; corrección *f*; etiqueta

format ['fɔːmæt] *n* formato ▷ *vt* (Comput) formatear

formation [fɔː'meɪʃən] *n* formación *f*

former ['fɔːmə*] *adj* anterior; (*earlier*) antiguo; (*ex*) ex; **the ~ ... the latter ...** aquél ... éste ...; **formerly** *adv* antes

formidable ['fɔːmɪdəbl] *adj* formidable

formula ['fɔːmjulə] *n* fórmula

fort [fɔːt] *n* fuerte *m*

forthcoming [fɔːθ'kʌmɪŋ] *adj* próximo, venidero; (*help, information*) disponible; (*character*) comunicativo

fortieth ['fɔːtɪɪθ] *adj* cuadragésimo

fortify ['fɔːtɪfaɪ] *vt* (*city*) fortificar; (*person*) fortalecer

fortnight ['fɔːtnaɪt] (BRIT) *n* quince días *mpl*; quincena; **fortnightly** *adj* de cada quince días, quincenal ▷ *adv* cada quince días, quincenalmente

fortress ['fɔːtrɪs] *n* fortaleza

fortunate ['fɔːtʃənɪt] *adj* afortunado; **it is ~ that ...** (es una) suerte que ...; **fortunately** *adv* afortunadamente

fortune ['fɔːtʃən] *n* suerte *f*; (*wealth*) fortuna; **fortune-teller** *n* adivino/a

forty ['fɔːtɪ] *num* cuarenta

forum ['fɔːrəm] *n* foro

forward ['fɔːwəd] *adj* (*movement, position*) avanzado; (*front*) delantero; (*in time*) adelantado; (*not shy*) atrevido ▷ *n* (Sport) delantero ▷ *vt* (*letter*) remitir; (*career*) promocionar; **to move ~** avanzar; **forwarding address** *n* destinatario; **forward(s)** *adv* (hacia) adelante; **forward slash** *n* barra diagonal

fossil ['fɔsl] *n* fósil *m*

foster ['fɔstə*] *vt* (*child*) acoger en una familia; fomentar; **foster child** *n* hijo/a adoptivo/a; **foster mother** *n* madre *f* adoptiva

fought [fɔːt] *pt, pp of* fight

foul [faul] *adj* sucio, puerco; (*weather, smell etc*) asqueroso; (*language*) grosero; (*temper*) malísimo ▷ *n* (Sport) falta ▷ *vt* (*dirty*) ensuciar; **foul play** *n* (Law) muerte *f* violenta

found [faund] *pt, pp of* find ▷ *vt* fundar; **foundation** [-'deɪʃən] *n* (*act*) fundación *f*; (*basis*) base *f*; (*also*: **foundation cream**) crema base; **foundations** *npl* (*of building*) cimientos *mpl*

founder ['faundə*] *n* fundador(a) *m/f* ▷ *vi* hundirse

fountain ['fauntɪn] *n* fuente *f*; **fountain pen** *n* (*pluma*) estilográfica (SP), pluma-fuente *f* (LAM)

four [fɔː*] *num* cuatro; **on all ~s** a gatas; **four-letter word** *n* taco; **four-poster** *n* (*also*: **four-poster bed**) cama de columnas; **fourteen** *num* catorce; **fourteenth** *adj* decimocuarto; **fourth** *num* cuarto; **four-wheel drive** *n* tracción *f* a las cuatro ruedas

fowl [faul] *n* ave *f* (de corral)

fox [fɔks] *n* zorro ▷ *vt* confundir

foyer ['fɔɪeɪ] *n* vestíbulo

fraction ['frækʃən] *n* fracción *f*

fracture ['fræktʃə*] *n* fractura

fragile ['frædʒaɪl] *adj* frágil

fragment ['frægmənt] *n* fragmento

fragrance ['freɪgrəns] *n* fragancia

frail [freɪl] *adj* frágil; (*person*) débil

frame [freɪm] *n* (Tech) armazón *m*; (*of person*) cuerpo; (*of picture, door etc*) marco; (*of spectacles: also*: **~s**) montura ▷ *vt* enmarcar; **framework** *n* marco

France [frɑːns] *n* Francia

franchise ['fræntʃaɪz] *n* (Pol) derecho de votar, sufragio; (Comm) licencia, concesión *f*

frank [fræŋk] *adj* franco ▷ *vt* (*letter*) franquear; **frankly** *adv* francamente

frantic ['fræntɪk] *adj* (*distraught*) desesperado; (*hectic*) frenético

fraud [frɔːd] n fraude m; (person) impostor(a) m/f
fraught [frɔːt] adj: ~ **with** lleno de
fray [freɪ] vi deshilacharse
freak [friːk] n (person) fenómeno m; (event) suceso anormal
freckle [ˈfrɛkl] n peca
free [friː] adj libre; (gratis) gratuito ▷ vt (prisoner etc) poner en libertad; (jammed object) soltar; ~ **(of charge)**, **for** ~ gratis; **freedom** n libertad f; **Freefone®** n número gratuito; **free gift** n prima; **free kick** n tiro libre; **freelance** adj independiente ▷ adv por cuenta propia; **freely** adv libremente; (liberally) generosamente; **Freepost®** n porte m pagado; **free-range** adj (hen, eggs) de granja; **freeway** (US) n autopista; **free will** n libre albedrío; **of one's own free will** por su propia voluntad
freeze [friːz] (pt **froze**, pp **frozen**) vi (weather) helar; (liquid, pipe, person) helarse, congelarse ▷ vt helar; (food, prices, salaries) congelar ▷ n helada; (on arms, wages) congelación f; **freezer** n congelador m, freezer m (SC)
freezing [ˈfriːzɪŋ] adj helado; **three degrees below** ~ tres grados bajo cero; **freezing point** n punto de congelación
freight [freɪt] n (goods) carga; (money charged) flete m; **freight train** (US) n tren m de mercancías
French [frɛntʃ] adj francés/esa ▷ n (Ling) francés m; **the French** npl los franceses; **French bean** n judía verde; **French bread** n pan m francés; **French dressing** n (Culin) vinagreta; **French fried potatoes**, **French fries** (US) npl patatas fpl (SP) or papas fpl (LAM) fritas; **Frenchman** (irreg) n francés m; **Frenchwoman** (irreg) n francesa; **French stick** n barra de pan; **French window** n puerta de cristal
frenzy [ˈfrɛnzɪ] n frenesí m
frequency [ˈfriːkwənsɪ] n frecuencia
frequent [adj ˈfriːkwənt, vb frɪˈkwɛnt] adj frecuente ▷ vt frecuentar; **frequently** [-əntlɪ] adv frecuentemente, a menudo
fresh [frɛʃ] adj fresco; (bread) tierno; (new) nuevo; **freshen** vi (wind, air) soplar más recio; **freshen up** vi (person) arreglarse, lavarse; **fresher** (BRIT: inf) n (Univ) estudiante mf de primer año; **freshly** adv (made, painted etc) recién; **freshman** (US: irreg) n = **fresher**; **freshwater** adj (fish) de agua dulce
fret [frɛt] vi inquietarse
Fri abbr (= Friday) vier
friction [ˈfrɪkʃən] n fricción f
Friday [ˈfraɪdɪ] n viernes m inv
fridge [frɪdʒ] (BRIT) n frigorífico (SP), nevera (SP), refrigerador m (LAM), heladera (RPL)
fried [fraɪd] adj frito
friend [frɛnd] n amigo/a; **friendly** adj simpático; (government) amigo; (place) acogedor(a); (match) amistoso; **friendship** n amistad f
fries [fraɪz] (esp US) npl = **French fried potatoes**
frigate [ˈfrɪgɪt] n fragata
fright [fraɪt] n (terror) terror m; (scare) susto; **to take** ~ asustarse; **frighten** vt asustar; **frightened** adj asustado; **frightening** adj espantoso; **frightful** adj espantoso, horrible
frill [frɪl] n volante m
fringe [frɪndʒ] n (BRIT: of hair) flequillo; (on lampshade etc) flecos mpl; (of forest etc) borde m, margen m
Frisbee® [ˈfrɪzbɪ] n frisbee® m
fritter [ˈfrɪtə*] n buñuelo

frivolous [ˈfrɪvələs] adj frívolo
fro [frəʊ] see **to**
frock [frɔk] n vestido
frog [frɒg] n rana; **frogman** (irreg) n hombre-rana m

Ⓞ KEYWORD

from [frɒm] prep **1** (indicating starting place) de, desde; **where do you come from?** ¿de dónde eres?; **from London to Glasgow** de Londres a Glasgow; **to escape from sth/sb** escaparse de algo/algn
2 (indicating origin etc) de; **a letter/telephone call from my sister** una carta/llamada de mi hermana; **tell him from me that …** dígale de mi parte que …
3 (indicating time): **from one o'clock to** or **until** or **till two** de(sde) la una a or hasta las dos; **from January (on)** a partir de enero
4 (indicating distance) de; **the hotel is 1 km from the beach** el hotel está a 1 km de la playa
5 (indicating price, number etc) de; **prices range from £10 to £50** los precios van desde £10 a or hasta £50; **the interest rate was increased from 9% to 10%** el tipo de interés fue incrementado de un 9% a un 10%
6 (indicating difference) de; **he can't tell red from green** no sabe distinguir el rojo del verde; **to be different from sb/sth** ser diferente a algn/algo
7 (because of, on the basis of): **from what he says** por lo que dice; **weak from hunger** debilitado por el hambre

front [frʌnt] n (foremost part) parte f delantera; (of house) fachada; (of dress) delantero; (promenade: also: **sea ~**) paseo marítimo; (Mil, Pol, Meteorology) frente m; (fig: appearances) apariencias fpl ▷ adj (wheel, leg) delantero; (row, line) primero; **in ~ (of)** delante (de); **front door** n puerta principal; **frontier** [ˈfrʌntɪə*] n frontera; **front page** n primera plana; **front-wheel drive** n tracción f delantera
frost [frɒst] n helada; (also: **hoar~**) escarcha; **frostbite** n congelación f; **frosting** (esp US: icing) glaseado; **frosty** adj (weather) de helada; (welcome etc) glacial
froth [frɒθ] n espuma
frown [fraʊn] vi fruncir el ceño
froze [frəʊz] pt of **freeze**
frozen [ˈfrəʊzn] pp of **freeze**
fruit [fruːt] n inv fruta; fruto; (fig) fruto; resultados mpl; **fruit juice** n zumo (SP) or jugo (LAM) de fruta; **fruit machine** (BRIT) n máquina f tragaperras; **fruit salad** n macedonia (SP) or ensalada (LAM) de frutas
frustrate [frʌsˈtreɪt] vt frustrar; **frustrated** adj frustrado
fry [fraɪ] (pt, pp **fried**) vt freír; **small ~** gente f menuda; **frying pan** n sartén f
ft. abbr = **foot**; **feet**
fudge [fʌdʒ] n (Culin) caramelo blando
fuel [fjʊəl] n (for heating) combustible m; (coal) carbón m; (wood) leña; (for engine) carburante m; **fuel tank** n depósito (de combustible)
fulfil [fʊlˈfɪl] vt (function) cumplir con; (condition) satisfacer; (wish, desire) realizar
full [fʊl] adj lleno; (fig) pleno; (complete) completo; (maximum) máximo; (information) detallado; (price) íntegro; (skirt) amplio ▷ adv: **to know ~ well that** saber perfectamente que; **I'm ~ (up)** no puedo más; ~ **employment** pleno empleo; **a ~ two hours** dos

horas completas; **at ~ speed** a máxima velocidad; **in ~** *(reproduce, quote)* íntegramente; **full length** *adj (novel etc)* entero; *(coat)* largo; *(portrait)* de cuerpo entero; **full moon** *n* luna llena; **full-scale** *adj (attack, war)* en gran escala; *(model)* de tamaño natural; **full stop** *n* punto; **full-time** *adj (work)* de tiempo completo ▷*adv*: **to work full-time** trabajar a tiempo completo; **fully** *adv* completamente; *(at least)* por lo menos

fumble ['fʌmbl] *vi*: **to ~ with** manejar torpemente
fume [fjuːm] *vi (rage)* estar furioso; **fumes** *npl* humo, gases *mpl*
fun [fʌn] *n (amusement)* diversión *f*; **to have ~** divertirse; **for ~** en broma; **to make ~ of** burlarse de
function ['fʌŋkʃən] *n* función *f* ▷*vi* funcionar
fund [fʌnd] *n* fondo; *(reserve)* reserva; **funds** *npl (money)* fondos *mpl*
fundamental [fʌndə'mɛntl] *adj* fundamental
funeral ['fjuːnərəl] *n (burial)* entierro; *(ceremony)* funerales *mpl*; **funeral director** *n* director(a) *m/f* de pompas fúnebres; **funeral parlour** *(BRIT)* *n* funeraria
funfair ['fʌnfɛə*] *(BRIT)* *n* parque *m* de atracciones
fungus ['fʌŋgəs] *(pl* fungi) *n* hongo; *(mould)* moho
funnel ['fʌnl] *n* embudo; *(of ship)* chimenea
funny ['fʌnɪ] *adj* gracioso, divertido; *(strange)* curioso, raro
fur [fəː*] *n* piel *f*; *(BRIT: in kettle etc)* sarro; **fur coat** *n* abrigo de pieles
furious ['fjuərɪəs] *adj* furioso; *(effort)* violento
furnish ['fəːnɪʃ] *vt* amueblar; *(supply)* suministrar; *(information)* facilitar; **furnishings** *npl* muebles *mpl*
furniture ['fəːnɪtʃə*] *n* muebles *mpl*; **piece of ~** mueble *m*
furry ['fəːrɪ] *adj* peludo
further ['fəːðə*] *adj (new)* nuevo, adicional ▷*adv* más lejos; *(more)* más; *(moreover)* además ▷*vt* promover, adelantar; **further education** *n* educación *f* superior; **furthermore** *adv* además
furthest ['fəːðɪst] *superlative of* **far**
fury ['fjuərɪ] *n* furia
fuse [fjuːz] *(US* fuze) *n* fusible *m*; *(for bomb etc)* mecha ▷*vt (metal)* fundir; *(fig)* fusionar ▷*vi* fundirse; fusionarse; *(BRIT Elec)*: **to ~ the lights** fundir los plomos; **fuse box** *n* caja de fusibles
fusion ['fjuːʒən] *n* fusión *f*
fuss [fʌs] *n (excitement)* conmoción *f*; *(trouble)* alboroto; **to make a ~** armar un lío or jaleo; **to make a ~ of sb** mimar a algn; **fussy** *adj (person)* exigente; *(too ornate)* recargado
future ['fjuːtʃə*] *adj* futuro; *(coming)* venidero ▷*n* futuro; *(prospects)* porvenir *m*; **in ~** de ahora en adelante; **futures** *npl (Comm)* operaciones *fpl* a término, futuros *mpl*
fuze [fjuːz] *(US)* = **fuse**
fuzzy ['fʌzɪ] *adj (Phot)* borroso; *(hair)* muy rizado

G [dʒiː] *n (Mus)* sol *m*
g. *abbr (= gram(s))* gr.
gadget ['gædʒɪt] *n* aparato
Gaelic ['geɪlɪk] *adj*, *n (Ling)* gaélico
gag [gæg] *n (on mouth)* mordaza; *(joke)* chiste *m* ▷*vt* amordazar
gain [geɪn] *n*: **~ (in)** aumento (de); *(profit)* ganancia ▷*vt* ganar ▷*vi (watch)* adelantarse; **to ~ from/by sth** sacar provecho de algo; **to ~ on sb** ganar terreno a algn; **to ~ 3 lbs (in weight)** engordar 3 libras
gal. *abbr* = **gallon**
gala ['gɑːlə] *n* fiesta
galaxy ['gæləksɪ] *n* galaxia
gale [geɪl] *n (wind)* vendaval *m*
gall bladder ['gɔːl-] *n* vesícula biliar
gallery ['gælərɪ] *n (also:* **art ~**: *public)* pinacoteca; *(: private)* galería de arte; *(for spectators)* tribuna
gallon ['gæln] *n* galón *m* (BRIT = 4,546 litros, US = 3,785 litros)
gallop ['gæləp] *n* galope *m* ▷*vi* galopar
gallstone ['gɔːlstəun] *n* cálculo biliario
gamble ['gæmbl] *n (risk)* riesgo ▷*vt* jugar, apostar ▷*vi (take a risk)* jugárselas; *(bet)* apostar; **to ~ on** apostar a; *(success etc)* contar con; **gambler** *n* jugador(a) *m/f*; **gambling** *n* juego
game [geɪm] *n* juego; *(match)* partido; *(of cards)* partida; *(Hunting)* caza ▷*adj (willing)*: **to be ~ for anything** atreverse a todo; **big ~** caza mayor; *(contest)* juegos; *(BRIT: Scol)* deportes *mpl*; **games console** [geɪmz-] *n* consola de juegos; **game show** *n* programa *m* concurso *m*, concurso
gammon ['gæmən] *n (bacon)* tocino ahumado; *(ham)* jamón *m* ahumado
gang [gæŋ] *n (of criminals)* pandilla; *(of friends etc)* grupo; *(of workmen)* brigada
gangster ['gæŋstə*] *n* gángster *m*
gap [gæp] *n* vacío (sp), hueco (LAM); *(in trees, traffic)* claro; *(in time)* intervalo; *(difference)*: **~ (between)** diferencia (entre)
gape [geɪp] *vi* mirar boquiabierto; *(shirt etc)* abrirse (completamente)
gap year *n* año sabático (antes de empezar a estudiar en la universidad)

garage ['gærɑ:ʒ] n garaje m; (for repairs) taller m;
garage sale n venta de objetos usados (en el jardín de
una casa particular)

garbage ['gɑ:bɪdʒ] (US) n basura; (inf: nonsense)
tonterías fpl; **garbage can** n cubo o bote m (MEX)
or tacho (SC) de la basura; **garbage collector** (US) n
basurero/a

garden ['gɑ:dn] n jardín m; **gardens** npl (park)
parque m; **garden centre** (BRIT) n centro de jardinería;
gardener n jardinero/a; **gardening** n jardinería

garlic ['gɑ:lɪk] n ajo

garment ['gɑ:mənt] n prenda (de vestir)

garnish ['gɑ:nɪʃ] vt (Culin) aderezar

garrison ['gærɪsn] n guarnición f

gas [gæs] n gas m; (fuel) combustible m; (US)
gasolina ▷ vt asfixiar con gas; **gas cooker** (BRIT) n
cocina de gas; **gas cylinder** n bombona de gas; **gas
fire** n estufa de gas

gasket ['gæskɪt] n (Aut) junta de culata

gasoline ['gæsəli:n] (US) n gasolina

gasp [gɑ:sp] n boqueada f; (of shock etc) grito sofocado
▷ vi (pant) jadear

gas: gas pedal n (esp US) acelerador m; **gas station**
(US) n gasolinera; **gas tank** (US) n (Aut) depósito
(de gasolina)

gate [geɪt] n puerta; (iron gate) verja

gateau ['gætəu] (pl -x) n tarta

gatecrash ['geɪtkræʃ] (BRIT) vt colarse en

gateway ['geɪtweɪ] n puerta

gather ['gæðə*] vt (flowers, fruit) coger (SP), recoger;
(assemble) reunir; (pick up) recoger; (Sewing) fruncir;
(understand) entender ▷ vi (assemble) reunirse; **to
~ speed** ganar velocidad; **gathering** n reunión f,
asamblea

gauge [geɪdʒ] n (instrument) indicador m ▷ vt medir;
(fig) juzgar

gave [geɪv] pt of **give**

gay [geɪ] adj (homosexual) gay; (joyful) alegre; (colour)
vivo

gaze [geɪz] n mirada fija ▷ vi: **to ~ at sth** mirar algo
fijamente

CB abbr = **Great Britain**

GCSE (BRIT) n abbr (= General Certificate of Secondary
Education) examen de reválida que se hace a los 16 años

gear [gɪə*] n equipo, herramientas fpl; (Tech)
engranaje m; (Aut) velocidad f, marcha ▷ vt
(fig: adapt): **to ~ sth to** adaptar or ajustar algo a; **top
or high** (US)/**low** - cuarta/primera velocidad; **in** -
en marcha; **gear up** vi prepararse; **gear box** n caja
de cambios; **gear lever** n palanca de cambio; **gear
shift** (US) n = **gear lever**; **gear stick** n (BRIT) palanca
de cambios

geese [gi:s] npl of **goose**

gel [dʒel] n gel m

gem [dʒem] n piedra preciosa

Gemini ['dʒemɪnaɪ] n Géminis m, Gemelos mpl

gender ['dʒendə*] n género

gene [dʒi:n] n gen(e)m

general ['dʒenərəl] n general m ▷ adj general; **in**
- en general; **general anaesthetic** (US **general
anesthetic**) n anestesia general; **general election**
n elecciones fpl generales; **generalize** vi generalizar;
generally adv generalmente, en general; **general
practitioner** n médico general; **general store** n
tienda (que vende de todo) (LAM, SP), almacén m (SC, SP)

generate ['dʒenəreɪt] vt (Elec) generar; (jobs, profits)

producir

generation [dʒenə'reɪʃən] n generación f

generator ['dʒenəreɪtə*] n generador m

generosity [dʒenə'rɒsɪtɪ] n generosidad f

generous ['dʒenərəs] adj generoso

genetic [dʒɪ'netɪk] adj: **~ engineering** ingeniería
genética; **~ fingerprinting** identificación f genética;
genetically modified adj transgénico; **genetics** n
genética

genitals ['dʒenɪtlz] npl (órganos mpl) genitales mpl

genius ['dʒi:nɪəs] n genio

genome ['dʒi:nəum] n genoma m

gent [dʒent] n abbr (BRIT inf) = **gentleman**

gentle ['dʒentl] adj apacible, dulce; (animal) manso;
(breeze, curve etc) suave

gentleman ['dʒentlmən] (irreg) n señor m; (well-bred
man) caballero

gently ['dʒentlɪ] adv dulcemente; suavemente

gents [dʒents] n aseos mpl (de caballeros)

genuine ['dʒenjuɪn] adj auténtico; (person) sincero;
genuinely adv sinceramente

geographic(al) [dʒɪə'græfɪk(l)] adj geográfico

geography [dʒɪ'ɒgrəfɪ] n geografía

geology [dʒɪ'ɒlədʒɪ] n geología

geometry [dʒɪ'ɒmətrɪ] n geometría

geranium [dʒɪ'reɪnjəm] n geranio

geriatric [dʒerɪ'ætrɪk] adj, n geriátrico/a m/f

germ [dʒə:m] n (microbe) microbio, bacteria; (seed,
fig) germen m

German ['dʒə:mən] adj alemán/ana ▷ n alemán/
ana m/f; (Ling) alemán m; **German measles** n rubéola

Germany ['dʒə:mənɪ] n Alemania

gesture ['dʒestjə*] n gesto; (symbol) muestra

○ **KEYWORD**

get [get] (pt, pp **got**, pp **gotten** (US)) vi
1 (become, be) ponerse, volverse; **to get old/tired**
envejecer/cansarse; **to get drunk** emborracharse; **to
get dirty** ensuciarse; **to get married** casarse; **when
do I get paid?** ¿cuándo me pagan or se me paga?; **it's
getting late** se está haciendo tarde

2 (go): **to get to/from** llegar a/de; **to get home** llegar
a casa

3 (begin) empezar a; **to get to know sb** (llegar a)
conocer a algn; **I'm getting to like him** me está
empezando a gustar; **let's get going or started!**
¡vamos (a empezar)!

4 (modal aux vb): **you've got to do it** tienes que hacerlo
▷ vt **1: to get sth done** (finish) terminar algo; (have
done) mandar hacer algo; **to get one's hair cut**
cortarse el pelo; **to get the car going or to go** arrancar
el coche; **to get sb to do sth** conseguir or hacer que
algn haga algo; **to get sth/sb ready** preparar algo/a
algn

2 (obtain: money, permission, results) conseguir; (find: job,
flat) encontrar; (fetch: person, doctor) buscar; (object) ir
a buscar, traer; **to get sth for sb** conseguir algo para
algn; **get me Mr Jones, please** (Tel) póngame (SP) or
comuníqueme (LAM) con el Sr. Jones, por favor; **can I
get you a drink?** ¿quieres algo de beber?

3 (receive: present, letter) recibir; (acquire: reputation)
alcanzar; (: prize) ganar; **what did you get for your
birthday?** ¿qué te regalaron or tu cumpleaños?; **how
much did you get for the painting?** ¿cuánto sacaste
por el cuadro?

4 (*catch*) coger (*SP*), agarrar (*LAM*); (*hit: target etc*) dar en; **to get sb by the arm/throat** coger or agarrar a algn por el brazo/cuello; **get him!** ¡cógelo! (*SP*), ¡atrápalo! (*LAM*); **the bullet got him in the leg** la bala le dio en la pierna

5 (*take, move*) llevar; **to get sth to sb** hacer llegar algo a algn; **do you think we'll get it through the door?** ¿crees que lo podremos meter por la puerta?

6 (*catch, take: plane, bus etc*) tomar (*LAM*); **where do I get the train for Birmingham?** ¿dónde se coge or se toma el tren para Birmingham?

7 (*understand*) entender; (*hear*) oír; **I've got it!** ¡ya lo tengo!, ¡eureka!; **I don't get your meaning** no te entiendo; **I'm sorry, I didn't get your name** lo siento, no cogí tu nombre

8 (*have, possess*): **to have got** tener
get away *vi* marcharse; (*escape*) escaparse
get away with *vt fus* hacer impunemente
get back *vi* (*return*) volver ▷ *vt* recobrar
get in *vi* entrar; (*train*) llegar; (*arrive home*) volver a casa, regresar
get into *vt fus* entrar en; (*vehicle*) subir a; **to get into a rage** enfadarse
get off *vi* (*from train etc*) bajar; (*depart: person, car*) marcharse ▷ *vt* (*remove*) quitar ▷ *vt fus* (*train, bus*) bajar de
get on *vi* (*at exam etc*): **how are you getting on?** ¿cómo te va?; (*agree*): **to get on (with)** llevarse bien (con) ▷ *vt fus* subir a
get out *vi* salir; (*of vehicle*) bajar ▷ *vt* sacar
get out of *vt fus* salir de; (*duty etc*) escaparse de
get over *vt fus* (*illness*) recobrarse de
get through *vi* (*Tel*) (*lograr*) comunicarse
get up *vi* (*rise*) levantarse ▷ *vt fus* subir

getaway ['gɛtəweɪ] *n* fuga
Ghana ['gɑːnə] *n* Ghana
ghastly ['gɑːstlɪ] *adj* horrible
ghetto ['gɛtəu] *n* gueto
ghost [gəust] *n* fantasma *m*
giant ['dʒaɪənt] *n* gigante *mf* ▷ *adj* gigantesco, gigante
gift [gɪft] *n* regalo; (*ability*) talento; **gifted** *adj* dotado; **gift shop** (*US* **gift store**) *n* tienda de regalos; **gift token, gift voucher** *n* vale *m* canjeable por un regalo
gig [gɪg] *n* (*inf: concert*) actuación *f*
gigabyte ['dʒɪgəbaɪt] *n* gigabyte *m*
gigantic [dʒaɪˈgæntɪk] *adj* gigantesco
giggle ['gɪgl] *vi* reírse tontamente
gills [gɪlz] *npl* (*of fish*) branquias *fpl*, agallas *fpl*
gilt [gɪlt] *adj*, *n* dorado
gimmick ['gɪmɪk] *n* truco
gin [dʒɪn] *n* ginebra
ginger ['dʒɪndʒə*] *n* jengibre *m*
gipsy ['dʒɪpsɪ] *n* = **gypsy**
giraffe [dʒɪˈrɑːf] *n* jirafa
girl [gəːl] *n* (*small*) niña; (*young woman*) chica, joven *f*, muchacha; (*daughter*) hija; **an English** = una (chica) inglesa; **girl band** *n* girl band *m* (*grupo musical de chicas*); **girlfriend** *n* (*of girl*) amiga; (*of boy*) novia; **Girl Scout** (*US*) = **Girl Guide**
gist [dʒɪst] *n* lo esencial
give [gɪv] (*pt* **gave**, *pp* **given**) *vt* dar; (*deliver*) entregar; (*as gift*) regalar ▷ *vi* (*break*) romperse; (*stretch: fabric*)

dar de sí; **to ~ sb sth, ~ sth to sb** dar algo a algn; **give away** *vt* (*give free*) regalar; (*betray*) traicionar; (*disclose*) revelar; **give back** *vt* devolver; **give in** *vi* ceder ▷ *vt* entregar; **give out** *vt* distribuir; **give up** *vi* rendirse, darse por vencido ▷ *vt* renunciar a; **to give up smoking** dejar de fumar; **to give o.s. up** entregarse
given ['gɪvn] *pp of* **give** (*fixed: time, amount*) determinado ▷ *conj*: **~ (that) ...** dado (que) ...; **~ the circumstances ...** dadas las circunstancias ...
glacier ['glæsɪə*] *n* glaciar *m*
glad [glæd] *adj* contento; **gladly** ['-lɪ] *adv* con mucho gusto
glamour ['glæmər] (*US* **glamor**) *n* encanto, atractivo; **glamorous** *adj* encantador(a), atractivo
glance [glɑːns] *n* ojeada, mirada ▷ *vi*: **to ~ at** echar una ojeada a
gland [glænd] *n* glándula
glare [glɛə*] *n* (*of anger*) mirada feroz; (*of light*) deslumbramiento, brillo; **to be in the ~ of publicity** ser el foco de la atención pública ▷ *vi* deslumbrar; **to ~ at** mirar con odio a; **glaring** *adj* (*mistake*) manifiesto
glass [glɑːs] *n* vidrio, cristal *m*; (*for drinking*) vaso; (*: with stem*) copa; **glasses** *npl* (*spectacles*) gafas *fpl*
glaze [gleɪz] *vt* (*window*) poner cristales a; (*pottery*) vidriar. ▷ *n* vidriado
gleam [gliːm] *vi* brillar
glen [glɛn] *n* cañada
glide [glaɪd] *vi* deslizarse; (*Aviat: birds*) planear; **glider** *n* (*Aviat*) planeador *m*
glimmer ['glɪmə*] *n* luz *f* tenue; (*of interest*) muestra; (*of hope*) rayo
glimpse [glɪmps] *n* vislumbre *m* ▷ *vt* vislumbrar, entrever
glint [glɪnt] *vi* centellear
glisten ['glɪsn] *vi* relucir, brillar
glitter ['glɪtə*] *vi* relucir, brillar
global ['gləubl] *adj* mundial; **globalization** *n* globalización *f*; **global warming** *n* (re)calentamiento global or de la tierra
globe [gləub] *n* globo; (*model*) globo terráqueo
gloom [gluːm] *n* oscuridad *f*; (*sadness*) tristeza; **gloomy** *adj* (*dark*) oscuro; (*sad*) triste; (*pessimistic*) pesimista
glorious ['glɔːrɪəs] *adj* glorioso; (*weather etc*) magnífico
glory ['glɔːrɪ] *n* gloria
gloss [glɔs] *n* (*shine*) brillo; (*paint*) pintura de aceite
glossary ['glɔsərɪ] *n* glosario
glossy ['glɔsɪ] *adj* lustroso; (*magazine*) de lujo
glove [glʌv] *n* guante *m*; **glove compartment** *n* (*Aut*) guantera
glow [gləu] *vi* brillar
glucose ['gluːkəus] *n* glucosa
glue [gluː] *n* goma (de pegar), cemento ▷ *vt* pegar
GM *adj abbr* (*= genetically modified*) transgénico
gm *abbr* (*= gram*) g
GMO *n abbr* (*= genetically modified organism*) organismo transgénico
GMT *abbr* (*= Greenwich Mean Time*) GMT
gnaw [nɔː] *vt* roer
go [gəu] (*pt* **went**, *pp* **gone**, *pl* **~es**) *vi* ir; (*travel*) viajar; (*depart*) irse, marcharse; (*work*) funcionar, marchar; (*be sold*) venderse; (*time*) pasar; (*fit, suit*) sentar ▷ *n*: **to have a ~ (at)** probar suerte (con); **to be on the ~** no parar; **whose ~ is it?** ¿a quién le toca?;

he's ~ing to do it va a hacerlo; **to ~ for a walk** ir de
paseo; **to ~ dancing** ir a bailar; **how did it ~?** ¿qué tal
salió o resultó?, ¿cómo ha ido?; **to ~ round the back**
pasar por detrás; **go ahead** vi seguir adelante; **go
away** vi irse, marcharse; **go back** vi volver; **go by**
(time) pasar ▷ vt fus guiarse por; **go down** vi bajar;
(ship) hundirse; (sun) ponerse ▷ vt fus bajar; **go for** vt
fus (fetch) ir por; (like) gustar; (attack) atacar; **go in** vi
entrar; **go into** vt fus entrar en; (investigate) investigar;
(embark on) dedicarse a; **go off** vi irse, marcharse;
(food) pasarse; (explode) estallar; (event) realizarse
▷ vt fus dejar de gustar; **I'm going off him/the idea**
ya no me gusta tanto él/la idea; **go on** vi (continue)
seguir, continuar; (happen) ocurrir; **to go on
doing sth** seguir haciendo algo; **go out** vi salir;
(fire, light) apagarse; **go over** vi (ship) zozobrar ▷ vt
fus (check) revisar; **go past** vi, vt fus pasar; **go round**
vi (circulate: news, rumour) correr; (suffice) alcanzar,
bastar; (revolve) girar, dar vueltas; (visit): **go round
(to sb's)** pasar a ver (a algn); **to go round (by)** (make
a detour) dar la vuelta (por); **go through** vt fus (town
etc) atravesar; **go up** vi, vt fus subir; **go with** vt fus
(accompany) ir con, acompañar a; **go without** vt fus
pasarse sin

go-ahead ['ɡəuəhɛd] adj (person) dinámico; (firm)
innovador(a) ▷ n luz f verde

goal [ɡəul] n meta; (score) gol m; **goalkeeper** n
portero; **goal-post** n poste m (de la portería)

goat [ɡəut] n cabra

gobble ['ɡɔbl] vt (also: **~ down, ~ up**) tragarse,
engullir

God [ɡɔd] n Dios m; **godchild** n ahijado/a;
goddaughter n ahijada; **goddess** n diosa;
godfather n padrino; **godmother** n madrina;
godson n ahijado

goggles ['ɡɔɡlz] npl gafas fpl

going ['ɡəuɪŋ] (conditions) estado del terreno
▷ adj: **the ~ rate** la tarifa corriente o en vigor

gold [ɡəuld] n oro ▷ adj (made of gold) de oro; **golden**
adj (made of gold) de oro; (in colour) dorado; **goldfish** n pez m
de colores; **goldmine** n (also fig) mina de oro; **gold-
plated** adj chapado en oro

golf [ɡɔlf] n golf m; **golf ball** n (for game) pelota de
golf; (on typewriter) esfera; **golf club** n club m de golf;
(stick) palo (de golf); **golf course** n campo de golf;
golfer n golfista mf

gone [ɡɔn] pp of **go**

gong [ɡɔŋ] n gong m

good [ɡud] adj bueno; (pleasant) agradable; (kind)
bueno, amable; (well-behaved) educado ▷ n bien m,
provecho; **goods** npl (Comm) mercancías fpl; **~!** ¡qué
bien!; **to be ~ at** tener aptitud para; **to be ~ for** servir
para; **it's ~ for you** te hace bien; **would you be ~
enough to ...?** ¿podría hacerme el favor de ...?, ¿sería
tan amable de ...?; **a ~ deal (of)** mucho; **a ~ many**
muchos; **to make ~** reparar; **it's no ~ complaining**
no vale la pena (de) quejarse; **for ~** para siempre,
definitivamente; **~ morning/afternoon!** ¡buenos
días/buenas tardes!; **~ evening!** ¡buenas noches!; **~
night!** ¡buenas noches!

goodbye [ɡud'baɪ] excl ¡adiós!; **to say ~ (to)** (person)
despedirse (de)

good: Good Friday n Viernes m Santo; **good-looking**
adj guapo; **good-natured** adj amable, simpático;
goodness n (of person) bondad f; **for goodness sake!**
¡por Dios!; **goodness gracious!** ¡Dios mío!; **goods**

---

train (BRIT) n tren m de mercancías; **goodwill** n
buena voluntad f

Google® ['ɡuːɡəl] n Google ® n ▷ vi hacer
búsquedas en Internet ▷ vt buscar información en
Internet sobre

goose [ɡuːs] (pl **geese**) n ganso, oca

gooseberry ['ɡuzbəri] n grosella espinosa; **to play ~**
hacer de carabina

goose bumps, goose pimples npl carne f de
gallina

gorge [ɡɔːdʒ] n barranco ▷ vr: **to ~ o.s. (on)** atracarse
(de)

gorgeous ['ɡɔːdʒəs] adj (thing) precioso; (weather)
espléndido; (person) guapísimo

gorilla [ɡə'rɪlə] n gorila m

gosh [ɡɔʃ] (inf) excl ¡cielos!

gospel ['ɡɔspl] n evangelio

gossip ['ɡɔsɪp] n (scandal) cotilleo, chismes mpl; (chat)
charla; (scandalmonger) cotilla m/f, chismoso/a ▷ vi
cotillear; **gossip column** n ecos mpl de sociedad

got [ɡɔt] pt, pp of **get**

gotten (us) ['ɡɔtn] pp of **get**

gourmet ['ɡuəmeɪ] n gastrónomo/a m/f

govern ['ɡʌvən] vt gobernar; (influence) dominar;
government n gobierno; **governor** n gobernador/a
m/f; (of school etc) miembro del consejo; (of jail)
director/a m/f

gown [ɡaun] n traje m; (of teacher, BRIT: of judge) toga

G.P. n abbr = **general practitioner**

grab [ɡræb] vt coger (SP), agarrar (LAM), arrebatar
▷ vi: **to ~ at** intentar agarrar

grace [ɡreɪs] n gracia ▷ vt honrar; (adorn) adornar;
5 days' ~ un plazo de 5 días; **graceful** adj grácil, ágil;
(style, shape) elegante, gracioso; **gracious** ['ɡreɪʃəs]
adj amable

grade [ɡreɪd] n (quality) clase f, calidad f; (in hierarchy)
grado; (Scol: mark) nota; (us: school class) curso ▷ vt
clasificar; **grade crossing** (us) n paso a nivel; **grade
school** (us) n escuela primaria

gradient ['ɡreɪdɪənt] n pendiente f

gradual ['ɡrædjuəl] adj paulatino; **gradually** adv
paulatinamente

graduate [n 'ɡrædjuit, vb 'ɡrædjueit] n (us: of
high school) graduado/a; (of university) licenciado/a
▷ vi graduarse; licenciarse; **graduation** [-'eɪʃən] n
(ceremony) entrega del título

graffiti [ɡrə'fiːtɪ] n pintadas fpl

graft [ɡrɑːft] n (Agr, Med) injerto; (BRIT: inf) trabajo
duro; (bribery) corrupción f ▷ vt injertar

grain [ɡreɪn] n (single particle) grano; (corn) granos
mpl, cereales mpl; (of wood) fibra

gram [ɡræm] n gramo

grammar ['ɡræmə*] n gramática; **grammar school**
(BRIT) ≈ instituto de segunda enseñanza, liceo (SP)

gramme [ɡræm] n = **gram**

gran [ɡræn] (inf) n (BRIT) abuelita

grand [ɡrænd] adj magnífico, imponente; (wonderful)
estupendo; (gesture etc) grandioso; **grandad** (inf) n =
granddad; **grandchild** (pl **grandchildren**) n nieto/a
m/f; **granddad** (inf) n yayo, abuelito; **granddaughter**
n nieta; **grandfather** n abuelo; **grandma** (inf) n
yaya, abuelita; **grandmother** n abuela; **grandpa** (inf)
n = **granddad**; **grandparents** npl abuelos mpl; **grand
piano** n piano de cola; **Grand Prix** ['ɡrɑː'priː] n (Aut)
gran premio, Grand Prix m; **grandson** n nieto

granite ['ɡrænɪt] n granito

granny ['grænɪ] (inf) n abuelita, yaya
grant [grɑːnt] vt (concede) conceder; (admit) reconocer ▷ n (Scol) beca; (Admin) subvención f; **to take sth/sb for ~ed** dar algo por sentado/no hacer ningún caso a algn
grape [greɪp] n uva
grapefruit ['greɪpfruːt] n pomelo (SP, SC), toronja (LAM)
graph [grɑːf] n gráfica; **graphic** ['græfɪk] adj gráfico; **graphics** n artes fpl gráficas ▷ npl (drawings) dibujos mpl
grasp [grɑːsp] vt agarrar, asir; (understand) comprender ▷ n (grip) asimiento; (understanding) comprensión f
grass [grɑːs] n hierba; (lawn) césped m; **grasshopper** n saltamontes m inv
grate [greɪt] n parrilla de chimenea ▷ vi: **to ~ (on)** chirriar (sobre) ▷ vt (Culin) rallar
grateful ['greɪtful] adj agradecido
grater ['greɪtə*] n rallador m
gratitude ['grætɪtjuːd] n agradecimiento
grave [greɪv] n tumba ▷ adj serio, grave
gravel ['grævl] n grava
gravestone ['greɪvstəun] n lápida
graveyard ['greɪvjɑːd] n cementerio
gravity ['grævɪtɪ] n gravedad f
gravy ['greɪvɪ] n salsa de carne
gray [greɪ] adj = **grey**
graze [greɪz] vi pacer ▷ vt (touch lightly) rozar; (scrape) raspar ▷ n (Med) abrasión f
grease [griːs] n (fat) grasa; (lubricant) lubricante m ▷ vt engrasar; lubricar; **greasy** adj grasiento
great [greɪt] adj grande; (inf) magnífico, estupendo; **Great Britain** n Gran Bretaña; **great-grandfather** n bisabuelo; **great-grandmother** n bisabuela; **greatly** adv muy; (with verb) mucho
Greece [griːs] n Grecia
greed [griːd] n (also: **-iness**) codicia, avaricia; (for food) gula; (for power etc) avidez f; **greedy** adj avaro; (for food) glotón/ona
Greek [griːk] adj griego ▷ n griego/a; (Ling) griego
green [griːn] adj (also Pol) verde; (inexperienced) novato ▷ n verde m; (stretch of grass) césped m; (Golf) green; m **greens** npl (vegetables) verduras fpl; **green card** n (Aut) carta verde; (US: work permit) permiso de trabajo para los extranjeros en EE. UU.; **greengage** n (ciruela) claudia; **greengrocer** (BRIT) n verdulero/a; **greenhouse** n invernadero; **greenhouse effect** n efecto invernadero
Greenland ['griːnlənd] n Groenlandia
green salad n ensalada f (de lechuga, pepino, pimiento verde, etc)
greet [griːt] vt (welcome) dar la bienvenida a; (receive: news) recibir; **greeting** n (welcome) bienvenida; **greeting(s) card** n tarjeta de felicitación
grew [gruː] pt of **grow**
grey [greɪ] (US **gray**) adj gris; (weather) sombrío; **grey-haired** adj canoso; **greyhound** n galgo
grid [grɪd] n reja; (Elec) red f; **gridlock** n (traffic jam) retención f
grief [griːf] n dolor m, pena
grievance ['griːvəns] n motivo de queja, agravio
grieve [griːv] vi afligirse, acongojarse ▷ vt dar pena a; **to ~ for** llorar por
grill [grɪl] n (on cooker) parrilla; (also: **mixed ~**) parrillada ▷ vt (BRIT) asar a la parrilla; (inf: question) interrogar

grille [grɪl] n reja; (Aut) rejilla
grim [grɪm] adj (place) sombrío; (situation) triste; (person) ceñudo
grime [graɪm] n mugre f, suciedad f
grin [grɪn] n sonrisa abierta ▷ vi sonreír abiertamente
grind [graɪnd] (pt, pp ground) vt (coffee, pepper etc) moler; (US: meat) picar; (make sharp) afilar ▷ n (work) rutina
grip [grɪp] n (hold) asimiento; (control) control m, dominio; (of tyre etc) agarre m: **to have a good/bad ~** agarrarse bien/mal; (handle) asidero; (holdall) maletín m ▷ vt agarrar; (viewer, reader) fascinar; **to get to ~s with** enfrentarse con; **gripping** adj absorbente
grit [grɪt] n gravilla; (courage) valor m ▷ vt (road) poner gravilla en; **to ~ one's teeth** apretar los dientes
grits [grɪts] (US) npl maíz msg a medio moler
groan [grəun] n gemido; quejido ▷ vi gemir; quejarse
grocer ['grəusə*] n tendero (de ultramarinos (SP)); **groceries** npl comestibles mpl; **grocer's (shop)** n tienda de comestibles or (MEX, CAM) abarrotes, almacén (SC); **grocery** n (shop) tienda de ultramarinos
groin [grɔɪn] n ingle f
groom [gruːm] n mozo/a de cuadra; (also: **bride~**) novio ▷ vt (horse) almohazar; (fig): **to ~ sb for** preparar a algn para; **well~ed** adj de buena presencia
groove [gruːv] n ranura, surco
grope [grəup] vi: **to ~ for** buscar a tientas
gross [grəus] adj (neglect, injustice) grave; (vulgar: behaviour) grosero; (: appearance) de mal gusto; (Comm) bruto; **grossly** adv (greatly) enormemente
grotesque [grə'tɛsk] adj grotesco
ground [graund] pt, pp of **grind** ▷ n suelo, tierra; (Sport) campo, terreno; (reason: gen pl) causa, razón f; (US: also: **~ wire**) tierra ▷ vt (plane) mantener en tierra; (US Elec) conectar con tierra; **grounds** npl (of coffee etc) poso; (gardens etc) jardines mpl, parque m; **on the ~** en el suelo; **to the ~** al suelo; **to gain/lose ~** ganar/perder terreno; **ground floor** n (BRIT) planta baja; **groundsheet** (BRIT) n tela impermeable; suelo; **groundwork** n preparación f
group [gruːp] n grupo; (musical) conjunto ▷ vt (also: **~ together**) agrupar ▷ vi (also: **~ together**) agruparse
grouse [graus] n inv (bird) urogallo ▷ vi (complain) quejarse
grovel ['grɔvl] vi (fig): **to ~ before** humillarse ante
grow [grəu] (pt **grew**, pp **grown**) vi crecer; (increase) aumentar; (expand) desarrollarse; (become) volverse; **to ~ rich/weak** enriquecerse/debilitarse ▷ vt cultivar; (hair, beard) dejar crecer; **grow on** vt fus: **that painting is growing on me** ese cuadro me gusta cada vez más; **grow up** vi crecer, hacerse hombre/mujer
growl [graul] vi gruñir
grown [grəun] pp of **grow**; **grown-up** n adulto/a, mayor mf
growth [grəuθ] n crecimiento, desarrollo; (what has grown) brote m; (Med) tumor m
grub [grʌb] n larva, gusano; (inf: food) comida
grubby ['grʌbɪ] adj sucio, mugriento
grudge [grʌdʒ] n (motivo de) rencor m ▷ vt: **to ~ sb sth** dar algo a algn de mala gana; **to bear sb a ~** guardar rencor a algn
gruelling ['gruəlɪŋ] (US **grueling**) adj penoso, duro
gruesome ['gruːsəm] adj horrible

grumble ['grʌmbl] vi refunfuñar, quejarse
grumpy ['grʌmpɪ] adj gruñón/ona
grunt [grʌnt] vi gruñir
guarantee [gærən'tiː] n garantía ▷vt garantizar
guard [gɑːd] n (squad) guardia; (one man) guardia
mf; (BRIT Rail) jefe m de tren; (on machine) dispositivo
de seguridad; (also: **fire~**) rejilla de protección ▷vt
guardar; (prisoner) vigilar; **to be on one's ~** estar alerta;
guardian n guardián/ana m/f; (of minor) tutor(a) m/f
guerrilla [gə'rɪlə] n guerrillero/a
guess [gɛs] vi adivinar; (US) suponer ▷vt adivinar;
suponer ▷n suposición f, conjetura; **to take** or **have a**
~ tratar de adivinar
guest [gɛst] n invitado/a; (in hotel) huésped mf; **guest**
house n casa de huéspedes, pensión f; **guest room** n
cuarto de huéspedes
guidance ['gaɪdəns] n (advice) consejos mpl
guide [gaɪd] n (person) guía mf; (book, fig) guía;
(also: **Girl ~**) guía ▷vt (round museum etc) guiar; (lead)
conducir; (direct) orientar; **guidebook** n guía; **guide**
dog n perro m guía; **guided tour** n visita f con guía;
guidelines npl (advice) directrices fpl
guild [gɪld] n gremio
guilt [gɪlt] n culpabilidad f; **guilty** adj culpable
guinea pig ['gɪnɪ-] n cobaya; (fig) conejillo de Indias
guitar [gɪ'tɑː*] n guitarra; **guitarist** n guitarrista
m/f
gulf [gʌlf] n golfo; (abyss) abismo
gull [gʌl] n gaviota
gulp [gʌlp] vi tragar saliva ▷vt (also: **~ down**)
tragarse
gum [gʌm] n (Anat) encía; (glue) goma, cemento;
(sweet) caramelo de goma; (also: **chewing-~**) chicle m
▷vt pegar con goma
gun [gʌn] n (small) pistola, revólver m; (shotgun)
escopeta; (rifle) fusil m; (cannon) cañón m; **gunfire** n
disparos mpl; **gunman** (irreg) n pistolero; **gunpoint**
n: **at gunpoint** a mano armada; **gunpowder** n
pólvora; **gunshot** n escopetazo
gush [gʌʃ] vi salir a raudales; (person) deshacerse en
efusiones
gust [gʌst] n (of wind) ráfaga
gut [gʌt] n intestino; **guts** npl (Anat) tripas fpl;
(courage) valor m
gutter ['gʌtə*] n (of roof) canalón m; (in street) cuneta
guy [gaɪ] n (also: **~rope**) cuerda; (inf: man) tío (SP),
tipo; (figure) monigote m
Guy Fawkes' Night [gaɪ'fɔːks-] n ver recuadro
gym [dʒɪm] n gimnasio; **gymnasium** n gimnasio m/f;
gymnast n gimnasta mf; **gymnastics** n gimnasia;
gym shoes npl zapatillas fpl (de deporte)
gynaecologist [gaɪnɪ'kɒlədʒɪst] n (US gynecologist)
n ginecólogo/a
gypsy ['dʒɪpsɪ] n gitano/a

haberdashery [hæbə'dæʃərɪ] (BRIT) n mercería
habit ['hæbɪt] n hábito, costumbre f; (drug habit)
adicción f; (costume) hábito
habitat ['hæbɪtæt] n hábitat m
hack [hæk] vt (cut) cortar; (slice) tajar ▷n (pej: writer)
escritor(a) m/f a sueldo; **hacker** n (Comput) pirata mf
informático/a
had [hæd] pt, pp of **have**
haddock ['hædək] (pl ~ or ~s) n especie de merluza
hadn't ['hædnt] = **had not**
haemorrhage ['hɛmərɪdʒ] (US **hemorrhage**) n
hemorragia
haemorrhoids ['hɛmərɔɪdz] (US **hemorrhoids**) npl
hemorroides fpl
haggle ['hægl] vi regatear
Hague [heɪg] n: **The ~** La Haya
hail [heɪl] n granizo; (fig) lluvia ▷vt saludar; (taxi)
llamar a; (acclaim) aclamar ▷vi granizar; **hailstone** n
(piedra de) granizo
hair [hɛə*] n pelo, cabellos mpl; (one hair) pelo,
cabello; (on legs etc) vello; **to do one's ~** arreglarse
el pelo; **to have grey ~** tener canas fpl; **hairband** n
cinta; **hairbrush** n cepillo (para el pelo); **haircut** n
corte (de pelo); **hairdo** n peinado; **hairdresser** n
peluquero/a; **hairdresser's** n peluquería; **hair dryer**
n secador m de pelo; **hair gel** n fijador; **hair spray** n
laca; **hairstyle** n peinado; **hairy** adj peludo; velludo;
(inf: frightening) espeluznante
hake [heɪk] (pl ~ or ~s) n merluza
half [hɑːf] (pl **halves**) n mitad f; (of beer) ~ caña (SP),
media pinta; (Rail, Bus) billete m de niño ▷adj medio
▷adv medio, a medias; **two and a ~** dos y media; **~ a**
dozen media docena; **~ a pound** media libra; **to cut**
sth in ~ cortar algo por la mitad; **half board** n (BRIT: in
hotel) media pensión; **half-brother** n hermanastro;
half day n medio día m, media jornada; **half fare**
n medio pasaje m; **half-hearted** adj indiferente,
poco entusiasta; **half-hour** n media hora; **half-price**
adj, adv a mitad de precio; **half term** (BRIT) n (Scol)
vacaciones de mediados del trimestre; **half-time** n
descanso; **halfway** adv a medio camino; **halfway**
through a mitad de
hall [hɔːl] n (for concerts) sala; (entrance way) hall m;

vestíbulo

hallmark ['hɔ:lmɑːk] n sello

hallo [hə'ləu] excl =**hello**

hall of residence n residencia

Hallowe'en [hæləu'iːn] n víspera de Todos los Santos

hallucination [həluːsɪ'neɪʃən] n alucinación f

hallway ['hɔ:lweɪ] n vestíbulo

halo ['heɪləu] n (of saint) halo, aureola

halt [hɔːlt] n (stop) alto, parada ▷ vt parar; interrumpir ▷ vi pararse

halve [hɑːv] vt partir por la mitad

halves [hɑːvz] npl of **half**

ham [hæm] n jamón m (cocido)

hamburger ['hæmbəːgə*] n hamburguesa

hamlet ['hæmlɪt] n aldea

hammer ['hæmə*] n martillo ▷ vt (nail) clavar; (force) > **to ~ an idea into sb/a message home** meter una idea en la cabeza a algn/machacar una idea ▷ vi dar golpes

hammock ['hæmək] n hamaca

hamper ['hæmpə*] vt estorbar ▷ n cesto

hamster ['hæmstə*] n hámster m

hamstring ['hæmstrɪŋ] n (Anat) tendón m de la corva

hand [hænd] n mano f; (of clock) aguja; (writing) letra; (worker) obrero ▷ vt dar, pasar; **to give** or **lend sb a ~** echar una mano a algn, ayudar a algn; **at ~** a mano; **in ~** (time) libre; (job etc) entre manos; **on ~** (person, services) a mano, al alcance; **to ~** (information etc) a mano; **on the one ~ ..., on the other ~ ...** por una parte ... por otra (parte) ...; **hand down** vt pasar, bajar; (tradition) transmitir; (heirloom) dejar en herencia; (us: sentence, verdict) imponer; **hand in** vt entregar; **hand out** vt distribuir; **hand over** vt (deliver) entregar; **handbag** n bolso (SP), cartera (LAM), bolsa (MEX); **hand baggage** =**hand luggage**; **handbook** n manual m; **handbrake** n freno de mano; **handcuffs** npl esposas fpl; **handful** n puñado

handicap ['hændɪkæp] n minusvalía; (disadvantage) desventaja; (Sport) handicap m ▷ vt estorbar; **to be mentally ~ped** ser mentalmente m/f discapacitado; **to be physically ~ped** ser minusválido/a

handkerchief ['hæŋkətʃɪf] n pañuelo

handle ['hændl] n (of door etc) tirador m; (of cup etc) asa; (of knife etc) mango; (for winding) manivela ▷ vt (touch) tocar; (deal with) encargarse de; (treat: people) manejar; **~ with care** "(manéjese) con cuidado"; **to fly off the ~** perder los estribos; **handlebar(s)** n(pl) manillar m

hand: hand luggage n equipaje m de mano; **handmade** adj hecho a mano; **handout** n (money etc) limosna; (leaflet) folleto; **hands-free** adj (phone) manos libres inv; **hands-free kit** n manos libres m inv

handsome ['hænsəm] adj guapo; (building) bello; (fig: profit) considerable

handwriting ['hændraɪtɪŋ] n letra

handy ['hændɪ] adj (close at hand) a la mano; (tool etc) práctico; (skilful) hábil, diestro

hang [hæŋ] (pt, pp hung) vt (suspend) colgar; (pp hanged) ahorcar ▷ vi (painting, coat etc) colgar; (hair, drapery) caer; **to get the ~ of sth** (inf) lograr dominar algo; **hang about** or **around** vi haraganear; **hang down** vi colgar, pender; **hang on** vi (wait) esperar; **hang out** vt (washing) tender, colgar ▷ vi (inf: live) vivir; (spend time) pasar el rato; **to hang out of sth**

hatchback ['hætʃbæk] n (Aut) tres o cinco puertas m

hate [heɪt] vt odiar, aborrecer ▷ n odio; **hatred**

colgar fuera de algo; **hang round** vi =**hang around**; **hang up** vi (Tel) colgar ▷ vt colgar

hanger ['hæŋə*] n percha

hang-gliding ['-glaɪdɪŋ] n vuelo libre

hangover ['hæŋəuvə*] n (after drinking) resaca

hankie, hanky ['hæŋkɪ] n abbr =**handkerchief**

happen ['hæpən] vi suceder, ocurrir; (chance): **he ~ed to hear/see** dió la casualidad de que oyó/vió; **as it ~s** da la casualidad de que

happily ['hæpɪlɪ] adv (luckily) afortunadamente; (cheerfully) alegremente

happiness ['hæpɪnɪs] n felicidad f; (cheerfulness) alegría

happy ['hæpɪ] adj feliz; (cheerful) alegre; **to be ~ (with)** estar contento (con); **to be ~ to do** estar encantado de hacer; **~ birthday!** ¡feliz cumpleaños!

harass ['hærəs] vt acosar, hostigar; **harassment** n persecución f

harbour ['hɑːbə*] (us **harbor**) n puerto ▷ vi (fugitive) dar abrigo a; (hope etc) abrigar

hard [hɑːd] adj duro; (difficult) difícil; (work) arduo; (person) severo; (fact) innegable ▷ adv (work) mucho, duro; (think) profundamente; **to look ~ at** clavar los ojos en; **to try ~** esforzarse; **no ~ feelings!** ¡sin rencor(es)!; **to be ~ of hearing** ser duro de oído; **to be ~ done by** ser tratado injustamente; **hardback** n libro en cartoné; **hardboard** n aglomerado m (de madera); **hard disk** n (Comput) disco duro o rígido; **harden** vt endurecer; (fig) curtir ▷ vi endurecerse; curtirse

hardly ['hɑːdlɪ] adv apenas; **~ ever** casi nunca

hard: hardship n privación f; **hard shoulder** (BRIT) n (Aut) arcén m; **hard-up** (inf) adj sin un duro (SP), pelado, sin un centavo (MEX), pato (SC); **hardware** n ferretería; (Comput) hardware m; (Mil) armamento; **hardware shop**, us **hardware store** ferretería; **hard-working** adj trabajador/a

hardy ['hɑːdɪ] adj fuerte; (plant) resistente

hare [hɛə*] n liebre f

harm [hɑːm] n daño, mal m ▷ vt (person) hacer daño a; (health, interests) perjudicar; (thing) dañar; **out of ~'s way** a salvo; **harmful** adj dañino; **harmless** adj (person) inofensivo; (joke etc) inocente

harmony ['hɑːmənɪ] n armonía

harness ['hɑːnɪs] n arreos mpl; (for child) arnés m; (safety harness) arneses mpl ▷ vt (horse) enjaezar; (resources) aprovechar

harp [hɑːp] n arpa ▷ vi: **to ~ on (about)** machacar (con)

harsh [hɑːʃ] adj (cruel) duro, cruel; (severe) severo; (sound) áspero; (light) deslumbrador/a

harvest ['hɑːvɪst] n (harvest time) siega; (of cereals etc) cosecha; (of grapes) vendimia ▷ vt cosechar

has [hæz] vb see **have**

hasn't ['hæznt] = **has not**

hassle ['hæsl] (inf) n lata

haste [heɪst] n prisa; **hasten** ['heɪsn] vt acelerar ▷ vi darse prisa; **hastily** adv de prisa; precipitadamente; **hasty** adj apresurado; (rash) precipitado

hat [hæt] n sombrero

hatch [hætʃ] n (Naut: also: ~**way**) escotilla; (also: **service ~**) ventanilla ▷ vi (bird) salir del cascarón ▷ vt incubar; (plot) tramar; **5 eggs have ~ed** han salido 5 pollos

['hɔːtrɪd] n odio
haul [hɔːl] vt tirar ▷ n (of fish) redada; (of stolen goods etc) botín m

haunt [hɔːnt] vt (ghost) aparecerse en; (obsess) obsesionar ▷ n guarida; **haunted** adj (castle etc) embrujado; (look) de angustia

○ **KEYWORD**

have [hæv] (pt, pp **had**) aux vb **1** (gen) haber; **to have arrived/eaten** haber llegado/comido; **having finished** or **when he had finished, he left** cuando hubo acabado, se fue

2 (in tag questions): **you've done it, haven't you?** lo has hecho, ¿verdad? or ¿no?

3 (in short answers and questions): **I haven't** no; **so I have** pues, es verdad; **we haven't paid – yes we have!** no hemos pagado – ¡sí que hemos pagado!; **I've been there before, have you?** he estado allí antes, ¿y tú?

▷ modal aux vb (be obliged): **to have (got) to do sth** tener que hacer algo; **you haven't to tell her** no hay que or no debes decírselo

▷ vt **1** (possess): **he has (got) blue eyes/dark hair** tiene los ojos azules/el pelo negro

2 (referring to meals etc): **to have breakfast/lunch/dinner** desayunar/comer/cenar; **to have a drink/a cigarette** tomar algo/fumar un cigarrillo

3 (receive) recibir; (obtain) obtener; **may I have your address?** ¿puedes darme tu dirección?; **you can have it for £5** te lo puedes quedar por £5; **I must have it by tomorrow** lo necesito para mañana; **to have a baby** tener un niño or bebé

4 (maintain, allow): **I won't have it/this nonsense!** ¡no lo permitiré!/¡no permitiré estas tonterías!; **we can't have that** no podemos permitir eso

5 **to have sth done** hacer or mandar hacer algo; **to have one's hair cut** cortarse el pelo; **to have sb do sth** hacer que algn haga algo

6 (experience, suffer): **to have a cold/flu** tener un resfriado/la gripe; **she had her bag stolen/her arm broken** le robaron el bolso/se rompió un brazo; **to have an operation** operarse

7 (+ noun): **to have a swim/walk/bath/rest** nadar/dar un paseo/darse un baño/descansar; **let's have a look** vamos a ver; **to have a meeting/party** celebrar una reunión/una fiesta; **let me have a try** déjame intentarlo

haven ['heɪvn] n puerto; (fig) refugio
haven't ['hævnt] = **have not**
havoc ['hævək] n estragos mpl
Hawaii [hə'waɪiː] n (Islas fpl) Hawai fpl
hawk [hɔːk] n halcón m
hawthorn ['hɔːθɔːn] n espino
hay [heɪ] n heno; **hay fever** n fiebre f del heno; **haystack** n almiar m
hazard ['hæzəd] n peligro ▷ vt aventurar; **hazardous** adj peligroso; **hazard warning lights** npl (Aut) señales fpl de emergencia
haze [heɪz] n neblina
hazel ['heɪzl] n (tree) avellano ▷ adj (eyes) color m de avellano; **hazelnut** n avellana
hazy ['heɪzɪ] adj brumoso; (idea) vago
he [hiː] pron él; ~ **who** ... él que ..., quien ...
head [hɛd] n cabeza; (leader) jefe a m/f; (of

school) director(a) m/f ▷ vt (list) encabezar; (group) capitanear; (company) dirigir; ~**s (or tails)** cara (o cruz); ~ **first** de cabeza; ~ **over heels** (in love) perdidamente; **to ~ the ball** cabecear (la pelota); **head for** vt fus dirigirse a; (disaster) ir camino de; **head off** vt (threat, danger) evitar; **headache** n dolor m de cabeza; **heading** n título; **headlamp** (BRIT) n = **headlight**; **headlight** n faro; **headline** n titular m; **head office** n oficina central, central f; **headphones** npl auriculares mpl; **headquarters** npl sede f central; (Mil) cuartel m general; **headroom** n (in car) altura interior; (under bridge) (límite m de) altura; **headscarf** n pañuelo; **headset** n cascos mpl; **headteacher** n director(directora) m/f; **head waiter** n maître m

heal [hiːl] vt curar ▷ vi cicatrizar
health [hɛlθ] n salud f; **health care** n asistencia sanitaria; **health centre** (BRIT) n ambulatorio, centro médico; **health food** n alimentos mpl orgánicos; **Health Service** (BRIT) n el servicio de salud pública, = el Insalud (SP); **healthy** adj sano, saludable
heap [hiːp] n montón m ▷ vt: **to ~ (up)** amontonar; **to ~ sth with** llenar algo hasta arriba de; **~s of** un montón de
hear [hɪə*] (pt, pp **~d**) vt (also Law) oír; (news) saber ▷ vi oír; **to ~ about** oír hablar de; **to ~ from sb** tener noticias de algn
heard [hɜːd] pt, pp of **hear**
hearing ['hɪərɪŋ] n (sense) oído; (Law) vista; **hearing aid** n audífono
hearse [hɜːs] n coche m fúnebre
heart [hɑːt] n corazón m; (fig) valor m; (of lettuce) cogollo; **hearts** npl (Cards) corazones mpl; **to lose/take ~** descorazonarse/cobrar ánimo; **at ~** en el fondo; **by ~** (learn, know) de memoria; **heart attack** n infarto (de miocardio); **heartbeat** n latido (del corazón); **heartbroken** adj: **she was heartbroken about it** esto le partió el corazón; **heartburn** n acedía; **heart disease** n enfermedad f cardíaca
hearth [hɑːθ] n (fireplace) chimenea
heartless ['hɑːtlɪs] adj despiadado
hearty ['hɑːtɪ] adj (person) campechano; (laugh) sano; (dislike, support) absoluto
heat [hiːt] n calor m; (Sport: also: **qualifying ~**) prueba eliminatoria ▷ vt calentar; **heat up** vi calentarse ▷ vt calentar; **heated** adj caliente; (fig) acalorado; **heater** n estufa; (in car) calefacción f
heather ['hɛðə*] n brezo
heating ['hiːtɪŋ] n calefacción f
heatwave ['hiːtweɪv] n ola de calor
heaven ['hɛvn] n cielo; (fig) una maravilla; **heavenly** adj celestial; (fig) maravilloso
heavily ['hɛvɪlɪ] adv pesadamente; (drink, smoke) con exceso; (sleep, sigh) profundamente; (depend) mucho
heavy ['hɛvɪ] adj pesado; (work, blow) duro; (sea, rain, meal) fuerte; (drinker, smoker) grande; (responsibility) grave; (schedule) ocupado; (weather) bochornoso
Hebrew ['hiːbruː] adj, n (Ling) hebreo
hectare ['hɛktɑː*] n (BRIT) hectárea
hectic ['hɛktɪk] adj agitado
he'd [hiːd] = **he would; he had**
hedge [hɛdʒ] n seto ▷ vi contestar con evasivas; **to ~ one's bets** (fig) cubrirse
hedgehog ['hɛdʒhɒg] n erizo
heed [hiːd] vt (also: **take ~**: pay attention to) hacer caso de
heel [hiːl] n talón m; (of shoe) tacón m ▷ vt (shoe)

poner tacón a

hefty ['heftɪ] *adj* (*person*) fornido; (*parcel, profit*) gordo

height [haɪt] *n* (*of person*) estatura; (*of building*) altura; (*high ground*) cerro; (*altitude*) altitud *f*; (*fig: of season*): **at the ~ of summer** en los días más calurosos del verano; (*: of power etc*) cúspide *f*; (*: of stupidity etc*) colmo; **heighten** *vt* elevar; (*fig*) aumentar

heir [ɛə*] *n* heredero; **heiress** *n* heredera

held [held] *pt, pp of* **hold**

helicopter ['helɪkɒptə*] *n* helicóptero

hell [hel] *n* infierno; **~!** (*inf*) ¡demonios!

he'll [hi:l] = **he will; he shall**

hello [hə'ləʊ] *excl* ¡hola!; (*to attract attention*) ¡oiga!; (*surprise*) ¡caramba!

helmet ['helmɪt] *n* casco

help [help] *n* ayuda; (*cleaner etc*) criada, asistenta ▷ *vt* ayudar; **~!** ¡socorro!; **~ yourself** sírvete; **he can't ~ it** no es culpa suya; **help out** *vi* ayudar, echar una mano a algn; **helper** *n* ayudante *mf*; **helpful** *adj* útil; (*person*) servicial; (*advice*) útil; **helping** *n* ración *f*; **helpless** *adj* (*incapable*) incapaz; (*defenceless*) indefenso; **helpline** *n* teléfono de asistencia al público

hem [hem] *n* dobladillo ▷ *vt* poner o coser el dobladillo a

hemisphere ['hemɪsfɪə*] *n* hemisferio

hemorrhage ['hemərɪdʒ] (*us*) *n* = **haemorrhage**

hemorrhoids ['hemərɔɪdz] (*us*) *npl* = **haemorrhoids**

hen [hen] *n* gallina; (*female bird*) hembra

hence [hens] *adv* (*therefore*) por lo tanto; **2 years ~** de aquí a 2 años

hen night, hen party *n* (*inf*) despedida de soltera

hepatitis [hepə'taɪtɪs] *n* hepatitis *f*

her [hə:*] *pron* (*direct*) la; (*indirect*) le; (*stressed, after prep*) ella ▷ *adj* su; *see also* **me; my**

herald ['herəld] *n* heraldo ▷ *vt* anunciar

herb [hə:b] *n* hierba; **herbal** *adj* de hierbas; **herbal tea** *n* infusión *f* de hierbas

herd [hə:d] *n* rebaño

here [hɪə*] *adv* aquí; (*at this point*) en este punto; **~!** (*present*) ¡presente!; **~ is/are** aquí está/están; **~ she is** aquí está

hereditary [hɪ'redɪtrɪ] *adj* hereditario

heritage ['herɪtɪdʒ] *n* patrimonio

hernia ['hə:nɪə] *n* hernia

hero ['hɪərəʊ] (*pl* **-es**) *n* héroe *m*; (*in book, film*) protagonista *m*; **heroic** [hɪ'rəʊɪk] *adj* heroico

heroin ['herəʊɪn] *n* heroína

heroine ['herəʊɪn] *n* heroína; (*in book, film*) protagonista

heron ['herən] *n* garza

herring ['herɪŋ] *n* arenque *m*

hers [hə:z] *pron* (el) suyo/(la) suya etc; *see also* **mine[1]**

herself [hə:'self] *pron* (*reflexive*) se; (*emphatic*) ella misma; (*after prep*) sí (misma); *see also* **oneself**

he's [hi:z] = **he is; he has**

hesitant ['hezɪtənt] *adj* vacilante

hesitate ['hezɪteɪt] *vi* vacilar; (*in speech*) titubear; (*be unwilling*) resistirse a; **hesitation** [-'teɪʃən] *n* indecisión *f*; titubeo; dudas *fpl*

heterosexual [hetərəʊ'seksjuəl] *adj* heterosexual

hexagon ['heksəgən] *n* hexágono

hey [heɪ] *excl* ¡oye!, ¡oiga!

heyday ['heɪdeɪ] *n*: **the ~ of** el apogeo de

HGV *n abbr* (= *heavy goods vehicle*) vehículo pesado

hi [haɪ] *excl* ¡hola!; (*to attract attention*) ¡oiga!

hibernate ['haɪbəneɪt] *vi* invernar

hiccough ['hɪkʌp] = **hiccup**

hiccup ['hɪkʌp] *vi* hipar

hid [hɪd] *pt of* **hide**

hidden ['hɪdn] *pp of* **hide** ▷ *adj*: **~ agenda** plan *m* encubierto

hide [haɪd] (*pt* **hid**, *pp* **hidden**) *n* (*skin*) piel *f* ▷ *vt* esconder, ocultar ▷ *vi*: **to ~ (from sb)** esconderse or ocultarse (de algn)

hideous ['hɪdɪəs] *adj* horrible

hiding ['haɪdɪŋ] *n* (*beating*) paliza; **to be in ~** (*concealed*) estar escondido

hi-fi ['haɪfaɪ] *n* estéreo, hifi *m* ▷ *adj* de alta fidelidad

high [haɪ] *adj* alto; (*speed, number*) grande; (*price*) elevado; (*wind*) fuerte; (*voice*) agudo ▷ *adv* alto, a gran altura; **it is 20 m ~** tiene 20 m de altura; **~ in the air** en las alturas; **highchair** *n* silla alta; **high-class** *adj* (*hotel*) de lujo; (*person*) distinguido, de categoría; (*food*) de alta categoría; **higher education** *n* educación *f* superior or enseñanza superior; **high heels** *npl* (*heels*) tacones *mpl* altos; (*shoes*) zapatos *mpl* de tacón; **high jump** *n* (*Sport*) salto de altura; **highlands** ['haɪləndz] *npl* tierras *fpl* altas; **the Highlands** (*in Scotland*) las Tierras Altas de Escocia; **highlight** *n* (*fig: of event*) punto culminante ▷ *vt* subrayar; **highlights** *npl* (*in hair*) reflejos *mpl*; **highlighter** *n* rotulador; **highly** *adv* (*paid*) muy bien; (*critical, confidential*) sumamente; (*a lot*): **to speak/ think highly of** hablar muy bien de/tener en mucho a; **highness** *n* altura; **Her/His Highness** Su Alteza; **high-rise** *n* (*also*: **high-rise block, high-rise building**) torre *f* de pisos; **high school** *n* = Instituto Nacional de Bachillerato (*sp*); **high season** (*brit*) *n* temporada alta; **high street** (*brit*) *n* calle *f* mayor; **high-tech** (*inf*) *adj* al-tec (*inf*), de alta tecnología; **highway** *n* carretera; (*us*) carretera nacional; autopista; **Highway Code** (*brit*) *n* código de la circulación

hijack ['haɪdʒæk] *vt* secuestrar; **hijacker** *n* secuestrador(a) *m/f*

hike [haɪk] *vi* (*go walking*) ir de excursión (a pie) ▷ *n* caminata; **hiker** *n* excursionista *mf*; **hiking** *n* senderismo

hilarious [hɪ'lɛərɪəs] *adj* divertidísimo

hill [hɪl] *n* colina; (*high*) montaña; (*slope*) cuesta; **hillside** *n* ladera; **hill walking** *n* senderismo (de montaña); **hilly** *adj* montañoso

him [hɪm] *pron* (*direct*) le, lo; (*indirect*) le; (*stressed, after prep*) él; *see also* **me**; **himself** *pron* (*reflexive*) se; (*emphatic*) él mismo; (*after prep*) sí (mismo); *see also* **oneself**

hind [haɪnd] *adj* posterior

hinder ['hɪndə*] *vt* estorbar, impedir

hindsight ['haɪndsaɪt] *n*: **with ~** en retrospectiva

Hindu ['hɪnduː] *n* hindú *mf*; **Hinduism** *n* (*Rel*) hinduismo

hinge [hɪndʒ] *n* bisagra, gozne *m* ▷ *vi* (*fig*): **to ~ on** depender de

hint [hɪnt] *n* indirecta; (*advice*) consejo; (*sign*) dejo ▷ *vt*: **to ~ that** insinuar que ▷ *vi*: **to ~ at** hacer alusión a

hip [hɪp] *n* cadera

hippie ['hɪpɪ] *n* hippie *m/f*, jipi *m/f*

hippo ['hɪpəʊ] (*pl* **~s**) *n* hipopótamo

hippopotamus [hɪpə'pɒtəməs] (*pl* **-es** or **hippopotami**) *n* hipopótamo

hippy ['hɪpɪ] *n* = **hippie**

hire ['haɪə*] *vt* (*brit: car, equipment*) alquilar; (*worker*) contratar ▷ *n* alquiler *m*; **for ~** se alquila; (*taxi*) libre; **hire(d) car** (*brit*) *n* coche *m* de alquiler; **hire purchase**

(BRIT) n compra a plazos

his [hɪz] pron (el) suyo/(la) suya) etc ▷ adj su; see also **mine¹; my**

Hispanic [hɪs'pænɪk] adj hispánico

hiss [hɪs] vi silbar

historian [hɪs'tɔːrɪən] n historiador(a) m/f

historic(al) [hɪs'tɔrɪk(l)] adj histórico

history ['hɪstərɪ] n historia

hit [hɪt] (pt, pp ~) vt (strike) golpear, pegar; (reach: target) alcanzar; (collide with: car) chocar contra; (fig: affect) afectar ▷ n golpe m; (success) éxito; (on website) visita; (in web search) correspondencia f; **to ~ it off with sb** llevarse bien con algn; **hit back** vi defenderse; (fig) devolver golpe por golpe

hitch [hɪtʃ] vt (fasten) atar, amarrar; (also: **~ up**) remangar ▷ n (difficulty) dificultad f; **to ~ a lift** hacer autostop

hitch-hike ['hɪtʃhaɪk] vi hacer autostop; **hitch-hiker** n autostopista m/f; **hitch-hiking** n autostop m

hi-tech ['haɪ'tɛk] adj de alta tecnología

hitman ['hɪtmæn] (irreg) n asesino a sueldo

HIV n abbr (= human immunodeficiency virus) VIH m; **~-negative/positive** VIH negativo/positivo

hive [haɪv] n colmena

hoard [hɔːd] n (treasure) tesoro; (stockpile) provisión f ▷ vt acumular; (goods in short supply) acaparar

hoarse [hɔːs] adj ronco

hoax [həʊks] n trampa

hob [hɔb] n quemador m

hobble [ˈhɔbl] vi cojear

hobby ['hɔbɪ] n pasatiempo, afición f

hobo ['həʊbəʊ] (US) n vagabundo

hockey ['hɔkɪ] n hockey m; **hockey stick** n palo m de hockey

hog [hɔg] n cerdo, puerco ▷ vt (fig) acaparar; **to go the whole ~** poner toda la carne en el asador

hoist [hɔɪst] n (crane) grúa ▷ vt levantar, alzar; (flag, sail) izar

hold [həʊld] (pt, pp **held**) vt sostener; (contain) contener; (have: power, qualification) tener; (keep back) retener; (believe) sostener; (consider) considerar; (keep in position) ▷ **to ~ one's head up** mantener la cabeza alta; (meeting) celebrar ▷ vi (withstand pressure) resistir; (be valid) valer ▷ n (grasp) asimiento; (fig) dominio; **~ the line!** (Tel) ¡no cuelgue!; **to ~ one's own** (fig) defenderse; **to catch or get (a) ~ of** agarrarse o asirse de; **hold back** vt retener; (secret) ocultar; **hold on** vi agarrarse bien; (wait) esperar; **hold on!** (Tel) ¡(espere) un momento!; **hold out** vt ofrecer ▷ vi (resist) resistir; **hold up** vt (raise) levantar; (support) apoyar; (delay) retrasar; (rob) asaltar; **holdall** (BRIT) n bolsa; **holder** n (container) receptáculo; (of ticket, record) poseedor(a) m/f; (of office, title etc) titular mf

hole [həʊl] n agujero

holiday ['hɔlɪdɪ] n vacaciones fpl; (public holiday) (día m de) fiesta, día m feriado; **on ~** de vacaciones; **holiday camp** n (BRIT: also: **holiday centre**) centro de vacaciones; **holiday job** n (BRIT) trabajillo extra para las vacaciones; **holiday-maker** (BRIT) n turista mf; **holiday resort** n centro turístico

Holland ['hɔlənd] n Holanda

hollow ['hɔləʊ] adj hueco; (claim) vacío; (eyes) hundido; (sound) sordo ▷ n hueco; (in ground) hoyo ▷ vt: **to ~ out** excavar

holly ['hɔlɪ] n acebo

Hollywood ['hɔlɪwʊd] n Hollywood m

holocaust ['hɔləkɔːst] n holocausto

holy ['həʊlɪ] adj santo, sagrado; (water) bendito

home [həʊm] n casa; (country) patria; (institution) asilo ▷ cpd (domestic) casero, de casa; (Econ, Pol) nacional ▷ adv (direction) a casa; (right in: nail etc) a fondo; **at ~** en casa; (in country) en el país; (fig) como pez en el agua; **to go/come ~** ir/volver a casa; **make yourself at ~** ¡estás en tu casa!; **home address** n domicilio; **homeland** n tierra natal; **homeless** adj sin hogar, sin casa; **homely** adj (simple) sencillo; **home-made** adj casero; **home match** n partido en casa; **Home Office** (BRIT) n Ministerio del Interior; **home owner** n propietario/a m/f de una casa; **home page** n página de inicio; **Home Secretary** (BRIT) n Ministro del Interior; **homesick** adj: **to be homesick** tener morriña, sentir nostalgia; **home town** n ciudad f natal; **homework** n deberes mpl

homicide ['hɔmɪsaɪd] (US) n homicidio

homoeopathic [həʊmɪɔ'pæθɪk] (US **homeopathic**) adj homeopático

homoeopathy [həʊmɪ'ɔpəθɪ] (US **homeopathy**) n homeopatía

homosexual [hɔməʊ'sɛksjuəl] adj, n homosexual mf

honest ['ɔnɪst] adj honrado; (sincere) franco, sincero; **honestly** adv honradamente; francamente; **honesty** n honradez f

honey ['hʌnɪ] n miel f; **honeymoon** n luna de miel; **honeysuckle** n madreselva

Hong Kong ['hɔŋ'kɔŋ] n Hong-Kong m

honorary ['ɔnərərɪ] adj (member, president) de honor; (title) honorífico; **~ degree** doctorado honoris causa

honour ['ɔnə*] (US **honor**) vt honrar; (commitment, promise) cumplir con ▷ n honor m, honra; **to graduate with ~s** licenciarse con matrícula (de honor); **honourable** (US **honorable**) adj honorable; **honours degree** n (Scol) título de licenciado con calificación alta

hood [hud] n capucha; (BRIT Aut) capota; (US Aut) capó m; (of cooker) campana de humos; **hoodie** n (top) jersey m con capucha

hoof [hu:f] (pl **hooves**) n pezuña

hook [huk] n gancho; (on dress) corchete m, broche m; (for fishing) anzuelo ▷ vt enganchar; (fish) pescar

hooligan ['hu:lɪgən] n gamberro

hoop [hu:p] n aro

hooray [hu:'reɪ] excl = **hurray**

hoot [hu:t] (BRIT) vi (Aut) tocar el pito, pitar; (siren) (hacer) sonar; (owl) ulular

Hoover® ['hu:və*] (BRIT) n aspiradora ▷ vt: **to hoover** pasar la aspiradora por

hooves [hu:vz] npl of **hoof**

hop [hɔp] vi saltar, brincar; (on one foot) saltar con un pie

hope [həʊp] vt, vi esperar ▷ n esperanza; **I ~ so/not** espero que sí/no; **hopeful** adj (person) optimista; (situation) prometedor(a); **hopefully** adv con esperanza; (one hopes): **hopefully he will recover** esperamos que se recupere; **hopeless** adj desesperado; (person): **to be hopeless** ser un desastre

hops [hɔps] npl lúpulo

horizon [hə'raɪzn] n horizonte m; **horizontal** [hɔrɪ'zɔntl] adj horizontal

hormone ['hɔːməʊn] n hormona

horn [hɔːn] n cuerno; (Mus: also: **French ~**) trompa; (Aut) pito, claxon m

horoscope ['hɔrəskəʊp] n horóscopo

horrendous [hɔ'rɛndəs] adj horrendo
horrible ['hɔrɪbl] adj horrible
horrid ['hɔrɪd] adj horrible, horroroso
horrific [hɔ'rɪfɪk] adj (accident) horroroso; (film) horripilante
horrifying ['hɔrɪfaɪɪŋ] adj horripilante
horror ['hɔrə*] n horror m; **horror film** n película de horror
hors d'œuvre [ɔ:'də:vrə] n entremeses mpl
horse [hɔ:s] n caballo; **horseback** n: **on horseback** a caballo; **horse chestnut** n (tree) castaño de Indias; (nut) castaña de Indias; **horsepower** n caballo (de fuerza); **horse-racing** n carreras fpl de caballos; **horseradish** n rábano picante; **horse riding** n (BRIT) equitación f
hose [hauz] n manguera; **hosepipe** n manguera
hospital ['hɔspɪtl] n hospital m
hospitality [hɔspɪ'tælɪtɪ] n hospitalidad f
host [haust] n anfitrión m; (TV, Radio) presentador m; (Rel) hostia; (large number): **a ~ of** multitud de
hostage ['hɔstɪdʒ] n rehén m
hostel ['hɔstl] n hostal m; (youth) ~ albergue m juvenil
hostess ['haustɪs] n anfitriona; (BRIT: air hostess) azafata; (TV, Radio) presentadora
hostile ['hɔstaɪl] adj hostil
hostility [hɔ'stɪlɪtɪ] n hostilidad f
hot [hɔt] adj caliente; (weather) caluroso, de calor; (as opposed to warm) muy caliente; (spicy) picante; **to be ~** (person) tener calor; (object) estar caliente; (weather) hacer calor; **hot dog** n perro caliente
hotel [hau'tɛl] n hotel m
hot-water bottle [hɔt'wɔ:tə*-] n bolsa de agua caliente
hound [haund] vt acosar ▷ n perro (de caza)
hour ['auə*] n hora; **hourly** adj (de) cada hora
house [n haus, pl 'hauzɪz, vb hauz] n (gen, firm) casa; (Pol) cámara; (Theatre) sala ▷ vt (person) alojar; (collection) albergar; **on the ~** (fig) la casa invita; **household** n familia; (home) casa; **householder** n propietario/a; (head of house) cabeza de familia; **housekeeper** n ama de llaves; **housekeeping** n (work) trabajos mpl domésticos; **housewife** (irreg) n ama de casa; **house wine** n vino m de la casa; **housework** n faenas fpl (de la casa)
housing ['hauzɪŋ] n (act) alojamiento; (houses) viviendas fpl; **housing development**, **housing estate** (BRIT) n urbanización f
hover ['hɔvə*] vi flotar (en el aire); **hovercraft** n aerodeslizador m
how [hau] adv (in what way) cómo; ~ **are you?** ¿cómo estás?; ~ **much milk/many people?** ¿cuánta leche/gente?; ~ **much does it cost?** ¿cuánto cuesta?; ~ **long have you been here?** ¿cuánto hace que estás aquí?; ~ **old are you?** ¿cuántos años tienes?; ~ **tall is he?** ¿cuánto es de alto?; ~ **is school?** ¿cómo (te) va (en) la escuela?; ~ **was the film?** ¿qué tal la película?; ~ **lovely/awful!** ¡qué bonito/horror!
however [hau'ɛvə*] adv: ~ **I do it** lo haga como lo haga; ~ **cold it is** por mucho frío que haga; ~ **fast he runs** por muy rápido que corra; ~ **did you do it?** ¿cómo lo hiciste? ▷ conj sin embargo, no obstante
howl [haul] n aullido ▷ vi aullar; (person) dar alaridos; (wind) ulular
H.P. n abbr = **hire purchase**
h.p. abbr = **horsepower**

HQ n abbr = **headquarters**
hr(s) abbr (= hour(s)) h
HTML n abbr (= hypertext markup language) lenguaje m de hipertexto
hubcap ['hʌbkæp] n tapacubos m inv
huddle ['hʌdl] vi: **to ~ together** acurrucarse
huff [hʌf] n: **in a ~** enojado
hug [hʌg] vt abrazar; (thing) apretar con los brazos
huge [hju:dʒ] adj enorme
hull [hʌl] n (of ship) casco
hum [hʌm] vt tararear, canturrear ▷ vi tararear, canturrear; (insect) zumbar
human ['hju:mən] adj, n humano
humane [hju:'meɪn] adj humano, humanitario
humanitarian [hju:mænɪ'tɛərɪən] adj humanitario
humanity [hju:'mænɪtɪ] n humanidad f
human rights npl derechos mpl humanos
humble ['hʌmbl] adj humilde
humid ['hju:mɪd] adj húmedo; **humidity** [-'mɪdɪtɪ] n humedad f
humiliate [hju:'mɪlɪeɪt] vt humillar
humiliating [hju:'mɪlɪeɪtɪŋ] adj humillante, vergonzoso
humiliation [hju:mɪlɪ'eɪʃən] n humillación f
hummus ['huməs] n paté de garbanzos
humorous ['hju:mərəs] adj gracioso, divertido
humour ['hju:mə*] (us humor) n humorismo, sentido del humor; (mood) humor m ▷ vt (person) complacer
hump [hʌmp] n (in ground) montículo; (camel's) giba
hunch [hʌntʃ] n (premonition) presentimiento
hundred ['hʌndrəd] num ciento; (before n) cien; ~ **s of** centenares de; **hundredth** [-ɪdθ] adj centésimo
hung [hʌŋ] pt, pp of **hang**
Hungarian [hʌŋ'gɛərɪən] adj, n húngaro/a m/f
Hungary ['hʌŋgərɪ] n Hungría
hunger ['hʌŋgə*] n hambre f ▷ vi: **to ~ for** (fig) tener hambre de, anhelar
hungry ['hʌŋgrɪ] adj: ~ **(for)** hambriento (de); **to be ~** tener hambre
hunt [hʌnt] vt (seek) buscar; (Sport) cazar ▷ vi (search): **to ~ (for)** buscar; (Sport) cazar ▷ n búsqueda; caza, cacería; **hunter** n cazador(a) m/f; **hunting** n caza
hurdle ['hə:dl] n (Sport) valla; (fig) obstáculo
hurl [hə:l] vt lanzar, arrojar
hurrah [hu'rɑ:] excl = **hurray**
hurray [hu'reɪ] excl ¡viva!
hurricane ['hʌrɪkən] n huracán m
hurry ['hʌrɪ] n prisa ▷ vi (also: ~ **up**: person) dar prisa a; (: work) apresurar, hacer de prisa; **to be in a ~** tener prisa; **hurry up** vi darse prisa, apurarse (LAM)
hurt [hə:t] (pt, pp ~) vt hacer daño a ▷ vi doler ▷ adj lastimado
husband ['hʌzbənd] n marido
hush [hʌʃ] n silencio ▷ vt hacer callar; ~! ¡chitón!, ¡cállate!
husky ['hʌskɪ] adj ronco ▷ n perro esquimal
hut [hʌt] n cabaña; (shed) cobertizo
hyacinth ['haɪəsɪnθ] n jacinto
hydrangea [haɪ'dreɪndʒə] n hortensia
hydrofoil ['haɪdrəfɔɪl] n aerodeslizador m
hydrogen ['haɪdrədʒən] n hidrógeno
hygiene ['haɪdʒi:n] n higiene f; **hygienic** [-'dʒi:nɪk] adj higiénico

hymn [hɪm] n himno
hype [haɪp] (inf) n bombardeo publicitario
hyphen ['haɪfn] n guión m
hypnotize ['hɪpnətaɪz] vt hipnotizar
hypocrite ['hɪpəkrɪt] n hipócrita mf
hypocritical [hɪpə'krɪtɪkl] adj hipócrita
hypothesis [haɪ'pɔθɪsɪs] (pl **hypotheses**) n hipótesis f inv
hysterical [hɪ'sterɪkl] adj histérico; (funny) para morirse de risa
hysterics [hɪ'sterɪks] npl histeria; **to be in ~** (fig) morirse de risa

I [aɪ] pron yo
ice [aɪs] n hielo; (ice cream) helado ▷ vt (cake) alcorzar ▷ vi (also: ~ **over**, ~ **up**) helarse; **iceberg** n iceberg m; **ice cream** n helado; **ice cube** n cubito de hielo; **ice hockey** n hockey m sobre hielo
Iceland ['aɪslənd] n Islandia; **Icelander** n islandés/esa m/f; **Icelandic** [aɪs'lændɪk] adj islandés/esa ▷ n (Ling) islandés m
ice: ice lolly (BRIT) n polo; **ice rink** n pista de hielo; **ice skating** n patinaje m sobre hielo
icing ['aɪsɪŋ] n (Culin) alcorza; **icing sugar** (BRIT) n azúcar m glas(eado)
icon ['aɪkɔn] n icono
ICT (BRIT: Scol) n abbr (= information and communications technology) informática
icy ['aɪsɪ] adj helado
I'd [aɪd] = **I would**; **I had**
ID card n (identity card) DNI m
idea [aɪ'dɪə] n idea
ideal [aɪ'dɪəl] n ideal m ▷ adj ideal; **ideally** [-dɪəlɪ] adv idealmente; **they're ideally suited** hacen una pareja ideal
identical [aɪ'dentɪkl] adj idéntico
identification [aɪdentɪfɪ'keɪʃən] n identificación f; **(means of) ~** documentos mpl personales
identify [aɪ'dentɪfaɪ] vt identificar
identity [aɪ'dentɪtɪ] n identidad f; **identity card** n carnet m de identidad; **identity theft** n robo de identidad
ideology [aɪdɪ'ɔlədʒɪ] n ideología
idiom ['ɪdɪəm] n modismo; (style of speaking) lenguaje m
idiot ['ɪdɪət] n idiota mf
idle ['aɪdl] adj (inactive) ocioso; (lazy) holgazán/ana; (unemployed) parado, desocupado; (machinery etc) parado; (talk etc) frívolo ▷ vi (machine) marchar en vacío
idol ['aɪdl] n ídolo
idyllic [ɪ'dɪlɪk] adj idílico
i.e. abbr (= that is) esto es
if [ɪf] conj si; **~ necessary** si fuera necesario, si hiciese falta; **~ I were you** yo en tu lugar; **~ so/not** de ser así/si no; **~ only I could!** ¡ojalá pudiera!; see also **as**; **even**

ignite [ɪɡ'naɪt] vt (set fire to) encender ▷ vi
encenderse

ignition [ɪɡ'nɪʃən] n (Aut: process) ignición f;
(: mechanism) encendido; **to switch on/off the ~**
arrancar/apagar el motor

ignorance ['ɪɡnərəns] n ignorancia

ignorant ['ɪɡnərənt] adj ignorante; **to be ~ of**
ignorar

ignore [ɪɡ'nɔː*] vt (person, advice) no hacer caso de;
(fact) pasar por alto

I'll [aɪl] = **I will; I shall**

ill [ɪl] adj enfermo, malo ▷ n mal m ▷ adv mal; **to be**
taken ~ ponerse enfermo

illegal [ɪ'liːɡl] adj ilegal

illegible [ɪ'lɛdʒɪbl] adj ilegible

illegitimate [ɪlɪ'dʒɪtɪmət] adj ilegítimo

ill health n mala salud f; **to be in ~** estar mal de salud

illiterate [ɪ'lɪtərət] adj analfabeto

illness ['ɪlnɪs] n enfermedad f

illuminate [ɪ'luːmɪneɪt] vt (room, street) iluminar,
alumbrar

illusion [ɪ'luːʒən] n ilusión f; (trick) truco

illustrate ['ɪləstreɪt] vt ilustrar

illustration [ɪlə'streɪʃən] n (act of illustrating)
ilustración f; (example) ejemplo, ilustración f; (in book)
lámina

I'm [aɪm] = **I am**

image ['ɪmɪdʒ] n imagen f

imaginary [ɪ'mædʒɪnərɪ] adj imaginario

imagination [ɪmædʒɪ'neɪʃən] n imaginación f;
(inventiveness) inventiva

imaginative [ɪ'mædʒɪnətɪv] adj imaginativo

imagine [ɪ'mædʒɪn] vt imaginarse

imbalance [ɪm'bæləns] n desequilibrio

imitate ['ɪmɪteɪt] vt imitar; **imitation** [ɪmɪ'teɪʃən] n
imitación f; (copy) copia

immaculate [ɪ'mækjulət] adj inmaculado

immature [ɪmə'tjuə*] adj (person) inmaduro

immediate [ɪ'miːdɪət] adj inmediato; (pressing)
urgente, apremiante; (nearest: family) próximo;
(: neighbourhood) inmediato; **immediately** adv
(at once) en seguida; (directly) inmediatamente;
immediately next to muy junto a

immense [ɪ'mɛns] adj inmenso, enorme;
(importance) enorme; **immensely** adv enormemente

immerse [ɪ'mɜːs] vt (submerge) sumergir; **to be ~d in**
(fig) estar absorto en

immigrant ['ɪmɪɡrənt] n inmigrante mf;
immigration [ɪmɪ'ɡreɪʃən] n inmigración f

imminent ['ɪmɪnənt] adj inminente

immoral [ɪ'mɔrl] adj inmoral

immortal [ɪ'mɔːtl] adj inmortal

immune [ɪ'mjuːn] adj: **~ (to)** inmune (a); **immune**
system n sistema m inmunitario

immunize ['ɪmjunaɪz] vt inmunizar

impact ['ɪmpækt] n impacto

impair [ɪm'pɛə*] vt perjudicar

impartial [ɪm'pɑːʃl] adj imparcial

impatience [ɪm'peɪʃəns] n impaciencia

impatient [ɪm'peɪʃənt] adj impaciente; **to get or**
grow ~ impacientarse

impeccable [ɪm'pɛkəbl] adj impecable

impending [ɪm'pɛndɪŋ] adj inminente

imperative [ɪm'pɛrətɪv] adj (tone) imperioso; (need)
imprescindible

imperfect [ɪm'pɜːfɪkt] adj (goods etc) defectuoso ▷ n

(Ling: also: **~ tense**) imperfecto

imperial [ɪm'pɪərɪəl] adj imperial

impersonal [ɪm'pɜːsənl] adj impersonal

impersonate [ɪm'pɜːsəneɪt] vt hacerse pasar por;
(Theatre) imitar

impetus ['ɪmpətəs] n ímpetu m; (fig) impulso

implant [ɪm'plɑːnt] n (Med) injertar, implantar;
(fig: idea, principle) inculcar

implement [n 'ɪmplɪmənt, vb 'ɪmplɪmɛnt] n
herramienta; (for cooking) utensilio ▷ vt (regulation)
hacer efectivo; (plan) realizar

implicate ['ɪmplɪkeɪt] vt (compromise) comprometer;
to ~ sb in sth comprometer a algn en algo

implication [ɪmplɪ'keɪʃən] n consecuencia f; **by ~**
indirectamente

implicit [ɪm'plɪsɪt] adj implícito; (belief, trust)
absoluto

imply [ɪm'plaɪ] vt (involve) suponer; (hint) dar a
entender que

impolite [ɪmpə'laɪt] adj mal educado

import [vb ɪm'pɔːt, n 'ɪmpɔːt] vt importar ▷ n
(Comm) importación f; (article) producto importado;
(meaning) significado, sentido

importance [ɪm'pɔːtəns] n importancia

important [ɪm'pɔːtənt] adj importante; **it's not ~**
no importa, no tiene importancia

importer [ɪm'pɔːtə*] n importador(a) m/f

impose [ɪm'pəuz] vt imponer ▷ vi: **to ~ on sb** abusar
de algn; **imposing** adj imponente, impresionante

impossible [ɪm'pɔsɪbl] adj imposible; (person)
insoportable

impotent ['ɪmpətənt] adj impotente

impoverished [ɪm'pɔvərɪʃt] adj necesitado

impractical [ɪm'præktɪkl] adj (person, plan) poco
práctico

impress [ɪm'prɛs] vt impresionar; (mark) estampar;
to ~ sth on sb hacer entender algo a algn

impression [ɪm'prɛʃən] n impresión f; (imitation)
imitación f; **to be under the ~ that** tener la impresión
de que

impressive [ɪm'prɛsɪv] adj impresionante

imprison [ɪm'prɪzn] vt encarcelar; **imprisonment** n
encarcelamiento; (term of imprisonment) cárcel f

improbable [ɪm'prɔbəbl] adj improbable,
inverosímil

improper [ɪm'prɔpə*] adj (unsuitable: conduct etc)
incorrecto; (: activities) deshonesto

improve [ɪm'pruːv] vt mejorar; (foreign language)
perfeccionar ▷ vi mejorarse; **improvement** n
mejoramiento; (in pupil etc) perfección f; progreso

improvise ['ɪmprəvaɪz] vt, vi improvisar

impulse ['ɪmpʌls] n impulso; **to act on ~** obrar sin
reflexión; **impulsive** [ɪm'pʌlsɪv] adj irreflexivo

○ **KEYWORD**

in [ɪn] prep **1** (indicating place, position, with place names)
en; **in the house/garden** en (la) casa/el jardín; **in**
here/there aquí/ahí or allí dentro; **in London/**
England en Londres/Inglaterra

2 (indicating time) en; **in spring** en (la) primavera; **in the**
afternoon por la tarde; **at 4 o'clock in the afternoon**
a las 4 de la tarde; **I did it in 3 hours/days** lo hice en 3
horas/días; **I'll see you in 2 weeks** or **in 2 weeks' time**
te veré dentro de 2 semanas

3 (indicating manner etc) en; **in a loud/soft voice** en voz

alta/baja; **in pencil/ink** a lápiz/bolígrafo; **the boy in the blue shirt** el chico de la camisa azul
4 (*indicating circumstances*): **in the sun/shade/rain** al sol/a la sombra/bajo la lluvia; **a change in policy** un cambio de política
5 (*indicating mood, state*): **in tears** en lágrimas, llorando; **in anger/despair** enfadado/desesperado; **to live in luxury** vivir lujosamente
6 (*with ratios, numbers*): **1 in 10 households, 1 household in 10** una de cada 10 familias; **20 pence in the pound** 20 peniques por libra; **they lined up in twos** se alinearon de dos en dos
7 (*referring to people, works*) en; entre; **the disease is common in children** la enfermedad es común entre los niños; **in (the works of) Dickens** en (las obras de) Dickens
8 (*indicating profession etc*): **to be in teaching** estar en la enseñanza
9 (*after superlative*) de; **the best pupil in the class** el(la) mejor alumno/a de la clase
10 (*with present participle*): **in saying this** al decir esto ▷ *adv*: **to be in** (*person: at home*) estar en casa; (*at work*) estar; (*train, ship, plane*) haber llegado; (*in fashion*) estar de moda; **she'll be in later today** llegará más tarde hoy; **to ask sb in** hacer pasar a algn; **to run/limp** *etc* **in** entrar corriendo/cojeando *etc*
▷ *n*: **the ins and outs** (*of proposal, situation etc*) los detalles

inability [ɪnəˈbɪlɪtɪ] *n*: **~ (to do)** incapacidad *f* (de hacer)
inaccurate [ɪnˈækjʊrət] *adj* inexacto, incorrecto
inadequate [ɪnˈædɪkwət] *adj* (*income, reply etc*) insuficiente; (*person*) incapaz
inadvertently [ɪnədˈvɜːtntlɪ] *adv* por descuido
inappropriate [ɪnəˈprəʊprɪət] *adj* inadecuado; (*improper*) poco oportuno
inaugurate [ɪˈnɔːgjʊreɪt] *vt* inaugurar; (*president, official*) investir
Inc. (*us*) *abbr* (= *incorporated*) S.A.
incapable [ɪnˈkeɪpəbl] *adj* incapaz
incense [*n* ˈɪnsens, *vb* ɪnˈsens] *n* incienso ▷ *vt* (*anger*) indignar, encolerizar
incentive [ɪnˈsentɪv] *n* incentivo, estímulo
inch [ɪntʃ] *n* pulgada; **to be within an ~ of** estar a dos dedos de; **he didn't give an ~** no dio concesión alguna
incidence [ˈɪnsɪdns] *n* (*of crime, disease*) incidencia
incident [ˈɪnsɪdnt] *n* incidente *m*
incidentally [ɪnsɪˈdentəlɪ] *adv* (*by the way*) a propósito
inclination [ɪnklɪˈneɪʃən] *n* (*tendency*) tendencia, inclinación *f*; (*desire*) deseo; (*disposition*) propensión *f*
incline [*n* ˈɪnklaɪn, *vb* ɪnˈklaɪn] *n* pendiente *m*, cuesta ▷ *vt* (*head*) poner de lado ▷ *vi* inclinarse; **to be ~d to** (*tend*) tener tendencia a hacer algo
include [ɪnˈkluːd] *vt* (*incorporate*) incluir; (*in letter*) adjuntar; **including** *prep* incluso, inclusive
inclusion [ɪnˈkluːʒən] *n* inclusión *f*
inclusive [ɪnˈkluːsɪv] *adj* inclusivo; **~ of tax** incluidos los impuestos
income [ˈɪnkʌm] *n* (*earned*) ingresos *mpl*; (*from property etc*) renta; (*from investment etc*) rédito; **income support** *n* (*BRIT*) ≈ ayuda familiar; **income tax** *n* impuesto sobre la renta
incoming [ˈɪnkʌmɪŋ] *adj* (*flight, government etc*)

entrante
incompatible [ɪnkəmˈpætɪbl] *adj* incompatible
incompetence [ɪnˈkɒmpɪtəns] *n* incompetencia
incompetent [ɪnˈkɒmpɪtənt] *adj* incompetente
incomplete [ɪnkəmˈpliːt] *adj* (*partial: achievement etc*) incompleto; (*unfinished: painting etc*) inacabado
inconsistent [ɪnkənˈsɪstənt] *adj* inconsecuente; (*contradictory*) incongruente; **~ with** (que) no concuerda con
inconvenience [ɪnkənˈviːnjəns] *n* inconvenientes *mpl*; (*trouble*) molestia, incomodidad *f* ▷ *vt* incomodar
inconvenient [ɪnkənˈviːnjənt] *adj* incómodo, poco práctico; (*time, place, visitor*) inoportuno
incorporate [ɪnˈkɔːpəreɪt] *vt* incorporar; (*contain*) comprender; (*add*) agregar
incorrect [ɪnkəˈrekt] *adj* incorrecto
increase [*n* ˈɪnkriːs, *vb* ɪnˈkriːs] *n* aumento ▷ *vi* aumentar; (*grow*) crecer; (*price*) subir ▷ *vt* aumentar; (*price*) subir; **increasingly** *adv* cada vez más, más y más
incredible [ɪnˈkredɪbl] *adj* increíble; **incredibly** *adv* increíblemente
incur [ɪnˈkɜː*] *vt* (*expenditure*) incurrir; (*loss*) sufrir; (*anger, disapproval*) provocar
indecent [ɪnˈdiːsnt] *adj* indecente
indeed [ɪnˈdiːd] *adv* efectivamente, en realidad; (*in fact*) en efecto; (*furthermore*) es más; **yes ~!** ¡claro que sí!
indefinitely [ɪnˈdefɪnɪtlɪ] *adv* (*wait*) indefinidamente
independence [ɪndɪˈpendns] *n* independencia; **Independence Day** (*us*) *n* Día de la Independencia
independent [ɪndɪˈpendənt] *adj* independiente; **independent school** *n* (*BRIT*) escuela *f* privada, colegio *m* privado
index [ˈɪndeks] (*pl* **-es**) *n* (*in book*) índice *m*; (: *in library etc*) catálogo; (*pl* **indices**: *ratio, sign*) exponente *m*
India [ˈɪndɪə] *n* la India; **Indian** *adj*, *n* indio/a; **Red Indian** piel roja *mf*
indicate [ˈɪndɪkeɪt] *vt* indicar; **indication** [-ˈkeɪʃə n] *n* indicio, señal *f*; **indicative** [ɪnˈdɪkətɪv] *adj*: **to be indicative of** indicar; **indicator** *n* indicador *m*; (*Aut*) intermitente *m*
indices [ˈɪndɪsiːz] *npl of* **index**
indict [ɪnˈdaɪt] *vt* acusar; **indictment** *n* acusación *f*
indifference [ɪnˈdɪfrəns] *n* indiferencia
indifferent [ɪnˈdɪfrənt] *adj* indiferente; (*mediocre*) regular
indigenous [ɪnˈdɪdʒɪnəs] *adj* indígena
indigestion [ɪndɪˈdʒestʃən] *n* indigestión *f*
indignant [ɪnˈdɪgnənt] *adj*: **to be ~ at sth/with sb** indignarse por algo/con algn
indirect [ɪndɪˈrekt] *adj* indirecto
indispensable [ɪndɪˈspensəbl] *adj* indispensable, imprescindible
individual [ɪndɪˈvɪdjuəl] *n* individuo ▷ *adj* individual; (*personal*) personal; (*particular*) particular; **individually** *adv* (*singly*) individualmente
Indonesia [ɪndəˈniːzɪə] *n* Indonesia
indoor [ˈɪndɔː*] *adj* (*swimming pool*) cubierto; (*plant*) de interior; (*sport*) bajo cubierta; **indoors** [ɪnˈdɔːz] *adv* dentro
induce [ɪnˈdjuːs] *vt* inducir, persuadir; (*bring about*) producir; (*labour*) provocar
indulge [ɪnˈdʌldʒ] *vt* (*whim*) satisfacer; (*person*) complacer; (*child*) mimar ▷ *vi*: **to ~ in** darse el gusto de; **indulgent** *adj* indulgente

industrial [ɪnˈdʌstrɪəl] *adj* industrial; **industrial estate** (BRIT) *n* polígono (SP) or zona (LAM) industrial; **industrialist** *n* industrial *mf*; **industrial park** (US) *n* = **industrial estate**

industry [ˈɪndəstrɪ] *n* industria; (*diligence*) aplicación *f*

inefficient [ɪnɪˈfɪʃənt] *adj* ineficaz, ineficiente

inequality [ɪnɪˈkwɒlɪtɪ] *n* desigualdad *f*

inevitable [ɪnˈɛvɪtəbl] *adj* inevitable; **inevitably** *adv* inevitablemente

inexpensive [ɪnɪkˈspɛnsɪv] *adj* económico

inexperienced [ɪnɪkˈspɪərɪənst] *adj* inexperto

inexplicable [ɪnɪkˈsplɪkəbl] *adj* inexplicable

infamous [ˈɪnfəməs] *adj* infame

infant [ˈɪnfənt] *n* niño/a; (*baby*) niño/a pequeño/a, bebé *mf*; (*pej*) aniñado

infantry [ˈɪnfəntrɪ] *n* infantería

infant school (BRIT) *n* parvulario

infect [ɪnˈfɛkt] *vt* (*wound*) infectar; (*food*) contaminar; (*person, animal*) contagiar; **infection** [ɪnˈfɛkʃən] *n* infección *f*; (*fig*) contagio; **infectious** [ɪnˈfɛkʃəs] *adj* (*also fig*) contagioso

infer [ɪnˈfəː*] *vt* deducir, inferir

inferior [ɪnˈfɪərɪə*] *adj, n* inferior *mf*

infertile [ɪnˈfəːtaɪl] *adj* estéril; (*person*) infecundo

infertility [ɪnfəˈtɪlɪtɪ] *n* esterilidad *f*; infecundidad *f*

infested [ɪnˈfɛstɪd] *adj*: **~ with** plagado de

infinite [ˈɪnfɪnɪt] *adj* infinito; **infinitely** *adv* infinitamente

infirmary [ɪnˈfəːmərɪ] *n* hospital *m*

inflamed [ɪnˈfleɪmd] *adj*: **to become ~** inflamarse

inflammation [ɪnfləˈmeɪʃən] *n* inflamación *f*

inflatable [ɪnˈfleɪtəbl] *adj* (*ball, boat*) inflable

inflate [ɪnˈfleɪt] *vt* (*tyre, price etc*) inflar; (*fig*) hinchar; **inflation** [ɪnˈfleɪʃən] *n* (*Econ*) inflación *f*

inflexible [ɪnˈflɛksəbl] *adj* (*rule*) rígido; (*person*) inflexible

inflict [ɪnˈflɪkt] *vt*: **to ~ sth on sb** infligir algo en algn

influence [ˈɪnfluəns] *n* influencia ▷ *vt* influir en, influenciar; **under the ~ of alcohol** en estado de embriaguez; **influential** [-ˈɛnʃl] *adj* influyente

influx [ˈɪnflʌks] *n* afluencia

info [ˈɪnfəu] (*inf*) *n* = **information**

inform [ɪnˈfɔːm] *vt*: **to ~ sb of sth** informar a algn sobre or de algo ▷ *vi*: **to ~ on sb** delatar a algn

informal [ɪnˈfɔːməl] *adj* (*manner, tone*) familiar; (*dress, interview, occasion*) informal; (*visit, meeting*) extraoficial

information [ɪnfəˈmeɪʃən] *n* información *f*; (*knowledge*) conocimientos *mpl*; **a piece of ~** dato; **information office** *n* información *f*; **information technology** *n* informática

informative [ɪnˈfɔːmətɪv] *adj* informativo

infra-red [ɪnfrəˈrɛd] *adj* infrarrojo

infrastructure [ˈɪnfrəstrʌktʃə*] *n* (*of system etc*) infraestructura

infrequent [ɪnˈfriːkwənt] *adj* infrecuente

infuriate [ɪnˈfjuərɪeɪt] *vt*: **to become ~d** ponerse furioso

infuriating [ɪnˈfjuərɪeɪtɪŋ] *adj* (*habit, noise*) enloquecedor(a)

ingenious [ɪnˈdʒiːnjəs] *adj* ingenioso

ingredient [ɪnˈgriːdɪənt] *n* ingrediente *m*

inhabit [ɪnˈhæbɪt] *vt* vivir en; **inhabitant** *n* habitante *m*

inhale [ɪnˈheɪl] *vt* inhalar ▷ *vi* (*breathe in*) aspirar; (*in smoking*) tragar; **inhaler** *n* inhalador *m*

inherent [ɪnˈhɪərənt] *adj*: **~ in** or **to** inherente a

inherit [ɪnˈhɛrɪt] *vt* heredar; **inheritance** *n* herencia; (*fig*) patrimonio

inhibit [ɪnˈhɪbɪt] *vt* inhibir, impedir; **inhibition** [-ˈbɪʃən] *n* cohibición *f*

initial [ɪˈnɪʃl] *adj* primero ▷ *n* inicial *f* ▷ *vt* firmar con las iniciales; **initials** *npl* (*as signature*) iniciales *fpl*; (*abbreviation*) siglas *fpl*; **initially** *adv* al principio

initiate [ɪˈnɪʃɪeɪt] *vt* iniciar; **to ~ proceedings against sb** (*Law*) entablar proceso contra algn

initiative [ɪˈnɪʃɪətɪv] *n* iniciativa

inject [ɪnˈdʒɛkt] *vt* inyectar; **to ~ sb with sth** inyectar algo a algn; **injection** [ɪnˈdʒɛkʃən] *n* inyección *f*

injure [ˈɪndʒə*] *vt* (*hurt*) herir, lastimar; (*fig: reputation etc*) perjudicar; **injured** (*person, arm*) herido, lastimado; **injury** *n* herida, lesión *f*; (*wrong*) perjuicio, daño

injustice [ɪnˈdʒʌstɪs] *n* injusticia

ink [ɪŋk] *n* tinta; **ink-jet printer** [ˈɪŋkdʒɛt-] *n* impresora de chorro de tinta

inland [*adj* ˈɪnlənd, *adv* ɪnˈlænd] *adj* (*waterway, port etc*) interior ▷ *adv* tierra adentro; **Inland Revenue** (BRIT) *n* departamento de impuestos ≈ Hacienda (SP)

in-laws [ˈɪnlɔːz] *npl* suegros *mpl*

inmate [ˈɪnmeɪt] *n* (*in prison*) preso/a, presidiario/a; (*in asylum*) internado/a

inn [ɪn] *n* posada, mesón *m*

inner [ˈɪnə*] *adj* (*courtyard, calm*) interior; (*feelings*) íntimo; **inner-city** *adj* (*schools, problems*) de las zonas céntricas pobres, de los barrios céntricos pobres

inning [ˈɪnɪŋ] *n* (*us: Baseball*) inning *m*, entrada; **~s** (*Cricket*) entrada, turno

innocence [ˈɪnəsns] *n* inocencia

innocent [ˈɪnəsnt] *adj* inocente

innovation [ɪnəuˈveɪʃən] *n* novedad *f*

innovative [ˈɪnəuveɪtɪv] *adj* innovador

in-patient [ˈɪnpeɪʃənt] *n* paciente *m/f* interno/a

input [ˈɪnput] *n* entrada; (*of resources*) inversión *f*; (*Comput*) entrada de datos

inquest [ˈɪnkwɛst] *n* (*coroner's*) encuesta judicial

inquire [ɪnˈkwaɪə*] *vi* preguntar ▷ *vt*: **to ~ whether** preguntar si; **to ~ about** (*person*) preguntar por; (*fact*) informarse de; **inquiry** *n* (*investigation*) investigación *f*, pesquisa; **"Inquiries"** "Información"

ins. *abbr* = **inches**

insane [ɪnˈseɪn] *adj* loco; (*Med*) demente

insanity [ɪnˈsænɪtɪ] *n* demencia, locura

insect [ˈɪnsɛkt] *n* insecto; **insect repellent** *n* loción *f* contra insectos

insecure [ɪnsɪˈkjuə*] *adj* inseguro

insecurity [ɪnsɪˈkjuərɪtɪ] *n* inseguridad *f*

insensitive [ɪnˈsɛnsɪtɪv] *adj* insensible

insert [*vb* ɪnˈsəːt, *n* ˈɪnsəːt] *vt* (*into sth*) introducir ▷ *n* encarte *m*

inside [ˈɪnsaɪd] *n* interior *m* ▷ *adj* interior, interno ▷ *adv* (*be*) (*por*) dentro; (*go*) hacia dentro ▷ *prep* dentro de; (*of time*): **~ 10 minutes** en menos de 10 minutos; **inside lane** *n* (*Aut: in Britain*) carril *m* izquierdo; (*: in US, Europe etc*) carril *m* derecho; **inside out** *adv* (*turn*) al revés; (*know*) a fondo

insight [ˈɪnsaɪt] *n* perspicacia

insignificant [ɪnsɪgˈnɪfɪknt] *adj* insignificante

insincere [ɪnsɪnˈsɪə*] *adj* poco sincero

insist [ɪnˈsɪst] *vi* insistir; **to ~ on** insistir en; **to ~ that** insistir en que; (*claim*) exigir que; **insistent** *adj* insistente; (noise, action) persistente

insomnia [ɪnˈsɒmnɪə] n insomnio

inspect [ɪnˈspɛkt] vt inspeccionar, examinar; (troops) pasar revista a; **inspection** [ɪnˈspɛkʃən] n inspección f, examen m; (of troops) revista f; **inspector** n inspector(a) m/f; (BRIT: on buses, trains) revisor(a) m/f

inspiration [ɪnspəˈreɪʃən] n inspiración f; **inspire** [ɪnˈspaɪə*] vt inspirar; **inspiring** adj inspirador(a)

instability [ɪnstəˈbɪlɪtɪ] n inestabilidad f

install [ɪnˈstɔːl] (us **instal**) vt instalar; (official) nombrar; **installation** [ɪnstəˈleɪʃən] n instalación f

instalment [ɪnˈstɔːlmənt] (us **installment**) n plazo; (of story) entrega; (of TV serial etc) capítulo; **in ~s** (pay, receive) a plazos

instance [ˈɪnstəns] n ejemplo, caso; **for ~** por ejemplo; **in the first ~** en primer lugar

instant [ˈɪnstənt] n instante m, momento ▷ adj inmediato; (coffee etc) instantáneo; **instantly** adv en seguida; **instant messaging** n mensajería instantánea

instead [ɪnˈstɛd] adv en cambio; **~ of** en lugar de, en vez de

instinct [ˈɪnstɪŋkt] n instinto; **instinctive** adj instintivo

institute [ˈɪnstɪtjuːt] n instituto; (professional body) colegio ▷ vt (begin) iniciar, empezar; (proceedings) entablar; (system, rule) establecer

institution [ɪnstɪˈtjuːʃən] n institución f; (Med: home) asilo; (: asylum) manicomio; (of system etc) establecimiento; (of custom) iniciación f

instruct [ɪnˈstrʌkt] vt: **to ~ sb in sth** instruir a algn or sobre algo; **to ~ sb to do sth** dar instrucciones a algn de hacer algo; **instruction** [ɪnˈstrʌkʃən] n (teaching) instrucción f; **instructions** npl (orders) órdenes fpl; **instructions (for use)** modo de empleo; **instructor** n instructor(a) m/f

instrument [ˈɪnstrəmənt] n instrumento; **instrumental** [-ˈmɛntl] adj (Mus) instrumental; **to be instrumental in** ser (el) artífice de

insufficient [ɪnsəˈfɪʃənt] adj insuficiente

insulate [ˈɪnsjuleɪt] vt aislar; **insulation** [-ˈleɪʃən] n aislamiento

insulin [ˈɪnsjulɪn] n insulina

insult [n ˈɪnsʌlt, vb ɪnˈsʌlt] n insulto ▷ vt insultar; **insulting** adj insultante

insurance [ɪnˈʃuərəns] n seguro; **fire/life ~** seguro contra incendios/sobre la vida; **insurance company** n compañía f de seguros; **insurance policy** n póliza (de seguros)

insure [ɪnˈʃuə*] vt asegurar

intact [ɪnˈtækt] adj íntegro; (unharmed) intacto

intake [ˈɪnteɪk] n (of food) ingestión f; (of air) consumo; (BRIT Scol): **an ~ of 200 a year** 200 matriculados al año

integral [ˈɪntɪɡrəl] adj (whole) íntegro; (part) integrante

integrate [ˈɪntɪɡreɪt] vt integrar ▷ vi integrarse

integrity [ɪnˈtɛɡrɪtɪ] n honradez f, rectitud f

intellect [ˈɪntəlɛkt] n intelecto; **intellectual** [-ˈlɛktjuəl] adj, n intelectual mf

intelligence [ɪnˈtɛlɪdʒəns] n inteligencia

intelligent [ɪnˈtɛlɪdʒənt] adj inteligente

intend [ɪnˈtɛnd] vt (gift etc): **to ~ sth for** destinar algo a; **to ~ to do sth** tener intención de or pensar hacer algo

intense [ɪnˈtɛns] adj intenso

intensify [ɪnˈtɛnsɪfaɪ] vt intensificar; (increase) aumentar

intensity [ɪnˈtɛnsɪtɪ] n (gen) intensidad f

intensive [ɪnˈtɛnsɪv] adj intensivo; **intensive care** n: **to be in intensive care** estar bajo cuidados intensivos; **intensive care unit** n unidad f de vigilancia intensiva

intent [ɪnˈtɛnt] n propósito; (Law) premeditación f ▷ adj (absorbed) absorto; (attentive) atento; **to all ~s and purposes** prácticamente; **to be ~ on doing sth** estar resuelto a hacer algo

intention [ɪnˈtɛnʃən] n intención f, propósito; **intentional** adj deliberado

interact [ɪntərˈækt] vi influirse mutuamente; **interaction** [ɪntərˈækʃən] n interacción f, acción f recíproca; **interactive** adj (Comput) interactivo

intercept [ɪntəˈsɛpt] vt interceptar; (stop) detener

interchange [ˈɪntətʃeɪndʒ] n intercambio; (on motorway) intersección f

intercourse [ˈɪntəkɔːs] n (sexual) relaciones fpl sexuales

interest [ˈɪntrɪst] n (also Comm) interés m ▷ vt interesar; **interested** adj interesado; **to be interested in** interesarse por; **interesting** adj interesante; **interest rate** n tipo or tasa de interés

interface [ˈɪntəfeɪs] n (Comput) junción f

interfere [ɪntəˈfɪə*] vi: **to ~ in** entrometerse en; **to ~ with** (hinder) estorbar; (damage) estropear

interference [ɪntəˈfɪərəns] n intromisión f; (Radio, TV) interferencia

interim [ˈɪntərɪm] n: **in the ~** en el ínterin ▷ adj provisional

interior [ɪnˈtɪərɪə*] n interior m ▷ adj interior; **interior design** n interiorismo, decoración f de interiores

intermediate [ɪntəˈmiːdɪət] adj intermedio

intermission [ɪntəˈmɪʃən] n intermisión f; (Theatre) descanso

intern [vb ɪnˈtəːn, n ˈɪntəːn] (us) vt internar ▷ n interno/a

internal [ɪnˈtəːnl] adj (layout, pipes, security) interior; (injury, structure, memo) internal; **Internal Revenue Service** (us) n departamento de impuestos, ≈ Hacienda (SP)

international [ɪntəˈnæʃənl] adj internacional ▷ n (BRIT: match) partido internacional

Internet [ˈɪntənɛt] n: **the ~** Internet m or f; **Internet café** n cibercafé m; **Internet Service Provider** n proveedor m de (acceso a) Internet; **Internet user** n internauta mf

interpret [ɪnˈtəːprɪt] vt interpretar; (translate) traducir; (understand) entender ▷ vi hacer de intérprete; **interpretation** [ɪntəːprɪˈteɪʃən] n interpretación f; traducción f; **interpreter** n intérprete mf

interrogate [ɪnˈtɛrəʊɡeɪt] vt interrogar; **interrogation** [-ˈɡeɪʃən] n interrogatorio

interrogative [ɪntəˈrɒɡətɪv] adj interrogativo

interrupt [ɪntəˈrʌpt] vt, vi interrumpir; **interruption** [-ˈrʌpʃən] n interrupción f

intersection [ɪntəˈsɛkʃən] n (of roads) cruce m

interstate [ˈɪntəsteɪt] (us) n carretera interestatal

interval [ˈɪntəvl] n intervalo; (BRIT Theatre, Sport) descanso; (Scol) recreo; **at ~s** a ratos, de vez en cuando

intervene [ɪntəˈviːn] vi intervenir; (event) interponerse; (time) transcurrir

interview ['ɪntəvjuː] n entrevista ▷ vt entrevistarse con; **interviewer** n entrevistador(a) m/f

intimate [adj 'ɪntɪmət, vb 'ɪntɪmeɪt] adj íntimo; (friendship) estrecho; (knowledge) profundo ▷ vt dar a entender

intimidate [ɪn'tɪmɪdeɪt] vt intimidar, amedrentar

intimidating [ɪn'tɪmɪdeɪtɪŋ] adj amedrentador, intimidante

into ['ɪntu:] prep en; (towards) a; (inside) hacia el interior de; **~ 3 pieces/French** en 3 pedazos/al francés

intolerant [ɪn'tɔlərənt] adj: **~ (of)** intolerante (con or para)

intranet ['ɪntrənet] n intranet f

intransitive [ɪn'trænsɪtɪv] adj intransitivo

intricate ['ɪntrɪkət] adj (design, pattern) intrincado

intrigue [ɪn'triːg] n intriga ▷ vt fascinar; **intriguing** adj fascinante

introduce [ɪntrə'djuːs] vt introducir, meter; (speaker, TV show etc) presentar; **to ~ sb (to sb)** presentar a algn (a algn); **to ~ sb to** (pastime, technique) introducir a algn a; **introduction** [-'dʌkʃən] n introducción f; (of person) presentación f; **introductory** [-'dʌktərɪ] adj introductorio; (lesson, offer) de introducción

intrude [ɪn'truːd] vi (person) entrometerse; **to ~ on** estorbar; **intruder** n intruso/a

intuition [ɪntjuː'ɪʃən] n intuición f

inundate ['ɪnʌndeɪt] vt: **to ~ with** inundar de

invade [ɪn'veɪd] vt invadir

invalid [n 'ɪnvəlɪd, adj ɪn'vælɪd] n (Med) minusválido/ a ▷ adj (not valid) inválido, nulo

invaluable [ɪn'væljuəbl] adj inestimable

invariably [ɪn'veərɪəblɪ] adv sin excepción, siempre; **she is ~ late** siempre llega tarde

invasion [ɪn'veɪʒən] n invasión f

invent [ɪn'vent] vt inventar; **invention** [ɪn'venʃən] n invento; (lie) ficción f, mentira; **inventor** n inventor(a) m/f

inventory ['ɪnvəntrɪ] n inventario

inverted commas [ɪn'vɜːtɪd-] (BRIT) npl comillas fpl

invest [ɪn'vest] vt invertir ▷ vi: **to ~ in** (company etc) invertir dinero en; (fig: sth useful) comprar

investigate [ɪn'vestɪgeɪt] vt investigar; **investigation** [-'geɪʃən] n investigación f, pesquisa

investigator [ɪn'vestɪgeɪtə*] n investigador(a) m/f; **private ~** investigador(a) m/f privado/a

investment [ɪn'vestmənt] n inversión f

investor [ɪn'vestə*] n inversionista mf

invisible [ɪn'vɪzɪbl] adj invisible

invitation [ɪnvɪ'teɪʃən] n invitación f

invite [ɪn'vaɪt] vt invitar; (opinions etc) solicitar, pedir; **inviting** adj atractivo; (food) apetitoso

invoice ['ɪnvɔɪs] n factura ▷ vt facturar

involve [ɪn'vɔlv] vt suponer, implicar; tener que ver con; (concern, affect) corresponder; **to ~ sb (in sth)** comprometer a algn (con algo); **involved** adj complicado; **to be involved in** (take part) tomar parte en; (be engrossed) estar muy metido en; **involvement** n participación f, dedicación f

inward ['ɪnwəd] adj (movement) interior, interno; (thought, feeling) íntimo; **inward(s)** adv hacia dentro

iPod ® ['aɪpɔd] n iPod ® f

IQ n abbr (= intelligence quotient) cociente m intelectual

IRA n abbr (= Irish Republican Army) IRA m

Iran [ɪ'rɑːn] n Irán m; **Iranian** [ɪ'reɪnɪən] adj, n iraní mf

Iraq [ɪ'rɑːk] n Iraq; **Iraqi** adj, n iraquí mf

Ireland ['aɪələnd] n Irlanda

iris ['aɪrɪs] (pl **~es**) n (Anat) iris m; (Bot) lirio

Irish ['aɪrɪʃ] adj irlandés/esa ▷ npl: **the ~** los irlandeses; **Irishman** (irreg) n irlandés m; **Irishwoman** (irreg) n irlandésa

iron ['aɪən] n hierro; (for clothes) plancha ▷ cpd de hierro ▷ vt (clothes) planchar

ironic(al) [aɪ'rɔnɪk(l)] adj irónico; **ironically** adv irónicamente

ironing ['aɪənɪŋ] n (activity) planchado; (clothes: ironed) ropa planchada; (: to be ironed) ropa por planchar; **ironing board** n tabla de planchar

irony ['aɪrənɪ] n ironía

irrational [ɪ'ræʃənl] adj irracional

irregular [ɪ'regjulə*] adj irregular; (surface) desigual; (action, event) anómalo; (behaviour) poco ortodoxo

irrelevant [ɪ'reləvənt] adj fuera de lugar, inoportuno

irresistible [ɪrɪ'zɪstɪbl] adj irresistible

irresponsible [ɪrɪ'spɔnsɪbl] adj (act) irresponsable, (person) poco serio

irrigation [ɪrɪ'geɪʃən] n riego

irritable ['ɪrɪtəbl] adj (person) de mal humor

irritate ['ɪrɪteɪt] vt fastidiar; (Med) picar; **irritating** adj fastidioso; **irritation** [-'teɪʃən] n fastidio; enfado; picazón f

IRS (us) n abbr = **Internal Revenue Service**

is [ɪz] vb see **be**

ISDN n abbr (= Integrated Services Digital Network) RDSI f

Islam ['ɪzlɑːm] n Islam m; **Islamic** [ɪz'læmɪk] adj islámico

island ['aɪlənd] n isla; **islander** n isleño/a

isle [aɪl] n isla

isn't ['ɪznt] = **is not**

isolated ['aɪsəleɪtɪd] adj aislado

isolation [aɪsə'leɪʃən] n aislamiento

ISP n abbr = **Internet Service Provider**

Israel ['ɪzreɪl] n Israel m; **Israeli** [ɪz'reɪlɪ] adj, n israelí mf

issue ['ɪsjuː] n (problem, subject) cuestión f; (outcome) resultado; (of banknotes etc) emisión f; (of newspaper etc) edición f ▷ vt (rations, equipment) distribuir, repartir; (orders) dar; (certificate, passport) expedir; (decree) promulgar; (magazine) publicar; (cheques) extender; (banknotes, stamps) emitir; **at ~** en cuestión; **to take ~ with sb (over)** estar en desacuerdo con algn (sobre); **to make an ~ of sth** hacer una cuestión de algo

IT n abbr = **information technology**

○ **KEYWORD**

it [ɪt] pron **1** (specific subject: not generally translated) él (ella); (: direct object) lo, la; (: indirect object) le; (after prep) él (ella); (abstract concept) ello; **it's on the table** está en la mesa; **I can't find it** no lo (or la) encuentro; **give it to me** dámelo (or dámela); **I spoke to him about it** le hablé del asunto; **what did you learn from it?** ¿qué aprendiste de él (or ella)?; **did you go to it?** (party, concert etc) ¿fuiste?

2 (impersonal): **it's raining** llueve, está lloviendo; **it's 6 o'clock/the 10th of August** son las 6/es el 10 de agosto; **how far is it? - it's 10 miles/2 hours on the train** ¿a qué distancia está? - a 10 millas/2 horas en tren; **who is it? - it's me** ¿quién es? - soy yo

Italian [ɪ'tæljən] adj italiano ▷ n italiano/a; (Ling)

italiano

italics [ɪˈtælɪks] *npl* cursiva
Italy [ˈɪtəlɪ] *n* Italia
itch [ɪtʃ] *n* picazón *f* ▷ *vi* (*part of body*) picar; **to ~ to do sth** rabiar por hacer algo; **itchy** *adj*: **my hand is itchy** me pica la mano
it'd [ˈɪtd] = **it would; it had**
item [ˈaɪtəm] *n* artículo; (*on agenda*) asunto (a tratar); (*also:* **news ~**) noticia
itinerary [aɪˈtɪnərərɪ] *n* itinerario
it'll [ˈɪtl] = **it will; it shall**
its [ɪts] *adj* su; sus *pl*
it's [ɪts] = **it is; it has**
itself [ɪtˈsɛlf] *pron* (*reflexive*) sí mismo/a; (*emphatic*) él mismo(ella misma)
ITV *n abbr* (BRIT: = *Independent Television*) cadena de televisión comercial independiente del Estado
I've [aɪv] = **I have**
ivory [ˈaɪvərɪ] *n* marfil *m*
ivy [ˈaɪvɪ] *n* (*Bot*) hiedra

J

jab [dʒæb] *vt*: **to ~ sth into sth** clavar algo en algo ▷ *n* (*inf: Med*) pinchazo
jack [dʒæk] *n* (*Aut*) gato; (*Cards*) sota
jacket [ˈdʒækɪt] *n* chaqueta, americana (SP), saco (LAM); (*of book*) sobrecubierta; **jacket potato** *n* patata asada (con piel)
jackpot [ˈdʒækpɔt] *n* premio gordo
Jacuzzi® [dʒəˈkuːzɪ] *n* jacuzzi® *m*
jagged [ˈdʒægɪd] *adj* dentado
jail [dʒeɪl] *n* cárcel *f* ▷ *vt* encarcelar; **jail sentence** *n* pena *f* de cárcel
jam [dʒæm] *n* mermelada; (*also:* **traffic ~**) embotellamiento; (*inf: difficulty*) apuro ▷ *vt* (*passage etc*) obstruir; (*mechanism, drawer etc*) atascar; (*Radio*) interferir ▷ *vi* atascarse, trabarse; **to ~ sth into sth** meter algo a la fuerza en algo
Jamaica [dʒəˈmeɪkə] *n* Jamaica
jammed [dʒæmd] *adj* atascado
Jan *abbr* (= *January*) ene
janitor [ˈdʒænɪtə*] *n* (*caretaker*) portero, conserje *m*
January [ˈdʒænjuərɪ] *n* enero
Japan [dʒəˈpæn] *n* (el) Japón; **Japanese** [dʒæpəˈniːz] *adj* japonés/esa ▷ *n inv* japonés/esa *m/f*; (*Ling*) japonés *m*
jar [dʒɑː*] *n* tarro, bote *m* ▷ *vi* (*sound*) chirriar; (*colours*) desentonar
jargon [ˈdʒɑːgən] *n* jerga
javelin [ˈdʒævlɪn] *n* jabalina
jaw [dʒɔː] *n* mandíbula
jazz [dʒæz] *n* jazz *m*
jealous [ˈdʒɛləs] *adj* celoso; (*envious*) envidioso; **jealousy** *n* celos *mpl*; envidia
jeans [dʒiːnz] *npl* vaqueros *mpl*, tejanos *mpl*
Jello® [ˈdʒɛləʊ] (US) *n* gelatina
jelly [ˈdʒɛlɪ] *n* (*jam*) jalea; (*dessert etc*) gelatina; **jellyfish** *n inv* medusa, aguaviva (RPL)
jeopardize [ˈdʒɛpədaɪz] *vt* arriesgar, poner en peligro
jerk [dʒəːk] *n* (*jolt*) sacudida; (*wrench*) tirón *m*; (*inf*) imbécil *mf* ▷ *vt* tirar bruscamente de ▷ *vi* (*vehicle*) traquetear
jersey [ˈdʒəːzɪ] *n* jersey *m*
jersey [ˈdʒəːzɪ] *n* jersey *m*; (*fabric*) (tejido de) punto

Jesus ['dʒiːzəs] n Jesús m

jet [dʒet] n (of gas, liquid) chorro m; (Aviat) avión m a reacción; **jet lag** n desorientación f después de un largo vuelo; **jet-ski** vi practicar el motociclismo acuático

jetty ['dʒɛtɪ] n muelle m, embarcadero

Jew [dʒuː] n judío/a

jewel ['dʒuːəl] n joya; (in watch) rubí m; **jeweller** (us **jeweler**) n joyero/a; **jeweller's (shop)** (us **jewelry store**) n joyería; **jewellery** (us **jewelry**) n joyas fpl, alhajas fpl

Jewish ['dʒuːɪʃ] adj judío

jigsaw ['dʒɪɡsɔː] n (also: **~ puzzle**) rompecabezas m inv, puzle m

job [dʒɔb] n (task) tarea; (post) empleo; **it's not my ~** no me incumbe a mí; **it's a good ~ that ...** menos mal que ...; **just the ~!** ¡estupendo!; **job centre** (BRIT) n oficina estatal de colocaciones; **jobless** adj sin trabajo

jockey ['dʒɔkɪ] n jockey mf ⊳ vi: **to ~ for position** maniobrar para conseguir una posición

jog [dʒɔɡ] vt empujar (ligeramente) ⊳ vi (run) hacer footing; **to ~ sb's memory** refrescar la memoria a algn; **jogging** n footing m

join [dʒɔɪn] vt (things) juntar, unir; (club) hacerse socio de; (Pol: party) afiliarse a; (queue) ponerse en; (meet: people) reunirse con ⊳ vi (roads) juntarse; (rivers) confluir ⊳ n juntura; **join in** vi tomar parte, participar ⊳ vt fus tomar parte o participar en; **join up** vi reunirse; (Mil) alistarse

joiner ['dʒɔɪnə*] (BRIT) n carpintero/a

joint [dʒɔɪnt] n (Tech) junta, unión f; (Anat) articulación f; (BRIT Culin) pieza de carne (para asar); (inf: place) tugurio; (of cannabis) porro ⊳ adj (common) común; (combined) combinado; **joint account** n (with bank etc) cuenta común; **jointly** adv (gen) en común; (together) conjuntamente

joke [dʒəuk] n chiste m; (also: **practical ~**) broma ⊳ vi bromear; **to play a ~ on** gastar una broma a algn ⊳ n (Cards) comodín m

jolly ['dʒɔlɪ] adj (merry) alegre; (enjoyable) divertido ⊳ adv (BRIT: inf) muy, terriblemente

jolt [dʒəult] n (jerk) sacudida; (shock) susto ⊳ vt (physically) sacudir; (emotionally) asustar

Jordan ['dʒɔːdən] n (country) Jordania; (river) Jordán m

journal ['dʒəːnl] n (magazine) revista; (diary) periódico, diario; **journalism** n periodismo; **journalist** n periodista mf, reportero/a

journey ['dʒəːnɪ] n viaje m; (distance covered) trayecto

joy [dʒɔɪ] n alegría; **joyrider** n gamberro que roba un coche para dar una vuelta y luego abandonarlo; **joy stick** n (Aviat) palanca de mando; (Comput) palanca de control

Jr abbr = **junior**

judge [dʒʌdʒ] n juez mf; (fig: expert) perito ⊳ vt juzgar; (consider) considerar

judo ['dʒuːdəu] n judo

jug [dʒʌɡ] n jarra

juggle ['dʒʌɡl] vi hacer juegos malabares; **juggler** n malabarista mf

juice [dʒuːs] n zumo (SP), jugo (LAM); **juicy** adj jugoso

Jul abbr (=July) jul

July [dʒuːˈlaɪ] n julio

jumble ['dʒʌmbl] n revoltijo ⊳ vt (also: **~ up**) revolver; **jumble sale** (BRIT) n venta de objetos usados con fines benéficos

jumbo ['dʒʌmbəu] n (also: **~ jet**) jumbo

jump [dʒʌmp] vi saltar, dar saltos; (with fear etc) pegar un bote; (increase) aumentar ⊳ vt saltar ⊳ n salto; aumento; **to ~ the queue** (BRIT) colarse

jumper ['dʒʌmpə*] n (BRIT: pullover) suéter m, jersey m; (us: dress) mandil m

jumper cables (us) npl = **jump leads**

jump leads (BRIT) npl cables mpl puente de batería

jun. abbr = **junior**

junction ['dʒʌŋkʃən] n (BRIT: of roads) cruce m; (Rail) empalme m

June [dʒuːn] n junio

jungle ['dʒʌŋɡl] n selva, jungla

junior ['dʒuːnɪə*] adj (in age) menor, más joven; (brother/sister etc): **seven years her ~** siete años menor que ella; (position) subalterno ⊳ n menor mf, joven mf; **junior high school** (us) n centro de educación secundaria; see also **high school**; **junior school** (BRIT) n escuela primaria

junk [dʒʌŋk] n (cheap goods) baratijas fpl; (rubbish) basura; **junk food** n alimentos preparados y envasados de escaso valor nutritivo

junkie ['dʒʌŋkɪ] (inf) n drogadicto/a, yonqui mf

junk mail n propaganda de buzón

Jupiter ['dʒuːpɪtə*] n (Mythology, Astrology) Júpiter m

jurisdiction [dʒuərɪsˈdɪkʃən] n jurisdicción f; **it falls or comes within/outside our ~** es/no es de nuestra competencia

jury ['dʒuərɪ] n jurado

just [dʒʌst] adj justo ⊳ adv (exactly) exactamente; (only) sólo, solamente; **he's ~ done it/left** acaba de hacerlo/irse; **~ right** perfecto; **~ two o'clock** las dos en punto; **she's ~ as clever as you** (ella) es tan lista como tú; **~ as well that ...** menos mal que ...; **~ as he was leaving** en el momento en que se marchaba; **~ before/enough** justo antes/lo suficiente; **~ here** aquí mismo; **he ~ missed** ha fallado por poco; **~ listen to this** escucha esto un momento

justice ['dʒʌstɪs] n justicia; (us: judge) juez mf; **to do ~ to** (fig) hacer justicia a

justification [dʒʌstɪfɪˈkeɪʃən] n justificación f

justify ['dʒʌstɪfaɪ] vt justificar; (text) alinear

jut [dʒʌt] vi (also: **~ out**) sobresalir

juvenile ['dʒuːvənaɪl] adj (court) de menores; (humour, mentality) infantil ⊳ n menor m de edad

k

K *abbr* (= *one thousand*) mil; (= *kilobyte*) kilobyte *m*, kilooocteto

kangaroo [kæŋgə'ruː] *n* canguro

karaoke [kɑːrə'əʊkɪ] *n* karaoke

karate [kə'rɑːtɪ] *n* karate *m*

kebab [kə'bæb] *n* pincho moruno

keel [kiːl] *n* quilla; **on an even ~** (*fig*) en equilibrio

keen [kiːn] *adj* (*interest, desire*) grande, vivo; (*eye, intelligence*) agudo; (*competition*) reñido; (*edge*) afilado; (*eager*) entusiasta; **to be ~ to do** *or* **on doing sth** tener muchas ganas de hacer algo; **to be ~ on sth/sb** interesarse por algo/algn

keep [kiːp] (*pt, pp* **kept**) *vt* (*preserve, store*) guardar; (*hold back*) quedarse con; (*maintain*) mantener; (*detain*) detener; (*shop*) ser propietario de; (*feed: family etc*) mantener; (*promise*) cumplir; (*chickens, bees etc*) criar; (*accounts*) llevar; (*diary*) escribir; (*prevent*): **to ~ sb from doing sth** impedir a algn hacer algo ▷ *vi* (*food*) conservarse; (*remain*) seguir, continuar ▷ *n* (*of castle*) torreón *m*; (*food etc*) comida, subsistencia; (*inf*): **for ~s** para siempre; **to ~ doing sth** seguir haciendo algo; **to ~ sb happy** tener a algn contento; **to ~ a place tidy** mantener un lugar limpio; **to ~ sth to o.s.** guardar algo para sí mismo; **to ~ sth (back) from sb** ocultar algo a algn; **to ~ time** (*clock*) mantener la hora exacta; **keep away** *vt*: **to keep sth/sb away from sb** mantener algo/a algn apartado de algn ▷ *vi*: **to keep away (from sb)** mantenerse apartado (de); **keep back** *vt* (*crowd, tears*) contener; (*money*) quedarse con; (*conceal: information*): **to keep sth back from sb** ocultar algo a algn ▷ *vi* hacerse a un lado; **keep off** *vt* (*dog, person*) mantener a distancia ▷ *vi*: **if the rain keeps off** so no llueve; **keep your hands off!** ¡no toques!; **"keep off the grass"** "prohibido pisar el césped"; **keep on** *vi*: **to keep on doing** seguir *or* continuar haciendo; **to keep on (about sth)** no parar de hablar (de algo); **keep out** *vi* (*stay out*) permanecer fuera; **"keep out"** prohibida la entrada"; **keep up** *vt* mantener, conservar ▷ *vi* no retrasarse; **to keep up with** (*pace*) ir al paso de; (*level*) mantenerse a la altura de; **keeper** *n* guardián/ana *m/f*; **keeping** *n* (*care*) cuidado; **in keeping with** de acuerdo con

kennel ['kɛnl] *n* perrera; **kennels** *npl* residencia canina

Kenya ['kɛnjə] *n* Kenia

kept [kɛpt] *pt, pp of* **keep**

kerb [kəːb] (*BRIT*) *n* bordillo

kerosene ['kɛrəsiːn] *n* keroseno

ketchup ['kɛtʃəp] *n* salsa de tomate, catsup *m*

kettle ['kɛtl] *n* hervidor *m* de agua

key [kiː] *n* llave *f*; (*Mus*) tono; (*of piano, typewriter*) tecla ▷ *adj* (*issue etc*) clave *inv* ▷ *vt* (*also*: **~ in**) teclear; **keyboard** *n* teclado; **keyhole** *n* ojo (de la cerradura); **keyring** *n* llavero

kg *abbr* (= *kilogram*) kg

khaki ['kɑːkɪ] *n* caqui

kick [kɪk] *vt* dar una patada *o* un puntapié a; (*inf: habit*) quitarse de ▷ *vi* (*horse*) dar coces ▷ *n* patada; puntapié *m*; (*of animal*) coz *f*; (*thrill*): **he does it for ~s** lo hace por pura diversión; **kick off** *vi* (*Sport*) hacer el saque inicial; **kick-off** *n* saque inicial; **the kick-off is at 10 o'clock** el partido empieza a las diez

kid [kɪd] *n* (*inf: child*) chiquillo/a; (*animal*) cabrito; (*leather*) cabritilla ▷ *vi* (*inf*) bromear

kidnap ['kɪdnæp] *vt* secuestrar; **kidnapping** *n* secuestro

kidney ['kɪdnɪ] *n* riñón *m*; **kidney bean** *n* judía, alubia

kill [kɪl] *vt* matar; (*murder*) asesinar ▷ *n* matanza; **to ~ time** matar el tiempo; **killer** *n* asesino/a; **killing** *n* (*one*) asesinato; (*several*) matanza; **to make a killing** (*fig*) hacer su agosto

kiln [kɪln] *n* horno

kilo ['kiːləʊ] *n* kilo; **kilobyte** *n* (*Comput*) kilobyte *m*, kilooocteto; **kilogram(me)** *n* kilo, kilogramo; **kilometre** ['kɪləmiːtə*] (*us* **kilometer**) *n* kilómetro; **kilowatt** *n* kilovatio

kilt [kɪlt] *n* falda escocesa

kin [kɪn] *n see* **next-of-kin**

kind [kaɪnd] *adj* amable, atento ▷ *n* clase *f*, especie *f*; (*species*) género; **in ~** (*Comm*) en especie; **a ~ of** una especie de; **to be two of a ~** ser tal para cual

kindergarten ['kɪndəgɑːtn] *n* jardín *m* de la infancia

kindly ['kaɪndlɪ] *adj* bondadoso; cariñoso ▷ *adv* bondadosamente, amablemente; **will you ~ ...** sea usted tan amable de ...

kindness ['kaɪndnɪs] *n* (*quality*) bondad *f*, amabilidad *f*; (*act*) favor *m*

king [kɪŋ] *n* rey *m*; **kingdom** *n* reino; **kingfisher** *n* martín *m* pescador; **king-size(d) bed** *n* cama de matrimonio extragrande

kiosk ['kiːɔsk] *n* quiosco; (*BRIT Tel*) cabina

kipper ['kɪpə*] *n* arenque *m* ahumado

kiss [kɪs] *n* beso ▷ *vt* besar; **to ~ (each other)** besarse; **kiss of life** *n* respiración *f* boca a boca

kit [kɪt] *n* (*equipment*) equipo; (*tools etc*) (caja de) herramientas *fpl*; (*assembly kit*) juego de armar

kitchen ['kɪtʃɪn] *n* cocina

kite [kaɪt] *n* (*toy*) cometa

kitten ['kɪtn] *n* gatito/a

kiwi ['kiːwiː] *n* (*also*: **~ fruit**) kiwi *m*

km *abbr* (= *kilometre*) km

km/h *abbr* (= *kilometres per hour*) km/h

knack [næk] *n*: **to have the ~ of doing sth** tener el don de hacer algo

knee [niː] *n* rodilla; **kneecap** *n* rótula

kneel [niːl] (*pt, pp* **knelt**) *vi* (*also*: **~ down**) arrodillarse

knelt [nɛlt] *pt, pp of* **kneel**

knew [njuː] *pt of* **know**

knickers ['nɪkəz] (BRIT) npl bragas fpl
knife [naɪf] (pl **knives**) n cuchillo ▷ vt acuchillar
knight [naɪt] n caballero; (Chess) caballo
knit [nɪt] vt tejer, tricotar ▷ vi hacer punto, tricotar; (bones) soldarse; **to ~ one's brows** fruncir el ceño; **knitting** n labor f de punto; **knitting needle** n aguja de hacer punto; **knitwear** n prendas fpl de punto
knives [naɪvz] npl of **knife**
knob [nɔb] n (of door) tirador m; (of stick) puño; (on radio, TV) botón m
knock [nɔk] vt (strike) golpear; (bump into) chocar contra; (inf) criticar ▷ vi (at door etc): **to ~ at/on** llamar a ▷ n golpe m; (on door) llamada; **knock down** vt atropellar; **knock off** vi (finish) salir del trabajo ▷ vt (from price) descontar; (inf: steal) birlar; **knock out** vt dejar sin sentido; (Boxing) poner fuera de combate, dejar K.O.; (in competition) eliminar; **knock over** vt (object) tirar; (person) atropellar; **knockout** n (Boxing) K.O. m, knockout m ▷ cpd (competition etc) eliminatorio
knot [nɔt] n nudo ▷ vt anudar
know [nəʊ] (pt **knew**, pp **known**) vt (facts) saber; (be acquainted with) conocer; (recognize) reconocer, conocer; **to ~ how to swim** saber nadar; **to ~ about or of sb/sth** saber de algn/algo; **know-all** n sabelotodo mf; **know-how** n conocimientos mpl; **knowing** adj (look) de complicidad; **knowingly** adv (purposely) adrede; (smile, look) con complicidad; **know-it-all** (US) n = **know-all**
knowledge ['nɔlɪdʒ] n conocimiento; (learning) saber m, conocimientos mpl; **knowledgeable** adj entendido
known [nəʊn] pp of **know** ▷ adj (thief, facts) conocido; (expert) reconocido
knuckle ['nʌkl] n nudillo
koala [kəʊ'ɑːlə] n (also: **~ bear**) koala m
Koran [kɔ'rɑːn] n Corán m
Korea [kə'rɪə] n Corea; **Korean** adj, n coreano/a m/f
kosher ['kəʊʃə*] adj autorizado por la ley judía
Kosovar ['kɔsəvɑː*], **Kosovan** ['kɔːsəvən] adj kosovar
Kosovo ['kɔsəvəʊ] n Kosovo
Kremlin ['krɛmlɪn] n: **the ~** el Kremlin
Kuwait [ku'weɪt] n Kuwait m

L (BRIT) abbr = **learner driver**
l. abbr (= litre) l
lab [læb] n abbr = **laboratory**
label ['leɪbl] n etiqueta ▷ vt poner etiqueta a
labor etc ['leɪbə*] (US) = **labour** etc
laboratory [lə'bɔrətərɪ] n laboratorio
Labor Day (US) n día m de los trabajadores (primer lunes de septiembre)
labor union (US) n sindicato
labour ['leɪbə*] (US **labor**) n (hard work) trabajo; (labour force) mano f de obra; (Med): **to be in ~** estar de parto ▷ vi: **to ~ (at sth)** trabajar (en algo) ▷ vt: **to ~ a point** insistir en un punto; **L~, the L~ party** (BRIT) el partido laborista, los laboristas mpl; **labourer** n peón m; **farm labourer** peón m; (day labourer) jornalero
lace [leɪs] n encaje m; (of shoe etc) cordón m ▷ vt (shoe: also: **~ up**) atarse (los zapatos)
lack [læk] n (absence) falta ▷ vt faltarle a algn, carecer de; **through** or **for ~ of** por falta de; **to be ~ing** faltar, no haber; **to be ~ing in sth** faltarle a algn algo
lacquer ['lækə*] n laca
lacy ['leɪsɪ] adj (of lace) de encaje; (like lace) como de encaje
lad [læd] n muchacho, chico
ladder ['lædə*] n escalera (de mano); (BRIT: in tights) carrera
ladle ['leɪdl] n cucharón m
lady ['leɪdɪ] n señora; (dignified, graceful) dama; **"ladies and gentlemen ..."** "señoras y caballeros ..."; **young ~** señorita; **the ladies' (room)** los servicios de señoras; **ladybird** (US **ladybug**) n mariquita
lag [læg] n retraso ▷ vi (also: **~ behind**) retrasarse, quedarse atrás ▷ vt (pipes) revestir
lager ['lɑːgə*] n cerveza (rubia)
lagoon [lə'guːn] n laguna
laid [leɪd] pt, pp of **lay**; **laid back** (inf) adj relajado
lain [leɪn] pp of **lie**
lake [leɪk] n lago
lamb [læm] n cordero; (meat) (carne f de) cordero
lame [leɪm] adj cojo; (excuse) poco convincente
lament [lə'mɛnt] n queja ▷ vt lamentarse de
lamp [læmp] n lámpara; **lamppost** (BRIT) n (poste m de) farol m; **lampshade** n pantalla

land [lænd] n tierra; (country) país m; (piece of land) terreno; (estate) tierras fpl, finca f ▷ vi (from ship) desembarcar; (Aviat) aterrizar; (fig: fall) caer, terminar ▷ vt (passengers, goods) desembarcar; **to ~ sb with sth** (inf) hacer cargar a algn con algo; **landing** n aterrizaje m; (of staircase) rellano; **landing card** n tarjeta de desembarque; **landlady** n (of rented house, pub etc) dueña; **landlord** n propietario; (of pub etc) patrón m; **landmark** n lugar m conocido; **to be a landmark** (fig) marcar un hito histórico; **landowner** n terrateniente mf; **landscape** n paisaje m; **landslide** n (Geo) corrimiento de tierras; (fig: Pol) victoria arrolladora

lane [leɪn] n (in country) camino; (Aut) carril m; (in race) calle f

language ['læŋgwɪdʒ] n lenguaje m; (national tongue) idioma m, lengua; **bad ~** palabrotas fpl; **language laboratory** n laboratorio de idiomas; **language school** n academia de idiomas

lantern ['læntn] n linterna, farol m

lap [læp] n (of track) vuelta; (of body) regazo ▷ vt (also: **~ up**) beber a lengüetadas ▷ vi (waves) chapotear; **to sit on sb's ~** sentarse en las rodillas de algn

lapel [lə'pel] n solapa

lapse [læps] n fallo; (moral) desliz m; (of time) intervalo ▷ vi (expire) caducar; (time) pasar, transcurrir; **to ~ into bad habits** caer en malos hábitos

laptop (computer) ['læptɒp-] n (ordenador m) portátil m

lard [lɑːd] n manteca (de cerdo)

larder ['lɑːdə*] n despensa

large [lɑːdʒ] adj grande; **at ~** (free) en libertad; (generally) en general; **largely** adv (mostly) en su mayor parte; (introducing reason) en gran parte; **large-scale** adj (map) en gran escala; (fig) importante

lark [lɑːk] n (bird) alondra; (joke) broma

laryngitis [lærɪn'dʒaɪtɪs] n laringitis f

lasagne [lə'zænjə] n lasaña

laser ['leɪzə*] n láser m; **laser printer** n impresora (por) láser

lash [læʃ] n latigazo; (also: **eye~**) pestaña ▷ vt azotar; (tie): **to ~ to** atar a/atar; **lash out** vi: **to lash out (at sb)** (hit) arremeter (contra algn); **to lash out against sb** caer en invectivas contra algn

lass [læs] (BRIT) n chica

last [lɑːst] adj último; (end: of series etc) final ▷ adv (most recently) la última vez; (finally) por último ▷ vi durar; (continue) continuar, seguir; **~ night** anoche; **~ week** la semana pasada; **at ~** por fin; **~ but one** penúltimo; **lastly** adv por último, finalmente; **last-minute** adj de última hora

latch [lætʃ] n pestillo; **latch onto** vt fus (person, group) pegarse a; (idea) agarrarse a

late [leɪt] adj (far on: in time, process etc) al final de; (not on time) tarde, atrasado; (dead) fallecido ▷ adv tarde; (behind time, schedule) con retraso; **of ~** últimamente; **~ at night** a última hora de la noche; **in ~ May** hacia fines de mayo; **the ~ Mr X** el difunto Sr X; **latecomer** n recién llegado/a; **lately** adv últimamente; **later** adj (date etc) posterior; (version etc) más reciente ▷ adv más tarde, después; **latest** ['leɪtɪst] adj último; **at the latest** a más tardar

lather ['lɑːðə*] n espuma (de jabón) ▷ vt enjabonar

Latin ['lætɪn] n latín m ▷ adj latino; **Latin America** n América latina; **Latin American** adj, n latinoamericano/a m/f

latitude ['lætɪtjuːd] n latitud f; (fig) libertad f

latter ['lætə*] adj último; (of two) segundo ▷ n: **the ~ el último, éste

laugh [lɑːf] n risa ▷ vi reír(se); **(to do sth) for a ~** (hacer algo) en broma; **laugh at** vt fus reírse de; **laughter** n risa

launch [lɔːntʃ] n lanzamiento; (boat) lancha ▷ vt (ship) botar; (rocket etc) lanzar; (fig) comenzar; **launch into** vt fus lanzarse a

launder ['lɔːndə*] vt lavar

Launderette® [lɔːn'dret] (BRIT) n lavandería (automática)

Laundromat® ['lɔːndrəmæt] (US) n **= Launderette**

laundry ['lɔːndrɪ] n (dirty) ropa sucia; (clean) colada; (room) lavadero

lava ['lɑːvə] n lava

lavatory ['lævətərɪ] n wáter m

lavender ['lævəndə*] n lavanda

lavish ['lævɪʃ] adj (amount) abundante; (person): **~ with** pródigo en ▷ vt: **to ~ sth on sb** colmar a algn de algo

law [lɔː] n ley f; (Scot) derecho; (a rule) regla; (professions connected with law) jurisprudencia; **lawful** adj legítimo, lícito; **lawless** adj (action) criminal

lawn [lɔːn] n césped m; **lawnmower** n cortacésped m

lawsuit ['lɔːsuːt] n pleito

lawyer ['lɔːjə*] n abogado/a; (for sales, wills etc) notario/a

lax [læks] adj laxo

laxative ['læksətɪv] n laxante m

lay [leɪ] (pt, pp **laid**) pt of **lie** ▷ adj laico; (not expert) lego ▷ vt (place) colocar; (eggs, table) poner; (cable) tender; (carpet) extender; **lay down** vt (pen etc) dejar; (rules etc) establecer; **to lay down the law** (pej) imponer las normas; **lay off** vt (workers) despedir; **lay on** vt (meal, facilities) proveer; **lay out** vt (spread out) disponer, exponer; **lay-by** n (BRIT Aut) área de aparcamiento

layer ['leɪə*] n capa

layman ['leɪmən] (irreg) n lego

layout ['leɪaʊt] n (design) plan m, trazado; (Press) composición f

lazy ['leɪzɪ] adj perezoso, vago; (movement) lento

lb. abbr = **pound** (weight)

lead¹ [liːd] (pt, pp **led**) n (front position) delantera; (clue) pista; (Elec) cable m; (for dog) correa; (Theatre) papel m principal ▷ vt (walk etc in front) ir a la cabeza de; (guide) conducir a; **to ~ to sb** somewhere conducir a algn a algún sitio; (be leader) dirigir; (start, guide: activity) protagonizar ▷ vi (road, pipe etc) conducir a; (Sport) ir primero; **to be in the ~** (Sport) llevar la delantera; (fig) ir a la cabeza; **to ~ the way** llevar la delantera; **lead up to** vt fus (events) conducir a; (in conversation) preparar el terreno para

lead² [led] n (metal) plomo; (in pencil) mina

leader ['liːdə*] n jefe/a m/f, líder mf; (Sport) líder mf; **leadership** n dirección f; (position) mando; (quality) iniciativa

lead-free ['ledfriː] adj sin plomo

leading ['liːdɪŋ] adj (main) principal; (first) primero; (front) delantero

lead singer [liːd-] n cantante mf

leaf [liːf] (pl **leaves**) n hoja ▷ vi: **to ~ through** hojear; **to turn over a new ~** reformarse

leaflet ['liːflɪt] n folleto

league [liːɡ] n sociedad f; (Football) liga; **to be in ~ with** haberse confabulado con

leak [liːk] n (of liquid, gas) escape m, fuga; (in pipe) agujero; (in roof) gotera; (in security) filtración f ▷ vi (shoes, ship) hacer agua; (pipe) tener (un) escape; (roof) gotear; (liquid, gas) escaparse, fugarse; (fig) divulgarse ▷ vt (fig) filtrar

lean [liːn] (pt, pp **-ed** or **~t**) adj (thin) flaco; (meat) magro ▷ vt: **to ~ sth on sth** apoyar algo en algo ▷ vi (slope) inclinarse; **to ~ against** apoyarse contra; **to ~ on** apoyarse en; **lean forward** vi inclinarse hacia adelante; **lean over** vi inclinarse; **leaning** n: **leaning (towards)** inclinación f (hacia)

leant [lɛnt] pt, pp of **lean**

leap [liːp] (pt, pp **-ed** or **~t**) n salto ▷ vi saltar

leapt [lɛpt] pt, pp of **leap**

leap year n año bisiesto

learn [ləːn] (pt, pp **-ed** or **~t**) vt aprender ▷ vi aprender; **to ~ about sth** enterarse de algo; **to ~ to do sth** aprender a hacer algo; **learner** n (BRIT: also: **learner driver**) principiante mf; **learning** n el saber m, conocimientos mpl

learnt [ləːnt] pp of **learn**

lease [liːs] n arriendo ▷ vt arrendar

leash [liːʃ] n correa

least [liːst] adj: **the ~** (slightest) el menor, el más pequeño; (smallest amount of) mínimo ▷ adv (+ vb) menos; (+ adj): **the ~ expensive** el (la) menos costoso; a **the ~ possible effort** el menor esfuerzo posible; **at ~** por lo menos, al menos; **you could at ~ have written** por lo menos podías haber escrito; **not in the ~** en absoluto

leather [ˈlɛðə*] n cuero

leave [liːv] (pt, pp **left**) vt dejar; (go away from) abandonar; (place etc: permanently) salir de ▷ vi irse; (train etc) salir ▷ n permiso; **to ~ sth to sb** (money etc) legar algo a algn; (responsibility etc) encargar a algn de algo; **to be left** quedar, sobrar; **there's some milk left over** sobra or queda algo de leche; **on ~** de permiso; **leave behind** vt (on purpose) dejar; (accidentally) dejarse; **leave out** vt omitir

leaves [liːvz] npl of **leaf**

Lebanon [ˈlɛbənən] n: **the ~** el Líbano

lecture [ˈlɛktʃə*] n conferencia; (Scol) clase f ▷ vi dar una clase ▷ vt (scold): **to ~ sb on** or **about sth** echar una reprimenda a algn por/acerca de; **to give a ~ on** dar una conferencia sobre; **lecture hall** n sala de conferencias; (Univ) aula; **lecturer** n conferenciante mf; (BRIT: at university) profesor(a) m/f; **lecture theatre** n =**lecture hall**

led [lɛd] pt, pp of **lead**[1]

ledge [lɛdʒ] n repisa; (of window) alféizar m; (of mountain) saliente m

leek [liːk] n puerro

left [lɛft] pt, pp of **leave** ▷ adj izquierdo; (remaining): **there are two ~** quedan dos ▷ n izquierda ▷ adv a la izquierda; **on** or **to the ~** a la izquierda; **the L~** (Pol) la izquierda; **left-hand** adj: **the left-hand side** la izquierda; **left-hand drive** adj: **a left-hand drive car** un coche con el volante a la izquierda; **left-handed** adj zurdo; **left-luggage locker** n (BRIT) consigna f automática; **left-luggage (office)** (BRIT) n consigna; **left-overs** npl sobras fpl; **left-wing** n (Pol) de izquierdas, izquierdista

leg [lɛɡ] n pierna; (of animal, chair) pata; (trouser leg) pernera; (Culin: of lamb) pierna; (: of chicken) pata; (of

journey) etapa

legacy [ˈlɛɡəsi] n herencia

legal [ˈliːɡl] adj (permitted by law) lícito; (of law) legal; **legal holiday** (US) n fiesta oficial; **legalize** vt legalizar; **legally** adv legalmente

legend [ˈlɛdʒənd] n (also fig: person) leyenda; **legendary** [-əri] adj legendario

leggings [ˈlɛɡɪnz] npl mallas fpl, leggins mpl

legible [ˈlɛdʒəbl] adj legible

legislation [lɛdʒɪsˈleɪʃən] n legislación f

legislative [ˈlɛdʒɪslətɪv] adj legislativo

legitimate [lɪˈdʒɪtɪmət] adj legítimo

leisure [ˈlɛʒə*] n ocio, tiempo libre; **at ~** con tranquilidad; **leisure centre** (BRIT) n centro de recreo; **leisurely** adj sin prisa; lento

lemon [ˈlɛmən] n limón m; **lemonade** n (fizzy) gaseosa; **lemon tea** n té m con limón

lend [lɛnd] (pt, pp **lent**) vt: **to ~ sth to sb** prestar algo a algn

length [lɛnθ] n (size) largo, longitud f; (distance): **the ~ of** todo lo largo de; (of swimming pool, cloth) largo; (of wood, string) trozo; (amount of time) duración f; **at ~** (at last) por fin, finalmente; (lengthily) largamente; **lengthen** vt alargar ▷ vi alargarse; **lengthways** adv a lo largo; **lengthy** adj largo, extenso

lens [lɛnz] n (of spectacles) lente f; (of camera) objetivo

Lent [lɛnt] n Cuaresma

lent [lɛnt] pt, pp of **lend**

lentil [ˈlɛntl] n lenteja

Leo [ˈliːəu] n Leo

leopard [ˈlɛpəd] n leopardo

leotard [ˈliːətɑːd] n mallas fpl

leprosy [ˈlɛprəsɪ] n lepra

lesbian [ˈlɛzbɪən] n lesbiana

less [lɛs] adj (in size, degree etc) menor; (in quality) menos ▷ pron, adv menos ▷ prep: **~ tax/10% discount** menos impuestos/el 10 por ciento de descuento; **~ than half** menos de la mitad; **~ than ever** menos que nunca; **~ and ~** cada vez menos; **the ~ he works … cuanto menos trabaja …; lessen** vi disminuir, reducirse ▷ vt disminuir, reducir; **lesser** [ˈlɛsə*] adj menor; **to a lesser extent** en menor grado

lesson [ˈlɛsn] n clase f; (warning) lección f

let [lɛt] (pt, pp **~**) vt (allow) dejar, permitir; (BRIT: lease) alquilar; **to ~ sb do sth** dejar que algn haga algo; **to ~ sb know sth** comunicar algo a algn; **~'s go** ¡vamos!; **~ him come** que venga; **"to ~"** se alquila; **let down** vt (tyre) desinflar; (disappoint) defraudar; **let in** vt dejar entrar; (visitor etc) hacer pasar; **let off** vt (culprit) dejar escapar; (gun) disparar; (bomb) accionar; (firework) hacer estallar; **let out** vt dejar salir; (sound) soltar

lethal [ˈliːθl] adj (weapon) mortífero; (poison, wound) mortal

letter [ˈlɛtə*] n (of alphabet) letra; (correspondence) carta; **letterbox** (BRIT) n buzón m

lettuce [ˈlɛtɪs] n lechuga

leukaemia [luːˈkiːmɪə] (US **leukemia**) n leucemia

level [ˈlɛvl] adj (flat) llano ▷ adv: **to draw ~ with** llegar a la altura de ▷ n nivel m; (height) altura ▷ vt nivelar; allanar; (destroy: building) derribar; (: forest) arrasar; **to be ~ with** estar a nivel de; **A ~s** (BRIT) = exámenes mpl de bachillerato superior, B.U.P.; **AS ~** (BRIT) asignatura aprobada entre los "GCSEs" y los "A levels"; **on the ~** (fig: honest) serio; **level crossing** (BRIT) n paso a nivel

lever [ˈliːvə*] n (also fig) palanca ▷ vt: **to ~ up** levantar con palanca; **leverage** n (using bar etc) apalancamiento; (fig: influence) influencia

levy ['lɛvɪ] n impuesto ▷ vt exigir, recaudar

liability [laɪə'bɪlətɪ] n (pej: person, thing) estorbo, lastre m; (Jur: responsibility) responsabilidad f

liable ['laɪəbl] adj (subject): **~ to** sujeto a; (responsible): **~ for** responsable de; (likely): **~ to do** propenso a hacer

liaise [lɪ'eɪz] vi: **to ~ with** enlazar con

liar ['laɪə*] n mentiroso/a

liberal ['lɪbərəl] adj liberal; (offer, amount etc) generoso; **Liberal Democrat** n (BRIT) demócrata m/f liberal

liberate ['lɪbəreɪt] vt (people: from poverty etc) librar; (prisoner) libertar; (country) liberar

liberation [lɪbə'reɪʃən] n liberación f

liberty ['lɪbətɪ] n libertad f; **to be at ~** (criminal) estar en libertad; **to be at ~ to do** estar libre para hacer; **to take the ~ of doing sth** tomarse la libertad de hacer algo

Libra ['liːbrə] n Libra

librarian [laɪ'brɛərɪən] n bibliotecario/a

library ['laɪbrərɪ] n biblioteca

Libya ['lɪbɪə] n Libia

lice [laɪs] npl of **louse**

licence ['laɪsəns] (US **license**) n licencia; (permit) permiso; (also: **driving ~**) carnet m de conducir (SP), licencia de manejo (LAM)

license ['laɪsəns] n (US) = **licence** ▷ vt autorizar, dar permiso a; **licensed** adj (for alcohol) autorizado para vender bebidas alcohólicas; (car) matriculado; **license plate** (US) n placa (de matrícula); **licensing hours** (BRIT) npl horas durante las cuales se permite la venta y consumo de alcohol (en un bar etc)

lick [lɪk] vt lamer; (inf: defeat) dar una paliza a; **to ~ one's lips** relamerse

lid [lɪd] n (of box, case) tapa; (of pan) tapadera

lie [laɪ] (pt **lay**, pp **lain**) vi (rest) estar echado, estar acostado; (of object: be situated) estar, encontrarse; (tell lies: pt, pp **lied**) mentir ▷ n mentira; **to ~ low** (fig) mantenerse a escondidas; **lie about** or **around** vi (things) estar tirado; (BRIT: people) estar tumbado; **lie down** vi echarse, tumbarse

Liechtenstein ['lɪktənstaɪn] n Liechtenstein m

lie-in [laɪɪn] (BRIT) n: **to have a ~** quedarse en la cama

lieutenant [lɛf'tɛnənt, US luː'tɛnənt] n (Mil) teniente mf

life [laɪf] (pl **lives**) n vida; **to come to ~** animarse; **life assurance** (BRIT) n seguro de vida; **lifeboat** n lancha de socorro; **lifeguard** n vigilante mf, socorrista mf; **life insurance** n = **life assurance**; **life jacket** n chaleco salvavidas; **lifelike** adj (model etc) que parece vivo; (realistic) realista; **life preserver** (US) n cinturón m/ chaleco salvavidas; **life sentence** n cadena perpetua; **lifestyle** n estilo de vida; **lifetime** n (of person) vida; (of thing) período de vida

lift [lɪft] vt levantar; (end: ban, rule) levantar, suprimir ▷ vi (fog) disiparse ▷ n (BRIT: machine) ascensor m; **to give sb a ~** (BRIT) llevar a algn en el coche; **lift up** vt levantar; **lift-off** n despegue m

light [laɪt] (pt, pp **~ed** or **lit**) n (gen) luz f; (lamp) luz f, lámpara; (Aut) faro; (for cigarette etc): **have you got a ~?** ¿tienes fuego? ▷ vt (candle, cigarette, fire) encender (SP), prender (LAM); (room) alumbrar ▷ adj (colour) claro; (not heavy, also fig) ligero; (room) con mucha luz; (gentle, graceful) ágil; **lights** npl (traffic lights) semáforos mpl; **to come to ~** salir a luz; **in the ~ of** (new evidence etc)

a la luz de; **light up** vi (smoke) encender un cigarrillo; (face) iluminarse ▷ vt (illuminate) iluminar, alumbrar; (set fire to) encender; **light bulb** n bombilla (SP), foco (MEX), bujía (CAM), bombita (RPL); **lighten** vt (make less heavy) aligerar; **lighter** n (also: **cigarette lighter**) encendedor m, mechero; **light-hearted** adj (person) alegre; (remark etc) divertido; **lighthouse** n faro; **lighting** n (system) alumbrado; **lightly** adv ligeramente; (not seriously) con poca seriedad; **to get off lightly** ser castigado con poca severidad

lightning ['laɪtnɪŋ] n relámpago, rayo

lightweight ['laɪtweɪt] adj (suit) ligero ▷ n (Boxing) peso ligero

like [laɪk] vt gustarle a algn ▷ prep como ▷ adj parecido, semejante ▷ vt (illuminate) ▷ n algo y otros por el estilo; **his ~s and dislikes** sus gustos y aversiones; **I would ~, I'd ~** me gustaría; (for purchase) quisiera; **would you ~ a coffee?** ¿te apetece un café?; **I ~ swimming** me gusta nadar; **she ~s apples** le gustan las manzanas; **to be** or **look ~ sb/sth** parecerse a algn/algo; **what does it look/taste/sound ~?** ¿cómo es/a qué sabe/cómo suena?; **that's just ~ him** es muy de él, es característico de él; **do it ~ this** hazlo así; **it is nothing ~ …** no tiene parecido alguno con …; **likeable** adj simpático, agradable

likelihood ['laɪklɪhʊd] n probabilidad f

likely ['laɪklɪ] adj probable; **he's ~ to leave** es probable que se vaya; **not ~!** ¡ni hablar!

likewise ['laɪkwaɪz] adv igualmente; **to do ~** hacer lo mismo

liking ['laɪkɪŋ] n: **~ (for)** (person) cariño (a); (thing) afición (a); **to be to sb's ~** ser del gusto de algn

lilac ['laɪlək] n (tree) lila; (flower) lila

Lilo® ['laɪləʊ] n colchoneta inflable

lily ['lɪlɪ] n lirio, azucena; **~ of the valley** lirio de los valles

limb [lɪm] n miembro

limbo ['lɪmbəʊ] n: **to be in ~** (fig) quedar a la expectativa

lime [laɪm] n (tree) limero; (fruit) lima; (Geo) cal f

limelight ['laɪmlaɪt] n: **to be in the ~** (fig) ser el centro de atención

limestone ['laɪmstəʊn] n piedra caliza

limit ['lɪmɪt] n límite m ▷ vt limitar; **limited** adj limitado; **to be limited to** limitarse a

limousine ['lɪməziːn] n limusina

limp [lɪmp] n: **to have a ~** tener cojera ▷ vi cojear ▷ adj flojo; (material) fláccido

line [laɪn] n línea; (rope) cuerda; (for fishing) sedal m; (wire) hilo; (row, series) fila, hilera; (of writing) renglón m, línea; (of song) verso; (on face) arruga; (Rail) vía ▷ vt (road etc) llenar; (Sewing) forrar; **to ~ the streets** llenar las aceras; **in ~ with** alineado con; (according to) de acuerdo con; **line up** vi hacer cola ▷ vt (prepare) disponer; organizar

linear ['lɪnɪə*] adj lineal

linen ['lɪnɪn] n ropa blanca; (cloth) lino

liner ['laɪnə*] n vapor m de línea, transatlántico; (for bin) bolsa (de basura)

line-up ['laɪnʌp] n (US: queue) cola, (Sport) alineación f

linger ['lɪŋɡə*] vi retrasarse, tardar en marcharse; (smell, tradition) persistir

lingerie ['læ̃ʒəriː] n lencería

linguist ['lɪŋɡwɪst] n lingüista mf; **linguistic** adj lingüístico

lining ['laɪnɪŋ] n forro; (Anat) (membrana) mucosa

link [lɪŋk] n (of a chain) eslabón m; (relationship) relación f, vínculo, (Internet) link m, enlace m ▷ vt vincular, unir; (associate): **to ~ with** or **to** relacionar con; **links** npl (Golf) campo de golf; **link up** vt acoplar ▷ vi unirse

lion ['laɪən] n león m; **lioness** n leona

lip [lɪp] n labio; **lipread** vi leer los labios; **lip salve** n crema protectora para labios; **lipstick** n lápiz m de labios, carmín m

liqueur [lɪ'kjuə*] n licor m

liquid ['lɪkwɪd] adj, n líquido; **liquidizer** [-aɪzə*] n licuadora

liquor ['lɪkə*] n licor m, bebidas fpl alcohólicas; **liquor store** (US) n bodega, tienda de vinos y bebidas alcohólicas

Lisbon ['lɪzbən] n Lisboa

lisp [lɪsp] n ceceo ▷ vi cecear

list [lɪst] n lista ▷ vt (mention) enumerar; (put on a list) poner en una lista

listen ['lɪsn] vi escuchar, oír; **to ~ to sb/sth** escuchar a algn/algo; **listener** n oyente mf; (Radio) radioyente mf

lit [lɪt] pt, pp of **light**

liter ['liːtə*] (US) n = **litre**

literacy ['lɪtərəsɪ] n capacidad f de leer y escribir

literal ['lɪtərl] adj literal; **literally** adv literalmente

literary ['lɪtərərɪ] adj literario

literate ['lɪtərət] adj que sabe leer y escribir; (educated) culto

literature ['lɪtərɪtʃə*] n literatura; (brochures etc) folletos mpl

litre ['liːtə*] (US **liter**) n litro

litter ['lɪtə*] n (rubbish) basura; (young animals) camada, cría; **litter bin** (BRIT) n papelera; **littered** adj: **littered with** (scattered) lleno de

little ['lɪtl] adj (small) pequeño; (not much) poco ▷ adv poco; **a ~** un poco (de); **~ house/bird** casita/pajarito; **a ~ bit** un poquito; **~ by ~** poco a poco; **little finger** n dedo meñique

live¹ [laɪv] adj (animal) vivo; (wire) conectado; (broadcast) en directo; (shell) cargado

live² [lɪv] vi vivir; **live together** vi vivir juntos; **live up to** vt fus (fulfil) cumplir con

livelihood ['laɪvlɪhud] n sustento

lively ['laɪvlɪ] adj vivo; (interesting: place, book etc) animado

liven up ['laɪvn-] vt animar ▷ vi animarse

liver ['lɪvə*] n hígado

lives [laɪvz] npl of **life**

livestock ['laɪvstɔk] n ganado

living ['lɪvɪŋ] adj (alive) vivo ▷ n: **to earn** or **make a ~** ganarse la vida; **living room** n sala (de estar)

lizard ['lɪzəd] n lagarto; (small) lagartija

load [ləud] n (gen) carga; (weight) peso ▷ vt (Comput) cargar; (also: **~ up**): **to ~ (with)** cargar (con or de); **a ~ of rubbish** (inf) tonterías fpl; **a ~ of**, **~s of** (fig) (gran) cantidad f, montones de; **loaded** adj (vehicle): **to be loaded with** estar cargado de

loaf [ləuf] (pl **loaves**) n (barra) de pan m

loan [ləun] n préstamo ▷ vt prestar; **on ~** prestado

loathe [ləuð] vt aborrecer; (person) odiar

loaves [ləuvz] npl of **loaf**

lobby ['lɔbɪ] n vestíbulo, sala de espera; (Pol: pressure group) grupo de presión ▷ vt presionar

lobster ['lɔbstə*] n langosta

local ['ləukl] adj local ▷ n (pub) the **locals**

npl los vecinos, los del lugar; **local anaesthetic** n (Med) anestesia local; **local authority** n municipio, ayuntamiento (SP); **local government** n gobierno municipal; **locally** adv en la vecindad; por aquí

locate [ləu'keɪt] vt (find) localizar; (situate): **to be ~d in** estar situado en

location [ləu'keɪʃən] n situación f; **on ~** (Cinema) en exteriores

loch [lɔx] n lago

lock [lɔk] n (of door, box) cerradura; (of canal) esclusa; (of hair) mechón m ▷ vt (with key) cerrar (con llave) ▷ vi (door etc) cerrarse (con llave); (wheels) trabarse; **lock in** vt encerrar; **lock out** vt (person) cerrar la puerta a; **lock up** vt (criminal) meter en la cárcel; (mental patient) encerrar; (house) cerrar (con llave) ▷ vi echar la llave

locker ['lɔkə*] n casillero; **locker-room** (US) n (Sport) vestuario

locksmith ['lɔksmɪθ] n cerrajero/a

locomotive [ləukə'məutɪv] n locomotora

lodge [lɔdʒ] n casa del guarda; (FREEMASONRY) logia ▷ vi (with): **to ~ (with)** alojarse (en casa de); (bullet, bone) incrustarse ▷ vt presentar; **lodger** n huésped mf

lodging ['lɔdʒɪŋ] n alojamiento, hospedaje m

loft [lɔft] n desván m

log [lɔg] n (of wood) leño, tronco; (written account) diario ▷ vt anotar; **log in**, **log on** vi (Comput) entrar en el sistema; **log off**, **log out** vi (Comput) salir del sistema

logic ['lɔdʒɪk] n lógica; **logical** adj lógico

logo ['ləugəu] n logotipo

lollipop ['lɔlɪpɔp] n pirulí m; **lollipop man/lady** (BRIT: irreg) n persona encargada de ayudar a los niños a cruzar la calle

lolly ['lɔlɪ] n (inf: ice cream) polo; (: lollipop) piruleta; (: money) guita

London ['lʌndən] n Londres; **Londoner** n londinense mf

lone [ləun] adj solitario

loneliness ['ləunlɪnɪs] n soledad f; aislamiento

lonely ['ləunlɪ] adj (situation) solitario; (person) solo; (place) aislado

long [lɔŋ] adj largo ▷ adv mucho tiempo, largamente ▷ vi: **to ~ for sth** anhelar algo; **so** or **as ~ as** mientras, con tal que; **don't be ~!** ¡no tardes!, ¡vuelve pronto!; **how ~ is the street?** ¿cuánto tiene la calle de largo?; **how ~ is the lesson?** ¿cuánto dura la clase?; **6 metres ~** que mide 6 metros, de 6 metros de largo; **6 months ~** que dura 6 meses, de 6 meses de duración; **all night ~** toda la noche; **he no ~er comes** ya no viene; **I can't stand it any ~er** no lo aguanto más; **~ before** mucho antes; **before ~** (+ future) dentro de poco; (+ past) poco tiempo después; **at ~ last** al fin, por fin; **long-distance** adj (race) de larga distancia; (call) interurbano; **long-haul** adj (flight) de larga distancia; **longing** n anhelo, ansia; (nostalgia) nostalgia ▷ adj anhelante

longitude ['lɔŋgɪtjuːd] n longitud f

long: **long jump** n salto de longitud; **long-life** adj (batteries) de larga duración; (milk) uperizado; **long-sighted** (BRIT) adj présbita; **long-standing** adj de mucho tiempo; **long-term** adj a largo plazo

loo [luː] (BRIT: inf) n wáter m

look [luk] vi mirar; (seem) parecer; (building etc): **to ~ south/on to the sea** dar al sur/al mar ▷ n (gen): **to have a ~** mirar; (glance) mirada; (appearance) aire m, aspecto; **looks** npl (good looks) belleza; **~ (here)!**

(expressing annoyance etc) ¡oye!; **~!** (expressing surprise) ¡mira!; **look after** vt fus (care for) cuidar a; (deal with) encargarse de; **look around** vi echar una mirada alrededor; **look at** vt fus mirar; (read quickly) echar un vistazo a; **look back** vi mirar hacia atrás; **look down on** vt fus (fig) despreciar, mirar con desprecio; **look for** vt fus buscar; **look forward to** vt fus esperar con ilusión; (in letters): **we look forward to hearing from you** quedamos a la espera de sus gratas noticias; **look into** vt investigar; **look out** vi (beware): **to look out (for)** tener cuidado (de); **look out for** vt fus (seek) buscar; (await) esperar; **look round** vi volver la cabeza; **look through** vt fus (examine) examinar; **look up** vi mirar hacia arriba; (improve) mejorar ▷ vt (word) buscar; **look up to** vt fus admirar; **lookout** n (tower etc) puesto de observación; (person) vigía mf; **to be on the lookout for** estar al acecho de algo

loom [luːm] vi: **~ (up)** (threaten) surgir, amenazar; (event: approach) aproximarse

loony ['luːnɪ] (inf) n, adj loco/a m/f

loop [luːp] n lazo ▷ vt: **to ~ sth round sth** pasar algo alrededor de algo; **loophole** n escapatoria

loose [luːs] adj suelto; (clothes) ancho; (morals, discipline) relajado; **to be at a ~ end** or **at ~ ends** (us) no saber qué hacer; **to be at a ~ end** or **at ~ ends** (us) no saber qué hacer; **loosely** adv libremente, aproximadamente; **loosen** vt aflojar

loot [luːt] n botín m ▷ vt saquear

lop-sided ['lɒp'saɪdɪd] adj torcido

lord [lɔːd] n señor m; **L~ Smith** Lord Smith; **the L~** el Señor; **my ~** (to bishop) Ilustrísima; (to noble etc) Señor; **good L~!** ¡Dios mío!; **Lords** npl (BRIT: Pol): **the (House of) Lords** la Cámara de los Lores

lorry ['lɒrɪ] (BRIT) n camión m; **lorry driver** (BRIT) n camionero/a

lose [luːz] (pt, pp **lost**) vt perder ▷ vi perder, ser vencido; **to ~ (time)** (clock) atrasarse; **lose out** vi salir perdiendo; **loser** n perdedor/a m/f

loss [lɒs] n pérdida; **heavy ~es** (Mil) grandes pérdidas; **to be at a ~** no saber qué hacer; **to make a ~** sufrir pérdidas

lost [lɒst] pt, pp of **lose** ▷ adj perdido; **lost property** (us **lost and found**) n objetos mpl perdidos

lot [lɒt] n (group: of things) grupo; (at auctions) lote m; **the ~** el todo, todos; **a ~** (large number: of books etc) muchos; (a great deal) mucho, bastante; **a ~ of**, **~s of** mucho(s) (pl); **I read a ~** leo bastante; **to draw ~s (for sth)** echar suertes (para decidir algo)

lotion ['ləʊʃən] n loción f

lottery ['lɒtərɪ] n lotería

loud [laʊd] adj (voice, sound) fuerte; (laugh, shout) estrepitoso; (condemnation etc) enérgico; (gaudy) chillón/ona ▷ adv (speak etc) fuerte; **out ~** en voz alta; **loudly** adv (noisily) fuerte; (aloud) en voz alta; **loudspeaker** n altavoz m

lounge [laʊndʒ] n salón m, sala (de estar); (at airport etc) sala; (BRIT: also: **~-bar**) salón-bar m ▷ vi (also: **~ about** or **around**) reposar, holgazanear

louse [laʊs] (pl **lice**) n piojo

lousy ['laʊzɪ] (inf) adj (bad quality) malísimo, asqueroso; (ill) fatal

love [lʌv] n (romantic, sexual) amor m; (kind, caring) cariño ▷ vt amar, querer; (thing, activity) encantarle a algn; **"~ from Anne"** (on letter) "un abrazo (de) Anne"; **to ~ to do** encantarle a algn hacer; **to be/fall in ~ with** estar enamorado/enamorarse de; **to make ~** hacer

el amor; **for the ~ of** por amor de; **"15 ~"** (Tennis) "15 a cero"; **I ~ you** te quiero; **I ~ paella** me encanta la paella; **love affair** n aventura sentimental; **love life** n vida sentimental

lovely ['lʌvlɪ] adj (delightful) encantador(a); (beautiful) precioso

lover ['lʌvə*] n amante mf; (person in love) enamorado; (amateur): **a ~ of** un(a) aficionado/a or un(a) amante de

loving ['lʌvɪŋ] adj amoroso, cariñoso; (action) tierno

low [ləʊ] adj, adv bajo ▷ n (Meteorology) área de baja presión; **to be ~ on** (supplies etc) andar mal de; **to feel ~** sentirse deprimido; **to turn (down) ~** bajar; **low-alcohol** adj de bajo contenido en alcohol; **low-calorie** adj bajo en calorías

lower ['ləʊə*] adj más bajo; (less important) menos importante ▷ vt bajar; (reduce) reducir ▷ vr: **to ~ o.s. to** (fig) rebajarse a

low-fat adj (milk, yoghurt) desnatado; (diet) bajo en calorías

loyal ['lɔɪəl] adj leal; **loyalty** n lealtad f; **loyalty card** n tarjeta cliente

L.P. n abbr (= long-playing record) elepé m

L-plates ['el'-] (BRIT) npl placas fpl de aprendiz de conductor

Lt abbr (= lieutenant) Tte.

Ltd abbr (= limited company) S.A.

luck [lʌk] n suerte f; **bad ~** mala suerte; **good ~!** ¡que tengas suerte!, ¡suerte!; **bad ~** or **hard ~!** ¡qué pena!; **luckily** adv afortunadamente; **lucky** adj afortunado; (at cards etc) con suerte; (object) que trae suerte

lucrative ['luːkrətɪv] adj lucrativo

ludicrous ['luːdɪkrəs] adj absurdo

luggage ['lʌgɪdʒ] n equipaje m; **luggage rack** n (on car) baca, portaequipajes m inv

lukewarm ['luːkwɔːm] adj tibio

lull [lʌl] n tregua ▷ vt: **to ~ sb to sleep** arrullar a algn; **to ~ sb into a false sense of security** dar a algn una falsa sensación de seguridad

lullaby ['lʌləbaɪ] n nana

lumber ['lʌmbə*] n (junk) trastos mpl viejos; (wood) maderos mpl

luminous ['luːmɪnəs] adj luminoso

lump [lʌmp] n terrón m; (fragment) trozo; (swelling) bulto ▷ vt (also: **~ together**) juntar; **lump sum** n suma global; **lumpy** adj (sauce) lleno de grumos; (mattress) lleno de bultos

lunatic ['luːnətɪk] adj loco

lunch [lʌntʃ] n almuerzo, comida ▷ vi almorzar; **lunch break**, **lunch hour** n hora del almuerzo; **lunch time** n hora de comer

lung [lʌŋ] n pulmón m

lure [luə*] n (attraction) atracción f ▷ vt tentar

lurk [ləːk] vi (person, animal) estar al acecho; (fig) acechar

lush [lʌʃ] adj exuberante

lust [lʌst] n lujuria; (greed) codicia

Luxembourg ['lʌksəmbəːg] n Luxemburgo

luxurious [lʌg'zjʊəriəs] adj lujoso

luxury ['lʌkʃəri] n lujo ▷ cpd de lujo

Lycra® ['laɪkrə] n licra®

lying ['laɪŋ] n mentiras fpl ▷ adj mentiroso

lyrics ['lɪrɪks] npl (of song) letra

m

m. *abbr* = **metre; mile; million**

M.A. *abbr* = **Master of Arts**

ma (*inf*) [mɑ:] *n* mamá

mac [mæk] (*BRIT*) *n* impermeable *m*

macaroni [mækə'rəʊnɪ] *n* macarrones *mpl*

Macedonia [mæsɪ'dəʊnɪə] *n* Macedonia; **Macedonian** [-'dəʊnɪən] *adj* macedonio ⊳ *n* macedonio/a; (*Ling*) macedonio

machine [mə'ʃiːn] *n* máquina ⊳ *vt* (*dress etc*) coser a máquina; (*Tech*) hacer a máquina; **machine gun** *n* ametralladora; **machinery** *n* maquinaria; (*fig*) mecanismo; **machine washable** *adj* lavable a máquina

macho ['mætʃəʊ] *adj* machista

mackerel ['mækrl] *n inv* caballa

mackintosh ['mækɪntɒʃ] (*BRIT*) *n* impermeable *m*

mad [mæd] *adj* loco; (*idea*) disparatado; (*angry*) furioso; (*keen*): **to be ~ about sth** volverle loco a algn algo

Madagascar [mædə'gæskə*] *n* Madagascar *m*

madam ['mædəm] *n* señora

mad cow disease *n* encefalopatía espongiforme bovina

made [meɪd] *pt, pp of* **make**; **made-to-measure** (*BRIT*) *adj* hecho a la medida; **made-up** ['meɪdʌp] (*story*) adj ficticio

madly ['mædlɪ] *adv* locamente

madman ['mædmən] (*irreg*) *n* loco

madness ['mædnɪs] *n* locura

Madrid [mə'drɪd] *n* Madrid *m*

Mafia ['mæfɪə] *n* Mafia

mag [mæg] *n abbr* (*BRIT inf*) = **magazine**

magazine [mægə'ziːn] *n* revista; (*Radio, TV*) programa *m* magazina

maggot ['mægət] *n* gusano

magic ['mædʒɪk] *n* magia ⊳ *adj* mágico; **magical** *adj* mágico; **magician** [mə'dʒɪʃən] *n* mago/a; (*conjurer*) prestidigitador(a) *m/f*

magistrate ['mædʒɪstreɪt] *n* juez *mf* (municipal)

magnet ['mægnɪt] *n* imán *m*; **magnetic** [-'nɛtɪk] *adj* magnético; (*personality*) atrayente

magnificent [mæg'nɪfɪsənt] *adj* magnífico

magnify ['mægnɪfaɪ] *vt* (*object*) ampliar; (*sound*) aumentar; **magnifying glass** *n* lupa

magpie ['mægpaɪ] *n* urraca

mahogany [mə'hɒgənɪ] *n* caoba

maid [meɪd] *n* criada, **old ~** (*pej*) solterona

maiden name *n* nombre *m* de soltera

mail [meɪl] *n* correo; (*letters*) cartas *fpl* ⊳ *vt* echar al correo; **mailbox** (*US*) *n* buzón *m*; **mailing list** *n* lista de direcciones; **mailman** (*US: irreg*) *n* cartero; **mail-order** *n* pedido postal

main [meɪn] *adj* principal, mayor ⊳ *n* (*pipe*) cañería maestra; (*US*) red *f* eléctrica ⊳ **the ~s** *npl* (*BRIT Elec*) la red eléctrica; **in the ~** en general; **main course** *n* (*Culin*) plato principal; **mainland** *n* tierra firme; **mainly** *adv* principalmente; **main road** *n* carretera; **mainstream** *n* corriente *f* principal; **main street** *n* calle *f* mayor

maintain [meɪn'teɪn] *vt* mantener; **maintenance** ['meɪntənəns] *n* mantenimiento; (*Law*) manutención *f*

maisonette [meɪzə'nɛt] *n* dúplex *m*

maize [meɪz] (*BRIT*) *n* maíz *m*, choclo (*SC*)

majesty ['mædʒɪstɪ] *n* majestad *f*; (*title*): **Your M~** Su Majestad

major ['meɪdʒə*] *n* (*Mil*) comandante *mf* ⊳ *adj* principal; (*Mus*) mayor

Majorca [mə'jɔːkə] *n* Mallorca

majority [mə'dʒɔrɪtɪ] *n* mayoría

make [meɪk] (*pt, pp* **made**) *vt* hacer; (*manufacture*) fabricar; (*mistake*) cometer; (*speech*) pronunciar; (*cause to be*): **to ~ sb sad** poner triste a algn; (*force*): **to ~ sb do sth** obligar a algn a hacer algo; (*earn*) ganar; (*equal*): **2 and 2 ~ 4** 2 y 2 son 4 ⊳ *n* marca; **to ~ the bed** hacer la cama; **to ~ a fool of sb** poner a algn en ridículo; **to ~ a profit/loss** obtener ganancias/sufrir pérdidas; **to ~ it** (*arrive*) llegar; (*achieve sth*) tener éxito; **what time do you ~ it?** ¿qué hora tienes?; **to ~ do with** contentarse con; **make off** *vi* largarse; **make out** *vt* (*decipher*) descifrar; (*understand*) entender; (*see*) distinguir; (*cheque*) extender; **make up** *vt* (*invent*) inventar; (*prepare*) hacer; (*constitute*) constituir ⊳ *vi* reconciliarse; (*with cosmetics*) maquillarse; **make up for** *vt fus* compensar; **makeover** ['meɪkəʊvə*] *n* (*by beautician*) sesión *f* de maquillaje y peluquería; (*change of image*) lavado de cara; **maker** *n* fabricante *mf*; (*of film, programme*) autor(a) *m/f*; **makeshift** *adj* improvisado; **make-up** *n* maquillaje *m*

making ['meɪkɪŋ] *n* (*fig*): **in the ~** en vías de formación; **to have the ~s of** (*person*) tener madera de

malaria [mə'lɛərɪə] *n* malaria

Malaysia [mə'leɪzɪə] *n* Malasia, Malaysia

male [meɪl] *n* (*Biol*) macho ⊳ *adj* (*sex, attitude*) masculino; (*child etc*) varón

malicious [mə'lɪʃəs] *adj* malicioso; rencoroso

malignant [mə'lɪgnənt] *adj* (*Med*) maligno

mall [mɔːl] (*US*) *n* (*also:* **shopping ~**) centro comercial

mallet ['mælɪt] *n* mazo

malnutrition [mælnjuː'trɪʃən] *n* desnutrición *f*

malpractice [mæl'præktɪs] *n* negligencia profesional

malt [mɔːlt] *n* malta; (*whisky*) whisky *m* de malta

Malta ['mɔːltə] *n* Malta; **Maltese** [-'tiːz] *adj, n inv* maltés/esa *m/f*

mammal ['mæml] *n* mamífero

mammoth ['mæməθ] *n* mamut *m* ⊳ *adj* gigantesco

man [mæn] (*pl* **men**) *n* hombre *m*; (*mankind*) el hombre *m* ⊳ *vt* (*Naut*) tripular; (*Mil*) guarnecer;

(operate: machine) manejar; **an old ~** un viejo; **~ and wife** marido y mujer

manage ['mænɪdʒ] *vi* arreglárselas, ir tirando ▷ *vt (be in charge of)* dirigir; *(control: person)* manejar; *(: ship)* gobernar; **manageable** *adj* manejable; **management** *n* dirección *f*; **manager** *n* director(a) *m/f*; *(of pop star)* mánager *mf*; *(Sport)* entrenador(a) *m/f*; **manageress** *n* directora; entrenadora; **managerial** [-ə'dʒɪərɪəl] *adj* directivo; **managing director** *n* director(a) *m/f* general

mandarin ['mændərɪn] *n (also: ~ orange)* mandarina; *(person)* mandarín *m*

mandate ['mændeɪt] *n* mandato

mandatory ['mændətərɪ] *adj* obligatorio

mane [meɪn] *n (of horse)* crin *f*; *(of lion)* melena

maneuver [mə'nu:və*] *(us)* = **manoeuvre**

mangetout [mɒnʒ'tu:] *n* tirabeque *m*

mango ['mæŋgəu] *(pl ~es)* *n* mango

man: manhole *n* agujero de acceso; **manhood** *n* edad *f* viril; *(state)* virilidad *f*

mania ['meɪnɪə] *n* manía; **maniac** ['meɪnɪæk] *n* maníaco/a; *(fig)* maniático

manic ['mænɪk] *adj* frenético

manicure ['mænɪkjuə*] *n* manicura

manifest ['mænɪfest] *vt* manifestar, mostrar ▷ *adj* manifiesto

manifesto [mænɪ'festəu] *n* manifiesto

manipulate [mə'nɪpjuleɪt] *vt* manipular

man: mankind [mæn'kaɪnd] *n* humanidad *f*, género humano; **manly** *adj* varonil; **man-made** *adj* artificial

manner ['mænə*] *n* manera, modo; *(behaviour)* conducta, manera de ser; *(type)*: **all ~ of things** toda clase de cosas; **manners** *npl (behaviour)* modales *mpl*; **bad ~s** mala educación

manoeuvre [mə'nu:və*] *(us* **maneuver)** *vt, vi* maniobrar ▷ *n* maniobra

manpower ['mænpauə*] *n* mano *f* de obra

mansion ['mænʃən] *n* palacio, casa grande

manslaughter ['mænslɔ:tə*] *n* homicidio no premeditado

mantelpiece ['mæntlpi:s] *n* repisa, chimenea

manual ['mænjuəl] *adj* manual ▷ *n* manual *m*

manufacture [mænju'fæktʃə*] *vt* fabricar ▷ *n* fabricación *f*; **manufacturer** *n* fabricante *mf*

manure [mə'njuə*] *n* estiércol *m*

manuscript ['mænjuskrɪpt] *n* manuscrito

many ['menɪ] *adj, pron* muchos/as; **a great ~** muchísimos, un buen número de; **~ a time** muchas veces

map [mæp] *n* mapa *m* ▷ **to ~ out** *vt* proyectar

maple ['meɪpl] *n* arce *m*, maple *m (LAM)*

Mar *abbr (= March)* mar

mar [mɑ:*] *vt* estropear

marathon ['mærəθən] *n* maratón *m*

marble ['mɑ:bl] *n* mármol *m*; *(toy)* canica

March [mɑ:tʃ] *n* marzo

march [mɑ:tʃ] *vi (Mil)* marchar; *(demonstrators)* manifestarse ▷ *n* marcha; *(demonstration)* manifestación *f*

mare [meə*] *n* yegua

margarine [mɑ:dʒə'ri:n] *n* margarina

margin ['mɑ:dʒɪn] *n* margen *m*; *(Comm: profit margin)* margen *m* de beneficios; **marginal** *adj* marginal; **marginally** *adv* ligeramente

marigold ['mærɪgəuld] *n* caléndula

marijuana [mærɪ'wɑ:nə] *n* marijuana

marina [mə'ri:nə] *n* puerto deportivo

marinade [mærɪ'neɪd] *n* adobo

marinate ['mærɪneɪt] *vt* marinar

marine [mə'ri:n] *adj* marino ▷ *n* soldado de marina

marital ['mærɪtl] *adj* matrimonial; **marital status** *n* estado civil

maritime ['mærɪtaɪm] *adj* marítimo

marjoram ['mɑ:dʒərəm] *n* mejorana

mark [mɑ:k] *n* marca, señal *f*; *(in snow, mud etc)* huella; *(stain)* mancha; *(BRIT Scol)* nota ▷ *vt* marcar; manchar; *(damage: furniture)* rayar; *(indicate: place etc)* señalar; *(BRIT Scol)* calificar, corregir; **to ~ time** marcar el paso; *(fig)* marcar(se) un ritmo; **marked** *adj (obvious)* marcado, acusado; **marker** *n (sign)* marcador *m*; *(bookmark)* señal *f* (de libro)

market ['mɑ:kɪt] *n* mercado ▷ *vt (Comm)* comercializar; **marketing** *n* márketing *m*; **marketplace** *n* mercado; **market research** *n* análisis *m inv* de mercados

marmalade ['mɑ:məleɪd] *n* mermelada de naranja

maroon [mə'ru:n] *vt*: **to be ~ed** quedar aislado; *(fig)* quedar abandonado ▷ *n (colour)* granate *m*

marquee [mɑ:'ki:] *n* entoldado

marriage ['mærɪdʒ] *n (relationship, institution)* matrimonio; *(wedding)* boda; *(act)* casamiento; **marriage certificate** *n* partida de casamiento

married ['mærɪd] *adj* casado; *(life, love)* conyugal

marrow ['mærəu] *n* médula; *(vegetable)* calabacín *m*

marry ['mærɪ] *vt* casarse con; *(father, priest etc)* casar ▷ *vi (also: get married)* casarse

Mars [mɑ:z] *n* Marte *m*

marsh [mɑ:ʃ] *n* pantano; *(salt marsh)* marisma

marshal ['mɑ:ʃl] *n (Mil)* mariscal *m*; *(at sports meeting etc)* oficial *m*; *(us: of police, fire department)* jefe/a *m/f* ▷ *vt (thoughts etc)* ordenar; *(soldiers)* formar

martyr ['mɑ:tə*] *n* mártir *mf*

marvel ['mɑ:vl] *n* maravilla, prodigio ▷ *vi*: **to ~ (at)** maravillarse (de); **marvellous** *(us* **marvelous)** *adj* maravilloso

Marxism ['mɑ:ksɪzəm] *n* marxismo

Marxist ['mɑ:ksɪst] *adj, n* marxista *mf*

marzipan ['mɑ:zɪpæn] *n* mazapán *m*

mascara [mæs'kɑ:rə] *n* rímel *m*

mascot ['mæskət] *n* mascota

masculine ['mæskjulɪn] *adj* masculino

mash [mæʃ] *vt* machacar; **mashed potato(es)** *n(pl)* puré *m* de patatas *(SP)* or papas *(LAM)*

mask [mɑ:sk] *n* máscara ▷ *vt (cover)*: **to ~ one's face** ocultarse la cara; *(hide: feelings)* enmascarar

mason ['meɪsn] *n (also: stone~)* albañil *m*; *(also: free~)* masón *m*; **masonry** *n (in building)* mampostería

mass [mæs] *n (people)* muchedumbre *f*; *(of air, liquid etc)* masa; *(of detail, hair etc)* gran cantidad *f*; *(Rel)* misa ▷ *cpd* masivo ▷ *vi* reunirse; concentrarse; **the masses** *npl* las masas; **~es of** *(inf)* montones de

massacre ['mæsəkə*] *n* masacre *f*

massage ['mæsɑ:ʒ] *n* masaje *m* ▷ *vt* dar masaje en

massive ['mæsɪv] *adj* enorme; *(support, changes)* masivo

mass media *npl* medios *mpl* de comunicación

mass-produce ['mæsprə'dju:s] *vt* fabricar en serie

mast [mɑ:st] *n (Naut)* mástil *m*; *(Radio etc)* torre *f*

master ['mɑ:stə*] *n (of servant)* amo; *(of situation)* dueño, maestro; *(in primary school)* maestro; *(in secondary school)* profesor *m*; *(title for boys)*: **M~ X** Señorito X ▷ *vt* dominar; **mastermind** *n* inteligencia

superior ▷ vt dirigir, planear; **Master of Arts/
Science** n licenciatura superior en Letras/Ciencias;
masterpiece n obra maestra

masturbate ['mæstəbeɪt] vi masturbarse

mat [mæt] n estera; (also: **door~**) felpudo; (also: **table
~**) salvamanteles m inv, posavasos m inv ▷ adj = **matt**

match [mætʃ] n cerilla, fósforo; (game) partido;
(equal) igual m/f ▷ vt (go well with) hacer juego con;
(equal) igualar; (correspond to) corresponderse con;
(pair: also: ~ **up**) casar con ▷ vi hacer juego; **to be a
good ~** hacer juego; **matchbox** n caja de cerillas;
matching adj que hace juego

mate [meɪt] n (workmate) colega mf; (inf: friend)
amigo/a; (animal) macho/hembra; (in merchant navy)
segundo de a bordo ▷ vi acoplarse, aparearse ▷ vt
aparear

material [mə'tɪərɪəl] n (substance) materia;
(information) material m; (cloth) tela, tejido ▷ adj
material; (important) esencial; **materials** npl
materiales mpl

materialize [mə'tɪərɪəlaɪz] vi materializarse

maternal [mə'tə:nl] adj maternal

maternity [mə'tə:nɪtɪ] n maternidad f; **maternity
hospital** n hospital m de maternidad; **maternity
leave** n baja por maternidad

math [mæθ] (US) n = **mathematics**

mathematical [mæθə'mætɪkl] adj matemático

mathematician [mæθəmə'tɪʃən] n matemático/a

mathematics [mæθə'mætɪks] n matemáticas fpl

maths [mæθs] (BRIT) n = **mathematics**

matinée ['mætɪneɪ] n sesión f de tarde

matron ['meɪtrən] n enfermera f jefe; (in school)
ama de llaves

matt [mæt] adj mate

matter ['mætə*] n cuestión f, asunto; (Physics)
sustancia, materia; (reading matter) material m;
(Med: pus) pus m ▷ vi importar; **matters** npl (affairs)
asuntos mpl, temas mpl; **it doesn't ~** no importa;
what's the ~? ¿qué pasa?; **no ~ what** pase lo que pase;
as a ~ of course por rutina; **as a ~ of fact** de hecho

mattress ['mætrɪs] n colchón m

mature [mə'tjuə*] adj maduro ▷ vi madurar;
mature student n estudiante de más de 21 años;
maturity n madurez f

maul [mɔ:l] vt magullar

mauve [məuv] adj de color malva (SP) or guinda (LAM)

max abbr = **maximum**

maximize ['mæksɪmaɪz] vt (profits etc) llevar al
máximo; (chances) maximizar

maximum ['mæksɪməm] (pl **maxima**) adj máximo
▷ n máximo

May [meɪ] n mayo

may [meɪ] (conditional **might**) vi (indicating
possibility): **he ~ come** puede que venga; (be allowed
to): **~ I smoke?** ¿puedo fumar?; (wishes): **~ God bless
you!** ¡que Dios le bendiga!; **you ~ as well go** bien
puedes irte

maybe ['meɪbiː] adv quizá(s)

May Day n el primero de Mayo

mayhem ['meɪhem] n caos m total

mayonnaise [meɪə'neɪz] n mayonesa

mayor ['mɛə*] n alcalde m; **mayoress** n alcaldesa

maze [meɪz] n laberinto

MD n abbr = **managing director**

me [miː] pron (direct) me; (stressed, after pron) mí; **can
you hear ~?** ¿me oyes?; **he heard ME** ¡me oyó a mí!; **it's**

~ soy yo; **give them to ~** dámelos/las; **with/without
~** conmigo/sin mí

meadow ['mɛdəu] n prado, pradera

meagre ['miːgə*] (US **meager**) adj escaso, pobre

meal [miːl] n comida; (flour) harina; **mealtime** n
hora de comer

mean [miːn] (pt, pp **~t**) adj (with money) tacaño;
(unkind) mezquino, malo; (shabby) humilde; (average)
medio ▷ vt (signify) querer decir, significar; (refer to)
referirse a; (intend): **to ~ to do sth** pensar or pretender
hacer algo ▷ n medio, término medio; **means** npl
(way) medio, manera; (money) recursos mpl, medios
mpl; **by ~s of** mediante, por medio de; **by all ~s!**
¡naturalmente!, ¡claro que sí!; **do you ~ it?** ¿lo dices en
serio?; **what do you ~?** ¿qué quiere decir?; **to be ~t for
sb/sth** ser para algn/algo

meaning ['miːnɪŋ] n significado, sentido; (purpose)
sentido, propósito; **meaningful** adj significativo;
meaningless adj sin sentido

meant [mɛnt] pt, pp of **mean**

meantime ['miːntaɪm] adv (also: **in the ~**) mientras
tanto

meanwhile ['miːnwaɪl] adv = **meantime**

measles ['miːzlz] n sarampión m

measure ['mɛʒə*] vt, vi medir ▷ n medida; (ruler)
regla; **measurement** ['mɛʒəmənt] n (measure)
medida; (act) medición f; **to take sb's measurements**
tomar las medidas a algn

meat [miːt] n carne f; **cold ~** fiambre m; **meatball** n
albóndiga

Mecca ['mɛkə] n La Meca

mechanic [mɪ'kænɪk] n mecánico/a; **mechanical**
adj mecánico

mechanism ['mɛkənɪzəm] n mecanismo

medal ['mɛdl] n medalla; **medallist** (US **medalist**) n
(Sport) medallista mf

meddle ['mɛdl] vi: **to ~ in** entrometerse en; **to ~ with
sth** manosear algo

media ['miːdɪə] npl medios mpl de comunicación
▷ npl of **medium**

mediaeval [mɛdɪ'iːvl] adj = **medieval**

mediate ['miːdɪeɪt] vi mediar

medical ['mɛdɪkl] adj médico ▷ n reconocimiento
médico; **medical certificate** n certificado m médico

medicated ['mɛdɪkeɪtɪd] adj medicinal

medication [mɛdɪ'keɪʃən] n medicación f

medicine ['mɛdsɪn] n medicina; (drug)
medicamento

medieval [mɛdɪ'iːvl] adj medieval

mediocre [miːdɪ'əukə*] adj mediocre

meditate ['mɛdɪteɪt] vi meditar

meditation [mɛdɪ'teɪʃən] n meditación f

Mediterranean [mɛdɪtə'reɪnɪən] adj
mediterráneo; **the ~ (Sea)** el (Mar) Mediterráneo

medium ['miːdɪəm] (pl **media**) adj mediano, regular
▷ n (means) medio; (pl **mediums**: person) médium mf;
medium-sized adj de tamaño mediano; (clothes) de
(la) talla mediana; **medium wave** n onda media

meek [miːk] adj manso, sumiso

meet [miːt] (pt, pp **met**) vt encontrar; (accidentally)
encontrarse con, tropezar con; (by arrangement)
reunirse con; (for the first time) conocer; (go and fetch)
ir a buscar; (opponent) enfrentarse con; (obligations)
cumplir; (encounter: problem) hacer frente a; (need)
satisfacer ▷ vi encontrarse; (in session) reunirse;
(join: objects) unirse; (for the first time) conocerse; **meet**

up vi: **to meet up with sb** reunirse con algn; **meet with** vt fus (difficulty) tropezar con; **to meet with success** tener éxito; **meeting** n encuentro; (arranged) cita, compromiso; (business meeting) reunión f; (Pol) mítin m; **meeting place** n lugar m de reunión or encuentro

megabyte ['megǝbaɪt] n (Comput) megabyte m, megaocteto

megaphone ['megǝfǝʊn] n megáfono

megapixel ['megǝpɪksl] n megapíxel m

melancholy ['melǝnkǝlɪ] n melancolía ▷ adj melancólico

melody ['melǝdɪ] n melodía

melon ['melǝn] n melón m

melt [melt] vi (metal) fundirse; (snow) derretirse ▷ vt fundir

member ['membǝ*] n (gen, Anat) miembro m; (of club) socio/a; **Member of Congress** (US) n miembro mf del Congreso; **Member of Parliament** n (BRIT) diputado/a m/f, parlamentario/a m/f; **Member of the European Parliament** n diputado/a m/f del Parlamento Europeo, eurodiputado/a m/f; **Member of the Scottish Parliament** (BRIT) diputado/a del Parlamento escocés; **membership** n (members) número de miembros; (state) filiación f; **membership card** n carnet m de socio

memento [mǝ'mentǝʊ] n recuerdo

memo ['memǝʊ] n apunte m, nota

memorable ['memǝrǝbl] adj memorable

memorandum [memǝ'rændǝm] n (pl **memoranda**) n apunte m, nota; (official note) acta

memorial [mɪ'mɔːrɪǝl] n monumento conmemorativo ▷ adj conmemorativo

memorize ['memǝraɪz] vt aprender de memoria

memory ['memǝrɪ] n (also: Comput) memoria; (instance) recuerdo; (of dead person): **in ~ of** a la memoria de; **memory card** n (for digital camera) tarjeta de memoria

men [men] npl of **man**

menace ['menǝs] n amenaza ▷ vt amenazar

mend [mend] vt reparar, arreglar; (darn) zurcir ▷ vi reponerse ▷ n arreglo, reparación f, zurcido ▷ v: **to be on the ~** ir mejorando; **to ~ one's ways** enmendarse

meningitis [menɪn'dʒaɪtɪs] n meningitis f

menopause ['menǝʊpɔːz] n menopausia

men's room (US) n: **the ~** el servicio de caballeros

menstruation [menstru'eɪʃǝn] n menstruación f

menswear ['menzweǝ*] n confección f de caballero

mental ['mentl] adj mental; **mental hospital** n (hospital m) psiquiátrico m; **mentality** [men'tælɪtɪ] n mentalidad f; **mentally** adv: **to be mentally ill** tener una enfermedad mental

menthol ['menθɔl] n mentol m

mention ['menʃǝn] n mención f ▷ vt mencionar; (speak) hablar de; **don't ~ it!** ¡de nada!

menu ['menjuː] n (set menu) menú m; (printed) carta; (Comput) menú m

MEP n abbr = **Member of the European Parliament**

mercenary ['mǝːsɪnǝrɪ] adj, n mercenario/a

merchandise ['mǝːtʃǝndaɪz] n mercancías fpl

merchant ['mǝːtʃǝnt] n comerciante mf; **merchant navy** (US), **merchant marine** n marina mercante

merciless ['mǝːsɪlɪs] adj despiadado

mercury ['mǝːkjʊrɪ] n mercurio

mercy ['mǝːsɪ] n compasión f; (Rel) misericordia; **at the ~ of** a la merced de

mere [mɪǝ*] adj simple, mero; **merely** adv simplemente, sólo

merge [mǝːdʒ] vt (join) unir ▷ vi unirse; (Comm) fusionarse; (colours etc) fundirse; **merger** n (Comm) fusión f

meringue [mǝ'ræŋ] n merengue m

merit ['merɪt] n mérito ▷ vt merecer

mermaid ['mǝːmeɪd] n sirena

merry ['merɪ] adj alegre; **M~ Christmas!** ¡Felices Pascuas!; **merry-go-round** n tiovivo

mesh [meʃ] n malla

mess [mes] n (muddle: of situation) confusión f; (: of room) revoltijo; (dirt) porquería; (Mil) comedor m; **mess about or around** (inf) vi perder el tiempo; (pass the time) entretenerse; **mess up** vt (spoil) estropear; (dirty) ensuciar; **mess with** (inf) vt fus (challenge, confront) meterse con (inf); (interfere with) interferir con

message ['mesɪdʒ] n recado, mensaje m

messenger ['mesɪndʒǝ*] n mensajero/a

Messrs abbr (on letters) (= Messieurs) Sres

messy ['mesɪ] adj (dirty) sucio; (untidy) desordenado

met [met] pt, pp of **meet**

metabolism [me'tæbǝlɪzǝm] n metabolismo

metal ['metl] n metal m; **metallic** [-'tælɪk] adj metálico

metaphor ['metǝfǝ*] n metáfora

meteor ['miːtɪǝ*] n meteoro; **meteorite** [-aɪt] n meteorito

meteorology [miːtɪǝ'rɔlǝdʒɪ] n meteorología

meter ['miːtǝ*] n (instrument) contador m; (US: unit) = **metre** ▷ vt (US Post) franquear

method ['meθǝd] n método; **methodical** [mɪ'θɔdɪkl] adj metódico

meths [meθs] n (BRIT) alcohol m metilado or desnaturalizado

meticulous [me'tɪkjʊlǝs] adj meticuloso

metre ['miːtǝ*] (US **meter**) n metro

metric ['metrɪk] adj métrico

metro ['metrǝʊ] n metro

metropolitan [metrǝ'pɔlɪtǝn] adj metropolitano; **the M~ Police** (BRIT) la policía londinense

Mexican ['meksɪkǝn] adj, n mexicano/a, mejicano/a

Mexico ['meksɪkǝʊ] n México, Méjico (SP)

mg abbr (= milligram) mg

mice [maɪs] npl of **mouse**

micro... [maɪkrǝʊ] prefix micro...; **microchip** n microplaqueta; **microphone** n micrófono; **microscope** n microscopio; **microwave** n (also: microwave oven) horno microondas

mid [mɪd] adj: **in ~ May** a mediados de mayo; **in ~ afternoon** a media tarde; **in ~ air** en el aire; **midday** n mediodía m

middle ['mɪdl] n centro; (half-way point) medio; (waist) cintura ▷ adj de en medio; (course, way) intermedio; **in the ~ of the night** en plena noche; **middle-aged** adj de mediana edad; **Middle Ages** npl: **the Middle Ages** la Edad Media; **middle-class** adj de clase media; **the middle class(es)** la clase media; **Middle East** n Oriente m Medio; **middle name** n segundo nombre; **middle school** n (US) colegio para niños de doce a catorce años; (BRIT) colegio para niños de ocho o nueve a trece años

midge [mɪdʒ] n mosquito

midget ['mɪdʒɪt] n enano/a

midnight ['mɪdnaɪt] n medianoche f

midst [mɪdst] *n*: **in the ~ of** (*crowd*) en medio de; (*situation, action*) en mitad de

midsummer [mɪd'sʌmə*] *n*: **in ~** en pleno verano

midway [mɪd'weɪ] *adj, adv*: **~ (between)** a medio camino (entre); **~ through** a la mitad (de)

midweek [mɪd'wiːk] *adv* entre semana

midwife [mɪdwaɪf] (*irreg*) *n* comadrona, partera

midwinter [mɪd'wɪntə*] *n*: **in ~** en pleno invierno

might [maɪt] *vb see* **may** ▷ *n* fuerza, poder *m*; **mighty** *adj* fuerte, poderoso

migraine [mi:greɪn] *n* jaqueca

migrant [maɪgrənt] *n, adj* (*bird*) migratorio/a; (*worker*) emigrante

migrate [maɪ'greɪt] *vi* emigrar

migration [maɪ'greɪʃən] *n* emigración *f*

mike [maɪk] *n abbr* (= *microphone*) micro

mild [maɪld] *adj* (*person*) apacible; (*climate*) templado; (*slight*) ligero, (*taste*) suave; (*illness*) leve; **mildly** [-lɪ] *adv* ligeramente; suavemente; **to put it mildly** para no decir más

mile [maɪl] *n* milla; **mileage** *n* número de millas ≈ kilometraje *m*; **mileometer** [maɪ'lɒmɪtə*] *n* ≈ cuentakilómetros *m inv*; **milestone** *n* mojón *m*

military [mɪlɪtərɪ] *adj* militar

militia [mɪ'lɪʃə] *n* milicia

milk [mɪlk] *n* leche *f* ▷ *vt* (*cow*) ordeñar; (*fig*) chupar; **milk chocolate** *n* chocolate *m* con leche; **milkman** (*irreg*) *n* lechero; **milky** *adj* lechoso

mill [mɪl] *n* (*windmill etc*) molino; (*coffee mill*) molinillo; (*factory*) fábrica ▷ *vt* moler ▷ *vi* (*also*: **~ about**) arremolinarse

millennium [mɪ'lenɪəm] (*pl* **~s** *or* **millennia**) *n* milenio, milenario

milli... [mɪlɪ] *prefix*: **milligram(me)** *n* miligramo; **millilitre** (*US* **milliliter**) [mɪlɪliːtə*] *n* mililitro; **millimetre** (*US* **millimeter**) *n* milímetro

million [mɪljən] *n* millón *m*; **a ~ times** un millón de veces; **millionaire** [-jə'neə*] *n* millonario/a; **millionth** [-θ] *adj* millonésimo

milometer [maɪ'lɒmɪtə*] (*BRIT*) *n* = **mileometer**

mime [maɪm] *n* mímica; (*actor*) mimo/a ▷ *vt* remedar ▷ *vi* actuar de mimo

mimic [mɪmɪk] *n* imitador(a) *m/f* ▷ *adj* mímico ▷ *vt* remedar, imitar

min. *abbr* = **minimum; minute(s)**

mince [mɪns] *vt* picar ▷ *n* (*BRIT Culin*) carne *f* picada; **mincemeat** *n* conserva de fruta picada; (*US*: *meat*) carne *f* picada; **mince pie** *n* empanadilla rellena de fruta picada

mind [maɪnd] *n* mente *f*; (*intellect*) intelecto; (*contrasted with matter*) espíritu *m* ▷ *vt* (*attend to, look after*) ocuparse de, cuidar; (*be careful*) tener cuidado con; (*object to*): **I don't ~ the noise** no me molesta el ruido; **it is on my ~** me preocupa; **to bear sth in ~** tomar o tener algo en cuenta; **to make up one's ~** decidirse; **I don't ~** me es igual; **~ you ...** te advierto que ...; **never ~** ¡es igual!, ¡no importa!; (*don't worry*) ¡no te preocupes!; **"~ the step"** "cuidado con el escalón"; **mindless** *adj* (*crime*) sin motivo; (*work*) de autómata

mine¹ [maɪn] *pron* el mío/la mía etc; **a friend of ~** un(a) amigo/a mío/mía ▷ *adj*: **this book is ~** este libro es mío

mine² [maɪn] *n* mina ▷ *vt* (*coal*) extraer; (*bomb: beach etc*) minar; **minefield** *n* campo de minas; **miner** *n* minero/a

mineral [mɪnərəl] *adj* mineral ▷ *n* mineral *m*; **mineral water** *n* agua mineral

mingle [mɪŋgl] *vi*: **to ~ with** mezclarse con

miniature [mɪnətʃə*] *adj* (en) miniatura ▷ *n* miniatura

minibar [mɪnɪbɑ:*] *n* minibar *m*

minibus [mɪnɪbʌs] *n* microbús *m*

minicab [mɪnɪkæb] *n* taxi *m* (*que sólo puede pedirse por teléfono*)

minimal [mɪnɪml] *adj* mínimo

minimize [mɪnɪmaɪz] *vt* minimizar; (*play down*) empequeñecer

minimum [mɪnɪməm] (*pl* **minima**) *n, adj* mínimo

mining [maɪnɪŋ] *n* explotación *f* minera

miniskirt [mɪnɪskɜːt] *n* minifalda

minister [mɪnɪstə*] *n* (*BRIT Pol*) ministro/a (*SP*), secretario/a (*LAM*); (*Rel*) pastor *m* ▷ *vi*: **to ~ to** atender a

ministry [mɪnɪstrɪ] *n* (*BRIT Pol*) ministerio, secretaría (*MEX*); (*Rel*) sacerdocio

minor [maɪnə*] *adj* (*repairs, injuries*) leve; (*poet, planet*) menor; (*Mus*) menor ▷ *n* (*Law*) menor *m* de edad

Minorca [mɪ'nɔːkə] *n* Menorca

minority [maɪ'nɒrɪtɪ] *n* minoría

mint [mɪnt] *n* (*plant*) menta, hierbabuena; (*sweet*) caramelo de menta ▷ *vt* (*coins*) acuñar; **the (Royal) M~, the (US) M~** la Casa de la Moneda; **in ~ condition** en perfecto estado

minus [maɪnəs] *n* (*also*: **~ sign**) signo de menos ▷ *prep* menos; **12 – 6 equals 6** 12 menos 6 son 6; **~ 24 °C** menos 24 grados

minute¹ [mɪnɪt] *n* minuto; (*fig*) momento; **minutes** *npl* (*of meeting*) actas *fpl*; **at the last ~** a última hora

minute² [maɪ'njuːt] *adj* diminuto; (*search*) minucioso

miracle [mɪrəkl] *n* milagro

miraculous [mɪ'rækjuləs] *adj* milagroso

mirage [mɪrɑːʒ] *n* espejismo

mirror [mɪrə*] *n* espejo; (*in car*) retrovisor *m*

misbehave [mɪsbɪ'heɪv] *vi* portarse mal

misc. *abbr* = **miscellaneous**

miscarriage [mɪskærɪdʒ] *n* (*Med*) aborto; **~ of justice** error *m* judicial

miscellaneous [mɪsɪ'leɪnɪəs] *adj* varios/as, diversos/as

mischief [mɪstʃɪf] *n* travesuras *fpl*, diabluras *fpl*; (*maliciousness*) malicia; **mischievous** [-ʃɪvəs] *adj* travieso

misconception [mɪskən'sepʃən] *n* idea equivocada; equivocación *f*

misconduct [mɪs'kɒndʌkt] *n* mala conducta; **professional ~** falta profesional

miser [maɪzə*] *n* avaro/a

miserable [mɪzərəbl] *adj* (*unhappy*) triste, desgraciado; (*unpleasant, contemptible*) miserable

misery [mɪzərɪ] *n* tristeza; (*wretchedness*) miseria, desdicha

misfortune [mɪs'fɔːtʃən] *n* desgracia

misgiving [mɪs'gɪvɪŋ] *n* (*apprehension*) presentimiento; **to have ~s about sth** tener dudas acerca de algo

misguided [mɪs'gaɪdɪd] *adj* equivocado

mishap [mɪshæp] *n* desgracia, contratiempo

misinterpret [mɪsɪn'tɜːprɪt] *vt* interpretar mal

misjudge [mɪs'dʒʌdʒ] *vt* juzgar mal

mislay [mɪs'leɪ] *vt* extraviar, perder

mislead [mɪs'liːd] *vt* llevar a conclusiones erróneas; **misleading** *adj* engañoso

misplace [mɪs'pleɪs] *vt* extraviar

misprint ['misprint] n errata, error m de imprenta
misrepresent [misrepri'zent] vt falsificar
Miss [mis] n Señorita
miss [mis] vt (train etc) perder; (fail to hit: target) errar; (regret the absence of): **I ~ him** (yo) le echo de menos or a faltar; (fail to see): **you can't ~ it** no tiene pérdida ▷ vi fallar ▷ n (shot) tiro fallido or perdido; **miss out** (BRIT) vt omitir; **miss out on** vt fus (fun, party, opportunity) perderse
missile ['misail] n (Aviat) mísil m; (object thrown) proyectil m
missing ['misin] adj (pupil) ausente; (thing) perdido; (Mil): **~ in action** desaparecido en combate
mission ['miʃən] n misión f; (official representation) delegación f; **missionary** n misionero/a
misspell [mis'spɛl] (pt, pp misspelt (BRIT) or **~ed**) vt escribir mal
mist [mist] n (light) neblina; (heavy) niebla; (at sea) bruma ▷ vi (eyes: also: **~ over, ~ up**) llenarse de lágrimas; (BRIT: windows: also: **~ over, ~ up**) empañarse
mistake [mis'teik] (vt: irreg) n error m ▷ vt entender mal; **by ~** por equivocación; **to make a ~** equivocarse; **to ~ A for B** confundir A con B; **mistaken** pp of **mistake** ▷ adj equivocado; **to be mistaken** equivocarse, engañarse
mister [mis'tə*] (inf) n señor m; see **Mr**
mistletoe ['misltəu] n muérdago
mistook [mis'tuk] pt of **mistake**
mistress ['mistris] n (lover) amante f; (of house) señora (de la casa); (BRIT: in primary school) maestra; (in secondary school) profesora; (of situation) dueña
mistrust [mis'trʌst] vt desconfiar de
misty ['misti] adj (day) de niebla; (glasses etc) empañado
misunderstand [misʌndə'stænd] (irreg) vt, vi entender mal; **misunderstanding** n malentendido
misunderstood [misʌndə'stud] pt, pp of **misunderstand** ▷ adj (person) incomprendido
misuse [n mis'ju:s, vb mis'ju:z] n mal uso; (of power) abuso; (of funds) malversación f ▷ vt abusar de; malversar
mitt(en) ['mit(n)] n manopla
mix [miks] vt mezclar; (combine) unir ▷ vi mezclarse; (people) llevarse bien ▷ n mezcla; **mix up** vt mezclar; (confuse) confundir; **mixed** adj mixto; (feelings etc) encontrado; **mixed grill** n (BRIT) parrillada mixta; **mixed salad** n ensalada mixta; **mixed-up** adj (confused) confuso, revuelto; **mixer** n (for food) licuadora; (for drinks) coctelera; (person): **he's a good mixer** tiene don de gentes; **mixture** n mezcla; (also: **cough mixture**) jarabe m; **mix-up** n confusión f
ml abbr (= millilitre(s)) ml
mm abbr (= millimetre) mm
moan [məun] n gemido ▷ vi gemir; (inf: complain): **to ~ (about)** quejarse (de)
moat [məut] n foso
mob [mɔb] n multitud f ▷ vt acosar
mobile ['məubail] adj móvil ▷ n móvil m; **mobile home** n caravana; **mobile phone** n teléfono móvil
mobility [məu'biliti] n movilidad f
mobilize ['məubilaiz] vt movilizar
mock [mɔk] vt (ridicule) ridiculizar; (laugh at) burlarse de ▷ adj fingido; **~ exam** examen preparatorio antes de los exámenes oficiales* (BRIT); **mocks** npl (Scot: inf) exámenes mpl de prueba; **mockery** n burla
mod cons ['mɔd'kɔnz] npl abbr (= modern

conveniences) see **convenience**
mode [məud] n modo
model ['mɔdl] n modelo; (fashion model, artist's model) modelo mf ▷ adj modelo ▷ vt (with clay etc) modelar; (copy): **to ~ o.s.** on tomar como modelo a ▷ vi ser modelo; **to ~ clothes** pasar modelos, ser modelo
modem ['məudəm] n modem m
moderate [adj 'mɔdərət, vb 'mɔdəreit] adj moderado/a ▷ vi moderarse, calmarse ▷ vt moderar
moderation [mɔdə'reiʃən] n moderación f; **in ~** con moderación
modern ['mɔdən] adj moderno; **modernize** vt modernizar; **modern languages** npl lenguas fpl modernas
modest ['mɔdist] adj modesto; (small) módico; **modesty** n modestia
modification [mɔdifi'keiʃən] n modificación f
modify ['mɔdifai] vt modificar
module ['mɔdju:l] n (unit, component, Space) módulo
mohair ['məuhɛə*] n mohair m
Mohammed [mə'hæmɛd] n Mahoma m
moist [mɔist] adj húmedo; **moisture** ['mɔistʃə*] n humedad f; **moisturizer** ['mɔistʃəraizə*] n crema hidratante
mold etc [məuld] (us) = **mould** etc
mole [məul] n (animal, spy) topo; (spot) lunar m
molecule ['mɔlikju:l] n molécula
molest [məu'lɛst] vt importunar; (assault sexually) abusar sexualmente de
molten ['məultən] adj fundido; (lava) líquido
mom [mɔm] (us) n = **mum**
moment ['məumənt] n momento; **at the ~** de momento, por ahora; **momentarily** ['məuməntrili] adv momentáneamente; (us: very soon) de un momento a otro; **momentary** adj momentáneo; **momentous** [-'mɛntəs] adj trascendental, importante
momentum [məu'mɛntəm] n momento; (fig) ímpetu m; **to gather ~** cobrar velocidad; (fig) ganar fuerza
mommy ['mɔmi] (us) n = **mummy**
Mon abbr (= Monday) lun
Monaco ['mɔnəkəu] n Mónaco m
monarch ['mɔnək] n monarca mf; **monarchy** n monarquía
monastery ['mɔnəstəri] n monasterio
Monday ['mʌndi] n lunes m inv
monetary ['mʌnitəri] adj monetario
money ['mʌni] n dinero; (currency) moneda; **to make ~** ganar dinero; **money belt** n riñonera; **money order** n giro
mongrel ['mʌngrəl] n (dog) perro mestizo
monitor ['mɔnitə*] n (Scol) monitor m; (also: **television ~**) receptor m de control; (of computer) monitor m ▷ vt controlar
monk [mʌnk] n monje m
monkey ['mʌnki] n mono
monologue ['mɔnəlɔg] n monólogo
monopoly [mə'nɔpəli] n monopolio
monosodium glutamate [mɔnə'səudiəm'glu:tə-meit] n glutamato monosódico
monotonous [mə'nɔtənəs] adj monótono
monsoon [mɔn'su:n] n monzón m
monster ['mɔnstə*] n monstruo
month [mʌnθ] n mes m; **monthly** adj mensual ▷ adv mensualmente

monument ['mɔnjumənt] n monumento

mood [muːd] n humor m; (of crowd, group) clima m; **to be in a good/bad** ~ estar de buen/mal humor; **moody** (changeable) de humor variable; (sullen) malhumorado

moon [muːn] n luna; **moonlight** n luz f de la luna

moor [muə*] n páramo ▷ vt (ship) amarrar ▷ vi echar las amarras

moose [muːs] n inv alce m

mop [mɔp] n fregona; (of hair) greña, melena ▷ vt fregar; **mop up** vt limpiar

mope [məup] vi estar o andar deprimido

moped ['məupεd] n ciclomotor m

moral ['mɔrl] adj moral n moraleja; **morals** npl moralidad f, moral f

morale [mɔ'rɑːl] n moral f

morality [mə'rælɪtɪ] n moralidad f

morbid ['mɔːbɪd] adj (interest) morboso, (Med) mórbido

○ **KEYWORD**

more [mɔː*] adj **1** (greater in number etc) más; **more people/work
than before** más gente/trabajo que antes
2 (additional) más; **do you want (some) more tea?** ¿quieres más té?; **is there any more wine?** ¿queda vino?; **it'll take a few more weeks** tardará unas semanas más; **it's 2 kms more to the house** faltan 2 kms para la casa; **more time/letters than we expected** más tiempo del que/más cartas de las que esperábamos
▷ pron (greater amount, additional amount) más; **more than 10** más de 10; **it cost more than the other one/than we expected** costó más que el otro/más de lo que esperábamos; **is there any more?** ¿hay más?; **many/much more** muchos(as)/mucho(a) más
▷ adv más; **more dangerous/easily (than)** más peligroso/fácilmente (que); **more and more expensive** cada vez más caro; **more or less** más o menos; **more than ever** más que nunca

moreover [mɔː'rəuvə*] adv además, por otra parte

morgue [mɔːg] n depósito de cadáveres

morning ['mɔːnɪŋ] n mañana; (early morning) madrugada ▷ cpd matutino, de la mañana; **in the** ~ por la mañana; **7 o'clock in the** ~ las 7 de la mañana; **morning sickness** n náuseas fpl matutinas

Moroccan [mə'rɔkən] adj, n marroquí m/f

Morocco [mə'rɔkəu] n Marruecos m

moron ['mɔːrɔn] (inf) n imbécil m/f

morphine ['mɔːfiːn] n morfina

Morse [mɔːs] n (also: ~ **code**) (código) Morse

mortal ['mɔːtl] adj, n mortal m

mortar ['mɔːtə*] n argamasa

mortgage ['mɔːgɪdʒ] n hipoteca ▷ vt hipotecar

mortician [mɔː'tɪʃən] (us) n director/a m/f de pompas fúnebres

mortified ['mɔːtɪfaɪd] adj: **I was** ~ me dio muchísima vergüenza

mortuary ['mɔːtjuərɪ] n depósito de cadáveres

mosaic [məu'zeɪɪk] n mosaico

Moslem ['mɔzləm] adj, n = **Muslim**

mosque [mɔsk] n mezquita

mosquito [mɔs'kiːtəu] (pl ~**es**) n mosquito (SP),

zancudo (LAM)

moss [mɔs] n musgo

most [məust] adj la mayor parte de, la mayoría de ▷ pron la mayor parte, la mayoría ▷ adv de lo más; (very) muy; **the** ~ (also: + adj) el más; ~ **of them** la mayor parte de ellos; **I saw the** ~ yo vi el que más; **at the (very)** ~ a lo sumo, todo lo más; **to make the** ~ **of** aprovechar (al máximo); **a** ~ **interesting book** un libro interesantísimo; **mostly** adv en su mayor parte, principalmente

MOT (BRIT) n abbr = **Ministry of Transport; the** ~ **(test)** inspección (anual) obligatoria de coches y camiones

motel [məu'tεl] n motel m

moth [mɔθ] n mariposa nocturna; (clothes moth) polilla

mother ['mʌðə*] n madre f ▷ adj materno ▷ vt (care for) cuidar (como una madre); **motherhood** n maternidad f; **mother-in-law** n suegra; **mother-of-pearl** n nácar m; **Mother's Day** n Día m de la Madre; **mother-to-be** n futura madre f; **mother tongue** n lengua materna

motif [məu'tiːf] n motivo

motion ['məuʃən] n movimiento; (gesture) ademán m, señal f; (at meeting) moción f ▷ vt, vi: **to ~ (to) sb to do sth** hacer señas a algn para que haga algo; **motionless** adj inmóvil; **motion picture** n película

motivate ['məutɪveɪt] vt motivar

motivation [məutɪ'veɪʃən] n motivación f

motive ['məutɪv] n motivo

motor ['məutə*] n motor m; (BRIT: inf: vehicle) coche m (SP), carro (LAM), automóvil m ▷ adj motor (f: motora or motriz); **motorbike** n moto f; **motorboat** n lancha motora; **motorcar** (BRIT) n coche m, carro, automóvil m; **motorcycle** n motocicleta; **motorcyclist** n motociclista m/f; **motoring** (BRIT) n automovilismo; **motorist** n conductor/a m/f, automovilista m/f; **motor racing** (BRIT) n carreras fpl de coches, automovilismo; **motorway** (BRIT) n autopista

motto ['mɔtəu] (pl ~**es**) n lema m; (watchword) consigna

mould [məuld] (us **mold**) n molde m; (mildew) moho ▷ vt moldear; (fig) formar; **mouldy** adj enmohecido

mound [maund] n montón m, montículo

mount [maunt] n monte m ▷ vt montar, subir a; (jewel) engarzar; (picture) enmarcar; (exhibition etc) organizar ▷ vi (increase) aumentar; **mount up** vi aumentar

mountain ['mauntɪn] n montaña ▷ cpd de montaña; **mountain bike** n bicicleta de montaña; **mountaineer** n alpinista m/f (SP, MEX), andinista m/f (LAM); **mountaineering** n alpinismo (SP, MEX), andinismo (LAM); **mountainous** adj montañoso; **mountain range** n sierra

mourn [mɔːn] vt llorar, lamentar ▷ vi: **to ~ for** llorar la muerte de; **mourner** n doliente m/f, dolorido/a; **mourning** n luto; **in mourning** de luto

mouse [maus] (pl **mice**) n (Zool, Comput) ratón m; **mouse mat** n (Comput) alfombrilla

moussaka [muːˈsɑːkə] n musaca

mousse [muːs] n (Culin) crema batida; (for hair) espuma (moldeadora)

moustache [məsˈtɑːʃ] (us **mustache**) n bigote m

mouth [mauθ, pl mauðz] n boca; (of river) desembocadura; **mouthful** n bocado; **mouth organ** n armónica; **mouthpiece** n (of musical instrument) boquilla; (spokesman) portavoz m/f; **mouthwash** n enjuague m

move [muːv] n (movement) movimiento; (in game) jugada; (: turn to play) turno; (change: of house) mudanza; (: of job) cambio de trabajo ▷ vt mover; (emotionally) conmover; (Pol: resolution etc) proponer ▷ vi moverse; (traffic) circular; (also: ~ house) trasladarse, mudarse; **to ~ sb to do sth** mover a algn a hacer algo; **to get a ~ on** darse prisa; **move back** vi retroceder; **move in** vi (to a house) instalarse; (police, soldiers) intervenir; **move off** vi ponerse en camino; **move on** vi ponerse en camino; **move out** vi (of house) mudarse; **move over** vi apartarse, hacer sitio; **move up** vi (employee) ser ascendido; **movement** n movimiento

movie [ˈmuːvɪ] n película; **to go to the ~s** ir al cine; **movie theater** (us) n cine m

moving [ˈmuːvɪŋ] adj (emotional) conmovedor(a); (that moves) móvil

mow [məʊ] (pt ~ed, pp mowed or mown) vt (grass, corn) cortar, segar; (also: **lawnmower**) cortacéspedes m inv

Mozambique [məʊzæmˈbiːk] n Mozambique m

MP n abbr = **Member of Parliament**

MP3 n MP3; **MP3 player** n reproductor m (de) MP3

mpg n abbr = **miles per gallon**

m.p.h. abbr = **miles per hour** (60 m.p.h. = 96 k.p.h.)

Mr [ˈmɪstə*] (us **Mr.**) n: **~ Smith** (el) Sr. Smith

Mrs [ˈmɪsɪz] (us **Mrs.**) n: **~ Smith** (la) Sra. Smith

Ms [mɪz] (us **Ms.**) n = **Miss** or **Mrs**; **~ Smith** (la) Sr(t)a. Smith

MSP n abbr = **Member of the Scottish Parliament**

Mt abbr (Geo) (= mount) m

much [mʌtʃ] adj mucho ▷ adv mucho; (before pp) muy ▷ n or pron mucho; **how ~ is it?** ¿cuánto es?, ¿cuánto cuesta?; **too ~** = demasiado; **it's not ~** no es mucho; **as ~ as** tanto como; **however ~ he tries** por mucho que se esfuerce

muck [mʌk] n suciedad f; **muck up** (inf) vt arruinar, estropear; **mucky** adj (dirty) sucio

mucus [ˈmjuːkəs] n mucosidad f, moco

mud [mʌd] n barro, lodo

muddle [ˈmʌdl] n desorden m, confusión f; (mix-up) embrollo, lío ▷ vt (also: **~ up**) embrollar, confundir

muddy [ˈmʌdɪ] adj fangoso, cubierto de lodo

mudguard [ˈmʌdɡɑːd] n guardabarros m inv

muesli [ˈmjuːzlɪ] n muesli m

muffin [ˈmʌfɪn] n panecillo dulce

muffled [ˈmʌfld] adj (noise etc) amortiguado, apagado

muffler (us) [ˈmʌflə*] n (Aut) silenciador m

mug [mʌɡ] n taza grande (sin platillo); (for beer) jarra; (inf: face) jeta ▷ vt (assault) asaltar; **mugger** [ˈmʌɡə*] n atracador(a) m/f; **mugging** n asalto

muggy [ˈmʌɡɪ] adj bochornoso

mule [mjuːl] n mula

multicoloured [ˈmʌltɪkʌləd], (us) **multicolored** adj multicolor

multimedia [ˈmʌltɪˈmiːdɪə] adj multimedia

multinational [mʌltɪˈnæʃənl] n multinacional f ▷ adj multinacional

multiple [ˈmʌltɪpl] adj múltiple ▷ n múltiplo; **multiple choice (test)** n examen m de tipo test; **multiple sclerosis** n esclerosis f múltiple

multiplex cinema [ˈmʌltɪpleks-] n multicines mpl

multiplication [mʌltɪplɪˈkeɪʃən] n multiplicación f

multiply [ˈmʌltɪplaɪ] vt multiplicar ▷ vi

multiplicarse

multistorey [mʌltɪˈstɔːrɪ] (BRIT) adj de muchos pisos

mum [mʌm] (BRIT: inf) n mamá ▷ adj: **to keep ~** mantener la boca cerrada

mumble [ˈmʌmbl] vt, vi hablar entre dientes, refunfuñar

mummy [ˈmʌmɪ] n (BRIT: mother) mamá; (embalmed) momia

mumps [mʌmps] n paperas fpl

munch [mʌntʃ] vt, vi mascar

municipal [mjuːˈnɪsɪpl] adj municipal

mural [ˈmjuərl] n (pintura) mural m

murder [ˈmɜːdə*] n asesinato; (in law) homicidio ▷ vt asesinar, matar; **murderer** n asesino

murky [ˈmɜːkɪ] adj (water) turbio; (street, night) lóbrego

murmur [ˈmɜːmə*] n murmullo ▷ vt, vi murmurar

muscle [ˈmʌsl] n músculo; (fig: strength) garra, fuerza; **muscular** [ˈmʌskjulə*] adj muscular; (person) musculoso

museum [mjuːˈzɪəm] n museo

mushroom [ˈmʌʃrum] n seta, hongo; (Culin) champiñón m ▷ vi crecer de la noche a la mañana

music [ˈmjuːzɪk] n música; **musical** adj musical; (sound) melodioso; (person) con talento musical ▷ n (show) comedia musical; **musical instrument** n instrumento musical; **musician** [-ˈzɪʃən] n músico/a

Muslim [ˈmʊzlɪm] adj, n musulmán/ana m/f

muslin [ˈmʌzlɪn] n muselina

mussel [ˈmʌsl] n mejillón m

must [mʌst] aux vb (obligation): **I ~ do it** debo hacerlo, tengo que hacerlo; (probability): **he ~ be there by now** ya debe (de) estar allí ▷ n: **it's a ~** es imprescindible

mustache [ˈmʌstæʃ] (us) n = **moustache**

mustard [ˈmʌstəd] n mostaza

mustn't [ˈmʌsnt] = **must not**

mute [mjuːt] adj, n mudo/a m/f

mutilate [ˈmjuːtɪleɪt] vt mutilar

mutiny [ˈmjuːtɪnɪ] n motín m ▷ vi amotinarse

mutter [ˈmʌtə*] vt, vi murmurar

mutton [ˈmʌtn] n carne f de cordero

mutual [ˈmjuːtʃuəl] adj mutuo; (interest) común

muzzle [ˈmʌzl] n hocico; (for dog) bozal m; (of gun) boca ▷ vt (dog) poner un bozal a

my [maɪ] adj mi(s); **~ house/brother/sisters** mi casa/mi hermano/mis hermanas; **I've washed ~ hair/cut ~ finger** me he lavado el pelo/cortado un dedo; **is this ~ pen or yours?** ¿es este bolígrafo mío o tuyo?

myself [maɪˈself] pron (reflexive) me; (emphatic) yo mismo; (after prep) mí (mismo); see also **oneself**

mysterious [mɪsˈtɪərɪəs] adj misterioso

mystery [ˈmɪstərɪ] n misterio

mystical [ˈmɪstɪkl] adj místico

mystify [ˈmɪstɪfaɪ] vt (perplex) dejar perplejo

myth [mɪθ] n mito; **mythology** [mɪˈθɒlədʒɪ] n mitología

n

n/a abbr (= not applicable) no interesa
nag [næg] vt (scold) regañar
nail [neɪl] n (human) uña; (metal) clavo ▷ vt clavar; **to ~ sth to sth** clavar algo en algo; **to ~ sb down to doing sth** comprometer a algn a que haga algo; **nailbrush** n cepillo para las uñas; **nailfile** n lima para las uñas; **nail polish** n esmalte m or laca para las uñas; **nail polish remover** n quitaesmalte m; **nail scissors** npl tijeras fpl para las uñas; **nail varnish** (BRIT) n = **nail polish**
naïve [naɪˈiːv] adj ingenuo
naked [ˈneɪkɪd] adj (nude) desnudo; (flame) expuesto al aire
name [neɪm] n nombre m; (surname) apellido; (reputation) fama, renombre m ▷ vt (child) poner nombre a; (criminal) identificar; (price, date etc) fijar; **what's your ~?** ¿cómo se llama?; **by ~** de nombre; **in the ~ of** en nombre de; **to give one's ~ and address** dar sus señas; **namely** adv a saber
nanny [ˈnænɪ] n niñera
nap [næp] n (sleep) sueñecito, siesta
napkin [ˈnæpkɪn] n (also: **table ~**) servilleta
nappy [ˈnæpɪ] (BRIT) n pañal m
narcotics npl (illegal drugs) estupefacientes mpl, narcóticos mpl
narrative [ˈnærətɪv] n narrativa ▷ adj narrativo
narrator [nəˈreɪtə*] n narrador(a) m/f
narrow [ˈnærəʊ] adj estrecho, angosto; (fig: majority etc) corto; (: ideas etc) estrecho ▷ vi (road) estrecharse; (diminish) reducirse; **to have a ~ escape** escaparse por los pelos; **narrow down** vt (search, investigation, possibilities) restringir, limitar; (list) reducir; **narrowly** adv (miss) por poco; **narrow-minded** adj de miras estrechas
nasal [ˈneɪzl] adj nasal
nasty [ˈnɑːstɪ] adj (remark) feo; (person) antipático; (revolting: taste, smell) asqueroso; (wound, disease etc) peligroso, grave
nation [ˈneɪʃən] n nación f
national [ˈnæʃənl] adj, n nacional m/f; **national anthem** n himno nacional; **national dress** n vestido nacional; **National Health Service** (BRIT) n servicio nacional de salud pública ≈ Insalud m (SP); **National Insurance** (BRIT) n seguro social

nacional; **nationalist** adj, n nacionalista mf; **nationality** [-ˈnælɪtɪ] n nacionalidad f; **nationalize** vt nacionalizar; **national park** (BRIT) n parque m nacional; **National Trust** n (BRIT) organización encargada de preservar el patrimonio histórico británico
nationwide [ˈneɪʃənwaɪd] adj en escala or a nivel nacional
native [ˈneɪtɪv] n (local inhabitant) natural mf, nacional mf ▷ adj (indigenous) indígena; (country) natal; (innate) natural, innato; **a ~ of Russia** un(a) natural mf de Rusia; **Native American** adj, n americano/a indígena, amerindio/a; **native speaker** n hablante mf nativo/a
NATO [ˈneɪtəʊ] n abbr (= North Atlantic Treaty Organization) OTAN f
natural [ˈnætʃrəl] adj natural; **natural gas** n gas m natural; **natural history** n historia natural; **naturally** adv (speak etc) naturalmente; (of course) desde luego, por supuesto; **natural resources** npl recursos mpl naturales
nature [ˈneɪtʃə*] n (also: **N~**) naturaleza; (group, sort) género, clase f; (character) carácter m, genio; **by ~** por or de naturaleza; **nature reserve** n reserva natural
naughty [ˈnɔːtɪ] adj (child) travieso
nausea [ˈnɔːsɪə] n náuseas fpl
naval [ˈneɪvl] adj naval, de marina
navel [ˈneɪvl] n ombligo
navigate [ˈnævɪɡeɪt] vt gobernar ▷ vi navegar; (Aut) ir de copiloto; **navigation** [-ˈɡeɪʃən] n (action) navegación f; (science) náutica
navy [ˈneɪvɪ] n marina de guerra; (ships) armada, flota
Nazi [ˈnɑːtsɪ] n nazi mf
NB abbr (= nota bene) nótese
near [nɪə*] adj (place, relation) cercano; (time) próximo ▷ adv cerca ▷ prep (also: **~ to**: space) cerca de, junto a; (: time) cerca de ▷ vt acercarse a, aproximarse a; **nearby** [nɪəˈbaɪ] adj cercano, próximo ▷ adv cerca; **nearly** adv casi, por poco; **I nearly fell** por poco me caigo; **near-sighted** adj miope, corto de vista
neat [niːt] adj (place) ordenado, bien cuidado; (person) pulcro; (plan) ingenioso; (spirits) solo; **neatly** adv (tidily) con esmero; (skilfully) ingeniosamente
necessarily [ˈnɛsɪsrɪlɪ] adv necesariamente
necessary [ˈnɛsɪsrɪ] adj necesario, preciso
necessity [nɪˈsɛsɪtɪ] n necesidad f
neck [nɛk] n (of person, garment, bottle) cuello; (of animal) pescuezo ▷ vi (inf) besuquearse; **~ and ~** parejos; **necklace** [ˈnɛklɪs] n collar m; **necktie** [ˈnɛktaɪ] n corbata
nectarine [ˈnɛktəriːn] n nectarina
need [niːd] n (lack) escasez f, falta; (necessity) necesidad f ▷ vt (require) necesitar; **I ~ to do it** tengo que or debo hacerlo; **you don't ~ to go** no hace falta que (te) vayas
needle [ˈniːdl] n aguja ▷ vt (fig: inf) picar, fastidiar
needless [ˈniːdlɪs] adj innecesario; **~ to say** huelga decir que
needlework [ˈniːdlwɜːk] n (activity) costura, labor f de aguja
needn't [ˈniːdnt] = **need not**
needy [ˈniːdɪ] adj necesitado
negative [ˈnɛɡətɪv] n (Phot) negativo; (Ling) negación f ▷ adj negativo
neglect [nɪˈɡlɛkt] vt (one's duty) faltar a, no cumplir con; (child) descuidar, desatender; (of house, garden etc) abandono; (of child) desatención f; (of duty)

incumplimiento

negotiate [nɪˈgəʊʃɪeɪt] vt (treaty, loan) negociar; (obstacle) franquear; (bend in road) tomar ▷ vi: **to ~ (with)** negociar (con)

negotiations [nɪgəʊʃɪˈeɪʃənz] pl n negociaciones

negotiator [nɪˈgəʊʃɪeɪtə*] n negociador(a) m/f

neighbour ['neɪbə*] (us **neighbor** etc) n vecino/a; **neighbourhood** n (place) vecindad f, barrio; (people) vecindario; **neighbouring** adj vecino

neither ['naɪðə*] adj ni ▷ conj: **I didn't move and ~ did John** no me he movido, ni Juan tampoco ▷ pron ninguno ▷ adv: **~ good nor bad** ni bueno ni malo; **~ is true** ninguno/a de los(las) dos es cierto/a

neon ['ni:ɔn] n neón m

Nepal [nɪˈpɔ:l] n Nepal m

nephew ['nevju:] n sobrino

nerve [nɜ:v] n (Anat) nervio m; (courage) valor m; (impudence) descaro, frescura (nervousness) nerviosismo msg, nervios mpl; **a fit of ~s** un ataque de nervios

nervous ['nɜ:vəs] adj (anxious, Anat) nervioso; (timid) tímido, miedoso; **nervous breakdown** n crisis f nerviosa

nest [nɛst] n (of bird) nido; (wasps' nest) avispero ▷ vi anidar

net [nɛt] n (gen) red f; (fabric) tul m ▷ adj (Comm) neto, líquido ▷ vt coger (SP) o agarrar (LAM) con red; (Sport) marcar; **netball** n básquet m

Netherlands ['nɛðələndz] npl: **the ~** los Países Bajos

nett [nɛt] adj =**net**

network ['nɛtwɜ:k] n red f

neurotic [njuəˈrɔtɪk] adj neurótico/a

neuter ['nju:tə*] adj (Ling) neutro ▷ vt castrar, capar

neutral ['nju:trəl] adj (person) neutral; (colour etc, Elec) neutro ▷ n (Aut) punto muerto

never ['nɛvə*] adv nunca, jamás; **I ~ went** no fui nunca; **~ in my life** jamás en la vida; see also **mind**; **never-ending** adj interminable, sin fin; **nevertheless** [nɛvəðəˈlɛs] adv sin embargo, no obstante

new [nju:] adj nuevo; (brand new) a estrenar; (recent) reciente; **New Age** n Nueva Era; **newborn** adj recién nacido; **newcomer** ['nju:kʌmə*] n recién venido/a or llegado/a; **newly** adv nuevamente, recién

news [nju:z] n noticias fpl; **a piece of ~** una noticia; **the ~** (Radio, TV) las noticias fpl; **news agency** n agencia de noticias; **newsagent** (BRIT) n vendedor(a) m/f de periódicos; **newscaster** n presentador(a) m/f, locutor(a) m/f; **news dealer** (US) n =**newsagent**; **newsletter** n hoja informativa, boletín m; **newspaper** n periódico, diario; **newsreader** n =**newscaster**

newt [nju:t] n tritón m

New Year n Año Nuevo; **New Year's Day** n Día m de Año Nuevo; **New Year's Eve** n Nochevieja

New Zealand [nju:ˈzi:lənd] n Nueva Zelanda; **New Zealander** n neozelandés/esa m/f

next [nɛkst] adj (house, room) vecino; (bus stop, meeting) próximo; (following: page etc) siguiente ▷ adv después; **the ~ day** el día siguiente; **~ time** la próxima vez; **~ year** el año próximo or que viene; **~ to** junto a, al lado de; **~ to nothing** casi nada; **~ please!** ¡el siguiente!; **next door** adv en la casa de al lado ▷ adj vecino, de al lado; **next-of-kin** n pariente m más cercano

NHS n abbr =**National Health Service**

nibble ['nɪbl] vt mordisquear, mordiscar

nice [naɪs] adj (likeable) simpático; (kind) amable; (pleasant) agradable; (attractive) bonito, lindo (LAM); **nicely** adv amablemente; bien

niche [ni:ʃ] n (Arch) nicho, hornacina

nick [nɪk] n (wound) rasguño; (cut, indentation) mella, muesca ▷ vt (inf) birlar, robar; **in the ~ of time** justo a tiempo

nickel ['nɪkl] n níquel m; (us) moneda de 5 centavos

nickname ['nɪkneɪm] n apodo, mote m ▷ vt apodar

nicotine ['nɪkəti:n] n nicotina

niece [ni:s] n sobrina

Nigeria [naɪˈdʒɪərɪə] n Nigeria

night [naɪt] n noche f; (evening) tarde f; **the ~ before last** anteanoche; **at ~, by ~** de noche, por la noche; **night club** n cabaret m; **nightdress** (BRIT) n camisón m; **nightie** ['naɪtɪ] n =**nightdress**; **nightlife** n vida nocturna; **nightly** adj de todas las noches ▷ adv todas las noches, cada noche; **nightmare** n pesadilla; **night school** n clase(s) f(pl) nocturna(s); **night shift** n turno nocturno or de noche; **night-time** n noche f

nil [nɪl] (BRIT) n (Sport) cero, nada

nine [naɪn] num nueve; **nineteen** num diecinueve, diez y nueve; **nineteenth** [naɪnˈti:nθ] adj decimonoveno, décimonono; **ninetieth** ['naɪntɪɪθ] adj nonagésimo; **ninety** num noventa

ninth [naɪnθ] adj noveno

nip [nɪp] vt (pinch) pellizcar; (bite) morder

nipple ['nɪpl] n (Anat) pezón m

nitrogen ['naɪtrədʒən] n nitrógeno

○ **KEYWORD**

no [nəʊ] (pl **noes**) adv (opposite of "yes") no; **are you coming? - no (I'm not)** ¿vienes? - no; **would you like some more? - no thank you** ¿quieres más? - no gracias ▷ adj (not any): **I have no money/time/books** no tengo dinero/tiempo/libros; **no other man would have done it** ningún otro lo hubiera hecho; **"no entry"** prohibido el paso; **"no smoking"** prohibido fumar

▷ n no m

nobility [nəʊˈbɪlɪtɪ] n nobleza

noble ['nəʊbl] adj noble

nobody ['nəʊbədɪ] pron nadie

nod [nɔd] vi saludar con la cabeza; (in agreement) decir que sí con la cabeza; (doze) dar cabezadas ▷ vt: **to ~ one's head** inclinar la cabeza ▷ n inclinación f de cabeza; **nod off** vi dar cabezadas

noise [nɔɪz] n ruido; (din) escándalo, estrépito; **noisy** adj ruidoso; (child) escandaloso

nominal ['nɔmɪnl] adj (nominal)

nominate ['nɔmɪneɪt] vt (propose) proponer; (appoint) nombrar; **nomination** [nɔmɪˈneɪʃən] n propuesta; nombramiento; **nominee** [-'ni:] n candidato/a

none [nʌn] pron ninguno/a ▷ adv de ninguna manera; **~ of you** ninguno de vosotros; **I've ~ left** no me queda ninguno/a; **he's ~ the worse for it** no le ha hecho ningún mal

nonetheless [nʌnðəˈlɛs] adv sin embargo, no obstante

non-fiction [nɔnˈfɪkʃən] n literatura no novelesca

nonsense ['nɔnsəns] n tonterías fpl, disparates fpl; **~!** ¡qué tonterías!

non: non-smoker n no fumador(a) m/f; **non-smoking** adj (de) no fumador; **non-stick** adj (pan, surface) antiadherente

noodles ['nuːdlz] npl tallarines mpl

noon [nuːn] n mediodía m

no-one ['nəʊwʌn] pron = **nobody**

nor [nɔː*] conj = **neither** ▷ adv see **neither**

norm [nɔːm] n norma

normal ['nɔːml] adj normal; **normally** adv normalmente

north [nɔːθ] n norte m ▷ adj del norte, norteño ▷ adv al o hacia el norte; **North America** n América del Norte; **North American** adj, n norteamericano/a m/f; **northbound** ['nɔːθbaʊnd] adj (traffic) que se dirige al norte; (carriageway) de dirección norte; **northeast** n nor(d)este m; **northeastern** adj nor(d)este, del nor(d)este; **northern** ['nɔːðən] adj norteño, del norte; **Northern Ireland** n Irlanda del Norte; **North Korea** n Corea del Norte; **North Pole** n Polo Norte; **North Sea** n Mar m del Norte; **northwest** n nor(d)oeste m; **northwestern** ['nɔːθ'westən] adj noroeste, del noroeste

Norway ['nɔːweɪ] n Noruega; **Norwegian** [-'wiːdʒən] adj noruego ▷ n noruego/a; (Ling) noruego

nose [nəʊz] n (Anat) nariz f; (Zool) hocico; (sense of smell) olfato ▷ vi: **to ~ about** curiosear; **nosebleed** n hemorragia nasal; **nosey** (inf) adj = **nosy**

nostalgia [nɔs'tældʒɪə] n nostalgia

nostalgic [nɔs'tældʒɪk] adj nostálgico

nostril ['nɔstrɪl] n ventana de la nariz

nosy ['nəʊzɪ] (inf) adj = **nosey**

not [nɔt] adv no; **~ that ...** no es que ...; **it's too late, isn't it?** es demasiado tarde, ¿verdad o no?; **~ yet/now** todavía/ahora no; **why ~?** ¿por qué no?; see also **all**; **only**

notable ['nəʊtəbl] adj notable; **notably** adv especialmente

notch [nɔtʃ] n muesca, corte m

note [nəʊt] n (Mus, record, letter) nota; (banknote) billete m; (tone) tono ▷ vt (observe) notar, observar; (write down) apuntar, anotar; **notebook** n libreta, cuaderno; **noted** ['nəʊtɪd] adj célebre, conocido; **notepad** n bloc m; **notepaper** n papel m para cartas

nothing ['nʌθɪŋ] n nada; (zero) cero; **he does ~** no hace nada; **~ new** nada nuevo; **~ much** no mucho; **for ~** (free) gratis, sin pago; (in vain) en balde

notice ['nəʊtɪs] n (announcement) anuncio; (warning) aviso; (dismissal) despido; (resignation) dimisión f; (period of time) plazo ▷ vt (observe) notar, observar; **to bring sth to sb's ~** (attention) llamar la atención de algn sobre algo; **to take ~ of** tomar nota de, prestar atención a; **at short ~** con poca anticipación; **until further ~** hasta nuevo aviso; **to hand in one's ~** dimitir; **noticeable** adj evidente, obvio

notify ['nəʊtɪfaɪ] vt: **to ~ sb (of sth)** comunicar (algo) a algn

notion ['nəʊʃən] n idea; (opinion) opinión f; **notions** npl (us) mercería

notorious [nəʊ'tɔːrɪəs] adj notorio

notwithstanding [nɔtwɪθ'stændɪŋ] adv no obstante, sin embargo; **~ this** a pesar de esto

nought [nɔːt] n cero

noun [naʊn] n nombre m, sustantivo

nourish ['nʌrɪʃ] vt nutrir; (fig) alimentar; **nourishment** n alimento, sustento

Nov. abbr (= November) nov

novel ['nɔvl] n novela ▷ adj (new) nuevo, original; (unexpected) insólito; **novelist** n novelista mf; **novelty** n novedad f

November [nəʊ'vembə*] n noviembre m

novice ['nɔvɪs] n (Rel) novicio/a

now [naʊ] adv (at the present time) ahora; (these days) actualmente, hoy día ▷ conj: **~ (that)** ya que, ahora que; **right ~** ahora mismo; **by ~** ya; **just ~** ahora mismo; **~ and then, ~ and again** de vez en cuando; **from ~ on** de ahora en adelante; **nowadays** ['naʊədeɪz] adv hoy (en) día, actualmente

nowhere ['nəʊwɛə*] adv (direction) a ninguna parte; (location) en ninguna parte

nozzle ['nɔzl] n boquilla

nr abbr (BRIT) = **near**

nuclear ['njuːklɪə*] adj nuclear

nucleus ['njuːklɪəs] (pl **nuclei**) n núcleo

nude [njuːd] adj, n desnudo/a m/f: **in the ~** desnudo

nudge [nʌdʒ] vt dar un codazo a

nudist ['njuːdɪst] n nudista mf

nudity ['njuːdɪtɪ] n desnudez f

nuisance ['njuːsns] n molestia, fastidio; (person) pesado, latoso; **what a ~!** ¡qué lata!

numb [nʌm] adj: **~ with cold/fear** entumecido por el frío/paralizado de miedo

number ['nʌmbə*] n número; (quantity) cantidad f ▷ vt (pages etc) numerar, poner número a; (amount to) sumar, ascender a; **to be ~ed among** figurar entre; **a ~ of** varios, algunos; **they were ten in ~** eran diez; **number plate** (BRIT) n matrícula, placa; **Number Ten** n (BRIT: 10 Downing Street) residencia del primer ministro

numerical [njuː'merɪkl] adj numérico

numerous ['njuːmərəs] adj numeroso

nun [nʌn] n monja, religiosa

nurse [nɜːs] n enfermero/a; (also: **~maid**) niñera ▷ vt (patient) cuidar, atender

nursery ['nɜːsərɪ] n (institution) guardería infantil; (room) cuarto de los niños; (for plants) criadero, semillero; **nursery rhyme** n canción f infantil; **nursery school** n parvulario, escuela de párvulos; **nursery slope** (BRIT) n (Ski) cuesta para principiantes

nursing ['nɜːsɪŋ] n (profession) profesión f de enfermera; (care) asistencia, cuidado; **nursing home** n clínica de reposo

nurture ['nɜːtʃə*] vt (child, plant) alimentar, nutrir

nut [nʌt] n (Tech) tuerca; (Bot) nuez f

nutmeg ['nʌtmeg] n nuez f moscada

nutrient ['njuːtrɪənt] adj nutritivo ▷ n elemento nutritivo

nutrition [njuː'trɪʃən] n nutrición f, alimentación f

nutritious [njuː'trɪʃəs] adj nutritivo, alimenticio

nuts [nʌts] (inf) adj loco

NVQ n abbr (BRIT) = **National Vocational Qualification**

nylon ['naɪlɔn] n nilón m ▷ adj de nilón

O

oath [əuθ] n juramento; (*swear word*) palabrota; **on** (*BRIT*) **or under ~** bajo juramento

oak [əuk] n roble ▷ *adj* de roble

O.A.P. (*BRIT*) n, *abbr* = **old-age pensioner**

oar [ɔ:*] n remo

oasis [əu'eɪsɪs] (*pl* **oases**) n oasis m *inv*

oath [əuθ] n juramento; (*swear word*) palabrota; **on** (*BRIT*) **or under ~** bajo juramento

oatmeal ['əutmi:l] n harina de avena

oats [əuts] *npl* avena

obedience [ə'bi:dɪəns] n obediencia

obedient [ə'bi:dɪənt] *adj* obediente

obese [əu'bi:s] *adj* obeso

obesity [əu'bi:sɪtɪ] n obesidad f

obey [ə'beɪ] vt obedecer; (*instructions, regulations*) cumplir

obituary [ə'bɪtjuərɪ] n necrología

object [n 'ɒbdʒɪkt, vb əb'dʒɛkt] n objeto; (*purpose*) objeto, propósito; (*Ling*) complemento ▷ vi: **to ~** estar en contra de; (*proposal*) oponerse a; **to ~ that** objetar que; **expense is no ~** no importa cuánto cuesta; **I ~!** ¡yo protesto!; **objection** [əb'dʒɛkʃən] n protesta; **I have no objection to ...** no tengo inconveniente en que ...; **objective** *adj, n* objetivo

obligation [ɒblɪ'ɡeɪʃən] n obligación f; (*debt*) deber m; **without ~** sin compromiso

obligatory [ə'blɪɡətərɪ] *adj* obligatorio

oblige [ə'blaɪdʒ] vt (*do a favour for*) complacer, hacer un favor a; **to ~ sb to do sth** forzar or obligar a algn a hacer algo; **expense is no ~** no importa cuánto **to be ~d to sb for sth** estarle agradecido a algn por algo

oblique [ə'bli:k] *adj* oblicuo; (*allusion*) indirecto

obliterate [ə'blɪtəreɪt] vt borrar

oblivious [ə'blɪvɪəs] *adj*: **~ of** inconsciente de

oblong ['ɒblɒŋ] *adj* rectangular ▷ n rectángulo

obnoxious [əb'nɒkʃəs] *adj* odioso, detestable; (*smell*) nauseabundo

oboe ['əubəu] n oboe m

obscene [əb'si:n] *adj* obsceno

obscure [əb'skjuə*] *adj* oscuro ▷ vt oscurecer; (*hide: sun*) esconder

observant [əb'zə:vnt] *adj* observador(a)

observation [ɒbzə'veɪʃən] n observación f; (*Med*) examen m

observatory [əb'zə:vətrɪ] n observatorio

observe [əb'zə:v] vt observar; (*rule*) cumplir; **observer** n observador(a) m/f

obsess [əb'sɛs] vt obsesionar; **obsession** [əb'sɛʃən] n obsesión f; **obsessive** *adj* obsesivo; obsesionante

obsolete ['ɒbsəli:t] *adj*: **to be ~** estar en desuso

obstacle ['ɒbstəkl] n obstáculo; (*nuisance*) estorbo

obstinate ['ɒbstɪnɪt] *adj* terco, porfiado; (*determined*) obstinado

obstruct [əb'strʌkt] vt obstruir; (*hinder*) estorbar, obstaculizar; **obstruction** [əb'strʌkʃən] n (*action*) obstrucción f; (*object*) estorbo, obstáculo

obtain [əb'teɪn] vt obtener; (*achieve*) conseguir

obvious ['ɒbvɪəs] *adj* obvio, evidente; **obviously** *adv* evidentemente, naturalmente; **obviously not** por supuesto que no

occasion [ə'keɪʒən] n oportunidad f, ocasión f; (*event*) acontecimiento; **occasional** *adj* poco frecuente, ocasional; **occasionally** *adv* de vez en cuando

occult [ɔ'kʌlt] *adj* (*gen*) oculto

occupant ['ɒkjupənt] n (*of house*) inquilino/a; (*of car*) ocupante mf

occupation [ɒkju'peɪʃən] n ocupación f; (*job*) trabajo; (*pastime*) ocupaciones fpl

occupy ['ɒkjupaɪ] vt (*seat, post, time*) ocupar; (*house*) habitar; **to ~ o.s. in doing** pasar el tiempo haciendo

occur [ə'kə:*] vi pasar, suceder; **to ~ to sb** ocurrírsele a algn; **occurrence** [ə'kʌrəns] n acontecimiento; (*existence*) existencia

ocean ['əuʃən] n océano

o'clock [ə'klɒk] *adv*: **it is 5 ~** son las 5

Oct. *abbr* (= *October*) oct

October [ɒk'təubə*] n octubre m

octopus ['ɒktəpəs] n pulpo

odd [ɒd] *adj* extraño, raro; (*number*) impar; (*sock, shoe etc*) suelto; **60-~** 60 y pico; **at ~ times** de vez en cuando; **to be the ~ one out** estar de más; **oddly** *adv* curiosamente, extrañamente; *see also* **enough**; **odds** *npl* (*in betting*) puntos mpl de ventaja; **it makes no odds** da lo mismo; **at odds** reñidos/as; **odds and ends** minucias fpl

odometer [ɔ'dɒmɪtə*] (*us*) n cuentakilómetros m *inv*

odour ['əudə*] (*us* **odor**) n olor m; (*unpleasant*) hedor m

○ KEYWORD

of [ɒv, əv] *prep* **1** (*gen*) de; **a friend of ours** un amigo nuestro; **a boy of 10** un chico de 10 años; **that was kind of you** eso fue muy amable por or de tu parte
2 (*expressing quantity, amount, dates etc*) de; **a kilo of flour** un kilo de harina; **there were three of them** había tres; **three of us went** tres de nosotros fuimos; **the 5th of July** el 5 de julio
3 (*from, out of*) de; **made of wood** (hecho) de madera

off [ɔf] *adj, adv* (*engine*) desconectado; (*light*) apagado; (*tap*) cerrado; (*BRIT: food: bad*) pasado, malo; (*: milk*) cortado; (*cancelled*) cancelado ▷ *prep* de; **to be ~** (*to leave*) irse, marcharse; **to be ~ sick** estar enfermo or de baja; **a day ~** un día libre or sin trabajar; **to have an ~ day** tener un día malo; **he had his coat ~** se había quitado el abrigo; **10% ~** (Comm) (con el) 10% de descuento; **5 km ~ (the road)** a 5 km (de la carretera); **~ the coast** frente a la costa; **I'm ~ meat** (no longer eat/ like it) paso de la carne; **on the ~ chance** por si acaso; **~ and on** de vez en cuando

offence [əˈfɛns] (US **offense**) n (crime) delito; **to take ~ at** ofenderse por

offend [əˈfɛnd] vt (person) ofender; **offender** n delincuente mf

offense [əˈfɛns] (US) n = **offence**

offensive [əˈfɛnsɪv] adj ofensivo; (smell etc) repugnante ▷ n (Mil) ofensiva

offer [ˈɔfə*] n oferta, ofrecimiento; (proposal) propuesta ▷ vt ofrecer; (opportunity) facilitar; **"on ~"** (Comm) "en oferta"

offhand [ɔfˈhænd] adj informal ▷ adv de improviso

office [ˈɔfɪs] n (place) oficina; (room) despacho; (position) carga, oficio; **doctor's ~** (US) consultorio; **to take ~** entrar en funciones; **office block** (US), **office building** n bloque m de oficinas; **office hours** npl horas fpl de oficina; (US Med) horas fpl de consulta

officer [ˈɔfɪsə*] n (Mil) oficial mf; (also: **police ~**) agente mf de policía; (of organization) director(a) m/f

office worker n oficinista mf

official [əˈfɪʃl] adj oficial, autorizado ▷ n funcionario/a, oficial mf

off-licence (BRIT) n (shop) bodega tienda de vinos y bebidas alcohólicas; **off-line** adj, adv (Comput) fuera de línea; **off-peak** adj (electricity) de banda económica; (ticket) billete de precio reducido por viajar fuera de las horas punta; **off-putting** (BRIT) adj (person) asqueroso; (remark) desalentador(a); **off-season** adj, adv fuera de temporada

offset [ˈɔfsɛt] vt contrarrestar, compensar

offshore [ɔfˈʃɔ*] adj (breeze, island) costera; (fishing) de bajura

offside [ˈɔfsaɪd] adj (Sport) fuera de juego; (Aut: in UK) del lado derecho; (: in US, Europe etc) del lado izquierdo

offspring [ˈɔfsprɪŋ] n inv descendencia

often [ˈɔfn] adv a menudo, con frecuencia; **how ~ do you go?** ¿cada cuánto vas?

oh [əu] excl ¡ah!

oil [ɔɪl] n aceite m; (petroleum) petróleo; (for heating) aceite m combustible ▷ vt engrasar; **oil filter** n (Aut) filtro de aceite; **oil painting** n pintura al óleo; **oil refinery** n refinería de petróleo; **oil rig** n torre f de perforación; **oil slick** n marea negra; **oil tanker** n petrolero; (truck) camión m cisterna; **oil well** n pozo (de petróleo); **oily** adj aceitoso; (food) grasiento

ointment [ˈɔɪntmənt] n ungüento

O.K., okay [ˈəuˈkeɪ] excl ¡O.K.!, ¡está bien!, ¡vale! (SP) ▷ adj bien ▷ vt dar el visto bueno a

old [əuld] adj viejo; (former) antiguo; **how ~ are you?** ¿cuántos años tienes?, ¿qué edad tienes?; **he's 10 years ~** tiene 10 años; **~er brother** hermano mayor; **old age** n vejez f; **old-age pension** n (BRIT) jubilación f, pensión f; **old-age pensioner** (BRIT) n jubilado/a; **old-fashioned** adj anticuado, pasado de moda; **old people's home** n (esp BRIT) residencia f de ancianos

olive [ˈɔlɪv] n (fruit) aceituna; (tree) olivo ▷ adj (also: **~-green**) verde oliva; **olive oil** n aceite m de oliva

Olympic [əuˈlɪmpɪk] adj olímpico; **the ~ Games, the ~s** las Olimpiadas

omelet(te) [ˈɔmlɪt] n tortilla francesa (SP), omelette f (LAM)

omen [ˈəumən] n presagio

ominous [ˈɔmɪnəs] adj de mal agüero, amenazador(a)

omit [əuˈmɪt] vt omitir

○ **KEYWORD**

on [ɔn] prep **1** (indicating position) en; sobre; **on the wall** en la pared; **it's on the table** está sobre o en la mesa; **on the left** a la izquierda

2 (indicating means, method, condition etc): **on foot** a pie; **on the train/plane** (go) en tren/avión; (be) en el tren/el avión; **on the radio/television/telephone** por or en la radio/ televisión/al teléfono; **to be on drugs** drogarse; (Med) estar a tratamiento; **to be on holiday/business** estar de vacaciones/en viaje de negocios

3 (referring to time): **on Friday** el viernes; **on Fridays** los viernes; **on June 20th** el 20 de junio; **a week on Friday** del viernes en una semana; **on arrival** al llegar; **on seeing this** al ver esto

4 (about, concerning) sobre, acerca de; **a book on physics** un libro or sobre física

▷ adv **1** (referring to dress): **to have one's coat on** tener or llevar el abrigo puesto; **she put her gloves on** se puso los guantes

2 (referring to covering): **"screw the lid on tightly"** "cerrar bien la tapa"

3 (further, continuously): **to walk etc on** seguir caminando etc

▷ adj **1** (functioning, in operation: machine, radio, TV, light) encendido/a (SP), prendido/a (LAM); (: tap) abierto/a; (: brakes) echado/a, puesto/a; **is the meeting still on?** (in progress) ¿todavía continúa la reunión?; (not cancelled) ¿va a haber reunión al fin?; **there's a good film on at the cinema** ponen una buena película en el cine

2 **that's not on!** (inf: not possible) ¡eso ni hablar!; (: not acceptable) ¡eso no se hace!

once [wʌns] adv una vez; (formerly) antiguamente ▷ conj una vez que; **~ he had left/it was done** una vez que se había marchado/se hizo; **at ~** en seguida, inmediatamente; (simultaneously) a la vez; **~ a week** una vez por semana; **~ more** otra vez; **~ and for all** de una vez por todas; **~ upon a time** érase una vez

oncoming [ˈɔnkʌmɪŋ] adj (traffic) que viene de frente

○ **KEYWORD**

one [wʌn] num uno/una; **one hundred and fifty** ciento cincuenta; **one by one** uno a uno

▷ adj **1** (sole) único; **the one book which** el único libro que; **the one man who** el único que

2 (same) mismo/a; **they came in the one car** vinieron en un solo coche

▷ pron **1** **this one** éste(ésta); **that one** ése(ésa); (more remote) aquél(aquella); **I've already got (a red) one** ya tengo uno/a rojo/a; **one by one** uno/a por uno/a

2 **one another** os (SP), se (: el uno al otro, unos a otros etc); **do you two ever see one another?** ¿vosotros dos os veis alguna vez? (SP), ¿se ven ustedes dos alguna vez?; **the boys didn't dare look at one another** los chicos no se atrevieron a mirarse (el uno al otro); **they all kissed one another** se besaron unos a otros

3 (impers): **one never knows** nunca se sabe; **to cut**

one's finger cortarse el dedo; **one needs to eat** hay que comer

one-off (BRIT: inf) n (event) acontecimiento único

oneself [wʌn'sɛlf] pron (reflexive) se; (after prep) sí; (emphatic) uno/a mismo/a; **to hurt ~** hacerse daño; **to keep sth for ~** guardarse algo; **to talk to ~** hablar solo
one: **one-shot** [wʌn'ʃɔt] (US) n =**one-off**; **one-sided** adj (argument) parcial; **one-to-one** adj (relationship) de dos; **one-way** adj (street) de sentido único

ongoing ['ɔngəʊɪŋ] adj continuo

onion ['ʌnjən] n cebolla

on-line ['ɔnlaɪn] adj, adv (Comput) en línea

onlooker ['ɔnlʊkə*] n espectador(a) m/f

only ['əʊnlɪ] adv solamente, sólo ▷ adj único, solo ▷ conj solamente que, pero; **an ~ child** un hijo único; **not ~ ... but also ...** no sólo ... sino también ...

on-screen [ɔn'skriːn] adj (Comput etc) en pantalla; (romance, kiss) cinematográfico

onset ['ɔnsɛt] n comienzo

onto ['ɔntu] prep = **on to**

onward(s) ['ɔnwəd(z)] adv (move) (hacia) adelante; **from that time ~** desde entonces en adelante

oops [ʊps] excl (also: **~-a-daisy!**) ¡huy!

ooze [uːz] vi rezumar

opaque [əʊ'peɪk] adj opaco

open ['əʊpn] adj abierto; (car) descubierto; (road, view) despejado; (meeting) público; (admiration) manifiesto ▷ vt abrir ▷ vi abrirse; (book etc: commence) comenzar; **in the ~ (air)** al aire libre; **open up** vt abrir; (blocked road) despejar ▷ vi abrirse, empezar; **open-air** al aire libre; **opening** n abertura; (start) comienzo; (opportunity) oportunidad f; **opening hours** npl horario de apertura; **open learning** n enseñanza flexible a tiempo parcial; **openly** adv abiertamente; **open-minded** adj imparcial; **open-necked** adj (shirt) desabrochado, sin corbata; **open-plan** adj: **open-plan office** gran oficina sin particiones; **Open University** n (BRIT) ≈ Universidad f Nacional de Enseñanza a Distancia, UNED f

opera ['ɔpərə] n ópera; **opera house** n teatro de la ópera; **opera singer** n cantante m/f de ópera

operate ['ɔpəreɪt] vt (machine) hacer funcionar; (company) dirigir ▷ vi funcionar; **to ~ on sb** (Med) operar a algn

operating room ['ɔpəreɪtɪŋ-] (US) n quirófano, sala de operaciones

operating theatre (BRIT) n sala de operaciones

operation [ɔpə'reɪʃən] n operación f; (of machine) funcionamiento; **to be in ~** estar funcionando or en funcionamiento; **to have an ~** (Med) ser operado; **operational** adj operacional, en buen estado

operative ['ɔpərətɪv] adj en vigor

operator ['ɔpəreɪtə*] n (of machine) maquinista m/f, operario/a; (Tel) operador(a) m/f, telefonista m/f

opinion [ə'pɪnɪən] n opinión f; **in my ~** en mi opinión, a mi juicio; **opinion poll** n encuesta, sondeo

opponent [ə'pəʊnənt] n adversario/a, contrincante m/f

opportunity [ɔpə'tjuːnɪtɪ] n oportunidad f; **to take the ~ of doing** aprovechar la ocasión para hacer

oppose [ə'pəʊz] vt oponerse a; **to be ~d to sth** oponerse a algo; **as ~d to** a diferencia de

opposite ['ɔpəzɪt] adj opuesto, contrario a; (house etc) de enfrente ▷ adv en frente ▷ prep en frente de, frente a ▷ n lo contrario

opposition [ɔpə'zɪʃən] n oposición f

oppress [ə'prɛs] vt oprimir

opt [ɔpt] vi: **to ~ for** optar por; **to ~ to do** optar por hacer; **opt out** vi: **to opt out of** optar por no hacer

optician [ɔp'tɪʃən] n óptico m/f

optimism ['ɔptɪmɪzəm] n optimismo

optimist ['ɔptɪmɪst] n optimista m/f; **optimistic** [-'mɪstɪk] adj optimista

optimum ['ɔptɪməm] adj óptimo

option ['ɔpʃən] n opción f; **optional** adj facultativo, discrecional

or [ɔː*] conj o; (before o, ho) u; (with negative): **he hasn't seen ~ heard anything** no ha visto ni oído nada; **~ else** si no

oral ['ɔːrəl] adj oral ▷ n examen m oral

orange ['ɔrɪndʒ] n (fruit) naranja ▷ adj color naranja; **orange juice** n jugo m de naranja, zumo m de naranja (SP); **orange squash** n naranjada

orbit ['ɔːbɪt] n órbita ▷ vt, vi orbitar

orchard ['ɔːtʃəd] n huerto

orchestra ['ɔːkɪstrə] n orquesta; (US: seating) platea

orchid ['ɔːkɪd] n orquídea

ordeal [ɔː'diːl] n experiencia horrorosa

order ['ɔːdə*] n orden m; (command) orden f; (good order) buen estado; (Comm) pedido ▷ vt (also: **put in ~**) arreglar, poner en orden; (Comm) pedir; (command) mandar, ordenar; **in ~** en orden; (of document) en regla; **in (working) ~** en funcionamiento; **in ~ to do/that** para hacer/que; **on ~** (Comm) pedido; **to be out of ~** estar desordenado; (not working) no funcionar; **to ~ sb to do sth** mandar a algn hacer algo; **order form** n hoja de pedido; **orderly** n (Mil) ordenanza m; (Med) enfermero/a (auxiliar) ▷ adj ordenado

ordinary ['ɔːdnrɪ] adj corriente, normal; (pej) común y corriente; **out of the ~** fuera de lo común

ore [ɔː*] n mineral m

oregano [ɔrɪ'gɑːnəʊ] n orégano

organ ['ɔːgən] n órgano; **organic** [ɔː'gænɪk] adj orgánico; **organism** n organismo

organization [ɔːgənaɪ'zeɪʃən] n organización f

organize ['ɔːgənaɪz] vt organizar; **organized** ['ɔːgənaɪzd] adj organizado; **organizer** n organizador(a) m/f

orgasm ['ɔːgæzəm] n orgasmo

orgy ['ɔːdʒɪ] n orgía

oriental [ɔːrɪ'ɛntl] adj oriental

orientation [ɔːrɪɛn'teɪʃən] n orientación f

origin ['ɔrɪdʒɪn] n origen m

original [ə'rɪdʒɪnl] adj original; (first) primero; (earlier) primitivo ▷ n original m; **originally** adv al principio

originate [ə'rɪdʒɪneɪt] vi: **to ~ from, to ~ in** surgir de, tener su origen en

Orkneys ['ɔːknɪz] npl: **the ~** (also: **the Orkney Islands**) las Orcadas

ornament ['ɔːnəmənt] n adorno; (trinket) chuchería; **ornamental** [-'mɛntl] adj decorativo, de adorno

ornate [ɔː'neɪt] adj muy ornado, vistoso

orphan ['ɔːfn] n huérfano/a

orthodox ['ɔːθədɔks] adj ortodoxo

orthopaedic [ɔːθə'piːdɪk] (US **orthopedic**) adj ortopédico

osteopath ['ɔstɪəpæθ] n osteópata m/f

ostrich ['ɔstrɪtʃ] n avestruz m

other ['ʌðə*] adj otro ▷ pron: **the ~ (one)** el(la)

otro/a ▷ *adv*: **~ than** aparte de; **otherwise** *adv* de otra manera ▷ *conj* (*if not*) si no

otter ['ɔtə*] *n* nutria

ouch [autʃ] *excl* ¡ay!

ought [ɔːt] (*pt* ~) *aux vb*: **I ~ to do it** debería hacerlo; **this ~ to have been corrected** esto debiera haberse corregido; **he ~ to win** (*probability*) debe or debiera ganar

ounce [auns] *n* onza (28.35g)

our ['auə*] *adj* nuestro; *see also* **my**; **ours** *pron* (el) nuestro/(la) nuestra etc; *see also* **mine¹**; **ourselves** *pron pl* (*reflexive, after prep*) nosotros; (*emphatic*) nosotros mismos; *see also* **oneself**

oust [aust] *vt* desalojar

out [aut] *adv* fuera, afuera; (*not at home*) fuera (de casa); (*light, fire*) apagado; **~ there** allí (fuera); **he's ~** (*absent*) no está, ha salido; **to be ~ in one's calculations** equivocarse en sus cálculos; **to run ~** salir corriendo; **~ loud** en alta voz, **~ of** (*outside*) fuera de; (*because of: anger etc*) por; **~ of petrol** sin gasolina; **"~ of order"** "no funciona"; **outback** *n* interior *m*; **outbound** *adj* (*flight*) de salida; (*flight: not return*) de ida; **outbreak** *n* (*of war*) comienzo *m*; (*of disease*) epidemia; (*of violence etc*) ola; (*of anger etc*) explosión *f*, arranque *m*, paria *m*f; **outcome** *n* resultado; **outcry** *n* protestas *fpl*; **outdated** *adj* anticuado, fuera de moda; **outdoor** *adj* exterior, de aire libre; (*clothes*) de calle; **outdoors** *adv* al aire libre

outer ['autə*] *adj* exterior, externo; **outer space** *n* espacio exterior

outfit ['autfit] *n* (*clothes*) conjunto

out: **outgoing** *adj* (*character*) extrovertido; (*retiring: president etc*) saliente; **outgoings** (BRIT) *npl* gastos *mpl*; **outhouse** *n* dependencia

outing ['autin] *n* excursión *f*, paseo

out: **outlaw** *n* proscrito ▷ *vt* proscribir; **outlay** *n* inversión *f*; **outlet** *n* salida; (*of pipe*) desagüe *m*; (*us Elec*) toma de corriente; (*also*: **retail outlet**) punto de venta; **outline** *n* (*shape*) contorno, perfil *m*; (*sketch, plan*) esbozo ▷ *vt* (*plan etc*) esbozar; **in outline** (*fig*) a grandes rasgos; **outlook** *n* (*fig: prospects*) perspectivas *fpl*; (*: for weather*) pronóstico; **outnumber** *vt* superar en número; **out-of-date** *adj* (*passport*) caducado; (*clothes*) pasado de moda; **out-of-doors** *adv* al aire libre; **out-of-the-way** *adj* apartado; **out-of-town** *adj* (*shopping centre etc*) en las afueras; **outpatient** *n* paciente *m*f externo/a; **outpost** *n* puesto avanzado; **output** *n* (*volumen m de*) producción *m*, rendimiento; (*Comput*) salida

outrage ['autreidʒ] *n* escándalo; (*atrocity*) atrocidad *f* ▷ *vt* ultrajar; **outrageous** [-'reidʒəs] *adj* monstruoso

outright [*adv* aut'rait, *adj* 'autrait] *adv* (*ask, deny*) francamente; (*refuse*) rotundamente; (*win*) de manera absoluta; (*be killed*) en el acto ▷ *adj* franco; rotundo

outset ['autset] *n* principio

outside [aut'said] *n* exterior *m* ▷ *adj* exterior, externo; *adv* fuera ▷ *prep* fuera de; (*beyond*) más allá de; **at the ~** (*fig*) a lo sumo; **outside lane** *n* (*Aut: in Britain*) carril *m* de la derecha; (*: in US, Europe etc*) carril *m* de la izquierda; **outside line** *n* (*Tel*) línea (exterior); **outsider** *n* (*stranger*) extraño, forastero

out: **outsize** *adj* (*clothes*) de talla grande; **outskirts** *npl* alrededores *mpl*, afueras *fpl*; **outspoken** *adj* muy franco; **outstanding** *adj* excepcional, destacado; (*remaining*) pendiente

outward ['autwəd] *adj* externo; (*journey*) de ida;

outwards *adv* (*esp* BRIT) = **outward**

outweigh [aut'wei] *vt* pesar más que

oval ['əuvl] *adj* ovalado ▷ *n* óvalo

ovary ['əuvəri] *n* ovario

oven ['ʌvn] *n* horno; **oven glove** *n* guante *m* para el horno, manopla para el horno; **ovenproof** *adj* resistente al horno; **oven-ready** *adj* listo para el horno

over ['əuvə*] *adv* encima, por encima ▷ *adj or adv* (*finished*) terminado; (*surplus*) de sobra ▷ *prep* (*por*) encima de; (*above*) sobre; (*on the other side of*) al otro lado de; (*more than*) más de; (*during*) durante; **~ here** (*por*) aquí; **~ there** (*por*) allí or allá; **all ~** (*everywhere*) por todas partes; **~ and ~ (again)** una y otra vez; **~ above** además de; **to ask sb ~** invitar a algn a casa; **to bend ~** inclinarse

overall [*adj, n* 'əuvərɔːl, *adv* əuvər'ɔːl] *adj* (*length etc*) total; (*study*) de conjunto ▷ *adv* sobre; (*in general*) en conjunto ▷ *n* (BRIT) guardapolvo; **overalls** *npl* (*boiler suit*) mono (SP) or overol *m* (LAM) (de trabajo)

overboard *adv* (*Naut*) por la borda

overcame [əuvə'keim] *pt of* **overcome**

overcast ['əuvəkɑːst] *adj* encapotado

overcharge [əuvə'tʃɑːdʒ] *vt*: **to ~ sb** cobrar un precio excesivo a algn

overcoat ['əuvəkəut] *n* abrigo, sobretodo

overcome [əuvə'kʌm] *vt* vencer; (*difficulty*) superar

over: **overcrowded** *adj* atestado de gente; (*city, country*) superpoblado; **overdo** (*irreg*) *vt* exagerar; (*overcook*) cocer demasiado; **to overdo it** (*work etc*) pasarse; **overdone** [əuvə'dʌn] *adj* (*vegetables*) recocido; (*steak*) demasiado hecho; **overdose** *n* sobredosis *f inv*; **overdraft** *n* saldo deudor; **overdrawn** [əuvə'drɔːn] *adj* (*account*) en descubierto; **overdue** *adj* retrasado; **overestimate** *vt* sobreestimar

overflow [*vb* əuvə'fləu, *n* 'əuvəfləu] *vi* desbordarse ▷ *n* (*also*: **~ pipe**) (cañería de) desagüe *m*

overgrown [əuvə'grəun] *adj* (*garden*) invadido por la vegetación

overhaul [*vb* əuvə'hɔːl, *n* 'əuvəhɔːl] *vt* revisar, repasar ▷ *n* revisión *f*

overhead [*adv* əuvə'hed, *adj, n* 'əuvəhed] *adv* por arriba or encima; (*cable*) aéreo ▷ *n* (US) = **overheads**; **overhead projector** *n* retroproyector; **overheads** *npl* (*expenses*) gastos *mpl* generales

over: **overhear** (*irreg*) *vt* oír por casualidad; **overheat** *vi* (*engine*) recalentarse; **overland** *adj, adv* por tierra; **overlap** [əuvə'læp] *vi* traslaparse; **overleaf** *adv* al dorso; **overload** *vt* sobrecargar; **overlook** *vt* (*have view of*) dar a, tener vistas a; (*miss: by mistake*) pasar por alto; (*excuse*) perdonar

overnight [əuvə'nait] *adv* durante la noche; (*fig*) de la noche a la mañana ▷ *adj* de noche; **to stay ~** pasar la noche; **overnight bag** *n* fin de semana, neceser *m* de viaje

overpass (US) ['əuvəpɑːs] *n* paso superior

overpower [əuvə'pauə*] *vt* dominar; (*fig*) embargar; **overpowering** *adj* (*heat*) agobiante; (*smell*) penetrante

over: **overreact** [əuvəri'ækt] *vi* reaccionar de manera exagerada; **overrule** *vt* (*decision*) anular; (*claim*) denegar; **overrun** (*irreg*) *vt* (*country*) invadir; (*time limit*) rebasar, exceder

overseas [əuvə'siːz] *adv* (*abroad: live*) en el extranjero; (*travel*) al extranjero ▷ *adj* (*trade*) exterior; (*visitor*) extranjero

oversee [əuvə'si:] (irreg) vt supervisar

overshadow [əuvə'ʃædəu] vt: **to be ~ed by** estar a la sombra de

oversight ['əuvəsaɪt] n descuido

oversleep [əuvə'sli:p] (irreg) vi quedarse dormido

overspend [əuvə'spend] (irreg) vi gastar más de la cuenta; **we have overspent by 5 pounds** hemos excedido el presupuesto en 5 libras

overt [əu'vɜːt] adj abierto

overtake [əuvə'teɪk] (irreg) vt sobrepasar; (BRIT Aut) adelantar

over: overthrow (irreg) vt (government) derrocar; **overtime** n horas fpl extraordinarias

overtook [əuvə'tuk] pt of **overtake**

over: overturn vt volcar; (fig: plan) desbaratar; (: government) derrocar ▷ vi volcar; **overweight** adj demasiado gordo or pesado; **overwhelm** vt aplastar; (emotion) sobrecoger; **overwhelming** adj (victory, defeat) arrollador(a); (feeling) irresistible

ow [au] excl ¡ay!

owe [əu] vt: **to ~ sb sth, to ~ sth to sb** deber algo a algn; **owing to** prep debido a, por causa de

owl [aul] n búho, lechuza

own [əun] vt tener, poseer ▷ adj propio; **a room of my ~** una habitación propia; **to get one's ~ back** tomar revancha; **on one's ~** solo, a solas; **own up** vi confesar; **owner** n dueño/a; **ownership** n posesión f

ox [ɔks] (pl ~en) n buey m

Oxbridge ['ɔksbrɪdʒ] n universidades de Oxford y Cambridge

oxen ['ɔksən] npl of **ox**

oxygen ['ɔksɪdʒən] n oxígeno

oyster ['ɔɪstə*] n ostra

oz. abbr = **ounce(s)**

ozone ['əuzəun] n ozono; **ozone friendly** adj que no daña la capa de ozono; **ozone layer** n capa f de ozono

P

p [pi:] abbr = **penny; pence**

P.A. n abbr = **personal assistant; public address system**

p.a. abbr = **per annum**

pace [peɪs] n paso ▷ vi: **to ~ up and down** pasearse de un lado a otro; **to keep ~ with** llevar el mismo paso que; **pacemaker** n (Med) regulador m cardíaco, marcapasos m inv; (Sport: also: **pacesetter**) liebre f

Pacific [pə'sɪfɪk] n: **the ~ (Ocean)** el (Océano) Pacífico

pacifier ['pæsɪfaɪə*] (us) n (dummy) chupete m

pack [pæk] n (packet) paquete m; (of hounds) jauría; (of people) manada, bando; (of cards) baraja; (bundle) fardo; (us: of cigarettes) paquete m; (back pack) mochila ▷ vt (fill) llenar; (in suitcase etc) meter, poner; (cram) llenar, atestar; **to ~ (one's bags)** hacerse la maleta; **to ~ sb off** despachar a algn; **pack in** vi (watch, car) estropearse ▷ vt (inf) dejar; **pack it in!** ¡para!, ¡basta ya!; **pack up** vi (inf: machine) estropearse; (person) irse ▷ vt (belongings, clothes) recoger; (goods, presents) empaquetar, envolver

package ['pækɪdʒ] n paquete m; (bulky) bulto; (also: ~ deal) acuerdo global; **package holiday** n vacaciones fpl organizadas; **package tour** n viaje m organizado

packaging ['pækɪdʒɪŋ] n envase m

packed [pækt] adj abarrotado; **packed lunch** n almuerzo frío

packet ['pækɪt] n paquete m

packing ['pækɪŋ] n embalaje m

pact [pækt] n pacto

pad [pæd] n (of paper) bloc m; (cushion) cojinete m; (inf: home) casa ▷ vt rellenar; **padded** adj (jacket) acolchado; (bra) reforzado

paddle ['pædl] n (oar) canalete m; (us: for table tennis) paleta ▷ vt impulsar con canalete ▷ vi (with feet) chapotear; **paddling pool** (BRIT) n estanque m de juegos

paddock ['pædək] n corral m

padlock ['pædlɔk] n candado

paedophile ['pi:dəufaɪl] (us pedophile) adj de pedófilos ▷ n pedófilo/a

page [peɪdʒ] n (of book) página; (of newspaper) plana; (also: ~ boy) paje m ▷ vt (in hotel etc) llamar por altavoz a

pager ['peɪdʒə*] n (Tel) busca m

paid [peɪd] pt, pp of **pay** ▷ adj (work) remunerado; (holiday) pagado; (official etc) a sueldo; **to put ~ to** (BRIT) acabar con

pain [peɪn] n dolor m; **to be in ~** sufrir; **to take ~s to do sth** tomarse grandes molestias en hacer algo; **painful** adj doloroso; (difficult) penoso; (disagreeable) desagradable; **painkiller** n analgésico; **painstaking** ['peɪnzteɪkɪŋ] adj (person) concienzudo, esmerado

paint [peɪnt] n pintura ▷ vt pintar; **to ~ the door blue** pintar la puerta de azul; **paintbrush** n (of artist) pincel m; (of decorator) brocha; **painter** n pintor(a) m/f; **painting** n pintura

pair [peə*] n (of shoes, gloves etc) par m; (of people) pareja; **a ~ of scissors** unas tijeras; **a ~ of trousers** unos pantalones, un pantalón

pajamas [pə'dʒɑːməz] (US) npl pijama m

Pakistan [pɑːkɪ'stɑːn] n Paquistán m; **Pakistani** adj, n paquistaní m

pal [pæl] (inf) n compinche mf, compañero/a

palace ['pæləs] n palacio

pale [peɪl] adj (gen) pálido; (colour) claro ▷ n: **to be beyond the ~** pasarse de la raya

Palestine ['pælɪstaɪn] n Palestina; **Palestinian** [-'tɪnɪən] adj, n palestino/a m/f

palm [pɑːm] n (Anat) palma; (also: **~ tree**) palmera, palma ▷ vt: **to ~ sth off on sb** (inf) encajar algo a algn

pamper ['pæmpə*] vt mimar

pamphlet ['pæmflət] n folleto

pan [pæn] n (also: **sauce~**) cacerola, cazuela, olla; (also: **frying~**) sartén f

pancake ['pænkeɪk] n crepe f

panda ['pændə] n panda m

pane [peɪn] n cristal m

panel ['pænl] n (of wood etc) panel m; (Radio, TV) panel m de invitados

panhandler ['pænhændlə*] (US) (inf) mendigo/a

panic ['pænɪk] n terror m pánico ▷ vi dejarse llevar por el pánico

panorama [pænə'rɑːmə] n panorama m

pansy ['pænzɪ] n (Bot) pensamiento; (inf, pej) maricón m

pant [pænt] vi jadear

panther ['pænθə*] n pantera

panties ['pæntɪz] npl bragas fpl, pantis mpl

pantomime ['pæntəmaɪm] (BRIT) n revista musical representada en Navidad, basada en cuentos de hadas

pants [pænts] n (BRIT: underwear: woman's) bragas fpl; (: man's) calzoncillos mpl; (US: trousers) pantalones mpl

paper ['peɪpə*] n papel m; (also: **news~**) periódico, diario; (academic essay) ensayo; (exam) examen m ▷ adj de papel ▷ vt empapelar, tapizar (MEX); **papers** npl (also: **identity ~s**) papeles mpl, documentos mpl; **paperback** n libro en rústica; **paper bag** n bolsa de papel; **paper clip** n clip m; **paper shop** (BRIT) n tienda de periódicos; **paperwork** n trabajo administrativo

paprika ['pæprɪkə] n pimentón m

par [pɑː*] n par f; (Golf) par m; **to be on a ~ with** estar a la par con

paracetamol [pærə'siːtəmɔl] (BRIT) n paracetamol m

parachute ['pærəʃuːt] n paracaídas m inv

parade [pə'reɪd] n desfile m ▷ vt (show) hacer alarde de ▷ vi desfilar; (Mil) pasar revista

paradise ['pærədaɪs] n paraíso

paradox ['pærədɔks] n paradoja

paraffin ['pærəfɪn] (BRIT) n (also: **~ oil**) parafina

paragraph ['pærəgrɑːf] n párrafo

parallel ['pærəlɛl] adj en paralelo; (fig) semejante ▷ n (line) paralelo; (fig, Geo) paralelo

paralysed ['pærəlaɪzd] adj paralizado

paralysis [pə'rælɪsɪs] n parálisis f inv

paramedic [pærə'mɛdɪk] n auxiliar m/f sanitario/a

paranoid ['pærənɔɪd] adj (person, feeling) paranoico

parasite ['pærəsaɪt] n parásito/a

parcel ['pɑːsl] n paquete m ▷ vt (also: **~ up**) empaquetar, embalar

pardon ['pɑːdn] n (Law) indulto ▷ vt perdonar; **~ me!, I beg your ~!** (I'm sorry!) ¡perdone usted!; **(I beg your) ~?, ~ me?** (US: what did you say?) ¿cómo?

parent ['pɛərənt] n (mother) madre f; (father) padre m; **parents** npl padres mpl; **parental** [pə'rɛntl] adj paternal/maternal

Paris ['pærɪs] n París

parish ['pærɪʃ] n parroquia

Parisian [pə'rɪzɪən] adj, n parisiense mf

park [pɑːk] n parque m ▷ vt aparcar, estacionar ▷ vi aparcar, estacionarse

parking ['pɑːkɪŋ] n aparcamiento, estacionamiento; **"no ~"** prohibido estacionarse"; **parking lot** (US) n parking m; **parking meter** n parquímetro; **parking ticket** n multa de aparcamiento

parkway ['pɑːkweɪ] (US) n alameda

parliament ['pɑːləmənt] n parlamento; (Spanish) Cortes fpl; **parliamentary** [-'mɛntərɪ] adj parlamentario

Parmesan [pɑːmɪ'zæn] n (also: **~ cheese**) queso parmesano

parole [pə'rəul] n: **on ~** libre bajo palabra

parrot ['pærət] n loro, papagayo

parsley ['pɑːslɪ] n perejil m

parsnip ['pɑːsnɪp] n chirivía

parson ['pɑːsn] n cura m

part [pɑːt] n (gen, Mus) parte f; (bit) trozo; (of machine) pieza; (Theatre etc) papel m; (of serial) entrega; (us: in hair) raya ▷ adv = **partly** ▷ vt separar ▷ vi (people) separarse; (crowd) apartarse; **to take ~ in** tomar parte or participar en; **to take sth in good ~** tomar algo en buena parte; **to take sb's ~** defender a algn; **for my ~** por mi parte; **for the most ~** en su mayor parte; **to ~ one's hair** hacerse la raya; **part with** vt fus ceder, entregar; (money) pagar; **part of speech** n parte f de la oración, categoría f gramatical

partial ['pɑːʃl] adj parcial; **to be ~ to** ser aficionado a

participant [pɑː'tɪsɪpənt] n (in competition) concursante mf; (in campaign etc) participante mf

participate [pɑː'tɪsɪpeɪt] vi: **to ~ in** participar en

particle ['pɑːtɪkl] n partícula; (of dust) grano

particular [pə'tɪkjulə*] adj (special) especial; (concrete) concreto; (given) determinado; (fussy) quisquilloso; (demanding) exigente; **in ~** en particular; **particularly** adv (in particular) sobre todo; (difficult, good etc) especialmente; **particulars** npl (information) datos mpl; (details) pormenores mpl

parting ['pɑːtɪŋ] n (act) separación f; (farewell) despedida; (BRIT: in hair) raya ▷ adj de despedida

partition [pɑː'tɪʃən] n (Pol) división f; (wall) tabique m

partly ['pɑːtlɪ] adv en parte

partner ['pɑːtnə*] n (Comm) socio/a; (Sport, at dance) pareja; (spouse) cónyuge mf; (lover) compañero/a; **partnership** n asociación f; (Comm) sociedad f

partridge ['pɑːtrɪdʒ] n perdiz f

part-time ['pɑːt'taɪm] adj, adv a tiempo parcial
party ['pɑːtɪ] n (Pol) partido; (celebration) fiesta; (group) grupo; (Law) parte f interesada ▷ cpd (Pol) de partido
pass [pɑːs] vt (time, object) pasar; (place) pasar por; (overtake) rebasar; (exam) aprobar; (approve) aprobar ▷ vi pasar; (Scol) aprobar, ser aprobado ▷ n (permit) permiso; (membership card) carnet m; (in mountains) puerto, desfiladero; (Sport) pase m; (Scol: also: ~ mark): **to get a ~ in** aprobar en; **to ~ sth through sth** pasar algo por algo; **to make a ~ at sb** (inf) hacer proposiciones a algn; **pass away** vi fallecer; **pass by** vi pasar ▷ vt (ignore) pasar por alto; **pass on** vt transmitir; **pass out** vi desmayarse; **pass over** vi, vt omitir, pasar por alto; **pass up** vt (opportunity) renunciar a; **passable** adj (road) transitable; (tolerable) pasable
passage ['pæsɪdʒ] n (also: ~way) pasillo; (act of passing) tránsito; (fare, in book) pasaje m; (by boat) travesía; (Anat) tubo
passenger ['pæsɪndʒə*] n pasajero/a, viajero/a
passer-by [pɑːsə'baɪ] n transeúnte mf
passing place n (Aut) apartadero
passion ['pæʃən] n pasión f; **passionate** adj apasionado; **passion fruit** n fruta de la pasión, granadilla
passive ['pæsɪv] adj (gen, also Ling) pasivo
passport ['pɑːspɔːt] n pasaporte m; **passport control** n control m de pasaporte; **passport office** n oficina de pasaportes
password ['pɑːswɜːd] n contraseña
past [pɑːst] prep (in front of) por delante de; (further than) más allá de; (later than) después de ▷ adj pasado; (president etc) antiguo ▷ n (time) pasado; (of person) antecedentes mpl; **he's ~ forty** tiene más de cuarenta años; **ten/quarter ~ eight** las ocho y diez/cuarto; **for the ~ few/3 days** durante los últimos días/últimos 3 días; **to run ~ sb** pasar a algn corriendo
pasta ['pæstə] n pasta
paste [peɪst] n pasta; (glue) engrudo ▷ vt pegar
pastel ['pæstl] adj pastel; (painting) al pastel
pasteurized ['pæstəraɪzd] adj pasteurizado
pastime ['pɑːstaɪm] n pasatiempo
pastor ['pɑːstə*] n pastor m
past participle [-'pɑːtɪsɪpl] n (Ling) participio m (de) pasado o (de) pretérito o pasivo
pastry ['peɪstrɪ] n (dough) pasta; (cake) pastel m
pasture ['pɑːstʃə*] n pasto
pasty¹ ['pæstɪ] n empanada
pasty² ['peɪstɪ] adj (complexion) pálido
pat [pæt] vt dar una palmadita a; (dog etc) acariciar
patch [pætʃ] n (of material, eye patch) parche m; (mended part) remiendo; (of land) terreno ▷ vt remendar; **(to go through) a bad ~** (pasar por) una mala racha; **patchy** adj desigual
pâté ['pæteɪ] n paté m
patent ['peɪtnt] n patente f ▷ vt patentar ▷ adj patente, evidente
paternal [pə'tɜːnl] adj paternal; (relation) paterno
paternity leave [pə'tɜːnɪtɪ-] n permiso m por paternidad, licencia por paternidad
path [pɑːθ] n camino, sendero; (trail, track) pista; (of missile) trayectoria
pathetic [pə'θetɪk] adj patético, lastimoso; (very bad) malísimo
pathway ['pɑːθweɪ] n sendero, vereda

patience ['peɪʃns] n paciencia; (BRIT Cards) solitario
patient ['peɪʃnt] n paciente mf ▷ adj paciente, sufrido
patio ['pætɪəʊ] n patio
patriotic [pætrɪ'ɒtɪk] adj patriótico
patrol [pə'trəʊl] n patrulla ▷ vt patrullar por; **patrol car** n coche m patrulla
patron ['peɪtrən] n (in shop) cliente mf; (of charity) patrocinador/a m/f; **~ of the arts** mecenas m
patronizing ['pætrənaɪzɪŋ] adj condescendiente
pattern ['pætən] n (Sewing) patrón m; (design) dibujo; **patterned** adj (material) estampado
pause [pɔːz] n pausa ▷ vi hacer una pausa
pave [peɪv] vt pavimentar; **to ~ the way for** preparar el terreno para
pavement ['peɪvmənt] n (BRIT) acera, banqueta (MEX), andén m (CAM), vereda (SC)
pavilion [pə'vɪljən] n (BRIT) caseta
paving ['peɪvɪŋ] n pavimento, enlosado
paw [pɔː] n pata
pawn [pɔːn] n (Chess) peón m; (fig) instrumento ▷ vt empeñar; **pawn broker** n prestamista mf
pay [peɪ] (pt, pp paid) n (wage etc) sueldo, salario ▷ vt pagar ▷ vi (be profitable) rendir; **to ~ attention (to)** prestar atención (a); **to ~ sb a visit** hacer una visita a algn; **to ~ one's respects to sb** presentar sus respetos a algn; **pay back** vt (money) reembolsar; (person) pagar; **pay for** vt fus pagar; **pay in** vt ingresar; **pay off** vt saldar ▷ vi (scheme, decision) dar resultado; **pay out** vt (money) gastar, desembolsar; **pay up** vt pagar (de mala gana); **payable** adj: **payable to** pagadero a; **pay day** n día m de paga; **pay envelope** (US) n =**pay packet**; **payment** n pago; **monthly payment** mensualidad f; **pay phone** n pago; (in competition) premio en metálico; **pay packet** (BRIT) n sobre m (de paga); **pay phone** n teléfono público; **payroll** n nómina; **pay slip** n recibo de sueldo; **pay television** n televisión f de pago
PC n abbr = **personal computer**; (BRIT) (= police constable) policía mf ▷ adv abbr = **politically correct**
p.c. abbr = **per cent**
PDA n abbr (= personal digital assistant) agenda electrónica
PE n abbr (= physical education) ed. física
pea [piː] n guisante m (SP), arveja (LAM), chícharo (MEX, CAM)
peace [piːs] n paz f; (calm) paz f, tranquilidad f; **peaceful** adj (gentle) pacífico; (calm) tranquilo, sosegado
peach [piːtʃ] n melocotón m (SP), durazno (LAM)
peacock ['piːkɒk] n pavo real
peak [piːk] n (of mountain) cumbre f, cima; (of cap) visera; (fig) cumbre f; **peak hours** npl horas fpl punta
peanut ['piːnʌt] n cacahuete m (SP), maní m (LAM), cacahuate m (MEX, CAM); **peanut butter** n manteca de cacahuete o maní
pear [pɛə*] n pera
pearl [pɜːl] n perla
peasant ['peznt] n campesino/a
peat [piːt] n turba
pebble ['pebl] n guijarro
peck [pek] vt (also: ~ at) picotear ▷ n picotazo; (kiss) besito; **peckish** (BRIT: inf) adj: **I feel peckish** tengo ganas de picar algo
peculiar [pɪ'kjuːlɪə*] adj (odd) extraño, raro; (typical) propio, característico; **~ to** propio de
pedal ['pedl] n pedal m ▷ vi pedalear

pedalo ['pedǝlǝu] n patín m a pedal

pedestal ['pedǝstl] n pedestal m

pedestrian [pɪ'destrɪǝn] n peatón/ona m/f ⊳ adj pedestre; **pedestrian crossing** (BRIT) n paso de peatones; **pedestrianized** adj: **a pedestrianized street** una calle peatonal; **pedestrian precinct** (US **pedestrian zone**) n zona peatonal

pedigree ['pedɪgriː] n genealogía; (of animal) raza, pedigrí m ⊳ cpd (animal) de raza, de casta

pedophile ['piːdǝufaɪl] (US) = **paedophile**

pee [piː] (inf) vi mear

peek [piːk] vi mirar a hurtadillas

peel [piːl] n piel f; (of orange, lemon) cáscara; (: removed) peladuras fpl ⊳ vt pelar ⊳ vi (paint etc) desconcharse; (wallpaper) despegarse, desprenderse; (skin) pelar

peep [piːp] n (BRIT: look) mirada furtiva; (sound) pío ⊳ vi (BRIT: look) mirar furtivamente

peer [pɪǝ*] vi: **to ~ at** esduriñar ⊳ n (noble) par m; (equal) igual m; (contemporary) contemporáneo/a

peg [peg] n (for coat etc) gancho, colgadero; (BRIT: also: **clothes ~**) pinza

pelican ['pelɪkǝn] n pelícano; **pelican crossing** (BRIT) n (Aut) paso de peatones señalizado

pelt [pelt] vt: **to ~ sb with sth** arrojarle algo a algn ⊳ vi (rain) llover a cántaros; (inf: run) correr ⊳ n pellejo

pelvis ['pelvɪs] n pelvis f

pen [pen] n (fountain pen) pluma; (ballpoint pen) bolígrafo; (for sheep) redil m

penalty ['penltɪ] n (gen) pena; (fine) multa

pence [pens] npl of **penny**

pencil ['pensl] n lápiz m; **pencil in** vt (appointment) apuntar con carácter provisional; **pencil case** n estuche m; **pencil sharpener** n sacapuntas m inv

pendant ['pendnt] n pendiente m

pending ['pendɪŋ] prep antes de ⊳ adj pendiente

penetrate ['penɪtreɪt] vt penetrar

penfriend ['penfrend] (BRIT) n amigo/a por carta

penguin ['peŋgwɪn] n pingüino

penicillin [penɪ'sɪlɪn] n penicilina

peninsula [pǝ'nɪnsjulǝ] n península

penis ['piːnɪs] n pene m

penitentiary [penɪ'tenʃǝrɪ] (US) n cárcel f, presidio

penknife ['pennaɪf] n navaja

penniless ['penɪlɪs] adj sin dinero

penny ['penɪ] n (pl **pennies** or **pence**) (BRIT) n penique m; (US) centavo

penpal ['penpæl] n amigo/a por carta

pension ['penʃǝn] n (state benefit) jubilación f; **pensioner** (BRIT) n jubilado/a

pentagon ['pentǝgǝn] (US) n: **the P~** (Pol) el Pentágono

penthouse ['penthaus] n ático de lujo

penultimate [pe'nʌltɪmǝt] adj penúltimo

people ['piːpl] npl gente f; (citizens) pueblo, ciudadanos mpl; (Pol): **the ~** el pueblo ⊳ n (nation, race) pueblo, nación f; **several ~ came** vinieron varias personas; **~ say that ...** dice la gente que ...

pepper ['pepǝ*] n (spice) pimienta; (vegetable) pimiento ⊳ vt: **to ~ with** (fig) salpicar de; **peppermint** n (sweet) pastilla de menta

per [pǝː*] prep por; **~ day/~son** por día/persona; **~ annum** al año

perceive [pǝ'siːv] vt percibir; (realize) darse cuenta de

per cent n por ciento

percentage [pǝ'sentɪdʒ] n porcentaje m

perception [pǝ'sepʃǝn] n percepción f; (insight)

perspicacia; (opinion etc) opinión f

perch [pǝːtʃ] n (fish) perca; (for bird) percha ⊳ vi: **to ~ (on)** (bird) posarse (en); (person) encaramarse (en)

percussion [pǝ'kʌʃǝn] n percusión f

perfect [adj, n 'pǝːfɪkt, vb pǝ'fekt] adj perfecto ⊳ n (also: **~ tense**) perfecto ⊳ vt perfeccionar; **perfection** [pǝ'fekʃǝn] n perfección f; **perfectly** ['pǝːfɪktlɪ] adv perfectamente

perform [pǝ'fɔːm] vt (carry out) realizar, llevar a cabo; (Theatre) representar; (piece of music) interpretar ⊳ vi (well, badly) funcionar; **performance** n (of a play) representación f; (of actor, athlete etc) actuación f; (of car, engine, company) rendimiento; (of economy) resultados mpl; **performer** n (actor) actor m, actriz f

perfume ['pǝːfjuːm] n perfume m

perhaps [pǝ'hæps] adv quizá(s), tal vez

perimeter [pǝ'rɪmɪtǝ*] n perímetro

period ['pɪǝrɪǝd] n período; (Scol) clase f; (full stop) punto; (Med) regla ⊳ adj (costume, furniture) de época; **periodical** [pɪǝrɪ'ɔdɪkl] n periódico; **periodically** adv de vez en cuando, cada cierto tiempo

perish ['perɪʃ] vi perecer; (decay) echarse a perder

perjury ['pǝːdʒǝrɪ] n (Law) perjurio

perk [pǝːk] n extra m

perm [pǝːm] n permanente f

permanent ['pǝːmǝnǝnt] adj permanente; **permanently** adv (lastingly) para siempre, de modo definitivo; (all the time) permanentemente

permission [pǝ'mɪʃǝn] n permiso

permit [n pǝ'mɪt, vt pǝ'mɪt] n permiso, licencia ⊳ vt permitir

perplex [pǝ'pleks] vt dejar perplejo

persecute ['pǝːsɪkjuːt] vt perseguir

persecution [pǝːsɪ'kjuːʃǝn] n persecución f

persevere [pǝːsɪ'vɪǝ*] vi persistir

Persian ['pǝːʃǝn] adj, n persa mf; **the ~ Gulf** el Golfo Pérsico

persist [pǝ'sɪst] vi: **to ~ (in doing sth)** persistir (en hacer algo); **persistent** adj persistente; (determined) porfiado

person ['pǝːsn] n persona; **in ~** en persona; **personal** adj personal; individual; (in person) en persona; **personal assistant** n ayudante mf personal; **personal computer** n ordenador m personal; **personality** [-'næltɪ] n personalidad f; **personally** adv personalmente; (in person) en persona; **to take sth personally** tomarse algo a mal; **personal organizer** n agenda; **personal stereo** n Walkman® m

personnel [pǝːsǝ'nel] n personal m

perspective [pǝ'spektɪv] n perspectiva

perspiration [pǝːspɪ'reɪʃǝn] n transpiración f

persuade [pǝ'sweɪd] vt: **to ~ sb to do sth** persuadir a algn para que haga algo

persuasion [pǝ'sweɪʒǝn] n persuasión f; (persuasiveness) persuasiva

persuasive [pǝ'sweɪsɪv] adj persuasivo

perverse [pǝ'vǝːs] adj perverso; (wayward) travieso

pervert [n 'pǝːvǝːt, vb pǝ'vǝːt] n pervertido/a ⊳ vt pervertir; (truth, sb's words) tergiversar

pessimism ['pesɪmɪzǝm] n pesimismo

pessimist ['pesɪmɪst] n pesimista mf; **pessimistic** [-'mɪstɪk] adj pesimista

pest [pest] n (insect) insecto nocivo; (fig) lata, molestia

pester ['pestǝ*] vt molestar, acosar

pesticide ['pestɪsaɪd] n pesticida m

pet [pet] *n* animal *m* doméstico ▷ *cpd* favorito ▷ *vt* acariciar; **teacher's ~** favorito/a (del profesor); **~ hate** manía

petal ['petl] *n* pétalo

petite [pə'tiːt] *adj* chiquita

petition [pə'tɪʃən] *n* petición *f*

petrified ['petrɪfaɪd] *adj* horrorizado

petrol ['petrəl] (BRIT) *n* gasolina

petroleum [pə'trəʊlɪəm] *n* petróleo

petrol: petrol pump (BRIT) *n* (*in garage*) surtidor *m* de gasolina; **petrol station** (BRIT) *n* gasolinera; **petrol tank** (BRIT) *n* depósito (de gasolina)

petticoat ['petɪkəʊt] *n* enaguas *fpl*

petty ['petɪ] *adj* (*mean*) mezquino; (*unimportant*) insignificante

pew [pjuː] *n* banco

pewter ['pjuːtə*] *n* peltre *m*

phantom ['fæntəm] *n* fantasma *m*

pharmacist ['fɑːməsɪst] *n* farmacéutico/a

pharmacy ['fɑːməsɪ] *n* farmacia

phase [feɪz] *n* fase *f*; **phase in** *vt* introducir progresivamente; **phase out** *vt* (*machinery, product*) retirar progresivamente; (*job, subsidy*) eliminar por etapas

Ph.D. *abbr* = **Doctor of Philosophy**

pheasant ['feznt] *n* faisán *m*

phenomena [fə'nɒmɪnə] *npl of* **phenomenon**

phenomenal [fɪ'nɒmɪnl] *adj* fenomenal, extraordinario

phenomenon [fə'nɒmɪnən] (*pl* **phenomena**) *n* fenómeno

Philippines ['fɪlɪpiːnz] *npl*: **the ~** las Filipinas

philosopher [fɪ'lɒsəfə*] *n* filósofo/a

philosophical [fɪlə'sɒfɪkl] *adj* filosófico

philosophy [fɪ'lɒsəfɪ] *n* filosofía

phlegm [flem] *n* flema

phobia ['fəʊbjə] *n* fobia

phone [fəʊn] *n* teléfono ▷ *vt, vi* telefonear, llamar por teléfono; **to be on the ~** tener teléfono; (*be calling*) estar hablando por teléfono; **phone back** *vt, vi* volver a llamar; **phone up** *vt, vi* llamar por teléfono; **phone book** *n* guía telefónica; **phone booth** *n* cabina telefónica; **phone box** (BRIT) *n* = **phone booth**; **phone call** *n* llamada (telefónica); **phonecard** *n* teletarjeta; **phone number** *n* número de teléfono

phonetics [fə'netɪks] *n* fonética

phoney ['fəʊnɪ] *adj* falso

photo ['fəʊtəʊ] *n* foto *f*; **photo album** *n* álbum *m* de fotos; **photocopier** *n* fotocopiadora; **photocopy** *n* fotocopia ▷ *vt* fotocopiar

photograph ['fəʊtəgrɑːf] *n* fotografía ▷ *vt* fotografiar; **photographer** [fə'tɒgrəfə*] *n* fotógrafo; **photography** [fə'tɒgrəfɪ] *n* fotografía

phrase [freɪz] *n* frase *f* ▷ *vt* expresar; **phrase book** *n* libro de frases

physical ['fɪzɪkl] *adj* físico; **physical education** *n* educación *f* física; **physically** *adv* físicamente

physician [fɪ'zɪʃən] *n* médico/a

physicist ['fɪzɪsɪst] *n* físico/a

physics ['fɪzɪks] *n* física

physiotherapist [fɪzɪəʊ'θerəpɪst] *n* fisioterapeuta

physiotherapy [fɪzɪəʊ'θerəpɪ] *n* fisioterapia

physique [fɪ'ziːk] *n* físico

pianist ['pɪənɪst] *n* pianista *mf*

piano [pɪ'ænəʊ] *n* piano

pick [pɪk] *n* (*tool: also*: **~-axe**) pico, piqueta ▷ *vt*

(*select*) elegir, escoger; (*gather*) coger (SP), recoger; (*remove, take out*) sacar, quitar; (*lock*) abrir con ganzúa; **take your ~** escoja lo que quiera; **the ~ of** lo mejor de; **to ~ one's nose/teeth** hurgarse las narices/limpiarse los dientes; **to ~ a quarrel with sb** meterse con algn; **pick on** *vt fus* (*person*) meterse con; **pick out** *vt* escoger; (*distinguish*) identificar; **pick up** *vi* (*improve: sales*) ir mejor; (: *patient*) reponerse; (*Finance*) recobrarse ▷ *vt* recoger; (*learn*) aprender; (*Police: arrest*) detener; (*person: for sex*) ligar; (*Radio*) captar; **to pick up speed** acelerarse; **to pick o.s. up** levantarse

pickle ['pɪkl] *n* (*also*: **~s**: *as condiment*) escabeche *m*; (*fig: mess*) apuro ▷ *vt* encurtir

pickpocket ['pɪkpɒkɪt] *n* carterista *mf*

pick-up ['pɪkʌp] *n* (*also*: **~ truck**) furgoneta, camioneta

picnic ['pɪknɪk] *n* merienda ▷ *vi* ir de merienda; **picnic area** *n* zona de picnic; (*Aut*) área de descanso

picture ['pɪktʃə*] *n* cuadro; (*painting*) pintura; (*photograph*) fotografía; (*TV*) imagen *f*; (*film*) película; (*fig: description*) descripción *f*; (: *situation*) situación *f* ▷ *vt* (*imagine*) imaginar; **pictures** *npl*: **the ~s** (BRIT) el cine; **picture frame** *n* marco; **picture messaging** *n* (envío de) mensajes con imágenes

picturesque [pɪktʃə'resk] *adj* pintoresco

pie [paɪ] *n* pastel *m*; (*open*) tarta; (*small: of meat*) empanada

piece [piːs] *n* pedazo, trozo; (*of cake*) trozo; (*item*): **a ~ of clothing/furniture/advice** una prenda (de vestir)/ un mueble/un consejo ▷ *vt*: **to ~ together** juntar; (*Tech*) armar; **to take to ~s** desmontar

pie chart *n* gráfico de sectores or tarta

pier [pɪə*] *n* muelle *m*, embarcadero

pierce [pɪəs] *vt* perforar; **pierced** *adj*: **I've got pierced ears** tengo los agujeros hechos en las orejas

pig [pɪg] *n* cerdo, chancho (LAM); (*pej: unkind person*) asqueroso; (: *greedy person*) glotón/ona *m/f*

pigeon ['pɪdʒən] *n* paloma; (*as food*) pichón *m*

piggy bank ['pɪgɪ-] *n* hucha (en forma de cerdito)

pigsty ['pɪgstaɪ] *n* pocilga

pigtail *n* (*girl's*) trenza

pike [paɪk] *n* (*fish*) lucio

pilchard ['pɪltʃəd] *n* sardina

pile [paɪl] *n* montón *m*; (*of carpet, cloth*) pelo; **pile up** *vi* +*adv* (*accumulate: work*) amontonarse, acumularse ▷ *vt* +*adv* (*put in a heap: books, clothes*) apilar, amontonar; (*accumulate*) acumular; **piles** *npl* (*Med*) almorranas *fpl*, hemorroides *mpl*; **pile-up** *n* (*Aut*) accidente *m* múltiple

pilgrimage ['pɪlgrɪmɪdʒ] *n* peregrinación *f*, romería

pill [pɪl] *n* píldora; **the ~** la píldora

pillar ['pɪlə*] *n* pilar *m*

pillow ['pɪləʊ] *n* almohada; **pillowcase** *n* funda

pilot ['paɪlət] *n* piloto ▷ *cpd* (*scheme etc*) piloto ▷ *vt* pilotar; **pilot light** *n* piloto

pimple ['pɪmpl] *n* grano

PIN *n abbr* (= *personal identification number*) número personal

pin [pɪn] *n* alfiler *m* ▷ *vt* prender (con alfiler); **~s and needles** hormigueo; **to ~ sb down** (*fig*) hacer que algn concrete; **to ~ sth on sb** (*fig*) colgarle a algn el sambenito de algo

pinafore ['pɪnəfɔː*] *n* delantal *m*

pinch [pɪntʃ] *n* (*of salt etc*) pizca ▷ *vt* pellizcar; (*inf: steal*) birlar; **at a ~** en caso de apuro

pine [paɪn] *n* (*also*: **~ tree**) pino ▷ *vi*: **to ~ for** suspirar por

pineapple ['paɪnæpl] n piña, ananás m
ping [pɪŋ] n (noise) sonido agudo; **ping-pong®** n pingpong® m
pink [pɪŋk] adj rosado, (color de) rosa ▷ n (colour) rosa; (Bot) clavel m, clavellina
pinpoint ['pɪnpɔɪnt] vt precisar
pint [paɪnt] n pinta (BRIT = 568cc, US = 473cc); (BRIT: inf: of beer) pinta de cerveza ≈ jarra (SP)
pioneer [paɪə'nɪə*] n pionero/a
pious ['paɪəs] adj piadoso, devoto
pip [pɪp] n (seed) pepita; **the ~s** (BRIT) la señal
pipe [paɪp] n tubo, caño; (for smoking) pipa ▷ vt conducir en cañerías; **pipeline** n (for oil) oleoducto; (for gas) gasoducto; **piper** n gaitero/a
pirate ['paɪərət] n pirata mf ▷ vt (cassette, book) piratear
Pisces ['paɪsiːz] n Piscis m
piss [pɪs] (inf!) vi mear; **pissed** (inf!) adj (drunk) borracho
pistol ['pɪstl] n pistola
piston ['pɪstən] n pistón m, émbolo
pit [pɪt] n hoyo; (also: **coal** ~) mina; (in garage) foso de inspección; (also: **orchestra** ~) platea ▷ vt: **to** ~ **one's wits against sb** medir fuerzas con algn
pitch [pɪtʃ] n (Mus) tono; (BRIT Sport) campo, terreno; (fig) punto; (tar) brea ▷ vt (throw) arrojar, lanzar ▷ vi (fall) caer(se); **to** ~ **a tent** montar una tienda (de campaña); **pitch-black** adj negro como boca de lobo
pitfall ['pɪtfɔːl] n riesgo
pith [pɪθ] n (of orange) médula
pitiful ['pɪtɪful] adj (touching) lastimoso, conmovedor(a)
pity ['pɪtɪ] n compasión f, piedad f ▷ vt compadecer(se de); **what a ~!** ¡qué pena!
pizza ['piːtsə] n pizza
placard ['plækɑːd] n letrero; (in march etc) pancarta
place [pleɪs] n lugar m, sitio; (seat) plaza, asiento; (post) puesto; (home): **at/to his** ~ en/a su casa; (role: in society etc) papel m ▷ vt (object) poner, colocar; (identify) reconocer; **to take** ~ tener lugar; **to be** ~**d** (in race, exam) colocarse; **out of** ~ (not suitable) fuera de lugar; **in the first** ~ en primer lugar; **to change** ~**s with sb** cambiarse de sitio con algn; ~ **of birth** lugar m de nacimiento; **place mat** n (wooden etc) salvamanteles m inv; (linen etc) mantel m individual; **placement** n (positioning) colocación f; (at work) emplazamiento
placid ['plæsɪd] adj apacible
plague [pleɪɡ] n plaga; (Med) peste f ▷ vt (fig) acosar, atormentar
plaice [pleɪs] n inv platija
plain [pleɪn] adj (unpatterned) liso; (clear) claro, evidente; (simple) sencillo; (not handsome) poco atractivo ▷ adv claramente ▷ n llano, llanura; **plain chocolate** n chocolate m amargo; **plainly** adv claramente
plaintiff ['pleɪntɪf] n demandante mf
plait [plæt] n trenza
plan [plæn] n (drawing) plano; (scheme) plan m, proyecto ▷ vt proyectar, planificar ▷ vi hacer proyectos; **to** ~ **to do** pensar hacer
plane [pleɪn] n (Aviat) avión m; (Math, fig) plano; (also: ~ **tree**) plátano; (tool) cepillo
planet ['plænɪt] n planeta m
plank [plæŋk] n tabla
planning ['plænɪŋ] n planificación f; **family ~** planificación familiar

plant [plɑːnt] n planta; (machinery) maquinaria; (factory) fábrica ▷ vt plantar; (field) sembrar; (bomb) colocar
plantation [plæn'teɪʃən] n plantación f; (estate) hacienda
plaque [plæk] n placa
plaster ['plɑːstə*] n (for walls) yeso; (also: ~ **of Paris**) yeso mate, escayola (SP); (BRIT: also: **sticking** ~) tirita (SP), curita (LAM) ▷ vt enyesar; (cover): **to** ~ **with** llenar o cubrir de; **plaster cast** n (Med) escayola (SP; model, statue) vaciado de yeso
plastic ['plæstɪk] n plástico ▷ adj de plástico; **plastic bag** n bolsa de plástico; **plastic surgery** n cirugía plástica
plate [pleɪt] n (dish) plato; (metal, in book) lámina; (dental plate) placa de dentadura postiza
plateau ['plætəʊ] (pl ~**s** or ~**x**) n meseta, altiplanicie f
platform ['plætfɔːm] n (Rail) andén m; (stage, BRIT: on bus) plataforma; (at meeting) tribuna; (Pol) programa m (electoral)
platinum ['plætɪnəm] adj, n platino
platoon [plə'tuːn] n pelotón m
platter ['plætə*] n fuente f
plausible ['plɔːzɪbl] adj verosímil; (person) convincente
play [pleɪ] n (Theatre) obra, comedia ▷ vt (game) jugar; (compete against) jugar contra; (instrument) tocar; (part: in play etc) hacer el papel de; (tape, record) poner ▷ vi jugar; (band) tocar; (tape, record) sonar; **to** ~ **safe** ir a lo seguro; **play back** vt (tape) poner; **play up** vi (cause trouble to) dar guerra; **player** n jugador/a m/f; (Theatre) actor(actriz) m/f; (Mus) músico/a; **playful** adj juguetón/ona; **playground** n (in school) patio de recreo; (in park) parque m infantil; **playgroup** n jardín m de niños; **playing card** n naipe m, carta; **playing field** n campo de deportes; **playschool** n = **playgroup**; **playtime** n (Scol) recreo; **playwright** n dramaturgo/a
plc abbr (= public limited company) ≈ S.A.
plea [pliː] n súplica, petición f; (Law) alegato, defensa
plead [pliːd] vt (Law): **to** ~ **sb's case** defender a algn; (give as excuse) poner como pretexto ▷ vi (Law) declararse; (beg): **to** ~ **with sb** suplicar o rogar a algn
pleasant ['plɛznt] adj agradable
please [pliːz] excl ¡por favor! ▷ vt (give pleasure to) dar gusto a, agradar ▷ vi (think fit): **do as you** ~ haz lo que quieras; ~ **yourself!** (inf) ¡haz lo que quieras!, ¡como quieras!; **pleased** adj (happy) alegre, contento; **pleased (with)** satisfecho (de); **pleased to meet you** ¡encantado!, ¡tanto gusto!
pleasure ['plɛʒə*] n placer m, gusto; **"it's a ~"** "el gusto es mío"
pleat [pliːt] n pliegue m
pledge [plɛdʒ] n (promise) promesa, voto ▷ vt prometer
plentiful ['plɛntɪful] adj copioso, abundante
plenty ['plɛntɪ] n: ~ **of** mucho(s)/a(s)
pliers ['plaɪəz] npl alicates mpl, tenazas fpl
plight [plaɪt] n situación f difícil
plod [plɒd] vi caminar con paso pesado; (fig) trabajar laboriosamente
plonk [plɒŋk] (inf) n (BRIT: wine) vino peleón ▷ vt: **to** ~ **sth down** dejar caer algo
plot [plɒt] n (scheme) complot m, conjura; (of story, play) argumento; (of land) terreno ▷ vt (mark out) trazar; (conspire) tramar, urdir ▷ vi conspirar

plough [plaʊ] (US **plow**) n arado ▷ vt (earth) arar; **to ~ money into** invertir dinero en; **ploughman's lunch** (BRIT) n almuerzo de pub a base de pan, queso y encurtidos

plow [plaʊ] (US) = **plough**

ploy [plɔɪ] n truco, estratagema

pluck [plʌk] vt (fruit) coger (SP), recoger (LAM); (musical instrument) puntear; (bird) desplumar; (eyebrows) depilar; **to ~ up courage** hacer de tripas corazón

plug [plʌg] n tapón m; (Elec) enchufe m, clavija; (Aut: also: **spark(ing) ~**) bujía ▷ vt (hole) tapar; (inf: advertise) dar publicidad a; **plug in** vt (Elec) enchufar; **plughole** n desagüe m

plum [plʌm] n (fruit) ciruela

plumber ['plʌmə*] n fontanero/a (SP, CAM), plomero/a (LAM)

plumbing ['plʌmɪŋ] n (trade) fontanería, plomería; (piping) cañería

plummet ['plʌmɪt] vi: **to ~ (down)** caer a plomo

plump [plʌmp] adj rechoncho, rollizo ▷ vi: **to ~ for** (inf: choose) optar por

plunge [plʌndʒ] n zambullida ▷ vt sumergir, hundir ▷ vi (fall) caer; (dive) saltar; (person) arrojarse; **to take the ~** lanzarse

plural ['plʊərəl] adj plural ▷ n plural m

plus [plʌs] n (also: **~ sign**) signo más ▷ prep más, y, además de; **ten/twenty ~** más de diez/veinte

ply [plaɪ] vt (a trade) ejercer ▷ vi (ship) ir y venir ▷ n (of wool, rope) cabo; **to ~ sb with drink** insistir en ofrecer a algn muchas copas; **plywood** n madera contrachapada

P.M. n abbr = **Prime Minister**

p.m. adv abbr (= post meridiem) de la tarde or noche

PMS n abbr (= premenstrual syndrome) SPM m

PMT n abbr (= premenstrual tension) SPM m

pneumatic drill [njuː'mætɪk-] n martillo neumático

pneumonia [njuː'məʊnɪə] n pulmonía

poach [pəʊtʃ] vt (cook) escalfar; (steal) cazar (or pescar) en vedado ▷ vi cazar (or pescar) en vedado; **poached** adj escalfado

P.O. Box n abbr (= Post Office Box) apdo., aptdo.

pocket ['pɒkɪt] n bolsillo; (fig: small area) bolsa ▷ vt meter en el bolsillo; (steal) embolsar; **to be out of ~** (BRIT) salir perdiendo; **pocketbook** (US) n cartera; **pocket money** n asignación f

pod [pɒd] n vaina

podiatrist [pɒ'diːətrɪst] (US) n pedicuro/a

podium ['pəʊdɪəm] n podio

poem ['pəʊɪm] n poema m

poet ['pəʊɪt] n poeta m/f; **poetic** [-'ɛtɪk] adj poético; **poetry** n poesía

poignant ['pɔɪnjənt] adj conmovedor(a)

point [pɔɪnt] n punto; (tip) punta; (purpose) fin m, propósito; (use) utilidad f; (significant part) lo significativo; (moment) momento; (Elec) toma (de corriente); (also: **decimal: ~ 2 → 3 (2.3)** dos coma tres (2.3) ▷ vt señalar; (gun etc) **to ~ sth at sb** apuntar algo a algn ▷ vi: **to ~ at** señalar; **points** npl (Aut) contactos mpl; (Rail) agujas fpl; **to be on the ~ of doing sth** estar a punto de hacer algo; **to make a ~ of** poner empeño en; **to get/miss the ~** comprender/no comprender; **to come to the ~** ir al meollo; **there's no ~ (in doing)** no tiene sentido (hacer); **point out** vt señalar; **point-blank** adv (say, refuse) sin más hablar; (also: **at point-blank range**) a quemarropa; **pointed** adj (shape) puntiagudo, afilado; (remark) intencionado; **pointer** n

(needle) aguja, indicador m; **pointless** adj sin sentido; **point of view** n punto de vista

poison ['pɔɪzn] n veneno ▷ vt envenenar; **poisonous** adj venenoso; (fumes etc) tóxico

poke [pəʊk] vt (jab with finger, stick etc) empujar; (put): **to ~ sth in(to)** introducir algo en; **poke about** or **around** vi fisgonear; **poke out** vi (stick out) salir

poker ['pəʊkə*] n atizador m; (Cards) póker m

Poland ['pəʊlənd] n Polonia

polar ['pəʊlə*] adj polar; **polar bear** n oso polar

Pole [pəʊl] n polaco/a

pole [pəʊl] n palo; (fixed) poste m; (Geo) polo; **pole bean** (US) n = judía verde; **pole vault** n salto con pértiga

police [pə'liːs] n policía ▷ vt vigilar; **police car** n coche-patrulla m; **police constable** (BRIT) n guardia m, policía m; **police force** n cuerpo de policía; **policeman** (irreg) n guardia m, guardia m; **police officer** n guardia m, policía m; **police station** n comisaría; **policewoman** (irreg) n mujer f policía

policy ['pɒlɪsɪ] n política; (also: **insurance ~**) póliza

polio ['pəʊlɪəʊ] n polio f

Polish ['pəʊlɪʃ] adj polaco ▷ n (Ling) polaco

polish ['pɒlɪʃ] n (for shoes) betún m; (for floor) cera (de lustrar); (shine) brillo, lustre m; (fig: refinement) educación f ▷ vt (shoes) limpiar; (make shiny) pulir, sacar brillo a; **polish off** vt (food) despachar; **polished** adj (fig: person) elegante

polite [pə'laɪt] adj cortés, atento; **politeness** n cortesía

political [pə'lɪtɪkl] adj político; **politically** adv políticamente; **politically correct** políticamente correcto

politician [pɒlɪ'tɪʃən] n político/a

politics ['pɒlɪtɪks] n política

poll [pəʊl] n (election) votación f; (also: **opinion ~**) sondeo, encuesta ▷ vt encuestar; (votes) obtener

pollen ['pɒlən] n polen m

polling station ['pəʊlɪŋ-] n centro electoral

pollute [pə'luːt] vt contaminar

pollution [pə'luːʃən] n polución f, contaminación f del medio ambiente

polo ['pəʊləʊ] n (sport) polo; **polo-neck** adj de cuello vuelto ▷ n (sweater) suéter m de cuello vuelto; **polo shirt** n polo, niqui m

polyester [pɒlɪ'ɛstə*] n poliéster m

polystyrene [pɒlɪ'staɪriːn] n poliestireno

polythene ['pɒlɪθiːn] (BRIT) n politeno; **polythene bag** n bolsa de plástico

pomegranate ['pɒmɪɡrænɪt] n granada

pompous ['pɒmpəs] adj pomposo

pond [pɒnd] n (natural) charca; (artificial) estanque m

ponder ['pɒndə*] vt meditar

pony ['pəʊnɪ] n poni m; **ponytail** n coleta; **pony trekking** n excursión f a caballo

poodle ['puːdl] n caniche m

pool [puːl] n (natural) charca; (also: **swimming ~**) piscina, alberca (MEX), pileta (RPL); (fig: of light) charco; (Sport) chapolín m ▷ vt juntar; **pools** npl quinielas fpl

poor [pʊə*] adj pobre; (bad) de mala calidad ▷ npl: **the ~** los pobres; **poorly** adj mal, enfermo ▷ adv mal

pop [pɒp] n (sound) ruido seco; (Mus) (música) pop m; (inf: father) papá m; (drink) gaseosa ▷ vt (put quickly) meter (de prisa) ▷ vi reventar; (cork) saltar; **pop in** vi entrar un momento; **pop out** vi salir un momento;

popcorn n palomitas fpl

poplar ['pɒplə*] n álamo

popper ['pɒpə*] (BRIT) n automático

poppy ['pɒpɪ] n amapola

Popsicle® ['pɒpsɪkl] (US) n polo

pop star n estrella del pop

popular ['pɒpjulə*] adj popular; **popularity** [pɒpjuˈlærɪtɪ] n popularidad f

population [pɒpjuˈleɪʃən] n población f

pop-up ['pɒpʌp] (Comput) adj (menu, window) emergente ▷ n ventana emergente, (ventana f) pop-up f

porcelain ['pɔːslɪn] n porcelana

porch [pɔːtʃ] n pórtico, entrada; (US) veranda

pore [pɔː*] n poro ▷ vi: **to ~ over** engolfarse en

pork [pɔːk] n carne f de cerdo or (LAM) chancho; **pork chop** n chuleta de cerdo; **pork pie** (BRIT: Culin) empanada de carne de cerdo

porn [pɔːn] adj (inf) porno inv ▷ n porno; **pornographic** [pɔːnəˈɡræfɪk] adj pornográfico; **pornography** [pɔːˈnɒɡrəfɪ] n pornografía

porridge ['pɒrɪdʒ] n gachas fpl de avena

port [pɔːt] n puerto; (Naut: left side) babor m; (wine) vino de Oporto; **~ of call** puerto de escala

portable ['pɔːtəbl] adj portátil

porter ['pɔːtə*] n (for luggage) maletero; (doorkeeper) portero/a, conserje m/f

portfolio [pɔːtˈfəulɪəu] n cartera

portion ['pɔːʃən] n porción f; (of food) ración f

portrait ['pɔːtreɪt] n retrato

portray [pɔːˈtreɪ] vt retratar; (actor) representar

Portugal ['pɔːtjuɡl] n Portugal m

Portuguese [pɔːtjuˈɡiːz] adj portugués/esa ▷ n inv portugués/esa m/f; (Ling) portugués m

pose [pəuz] n postura, actitud f ▷ vi (pretend): **to ~ as** hacerse pasar por ▷ vt (question) plantear; **to ~ for** posar para

posh [pɒʃ] (inf) adj elegante, de lujo

position [pəˈzɪʃən] n posición f; (job) puesto; (situation) situación f ▷ vt colocar

positive ['pɒzɪtɪv] adj positivo; (certain) seguro; (definite) definitivo; **positively** adv (affirmatively, enthusiastically) de forma positiva; (inf: really) absolutamente

possess [pəˈzɛs] vt poseer; **possession** [pəˈzɛʃən] n posesión f; **possessions** npl (belongings) pertenencias fpl; **possessive** adj posesivo

possibility [pɒsɪˈbɪlɪtɪ] n posibilidad f

possible ['pɒsɪbl] adj posible; **as big as ~** lo más grande posible; **possibly** adv posiblemente; **I cannot possibly come** me es imposible venir

post [pəust] n (BRIT: system) correos mpl; (BRIT: letters, delivery) correo; (job, situation) puesto; (pole) poste m ▷ vt (BRIT: send by post) echar al correo; (BRIT: appoint): **to ~ to** enviar a; **postage** n porte m, franqueo; **postal** adj postal, de correos; **postal order** n giro postal; **postbox** (BRIT) n buzón m; **postcard** n tarjeta postal; **postcode** (BRIT) n código postal

poster ['pəustə*] n cartel m

postgraduate ['pəustˈɡrædjuət] n posgraduado/a

postman ['pəustmən] (BRIT: irreg) n cartero

postmark ['pəustmɑːk] n matasellos m inv

post-mortem [-ˈmɔːtəm] n autopsia

post office n (building) (oficina de) correos m; (organization): **the Post Office** Correos m inv (SP), Dirección f General de Correos (LAM)

postpone [pəsˈpəun] vt aplazar

posture ['pɒstʃə*] n postura, actitud f

postwoman ['pəustwumən] (BRIT: irreg) n cartera

pot [pɒt] n (for cooking) olla; (teapot) tetera; (coffeepot) cafetera; (for flowers) maceta; (for jam) tarro, pote m; (inf: marijuana) chocolate m ▷ vt (plant) poner en tiesto; **to go to ~** (inf) irse al traste

potato [pəˈteɪtəu] (pl **-es**) n patata (SP), papa (LAM); **potato peeler** n pelapatatas m inv

potent ['pəutnt] adj potente, poderoso; (drink) fuerte

potential [pəˈtɛnʃl] adj potencial, posible ▷ n potencial m

pothole ['pɒthəul] n (in road) bache m; (BRIT: underground) gruta

pot plant ['pɒtplɑːnt] n planta de interior

potter ['pɒtə*] n alfarero/a ▷ vi: **to ~ around** or **about** (BRIT) hacer trabajitos; **pottery** n cerámica; (factory) alfarería

potty ['pɒtɪ] n orinal m de niño

pouch [pautʃ] n (Zool) bolsa; (for tobacco) petaca

poultry ['pəultrɪ] n aves fpl de corral; (meat) pollo

pounce [pauns] vi: **to ~ on** precipitarse sobre

pound [paund] n libra (weight = 453g or 16oz; money = 100 pence) ▷ vt (beat) golpear; (crush) machacar ▷ vi (heart) latir; **pound sterling** n libra esterlina

pour [pɔː*] vt echar; (tea etc) servir ▷ vi correr, fluir; **to ~ sb a drink** servirle a algún una copa; **pour in** vi (people) entrar en tropel; **pour out** vi salir en tropel ▷ vt (drink) echar, servir; (fig): **to pour out one's feelings** desahogarse; **pouring** adj: **pouring rain** lluvia torrencial

pout [paut] vi hacer pucheros

poverty ['pɒvətɪ] n pobreza, miseria

powder ['paudə*] n polvo; (also: **face ~**) polvos mpl ▷ vt polvorear; **to ~ one's face** empolvarse la cara; **powdered milk** n leche f en polvo

power ['pauə*] n poder m; (strength) fuerza; (nation, Tech) potencia; (drive) empuje m; (Elec) fuerza, energía ▷ vt impulsar; **to be in ~** (Pol) estar en el poder; **power cut** (BRIT) n apagón m; **power failure** n = **power cut**; **powerful** adj poderoso; (engine) potente; (speech etc) convincente; **powerless** adj; **powerless (to do)** incapaz (de hacer); **power point** (BRIT) n enchufe m; **power station** n central f eléctrica

p.p. abbr (= per procurationem): **p.p.J. Smith** p.p. (por poder de) J. Smith; (= pages) págs

PR n abbr = **public relations**

practical ['præktɪkl] adj práctico; **practical joke** n broma pesada; **practically** adv (almost) casi

practice ['præktɪs] n (habit) costumbre f; (exercise) práctica, ejercicio; (training) adiestramiento; (Med: of profession) práctica, ejercicio; (Med, Law: business) consulta ▷ vt, vi (US) = **practise**; **in ~** (in reality) en la práctica; **out of ~** desentrenado

practise ['præktɪs] (US **practice**) vt (carry out) practicar; (profession) ejercer; (train at) practicar ▷ vi ejercer; (train) practicar; **practising** adj (Christian etc) practicante; (lawyer) en ejercicio

practitioner [prækˈtɪʃənə*] n (Med) médico/a

pragmatic [præɡˈmætɪk] adj pragmático

prairie ['prɛərɪ] n pampa

praise [preɪz] n alabanza f(pl), elogio(s) m(pl) ▷ vt alabar, elogiar

pram [præm] (BRIT) n cochecito de niño

prank [præŋk] n travesura

prawn [prɔːn] n gamba; **prawn cocktail** n cóctel

m de gambas

pray [preɪ] *vi* rezar; **prayer** [preə*] *n* oración *f*, rezo; (*entreaty*) ruego, súplica

preach [priːtʃ] *vi* predicar; **preacher** *n* predicador(a) *m/f*

precarious [prɪˈkɛərɪəs] *adj* precario

precaution [prɪˈkɔːʃən] *n* precaución *f*

precede [prɪˈsiːd] *vt, vi* preceder; **precedent** [ˈprɛsɪdənt] *n* precedente *m*; **preceding** [prɪˈsiːdɪŋ] *adj* anterior

precinct [ˈpriːsɪŋkt] *n* recinto

precious [ˈprɛʃəs] *adj* precioso

precise [prɪˈsaɪs] *adj* preciso, exacto; **precisely** *adv* precisamente, exactamente

precision [prɪˈsɪʒən] *n* precisión *f*

predator [ˈprɛdətə*] *n* depredador *m*

predecessor [ˈpriːdɪsɛsə*] *n* antecesor(a) *m/f*

predicament [prɪˈdɪkəmənt] *n* apuro

predict [prɪˈdɪkt] *vt* pronosticar; **predictable** *adj* previsible; **prediction** [ˈdɪkʃən] *n* predicción *f*

preface [ˈprɛfəs] *n* prefacio

prefect [ˈpriːfɛkt] (BRIT) *n* (*in school*) monitor(a) *m/f*

prefer [prɪˈfəː*] *vt* preferir; **to ~ doing** or **to do** preferir hacer; **preferable** [ˈprɛfrəbl] *adj* preferible; **preferably** [ˈprɛfrəblɪ] *adv* de preferencia; **preference** [ˈprɛfrəns] *n* preferencia; (*priority*) prioridad *f*

prefix [ˈpriːfɪks] *n* prefijo

pregnancy [ˈprɛɡnənsɪ] *n* (*of woman*) embarazo; (*of animal*) preñez *f*

pregnant [ˈprɛɡnənt] *adj* (*woman*) embarazada; (*animal*) preñada

prehistoric [ˈpriːhɪsˈtɔrɪk] *adj* prehistórico

prejudice [ˈprɛdʒʊdɪs] *n* prejuicio; **prejudiced** (*person*) predispuesto

preliminary [prɪˈlɪmɪnərɪ] *adj* preliminar

prelude [ˈprɛljuːd] *n* preludio

premature [ˈprɛmətʃʊə*] *adj* prematuro

premier [ˈprɛmɪə*] *adj* primero, principal ▷ *n* (*Pol*) primer(a) ministro/a

première [ˈprɛmɪɛə*] *n* estreno

Premier League [premɪəˈliːɡ] *n* primera división

premises [ˈprɛmɪsɪz] *npl* (*of business etc*) local *m*; **on the ~** en el lugar mismo

premium [ˈpriːmɪəm] *n* premio; (*insurance*) prima; **to be at a ~** ser muy solicitado

premonition [prɛməˈnɪʃən] *n* presentimiento

preoccupied [priːˈɔkjupaɪd] *adj* ensimismado

prepaid [priːˈpeɪd] *adj* porte pagado

preparation [prɛpəˈreɪʃən] *n* preparación *f*; **preparations** *npl* preparativos *mpl*

preparatory school [prɪˈpærətərɪ–] *n* escuela preparatoria

prepare [prɪˈpɛə*] *vt* preparar, disponer ▷ *vi*: **to ~ for** (*action*) prepararse or disponerse para; (*event*) hacer preparativos para; **~d to** dispuesto a; **~d for** listo para

preposition [prɛpəˈzɪʃən] *n* preposición *f*

prep school [prɛp–] *n* = **preparatory school**

prerequisite [priːˈrɛkwɪzɪt] *n* requisito

preschool [ˈpriːskuːl] *adj* preescolar

prescribe [prɪˈskraɪb] *vt* (*Med*) recetar

prescription [prɪˈskrɪpʃən] *n* (*Med*) receta

presence [ˈprɛzns] *n* presencia; **in sb's ~** en presencia de algn; **~ of mind** aplomo

present [*adj, n* ˈprɛznt, *vb* prɪˈzɛnt] *adj* (*in attendance*) presente; (*current*) actual ▷ *n* (*gift*) regalo; (*actuality*): **the ~** la actualidad, el presente ▷ *vt* (*introduce, describe*) presentar; (*expound*) exponer; presentar, dar, ofrecer; (*Theatre*) representar; **to give sb a ~** regalar algo a algn; **at ~** actualmente; **presentable** [prɪˈzɛntəbl] *adj*: **to make o.s. presentable** arreglarse; **presentation** [–ˈteɪʃən] *n* presentación *f*; (*of report etc*) exposición *f*; (*formal ceremony*) entrega de un regalo; **present-day** *adj* actual; **presenter** [prɪˈzɛntə*] *n* (*Radio, TV*) locutor(a) *m/f*; **presently** *adv* (*soon*) dentro de poco; (*now*) ahora; **present participle** *n* participio (de) presente

preservation [prɛzəˈveɪʃən] *n* conservación *f*

preservative [prɪˈzɜːvətɪv] *n* conservante *m*

preserve [prɪˈzɜːv] *vt* (*keep safe*) mantener, proteger; (*maintain*) mantener; (*food*) conservar ▷ *n* (*for game*) coto, vedado; (*often pl: jam*) conserva, confitura

preside [prɪˈzaɪd] *vi* presidir

president [ˈprɛzɪdənt] *n* presidente *m/f*; **presidential** [–ˈdɛnʃl] *adj* presidencial

press [prɛs] *n* (*newspapers*): **the P~** la prensa; (*printer's*) imprenta; (*of button*) pulsación *f* ▷ *vt* empujar; (*button etc*) apretar; (*clothes: iron*) planchar; (*put pressure on: person*) presionar a; (*insist*): **to ~ sth on sb** insistir en que algn acepte algo ▷ *vi* (*squeeze*) apretar; (*pressurize*): **to ~ for** presionar por; **we are ~ed for time/money** estamos apurados de tiempo/dinero; **press conference** *n* rueda de prensa; **pressing** *adj* apremiante; **press stud** (BRIT) *n* botón *m* de presión; **press-up** (BRIT) *n* plancha

pressure [ˈprɛʃə*] *n* presión *f*; **to put ~ on sb** presionar a algn; **pressure cooker** *n* olla a presión; **pressure group** *n* grupo de presión

prestige [prɛsˈtiːʒ] *n* prestigio

prestigious [prɛsˈtɪdʒəs] *adj* prestigioso

presumably [prɪˈzjuːməblɪ] *adv* es de suponer que, cabe presumir que

presume [prɪˈzjuːm] *vt*: **to ~ (that)** presumir (que), suponer (que)

pretence [prɪˈtɛns] (*us* **pretense**) *n* fingimiento; **under false ~s** con engaños

pretend [prɪˈtɛnd] *vt, vi* (*feign*) fingir

pretense [prɪˈtɛns] (*us*) *n* = **pretence**

pretentious [prɪˈtɛnʃəs] *adj* presumido; (*ostentatious*) ostentoso, aparatoso

pretext [ˈpriːtɛkst] *n* pretexto

pretty [ˈprɪtɪ] *adj* bonito, lindo (LAM) ▷ *adv* bastante

prevail [prɪˈveɪl] *vi* (*gain mastery*) prevalecer; (*be current*) predominar; **prevailing** *adj* (*dominant*) predominante

prevalent [ˈprɛvələnt] *adj* (*widespread*) extendido

prevent [prɪˈvɛnt] *vt*: **to ~ sb from doing sth** impedir a algn hacer algo; **to ~ sth from happening** evitar que ocurra algo; **prevention** [prɪˈvɛnʃən] *n* prevención *f*; **preventive** *adj* preventivo

preview [ˈpriːvjuː] *n* (*of film*) preestreno

previous [ˈpriːvɪəs] *adj* previo, anterior; **previously** *adv* antes

prey [preɪ] *n* presa ▷ *vi*: **to ~ on** (*feed on*) alimentarse de; **it was ~ing on his mind** le preocupaba, le obsesionaba

price [praɪs] *n* precio ▷ *vt* (*goods*) fijar el precio de; **priceless** *adj* que no tiene precio; **price list** *n* tarifa

prick [prɪk] *n* (*sting*) picadura ▷ *vt* pinchar; (*hurt*) picar; **to ~ up one's ears** aguzar el oído

prickly ['prɪklɪ] adj espinoso; (fig: person) enojadizo

pride [praɪd] n orgullo; (pej) soberbia ▷ vt: **to ~ o.s. on** enorgullecerse de

priest [priːst] n sacerdote m

primarily ['praɪmərɪlɪ] adv ante todo

primary ['praɪmərɪ] adj (first in importance) principal ▷ n (us Pol) elección f primaria; **primary school** (BRIT) n escuela primaria

prime [praɪm] adj primero, principal; (excellent) selecto, de primera clase ▷ n: **in the ~ of life** en la flor de la vida ▷ vt (wood: fig) preparar; **~ example** ejemplo típico; **Prime Minister** n primer(a) ministro/a

primitive ['prɪmɪtɪv] adj primitivo; (crude) rudimentario

primrose ['prɪmrəuz] n primavera, prímula

prince [prɪns] n príncipe m

princess [prɪn'sɛs] n princesa

principal ['prɪnsɪpl] adj principal, mayor ▷ n director(a) m/f; **principally** adv principalmente

principle ['prɪnsɪpl] n principio; **in ~** en principio; **on ~** por principio

print [prɪnt] n (footprint) huella; (fingerprint) huella dactilar; (letters) letra de molde; (fabric) estampado; (Art) grabado; (Phot) impresión f ▷ vt imprimir; (cloth) estampar; (write in capitals) escribir en letras de molde; **out of ~** agotado; **print out** vt (Comput) imprimir; **printer** n (person) impresor(a) m/f; (machine) impresora; **printout** n (Comput) impresión f

prior ['praɪə*] adj anterior, previo; (more important) más importante; **~ to** antes de

priority [praɪ'ɒrɪtɪ] n prioridad f; **to have ~ (over)** tener prioridad (sobre)

prison ['prɪzn] n cárcel f, prisión f ▷ cpd carcelario; **prisoner** n (in prison) preso/a; (captured person) prisionero; **prisoner-of-war** n prisionero de guerra

pristine ['prɪstiːn] adj prístino

privacy ['prɪvəsɪ] n intimidad f

private ['praɪvɪt] adj (personal) particular; (property, industry, discussion etc) privado; (person) reservado; (place) tranquilo ▷ n soldado raso; **"~"** (on envelope) "confidencial"; (on door) "prohibido el paso"; **in ~** en privado; **privately** adv en privado; (in o.s.) en secreto; **private property** n propiedad f privada; **private school** n colegio particular

privatize ['praɪvɪtaɪz] vt privatizar

privilege ['prɪvɪlɪdʒ] n privilegio; (prerogative) prerrogativa

prize [praɪz] n premio ▷ adj de primera clase ▷ vt apreciar, estimar; **prize-giving** n distribución f de premios; **prizewinner** n premiado/a

pro [prəu] n (Sport) profesional m/f ▷ prep a favor de; **the ~s and cons** los pros y los contras

probability [prɒbə'bɪlɪtɪ] n probabilidad f; **in all ~** con toda probabilidad

probable ['prɒbəbl] adj probable

probably ['prɒbəblɪ] adv probablemente

probation [prə'beɪʃən] n: **on ~** (employee) a prueba; (Law) en libertad condicional

probe [prəub] n (Med, Space) sonda; (enquiry) encuesta, investigación f ▷ vt sondar; (investigate) investigar

problem ['prɒbləm] n problema m

procedure [prə'siːdʒə*] n procedimiento; (bureaucratic) trámites mpl

proceed [prə'siːd] vi (do afterwards): **to ~ to do sth** proceder a hacer algo; (continue): **to ~ (with)** continuar

or seguir (con); **proceedings** npl acto(s) (pl); (Law) proceso; **proceeds** ['prəusiːdz] npl (money) ganancias fpl, ingresos mpl

process ['prəusɛs] n proceso ▷ vt tratar, elaborar

procession [prə'sɛʃən] n desfile m; **funeral ~** cortejo fúnebre

proclaim [prə'kleɪm] vt (announce) anunciar

prod [prɒd] vt empujar ▷ n empujón m

produce [n 'prɒdjuːs, vt prə'djuːs] n (Agr) productos mpl agrícolas ▷ vt producir; (play, film, programme) presentar; **producer** n productor(a) m/f; (of film, programme) director(a) m/f; (of record) productor(a) m/f

product ['prɒdʌkt] n producto; **production** [prə'dʌkʃən] n producción f; (Theatre) presentación f; **productive** [prə'dʌktɪv] adj productivo; **productivity** [prɒdʌk'tɪvɪtɪ] n productividad f

Prof. [prɒf] abbr (= professor) Prof

profession [prə'fɛʃən] n profesión f; **professional** adj profesional ▷ n profesional mf; (skilled person) perito

professor [prə'fɛsə*] n (BRIT) catedrático/a; (US, CANADA) profesor/a m/f

profile ['prəufaɪl] n perfil m

profit ['prɒfɪt] n (Comm) ganancia ▷ vi: **to ~ by or from** aprovechar or sacar provecho de; **profitable** adj (Econ) rentable

profound [prə'faund] adj profundo

programme ['prəugræm] (US **program**) n programa m ▷ vt programar; **programmer** (US **programer**) n programador/a m/f; **programming** (US **programing**) n programación f

progress [n 'prəugrɛs, vi prə'grɛs] n progreso; (development) desarrollo ▷ vi progresar, avanzar; **in ~** en curso; **progressive** [-'grɛsɪv] adj progresivo; (person) progresista

prohibit [prə'hɪbɪt] vt prohibir; **to ~ sb from doing sth** prohibir a algn hacer algo

project [n 'prɒdʒɛkt, vb prə'dʒɛkt] n proyecto ▷ vt proyectar ▷ vi (stick out) salir, sobresalir; **projection** [prə'dʒɛkʃən] n proyección f; (overhang) saliente m; **projector** [prə'dʒɛktə*] n proyector m

prolific [prə'lɪfɪk] adj prolífico

prolong [prə'lɒŋ] vt prolongar, extender

prom [prɒm] n abbr = **promenade** (us: ball) baile m de gala; **the P~s** ver recuadro

promenade [prɒmə'nɑːd] n (by sea) paseo marítimo

prominent ['prɒmɪnənt] adj (standing out) saliente; (important) eminente, importante

promiscuous [prə'mɪskjuəs] adj (sexually) promiscuo

promise ['prɒmɪs] n promesa ▷ vt, vi prometer; **promising** adj prometedor/a

promote [prə'məut] vt (employee) ascender; (product, pop star) hacer propaganda por; (ideas) fomentar; **promotion** [-'məuʃən] n (advertising campaign) campaña f de promoción; (in rank) ascenso

prompt [prɒmpt] adj rápido ▷ adv: **at 6 o'clock ~** a las seis en punto ▷ n (Comput) aviso ▷ vt (urge) mover, incitar; (when talking) instar; (Theatre) apuntar; **to ~ sb to do sth** instar a algn a hacer algo; **promptly** adv rápidamente; (exactly) puntualmente

prone [prəun] adj (lying) postrado; **~ to** propenso a

prong [prɒŋ] n diente m, punta

pronoun ['prəunaun] n pronombre m

pronounce [prə'nauns] vt pronunciar

pronunciation [prənʌnsɪˈeɪʃən] n pronunciación f
proof [pruːf] n prueba ▷ adj: **~ against** a prueba de
prop [prɒp] n apoyo; (fig) sostén m accesorios mpl; at(t)rezzo msg; **prop up** vt (roof, structure) apuntalar; (economy) respaldar
propaganda [prɒpəˈgændə] n propaganda
propeller [prəˈpɛlə] n hélice f
proper [ˈprɒpə] adj (suited, right) propio; (exact) justo; (seemly) correcto, decente; (authentic) verdadero; (referring to place): **the village ~** el pueblo mismo; **properly** adv (adequately) correctamente; (decently) decentemente; **proper noun** n nombre m propio
property [ˈprɒpətɪ] n propiedad f; (personal) bienes mpl muebles
prophecy [ˈprɒfɪsɪ] n profecía
prophet [ˈprɒfɪt] n profeta m
proportion [prəˈpɔːʃən] n proporción f; (share) parte f; **proportions** npl (size) dimensiones fpl; **proportional** adj: **proportional (to)** en proporción (con)
proposal [prəˈpəuzl] n (offer of marriage) oferta de matrimonio; (plan) proyecto
propose [prəˈpəuz] vt proponer ▷ vi declararse; **to ~ to do** tener intención de hacer
proposition [prɒpəˈzɪʃən] n propuesta
proprietor [prəˈpraɪətə] n propietario/a, dueño/a
prose [prəuz] n prosa
prosecute [ˈprɒsɪkjuːt] vt (Law) procesar; **prosecution** [-ˈkjuːʃən] n proceso, causa; (accusing side) acusación f; **prosecutor** n acusador/a m/f; (also: **public prosecutor**) fiscal mf
prospect [n ˈprɒspɛkt, vb prəˈspɛkt] n (possibility) posibilidad f; (outlook) perspectiva ▷ vi: **to ~ for** buscar; **prospects** npl (for work etc) perspectivas fpl; **prospective** [prəˈspɛktɪv] adj futuro
prospectus [prəˈspɛktəs] n prospecto
prosper [ˈprɒspə] vi prosperar; **prosperity** [-ˈspɛrɪtɪ] n prosperidad f; **prosperous** adj próspero
prostitute [ˈprɒstɪtjuːt] n prostituta f; (male) hombre que se dedica a la prostitución
protect [prəˈtɛkt] vt proteger; **protection** [-ˈtɛkʃən] n protección f; **protective** adj protector(a)
protein [ˈprəutiːn] n proteína
protest [n ˈprəutɛst, vb prəˈtɛst] n protesta ▷ vi: **to ~ about** or **at/against** protestar de/contra ▷ vt (insist): **to ~ (that)** insistir en (que)
Protestant [ˈprɒtɪstənt] adj, n protestante mf
protester [prəˈtɛstə] n manifestante mf
protractor [prəˈtræktə] n (Geom) transportador m
proud [praud] adj orgulloso; (pej) soberbio, altanero
prove [pruːv] vt probar; (show) demostrar ▷ vi: **to ~ (to be) correct** resultar correcto; **to ~ o.s.** probar su valía
proverb [ˈprɒvɜːb] n refrán m
provide [prəˈvaɪd] vt proporcionar, dar; **to ~ sb with sth** proveer a algn de algo; **provide for** vt fus (person) mantener a; (problem etc) tener en cuenta; **provided** conj: **provided (that)** con tal de que, a condición de que; **providing** [prəˈvaɪdɪŋ] conj: **providing (that)** a condición de que, con tal de que
province [ˈprɒvɪns] n provincia; (fig) esfera; **provincial** [prəˈvɪnʃəl] adj provincial; (pej) provinciano
provision [prəˈvɪʒən] n (supplying) suministro, abastecimiento; (of contract etc) disposición f; **provisions** npl (food) comestibles mpl; **provisional** adj provisional

provocative [prəˈvɒkətɪv] adj provocativo
provoke [prəˈvəuk] vt (cause) provocar, incitar; (anger) enojar
prowl [praul] vi (also: **~ about**, **~ around**) merodear ▷ n: **on the ~** de merodeo
proximity [prɒkˈsɪmɪtɪ] n proximidad f
proxy [ˈprɒksɪ] n: **by ~** por poderes
prudent [ˈpruːdənt] adj prudente
prune [pruːn] n ciruela pasa ▷ vt podar
pry [praɪ] vi: **to ~ (into)** entrometerse (en)
PS n abbr (= postscript) P.D.
pseudonym [ˈsjuːdəunɪm] n seudónimo
PSHE (BRIT: Scol) n abbr (= personal, social and health education) formación social y sanitaria
psychiatric [saɪkɪˈætrɪk] adj psiquiátrico
psychiatrist [saɪˈkaɪətrɪst] n psiquiatra mf
psychic [ˈsaɪkɪk] adj (also: **-al**) psíquico
psychoanalysis [saɪkəuəˈnælɪsɪs] n psicoanálisis m inv
psychological [saɪkəˈlɒdʒɪkl] adj psicológico
psychologist [saɪˈkɒlədʒɪst] n psicólogo/a
psychology [saɪˈkɒlədʒɪ] n psicología
psychotherapy [saɪkəuˈθɛrəpɪ] n psicoterapia
pt abbr = **pint(s)**; **point(s)**
PTO abbr (= please turn over) sigue
pub [pʌb] n abbr (= public house) pub m, bar m
puberty [ˈpjuːbətɪ] n pubertad f
public [ˈpʌblɪk] adj público ▷ n: **the ~** el público; **in ~** en público; **to make ~** hacer público
publication [pʌblɪˈkeɪʃən] n publicación f
public: public company n sociedad f anónima; **public convenience** (BRIT) n aseos mpl públicos (SP), sanitarios mpl (LAM); **public holiday** n (día m de) fiesta (SP), (día m) feriado (LAM); **public house** (BRIT) n bar m, pub m
publicity [pʌbˈlɪsɪtɪ] n publicidad f
publicize [ˈpʌblɪsaɪz] vt publicitar
public: public limited company n sociedad f anónima (S.A.); **publicly** adv públicamente, en público; **public opinion** n opinión f pública; **public relations** n relaciones fpl públicas; **public school** n (BRIT) escuela privada; (US) instituto; **public transport** n transporte m público
publish [ˈpʌblɪʃ] vt publicar; **publisher** n (person) editor(a) m/f; (firm) editorial f; **publishing** n (industry) industria del libro
pub lunch n almuerzo que se sirve en un pub; **to go for a ~** almorzar o comer en un pub
pudding [ˈpudɪŋ] n pudín m; (BRIT: dessert) postre m; **black ~** morcilla
puddle [ˈpʌdl] n charco
Puerto Rico [pwɛːtəuˈriːkəu] n Puerto Rico
puff [pʌf] n soplo; (of smoke, air) bocanada; (of breathing) resoplido ▷ vt: **to ~ one's pipe** chupar la pipa ▷ vi (pant) jadear; **puff pastry** n hojaldre m
pull [pul] n (tug): **to give sth a ~** dar un tirón a algo ▷ vt tirar de; (press: trigger) apretar; (haul) tirar, arrastrar; (close: curtain) echar ▷ vi tirar; **to ~ to pieces** hacer pedazos; **not to ~ one's punches** no andarse con bromas; **to ~ one's weight** hacer su parte; **to ~ o.s. together** sobreponerse; **to ~ sb's leg** tomar el pelo a algn; **pull apart** vt (break) romper; **pull away** vi (vehicle: move off) salir, arrancar; (draw back) apartarse bruscamente; **pull back** vt (lever etc) tirar hacia sí; (curtains) descorrer ▷ vi (refrain) contenerse; (Mil: withdraw) retirarse; **pull down** vt (building)

derribar; **pull in** vi (car etc) parar (junto a la acera); (train) llegar a la estación; **pull off** vt (deal etc) cerrar; **pull out** vi (car, train etc) salir ▷ vt sacar, arrancar; **pull over** vi (Aut) hacerse a un lado; **pull up** vi (stop) parar ▷ vt (raise) levantar; (uproot) arrancar, desarraigar

pulley ['pʊlɪ] n polea

pullover ['pʊləʊvə*] n jersey m, suéter m

pulp [pʌlp] n (of fruit) pulpa

pulpit ['pʊlpɪt] n púlpito

pulse [pʌls] n (Anat) pulso; (rhythm) pulsación f; (Bot) legumbre f; **pulses** pl n legumbres

puma ['pjuːmə] n puma m

pump [pʌmp] n bomba; (shoe) zapatilla ▷ vt sacar con una bomba; **pump up** vt inflar

pumpkin ['pʌmpkɪn] n calabaza

pun [pʌn] n juego de palabras

punch [pʌntʃ] n (blow) golpe m, puñetazo; (tool) punzón m; (drink) ponche m ▷ vt (hit): **to ~ sb/sth** dar un puñetazo or golpear a algn/algo; **punch-up** (BRIT: inf) n riña

punctual ['pʌŋktjuəl] adj puntual

punctuation [pʌŋktjuˈeɪʃən] n puntuación f

puncture ['pʌŋktʃə*] (BRIT) n pinchazo ▷ vt pinchar

punish ['pʌnɪʃ] vt castigar; **punishment** n castigo

punk [pʌŋk] n (also: ~ rocker) punki mf; (also: ~ rock) música punk; (us: inf: hoodlum) rufián m

pup [pʌp] n cachorro

pupil ['pjuːpl] n alumno/a; (of eye) pupila

puppet ['pʌpɪt] n títere m

puppy ['pʌpɪ] n cachorro, perrito

purchase ['pəːtʃɪs] n compra ▷ vt comprar

pure [pjuə*] adj puro; **purely** adv puramente

purify ['pjuərɪfaɪ] vt purificar, depurar

purity ['pjuərɪtɪ] n pureza

purple ['pəːpl] adj purpúreo; morado

purpose ['pəːpəs] n propósito; **on ~** a propósito, adrede

purr [pəː*] vi ronronear

purse [pəːs] n monedero; (us: handbag) bolso (SP), cartera (LAM), bolsa (MEX) ▷ vt fruncir

pursue [pəˈsjuː] vt seguir

pursuit [pəˈsjuːt] n (chase) caza; (occupation) actividad f

pus [pʌs] n pus m

push [pʊʃ] n empuje m, empujón m; (of button) presión f; (drive) empuje m ▷ vt empujar; (button) apretar; (promote) promover ▷ vi empujar; (demand): **to ~ for** luchar por; **push in** vi colarse; **push off** (inf) vi largarse; **push on** vi seguir adelante; **push over** vt (cause to fall) hacer caer, derribar; (knock over) volcar; **push through** vi (crowd) abrirse paso a empujones ▷ vt (measure) despachar; **pushchair** (BRIT) n sillita de ruedas; **pusher** n (drug pusher) traficante mf de drogas; **push-up** (us) n plancha

pussy(-cat) ['pʊsɪ-] (inf) n minino (inf)

put [pʊt] (pt, pp ~) vt (place) poner, colocar; (put into) meter; (say) expresar; (a question) hacer; (estimate) estimar; **put aside** vt (lay down: book etc) dejar or poner a un lado; (save) ahorrar; (in shop) guardar; **put away** vt (store) guardar; **put back** vt (replace) devolver a su lugar; (postpone) aplazar; **put by** vt (money) guardar; **put down** vt (on ground) poner en el suelo; (animal) sacrificar; (in writing) apuntar; (revolt etc) sofocar; (attribute): **to put sth down to** atribuir algo a; **put forward** vt (ideas) presentar, proponer; **put in** vt (complaint) presentar; (time) dedicar; **put**

off vt (postpone) aplazar; (discourage) desanimar; **put on** vt ponerse; (light etc) encender; (play etc) presentar; (gain): **to put on weight** engordar; (brake) echar; (record, kettle etc) poner; (assume) adoptar; **put out** vt (fire, light) apagar; (rubbish etc) sacar; (cat etc) echar; (one's hand) alargar; (inf: person): **to be put out** alterarse; **put through** vt (Tel) poner; (plan etc) hacer aprobar; **put together** vt unir, reunir; (assemble: furniture) armar, montar; (meal) preparar; **put up** vt (raise) levantar, alzar; (hang) colgar; (build) construir; (increase) aumentar; (accommodate) alojar; **put up with** vt fus aguantar

putt [pʌt] n putt m, golpe m corto; (putting green n green m; minigolf m

puzzle ['pʌzl] n rompecabezas m inv; (also: **crossword ~**) crucigrama m; (mystery) misterio ▷ vt dejar perplejo, confundir ▷ vi: **to ~ over sth** devanarse los sesos con algo; **puzzled** adj perplejo; **puzzling** adj misterioso, extraño

pyjamas [pɪˈdʒɑːməz] (BRIT) npl pijama m

pylon ['paɪlən] n torre f de conducción eléctrica

pyramid ['pɪrəmɪd] n pirámide f

q

quack [kwæk] n graznido; (pej: doctor) curandero/a

quadruple [kwɒˈdrupl] vt, vi cuadruplicar

quail [kweɪl] n codorniz f ▷ vi: **to ~ at** or **before** amedrentarse ante

quaint [kweɪnt] adj extraño; (picturesque) pintoresco

quake [kweɪk] vi temblar ▷ n abbr = **earthquake**

qualification [kwɒlɪfɪˈkeɪʃən] n (ability) capacidad f; (often pl: diploma etc) título; (reservation) salvedad f

qualified [ˈkwɒlɪfaɪd] adj capacitado; (professionally) titulado; (limited) limitado

qualify [ˈkwɒlɪfaɪ] vt (make competent) capacitar; (modify) modificar ▷ vi (in competition): **to ~ (for)** calificarse (para); (pass examination(s): **to ~ (as)** calificarse (de), graduarse (en); (be eligible): **to ~ (for)** reunir los requisitos (para)

quality [ˈkwɒlɪtɪ] n calidad f; (of person) cualidad f

qualm [kwɑːm] n escrúpulo

quantify [ˈkwɒntɪfaɪ] vt cuantificar

quantity [ˈkwɒntɪtɪ] n cantidad f; **in ~** en grandes cantidades

quarantine [ˈkwɒrəntiːn] n cuarentena

quarrel [ˈkwɒrl] n riña, pelea ▷ vi reñir, pelearse

quarry [ˈkwɒrɪ] n cantera

quart [kwɔːt] n ≈ litro

quarter [ˈkwɔːtə*] n cuarto, cuarta parte f; (us: coin) moneda de 25 centavos; (of year) trimestre m; (district) barrio ▷ vt dividir en cuartos; (Mil: lodge) alojar; **quarters** npl (barracks) cuartel m; (living quarters) alojamiento; **a ~ of an hour** un cuarto de hora; **quarter final** n cuarto de final; **quarterly** adj trimestral ▷ adv cada 3 meses, trimestralmente

quartet(te) [kwɔːˈtɛt] n cuarteto

quartz [kwɔːts] n cuarzo

quay [kiː] n (also: **~side**) muelle m

queasy [ˈkwiːzɪ] adj: **to feel ~** tener náuseas

queen [kwiːn] n reina; (Cards etc) dama

queer [kwɪə*] adj raro, extraño ▷ n (inf: highly offensive) maricón m

quench [kwɛntʃ] vt: **to ~ one's thirst** apagar la sed

query [ˈkwɪərɪ] n (question) pregunta ▷ vt dudar de

quest [kwɛst] n busca, búsqueda

question [ˈkwɛstʃən] n pregunta; (doubt) duda; (matter) asunto, cuestión f ▷ vt (doubt) dudar de; (interrogate) interrogar, hacer preguntas a; **beyond ~** fuera de toda duda; **out of the ~** imposible; ni hablar; **questionable** adj dudoso; **question mark** n punto de interrogación; **questionnaire** [-ˈnɛə*] n cuestionario

queue [kjuː] (BRIT) n cola ▷ vi (also: **~ up**) hacer cola

quiche [kiːʃ] n quiche m

quick [kwɪk] adj rápido; (agile) ágil; (mind) listo ▷ n: **cut to the ~** (fig) herido en lo vivo; **be ~!** ¡date prisa!; **quickly** adv rápidamente, de prisa

quid [kwɪd] (BRIT: inf) n inv libra

quiet [ˈkwaɪət] adj (voice, music etc) bajo; (person, place) tranquilo; (ceremony) íntimo ▷ n silencio; (calm) tranquilidad f ▷ vt, vi (us): **quieten**; **quietly** adv tranquilamente; (silently) silenciosamente

quilt [kwɪlt] n edredón m

quirky [ˈkwɜːkɪ] adj raro, estrafalario

quit [kwɪt] (pt, pp ~ or ~**ted**) vt dejar, abandonar; (premises) desocupar ▷ vi (give up) renunciar; (resign) dimitir

quite [kwaɪt] adv (rather) bastante; (entirely) completamente; **that's not ~ big enough** no acaba de ser lo bastante grande; **~ a few of them** un buen número de ellos; **~ (so)!** ¡así es!, ¡exactamente!

quits [kwɪts] adj: **~ (with)** en paz (con); **let's call it ~** dejémoslo en tablas

quiver [ˈkwɪvə*] vi estremecerse

quiz [kwɪz] n concurso ▷ vt interrogar

quota [ˈkwəʊtə] n cuota

quotation [kwəʊˈteɪʃən] n cita; (estimate) presupuesto; **quotation marks** npl comillas fpl

quote [kwəʊt] n cita; (estimate) presupuesto ▷ vt citar; (price) cotizar ▷ vi: **to ~ from** citar de; **quotes** npl (inverted commas) comillas fpl

r

rabbi ['ræbaɪ] n rabino

rabbit ['ræbɪt] n conejo

rabies ['reɪbiːz] n rabia

RAC (BRIT) n abbr (= Royal Automobile Club) ≈ RACE m

rac(c)oon [rəˈkuːn] n mapache m

race [reɪs] n carrera; (species) raza ▷ vt (horse) hacer correr; (engine) acelerar ▷ vi (compete) competir; (run) correr; (pulse) latir a ritmo acelerado; **race car** (US) n = **racing car**; **racecourse** n hipódromo; **racehorse** n caballo de carreras; **racetrack** n pista; (for cars) autódromo

racial ['reɪʃl] adj racial

racing ['reɪsɪŋ] n carreras fpl; **racing car** (BRIT) n coche m de carreras; **racing driver** (BRIT) n piloto mf de carreras

racism ['reɪsɪzəm] n racismo; **racist** [-sɪst] adj, n racista mf

rack [ræk] n (also: **luggage ~**) rejilla; (shelf) estante m; (also: **roof ~**) baca, portaequipajes m inv; (dish rack) escurreplatos m inv; (clothes rack) percha ▷ vt atormentar; **to ~ one's brains** devanarse los sesos

racket ['rækɪt] n (for tennis) raqueta; (noise) ruido, estrépito; (swindle) estafa, timo

racquet ['rækɪt] n raqueta

radar ['reɪdɑː*] n radar m

radiation [reɪdɪˈeɪʃən] n radiación f

radiator ['reɪdɪeɪtə*] n radiador m

radical ['rædɪkl] adj radical

radio ['reɪdɪəu] n radio f; **on the ~** por radio; **radioactive** adj radioactivo; **radio station** n emisora

radish ['rædɪʃ] n rábano

RAF n abbr (= Royal Air Force) las Fuerzas Aéreas Británicas

raffle ['ræfl] n rifa, sorteo

raft [rɑːft] n balsa; (also: **life ~**) balsa salvavidas

rag [ræg] n (piece of cloth) trapo; (torn cloth) harapo; (pej: newspaper) periodicucho; (for charity) actividades estudiantiles benéficas; **rags** npl (torn clothes) harapos mpl

rage [reɪdʒ] n rabia, furor m ▷ vi (person) rabiar, estar furioso; (storm) bramar; **it's all the ~** (very fashionable) está muy de moda

ragged ['rægɪd] adj (edge) desigual, mellado; (appearance) andrajoso, harapiento

raid [reɪd] n (Mil) incursión f; (criminal) asalto; (by police) redada ▷ vt invadir, atacar; asaltar

rail [reɪl] n (on stair) barandilla, pasamanos m inv; (on bridge, balcony) pretil m; (of ship) barandilla; (also: **towel ~**) toallero; **railcard** n (BRIT) tarjeta para obtener descuentos en el tren; **railing(s)** n(pl) vallado; **railroad** (US) n = **railway**; **railway** (BRIT) n ferrocarril m, vía férrea; **railway line** (BRIT) n línea (de ferrocarril); **railway station** (BRIT) n estación f de ferrocarril

rain [reɪn] n lluvia ▷ vi llover; **in the ~** bajo la lluvia; **it's ~ing** llueve, está lloviendo; **rainbow** n arco iris; **raincoat** n impermeable m; **raindrop** n gota de lluvia; **rainfall** n lluvia; **rainforest** n selvas fpl tropicales; **rainy** adj lluvioso

raise [reɪz] n aumento ▷ vt levantar; (increase) aumentar; (improve: morale) subir; (: standards) mejorar; (doubts) suscitar; (a question) plantear; (cattle, family) criar; (crop) cultivar; (army) reclutar; (loan) obtener; **to ~ one's voice** alzar la voz

raisin ['reɪzn] n pasa de Corinto

rake [reɪk] n (tool) rastrillo; (person) libertino ▷ vt (garden) rastrillar

rally ['rælɪ] n (Pol etc) reunión f, mitin m; (Aut) rallye m; (Tennis) peloteo ▷ vt reunir ▷ vi recuperarse

RAM [ræm] n abbr (= random access memory) RAM f

ram [ræm] n carnero; (also: **battering ~**) ariete m ▷ vt (crash into) dar contra, chocar con; (push: fist etc) empujar con fuerza

Ramadan [ræməˈdæn] n ramadán m

ramble ['ræmbl] n caminata, excursión f en el campo ▷ vi (pej: also: **~ on**) divagar; **rambler** n excursionista mf; (Bot) trepadora; **rambling** adj (speech) inconexo; (house) laberíntico; (Bot) trepador(a)

ramp [ræmp] n rampa; **on/off ~** (US Aut) vía de acceso/salida

rampage [ræmˈpeɪdʒ] n: **to be on the ~** desmandarse ▷ vi: **they went rampaging through the town** recorrieron la ciudad armando alboroto

ran [ræn] pt of **run**

ranch [rɑːntʃ] n hacienda, estancia

random ['rændəm] adj fortuito, sin orden; (Comput, Math) aleatorio ▷ n: **at ~** al azar

rang [ræŋ] pt of **ring**

range [reɪndʒ] n (of mountains) cadena de montañas, cordillera; (of missile) alcance m; (of voice) registro; (series) serie f; (of products) surtido; (Mil: also: **shooting ~**) campo de tiro; (also: **kitchen ~**) fogón m ▷ vt (place) colocar; (arrange) arreglar ▷ vi: **to ~ over** (extend) extenderse por; **to ~ from ... to ...** oscilar entre ... y ...

ranger ['reɪndʒə*] n guardabosques mf inv

rank [ræŋk] n (row) fila; (Mil) rango; (status) categoría; (BRIT: also: **taxi ~**) parada de taxis ▷ vi: **to ~ among** figurar entre ▷ adj fétido, rancio; **the ~ and file** (fig) la base

ransom ['rænsəm] n rescate m; **to hold to ~** (fig) hacer chantaje a

rant [rænt] vi divagar, desvariar

rap [ræp] vt golpear, dar un golpecito en ▷ n (music) rap m

rape [reɪp] n violación f; (Bot) colza ▷ vt violar

rapid ['ræpɪd] adj rápido; **rapidly** adv rápidamente; **rapids** npl (Geo) rápidos mpl

rapist ['reɪpɪst] n violador m

rapport [ræˈpɔː*] n simpatía

rare [reə*] adj raro, poco común; (Culin: steak) poco hecho; **rarely** adv pocas veces

rash [ræʃ] adj imprudente, precipitado ▷ n (Med) sarpullido, erupción f (cutánea); (of events) serie f

rasher ['ræʃə*] n lonja

raspberry ['rɑːzbəri] n frambuesa

rat [ræt] n rata

rate [reɪt] n (ratio) razón f; (price) precio; (: of hotel etc) tarifa; (of interest) tipo; (speed) velocidad f ▷ vt (value) tasar; (estimate) estimar; **rates** npl (BRIT: property tax) impuesto municipal; (fees) tarifa; **to ~ sth/sb as** considerar algo/a algn como

rather ['rɑːðə*] adv **it's ~ expensive** es algo caro; (too much) es demasiado caro; (to some extent) más bien; **there's ~ a lot** hay bastante; **I would** or **I'd ~ go** preferiría ir; **or ~** mejor dicho

rating ['reɪtɪŋ] n tasación f; (score) índice m; (of ship) clase f; **ratings** npl (Radio, TV) niveles mpl de audiencia

ratio ['reɪʃiəu] n razón f; **in the ~ of 100 to 1** a razón de 100 a 1

ration ['ræʃən] n ración f ▷ vt racionar; **rations** npl víveres mpl

rational ['ræʃənl] adj (solution, reasoning) lógico, razonable; (person) cuerdo, sensato

rattle ['rætl] n golpeteo; (of train etc) traqueteo; (for baby) sonaja, sonajero ▷ vi castañetear; (car, bus): **to ~ along** traquetear ▷ vt hacer sonar agitando

rave [reɪv] vi (in anger) encolerizarse; (with enthusiasm) entusiasmarse; (Med) delirar, desvariar ▷ n (inf: party) rave m

raven ['reɪvən] n cuervo

ravine [rə'viːn] n barranco

raw [rɔː] adj crudo; (not processed) bruto; (sore) vivo; (inexperienced) novato, inexperto; **~ materials** materias primas

ray [reɪ] n rayo; **~ of hope** (rayo de) esperanza

razor ['reɪzə*] n (open) navaja; (safety razor) máquina de afeitar; (electric razor) máquina (eléctrica) de afeitar; **razor blade** n hoja de afeitar

Rd abbr = **road**

RE n abbr (BRIT) = **religious education**

re [riː] prep con referencia a

reach [riːtʃ] n alcance m; (of river etc) extensión f entre dos recodos ▷ vt alcanzar, llegar a; (achieve) lograr ▷ vi extenderse; **within ~** al alcance (de la mano); **out of ~** fuera del alcance; **reach out** vt (hand) tender ▷ vi: **to reach out for sth** alargar or tender la mano para tomar algo

react [riː'ækt] vi reaccionar; **reaction** [-'ækʃən] n reacción f; **reactor** [riː'æktə*] n (also: **nuclear reactor**) reactor m (nuclear)

read [riːd, pt, pp red] (pt, pp ~) vi leer ▷ vt leer; (understand) entender; (study) estudiar; **read out** vt leer en alta voz; **reader** n lector(a) m/f; (BRIT: at university) profesor(a) m/f adjunto/a

readily ['redɪlɪ] adv (willingly) de buena gana; (easily) fácilmente; (quickly) en seguida

reading ['riːdɪŋ] n lectura; (understanding) indicación f

ready ['redɪ] adj listo, preparado; (willing) dispuesto; (available) disponible ▷ adv: **~-cooked** listo para comer ▷ n: **at the ~** (Mil) listo para tirar ▷ **to get ~** vi prepararse ▷ **to get ~** vt preparar; **ready-made** adj confeccionado

real [rɪəl] adj verdadero, auténtico; **in ~ terms** en términos reales; **real ale** n cerveza elaborada tradicionalmente; **real estate** n bienes mpl raíces;

realistic [-'lɪstɪk] adj realista; **reality** [riː'ælɪtɪ] n realidad f; **reality TV** n telerrealidad f

realization [rɪəlaɪ'zeɪʃən] n comprensión f; (fulfilment, Comm) realización f

realize ['rɪəlaɪz] vt (understand) darse cuenta de

really ['rɪəlɪ] adv realmente; (for emphasis) verdaderamente; (actually): **what ~ happened** lo que pasó en realidad; **~?** ¿de veras?; **~!** (annoyance) ¡vamos!, ¡por favor!

realm [relm] n reino; (fig) esfera

realtor ['rɪəltɔː*] (US) n agente mf inmobiliario/a

reappear [riːə'pɪə*] vi reaparecer

rear [rɪə*] adj trasero ▷ n parte f trasera ▷ vt (cattle, family) criar ▷ vi (also: **~ up**: animal) encabritarse

rearrange [riːə'reɪndʒ] vt ordenar or arreglar de nuevo

rear: rear-view mirror n (Aut) (espejo) retrovisor m; **rear-wheel drive** n tracción f trasera

reason ['riːzn] n razón f ▷ vi: **to ~ with sb** tratar de que algn entre en razón; **it stands to ~ that ...** es lógico que ...; **reasonable** adj razonable; (sensible) sensato; **reasonably** adv razonablemente; **reasoning** n razonamiento, argumentos mpl

reassurance [riːə'ʃuərəns] n consuelo

reassure [riːə'ʃuə*] vt tranquilizar, alentar; **to ~ sb that ...** tranquilizar a algn asegurando que ...

rebate ['riːbeɪt] n (on tax etc) desgravación f

rebel [n 'rebl, vi ri'bel] n rebelde mf ▷ vi rebelarse, sublevarse; **rebellion** [ri'beljan] n rebelión f, sublevación f; **rebellious** [ri'beljas] adj rebelde; (child) revoltoso

rebuild [riː'bɪld] vt reconstruir

recall [vb ri'kɔːl, n ri'kɔːl] vt (remember) recordar; (ambassador etc) retirar ▷ n recuerdo; retirada

rec'd abbr (= received) rbdo

receipt [ri'siːt] n (document) recibo; (for parcel etc) acuse m de recibo; (act of receiving) recepción f; **receipts** npl (Comm) ingresos mpl

receive [ri'siːv] vt recibir; (guest) acoger; (wound) sufrir; **receiver** n (Tel) auricular m; (Radio) receptor m; (of stolen goods) perista mf; (Comm) administrador m jurídico

recent ['riːsnt] adj reciente; **recently** adv recientemente; **recently arrived** recién llegado

reception [ri'sepʃən] n recepción f; (welcome) acogida; **reception desk** n recepción f; **receptionist** n recepcionista mf

recession [ri'seʃən] n recesión f

recharge [riː'tʃɑːdʒ] vt (battery) recargar

recipe ['resɪpɪ] n receta; (for disaster, success) fórmula

recipient [ri'sɪpɪənt] n recibidor(a) m/f; (of letter) destinatario/a

recital [ri'saɪtl] n recital m

recite [ri'saɪt] vt (poem) recitar

reckless ['reklas] adj temerario, imprudente; (driving, driver) peligroso

reckon ['rekən] vt calcular; (consider) considerar; (think): **I ~ that ...** me parece que ...

reclaim [ri'kleɪm] vt (land, waste) recuperar; (land: from sea) rescatar; (demand back) reclamar

recline [ri'klaɪn] vi reclinarse

recognition [rekəg'nɪʃən] n reconocimiento; **transformed beyond ~** irreconocible

recognize ['rekəgnaɪz] vt: **to ~ (by/as)** reconocer (por/como)

recollection [rekə'lekʃən] n recuerdo

recommend [rekə'mend] vt recomendar; **recommendation** [rekəmen'deɪʃən] n recomendación f

reconcile ['rekənsaɪl] vt (two people) reconciliar; (two facts) compaginar; **to ~ o.s. to sth** conformarse a algo

reconsider [ri:kən'sɪdə*] vt repensar

reconstruct [ri:kən'strʌkt] vt reconstruir

record [n, adj 'rekɔ:d, vt rɪ'kɔ:d] n (Mus) disco; (of meeting etc) acta; (register) registro, partida; (file) archivo; (also: **criminal ~**) antecedentes mpl; (written) expediente m; (Sport, Comput) récord m ▷ adj récord, sin precedentes ▷ vt registrar; (Mus: song etc) grabar; **in ~ time** en un tiempo récord; **off the ~** adj no oficial ▷ adv confidencialmente; **recorded delivery** (BRIT) n (Post) entrega con acuse de recibo; **recorder** n (Mus) flauta de pico; **recording** n (Mus) grabación f; **record player** n tocadiscos m inv

recount [rɪ'kaunt] vt contar

recover [rɪ'kʌvə*] vt recuperar ▷ vi (from illness, shock) recuperarse, **recovery** n recuperación f

recreate [ri:krɪ'eɪt] vt recrear

recreation [rekrɪ'eɪʃən] n recreo; **recreational vehicle** (US) n caravan or rulota pequeña; **recreational drug** droga recreativa

recruit [rɪ'kru:t] n recluta mf ▷ vt reclutar; (staff) contratar; **recruitment** n reclutamiento

rectangle ['rektæŋgl] n rectángulo; **rectangular** [-'tæŋgjulə*] adj rectangular

rectify ['rektɪfaɪ] vt rectificar

rector ['rektə*] n (Rel) párroco

recur [rɪ'kə:*] vi repetirse; (pain, illness) producirse de nuevo; **recurring** adj (problem) repetido, constante

recyclable [ri:'saɪkləbl] adj reciclable

recycle [ri:'saɪkl] vt reciclar

recycling [ri:'saɪklɪŋ] n reciclaje

red [red] n rojo ▷ adj rojo; (hair) pelirrojo; (wine) tinto; **to be in the ~** (account) estar en números rojos; (business) tener un saldo negativo; **to give sb the ~ carpet treatment** recibir a algn con todos los honores; **Red Cross** n Cruz f Roja; **redcurrant** n grosella roja

redeem [rɪ'di:m] vt (promises) cumplir; (sth in pawn) desempeñar; (fig, also Rel) rescatar

red-haired adj pelirrojo; **redhead** n pelirrojo/a; **red-hot** adj candente; **red light**: **to go through a red light** (Aut) pasar la luz roja; **red-light district** n barrio chino

red meat n carne f roja

reduce [rɪ'dju:s] vt reducir; **to ~ sb to tears** hacer llorar a algn; **"~ speed now"** (Aut) "reduzca la velocidad"; **reduced** adj (decreased) reducido, rebajado; **at a reduced price** con rebaja or descuento; **"greatly reduced prices"** "grandes rebajas"; **reduction** [rɪ'dʌkʃən] n reducción f; (of price) rebaja; (discount) descuento; (smaller-scale copy) copia reducida

redundancy [rɪ'dʌndənsɪ] n (dismissal) despido; (unemployment) desempleo

redundant [rɪ'dʌndnt] adj (BRIT: worker) parado, sin trabajo; (detail, object) superfluo; **to be made ~** quedar(se) sin trabajo

reed [ri:d] n (Bot) junco, caña; (Mus) lengüeta

reef [ri:f] n (at sea) arrecife m

reel [ri:l] n carrete m, bobina; (of film) rollo; (dance) baile escocés ▷ vt (also: **~ up**) devanar; (also: **~ in**) sacar ▷ vi (sway) tambalear(se)

ref [ref] (inf) n abbr = **referee**

refectory [rɪ'fektərɪ] n comedor m

refer [rɪ'fə:*] vt (send: patient) referir; (: matter) remitir ▷ vi: **to ~ to** (allude to) referirse a, aludir a; (apply to) relacionarse con; (consult) consultar

referee [refə'ri:] n árbitro; (BRIT: for job application): **to be a ~ for sb** proporcionar referencias a algn ▷ vt (match) arbitrar en

reference ['refrəns] n referencia; (for job application: letter) carta de recomendación; **with ~ to** (Comm: in letter) me remito a; **reference number** n número de referencia

refill [vt ri:'fɪl, n 'ri:fɪl] vt rellenar ▷ n repuesto, recambio

refine [rɪ'faɪn] vt refinar; **refined** adj (person) fino; **refinery** n refinería f

reflect [rɪ'flekt] vt reflejar ▷ vi (think) reflexionar, pensar; **it ~s badly/well on him** le perjudica/le hace honor; **reflection** [-'flekʃən] n (act) reflexión f; (image) reflejo; (criticism) crítica; **on reflection** pensándolo bien

reflex ['ri:fleks] adj, n reflejo

reform [rɪ'fɔ:m] n reforma ▷ vt reformar

refrain [rɪ'freɪn] vi: **to ~ from doing** abstenerse de hacer ▷ n estribillo

refresh [rɪ'freʃ] vt refrescar; **refreshing** adj refrescante; **refreshments** npl refrescos mpl

refrigerator [rɪ'frɪdʒəreɪtə*] n frigorífico (SP), nevera (SP), refrigerador m (LAM), heladera (RPL)

refuel [ri:'fjuəl] vt repostar (combustible)

refuge ['refju:dʒ] n refugio, asilo; **to take ~ in** refugiarse en; **refugee** [refju'dʒi:] n refugiado/a

refund [n 'ri:fʌnd, vb rɪ'fʌnd] n reembolso ▷ vt devolver, reembolsar

refurbish [ri:'fə:bɪʃ] vt restaurar, renovar

refusal [rɪ'fju:zəl] n negativa; **to have first ~ on** tener la primera opción a

refuse[1] ['refju:s] n basura

refuse[2] [rɪ'fju:z] vt rechazar; (invitation) declinar; (permission) denegar ▷ vi: **to ~ to do sth** negarse a hacer algo; (horse) rehusar

regain [rɪ'geɪn] vt recobrar, recuperar

regard [rɪ'gɑ:d] n mirada; (esteem) respeto; (attention) consideración f ▷ vt (consider) considerar; **to give one's ~s to** saludar de su parte a; **"with kindest ~s"** "con muchos recuerdos"; **as ~s**, **with ~ to** con respecto a, en cuanto a; **regarding** prep con respecto a, en cuanto a; **regardless** adv a pesar de todo; **regardless of** sin reparar en

regenerate [rɪ'dʒenəreɪt] vt regenerar

reggae ['regeɪ] n reggae m

regiment ['redʒɪmənt] n regimiento

region ['ri:dʒən] n región f; **in the ~ of** (fig) alrededor de; **regional** adj regional

register ['redʒɪstə*] n registro ▷ vt registrar; (birth) declarar; (car) matricular; (letter) certificar; (instrument) marcar, indicar ▷ vi (at hotel) registrarse; (as student) matricularse; (make impression) producir impresión; **registered** adj (letter, parcel) certificado

registrar ['redʒɪstrɑ:*] n secretario/a (del registro civil)

registration [redʒɪs'treɪʃən] n (act) declaración f; (Aut: also: **~ number**) matrícula

registry office ['redʒɪstrɪ-] (BRIT) n registro civil; **to get married in a ~** casarse por lo civil

regret [rɪ'gret] n sentimiento, pesar m ▷ vt sentir, lamentar; **regrettable** adj lamentable

regular ['regjulə*] adj regular; (soldier) profesional;

(*usual*) habitual; (: *doctor*) de cabecera ▷ *n* (*client etc*) cliente/a *m/f* habitual; **regularly** *adv* con regularidad; (*often*) repetidas veces

regulate ['regjuleit] *vt* controlar; **regulation** [-'leiʃə n] *n* (*rule*) regla, reglamento

rehabilitation ['ri:əbili'teiʃən] *n* rehabilitación *f*

rehearsal [ri'hə:səl] *n* ensayo

rehearse [ri'hə:s] *vt* ensayar

reign [rein] *n* reinado; (*fig*) predominio ▷ *vi* reinar; (*fig*) imperar

reimburse [ri:im'bə:s] *vt* reembolsar

rein [rein] *n* (*for horse*) rienda

reincarnation [ri:inka:'neiʃən] *n* reencarnación *f*

reindeer ['reindiə*] *n inv* reno

reinforce [ri:in'fo:s] *vt* reforzar; **reinforcements** *npl* (*Mil*) refuerzos *mpl*

reinstate [ri:in'steit] *vt* reintegrar; (*tax, law*) reinstaurar

reject [*n* 'ri:dʒekt, *vb* ri'dʒekt] *n* (*thing*) desecho ▷ *vt* rechazar; (*suggestion*) descartar; (*coin*) expulsar; **rejection** [ri'dʒekʃən] *n* rechazo

rejoice [ri'dʒɔis] *vi:* **to ~ at** or **over** regocijarse or alegrarse de

relate [ri'leit] *vt* (*tell*) contar, relatar; (*connect*) relacionar ▷ *vi* relacionarse; **related** *adj* afín; (*person*) emparentado; **related to** (*subject*) relacionado con; **relating to** *prep* referente a

relation [ri'leiʃən] *n* (*person*) familiar *m f*, pariente *m f*; (*link*) relación *f*; **relations** *npl* (*relatives*) familiares *mpl*; **relationship** *n* relación *f*; (*personal*) relaciones *fpl*; (*also:* **family relationship**) parentesco

relative ['relativ] *n* pariente *m f*, familiar *m f* ▷ *adj* relativo; **relatively** *adv* (*comparatively*) relativamente

relax [ri'læks] *vi* descansar; (*unwind*) relajarse ▷ *vt* (*one's grip*) soltar, aflojar; (*control*) relajar; (*mind, person*) descansar; **relaxation** [ri:læk'seiʃən] *n* descanso; (*of rule, control*) relajamiento; (*entertainment*) diversión *f*; **relaxed** *adj* relajado; (*tranquil*) tranquilo; **relaxing** *adj* relajante

relay ['ri:lei] *n* (*race*) carrera de relevos ▷ *vt* (*Radio, TV*) retransmitir

release [ri'li:s] *n* (*liberation*) liberación *f*; (*from prison*) puesta en libertad; (*of gas etc*) escape *m*; (*of film etc*) estreno; (*of record*) lanzamiento ▷ *vt* (*prisoner*) poner en libertad; (*gas*) despedir, arrojar; (*from wreckage*) soltar; (*catch, spring etc*) desenganchar; (*film*) estrenar; (*book*) publicar; (*news*) difundir

relegate ['relegeit] *vt* relegar; (*BRIT Sport*) **to be ~d to** bajar a

relent [ri'lent] *vi* ablandarse; **relentless** *adj* implacable

relevant ['relevant] *adj* (*fact*) pertinente; **~ to** relacionado con

reliable [ri'laiabl] *adj* (*person, firm*) de confianza, de fiar; (*method, machine*) seguro; (*source*) fidedigno

relic ['relik] *n* (*Rel*) reliquia; (*of the past*) vestigio

relief [ri'li:f] *n* (*from pain, anxiety*) alivio; (*help, supplies*) socorro, ayuda; (*Art, Geo*) relieve *m*

relieve [ri'li:v] *vt* (*pain*) aliviar; (*bring help to*) ayudar, socorrer; (*take over from*) sustituir; (: *guard*) relevar; **to ~ sb of sth** quitar algo a algn; **to ~ o.s.** hacer sus necesidades; **relieved** *adj:* **to be relieved** sentir un gran alivio

religion [ri'lidʒən] *n* religión *f*

religious [ri'lidʒəs] *adj* religioso; **religious education** *n* educación *f* religiosa

relish ['reliʃ] *n* (*Culin*) salsa; (*enjoyment*) entusiasmo ▷ *vt* (*food etc*) saborear; (*enjoy*): **to ~ sth** hacerle mucha ilusión a algn algo

relocate [ri:ləu'keit] *vt* cambiar de lugar, mudar ▷ *vi* mudarse

reluctance [ri'lʌktəns] *n* renuencia

reluctant [ri'lʌktənt] *adj* renuente; **reluctantly** *adv* de mala gana

rely on [ri'lai-] *vt fus* depender de; (*trust*) contar con

remain [ri'mein] *vi* (*survive*) quedar; (*be left*) sobrar; (*continue*) quedar(se), permanecer; **remainder** *n* resto; **remaining** *adj* que queda(n); (*surviving*) restante(s); **remains** *npl* restos *mpl*

remand [ri'ma:nd] *n:* **on ~** detenido (bajo custodia) ▷ *vt:* **to be ~ed in custody** quedar detenido bajo custodia

remark [ri'ma:k] *n* comentario ▷ *vt* comentar; **remarkable** *adj* (*outstanding*) extraordinario

remarry [ri:'mæri] *vi* volver a casarse

remedy ['remədi] *n* remedio ▷ *vt* remediar, curar

remember [ri'membə*] *vt* recordar, acordarse de; (*bear in mind*) tener presente; (*send greetings to*): **~ me to him** dale recuerdos de mi parte; **Remembrance Day** *n* = día en el que se recuerda a los caídos en las dos guerras mundiales

remind [ri'maind] *vt:* **to ~ sb to do sth** recordar a algn que haga algo; **to ~ sb of sth** (*of fact*) recordar algo a algn; **she ~s me of her mother** me recuerda a su madre; **reminder** *n* notificación *f*; (*memento*) recuerdo

reminiscent [remi'nisnt] *adj:* **to be ~ of sth** recordar algo

remnant ['remnənt] *n* resto; (*of cloth*) retal *m*

remorse [ri'mɔ:s] *n* remordimientos *mpl*

remote [ri'məut] *adj* (*distant*) lejano; (*person*) distante; **remote control** *n* telecontrol *m*; **remotely** *adv* remotamente; (*slightly*) levemente

removal [ri'mu:vəl] *n* (*taking away*) el quitar; (*BRIT: from house*) mudanza; (*from office: dismissal*) destitución *f*; (*Med*) extirpación *f*; **removal man** (*irreg*) *n* (*BRIT*) mozo de mudanzas; **removal van** (*BRIT*) *n* camión *m* de mudanzas

remove [ri'mu:v] *vt* quitar; (*employee*) destituir; (*name: from list*) tachar, borrar; (*doubt*) disipar; (*abuse*) suprimir, acabar con; (*Med*) extirpar

Renaissance [ri'neisāns] *n:* **the ~** el Renacimiento

rename [ri:'neim] *vt* poner nuevo nombre a

render ['rendə*] *vt* (*thanks*) dar; (*aid*) proporcionar, prestar; (*make*): **to ~ sth useless** hacer algo inútil

rendezvous ['rɔndivu:] *n* cita

renew [ri'nju:] *vt* renovar; (*resume*) reanudar; (*loan etc*) prorrogar

renovate ['renəveit] *vt* renovar

renowned [ri'naund] *adj* renombrado

rent [rent] *n* (*for house*) arriendo, renta ▷ *vt* alquilar; **rental** *n* (*for television, car*) alquiler *m*

reorganize [ri:'ɔ:gənaiz] *vt* reorganizar

rep [rep] *n abbr* = **representative**

repair [ri'peə*] *n* reparación *f*, compostura ▷ *vt* reparar, componer; (*shoes*) remendar; **in good/bad ~** en buen/mal estado; **repair kit** *n* caja de herramientas

repay [ri:'pei] *vt* (*money*) devolver, reembolsar; (*person: again*) pagar; (*debt*) liquidar; (*sb's efforts*) devolver, corresponder a; **repayment** *n* reembolso, devolución *f*; (*sum of money*) recompensa

repeat [ri'pi:t] *n* (*Radio, TV*) reposición *f* ▷ *vt* repetir

▷ vi repetirse; **repeatedly** adv repetidas veces;
repeat prescription n (BRIT) receta renovada
repellent [rɪ'pelənt] adj repugnante ▷ n: **insect ~** crema ór loción f anti-insectos
repercussions [ri:pə'kʌʃənz] npl consecuencias fpl
repetition [repɪ'tɪʃən] n repetición f
repetitive [rɪ'petɪtɪv] adj repetitivo
replace [rɪ'pleɪs] vt (put back) devolver a su sitio; (take the place) reemplazar, sustituir; **replacement** n (act) reposición f; (thing) recambio; (person) suplente mf
replay ['ri:pleɪ] n (Sport) desempate m; (of tape, film) repetición f
replica ['replɪkə] n copia, reproducción f (exacta)
reply [rɪ'plaɪ] n respuesta, contestación f ▷ vi contestar, responder
report [rɪ'pɔːt] n informe m; (Press etc) reportaje m; (BRIT: also: **school ~**) boletín m escolar; (of gun) estallido ▷ vt informar de; (Press etc) hacer un reportaje sobre; (notify: accident, culprit) denunciar ▷ vi (make a report) presentar un informe; (present o.s.): **to ~ (to sb)** presentarse (ante algn); **report card** n (US, SCOTTISH) cartilla escolar; **reportedly** adv según se dice; **reporter** n periodista mf
represent [reprɪ'zent] vt representar; (Comm) ser agente de; (describe): **to ~ sth as** describir algo como; **representation** [-'teɪʃən] n representación f; **representative** n representante mf; (US Pol) diputado/a m/f ▷ adj representativo
repress [rɪ'pres] vt reprimir; **repression** [-'preʃən] n represión f
reprimand ['reprɪmɑːnd] n reprimenda ▷ vt reprender
reproduce [ri:prə'djuːs] vt reproducir ▷ vi reproducirse; **reproduction** [-'dʌkʃən] n reproducción f
reptile ['reptaɪl] n reptil m
republic [rɪ'pʌblɪk] n república; **republican** adj, n republicano/a m/f
reputable ['repjutəbl] adj (make etc) de renombre
reputation [repju'teɪʃən] n reputación f
request [rɪ'kwest] n petición f; (formal) solicitud f ▷ vt: **to ~ sth of or from sb** solicitar algo a algn; **request stop** (BRIT) n parada discrecional
require [rɪ'kwaɪə*] vt (need: person) necesitar, tener necesidad de; (: thing, situation) exigir; (want) pedir; **to ~ sb to do sth** pedir a algn que haga algo; **requirement** n requisito; (need) necesidad f
resat [riːˈsæt] pt, pp of **resit**
rescue ['reskjuː] n rescate m ▷ vt rescatar
research [rɪ'səːtʃ] n investigaciones fpl ▷ vt investigar
resemblance [rɪ'zembləns] n parecido
resemble [rɪ'zembl] vt parecerse a
resent [rɪ'zent] vt tomar a mal; **resentful** adj resentido; **resentment** n resentimiento
reservation [rezə'veɪʃən] n reserva; **reservation desk** (US) n (in hotel) recepción f
reserve [rɪ'zəːv] n reserva; (Sport) suplente mf ▷ vt (seats etc) reservar; **reserved** adj reservado
reservoir ['rezəvwɑː*] n (artificial lake) embalse m, tank; (small) depósito
residence ['rezɪdəns] n (formal: home) domicilio; (length of stay) permanencia; **residence permit** (BRIT) n permiso de permanencia
resident ['rezɪdənt] n (of area) vecino/a; (in hotel) huésped mf ▷ adj (population) permanente; (doctor)

residente; **residential** [-'denʃəl] adj residencial
residue ['rezɪdjuː] n resto
resign [rɪ'zaɪn] vt renunciar a ▷ vi dimitir; **to ~ o.s. to** (situation) resignarse a; **resignation** [rezɪg'neɪʃən] n dimisión f; (state of mind) resignación f
resin ['rezɪn] n resina
resist [rɪ'zɪst] vt resistir, oponerse a; **resistance** n resistencia
resit [rɪ'sɪt] (BRIT) (pt, pp **resat**) vt (exam) volver a presentarse a; (subject) recuperar, volver a examinarse de (SP)
resolution [rezə'luːʃən] n resolución f
resolve [rɪ'zɔlv] n resolución f ▷ vt resolver ▷ vi: **to do** resolver hacer
resort [rɪ'zɔːt] n (town) centro turístico; (recourse) recurso ▷ vi: **to ~ to** recurrir a; **in the last ~** como último recurso
resource [rɪ'sɔːs] n recurso; **resourceful** adj despabilado, ingenioso
respect [rɪs'pekt] n respeto ▷ vt respetar; **respectable** adj respetable; (large: amount) apreciable; (passable) tolerable; **respectful** adj respetuoso; **respective** adj respectivo; **respectively** adv respectivamente
respite ['respaɪt] n respiro
respond [rɪs'pɔnd] vi responder; (react) reaccionar; **response** [-'pɔns] n respuesta; reacción f
responsibility [rɪspɔnsɪ'bɪlɪtɪ] n responsabilidad f
responsible [rɪs'pɔnsɪbl] adj (character) serio, formal; (job) de confianza; (liable): **~ (for)** responsable (de); **responsibly** adv con seriedad
responsive [rɪs'pɔnsɪv] adj sensible
rest [rest] n descanso, reposo; (Mus: pause) pausa, silencio; (support) apoyo; (remainder) resto ▷ vi descansar; (be supported): **to ~ on** descansar sobre ▷ vt: **to ~ sth on/against** apoyar algo en o sobre/contra; **the ~ of them** (people, objects) los demás; **it ~s with him to ...** depende de él el que ...
restaurant ['restərɔŋ] n restaurante m; **restaurant car** (BRIT) n (Rail) coche-comedor m
restless ['restlɪs] adj inquieto
restoration [restə'reɪʃən] n restauración f; devolución f
restore [rɪ'stɔː*] vt (building) restaurar; (sth stolen) devolver; (health) restablecer; (to power) volver a poner a
restrain [rɪs'treɪn] vt (feeling) contener, refrenar; (person): **to ~ (from doing)** disuadir (de hacer); **restraint** n (restriction) restricción f; (moderation) moderación f; (of manner) reserva
restrict [rɪs'trɪkt] vt restringir, limitar; **restriction** [-kʃən] n restricción f, limitación f
rest room (US) n aseos mpl
restructure [riː'strʌktʃə*] vt reestructurar
result [rɪ'zʌlt] n resultado ▷ vi: **to ~ in** terminar en, tener por resultado; **as a ~ of** a consecuencia de
resume [rɪ'zjuːm] vt reanudar ▷ vi comenzar de nuevo
résumé ['reɪzjuːmeɪ] n resumen m; (US) currículum m
resuscitate [rɪ'sʌsɪteɪt] vt (Med) resucitar
retail ['riːteɪl] adj, adv al por menor; **retailer** n detallista mf
retain [rɪ'teɪn] vt (keep) retener, conservar
retaliation [rɪtælɪ'eɪʃən] n represalias fpl
retarded [rɪ'tɑːdɪd] adj retrasado
retire [rɪ'taɪə*] vi (give up work) jubilarse; (withdraw) retirarse; (go to bed) acostarse; **retired** adj (person)

jubilado; retirement n (giving up work: state) retiro; (: act) jubilación f

retort [rɪ'tɔːt] vi contestar

retreat [rɪ'triːt] n (place) retiro; (Mil) retirada ▷vi retirarse

retrieve [rɪ'triːv] vt recobrar; (situation, honour) salvar; (Comput) recuperar; (error) reparar

retrospect ['rɛtrəspɛkt] n: **in ~** retrospectivamente; **retrospective** [-'spɛktɪv] adj retrospectivo; (law) retroactivo

return [rɪ'təːn] n (going or coming back) vuelta, regreso; (of sth stolen etc) devolución f; (Finance: from land, shares) ganancia, ingresos mpl ▷cpd (journey) de regreso; (BRIT: ticket) de ida y vuelta; (match) de vuelta ▷vi (person etc: come or go back) volver, regresar; (symptoms etc) reaparecer; (regain) **to ~ to** recuperar ▷vt devolver; (favour, love etc) corresponder a; (verdict) pronunciar; (Pol: candidate) elegir; **returns** npl (Comm) ingresos mpl; **in ~ (for)** a cambio (de), **by ~ of post** a vuelta de correo; **many happy ~s (of the day)!** ¡feliz cumpleaños!; **return ticket** n (esp BRIT) billete m (SP) or boleto m (LAM) de ida y vuelta, billete m redondo (MEX)

reunion [riː'juːnɪən] n (of family) reunión f; (of two people, school) reencuentro

reunite [riːjuː'naɪt] vt reunir; (reconcile) reconciliar

revamp [riː'væmp] vt renovar

reveal [rɪ'viːl] vt revelar; **revealing** adj revelador(a)

revel ['rɛvl] vi: **to ~ in sth/in doing sth** gozar de algo/con hacer algo

revelation [rɛvə'leɪʃən] n revelación f

revenge [rɪ'vɛndʒ] n venganza; **to take ~ on** vengarse de

revenue ['rɛvənjuː] n ingresos mpl, rentas fpl

Reverend ['rɛvərənd] adj (in titles): **the ~ John Smith** (Anglican) el Reverendo John Smith; (Catholic) el Padre John Smith; (Protestant) el Pastor John Smith

reversal [rɪ'vəːsl] n (of order) inversión f; (of cloth, policy) cambio; (of decision) revocación f

reverse [rɪ'vəːs] n (opposite) contrario; (back: of cloth) revés m; (: of coin) reverso; (of paper) dorso; (Aut: also: **~ gear**) marcha atrás, revés m ▷adj (order) inverso; (direction) contrario; (process) opuesto ▷vt (decision, Aut) dar marcha atrás a; (position, function) invertir ▷vi (BRIT Aut) dar marcha atrás; **reverse-charge call** (BRIT) n llamada a cobro revertido; **reversing lights** (BRIT) npl (Aut) luces fpl de retroceso

revert [rɪ'vəːt] vi: **to ~ to** volver a

review [rɪ'vjuː] n (magazine, Mil) revista; (of book, film) reseña; (US: examination) repaso, examen m ▷vt repasar, examinar; (Mil) pasar revista a; (book, film) reseñar

revise [rɪ'vaɪz] vt (manuscript) corregir; (opinion) modificar; (price, procedure) revisar ▷vi (study) repasar; **revision** [rɪ'vɪʒən] n corrección f; modificación f; (for exam) repaso

revival [rɪ'vaɪvl] n (recovery) reanimación f; (of interest) renacimiento; (Theatre) reestreno; (of faith) despertar m

revive [rɪ'vaɪv] vt resucitar; (custom) restablecer; (hope) despertar; (play) reestrenar ▷vi (unconscious) volver en sí; (business) reactivarse

revolt [rɪ'vəult] n rebelión f ▷vi rebelarse, sublevarse ▷vt dar asco a, repugnar; **revolting** adj asqueroso, repugnante

revolution [rɛvə'luːʃən] n revolución f;

revolutionary adj, n revolucionario/a m/f

revolve [rɪ'vɔlv] vi dar vueltas, girar; (life, discussion): **to ~ (a)round** girar en torno a

revolver [rɪ'vɔlvə*] n revólver m

reward [rɪ'wɔːd] n premio, recompensa ▷vt: **to ~ (for)** recompensar o premiar (por); **rewarding** adj (fig) valioso

rewind [riː'waɪnd] vt rebobinar

rewritable [riː'raɪtəbl] adj (CD, DVD) reescribible

rewrite [riː'raɪt] (pt rewrote, pp rewritten) vt reescribir

rheumatism ['ruːmətɪzəm] n reumatismo, reúma m

rhinoceros [raɪ'nɔsərəs] n rinoceronte m

rhubarb ['ruːbɑːb] n ruibarbo

rhyme [raɪm] n rima; (verse) poesía

rhythm ['rɪðm] n ritmo

rib [rɪb] n (Anat) costilla ▷vt (mock) tomar el pelo a

ribbon ['rɪbən] n cinta; **in ~s** (torn) hecho trizas

rice [raɪs] n arroz m; **rice pudding** n arroz m con leche

rich [rɪtʃ] adj (soil) fértil; (food) pesado; (: sweet) empalagoso; (abundant): **~ in** (minerals etc) rico en

rid [rɪd] (pt, pp rid) vt: **to ~ sb of sth** librar a algn de algo; **to get ~ of** deshacerse or desembarazarse de

riddle ['rɪdl] n (puzzle) acertijo; (mystery) enigma m, misterio ▷vt: **to be ~d with** ser lleno or plagado de

ride [raɪd] (pt rode, pp ridden) n paseo; (distance covered) viaje m, recorrido ▷vi (as sport) montar; (go somewhere: on horse, bicycle) dar un paseo, pasearse; (travel: on bicycle, motorcycle, bus) viajar ▷vt (a horse) montar a; (a bicycle, motorcycle) andar en; (distance) recorrer; **to take sb for a ~** (fig) engañar a algn; **rider** n (on horse) jinete mf; (on bicycle) ciclista mf; (on motorcycle) motociclista mf

ridge [rɪdʒ] n (of hill) cresta; (of roof) caballete m; (wrinkle) arruga

ridicule ['rɪdɪkjuːl] n irrisión f, burla ▷vt poner en ridículo, burlarse de; **ridiculous** [-'dɪkjuləs] adj ridículo

riding ['raɪdɪŋ] n equitación f; **I like ~** me gusta montar a caballo; **riding school** n escuela de equitación

rife [raɪf] adj: **to be ~** ser muy común; **to be ~ with** abundar en

rifle ['raɪfl] n rifle m, fusil m ▷vt saquear

rift [rɪft] n (in clouds) claro; (fig: disagreement) desavenencia

rig [rɪg] n (also: **oil ~**: at sea) plataforma petrolera ▷vt (election etc) amañar

right [raɪt] adj (correct) correcto, exacto; (suitable) indicado, debido; (proper) apropiado; (just) justo; (morally good) bueno; (not left) derecho ▷n bueno; (title, claim) derecho; (not left) derecha ▷adv bien, correctamente; (not left) a la derecha; (exactly): **~ now** ahora mismo ▷vt enderezar; (correct) corregir ▷excl ¡bueno!, ¡está bien!; **to be ~** (person) tener razón; (answer) ser correcto; **is that the ~ time?** (of clock) ¿es esa la hora buena?; **by ~s** en justicia; **on the ~** a la derecha; **to be in the ~** tener razón; **~ away** en seguida; **~ in the middle** exactamente en el centro; **right angle** n ángulo recto; **rightful** adj legítimo; **right-hand** adj: **right-hand drive** conducción f por la derecha; **the right-hand side** derecha; **right-handed** adj diestro; **rightly** adv correctamente, debidamente; (with reason) con razón; **right of way** n (on path etc) derecho de paso; (Aut) prioridad f; **right-wing** adj (Pol) derechista

rigid ['rɪdʒɪd] *adj* rígido; *(person, ideas)* inflexible

rigorous ['rɪɡərəs] *adj* riguroso

rim [rɪm] *n* borde *m*; *(of spectacles)* aro; *(of wheel)* llanta

rind [raɪnd] *n* *(of bacon)* corteza; *(of lemon etc)* cáscara; *(of cheese)* costra

ring [rɪŋ] *(pt* **rang***, pp* **rung)** *n* *(of finger)* anillo; *(of people)* corro; *(of objects)* círculo; *(gang)* banda; *(for boxing)* cuadrilátero; *(of circus)* pista; *(bull ring)* ruedo, plaza; *(sound of bell)* toque *m* ▷ *vi* *(on telephone)* llamar por teléfono; *(bell)* repicar; *(doorbell, phone)* sonar; *(also:* ~ **out)** sonar; *(ears)* zumbar ▷ *vt* *(BRIT Tel)* llamar, telefonear; *(bell etc)* hacer sonar; *(doorbell)* tocar; **to give sb a** ~ *(BRIT Tel)* llamar o telefonear a algn; **ring back** *(BRIT)* *vt, vi (Tel)* devolver la llamada; **ring off** *(BRIT)* *vi (Tel)* colgar, cortar la comunicación; **ring up** *(BRIT)* *vt (Tel)* llamar, telefonear; **ringing tone** *n (Tel)* tono de llamada; **ringleader** *n (of gang)* cabecilla *m*; **ring road** *(BRIT)* *n* carretera periférica o de circunvalación; **ringtone** *n (on mobile)* tono de llamada

rink [rɪŋk] *n (also:* **ice** ~**)** pista de hielo

rinse [rɪns] *n* aclarado; *(dye)* tinte *m* ▷ *vt* aclarar; *(mouth)* enjuagar

riot ['raɪət] *n* motín *m*, disturbio ▷ *vi* amotinarse; **to run** ~ desmandarse

rip [rɪp] *n* rasgón *m*, rasgadura ▷ *vt* rasgar, desgarrar ▷ *vi* rasgarse, desgarrarse; **rip off** *vt (inf: cheat)* estafar; **rip up** *vt* hacer pedazos

ripe [raɪp] *adj* maduro

rip-off ['rɪpɔf] *n (inf)*: **it's a** ~! ¡es una estafa!, ¡es un timo!

ripple ['rɪpl] *n* onda, rizo; *(sound)* murmullo ▷ *vi* rizarse

rise [raɪz] *(pt* **rose***, pp* **risen)** *n (slope)* cuesta, pendiente *f*; *(hill)* altura; *(BRIT: in wages)* aumento; *(in prices, temperature)* subida; *(fig: to power etc)* ascenso ▷ *vi* subir; *(waters)* crecer; *(sun, moon)* salir; *(person: from bed etc)* levantarse; *(also:* ~ **up: rebel)** sublevarse; *(in rank)* ascender; **to give** ~ **to** dar lugar or origen a; **to** ~ **to the occasion** ponerse a la altura de las circunstancias; **risen** ['rɪzn] *pp of* **rise**; **rising** *adj (increasing: number)* creciente; *(: prices)* en aumento or alza; *(tide)* creciente; *(sun, moon)* naciente

risk [rɪsk] *n* riesgo, peligro ▷ *vt* arriesgar; *(run the risk of)* exponerse a; **to take** or **run the** ~ **of doing** correr el riesgo de hacer; **at** ~ en peligro; **at one's own** ~ bajo su propia responsabilidad; **risky** *adj* arriesgado, peligroso

rite [raɪt] *n* rito; **last** ~**s** exequias *fpl*

ritual ['rɪtjuəl] *adj* ritual ▷ *n* ritual *m*, rito

rival ['raɪvl] *n* rival *m/f*; *(in business)* competidor(a) *m/f* ▷ *adj* rival, opuesto ▷ *vt* competir con; **rivalry** *n* competencia

river ['rɪvə*] *n* río ▷ *cpd (port)* de río; *(traffic)* fluvial; **up/down~** río arriba/abajo; **riverbank** *n* orilla (del río)

rivet ['rɪvɪt] *n* roblón *m*, remache *m* ▷ *vt (fig)* captar

road [rəud] *n* camino; *(motorway etc)* carretera; *(in town)* calle *f* ▷ *cpd (accident)* de tráfico; **major/minor** ~ carretera principal/secundaria; **roadblock** *n* barricada; **road map** *n* mapa *m* de carreteras; **road rage** *n* agresividad en la carretera; **road safety** *n* seguridad *f* vial; **roadside** *n* borde *m* (del camino); **roadsign** *n* señal *f* de tráfico; **road tax** *(BRIT)* *n* impuesto de rodaje; **roadworks** *npl* obras *fpl*

279 | **rope**

roam [rəum] *vi* vagar

roar [rɔ:*] *n* rugido; *(of vehicle, storm)* estruendo; *(of laughter)* carcajada ▷ *vi* rugir; hacer estruendo; **to** ~ **with laughter** reírse a carcajadas; **to do a ~ing trade** hacer buen negocio

roast [rəust] *n* carne *f* asada, asado ▷ *vt* asar; *(coffee)* tostar; **roast beef** *n* rosbif *m*

rob [rɔb] *vt* robar; **to** ~ **sb of sth** robar algo a algn; *(fig: deprive)* quitar algo a algn; **robber** *n* ladrón/ona *m/f*; **robbery** *n* robo

robe [rəub] *n (for ceremony etc)* toga; *(also:* **bath~)** albornoz *m*

robin ['rɔbɪn] *n* petirrojo

robot ['rəubɔt] *n* robot *m*

robust [rəu'bʌst] *adj* robusto, fuerte

rock [rɔk] *n* roca; *(boulder)* peña, peñasco; *(us: small stone)* piedrecita; *(BRIT: sweet)* ≈ pirulí ▷ *vt (swing gently: cradle)* balancear, mecer; *(: child)* arrullar; *(shake)* sacudir ▷ *vi* mecerse, balancearse; sacudirse; **on the ~s** *(drink)* con hielo; *(marriage etc)* en ruinas; **rock and roll** *n* rocanrol *m*; **rock climbing** *n (Sport)* escalada

rocket ['rɔkɪt] *n* cohete *m*; **rocking chair** ['rɔkɪŋ-] *n* mecedora

rocky ['rɔkɪ] *adj* rocoso

rod [rɔd] *n* vara, varilla; *(also:* **fishing ~)** caña

rode [rəud] *pt of* **ride**

rodent ['rəudnt] *n* roedor *m*

rogue [rəuɡ] *n* pícaro, pillo

role [rəul] *n* papel *m*; **role-model** *n* modelo a imitar

roll [rəul] *n* rollo; *(of bank notes)* fajo; *(also:* **bread ~)** panecillo; *(register, list)* lista, nómina; *(sound of drums etc)* redoble *m* ▷ *vt* hacer rodar; *(also:* ~ **up: string)** enrollar; *(cigarette)* liar; *(also:* ~ **out: pastry)** aplanar; *(flatten: road, lawn)* apisonar ▷ *vi* rodar; *(drum)* redoblar; *(ship)* balancearse; **roll over** *vi* dar una vuelta; **roll up** *vi (inf: arrive)* aparecer ▷ *vt (carpet)* arrollar; *(: sleeves)* arremangar; **roller** *n* rodillo; *(wheel)* rueda; *(for road)* apisonadora; *(for hair)* rulo; **Rollerblades®** *npl* patines *mpl* en línea; **roller coaster** *n* montaña rusa; **roller skates** *npl* patines *mpl* de rueda; **roller-skating** *n* patinaje sobre ruedas; **to go roller-skating** ir a patinar *(sobre ruedas)*; **rolling pin** *n* rodillo (de cocina)

ROM [rɔm] *n abbr (Comput* = *read only memory)* ROM *f*

Roman ['rəumən] *(irreg) adj* romano/a; **Roman Catholic** *(irreg) adj, n* católico/a *m/f* (romano/a)

romance [rə'mæns] *n (love affair)* amor *m*; *(charm)* lo romántico; *(novel)* novela de amor

Romania *etc* [ru:'meɪnɪə] *n* = **Rumania** *etc*

Roman numeral *n* número romano

romantic [rə'mæntɪk] *adj* romántico

Rome [rəum] *n* Roma

roof [ru:f] *(pl* ~**s)** *n* techo; *(of house)* techo, tejado ▷ *vt* techar, poner techo a; **the** ~ **of the mouth** el paladar; **roof rack** *n (Aut)* baca, portaequipajes *m inv*

rook [ruk] *n (bird)* graja; *(Chess)* torre *f*

room [ru:m] *n* cuarto, habitación *f*; *(also:* **bed~)** dormitorio, recámara *(MEX)*, pieza *(sc)*; *(in school etc)* sala; *(space, scope)* sitio, cabida; **roommate** *n* compañero/a de cuarto; **room service** *n* servicio de habitaciones; **roomy** *adj* espacioso; *(garment)* amplio

rooster ['ru:stə*] *n* gallo

root [ru:t] *n* raíz *f* ▷ *vi* arraigarse

rope [rəup] *n* cuerda; *(Naut)* cable *m* ▷ *vt (tie)* atar or amarrar con (una) cuerda; *(climbers: also:* ~ **together)** encordarse; *(an area: also:* ~ **off)** acordonar; **to know**

the ~s (fig) conocer los trucos (del oficio)
rose [rəʊz] pt of **rise** ▷ n rosa; (shrub) rosal m; (on watering can) roseta
rosé ['rəʊzeɪ] n vino rosado
rosemary ['rəʊzmərɪ] n romero
rosy ['rəʊzɪ] adj rosado, sonrosado; **a ~ future** un futuro prometedor
rot [rɒt] n podredumbre f; (fig: pej) tonterías fpl ▷ vt pudrir ▷ vi pudrirse
rota ['rəʊtə] n (sistema m de) turnos m
rotate ['rəʊteɪt] vt (revolve) hacer girar, dar vueltas a; (jobs) alternar ▷ vi girar, dar vueltas
rotten ['rɒtn] adj podrido; (dishonest) corrompido; (inf: bad) pocho; **to feel ~** (ill) sentirse fatal
rough [rʌf] adj (skin, surface) áspero; (terrain) quebrado; (road) desigual; (voice) bronco; (person, manner) tosco, grosero; (weather) borrascoso; (treatment) brutal; (sea) picado; (town, area) peligroso; (cloth) basto; (plan) preliminar; (guess) aproximado ▷ n (Golf): **in the ~** en las hierbas altas; **to ~ it** vivir sin comodidades; **to sleep ~** (BRIT) pasar la noche al raso; **roughly** adv (handle) torpemente; (make) toscamente; (speak) groseramente; (approximately) aproximadamente
roulette [ru:'let] n ruleta
round [raʊnd] adj redondo ▷ n círculo; (BRIT: of toast) rebanada; (of policeman) ronda; (of milkman) recorrido; (of doctor) visitas fpl; (game: of cards, in competition) partida; (of ammunition) cartucho; (Boxing) asalto; (of talks) ronda ▷ vt (corner) doblar ▷ prep alrededor de; (surrounding): **~ his neck/the table** en su cuello/alrededor de la mesa; (in a circular movement): **to move ~ the room/sail ~ the world** dar una vuelta a la habitación/circunnavegar el mundo; (in various directions): **to move ~ a room/house** moverse por toda la habitación/casa; (approximately) alrededor de ▷ adv: **all ~** por todos lados; **the long way ~** por el camino menos directo; **all (the) year ~** durante todo el año; **it's just ~ the corner** (fig) está a la vuelta de la esquina; **~ the clock** adv las 24 horas; **to go ~ to sb's (house)** ir a casa de algn; **to go ~ the back** pasar por atrás; **enough to go ~** bastante (para todos); **a ~ of applause** una salva de aplausos; **a ~ of drinks/sandwiches** una ronda de bebidas/bocadillos; **round off** vt (speech etc) acabar, poner término a; **round up** vt (cattle) acorralar; (people) reunir; (price) redondear; **roundabout** (BRIT) n (Aut) isleta; (at fair) tiovivo ▷ adj (route, means) indirecto; **round trip** n viaje m de ida y vuelta; **roundup** n rodeo; (of criminals) redada; (of news) resumen m
rouse [raʊz] vt (wake up) despertar; (stir up) suscitar
route [ru:t] n ruta, camino; (of bus) recorrido; (of shipping) derrota
routine [ru:'ti:n] adj rutinario ▷ n rutina; (Theatre) número
row¹ [rəʊ] n (line) fila, hilera; (Knitting) pasada ▷ vi (in boat) remar ▷ vt conducir remando; **4 days in a ~** 4 días seguidos
row² [raʊ] n (racket) escándalo; (dispute) bronca, pelea; (scolding) regaño ▷ vi pelear(se)
rowboat ['rəʊbəʊt] (US) = **rowing boat**
rowing ['rəʊɪŋ] n remo; **rowing boat** (BRIT) n bote m de remos
royal ['rɔɪəl] adj real; **royalty** n (royal persons) familia real; (payment to author) derechos mpl de autor
rpm abbr (= revs per minute) r.p.m.

R.S.V.P. abbr (= répondez s'il vous plaôt) SRC
Rt. Hon. abbr (BRIT) (= Right Honourable) título honorífico de diputado
rub [rʌb] vt frotar; (scrub) restregar ▷ n: **to give sth a ~** frotar algo; **to ~ sb up** or **~ sb** (US) **the wrong way** entrarle algn por mal ojo; **rub in** vt (ointment) aplicar frotando; **rub off** vi borrarse; **rub out** vt borrar
rubber ['rʌbə*] n caucho, goma; (BRIT: eraser) goma de borrar; **rubber band** n goma, gomita; **rubber gloves** npl guantes mpl de goma
rubbish ['rʌbɪʃ] (BRIT) n basura; (waste) desperdicios mpl; (fig: pej) tonterías fpl; (junk) pacotilla; **rubbish bin** (BRIT) n cubo o bote m (MEX) o tacho (SC) de la basura; **rubbish dump** (BRIT) n vertedero, basurero
rubble ['rʌbl] n escombros mpl
ruby ['ru:bɪ] n rubí m
rucksack ['rʌksæk] n mochila
rudder ['rʌdə*] n timón m
rude [ru:d] adj (impolite: person) mal educado; (: word, manners) grosero; (crude) crudo; (indecent) indecente
ruffle ['rʌfl] vt (hair) despeinar; (clothes) arrugar; **to get ~d** (fig: person) alterarse
rug [rʌg] n alfombra; (for knees) manta
rugby ['rʌgbɪ] n rugby m
rugged ['rʌgɪd] adj (landscape) accidentado; (features) robusto
ruin ['ru:ɪn] n ruina ▷ vt arruinar; (spoil) estropear; **ruins** npl ruinas fpl, restos mpl
rule [ru:l] n (norm) norma, costumbre f; (regulation, ruler) regla; (government) dominio ▷ vt (country, person) gobernar ▷ vi gobernar; (Law) fallar; **as a ~** por regla general; **rule out** vt excluir; **ruler** n (sovereign) soberano; (for measuring) regla; **ruling** adj (party) gobernante; (class) dirigente ▷ n (Law) fallo, decisión f
rum [rʌm] n ron m
Rumania [ru:'meɪnɪə] n Rumanía; **Rumanian** adj rumano/a ▷ n rumano/a m/f; (Ling) rumano
rumble ['rʌmbl] n (noise) ruido sordo ▷ vi retumbar, hacer un ruido sordo; (stomach, pipe) sonar
rumour ['ru:mə*] (US **rumor**) n rumor m ▷ vt: **it is ~ed that ...** se rumorea que ...
rump steak n filete m de lomo
run [rʌn] (pt ran, pp run) n (fast pace): **at a ~** corriendo; (Sport, in tights) carrera; (outing) paseo, excursión f; (distance travelled) trayecto; (series) serie f; (Theatre) temporada; (Ski) pista ▷ vt correr; (operate: business) dirigir; (: competition, course) organizar; (: hotel, house) administrar, llevar; (Comput) ejecutar; (pass: hand) pasar; (Press: feature) publicar ▷ vi correr; (work: machine) funcionar, marchar; (bus, train: operate) circular; (: travel) ir; (continue: play) seguir; (contract) ser válido; (flow: river) fluir; (colours, washing) desteñirse; (in election) ser candidato; **there was a ~ on** (meat, tickets) hubo mucha demanda de; **in the long ~ a la larga; on the ~** en fuga; **I'll ~ you to the station** te llevaré a la estación (en coche); **to ~ a risk** correr un riesgo; **to ~ a bath** llenar la bañera; **run after** vt fus (to catch up) correr tras; (chase) perseguir; **run away** vi huir; **run down** vt (production) ir reduciendo; (factory) ir restringiendo la producción en; (car) atropellar; (criticize) criticar; **to be ~** (person: tired) estar debilitado; **run into** vt fus (meet: person, trouble) tropezar con; (collide with) chocar con; **run off** vt (water) dejar correr; (copies) sacar ▷ vi huir corriendo; **run out** vi (person) salir corriendo; (liquid) irse; (lease) caducar, vencer; (money etc) acabarse; **run out of** vt fus

quedar sin; **run over** vt (Aut) atropellar ▷ vt fus (revise)
repasar; **run through** vt fus (instructions) repasar; **run
up** vt (debt) contraer; **to run up against** (difficulties)
tropezar con; **runaway** adj (horse) desbocado; (truck)
sin frenos; (child) escapado de casa
rung [rʌŋ] pp of **ring** ▷ n (of ladder) escalón m, peldaño
runner ['rʌnə*] n (in race: person) corredor(a) m/f;
(: horse) caballo; (on sledge) patín m; **runner bean** (BRIT)
n = judía verde; **runner-up** n subcampeón/ona m/f
running ['rʌnɪŋ] n (sport) atletismo; (of business)
administración f ▷ adj (water, costs) corriente;
(commentary) continuo; **to be in/out of the ~ for sth**
tener/no tener posibilidades de ganar algo; **6 days ~**
6 días seguidos
runny ['rʌnɪ] adj fluido; (nose, eyes) gastante
run-up ['rʌnʌp] n: **~ to** (election etc) período previo a
runway ['rʌnweɪ] n (Aviat) pista de aterrizaje
rupture ['rʌptʃə*] n (Med) hernia ▷ vt: **to ~ o.s**
causarse una hernia
rural ['ruərl] adj rural
rush [rʌʃ] n ímpetu m; (hurry) prisa; (Comm) demanda
repentina; (current) corriente f fuerte; (of feeling)
torrente m; (Bot) junco ▷ vt apresurar; (work) hacer
de prisa ▷ vi correr, precipitarse; **rush hour** n horas
fpl punta
Russia ['rʌʃə] n Rusia; **Russian** adj ruso/a ▷ n
ruso/a m/f; (Ling) ruso
rust [rʌst] n herrumbre f, moho ▷ vi oxidarse
rusty ['rʌstɪ] adj oxidado
ruthless ['ruːθlɪs] adj despiadado
RV (US) n abbr = **recreational vehicle**
rye [raɪ] n centeno

S

Sabbath ['sæbəθ] n domingo; (Jewish) sábado
sabotage ['sæbətɑːʒ] n sabotaje m ▷ vt sabotear
saccharin(e) ['sækərɪn] n sacarina
sachet ['sæʃeɪ] n sobrecito
sack [sæk] n (bag) saco, costal m ▷ vt (dismiss)
despedir; (plunder) saquear; **to get the ~** ser despedido
sacred ['seɪkrɪd] adj sagrado, santo
sacrifice ['sækrɪfaɪs] n sacrificio ▷ vt sacrificar
sad [sæd] adj (unhappy) triste; (deplorable) lamentable
saddle ['sædl] n silla (de montar); (of cycle) sillín
m ▷ vt (horse) ensillar; **to be ~d with sth** (inf) quedar
cargado con algo
sadistic [sə'dɪstɪk] adj sádico
sadly ['sædlɪ] adv lamentablemente; **to be ~ lacking
in** estar por desgracia carente de
sadness ['sædnɪs] n tristeza
s.a.e. abbr (= stamped addressed envelope) sobre con las
propias señas de uno y con sello
safari [sə'fɑːrɪ] n safari m
safe [seɪf] adj (out of danger) fuera de peligro; (not
dangerous, sure) seguro; (unharmed) ileso ▷ n caja de
caudales, caja fuerte; **~ and sound** sano y salvo; **(just)
to be on the ~ side** para mayor seguridad; **safely** adv
seguramente, con seguridad; **to arrive safely** llegar
bien; **safe sex** n sexo seguro or sin riesgo
safety ['seɪftɪ] n seguridad f; **safety belt** n cinturón
m (de seguridad); **safety pin** n imperdible m, seguro
(MEX), alfiler m de gancho (SC)
saffron ['sæfrən] n azafrán m
sag [sæg] vi aflojarse
sage [seɪdʒ] n (herb) salvia; (man) sabio
Sagittarius [sædʒɪ'tɛərɪəs] n Sagitario
Sahara [sə'hɑːrə] n: **the ~ (Desert)** el (desierto del)
Sáhara
said [sed] pt, pp of **say**
sail [seɪl] n (on boat) vela; (trip): **to go for a ~** dar un
paseo en barco ▷ vt (boat) gobernar ▷ vi (travel: ship)
navegar; (Sport) hacer vela; (begin voyage) salir; **they
~ed into Copenhagen** arribaron a Copenhague;
sailboat (US) n = **sailing boat**; **sailing** n (Sport) vela;
to go sailing hacer vela; **sailing boat** n barco de vela;
sailor n marinero, marino
saint [seɪnt] n santo

sake [seɪk] n: **for the ~ of** por

salad ['sæləd] n ensalada; **salad cream** (BRIT) n (especie f de) mayonesa; **salad dressing** n aliño

salami [sə'lɑːmɪ] n salami m, salchichón m

salary ['sælərɪ] n sueldo

sale [seɪl] n venta; (at reduced prices) liquidación f, saldo; (auction) subasta; **sales** npl (total amount sold) ventas fpl, facturación f; **"for ~"** "se vende"; **on ~** en venta; **on ~ or return** (goods) venta por reposición; **sales assistant** (US), **sales clerk** n dependiente/a m/f; **salesman/woman** (irreg) n (in shop) dependiente/a m/f; **salesperson** (irreg) n vendedor(a) m/f, dependiente/a m/f; **sales rep** n representante mf, agente mf comercial

saline ['seɪlaɪn] adj salino

saliva [sə'laɪvə] n saliva

salmon ['sæmən] n inv salmón m

salon ['sælɔn] n (hairdressing salon) peluquería; (beauty salon) salón m de belleza

saloon [sə'luːn] n (US) bar m, taberna; (BRIT AUT) coche m (de) turismo; (ship's lounge) cámara, salón m

salt [sɔːlt] n sal f; (put salt on) poner sal en; **saltwater** adj de agua salada; **salty** adj salado

salute [sə'luːt] n saludo; (of guns) salva ▷vt saludar

salvage ['sælvɪdʒ] n (saving) salvamento, recuperación f; (things saved) objetos mpl salvados ▷vt salvar

Salvation Army [sæl'veɪʃən-] n Ejército de Salvación

same [seɪm] adj mismo ▷pron: **the ~** el(la) mismo/a, los(las) mismos/as; **the ~ book as** el mismo libro que; **at the ~ time** (at the same moment) al mismo tiempo; (yet) sin embargo; **all** or **just the ~** sin embargo, aun así; **to do the ~ (as sb)** hacer lo mismo (que algn); **the ~ to you!** ¡igualmente!

sample ['sɑːmpl] n muestra ▷vt (food) probar; (wine) catar

sanction ['sæŋkʃən] n aprobación f ▷vt sancionar; aprobar; **sanctions** npl (Pol) sanciones fpl

sanctuary ['sæŋktjuərɪ] n santuario; (refuge) asilo, refugio; (for wildlife) reserva

sand [sænd] n arena; (beach) playa ▷vt (also: ~ down) lijar

sandal ['sændl] n sandalia

sand: sandbox (US) n =**sandpit**; **sandcastle** n castillo de arena; **sand dune** n duna; **sandpaper** n papel m de lija; **sandpit** n (for children) cajón m de arena; **sands** npl playa sg de arena; **sandstone** ['sændstəun] n piedra arenisca

sandwich ['sændwɪtʃ] n sándwich m ▷vt intercalar; **~ed between** apretujado entre; **cheese/ham ~** sándwich de queso/jamón

sandy ['sændɪ] adj arenoso; (colour) rojizo

sane [seɪn] adj cuerdo; (sensible) sensato

sang [sæŋ] pt of **sing**

sanitary towel (US **sanitary napkin**) n paño higiénico, compresa

sanity ['sænɪtɪ] n cordura; (of judgment) sensatez f

sank [sæŋk] pt of **sink**

Santa Claus [sæntə'klɔːz] n San Nicolás, Papá Noel

sap [sæp] n (of plants) savia ▷vt (strength) minar, agotar

sapphire ['sæfaɪə*] n zafiro

sarcasm ['sɑːkæzm] n sarcasmo

sarcastic [sɑː'kæstɪk] adj sarcástico

sardine [sɑː'diːn] n sardina

SASE (US) n abbr (= self-addressed stamped envelope) sobre con las propias señas de uno y con sello

Sat. abbr (= Saturday) sáb

sat [sæt] pt, pp of **sit**

satchel ['sætʃl] n (child's) mochila, cartera (SP)

satellite ['sætəlaɪt] n satélite m; **satellite dish** n antena de televisión por satélite; **satellite television** n televisión f vía satélite

satin ['sætɪn] n raso ▷adj de raso

satire ['sætaɪə*] n sátira

satisfaction [sætɪs'fækʃən] n satisfacción f

satisfactory [sætɪs'fæktərɪ] adj satisfactorio

satisfied ['sætɪsfaɪd] adj satisfecho; **to be ~ (with sth)** estar satisfecho (de algo)

satisfy ['sætɪsfaɪ] vt satisfacer; (convince) convencer

Saturday ['sætədɪ] n sábado

sauce [sɔːs] n salsa; (sweet) crema; jarabe m; **saucepan** n cacerola, olla

saucer ['sɔːsə*] n platillo; **Saudi Arabia** n Arabia Saudí or Saudita

sauna ['sɔːnə] n sauna

sausage ['sɔsɪdʒ] n salchicha; **sausage roll** n empanadita de salchicha

sautéed ['səuteɪd] adj salteado

savage ['sævɪdʒ] adj (cruel, fierce) feroz, furioso; (primitive) salvaje ▷n salvaje mf ▷vt (attack) embestir

save [seɪv] vt (rescue) salvar, rescatar; (money, time) ahorrar; (put by, keep: seat) guardar; (Comput) salvar (y guardar); (avoid: trouble) evitar; (Sport) parar ▷vi (also: ~ up) ahorrar ▷n (Sport) parada ▷prep salvo, excepto

savings ['seɪvɪŋz] npl ahorros mpl; **savings account** n cuenta de ahorros; **savings and loan association** (US) n sociedad f de ahorro y préstamo

savoury ['seɪvərɪ] (US **savory**) adj sabroso; (dish: not sweet) salado

saw [sɔː] (pt **~ed**, pp **~ed** or **~n**) pt of **see** ▷n (tool) sierra ▷vt serrar; **sawdust** n (a)serrín m

sawn [sɔːn] pp of **saw**

saxophone ['sæksəfəun] n saxófono

say [seɪ] (pt, pp **said**) n: **to have one's ~** expresar su opinión ▷vt decir; **to have a** or **some ~ in sth** tener voz or tener que ver en algo; **to ~ yes/no** decir que sí/no; **could you ~ that again?** ¿podría repetir eso?; **that is to ~** es decir; **that goes without ~ing** ni que decir tiene; **saying** n dicho, refrán m

scab [skæb] n costra; (pej) esquirol m

scaffolding ['skæfəldɪŋ] n andamio, andamiaje m

scald [skɔːld] n escaldadura ▷vt escaldar

scale [skeɪl] n (gen, Mus) escala; (of fish) escama; (of salaries, fees etc) escalafón m ▷vt (mountain) escalar; (tree) trepar; **scales** npl (for weighing: small) balanza; (: large) báscula; **on a large ~** en gran escala; **~ of charges** tarifa, lista de precios

scallion ['skæljən] (US) n cebolleta

scallop ['skɔləp] n (Zool) venera; (Sewing) festón m

scalp [skælp] n cabellera ▷vt escalpar

scalpel ['skælpl] n bisturí m

scam [skæm] n (inf) estafa, timo

scampi ['skæmpɪ] npl gambas fpl

scan [skæn] vt (examine) escudriñar; (glance at quickly) dar un vistazo a; (TV, Radar) explorar, registrar ▷n (Med): **to have a ~** pasar por el escáner

scandal ['skændl] n escándalo; (gossip) chismes mpl

Scandinavia [skændɪ'neɪvɪə] n Escandinavia; **Scandinavian** adj, n escandinavo/a m/f

scanner ['skænə*] n (Radar, Med) escáner m

scapegoat ['skeɪpgəut] n cabeza de turco, chivo expiatorio

scar [skɑ:] n cicatriz f; (fig) señal f ▷ vt dejar señales en

scarce [skeəs] adj escaso; **to make o.s. ~** (inf) esfumarse; **scarcely** adv apenas

scare [skeə*] n susto, sobresalto; (panic) pánico ▷ vt asustar, espantar; **to ~ sb stiff** dar a algn un susto de muerte; **bomb ~** amenaza de bomba; **scarecrow** n espantapájaros m inv; **scared** adj: **to be scared** estar asustado

scarf [skɑ:f] (pl **~s** or **scarves**) n (long) bufanda; (square) pañuelo

scarlet ['skɑ:lɪt] adj escarlata

scarves [skɑ:vz] npl of **scarf**

scary ['skɛərɪ] (inf) adj espeluznante

scatter ['skætə*] vt (spread) esparcir, desparramar; (put to flight) dispersar ▷ vi desparramarse; dispersarse

scenario [sɪ'nɑ:rɪəu] n (Theatre) argumento; (Cinema) guión m; (fig) escenario

scene [si:n] n (Theatre, fig etc) escena; (of crime etc) escenario; (view) panorama m; (fuss) escándalo; **scenery** n (Theatre) decorado; (landscape) paisaje m; **scenic** adj pintoresco

scent [sɛnt] n perfume m, olor m; (fig: track) rastro, pista

sceptical ['skɛptɪkl] adj escéptico

schedule ['ʃɛdju:l] (us) ['skɛdju:l] n (timetable) horario; (of events) programa m; (list) lista ▷ vt (visit) fijar la hora de; **to arrive on ~** llegar a la hora debida; **to be ahead of/behind ~** estar adelantado/en retraso; **scheduled flight** n vuelo regular

scheme [ski:m] n (plan) plan m, proyecto; (plot) intriga; (arrangement) disposición f; (pension scheme etc) sistema m ▷ vi (intrigue) intrigar

schizophrenic [skɪtsə'frɛnɪk] adj esquizofrénico

scholar ['skɔlə*] n (pupil) alumno/a; (learned person) sabio/a, erudito/a; **scholarship** n erudición f; (grant) beca

school [sku:l] n escuela, colegio; (in university) facultad f ▷ cpd escolar; **schoolbook** n libro de texto; **schoolboy** n alumno; **school children** npl alumnos mpl; **schoolgirl** n alumna; **schooling** n enseñanza; **schoolteacher** n (primary) maestro/a; (secondary) profesor(a) m/f

science ['saɪəns] n ciencia; **science fiction** n ciencia-ficción f; **scientific** [-'tɪfɪk] adj científico; **scientist** n científico/a

sci-fi ['saɪfaɪ] n abbr (inf) = **science fiction**

scissors ['sɪzəz] npl tijeras fpl; **a pair of ~** unas tijeras

scold [skəuld] vt regañar

scone [skɔn] n pastel de pan

scoop [sku:p] n (for flour etc) pala; (Press) exclusiva

scooter ['sku:tə*] n moto f; (toy) patinete m

scope [skəup] n (of plan) ámbito; (of person) competencia; (opportunity) libertad f (de acción)

scorching ['skɔ:tʃɪŋ] adj (heat, sun) abrasador(a)

score [skɔ:*] n (points etc) puntuación f; (Mus) partitura f; (twenty) veintena ▷ vt (goal, point) ganar; (mark) rayar; (achieve: success) conseguir ▷ vi marcar un tanto; (Football) marcar (un) gol; (keep score) llevar el tanteo; **~s** (lots of) decenas de; **on that ~** en lo que se refiere a eso; **to ~ 6 out of 10** obtener una puntuación de 6 sobre 10; **score out** vt tachar; **scoreboard** n

marcador m; **scorer** n marcador m; (keeping score) encargado/a del marcador

scorn [skɔ:n] n desprecio

Scorpio ['skɔ:pɪəu] n Escorpión m

scorpion ['skɔ:pɪən] n alacrán m

Scot [skɔt] n escocés/esa m/f

Scotch tape® (us) n cinta adhesiva, celo, scotch® m

Scotland ['skɔtlənd] n Escocia

Scots [skɔts] adj escocés/esa; **Scotsman** (irreg) n escocés; **Scotswoman** (irreg) n escocesa; **Scottish** ['skɔtɪʃ] adj escocés/esa; **Scottish Parliament** n Parlamento escocés

scout [skaut] n (Mil: also: **boy ~**) explorador m; **girl ~** (us) niña exploradora

scowl [skaul] vi fruncir el ceño; **to ~ at sb** mirar con ceño a algn

scramble ['skræmbl] n (climb) subida (difícil); (struggle) pelea ▷ vi: **to ~ through/out** abrirse paso(-); salir con dificultad; **to ~ for** pelear por; **scrambled eggs** npl huevos mpl revueltos

scrap [skræp] n (bit) pedacito; (fig) pizca; (fight) riña, bronca; (also: **~ iron**) chatarra, hierro viejo ▷ vt (discard) desechar, descartar ▷ vi reñir, armar una bronca; **scraps** npl (waste) sobras fpl, desperdicios mpl; **scrapbook** n álbum m de recortes

scrape [skreɪp] n: **to get into a ~** meterse en un lío ▷ vt raspar; (skin etc) rasguñar; (scrape against) rozar ▷ vi: **to ~ through** (exam) aprobar por los pelos; **scrap paper** n pedazos mpl de papel

scratch [skrætʃ] n rasguño; (from claw) arañazo ▷ vt (paint, car) rayar; (with claw, nail) rasguñar, arañar; (rub: nose etc) rascarse ▷ vi rascarse; **to start from ~** partir de cero; **to be up to ~** cumplir con los requisitos; **scratch card** n (BRIT) tarjeta f de "rasque y gane"

scream [skri:m] n chillido ▷ vi chillar

screen [skri:n] n (Cinema, TV) pantalla; (movable barrier) biombo ▷ vt (conceal) tapar; (from the wind etc) proteger; (film) proyectar; (candidates etc) investigar a; **screening** n (Med) investigación f médica; **screenplay** n guión m; **screen saver** n (Comput) protector m de pantalla

screw [skru:] n tornillo ▷ vt (also: **~ in**) atornillar; **screw up** vt (paper etc) arrugar; **to screw up one's eyes** arrugar el entrecejo; **screwdriver** n destornillador m

scribble ['skrɪbl] n garabatos mpl ▷ vt, vi garabatear

script [skrɪpt] n (Cinema etc) guión m; (writing) escritura, letra

scroll [skrəul] n rollo

scrub [skrʌb] n (land) maleza ▷ vt fregar, restregar; (inf: reject) cancelar, anular

scruffy ['skrʌfɪ] adj desaliñado, piojoso

scrum(mage) ['skrʌm(mɪdʒ)] n (Rugby) melée f

scrutiny ['skru:tɪnɪ] n escrutinio, examen m

scuba diving ['sku:bə'daɪvɪŋ] n submarinismo

sculptor ['skʌlptə*] n escultor(a) m/f

sculpture ['skʌlptʃə*] n escultura

scum [skʌm] n (on liquid) espuma; (pej: people) escoria

scurry ['skʌrɪ] vi correr; **to ~ off** escabullirse

sea [si:] n mar m or f ▷ cpd de mar, marítimo; **by ~** (travel) en barco; **on the ~** (boat) en el mar; (town) junto al mar; **to be all at ~** (fig) estar despistado; **out to ~**, **at ~** en alta mar; **seafood** n mariscos mpl; **sea front** n paseo marítimo; **seagull** n gaviota

seal [si:l] n (animal) foca; (stamp) sello ▷ vt (close) cerrar; **seal off** vt (area) acordonar

sea level n nivel m del mar
seam [siːm] n costura; (of metal) juntura; (of coal) veta, filón m
search [sɔːtʃ] n (for person, thing) busca, búsqueda; (Comput) búsqueda; (inspection: of sb's home) registro ▷ vt (look in) buscar en; (examine) examinar; (person, place) registrar ▷ vi: to ~ for buscar; in ~ of en busca de; **search engine** n (Comput) buscador m; **search party** n pelotón m de salvamento
sea: seashore n playa, orilla del mar; **seasick** adj mareado; **seaside** n playa, orilla del mar; **seaside resort** n centro turístico costero
season ['siːzn] n (of year) estación f; (sporting etc) temporada; (of films etc) ciclo ▷ vt (food) sazonar; **in/out of ~** en sazón/fuera de temporada; **seasonal** adj estacional; **seasoning** n condimento, aderezo; **season ticket** n abono
seat [siːt] n (in bus, train) asiento; (chair) silla; (Parliament) escaño; (buttocks) culo, trasero; (of trousers) culera ▷ vt sentar; (have room for) tener cabida para; **to be ~ed** sentarse; **seat belt** n cinturón m de seguridad; **seating** n asientos mpl
sea: sea water n agua del mar; **seaweed** n alga marina
sec. abbr = **second(s)**
secluded [sɪ'kluːdɪd] adj retirado
second ['sekənd] adj segundo ▷ adv en segundo lugar ▷ n (Aut: also: ~ gear) segunda; (Comm) artículo con algún desperfecto; (Brit Scol: degree) título de licenciado con calificación de notable ▷ vt (motion) apoyar; **secondary** adj secundario; **secondary school** n escuela secundaria; **second-class** adj de segunda clase ▷ adv (Rail) en segunda; **secondhand** adj de segunda mano, usado; **secondly** adv en segundo lugar; **second-rate** adj de segunda categoría; **second thoughts**: **to have second thoughts** cambiar de opinión; **on second thoughts** or **thought** (us) pensándolo bien
secrecy ['siːkrəsɪ] n secreto
secret ['siːkrɪt] adj, n secreto; **in ~** en secreto
secretary ['sekrətərɪ] n secretario/a; **S~ of State (for)** (Brit Pol) Ministro (de)
secretive [sɪ'kriːtɪv] adj reservado, sigiloso
secret service n servicio secreto
sect [sekt] n secta
section ['sekʃən] n sección f; (part) parte f; (of document) artículo; (of opinion) sector m; (cross-section) corte m transversal
sector ['sektə*] n sector m
secular ['sekjulə*] adj secular, seglar
secure [sɪ'kjuə*] adj seguro; (firmly fixed) firme, fijo ▷ vt (fix) asegurar, afianzar; (get) conseguir
security [sɪ'kjuərɪtɪ] n seguridad f; (for loan) fianza; (: object) prenda; **securities** npl (Comm) valores mpl, títulos mpl; **security guard** n guardia m/f de seguridad
sedan [sɪ'dæn] (us) n (Aut) sedán m
sedate [sɪ'deɪt] adj tranquilo ▷ vt tratar con sedantes
sedative ['sedɪtɪv] n sedante m, sedativo
seduce [sɪ'djuːs] vt seducir; **seductive** [-'dʌktɪv] adj seductor/a
see [siː] (pt saw, pp seen) vt ver; (accompany): **to ~ sb to the door** acompañar a algn a la puerta; (understand) ver, comprender ▷ vi ver ▷ n (arz)obispado; **to ~ that** (ensure) asegurar que; **~ you soon!** ¡hasta pronto!;

see off vt despedir; **see out** vt (take to the door) acompañar hasta la puerta; **see through** vt fus (fig) calar ▷ vt (plan) llevar a cabo; **see to** vt fus atender a, encargarse de
seed [siːd] n semilla; (in fruit) pepita; (fig: gen pl) germen m; (Tennis etc) preseleccionado/a; **to go to ~** (plant) granar; (fig) descuidarse
seeing ['siːɪŋ] conj: ~ **(that)** visto que, en vista de que
seek [siːk] (pt, pp **sought**) vt buscar; (post) solicitar
seem [siːm] vi parecer; **there ~s to be** ... parece que hay ...; **seemingly** adv aparentemente, según parece
seen [siːn] pp of **see**
seesaw ['siːsɔː] n subibaja
segment ['segmənt] n (part) sección f; (of orange) gajo
segregate ['segrɪgeɪt] vt segregar
seize [siːz] vt (grasp) agarrar, asir; (take possession of) secuestrar; (: territory) apoderarse de; (opportunity) aprovecharse de
seizure ['siːʒə*] n (Med) ataque m; (Law, of power) incautación f
seldom ['seldəm] adv rara vez
select [sɪ'lekt] adj selecto, escogido ▷ vt escoger, elegir; (Sport) seleccionar; **selection** n selección f, elección f; (Comm) surtido; **selective** adj selectivo
self [self] (pl selves) n uno mismo; **the ~** el yo ▷ prefix auto...; **self-assured** adj seguro de sí mismo; **self-catering** (Brit) adj (flat etc) con cocina; **self-centred** (us **self-centered**) adj egocéntrico; **self-confidence** n confianza en sí mismo; **self-confident** adj seguro de sí (mismo), lleno de confianza en sí mismo; **self-conscious** adj cohibido; **self-contained** adj (flat) con entrada particular; **self-control** n autodominio; **self-defence** (us **self-defense**) n defensa propia; **self-drive** (Brit) n chofer or (sp) chófer; **self-employed** adj que trabaja por cuenta propia; **self-esteem** n amor m propio; **self-indulgent** adj autocomplaciente; **self-interest** n egoísmo; **selfish** adj egoísta; **self-pity** n lástima de sí mismo; **self-raising** [self'reɪzɪŋ] (us **self-rising**) adj: **self-raising flour** harina con levadura; **self-respect** n amor m propio; **self-service** adj de autoservicio
sell [sel] (pt, pp **sold**) vt vender; **to ~ at** or **for £10** venderse a 10 libras; **sell off** vt liquidar; **sell out** vi: **to sell out of tickets/milk** vender todas las entradas/toda la leche; **sell-by date** n fecha de caducidad; **seller** n vendedor(a) m/f
Sellotape® ['seləuteɪp] (Brit) n celo (sp), cinta Scotch® (lam) or Dúrex® (mex, arg)
selves [selvz] npl of **self**
semester [sɪ'mestə*] (us) n semestre m
semi... [semɪ] prefix semi..., medio...; **semicircle** n semicírculo; **semidetached (house)** n (casa) semiseparada; **semi-final** n semi-final m
seminar ['semɪnɑː*] n seminario
semi-skimmed [semɪ'skɪmd] adj semidesnatado; **semi-skimmed (milk)** n leche semidesnatada
senate ['senɪt] n senado; **the S~** (us) el Senado; **senator** n senador(a) m/f
send [send] (pt, pp **sent**) vt mandar, enviar; (signal) transmitir; **send back** vt devolver; **send for** vt fus mandar traer; **send in** vt (report, application, resignation) mandar; **send off** vt (goods) despachar; (Brit Sport: player) expulsar; **send on** vt (letter, luggage) remitir; (person) mandar; **send out** vt (invitation) mandar; (signal) emitir; **send up** vt (person, price) hacer

subir; (BRIT: parody) parodiar; **sender** n remitente mf; **send-off** n: **a good send-off** una buena despedida
senile ['si:naɪl] adj senil
senior ['si:nɪə*] adj (older) mayor, más viejo; (: on staff) de más antigüedad; (of higher rank) superior; **senior citizen** n persona de la tercera edad; **senior high school** (US) n = instituto de enseñanza media; see also **high school**
sensation [sen'seɪʃən] n sensación f; **sensational** adj sensacional
sense n (faculty, meaning) sentido; (feeling) sensación f; (good sense) sentido común, juicio ▷vt sentir, percibir; **it makes ~** tiene sentido; **senseless** adj estúpido, insensato; (unconscious) sin conocimiento; **sense of humour** (BRIT) n sentido del humor
sensible ['sensɪbl] adj sensato; (reasonable) razonable, lógico
sensitive ['sensɪtɪv] adj sensible; (touchy) susceptible
sensual ['sensjuəl] adj sensual
sensuous ['sensjuəs] adj sensual
sent [sent] pt, pp of **send**
sentence ['sentns] n (Ling) oración f; (Law) sentencia, fallo ▷vt: **to ~ sb to death/to 5 years (in prison)** condenar a algn a muerte/a 5 años de cárcel
sentiment ['sentɪmənt] n sentimiento; (opinion) opinión f; **sentimental** [-'mentl] adj sentimental
Sep. abbr (= September) sep., set.
separate [adj 'seprɪt, vb 'sepəreɪt] adj separado; (distinct) distinto ▷vt separar; (part) dividir ▷vi separarse; **separately** adv por separado; **separates** npl (clothes) coordinados mpl; **separation** [-'reɪʃən] n separación f
September [sep'tembə*] n se(p)tiembre m
septic ['septɪk] adj séptico; **septic tank** n fosa séptica
sequel ['si:kwl] n consecuencia, resultado; (of story) continuación f
sequence ['si:kwəns] n sucesión f, serie f; (Cinema) secuencia
sequin ['si:kwɪn] n lentejuela
Serb [sə:b] adj, n = **Serbian**
Serbian ['sə:bɪən] adj serbio ▷n serbio/a; (Ling) serbio
sergeant ['sɑ:dʒənt] n sargento
serial ['sɪərɪəl] n (TV) telenovela, serie f televisiva; (Book) serie f; **serial killer** n asesino/a múltiple; **serial number** n número de serie
series ['sɪəri:s] n inv serie f
serious ['sɪərɪəs] adj serio; (grave) grave; **seriously** adv en serio; (ill, wounded etc) gravemente
sermon ['sə:mən] n sermón m
servant ['sə:vənt] n servidor(a) m/f; (house servant) criado/a
serve [sə:v] vt servir; (customer) atender; (train) pasar por; (apprenticeship) hacer; (prison term) cumplir ▷vi (at table) servir; (Tennis) sacar; **to ~ as/for/to do** servir de/para/para hacer ▷n (Tennis) saque m; **it ~s him right** se lo tiene merecido; **server** n (Comput) servidor m
service ['sə:vɪs] n servicio; (Rel) misa; (Aut) mantenimiento; (dishes etc) juego ▷vt (car etc) revisar; (: repair) reparar; **to be of ~ to sb** ser útil a algn; **~ included/not included** servicio incluido/no incluido (Econ: tertiary sector) sector m terciario or (de) servicios; (BRIT: on motorway) área de servicio; (Mil): **the S~s** las fuerzas armadas; **service area** n (on motorway)

área de servicio; **service charge** (BRIT) n servicio; **serviceman** (irreg) n militar m; **service station** n estación f de servicio
serviette [sə:vɪ'et] (BRIT) n servilleta
session ['seʃən] n sesión f; **to be in ~** estar en sesión
set [set] (pt, pp ~) n juego; (Radio) aparato; (TV) televisor m; (of utensils) batería; (of cutlery) cubierto; (of books) colección f; (Tennis) set m; (group of people) grupo; (Cinema) plató m; (Theatre) decorado; (Hairdressing) marcado ▷adj (fixed) fijo; (ready) listo ▷vt (place) poner, colocar; (fix) fijar; (adjust) ajustar, arreglar; (decide: rules etc) establecer, decidir ▷vi (sun) ponerse; (jam, jelly) cuajarse; (concrete) fraguar; (bone) componerse; **to be ~ on doing sth** estar empeñado en hacer algo; **to ~ music** poner música a; **to ~ on fire** incendiar, poner fuego a; **to ~ free** poner en libertad; **to ~ sth going** poner algo en marcha; **to ~ sail** zarpar, hacerse a la vela; **set aside** vt poner aparte, dejar de lado; (money, time) reservar; **set down** vt (bus, train) dejar; **set in** vi (infection) declararse; (complications) comenzar; **the rain has set in for the day** parece que va a llover todo el día; **set off** vi partir ▷vt (bomb) hacer estallar; (events) poner en marcha; (show up well) hacer resaltar; **set out** vi partir ▷vt (arrange) disponer; (state) exponer; **to set out to do sth** proponerse hacer algo; **set up** vt establecer; **setback** n revés m, contratiempo; **set menu** n menú m
settee [se'ti:] n sofá m
setting ['setɪŋ] n (scenery) marco; (position) disposición f; (of sun) puesta; (of jewel) engaste m, montadura
settle ['setl] vt (argument) resolver; (accounts) ajustar, liquidar; (Med: calm) calmar, sosegar ▷vi (dust etc) depositarse; (weather) serenarse; **to ~ for sth** convenir en aceptar algo; **to ~ on sth** decidirse por algo; **settle down** vi (get comfortable) ponerse cómodo, acomodarse; (calm down) calmarse, tranquilizarse; (live quietly) echar raíces; **settle in** vi instalarse; **settle up** vi: **to settle up with sb** ajustar cuentas con algn; **settlement** n (payment) liquidación f; (agreement) acuerdo, convenio; (village etc) pueblo
setup ['setʌp] n sistema m; (situation) situación f
seven ['sevn] num siete; **seventeen** num diez y siete, diecisiete; **seventeenth** [sevn'ti:nθ] adj decimoséptimo; **seventh** num séptimo; **seventieth** ['sevntɪɪθ] adj septuagésimo; **seventy** num setenta
sever ['sevə*] vt cortar; (relations) romper
several ['sevrəl] adj, pron varios as m/fpl, algunos/as m/fpl; **~ of us** varios de nosotros
severe [sɪ'vɪə*] adj severo; (serious) grave; (hard) duro; (pain) intenso
sew [səu] (pt ~ed, pp ~n) vt, vi coser
sewage ['su:ɪdʒ] n aguas fpl residuales
sewer ['su:ə*] n alcantarilla, cloaca
sewing ['səuɪŋ] n costura; **sewing machine** n máquina de coser
sewn [səun] pp of **sew**
sex [seks] n sexo; (lovemaking): **to have ~** hacer el amor; **sexism** ['seksɪzəm] n sexismo; **sexist** adj, n sexista mf; **sexual** ['seksjuəl] adj sexual; **sexual intercourse** n relaciones fpl sexuales; **sexuality** [seksju'ælɪtɪ] n sexualidad f; **sexy** adj sexy
shabby ['ʃæbɪ] adj (person) desharrapado; (clothes) raído, gastado; (behaviour) ruin inv
shack [ʃæk] n choza, chabola
shade [ʃeɪd] n sombra; (for lamp) pantalla; (for eyes)

visera; (of colour) matiz m, tonalidad f; (small quantity): **a ~ (too big/more)** un poquitín (grande/más) ▷ vt dar sombra a; (eyes) proteger del sol; **in the ~** en la sombra; **shades** npl (sunglasses) gafas fpl de sol

shadow ['ʃædəʊ] n sombra f ▷ vt (follow) seguir y vigilar; **shadow cabinet** (BRIT) n (Pol) gabinete paralelo formado por el partido de oposición

shady ['ʃeɪdɪ] adj sombreado; (fig: dishonest) sospechoso; (: deal) turbio

shaft [ʃɑːft] n (of arrow, spear) astil m; (Aut, Tech) eje m, árbol m; (of mine) pozo; (of lift) hueco, caja; (of light) rayo

shake [ʃeɪk] (pt **shook**, pp **shaken**) vt sacudir; (building) hacer temblar; (bottle, cocktail) agitar ▷ vi (tremble) temblar; **to ~ one's head** (in refusal) negar con la cabeza; (in dismay) mover o menear la cabeza, incrédulo; **to ~ hands with sb** estrechar la mano a algn; **shake off** vt sacudirse; (fig) deshacerse de; **shake up** vt agitar; (fig) reorganizar; **shaky** adj (hand, voice) trémulo; (building) inestable

shall [ʃæl] aux vb: **~ I help you?** ¿quieres que te ayude?; **I'll buy three, ~ I?** compro tres, ¿no te parece?

shallow ['ʃæləʊ] adj poco profundo; (fig) superficial

sham [ʃæm] n fraude m, engaño

shambles ['ʃæmblz] n confusión f

shame [ʃeɪm] n vergüenza f ▷ vt avergonzar; **it is a ~ that/to do** es una lástima que/hacer; **what a ~!** ¡qué lástima!; **shameful** adj vergonzoso; **shameless** adj desvergonzado

shampoo [ʃæm'puː] n champú m ▷ vt lavar con champú

shandy ['ʃændɪ] n mezcla de cerveza con gaseosa

shan't [ʃɑːnt] = **shall not**

shape [ʃeɪp] n forma f ▷ vt formar, dar forma a; (sb's ideas) formar; (sb's life) determinar; **to take ~** tomar forma

share [ʃeə*] n (part) parte f, porción f; (contribution) cuota; (Comm) acción f ▷ vt dividir; (have in common) compartir; **to ~ out (among or between)** repartir (entre); **shareholder** (BRIT) n accionista mf

shark [ʃɑːk] n tiburón m

sharp [ʃɑːp] adj (blade, nose) afilado; (point) puntiagudo; (outline) definido; (pain) intenso; (Mus) desafinado; (contrast) marcado; (voice) agudo; (person: quick-witted) astuto; (: dishonest) poco escrupuloso ▷ n (Mus) sostenido ▷ adv: **at 2 o'clock ~** a las 2 en punto; **sharpen** vt afilar; (pencil) sacar punta a; (fig) aguzar; **sharpener** n (also: **pencil sharpener**) sacapuntas m inv; **sharply** adv (turn, stop) bruscamente; (stand out, contrast) claramente; (criticize, retort) severamente

shatter ['ʃætə*] vt hacer añicos o pedazos; (fig: ruin) destruir, acabar con ▷ vi hacerse añicos; **shattered** adj (grief-stricken) destrozado, deshecho; (exhausted) agotado, hecho polvo

shave [ʃeɪv] vt afeitar, rasurar ▷ vi afeitarse, rasurarse n **to have a ~** afeitarse; **shaver** n (also: **electric shaver**) máquina de afeitar (eléctrica)

shavings ['ʃeɪvɪŋz] npl (of wood etc) virutas fpl

shaving cream ['ʃeɪvɪŋ~] n crema de afeitar

shaving foam n espuma de afeitar

shawl [ʃɔːl] n chal m

she [ʃiː] pron ella

sheath [ʃiːθ] n vaina; (contraceptive) preservativo

shed [ʃed] (pt, pp **~**) n cobertizo ▷ vt (skin) mudar; (tears, blood) derramar; (load) derramar; (workers) despedir

she'd [ʃiːd] = **she had; she would**

sheep [ʃiːp] n inv oveja; **sheepdog** n perro pastor; **sheepskin** n piel f de carnero

sheer [ʃɪə*] adj (utter) puro, completo; (steep) escarpado; (material) diáfano ▷ adv verticalmente

sheet [ʃiːt] n (on bed) sábana f; (of paper) hoja; (of glass, metal) lámina; (of ice) capa

sheik(h) [ʃeɪk] n jeque m

shelf [ʃelf] (pl **shelves**) n estante m

shell [ʃel] n (on beach) concha; (of egg, nut etc) cáscara; (explosive) proyectil m, obús m; (of building) armazón f ▷ vt (peas) desenvainar; (Mil) bombardear

she'll [ʃiːl] = **she will; she shall**

shellfish ['ʃelfɪʃ] n inv crustáceo; (as food) mariscos mpl

shelter ['ʃeltə*] n abrigo, refugio ▷ vt (aid) amparar, proteger; (give lodging to) abrigar ▷ vi abrigarse, refugiarse; **sheltered** adj (life) protegido; (spot) abrigado

shelves [ʃelvz] npl of **shelf**

shelving ['ʃelvɪŋ] n estantería

shepherd ['ʃepəd] n pastor m ▷ vt (guide) guiar, conducir; **shepherd's pie** (BRIT) n pastel de carne y patatas

sheriff ['ʃerɪf] (US) n sheriff m

sherry ['ʃerɪ] n jerez m

she's [ʃiːz] = **she is; she has**

Shetland ['ʃetlənd] n (also: **the ~s, the ~ Isles**) las Islas de Zetlandia

shield [ʃiːld] n escudo; (protection) blindaje m ▷ vt: **to ~ (from)** proteger (de)

shift [ʃɪft] n (change) cambio; (at work) turno ▷ vt trasladar; (remove) quitar ▷ vi moverse

shin [ʃɪn] n espinilla

shine [ʃaɪn] (pt, pp **shone**) n brillo, lustre m ▷ vi brillar, relucir ▷ vt (shoes) lustrar, sacar brillo a; **to ~ a torch on sth** dirigir una linterna hacia algo

shingles ['ʃɪŋglz] n (Med) herpes mpl or fpl

shiny ['ʃaɪnɪ] adj brillante, lustroso

ship [ʃɪp] n buque m, barco ▷ vt (goods) embarcar; (send) transportar o enviar por vía marítima; **shipment** n (goods) envío; **shipping** n (act) embarque m; (traffic) buques mpl; **shipwreck** n naufragio ▷ vt: **to be shipwrecked** naufragar; **shipyard** n astillero

shirt [ʃəːt] n camisa; **in (one's) ~ sleeves** en mangas de camisa

shit [ʃɪt] (infl) excl ¡mierda! (!)

shiver ['ʃɪvə*] n escalofrío ▷ vi temblar, estremecerse; (with cold) tiritar

shock [ʃɔk] n (impact) choque m; (Elec) descarga (eléctrica); (emotional) conmoción f; (start) sobresalto, susto; (Med) postración f nerviosa ▷ vt dar un susto a; (offend) escandalizar; **shocking** adj (awful) espantoso; (outrageous) escandaloso

shoe [ʃuː] (pt, pp **shod**) n zapato; (for horse) herradura ▷ vt (horse) herrar; **shoelace** n cordón m; **shoe polish** n betún m; **shoeshop** n zapatería

shone [ʃɔn] pt, pp of **shine**

shook [ʃuk] pt of **shake**

shoot [ʃuːt] (pt, pp **shot**) n (on branch, seedling) retoño, vástago ▷ vt disparar; (kill) matar a tiros; (execute) fusilar; (film) rodar, filmar ▷ vi (Football) chutar; **shoot down** vt (plane) derribar; **shoot up** vi (prices) dispararse; **shooting** n (shots) tiros mpl; (Hunting) caza con escopeta

shop [ʃɔp] n tienda; (workshop) taller m ▷ vi (also: **go**

~ping) ir de compras; **shop assistant** (BRIT) n dependiente/a m/f; **shopkeeper** n tendero/a; **shoplifting** n mechería; **shopping** n (goods) compras fpl; **shopping bag** n bolsa (de compras); **shopping centre** (US **shopping center**) n centro comercial; **shopping mall** n centro comercial; **shopping trolley** n (BRIT) carrito de la compra; **shop window** n escaparate m (SP), vidriera (LAM)

shore [ʃɔ:*] n orilla f ▷ vt: **to ~ (up)** reforzar; **on ~** en tierra

short [ʃɔ:t] adj corto; (in time) breve, de corta duración; (person) bajo; (curt) brusco, seco; (insufficient) insuficiente; **(a pair of) ~s** (unos) pantalones mpl cortos; **to be ~ of sth** estar falto de algo; **in ~** en pocas palabras; **~ of doing ...** fuera de hacer ...; **it is ~ for** es la forma abreviada de; **to cut ~** (speech, visit) interrumpir, terminar inesperadamente; **everything ~ of ...** todo menos ...; **to fall ~ of** no alcanzar; **to run ~ of** quedarse a algn poco, **to stop ~** parar en seco; **to stop ~ of** detenerse antes de; **shortage** n: **a shortage of** una falta de; **shortbread** n especie de mantecada; **shortcoming** n defecto, deficiencia; **short(crust) pastry** n pasta quebradiza; **shortcut** n atajo; **shorten** vt acortar; (visit) interrumpir; **shortfall** n déficit m; **shorthand** (BRIT) n taquigrafía; **short-lived** adj efímero; **shortly** adv en breve, dentro de poco; **shorts** npl pantalones mpl cortos; (US) calzoncillos mpl; **short-sighted** (BRIT) adj miope; (fig) imprudente; **short-sleeved** adj de manga corta; **short story** n cuento; **short-tempered** adj enojadizo; **short-term** adj (effect) a corto plazo

shot [ʃɔt] pt, pp of **shoot** ▷ n (sound) tiro, disparo; (try) tentativa; (injection) inyección f; (Phot) toma, fotografía; **to be a good/poor ~** (person) tener buena/mala puntería; **like a ~** (without any delay) como un rayo; **shotgun** n escopeta

should [ʃud] aux vb: **I ~ go now** debo irme ahora; **he ~ be there now** debe de haber llegado (ya); **I ~ go if I were you** yo en tu lugar me iría; **I ~ like to** me gustaría

shoulder ['ʃəʊldə*] n hombro ▷ vt (fig) cargar con; **shoulder blade** n omóplato

shouldn't ['ʃudnt] = **should not**

shout [ʃaut] n grito ▷ vt gritar ▷ vi gritar, dar voces

shove [ʃʌv] n empujón m ▷ vt empujar; (inf: put): **to ~ sth in** meter a algo a empellones

shovel ['ʃʌvl] n pala; (mechanical) excavadora ▷ vt mover con pala

show [ʃəʊ] (pt **-ed**, pp **-n**) n (of emotion) demostración f; (semblance) apariencia; (exhibition) exposición f; (Theatre) función f, espectáculo; (TV) show m ▷ vt mostrar, enseñar; (courage etc) mostrar, manifestar; (exhibit) exponer; (film) proyectar ▷ vi mostrarse; (appear) aparecer; **for ~** para impresionar; **on ~** (exhibits etc) expuesto; **show in** vt (person) hacer pasar; **show off** vi (pej) presumir ▷ vt (display) lucir; **show out** vt: **to show sb out** acompañar a algn a la puerta; **show up** vi (stand out) destacar; (inf: turn up) aparecer ▷ vt (unmask) desenmascarar; **show business** n mundo del espectáculo

shower ['ʃaʊə*] n (rain) chaparrón m, chubasco; (of stones etc) lluvia; (for bathing) ducha, regadera (MEX) ▷ vi llover ▷ vt (fig): **to ~ sb with sth** colmar a algn de algo; **to have a ~** ducharse; **shower cap** n gorro de baño; **shower gel** n gel m de ducha

showing ['ʃəʊɪŋ] n (of film) proyección f

show jumping n hípica

shown [ʃəʊn] pp of **show**

show: **show-off** (inf) n (person) presumido/a; **showroom** n sala de muestras

shrank [ʃræŋk] pt of **shrink**

shred [ʃred] n (gen pl) triza, jirón m ▷ vt hacer trizas; (Culin) desmenuzar

shrewd [ʃru:d] adj astuto

shriek [ʃri:k] n chillido ▷ vi chillar

shrimp [ʃrɪmp] n camarón m

shrine [ʃraɪn] n santuario, sepulcro

shrink [ʃrɪŋk] (pt **shrank**, pp **shrunk**) vi encogerse; (be reduced) reducirse; (also: **~ away**) retroceder ▷ vt encoger ▷ n (inf, pej) loquero/a; **to ~ from (doing) sth** no atreverse a hacer algo

shrivel ['ʃrɪvl] (also: **~ up**) vt (dry) secar ▷ vi secarse

shroud [ʃraʊd] n sudario ▷ vt: **~ed in mystery** envuelto en el misterio

Shrove Tuesday ['ʃrəʊv~] n martes m de carnaval

shrub [ʃrʌb] n arbusto

shrug [ʃrʌg] n encogimiento de hombros ▷ vt, vi: **to ~ (one's shoulders)** encogerse de hombros; **shrug off** vt negar importancia a

shrunk [ʃrʌŋk] pp of **shrink**

shudder ['ʃʌdə*] n estremecimiento, escalofrío ▷ vi estremecerse

shuffle ['ʃʌfl] vt (cards) barajar ▷ vi: **to ~ (one's feet)** arrastrar los pies

shun [ʃʌn] vt rehuir, esquivar

shut [ʃʌt] (pt, pp **~**) vt cerrar ▷ vi cerrarse; **shut down** vt, vi cerrar; **shut up** vi (inf: keep quiet) callarse ▷ vt (close) cerrar; (silence) hacer callar; **shutter** n contraventana; (Phot) obturador m

shuttle ['ʃʌtl] n lanzadera; (also: **~ service**) servicio rápido y continuo entre dos puntos; (Aviat) puente m aéreo; **shuttlecock** n volante m

shy [ʃaɪ] adj tímido

sibling ['sɪblɪŋ] n (formal) hermano/a

Sicily ['sɪsɪlɪ] n Sicilia

sick [sɪk] adj (ill) enfermo; (nauseated) mareado; (humour) negro; (vomiting): **to be ~** (BRIT) vomitar; **to feel ~** tener náuseas; **to be ~ of** (fig) estar harto de; **sickening** adj (fig) asqueroso; **sick leave** n baja por enfermedad; **sickly** adj enfermizo; (smell) nauseabundo; **sickness** n enfermedad f, mal m; (vomiting) náuseas fpl

side [saɪd] n (gen) lado; (of body) costado; (of lake) orilla; (of hill) ladera; (team) equipo ▷ adj (door, entrance) lateral ▷ vi: **to ~ with sb** tomar el partido de algn; **by the ~ of** al lado de; **~ by ~** juntos/as; **from ~ to ~** de un lado para otro; **from all ~s** de todos lados; **to take ~s (with)** tomar partido (con); **sideboard** n aparador m; **sideboards** (BRIT) npl = **sideburns**; **sideburns** npl patillas fpl; **sidelight** n (Aut) luz f lateral; **sideline** n (Sport) línea de banda; (fig) empleo suplementario; **side order** n plato de acompañamiento; **side road** n (BRIT) calle f lateral; **side street** n calle f lateral; **sidetrack** vt (fig) desviar (de su propósito); **sidewalk** (US) n acera; **sideways** adv de lado

siege [si:dʒ] n cerco, sitio

sieve [sɪv] n colador m ▷ vt cribar

sift [sɪft] vt cribar; (fig: information) escudriñar

sigh [saɪ] n suspiro ▷ vi suspirar

sight [saɪt] n (faculty) vista; (spectacle) espectáculo; (on gun) mira, alza ▷ vt divisar; **in ~** a la vista; **out of ~** fuera de (la) vista; **on ~** (shoot) sin previo aviso; **sightseeing** n excursionismo, turismo; **to go**

sightseeing hacer turismo

sign [saɪn] n (with hand) señal f, seña; (trace) huella, rastro; (notice) letrero; (written) signo ▷ vt firmar; (Sport) fichar; **to ~ sth over to sb** firmar el traspaso de algo a algn; **sign for** vt fus (item) firmar el recibo de; **sign in** vi firmar el registro (al entrar); **sign on** vi (BRIT: as unemployed) registrarse como desempleado; (for course) inscribirse ▷ vt (Mil) alistar; (employee) contratar; **sign up** vi (Mil) alistarse; (for course) inscribirse ▷ vt (player) fichar

signal ['sɪgnl] n señal f ▷ vi señalizar ▷ vt (person) hacer señas a; (message) comunicar por señales

signature ['sɪgnətʃə*] n firma

significance [sɪg'nɪfɪkəns] n (importance) trascendencia

significant [sɪg'nɪfɪkənt] adj significativo; (important) trascendente

signify ['sɪgnɪfaɪ] vt significar

sign language n lenguaje m para sordomudos

signpost ['saɪnpəust] n indicador m

Sikh [si:k] adj, n sij mf

silence ['saɪləns] n silencio ▷ vt acallar; (guns) reducir al silencio

silent ['saɪlnt] adj silencioso; (not speaking) callado; (film) mudo; **to remain ~** guardar silencio

silhouette [sɪluː'et] n silueta

silicon chip ['sɪlɪkən-] n plaqueta de silicio

silk [sɪlk] n seda ▷ adj de seda

silly ['sɪlɪ] adj (person) tonto; (idea) absurdo

silver ['sɪlvə*] n plata; (money) moneda suelta ▷ adj de plata; (colour) plateado; **silver-plated** adj plateado

similar ['sɪmɪlə*] adj: **~ (to)** parecido or semejante (a); **similarity** [-'lærɪtɪ] n semejanza; **similarly** adv del mismo modo

simmer ['sɪmə*] vi hervir a fuego lento

simple ['sɪmpl] adj (easy) sencillo; (foolish, Comm: interest) simple; **simplicity** [-'plɪsɪtɪ] n sencillez f; **simplify** ['sɪmplɪfaɪ] vt simplificar; **simply** adv (live, talk) sencillamente; (just, merely) sólo

simulate ['sɪmjuleɪt] vt fingir, simular

simultaneous [sɪmʌl'teɪnɪəs] adj simultáneo; **simultaneously** adv simultáneamente

sin [sɪn] n pecado ▷ vi pecar

since [sɪns] adv desde entonces, después ▷ prep desde ▷ conj (time) desde que; (because) ya que, puesto que; **~ then, ever ~** desde entonces

sincere [sɪn'sɪə*] adj sincero; **sincerely** adv: **yours sincerely** (in letters) le saluda atentamente

sing [sɪŋ] (pt **sang**, pp **sung**) vt, vi cantar

Singapore [sɪŋə'pɔː*] n Singapur m

singer ['sɪŋə*] n cantante mf

singing ['sɪŋɪŋ] n canto

single ['sɪŋgl] adj único, solo; (unmarried) soltero; (not double) simple, sencillo ▷ n (BRIT: also: **~ ticket**) billete m sencillo; (record) sencillo, single m; **singles** npl (Tennis) individual m; **single out** vt (choose) escoger; **single bed** n cama individual; **single file** n: **in single file** en fila de uno; **single-handed** adv sin ayuda; **single-minded** adj resuelto, firme; **single parent** n padre m soltero, madre f soltera (o divorciado etc); **single parent family** familia monoparental; **single room** n cuarto individual

singular ['sɪŋgjulə*] adj (odd) raro, extraño; (outstanding) excepcional ▷ n (Ling) singular m

sinister ['sɪnɪstə*] adj siniestro

sink [sɪŋk] (pt **sank**, pp **sunk**) n fregadero ▷ vt (ship)

hundir, echar a pique; (foundations) excavar ▷ vi hundirse; **to ~ sth into** hundir algo en; **sink in** vi (fig) penetrar, calar

sinus ['saɪnəs] n (Anat) seno

sip [sɪp] n sorbo ▷ vt sorber, beber a sorbitos

sir [sə*] n señor m; **S~ John Smith** Sir John Smith; **yes ~** sí, señor

siren ['saɪərn] n sirena

sirloin ['sə:lɔɪn] n (also: **~ steak**) solomillo

sister ['sɪstə*] n hermana; (BRIT: nurse) enfermera jefe; **sister-in-law** n cuñada

sit [sɪt] (pt, pp **sat**) vi sentarse; (be sitting) estar sentado; (assembly) reunirse; (for painter) posar ▷ vt (exam) presentarse a; **sit back** vi (in seat) recostarse; **sit down** vi sentarse; **sit on** vt fus (jury, committee) ser miembro de, formar parte de; **sit up** vi incorporarse; (not go to bed) velar

sitcom ['sɪtkɔm] n abbr (= situation comedy) comedia de situación

site [saɪt] n sitio; (also: **building ~**) solar m ▷ vt situar

sitting ['sɪtɪŋ] n (of assembly etc) sesión f; (in canteen) turno; **sitting room** n sala de estar

situated ['sɪtjueɪtɪd] adj situado

situation [sɪtju'eɪʃən] n situación f; **"~s vacant"** (BRIT) "ofrecen trabajo"

six [sɪks] num seis; **sixteen** num diez y seis, dieciséis; **sixteenth** [sɪks'ti:nθ] adj decimosexto; **sixth** [sɪksθ] num sexto; **sixth form** (BRIT) clase f de alumnos del sexto año (de 16 a 18 años de edad); **sixth-form college** n instituto m para alumnos de 16 a 18 años; **sixtieth** ['sɪkstɪɪθ] adj sexagésimo; **sixty** num sesenta

size [saɪz] n tamaño; (extent) extensión f; (of clothing) talla; (of shoes) número; **sizeable** adj importante, considerable

sizzle ['sɪzl] vi crepitar

skate [skeɪt] n patín m; (fish: pl inv) raya ▷ vi patinar; **skateboard** n monopatín m; **skateboarding** n monopatín m; **skater** n patinador(a) m/f; **skating** n patinaje m; **skating rink** n pista de patinaje

skeleton ['skelɪtn] n esqueleto; (Tech) armazón f; (outline) esquema m

skeptical ['skeptɪkl] (US) = **sceptical**

sketch [sketʃ] n (drawing) dibujo; (outline) esbozo, bosquejo; (Theatre) sketch m ▷ vt dibujar; (plan etc: also: **~ out**) esbozar

skewer ['skju:ə*] n broqueta

ski [ski:] n esquí m ▷ vi esquiar; **ski boot** n bota de esquí

skid [skɪd] n patinazo ▷ vi patinar

ski: skier n esquiador(a) m/f; **skiing** n esquí m

skilful ['skɪlful] (US **skillful**) adj diestro, experto

ski lift n telesilla m, telesquí m

skill [skɪl] n destreza, pericia, técnica; **skilled** adj hábil, diestro; (worker) cualificado

skim [skɪm] vt (milk) desnatar; (glide over) rozar, rasar ▷ vi: **to ~ through** (book) hojear; **skimmed milk** (US **skim milk**) n leche f desnatada

skin [skɪn] n piel f; (complexion) cutis m; (of fruit etc) pelar; (animal) despellejar; **skinhead** n cabeza m/f rapada, skin(head) m/f; **skinny** adj flaco

skip [skɪp] n brinco, salto; (BRIT: container) contenedor m ▷ vi brincar; (with rope) saltar a la comba ▷ vt saltarse

ski: ski pass n forfait m (de esquí); **ski pole** n bastón m de esquiar

skipper ['skɪpə*] n (Naut, Sport) capitán m

skipping rope ['skɪpɪŋ-] (*us* **skip rope**) *n* comba
skirt [skɜːt] *n* falda, pollera (sc) ▷ *vt* (*go round*) ladear
skirting board ['skɜːtɪŋ-] (*BRIT*) *n* rodapié *m*
ski slope *n* pista de esquí
ski suit *n* traje *m* de esquiar
skull [skʌl] *n* calavera; (*Anat*) cráneo
skunk [skʌŋk] *n* mofeta
sky [skaɪ] *n* cielo; **skyscraper** *n* rascacielos *m inv*
slab [slæb] *n* (*stone*) bloque *m*; (*flat*) losa; (*of cake*) trozo
slack [slæk] *adj* (*loose*) flojo; (*slow*) de poca actividad;
(*careless*) descuidado; **slacks** *npl* pantalones *mpl*
slain [sleɪn] *pp of* **slay**
slam [slæm] *vt* (*throw*) arrojar (violentamente);
(*criticize*) criticar duramente ▷ *vi* (*door*) cerrarse de
golpe; **to ~ the door** dar un portazo
slander ['slɑːndə*] *n* calumnia, difamación *f*
slang [slæŋ] *n* argot *m*; (*jargon*) jerga
slant [slɑːnt] *n* sesgo, inclinación *f*; (*fig*)
interpretación *f*
slap [slæp] *n* palmada; (*in face*) bofetada ▷ *vt* dar
una palmada o bofetada a; (*paint etc*): **to ~ sth
on sth** embadurnar algo con algo ▷ *adv* (*directly*)
exactamente, directamente
slash [slæʃ] *vt* acuchillar; (*fig: prices*) fulminar
slate [sleɪt] *n* pizarra ▷ *vt* (*fig: criticize*) criticar
duramente
slaughter ['slɔːtə*] *n* (*of animals*) matanza; (*of people*)
carnicería ▷ *vt* matar; **slaughterhouse** *n* matadero
Slav [slɑːv] *adj* eslavo
slave [sleɪv] *n* esclavo/a ▷ *vi* (*also*: **~ away**) sudar
tinta; **slavery** *n* esclavitud *f*
slay [sleɪ] (*pt* **slew**, *pp* **slain**) *vt* matar
sleazy ['sliːzɪ] *adj* de mala fama
sled [sled] (*us*) = **sledge**
sledge [sledʒ] *n* trineo
sleek [sliːk] *adj* (*shiny*) lustroso; (*car etc*) elegante
sleep [sliːp] (*pt*, *pp* **slept**) *n* sueño ▷ *vi* dormir; **to
go to ~** quedarse dormido; **sleep in** *vi* (*oversleep*)
quedarse dormido; **sleep together** *vi* (*have sex*)
acostarse juntos; **sleeper** *n* (*person*) durmiente *mf*;
(*BRIT Rail: on track*) traviesa; (: *train*) coche-cama *m*;
sleeping bag *n* saco de dormir; **sleeping car** *n*
coche-cama *m*; **sleeping pill** *n* somnífero; **sleepover**
n: **we're having a sleepover at Jo's** nos vamos a
quedar a dormir en casa de Jo; **sleepwalk** *vi* caminar
dormido; (*habitually*) ser sonámbulo; **sleepy** *adj*
soñoliento; (*place*) soporífero
sleet [sliːt] *n* aguanieve *f*
sleeve [sliːv] *n* manga; (*Tech*) manguito; (*of record*)
portada; **sleeveless** *adj* sin mangas
sleigh [sleɪ] *n* trineo
slender ['slendə*] *adj* delgado; (*means*) escaso
slept [slept] *pt*, *pp of* **sleep**
slew [sluː] *pt of* **slay** ▷ *vi* (*BRIT: veer*) torcerse
slice [slaɪs] *n* (*of meat*) tajada; (*of bread*) rebanada;
(*of lemon*) rodaja; (*utensil*) pala ▷ *vt* cortar (en tajos),
rebanar
slick [slɪk] *adj* (*skilful*) hábil, diestro; (*clever*) astuto ▷ *n*
(*also*: **oil ~**) marea negra
slide [slaɪd] (*pt*, *pp* **slid**) *n* (*movement*) descenso,
desprendimiento; (*in playground*) tobogán *m*; (*Phot*)
diapositiva; (*BRIT: also*: **hair ~**) pasador *m* ▷ *vt* correr,
deslizar ▷ *vi* (*slip*) resbalarse; (*glide*) deslizarse; **sliding**
adj (*door*) corredizo
slight [slaɪt] *adj* (*slim*) delgado; (*frail*) delicado; (*pain
etc*) leve; (*trivial*) insignificante; (*small*) pequeño ▷ *n*

desaire *m* ▷ *vt* (*insult*) ofender, desairar; **not in the
~est** en absoluto; **slightly** *adv* ligeramente, un poco
slim [slɪm] *adj* delgado, esbelto; (*fig: chance*) remoto
▷ *vi* adelgazar; **slimming** *n* adelgazamiento
slimy ['slaɪmɪ] *adj* cenagoso
sling [slɪŋ] *n* (*Med*) cabestrillo; (*weapon*)
honda ▷ *vt* tirar, arrojar
slip [slɪp] *n* (*slide*) resbalón *m*; (*mistake*) descuido;
(*underskirt*) combinación *f*; (*of paper*) papelito ▷ *vt*
(*slide*) deslizar ▷ *vi* deslizarse; (*stumble*) resbalar(se);
(*decline*) decaer; (*move smoothly*): **to ~ into/out of** (*room
etc*) introducirse en/salirse de; **to give sb the ~** eludir
a algn; **a ~ of the tongue** un lapsus; **~ sth on/off**
ponerse/quitarse algo; **slip up** *vi* (*make mistake*)
equivocarse; meter la pata
slipper ['slɪpə*] *n* zapatilla, pantufla
slippery ['slɪpərɪ] *adj* resbaladizo; **slip road** (*BRIT*) *n*
carretera de acceso
slit [slɪt] (*pt*, *pp* **~**) *n* raja; (*cut*) corte *m* ▷ *vt* rajar;
cortar
slog [slɔg] (*BRIT*) *vi* sudar tinta; **it was a ~** costó
trabajo (hacerlo)
slogan ['sləugən] *n* eslogan *m*, lema *m*
slope [sləup] *n* (*up*) cuesta, pendiente *f*; (*down*)
declive *m*; (*side of mountain*) falda, vertiente *m* ▷ *vi*: **to ~
down** estar en declive; **to ~ up** inclinarse; **sloping** *adj*
en pendiente; en declive; (*writing*) inclinado
sloppy ['slɔpɪ] *adj* (*work*) descuidado; (*appearance*)
desaliñado
slot [slɔt] *n* ranura ▷ *vt*: **to ~ into** encajar en; **slot
machine** *n* (*BRIT: vending machine*) distribuidor *m*
automático; (*for gambling*) tragaperras *m inv*
Slovakia [sləu'vækɪə] *n* Eslovaquia
Slovene [sləu'viːn] *adj* esloveno ▷ *n* esloveno/a;
(*Ling*) esloveno; **Slovenia** [sləu'viːnɪə] *n* Eslovenia;
Slovenian *adj*, *n* = **Slovene**
slow [sləu] *adj* lento; (*not clever*) lerdo; (*watch*): **to be ~**
atrasar ▷ *adv* lentamente, despacio ▷ *vt*, *vi* retardar;
"~" (*road sign*) "disminuir velocidad"; **slow down** *vi*
reducir la marcha; **slowly** *adv* lentamente, despacio;
slow motion *n*: **in slow motion** a cámara lenta
slug [slʌg] *n* babosa; (*bullet*) posta; **sluggish** *adj*
lento; (*person*) perezoso
slum [slʌm] *n* casucha
slump [slʌmp] *n* (*economic*) depresión *f* ▷ *vi*
hundirse; (*prices*) caer en picado
slung [slʌŋ] *pt*, *pp of* **sling**
slur [slɜː*] *n*: **to cast a ~ on** insultar ▷ *vt* (*speech*)
pronunciar mal
sly [slaɪ] *adj* astuto; (*smile*) taimado
smack [smæk] *n* bofetada ▷ *vt* dar con la mano a;
(*child, on face*) abofetear ▷ *vi*: **to ~ of** saber a, oler a
small [smɔːl] *adj* pequeño; **small ads** (*BRIT*) *npl*
anuncios *mpl* por palabras; **small change** *n* suelto,
cambio
smart [smɑːt] *adj* elegante; (*clever*) listo, inteligente;
(*quick*) rápido, vivo ▷ *vi* escocer, picar; **smartcard** *n*
tarjeta inteligente
smash [smæʃ] *n* (*also*: **~-up**) choque *m*; (*Mus*)
exitazo ▷ *vt* (*break*) hacer pedazos; (*car etc*) estrellar;
(*Sport: record*) batir ▷ *vi* hacerse pedazos; (*against wall
etc*) estrellarse; **smashing** (*inf*) *adj* estupendo
smear [smɪə*] *n* mancha; (*Med*) frotis *m inv* ▷ *vt*
untar; **smear test** *n* (*Med*) citología, frotis *m inv*
(*cervical*)
smell [smɛl] (*pt*, *pp* **smelt** *or* **~ed**) *n* olor *m*; (*sense*)

olfato ▷ vi oler; **smelly** adj maloliente
smelt [smɛlt] pt, pp of **smell**
smile [smaɪl] n sonrisa ▷ vi sonreír
smirk [smə:k] n sonrisa falsa or afectada
smog [smɔg] n esmog m
smoke [sməʊk] n humo ▷ vi fumar; (chimney)
echar humo ▷ vt (cigarettes) fumar; **smoke alarm** n
detector m de humo, alarma contra incendios; **smoked**
adj (bacon, glass) ahumado; **smoker** n fumador(a) m/f;
(Rail) coche m fumador; **smoking** n: "**no smoking**"
"prohibido fumar"; **smoky** adj (room) lleno de humo;
(taste) ahumado
smooth [smu:ð] adj liso; (flavour,
movement) suave; (sauce) fino; (person: pej) meloso ▷ vt
(also: ~ out) alisar; (creases, difficulties) allanar
smother ['smʌðə*] vt sofocar; (repress) contener
SMS n abbr (= short message service) (servicio) SMS; **SMS
message** n (mensaje m) SMS
smudge [smʌdʒ] n mancha ▷ vt manchar
smug [smʌg] adj presumido; orondo
smuggle ['smʌgl] vt pasar de contrabando;
smuggling n contrabando
snack [snæk] n bocado; **snack bar** n cafetería
snag [snæg] n problema m
snail [sneɪl] n caracol m
snake [sneɪk] n serpiente f
snap [snæp] n (sound) chasquido; (photograph) foto
f ▷ adj (decision) instantáneo ▷ vt (break) quebrar;
(fingers) castañetear ▷ vi quebrarse; (fig: speak sharply)
contestar bruscamente; **to ~ shut** cerrarse de golpe;
snap at vt fus (dog) intentar morder; **snap up** vt
agarrar; **snapshot** n foto f (instantánea)
snarl [snɑ:l] vi gruñir
snatch [snætʃ] n (small piece) fragmento ▷ vt
(snatch away) arrebatar; (fig) agarrar; **to ~ some sleep**
encontrar tiempo para dormir
sneak [sni:k] (pt (us) **snuck**) vi: **to ~ in/out** entrar/
salir a hurtadillas ▷ n (inf) soplón/ona m/f; **to ~ up
on sb** aparecérsele de improviso a algn; **sneakers** npl
zapatos mpl de lona
sneer [snɪə*] vi reír con sarcasmo; (mock) **to ~ at**
burlarse de
sneeze [sni:z] vi estornudar
sniff [snɪf] vi sollozar ▷ vt husmear, oler; (drugs)
esnifar
snigger ['snɪgə*] vi reírse con disimulo
snip [snɪp] n tijeretazo; (BRIT: inf: bargain) ganga ▷ vt
tijeretear
sniper ['snaɪpə*] n francotirador(a) m/f
snob [snɔb] n (e)snob m/f
snooker ['snu:kə*] n especie de billar
snoop [snu:p] vi: **to ~ about** fisgonear
snooze [snu:z] n siesta ▷ vi echar una siesta
snore [snɔ:*] vi roncar ▷ n ronquido
snorkel ['snɔ:kl] n (tubo) respirador m
snort [snɔ:t] n bufido ▷ vi bufar
snow [snəʊ] n nieve f ▷ vi nevar; **snowball** n bola
de nieve ▷ vi (fig) agrandarse, ampliarse; **snowstorm**
n nevada, nevasca
snub [snʌb] vt (person) desairar ▷ n desaire m,
repulsa
snug [snʌg] adj (cosy) cómodo; (fitted) ajustado

🔑 **KEYWORD**

so [səʊ] adv **1** (thus, likewise) así, de este modo; **if so** de

ser así; **I like swimming – so do I** a mí me gusta nadar
– a mí también; **I've got work to do – so has Paul**
tengo trabajo que hacer – Paul también; **it's 5 o'clock
– so it is!** son las cinco – ¡pues es verdad!; **I hope/think
so** espero/creo que sí; **so far** hasta ahora; (in past)
hasta este momento
2 (in comparisons etc: to such a degree) tan; **so quickly
(that)** tan rápido (que); **so big (that)** tan grande (que);
she's not so clever as her brother no es
tan lista como su hermano; **we were so worried**
estábamos preocupadísimos
3: **so much** adj, adv tanto; **so many** tantos/as
4 (phrases): **10 or so** unos 10, 10 o así; **so long!**
(inf: goodbye) ¡hasta luego!
▷ conj **1** (expressing purpose): **so as to do** para hacer; **so
(that)** para que +subjun
2 (expressing result) así que; **so you see, I could have
gone** así que ya ves, (yo) podría haber ido

soak [səʊk] vt (drench) empapar; (steep in water)
remojar ▷ vi empaparse, estar a remojo; **soak up** vt
absorber; **soaking** adj (also: **soaking wet**) calado or
empapado (hasta los huesos or el tuétano)
so-and-so ['səʊənsəʊ] n (somebody) fulano/a de tal
soap [səʊp] n jabón m; **soap opera** n telenovela;
soap powder n jabón m en polvo
soar [sɔ:*] vi (on wings) remontarse; (rocket: prices)
dispararse; (building etc) elevarse
sob [sɔb] n sollozo ▷ vi sollozar
sober ['səʊbə*] adj (serious) serio; (not drunk)
sobrio; (colour, style) discreto; **sober up** vt quitar la
borrachera
so-called ['səʊ'kɔ:ld] adj así llamado
soccer ['sɔkə*] n fútbol m
sociable ['səʊʃəbl] adj sociable
social ['səʊʃl] adj social ▷ n velada, fiesta; **socialism**
n socialismo; **socialist** adj, n socialista mf; **socialize**
vi: **to socialize (with)** alternar (con); **social life** n vida
social; **socially** adv socialmente; **social security**
n seguridad f social; **social services** npl servicios
mpl sociales; **social work** n asistencia social; **social
worker** n asistente/a m/f social
society [sə'saɪətɪ] n sociedad f; (club) asociación f;
(also: **high ~**) alta sociedad
sociology [səʊsɪ'ɔlədʒɪ] n sociología
sock [sɔk] n calcetín m
socket ['sɔkɪt] n cavidad f; (BRIT Elec) enchufe m
soda ['səʊdə] n (Chem) sosa; (also: **~ water**) soda;
(us: also: **~ pop**) gaseosa
sodium ['səʊdɪəm] n sodio
sofa ['səʊfə] n sofá m; **sofa bed** n sofá-cama m
soft [sɔft] adj (lenient, not hard) blando; (gentle, not
bright) suave; **soft drink** n bebida no alcohólica;
soft drugs npl drogas fpl blandas; **soften** ['sɔfn]
vt ablandar; suavizar; (effect) amortiguar ▷ vi
ablandarse; suavizarse; **softly** adv suavemente;
(gently) delicadamente, con delicadeza; **software** n
(Comput) software m
soggy ['sɔgɪ] adj empapado
soil [sɔɪl] n (earth) tierra, suelo ▷ vt ensuciar
solar ['səʊlə*] adj solar; **solar power** n energía solar;
solar system n sistema m solar
sold [səʊld] pt, pp of **sell**
soldier ['səʊldʒə*] n soldado; (army man) militar m
sold out adj (Comm) agotado

sole [səʊl] n (of foot) planta; (of shoe) suela; (fish: pl inv) lenguado ▷ adj único; **solely** adv únicamente, sólo, solamente; **I will hold you solely responsible** le consideraré el único responsable
solemn ['sɒləm] adj solemne
solicitor [sə'lɪsɪtə*] (BRIT) n (for wills etc) ≈ notario/a; (in court) abogado/a
solid ['sɒlɪd] adj sólido; (gold etc) macizo ▷ n sólido
solitary ['sɒlɪtərɪ] adj solitario, solo
solitude ['sɒlɪtjuːd] n soledad f
solo ['səʊləʊ] n solo ▷ adv (fly) en solitario; **soloist** n solista m/f
soluble ['sɒljʊbl] adj soluble
solution [sə'luːʃən] n solución f
solve [sɒlv] vt resolver, solucionar
solvent ['sɒlvənt] adj (Comm) solvente ▷ n (Chem) solvente m
sombre ['sɒmbə*] (US **somber**) adj sombrío

○ **KEYWORD**

some [sʌm] adj **1** (a certain amount or number): **some tea/water/biscuits** té/agua/(unas) galletas; **there's some milk in the fridge** hay leche en el frigo; **there were some people outside** había algunas personas fuera; **I've got some money, but not much** tengo algo de dinero, pero no mucho
2 (certain: in contrasts) algunos/as; **some people say that …** hay quien dice que …; **some films were excellent, but most were mediocre** hubo películas excelentes, pero la mayoría fueron mediocres
3 (unspecified): **some woman was asking for you** una mujer estuvo preguntando por ti; **he was asking for some book (or other)** pedía un libro; **some day** algún día; **some day next week** un día de la semana que viene
▷ pron **1** (a certain number): **I've got some** (books etc) tengo algunos/as
2 (a certain amount) algo; **I've got some** (money, milk) tengo algo; **could I have some of that cheese?** ¿me puede dar un poco de ese queso?; **I've read some of the book** he leído parte del libro
▷ adv: **some 10 people** unas 10 personas, una decena de personas

some: somebody ['sʌmbədɪ] pron = **someone**; **somehow** adv de alguna manera; (for some reason) por una u otra razón; **someone** pron alguien; **someplace** (US) adv = **somewhere**; **something** pron algo; **would you like something to eat/drink?** ¿te gustaría cenar/tomar algo?; **sometime** adv (in future) algún día, en algún momento; (in past): **sometime last month** durante el mes pasado; **sometimes** adv a veces; **somewhat** adv algo; **somewhere** adv (be) en alguna parte; (go) a alguna parte; **somewhere else** (be) en otra parte; (go) a otra parte
son [sʌn] n hijo
song [sɒŋ] n canción f
son-in-law ['sʌnɪnlɔː] n yerno
soon [suːn] adv pronto, dentro de poco; ~ **afterwards** poco después; see also **as**; **sooner** adv (time) antes, más temprano; (preference: rather): **I would sooner do that** preferiría hacer eso; **sooner or later** tarde o temprano
soothe [suːð] vt tranquilizar; (pain) aliviar

sophisticated [sə'fɪstɪkeɪtɪd] adj sofisticado
sophomore ['sɒfəmɔː*] (US) n estudiante m/f de segundo año
soprano [sə'prɑːnəʊ] n soprano f
sorbet ['sɔːbeɪ] n sorbete m
sordid ['sɔːdɪd] adj (place etc) sórdido; (motive etc) mezquino
sore [sɔː*] adj (painful) doloroso, que duele ▷ n llaga
sorrow ['sɒrəʊ] n pena, dolor m
sorry ['sɒrɪ] adj (regretful) arrepentido; (condition, excuse) lastimoso; ~! ¡perdón!, ¡perdone!; ~? ¿cómo?; **to feel ~ for sb** tener lástima a algn; **I feel ~ for him** me da lástima
sort [sɔːt] n clase f, género, tipo; **sort out** vt (papers) clasificar; (organize) ordenar, organizar; (resolve: problem, situation etc) arreglar, solucionar
SOS n SOS m
so-so ['səʊsəʊ] adv regular, así así
sought [sɔːt] pt, pp of **seek**
soul [səʊl] n alma
sound [saʊnd] n (noise) sonido, ruido; (volume: on TV etc) volumen m; (Geo) estrecho ▷ adj (healthy) sano; (safe, not damaged) en buen estado; (reliable: person) digno de confianza; (sensible) sensato, razonable; (secure: investment) seguro ▷ adv: ~ **asleep** profundamente dormido ▷ vt (alarm) sonar ▷ vi sonar, resonar; (fig: seem) parecer; **to ~ like** sonar a; **soundtrack** n (of film) banda sonora
soup [suːp] n (thick) sopa; (thin) caldo
sour [saʊə*] adj agrio; (milk) cortado; **it's ~ grapes** (fig) están verdes
source [sɔːs] n fuente f
south [saʊθ] n sur m ▷ adj del sur, sureño ▷ adv al sur, hacia el sur; **South Africa** n África del Sur; **South African** adj, n sudafricano/a m/f; **South America** n América del Sur, Sudamérica; **South American** adj, n sudamericano/a m/f; **southbound** adj (con) rumbo al sur; **southeast** n sureste, sudeste; **southeastern** adj ['saʊθi:stən] adj sureste, del sureste; **southern** ['sʌðən] adj del sur, meridional; **South Korea** n Corea del Sur; **South Pole** n Polo Sur; **southward(s)** adv hacia el sur; **south-west** n suroeste; **southwestern** [saʊθ'westən] adj suroeste
souvenir [suːvə'nɪə*] n recuerdo
sovereign ['sɒvrɪn] adj, n soberano/a m/f
sow¹ [səʊ] (pt ~**ed**, pp sown) vt sembrar
sow² [saʊ] n cerda, puerca
soya ['sɔɪə] (BRIT) n soja
spa [spɑː] n balneario
space [speɪs] n espacio; (room) sitio ▷ cpd espacial ▷ vt (also: ~ **out**) espaciar; **spacecraft** n nave f espacial; **spaceship** n = **spacecraft**
spacious ['speɪʃəs] adj amplio
spade [speɪd] n (tool) pala, laya; **spades** npl (Cards: British) picas fpl; (: Spanish) espadas fpl
spaghetti [spə'getɪ] n espaguetis mpl, fideos mpl
Spain [speɪn] n España
spam [spæm] n (junk e-mail) spam m
span [spæn] n (of bird, plane) envergadura; (of arch) luz f; (in time) lapso ▷ vt extenderse sobre, cruzar; (fig) abarcar
Spaniard ['spænjəd] n español(a) m/f
Spanish ['spænɪʃ] adj español(a) ▷ n (Ling) español m, castellano; **the Spanish** npl los españoles
spank [spæŋk] vt zurrar
spanner ['spænə*] (BRIT) n llave f (inglesa)

spare [speə*] *adj* de reserva; (*surplus*) sobrante, de más ▷ *n* = **spare part** ▷ *vt* (*do without*) pasarse sin; (*refrain from hurting*) perdonar; **to ~** (*surplus*) sobrante, de sobra; **spare part** *n* pieza de repuesto; **spare room** *n* cuarto de los invitados; **spare time** *n* tiempo libre; **spare tyre** (US **spare tire**) *n* (*Aut*) neumático or llanta (LAM) de recambio; **spare wheel** *n* (*Aut*) rueda de recambio

spark [spɑːk] *n* chispa; (*fig*) chispazo; **spark(ing) plug** *n* bujía

sparkle [ˈspɑːkl] *n* centelleo, destello ▷ *vi* (*shine*) relucir, brillar

sparrow [ˈspærəu] *n* gorrión *m*

sparse [spɑːs] *adj* esparcido, escaso

spasm [ˈspæzəm] *n* (*Med*) espasmo

spat [spæt] *pt, pp of* **spit**

spate [speit] *n* (*fig*): **a ~ of** un torrente de

spatula [ˈspætjulə] *n* espátula

speak [spiːk] (*pt* **spoke**, *pp* **spoken**) *vt* (*language*) hablar; (*truth*) decir ▷ *vi* hablar; (*make a speech*) intervenir; **to ~ to sb/of** *or* **about sth** hablar con algn/de o sobre algo; **~ up!** ¡habla fuerte!; **speaker** *n* (*in public*) orador/a *m/f*; (*also*: **loudspeaker**) altavoz *m*; (*for stereo etc*) bafle *m*; (*Pol*): **the Speaker** (BRIT) el Presidente de la Cámara de los Comunes; (US) el Presidente del Congreso

spear [spiə*] *n* lanza ▷ *vt* alancear

special [ˈspeʃl] *adj* especial; (*edition etc*) extraordinario; (*delivery*) urgente; **special delivery** *n* (*Post*): **by special delivery** por entrega urgente; **special effects** *npl* (*Cine*) efectos *mpl* especiales; **specialist** *n* especialista *mf*; **speciality** [speʃiˈælɪtɪ] (BRIT) *n* especialidad *f*; **specialize** *vi*: **to specialize (in)** especializarse (en); **specially** *adv* sobre todo, en particular; **special needs** *npl* (BRIT): **children with special needs** niños que requieren una atención diferenciada; **special offer** *n* (*Comm*) oferta especial; **special school** *n* (BRIT) colegio *m* de educación especial; **specialty** (US) *n* = **speciality**

species [ˈspiːʃiːz] *n inv* especie *f*

specific [spəˈsɪfɪk] *adj* específico; **specifically** *adv* específicamente

specify [ˈspesɪfaɪ] *vt, vi* especificar, precisar

specimen [ˈspesɪmən] *n* ejemplar *m*; (*Med: of urine*) espécimen *m*; (: *of blood*) muestra

speck [spek] *n* grano, mota

spectacle [ˈspektəkl] *n* espectáculo; **spectacles** *npl* (BRIT: *glasses*) gafas *fpl* (SP), anteojos *mpl*; **spectacular** [-ˈtækjulə*] *adj* espectacular; (*success*) impresionante

spectator [spekˈteɪtə*] *n* espectador/a *m/f*

spectrum [ˈspektrəm] (*pl* **spectra**) *n* espectro

speculate [ˈspekjuleɪt] *vi*: **to ~ (on)** especular (en)

sped [sped] *pt, pp of* **speed**

speech [spiːtʃ] *n* (*faculty*) habla; (*formal talk*) discurso; (*spoken language*) lenguaje *m*; **speechless** *adj* mudo, estupefacto

speed [spiːd] *n* velocidad *f*; (*haste*) prisa; (*promptness*) rapidez *f*; **at full** *or* **top ~** a máxima velocidad; **speed up** *vi* acelerarse ▷ *vt* acelerar; **speedboat** *n* lancha motora; **speeding** *n* (*Aut*) exceso de velocidad; **speed limit** *n* límite *m* de velocidad, velocidad *f* máxima; **speedometer** [spɪˈdɔmɪtə*] *n* velocímetro; **speedy** *adj* (*fast*) veloz, rápido; (*prompt*) pronto

spell [spel] (*pt, pp* **spelt** *or* **~ed**) *n* (*also*: **magic ~**) encanto, hechizo; (*period of time*) rato, período ▷ *vt* deletrear; (*fig*) anunciar, presagiar; **to cast a ~ on sb**

hechizar a algn; **he can't ~** pone faltas de ortografía; **spell out** *vt* (*explain*): **to spell sth out for sb** explicar algo a algn en detalle; **spellchecker** [ˈspeltʃekə*] *n* corrector *m* ortográfico; **spelling** *n* ortografía

spelt [spelt] *pt, pp of* **spell**

spend [spend] (*pt, pp* **spent**) *vt* (*money*) gastar; (*time*) pasar; (*life*) dedicar; **spending** *n*: **government spending** gastos *mpl* del gobierno

spent [spent] *pt, pp of* **spend** ▷ *adj* (*cartridge, bullets, match*) usado

sperm [spəːm] *n* esperma

sphere [sfɪə*] *n* esfera

spice [spaɪs] *n* especia ▷ *vt* condimentar

spicy [ˈspaɪsɪ] *adj* picante

spider [ˈspaɪdə*] *n* araña

spike [spaɪk] *n* (*point*) punta; (*Bot*) espiga

spill [spɪl] (*pt, pp* **spilt** *or* **~ed**) *vt* derramar, verter ▷ *vi* derramarse; **to ~ over** desbordarse

spin [spɪn] (*pt, pp* **spun**) *n* (*Aviat*) barrena; (*trip in car*) paseo (en coche); (*on ball*) efecto ▷ *vt* (*wool etc*) hilar; (*ball etc*) hacer girar ▷ *vi* girar, dar vueltas

spinach [ˈspɪnɪtʃ] *n* espinaca; (*as food*) espinacas *fpl*

spinal [ˈspaɪnl] *adj* espinal

spin doctor *n* informador(a) parcial al servicio de un partido político etc

spin-dryer (BRIT) *n* secador *m* centrífugo

spine [spaɪn] *n* espinazo, columna vertebral; (*thorn*) espina

spiral [ˈspaɪərl] *n* espiral *f* ▷ *vi* (*fig: prices*) subir desorbitadamente

spire [ˈspaɪə*] *n* aguja, chapitel *m*

spirit [ˈspɪrɪt] *n* (*soul*) alma; (*ghost*) fantasma *m*; (*attitude, sense*) espíritu *m*; (*courage*) valor *m*, ánimo; **spirits** *npl* (*drink*) licor(es) *m*(*pl*); **in good ~s** alegre, de buen ánimo

spiritual [ˈspɪrɪtjuəl] *adj* espiritual ▷ *n* espiritual *m*

spit [spɪt] *n* (*for roasting*) asador *m*, espetón *m*; (*saliva*) saliva ▷ *vi* escupir; (*sound*) chisporrotear; (*rain*) lloviznar

spite [spaɪt] *n* rencor *m*, ojeriza ▷ *vt* causar pena a, mortificar; **in ~ of** a pesar de, pese a; **spiteful** *adj* rencoroso, malévolo

splash [splæʃ] *n* (*sound*) chapoteo; (*of colour*) mancha ▷ *vt* salpicar ▷ *vi* (*also*: **~ about**) chapotear; **splash out** *vi* (BRIT) derrochar dinero

splendid [ˈsplendɪd] *adj* espléndido

splinter [ˈsplɪntə*] *n* (*of wood etc*) astilla; (*in finger*) espigón *m* ▷ *vi* astillarse, hacer astillas

split [splɪt] (*pt, pp* **~**) *n* hendedura, raja; (*fig*) división *f*; (*Pol*) escisión *f* ▷ *vt* partir, rajar; (*party*) dividir; (*share*) repartir ▷ *vi* dividirse, escindirse; **split up** *vi* (*couple*) separarse; (*meeting*) acabarse

spoil [spɔɪl] (*pt, pp* **~t** *or* **~ed**) *vt* (*damage*) dañar; (*mar*) estropear; (*child*) mimar, consentir

spoilt [spɔɪlt] *pt, pp of* **spoil** ▷ *adj* (*child*) mimado, consentido; (*ballot paper*) invalidado

spoke [spəuk] *pt of* **speak** ▷ *n* rayo, radio

spoken [ˈspəukn] *pp of* **speak**

spokesman [ˈspəuksmən] (*irreg*) *n* portavoz *m*

spokesperson [ˈspəukspəːsn] (*irreg*) *n* portavoz *m/f*, vocero/a (LAM)

spokeswoman [ˈspəukswumən] (*irreg*) *n* portavoz *f*

sponge [spʌndʒ] *n* esponja; (*also*: **~ cake**) bizcocho ▷ *vt* (*wash*) lavar con esponja ▷ *vi*: **to ~ off** *or* **on sb** vivir a costa de algn; **sponge bag** (BRIT) *n* esponjera

sponsor [ˈsponsə*] *n* patrocinador(a) *m/f* ▷ *vt*

(applicant, proposal etc) proponer; **sponsorship** n patrocinio

spontaneous [spɒnˈteɪnɪəs] adj espontáneo

spooky [ˈspuːkɪ] *(inf)* adj espeluznante, horripilante

spoon [spuːn] n cuchara; **spoonful** n cucharada

sport [spɔːt] n deporte m; *(person)*: **to be a good ~** ser muy majo ▷ vt *(wear)* lucir, ostentar; **sport jacket** *(US)* n = **sports jacket**; **sports car** n coche m deportivo; **sports centre** *(BRIT)* n polideportivo; **sports jacket** *(BRIT)* n chaqueta deportiva; **sportsman** *(irreg)* n deportista m; **sports utility vehicle** n todoterreno m inv; **sportswear** n trajes mpl de deporte or sport; **sportswoman** *(irreg)* n deportista f; **sporty** adj deportista

spot [spɒt] n sitio, lugar m; *(dot: on pattern)* punto, mancha; *(pimple)* grano; *(Radio)* cuña publicitaria; *(TV)* espacio publicitario; *(small amount)*: **a ~ of** un poquito de ▷ vt *(notice)* notar, observar; **on the ~** allí mismo; **spotless** adj perfectamente limpio; **spotlight** n foco, reflector m; *(Aut)* faro auxiliar

spouse [spauz] n cónyuge mf

sprain [spreɪn] n torcedura ▷ vt: **to ~ one's ankle/wrist** torcerse el tobillo/la muñeca

sprang [spræŋ] pt of **spring**

sprawl [sprɔːl] vi tumbarse

spray [spreɪ] n rociada; *(of sea)* espuma; *(container)* atomizador m; *(for paint etc)* pistola rociadora; *(of flowers)* ramita ▷ vt rociar; *(crops)* regar

spread [spred] *(pt, pp ~)* n extensión f; *(for bread etc)* pasta para untar; *(inf: meal)* comilona ▷ vt extender; *(butter)* untar; *(wings, sails)* desplegar; *(work, wealth)* repartir; *(scatter)* esparcir ▷ vi *(also: ~ out)* (*move apart*) separarse; **spreadsheet** n hoja electrónica or de cálculo

spree [spriː] n: **to go on a ~** ir de juerga

spring [sprɪŋ] *(pt* **sprang**, *pp* **sprung**) n *(season)* primavera; *(leap)* salto, brinco; *(coiled metal)* resorte m; *(of water)* fuente f, manantial m ▷ vi saltar, brincar; **spring up** vi *(thing: appear)* aparecer; *(problem)* surgir; **spring onion** n cebolleta

sprinkle [ˈsprɪŋkl] vt *(pour: liquid)* rociar; *(: salt, sugar)* espolvorear; **to ~ water etc on, ~ with water** etc rociar or salpicar de agua etc

sprint [sprint] n esprint m ▷ vi esprintar

sprung [sprʌŋ] pp of **spring**

spun [spʌn] pt, pp of **spin**

spur [spəː*] n espuela; *(fig)* estímulo, aguijón m ▷ vt *(also: ~ on)* estimular, incitar; **on the ~ of the moment** de improviso

spurt [spəːt] n chorro; *(of energy)* arrebato ▷ vi chorrear

spy [spaɪ] n espía m ▷ vi: **to ~ on** espiar a ▷ vt *(see)* divisar, lograr ver

sq. abbr = **square**

squabble [ˈskwɒbl] vi reñir, pelear

squad [skwɒd] n *(Mil)* pelotón m; *(Police)* brigada; *(Sport)* equipo

squadron [ˈskwɒdrn] n *(Mil)* escuadrón m; *(Aviat, Naut)* escuadra

squander [ˈskwɒndə*] vt *(money)* derrochar, despilfarrar; *(chances)* desperdiciar

square [skwɛə*] n *(in town)* plaza; *(inf: person)* carca m/f ▷ adj cuadrado; *(inf: ideas, tastes)* trasnochado ▷ vt *(arrange)* arreglar; *(Math)* cuadrar; *(reconcile)* compaginar; **all ~** igual(es); **to have a ~**

meal comer caliente; **2 metres ~** 2 metros en cuadro; **2 ~ metres** 2 metros cuadrados; **square root** n raíz f cuadrada

squash [skwɒʃ] n *(BRIT: drink)*: **lemon/orange ~** zumo *(SP)* or jugo *(LAM)* de limón/naranja; *(US Bot)* calabacín m; *(Sport)* squash m ▷ vt aplastar

squat [skwɒt] adj achaparrado ▷ vi *(also: ~ down)* agacharse, sentarse en cuclillas; **squatter** n okupa mf *(SP)*

squeak [skwiːk] vi *(hinge)* chirriar, rechinar; *(mouse)* chillar

squeal [skwiːl] vi chillar, dar gritos agudos

squeeze [skwiːz] n presión f; *(of hand)* apretón m; *(Comm)* restricción f ▷ vt *(hand, arm)* apretar

squid [skwɪd] n inv calamar m; *(Culin)* calamares mpl

squint [skwɪnt] vi bizquear, ser bizco ▷ n *(Med)* estrabismo

squirm [skwəːm] vi retorcerse, revolverse

squirrel [ˈskwɪrəl] n ardilla

squirt [skwəːt] vi salir a chorros ▷ vt chiscar

Sr abbr = **senior**

Sri Lanka [srɪˈlæŋkə] n Sri Lanka m

St abbr = **saint; street**

stab [stæb] n *(with knife)* puñalada; *(of pain)* pinchazo; *(inf: try)*: **to have a ~ at (doing) sth** intentar (hacer) algo ▷ vt apuñalar

stability [stəˈbɪlɪtɪ] n estabilidad f

stable [ˈsteɪbl] adj estable ▷ n cuadra, caballeriza

stack [stæk] n montón m, pila ▷ vt amontonar, apilar

stadium [ˈsteɪdɪəm] n estadio

staff [stɑːf] n *(work force)* personal m, plantilla; *(BRIT Scol)* cuerpo docente ▷ vt proveer de personal

stag [stæg] n ciervo, venado

stage [steɪdʒ] n escena; *(point)* etapa; *(platform)* plataforma; *(profession)*: **the ~** el teatro ▷ vt *(play)* poner en escena, representar; *(organize)* montar, organizar; **in ~s** por etapas

stagger [ˈstægə*] vi tambalearse ▷ vt *(amaze)* asombrar; *(hours, holidays)* escalonar; **staggering** adj asombroso

stagnant [ˈstægnənt] adj estancado

stag night, stag party n despedida de soltero

stain [steɪn] n mancha; *(colouring)* tintura ▷ vt manchar; *(wood)* teñir; **stained glass** n vidrio m de color; **stainless steel** n acero inoxidable

staircase [ˈstɛəkeɪs] n = **stairway**

stairs [stɛəz] npl escaleras fpl

stairway [ˈstɛəweɪ] n escalera

stake [steɪk] n estaca, poste m; *(Comm)* interés m; *(Betting)* apuesta ▷ vt *(money)* apostar; *(life)* arriesgar; *(reputation)* poner en juego; *(claim)* presentar una reclamación; **to be at ~** estar en juego

stale [steɪl] adj *(bread)* duro; *(food)* pasado; *(smell)* rancio; *(beer)* agrio

stalk [stɔːk] n tallo, caña ▷ vt acechar, cazar al acecho

stall [stɔːl] n *(in market)* puesto; *(in stable)* casilla (de establo) ▷ vt *(Aut)* calar; *(fig)* dar largas a ▷ vi *(Aut)* calarse; *(fig)* andarse con rodeos

stamina [ˈstæmɪnə] n resistencia

stammer [ˈstæmə*] n tartamudeo ▷ vi tartamudear

stamp [stæmp] n sello *(SP)*, estampilla *(LAM)*, timbre m *(MEX)*; *(mark)* marca, huella; *(on document)* timbre m ▷ vi *(also: ~ one's foot)* patear ▷ vt *(mark)* marcar;

(letter) franquear; *(with rubber stamp)* sellar; **stamp out** *vt (fire)* apagar con el pie; *(crime, opposition)* acabar con; **stamped addressed envelope** *n (BRIT)* sobre *m* sellado con las señas propias

stampede [stæm'piːd] *n* estampida

stance [stæns] *n* postura

stand [stænd] *(pt, pp* **stood)** *n (position)* posición *f,* postura; *(for taxis)* parada; *(hall stand)* perchero; *(music stand)* atril *m; (Sport)* tribuna; *(at exhibition)* stand *m* ▷ *vi (be)* estar, encontrarse; *(be on foot)* estar de pie; *(rise)* levantarse; *(remain)* quedar en pie; *(in election)* presentar candidatura ▷ *vt (place)* poner, colocar; *(withstand)* aguantar, soportar; *(invite to)* invitar; **to make a ~** *(fig)* mantener una postura firme; **to ~ for parliament** *(BRIT)* presentarse (como candidato) a las elecciones; **stand back** *vi* retirarse; **stand by** *vi (be ready)* estar listo *▷ vt fus (opinion)* aferrarse a; *(person)* apoyar; **stand down** *vi (withdraw)* ceder el puesto; **stand for** *vt fus (signify)* significar; *(tolerate)* aguantar, permitir; **stand in for** *vt fus* suplir a; **stand out** *vi* destacarse; **stand up** *vi* levantarse, ponerse de pie; **stand up for** *vt fus* defender; **stand up to** *vt fus* hacer frente a

standard ['stændəd] *n* patrón *m,* norma; *(level)* nivel *m; (flag)* estandarte *m ▷ adj (size etc)* normal, corriente; *(text)* básico; **standards** *npl (morals)* valores *mpl* morales; **standard of living** *n* nivel *m* de vida

standing ['stændɪŋ] *adj (on foot)* de pie, en pie; *(permanent)* permanente *▷ n* reputación *f;* **of many years' ~** que lleva muchos años; **standing order** *(BRIT) n (at bank)* orden *f* de pago permanente

stand: standpoint *n* punto de vista; **standstill** *n:* **at a standstill** *(industry, traffic)* paralizado; *(car)* parado; **to come to a standstill** quedar paralizado; pararse

stank [stæŋk] *pt of* **stink**

staple ['steɪpl] *n (for papers)* grapa *▷ adj (food etc)* básico *▷ vt* grapar

star [staː*] *n* estrella; *(celebrity)* estrella, astro *▷ vt (Theatre, Cinema)* ser el/la protagonista de; **the stars** *npl (Astrology)* el horóscopo

starboard ['staːbəd] *n* estribor *m*

starch [staːtʃ] *n* almidón *m*

stardom ['staːdəm] *n* estrellato

stare [stɛə*] *n* mirada fija *▷ vi:* **to ~ at** mirar fijo

stark [staːk] *adj (bleak)* severo, escueto *▷ adv:* **~ naked** en cueros

start [staːt] *n* principio, comienzo; *(departure)* salida; *(sudden movement)* salto, sobresalto; *(advantage)* ventaja *▷ vt* empezar, comenzar; *(cause)* causar; *(found)* fundar; *(engine)* poner en marcha *▷ vi* comenzar, empezar; *(with fright)* asustarse, sobresaltarse; *(train etc)* salir; **to ~ doing or to do sth** empezar a hacer algo; **start off** *vi* empezar, comenzar; *(leave)* salir, ponerse en camino; **start out** *vi (begin)* empezar; *(set out)* partir, salir; **start up** *vi* comenzar; *(car)* ponerse en marcha *▷ vt* comenzar; poner en marcha; **starter** *n (Aut)* botón *m* de arranque; *(Sport: official)* juez *mf* de salida; *(BRIT Culin)* entrante *m;* **starting point** *n* punto de partida

startle ['staːtl] *vt* asustar, sobrecoger; **startling** *adj* alarmante

starvation [staː'veɪʃən] *n* hambre *f*

starve [staːv] *vi* tener mucha hambre; *(to death)* morir de hambre *▷ vt* hacer pasar hambre

state [steɪt] *n* estado *▷ vt (say, declare)* afirmar; **the S~s** los Estados Unidos; **to be in a ~** estar agitado; **statement** *n* afirmación *f;* **state school** *n* escuela or

colegio estatal; **statesman** *(irreg) n* estadista *m*

static ['stætɪk] *n (Radio)* parásitos *mpl ▷ adj* estático

station ['steɪʃən] *n* estación *f; (Radio)* emisora; *(rank)* posición *f* social *▷ vt* colocar, situar; *(Mil)* apostar

stationary ['steɪʃnərɪ] *adj* estacionario, fijo

stationer's (shop) *(BRIT) n* papelería

stationery [-nərɪ] *n* papel *m* de escribir, artículos *mpl* de escritorio

station wagon *(us) n* ranchera

statistic [stə'tɪstɪk] *n* estadística; **statistics** *n (science)* estadística

statue ['stætjuː] *n* estatua

stature ['stætʃə*] *n* estatura; *(fig)* talla

status ['steɪtəs] *n* estado; *(reputation)* estatus *m;* **status quo** *n* (e)statu quo *m*

statutory ['stætjutrɪ] *adj* estatutario

staunch [stɔːntʃ] *adj* leal, incondicional

stay [steɪ] *n* estancia *▷ vi* quedar(se); *(as guest)* hospedarse; **to ~ put** seguir en el mismo sitio; **to ~ the night/5 days** pasar la noche/estar 5 días; **stay away** *vi (from person, building)* no acercarse; *(from event)* no acudir; **stay behind** *vi* quedar atrás; **stay in** *vi* quedarse en casa; **stay on** *vi* quedarse; **stay out** *vi (of house)* no volver a casa; *(on strike)* permanecer en huelga; **stay up** *vi (at night)* velar, no acostarse

steadily ['stedɪlɪ] *adv* constantemente; *(firmly)* firmemente; *(work, walk)* sin parar; *(gaze)* fijamente

steady ['stedɪ] *adj (firm)* firme; *(regular)* regular; *(person, character)* sensato, juicioso; *(boyfriend)* formal; *(look, voice)* tranquilo *▷ vt (stabilize)* estabilizar; *(nerves)* calmar

steak [steɪk] *n* filete *m; (beef)* bistec *m*

steal [stiːl] *(pt* **stole,** *pp* **stolen)** *vt* robar *▷ vi* robar; *(move secretly)* andar a hurtadillas

steam [stiːm] *n* vapor *m; (mist)* vaho, humo *▷ vt (Culin)* cocer al vapor *▷ vi* echar vapor; **steam up** *vi (window)* empañarse; **to get steamed up about sth** *(fig)* ponerse negro por algo; **steamy** *adj (room)* lleno de vapor; *(window)* empañado; *(heat, atmosphere)* bochornoso

steel [stiːl] *n* acero *▷ adj* de acero

steep [stiːp] *adj* escarpado, abrupto; *(stair)* empinado; *(price)* exorbitante, excesivo *▷ vt* empapar, remojar

steeple ['stiːpl] *n* aguja

steer [stɪə*] *vt (car)* conducir *(sp),* manejar *(LAM); (person)* dirigir *▷ vi* conducir, manejar; **steering** *n (Aut)* dirección *f;* **steering wheel** *n* volante *m*

stem [stem] *n (of plant)* tallo; *(of glass)* pie *m ▷ vt* detener; *(blood)* restañar

step [step] *n* paso; *(on stair)* peldaño, escalón *m ▷ vi:* **to ~ forward/back** dar un paso adelante/hacia atrás; **steps** *npl (BRIT)* = **stepladder; in/out of ~ (with)** acorde/en disonancia *(con);* **step down** *vi (fig)* retirarse; **step in** *vi* entrar; *(fig)* intervenir; **step up** *vt (increase)* aumentar; **stepbrother** *n* hermanastro; **stepchild** *(pl* **stepchildren)** *n* hijastro/a *m/f;* **stepdaughter** *n* hijastra; **stepfather** *n* padrastro; **stepladder** *n* escalera doble or de tijera; **stepmother** *n* madrastra; **stepsister** *n* hermanastra; **stepson** *n* hijastro

stereo ['stɛrɪəu] *n* estéreo *▷ adj (also:* **~phonic)** estéreo, estereofónico

stereotype ['stɪərɪətaɪp] *n* estereotipo *▷ vt* estereotipar

sterile ['stɛraɪl] *adj* estéril; **sterilize** ['stɛrɪlaɪz] *vt* esterilizar

sterling ['stɜːlɪŋ] *adj* (*silver*) de ley ▷ *n* (*Econ*) libras *fpl* esterlinas *fpl*; **one pound ~** una libra esterlina

stern [stɜːn] *adj* severo, austero ▷ *n* (*Naut*) popa

steroid ['stɪərɔɪd] *n* esteroide *m*

stew [stjuː] *n* estofado, guiso ▷ *vt* estofar, guisar; (*fruit*) cocer

steward ['stjuːəd] *n* camarero; **stewardess** *n* (*esp on plane*) azafata

stick [stɪk] (*pt, pp* **stuck**) *n* palo; (*of dynamite*) barreno; (*as weapon*) porra; (*also*: **walking ~**) bastón *m* ▷ *vt* (*glue*) pegar; (*inf*: *put*) meter; (*: tolerate*) aguantar, soportar; (*thrust*): **to ~ sth into** clavar or hincar algo en ▷ *vi* pegarse; (*be unmoveable*) quedarse parado; (*in mind*) quedarse grabado; **stick out** *vi* sobresalir; **stick up** *vi* sobresalir; **stick up for** *vt fus* defender; **sticker** *n* (*label*) etiqueta engomada; (*with slogan*) pegatina; **sticking plaster** *n* esparadrapo; **stick shift** (*US*) *n* (*Aut*) palanca de cambios

sticky ['stɪkɪ] *adj* pegajoso; (*label*) engomado; (*fig*) difícil

stiff [stɪf] *adj* rígido, tieso; (*hard*) duro; (*manner*) estirado; (*difficult*) difícil; (*person*) inflexible; (*price*) exorbitante ▷ *adv*: **scared/bored ~** muerto de miedo/aburrimiento

stifling ['staɪflɪŋ] *adj* (*heat*) sofocante, bochornoso

stigma ['stɪgmə] *n* (*fig*) estigma *m*

stiletto [stɪ'letəu] (*BRIT*) *n* (*also*: **~ heel**) tacón *m* de aguja

still [stɪl] *adj* inmóvil, quieto ▷ *adv* todavía; (*even aun*); (*nonetheless*) sin embargo, aun así

stimulate ['stɪmjuleɪt] *vt* estimular

stimulus ['stɪmjuləs] (*pl* **stimuli**) *n* estímulo, incentivo

sting [stɪŋ] (*pt, pp* **stung**) *n* picadura; (*pain*) escozor *m*, picazón *f*; (*organ*) aguijón *m* ▷ *vt*, *vi* picar

stink [stɪŋk] (*pt* **stank**, *pp* **stunk**) *n* hedor *m*, tufo ▷ *vi* heder, apestar

stir [stɜː*] *n* (*fig*: *agitation*) conmoción *f* ▷ *vt* (*tea etc*) remover; (*fig*: *emotions*) provocar ▷ *vi* moverse; **stir up** *vt* (*trouble*) fomentar; **stir-fry** *vt* sofreír removiendo ▷ *n* plato preparado sofriendo y removiendo los ingredientes

stitch [stɪtʃ] *n* (*Sewing*) puntada; (*Knitting*) punto; (*Med*) punto (de sutura); (*pain*) punzada ▷ *vt* coser; (*Med*) suturar

stock [stɔk] *n* (*Comm*: *reserves*) existencias *fpl*, stock *m*; (*: selection*) surtido; (*Agr*) ganado, ganadería; (*Culin*) caldo; (*descent*) raza, estirpe *f*; (*Finance*) capital *m* ▷ *adj* (*fig*: *reply etc*) clásico ▷ *vt* (*have in stock*) tener existencias de; **~s and shares** acciones y valores; **in ~** en existencia or almacén; **out of ~** agotado; **to take ~ of** (*fig*) asesorar, examinar; **stockbroker** ['stɔkbrəukə*] *n* agente *mf* or corredor *mf* de bolsa(a); **stock cube** (*BRIT*) *n* pastilla de caldo; **stock exchange** *n* bolsa; **stockholder** ['stɔkhəuldə*] (*US*) *n* accionista *m/f*

stocking ['stɔkɪŋ] *n* media

stock market *n* bolsa (de valores)

stole [stəul] *pt of* **steal** ▷ *n* estola

stolen ['stəuln] *pp of* **steal**

stomach ['stʌmək] *n* (*Anat*) estómago; (*belly*) vientre *m* ▷ *vt* tragar, aguantar; **stomachache** *n* dolor *m* de estómago

stone [stəun] *n* piedra; (*in fruit*) hueso (= 6.348 *kg*; 14 *libras*) ▷ *adj* de piedra ▷ *vt* apedrear; (*fruit*) deshuesar

stood [stud] *pt, pp of* **stand**

stool [stuːl] *n* taburete *m*

stoop [stuːp] *vi* (*also*: **~ down**) doblarse, agacharse; (*also*: **have a ~**) ser cargado de espaldas

stop [stɔp] *n* parada; (*in punctuation*) punto ▷ *vt* parar, detener; (*break*) suspender; (*block*: *pay*) suspender; (*: cheque*) invalidar; (*also*: **put a ~ to**) poner término a ▷ *vi* pararse, detenerse; (*end*) acabarse; **to ~ doing sth** dejar de hacer algo; **stop by** *vi* pasar por; **stop off** *vi* interrumpir el viaje; **stopover** *n* parada, (*Aviat*) escala; **stoppage** *n* (*strike*) paro; (*blockage*) obstrucción *f*

storage ['stɔːrɪdʒ] *n* almacenaje *m*

store [stɔː*] *n* (*stock*) provisión *f*; (*depot*, *BRIT*: *large shop*) almacén *m*; (*US*) tienda; (*reserve*) reserva, repuesto ▷ *vt* almacenar; **stores** *npl* víveres *mpl*; **to be in ~ for sb** (*fig*) esperarle a algn; **storekeeper** (*US*) *n* tendero/a

storey ['stɔːrɪ] (*US* **story**) *n* piso

storm [stɔːm] *n* tormenta; (*fig*: *of applause*) salva; (*: of criticism*) nube *f* ▷ *vi* (*fig*) rabiar ▷ *vt* tomar por asalto; **stormy** *adj* tempestuoso

story ['stɔːrɪ] *n* historia; (*lie*) mentira; (*US*) = **storey**

stout [staut] *adj* (*strong*) sólido; (*fat*) gordo, corpulento; (*resolute*) resuelto ▷ *n* cerveza negra

stove [stəuv] *n* (*for cooking*) cocina; (*for heating*) estufa

straight [streɪt] *adj* recto, derecho; (*frank*) franco, directo; (*simple*) sencillo ▷ *adv* derecho, directamente; (*drink*) sin mezcla; **to put** or **get sth ~** dejar algo en claro; **~ away**, **~ off** en seguida; **straighten** *vt* (*also*: **straighten out**) enderezar, poner derecho ▷ *vi* (*also*: **straighten up**) enderezarse, ponerse derecho; **straightforward** *adj* (*simple*) sencillo; (*honest*) honrado, franco

strain [streɪn] *n* tensión *f*; (*Tech*) presión *f*; (*Med*) torcedura; (*breed*) tipo, variedad *f* ▷ *vt* (*back etc*) torcerse; (*resources*) agotar; (*stretch*) estirar; (*food, tea*) colar; **strained** *adj* (*muscle*) torcido; (*laugh*) forzado; (*relations*) tenso; **strainer** *n* colador *m*

strait [streɪt] *n* (*Geo*) estrecho (*fig*): **to be in dire ~s** estar en un gran apuro

strand [strænd] *n* (*of thread*) hebra; (*of hair*) trenza; (*of rope*) ramal *m*; **stranded** *adj* (*person*: *without money*) desamparado; (*: without transport*) colgado

strange [streɪndʒ] *adj* (*not known*) desconocido; (*odd*) extraño, raro; **strangely** *adv* de un modo raro; **stranger** *n* desconocido/a; (*from another area*) forastero/a

strangle ['stræŋgl] *vt* estrangular

strap [stræp] *n* correa; (*of slip, dress*) tirante *m*

strategic [strə'tiːdʒɪk] *adj* estratégico

strategy ['strætɪdʒɪ] *n* estrategia

straw [strɔː] *n* paja; (*drinking straw*) caña, pajita; **that's the last ~!** ¡eso es el colmo!

strawberry ['strɔːbərɪ] *n* fresa, frutilla (*sc*)

stray [streɪ] *adj* (*animal*) extraviado; (*bullet*) perdido; (*scattered*) disperso ▷ *vi* extraviarse, perderse

streak [striːk] *n* raya; (*in hair*) raya ▷ *vt* rayar ▷ *vi*: **to ~ past** pasar como un rayo

stream [striːm] *n* riachuelo, arroyo; (*of people, vehicles*) riada, caravana; (*of smoke, insults etc*) chorro ▷ *vt* (*Scol*) dividir en grupos por habilidad ▷ *vi* correr, fluir; **to ~ in/out** (*people*) entrar/salir en tropel

street [striːt] *n* calle *f*; **streetcar** (*US*) *n* tranvía *m*; **street light** *n* farol *m* (*LAM*), farola (*SP*); **street map** *n* plano (de la ciudad); **street plan** *n* plano

strength [streŋθ] *n* fuerza; (*of girder, knot etc*) resistencia; (*fig*: *power*) poder *m*; **strengthen** *vt* fortalecer, reforzar

strenuous ['strɛnjuəs] adj (energetic, determined) enérgico

stress [strɛs] n presión f; (mental strain) estrés m; (accent) acento ▷ vt subrayar, recalcar; (syllable) acentuar; **stressed** adj (tense) estresado, agobiado; (syllable) acentuado; **stressful** adj (job) estresante

stretch [strɛtʃ] n (of sand etc) trecho ▷ vi estirarse; (extend) **to ~ to** or **as far as** extenderse hasta ▷ vt extender, estirar; (make demands) exigir el máximo esfuerzo a; **stretch out** vi tenderse ▷ vt (arm etc) extender; (spread) estirar

stretcher ['strɛtʃə*] n camilla

strict [strɪkt] adj severo; (exact) estricto; **strictly** adv severamente; estrictamente

stride [straɪd] (pt **strode**, pp **stridden**) n zancada, tranco ▷ vi dar zancadas, andar a trancos

strike [straɪk] (pt, pp **struck**) n huelga; (of oil etc) descubrimiento; (attack) ataque m ▷ vt golpear, pegar; (oil etc) descubrir; (bargain, deal) cerrar ▷ vi (go on strike) declarar la huelga; (attack) atacar; (clock) dar la hora; **on ~** (workers) en huelga; **to ~ a match** encender un fósforo; **striker** n huelguista mf; (Sport) delantero; **striking** adj llamativo

string [strɪŋ] (pt, pp **strung**) n cuerda; (row) hilera ▷ vt: **to ~ together** ensartar; **to ~ out** extenderse; **the strings** npl (Mus) los instrumentos de cuerda; **to pull ~s** (fig) mover palancas

strip [strɪp] n tira; (of land) franja; (of metal) cinta, lámina ▷ vt desnudar; (paint) quitar; (also: **~ down**) desmontar ▷ vi desnudarse; **strip off** vt (paint etc) quitar ▷ vi (person) desnudarse

stripe [straɪp] n raya; (Mil) galón m; **striped** adj a rayas, rayado

stripper ['strɪpə*] n artista mf de striptease

strip-search ['strɪpsəːtʃ] vt: **to ~ sb** desnudar y registrar a algn

strive [straɪv] (pt **strove**, pp **striven**) vi: **to ~ for sth/to do sth** luchar por conseguir/hacer algo

strode [strəud] pt of **stride**

stroke [strəuk] n (blow) golpe m; (Swimming) brazada; (Med) apoplejía; (of paintbrush) toque m ▷ vt acariciar; **at a ~** de un solo golpe

stroll [strəul] n paseo, vuelta ▷ vi dar un paseo or una vuelta; **stroller** (us) n (for child) sillita de ruedas

strong [strɔŋ] adj fuerte; **they are 50 ~** son 50; **stronghold** n fortaleza; (fig) baluarte m; **strongly** adv fuertemente, con fuerza; (believe) firmemente

strove [strəuv] pt of **strive**

struck [strʌk] pt, pp of **strike**

structure ['strʌktʃə*] n estructura; (building) construcción f

struggle ['strʌgl] n lucha ▷ vi luchar

strung [strʌŋ] pt, pp of **string**

stub [stʌb] n (of ticket etc) talón m; (of cigarette) colilla; **to ~ one's toe on sth** dar con el dedo (del pie) contra algo; **stub out** vt apagar

stubble ['stʌbl] n rastrojo; (on chin) barba (incipiente)

stubborn ['stʌbən] adj terco, testarudo

stuck [stʌk] pt, pp of **stick** ▷ adj (jammed) atascado

stud [stʌd] n (shirt stud) corchete m; (of boot) taco; (earring) pendiente m (de bolita); (also: **~ farm**) caballeriza; (also: **~ horse**) caballo semental ▷ vt (fig): **~ded with** salpicado de

student ['stjuːdənt] n estudiante mf ▷ adj estudiantil; **student driver** (us) n conductor(a) mf

en prácticas; **students' union** n (building) centro de estudiantes; (BRIT: association) federación f de estudiantes

studio ['stjuːdɪəu] n estudio; (artist's) taller m; **studio flat** n estudio

study ['stʌdɪ] n estudio ▷ vt estudiar; (examine) examinar, investigar ▷ vi estudiar

stuff [stʌf] n materia; (substance) material m, sustancia; (things) cosas fpl ▷ vt llenar; (Culin) rellenar; (animals) disecar; (inf: push) meter; **stuffing** n relleno; **stuffy** adj (room) mal ventilado; (person) de miras estrechas

stumble ['stʌmbl] vi tropezar, dar un traspié; **to ~ across, ~ on** (fig) tropezar con

stump [stʌmp] n (of tree) tocón m; (of limb) muñón m ▷ vt: **to be ~ed for an answer** no saber qué contestar

stun [stʌn] vt dejar sin sentido

stung [stʌŋ] pt, pp of **sting**

stunk [stʌŋk] pp of **stink**

stunned [stʌnd] adj (dazed) aturdido, atontado; (amazed) pasmado; (shocked) anonadado

stunning ['stʌnɪŋ] adj (fig: news) pasmoso; (: outfit etc) sensacional

stunt [stʌnt] n (in film) escena peligrosa; (publicity stunt) truco publicitario

stupid ['stjuːpɪd] adj estúpido, tonto; **stupidity** [-'pɪdɪtɪ] n estupidez f

sturdy ['stəːdɪ] adj robusto, fuerte

stutter ['stʌtə*] n tartamudeo ▷ vi tartamudear

style [staɪl] n estilo; **stylish** adj elegante, a la moda; **stylist** n (hair stylist) peluquero/a

sub... [sʌb] prefix sub...; **subconscious** adj subconsciente

subdued [səb'djuːd] adj (light) tenue; (person) sumiso, manso

subject [n 'sʌbdʒɪkt, vb səb'dʒɛkt] n súbdito; (Scol) asignatura; (matter) tema m; (Grammar) sujeto ▷ vt: **to ~ sb to sth** someter a algn a algo; **to be ~ to** (law) estar sujeto a; (person) ser propenso a; **subjective** [-'dʒɛktɪv] adj subjetivo; **subject matter** n (content) contenido

subjunctive [səb'dʒʌŋktɪv] adj, n subjuntivo

submarine [sʌbmə'riːn] n submarino

submission [səb'mɪʃən] n sumisión f

submit [səb'mɪt] vt someter ▷ vi: **to ~ to sth** someterse a algo

subordinate [sə'bɔːdɪnət] adj, n subordinado/a m/f

subscribe [səb'skraɪb] vi suscribir; **to ~ to** (opinion, fund) suscribir, aprobar; (newspaper) suscribirse a

subscription [səb'skrɪpʃən] n abono; (to magazine) suscripción f

subsequent ['sʌbsɪkwənt] adj subsiguiente, posterior; **subsequently** adv posteriormente, más tarde

subside [səb'saɪd] vi hundirse; (flood) bajar; (wind) amainar

subsidiary [səb'sɪdɪərɪ] adj secundario ▷ n sucursal f, filial f

subsidize ['sʌbsɪdaɪz] vt subvencionar

subsidy ['sʌbsɪdɪ] n subvención f

substance ['sʌbstəns] n sustancia

substantial [səb'stænʃl] adj sustancial, sustancioso; (fig) importante

substitute ['sʌbstɪtjuːt] n (person) suplente mf; (thing) sustituto ▷ vt: **to ~ A for B** sustituir A por B, reemplazar B por A; **substitution** n sustitución f

subtle ['sʌtl] adj sutil

subtract [səb'trækt] vt restar, sustraer

suburb ['sʌbə:b] n barrio residencial; **the ~s** las afueras (de la ciudad); **suburban** [sə'bə:bən] adj suburbano; (train etc) de cercanías

subway ['sʌbweɪ] n (BRIT) paso subterráneo or inferior; (US) metro

succeed [sək'si:d] vi (person) tener éxito; (plan) salir bien ▷ vt suceder a; **to ~ in doing** lograr hacer

success [sək'sɛs] n éxito; **successful** adj exitoso; (business) próspero; **to be successful (in doing)** lograr (hacer); **successfully** adv con éxito

succession [sək'sɛʃən] n sucesión f, serie f

successive [sək'sɛsɪv] adj sucesivo, consecutivo

successor [sək'sɛsə*] n sucesor(a) m/f

succumb [sə'kʌm] vi sucumbir

such [sʌtʃ] adj tal, semejante; (of that kind): **~ a book** tal libro; (so much): **~ courage** tanto valor ▷ adv tan; **~ a long trip** un viaje tan largo; **~ a lot of** tanto(s)/a(s); **~ as** (like) tal como; **as ~** como tal; **such and-such** adj tal o cual

suck [sʌk] vt chupar; (bottle) sorber; (breast) mamar

Sudan [su'dæn] n Sudán m

sudden ['sʌdn] adj (rapid) repentino, súbito; (unexpected) imprevisto; **all of a ~** de repente; **suddenly** adv de repente

sue [su:] vt demandar

suede [sweɪd] n ante m, gamuza

suffer ['sʌfə*] vt sufrir, padecer; (tolerate) aguantar, soportar ▷ vi sufrir; **to ~ from** (illness etc) padecer; **suffering** n sufrimiento

suffice [sə'faɪs] vi bastar, ser suficiente

sufficient [sə'fɪʃənt] adj suficiente, bastante

suffocate ['sʌfəkeɪt] vi ahogarse, asfixiarse

sugar ['ʃugə*] n azúcar m ▷ vt echar azúcar a, azucarar

suggest [sə'dʒɛst] vt sugerir; **suggestion** [-'dʒɛstʃən] n sugerencia

suicide ['suɪsaɪd] n suicidio; (person) suicida mf; see also **commit**; **suicide attack** n atentado suicida; **suicide bomber** n terrorista mf suicida; **suicide bombing** n atentado suicida

suit [su:t] n (man's) traje m; (woman's) conjunto m; (Law) pleito; (Cards) palo ▷ vt convenir; (clothes) sentar a, ir bien a; (adapt): **to ~ sth to** adaptar or ajustar algo a; **well ~ed** (well matched: couple) hecho el uno para el otro; **suitable** adj conveniente; (apt) indicado; **suitcase** n maleta, valija (RPL)

suite [swi:t] n (of rooms, Mus) suite f; (furniture): **bedroom/dining room ~** (juego de) dormitorio/comedor; see also **three-piece suite**

sulfur ['sʌlfə*] (US) n = **sulphur**

sulk [sʌlk] vi estar de mal humor

sulphur ['sʌlfə*] (US **sulfur**) n azufre m

sultana [sʌl'tɑ:nə] n (fruit) pasa de Esmirna

sum [sʌm] n suma; (total) total m; **sum up** vt resumir ▷ vi hacer un resumen

summarize ['sʌmə raɪz] vt resumir

summary ['sʌmərɪ] n resumen m ▷ adj (justice) sumario

summer ['sʌmə*] n verano ▷ cpd de verano; **in ~** en verano; **summer holidays** npl vacaciones fpl de verano; **summertime** n (season) verano

summit ['sʌmɪt] n cima, cumbre f; (also: **~ conference, ~ meeting**) (conferencia) cumbre f

summon ['sʌmən] vt (person) llamar; (meeting) convocar; (Law) citar

Sun. abbr (= Sunday) dom

sun [sʌn] n sol m; **sunbathe** vi tomar el sol; **sunbed** n cama solar; **sunblock** n filtro solar; **sunburn** n (painful) quemadura; (tan) bronceado; **sunburned, sunburnt** adj (painfully) quemado por el sol; (tanned) bronceado

Sunday ['sʌndɪ] n domingo

sunflower ['sʌnflauə*] n girasol m

sung [sʌŋ] pp of **sing**

sunglasses ['sʌnglɑ:sɪz] npl gafas fpl (SP) or anteojos fpl (LAM) de sol

sunk [sʌŋk] pp of **sink**

sun: sunlight n luz f del sol; **sun lounger** n tumbona, perezosa (LAM) soleado; (day) de sol; (fig) alegre; **sunrise** n salida del sol; **sun roof** n (Aut) techo corredizo; **sunscreen** n protector m solar; **sunset** n puesta del sol; **sunshade** n (over table) sombrilla; **sunshine** n sol m; **sunstroke** n insolación f; **suntan** n bronceado; **suntan lotion** n bronceador m; **suntan oil** n aceite m bronceador

super ['su:pə*] (inf) adj genial

superb [su:'pə:b] adj magnífico, espléndido

superficial [su:pə'fɪʃəl] adj superficial

superintendent [su:pərɪn'tɛndənt] n director(a) m/f; (Police) subjefe/a m/f

superior [su'pɪərɪə*] adj superior; (smug) desdeñoso ▷ n superior m

superlative [su'pə:lətɪv] n superlativo

supermarket ['su:pəmɑ:kɪt] n supermercado

supernatural [su:pə'nætʃərəl] adj sobrenatural ▷ n: **the ~** lo sobrenatural

superpower ['su:pəpauə*] n (Pol) superpotencia

superstition [su:pə'stɪʃən] n superstición f

superstitious [su:pə'stɪʃəs] adj supersticioso

superstore ['su:pəstɔ:*] n (BRIT) hipermercado

supervise ['su:pəvaɪz] vt supervisar; **supervision** [-'vɪʒən] n supervisión f; **supervisor** n supervisor(a) m/f

supper ['sʌpə*] n cena

supple ['sʌpl] adj flexible

supplement [n 'sʌplɪmənt, vb sʌplɪ'mɛnt] n suplemento ▷ vt suplir

supplier [sə'plaɪə*] n (Comm) distribuidor(a) m/f

supply [sə'plaɪ] vt (provide) suministrar; (equip): **to ~ (with)** proveer (de) ▷ n provisión f; (of gas, water etc) suministro; **supplies** npl (food) víveres mpl; (Mil) pertrechos mpl

support [sə'pɔ:t] n apoyo; (Tech) soporte m ▷ vt apoyar; (financially) mantener; (uphold, Tech) sostener; **supporter** n (Pol etc) partidario/a; (Sport) aficionado/a

suppose [sə'pəuz] vt suponer; (imagine) imaginarse; (duty): **to be ~d to do sth** deber hacer algo; **supposedly** [sə'pəuzɪdlɪ] adv según cabe suponer; **supposing** conj en caso de que

suppress [sə'prɛs] vt suprimir; (yawn) ahogar

supreme [su'pri:m] adj supremo

surcharge ['sə:tʃɑ:dʒ] n sobretasa, recargo

sure [ʃuə*] adj seguro; (definite, convinced) cierto; **to make ~ of sth/that** asegurarse de algo/asegurar que; **~!** (of course) ¡claro!, ¡por supuesto!; **~ enough** efectivamente; **surely** adv (certainly) seguramente

surf [sə:f] n olas fpl ▷ vt: **to ~ the Net** navegar por Internet

surface ['sə:fɪs] n superficie f ▷ vt (road) revestir ▷ vi salir a la superficie; **by ~ mail** por vía terrestre

surfboard ['sɜːfbɔːd] n tabla (de surf)
surfer ['sɜːfə*] n (in sea) surfista mf; **web** or **net ~** internauta mf
surfing ['sɜːfɪŋ] n surf m
surge [sɜːdʒ] n oleada, oleaje m ▷ vi (wave) romper; (people) avanzar en tropel
surgeon ['sɜːdʒən] n cirujano/a
surgery ['sɜːdʒərɪ] n cirugía; (BRIT: room) consultorio
surname ['sɜːneɪm] n apellido
surpass [sɜː'pɑːs] vt superar, exceder
surplus ['sɜːpləs] n excedente m; (Comm) superávit m ▷ adj excedente, sobrante
surprise [sə'praɪz] n sorpresa ▷ vt sorprender; **surprised** adj (look, smile) de sorpresa; **to be surprised** sorprenderse; **surprising** adj sorprendente; **surprisingly** adv: **it was surprisingly easy** me etc sorprendió lo fácil que fue
surrender [sə'rendə*] n rendición f, entrega f ▷ vi rendirse, entregarse
surround [sə'raund] vt rodear, circundar; (Mil etc) cercar; **surrounding** adj circundante; **surroundings** npl alrededores mpl, cercanías fpl
surveillance [sɜː'veɪləns] n vigilancia
survey [n 'sɜːveɪ, vb sɜː'veɪ] n inspección f, reconocimiento; (inquiry) encuesta ▷ vt examinar, inspeccionar; (look at) mirar, contemplar; **surveyor** n agrimensor(a) m/f
survival [sə'vaɪvl] n supervivencia
survive [sə'vaɪv] vi sobrevivir; (custom etc) perdurar ▷ vt sobrevivir a; **survivor** n superviviente mf
suspect [adj, n 'sʌspekt, vb səs'pekt] adj, n sospechoso/a m/f ▷ vt (person) sospechar de; (think) sospechar
suspend [səs'pend] vt suspender; **suspended sentence** n (Law) libertad f condicional; **suspenders** npl (BRIT) ligas fpl; (US) tirantes mpl
suspense [səs'pens] n incertidumbre f, duda; (in film etc) suspense m; **to keep sb in ~** mantener a algn en suspense
suspension [səs'penʃən] n (gen, Aut) suspensión f; (of driving licence) privación f; **suspension bridge** n puente m colgante
suspicion [səs'pɪʃən] n sospecha; (distrust) recelo; **suspicious** adj receloso; (causing suspicion) sospechoso
sustain [səs'teɪn] vt sostener, apoyar; (suffer) sufrir, padecer
SUV (esp US) n abbr (= sports utility vehicle) todoterreno m inv, 4x4 m
swallow ['swɒləu] n (bird) golondrina ▷ vt tragar; (fig.: pride) tragarse
swam [swæm] pt of **swim**
swamp [swɒmp] n pantano, ciénaga ▷ vt (with water etc) inundar; (fig) abrumar, agobiar
swan [swɒn] n cisne m
swap [swɒp] n canje m, intercambio ▷ vt: **to ~ (for)** cambiar (por)
swarm [swɔːm] n (of bees) enjambre m; (fig) multitud f ▷ vi (bees) formar un enjambre; (people) pulular; **to be ~ing with** ser un hervidero de
sway [sweɪ] vi mecerse, balancearse ▷ vt (influence) mover, influir en
swear [swɛə*] (pt **swore**, pp **sworn**) vi (curse) maldecir; (promise) jurar ▷ vt jurar; **swear in** vt: **to be sworn in** prestar juramento; **swearword** n taco, palabrota

sweat [swɛt] n sudor m ▷ vi sudar
sweater ['swɛtə*] n suéter m
sweatshirt ['swɛtʃɜːt] n suéter m
sweaty ['swɛtɪ] adj sudoroso
Swede [swiːd] n sueco/a
swede [swiːd] (BRIT) n nabo
Sweden ['swiːdn] n Suecia; **Swedish** ['swiːdɪʃ] adj sueco ▷ n (Ling) sueco
sweep [swiːp] (pt, pp **swept**) n (act) barrido; (also: **chimney ~**) deshollinador(a) m/f ▷ vt barrer; (with arm) empujar; (current) arrastrar ▷ vi barrer; (arm etc) moverse rápidamente; (wind) soplar con violencia
sweet [swiːt] n (candy) dulce m, caramelo; (BRIT: pudding) postre m ▷ adj dulce; (fig: kind) dulce, amable; (: attractive) mono; **sweetcorn** n maíz m; **sweetener** ['swiːtnə*] n (Culin) edulcorante m; **sweetheart** n novio/a; **sweetshop** n (BRIT) confitería, bombonería
swell [swɛl] (pt **~ed**, pp **swollen** or **~ed**) n (of sea) marejada, oleaje m ▷ adj (us: inf: excellent) estupendo, fenomenal ▷ vt hinchar, inflar ▷ vi (also: **~ up**) hincharse; (numbers) aumentar; (sound, feeling) ir aumentando; **swelling** n (Med) hinchazón f
swept [swɛpt] pt, pp of **sweep**
swerve [swɜːv] vi desviarse bruscamente
swift [swɪft] n (bird) vencejo ▷ adj rápido, veloz
swim [swɪm] (pt **swam**, pp **swum**) n: **to go for a ~** ir a nadar or a bañarse ▷ vi nadar; (head, room) dar vueltas ▷ vt nadar; (the Channel etc) cruzar a nado; **swimmer** n nadador/a m/f; **swimming** n natación f; **swimming costume** (BRIT) n bañador m, traje m de baño; **swimming pool** n piscina, alberca (MEX), pileta (RPL); **swimming trunks** npl bañador m (de hombre); **swimsuit** n = **swimming costume**
swing [swɪŋ] (pt, pp **swung**) n (in playground) columpio; (movement) balanceo, vaivén m; (change of direction) viraje m; (rhythm) ritmo ▷ vt balancear; (also: **~ round**) voltear, girar ▷ vi balancearse, columpiarse; (also: **~ round**) dar media vuelta; **to be in full ~** estar en plena marcha
swipe card [swaɪp-] n tarjeta magnética deslizante, tarjeta swipe
swirl [swɜːl] vi arremolinarse
Swiss [swɪs] adj, n inv suizo/a m/f
switch [swɪtʃ] n (for light etc) interruptor m; (change) cambio ▷ vt (change) cambiar de; **switch off** vt apagar; (engine) parar; **switch on** vt encender (SP), prender (LAM); (engine, machine) arrancar; **switchboard** n (Tel) centralita (SP), conmutador m (LAM)
Switzerland ['swɪtsələnd] n Suiza
swivel ['swɪvl] vi (also: **~ round**) girar
swollen ['swəulən] pp of **swell**
swoop [swuːp] n (by police etc) redada ▷ vi (also: **~ down**) calarse
swop [swɒp] = **swap**
sword [sɔːd] n espada; **swordfish** n pez m espada
swore [swɔː*] pt of **swear**
sworn [swɔːn] pp of **swear** ▷ adj (statement) bajo juramento; (enemy) implacable
swum [swʌm] pp of **swim**
swung [swʌŋ] pt, pp of **swing**
syllable ['sɪləbl] n sílaba
syllabus ['sɪləbəs] n programa m de estudios
symbol ['sɪmbl] n símbolo; **symbolic(al)** [sɪm'bɒlɪk(l)] adj simbólico; **to be symbolic(al) of sth** simbolizar algo

symmetrical [sɪˈmetrɪkl] *adj* simétrico
symmetry [ˈsɪmɪtrɪ] *n* simetría
sympathetic [sɪmpəˈθetɪk] *adj* (*understanding*) comprensivo; (*showing support*): **~ to(wards)** bien dispuesto hacia
sympathize [ˈsɪmpəθaɪz] *vi*: **to ~ with** (*person*) compadecerse de; (*feelings*) comprender; (*cause*) apoyar
sympathy [ˈsɪmpəθɪ] *n* (*pity*) compasión f
symphony [ˈsɪmfənɪ] *n* sinfonía
symptom [ˈsɪmptəm] *n* síntoma m, indicio
synagogue [ˈsɪnəgɔg] *n* sinagoga
syndicate [ˈsɪndɪkɪt] *n* sindicato; (*of newspapers*) agencia (de noticias)
syndrome [ˈsɪndrəʊm] *n* síndrome m
synonym [ˈsɪnənɪm] *n* sinónimo
synthetic [sɪnˈθetɪk] *adj* sintético
Syria [ˈsɪrɪə] *n* Siria
syringe [sɪˈrɪndʒ] *n* jeringa
syrup [ˈsɪrəp] *n* jarabe m; (*also*: **golden ~**) almíbar m
system [ˈsɪstəm] *n* sistema m; (*Anat*) organismo; **systematic** [-ˈmætɪk] *adj* sistemático, metódico; **systems analyst** *n* analista mf de sistemas

ta [tɑ:] (*BRIT: inf*) *excl* ¡gracias!
tab [tæb] *n* lengüeta; (*label*) etiqueta; **to keep ~s on** (*fig*) vigilar
table [ˈteɪbl] *n* mesa; (*of statistics etc*) cuadro, tabla ▷ *vt* (*BRIT: motion etc*) presentar; **to lay** *or* **set the ~** poner la mesa; **tablecloth** *n* mantel m; **table d'hôte** [tɑ:blˈdəʊt] *adj* del menú; **table lamp** *n* lámpara de mesa; **tablemat** *n* (*for plate*) posaplatos m inv; (*for hot dish*) salvamantel m; **tablespoon** *n* cuchara de servir; (*also*: **tablespoonful**: *as measurement*) cucharada
tablet [ˈtæblɪt] *n* (*Med*) pastilla, comprimido; (*of stone*) lápida
table tennis *n* ping-pong m, tenis m de mesa
tabloid [ˈtæblɔɪd] *n* periódico popular sensacionalista
taboo [təˈbu:] *adj, n* tabú m
tack [tæk] *n* (*nail*) tachuela; (*fig*) rumbo ▷ *vt* (*nail*) clavar con tachuelas; (*stitch*) hilvanar ▷ *vi* virar
tackle [ˈtækl] *n* (*fishing tackle*) aparejo (de pescar); (*for lifting*) aparejo ▷ *vt* (*difficulty*) enfrentarse con; (*challenge: person*) hacer frente a; (*grapple with*) agarrar; (*Football*) cargar; (*Rugby*) placar
tacky [ˈtækɪ] *adj* pegajoso; (*pej*) cutre
tact [tækt] *n* tacto, discreción f; **tactful** *adj* discreto, diplomático
tactics [ˈtæktɪks] *npl* táctica
tactless [ˈtæktlɪs] *adj* indiscreto
tadpole [ˈtædpəʊl] *n* renacuajo
taffy [ˈtæfɪ] (*us*) *n* melcocha
tag [tæg] *n* (*label*) etiqueta
tail [teɪl] *n* cola; (*of shirt, coat*) faldón m ▷ *vt* (*follow*) vigilar a; **tails** *npl* (*formal suit*) levita
tailor [ˈteɪlə*] *n* sastre m
Taiwan [taɪˈwɑ:n] *n* Taiwán m; **Taiwanese** [taɪwɑˈni:z] *adj, n* taiwanés/esa m/f
take [teɪk] (*pt* **took**, *pp* **taken**) *vt* tomar; (*grab*) coger (*SP*), agarrar (*LAM*); (*gain: prize*) ganar; (*require: effort, courage*) exigir; (*tolerate: pain etc*) aguantar; (*hold: passengers etc*) tener cabida para; (*accompany, bring, carry*) llevar; (*exam*) presentarse a; **to ~ sth from** (*drawer etc*) sacar algo de; (*person*) quitar algo a; **I ~ it that ...** supongo que ...; **take after** *vt fus* parecerse a; **take apart** *vt* desmontar; **take away** *vt* (*remove*)

quitar; *(carry)* llevar; *(Math)* restar; **take back** vt *(return)* devolver; *(one's words)* retractarse de; **take down** vt *(building)* derribar; *(letter etc)* apuntar; **take in** vt *(deceive)* engañar; *(understand)* entender; *(include)* abarcar; *(lodger)* acoger, recibir; **take off** vi *(Aviat)* despegar ▷ vt *(remove)* quitar; **take on** vt *(work)* aceptar; *(employee)* contratar; *(opponent)* desafiar; **take out** vt sacar; **take over** vt *(business)* tomar posesión de; *(country)* tomar el poder ▷ vi: **to take over from sb** reemplazar a algn; **take up** vt *(a dress)* acortar; *(occupy: time, space)* ocupar; *(engage in: hobby etc)* dedicarse a; *(accept)*: **to take sb up on** aceptar algo de algn; **takeaway** *(BRIT) adj (food)* para llevar ▷ n tienda o restaurante de comida para llevar; **taken** pp of **take**; **takeoff** n *(Aviat)* despegue m; **takeout** *(US)* n =**takeaway**; **takeover** n *(Comm)* absorción f; **takings** npl *(Comm)* ingresos mpl

talc [tælk] n *(also:* **~um powder**) polvos de talco

tale [teɪl] n *(story)* cuento; *(account)* relación f; **to tell ~s** *(fig)* chivarse

talent ['tælnt] n talento; **talented** adj de talento

talk [tɔːk] n charla; *(conversation)* conversación f; *(gossip)* habladurías fpl, chismes mpl ▷ vi hablar; **talks** npl *(Pol etc)* conversaciones fpl; **to ~ about** hablar de; **to ~ sb into doing sth** convencer a algn para que haga algo; **to ~ sb out of doing sth** disuadir a algn de que haga algo; **to ~ shop** hablar del trabajo; **talk over** vt discutir; **talk show** n programa m de entrevistas

tall [tɔːl] adj alto; *(object)* grande; **to be 6 feet ~** *(person)* ≈ medir 1 metro 80

tambourine [tæmbəˈriːn] n pandereta

tame [teɪm] adj domesticado; *(fig)* mediocre

tamper ['tæmpə*] vi: **to ~ with** tocar, andar con

tampon ['tæmpən] n tampón m

tan [tæn] n *(also:* **sun~**) bronceado ▷ vi ponerse moreno ▷ adj *(colour)* marrón

tandem ['tændəm] n tándem m

tangerine [tændʒəˈriːn] n mandarina

tangle ['tæŋgl] n enredo; **to get in(to) a ~** enredarse

tank [tæŋk] n *(water tank)* depósito, tanque m; *(for fish)* acuario; *(Mil)* tanque m

tanker ['tæŋkə*] n *(ship)* buque m, cisterna; *(truck)* camión m cisterna

tanned [tænd] adj *(skin)* moreno

tantrum ['tæntrəm] n rabieta

Tanzania [tænzəˈnɪə] n Tanzania

tap [tæp] n *(BRIT: on sink etc)* grifo *(SP)*, llave f, canilla *(RPL)*; *(gas tap)* llave f; *(gentle blow)* golpecito ▷ vt *(hit gently)* dar golpecitos en; *(resources)* utilizar, explotar; *(telephone)* intervenir; **on ~** *(fig: resources)* a mano; **tap dancing** n claqué m

tape [teɪp] n *(also:* **magnetic ~**) cinta magnética; *(cassette)* cassette f, cinta; *(sticky tape)* cinta adhesiva; *(for tying)* cinta ▷ vt *(record)* grabar (en cinta); *(stick with tape)* pegar con cinta adhesiva; **tape measure** n cinta métrica, metro; **tape recorder** n grabadora

tapestry ['tæpɪstrɪ] n *(object)* tapiz m; *(art)* tapicería

tar [tɑː] n alquitrán m, brea

target ['tɑːgɪt] n blanco

tariff ['tærɪf] n *(on goods)* arancel m; *(BRIT: in hotels etc)* tarifa

tarmac ['tɑːmæk] n *(BRIT: on road)* asfaltado; *(Aviat)* pista de aterrizaje

tarpaulin [tɑːˈpɔːlɪn] n lona impermeabilizada

tarragon ['tærəgən] n estragón m

tart [tɑːt] n *(Culin)* tarta; *inf: prostitute)* puta

▷ adj agrio, ácido

tartan ['tɑːtn] n tejido escocés m

tartar(e) sauce ['tɑːtə-] n salsa tártara

task [tɑːsk] n tarea; **to take sb to ~** reprender

taste [teɪst] n *(sense)* gusto; *(flavour)* sabor m; *(sample)*: **have a ~!** ¡prueba un poquito!; *(fig)* muestra, idea ▷ vt probar ▷ vi: **to ~ of o like** *(fish, garlic etc)* saber a; **you can ~ the garlic (in it)** se nota el sabor a ajo; **in good/bad ~** de buen/mal gusto; **tasteful** adj de buen gusto; **tasteless** adj *(food)* soso; *(remark etc)* de mal gusto; **tasty** adj sabroso, rico

tatters ['tætəz] npl: **in ~** hecho jirones

tattoo [tə'tuː] n tatuaje m; *(spectacle)* espectáculo militar ▷ vt tatuar

taught [tɔːt] pt, pp of **teach**

taunt [tɔːnt] n burla ▷ vt burlarse de

Taurus ['tɔːrəs] n Tauro

taut [tɔːt] adj tirante, tenso

tax [tæks] n impuesto ▷ vt gravar (con un impuesto); *(fig: memory)* poner a prueba; *(: patience)* agotar; **tax-free** adj libre de impuestos

taxi ['tæksɪ] n taxi m ▷ vi *(Aviat)* rodar por la pista; **taxi driver** n taxista mf; **taxi rank** *(BRIT)* n =**taxi stand**; **taxi stand** n parada de taxis

tax payer n contribuyente mf

TB n abbr =**tuberculosis**

tea [tiː] n té m; *(BRIT: meal)* ≈ merienda *(SP)*; cena; **high ~** *(BRIT)* merienda-cena *(SP)*; **tea bag** n bolsita de té; **tea break** *(BRIT)* n descanso para el té

teach [tiːtʃ] *(pt, pp* **taught**) vt: **to ~ sb sth**, **~ sth to sb** enseñar algo a algn ▷ vi *(be a teacher)* ser profesor(a), enseñar; **teacher** n *(in secondary school)* profesor(a) m/f; *(in primary school)* maestro/a, profesor(a) de EGB; **teaching** n enseñanza

tea: tea cloth n *(BRIT)* paño de cocina, trapo de cocina *(LAM)*; **teacup** n taza para el té

tea leaves npl hojas de té

team [tiːm] n equipo; *(of horses)* tiro; **team up** vi asociarse

teapot ['tiːpɔt] n tetera

tear¹ [tɪə*] n lágrima; **in ~s** llorando

tear² [tɛə*] *(pt* **tore**, *pp* **torn**) n rasgón m, desgarrón m ▷ vt romper, rasgar ▷ vi rasgarse; **tear apart** vt *(also fig)* hacer pedazos; **tear down** vt +adv *(building, statue)* derribar; *(poster, flag)* arrancar; **tear off** vt *(sheet of paper etc)* arrancar; *(one's clothes)* quitarse a tirones; **tear up** vt *(sheet of paper etc)* romper

tearful ['tɪəfəl] adj lloroso

tear gas [tɪə-] n gas m lacrimógeno

tearoom ['tiːruːm] n salón m de té

tease [tiːz] vt tomar el pelo a

tea: teaspoon n cucharita; *(also:* **teaspoonful:** as measurement) cucharadita; **teatime** n hora del té; **tea towel** *(BRIT)* n paño de cocina

technical ['tɛknɪkl] adj técnico

technician [tɛk'nɪʃn] n técnico/a

technique [tɛk'niːk] n técnica

technology [tɛk'nɔlədʒɪ] n tecnología

teddy (bear) ['tɛdɪ-] n osito de felpa

tedious ['tiːdɪəs] adj pesado, aburrido

tee [tiː] n *(Golf)* tee m

teen [tiːn] adj =**teenage** ▷ n *(US)* =**teenager**

teenage ['tiːneɪdʒ] adj *(fashions etc)* juvenil; *(children)* quinceañero; **teenager** n adolescente mf

teens [tiːnz] npl: **to be in one's ~** ser adolescente

teeth [tiːθ] npl of **tooth**

teetotal ['ti:'təutl] *adj* abstemio
telecommunications [tɛlɪkəmju:·nɪ'keɪʃənz] *n* telecomunicaciones *fpl*
telegram ['tɛlɪgræm] *n* telegrama *m*
telegraph pole ['tɛlɪgrɑ:f-] *n* poste *m* telegráfico
telephone ['tɛlɪfəun] *n* teléfono *⊳ vt* llamar por teléfono, telefonear; (*message*) dar por teléfono; **to be on the ~** (*talking*) hablar por teléfono; (*possessing telephone*) tener teléfono; **telephone book** *n* guía *f* telefónica; **telephone booth, telephone box** (BRIT) *n* cabina telefónica; **telephone call** *n* llamada (telefónica); **telephone directory** *n* guía (telefónica); **telephone number** *n* número de teléfono
telesales ['tɛlɪseɪlz] *npl* televenta(s) (*f(pl)*)
telescope ['tɛlɪskəup] *n* telescopio
televise ['tɛlɪvaɪz] *vt* televisar
television ['tɛlɪvɪʒən] *n* televisión *f*; **on ~** en la televisión; **television programme** *n* programa *m* de televisión
tell [tɛl] (*pt, pp* **told**) *vt* decir; (*relate: story*) contar; (*distinguish*): **to ~ sth from** distinguir algo de *⊳ vi* (*talk*): **to ~ (of)** contar; (*have effect*) tener efecto; **to ~ sb to do sth** mandar a algn hacer algo; **tell off** *vt*: **to tell sb off** regañar a algn; **teller** *n* (*in bank*) cajero/a
telly ['tɛlɪ] (BRIT: *inf*) *n abbr* (=*television*) tele *f*
temp [tɛmp] *n abbr* (BRIT) (=*temporary*) temporero/a
temper ['tɛmpə*] *n* (*nature*) carácter *m*; (*mood*) humor *m*; (*bad temper*) (mal) genio; (*fit of anger*) acceso de ira *⊳ vt* (*moderate*) moderar; **to be in a ~** estar furioso; **to lose one's ~** enfadarse, enojarse
temperament ['tɛmprəmənt] *n* (*nature*) temperamento; **temperamental** [tɛmprə'mɛntl] *adj* temperamental
temperature ['tɛmprətʃə*] *n* temperatura; **to have** *or* **run a ~** tener fiebre
temple ['tɛmpl] *n* (*building*) templo; (*Anat*) sien *f*
temporary ['tɛmpərərɪ] *adj* provisional; (*passing*) transitorio; (*worker*) temporero; (*job*) temporal
tempt [tɛmpt] *vt* tentar; **to ~ sb into doing sth** tentar *or* inducir a algn a hacer algo; **temptation** *n* tentación *f*; **tempting** *adj* tentador(a); (*food*) apetitoso/a
ten [tɛn] *num* diez
tenant ['tɛnənt] *n* inquilino/a
tend [tɛnd] *vt* cuidar *⊳ vi*: **to ~ to do sth** tener tendencia a hacer algo; **tendency** ['tɛndənsɪ] *n* tendencia
tender ['tɛndə*] *adj* (*person, care*) tierno, cariñoso; (*meat*) tierno; (*sore*) sensible *⊳ n* (*Comm: offer*) oferta; (*money*): **legal ~** moneda de curso legal *⊳ vt* ofrecer
tendon ['tɛndən] *n* tendón *m*
tenner ['tɛnə*] *n* (*inf*) (billete *m* de) diez libras *m*
tennis ['tɛnɪs] *n* tenis *m*; **tennis ball** *n* pelota de tenis; **tennis court** *n* cancha de tenis; **tennis match** *n* partido de tenis; **tennis player** *n* tenista *mf*; **tennis racket** *n* raqueta de tenis
tenor ['tɛnə*] *n* (*Mus*) tenor *m*
tenpin bowling ['tɛnpɪn-] *n* (juego de los) bolos
tense [tɛns] *adj* (*person*) nervioso; (*moment, atmosphere*) tenso; (*muscle*) tenso, en tensión *⊳ n* (*Ling*) tiempo
tension ['tɛnʃən] *n* tensión *f*
tent [tɛnt] *n* tienda (de campaña) (SP), carpa (LAM)
tentative ['tɛntətɪv] *adj* (*person, smile*) indeciso; (*conclusion, plans*) provisional

tent: **tent peg** *n* clavija, estaca; **tent pole** *n* mástil *m*
tepid ['tɛpɪd] *adj* tibio
term [tə:m] *n* (*word*) término; (*period*) período; (*Scol*) trimestre *m ⊳ vt* llamar; **terms** *npl* (*conditions, Comm*) condiciones *fpl*; **in the short/long ~** a corto/largo plazo; **to be on good ~s with sb** llevarse bien con algn; **to come to ~s with** (*problem*) aceptar
terminal ['tə:mɪnl] *adj* (*disease*) mortal; (*patient*) terminal *⊳ n* (*Elec*) borne *m*; (*Comput*) terminal *m*; (*also:* **air ~**) terminal *f*; (BRIT: *also:* **coach ~**) estación *f* terminal *f*
terminate ['tə:mɪneɪt] *vt* terminar
termini ['tə:mɪnaɪ] *npl of* **terminus**
terminology [tə:mɪ'nɔlədʒɪ] *n* terminología
terminus ['tə:mɪnəs] (*pl* **termini**) *n* término, (estación *f*) terminal *f*
terrace ['tɛrəs] *n* terraza; (BRIT: *row of houses*) hilera de casas adosadas; **the ~s** (BRIT *Sport*) las gradas *fpl*; **terraced** *adj* (*garden*) en terrazas; (*house*) adosado
terrain [tɛ'reɪn] *n* terreno
terrestrial [tɪ'rɛstrɪəl] *adj* (*life*) terrestre; (BRIT: *channel*) de transmisión (por) vía terrestre
terrible ['tɛrɪbl] *adj* terrible, horrible; (*inf*) atroz; **terribly** *adv* terriblemente; (*very badly*) malísimamente
terrier ['tɛrɪə*] *n* terrier *m*
terrific [tə'rɪfɪk] *adj* (*very great*) tremendo; (*wonderful*) fantástico, fenomenal
terrified ['tɛrɪfaɪd] *adj* aterrorizado
terrify ['tɛrɪfaɪ] *vt* aterrorizar; **terrifying** *adj* aterrador(a)
territorial [tɛrɪ'tɔ:rɪəl] *adj* territorial
territory ['tɛrɪtərɪ] *n* territorio
terror ['tɛrə*] *n* terror *m*; **terrorism** *n* terrorismo; **terrorist** *n* terrorista *mf*; **terrorist attack** *n* atentado (terrorista)
test [tɛst] *n* (*gen, Chem*) prueba; (*Med*) examen *m*; (*Scol*) examen *m*, test *m*; (*also:* **driving ~**) examen *m* de conducir *⊳ vt* probar, poner a prueba; (*Med, Scol*) examinar
testicle ['tɛstɪkl] *n* testículo
testify ['tɛstɪfaɪ] *vi* (*Law*) prestar declaración; **to ~ to sth** atestiguar algo
testimony ['tɛstɪmənɪ] *n* (*Law*) testimonio
test: **test match** *n* (*Cricket, Rugby*) partido internacional; **test tube** *n* probeta
tetanus ['tɛtənəs] *n* tétano
text [tɛkst] *n* texto; (*on mobile phone*) mensaje *m* de texto *⊳ vt*: **to ~ sb** (*inf*) enviar un mensaje (de texto) *or* un SMS a algn; **textbook** *n* libro de texto
textile ['tɛkstaɪl] *n* textil *m*, tejido
text message *n* mensaje *m* de texto
text messaging [-'mɛsɪdʒɪŋ] *n* (envío de) mensajes *mpl* de texto
texture ['tɛkstʃə*] *n* textura
Thai [taɪ] *adj, n* tailandés/esa *m/f*
Thailand ['taɪlænd] *n* Tailandia
than [ðæn, ðən] *conj* (*in comparisons*):
more ~ 10/once más de 10/una vez; **I have more/less ~ you/Paul** tengo más/menos que tú/Paul; **she is older ~ you think** es mayor de lo que piensas
thank [θæŋk] *vt* dar las gracias a, agradecer; **~ you (very much)** muchas gracias; **~ God!** ¡gracias a Dios! *⊳ excl* (*also:* **many ~s, ~s a lot**) ¡gracias! *⊳* **~s to** *prep* gracias a; **thanks** *npl* gracias *fpl*; **thankfully** *adv* (*fortunately*) afortunadamente; **Thanksgiving (Day)** *n*

día m de Acción de Gracias

○ **KEYWORD**

that [ðæt] *(pl* **those)** *adj (demonstrative)* ese/a; *(pl)* esos/as; *(more remote)* aquel(aquella); *(pl)* aquellos/as; **leave those books on the table** deja esos libros sobre la mesa; **that one** ése(ésa); *(more remote)* aquél(aquélla); **that one over there** ése(ésa) de ahí; aquél(aquélla) de allí
▷ *pron* **1** *(demonstrative)* ese/a; *(pl)* ésos/as; *(neuter)* eso; *(more remote)* aquél(aquélla); *(pl)* aquéllos/as; *(neuter)* aquello; **what's that?** ¿qué es eso (or aquello)?; **who's that?** ¿quién es ése/a (or aquél(aquella))?; **is that you?** ¿eres tú?; **will you eat all that?** ¿vas a comer todo eso?; **that's my house** ésa es mi casa; **that's what he said** eso es lo que dijo; **that is (to say)** es decir
2 *(relative: subject, object)* que; *(with preposition)* (el (la)) que *etc*, el/la) cual *etc*; **the book (that) I read** el libro que leí; **the books that are in the library** los libros que están en la biblioteca; **all (that) I have** todo lo que tengo; **the box (that) I put it in** la caja en la que or donde lo puse; **the people (that) I spoke to** la gente con la que hablé
3 *(relative: of time)* que; **the day (that) he came** el día (en) que vino
▷ *conj* que; **he thought that I was ill** creyó que yo estaba enfermo
▷ *adv (demonstrative)*: **I can't work that much** no puedo trabajar tanto; **I didn't realise it was that bad** no creí que fuera tan malo; **that high** así de alto

thatched [θætʃt] *adj (roof)* de paja; *(cottage)* con tejado de paja

thaw [θɔ:] *n* deshielo ▷ *vi (ice)* derretirse; *(food)* descongelarse ▷ *vt (food)* descongelar

○ **KEYWORD**

the [ði:, ðə] *def art* **1** *(gen)* el *f*, la *pl*, los *fpl*, las *(NB 'el' immediately before f n beginning with stressed (h)a; a+el =al; de+el = del)*: **the boy/girl** el chico/la chica; **the books/flowers** los libros/las flores; **to the postman/from the drawer** al cartero/del cajón; **I haven't the time/money** no tengo tiempo/dinero
2 *(+adj to form n)* los; **the rich and the poor** los ricos y los pobres; **to attempt the impossible** intentar lo imposible
3 *(in titles)*: **Elizabeth the First** Isabel primera; **Peter the Great** Pedro el Grande
4 *(in comparisons)*: **the more he works the more he earns** cuanto más trabaja más gana

theatre ['θɪətə*]* (*us* **theater)** *n* teatro; *(also:* **lecture ~)** aula; *(Med: also:* **operating ~)** quirófano
theft [θeft] *n* robo
their [ðeə*]* *adj* su; **theirs** *pron* (el) suyo/(la) suya *etc*); *see also* **my; mine¹**
them [ðem, ðəm] *pron (direct)* los/las; *(indirect)* les; *(stressed, after prep)* ellos(ellas); *see also* **me**
theme [θi:m] *n* tema *m*; **theme park** *n* parque de atracciones *(en torno a un tema central)*
themselves [ðəm'selvz] *pl pron (subject)* ellos mismos(ellas mismas); *(complement)* se; *(after prep)* sí

(mismos(as)); see also **oneself**

then [ðen] *adv (at that time)* entonces; *(next)* después; *(later)* luego, después; *(and also)* además ▷ *conj (therefore)* en ese caso, entonces ▷ *adj*: **the ~ president** el entonces presidente; **by ~** para entonces; **from ~ on** desde entonces

theology [θɪˈɒlədʒɪ] *n* teología
theory ['θɪərɪ] *n* teoría
therapist ['θerəpɪst] *n* terapeuta *mf*
therapy ['θerəpɪ] *n* terapia

○ **KEYWORD**

there ['ðeə*]* *adv* **1 there is, there are** hay; **there is no-one here/no bread left** no hay nadie aquí/no queda pan; **there has been an accident** ha habido un accidente
2 *(referring to place)* ahí; *(distant)* allí; **it's there** está ahí; **put it in/on/up/down there** ponlo ahí dentro/ encima/arriba/abajo; **I want that book there** quiero ese libro de ahí; **there he is!** ¡ahí está!
3 there, there *(esp to child)* ea, ea

there: thereabouts *adv* por ahí; **thereafter** *adv* después; **thereby** *adv* así, de ese modo; **therefore** *adv* por lo tanto; **there's = there is; there has**
thermal ['θə:ml] *adj* termal; *(paper)* térmico
thermometer [θəˈmɒmɪtə*]* *n* termómetro
thermostat ['θə:məustæt] *n* termostato
these [ði:z] *pl adj* estos/as ▷ *pl pron* éstos/as, éstas
thesis ['θi:sɪs] *(pl* **theses)** *n* tesis *f inv*
they [ðeɪ] *pl pron* ellos(ellas); *(stressed)* ellos (mismos/ellas mismas); **~ say that ...** *(it is said that)* se dice que ...; **they'd = they had; they would; they'll = they shall; they will; they're = they are; they've = they have**
thick [θɪk] *adj (in consistency)* espeso; *(in size)* grueso; *(stupid)* torpe ▷ *n*: **in the ~ of the battle** en lo más reñido de la batalla; **it's 20 cm ~** tiene 20 cm de espesor; **thicken** *vi* espesarse ▷ *vt (sauce etc)* espesar; **thickness** *n* espesor *m*; grueso
thief [θi:f] *(pl* **thieves)** *n* ladrón/ona *m/f*
thigh [θaɪ] *n* muslo
thin [θɪn] *adj (person, animal)* flaco; *(in size)* delgado; *(in consistency)* poco espeso; *(hair, crowd)* escaso ▷ *vt*: **to ~ (down)** diluir
thing [θɪŋ] *n* cosa; *(object)* objeto, artículo; *(matter)* asunto; *(mania)*: **to have a ~** estar obsesionado con algn/algo; **things** *npl (belongings)* efectos *mpl (personales);* **the best ~ would be to ...** lo mejor sería ...; **how are ~s?** ¿qué tal?
think [θɪŋk] *(pt, pp* **thought)** *vi* pensar ▷ *vt* pensar, creer; **what did you ~ of them?** ¿qué te parecieron?; **to ~ about sth/sb** pensar en algo/algn; **I'll ~ about it** lo pensaré; **to ~ of doing sth** pensar en hacer algo; **I ~ so/not** creo que sí/no; **to ~ well of sb** tener buen concepto de algn; **think over** *vt* reflexionar sobre, meditar; **think up** *vt (plan etc)* idear
third [θə:d] *adj (before n)* tercer(a); *(following n)* tercero/a ▷ *n* tercero/a; *(fraction)* tercio; *(BRIT Scol: degree)* título de licenciado con calificación de aprobado; **thirdly** *adv* en tercer lugar; **third party insurance** *(BRIT)* *n* seguro contra terceros; **Third World** *n* Tercer Mundo
thirst [θə:st] *n* sed *f*; **thirsty** *adj (person, animal)*

sediento; (work) que da sed; **to be thirsty** tener sed

thirteen [θɜːˈtiːn] num trece; **thirteenth** [-ˈtiːnθ] adj decimotercero

thirtieth [ˈθɜːtɪəθ] adj trigésimo

thirty [ˈθɜːtɪ] num treinta

○ **KEYWORD**

this [ðɪs] (pl **these**) adj
(demonstrative) este/a pl; estos/as; (neuter) esto; **this man/woman** este hombre/esta mujer; **these children/flowers** estos chicos/estas flores; **this one (here)** éste/a, esto (de aquí)
▷ pron (demonstrative) éste/a pl, éstos/as; (neuter) esto; **who is this?** ¿quién es éste/ésta?; **what is this?** ¿qué es esto?; **this is where I live** aquí vivo; **this is what he said** esto es lo que dijo; **this is Mr Brown** (in introductions) le presento al Sr. Brown; (photo) éste es el Sr. Brown; (on telephone) habla el Sr. Brown
▷ adv (demonstrative): **this high/long** etc así de alto/largo etc; **this far** hasta aquí

thistle [ˈθɪsl] n cardo

thorn [θɔːn] n espina

thorough [ˈθʌrə] adj (search) minucioso; (wash) a fondo; (knowledge, research) profundo; (person) meticuloso; **thoroughly** adv (search) minuciosamente; (study) profundamente; (wash) a fondo; (utterly: bad, wet etc) completamente, totalmente

those [ðəuz] pl adj esos(esas); (more remote) aquellos/as

though [ðəu] conj aunque ▷ adv sin embargo

thought [θɔːt] pt, pp of **think** ▷ n pensamiento; (opinion) opinión f; **thoughtful** adj pensativo; (serious) serio; (considerate) atento; **thoughtless** adj desconsiderado

thousand [ˈθauzənd] num mil; **two ~** dos mil; **~s of** miles de; **thousandth** num milésimo

thrash [θræʃ] vt azotar; (defeat) derrotar

thread [θrɛd] n hilo; (of screw) rosca ▷ vt (needle) enhebrar

threat [θrɛt] n amenaza; **threaten** vi amenazar ▷ vt: **to threaten sb with/to do** amenazar a algn con/con hacer; **threatening** adj amenazador(a), amenazante

three [θriː] num tres; **three-dimensional** adj tridimensional; **three-piece suite** n tresillo; **three-quarters** npl tres cuartas partes; **three-quarters full** tres cuartas partes lleno

threshold [ˈθrɛʃhəuld] n umbral m

threw [θruː] pt of **throw**

thrill [θrɪl] n (excitement) emoción f; (shudder) estremecimiento ▷ vt emocionar; **to be ~ed** (with gift etc) estar encantado; **thrilled** adj: **I was thrilled** Estaba emocionada; **thriller** n novela (u obra or película) de suspense; **thrilling** adj emocionante

thriving [ˈθraɪvɪŋ] adj próspero

throat [θrəut] n garganta; **to have a sore ~** tener dolor de garganta

throb [θrɔb] vi latir; dar puntadas; vibrar

throne [θrəun] n trono

through [θruː] prep por, a través de; (time) durante; (by means of) por medio de, mediante; (owing to) gracias a ▷ adj (ticket, train) directo ▷ adv completamente,

de parte a parte; de principio a fin; **to put sb ~ to sb** (Tel) poner or pasar a algn con algn; **to be ~** (Tel) tener comunicación; (have finished) haber terminado; **"no ~ road"** (BRIT) "calle sin salida"; **throughout** prep (place) por todas partes de, por todo; (time) durante todo ▷ adv por or en todas partes

throw [θrəu] (pt **threw**, pp **thrown**) n tiro; (Sport) lanzamiento ▷ vt tirar, echar; (Sport) lanzar; (rider) derribar; (fig) desconcertar; **to ~ a party** dar una fiesta; **throw away** vt tirar; (money) derrochar; **throw in** vt (Sport: ball) sacar; (include) incluir; **throw off** vt deshacerse de; **throw out** vt tirar; (person) echar; expulsar; **throw up** vi vomitar

thru [θruː] (US) = **through**

thrush [θrʌʃ] n zorzal m, tordo

thrust [θrʌst] (pt, pp ~) vt empujar con fuerza

thud [θʌd] n golpe m sordo

thug [θʌg] n gamberro/a

thumb [θʌm] n (Anat) pulgar m; **to ~ a lift** hacer autostop; **thumbtack** (US) n chincheta (SP)

thump [θʌmp] n golpe m; (sound) ruido seco or sordo ▷ vt golpear ▷ vi (heart etc) palpitar

thunder [ˈθʌndə*] n trueno ▷ vi tronar; (train etc): **to ~ past** pasar como un trueno; **thunderstorm** n tormenta

Thur(s). abbr (= Thursday) juev

Thursday [ˈθɜːzdɪ] n jueves m inv

thus [ðʌs] adv así, de este modo

thwart [θwɔːt] vt frustrar

thyme [taɪm] n tomillo

Tibet [tɪˈbɛt] n el Tibet

tick [tɪk] n (sound: of clock) tictac m; (mark) palomita; (Zool) garrapata; (BRIT: inf): **in a ~** en un instante ▷ vi hacer tictac ▷ vt marcar; **tick off** vt marcar; (person) reñir

ticket [ˈtɪkɪt] n billete m (SP), boleto (LAM); (for cinema etc) entrada; (in shop: on goods) etiqueta; (for raffle) papeleta; (for library) tarjeta; (parking ticket) multa de aparcamiento (SP) or por estacionamiento (indebido) (LAM); **ticket barrier** n (BRIT: Rail) barrera más allá de la cual se necesita billete/boleto; **ticket collector** n revisor(a) m/f; **ticket inspector** n revisor(a) m/f, inspector(a) m/f de boletos (LAM); **ticket machine** n máquina de billetes (SP) or boletos (LAM); **ticket office** n (Theatre) taquilla (SP), boletería (LAM); (Rail) mostrador m de billetes (SP) or boletos (LAM)

tickle [ˈtɪkl] vt hacer cosquillas a ▷ vi hacer cosquillas; **ticklish** adj (person) cosquilloso; (problem) delicado

tide [taɪd] n marea; (fig: of events) curso, marcha

tidy [ˈtaɪdɪ] adj (room etc) ordenado; (dress, work) limpio; (person) (bien) arreglado ▷ vt (also: **~ up**) poner en orden

tie [taɪ] n (string etc) atadura; (BRIT: also: **neck~**) corbata; (fig: link) vínculo, lazo; (Sport etc: draw) empate m ▷ vt atar ▷ vi (Sport) empatar; **to ~ in a bow** atar con un lazo; **to ~ a knot in sth** hacer un nudo en algo; **tie down** vt (fig: person: restrict) atar; (: to fix: date etc) obligar a; **tie up** vt (dog, person) atar; (arrangements) concluir; **to be tied up** (busy) estar ocupado

tier [tɪə*] n grada; (of cake) piso

tiger [ˈtaɪgə*] n tigre m

tight [taɪt] adj (rope) tirante; (money) escaso; (clothes) ajustado; (bend) cerrado; (shoes, schedule) apretado; (budget) ajustado; (security) estricto; (inf: drunk) borracho ▷ adv (squeeze) muy fuerte; (shut) bien;

tighten vt (rope) estirar; (screw, grip) apretar; (security) reforzar ▷vi estirarse; apretarse; **tightly** adv (grasp) muy fuerte; **tights** (BRIT) npl panti mpl

tile [taɪl] n (on roof) teja; (on floor) baldosa; (on wall) azulejo

till [tɪl] n caja (registradora) ▷vt (land) cultivar ▷prep, conj = until

tilt [tɪlt] vt inclinar ▷vi inclinarse

timber [ˈtɪmbə*] n (material) madera

time [taɪm] n tiempo; (epoch: often pl) época; (by clock) hora; (moment) momento; (occasion) vez f; (Mus) compás m ▷vt calcular o medir el tiempo de; (race) cronometrar; (remark, visit etc) elegir el momento para; **a long ~** mucho tiempo; **4 at a ~** de 4 en 4; 4 a la vez; **for the ~ being** de momento, por ahora; **from ~ to ~** de vez en cuando; **at ~s** a veces; **in ~** (soon enough) a tiempo; (after some time) con el tiempo; (Mus) al compás; **in a week's ~** dentro de una semana; **in no ~** en un abrir y cerrar de ojos; **any ~** cuando sea; **on ~** a la hora; **5 ~s 5** 5 por 5; **what ~ is it?** ¿qué hora es?; **to have a good ~** pasarlo bien, divertirse; **time limit** n plazo; **timely** adj oportuno; **timer** n (in kitchen etc) programador m horario; **time-share** n apartamento (or casa) a tiempo compartido; **timetable** n horario; **time zone** n huso horario

timid [ˈtɪmɪd] adj tímido

timing [ˈtaɪmɪŋ] n (Sport) cronometraje m; **the ~ of his resignation** el momento que eligió para dimitir

tin [tɪn] n estaño; (also: **~ plate**) hojalata; (BRIT: can) lata; **tinfoil** n papel m de estaño

tingle [ˈtɪŋɡl] vi (person): **to ~ (with)** estremecerse (de); (hands etc) hormiguear

tinker [ˈtɪŋkə*]: **~ with** vt fus jugar con, tocar

tinned [tɪnd] (BRIT) adj (food) en lata, en conserva

tin opener [-ˈəʊpnə*] (BRIT) n abrelatas m inv

tint [tɪnt] n matiz m; (for hair) tinte m; **tinted** adj (hair) teñido; (glass, spectacles) ahumado

tiny [ˈtaɪnɪ] adj minúsculo, pequeñito

tip [tɪp] n (end) punta; (gratuity) propina; (BRIT: for rubbish) vertedero; (advice) consejo ▷vt (waiter) dar una propina a; (tilt) inclinar; (empty: also: **~ out**) vaciar, echar; (overturn: also: **~ over**) volcar; **tip off** vt avisar, poner sobre aviso a

tiptoe [ˈtɪptəʊ] n: **on ~** de puntillas

tire [ˈtaɪə*] n (US) = **tyre** ▷vt cansar ▷vi cansarse; (become bored) aburrirse; **tired** adj cansado; **to be tired of sth** estar harto de algo; **tire pressure** (US) = **tyre pressure**; **tiring** adj cansado

tissue [ˈtɪʃuː] n tejido; (paper handkerchief) pañuelo de papel, kleenex®m; **tissue paper** n papel m de seda

tit [tɪt] n (bird) herrerillo común; **to give ~ for tat** dar ojo por ojo

title [ˈtaɪtl] n título

T-junction [ˈtiːdʒʌŋkʃən] n cruce m en T

TM abbr = **trademark**

○ **KEYWORD**

to [tuː, tə] prep 1 (direction) a; **to go to France/London/school/the station** ir a Francia/Londres/al colegio/a la estación; **to go to Claude's/the doctor's** ir a casa de Claude/al médico; **the road to Edinburgh** la carretera de Edimburgo

2 (as far as) hasta; **from here to London** de aquí o hasta Londres; **to count to 10** contar hasta 10; **from 40 to 50 people** entre 40 y 50

personas

3 (with expressions of time): **a quarter/twenty to 5** las 5 menos cuarto/veinte

4 (for, of): **the key to the front door** la llave de la puerta principal; **she is secretary to the director** es la secretaria del director; **a letter to his wife** una carta a or para su mujer

5 (expressing indirect object) a; **to give sth to sb** darle algo a algn; **to talk to sb** hablar con algn; **to be a danger to sb** ser un peligro para algn; **to carry out repairs to sth** hacer reparaciones en algo

6 (in relation to): **3 goals to 2** 3 goles a 2; **30 miles to the gallon** ≈ 94 litros a los cien (kms)

7 (purpose, result): **to come to sb's aid** venir en auxilio or ayuda de algn; **to sentence sb to death** condenar a algn a muerte; **to my great surprise** con gran sorpresa mía

▷with vb 1 (simple infin): **to go/eat** ir/comer

2 (following another vb): **to want/try/start to do** querer/intentar/empezar a hacer

3 (with vb omitted): **I don't want to** no quiero

4 (purpose, result) para; **I did it to help you** lo hice para que ayudarte; **he came to see you** vino a verte

5 (equivalent to relative clause): **I have things to do** tengo cosas que hacer; **the main thing is to try** lo principal es intentarlo

6 (after adj etc): **ready to go** listo para irse; **too old to ...** demasiado viejo (como) para ...

▷adv: **pull/push the door to** tirar de/empujar la puerta

toad [təʊd] n sapo; **toadstool** n hongo venenoso

toast [təʊst] n (Culin) tostada; (drink, speech) brindis m ▷vt (Culin) tostar; (drink to) brindar por; **toaster** n tostador m

tobacco [təˈbækəʊ] n tabaco

toboggan [təˈbɒɡən] n tobogán m

today [təˈdeɪ] adv, n (also fig) hoy m

toddler [ˈtɒdlə*] n niño/a que empieza a andar

toe [təʊ] n dedo (del pie); (of shoe) punta; **to ~ the line** (fig) conformarse; **toenail** n uña del pie

toffee [ˈtɒfɪ] n toffee m

together [təˈɡeðə*] adv juntos; (at same time) al mismo tiempo, a la vez; **~ with** junto con

toilet [ˈtɔɪlət] n inodoro; (BRIT: room) (cuarto de baño, servicio ▷cpd (soap etc) de aseo; **toilet bag** n neceser m, bolsa de aseo; **toilet paper** n papel m higiénico; **toiletries** npl artículos mpl de tocador; **toilet roll** n rollo de papel higiénico

token [ˈtəʊkən] n (sign) señal f, muestra; (souvenir) recuerdo; (disc) ficha ▷adj (strike, payment etc) simbólico; **book/record ~** (BRIT) vale m para comprar libros/discos; **gift ~** (BRIT) vale-regalo

Tokyo [ˈtəʊkjəʊ] n Tokio, Tokío

told [təʊld] pt, pp of **tell**

tolerant [ˈtɒlərnt] adj: **~ of** tolerante con

tolerate [ˈtɒləreɪt] vt tolerar

toll [təʊl] n (of casualties) número de víctimas; (tax, charge) peaje m ▷vi (bell) doblar; **toll call** n (US Tel) conferencia, llamada interurbana; **toll-free** (US) adj, adv gratis

tomato [təˈmɑːtəʊ] (pl **~es**) n tomate m; **tomato sauce** n salsa de tomate

tomb [tuːm] n tumba; **tombstone** n lápida

tomorrow [təˈmɒrəʊ] adv, n (also: fig) mañana; **the**

day after ~ pasado mañana; **~ morning** mañana por la mañana

ton [tʌn] n tonelada (BRIT = 1016 kg, US = 907 kg); (metric ton) tonelada métrica; **~s of** (inf) montones de

tone [təun] n tono ⊳ vi (also: **~ in**) armonizar; **tone down** vt (criticism) suavizar; (colour) atenuar

tongs [tɒŋz] npl (for coal) tenazas fpl; (curling tongs) tenacillas fpl

tongue [tʌŋ] n lengua; **~ in cheek** irónicamente

tonic ['tɒnɪk] n (Med) tónico; (also: **~ water**) (agua) tónica

tonight [tə'naɪt] adv, n esta noche; esta tarde

tonne [tʌn] n tonelada (métrica) (1.000kg)

tonsil ['tɒnsl] n amígdala; **tonsillitis** [-'laɪtɪs] n amigdalitis f

too [tu:] adv (excessively) demasiado; (also) también; **~ much** demasiado; **~ many** demasiados/as

took [tʊk] pt of **take**

tool [tu:l] n herramienta; **tool box** n caja de herramientas; **tool kit** n juego de herramientas

tooth [tu:θ] (pl teeth) n (Anat, Tech) diente m; (molar) muela; **toothache** n dolor m de muelas; **toothbrush** n cepillo de dientes; **toothpaste** n pasta de dientes; **toothpick** n palillo

top [tɒp] n (of mountain) cumbre f, cima; (of tree) copa; (of head) coronilla; (of ladder, page) lo alto; (of table) superficie f; (of cupboard) parte f de arriba; (lid: of box) tapa; (: of bottle, jar) tapón m; (of list etc) cabeza; (toy) peonza; (garment) blusa; camiseta ⊳ adj de arriba; (in rank) principal, primero; (best) mejor ⊳ vt (exceed) exceder; (be first in) encabezar; **on ~ of** (above) sobre, encima de; (in addition to) además de; **from ~ to bottom** de pies a cabeza; **top up** vt llenar; (mobile phone) recargar (el saldo de); **top floor** n último piso; **top hat** n sombrero de copa

topic ['tɒpɪk] n tema m; **topical** adj actual

topless ['tɒplɪs] adj (bather, bikini) topless inv

topping ['tɒpɪŋ] n (Culin): **with a ~ of cream** con nata por encima

topple ['tɒpl] vt derribar ⊳ vi caerse

top-up card n (for mobile phone) tarjeta prepago

torch [tɔ:tʃ] n antorcha; (BRIT: electric) linterna

tore [tɔ:*] pt of **tear²**

torment [n 'tɔ:mɛnt, vt tɔ:'mɛnt] n tormento ⊳ vt atormentar; (fig: annoy) fastidiar

torn [tɔ:n] pp of **tear²**

tornado [tɔ:'neɪdəu] (pl ~es) n tornado

torpedo [tɔ:'pi:dəu] (pl ~es) n torpedo

torrent ['tɒrnt] n torrente m; **torrential** [tɔ'rɛnʃl] adj torrencial

tortoise ['tɔ:təs] n tortuga

torture ['tɔ:tʃə*] n tortura ⊳ vt torturar; (fig) atormentar

Tory ['tɔ:rɪ] (BRIT) adj, n (Pol) conservador(a) m/f

toss [tɒs] vt tirar, echar; (one's head) sacudir; **to ~ a coin** echar a cara o cruz; **to ~ up for sth** jugar a cara o cruz algo; **to ~ and turn** (in bed) dar vueltas

total ['təutl] adj total, entero; (emphatic: failure etc) completo, total ⊳ n total m, suma ⊳ vt (add up) sumar; (amount to) ascender a

totalitarian [təutælɪ'tɛərɪən] adj totalitario

totally ['təutəlɪ] adv totalmente

touch [tʌtʃ] n (sense) tacto; (contact) contacto ⊳ vt tocar; (emotionally) conmover; **a ~ of** (fig) un poquito de; **to get in ~ with sb** ponerse en contacto con algn; **to lose ~** (friends) perder contacto; **touch down** vi (on

land) aterrizar; **touchdown** n aterrizaje m; (on sea) amerizaje m; (us Football) ensayo; **touched** adj (moved) conmovido; **touching** adj (moving) conmovedor(a); **touchline** n (Sport) línea de banda; **touch-sensitive** adj sensible al tacto

tough [tʌf] adj (material) resistente; (meat) duro; (problem etc) difícil; (policy, stance) inflexible; (person) fuerte

tour [tuə*] n viaje m, vuelta; (also: **package ~**) viaje m todo comprendido; (of town, museum) visita; (by band etc) gira ⊳ vt recorrer, visitar; **tour guide** n guía mf turístico/a

tourism ['tuərɪzm] n turismo

tourist ['tuərɪst] n turista mf ⊳ cpd turístico; **tourist office** n oficina de turismo

tournament ['tuənəmənt] n torneo

tour operator n touroperador(a) m/f, operador(a) m/f turístico/a

tow [təu] vt remolcar; **"on** or **in** (US) **~"** (Aut) "a remolque"; **tow away** vt llevarse a remolque

toward(s) [tə'wɔ:d(z)] prep hacia; (attitude) respecto a, con; (purpose) para

towel ['tauəl] n toalla; **towelling** n (fabric) felpa

tower ['tauə*] n torre f; **tower block** (BRIT) n torre f (de pisos)

town [taun] n ciudad f; **to go to ~** ir a la ciudad; (fig) echar la casa por la ventana; **town centre** (BRIT) n centro de la ciudad; **town hall** n ayuntamiento

tow truck (US) n camión m grúa

toxic ['tɒksɪk] adj tóxico

toy [tɔɪ] n juguete m; **toy with** vt fus jugar con; (idea) acariciar; **toyshop** n juguetería

trace [treɪs] n rastro ⊳ vt (draw) trazar, delinear; (locate) encontrar; (follow) seguir la pista de

track [træk] n (mark) huella, pista; (path: gen) camino, senda; (: of bullet etc) trayectoria; (: of suspect, animal) pista, rastro; (Rail) vía; (Sport) pista; (on tape, record) canción f ⊳ vt seguir la pista de; **to keep ~ of** mantenerse al tanto de, seguir; **track down** vt (prey) seguir el rastro de; (sth lost) encontrar; **tracksuit** n chandal m

tractor ['træktə*] n tractor m

trade [treɪd] n comercio; (skill, job) oficio ⊳ vi negociar, comerciar ⊳ vt (exchange): **to ~ sth (for sth)** cambiar algo (por algo); **trade in** vt (old car etc) ofrecer como parte del pago; **trademark** n marca de fábrica; **trader** n comerciante mf; **tradesman** (irreg) n (shopkeeper) tendero; **trade union** n sindicato

trading ['treɪdɪŋ] n comercio

tradition [trə'dɪʃən] n tradición f; **traditional** adj tradicional

traffic ['træfɪk] n (gen, Aut) tráfico, circulación f ⊳ vi: **to ~ in** (pej: liquor, drugs) traficar en; **traffic circle** (US) n isleta; **traffic island** n refugio, isleta; **traffic jam** n embotellamiento; **traffic lights** npl semáforo; **traffic warden** n guardia mf de tráfico

tragedy ['trædʒədɪ] n tragedia

tragic ['trædʒɪk] adj trágico

trail [treɪl] n (tracks) rastro, pista; (path) camino, sendero; (dust, smoke) estela ⊳ vt (drag) arrastrar; (follow) seguir la pista de ⊳ vi arrastrar; (in contest etc) ir perdiendo; **trailer** n (Aut) remolque m; (caravan) caravana; (Cinema) trailer m, avance m

train [treɪn] n tren m; (of dress) cola; (series) serie f ⊳ vt (educate, teach skills to) formar; (sportsman) entrenar; (dog) adiestrar; (point: gun etc): **to ~ on**

apuntar a ▷ vi (Sport) entrenarse; (learn a skill): **to ~ as a teacher** etc estudiar para profesor etc; **one's ~ of thought** el razonamiento de algn; **trainee** ['treɪni:] n aprendiz(a) m/f; **trainer** n (Sport: coach) entrenador(a) m/f; (of animals) domador(a) m/f; **trainers** npl (shoes) zapatillas fpl (de deporte); **training** n formación f; entrenamiento; **to be in training** (Sport) estar entrenando; **training course** n curso de formación; **training shoes** npl zapatillas fpl (de deporte)

trait [treɪt] n rasgo

traitor ['treɪtə*] n traidor(a) m/f

tram [træm] (BRIT) n (also: ~car) tranvía m

tramp [træmp] n (person) vagabundo/a; (inf, pej: woman) puta

trample ['træmpl] vt: **to ~ (underfoot)** pisotear

trampoline ['træmpəli:n] n trampolín m

tranquil ['træŋkwɪl] adj tranquilo; **tranquillizer** (US **tranquilizer**) n (Med) tranquilizante m

transaction [træn'zækʃən] n transacción f, operación f

transatlantic ['trænzət'læntɪk] adj transatlántico

transcript ['trænskrɪpt] n copia

transfer [n 'trænsfə:*, vb træns'fə:*] n (of employees) traslado; (of money, power) transferencia; (Sport) traspaso; (picture, design) calcomanía ▷ vt trasladar; transferir; **to ~ the charges** (BRIT Tel) llamar a cobro revertido

transform [træns'fɔ:m] vt transformar; **transformation** n transformación f

transfusion [træns'fju:ʒən] n transfusión f

transit ['trænzɪt] n: **in ~** en tránsito

transition [træn'zɪʃən] n transición f

transitive ['trænzɪtɪv] adj (Ling) transitivo

translate [trænz'leɪt] vt traducir; **translation** [-'leɪʃən] n traducción f; **translator** n traductor(a) m/f

transmission [trænz'mɪʃən] n transmisión f

transmit [trænz'mɪt] vt transmitir; **transmitter** n transmisor m

transparent [træns'pærnt] adj transparente

transplant ['trænsplɑ:nt] n (Med) transplante m

transport [n 'trænspɔ:t, vt træns'pɔ:t] n transporte m; (car) coche m (SP), carro (LAM), automóvil m ▷ vt transportar; **transportation** [-'teɪʃən] n transporte m

transvestite [trænz'vestaɪt] n travestí mf

trap [træp] n (snare, trick) trampa; (carriage) cabriolé m ▷ vt coger (SP) o agarrar (LAM) (en una trampa); (trick) engañar; (confine) atrapar

trash [træʃ] n (rubbish) basura; (nonsense) tonterías fpl; (pej): **the book/film is ~** el libro/la película no vale nada; **trash can** (US) n cubo o bote m (MEX) o tacho (SC) de la basura

trauma ['trɔ:mə] n trauma m; **traumatic** [trɔ:'mætɪk] adj traumático

travel ['trævl] n viaje m ▷ vi viajar ▷ vt (distance) recorrer; **travel agency** n agencia de viajes; **travel agent** n agente mf de viajes; **travel insurance** n seguro de viaje; **traveller** (US **traveler**) n viajero/a; **traveller's cheque** (US **traveler's check**) n cheque m de viajero; **travelling** (US **traveling**) n los viajes, el viajar; **travel-sick** adj: **to get travel-sick** marearse al viajar; **travel sickness** n mareo

tray [treɪ] n bandeja; (on desk) cajón m

treacherous ['tretʃərəs] adj traidor, traicionero; (dangerous) peligroso

treacle ['tri:kl] (BRIT) n melaza

tread [tred] (pt trod, pp trodden) n (step) paso, pisada; (sound) ruido de pasos; (of stair) escalón m; (of tyre) banda de rodadura ▷ vi pisar; **tread on** vt fus pisar

treasure ['treʒə*] n tesoro ▷ vt (value: object, friendship) apreciar; (: memory) guardar; **treasurer** n tesorero/a

treasury ['treʒərɪ] n: **the T~** el Ministerio de Hacienda

treat [tri:t] n (present) regalo ▷ vt tratar; **to ~ sb to sth** invitar a algn a algo; **treatment** n tratamiento

treaty ['tri:tɪ] n tratado

treble ['trebl] adj triple ▷ vt triplicar ▷ vi triplicarse

tree [tri:] n árbol m; **~ trunk** tronco (de árbol)

trek [trek] n (long journey) viaje m largo y difícil; (tiring walk) caminata

tremble ['trembl] vi temblar

tremendous [trɪ'mendəs] adj tremendo, enorme; (excellent) estupendo

trench [trentʃ] n zanja

trend [trend] n (tendency) tendencia; (of events) curso; (fashion) moda; **trendy** adj de moda

trespass ['trespəs] vi: **to ~ on** entrar sin permiso en; **"no ~ing"** "prohibido el paso"

trial ['traɪəl] n (Law) juicio, proceso; (test: of machine etc) prueba; **trial period** n periodo de prueba

triangle ['traɪæŋgl] n (Math, Mus) triángulo

triangular [traɪ'æŋgjulə*] adj triangular

tribe [traɪb] n tribu f

tribunal [traɪ'bju:nl] n tribunal m

tribute ['trɪbju:t] n homenaje m, tributo; **to pay ~ to** rendir homenaje a

trick [trɪk] n (skill, knack) tino, truco; (conjuring trick) truco; (joke) broma; (Cards) baza ▷ vt engañar; **to play a ~ on sb** gastar una broma a algn; **that should do the ~** a ver si funciona así

trickle ['trɪkl] n (of water etc) goteo ▷ vi gotear

tricky ['trɪkɪ] adj difícil; delicado

tricycle ['traɪsɪkl] n triciclo

trifle ['traɪfl] n bagatela; (Culin) dulce de bizcocho borracho, gelatina, fruta y natillas ▷ adv: **a ~ long** un poquito largo

trigger ['trɪgə*] n (of gun) gatillo

trim [trɪm] adj (house, garden) en buen estado; (person, figure) esbelto ▷ vt (haircut etc) recorte m; (on car) guarnición f ▷ vt (neaten) arreglar; (cut) recortar; (decorate) adornar; (Naut: a sail) orientar

trio ['tri:əu] n trío

trip [trɪp] n viaje m; (excursion) excursión f; (stumble) traspié m ▷ vi (stumble) tropezar; (go lightly) andar a paso ligero; **on a ~** de viaje; **trip up** vi tropezar, caerse ▷ vt hacer tropezar o caer

triple ['trɪpl] adj triple

triplets ['trɪplɪts] npl trillizos/as mpl/fpl

tripod ['traɪpɒd] n trípode m

triumph ['traɪʌmf] n triunfo ▷ vi: **to ~ (over)** vencer; **triumphant** [traɪ'ʌmfənt] adj (team etc) vencedor(a); (wave, return) triunfal

trivial ['trɪvɪəl] adj insignificante; (commonplace) banal

trod [trɒd] pt of tread

trodden ['trɒdn] pp of tread

trolley ['trɒlɪ] n carrito; (also: ~ bus) trolebús m

trombone [trɒm'bəun] n trombón m

troop [tru:p] n grupo, banda; **troops** npl (Mil)

tropas fpl
trophy ['trəufi] n trofeo
tropical ['trɒpɪkl] adj tropical
trot [trɒt] n trote m ▷ vi trotar; **on the ~** (BRIT: fig) seguidos/as
trouble ['trʌbl] n problema m, dificultad f; (worry) preocupación f; (bother, effort) molestia, esfuerzo; (unrest) inquietud f; (Med): **stomach etc ~** problemas mpl gástricos etc ▷ vt (disturb) molestar; (worry) preocupar, inquietar ▷ vi: **to ~ to do sth** molestarse en hacer algo; **troubles** npl (Pol etc) conflictos mpl; (personal) problemas mpl; **to be in ~** estar en un apuro; **it's no ~!** ¡no es molestia (ninguna)!; **what's the ~?** (with broken TV etc) ¿cuál es el problema?; (doctor to patient) ¿qué pasa?; **troubled** adj (person) preocupado; (country, epoch, life) agitado; **troublemaker** n agitador(a) m/f; (child) alborotador m; **troublesome** adj molesto
trough [trɒf] n (also: **drinking ~**) abrevadero; (also: **feeding ~**) comedero; (depression) depresión f
trousers ['trauzəz] npl pantalones mpl; **short ~** pantalones mpl cortos
trout [traut] n inv trucha
trowel ['trauəl] n (of gardener) palita; (of builder) paleta
truant ['truənt] n: **to play ~** (BRIT) hacer novillos
truce [truːs] n tregua
truck [trʌk] n (lorry) camión m; (Rail) vagón m; **truck driver** n camionero
true [truː] adj verdadero; (accurate) exacto; (genuine) auténtico; (faithful) fiel; **to come ~** realizarse
truly ['truːli] adv (really) realmente; (truthfully) verdaderamente; (faithfully): **yours ~** (in letter) le saluda atentamente
trumpet ['trʌmpɪt] n trompeta
trunk [trʌŋk] n (of tree, person) tronco; (of elephant) trompa; (case) baúl m; (us Aut) maletero; **trunks** npl (also: **swimming ~s**) bañador m (de hombre)
trust [trʌst] n confianza; (responsibility) responsabilidad f; (Law) fideicomiso m ▷ vt (rely on) tener confianza en; (hope) esperar; (entrust): **to ~ sth to sb** confiar algo a algn; **to take sth on ~** fiarse de algo; **trusted** adj de confianza; **trustworthy** adj digno de confianza
truth [truːθ] n verdad f; **truthful** adj veraz
try [traɪ] n tentativa, intento; (Rugby) ensayo ▷ vt (attempt) intentar; (test: also: **~ out**) probar, someter a prueba; (Law) juzgar, procesar; (strain: patience) hacer perder ▷ vi probar; **to have a ~** probar suerte; **to ~ to do sth** intentar hacer algo; **~ again!** ¡vuelve a probar!; **~ harder!** ¡esfuérzate más!; **well, I tried** al menos lo intenté; **try on** vt (clothes) probarse; **trying** adj (experience) cansado; (person) pesado
T-shirt ['tiːʃəːt] n camiseta
tub [tʌb] n cubo (SP), cubeta (SP, MEX), balde m (LAM); (bath) bañera (SP), tina (LAM), bañadera (RPL)
tube [tjuːb] n tubo; (BRIT: underground) metro; (for tyre) cámara de aire
tuberculosis [tjubəːkjuˈləusɪs] n tuberculosis f inv
tube station (BRIT) n estación f de metro
tuck [tʌk] vt (put) poner; **tuck away** vt (money) guardar; (building): **to be tucked away** esconderse, ocultarse; **tuck in** vt meter dentro; (child) arropar ▷ vi (eat) comer con apetito; **tuck shop** n (Scol) tienda = bar m (del colegio) (SP)
Tue(s). abbr (= Tuesday) mart

Tuesday ['tjuːzdɪ] n martes m inv
tug [tʌg] n (ship) remolcador m ▷ vt tirar de
tuition [tjuˈɪʃən] n (BRIT) enseñanza; (: private tuition) clases fpl particulares; (us: school fees) matrícula
tulip ['tjuːlɪp] n tulipán m
tumble ['tʌmbl] n (fall) caída ▷ vi caer; **to ~ to sth** (inf) caer en la cuenta de algo; **tumble dryer** (BRIT) n secadora
tumbler ['tʌmblə*] n (glass) vaso
tummy ['tʌmɪ] (inf) n barriga, tripa
tumour ['tjuːmə*] (us **tumor**) n tumor m
tuna ['tjuːnə] n inv (also: **~ fish**) atún m
tune [tjuːn] n melodía ▷ vt (Mus) afinar; (Radio, TV, Aut) sintonizar; **to be in/out of ~** (instrument) estar afinado/desafinado; (singer) cantar afinadamente/ desafinar; **to be in/out of ~ with** (fig) estar de acuerdo/en desacuerdo con; **tune in** vi: **to tune in (to)** (Radio, TV) sintonizar (con); **tune up** vi (musician) afinar (su instrumento)
tunic ['tjuːnɪk] n túnica
Tunisia [tjuˈnɪzɪə] n Túnez m
tunnel ['tʌnl] n túnel m; (in mine) galería ▷ vi construir un túnel/una galería
turbulence ['təːbjuləns] n (Aviat) turbulencia
turf [təːf] n césped m; (clod) tepe m ▷ vt cubrir con césped
Turk [təːk] n turco/a
Turkey ['təːkɪ] n Turquía
turkey ['təːkɪ] n pavo
Turkish ['təːkɪʃ] adj, n turco; (Ling) turco
turmoil ['təːmɔɪl] n: **in ~** revuelto
turn [təːn] n turno; (in road) curva; (of mind, events) rumbo; (Theatre) número; (Med) ataque m ▷ vt girar, volver; (collar, steak) dar la vuelta a; (page) pasar; (change): **to ~ sth into** convertir algo en ▷ vi volver; (person: look back) volverse; (reverse direction) dar la vuelta; (milk) cortarse; (become): **to ~ nasty/forty** ponerse feo/cumplir los cuarenta; **a good ~** un favor; **it gave me quite a ~** me dio un susto; **"no left ~"** (Aut) "prohibido girar a la izquierda"; **it's your ~** te toca a ti; **in ~** por turnos; **to take ~s (at)** turnarse (en); **turn around** vi (person) volverse, darse la vuelta ▷ vt (object) dar la vuelta a, voltear (LAM); **turn away** vi apartar la vista ▷ vi rechazar; **turn back** vi volverse atrás ▷ vt hacer retroceder; (clock) retrasar; **turn down** vt (refuse) rechazar; (reduce) bajar; (fold) doblar; **turn in** vi (inf: go to bed) acostarse ▷ vt (fold) doblar hacia dentro; **turn off** vi (from road) desviarse ▷ vt (light, radio etc) apagar; (tap) cerrar; (engine) parar; **turn on** vt (light, radio etc) encender, prender (LAM); (tap) abrir; (engine) poner en marcha; **turn out** vt (light, gas) apagar; (produce) producir ▷ vi (voters) concurrir; **to turn out to be ...** resultar ser ...; **turn over** vi (person) volverse ▷ vt (object) dar la vuelta a; (page) volver; **turn round** vi volverse; (rotate) girar; **turn to** vt fus: **to turn to sb** acudir a algn; **turn up** vi (person) llegar, presentarse; (lost object) aparecer ▷ vt (gen) subir; **turning** n (in road) vuelta; **turning point** n (fig) momento decisivo
turnip ['təːnɪp] n nabo
turn: turnout n concurrencia; **turnover** n (Comm: amount of money) volumen m de ventas; (: of goods) movimiento; **turnstile** n torniquete m; **turn-up** (BRIT) n (on trousers) vuelta
turquoise ['təːkwɔɪz] n (stone) turquesa ▷ adj color turquesa

turtle ['tɜːtl] n galápago; **turtleneck (sweater)** n jersey m de cuello vuelto

tusk [tʌsk] n colmillo

tutor ['tjuːtə*] n profesor(a) m/f; **tutorial** [-'tɔːrɪəl] n (Scol) seminario

tuxedo [tʌk'siːdəu] (US) n smóking m, esmoquin m

TV [tiː'viː] n abbr (= television) tele f

tweed [twiːd] n tweed m

tweezers ['twiːzəz] npl pinzas fpl (de depilar)

twelfth [twelfθ] num duodécimo

twelve [twelv] num doce; **at ~ o'clock** (midday) a mediodía; (midnight) a medianoche

twentieth ['twentiiθ] adj vigésimo

twenty ['twenti] num veinte

twice [twais] adv dos veces; **~ as much** dos veces más

twig [twig] n ramita

twilight ['twailait] n crepúsculo

twin [twin] adj, n gemelo/a m/f ▷ vt hermanar; **twin(-bedded) room** n habitación f doble; **twin beds** npl camas fpl gemelas

twinkle ['twiŋkl] vi centellear; (eyes) brillar

twist [twist] n (action) torsión f; (in road, coil) vuelta; (in wire, flex) doblez f; (in story) giro ▷ vt torcer; (weave) trenzar; (roll around) enrollar; (fig) deformar ▷ vi serpentear

twit [twit] (inf) n tonto

twitch [twitʃ] n (pull) tirón m; (nervous) tic m ▷ vi crisparse

two [tuː] num dos; **to put ~ and ~ together** (fig) atar cabos

type [taip] n (category) tipo, género; (model) tipo; (Typ) tipo, letra ▷ vt (letter etc) escribir a máquina; **typewriter** n máquina de escribir

typhoid ['taifɔid] n tifoidea

typhoon [tai'fuːn] n tifón m

typical ['tipikl] adj típico; **typically** adv típicamente

typing ['taipiŋ] n mecanografía

typist ['taipist] n mecanógrafo/a

tyre ['taiə*] (US **tire**) n neumático, llanta (LAM); **tyre pressure** (BRIT) n presión f de los neumáticos

u

UFO ['juːfəu] n abbr (= unidentified flying object) OVNI m

Uganda [juːˈɡændə] n Uganda

ugly ['ʌɡlɪ] adj feo; (dangerous) peligroso

UHT abbr (= UHT milk) leche f UHT, leche f uperizada

UK n abbr = **United Kingdom**

ulcer ['ʌlsə*] n úlcera; (mouth ulcer) llaga

ultimate ['ʌltɪmət] adj último, final; (greatest) máximo; **ultimately** adv (in the end) por último, al final; (fundamentally) a or en fin de cuentas

ultimatum [ʌltɪˈmeɪtəm] (pl **~s** or **ultimata**) n ultimátum m

ultrasound ['ʌltrəsaund] n (Med) ultrasonido

ultraviolet ['ʌltrəˈvaɪəlɪt] adj ultravioleta

umbrella [ʌmˈbrelə] n paraguas m inv; (for sun) sombrilla

umpire ['ʌmpaɪə*] n árbitro

UN n abbr (= United Nations) NN. UU.

unable [ʌnˈeɪbl] adj: **to be ~ to do sth** no poder hacer algo

unacceptable [ʌnəkˈseptəbl] adj (proposal, behaviour, price) inaceptable; **it's ~ that** no se puede aceptar que

unanimous [juːˈnænɪməs] adj unánime

unarmed [ʌnˈɑːmd] adj (defenceless) inerme; (without weapon) desarmado

unattended [ʌnəˈtendɪd] adj desatendido

unattractive [ʌnəˈtræktɪv] adj poco atractivo

unavailable [ʌnəˈveɪləbl] adj (article, room, book) no disponible; (person) ocupado

unavoidable [ʌnəˈvɔɪdəbl] adj inevitable

unaware [ʌnəˈweə*] adj: **to be ~ of** ignorar; **unawares** adv: **to catch sb unawares** pillar a algn desprevenido

unbearable [ʌnˈbeərəbl] adj insoportable

unbeatable [ʌnˈbiːtəbl] adj (team) invencible; (price) inmejorable; (quality) insuperable

unbelievable [ʌnbɪˈliːvəbl] adj increíble

unborn [ʌnˈbɔːn] adj que va a nacer

unbutton [ʌnˈbʌtn] vt desabrochar

uncalled-for [ʌnˈkɔːldfɔː*] adj gratuito, inmerecido

uncanny [ʌnˈkænɪ] adj extraño

uncertain [ʌnˈsɜːtn] adj incierto; (indecisive) indeciso; **uncertainty** n incertidumbre f

unchanged [ʌn'tʃeɪndʒd] *adj* igual, sin cambios
uncle ['ʌŋkl] *n* tío
unclear [ʌn'klɪə*] *adj* poco claro; **I'm still ~ about what I'm supposed to do** todavía no tengo muy claro lo que tengo que hacer
uncomfortable [ʌn'kʌmfətəbl] *adj* incómodo; (*uneasy*) inquieto
uncommon [ʌn'kɒmən] *adj* poco común, raro
unconditional [ʌnkən'dɪʃənl] *adj* incondicional
unconscious [ʌn'kɒnʃəs] *adj* sin sentido; (*unaware*): **to be ~ of** no darse cuenta de ▷ *n*: **the ~ el** inconsciente
uncontrollable [ʌnkən'trəʊləbl] *adj* (*child etc*) incontrolable; (*temper*) indomable; (*laughter*) incontenible
unconventional [ʌnkən'venʃənl] *adj* poco convencional
uncover [ʌn'kʌvə*] *vt* descubrir; (*take lid off*) destapar
undecided [ʌndɪ'saɪdɪd] *adj* (*character*) indeciso; (*question*) sin resolver
undeniable [ʌndɪ'naɪəbl] *adj* innegable
under ['ʌndə*] *prep* debajo de; (*less than*) menos de; (*according to*) según, de acuerdo con; (*sb's leadership*) bajo ▷ *adv* debajo, abajo; **~ there** allí abajo; **~ repair** en reparación; **undercover** *adj* clandestino; **underdone** *adj* (*Culin*) poco hecho; **underestimate** *vt* subestimar; **undergo** (*irreg*) *vt* sufrir; (*treatment*) recibir; **undergraduate** *n* estudiante *mf*; **underground** *n* (*BRIT: railway*) metro; (*Pol*) movimiento clandestino ▷ *adj* (*car park*) subterráneo ▷ *adv* (*work*) en la clandestinidad; **undergrowth** *n* maleza; **underline** *vt* subrayar; **undermine** *vt* socavar, minar; **underneath** [ʌndə'niːθ] *adv* debajo ▷ *prep* debajo de, bajo; **underpants** *npl* calzoncillos *mpl*; **underpass** (*BRIT*) *n* paso subterráneo; **underprivileged** *adj* desposeído; **underscore** *vt* subrayar; **undershirt** (*US*) *n* camiseta; **underskirt** (*BRIT*) *n* enaguas *fpl*
understand [ʌndə'stænd] *vt, vi* entender, comprender; (*assume*) tener entendido; **understandable** *adj* comprensible; **understanding** *adj* comprensivo ▷ *n* comprensión *f*, entendimiento; (*agreement*) acuerdo
understatement ['ʌndəsteɪtmənt] *n* modestia (excesiva); **that's an ~!** ¡eso es decir poco!
understood [ʌndə'stʊd] *pt, pp of* **understand** ▷ *adj* (*agreed*) acordado; (*implied*): **it is ~ that** se sobreentiende que
undertake [ʌndə'teɪk] (*irreg*) *vt* emprender; **to ~ to do sth** comprometerse a hacer algo
undertaker ['ʌndəteɪkə*] *n* director(a) *m/f* de pompas fúnebres
undertaking ['ʌndəteɪkɪŋ] *n* empresa; (*promise*) promesa
under: **underwater** *adv* bajo el agua ▷ *adj* submarino; **underway** *adj*: **to be underway** (*meeting*) estar en marcha; (*investigation*) estar llevándose a cabo; **underwear** *n* ropa interior; **underwent** *vb see* **undergo**; **underworld** *n* (*of crime*) hampa, inframundo
undesirable [ʌndɪ'zaɪrəbl] *adj* (*person*) indeseable; (*thing*) poco aconsejable
undisputed [ʌndɪ'spjuːtɪd] *adj* incontestable
undo [ʌn'duː] (*irreg*) *vt* (*laces*) desatar; (*button etc*) desabrochar; (*spoil*) deshacer

undone [ʌn'dʌn] *pp of* **undo** ▷ *adj*: **to come ~** (*clothes*) desabrocharse; (*parcel*) desatarse
undoubtedly [ʌn'daʊtɪdlɪ] *adv* indudablemente, sin duda
undress [ʌn'dres] *vi* desnudarse
unearth [ʌn'ɜːθ] *vt* desenterrar
uneasy [ʌn'iːzɪ] *adj* intranquilo, preocupado; (*feeling*) desagradable; (*peace*) inseguro
unemployed [ʌnɪm'plɔɪd] *adj* parado, sin trabajo ▷ *npl*: **the ~** los parados
unemployment [ʌnɪm'plɔɪmənt] *n* paro, desempleo; **unemployment benefit** *n* (*BRIT*) subsidio de desempleo o paro
unequal [ʌn'iːkwəl] *adj* (*unfair*) desigual; (*size, length*) distinto
uneven [ʌn'iːvən] *adj* desigual; (*road etc*) lleno de baches
unexpected [ʌnɪk'spektɪd] *adj* inesperado; **unexpectedly** *adv* inesperadamente
unfair [ʌn'fɛə*] *adj*: **~ (to sb)** injusto (con algn)
unfaithful [ʌn'feɪθful] *adj* infiel
unfamiliar [ʌnfə'mɪlɪə*] *adj* extraño, desconocido; **to be ~ with** desconocer
unfashionable [ʌn'fæʃnəbl] *adj* pasado o fuera de moda
unfasten [ʌn'fɑːsn] *vt* (*knot*) desatar; (*dress*) desabrochar; (*open*) abrir
unfavourable [ʌn'feɪvərəbl] (*US* **unfavorable**) *adj* desfavorable
unfinished [ʌn'fɪnɪʃt] *adj* inacabado, sin terminar
unfit [ʌn'fɪt] *adj* bajo de forma; (*incompetent*): **~ (for)** incapaz (de); **~ for work** no apto para trabajar
unfold [ʌn'fəʊld] *vt* desdoblar ▷ *vi* abrirse
unforgettable [ʌnfə'getəbl] *adj* inolvidable
unfortunate [ʌn'fɔːtʃnət] *adj* desgraciado; (*event, remark*) inoportuno; **unfortunately** *adv* desgraciadamente
unfriendly [ʌn'frendlɪ] *adj* antipático; (*behaviour, remark*) hostil, poco amigable
unfurnished [ʌn'fɜːnɪʃt] *adj* sin amueblar
unhappiness [ʌn'hæpɪnɪs] *n* tristeza, desdicha
unhappy [ʌn'hæpɪ] *adj* (*sad*) triste; (*unfortunate*) desgraciado; (*childhood*) infeliz; **~ about/with** (*arrangements etc*) poco contento con, descontento de
unhealthy [ʌn'helθɪ] *adj* (*place*) malsano; (*person*) enfermizo; (*fig: interest*) morboso
unheard-of [ʌn'hɜːdɔv] *adj* inaudito, sin precedente
unhelpful [ʌn'helpful] *adj* (*person*) poco servicial; (*advice*) inútil
unhurt [ʌn'hɜːt] *adj* ileso
unidentified [ʌnaɪ'dentɪfaɪd] *adj* no identificado, sin identificar; *see also* **UFO**
uniform ['juːnɪfɔːm] *n* uniforme *m* ▷ *adj* uniforme
unify ['juːnɪfaɪ] *vt* unificar, unir
unimportant [ʌnɪm'pɔːtənt] *adj* sin importancia
uninhabited [ʌnɪn'hæbɪtɪd] *adj* desierto
unintentional [ʌnɪn'tenʃənəl] *adj* involuntario
union ['juːnjən] *n* unión *f*; (*also:* **trade ~**) sindicato ▷ *cpd* sindical; **Union Jack** *n* bandera del Reino Unido
unique [juː'niːk] *adj* único
unisex ['juːnɪseks] *adj* unisex
unit ['juːnɪt] *n* unidad *f*; (*section: of furniture etc*) elemento; (*team*) grupo; **kitchen ~** módulo de cocina
unite [juː'naɪt] *vt* unir ▷ *vi* unirse; **united** *adj* unido; (*effort*) conjunto; **United Kingdom** *n* Reino Unido; **United Nations (Organization)** *n* Naciones

fpl Unidas; **United States (of America)** *n* Estados *mpl* Unidos

unity ['ju:nɪtɪ] *n* unidad *f*

universal [ju:nɪ'vɜ:sl] *adj* universal

universe ['ju:nɪvɜ:s] *n* universo

university [ju:nɪ'vɜ:sɪtɪ] *n* universidad *f*

unjust [ʌn'dʒʌst] *adj* injusto

unkind [ʌn'kaɪnd] *adj* poco amable; (*behaviour, comment*) cruel

unknown [ʌn'nəʊn] *adj* desconocido

unlawful [ʌn'lɔ:ful] *adj* ilegal, ilícito

unleaded [ʌn'ledɪd] *adj* (*petrol, fuel*) sin plombo

unleash [ʌn'li:ʃ] *vt* desatar

unless [ʌn'les] *conj* a menos que; **~ he comes** a menos que venga; **~ otherwise stated** salvo indicación contraria

unlike [ʌn'laɪk] *adj* (*not alike*) distinto de or a; (*not like*) poco propio de ▷ *prep* a diferencia de

unlikely [ʌn'laɪklɪ] *adj* improbable; (*unexpected*) inverosímil

unlimited [ʌn'lɪmɪtɪd] *adj* ilimitado

unlisted [ʌn'lɪstɪd] (*us*) *adj* (*Tel*) que no consta en la guía

unload [ʌn'ləʊd] *vt* descargar

unlock [ʌn'lɔk] *vt* abrir (con llave)

unlucky [ʌn'lʌkɪ] *adj* desgraciado; (*object, number*) que da mala suerte; **to be ~** tener mala suerte

unmarried [ʌn'mærɪd] *adj* soltero

unmistak(e)able [ʌnmɪs'teɪkəbl] *adj* inconfundible

unnatural [ʌn'nætʃrəl] *adj* (*gen*) antinatural; (*manner*) afectado; (*habit*) perverso

unnecessary [ʌn'nesəsərɪ] *adj* innecesario, inútil

UNO ['ju:nəʊ] *n abbr* (= *United Nations Organization*) ONU *f*

unofficial [ʌnə'fɪʃl] *adj* no oficial; (*news*) sin confirmar

unpack [ʌn'pæk] *vi* deshacer las maletas ▷ *vt* deshacer

unpaid [ʌn'peɪd] *adj* (*bill, debt*) sin pagar, impagado; (*Comm*) pendiente; (*holiday*) sin sueldo; (*work*) sin pago, voluntario

unpleasant [ʌn'pleznt] *adj* (*disagreeable*) desagradable; (*person, manner*) antipático

unplug [ʌn'plʌg] *vt* desenchufar, desconectar

unpopular [ʌn'pɒpjulə*] *adj* impopular, poco popular

unprecedented [ʌn'presɪdəntɪd] *adj* sin precedentes

unpredictable [ʌnprɪ'dɪktəbl] *adj* imprevisible

unprotected ['ʌnprə'tektɪd] *adj* (*sex*) sin protección

unqualified [ʌn'kwɔlɪfaɪd] *adj* sin título, no cualificado; (*success*) total

unravel [ʌn'rævl] *vt* desenmarañar

unreal [ʌn'rɪəl] *adj* irreal; (*extraordinary*) increíble

unrealistic [ʌnrɪə'lɪstɪk] *adj* poco realista

unreasonable [ʌn'ri:znəbl] *adj* irrazonable; (*demand*) excesivo

unrelated [ʌnrɪ'leɪtɪd] *adj* sin relación; (*family*) no emparentado

unreliable [ʌnrɪ'laɪəbl] *adj* (*person*) informal; (*machine*) poco fiable

unrest [ʌn'rest] *n* inquietud *f*, malestar *m*; (*Pol*) disturbios *mpl*

unroll [ʌn'rəʊl] *vt* desenrollar

unruly [ʌn'ru:lɪ] *adj* indisciplinado

unsafe [ʌn'seɪf] *adj* peligroso

unsatisfactory ['ʌnsætɪs'fæktərɪ] *adj* poco satisfactorio

unscrew [ʌn'skru:] *vt* destornillar

unsettled [ʌn'setld] *adj* inquieto, intranquilo; (*weather*) variable

unsettling [ʌn'setlɪŋ] *adj* perturbador(a), inquietante

unsightly [ʌn'saɪtlɪ] *adj* feo

unskilled [ʌn'skɪld] *adj* (*work*) no especializado; (*worker*) no cualificado

unspoiled ['ʌn'spɔɪld], **unspoilt** ['ʌn'spɔɪlt] *adj* (*place*) que no ha perdido su belleza natural

unstable [ʌn'steɪbl] *adj* inestable

unsteady [ʌn'stedɪ] *adj* inestable

unsuccessful [ʌnsək'sesful] *adj* (*attempt*) infructuoso; (*writer, proposal*) sin éxito; **to be ~** (*in attempting sth*) no tener éxito, fracasar

unsuitable [ʌn'su:təbl] *adj* inapropiado; (*time*) inoportuno

unsure [ʌn'ʃuə*] *adj* inseguro, poco seguro

untidy [ʌn'taɪdɪ] *adj* (*room*) desordenado; (*appearance*) desaliñado

untie [ʌn'taɪ] *vt* desatar

until [ən'tɪl] *prep* hasta ▷ *conj* hasta que; **~ he comes** hasta que venga; **~ now** hasta ahora; **~ then** hasta entonces

untrue [ʌn'tru:] *adj* (*statement*) falso

unused [ʌn'ju:zd] *adj* sin usar

unusual [ʌn'ju:ʒuəl] *adj* insólito, poco común; (*exceptional*) inusitado; **unusually** *adv* (*exceptionally*) excepcionalmente; **he arrived unusually early** llegó más temprano que de costumbre

unveil [ʌn'veɪl] *vt* (*statue*) descubrir

unwanted [ʌn'wɒntɪd] *adj* (*clothing*) viejo; (*pregnancy*) no deseado

unwell [ʌn'wel] *adj*: **to be/feel ~** estar indispuesto/ sentirse mal

unwilling [ʌn'wɪlɪŋ] *adj*: **to be ~ to do sth** estar poco dispuesto a hacer algo

unwind [ʌn'waɪnd] (*irreg*) *vt* desenvolver ▷ *vi* (*relax*) relajarse

unwise [ʌn'waɪz] *adj* imprudente

unwittingly [ʌn'wɪtɪŋlɪ] *adv* inconscientemente, sin darse cuenta

unwrap [ʌn'ræp] *vt* desenvolver

unzip [ʌn'zɪp] *vt* abrir la cremallera de; (*Comput*) descomprimir

---

○ KEYWORD

up [ʌp] *prep*: **to go/be up sth** subir/estar subido en algo; **he went up the stairs/the hill** subió las escaleras/la colina; **we walked/climbed up the hill** subimos la colina; **they live further up the street** viven más arriba en la calle; **go up that road and turn left** sigue por esa calle y gira a la izquierda

▷ *adv* **1** (*upwards, higher*) más arriba; **up in the mountains** en lo alto (de la montaña); **put it a bit higher up** ponlo un poco más arriba or alto; **up there** ahí or allí arriba; **up above** en lo alto, por encima, arriba

2: **to be up** (*out of bed*) estar levantado; (*prices, level*) haber subido

3: **up to** (*as far as*) hasta; **up to now** hasta ahora or la fecha

4: **to be up to**: **it's up to you** (*depending on*) depende de ti; **he's not up to it** (*job, task etc*) no es capaz de hacerlo; **his work is not up to the required standard** su trabajo no da la talla; (*inf: be doing*): **what is he up to?** ¿que estará tramando?
▷ *n*: **ups and downs** altibajos *mpl*

up-and-coming [ʌpənd'kʌmɪŋ] *adj* prometedor(a)
upbringing ['ʌpbrɪŋɪŋ] *n* educación *f*
update [ʌp'deɪt] *vt* poner al día
upfront [ʌp'frʌnt] *adj* claro, directo ▷ *adv* a las claras; (*pay*) por adelantado; **to be ~ about sth** admitir algo claramente
upgrade [ʌp'greɪd] *vt* (*house*) modernizar; (*employee*) ascender
upheaval [ʌp'hiːvl] *n* trastornos *mpl*; (*Pol*) agitación *f*
uphill [ʌp'hɪl] *adj* cuesta arriba; (*fig: task*) penoso, difícil ▷ *adv*: **to go ~** ir cuesta arriba
upholstery [ʌp'həulstərɪ] *n* tapicería
upmarket [ʌp'mɑːkɪt] *adj* (*product*) de categoría
upon [ə'pɒn] *prep* sobre
upper ['ʌpə*] *adj* superior, de arriba ▷ *n* (*of shoe: also*: **~s**) empeine *m*; **upper-class** *adj* de clase alta
upright ['ʌpraɪt] *adj* derecho; (*vertical*) vertical; (*fig*) honrado
uprising ['ʌpraɪzɪŋ] *n* sublevación *f*
uproar ['ʌprɔ:*] *n* escándalo
upset [*n* 'ʌpsɛt, *vb, adj* ʌp'sɛt] *n* (*to plan etc*) revés *m*, contratiempo; (*Med*) trastorno ▷ *vt irreg* (*glass etc*) volcar; (*plan*) alterar; (*person*) molestar, disgustar ▷ *adj* molesto, disgustado; (*stomach*) revuelto
upside-down [ʌpsaɪd'daun] *adv* al revés; **to turn a place ~** (*fig*) revolverlo todo
upstairs [ʌp'stɛəz] *adv* arriba ▷ *adj* (*room*) de arriba ▷ *n* el piso superior
up-to-date ['ʌptə'deɪt] *adj* al día
uptown ['ʌptaun] (*US*) *adv* hacia las afueras ▷ *adj* exterior, de las afueras
upward ['ʌpwəd] *adj* ascendente; **upward(s)** *adv* hacia arriba; (*more than*): **upward(s) of** más de
uranium [juə'reɪnɪəm] *n* uranio
Uranus [juə'reɪnəs] *n* Urano
urban ['ə:bən] *adj* urbano
urge [ə:dʒ] *n* (*desire*) deseo ▷ *vt*: **to ~ sb to do sth** animar a algn a hacer algo
urgency ['ə:dʒənsɪ] *n* urgencia
urgent ['ə:dʒənt] *adj* urgente; (*voice*) perentorio
urinal ['juərɪnl] *n* (*building*) urinario; (*vessel*) orinal *m*
urinate ['juərɪneɪt] *vi* orinar
urine ['juərɪn] *n* orina, orines *mpl*
US *n abbr* (= *United States*) EE. UU.
us [ʌs] *pron* nos; (*after prep*) nosotros/as; *see also* **me**
USA *n abbr* (= *United States (of America)*) EE. UU.
use [*n* ju:s, *vb* ju:z] *n* uso, empleo; (*usefulness*) utilidad *f* ▷ *vt* usar, emplear; **she ~d to do it** (*ella*) solía or acostumbraba hacerlo; **in ~** en uso; **out of ~** en desuso; **to be of ~** servir; **it's no ~** (*pointless*) es inútil; (*not useful*) no sirve; **to be ~d to** estar acostumbrado a, acostumbrar; **use up** *vt* (*food*) consumir; (*money*) gastar; **used** [ju:zd] *adj* (*car*) usado; **useful** *adj* útil; **useless** *adj* (*unusable*) inservible; (*pointless*) inútil; (*person*) inepto; **user** *n* usuario/a; **user-friendly** *adj* (*computer*) amistoso
usual ['ju:ʒuəl] *adj* normal, corriente; **as ~** como de costumbre; **usually** *adv* normalmente

utensil [ju:'tɛnsl] *n* utensilio; **kitchen ~s** batería de cocina
utility [ju:'tɪlɪtɪ] *n* utilidad *f*; (*public utility*) (empresa de) servicio público
utilize ['ju:tɪlaɪz] *vt* utilizar
utmost ['ʌtməust] *adj* mayor ▷ *n*: **to do one's ~** hacer todo lo posible
utter ['ʌtə*] *adj* total, completo ▷ *vt* pronunciar, proferir; **utterly** *adv* completamente, totalmente
U-turn ['ju:'tə:n] *n* viraje *m* en redondo

V

v. *abbr* = **verse; versus;** (= *volt*) v; (= *vide*) véase

vacancy ['veɪkənsɪ] *n* (*BRIT: job*) vacante *f*; (*room*) habitación *f* libre; **"no vacancies"** "completo"

vacant ['veɪkənt] *adj* desocupado, libre; (*expression*) distraído

vacate [vəˈkeɪt] *vt* (*house, room*) desocupar; (*job*) dejar (vacante)

vacation [vəˈkeɪʃən] *n* vacaciones *fpl*; **vacationer** (*US* **vacationist**) *n* turista *m/f*

vaccination [væksɪˈneɪʃən] *n* vacunación *f*

vaccine ['væksiːn] *n* vacuna *f*

vacuum ['vækjum] *n* vacío *m*; **vacuum cleaner** *n* aspiradora

vagina [vəˈdʒaɪnə] *n* vagina

vague [veɪg] *adj* vago; (*memory*) borroso; (*ambiguous*) impreciso; (*person: absent-minded*) distraído; (*: evasive*): **to be** ~ no decir las cosas claramente

vain [veɪn] *adj* (*conceited*) presumido; (*useless*) vano, inútil; **in** ~ en vano

Valentine's Day ['vælentaɪnzdeɪ] *n* día de los enamorados

valid ['vælɪd] *adj* válido; (*ticket*) valedero; (*law*) vigente

valley ['vælɪ] *n* valle *m*

valuable ['væljuəbl] *adj* (*jewel*) de valor; (*time*) valioso; **valuables** *npl* objetos *mpl* de valor

value ['væljuː] *n* valor *m*; (*importance*) importancia *▷ vt* (*fix price of*) tasar, valorar; (*esteem*) apreciar; **values** *npl* (*principles*) principios *mpl*

valve [vælv] *n* válvula

vampire ['væmpaɪə*] *n* vampiro

van [væn] *n* (*Aut*) furgoneta, camioneta

vandal ['vændl] *n* vándalo/a; **vandalism** *n* vandalismo; **vandalize** *vt* dañar, destruir

vanilla [vəˈnɪlə] *n* vainilla

vanish ['vænɪʃ] *vi* desaparecer

vanity ['vænɪtɪ] *n* vanidad *f*

vapour ['veɪpə*] (*US* **vapor**) *n* vapor *m*; (*on breath, window*) vaho

variable ['veərɪəbl] *adj* variable

variant ['veərɪənt] *n* variante *f*

variation [veərɪˈeɪʃən] *n* variación *f*

varied ['veərɪd] *adj* variado

variety [vəˈraɪətɪ] *n* (*diversity*) diversidad *f*; (*type*) variedad *f*

various ['veərɪəs] *adj* (*several: people*) varios/as; (*reasons*) diversos/as

varnish ['vɑːnɪʃ] *n* barniz *m*; (*nail varnish*) esmalte *m* *▷ vt* barnizar; (*nails*) pintar (con esmalte)

vary ['veərɪ] *vt* variar; (*change*) cambiar *▷ vi* variar

vase [vɑːz] *n* jarrón *m*

Vaseline® ['væsɪliːn] *n* vaselina®

vast [vɑːst] *adj* enorme

VAT [væt] (*BRIT*) *n abbr* (= *value added tax*) IVA *m*

vault [vɔːlt] *n* (*of roof*) bóveda; (*tomb*) panteón *m*; (*in bank*) cámara acorazada *▷ vt* (*also*: ~ **over**) saltar (por encima de)

VCR *n abbr* = **video cassette recorder**

VDU *n abbr* (= *visual display unit*) UPV *f*

veal [viːl] *n* ternera

veer [vɪə*] *vi* (*vehicle*) virar; (*wind*) girar

vegan ['viːgən] *n* vegetariano/a estricto/a, vegetaliano/a

vegetable ['vedʒtəbl] *n* (*Bot*) vegetal *m*; (*edible plant*) legumbre *f*, hortaliza *▷ adj* vegetal

vegetarian [vedʒɪˈteərɪən] *adj*, *n* vegetariano/a *m/f*

vegetation [vedʒɪˈteɪʃən] *n* vegetación *f*

vehicle ['viːɪkl] *n* vehículo; (*fig*) medio

veil [veɪl] *n* velo *▷ vt* velar

vein [veɪn] *n* vena; (*of ore etc*) veta

Velcro® ['velkrəʊ] *n* velcro® *m*

velvet ['velvɪt] *n* terciopelo

vending machine ['vendɪŋ-] *n* distribuidor *m* automático

vendor ['vendə*] *n* vendedor(a) *m/f*; **street** ~ vendedor(a) *m/f* callejero/a

vengeance ['vendʒəns] *n* venganza; **with a** ~ (*fig*) con creces

venison ['venɪsn] *n* carne *f* de venado

venom ['venəm] *n* veneno; (*bitterness*) odio

vent [vent] *n* (*in jacket*) respiradero; (*in wall*) rejilla (de ventilación) *▷ vt* (*fig: feelings*) desahogar

ventilation [ventɪˈleɪʃən] *n* ventilación *f*

venture ['ventʃə*] *n* empresa *▷ vt* (*opinion*) ofrecer *▷ vi* arriesgarse, lanzarse; **business** ~ empresa comercial

venue ['venjuː] *n* lugar *m*

Venus ['viːnəs] *n* Venus *m*

verb [vəːb] *n* verbo; **verbal** *adj* verbal

verdict ['vəːdɪkt] *n* veredicto, fallo; (*fig*) opinión *f*, juicio

verge [vəːdʒ] *n* borde *m*; **"soft ~s"** (*Aut*) "arcén *m* no asfaltado"; **to be on the ~ of doing sth** estar a punto de hacer algo

verify ['verɪfaɪ] *vt* comprobar, verificar

versatile ['vəːsətaɪl] *adj* (*person*) polifacético; (*machine, tool etc*) versátil

verse [vəːs] *n* poesía; (*stanza*) estrofa; (*in bible*) versículo

version ['vəːʃən] *n* versión *f*

versus ['vəːsəs] *prep* contra

vertical ['vəːtɪkl] *adj* vertical

very ['verɪ] *adv* muy *▷ adj*: **the** ~ **book which** el mismo libro que; **the** ~ **last** el último de todos; **at the** ~ **least** al menos; ~ **much** muchísimo

vessel ['vesl] *n* (*ship*) barco; (*container*) vasija; *see* **blood**

vest [vest] *n* (*BRIT*) camiseta; (*US: waistcoat*) chaleco

vet [vet] *vt* (*candidate*) investigar *▷ n abbr* (*BRIT*) =

veterinary surgeon
veteran ['vɛtərn] n excombatiente mf, veterano/a
veterinary surgeon ['vɛtrɪnərɪ-] (US **veterinarian**) n veterinario/a m/f
veto ['viːtəu] (pl **~es**) n veto ▷vt prohibir, poner el veto a
via ['vaɪə] prep por, por medio de
viable ['vaɪəbl] adj viable
vibrate [vaɪ'breɪt] vi vibrar
vibration [vaɪ'breɪʃən] n vibración f
vicar ['vɪkə*] n párroco (de la Iglesia Anglicana)
vice [vaɪs] n (evil) vicio; (Tech) torno de banco; **vice-chairman** (irreg) n vicepresidente m
vice versa ['vaɪsɪ'vəːsə] adv viceversa
vicinity [vɪ'sɪnɪtɪ] n: **in the ~ (of)** cercano (a)
vicious ['vɪʃəs] adj (attack) violento; (words) cruel; (horse, dog) resabido
victim ['vɪktɪm] n víctima
victor ['vɪktə*] n vencedor(a) m/f
Victorian [vɪk'tɔːrɪən] adj victoriano
victorious [vɪk'tɔːrɪəs] adj vencedor(a)
victory ['vɪktərɪ] n victoria
video ['vɪdɪəu] n vídeo (SP), video (LAM); **video call** n videollamada; **video camera** n videocámara, cámara de vídeo; **video (cassette) recorder** n vídeo (SP), video (LAM); **video game** n videojuego; **videophone** n videoteléfono; **video shop** n videoclub m; **video tape** n cinta de vídeo
vie [vaɪ] vi: **to ~ (with sb for sth)** competir (con algn por algo)
Vienna [vɪ'ɛnə] n Viena
Vietnam [vjɛt'næm] n Vietnam m; **Vietnamese** [-nə'miːz] adj n inv, adj vietnamita mf
view [vjuː] n (sight), (outlook) perspectiva; (opinion) opinión f, criterio ▷vt (look at) mirar; (fig) considerar; **on ~** (in museum etc) expuesto; **in full ~ (of)** en plena vista de; **in ~ of the weather/the fact that** en vista del tiempo/del hecho de que; **in my ~** en mi opinión; **viewer** n espectador(a) m/f; (TV) telespectador(a) m/f; **viewpoint** n (attitude) punto de vista; (place) mirador m
vigilant ['vɪdʒɪlənt] adj vigilante
vigorous ['vɪɡərəs] adj enérgico, vigoroso
vile [vaɪl] adj vil, infame; (smell) asqueroso; (temper) endemoniado
villa ['vɪlə] n (country house) casa de campo; (suburban house) chalet m
village ['vɪlɪdʒ] n aldea; **villager** n aldeano/a
villain ['vɪlən] n (scoundrel) malvado/a; (in novel) malo; (BRIT: criminal) maleante m
vinaigrette [vɪneɪ'ɡrɛt] n vinagreta
vine [vaɪn] n vid f
vinegar ['vɪnɪɡə*] n vinagre m
vineyard ['vɪnjɑːd] n viña, viñedo
vintage ['vɪntɪdʒ] n (year) vendimia, cosecha ▷cpd de época
vinyl ['vaɪnl] n vinilo
viola [vɪ'əulə] n (Mus) viola
violate ['vaɪəleɪt] vt violar
violation [vaɪə'leɪʃən] n violación f; **in ~ of sth** en violación de algo
violence ['vaɪələns] n violencia
violent ['vaɪələnt] adj violento; (intense) intenso
violet ['vaɪələt] adj violado, violeta ▷n (plant) violeta
violin [vaɪə'lɪn] n violín m
VIP n abbr (= very important person) VIP m

virgin ['vəːdʒɪn] n virgen f
Virgo ['vəːɡəu] n Virgo
virtual ['vəːtjuəl] adj virtual; **virtually** adv prácticamente; **virtual reality** n (Comput) mundo or realidad f virtual
virtue ['vəːtjuː] n virtud f; (advantage) ventaja; **by ~ of** en virtud de
virus ['vaɪərəs] n (also Comput) virus m inv
visa ['viːzə] n visado (SP), visa (LAM)
vise [vaɪs] n (US) (Tech) = **vice**
visibility [vɪzɪ'bɪlɪtɪ] n visibilidad f
visible ['vɪzəbl] adj visible
vision ['vɪʒən] n (sight) vista; (foresight, in dream) visión f
visit ['vɪzɪt] n visita ▷vt (person (US: also: **~ with**) visitar, hacer una visita a; (place) ir a, (ir a) conocer; **visiting hours** npl (in hospital etc) horas fpl de visita; **visitor** n (in museum) visitante mf; (invited to house) visita; (tourist) turista mf; **visitor centre** (US **visitor center**) n centro m de información
visual ['vɪzjuəl] adj visual; **visualize** vt imaginarse
vital ['vaɪtl] adj (essential) esencial, imprescindible; (dynamic) dinámico; (organ) vital
vitality [vaɪ'tælɪtɪ] n energía, vitalidad f
vitamin ['vɪtəmɪn] n vitamina
vivid ['vɪvɪd] adj (account) gráfico; (light) intenso; (imagination, memory) vivo
V-neck ['viːnɛk] n cuello de pico
vocabulary [vəu'kæbjulərɪ] n vocabulario
vocal ['vəukl] adj vocal; (articulate) elocuente
vocational [vəu'keɪʃənl] adj profesional
vodka ['vɒdkə] n vodka m
vogue [vəuɡ] n: **in ~** en boga
voice [vɔɪs] n voz f ▷vt expresar; **voice mail** n fonobuzón m
void [vɔɪd] n vacío; (hole) hueco ▷adj (invalid) nulo, inválido; (empty): **~ of** carente o desprovisto de
volatile ['vɒlətaɪl] adj (situation) inestable; (person) voluble; (liquid) volátil
volcano [vɒl'keɪnəu] (pl **~es**) n volcán m
volleyball ['vɒlɪbɔːl] n vol(e)ibol m
volt [vəult] n voltio; **voltage** n voltaje m
volume ['vɒljuːm] n (gen) volumen m; (book) tomo
voluntarily ['vɒləntrɪlɪ] adv libremente, voluntariamente
voluntary ['vɒləntərɪ] adj voluntario
volunteer [vɒlən'tɪə*] n voluntario/a ▷vt (information) ofrecer ▷vi ofrecerse (de voluntario); **to ~ to do** ofrecerse a hacer
vomit ['vɒmɪt] n vómito ▷vt, vi vomitar
vote [vəut] n voto; (votes cast) votación f; (right to vote) derecho de votar; (franchise) sufragio ▷vt (elect) elegir; (propose): **to ~ that** proponer que ▷vi votar, ir a votar; **~ of thanks** voto de gracias; **voter** n votante mf; **voting** n votación f
voucher ['vautʃə*] n (for meal, petrol) vale m
vow [vau] n voto ▷vt: **to ~ to do/that** hacer/que
vowel ['vauəl] n vocal f
voyage ['vɔɪɪdʒ] n viaje m
vulgar ['vʌlɡə*] adj (rude) ordinario, grosero; (in bad taste) de mal gusto
vulnerable ['vʌlnərəbl] adj vulnerable
vulture ['vʌltʃə*] n buitre m

W

waddle ['wɔdl] vi anadear

wade [weɪd] vi: **to ~ through** (water) vadear; (fig: book) leer con dificultad

wafer ['weɪfə*] n galleta, barquillo

waffle ['wɔfl] n (Culin) gofre m ▷ vi dar el rollo

wag [wæg] vt menear, agitar ▷ vi moverse, menearse

wage [weɪdʒ] n (also: **~s**) sueldo, salario ▷ vt: **to ~ war** hacer la guerra

wag(g)on ['wægən] n (horse-drawn) carro; (BRIT Rail) vagón m

wail [weɪl] n gemido ▷ vi gemir

waist [weɪst] n cintura, talle m; **waistcoat** (BRIT) n chaleco

wait [weɪt] n (interval) pausa ▷ vi esperar; **to lie in ~ for** acechar a; **I can't ~ to** (fig) estoy deseando; **to ~ for** esperar (a); **wait on** vt fus servir a; **waiter** n camarero; **waiting list** n lista de espera; **waiting room** n sala de espera; **waitress** ['weɪtrɪs] n camarera

waive [weɪv] vt suspender

wake [weɪk] (pt **woke** or **~d**, pp **woken** or **~d**) vt (also: **~ up**) despertar ▷ vi (also: **~ up**) despertarse ▷ n (for dead person) vela, velatorio; (Naut) estela

Wales [weɪlz] n País m de Gales; **the Prince of ~** el príncipe de Gales

walk [wɔːk] n (stroll) paseo; (hike) excursión f a pie, caminata; (gait) paso, andar m; (in park etc) paseo, alameda ▷ vi andar, caminar; (for pleasure, exercise) pasear ▷ vt (distance) recorrer a pie, andar; (dog) pasear; **10 minutes' ~ from here** a 10 minutos de aquí andando; **people from all ~s of life** gente de todas las esferas; **walk out** vi (audience) salir; (workers) declararse en huelga; **walker** n (person) paseante mf, caminante mf; **walkie-talkie** ['wɔːkɪ'tɔːkɪ] n walkie-talkie m; **walking** n el andar; **walking shoes** npl zapatos npl para andar; **walking stick** n bastón m; **Walkman**® n Walkman® m; **walkway** n paseo

wall [wɔːl] n pared f; (exterior) muro; (city wall etc) muralla

wallet ['wɔlɪt] n cartera, billetera

wallpaper ['wɔːlpeɪpə*] n papel m pintado ▷ vt empapelar

walnut ['wɔːlnʌt] n nuez f; (tree) nogal m

walrus ['wɔːlrəs] (pl **~** or **~es**) n morsa

waltz [wɔːlts] n vals m ▷ vi bailar el vals

wand [wɔnd] n (also: **magic ~**) varita (mágica)

wander ['wɔndə*] vi (person) vagar; deambular; (thoughts) divagar ▷ vt recorrer, vagar por

want [wɔnt] vt querer, desear; (need) necesitar ▷ n: **for ~ of** por falta de; **wanted** adj (criminal) buscado; **"wanted"** (in advertisements) "se busca"

war [wɔː*] n guerra; **to make ~ (on)** declarar la guerra (a)

ward [wɔːd] n (in hospital) sala; (Pol) distrito electoral; (Law: child: also: **~ of court**) pupilo/a

warden ['wɔːdn] n (BRIT: of institution) director(a) m/f; (of park, game reserve) guardián/ana m/f; (BRIT: also: **traffic ~**) guardia mf

wardrobe ['wɔːdrəub] n armario, ropero; (clothes) vestuario

warehouse ['wɛəhaus] n almacén m, depósito

warfare ['wɔːfɛə*] n guerra

warhead ['wɔːhɛd] n cabeza armada

warm [wɔːm] adj caliente; (thanks) efusivo; (clothes etc) abrigado; (welcome, day) caluroso; **it's ~** hace calor; **I'm ~** tengo calor; **warm up** vi (room) calentarse; (person) entrar en calor; (athlete) hacer ejercicios de calentamiento ▷ vt calentar; **warmly** adv afectuosamente; **warmth** n calor m

warn [wɔːn] vt avisar, advertir; **warning** n aviso, advertencia; **warning light** n luz f de advertencia

warrant ['wɔrnt] n autorización f; (Law: to arrest) orden f de detención; (: to search) mandamiento de registro

warranty ['wɔrəntɪ] n garantía

warrior ['wɔrɪə*] n guerrero/a

Warsaw ['wɔːsɔː] n Varsovia

warship ['wɔːʃɪp] n buque m or barco de guerra

wart [wɔːt] n verruga

wartime ['wɔːtaɪm] n: **in ~** en tiempos de guerra, en la guerra

wary ['wɛərɪ] adj cauteloso

was [wɔz] pt of **be**

wash [wɔʃ] vt lavar ▷ vi lavarse; (sea etc): **to ~ against/over sth** llegar hasta/cubrir algo ▷ n (clothes etc) lavado; (of ship) estela; **to have a ~** lavarse; **wash up** vi (BRIT) fregar los platos; (US) lavarse; **washbasin** (US) n lavabo; **wash cloth** (US) n manopla; **washer** n (Tech) arandela; **washing** n (dirty) ropa sucia; (clean) colada; **washing line** n cuerda de (colgar) la ropa; **washing machine** n lavadora; **washing powder** (BRIT) n detergente m (en polvo)

Washington ['wɔʃɪŋtən] n Washington m

wash: washing-up (BRIT) n fregado, platos mpl (para fregar); **washing-up liquid** (BRIT) n líquido lavavajillas; **washroom** (US) n servicios mpl

wasn't ['wɔznt] = **was not**

wasp [wɔsp] n avispa

waste [weɪst] n derroche m, despilfarro; (of time) pérdida; (food) sobras fpl; (rubbish) basura, desperdicios mpl ▷ adj (material) de desecho; (left over) sobrante; (land) baldío, descampado ▷ vt malgastar, derrochar; (time) perder; (opportunity) desperdiciar; **waste ground** (BRIT) n terreno baldío; **wastepaper basket** n papelera

watch [wɔtʃ] n (also: **wrist ~**) reloj m; (Mil: group of guards) centinela m; (act) vigilancia; (Naut: spell of duty) guardia ▷ vt (look at) mirar, observar; (: match, *programme*) ver; (*spy on, guard*) vigilar; (*be careful of*) cuidarse de, tener cuidado de ▷ *vt* ver, mirar; (*keep guard*) montar guardia; **watch out** *vi* cuidarse, tener cuidado; **watchdog** *n* perro guardián; (*fig*) persona u organismo encargado de asegurarse de que las empresas u organismo dentro de la legalidad; **watch strap** *n* pulsera f (de reloj)

water ['wɔːtə*] *n* agua f ▷ *vt* (*plant*) regar ▷ *vi* (*eyes*) llorar; (*mouth*) hacerse la boca agua; **water down** *vt* (*milk etc*) aguar; (*fig: story*) dulcificar, diluir; **watercolour** (*us* **watercolor**) *n* acuarela; **watercress** *n* berro; **waterfall** *n* cascada, salto de agua; **watering can** *n* regadera; **watermelon** *n* sandía; **waterproof** *adj* impermeable; **water-skiing** *n* esquí m acuático

watt [wɔt] *n* vatio m

wave [weiv] *n* (*of hand*) señal f con la mano; (*on water*) ola; (*Radio, in hair*) onda; (*fig*) oleada ▷ *vi* agitar la mano; (*flag etc*) ondear ▷ *vt* (*handkerchief, gun*) agitar; **wavelength** *n* longitud f de onda

waver ['weivə*] *vi* (*voice, love etc*) flaquear; (*person*) vacilar

wavy ['weivi] *adj* ondulado

wax [wæks] *n* cera ▷ *vt* encerar ▷ *vi* (*moon*) crecer

way [wei] *n* camino; (*distance*) trayecto, recorrido; (*direction*) dirección f, sentido; (*manner*) modo, manera; (*habit*) costumbre f; **which ~? - this ~** ¿por dónde? o ¿en qué dirección? - por aquí; **on the ~** (*en route*) en (el) camino; **to be on one's ~** estar en camino; **to be in the ~** bloquear el camino; (*fig*) estorbar; **to go out of one's ~ to do sth** desvivirse por hacer algo; **under ~** en marcha; **to lose one's ~** extraviarse; **in a ~** en cierto modo o sentido; **no ~!** (*inf*) ¡de eso nada!; **by the ~** ... a propósito ...; **"~ in"** (*BRIT*) "entrada"; **"~ out"** (*BRIT*) "salida"; **the ~ back** el camino de vuelta; **"give ~"** (*BRIT Aut*) "ceda el paso"

W.C. *n* (*BRIT*) wáter m

we [wiː] *pl pron* nosotros/as

weak [wiːk] *adj* débil, flojo; (*tea etc*) claro; **weaken** *vi* debilitarse; (*give way*) ceder ▷ *vt* debilitar; **weakness** *n* debilidad f; (*fault*) punto débil; **to have a weakness for** tener debilidad por

wealth [wɛlθ] *n* riqueza; (*of details*) abundancia; **wealthy** *adj* rico

weapon ['wɛpən] *n* arma; **~s of mass destruction** armas de destrucción masiva

wear [wɛə*] (*pt* **wore**, *pp* **worn**) *n* (*use*) uso; (*deterioration through use*) desgaste m ▷ *vt* (*clothes*) llevar; (*shoes*) calzar; (*damage: through use*) gastar, usar ▷ *vi* (*last*) durar; (*rub through etc*) desgastarse; **evening ~** ropa de etiqueta; **sports~/baby~** ropa de deportes/ de niños; **wear off** *vi* (*pain etc*) pasar, desaparecer; **wear out** *vt* desgastar; (*person, strength*) agotar

weary ['wiəri] *adj* cansado; (*dispirited*) abatido ▷ *vi* **to ~ of** cansarse de

weasel ['wiːzl] *n* (*Zool*) comadreja

weather ['wɛðə*] *n* tiempo ▷ *vt* (*storm, crisis*) hacer frente a; **under the ~** (*fig: ill*) indispuesto, pachucho; **weather forecast** *n* boletín m meteorológico

weave [wiːv] (*pt* **wove**, *pp* **woven**) *vt* (*cloth*) tejer; (*fig*) entretejer

web [wɛb] *n* (*of spider*) telaraña; (*on duck's foot*) membrana; (*network*) red f; **the (World Wide) W~** la Red; **web address** *n* dirección f de Internet; **webcam** *n* webcam f; **web page** *n* (página) web m o f; **website** *n* sitio web

Wed. *abbr* (= *Wednesday*) miérc

wed [wɛd] (*pt*, *pp* **~ded**) *vt* casar ▷ *vi* casarse

we'd [wiːd] = **we had; we would**

wedding ['wɛdɪŋ] *n* boda, casamiento; **silver/ golden ~ (anniversary)** bodas *fpl* de plata/de oro; **wedding anniversary** *n* aniversario de boda; **wedding day** *n* día m de la boda; **wedding dress** *n* traje m de novia; **wedding ring** *n* alianza

wedge [wɛdʒ] *n* (*of wood etc*) cuña; (*of cake*) trozo ▷ *vt* acuñar; (*push*) apretar

Wednesday ['wɛnzdɪ] *n* miércoles m inv

wee [wiː] (*SCOTTISH*) *adj* pequeñito

weed [wiːd] *n* mala hierba, maleza ▷ *vt* escardar, desherbar; **weedkiller** *n* herbicida m

week [wiːk] *n* semana; **a ~ today/on Friday** de hoy/del viernes en ocho días; **weekday** *n* día m laborable; **weekend** *n* fin m de semana; **weekly** *adv* semanalmente, cada semana ▷ *adj* semanal ▷ *n* semanario

weep [wiːp] (*pt*, *pp* **wept**) *vi*, *vt* llorar

weigh [wei] *vt*, *vi* pesar; **to ~ anchor** levar anclas; **weigh up** *vt* sopesar

weight [weit] *n* peso; (*metal weight*) pesa; **to lose/put on ~** adelgazar/engordar; **weightlifting** *n* levantamiento de pesas

weir [wiə*] *n* presa

weird [wiəd] *adj* raro, extraño

welcome ['wɛlkəm] *adj* bienvenido ▷ *n* bienvenida ▷ *vt* dar la bienvenida a; (*be glad of*) alegrarse de; **thank you - you're ~** gracias - de nada

weld [wɛld] *n* soldadura ▷ *vt* soldar

welfare ['wɛlfɛə*] *n* bienestar m; (*social aid*) asistencia social; **welfare state** *n* estado del bienestar

well [wɛl] *n* fuente f, pozo ▷ *adv* bien ▷ *adj*: **to be ~** estar bien (de salud) ▷ *excl* ¡vaya!, ¡bueno!; **as ~** también; **as ~ as** además de; **~ done!** ¡bien hecho!; **get ~ soon!** ¡que te mejores pronto!; **to do ~** (*business*) ir bien; (*person*) tener éxito

we'll [wiːl] = **we will; we shall**

well: well-behaved *adj* bueno; **well-built** *adj* (*person*) fornido; **well-dressed** *adj* bien vestido

wellies ['wɛlɪz] (*inf*) *npl* (*BRIT*) botas f de goma

well: well-known *adj* (*person*) conocido; **well-off** *adj* acomodado; **well-paid** [wɛl'peid] *adj* bien pagado, bien retribuido

Welsh [wɛlʃ] *adj* galés/esa ▷ *n* (*Ling*) galés m; **Welshman** (*irreg*) *n* galés m; **Welshwoman** (*irreg*) *n* galesa

went [wɛnt] *pt of* **go**

wept [wɛpt] *pt*, *pp of* **weep**

were [wəː*] *pt of* **be**

we're [wiə*] = **we are**

weren't [wəːnt] = **were not**

west [wɛst] *n* oeste m ▷ *adj* occidental, del oeste ▷ *adv* al o hacia el oeste; **the W~** el Oeste, el Occidente; **westbound** ['wɛstbaund] *adj* (*traffic, carriageway*) con rumbo al oeste; **western** *adj* occidental ▷ *n* (*Cinema*) película del oeste; **West Indian** *adj*, *n* antillano/a m/f

wet [wɛt] *adj* (*damp*) húmedo; (*soaked*) mojado; (*rainy*) lluvioso ▷ *n* (*BRIT: Pol*) conservador(a) m/f moderado/a; **to get ~** mojarse; **"~ paint"** "recién pintado"; **wetsuit** *n* traje m térmico

we've [wiːv] = **we have**

whack [wæk] *vt* dar un buen golpe a

whale [weil] *n* (*Zool*) ballena

wharf [wɔːf] (pl **wharves**) n muelle m

○ **KEYWORD**

what [wɒt] adj 1 (in direct/indirect questions) qué; **what size is he?** ¿qué talla usa?; **what colour/shape is it?** ¿de qué color/forma es?
2 (in exclamations): **what a mess!** ¡qué desastre!; **what a fool I am!** ¡qué tonto soy!
▷ pron 1 (interrogative) qué; **what are you doing?** ¿qué haces or estás haciendo?; **what is happening?** ¿qué pasa or está pasando?; **what is it called?** ¿cómo se llama?; **what about me?** ¿y yo qué?; **what about doing …?** ¿qué tal si hacemos …?
2 (relative) lo que; **I saw what you did/was on the table** vi lo que hiciste/había en la mesa
▷ excl (disbelieving) ¡cómo!; **what, no coffee!** ¡que no hay café!

whatever [wɒtˈevə*] adj: **~ book you choose** cualquier libro que elijas ▷ pron: **do ~ is necessary** haga lo que sea necesario; **~ happens** pase lo que pase; **no reason ~** or **whatsoever** ninguna razón sea la que sea; **nothing ~** nada en absoluto
whatsoever [wɒtsəʊˈevə*] adj see **whatever**
wheat [wiːt] n trigo
wheel [wiːl] n rueda; (Aut: also: **steering ~**) volante m; (Naut) timón m ▷ vt (pram etc) empujar ▷ vi (also: **~ round**) dar la vuelta, girar; **wheelbarrow** n carretilla; **wheelchair** n silla de ruedas; **wheel clamp** n (Aut) cepo
wheeze [wiːz] vi resollar

○ **KEYWORD**

when [wɛn] adv cuando; **when did it happen?** ¿cuándo ocurrió?; **I know when it happened** sé cuándo ocurrió
▷ conj 1 (at, during, after the time that) cuando; **be careful when you cross the road** ten cuidado al cruzar la calle; **that was when I needed you** fue entonces que te necesité
2 (on, at which): **on the day when I met him** el día en que le conocí
3 (whereas) cuando

whenever [wɛnˈevə*] conj cuando; (every time that) cada vez que ▷ adv cuando sea
where [wɛə*] adv dónde ▷ conj donde; **this is ~** aquí es donde; **whereabouts** adv dónde ▷ n: **nobody knows his whereabouts** nadie conoce su paradero; **whereas** conj visto que, mientras; **whereby** pron por lo cual; **wherever** conj dondequiera que; (interrogative) dónde
whether [ˈwɛðə*] conj si; **I don't know ~ to accept or not** no sé si aceptar o no; **~ you go or not** vayas o no vayas

○ **KEYWORD**

which [wɪtʃ] adj 1 (interrogative: direct, indirect) qué; **which picture(s) do you want?** ¿qué cuadro(s) quieres?; **which one?** ¿cuál?
2 **in which case** en cuyo caso; **we got there at 8 pm, by which time the cinema was full** llegamos allí a las

8, cuando el cine estaba lleno
▷ pron 1 (interrogative) cuál; **I don't mind which** el/la que sea
2 (relative: replacing noun) que; (: replacing clause) lo que; (: after preposition) (el(la)) que or el/la cual etc; **the apple which you ate/which is on the table** la manzana que comiste/que está en la mesa; **the chair on which you are sitting** la silla en la que estás sentado; **he said he knew, which is true/I feared** dijo que lo sabía, lo cual or lo que es cierto/me temía

whichever [wɪtʃˈevə*] adj: **take ~ book you prefer** coja (SP) el libro que prefiera; **~ book you take** cualquier libro que coja
while [waɪl] n rato, momento ▷ conj mientras; (although) aunque; **for a ~** durante algún tiempo
whilst [waɪlst] conj = **while**
whim [wɪm] n capricho
whine [waɪn] n (of pain) gemido; (of engine) zumbido; (of siren) aullido ▷ vi gemir; zumbar; (fig: complain) gimotear
whip [wɪp] n látigo; (Pol: person) encargado de la disciplina partidaria en el parlamento ▷ vt azotar; (Culin) batir; (move quickly): **to ~ sth out/off** sacar/quitar algo de un tirón; **whipped cream** n nata or crema montada
whirl [wɜːl] vt hacer girar, dar vueltas a ▷ vi girar, dar vueltas; (leaves etc) arremolinarse
whisk [wɪsk] n (Culin) batidor m ▷ vt (Culin) batir; **to ~ sb away** or **off** llevar volando a algn
whiskers [ˈwɪskəz] npl (of animal) bigotes mpl; (of man) patillas fpl
whiskey [ˈwɪskɪ] (US, IRELAND) n = **whisky**
whisky [ˈwɪskɪ] n whisky m
whisper [ˈwɪspə*] n susurro ▷ vi, vt susurrar
whistle [ˈwɪsl] n (sound) silbido; (object) silbato ▷ vi silbar
white [waɪt] adj blanco; (pale) pálido ▷ n blanco; (of egg) clara; **whiteboard** n pizarra blanca; **interactive whiteboard** pizarra interactiva; **White House** (US) n Casa Blanca; **whitewash** n (paint) jalbegue m, cal f ▷ vt blanquear
whiting [ˈwaɪtɪŋ] n inv (fish) pescadilla
Whitsun [ˈwɪtsn] n pentecostés m
whittle [ˈwɪtl] vt: **to ~ away**, **~ down** ir reduciendo
whizz [wɪz] vi: **to ~ past** or **by** pasar a toda velocidad

○ **KEYWORD**

who [huː] pron 1 (interrogative) quién; **who is it?**, **who's there?** ¿quién es?; **who are you looking for?** ¿a quién buscas?; **I told her who I was** le dije quién era yo
2 (relative) que; **the man/woman who spoke to me** el hombre/la mujer que habló conmigo; **those who can swim** los que saben or sepan nadar

whoever [huːˈevə*] pron: **~ finds it** cualquiera or quienquiera que lo encuentre; **ask ~ you like** pregunta a quien quieras; **~ he marries** no importa con quién se case
whole [həʊl] adj (entire) todo, entero; (not broken) intacto ▷ n todo; (all): **the ~ of the town** toda la ciudad, la ciudad entera ▷ n (total) total m; (sum) conjunto; **on the ~**, **as a ~** en general; **wholefood(s)**

n(pl) alimento(s) m(pl) integral(es); **wholeheartedly**
[həul'hɑ:tɪdlɪ] adv con entusiasmo; **wholemeal** adj
integral; **wholesale** n venta al por mayor ▷ adj al por
mayor; (fig: destruction) sistemático; **wholewheat** adj
= **wholemeal**; **wholly** adv totalmente,
enteramente

○ KEYWORD

whom [hu:m] pron 1 (interrogative):
whom did you see? ¿a quién viste?; **to whom did you
give it?** ¿a quién se lo diste?; **tell me from whom you
received it** dígame de quién lo recibió
2 (relative) que; **to whom** a quien(es); **of whom** de
quien(es), del/de la que etc; **the man whom I saw/to
whom I wrote** el hombre que vi/a quien escribí; **the
lady about/with whom I was talking** la señora de (la)
que/con quien o (la) que hablaba

whore [hɔ:*] (inf, pej) n puta

○ KEYWORD

whose [hu:z] adj 1 (possessive: interrogative): **whose
book is this?, whose is this book?** ¿de quién es este
libro?; **whose pencil have you taken?** ¿de quién es el
lápiz que has cogido?; **whose daughter are you?** ¿de
quién eres hija?
2 (possessive: relative) cuyo/a, pl cuyos/as; **the man
whose son you rescued** el hombre cuyo hijo
rescataste; **the woman whose passports I have** aquellas
personas cuyos pasaportes tengo; **the woman whose
car was stolen** la mujer a quien le robaron el coche
▷ pron de quién; **whose is this?** ¿de quién es esto?; **I
know whose it is** sé de quién es

○ KEYWORD

why [waɪ] adv por qué; **why not?** ¿por qué no?; **why
not do it now?** ¿por qué no lo haces (or hacemos
etc) ahora? ▷ conj: **I wonder why he said that** me
pregunto por qué dijo eso; **that's not why I'm here**
no es por eso (por lo) que estoy aquí; **the reason why**
la razón por la que
▷ excl (expressing surprise, shock, annoyance) ¡hombre!,
¡vaya!; (explaining): **why, it's you!** ¡hombre, eres tú!;
why, that's impossible ¡pero si eso es imposible!

wicked ['wɪkɪd] adj malvado, cruel
wicket ['wɪkɪt] n (Cricket: stumps) palos mpl; (: grass
area) terreno de juego
wide [waɪd] adj ancho; (area, knowledge) vasto,
grande; (choice) amplio ▷ adv: **to open ~** abrir de par
en par; **to shoot ~** errar el tiro; **widely** adv (travelled)
mucho; (spaced) muy; **it is widely believed/known
that ...** mucha gente piensa/sabe que ...; **widen** vt
ensanchar; (experience) ampliar ▷ vi ensancharse;
wide open adj abierto de par en par; **widespread** adj
extendido, general
widow ['wɪdəu] n viuda; **widower** n viudo
width [wɪdθ] n anchura; (of cloth) ancho
wield [wi:ld] vt (sword) blandir; (power) ejercer
wife [waɪf] (pl **wives**) n mujer f, esposa

wig [wɪg] n peluca
wild [waɪld] adj (animal) salvaje; (plant) silvestre;
(person) furioso, violento; (idea) descabellado,
(rough: sea) bravo; (: land) agreste; (: weather) muy
revuelto; **wilderness** ['wɪldənɪs] n desierto; **wildlife**
n fauna; **wildly** adv (behave) locamente; (lash out)
a diestro y siniestro; (guess) a lo loco; (happy) a más
no poder

○ KEYWORD

will [wɪl] aux vb 1 (forming future tense): **I will finish it
tomorrow** lo terminaré o voy a terminar mañana; **I
will have finished it by tomorrow** lo habré terminado
para mañana; **will you do it? – yes I will/no I won't**
¿lo harás? – sí/no
2 (in conjectures, predictions): **he will** or **he'll be there by
now** ya habrá o debe (de) haber llegado; **that will be
the postman** será o debe ser el cartero
3 (in commands, requests, offers): **will you be quiet!**
¿quieres callarte?; **will you help me?** ¿quieres
ayudarme?; **will you have a cup of tea?** ¿te apetece
un té?; **I won't put up with it!** ¡no lo soporto! ▷ vt (pt,
pp **willed**): **to will sb to do sth** desear que algn haga
algo; **he willed himself to go on** con gran fuerza de
voluntad, continuó
▷ n voluntad f; (testament) testamento

willing ['wɪlɪŋ] adj (with goodwill) de buena voluntad;
(enthusiastic) entusiasta; **he's ~ to do it** está dispuesto
a hacerlo; **willingly** adv con mucho gusto
willow ['wɪləu] n sauce m
willpower ['wɪlpauə*] n fuerza de voluntad
wilt [wɪlt] vi marchitarse
win [wɪn] (pt, pp **won**) n victoria, triunfo ▷ vt ganar;
(obtain) conseguir, lograr ▷ vi ganar; **win over** vt
convencer a
wince [wɪns] vi encogerse
wind[1] [wɪnd] n viento; (Med) gases mpl ▷ vt (take
breath away from) dejar sin aliento a
wind[2] [waɪnd] (pt, pp **wound**) vt enrollar; (wrap)
envolver; (clock, toy) dar cuerda a ▷ vi (road, river)
serpentear; **wind down** vt (car window) bajar;
(fig: production, business) disminuir; **wind up** vt (clock)
dar cuerda a; (debate, meeting) concluir, terminar
windfall ['wɪndfɔ:l] n golpe m de suerte
winding ['waɪndɪŋ] adj (road) tortuoso; (staircase)
de caracol
windmill ['wɪndmɪl] n molino de viento
window ['wɪndəu] n ventana; (in car, train)
ventanilla; (in shop etc) escaparate m (SP), vidriera
(LAM); **window box** n jardinera de ventana; **window
cleaner** n (person) limpiacristales mf inv; **window
pane** n cristal m; **window seat** n asiento junto a la
ventana; **windowsill** n alféizar m, repisa
windscreen ['wɪndskri:n] (US **windshield**) n
parabrisas m inv; **windscreen wiper** (US **windshield
wiper**) n limpiaparabrisas m inv
windsurfing ['wɪndsə:fɪŋ] n windsurf m
windy ['wɪndɪ] adj de mucho viento; **it's ~** hace
viento
wine [waɪn] n vino; **wine bar** n enoteca; **wine glass**
n copa (para vino); **wine list** n lista de vinos; **wine
tasting** n degustación f de vinos
wing [wɪŋ] n ala; (Aut) aleta; **wing mirror** n (espejo)

retrovisor m

wink [wɪŋk] n guiño, pestañeo ⊳ vi guiñar, pestañear

winner ['wɪnə*] n ganador(a) m/f

winning ['wɪnɪŋ] adj (team) ganador(a); (goal) decisivo; (smile) encantador(a)

winter ['wɪntə*] n invierno ⊳ vi invernar; **winter sports** npl deportes mpl de invierno; **wintertime** n invierno

wipe [waɪp] n: **to give sth a ~** pasar un trapo sobre algo ⊳ vt limpiar; (tape) borrar; **wipe out** vt (debt) liquidar; (memory) borrar; (destroy) destruir; **wipe up** vt limpiar

wire ['waɪə*] n alambre m; (Elec) cable m (eléctrico); (Tel) telegrama m ⊳ vt (house) poner la instalación eléctrica en; (also: ~ **up**) conectar; (person: telegram) telegrafiar

wiring ['waɪərɪŋ] n instalación f eléctrica

wisdom ['wɪzdəm] n sabiduría, saber m; (good sense) cordura; **wisdom tooth** n muela del juicio

wise [waɪz] adj sabio; (sensible) juicioso

wish [wɪʃ] n deseo ⊳ vt querer; **best ~es** (on birthday etc) felicidades fpl; **with best ~es** (in letter) saludos mpl, recuerdos mpl; **to ~ sb goodbye** despedirse de algn; **he ~ed me well** me deseó mucha suerte; **to ~ to do/sb to do sth** querer hacer/que algn haga algo; **to ~ for** desear

wistful ['wɪstful] adj pensativo

wit [wɪt] n ingenio, gracia; (also: ~s) inteligencia; (person) chistoso/a

witch [wɪtʃ] n bruja

○ **KEYWORD**

with [wɪð, wɪθ] prep **1** (accompanying, in the company of) con (con +mí, ti, sí = conmigo, contigo, consigo); **I was with him** estaba con él; **we stayed with friends** nos quedamos en casa de unos amigos; **I'm (not) with you** (don't understand) (no) te entiendo; **to be with it** (inf: person: up-to-date) estar al tanto; (: alert) ser despabilado

2 (descriptive, indicating manner etc) con; de; **a room with a view** una habitación con vistas; **the man with the grey hat/blue eyes** el hombre del sombrero gris/de los ojos azules; **red with anger** rojo de ira; **to shake with fear** temblar de miedo; **to fill sth with water** llenar algo de agua

withdraw [wɪð'drɔː] vt retirar, sacar ⊳ vi retirarse; **to ~ money (from the bank)** retirar fondos (del banco); **withdrawal** n retirada; (of money) reintegro; **withdrawn** pp of **withdraw** ⊳ adj (person) reservado, introvertido

withdrew [wɪð'druː] pt of **withdraw**

wither ['wɪðə*] vi marchitarse

withhold [wɪð'həuld] vt (money) retener; (decision) aplazar; (permission) negar; (information) ocultar

within [wɪð'ɪn] prep dentro de ⊳ adv dentro; **~ reach (of)** al alcance (de); **~ sight (of)** a la vista (de); **~ the week** antes de acabar la semana; **~ a mile (of)** a menos de una milla (de)

without [wɪð'aut] prep sin; **to go ~ sth** pasar sin algo

withstand [wɪθ'stænd] vt resistir a

witness ['wɪtnɪs] n testigo mf ⊳ vt (event) presenciar; (document) atestiguar la veracidad de; **to**

bear ~ to (fig) ser testimonio de

witty ['wɪtɪ] adj ingenioso

wives [waɪvz] npl of **wife**

wizard ['wɪzəd] n hechicero

wk abbr = **week**

wobble ['wɔbl] vi temblar; (chair) cojear

woe [wəu] n desgracia

woke [wəuk] pt of **wake**

woken ['wəukən] pp of **wake**

wolf [wulf] n lobo

woman ['wumən] (pl **women**) n mujer f

womb [wuːm] n matriz f, útero

women ['wɪmɪn] npl of **woman**

won [wʌn] pt, pp of **win**

wonder ['wʌndə*] n maravilla, prodigio; (feeling) asombro ⊳ vi: **to ~ whether/why** preguntarse si/por qué; **to ~ at** asombrarse de; **to ~ about** pensar sobre or en; **it's no ~ (that)** no es de extrañarse (que +subjun); **wonderful** adj maravilloso

won't [wəunt] = **will not**

wood [wud] n (timber) madera; (forest) bosque m; **wooden** adj de madera; (fig) inexpresivo; **woodwind** n (Mus) instrumentos mpl de viento de madera; **woodwork** n carpintería

wool [wul] n lana; **to pull the ~ over sb's eyes** (fig) engatusar a algn; **woollen** (us **woolen**) adj de lana; **woolly** (us **wooly**) adj lanudo, de lana; (fig: ideas) confuso

word [wəːd] n palabra; (news) noticia; (promise) palabra (de honor) ⊳ vt redactar; **in other ~s** en otras palabras; **to break/keep one's ~** faltar a la palabra/ cumplir la promesa; **to have ~s with sb** reñir con algn; **wording** n redacción f; **word processing** n proceso de textos; **word processor** n procesador m de textos

wore [wɔː*] pt of **wear**

work [wəːk] n trabajo; (job) empleo, trabajo; (Art, Literature) obra ⊳ vi trabajar; (mechanism) funcionar, marchar; (medicine) ser eficaz, surtir efecto ⊳ vt (shape) trabajar; (stone etc) tallar; (mine etc) explotar; (machine) manejar, hacer funcionar ⊳ npl (of clock, machine) mecanismo; **to be out of ~** estar parado, no tener trabajo; **to ~ loose** (part) desprenderse; (knot) aflojarse; **works** n (BRIT: factory) fábrica; **work out** vi (plans etc) salir bien, funcionar; **works** vt (problem) resolver; (plan) elaborar; **it works out at £100** suma 100 libras; **worker** n trabajador(a) m/f, obrero/a; **work experience** n: **I'm going to do my work experience in a factory** voy a hacer las prácticas en una fábrica; **workforce** n mano de obra; **working class** n clase f obrera ⊳ adj: **working-class** obrero; **working week** n semana laboral; **workman** (irreg) n obrero; **work of art** n obra de arte; **workout** n (Sport) sesión f de ejercicios; **work permit** n permiso de trabajo; **workplace** n lugar m de trabajo; **worksheet** n (Scol) hoja de ejercicios; **workshop** n taller m; **work station** n puesto or estación f de trabajo; **work surface** n encimera; **worktop** n encimera

world [wəːld] n mundo ⊳ cpd (champion) del mundo; (power, war) mundial; **to think the ~ of sb** (fig) tener un concepto muy alto de algn; **World Cup** n (Football): **the World Cup** el Mundial, los Mundiales; **world-wide** adj mundial, universal; **World-Wide Web** n: **the World-Wide Web** el World-Wide Web

worm [wəːm] n (also: **earth ~**) lombriz f

worn [wɔːn] pp of **wear** ⊳ adj usado; **worn-out** adj (object) gastado; (person) rendido, agotado

worried ['wʌrɪd] adj preocupado
worry ['wʌrɪ] n preocupación f ▷ vt preocupar, inquietar ▷ vi preocuparse; **worrying** adj inquietante
worse [wəːs] adj, adv peor ▷ n lo peor; **a change for the ~** un empeoramiento; **worsen** vt, vi empeorar; **worse off** adj (financially): **to be worse off** tener menos dinero; (fig): **you'll be worse off this way** de esta forma estarás peor que nunca
worship ['wəːʃɪp] n adoración f ▷ vt adorar; **Your W~** (BRIT: to mayor) señor alcalde; (: to judge) señor juez
worst [wəːst] adj, adv peor ▷ n lo peor; **at ~** en lo peor de los casos
worth [wəːθ] n valor m ▷ adj: **to be ~** valer; **it's ~ it** vale or merece la pena; **to be ~ one's while (to do)** merecer la pena (hacer); **worthless** adj sin valor; (useless) inútil; **worthwhile** adj (activity) que merece la pena; (cause) loable
worthy ['wəːðɪ] adj respetable; (motive) honesto; **~ of** digno de

○ **KEYWORD**

would [wud] aux vb 1 (conditional tense): **if you asked him he would do it** si se lo pidieras, lo haría; **if you had asked him he would have done it** si se lo hubieras pedido, lo habría or hubiera hecho
2 (in offers, invitations, requests): **would you like a biscuit?** ¿quieres una galleta?; (formal) ¿querría una galleta?; **would you ask him to come in?** ¿quiere hacerle pasar?; **would you open the window please?** ¿quiere or podría abrir la ventana, por favor?
3 (in indirect speech): **I said I would do it** dije que lo haría
4 (emphatic): **it would have to snow today!** ¡tenía que nevar precisamente hoy!
5 (insistence): **she wouldn't behave** no quiso comportarse bien
6 (conjecture): **it would have been midnight** sería medianoche; **it would seem so** parece ser que sí
7 (indicating habit): **he would go there on Mondays** iba allí los lunes

wouldn't ['wudnt] = **would not**
wound¹ [wuːnd] n herida f ▷ vt herir
wound² [waund] pt, pp of **wind²**
wove [wəuv] pt of **weave**
woven ['wəuvən] pp of **weave**
wrap [ræp] vt (also: **~ up**) envolver; (gift) envolver, abrigar ▷ vi (dress warmly) abrigarse; **wrapper** n (on chocolate) papel m; (BRIT: of book) sobrecubierta; **wrapping** n envoltura, envase m; **wrapping paper** n papel m de envolver; (fancy) papel m de regalo
wreath [riːθ, pl riːðz] n (funeral wreath) corona
wreck [rɛk] n (ship: destruction) naufragio; (: remains) restos mpl del barco; (pej: person) ruina ▷ vt destrozar; (chances) arruinar; **wreckage** n restos mpl; (of building) escombros mpl
wren [rɛn] n (Zool) reyezuelo
wrench [rɛntʃ] n (Tech) llave f inglesa; (tug) tirón m; (fig) dolor m ▷ vt arrancar; **to ~ sth from sb** arrebatar algo violentamente a algn
wrestle ['rɛsl] vi: **to ~ (with sb)** luchar (con or contra algn); **wrestler** n luchador(a) m/f (de lucha libre); **wrestling** n lucha libre
wretched ['rɛtʃɪd] adj miserable

wriggle ['rɪgl] vi (also: **~ about**) menearse, retorcerse
wring [rɪŋ] (pt, pp **wrung**) vt retorcer; (wet clothes) escurrir; (fig): **to ~ sth out of sb** sacar algo por la fuerza a algn
wrinkle ['rɪŋkl] n arruga ▷ vt arrugar ▷ vi arrugarse
wrist [rɪst] n muñeca
writable ['raɪtəbl] adj (CD, DVD) escribible
write [raɪt] (pt **wrote**, pp **written**) vt escribir; (cheque) extender ▷ vi escribir; **write down** vt escribir; (note) apuntar; **write off** vt (debt) borrar (como incobrable); (fig) desechar por inútil; **write out** vt escribir; **write-off** n siniestro total; **writer** n escritor(a) m/f
writing ['raɪtɪŋ] n escritura; (hand-writing) letra; (of author) obras fpl; **in ~** por escrito; **writing paper** n papel m de escribir
written ['rɪtn] pp of **write**
wrong [rɔŋ] adj (wicked) malo; (unfair) injusto; (incorrect) equivocado, incorrecto; (not suitable) inoportuno, inconveniente, (reverse) del revés ▷ adv equivocadamente ▷ n injusticia ▷ vt ser injusto con; **you are ~ to do it** haces mal en hacerlo; **you are ~ about that, you've got it ~** en eso estás equivocado; **to be in the ~** no tener razón, tener la culpa; **what's ~?** ¿qué pasa?; **to go ~** (person) equivocarse; (plan) salir mal; (machine) estropearse; **wrongly** adv mal, incorrectamente; (by mistake) por error; **wrong number** n (Tel): **you've got the wrong number** se ha equivocado de número
wrote [rəut] pt of **write**
wrung [rʌŋ] pt, pp of **wring**
WWW n abbr (= World Wide Web) WWW m

XL *abbr* = **extra large**

Xmas ['eksməs] *n abbr* = **Christmas**

X-ray ['eksreɪ] *n* radiografía ▷ *vt* radiografiar, sacar radiografías de

xylophone ['zaɪləfəun] *n* xilófono

---

yacht [jɔt] *n* yate *m*; **yachting** *n* (*sport*) balandrismo

yard [jɑːd] *n* patio; (*measure*) yarda; **yard sale** (*us*) *n* venta de objetos usados (*en el jardín de una casa particular*)

yarn [jɑːn] *n* hilo; (*tale*) cuento, historia

yawn [jɔːn] *n* bostezo ▷ *vi* bostezar

yd. *abbr* (= *yard*) yda

yeah [jeə] (*inf*) *adv* sí

year [jɪə*] *n* año; **to be 8 ~s old** tener 8 años; **an eight-~-old child** un niño de ocho años (de edad); **yearly** *adj* anual ▷ *adv* anualmente, cada año

yearn [jəːn] *vi*: **to ~ for sth** añorar algo, suspirar por algo

yeast [jiːst] *n* levadura

yell [jel] *n* grito, alarido ▷ *vi* gritar

yellow ['jeləu] *adj* amarillo; **Yellow Pages®** *npl* páginas *fpl* amarillas

yes [jes] *adv* sí ▷ *n* sí *m*; **to say/answer ~** decir/contestar que sí

yesterday ['jestədɪ] *adv* ayer ▷ *n* ayer *m*; **~ morning/evening** ayer por la mañana/tarde; **all day ~** todo el día de ayer

yet [jet] *adv* ya; (*negative*) todavía ▷ *conj* sin embargo, a pesar de todo; **it is not finished ~** todavía no está acabado; **the best ~** el/la mejor hasta ahora; **as ~** hasta ahora, todavía

yew [juː] *n* tejo

Yiddish ['jɪdɪʃ] *n* yiddish *m*

yield [jiːld] *n* (*Agr*) cosecha; (*Comm*) rendimiento ▷ *vt* ceder; (*results*) producir, dar; (*profit*) rendir ▷ *vi* rendirse, ceder; (*us Aut*) ceder el paso

yob(bo) ['jɔb(bəu)] *n* (*BRIT inf*) gamberro

yoga ['jəugə] *n* yoga *m*

yog(h)ourt ['jəugət] *n* yogur *m*

yog(h)urt ['jəugət] *n* = **yog(h)ourt**

yolk [jəuk] *n* yema (de huevo)

⭕ **KEYWORD**

you [juː] *pron* **1** (*subject: familiar*) tú; (*pl*) vosotros/as (*SP*), ustedes (*LAM*); (*polite*) usted; (*pl*) ustedes; **you are very kind** eres/es *etc* muy amable; **you Spanish enjoy your food** a vosotros (*or* ustedes) los españoles os

(*or* les) gusta lacomida; **you and I will go** iremos tú y yo
2 (*object: direct: familiar*) te; (*pl*) os (*SP*), les (*LAM*); (*polite*)
le; (*pl*) les; (*f*) la; (*pl*) las; **I know you** te/le etc conozco
3 (*object: indirect: familiar*) te; (*pl*) les (*SP*), les (*LAM*); (*polite*)
le; (*pl*) les; **I gave the letter to you yesterday** te/os
etc di la carta ayer
4 (*stressed*): **I told you to do it** te dije a ti que lo
hicieras, es a ti a quien dije que lo hicieras; *see also* **3; 5**
5 (*after prep*: NB: con +ti = contigo: *familiar*) ti; (*pl*)
vosotros/as (*SP*), ustedes (*LAM*); (: *polite*) usted; (*pl*)
ustedes; **it's for you** es para ti/vosotros *etc*
6 (*comparisons: familiar*) tú; (*pl*) vosotros/as (*SP*), ustedes
(*LAM*); (: *polite*) usted; (*pl*) ustedes; **she's younger than
you** es más joven que tú/vosotros etc
7 (*impersonal one*): **fresh air does you good** el aire puro
(te) hace bien; **you never know** nunca se sabe; **you
can't do that!** ¡eso no se hace!

you'd [juːd] = **you had; you would**
you'll [juːl] = **you will; you shall**
young [jʌŋ] *adj* joven ▷ *npl* (*of animal*) cría;
(*people*): **the ~** los jóvenes, la juventud; **youngster**
n joven *mf*
your [jɔː*] *adj* tu; (*pl*) vuestro; (*formal*) su; *see also* **my**
you're [juə*] = **you are**
yours [jɔːz] *pron* tuyo (*pl*), vuestro; (*formal*) suyo; *see
also* **faithfully; mine**[1] *see also* **sincerely**
yourself [jɔːˈsɛlf] *pron* tú mismo (*complement*)
te; (*after prep*) tí (mismo); (*formal*) usted mismo;
(: *complement*) se; (: *after prep*) sí (mismo); **yourselves** *pl
pron* vosotros mismos; (*after prep*) vosotros (mismos);
(*formal*) ustedes (mismos); (: *complement*) se; (: *after
prep*) sí mismos; *see also* **oneself**
youth [*pl* juːðz *n* juventud *f*; (*young man*) joven *m*;
youth club *n* club *m* juvenil; **youthful** *adj* juvenil;
youth hostel *n* albergue *m* de juventud
you've [juːv] = **you have**

Z

zeal [ziːl] *n* celo, entusiasmo
zebra [ˈziːbrə] *n* cebra; **zebra crossing** (*BRIT*) *n* paso
de peatones
zero [ˈzɪərəu] *n* cero
zest [zɛst] *n* ánimo, vivacidad *f*; (*of orange*) piel *f*
zigzag [ˈzɪgzæg] *n* zigzag *m* ▷ *vi* zigzaguear, hacer
eses
Zimbabwe [zɪmˈbɑːbwɪ] *n* Zimbabwe *m*
zinc [zɪŋk] *n* cinc *m*, zinc *m*
zip [zɪp] *n* (*also*: ~ **fastener,** (*US*) ~**per**) cremallera
(*SP*), cierre (*AM*) *m*, zíper *m* (*MEX, CAM*) ▷ *vt* (*also*: ~
up) cerrar la cremallera de; (*file*) comprimir; **zip code**
(*US*) *n* código postal; **zip file** *n* (*Comput*) archivo
comprimido; **zipper** (*US*) *n* cremallera
zit [zɪt] *n* grano
zodiac [ˈzəudiæk] *n* zodíaco
zone [zəun] *n* zona
zoo [zuː] *n* (jardín *m*) zoo *m*
zoology [zuːˈɔlədʒɪ] *n* zoología
zoom [zuːm] *vi*: **to ~ past** pasar zumbando; **zoom
lens** *n* zoom *m*
zucchini [zuːˈkiːnɪ] (*US*) *n*(*pl*) calabacín(ines) *m*(*pl*)